The Concise Oxford
Dictionary of
Art and Artists

THE
CONCISE OXFORD
DICTIONARY OF
ART AND
ARTISTS

EDITED BY
IAN CHILVERS

Oxford   New York
OXFORD UNIVERSITY PRESS
1990

Oxford University Press, Walton Street, Oxford OX2 6DP
Oxford New York Toronto
Delhi Bombay Calcutta Madras Karachi
Petaling Jaya Singapore Hong Kong Tokyo
Nairobi Dar es Salaam Cape Town
Melbourne Auckland
and associated companies in
Berlin Ibadan

Oxford is a trade mark of Oxford University Press

British Library Cataloguing in Publication Data
The Concise Oxford Dictionary of Art and Artists.
1. Visual arts—Encylopaedias
I. Chilvers, Ian   II. The Oxford Dictionary of Art.
703'.21
ISBN 0-19-866166-5
ISBN 0-19-282676-X

Text processing by the Oxford Text System
Printed in Great Britain by
Richard Clay Ltd.
Bungay, Suffolk

PREFACE

The Concise Oxford Dictionary of Art and Artists is a revised, updated, and condensed version of *The Oxford Dictionary of Art*, which was published in 1988. It is about a fifth shorter than the parent work, but the majority of the entries are unchanged or amended only slightly; the reduction in length has been achieved not by trying to condense each entry by an average amount, but by recasting the longer, discursive articles (such as those on printmaking techniques) in much pithier form and by dropping certain marginal classes of entry. These include, for example, all entries on book-printing, unless there is a very close connection with a major artist or artists; so the Kelmscott Press still finds a place, but the Aldine Press does not. In this way, *The Concise Oxford Dictionary of Art and Artists* is more sharply focused than its parent as a reference book to Western and Western-inspired painting, sculpture, and graphic art. Architecture is excluded, although there are entries on individuals who were active chiefly as architects but who made significant contributions to other fields of the visual arts (Bramante and Brunelleschi, for example). Oriental art, too, is omitted, although there is an entry on Ukiyo-e, as the subject of Japanese prints occurs so frequently in the discussion of late nineteenth-century French painting.

The time span of the book is from the 5th century BC (the Classical age of Greek art) to the present day; an arbitrary cut-off point has been adopted for contemporary art, in that no artist born after 1945 is included. As well as biographies of artists, the book has entries on techniques, groups, styles, movements, writers, patrons, dealers, collectors, museums, and galleries. Also included are the celebrated antique statues (such as the *Apollo Belvedere*, the *Belvedere Torso*, and the *Laocoön*) that were so influential on European art from the Renaissance onwards, and one or two (such as the *Venus de Milo*) whose fame is more recent.

The length of individual entries is roughly correlated to the importance of the subject, but with many qualifications, some artists' lives being much more easily summarized than others. Those who travelled a great deal, or had fingers in many pies, or who for one reason or another led especially interesting lives are likely to have longer entries than equally accomplished artists who stayed at home and devoted themselves to one speciality. It is of course tempting to write more about one's own favourites, but I hope this kind of personal bias (for or against) has intruded only rarely.

There is no system of alphabetizing artists' names that will satisfy logic but not offend against usage. Thus, one says 'van Dyck' or 'van Gogh', rather than 'Dyck' of 'Gogh', but they are almost invariably indexed under D and G (as they are here) rather than V. Cross-references are given when there is likely to be doubt about where an artist will be found, but the following general rules may be taken as guidelines. Prefixes such as 'de', 'van', and 'von' are generally ignored, but an exception is 'La' or 'Le' (thus La Tour, Georges de). There are certain names where usage goes against this principle—thus Willem de Kooning and Peter De Wint are found under D. Italian Old Masters whose names include 'da', 'del', or 'di' are usually found under their first name (Leonardo da Vinci, rather than Vinci, Leonardo da), but again usage occasionally dictates otherwise; thus Andrea del Verrocchio is found under Verrocchio, not Andrea. For purposes of alphabetization 'Mc' is treated as 'Mac' and 'St' as 'Saint'. Artists from the same family are usually covered in one composite entry, except where it seemed more reasonable to treat major and distinct personalitites separately. In line with the practice of the National Gallery in London and the Witt Library at the Courtauld Institute of Art, artists from the Low Countries are called Netherlandish up to about 1600; they are then distinguished as either Dutch or Flemish; and after about 1830 'Flemish' becomes 'Belgian'.

Artists' names are given in the form most commonly used; so various elements of full names have sometimes been dropped, and nicknames or pseudonyms are used as the heading where these are better known than the artist's real name. Thus Delacroix's Christian name is given as Eugène rather Ferdinand-Victor-Eugène, Velázquez, is called Diego Velázquez rather than Diego Rodriquez de Silva y Velázquez, and Giovanni Francesco Barbieri appears under his nickname Guercino.

Names of galleries are also sometimes given in slightly shortened form; thus the Museum Boymans-van Beuningen in Rotterdam is generally referred to as 'Boymans Museum'. When a gallery is mentioned more than once within the same entry, the town in which it is located is generally omitted after the first mention. Locations are not given for prints unless they are known to be exceptionally rare (see, for example, Bramante).

Cross-references from one article to another are indicated by an asterisk (*) within the main part of the text or by the use of small capitals when the formula 'see so-and-so' is used. Names of all people who have their own entries are automatically asterisked on their first mention in another entry, but cross-references are used selectively for art media, styles, terms, etc., and given only when further elucidation under that heading might be helpful.

*   *   *   *   *   *   *   *   *   *

Dr Johnson defined a lexicographer as 'a writer of dictionaries, a harmless drudge'. I can vouch for the drudgery, but there is also much satisfaction involved in compiling a dictionary such as this, and I should like to thank the various people who have helped to make the task often such an enjoyable one. My chief indebtedness is to Dr Dennis Farr, who read all the copy for *The Oxford Dictionary of Art*, making numerous corrections and a great many suggestions for improvements to both content and style, and now has commented wisely and wittily on the deletions, additions, and modifications that have transformed it into *The Concise Oxford Dictionary of Art and Artists*.

At the Oxford University Press, I am grateful to everyone who worked on the book—for their enthusiasm and encouragement no less than for their skills. To the names of Pam Coote, Betty Palmer, and Nicholas Wilson, editors on *The Oxford Dictionary of Art*, I now add those of Hilary McGlynn and Thomas Webster, their counterparts on the present book.

In a more general sense, I should like to say what a comfort it is to anyone involved in the field of reference books to be able to draw on the resources and tradition of the OUP. I have been able to use the various members of the family of Oxford English Dictionaries to help with definitions, and I have taken much information from *The Dictionary of National Biography* and the various *Oxford Companions* outside the field of art. Margaret Drabble's new edition of *The Oxford Companion to English Literature*, for example, contains many excellent entries (by Helen Langdon) on artists and their relationship to literature, and I have also made frequent use of the *Oxford Companions* to *French Literature* and *German Literature*, and of *The Oxford Classical Dictionary* and the *Oxford Dictionary of the Christian Church*. The *Oxford Companions* to *Film*, *Music*, and the *Theatre* have likewise proved helpful when their fields overlapped with mine, and, less obviously, I have also benefited from the *Oxford Companion to Ships and the Sea* (in relation to Clarkson Stanfield) and from the *Oxford Companion to Chess* (for some information concerning a Lucas van Leyden painting and for the delightful anecdote in the Duchamp entry).

On a more personal note, I should like to thank my sister, Doreen Chilvers, for undertaking the tedious task of pasting up the slips from *The Oxford Dictionary of Art* that formed the raw material of this book, and my nephew, Gavin Chilvers, for some valuable help at the proof-reading stage. Many friends and former colleagues have given me advice, information, or encouragement, and several have read and commented on entries in fields in which they have specialist knowledge. Among them are: Jonathan Alden, Tim Ayers, Chris Barker, Georgina Barker, Judy Binning, Alison Bolus, Jo Bourne, Claudia Brigg, Caroline Bugler, Veneta Bullen, Penelope Byrde, Vanessa Cawley, Caroline Christian, Sue Churchill, Alison Cole, Nic Dean, Celia de la Hey, Vanessa Fletcher, Emma Foa, Janet Furze-Lewis, John Gaisford, John Glaves-Smith, Bina Goldman, Sylvia Goulding, Arabella Grazebrook, Clive Gregory, Julia Hanson, Flavia Howard, James Hughes, Miranda Innes, Annette Jacobs, Dr Michael Jacobs, Stuart John, Jessica Johnson, Frances Kelly, Blaise Keogh, Jon Kirkwood, Frank Landamore, Robin Loerch, Anne Lyons, Geraldine McCaughrean, Margaret Mauger, Jenny Mohammadi, Sir Felix Moore, Anna Morter, Jenny Mulherin, Nigel O'Gorman, Alice Peebles, Maggie Ramsay, Clare Randall, Benedict Read, John Roberts, Carolyn Rogers, Antonia Spowers, Kate Sprawson, Julie Staniland, Ruth Taylor, Jack Tresidder, Nicholas Turner, Trevor Vertigan, Dr Malcolm Warner, Christine Webb, Jude Welton, Reg Wright, and Iain Zaczec. I am also grateful to the staff of the Tate Gallery Archive, who allowed me access to their press cutting files to try to ensure that the book was as up to date as reasonably possible in recording the deaths of recently deceased artists. Branches of the OUP in Australia, Canada, and the USA similarly provided up-to-date information on artists in those countries. Finally, for inspiration from afar, thanks to Deborah Lambert, Victoria Kirkham, and G.G.

Jesmond, Newcastle upon Tyne   IAN CHILVERS
August 1989

ABBREVIATIONS

Bib.	Bibliothèque or Biblioteca
Bib. Nat.	Bibliothèque Nationale
BL	British Library
BM	British Museum
Coll.	Collection
Gal.	Gallery
Inst.	Institute
Met. Mus.	Metropolitan Museum
MOMA	Museum of Modern Art
Mus.	Museum or Museo
NG	National Gallery
NPG	National Portrait Gallery
OED	*The Oxford English Dictionary*
V&A	Victoria and Albert Museum

A

Aachen, Hans von (1552–1615). German painter, born in Cologne (in spite of his name) and active in the Netherlands, Italy (1574–88), and most notably Prague, where in 1597 he became court painter to the emperor Rudolf II. On Rudolf's death (1612) he worked for the emperor Matthias. His paintings, featuring elegant, elongated figures, are leading examples of the sophisticated *Mannerist art then in vogue at the courts of Northern Europe, and he was particularly good with playfully erotic nudes (*The Triumph of Truth*, Alte Pinakothek, Munich, 1598). Engravings after his work gave his style wide influence.

Aaltonen, Wäinö (1894–1966). Finnish sculptor, the personification of the patriotic spirit of his country in the years following the declaration of independence from Russia (1917). The bronze monument to the runner Paavo Nurmi (1925) outside the athletics stadium in Helsinki and the bust of the composer Sibelius (1928, various casts exist) are among his portrayals of national heroes.

Abbate, Niccolò dell' (c.1512–71). Italian *Mannerist painter. He was trained in the tradition of his birthplace, Modena, but he developed his mature style in Bologna (1548–52). There he decorated palaces, combining painted stucco with figure compositions and landscapes (Palazzo Pozzi, now Palazzo dell' Università), and painted some portraits in the manner of *Pontormo. He was invited to France in 1552, probably at the suggestion of *Primaticcio, under whom he worked at *Fontainebleau, and he remained in France for the rest of his life. Most of his work in the palace itself has been lost, and he is now considered most important for his landscapes with figures from mythological stories (*Landscape with the Death of Eurydice*, NG, London). In these he was the direct precursor of *Claude and *Poussin in the long-lived tradition of French classical landscape.

Abbey, Edwin Austin (1852–1911). American painter, etcher, and book illustrator, highly successful in England (where he settled in 1880) as well as his own country. He specialized in historical scenes and had several large and prestigious commissions, most notably a set of murals representing *The Quest of the Holy Grail* (1902) in Boston Public Library and the official painting commemorating Edward VII's coronation in 1902 (Buckingham Palace, London). Such paintings now seem rather overblown and ponderous, and he is most highly esteemed for his lively book illustrations. He was particularly prolific for *Harper's Weekly*, his association with the magazine lasting from 1870 until his death. Although he always remained an American citizen, Abbey was extremely fond of cricket and had a private ground at his house in Gloucestershire.

Abbot, Lemuel Francis (c.1760–1802). English portrait painter. His clientele included many naval officers and he is best known for his portrayals of Lord Nelson, of whom he did several portraits with slight variations (1797–8). In 1798 Abbot became insane, and his unfinished works were completed by other hands.

Abildgaard, Nicolai Abraham (1743–1809). Danish *Neoclassical painter. From 1772 to 1777 he studied in Rome, where his friendship with *Fuseli helped to form his *eclectic early style. On his return to Denmark his work became more purely Classical, as is best seen in his cycles of paintings illustrating Apuleius and Terence (Statens Mus. for Kunst, Copenhagen). He became one of the leading figures in Danish art and had great influence as Director of the Copenhagen Academy (1789–91 and 1801–09), where his pupils included *Runge and *Thorvaldsen. Abildgaard occasionally worked as an architect, sculptor, and designer, and he also wrote on art. His most ambitious work, a huge decorative scheme at Christianborg Palace, was destroyed by fire in 1794.

abstract art. Term that can in its broadest sense be applied to any art that does not represent recognizable objects (much decorative art, for example), but which is most commonly applied to those forms of 20th-cent. art in which the traditional European conception of art as the imitation of nature is abandoned. *Kandinsky is usually credited with having made the first entirely non-representational picture around 1910, and since then modern abstract art has developed into many different movements and 'isms'. However, two basic tendencies are recognizable within it: (i) the reduction of natural appearances to radically simplified forms, exemplified in the work of *Brancusi; and (ii) the construction of art objects from non-representational basic forms, as in Ben *Nicholson's *reliefs.

Abstract Expressionism. Movement in *abstract art that developed in New York in the 1940s. The same term had earlier been used in connection with some of *Kandinsky's early abstract paintings, but first came into vogue when applied to the work of Arshile *Gorky and Jackson *Pollock. It was soon extended to the work of other New York painters, even when it was neither abstract (*de Kooning, *Gottlieb) nor *Expressionist (*Rothko, *Kline). The painters embraced by the term shared a similarity of outlook rather than of style—an outlook characterized by a spirit of revolt against tradition and a demand for spontaneous freedom of expression. This spontaneity is seen most clearly in the *Action painting made famous by Pollock. The movement has affinities with *Tachisme and made a strong impact in several European countries—the first American movement to do so.

Abstraction-Création. The name taken by a group of abstract painters and sculptors formed in Paris in February 1931, a successor to *Cercle et Carré. The group was open to artists of all nationalities and the organization was loose, so that at one time its numbers rose to as many as 400. It operated by arranging group exhibitions and by publishing an illustrated annual (1932–6) called *Abstraction-Création: Art non-figuratif*. Within this general principle the association was extremely catholic in its outlook and embraced many kinds of non-figurative art, although the emphasis fell increasingly upon geometrical rather than expressive or *lyrical abstraction.

After c.1936 the activities of the association dwindled as some of the leading Constructivists moved from France to England.

academy. Association of artists, scholars, etc., arranged in a professional institution. Although the name was applied to various informal gatherings of artists from c.1500, the first formal art academy was not set up until 1563, when Duke Cosimo de' *Medici founded the Accademia del Disegno in Florence. The prime mover was Giorgio *Vasari, whose aim was to emancipate artists from control by the guilds, and to confirm the rise in social standing they had achieved during the previous hundred years. *Michelangelo, who more than anyone else embodied this change of status, was made one of the two heads and Duke Cosimo was the other. The next important step was taken in Rome, where the Accademia di S. Luca was founded in 1593, with Federico *Zuccaro as its first president. More stress was laid on practical instruction than at Florence, but the Academy was not at all successful in its war against the guilds until the powerful support it received from Pope Urban VIII (Maffeo *Barberini) in 1627 and 1633. Thereafter it grew in wealth and prestige. The only other similar organization in Italy was the Academy established in Milan by Cardinal Federico Borromeo in 1620. But meanwhile the word was very frequently used of private institutions where artists met to draw from life. The most famous example of this kind was organized by the *Carracci in Bologna.

In France a group of painters, moved by the same reasons of prestige as had earlier inspired the Italians, persuaded Louis XIV to found the Académie Royale de Peinture et de Sculpture in 1648. Here too the guilds put up powerful opposition, and its supremacy was not assured until *Louis' chief minister, Jean-Baptiste Colbert, was elected Vice-Protector in 1661 and found in the Académie an instrument for imposing official standards and principles of taste. Colbert and *Lebrun, the Director, envisaged dictatorship of the arts, and for the first time in history the expression 'academic art' acquired a precise significance. The Académie assumed a virtual monopoly of teaching and of exhibition, and an orthodoxy of artistic and aesthetic doctrine obtained official sanction. Implicit in the academic theory and teaching was the assumption that everything to do with art can be brought within the scope of rational understanding and reduced to logical precepts that can be taught and studied.

Other art academies were founded in Germany, Spain, and other countries after the middle of the 17th cent., and by the end of the 18th cent. well over a hundred were flourishing throughout Europe. Among these was the *Royal Academy in London, founded in 1768. Everywhere the academies made themselves champions of *Neoclassicism in opposition to the surviving styles of *Baroque and *Rococo. There was some opposition to these bodies from the start. Towards the end of the 18th cent. French Revolutionary sentiment was especially bitter about the exclusive privileges enjoyed by members of the Académie, and many artists, with *David in the lead, demanded its dissolution. This step was taken in 1793, and the Ecole des *Beaux-Arts was set up in 1795. While this looked after practical instruction, social functions were left to the fine arts section of the Institut de France, which in 1816 was reconstituted as the Académie des Beaux-Arts.

The principal threat to academies, however, came from the *Romantic notion of the artist as a genius who produces his masterpieces by the light of inspiration which cannot be taught or subjected to rule. Virtually all the most creative artists of the 19th cent. stood outside the academies and sought alternative channels for exhibiting their works, although *Manet for example, always craved traditional success at the *Salon. Academies still retained prestige in conservative cities, but they were condemned out of hand by the adventurous, and in 1898, in his book *Modern Painting*, the novelist and critic George Moore wrote 'that nearly all artists dislike and despise the Royal Academy is a matter of common knowledge.' Gradually compromises were made on both sides, and academies became more liberal in the face of competition from rival teaching institutions and artists' groups (the *Slade School and *New English Art Club, in England for example, and the *Sezessionen in Germany and Austria). In spite of this liberalization, however, the word 'academic' now almost always carries a pejorative meaning, and is associated with mediocrity and lack of originality.

academy board. A pasteboard used for painting, especially in oils, since the early 19th cent. It is made of sheets of paper sized and pressed together, treated with a *ground, and sometimes embossed with an imitation canvas grain. Because it is fairly inexpensive, academy board is a popular *support with amateur painters, and it is also used by professional artists for sketches and studies.

academy figure. A careful painting or drawing (usually about half life-size) from the nude made as an exercise. The figure is usually depicted in a heroic pose, and there is a tradition of suitable postures which goes back to the *Carracci.

Achilles Painter. Greek vase painter, active in Athens in the mid 5th cent. BC, named after an amphora decorated with a figure of Achilles (Vatican Museums). He was a contemporary of *Phidias and his paintings have some of the nobility associated with the great sculptor's work. His compositions are simple (usually limited to one or two figures) and his figures are serene and graceful.

acrylic paint. A synthetic paint combining some of the properties of *oils and *watercolour. It is soluble in water, quick-drying, apparently permanent, and can be used on a wide variety of surfaces to create effects ranging from thin washes to rich *impasto. The finish it produces can be matt or gloss. First used by artists in the 1940s, it is now a serious rival to oil paint and has been much favoured by, for example, David *Hockney.

Action painting. A technique and style of painting made famous by Jackson *Pollock—in which paint is dribbled, splashed, and poured over the canvas, which is often laid on the floor rather than placed upright. The term was first used in 1952 by the art critic Harold Rosenberg. It is sometimes used as an alternative name for *Abstract Expressionism, but such usage is inexact, as Action painting represents only one form of Abstract Expressionism. See also GESTURAL PAINTING.

Adam, François-Gérard (1710–61); **Lambert-Sigisbert** (1700–59); **Nicolas-Sébastien** (1705–78). French sculptors from Nancy, brothers. All three went to Rome after training with their father **Jacob-Sigisbert** (1670–1747), and on their return adapted the Roman *Baroque style to French *Rococo taste. Lambert-Sigisbert was the most distinguished member of the family. His masterpiece is the *Neptune Fountain* (1740) at Versailles, a work showing the influence of *Bernini in its exuberant movement. Nicolas-Sébastien is remembered mainly for the monument of Queen Catharina Opalinska (1749) in the church of Notre Dame de Bon Secours in Nancy. François-Gérard's best works are probably his garden statues for Frederick the Great of Prussia at Sanssouci, Potsdam. Better known than any of the three brothers is their nephew *Clodion.

Aelst, Willem van (1625–c.1683). Dutch painter of lavish flower pieces and still lifes, a pupil of his uncle **Evert van Aelst** (1602–57). He worked in Paris, Florence, and Rome (he was court painter to Ferdinando de' *Medici, Grand Duke of Tuscany), before settling in Amsterdam in 1657. His pupils included Rachel *Ruysch.

aerial perspective. Term describing the means of producing a sense of depth in a painting by imitating the effect of atmosphere whereby objects look paler and bluer the further away they are from the viewer. Dust and large moisture particles in the atmosphere cause some scattering of light as it passes through it, the amount of scattering depending on the wavelength (hence colour) of the light. Short wavelength (blue) light is scattered most and long wavelength (red) is scattered least. This is the reason why the sky is blue and why distant dark objects appear to lie behind a veil of blue. The term 'aerial perspective' was invented by *Leonardo, but the device was used by Roman painters, for example at Pompeii. In the work of Italian painters of Leonardo's time, backgrounds sometimes look artificially blue, and in general aerial perspective has been more subtly exploited in Northern Europe, where the atmosphere tends to be hazier. No one used it more beautifully than *Turner, in some of whose late works it is virtually the subject of the painting.

Aertsen, Pieter (1508/9–75). Netherlandish painter, active in his native Amsterdam and in Antwerp. A pioneer of still life and *genre painting, he is best known for scenes that at first glance look like pure examples of these types, but which in fact have a religious scene incorporated in them (*Butcher's Shop with the Flight into Egypt*, Univ. of Uppsala, 1551). Aertsen was the head of a long dynasty of painters, of whom the most talented was his nephew and pupil Joachim *Bueckelaer.

Aestheticism. A term applied to various exaggerations of the doctrine that art is self-sufficient and need serve no ulterior purpose, whether moral, political, or religious. Both the doctrine and its exaggerations have found expression in the phrase 'art for art's sake', which in England became the catchword of the 'Aesthetic Movement' in the late 19th-cent. Central figures of the movement included *Whistler and Oscar Wilde, both of them notorious dandies, and the movement was frequently ridiculed for its tendency towards preciousness and affectation, most notably in Gilbert and Sullivan's *Patience* (1881). Nevertheless, the movement helped to focus attention on the formal qualities of works of art, and so contributed to the critical outlook of writers such as *Berenson and *Fry.

aesthetics. The branch of philosophy that deals with questions of beauty and taste. The term, which derives from a Greek word meaning 'to perceive', was coined by the German philosopher Alexander Gottlieb Baumgarten (1714–62), the author of a two-volume Latin treatise called *Aesthetica* (1750–8). It is usually used in connection with the arts, but it can also embrace beauty in nature.

Agam, Yaacov (Jacob Gipstein) (1928–   ). Israeli sculptor and experimental artist, based in Paris from 1951. In 1955 Agam participated, with *Bury, *Tinguely, *Calder, and other artists, in the exhibition 'Le Mouvement' at the Denise René Gallery, considered the definitive exhibition for the *Kinetic movement, and from this time he was recognized as a pioneer in those branches of non-figurative art which lay stress on movement and spectator participation. Agam often uses light and sound effects in conjunction with his sculptures, and sometimes the components of his works can be rearranged by the spectator. He has made works for major public buildings in France and elsewhere.

Agasse, Jacques-Laurent (1767–1849). Swiss-born animal painter who settled permanently in England in 1800 and became one of the principal successors to *Stubbs. He studied veterinary science in Paris as well as painting (with J.-L. *David) and his work is distinguished by anatomical accuracy as well as grace of line. Although Agasse was initially successful in England (George IV was among his patrons), he died poor and virtually forgotten. The Musée d'Art et d'Histoire in his native Geneva has the best collection of his work.

Agostino di Duccio (1418–81). Florentine sculptor and architect. He was the most original if not the greatest sculptor of his time, and the only 15th-cent. sculptor born at Florence who owed little to *Donatello or *Ghiberti. His fresh and lively style was linear and graceful, with distinctive swirling draperies. *Reliefs at Modena Cathedral executed by 1442 are accepted as his earliest work. Some have seen in them indications of a debt to Jacopo della *Quercia, and others of possible training by Luca della *Robbia. In 1446 he was banished from Florence for theft and from c.1450 to 1457 he worked on the sculptural reliefs for the Tempio Malatestiano at Rimini (see MALATESTA). His other memorable large work is the series of reliefs, partly in *terracotta, on the façade of the Oratory of S. Bernadino at Perugia, on which he worked c.1457–61, as architect as well as sculptor. Agostino also executed several delightful reliefs of the Virgin and Child.

air brush. An instrument for spraying paint or varnish by means of compressed air. It looks rather like an outsize fountain pen and is operated in a similar fashion, the pressure of the forefinger on a lever regulating the air supply. It can be controlled so as to give large areas of flat colour, delicate gradations of tone, or a fairly fine line. Although most often associated with commercial artists, it is also used by painters such as *Hard Edge Abstractionists and *Superrealists, who require a very smooth finish.

alabaster. Soft, semi-transparent stone (a form of gypsum) extensively used in sculpture in the later Middle Ages. Its most notable use was in small *retables, which were made in great numbers in England, many of them for export—they were sent even as far as Italy, Spain, and Russia. The best collection of such retables is in the Victoria and Albert Museum, London, and other fine examples are in the Castle Museum at Nottingham, a town that was famed for its 'alabastermen'. The production of religious images was cut off abruptly by the Reformation, but some tombs continued to be carved in alabaster until the 18th cent. Some modern sculptors, for example Henry *Moore, have used alabaster for small-scale sculptures.

Albani, Cardinal Alessandro (1692–1779). Italian churchman, the leading collector and art patron in Rome in his day. He came from a distinguished family that included several cardinals and also Pope Clement XI, but he led a worldly life and was notorious for his lucrative dealings in the art market, not hesitating to have works heavily restored if it made them sell better. With the help of his librarian *Winckelmann, he made a fine collection of *antique sculpture, much of which is now in the Glyptothek at Munich. It was housed in his villa in Rome, where *Mengs painted his famous ceiling painting *Parnassus* (1761), one of the key works of *Neoclassicism.

Albani (or **Albano**), **Francesco** (1578–1660). Bolognese painter. After a period in the studio of Denis *Calvaert and subsequently in the *Carracci academy, he moved to Rome (c.1600), where he collaborated with Annibale Carracci and *Domenichino on various decorative schemes, including work in the Palazzo Farnese. In 1616 he returned to Bologna and produced, besides altarpieces, many allegorical paintings and idyllic landscapes in a charmingly light-hearted style which proved very popular in England in the 18th cent.

Albers, Josef (1888–1976). German-American painter and designer. He studied and taught at the *Bauhaus, where his activities embraced stained glass, typography, and designing furniture and utility objects. When the Bauhaus closed in 1933 he made his first visit to the newly founded experimental Black Mountain College in North Carolina. Albers was one of the first of the Bauhaus teachers to emigrate to the USA (he became an American citizen in 1939) and one of the most active in propagating Bauhaus ideas there, teaching at Harvard and Yale as well as Black Mountain College. As a painter Albers was best known for his long series, begun in 1950, entitled *Homage to the Square*. The paintings in this series consisted of squares within squares of closely calculated sizes and subtly varied hues. The research into colour which they embodied was published in *Interaction of Color* (1963), and his disciplined ideas and techniques were influential on *Op art.

Alberti, Leon Battista (1404–72). Italian architect, sculptor, painter, and writer, the most important art theorist of the *Renaissance. Born in Genoa, the illegitimate son of an exiled Florentine merchant, he was educated at Padua and Bologna, and proved himself a precocious scholar. In about 1428 he went to Florence and became a friend of the most advanced artists—*Brunelleschi, *Donatello, *Ghiberti, Luca della *Robbia, and *Masaccio. To all these, jointly, he dedicated his first theoretical work on the arts, *Della Pittura* (1436). (This was initially written in Latin as *De Pictura*, but Alberti translated it into Italian for Brunelleschi's benefit.) Alberti wrote on a wide variety of other topics, complementing *Della Pittura* with treatises on architecture (*De Re Aedificatoria*) and sculpture (*De Statua*). He worked on *De Re Aedificatoria* until his death and it became the first printed book on architecture in 1485: *De Statua* is generally dated to the 1460s. In these works Alberti turned away from the medieval outlook in which art was considered a symbolic expression of theological truths. Instead he emphasized the rational basis of the arts, and the necessity for the artist to have a thorough grounding in such 'sciences' as history, poetry, and mathematics. Alberti spent most of his life in Florence and Rome (he held a secretarial post in the papal court from 1432 to 1464), and he worked as an architect in both these places as well as in Mantua and Rimini. His buildings—among them the churches of S. Andrea and S. Sebastiano in Mantua, and the façade of Sta. Maria Novella and the Palazzo Rucellai

in Florence—are among the outstanding architectural works of the early Renaissance, but almost no trace survives of his work as a painter or sculptor. Two self-portrait plaques are attributed to him (Louvre, Paris, and NG, Washington), but no paintings are extant.

Albertinelli, Mariotto (1474–1515). Florentine painter, trained by Cosimo *Rosselli, in whose studio he met Fra *Bartolommeo. The two went into partnership in 1508, but soon after this Albertinelli abandoned painting to become an inn keeper, saying (according to *Vasari) that he was fed up with criticism and wanted a 'less difficult and more cheerful craft'. His paintings are elegant but rather insipid.

Albright, Ivan Le Lorraine (1897–1983). American painter, the son of **Adam Emery Albright** (1862–1957), a painter who had studied under *Eakins. During the First World War Albright served in France as a medical draughtsman and worked with a meticulous detail and clinical precision that anticipated his later style, which shows a morbid obsession with death and corruption evoking a poignant impression of melancholy for a beauty that is past. Two of the paintings that Albright considered among his most important works are in the Art Institute of Chicago: *That Which I Should Have Done I Did Not Do* (1931–41) and *Portrait of Mary Block* (1955–6). In the same collection is the painting Albright did for the Hollywood film (1943) of Oscar Wilde's *The Picture of Dorian Gray*, showing the loathsomely corrupted title figure; Albright's identical twin brother, **Malvin Marr Albright** (1897–), did the portrait of the young and beautiful Dorian for this film.

Aldegrever, Heinrich (1502–c.1555). German engraver and painter, one of the leading artists in the Westphalia of his day. His numerous engravings, usually of religious subjects, betray the all-pervading influence of *Dürer. Little is known of his activity as a painter.

Alechinsky, Pierre (1927–). Belgian painter and graphic artist. In 1947 he became a member of *Jeune Peinture Belge and in 1949 joined the *Cobra group. He left Cobra in 1951 and settled in Paris, where he studied graphic techniques under S. W. *Hayter. In 1955 he travelled to the Far East and produced a film *Calligraphie japonaise*. Alechinsky paints in a style of vigorous, even violent, expressive abstraction which has close affinities with Nordic *Expressionism. Residual figurative motifs remained constant to his work, and these were redolent of a turbulent fantasy, often approaching *Surrealism and also showing a strong debt to *Ensor.

Algardi, Alessandro (1598–1654). Italian sculptor, born in Bologna, where he had his initial training in the *Carracci academy. He settled in Rome in 1625 and became, apart from *Bernini, the most outstanding sculptor in the city. During the pontificate of Innocent X (1644–55) Bernini was out of favour and Algardi replaced him at the papal court. His principal works are the tomb of Leo XI (Alessandro de' *Medici) (1634–44) and the huge relief of *Pope Leo driving Attila from Rome* (1646–53), both in St Peter's, Rome, and the free-standing group of *The Decapitation of St Paul* (1641–7) in S. Paolo, Bologna. He was a prolific sculptor of portrait *busts, and these are his works that are now generally most admired—indeed he ranks as one of the greatest portrait sculptors of all time. His style was generally more sober and Classical than Bernini's (although portraits have occasionally been disputed between them), reflecting his Bolognese upbringing, his work as a restorer of antique statuary, and his friendship with artists such as *Domenichino, *Duquesnoy, *Poussin, and *Sacchi.

Algarotti, Francesco (1712–64). The foremost Italian art critic of his day, a cosmopolitan snob of great charm, whose friendship with some of the leading men of Europe—notably the French philosopher Voltaire and Frederick the Great of Prussia—played a part in spreading Venetian culture. His writings proclaimed a watered-down version of the *Neoclassicism which was then gaining ground in Europe (though not yet in Venice). For some years he influenced the practice of his friends *Tiepolo ('restraining his wilder fantasies' as he claimed) and *Canaletto (encouraging his architectural *capricci), as well as *Piazzetta and other Venetian

painters. He was also a notable collector of paintings and drawings.

Alken. Family of British sporting artists of Danish origin. **Samuel Alken** senior (1750–1815) did hunting and sporting landscapes in the manner of *Stubbs. He was the father of **Samuel** junior (1784–1825) and of **Henry** (1785–1851), the latter of whom became one of the most prolific sporting painters and illustrators of his time. His gaunt but sprightly style was already archaic in his day, but he excelled at representing the life and movement of the hunting field. The great popularity of coloured *aquatints after his paintings (some of them produced under the name 'Ben Tally-Ho') has persisted. His publications included *National Sports of Great Britain* (1820) and *The Art and Practice of Etching* (1849). He had four sons, among them **Henry Gordon Alken** (1810–92), with whose work his own is often confused.

Allan, David (1744–96). Scottish portrait and *genre painter. He was in Italy 1764–7, studying with Gavin *Hamilton and winning a prize for history painting at the Academy of St Luke in Rome. In 1770–80 he worked in London, then settled in Edinburgh as a painter of portraits and *conversation pieces. When abroad he had made studies of French and Italian peasants and he painted scenes of Scottish life in a similar vein, which earned him the misleading title of 'the Scottish *Hogarth'. Such works influenced *Wilkie.

Allan, Sir William (1782–1850). Scottish historical painter, who travelled extensively in Russia, the Middle East, and elsewhere, before settling in Edinburgh in 1814. His accuracy of detail and exotic subject matter satisfied the same appetite as did the novels of Sir Walter Scott, who was Allan's enthusiastic supporter. *The Black Dwarf* (NG, Edinburgh) is an illustration to Scott's novel of that name. With *Wilkie, Allan did much to establish the vogue for historical *genre painting in Scotland.

alla prima. Method of painting, primarily in oils, in which the paint is applied directly to the ground, without underpainting, and the finished surface is achieved with a single application of *pigments. *Alla prima* is Italian for 'at first'; synonymous terms are 'direct painting', 'wet on wet', and the

French *au premier coup* (at first stroke). Direct painting was practised from the 17th cent. (for example by *Hals), but it was not until the middle of the 19th cent. that it became the chief method in oil painting. Its growing popularity was connected with the availability of commercial paints of a buttery consistency, as well as with Romantic ideas about spontaneity of expression.

Allied Artists' Association. A group of British artists formed in 1908 by the critic Frank Rutter and artists in *Sickert's circle for the purpose of organizing annual exhibitions of independent progressive painters in the jury-free manner of the French *Salon des Indépendants. *Brancusi, *Kandinsky and *Zadkine received the first British showing of their works at these exhibitions. In addition to *Sickert, the Association included Spencer *Gore, Harold *Gilman, Lucien *Pissarro, Augustus *John, Henry *Lamb, and Charles *Ginner. It was from the Allied Artists' Association that the *Camden Town Group emerged in 1911.

Allori, Alessandro (1535–1607). Florentine painter, the pupil and adopted son of *Bronzino. An early visit to Rome added the influence of late *Michelangelo paintings to that of his master's courtly *Mannerism. *The Pearl Fishers* (Studiolo of Francesco I, Palazzo Vecchio, Florence, *c.*1570) is generally considered his masterpiece; playful and full of artifice, it combines nude figures obviously drawn from Michelangelo with Bronzino's svelteness and enamelled colouring. His son **Cristofano** (1577–1621) was one of the leading Florentine painters of his period. He is remembered primarily for one work, *Judith with the Head of Holofernes* (*c.*1615, Pitti, Florence, and other versions), in which his *femme fatale* mistress is portrayed as Judith and he has depicted his own features in Holofernes' severed head. The Ashmolean Museum in Oxford possesses portraits by both Alessandro and Cristofano Allori.

All-over painting. A type of painting in which the whole surface of the canvas is treated in a relatively uniform manner and traditional ideas of composition—of the picture having a top, bottom, or centre—are abandoned. First used of the 'drip' paintings of Jackson *Pollock, the term

has since been applied to pictures where the overall treatment of the canvas is relatively uniform, whether relying on texture or on 'scribbled' material as with Cy *Twombly or on colour as with the *Colour Field painters.

Allston, Washington (1779–1843). American painter and writer, considered the most important artistic personality of the first generation of *Romanticism in the USA. Samuel Taylor Coleridge, who met him in Rome and whose portrait Allston painted (NPG, London), considered him 'a man of . . . high and rare genius . . . whether I contemplate him in the character of a Poet, a Painter, or a Philosophic Analyst'. Allston spent his working life in Boston apart from two lengthy visits to Europe: during the first, 1801–8, he studied under Benjamin *West at the *Royal Academy, subsequently visiting France with John *Vanderlyn; the second stay in England was from 1811 to 1818. Up to *c.*1818 his Romanticism expressed itself in the grandiose and dramatic, and his large canvases exploited the mysterious, monumental, and terrific aspects of nature (*The Rising of a Thunderstorm at Sea*, Mus. of Fine Arts, Boston, 1804). In his later period he was a forerunner of the subjective and visionary trend in American landscape painting, which relied more upon mood and reverie than upon observation or drama, as in his famous *Moonlight Landscape* (Mus. of Fine Arts, Boston, 1819). Through his pupil *Morse his art of poetic mood became indigenous in the USA. Allston's writing included poetry, a Gothic novel entitled *Monaldi* (1841), and the posthumously published *Lectures on Art* (1850).

Alma-Tadema, Sir Lawrence (1836–1912). Dutch painter who settled in London in 1870 and took British nationality in 1873. He specialized in historical genre scenes, beginning with medieval subjects, but then—following a visit to Pompeii in 1863—turning to the ancient world. His paintings evoke a Hollywood vision of ancient Greece and Rome (and sometimes Egypt), with their sensuous depiction of beautiful women, exotic costumes, and marbled settings—*Punch* called him a 'marbellous artist'. They were enormously successful and he had a sumptuous lifestyle in his house in St John's Wood, which had previously been owned by *Tissot and which Alma-Tadema remodelled as a Roman villa. He was knighted in 1899 and received the Order of Merit in 1905. His success encouraged several imitators, including his wife **Laura** (1852–1909), his daughter **Anna** (d. 1943), and painters such as John William Godward (1861–1922) and Edwin Long (1829–91). However, Alma-Tadema's work went completely out of favour after his death, and his reputation has only recently revived.

altarpiece. A picture, sculpture, screen, or decorated wall standing on or behind an altar in a Christian church. They vary enormously in size and conception, from tiny portable pictures to huge structures embracing the arts of architecture, sculpture, and painting. They do, however, divide into two main types: the reredos, which rises from ground level behind the altar; and the retable, which stands either on the back of the altar itself or on a pedestal behind it. Many altars have both.

Altdorfer, Albrecht (c.1480–1538). German painter and graphic artist working in Regensburg, of which town he was a citizen from 1505 onwards, the leading artist of the so-called *Danube School. His training is unknown, but his early work was influenced by *Cranach and *Dürer's art too was known to him through the woodcuts and engravings. Mingled with these German impressions was a knowledge of the art of *Mantegna, perhaps through the mediation of Michael *Pacher. Yet in spite of these varied influences Altdorfer's style always remained personal. Most of his paintings are religious works, but he was one of the first artists to show an interest in landscape as an independent genre. In works such as the altar for S. Florian near Linz (1518) or the *Christ Taking Leave of His Mother* (NG, London) he achieved a wonderful unity of mood between action and landscape, and two pure landscape paintings (without any figures) by him are known (NG, London, and Alte Pinakothek, Munich). His patrons included the emperor Maximilian and Louis X, Duke of Bavaria, for whom he painted the celebrated *Battle of Issus* (Alte Pinakothek, Munich, 1529), which formed part of a large series of famous battle-pieces from Classical antiquity. With its dazzling light effects, teeming figures, and brilliant colours, it is one of the finest examples of Altdorfer's rich imaginative powers. From 1526 until his death Altdorfer was employed as town architect of Regensburg. No architectural work by him is known, but his interest in architecture and his skill in handling intricate problems of *perspective are demonstrated by his *Birth of the Virgin* (Alte Pinakothek, Munich).

Altichiero (active 1372–84). Italian painter. He probably came from Zevio near Verona and is sometimes considered to be the founder of the Veronese School, although the only surviving example of his work in that town is a fresco in Sta Anastasia. Most of his surviving work is in Padua, where he had a hand in fresco cycles in the Basilica of St Anthony (between 1372 and 1379) and in the Oratory of St George (between 1377 and 1384), in the latter of which he collaborated with an artist called Avanzo, who is otherwise unknown and whose contribution to the work is uncertain. Altichiero's gravity and the solidity and voluminousness of his figures clearly reveal his debt to *Giotto's frescos in the Arena Chapel of Padua. But his pageant-like scenes with their elaborate architectural views express the taste of the late 14th cent. for *Gothic intricacy, while his naturalism in the study of plants and animals formed the point of departure for a new style which is reflected in *Pisanello.

Álvarez y Cubero, José (1768–1827). The leading Spanish sculptor of the *Neoclassical period, sometimes called 'the Spanish *Canova'. After studying at Granada, Madrid, and Paris he settled in Rome (1805–25), where Canova befriended him. He preferred Classical themes such as *Nestor and Antilochus* (Modern Art Mus., Madrid, 1818), but was also an accomplished portrait sculptor.

Amberger, Christoph (d. 1562). German portrait painter. He worked in Augsburg, which had many cultural and economic ties with Italy (he met *Titian when he visited the city in 1548), and his style emulates the grand manner of the Venetian School, paying as much attention to rich effects of dress and jewellery as to psychological subtlety (*Charles V*, Staatliche Museen, Berlin, c.1532). His rare figure compositions (*Virgin and Child between Saints Ulrich and Afra*, Augsburg Cathedral, 1554) are less distinguished.

American Abstract Artists. An association of American abstract painters and sculptors formed in 1936 with the aims of making New York a centre for *abstract art. The group held annual exhibitions and disseminated the principles of abstract art by lectures, publications, etc. Among the early members were: Josef *Albers, Willem *de Kooning, and David *Smith. By the mid 1940s the battle was won, and the activities of the association dwindled. In the 1950s, however, it became active again with more than 200 members.

American Scene painting. Term applied to the work of various painters who in the 1920s and 1930s depicted aspects of American life and landscape in a naturalistic, descriptive style. The term does not signify an organized movement, but rather an aspect of a broad tendency for American artists to move away from abstraction and the avant-garde in the period between the two world wars. *Burchfield and *Hopper are among the best known exponents of American Scene painting, and the *Regionalists, who were more self-conscious in their nationalism, are also embraced by the term.

Amigoni, Jacopo (c.1682–1752). Italian *Rococo decorative painter and portraitist. He was born in Naples, formed his style in Venice, and had an international career, working in Bavaria, England, Flanders, France, and Spain. His English sojourn lasted from 1730 to 1739 (with a break for a visit to Paris in 1736), his finest surviving work from this period being a series of four paintings on the Story of Jupiter and Io at Moor Park (now Moor Park Golf Club) in Hertfordshire. He was the last of the Venetian decorators to come to England, in the wake of *Pellegrini and the *Ricci, for the demand for large-scale decorative painting was fairly short-lived. Amigoni, however, earned a good living with his portraits, and it was he who persuaded *Canaletto to try his fortune in England.

Amman, Jost (1539–91). Swiss engraver, born in Zurich and active mainly in Nuremberg, Germany. He was perhaps the most prolific book illustrator of his day and one of his pupils boasted that he produced more drawings in four years than could be carted away in a hay-wagon.

His woodcuts and engravings are more important as documents of contemporary life than for their artistic value and his Panoplia Omnium Artium (1568) in particular contains a wealth of evidence on contemporary crafts.

Ammanati, Bartolommeo (1511–92). Florentine *Mannerist architect and sculptor, strongly influenced by *Michelangelo and by *Sansovino, on whose Library in Venice he worked. His best-known works in Florence are the Ponte Sta Trinità (1567–70), destroyed during the Second World War, but rebuilt, and his additions to the *Pitti Palace (1558–70), including the rusticated courtyard. In sculpture his chief work is the rather ponderous fountain (1560–75) in the Piazza della Signoria, Florence, with its marble Neptune and bronze Nymphs. Ammanati beat several sculptors, including *Cellini and *Giambologna, in a competition for this commission, but the work was not well received. In old age, influenced by Counter-Reformation piety, he wrote a recantation of his secular works and destroyed some. He was married to Laura Battiferri, a poet who was the subject of a memorable portrait by *Bronzino.

anamorphosis. A picture (or a part of one) executed in such a way that it gives a distorted image of the object represented until it is seen from a particular angle or by means of a special lens or mirror, when it appears in lifelike aspect. Anamorphosis is first mentioned in the notes of *Leonardo da Vinci, and probably the most famous example of its use is in *Holbein's The Ambassadors (NG, London, 1533), which features a distorted skull, probably a symbol of the brevity of life. Generally, however, the purpose of anamorphosis was to mystify or amuse, and it rarely occurs in major works such as this.

Ancients. Group of English *Romantic artists active for about a decade in the 1820s and 1830s. The leading member of the group was Samuel *Palmer; others included Edward *Calvert and George *Richmond. The name derives from their passion for the medieval world, but they concentrated on pastoral subjects, sharing the mystical outlook of their inspiration, William *Blake.

Andre, Carl (1935–). American *Minimal sculptor. He produces his works by stacking identical ready-made commercial units such as bricks, cement blocks, etc., according to a mathematically imposed modular system. From *c.*1965 he abjured height and made his arrangements as horizontal configurations on the ground. He also became one of the pioneers of *Earthwork art. In England Andre is best known for the sensational publicity accompanying 'the Tate bricks' incident in 1976. His *Equivalent VIII* (1966) (consisting of 120 bricks arranged two deep in a rectangle) was vandalized and there was an outcry about the alleged wastage of public money on its purchase by the Tate Gallery.

Andrea da Firenze (Andrea Bonaiuti) (active *c.*1343–77). Florentine painter, responsible for the remarkable frescos in the Spanish Chapel of Sta Maria Novella, a church of the Dominican Order. The frescos illustrate the Triumph of the Faith and the Dominican doctrine, and both their severity and their meticulous detail accorded with the expository style of the Dominican preaching friars. Andrea is last recorded in 1377 working on frescos of the *Life of St Raynerius* in the Campo Santo at Pisa.

Andrea del Castagno (Andrea di Bartolo di Bargilla) (*c.*1421–57). One of the most powerful Florentine painters in the generation after *Masaccio. In 1440 he is said to have painted frescos at the Palazzo del Podestà of rebels against Cosimo de' *Medici who were sentenced to be hanged by the heels after the Battle of Anghiari, earning him the sobriquet Andreino degli Impiccati (of the hanged men). These have been destroyed, and Andrea's earliest known surviving works are frescos in the church of Sta Zaccaria in Venice (1442). By 1444 he was back in Florence, designing a stained-glass window for the cathedral, and soon after he began his greatest work, a series of frescos on Christ's Passion for the monastery of Sta Apollonia (now a Castagno Mus.), dominated by one of the most celebrated of all portrayals of The Last Supper. In their emotional vigour and sinewy realism these paintings have been regarded as the pictorial equivalent of the sculpture of *Donatello, but they also have something of Masaccio's monumentality.

Andrea's other noteworthy works in Florence include the *St Julian* (SS. Annunziata, 1454–5), an equestrian portrait—*Niccolò da Tolentino*—a pendant to *Uccello's earlier fresco of Sir John Hawkwood in the cathedral, and an extraordinarily intense pair of altar frescos for SS. Annunziata (*c.*1455). *Vasari started the rumour that Castagno murdered his friend *Domenico Veneziano, and it was not until the 19th cent. that it was discovered that Castagno had died early of the plague and that Domenico in fact had outlived him. The story, however, makes it easy to believe that the intensity of his work reflected a fierce temperament.

Andrea del Sarto (1486–1530). Florentine painter. The epithet 'del sarto' (of the tailor) is derived from his father's profession; his real name was Andrea d'Agnolo di Francesco. After an apprenticeship under *Piero di Cosimo he soon absorbed the poised and graceful style developed by Fra *Bartolommeo and *Raphael in Florence during the first decade of the 16th cent., and following the departures of *Leonardo, Raphael, and *Michelangelo (all of whom had left Florence by 1509) he became established with Bartolommeo as the leading painter of the city. Apart from a visit to France in 1518–19, Andrea was based in Florence all his life, although he probably visited Rome soon after his return from France, and made short visits elsewhere. He excelled as a fresco decorator (there are outstanding examples in Florence in SS. Annunziata and the Chiostro dello Scalzo), and he also painted superb altarpieces (*The Madonna of the Harpies*, Uffizi, Florence, 1517) and portraits (*A Young Man*, NG, London). His reputation was largely made and marred by *Vasari, who said that Andrea's works were 'faultless' but represented him as a weakling completely under the thumb of his wicked wife. In Robert Browning's poem on the painter (1855) and in a psychoanalytic essay by Freud's disciple Ernest Jones (1913) attempts are made to link a supposed lack of vigour in his mellifluous art with these traits of character. This, however, is hardly just and a good deal of Vasari's account of Andrea's private life has been shown to be factually inaccurate (the scandal-mongering is mainly in the 1550 edition of his book and was suppressed in the 1568 edition). Andrea has suffered from being the contemporary of such giants as Michelangelo and Raphael, but he undoubtedly ranks as one of the greatest masters of his time. In grandeur and gracefulness he approaches Raphael, and he had a feel for colour and atmosphere that was unrivalled among Florentine painters of his period. He also numbers among the finest draughtsmen of the Renaissance (the best collection of his drawings is in the Uffizi). Certain features of his art foreshadow the *Mannerist experiments of his great pupils *Pontormo and *Rosso Fiorentino.

Angelico, Fra (Guido di Pietro) (c.1400–55). Florentine painter, a Dominican friar. Although in popular tradition he has been seen as 'not an artist properly so-called but an inspired saint' (*Ruskin), Angelico was in fact a highly professional artist, who was in touch with the most advanced developments in contemporary Florentine art and in later life travelled extensively for prestigious commissions. He probably began his career as a manuscript *illuminator, and his early paintings are strongly influenced by *International Gothic. But even in the most lavishly decorative of them all—the *Annunciation* in the Diocesan Museum in Cortona—*Masaccio's influence is evident in the insistent perspective of the architecture. For most of his career Angelico was based in S. Domenico in Fiesole (he became Prior there in 1450), but his most famous works were painted at S. Marco in Florence (now an Angelico museum), a Sylvestrine monastery which was taken over by his Order in 1436. He and his assistants painted about fifty frescos in the friary (c.1438–45) that are at once the expression of and a guide to the spiritual life of the community. Many of the frescos are in the friars' cells and were intended as aids to devotion; with their immaculate colouring, their economy in drawing and composition, and their freedom from the accidents of time and place, they attain a sense of blissful serenity. In the last decade of his life Angelico also worked in Orvieto and Perugia, and most importantly in Rome, where he frescoed the private chapel of Pope Nicholas V in the Vatican with *Scenes from the Lives of SS. Stephen and Lawrence* (1447–50). These differ considerably from the S. Marco frescos, with new emphasis on the story and on circumstantial detail, bringing Angelico more clearly into the

mainstream of 15th-cent. Italian fresco painting. Angelico died in Rome and was buried in the church of S. Maria sopra Minerva, where his tombstone still exists. His most important pupil was Benozzo *Gozzoli and he had considerable influence on Italian painting. His particular grace and sweetness stimulated the school of Perugia, and Fra *Bartolommeo, who followed him into the Convento di S. Marco in 1500, had something of his restraint and grandeur. *Vasari, who referred to Fra Giovanni as 'a simple and most holy man', popularized the use of the name Angelico for him, but he says it is the name by which he was always known, and it was certainly used as early as 1469. The painter has long been called 'Beato Angelico' (the Blessed Angelico), but his beatification was not made official by the Vatican until 1984.

Angry Penguins. An Australian avant-garde journal (1940–6) devoted to arts and letters. It provided support for an Australian type of *Expressionism with allegorical and regional qualities, and fostered the early work of such artists as Sidney *Nolan and Arthur *Boyd. In 1944 the journal was the victim of a celebrated hoax when it devoted an issue to the poems of the non-existent 'Ern Malley', whose works were concocted from arbitrarily selected quotations.

Anguier, François (c.1604–69) and **Michel** (c.1613–86). French sculptors, brothers, who stood apart from the mainstream which in the middle of the 17th cent. was dominated by *Sarrazin. They went to Rome about 1641 and joined the studio of *Algardi. On their return to France (François in 1643, Michel in 1651), the brothers collaborated on the tomb of Henry de Montmorency in the chapel of the Lycée at Moulins (1648–52), which reveals the new Roman influence they introduced into France. Later the two brothers worked mainly apart, Michel having the more interesting career. His work includes the decoration of the interior of the church of the Val-de-Grâce, Paris (1662–7), and the Nativity group in St Roch, Paris (1665).

Anguisciola, Sofonisba (c.1530–1625). Italian portrait painter, one of six painter-sisters from Cremona. She was the first woman artist to achieve international renown, being called to Spain by Philip II and visited by van *Dyck in Genoa in 1623, when she was in her nineties. Her self-portraits and portraits of her family are considered her finest works; they are somewhat stiff, but can have great charm.

Angus, Rita (1908–70). New Zealand painter, mainly of portraits and landscapes. She was considered one of the leading figures in New Zealand art, particularly in the 1940s. Working in both oils and water-colours, she painted in a forthright, brightly coloured style. She also painted under her married name, Rita Cook.

Annigoni, Pietro (1910–88). Italian painter. Although he valued his religious and allegorical works most highly, he became internationally famous for his portraits, particularly those of members of the British royal family. They are generally dismissed by critics as tasteless and portentously inflated, but they are enormously popular with the general public. His meticulous technique was based on Italian *Renaissance art and he often worked in *tempera and (for his church decorations) in *fresco.

Anquetin, Louis (1861–1932). French painter. He was a friend of Van *Gogh and *Toulouse-Lautrec (fellow-students in *Cormon's studio), and with *Bernard he was one of the pioneers of *cloisonnism. After about 1890, however, Anquetin's work was much more traditional, and he became interested in research into the techniques of the Old Masters, notably *Rubens.

Antal, Frederick (1887–1954). Hungarian-born art historian who settled in England in 1933 and became a British citizen in 1946. He was deeply interested in historical methodology, and is regarded as the leading exponent of an approach that attempted to apply the Marxist interpretation of history to the arts. His views are most fully expressed in *Florentine Painting and its Social Background* (1948), in which he argues that developments in style and subject matter were directly influenced by social and political changes. The book was widely admired, but it was also attacked as being over-rigid in the way it linked

artistic phenomena with social and economic causes. Antal's other books include the posthumously published *Hogarth and his Place in European Art* (1962), in which he applied his methods more subtly and flexibly, revealing his fascination with *Hogarth as an expression of English middle-class morality and culture. A collection of his articles, *Classicism and Romanticism, with Other Studies in Art History* (1966), includes 'Remarks on the Method of Art History', which is a statement of his own credo. Antal never held a regular teaching post in England (he occasionally lectured at the *Courtauld Institute), but he was an influential figure.

Antelami, Benedetto (active late 12th cent.). Italian *Romanesque sculptor, the most notable figure in the history of Italian sculpture before Nicola *Pisano. His name first appears on a marble panel representing the *Descent from the Cross* (1178) in Parma Cathedral. He is chiefly known for his *reliefs on the doors of the Baptistery at Parma, which was begun in 1196, and it has been suggested that he may have overseen the whole structure as architect as well as sculptor. On stylistic grounds he has also been credited with a hand in the sculptural decorations of Fidenza Cathedral (formerly Borgo San Donnino) and of S. Andrea at Vercelli. His elongated figures, compact compositions, and skilful use of drapery folds give his work a gravity and dramatic expressiveness hitherto unknown to north Italian sculpture.

Anthonisz., Cornelis (c.1499–after 1556). Netherlandish painter, etcher, and designer of woodcuts. He was active in Amsterdam and in 1544 made a large map of that city, now in the Weigh House there. He worked as a cartographer in the service of the emperor Charles V and also painted group portraits, most notably *The Civic Guard* (Historical Mus., Amsterdam, 1533), an early example of a type in which *Hals was later to specialize.

Antico (Pier Jacopo Alari Bonacolsi) (c.1460–1528). Italian sculptor, goldsmith, and medallist. His nickname derived from his Classically inspired statuettes, which won him great popularity (he also restored ancient sculpture). He visited Rome in the 1490s, but worked mainly in and around his native Mantua, particularly for the *Gonzaga family and Isabella d' *Este.

Antinous. A representation in sculpture of the beautiful youth of this name who was a favourite of the emperor Hadrian. After Antinous was drowned while accompanying Hadrian up the Nile in AD 130 his name became surrounded by romantic legend, and the grief-stricken emperor commemorated him in lavish fashion. He founded a city called Antinoöpolis in Egypt, erected temples in his memory, and had him honoured in festivals. Antinous was frequently represented in sculpture, sometimes as Apollo or Dionysus, and several examples survive; typically he is shown with curly hair and a sad-sweet expression, although the identification is not always certain, and the title 'Antinous' has sometimes been given generally to figures of beautiful and graceful youths. Particularly famous were the *Belvedere Antinous* (Vatican Museums), which was regarded as one of the standards of male beauty (for *Bernini's views on it, see ANTIQUE), and a relief (Villa Albani, Rome) excavated at Hadrian's Villa at Tivoli in 1735. It was one of the greatest treasures of Cardinal *Albani and was regarded by his librarian *Winckelmann as one of the peaks of ancient art.

Antipodeans. The name adopted by a group of Australian painters who held an exhibition and published a manifesto in 1959 which championed the figurative image and was critical of abstract art. The best-known member of the group was Arthur *Boyd.

antique, the. The physical remains of the Greek and Roman world, or more particularly the remains of antique sculpture, which have been for later artists an inspiration, a challenge, and a canon of perfection. Such remains have never been totally absent and seldom totally disregarded. Memories of Classical ornament or drapery forms recur throughout the Middle Ages, but it was in Renaissance Italy that the recovery of the Classical antique as a Golden Age in the past became a deliberate ideal. *Ghiberti's writings, for example, testify to his admiration for antique statues and *cameos and much of *Donatello's work would be unthinkable without a close study of the antique.

*Vasari attributed the attainment of perfection by the generation of *Leonardo, *Michelangelo, and *Raphael in no small measure to the discovery of the famous antiques of the Vatican collection, notably the *Apollo Belvedere* and the *Laocöon* (found 1506), though it was mainly the next generation, particularly visitors from northern Europe (*Heemskerck for example), who systematically drew after the antique. Towards the middle of the 16th cent. the role of the antique in the curriculum of artists became firmly established. Giovanni Armenini in his *De' Veri Precetti della Pittura* (1587) already gives a list of 'canonic' antiques, including the famous *Belvedere Torso*, and such works were carried by means of engravings, casts, and copies into every artist's studio. The philosophical justification for this dependence on antique models was given in *Bellori's famous oration, *Idea* (1664), where he claimed in the ancient statuary a revelation of an absolute beauty that had been discovered once and for all (see IDEAL). To the followers of the academic doctrine each of the great antiques, to which now had to be added the *Farnese Hercules*, the *Borghese Warrior*, the *Medici Venus*, and the *Barberini Faun*, represented a type of physique that could serve as a permanent standard for the artist. Nor was antique influence confined to those artists whose work was most obviously Classical (such as *Poussin). *Bernini, for example, when he addressed the Academy in Paris in 1666, said 'In my early youth I drew a great deal from Classical figures, and when I was in difficulties with my first statue I turned to the *Antinous* as to the oracle.' Reverence for the antique was given a new lease of life when the *Neoclassical movement reacted against the frivolities of *Rococo fashions. In opposition to earlier ideas, *Winckelmann preached the belief that Classical artists had deliberately avoided representing extreme passions, and he regarded the antique less as a source of expressive formulas than as a model of noble restraint. The authority of the antique declined with the onset of *Romanticism, with its stress on self-expression, but its influence has still continued. Drawing from casts of antique sculpture remained a part of most official art training into the 20th cent., and *Picasso, for example, often drew on Classical art as a source of inspiration; in particular, his

'Neoclassical' paintings of the 1920s owed much to visits to the Archaeological Museum in Naples.

Antolínez, José (1635–75). Spanish painter, born and active in Madrid. Like *Murillo in Seville, he had a penchant for paintings of the Immaculate Conception, and his colourful, sweet style has much in common with Murillo's. His temperament was anything but sweet, however, for he was renowned for his arrogance and died of wounds received in a duel.

Antonello da Messina (c.1430–79). Italian painter, from Messina in Sicily, a pioneer of *oil painting in Italy. According to *Vasari he was a pupil of Jan van *Eyck, but he is most unlikely to have visited northern Europe. He probably acquired his knowledge of northern techniques in Naples, then artistically dominated by the Netherlands, and the simplified, rounded, sculptural modelling characteristic of Antonello's style was perhaps influenced by the visit to Sicily of the sculptor Francesco *Laurana. In 1475–6 Antonello visited Venice, where he painted the S. Cassiano altarpiece, of which two fragments only remain, both in the Kunsthistorisches Museum, Vienna. *Vasari says that Antonello brought the 'secret' of oil painting to Venice, and while this is untrue, his altarpiece was certainly influential, for several younger Venetian artists borrowed directly from it and Giovanni *Bellini admired the modelling of its figures. Antonello's bust portraits—in three-quarter view, of Flemish type—also enjoyed a notable vogue in Venice: their expressions were more lively than in the portraits by *Memlinc then being imported and, like Antonello's religious works, they show a remarkable ability to combine Northern particularity of detail with the Italian tradition of grandeur and clarity of form. Good examples of Antonello's portraits are in the National Gallery, London (this one is often considered a self-portrait), and in the Louvre, Paris.

Apelles. Greek painter active in the 4th cent. BC, born at Colothon on the island of Cos. Apelles was reckoned in antiquity to be the greatest of Greek painters, renowned particularly for his gracefulness, but none of his work remains. He was court painter to Philip of Macedon and his

son Alexander the Great, and one of the many anecdotes about Apelles tells how Alexander gave him his mistress Pancaspe after the artist had fallen in love with her while painting her in the nude. Among his recorded subjects are portraits of Alexander the Great (particularly famous was one for the temple of Artemis at Ephesus), *Aphrodite Anadyomene* (Venus rising from the sea) made for the temple of Asclepius at Cos, brought to Rome by Augustus, and set up in the temple of Caesar, and *Calumny*. Descriptions of his work by Classical authors were well known during the *Renaissance and inspired several major artists to attempt to emulate them. *Botticelli made a painting and *Mantegna a drawing of *Calumny* (Uffizi, Florence, and BM, London, respectively), and *Titian painted an *Aphrodite Anadyomene* (NG, Edinburgh, on loan from Ellesmere collection).

Aphrodite of Cnidus. Statue by *Praxiteles, made for the people of Cnidus. It is now lost, but it was his most famous work in antiquity (*Pliny thought it was the finest statue in the world), and was the ancestress of the modern female nude—the first life-size statue showing the goddess completely naked. Several Roman copies survive (for example in the Vatican): they show the goddess in a gently twisted pose, with right hand casually masking the pudenda and left hand dropping her robe over an urn. The statue was placed in an open shrine so it could be seen from all four sides, each view being equally admired.

Apollinaire, Guillaume (1880–1918). French poet and art critic, an active influence in shaping most of the aesthetic movements which dominated Paris artists during the early 20th cent. He was among the first to acclaim *Picasso (in 1905), praised *Matisse in 1907, *Braque in 1908, and led the way in doing honour to Henri *Rousseau. One of the earliest champions of the *Cubist movement, he published *Les peintres cubistes* in 1913, and helped to found the offshoot group *Section d'Or. Apollinaire was also a friend of the *Futurists and composed one of the Futurist Manifestos. He coined the word 'surrealist' in 1917 and through André *Breton he influenced the views of the *Surrealist school. His early death was hastened by wounds sustained fighting in the trenches in the First World War.

Apollo Belvedere. Marble statue (Vatican Museums) of the Greek god Apollo, discovered towards the end of the 15th cent. and long regarded as one of the supreme masterpieces of world art and the absolute standard for male beauty (it is named after the Belvedere Court in the Vatican, in which it was once displayed). The statue is a copy from the Roman period of a *Classical or *Hellenistic Greek bronze, and *Leochares has been proposed as the sculptor of the lost original. It was often copied or adapted, as when *Reynolds painted his *Commodore Keppel* in the posture of the statue but in 18th-cent. dress, and *Winckelmann's rapturous description of it had a profound influence on *Neoclassical sculptors such as *Canova and *Thorvaldsen. Since the revelation of the Parthenon sculptures (SEE ELGIN MARBLES) and the aesthetic discovery of *Archaic Greek sculpture the *Apollo Belvedere* has seemed cold and academic, and has lost much of its appeal. Whereas to Winckelmann it appeared 'the highest ideal of art among all the works of antiquity', to Kenneth *Clark it seemed that 'in no other famous work of art are idea and execution more distressingly divorced'.

Apollonio di Giovanni. See CASSONE.

Appel, Karel (1921–). Dutch abstract painter, sculptor, and graphic artist, regarded as the most powerful of the post-war generation of Dutch artists. In 1948 he was a founder of the *Cobra group. He moved to Paris in 1950 and during the 1950s gained an international reputation, spending much of his time in the USA. In his Cobra period Appel was among the most energetic exponents of expressive abstraction, anticipating *Art Informel. His work, executed in very thick impasto and violent colours, had the restless, agitated character of northern *Expressionism rather than the more restrained Classicism of the French: in the words of Herbert *Read, looking at his pictures one has the impression 'of a spiritual tornado that has left these images of its passage'. Latterly he has often painted with a rather smoother facture and in a style somewhat closer to *Hard Edge.

Appiani, Andrea (1754–1817). Italian painter. He was the leading Italian painter of the *Neoclassical period, but more on account of the lack of native competition than because of the quality of his work, which generally looks like a rather tired imitation of *David. Most of his career was spent in his native Milan, where he did large decorative schemes at Sta Maria presso S. Celso (1792–8) and the Palazzo Reale (1808). He also painted numerous portraits, which are generally more accomplished than his decorative work.

applied art. Term describing the design or decoration of functional objects so as to make them aesthetically pleasing. It is used in distinction to *fine art, although there is often no clear dividing line between the two terms.

Apt, Ulrich the Elder (d. 1532). German painter, the best-known member of a family of artists. He worked in Augsburg, where he is recorded from 1481, painting altarpieces, portraits, and in 1516 a series of wall-paintings in Augsburg Town Hall in collaboration with his pupil Jörg *Breu.

aquarelle. The French term for true *water-colour painting in transparent washes of colour, as distinct from opaque *gouache.

aquatint. An engraving method related to *etching but producing finely granulated tonal areas rather than lines. The term applies also to a print made by this method. There are several variants of the technique, but in essence the process is as follows. A metal plate is sprinkled with acid-resistant varnish, which is fused to the plate by heating, and when the plate is immersed in an acid bath the acid bites between the tiny particles of resin and produces an evenly granulated surface. The design is created by drawing on the plate with acid-resistant varnish, and great variety of tone can be obtained by immersing in acid and varnishing in turn (the longer the acid bites, the darker the tone). Aquatint was invented around the middle of the 18th cent., and in the late 18th and early 19th cents. was highly popular in England for reproducing watercolours (colour could be added by hand or by using several plates with different coloured inks). It has also been used as an original creative medium (sometimes in conjunction with other graphic techniques) by many distinguished artists, including *Goya, *Degas, *Picasso, and *Rouault.

Archaic art. Term applied to Greek art in the period before the *Classical period, roughly from about 650 BC until about 480 BC (the date of the Persian sack of Athens). The Archaic period is marked by the development of the life-size stone statue (the *kouros and *kore) and by the change from *black-figure vase-painting to *red-figure.

Archipenko, Alexander (1887–1964). Russian-born sculptor who took American nationality in 1928. In 1908 he moved to Paris and played a part in the development of the *Cubist movement. In sculptures such as *Walking Woman* (Denver Art Mus., 1912), he analysed the human figure into geometrical forms and opened parts of it up with holes and concavities to create a contrast of solid and void, issuing in a new idiom in modern sculpture. In 1913 he was connected with the German *Sturm group and he taught in Berlin between 1921 and 1923, when he settled in the USA. He taught in various places, but principally in New York, where he opened his own school of sculpture in 1939. Archipenko pursued an independent course, and was inventive in technique. He created sculpto-painting, in which forms project from and develop a painted background, and he was a pioneer in the revival of *polychromy in sculpture. In 1924 he invented the *Archipentura*, an attempt to make movable paintings, and from c.1946 he experimented with 'light' sculpture, making structures of Plexiglas lit from within. Archipenko had a considerable influence on the course of sculpture both in Europe and in America, particularly in the use of new materials and in pointing a course away from the sculpture of solid form towards one of space and light.

Arcimboldo, Giuseppe (1527–93). Milanese painter famous for his *grotesque symbolical compositions of fruits or animals, landscapes or implements arranged into human forms. He began his career as a designer of stained-glass windows for Milan Cathedral, but in 1562 he moved to Prague and became court painter to the emperors Ferdinand I and Rudolf II. He

returned to Milan in 1587. His paintings, though much imitated, were generally regarded as curiosities in very poor taste until the *Surrealists revived interest in 'visual punning'.

Arman (Armand Fernandez) (1928–). French-born artist who became an American citizen in 1972. In 1957, with his friend Yves *Klein, he decided to be known by his first name only, and the form 'Arman' was adopted in 1958 as a result of a printer's error on the cover of a catalogue. He is best known for his assemblages of junk material (*Accumulation of Sliced Teapots*, Walker Art Center, Minneapolis, 1964).

armature. A framework or skeleton round which a figure of clay, plaster, or other similar material can be modelled. The term is also applied to the iron framework of *stained glass windows.

Armitage, Kenneth (1916–). British sculptor. He first exhibited in 1952, and very rapidly established an international reputation. His characteristic work began in the mid 1940s, when he destroyed his pre-war carvings and began to model in plaster round an *armature. Though not naturalistic, his sculpture was figurative and humanistic, capturing typical gesture and attitude, as for example in *People in the Wind* (Tate, London, 1951). At the same time all his work gave great prominence to the qualities of the material—usually at this period bronze—in which the sculptures were cast. From the mid 1950s his figures became more impersonal in character and often larger in scale, and a new phase began in 1969, when he began to combine sculpture and drawing in figures of wood, plaster, and paper.

Armory Show. An art exhibition (officially entitled the International Exhibition of Modern Art) held in New York, 17 February–15 March 1913, at the Sixty-ninth Regiment Armory. The initiative came from a group of artists, several of them from the circle of Robert *Henri, who formed the Association of American Painters and Sculptors to organize the show. The breadth of conception with which the project was envisaged and conceived was largely due to the president, Arthur B. *Davies. It was both a mammoth exhibition in sheer quantity (estimated at 1,600 works) and a daring presentation of new and still controversial art. The American portion gave a cross-section of contemporary US art heavily weighted in favour of the younger and more radical groups. The foreign section traced the evolution of modern art, showing works by *Goya, *Delacroix, *Courbet, and the *Impressionists and *Post-Impressionists, as well as leading contemporary artists such as *Duchamp and *Kandinsky. From New York the show went to Chicago (Art Institute) and Boston (Copley Hall). It was estimated that over a quarter of a million visitors paid to see it, and its impact was enormous. Though the first reactions were ridicule or shocked indignation, the effect of the show was momentous, and it has become a commonplace to speak of the Armory Show as the beginning of an interest in progressive art in the USA.

Arnolfo di Cambio (d. probably 1302, certainly before 1310). Italian sculptor and architect. He is first mentioned in 1265 as Nicola *Pisano's assistant on the pulpit for Siena Cathedral. In 1277 he went to Rome, where he was in the service of Charles of Anjou: his portrait of Charles (Capitoline Mus., Rome) is one of the earliest portrait-statues since the ancient world. His most important surviving work, however, is the tomb of Cardinal de Braye (d. 1282), in S. Domenico at Orvieto, which set the type of wall tomb for more than a century. The most distinguished piece of sculpture attributed to him is the famous bronze statue of St Peter in St Peter's, Rome. As an architect, Arnolfo had a great reputation in his day and began the building of Florence Cathedral. No other buildings are documented as being by him, but several other important Florentine buildings, including Sta Croce and the Palazzo Vecchio, have been attributed to him, notably by *Vasari. If they really are to be credited to Arnolfo, he must rank as one of the greatest architects of the Middle Ages, as well as a distinguished sculptor.

Arp, Jean (or **Hans**) (1887–1966). French sculptor, painter, and poet who was involved with several of the most important movements in European art in the first half of the 20th cent. He was born in Strasburg, then under German rule, and before the First World War he came into contact with the *Blaue Reiter group in Munich and participated in their second exhibition (1912), where he met Robert *Delaunay. During the war he met Max *Ernst in Cologne, and was a member of a circle in Paris which included *Modigliani, *Apollinaire, and *Picasso. In 1915 he met Sophie *Taeuber (whom he married in 1922) at Zurich and collaborated with her in experiments with cut-paper compositions and *collages. He helped to found the *Dada movement and made illustrations for Dada publications 1916–19, during which years he also made his first abstract polychrome *relief carvings in wood (*Dada Relief*, Kunsthaus, Basle, 1916). In 1919–20 he worked with Max Ernst at Cologne and met *Schwitters in Berlin. During the 1920s he settled at Meudon near Paris and was associated with the *Surrealist movement, participating in the first Surrealist exhibition in 1925. He joined *Cercle et Carré in 1930 and was a founder member of *Abstraction-Création in 1931. In the 1930s he turned to sculpture, and produced what are now his most familiar and distinctive works—sensuous abstract pieces that convey a suggestion of organic forms and growth without reproducing actual plant or animal shapes (*Hybrid Fruit called Pagoda*, Tate, London, 1934). During the 1940s he lived first at Grasse with Sophie Taeuber, Sonia *Delaunay, and Alberto *Magnelli, then in Switzerland. He returned to Meudon in 1946. In his final years he won honours and prestigious public commissions, including a relief for the Unesco building in Paris (1958), but he did not seriously add to his earlier achievements.

Arpino, Cavaliere d'. See CESARI, GIUSEPPE.

arriccio (or **arricciato**). In *fresco painting, the rough coating of lime and sand plaster to which the final layer of plaster forming the painting surface (the *intonaco*) is applied.

Art Autre. A name for expressive or non-geometrical abstraction, virtually synonymous with *Tachisme and *Art Informel. The expression originated with the critic Michel Tapié, who in 1952 published a book entitled *Un art autre*. Tapié emphasized the spontaneous, unorganized character of *Art Informel*—art without form. He cited among others *Dubuffet, *Mathieu, *Wols, and *Matta as representatives of *Art Autre*.

Art Brut. Term coined by Jean *Dubuffet for the art produced by people outside the established art world—solitaries, the maladjusted, patients in psychiatric hospitals, prisoners, and fringe-dwellers of all kinds. Dubuffet claimed that such art— 'springing from pure invention and in no way based, as cultural art constantly is, on chameleon- or parrot-like processes'—is evidence of a power of originality that all people possess but which in most has been stifled by educational training and social constraints. In 1945 he began to make a collection of works free from cultural norms, and in 1972 his collection, by then numbering more than 5,000 items, was presented to the city of Lausanne, where it was inaugurated at the Château de Beaulieu in 1976. Although nearly half the collection was produced by patients, usually schizophrenics, in psychiatric hospitals, Dubuffet repudiated the concept of psychiatric art, claiming that 'there is no art of the insane any more than there is an art of dyspeptics or an art of people with knee complaints'. He also distinguished Art Brut from *naïve art on the more dubious ground that the naïve or 'primitive' painters remain within the mainstream of painting proper, hoping for public if not official recognition, whereas the *Art Brut* artists create their works for their own use as a kind of private theatre.

Arte Povera. Term coined by the Italian art critic Germano Celant to unite certain aspects of *Conceptual, *Minimal, and *Performance art. Celant, who organized an exhibition of Arte Povera at the Museo Civico, Turin, in 1970 and edited a book on the subject (*Arte Povera: conceptual, actual or impossible art?*, 1969), hoped that the use of 'worthless' materials such as soil and the avoidance of the traditional idea of art as a collectable 'product' would undermine the art world's commercialism. However, dealers have shown that even this kind of art can be commercially exploited.

Arthois, Jacques d' (1613–86). Flemish landscape painter active at Brussels. He specialized in large wooded landscapes, with figures that were often added by other artists, notably *Teniers the Younger. Few

dated works exist, the development of his style is not easily followed, and the work of his brother, **Nicolas**, and his son, **Jean-Baptiste**, is sometimes indistinguishable from his. D'Arthois led an unstable life, being imprisoned for debt, and dying in poverty despite his successful career. Paintings from his busy studio were often used to decorate churches; examples are in Brussels Cathedral.

Art Informel. Term coined by the French critic Michel Tapié in his book *Un art autre* (1952) to describe a type of spontaneous abstract painting prominent among European artists in the 1940s and 1950s. The term is more or less synonymous with *Tachisme. Tapié devised the word 'informel', which might be translated as 'without form' rather than 'informal'. The phrase *'Art Autre' ('other art'), from the title of his book, has also been used to cover the same style. In using it Tapié claimed that post-war art showed a complete break with the past.

Art Nouveau. Decorative style flourishing in most of western Europe and the USA from about 1890 to the First World War. It was a deliberate attempt to create a new style in reaction to the academic 'historicism' of much 19th-cent. art, its most characteristic theme being the use of sinuous asymmetrical lines based on plant forms. Primarily an art of ornament, its most typical manifestations occurred in the practical and applied arts, *graphic work, and illustration. The style takes its name from a gallery called L'Art Nouveau opened in Paris in 1895 by the art dealer Siegfried (not Samuel) Bing, a leading propagandist for modern design. However, the roots of the style were in England, where the *Arts and Crafts movement had established a tradition of vitality in the applied arts, and it spread to the Continent chiefly from London. In France, indeed, Art Nouveau is sometimes known by the name 'Modern Style', reflecting its English origin. In Germany the style was called Jugendstil (a name connected with the popular review *Die Jugend* founded in 1896); in Austria it was called Sezessionstil (see SEZESSION); in Italy Stile Liberty after the Regent Street store which had played so large a part in the dissemination of designs; and in Spain Modernista. Although not primarily associated with painting and sculpture, the influence of Art Nouveau can clearly be seen in these fields, for example, in the work of Alfred *Gilbert and Jan *Toorop.

Arts and Crafts Movement. English social and aesthetic movement of the latter half of the 19th cent. that aimed to reassert the importance of craftsmanship in the face of increasing mechanization and mass production. The name derives from the Arts and Crafts Exhibition Society founded in 1888, but the movement had its basis in the ideas of *Ruskin and the architect A. W. N. Pugin. They were the most eloquent and influential of the writers who deplored the aesthetic as well as the social effects of industrialization and nostalgically longed for the standards of craftsmanship of the medieval guilds, but it was left to the businesslike genius of William *Morris to translate their ideas into practical activity. Morris set about the re-creation of hand industry in a machine age, producing hand-printed, hand-woven, hand-dyed textiles, printed books, wallpaper, furniture, and so forth. Aesthetically his work was highly successful, but his ideal of producing art for the masses failed for the simple reason that his products were necessarily expensive. Nevertheless, his ideas had great influence on craftsmen, teachers, and propagandists. In the 1890s the Arts and Crafts Movement was connected with the International style of *Art Nouveau. It spread abroad in the early years of this century, being particularly successful in Germany, Austria, the Low Countries, and Scandinavia, where it is still influential. In Germany it came to terms with the machine and may be considered an ancestor of the *Bauhaus. The movement died out, or rather was transformed by the acceptance of modern industrial methods, but it has had a lasting legacy.

Arundel, Thomas Howard, 2nd Earl of (1586–1646). English collector and patron of the arts. With Inigo *Jones, he carried out archaeological investigations in Italy, and later British ambassadors as well as his own agents sought out antiquities which he could import from all over Europe and even the Levant. He patronized living artists, notably *Rubens and van *Dyck (both of whom painted him), and he brought *Hollar to England. Of the Old Masters, he collected especially works by *Holbein and *Dürer. His great collections were gradually dispersed after his death, but much of his collection of Classical sculpture is in the *Ashmolean Museum, Oxford.

Asam, Cosmas Damian (1686–1739) and **Egid Quirin** (1692–1750). Bavarian architects and decorators, brothers. They studied in Rome (1711–14) and developed further the dramatic effects of light and illusionism with which Italian *Baroque artists, notably *Bernini and *Pozzo, had experimented. Both men worked as architects, but Cosmas Damian was also a prolific fresco painter, and Egid Quirin was a sculptor and *stuccoist. They worked best as a team, and their ecclesiastical buildings were the supreme expression of the Bavarian delight in decorative display; architecture, painting, and sculpture unite to set a scene in which light and colour are the chief actors. The best known of their churches is that of St John Nepomuk, Munich (1733–46). The brothers paid for the building (which is attached to their house) themselves, and it is often referred to simply as the 'Asamkirche'.

Ash-can School. Group of American painters active from about 1908 until the First World War. It was inspired largely by Robert *Henri and its nucleus was formed by the group of The *Eight, which he founded. The core of the school were the four artists—*Glackens, *Sloan, *Luks, and *Shinn—who had gathered round Henri at his studio in Philadelphia, and who afterwards joined him in New York. All four had been artist-reporters on the *Philadelphia Press* and so had been used to making rapid sketches of scenes of everyday life. In style and technique the artists of the Ash-can School are now seen to have differed less from contemporary academic painting than they themselves believed. Although they often painted slum life and outcasts, they were interested more in the picturesque aspects of these subjects than in the social issues they raised. *Bellows and *Hopper are among the other artists associated with the group.

Ashmolean Museum, Oxford. The most important of the museums belonging to the University of Oxford. The nucleus of the Ashmolean collection was formed by the 'closet of rarities' (a collection of curiosities rather than works of art) assembled by the traveller and gardener John Tradescant (1608–62) and given in 1659 to the antiquary Elias Ashmole (1617–92), who offered it to Oxford University in 1675. The original Ashmolean Museum was built by the University to the design of the mason and sculptor Thomas Wood to house this collection and was opened in 1683—the first public museum in Great Britain. The new building in Beaumont Street by Charles Robert Cockerell was opened in 1845, and this was enlarged in 1894. In 1899 the designation 'Ashmolean Museum' was transferred to the new building and the original museum of Thomas Wood became known as the 'Old Ashmolean Building'. It now houses the Museum of the History of Science. The collections of the Ashmolean are large and varied. It is particularly rich in works from the ancient world (including marbles from the collection formed by Thomas *Arundel in the 17th cent.) and in Italian *Renaissance paintings. Also outstanding are the collections of coins and of Old Master drawings, the latter including a superlative representation of *Michelangelo and *Raphael from the collection of Sir Thomas *Lawrence.

Aspertini, Amico (c.1475–1552). Italian *Mannerist painter from Bologna, where he was a pupil of *Francia. *Vasari describes him as having an eccentric personality and this comes out in his paintings, which are often bizarre in expression: *The Holy Family with Saints* (St Nicolas aux Champs, Paris) is described by S. J. Freedberg (*Painting in Italy: 1500–1600*) as 'suggesting to the spectator the image of what he would expect from a demented Michelangelo'. Aspertini was in Rome 1500–3 and his sketchbooks of Roman remains (BM, London) are important sources about contemporary knowledge of the *antique.

Asselyn, Jan (c.1615–52). Dutch landscape artist who specialized in painting real and imaginary scenes of the Roman Campagna. He studied in Italy in the 1630s and 1640s and his glowing light effects owe much to *Claude Lorraine. His most famous painting, however, is not a landscape, but *The Threatened Swan* (Rijksmuseum, Amsterdam), an unusual work that is said to be an allegory of Dutch nationalism.

*Rembrandt, who was Asselyn's friend, etched his portrait. Because of a crippled hand he was nicknamed 'Crabbetje' (Little Crab).

assemblage. Term coined in the 1950s by Jean *Dubuffet to describe works of art made from fragments of natural or preformed materials, such as household debris. The term is not usually employed with any precision and has been used to embrace *photomontage at one extreme and room *environments at the other. It gained wide currency with an exhibition called 'The Art of Assemblage' staged at the Museum of Modern Art, New York, in 1961.

Ast, Balthasar van der (1593/4–1657). Dutch still-life painter, the brother-in-law of Ambrosius *Bosschaert the Elder, with whom he trained in Middelburgh. He worked in Utrecht before settling in Delft in 1632. His touch was less exquisite than Bosschaert's, but his range was wider, his paintings often including fruit and shells as well as flowers. Jan Davidsz. de *Heem was his pupil in Utrecht.

atelier. French term for an artist's workshop or studio. In the 19th cent., certain informal academies called 'ateliers libres' became centres for avant-garde artists. A model was provided, but there was no (or very little) supervision or formal instruction.

atlas (pl. atlantes). A sculpted male figure used in place of a column or other supporting feature in architecture. In Greek mythology, Atlas was the giant who supported the sky, and atlantes are often depicted so as to suggest the strain of carrying a huge weight on the shoulders. The female equivalent—the *caryatid—is, in contrast, shown standing serenely upright.

atmospheric perspective. An alternative term for *aerial perspective.

Audran, Claude III (1658–1734). The best-known member of a family of French painters and decorators. He was one of the most prominent decorators of the time, but most of his work has been destroyed or obscured by later additions. A great number of drawings survive, however, and these show him to have been one of the leading figures in the creation of the *Rococo style. In 1704 he was appointed curator at the Luxembourg, where *Rubens's *Marie de Médicis* cycle was then housed, and he introduced his pupil *Watteau to this masterpiece by an artist who was to have an enormous influence on his work.

Audubon, John James (1785–1851). American painter-naturalist. Born at Haiti, the illegitimate son of a chambermaid and a French sea captain, he was educated in France and received instruction in drawing from J.-L. *David. He moved to the USA in 1803 to avoid conscription in Napoleon's army and lived as a naturalist, hunter, and taxidermist, also earning some money as a portraitist and drawing master. His combined interests in art and ornithology grew into a plan to make a complete pictorial record of all the bird species of North America. He was unable to find a publisher in America, so he went to England in 1826. His *The Birds of America, from Original Drawings, with 435 Plates Showing 1,065 Figures* was published in four volumes of hand-tinted aquatints (1827–38) and now ranks among the most famous and prized books of the world. The engraver and publisher was the London firm of Robert Havell and Son. It was followed by *The Viviparous Quadrupeds of America* (1845–8), which was completed by his son **John Woodhouse Audubon** (1812–62) after his sight failed in 1846. His other son, **Victor Gifford Audubon** (1809–60), also assisted his father. Many of Audubon's original drawings are in the New-York Historical Society.

Auerbach, Frank (1931–   ). German-born painter who came to Britain in 1939 and adopted British nationality in 1947. His work (characteristically nudes and townscapes) is remarkable for its use of extreme *impasto, so thick that the paint at times seems modelled rather than brushed.

Auto-destructive art. Term applied to works of art deliberately intended to self-destruct. Works of art not made to endure are not unique to the 20th cent. (witness the butter sculptures of Tibet and the sand paintings of some North American Indian tribes), but the originator of the modern concept of auto-destructive art is Gustav Metzger (1926–   ), who is best known for painting with acid on nylon cloth in front of an audience. The most famous of all auto-destructive works was Jean *Tinguely's *Homage to New York*, which blew itself up at the Museum of Modern Art, New York, in 1960, watched by a distinguished audience.

automatism. Method of producing paintings or drawings in which the artist suppresses conscious control over the movements of the hand, allowing the subconscious mind to take over. The idea is anticipated to some extent in Alexander *Cozens's *blot drawings, but automatism in its fully developed form is associated particularly with the *Surrealists and *Abstract Expressionists. With *Action painters such as Jackson *Pollock, the automatic process in principle permeated the whole process of composition, but with the Surrealists, once an interesting image or form or texture had been achieved by automatic or chance means it was often exploited with fully conscious purpose.

Automatistes, Les. A radical group of seven Montreal abstract painters active c.1946–51. The oldest of them, mainly responsible for the formation of the group, was Paul-Émile *Borduas, and the other outstanding member was Jean-Paul *Riopelle. Members of the group were influenced by the *Surrealists, from whom they took over their techniques of *automatism. Their first exhibition, in 1946, was the first exhibition by a group of abstract painters to be held in Canada.

Avercamp, Hendrick (1585–1634). Dutch painter, active in Kampen, the most famous exponent of the winter landscape. He was deaf and dumb and known as 'de Stomme van Kampen' (the mute of Kampen). His paintings are colourful and lively, with carefully observed skaters, tobogganers, golfers, and pedestrians. Avercamp's work enjoyed great popularity and he sold his drawings, many of which are tinted with water-colour, as finished pictures to be pasted into the albums of collectors (an outstanding collection is at Windsor Castle). His nephew and pupil **Barent Avercamp** (1612–79) carried on his style in an accomplished manner.

Avery, Milton (1893–1965). American painter. Through the 1930s and 1940s he perpetuated in America *Matisse's post-*Fauvist style of figure painting, with flat areas of restrained but scintillating colour enclosed in flowing outlines. His favourite subjects included landscapes and beach scenes. Avery was the main and practically the only channel through whom Matisse's sophisticated innovations in the decorative use of colour survived in America until new interest was taken in them by younger artists such as *Rothko (his close friend) and *Gottlieb.

Avignon, School of. School of painting associated with the city of Avignon originating during the period when the papal court was transferred there from Rome (1309–77). The presence of this great source of patronage drew many artists to the city, mainly Italian masters, including *Simone Martini. After the departure of the popes Avignon became the centre of a school of painting which amalgamated Italian with northern Flemish influences (see FROMENT, CHARONTON). The greatest single work which the School produced is the *Pietà* from Villeneuve-lés Avignon (Louvre, Paris, c.1460), now generally attributed to Charonton. Several 14th-cent. frescos survive in the Palace of the Popes, but many works which were at one time attributed to the School of Avignon have since been reassigned and the School is no longer a clearly defined stylistic entity.

Ayrton, Michael (1921–75). British painter, sculptor, theatre designer, book illustrator, and writer on art. He was an erudite, inventive, and highly individual artist, much of whose work revolved around his obsession with the myth of Daedalus and Icarus, which he treated as analogous to his own artistic endeavours. The most extreme expression of his obsession is the enormous maze of brick and stone he built at Arkville in New York State, imitating the labyrinth Daedalus built for King Minos of Crete at Knossos.

B

Baburen, Dirck van (*c.*1595?–1624). Dutch painter of religious works and *genre scenes. After training in Utrecht with *Moreelse, he went (*c.*1612) to Rome, where his style became strongly influenced by *Caravaggio. He returned to the Netherlands in about 1621 and although he died only a few years after this he played a leading role, with *Honthorst and *Terbrugghen, in establishing Utrecht as a stronghold of the Caravaggesque style. His best-known work is *The Procuress* (Mus. of Fine Arts, Boston, 1622). This picture is seen in the background of two paintings by *Vermeer, whose mother-in-law apparently owned it.

Baciccio, Il (Giovanni Battista Gaulli) (1639–1709). Italian painter, born in Genoa and active mainly in Rome, where he settled in 1657 and became a protégé of *Bernini. He achieved success as a painter of altarpieces and portraits (he painted each of the seven popes from Alexander VII to Clement XI), but is remembered mainly for his decorative work and above all for his *Adoration of the Name of Jesus* (1674–9) on the ceiling of the nave of the Gesù. This is one of the supreme masterpieces of *illusionistic decoration, ranking alongside *Pozzo's slightly later ceiling in S. Ignazio. The *stucco figures that are so brilliantly combined with the painted decoration (from the ground it is not always possible to tell which is which) are the work of Bernini's pupil Antonio Raggi (1624–86).

Backer, Jacob Adriaensz. (1608–51). Dutch portrait and history painter, active mainly in Amsterdam, where he had a prosperous career. He studied briefly with *Rembrandt, and imitated his style so successfully that attributions have sometimes been disputed between them (see BOL). His best-known painting is the beautiful *Portrait of a Boy in Grey* (Mauritshuis, The Hague, 1634).

Bacon, Francis (1909–). British painter, born in Dublin of English parents. He came to London in 1925, setting up for a while as an interior decorator, and had no formal training as a painter. In the 1930s he began exhibiting in London commercial galleries, but he destroyed much of his early work and dropped out of sight until 1945, when his *Three Studies for Figures at the Base of a Crucifixion* (Tate, London), painted in the previous year, was exhibited at the Lefevre Gallery and made him overnight the most controversial painter in post-war England. John Russell has written of this *triptych: 'British art has never been quite the same since the day in April . . . when three of the strangest pictures ever put on show in London were slipped without warning into an exhibition at the Lefevre Gallery. Visitors . . . were brought up short by images so unrelievedly awful that the mind shut with a snap at the sight of them . . .' The emotional impact that Bacon's work makes depends not only on his imagery characteristically single figures in isolation and despair—but also on his handling of paint, by means of which he smudges and twists faces and bodies into ill-defined jumbled protuberances suggestive of formless, slug-like creatures from some nightmare fantasy: 'I would like my pictures to look as if a human being had passed between them, like a snail, leaving a trail of the human presence and memory trace of past events as the snail leaves its slime.' Bacon's work has won him an international reputation as one of the giants of contemporary art. In the catalogue of a major retrospective exhibition of his work held at the Tate Gallery in 1985, the Director of the gallery, Alan Bowness, called Bacon the 'greatest living painter', a judgement in which many critics would concur.

Bacon, John (1740–99). English sculptor. He started work as a modeller in a porcelain factory and this experience left a permanent mark on his style as a sculptor, as his work, even in marble, is soft, often showing much pretty detail. The favour of George III gained him the important commission for the monument to the Earl of Chatham (the Elder Pitt) (Westminster Abbey, 1779–83), and he also carried out much sculpture at Somerset House, but his finest work is the monument to Thomas Guy (Guy's Hospital, 1779), showing the founder succouring a sick man. His practice was carried on by his son **John** (1777–1859).

Bacon, Sir Nathaniel (1585–1627). The first English amateur painter of note. He was a high-born country gentleman, nephew of the Lord Chancellor Francis Bacon. Only a handful of paintings survive (mainly at Gorhambury House, Herts.); with the exception of a miniature landscape on copper in the manner of *Bril, described as the earliest British landscape (Ashmolean, Oxford), they are either portraits or kitchen still lifes. His ambitious full-length self-portrait at Gorhambury displays a more coherent realization of space, greater subtlety of colouring, and acuter sense of characterization than had hitherto been achieved in English portraiture and shows he was the equal of *Mytens or Cornelius *Johnson, the finest portraitists in England before the arrival of van *Dyck.

Baglione, Giovanni (c.1566–1643). Italian painter and writer, born and mainly active in Rome. He is of little account as a painter and is remembered as the author of *Le vite de' pittori, scultori, ed architetti . . .*, published in 1642. One of the fundamental sources of information for the period covered (1572–1642), this collection of biographies deals mainly with Roman artists but also discusses foreign artists working in the city such as *Bril and *Rubens. In 1603 Baglione sued *Caravaggio and three other painters for circulating coarse satirical poems about him. His hatred of Caravaggio comes out in the biography devoted to him in his *Vite*, but ironically his best pictures are his most Caravaggesque.

Baily, Edward Hodges (1788–1867). English sculptor, the son of a carver of ships' figure-heads at Bristol and *Flaxman's favourite pupil. His two most conspicuous works are also his most inaccessible—the statues at the top of Nelson's Column in Trafalgar Square (1843) and the almost equally tall Grey's Monument in Newcastle upon Tyne (1837). *Eve at the Fountain* (City Art Gal., Bristol, 1822) was highly regarded by his contemporaries. His prolific output of portrait busts included many of fellow artists (examples are in the NPG, London).

Bakhuyzen, Ludolf (1631–1708). Dutch marine painter, active mainly in Amsterdam. After the van de *Veldes moved to England in 1672 Bakhuyzen became the most popular marine painter in Holland. He captures the drama and movement of ships, but seldom achieves the poetic effects of either van de Velde the Younger or Jan van de *Cappelle.

Bakst, Léon (Lev) (1866–1924). Russian painter and stage designer, a member of the *Mir Iskusstva (World of Art) group. In 1909 he joined the ballet impresario *Diaghilev in Paris and played a major role in the impact that the *Ballets Russes* made in Europe. The uninhibited splendour of his spectacles revolutionized European stage design with their combination of oriental magnificence and the gaudy colour of Russian peasant art.

baldachin (or **baldacchino**). A canopy over an altar or other hallowed object; it may be portable for use in processions or fixed, and in the latter case it may be supported on columns or suspended from the ceiling. The most famous baldacchino is that designed by *Bernini for St Peter's in Rome. This type, often with twisted columns and fringed canopy, became usual in *Baroque churches.

Baldinucci, Filippo (1624–96). Florentine artist, art historian, antiquarian, and philologian. His *Notizie de' professori del disegno* (1681–1728), lives of artists from *Cimabue to his own time, is valuable for the information it gives about 16th-cent. Florentine artists as well as about his own contemporaries. He was an innovator as an art historian in making use of every kind of document. Apart from the *Notizie*, his most important work is his biography of *Bernini (1682), the primary source for the artist's life.

Baldovinetti, Alesso (c.1426–99). Florentine painter, mosaicist, and worker in stained glass. His training is unknown, but his graceful and refined style shows the influence of *Domenico Veneziano and Fra *Angelico. His finest works include a damaged but still enchanting fresco of the

Nativity (1460–2) in the forecourt of the SS. Annunziata, Florence, a *Madonna and Child* (c.1460) in the Louvre, and an *Annunciation* (c.1460) in the Uffizi. They show his remarkable sensitivity to light and landscape and his engaging blend of naïvety and sophistication. In his *History of Italian Renaissance Art*, Frederick Hartt writes that Baldovinetti was 'the finest painter in Florence' in the 1460s, and considers him 'a very gifted master who somehow never quite seemed to fulfil his great initial promise'.

Baldung Grien, Hans (1484/5–1545). German painter and graphic artist. He probably trained with *Dürer in Nuremberg, but his brilliant colour, expressive use of distortion, and taste for the gruesome bring him closer in spirit to his other great German contemporary, *Grünewald. His output was varied and extensive, including religious works, allegories and mythologies, portraits, designs for stained glass and tapestries, and a large body of graphic work, particularly book illustrations. He was active mainly in Strasburg, but from 1512 to 1517 he lived in Freiburg-im-Breisgau, where he worked on his masterpiece, the high altar for Freiburg Cathedral, the centre panel of which is a radiant *Coronation of the Virgin*. His most characteristic paintings, however, are fairly small in scale—erotic allegories such as *Death and the Maiden*, a subject he treated several times. Eroticism is often strongly present in his engravings, the best known of which is *The Bewitched Stable Boy* (1544), which has been interpreted as an allegory of lust.

Balen, Hendrick van (1575?–1632). Flemish *Mannerist painter, active mainly in his native Antwerp. He was in Italy in the 1590s. His speciality was mythological scenes painted in the highly finished manner of Jan *Brueghel, one of the numerous artists with whom he collaborated. Van Balen was a popular teacher, his most important pupil being Van *Dyck. He also had three painter sons.

Balla, Giacomo (1871–1958). Italian painter and sculptor, one of the leading *Futurist artists. From a visit to Paris in 1900 Balla brought back to Italy a feeling for *divisionism and for colour and light, which he passed on to *Boccioni and

*Severini, whom he taught in Rome. In 1910 he was converted to Futurism and in the immediately following years his paintings show a preoccupation with the characteristic Futurist aim of portraying movement. Unlike the other Futurists, however, Balla was not interested in machines and violence and his paintings tend towards the lyrical and the witty. The most famous is the delightful *Dynamism of a Dog on a Leash* (Albright-Knox Art Gal., Buffalo, 1912), in which the multiple impressions of the dog's legs and tail convey movement in a manner that later became a cartoon convention. In 1913–16 Balla went beyond the principles of the Futurist manifesto, painting more abstract pictures that nevertheless originated in observations of reality. After the First World War, Balla stayed true to the ideals of Futurism after his colleagues had abandoned them, but he turned to a more conventional style in the 1930s.

Balthus (Count Balthasar Klossowski de Rola) (1908–   ). French painter, born in Paris of aristocratic Polish parents, both of whom painted. He had no formal training but had the reputation of being an infant prodigy and was encouraged by the family friends *Bonnard and *Derain (of whom Balthus painted a memorable portrait, MOMA, New York, 1936). Since the late 1930s Balthus has been obsessed with the theme of the adolescent girl awakening to sexual consciousness, usually depicted in languid but powerful interiors such as *The Living Room* (Minneapolis Inst. of Arts, 1941–3). Although he has spent most of his life living in seclusion outside Paris and shunning all publicity, Balthus has become internationally famous and his distinctive and poignantly erotic work has made him something of a cult figure.

bambocciate. See LAER, PIETER VAN.

Bandinelli, Baccio (1493–1560). Florentine sculptor, painter, and draughtsman. He was a favourite of the *Medici family, but he is remembered more for his unattractive character and the antipathy of his contemporaries than for the quality of his work. His most famous and conspicuous sculpture is *Hercules and Cacus* (Piazza della Signoria, Florence, finished 1534), a pendant to *Michelangelo's *David*. The commission had originally been intended for Michelangelo himself, and Bandinelli's ponderous figure, which he had boasted would surpass *David*, was ridiculed by *Cellini and others. Bandinelli had a habit of failing to fulfil his commissions and Cellini's accusations of incompetence had much justification. In return, Bandinelli attempted to sabotage Cellini's career, as he also did with another rival, *Ammanati. Bandinelli was a fine draughtsman. His paintings include a pompous self-portrait in the Isabella Stewart Gardner Museum, Boston.

Banks, Thomas (1735–1805). English sculptor. He studied in Rome 1772–9 and in 1781 was employed by Catherine the Great in Russia. Back in England, he became with *Flaxman the leader of the *Neoclassical movement in sculpture. He had a very high reputation with his contemporaries: *Reynolds called him 'the first British sculptor who has produced works of classic grace' and Queen Charlotte (queen consort of George III) is said to have wept when she saw his most famous work, the monument to Penelope Boothby (Ashbourne Church, Derbyshire, 1793), in which the child is shown sleeping rather than dead. Small monuments such as this show Banks at his best, and his few surviving portrait busts demonstrate a gift for characterization. His larger monuments, however, are somewhat ponderous.

Barbari, Jacopo de' (active *c*.1497, d. 1516?). Venetian painter and engraver. His early career is obscure and he is first documented in 1500 in connection with his huge (nearly 3 m. wide) woodcut view of Venice, which had taken three years to complete. Most of his known career was spent in northern Europe, where he worked for several royal patrons. His delicate engravings, many of mythological figures, helped to spread the Italian conception of the nude in northern Europe. As a painter he is best known for his *Dead Bird* (Alte Pinakothek, Munich, 1504), an early example of still life.

Barberini. Tuscan family who came to prominence with the election of Maffeo (1568–1644) as Pope Urban VIII in 1623 and became the chief patrons of *Baroque art in 17th-cent. Rome. Urban commissioned the *baldacchino and the statue of St Longinus (both in St Peter's) from

*Bernini, and the Barberini also employed Pietro da *Cortona, *Romanelli, Andrea *Sacchi, and others in the decoration of the family palace and of St Peter's. The Palazzo Barberini, in the design of which Bernini and two other great contemporary architects—Carlo Maderna and Francesco Borromini—all played parts, now houses part of the national art collection.

Barberini Faun (*Sleeping Satyr*). *Hellenistic marble statue of a satyr sprawled in drunken sleep (Glyptothek, Munich). It has been several times restored, sometimes with substantial changes to its posture. It is first recorded in the possession of Cardinal Francesco *Barberini in 1628, and in the 17th and particularly the 18th cent. it was generally regarded as one of the greatest works of antiquity. It is still an admired work (unlike most once celebrated antique statues) and is considered by some authorities to be an original work of around 200 BC, although others believe it to be a good copy.

Barbizon School. Group of French landscape painters who took their name from a small village on the outskirts of the Forest of Fontainebleau, where its leader, Théodore *Rousseau, and several of his followers settled in the latter half of the 1840s. The other main members of the group included Charles-François *Daubigny, Narcisse-Virgile *Diaz, and Constant *Troyon. They were united in their attitude of opposition to Classical conventions and by their interest in landscape painting for its own sake, a fairly new development in French art. The inspiration came partly from England (particularly *Constable and *Bonington) and partly from the 17th-cent. Dutch painters on whom the English tradition was founded. They were advocates of painting direct from nature, but unlike the *Impressionists, they usually painted only studies in the open air; their finished pictures were almost always done in the studio. Their feeling for nature, amounting almost to a cult, may be regarded as a form of *Romantic revolt from the drabness of urban life and coincided with a longing among the urban population in expanding cities to renew the contact with nature. *Corot is often associated with the group, but his work has a poetic and literary quality which sets him somewhat apart. *Millet is also often linked with the School, as he settled in Barbizon in 1849 and during his last period painted pure landscape.

Bargello. Museum in Florence housing an unrivalled collection of Italian *Renaissance sculpture. The building was originally the Palazzo del Podestà, begun in 1255 as the residence of the chief magistrate of the city. In 1574 it was converted into a prison and assigned to the head of the Police, the 'Bargello'. In 1857–65 it was restored and fitted up as a museum. The collection contains works by virtually all the leading Italian Renaissance sculptors (including the celebrated statues of David by *Donatello and *Verrocchio) and also has an extensive collection of minor arts, including armour, *enamels, ivories, medals, and tapestries.

Barker, Thomas (1769–1847). English landscape and *genre painter, called 'Barker of Bath' from his main place of work, where he enjoyed a successful career. He was entirely self-taught, but was clearly influenced by the landscapes and *fancy pictures of *Gainsborough, and made his name mainly as a painter of rustic scenes. His brother **Benjamin** (1776–1838) and his son **Thomas Jones Barker** (1815–82) were also painters.

Barlach, Ernst (1870–1938). German sculptor, graphic artist, and writer. Until he reached his thirties Barlach was as much attracted to ceramics as he was to sculpture, but he found his personal style during a visit to southern Russia in 1906, when the sturdy peasant type led him to an interest in medieval German carving, with which he recognized both a spiritual and a technical affinity—even when they are modelled and cast in bronze his figures have the broad planes and sharp edges typical of wood-carving. In 1910 he settled at Güstrow and passed the rest of his life there. Barlach exemplified the sense of man's alienation which was typical of German *Expressionism, believing that, through the creation of visible artistic forms from the 'unknown darkness' within, man can rediscover himself and his lost God. He executed a number of war memorials under the Weimar Republic, including one at the cathedral of Güstrow which was destroyed when his art was condemned as *degenerate in 1938 by the National Socialist regime; it was subsequently restored and a replica made for the Antoniterkirche in Cologne. After his death his studio at Güstrow was made a permanent museum; there is another museum devoted to his work in Hamburg. Barlach also wrote Expressionist plays, which he illustrated with woodcuts and lithographs, and published an autobiography in 1928.

Barlow, Francis (1626?–1704). English painter and illustrator of animal subjects, known as 'the father of British sporting painting'. He painted numerous large canvases for decorative schemes (examples are at Ham House in London and Clandon Park in Surrey) and was also a prolific book illustrator, his etchings for an edition of Aesop's *Fables* published in 1666 being particularly well known. His work is vividly observed, with an almost naïve charm.

Barna da Siena. Sienese painter of the second half of the 14th cent. Nothing is known for certain of his life and no documented works survive, but he was probably the leading Sienese painter of his period. *Ghiberti's *Commentarii* associated him with frescos in the Collegiata at S. Gimignano, and the series on The Life of Christ there (c.1350–5) is the core around which his work has been reconstructed. As with *Simone Martini (traditionally Barna's master) and Lippo *Memmi, drawing plays a predominant part in his work; where their line is a graceful arabesque, however, Barna's is direct and thrusting, his figures having a more dramatic vigour than any in previous Sienese painting. Other works given to Barna include Christ Carrying the Cross in the Frick Collection, New York. Tradition has it that Barna died in a fall from scaffolding.

Barnes, Dr Albert C. (1872–1951). American drug manufacturer and art collector. He made a fortune with the antiseptic Argyrol, which he created in 1901, and by 1913 was devoting his life to collecting. His greatest interest was in modern French painting, but he also collected Old Masters and primitive art. In 1922 he established the Barnes Foundation at Merion, Pennsylvania, to house his collection and to provide education in art appreciation. Barnes commissioned *Matisse to paint a mural decoration for the Foundation in

1931, and when it turned out to be unusable because of an error in the measurements he had been given, Matisse did a new version. The abortive scheme, *The Dance I* (1931–2) is in the Musée d'Art Moderne de la Ville de Paris, and the second scheme, *The Dance II* (1932–3), is *in situ* in the Barnes Foundation. The museum Barnes created was closed to the public during his lifetime, and after his death the trustees engaged in litigation over whether it should be opened. An agreement was reached in 1960 allowing restricted public access. The collection of Matisse's work is one of the best in the world, and *Cézanne, *Picasso, and *Renoir are among the other artists who are particularly well represented.

Barocci (or **Baroccio**), **Federico** (*c.*1535–1612). Italian painter. Barocci was born in Urbino and apart from two trips to Rome early in his career was based there all his life. He is said to have abandoned his frescos in the Casino of Pius IV in the Vatican Gardens (1561–3) for fear that rivals were trying to poison him, and the hypersensitive temperament this suggests comes out in his work. It consists mainly of religious paintings, which combine the influence of *Correggio and *Raphael (also a native of Urbino) in a highly individual and sensitive manner. His colour harmonies are sharp but subtle and, although his paintings often convey a feeling of intimate tenderness, his handling has great vigour. Despite the fact that he worked away from the main centres of art, his work was much sought after, his patrons including the emperor Rudolf II. And although Barocci constantly claimed to be ill, he had a long and productive career; he was prolific as a draughtsman as well as a painter and was one of the first artists to make extensive use of coloured *chalks. Barocci is generally considered the greatest and most individual painter of his time in central Italy; certain features of his work are thoroughly in the *Mannerist tradition (his rather indefinite treatment of space, for example, and his delight in fluttering draperies), but in his directness and freshness he looked forward to the *Baroque. *Bellori, the pre-eminent biographer of the Baroque age, considered him the finest Italian painter of his period and lamented that he had 'languished in Urbino'.

Baroque. A term used in the literature of the arts with both historical and critical meanings and as both an adjective and a noun. The word has a long, complex, and controversial history (it possibly derives from a Portuguese word for a misshapen pearl, and until the late 19th cent. it was used mainly as a synonym for 'absurd' or 'grotesque'), but in English it is now current with three principal meanings. Primarily, it designates the dominant style of European art between *Mannerism and *Rococo. This style originated in Rome and is associated with the Catholic Counter-Reformation, its salient characteristics—overt rhetoric and dynamic movement—being well suited to expressing the self-confidence and proselytizing spirit of the reinvigorated Catholic Church. It is by no means exclusively associated with religious art, however, and aspects of the Baroque can be seen even in works that have nothing to do with emotional display—for example in the dynamic lines of certain Dutch still-life paintings. Secondly, it is used as a general label for the period when this style flourished, broadly speaking, the 17th cent. and in certain areas much of the 18th cent. Hence such phrases as 'the age of Baroque', 'Baroque politics', 'Baroque science', and so on. Thirdly, the term 'Baroque' (often written without the initial capital) is applied to art of any time or place that shows the qualities of vigorous movement and emotional intensity associated with Baroque art in its primary meaning. Much *Hellenistic sculpture could therefore be described as 'baroque'. The older meaning of the word, as a synonym for 'capricious', 'overwrought', or 'florid', still has some currency, but not in serious criticism.

*Caravaggio and Annibale *Carracci are the two great figures who stand at the head of the Baroque tradition, bringing a new solidity and weightiness to Italian painting, which in the late 16th cent. had generally been artificial and often convoluted in style. In doing so they looked back to some extent to the dignified and harmonious art of the High *Renaissance, but Annibale's work has an exuberance that is completely his own, and Caravaggio created figures with an unprecedented sense of sheer physical presence. From the Mannerist style the Baroque inherited movement and fervent emotion, and from the Renaissance style solidity and grandeur, fusing the two influences into a new and dynamic whole. The supreme genius of Baroque art was Gianlorenzo *Bernini, an artist of boundless energy and the utmost virtuosity, whose work— imbued with total spiritual conviction— dominates the period sometimes called the 'High Baroque' (c.1625–75). Slightly later, Andrea *Pozzo marks the culmination in Italy of the Baroque tendency towards overwhelmingly grandiose display.

In the 17th cent. Rome was the artistic capital of Europe, and the Baroque style soon spread outwards from it, undergoing modification in each of the countries to which it migrated, as it encountered different tastes and outlooks and merged with local traditions. In some areas it became more extravagant (notably in the fervent religious atmosphere of Spain and Latin America) and in others it was toned down to suit more conservative tastes. In Catholic Flanders it had one of its finest flowerings in the work of *Rubens, but in neighbouring Holland, a predominantly Protestant country, the Baroque made comparatively slight inroads; nor did it ever take firm root in England. In France the Baroque found its greatest expression in the service of the monarchy rather than the church. Louis XIV realized the importance of the arts as a propaganda medium in promoting the idea of his regal glory, and his palace at Versailles—with its grandiose combination of architecture, sculpture, painting, decoration, and (not least) the art of the gardener—represents one of the supreme examples of the Baroque fusion of the arts to create an overwhelmingly impressive whole. (The German term Gesamtkunstwerk—'total work of art'—has been applied to this ideal.) In France, as in other countries, the Baroque style merged imperceptibly with the Rococo style that followed it.

Barr, Alfred H. jun. (1902–81). American art historian, first Director of the *Museum of Modern Art in New York from 1929 until his retirement in 1967. He not only built up the museum's collections to become the finest in the world in their field, but also organized more than 100 exhibitions and wrote several books that are still considered standard works.

Barret, George (1732?–84). Irish landscape painter in oils and water-colour. He came to London in 1762 and quickly made a reputation as a painter of views and *panoramas and was a foundation member of the *Royal Academy. Though he sometimes imitated the Classical manner of his rival Richard *Wilson (who described Barret's foliage as 'spinach and eggs'), his natural gift was for topographical landscape. His most famous work in his day was a panorama of the Lake District painted in *distemper on the walls of a room at Norbury Park in Surrey (c.1780; still in situ). He initially had a successful career, but he had an improvident nature and became bankrupt. Barrett had three painter sons, **George Jun.**, **James**, and **Joseph**, and his daughter **Mary** was a *miniaturist.

Barry, James (1741–1806). Irish history painter. The statesman Edmund Burke brought him to London in 1764 and provided money for him to travel to Italy (1766–71). The work of the great masters of the *Renaissance had an overwhelming effect on Barry, and he was the only British painter who adhered consistently to *Reynolds's precepts for history painting in the *Grand Manner. His scheme of large decorative paintings on The Progress of Human Culture (1777–83), for the Great Room of the Society of Arts, London, is the most ambitious achievement of this kind by any artist of the British School, but its weak draughtsmanship and flabby rhetoric show that his ambitions far outstripped his talent. Barry was elected Professor of Painting at the *Royal Academy in 1782, but after a series of quarrels was expelled in 1799. His truculent nature and uncompromising belief in his own genius come out in his numerous self-portraits.

Bartolommeo, Fra (Baccio della Porta) (1472/5–1517). Florentine painter. After training with Cosimo *Rosselli, he was deeply influenced by the preaching of Savonarola and entered the Dominican Order in 1500, giving up painting until 1504. From then until 1508 he developed parallel with *Raphael—though Raphael's was the more imaginative genius—each contributing something to the new High *Renaissance type of Madonna with Saints, in which the figure of the Madonna acts not merely as a centre but as a pivot about which the whole composition turns. The two artists also evolved a new treatment, first adumbrated by *Leonardo, of the theme of the *Madonna and Child with the Infant St John in a Landscape*. Raphael, *Michelangelo, and Leonardo had all left Florence by 1509 and in the second decade of the century Fra Bartolommeo was rivalled only by *Andrea del Sarto as the leading painter in the city, which he left only briefly for visits to Venice in 1508 and Rome in 1514. His style acquired a solemn restraint and monumentality that made him one of the purest representatives of the High Renaissance (*The Mystical Marriage of St Catherine*, Louvre, Paris, 1511). Fra Bartolommeo was a brilliant draughtsman and the mystical element in his nature found clearer expression in his drawings, which escape the tendency to empty rhetoric occasionally shown in his later paintings. His drawings include not only figure studies, but also landscape and nature studies.

Bartolozzi, Francesco (1727–1815). Italian engraver, active mainly in England. He was one of the most accomplished engravers of his period, achieving success in Italy, in England, where he became Engraver to George III in 1764, and in Portugal, where he moved in 1802 to become Director of the National Academy in Lisbon. Bartolozzi became a founder member of the *Royal Academy in 1768 and engraved the works of many of his leading contemporaries, such as *Copley, *Kauffmann, and *Reynolds, but he was also celebrated for engravings after the Old Masters.

Barye, Antoine-Louis (1796–1875). French sculptor, celebrated for his portrayal of animals. He laid the basis of his extensive knowledge of animal forms while employed by a goldsmith making models of animals in the Jardin des Plantes, Paris (1823–31). His work was in the spirit of the *Romantic movement, particularly his preference for rendering violent movement and tense posture. He also did the pediment *Napoleon dominating History and the Arts* on the Pavillon de l'Horloge of the *Louvre and an equestrian statue of Napoleon at Ajaccio, the Emperor's birthplace in Corsica.

Baschenis, Evaristo (1617–77). Italian painter, the most prominent of a family of artists recorded from 1400. He was ordained c.1647 and painted a few religious subjects, but his fame rests chiefly on his beautifully poised and polished still lifes of musical instruments. His predilection for the subject may have been associated with the contemporary fame of the Amati family of violin-makers of Cremona, which is near to Baschenis's native town of Bergamo. The Accademia Carrara there has the best collection of his paintings.

Baselitz, Georg (1938–). East German-born painter and sculptor, active in the West. He is regarded as one of the leading contemporary *Expressionist artists and his work has often been the subject of controversy, particularly since, in 1969, he began painting the images in his pictures upside down.

Bassa, Ferrer (c.1285/90–1348). Spanish painter and *miniaturist who worked for the Aragon court. He is considered the founder of the Catalan School, but the only certain surviving work by his hand is a series of *frescos in the chapel of S. Miguel at the convent of Pedralbes near Barcelona, executed in 1345–6 and strongly Italianate in style.

Bassano, Jacopo (Jacopo da Ponte) (c.1510/18–92). Italian painter, the most celebrated member of a family of artists who took their name from the small town of Bassano, about 65 km. from Venice. Apart from a period in the 1530s when he trained with *Bonifazio Veronese in Venice, Jacopo worked in Bassano all his life. His father, **Francesco the Elder** (c.1475–1539), was a village painter and Jacopo always retained something of the peasant artist, even though the influence of, for example, the fashionable etchings of *Parmigianino is evident in his work. He treated biblical themes in the manner of rustic genre scenes, using genuine country types and portraying animals with real interest. In this way he helped to develop the taste for paintings in which the *genre or still-life element assumes greater importance than the ostensible religious subject. From around 1560 his work became vested with a more exaggerated search for novel effects of light, taking on something of the iridescent colouring of *Tintoretto. Bassano had four painter sons who continued his style—**Francesco the Younger** (1549–92), **Gerolamo** (1566–1621), **Giovanni Battista** (1553–1613), and **Leandro**

(1557–1622). Francesco (who committed suicide by throwing himself out of a window) and Leandro both acquired some distinction and popularity working in Venice. The work of the family is well represented in the Museo Civico at Bassano.

Bastien-Lepage, Jules (1848–84). French painter, best known for his sentimental scenes of rural life such as *The Haymakers* (Musée d'Orsay, Paris, 1877). Émile Zola described Bastien-Lepage's work as 'Impressionism corrected, sweetened and adapted to the taste of the crowd', and his work had considerable success and influence not only in France, but also in England and Scotland, and even—via Tom *Roberts—in Australia. He was also much admired as a portraitist.

Batoni, Pompeo (1708–87). Italian painter, the last great Italian personality in the history of painting at Rome. He carried out prestigious church commissions and painted numerous fine mythological canvases, many for eminent foreign patrons, but he is famous above all as a portraitist. After *Mengs left Rome for Madrid in 1761 his pre-eminence in this field was unchallenged, and he was particularly favoured by foreign visitors making the *Grand Tour, whom he often portrayed in an *antique setting. His style was a polished and learned distillation from the *antique, the works of *Raphael, academic French painting, and the teaching of his master Sebastiano *Conca. His characterization is not profound, but it is usually vivid, and he presented his sitters with poise and dignity. Batoni was also an outstanding draughtsman, his drawings after the antique being particularly memorable. He was curator of the papal collections and his house was a social, intellectual, and artistic centre, *Winckelmann being among his friends.

Battistello. See CARACCIOLO.

Bauchant, André (1873–1958). French *naïve painter, a market gardener until he devoted himself full time to painting in 1918. He worked in the meticulously realistic manner which is characteristic of most *naïve artists, devoting himself for preference to historical or mythological themes for which he found inspiration in old illustrated books (*Greek Dance in a*

Landscape, Tate, London, 1937). Bauchant became part of the cult for naïve painting when he was promoted by Wilhelm *Uhde. Among his other admirers and patrons were *Diaghilev, *Le Corbusier, *Lipchitz, and *Ozenfant.

Baudelaire, Charles (1821–67). French poet and critic. As well as being a major poet, Baudelaire was one of the foremost art critics of his day. He held that there is no absolute and universal beauty but a different beauty for different peoples and cultures. Moreover, the individuality of the artist is essential to the creation of beauty and if it is suppressed or regimented, art becomes banal: 'the beautiful is always bizarre' was a favourite maxim. Baudelaire resisted the claims that art should serve social or moral purposes and was one of the leaders of the 'art for art's sake' school (see AESTHETICISM). He sought to assess the stature of an artist by his ability to portray the 'heroism' of modern life. *Delacroix, to whom he devoted some of his most perceptive essays, he found unsuitable owing to his predilection for *Romantic and exotic subject matter. *Courbet seemed to him too materialistic and he finally chose the relatively minor painter Constantin *Guys as the representative *par excellence* of contemporary society, and wrote a long appreciation of his work entitled *Le Peintre de la vie moderne* (1863). He was a friend and supporter of *Manet and he is one of the persons depicted in Manet's *Music in the Tuileries Gardens* (NG, London, 1863) as well as in Courbet's *The Painter's Studio* (Musée d'Orsay, Paris, 1854–5). His writings later had great influence on the *Symbolists.

Baugin, Lubin (c. 1610–63). French painter, active in Paris. He painted religious works and has earned the nickname 'Le Petit Guide' (Little Guido) because he was strongly influenced by Guido *Reni. This suggests that he visited Italy, but there is no firm evidence. A small group of strikingly austere still lifes, signed simply 'Baugin' (examples are in the Louvre), has also been attributed to him, although there is little in common between these pictures and the religious works.

Bauhaus. A school of architecture and the applied arts which became the centre of modern design in Germany during the

1920s and played a key role in establishing the relationship between design and industrial techniques. The Bauhaus was founded in 1919 by the fusion under Walter *Gropius of the old Weimar Academy of Fine Arts and the Weimar School of Arts and Crafts. Although the emphasis was on architecture and design, the teachers in the early days were mostly painters, among them *Kandinsky and *Klee. A close relationship was established with industry and many products of the studios (furniture, textiles, and electric-light fittings in particular) were adopted for large-scale manufacture. The characteristic Bauhaus style was impersonal, geometrical, and severe, but with a refinement of line and shape that came from a strict economy of means and a close study of the nature of the materials. In 1925 the Bauhaus moved from Weimar to Dessau, where it was housed in a group of new buildings designed as a co-operative effort by Gropius and his staff and students. In 1928 Gropius left the Bauhaus to concentrate on his own architectural practice and was succeeded as director by the Swiss architect Hannes Meyer. He in turn was replaced by another architect, Ludwig Mies van der Rohe, in 1930. Two years later the Bauhaus moved to Berlin, where it was closed down by the Nazis in 1933. Following this dissolution, the emigration of staff and students helped to disseminate Bauhaus ideas in many countries, and they have had an enormous influence on art education throughout the Western world. László *Moholy-Nagy, who taught at the Bauhaus from 1923 to 1928, founded the New Bauhaus (which became the Institute of Design) in Chicago in 1937.

Baumeister, Willi (1889–1955). German abstract painter. Unlike most significant German painters of his time he stood outside the ambit of *Expressionism and is regarded as the most 'European' in spirit of all contemporary German artists. He visited Paris in 1912 and again in 1914 with his close friend Oskar *Schlemmer, and became interested both in the *Neo-Impressionists and in *Cubism. His own style matured c.1920, after he had served in the First World War, and found its first expression in a series of Wall paintings (*Mauerbilder*), so called because he added sand, putty, etc., to his pigments to give a texture suggesting a wall. He also did sculpturesque Wall paintings with geometrically simplified objects in a manner akin to that of the French *Purists, and in 1924 he met *Ozenfant, *Léger, and *Le Corbusier. In 1933 he was dismissed from his teaching post at Frankfurt by the Nazis and forbidden to exhibit; after the Second World War he was reinstated and from 1946 taught at the Stuttgart Academy. Baumeister's method during the 1930s of using pictorial signs from the deep subconscious had analogies in *Picasso, *Klee, and others and was described by him in a book *Das Unbekannte in der Kunst* (*The Unknown in Art*), published in 1947.

Baxter, George (1804–67). English engraver and printer. In 1835 he patented a method of making colour prints using oil colours, and around the middle of the century 'Baxter prints' enjoyed a great vogue, making coloured reproductions of paintings widely available. Baxter licensed other firms to employ the process and did not himself profit greatly from the invention, which was eventually supplanted by cheap coloured *lithographs.

Bayeu y Subías, Francisco (1734–95). Spanish painter. He had an eminently successful career, becoming court painter to Charles IV and director of the Academy of San Fernando, but he is now remembered almost solely because he was the brother-in-law of *Goya, who spent some time in Bayeu's studio in the 1760s and later painted a memorable portrait of him (Prado, Madrid, 1795). Bayeu painted portraits and also did much decorative work, particularly making *cartoons for the royal tapestry factory, where he succeeded *Mengs as director in 1777.

Bazille, Frédéric (1841–70). French painter, one of the early *Impressionist group. As a student in *Gleyre's studio in Paris (1862) he befriended *Monet, *Renoir, and *Sisley, with whom he painted out of doors at Fontainebleau and in Normandy. He was, however, primarily a figure painter rather than a landscapist, his best-known work being the large *Family Reunion* (Musée d'Orsay, Paris, 1867–8). Bazille was killed in action during the Franco-Prussian War, cutting short a promising career. He came from a wealthy family and had given generous financial support to Monet and Renoir.

Baziotes, William (1912–63). American painter, one of the leading *Abstract Expressionists. From 1936 to 1941 he worked for the *Federal Art Project, and during the war he was attracted to *Surrealism and experimented with various types of *automatism. In the early 1950s he attained his characteristic style, which was not fully abstract but used strange *biomorphic shapes, akin to those of *Miró, suggesting animal or plant forms in an underwater setting (*Mammoth*, Tate, London, 1957). He said, 'It is the mysterious that I love in painting. It is the stillness and the silence. I want my pictures to take effect very slowly, to obsess and to haunt.'

Beale, Mrs Mary (1633–99). English portrait painter and copyist. Her portraits, often of clergymen, are dull derivations from her friend *Lely, but the diaries of her painting activities kept by her husband Charles, an artist's colourman, afford an interesting picture of contemporary artistic practice. Several examples from her prolific output are in the National Portrait Gallery, London. A son, **Charles** (b. 1660), was mainly a *miniaturist.

Beardsley, Aubrey (1872–98). English illustrator, a leading figure of *Aestheticism and of *Art Nouveau. Beardsley had little formal training, but he read voraciously and studied the art of the past and present, and his highly distinctive style was based on sources including *Burne Jones (who encouraged him) and Japanese prints (see UKIYO-E). He made a name for himself in 1893 with illustrations for an edition of Malory's *Morte d'Arthur*, and in the following year he became the rage with the publication of his illustrations to the English version of Oscar Wilde's *Salome* and the appearance of the first issue of *The Yellow Book*, a quarterly periodical of which he was art editor. Owing perhaps partly to the tuberculosis which carried him off at the age of 25, his work had a morbid suggestion of depravity which made it the most controversial illustration of its day. Some of his work was frankly pornographic, including illustrations for his own *Story of Venus and Tannhauser* (he wrote poetry as well as prose), which was privately published in an unexpurgated edition in 1907. In spite of his ill health and early death, however, Beardsley's output was prodigious.

Beaumont, Sir George (1753–1827). English collector, connoisseur, and amateur painter, the friend of numerous artists and men of letters; his most celebrated work, *Peel Castle in a Storm* (Leicestershire Museum and Art Gallery, Leicester), moved Wordsworth to a sonnet. Beaumont had much to do with the foundation of the *National Gallery, to which he presented the best part of his collection in 1826. His favourite painting was *Claude's *Hagar and the Angel* (NG, London), which he frequently took with him when he travelled and which had a great impact on his friend *Constable. Constable's famous painting *The Cenotaph* (NG, London) shows the memorial to Sir Joshua *Reynolds that Beaumont had erected in the grounds of his house at Coleorton, Leicestershire.

Beauneveu, André (active 1360–1403/13). French sculptor and *illuminator from Valenciennes, who worked for the French court, Louis de Mâle, Count of Flanders, and the Duc de Berry. Four of the royal effigies in Saint-Denis came from his workshop (Philip VI; John II, ordered 1364; and Charles V and his queen, both ordered 1367). The only illuminations certainly by him are the Prophets and Apostles of the Duc de Berry's *Psalter* (Bib. Nat., Paris, 1380–5). Beauneveu's style in sculpture and painting looked forward to the general northern European trend towards naturalism in the 15th cent.

Beaux-Arts, École Nationale Supérieure des. The chief of the official art schools of France. The origins of the École des Beaux-Arts go back to 1648, the foundation date of the Académie Royale de Peinture et de Sculpture (see ACADEMY), but it was not established as a separate institution until 1795, during the administrative reforms of the French Revolution. It controlled the path to traditional success with its awards and state commissions, notably the prestigious *Prix de Rome, and teaching remained conservative until after the Second World War. Entry was difficult—among the artists who failed were *Rodin and *Vuillard—and students often preferred the private academies. Many progressive artists, however, obtained a sound technical grounding there—*Degas, *Manet, *Matisse, *Monet, and *Renoir all attended. The

BECCAFUMI, DOMENICO 36

École, which is housed in a complex of early 19th-cent. buildings in Paris, has a large and varied collection of works of art. Many of them are primarily of historical interest, but the collection of drawings is of high quality.

Beccafumi, Domenico (c.1486–1551). Italian painter, generally considered the outstanding Sienese *Mannerist. He was alive to the developments of Fra *Bartolommeo, *Michelangelo, and *Raphael and combined the new ideas with the bright and decorative colouring of the Sienese tradition. His work is noteworthy for its sense of fantasy and striking effects of light, as in *The Birth of the Virgin* (c.1543), one of several outstanding examples of his work in the Pinacoteca, Siena.

Becerra, Gaspar (c.1520–68/70). Spanish *Mannerist sculptor and painter. He studied at Rome and assisted *Vasari in the decoration of the Cancelleria. Soon after 1556 he returned to Spain and in 1558 contracted for the main *reredos of Astorga Cathedral, his most important work as a sculptor. In 1563 he was appointed court painter to Philip II and began mythological ceiling paintings at the palace of El Pardo, near Madrid. His up-to-date knowledge of Italian art gave him a high contemporary reputation.

Beckford, William (1760–1844). English collector, writer, and eccentric. A pampered millionaire from boyhood (at the age of 5 he had piano lessons from the 8-year-old Mozart), he became a legendary figure in his own lifetime. One of his cousins referred to him as 'a second Lucifer' (a reference to both his youthful beauty and his depravity), and in 1784 he left England after a homosexual scandal involving a 13-year-old boy. For the next decade he travelled widely on the Continent and after his return to England he lived in eccentric seclusion at Fonthill in Wiltshire, where the architect James Wyatt built for him Fonthill Abbey (1796–1807, now destroyed), a huge mansion dressed in ecclesiastical garb. He formed an excellent library and a vast collection of objects of every kind, both natural and artificial; it drew from William *Hazlitt the wry comment that 'the only proof of taste he has shown in this collection is his getting rid of it', but it included some outstanding

paintings (twenty of them are now in the National Gallery, London). In 1826 when his fortunes had declined Beckford built Lansdowne Tower, Bath, a lesser but still highly impressive *Classical folly which now enlivens a cemetery. Beckford's most famous literary work was the fantastic oriental tale *Vathek*, written in French, but published first in English in 1786, a successor to Horace *Walpole's *The Castle of Otranto* in the vogue for the Gothic novel. The nightmarish visions of Beckford's book were inspired partly, as he himself said, by *Piranesi's engravings.

Beckmann, Max (1884–1950). German *Expressionist painter and graphic artist. At the beginning of his career Beckmann was artistically conservative, a German *Impressionist, but his experiences as a medical orderly in the First World War completely changed his outlook and his style. His work became full of horrifying imagery, and his forms were expressively distorted in a manner that reflected the influence of German *Gothic art. The combination of brutal realism and social criticism in his work led him to be classified for a time with the artists of the *Neue Sachlichkeit, but Beckmann differed from such artists as *Dix and *Grosz in his concern for allegory and symbolism. His paintings were intended as depictions of lust, sadism, cruelty, etc., rather than illustrations of specific instances of those qualities at work, and he ceased to regard painting as a purely aesthetic matter, and thought of it as an ethical necessity. In 1933 Beckmann was dismissed by the Nazis from his professorship at the Städelsches Kunstinstitut in Frankfurt, and in that year he began *Departure* (MOMA, New York), the first of a series of nine great *triptychs painted between then and his death in which he expressed his philosophy of life and society, and his horror at man's cruelty. He moved to the Netherlands in 1937 (the year in which his work was included in the infamous Nazi exhibition of *Degenerate Art), settling in Amsterdam until 1947. The last three years of his life were spent in the USA, where he taught in Washington and New York. Beckmann's philosophical outlook, which he expressed in his lecture *My Theory of Painting* in 1937, is somewhat incoherent, but his work has been hailed as the most authentic comment of German culture on the disorientation of the modern world.

Beechey, Sir William (1753–1839). English portrait painter. Beechey's careful, somewhat insipid style changed little throughout his successful career. He was appointed Portrait Painter to Queen Charlotte (queen consort of George III) in 1793 and was knighted in 1798 in recognition of his most ambitious painting, *A Review of the Horse Guard with King George III and the Prince of Wales* (Royal Collection).

Beert, Osias (*c.*1580–1623/4). Flemish painter of still life and flower pieces. Beert became a master in Antwerp in 1602 and also carried on business as a cork merchant. He is specially noted for his paintings of oysters, which show a masterly feeling for colour and texture.

Beggarstaff Brothers. Pseudonym used by the brothers-in-law William *Nicholson and James *Pryde for their poster designs.

Beham, Hans Sebald (1500–50) and **Bartel** (1502–40). German engravers, brothers. They were expelled from their native city of Nuremberg in 1525 for their extreme Protestant views. Hans settled in Frankfurt and Bartel worked for Duke William IV of Bavaria. Both brothers produced a great number of illustrations to the Bible, mythology, and history, strongly influenced by *Dürer. Bartel was also a painter, primarily of portraits.

Bell, Clive (1881–1964). English critic and writer on art. With Roger *Fry he was largely instrumental in propagating in Great Britain an appreciation of the *Post-Impressionist painters and particularly *Cézanne. Bell chose the British section of Fry's second Post-Impressionist exhibition (1912), including work by his wife Vanessa *Bell, Fry himself, and Duncan *Grant among *Bloomsbury Group artists, with Spencer *Gore and Wyndham *Lewis representing the more radical wing. His aesthetic ideas were set forth in his book *Art* (1914) and were much concerned with his theory of 'significant form'. He invented this term to denote 'the quality that distinguishes works of art from all other classes of objects'—a quality never found in nature but common to all works of

art and existing independently of representational or symbolic content. The philosophical merit of Bell's theory has been much challenged, but there can be no doubt that his ideas were important in spreading an attitude that demanded greater attention to the formal qualities of a work of art.

Bell, Graham (1910–43). British painter, born in South Africa. He came to England in 1931 and was a pupil of Duncan *Grant and a friend of William *Coldstream. In the early 1930s he painted abstracts, but then reverted to a sober naturalism and became a teacher at the *Euston Road School in 1938. He was killed in action in the Second World War.

Bell, Vanessa (1879–1961). British painter and designer. She married Clive *Bell in 1907 and like him and her sister, Virginia Woolf, was a central figure of the *Bloomsbury Group. Her early work, up to about 1910, and her paintings produced after the First World War are tasteful and fairly conventional, in the tradition of the *New English Art Club, but in the intervening years she was briefly in the vanguard of progressive ideas in British art. At this time, stimulated by Roger *Fry's *Post-Impressionist exhibitions, she worked with bright colours and bold designs and by 1914 was painting completely abstract pictures. Her designs for Fry's *Omega Workshops included a folding screen (V&A, London, 1913–14) clearly showing the influence of *Matisse. From about 1914 she lived with Duncan *Grant.

Della, Stefano della (1610–64). Italian engraver. His delicate, mannered style was early formed on that of *Callot and remained close to it. Most of his career was spent in his native Florence, where he worked chiefly for the Grand Duke of Tuscany, but he spent a period in Paris (1639–49), where he was patronized by Richelieu, and in 1647 visited the Netherlands, where he admired *Rembrandt's etchings. His output as an engraver was enormous—masque-designs, battle-pieces, animals, landscapes—and he was also a prolific draughtsman.

Bellange, Jacques (active 1600–17). French painter, etcher, and decorator, active in the Duchy of Lorraine. His reputation now rests on his etchings and drawings, as all his decorative work and almost all his paintings have disappeared. His highly individual style represents a last stage of the development of *Mannerist art in Europe. Exaggerating the tradition initiated by *Parmigianino, he expressed a personal religious mysticism through the artificial conventions of aristocratic elegance.

Bellechose, Henri (d. 1440/4). Netherlandish painter from Brabant, who succeeded *Malouel as court painter to the Duke of Burgundy at Dijon in 1415. He is documented in 1416 as completing an altarpiece left unfinished by Malouel, which can be identified as *The Martyrdom of St Denis* in the Louvre. This painting appears to be the work of two hands, and the more naturalistic, less elegant parts are given to Bellechose.

Bellini. Family of Venetian painters who played a dominant role in the art of their city for three-quarters of a century. **Jacopo** (c.1400–70/1) was the father of Gentile and Giovanni and father-in-law of *Mantegna. He was trained by *Gentile da Fabriano and achieved early popularity both in Venice and elsewhere. His most notable paintings have disappeared, however, and it is not easy to form an assessment from those that survive—mainly fairly simple and traditional representations of the Madonna and Child. Although he has the grace of the late *Gothic, there is a certain dryness and stiffness in his figures. Yet he was obviously keenly alert to contemporary ideas and shared the fashionable interests in archaeology, *perspective, and anatomy. His artistic personality is manifested best in his two surviving sketchbooks (Louvre, Paris, and BM, London), containing more than 230 drawings in all, many of them remarkable for bold perspective effects conveying an exhilarating sense of space.

Gentile (1429?–1507) inherited his father's sketchbooks and took over as head of his studio, so he was presumably the elder son. He carried on the reputation of his father and was greatly admired in his time, but many of his major works have perished. They included erotic scenes painted for the harem of Sultan Mehmet II, when Gentile worked at the court of Constantinople in 1479–81; his portrait of Mehmet, however, survives in the National

Gallery, London. The most famous of his extant works are probably the *Procession of the Relic of the True Cross* (1496) and the *Miracle at Ponte di Lorenzo* (1500), two huge canvases crowded with anecdotal detail of contemporary Venetian life. Both are in the Accademia, Venice.

Giovanni (called Giambellino) (c.1430/ 40–1516) was the greatest artist of the family and during his long and prolific career transformed Venice from an artistically provincial city into a *Renaissance centre rivalling Florence and Rome in importance. He was trained by his father Jacopo, but the major influence on his formative years was that of his brother-in-law, Mantegna. This and Bellini's own originality are made clear by a comparison of their pictures of the *Agony in the Garden*, both painted about 1460 and both now in the National Gallery, London. The compositions are clearly related, both deriving from a drawing in one of Jacopo's sketchbooks, but there is great difference in treatment, particularly of the landscape. Mantegna's is sharp, precise, and analytical, Bellini's is lyrical and spacious. To Mantegna's influence was later added that of *Antonello da Messina, who was in Venice in 1475–6. Like him, Bellini became one of the great early masters of the *oil technique, the linear style of his early work mellowing into one of masterly breadth, initiating the characteristically Venetian conception of painting in which colour and light were the primary means of expression. Bellini was remarkably inventive *iconographically and to the end of his long life he continued to learn from new ideas. From the year before his death dates the dreamy *Woman with a Mirror* (Kunsthistorisches Museum, Vienna), which is strongly influenced by his pupil *Giorgione, who predeceased him; it shows that his genius remained undiminished by advancing years, and it is easy to appreciate the remark made by *Dürer on his visit to Venice in 1505–7 that although Bellini was 'very old' he was still 'the best painter'. He painted excellent portraits, of which the *Doge Leonardo Loredan* (NG, London, c.1501) is the best-known example, and a few mythologies and allegories, notably *The Feast of the Gods* (NG, Washington, 1514, altered after his death by his greatest pupil, *Titian), but he was above all a religious painter. His most characteristic subject was the

Madonna and Child, and only *Raphael has rivalled his treatment of the theme, which ranges from the wistful melancholy of *The Madonna of the Meadow* (NG, London, *c.*1510), one of the most marvellous examples of his ability to bring together figures and landscape in perfect harmony, to the monumentality of the San Zaccaria Altarpiece (S. Zaccaria, Venice, 1505), perhaps the grandest of all *sacra conversazioni*. His influence on Venetian painting was enormous. As well as Giorgione and Titian, almost all the other outstanding Venetian painters of their generation trained in his workshop.

Bellmer, Hans (1902–75). Polish-French painter and graphic artist, renowned for the erotic quality of his work. In 1923 he began to construct jointed and articulated dolls in the form of adolescent girls and photographed them in a variety of erotic postures. These photographs came into the hands of the Paris *Surrealists and their reception encouraged him to join the Surrealist movement. In 1938 he settled in Paris and after the war he turned to etching, devoting a superb technique to his obsession with the female body, which he treated in a fantastic manner evocative of the erotic yearnings of adolescence.

Bellori, Giovanni Pietro (1615–96). Italian biographer, art theorist, antiquarian, and collector. His most important work—a basic source for the history of the *Baroque period—is *Vite de' pittori, scultori et architetti moderni* (1672), in the preparation of which he was helped by his friend *Poussin. In contrast to former biographers, his method was to concentrate on artists selected for their importance and only these received comprehensive treatment. The Preface to the work was a lecture given in 1664 to the Academy of St Luke at Rome, which became the seminal statement of the concept of *ideal art. In the prominence he gave to *Raphael, Annibale *Carracci, and Poussin, his rational Platonism, and his acceptance of the *antique as the model of excellence, his formulation expressed the ideals of the Roman Academy and proved a decisive influence on French academic theory. It later became the theoretical basis of the *Neoclassicism that was preached by *Winckelmann.

Bellotto, Bernardo (1720–80). Italian painter, nephew, pupil, and assistant of *Canaletto in Venice. Bellotto left Italy for good in 1747, to spend the rest of his life working at various European courts, notably Dresden and Warsaw, where he died. He called himself Canaletto, and this caused confusion (perhaps deliberate) between his work and his uncle's, particularly in views of Venice. Bellotto's style, however, is distinguished from his uncle's by an almost Dutch interest in massed clouds, cast shadows, and rich foliage. His colouring is also generally more sombre, much of his work being characterized by a steely grey. The best collections of his work are in Dresden (Gemäldegalerie) and Warsaw (National Museum). In the rebuilding of Warsaw after the Second World War his pictures were used as guides, even in the reconstruction of architectural ornament.

Bellows, George Wesley (1882–1925). American painter and lithographer. He was a pupil of Robert *Henri and became associated with the *Ash-can School. An outstanding athlete during his youth and noted for his hearty, outgoing character, Bellows is best known for his boxing scenes and sprang to fame with his *Stag at Sharkey's* (Cleveland Mus. of Art, 1907), a vividly impressionistic picture of an illegal boxing match. After the *Armory Show, which he helped to organize, his work became less directly impressionistic and began to show more attention to formal balance. This is apparent in *Dempsey and Firpo* (1924), one of the best-known of his lithographs. In the last five years of his life he turned with great success to portraiture.

Belvedere Torso. A marble torso of a powerful male figure seated on a rock, now in the Vatican Museums and named after the Belvedere Court in the Vatican in which it was once displayed. It is signed by a Greek sculptor 'Apollonius, son of Nestor, Athenian', about whom nothing is known, and there is scholarly dispute as to whether it is an original *Hellenistic work or a Roman copy. (It is sometimes alleged that the signature of Apollonius occurs also on the famous and stylistically similar bronze figure of a seated boxer in the Terme Museum in Rome, but most authorities now consider that this is a mirage.) The date of the discovery of the torso is uncertain, but it is first mentioned in the 1430s. It had become well known by 1500 and had a profound influence on *Michelangelo among other *Renaissance artists. From then until the early 19th cent. it was widely regarded as one of the greatest works of art in the world, rivalled in status probably only by the *Apollo Belvedere and the *Laocoön among ancient sculptures, although its fame was generally more academic than popular. It was often referred to simply as 'the Torso'. Unusually, the figure has always been left unrestored, but various artists have attempted to reconstruct the statue, notably *Flaxman, who made of it a group as Hercules and Hebe (University College, London, on loan to V&A, 1792). Between 1798 and 1815 the Belvedere Torso was in Paris, one of the many antique statues taken there by Napoleon.

Benedetto da Maiano (1442–97). Florentine sculptor, who carried over into the second half of the 15th cent. many of the motifs and stylistic features characteristic of the first half. His marble tomb designs are variants on patterns established by his master, Antonio *Rossellino; his pictorial *relief style, which found its most eloquent expression in a pulpit executed between 1472 and 1475 in Sta Croce, Florence, belongs to the narrative tradition associated with *Ghiberti and *Donatello. Perhaps his most memorable achievement lay not in his figures or reliefs but in the decorative architectural settings in which they were placed. In the design and execution of the exquisite pilasters, capitals, friezes, niches, and so on which form these settings he was often assisted by his brothers **Giovanni** (1438–78) and **Giuliano** (1432–90), who was primarily an architect. Benedetto's other work includes two outstanding portrait busts—of Pietro Mellini (Bargello, Florence, 1474) and of Filippo Strozzi (Louvre, Paris, c.1490).

Bening (or **Benig**). The name of two Netherlandish book *illuminators, father and son. **Sanders** (sometimes called Alexander) (d. 1519) worked in Ghent and Bruges. No documented works by him are known, but attempts have been made to identify him with the *Master of Mary of Burgundy, which would give him an artistic status appropriate to the success he seems to have enjoyed. **Simon** (1483/4–

1561) worked in Bruges and represents one of the final sparks of the tradition of illumination as the manuscript was overtaken by the printed book. There is a self-portrait *miniature by Simon in the Victoria and Albert Museum, London. His daughter **Levina Teerlinc** (d. 1576) was also a miniaturist. She settled in London in 1546 and worked at the English court.

Benois, Alexandre (1870–1960). Russian painter, stage designer, art historian, and critic, a leader and spokesman of the *Mir Iskusstva (World of Art) group. Benois became famous through his stage designs in which the tradition of Russian *folk art is harmonized with French *Rococo elements. He was a close friend and collaborator of *Diaghilev, both in Russia and later in Paris with the Ballets Russes, for which he designed among others Les Sylphides, and Petrushka (1909–11). His writings include a History of Russian Painting (1904), and after the Revolution he was made curator of the paintings in the *Hermitage. In 1928 he settled in Paris, where he died.

Benson, Ambrosius (d. 1550). Netherlandish painter of religious works and portraits. He was born in Italy, but from 1519 worked in Bruges, where he continued the tradition of Gerard *David. Many of his pictures were done for the export trade to Italy and Spain, and he evidently had a flourishing business. There is a slightly southern flavour to his compositions and for a long time many of them were thought to be by an anonymous Spanish painter known as the Master of Segovia.

Benton, Thomas Hart (1889–1975). American painter. After working as a newspaper cartoonist, in 1908 he went to Paris, where he remained for three years and became a friend of Stanton *Macdonald-Wright. Back in New York in 1912, he continued for some years painting in Macdonald-Wright's abstract *Synchromist style, but having failed to win success in avant-garde styles of painting, he abandoned modernism around 1920 and gained fame as the mouthpiece of the *Regionalist group of *American Scene painters. His work included several murals, notably the scenes of American life (1930–1) at the New School for Social Research in New York. Some of his later work introduced American types into representations of Greek myths or biblical stories. His most famous pupil was Jackson *Pollock, whose early work reflected something of Benton's restlessly energetic rhythms.

Bentveughels. See SCHILDERSBENT.

Berchem, Nicolaes (1620–83). Dutch painter of pastoral landscapes in the Italianate manner, principally active in Haarlem. Berchem was the son of the still-life painter Pieter *Claesz., with whom he first studied, but although he tried his hand at most subjects, no still lifes by him are known. He visited Italy in the 1640s and perhaps again in the 1650s and became, with Jan *Both, the most highly regarded exponent of the Italianate landscape. Successful and well rewarded in his lifetime, he had numerous pupils and his influence on 18th-cent. English and French landscape painters was considerable, *Gainsborough and *Watteau being among the artists who particularly admired his work. His prolific output is well represented in British galleries.

Berckheyde, Gerrit Adriaensz. (1638–98). Dutch painter of architectural views, active in Haarlem (his native city), Amsterdam, and The Hague. His representations of those cities have documentary accuracy, but they are never dry, achieving a poetic harmony by a subtle use of light and shade (three of his views of Haarlem are in the NG, London). The work of Gerrit's elder brother, **Job Adriaensz.** (1630–93), is very similar; it is also rarer and more varied, including *genre and biblical scenes.

Berenson, Bernard (1865–1959). American art historian, critic, and connoisseur, born in Lithuania and resident in Italy for most of his life. He built up a formidable reputation as an authority on Italian *Renaissance painting and was associated with several prominent dealers and collectors, notably Lord *Duveen and Isabella Stewart Gardner (founder of the Gardner Museum in Boston), advising them on purchases. The fortune he earned in the picture trade has caused his impartiality to be questioned, and many of his attributions have been downgraded, but his lists of the work of Renaissance painters formed a basis for further work for many years. His most enduring work of scholarship is *The Drawings of the Florentine Painters* (1903, 2nd edn. 1938, 3rd edn.—in Italian—1961). He amassed a huge library of books and photographs and a fine art collection at his villa, I Tatti, at Settignano near Florence, which he left to Harvard University. In 1961 it opened as the Harvard University Center for Italian Renaissance Studies. Dapper and polylingual, Berenson often played host to visiting art historians and intellectuals at I Tatti and was a renowned conversationalist, diarist, and bon vivant. See also TACTILE VALUES.

Berlinghieri. A family of Italian painters active at Lucca in the 13th cent. **Berlinghiero Berlinghieri**, the founder of the family, is called 'Milanese' in a document of 1228, which also mentions three sons, **Marco**, **Barone**, and **Bonaventura**. He is not otherwise known, but a painted *Crucifix* (now in the Lucca Pinacoteca) signed 'Berlingeri' without Christian name is attributed to him. A *Crucifix* in the Accademia, Florence, is also sometimes assigned to him. Bonaventura, the most talented of his sons, is known chiefly for his signed and dated altarpiece in the church of S. Francesco at Pescia (1235), which with its combination of solemn images and homely detail has been regarded as one of the most original, as it is one of the earliest, pictorial representations of Franciscan ideas. The *Scenes from the Life of St Francis* in Sta Croce, Florence, and the *St Francis receiving the Stigmata* in the Accademia, Florence, have also been attributed to him.

Berman, Eugene (1899–1972). Russian-born American painter and stage designer. He fled with his family to Paris in 1918 during the Russian Revolution and became friendly with *Tchelitchew and a group of painters who became known as *'Neo-Romantics', painting dreamlike scenes with mournful, drooping figures. In 1935 he emigrated to the USA and became an American citizen in 1937.

Bermejo, Bartolomé (active 1474–98). Spanish painter and stained-glass designer, born in Cordova, but active in northern Spain—in Aragon and then in Barcelona from 1486. His *Pietà* in Barcelona Cathedral, signed and dated 1490, is one of the earliest Spanish *oil paintings and one of the masterpieces of Spanish art of this period. Its intense naturalism recalls Nuño *Gonçalves.

Bernard, Émile (1868–1941). French painter and writer. In 1884 he entered the studio of Fernand *Cormon, where he was a contemporary of van *Gogh and *Toulouse-Lautrec, and also of Louis *Anquetin, with whom he developed *Cloisonnism. He then joined *Gauguin at *Pont-Aven and later claimed that it was he who in 1888 introduced Gauguin to the *Synthetist manner: certainly the two worked closely together between 1888 and 1891 in Pont Aven and Paris, and Bernard seems to have had a stimulating effect on his great colleague. Thereafter, however, Bernard's work as a painter greatly declined in importance, and he became of interest chiefly for his activities as a writer, playing a significant role as a sponsor of *Post-Impressionism.

Bernini, Gianlorenzo (1598–1680). Italian sculptor, architect, painter, and designer, the outstanding figure of the Italian *Baroque. His father, **Pietro** (1562–1629), was a *Mannerist sculptor of some distinction, active in Naples and then in Rome, and Gianlorenzo owed to him not only his early training in the handling of marble but also his introduction to the group of powerful patrons, the *Borghese and the *Barberini, who so promptly fostered his genius. He executed a series of life-size marble sculptures for Cardinal Scipione Borghese which showed an astonishingly precocious virtuosity in the handling of the material, and in their dramatic vigour and movement made a complete break with the Mannerist tradition. These are *Aeneas, Anchises and Ascanius* (1618–19), the *Rape of Proserpine* (1621–2), *David* (1623), and *Apollo and Daphne* (1622–5), all in the Borghese Gallery in Rome. After the election of Maffeo Barberini as Pope Urban VIII (1623) Bernini became the principal artist in the papal court and in Rome. In 1629 he was appointed architect to St Peter's, for which his work included the great *baldacchino over the High Altar (1624–33), and the huge statue of *St Longinus* (1629–38), which stands in a niche in one of the piers of the crossing. But on Urban's death in 1644 Bernini fell under a cloud,

partly owing to his failure in the construction of the lateral towers for St Peter's but as much because of the different artistic tastes of the new pope, Innocent X, who favoured Bernini's rival, *Algardi. During Innocent's papacy Bernini worked mainly for private patrons. The Cornaro Chapel, with the celebrated marble group of the *Ecstasy of St Teresa*, in Sta Maria della Vittoria dates from this period (1645–52). It is a comparatively small work, but an excellent example of Bernini's aims and achievement in the fusion of sculpture, architecture, and painting into a magnificent decorative whole. Bernini did, however, do some work for Innocent X, including the *Fountain of the Four Rivers* (1648–51) in the Piazza Navona. This is the most celebrated and spectacular of Bernini's fountains, and with these, his buildings, and his outdoor statuary he has had a greater effect on the face of Rome than any other artist. After Innocent's death in 1655 and the accession of Alexander VII Bernini was restored to full favour. At Alexander's order he decorated the apse of St Peter's with the group of the Fathers of the Church supporting the *Cathedra Petri* against an illusionistic background which, when viewed as the artist intended through the columns of the baldacchino, is intensely dramatic. Both this and the vast colonnade round the piazza in front of the church were begun by Bernini in 1656.

In 1665 Louis XIV invited Bernini to Paris to build the east front of the *Louvre, but his plans were abandoned in favour of a French design, and the trip—which he had made unwillingly—was not a success. He returned to Rome in 1666 and continued to be extremely active into his old age. His late religious works were intensely spiritual, reflecting his own devout way of life (*The Blessed Lodovica Albertoni*, S. Francesco a Ripa, Rome, 1671–4). As an architect his late work included important secular as well as religious buildings, notably the Palazzo Chigi-Odescalchi (begun 1664), which had great influence on Baroque palace design throughout Europe, and S. Andrea al Quirinale (1658–70), a fairly small church but one of his most sophisticated creations in its use of rich architectural and sculptural decoration to create an appropriate setting for the mysteries of the Catholic faith. In addition to large works of sculpture and architecture, Bernini executed many portrait busts, among the finest of which are those of his mistress Costanza Buonarelli (*c.*1645), in the Bargello, Florence, and Louis XIV (1665) at Versailles. Besides being the official entrepreneur of the papacy in a period of its political ascendancy, Bernini was also a brilliant wit, a writer of comedies, a *caricaturist, and—for his private pleasure—a painter of such high quality that his rare surviving works (which include several self-portraits) have sometimes been attributed to *Velázquez. Examples of his paintings are in the National Gallery, London, and the Ashmolean Museum, Oxford.

Bernini accurately predicted that his reputation would decline after his death. To the *Neoclassical taste of the 18th cent. his approach to sculpture was anathema, to *Ruskin in the 19th cent. it seemed 'impossible for false taste and base feeling to sink lower', and to the devotees of the idea of 'truth to materials' in the 20th cent. he appeared, in the words of his most distinguished apologist, Rudolf *Wittkower, as 'Antichrist personified'. It is only fairly recently that he has come to enjoy a reputation, comparable with his status in his lifetime, as the greatest sculptor since *Michelangelo and one of the giants of Baroque architecture.

Bernward of Hildesheim (*c.*960–1022). German ecclesiastic and art patron. He was abbot of the Benedictine monastery at Hildesheim in Saxony from 993 until his death, and for the church of St Michael there (begun 1001) he commissioned the famous bronze doors (*c.*1008–15) and a great bronze column (*c.*1018–20) probably intended to support the paschal candle. They are important not only for being among the outstanding European works of their period, but also for marking the revival of the *cire-perdue* technique of casting, which had virtually disappeared since the time of Charlemagne. A contemporary biographer records that Bernward himself practised metalwork and manuscript *illumination, but no work can be attributed to him. He was canonized in 1192 and is the patron saint of goldsmiths.

Berruguete. The name of two Castilian artists, father and son, who are respectively associated with the beginnings of the *Renaissance and *Mannerist styles in Spain. **Pedro** (d. 1504) was court painter to

Ferdinand and Isabella. He may have been the 'Pietro Spagnuolo' employed in 1477 with *Melozzo da Forlì and *Joos van Wassenhove on the decoration of the palace library at Urbino. He was working at Toledo from 1483. Ten panels from the Dominican convent at Avila, now in the Prado, demonstrate that his Renaissance style was then modified by the Flemish influences then prevailing in Spain. **Alonso** (*c.*1488–1561), sculptor and painter, was the son and probably pupil of Pedro. For some years, between 1504 and 1517, he was in Italy, where he completed Filippino *Lippi's *Coronation of the Virgin* (Louvre, Paris). Berruguete was back in Spain by 1518; in that year he was appointed court painter to Charles V, but his career flourished mainly as a sculptor. He worked in Valladolid and Toledo, his finest works including the *reredos of the monastery church of S. Benito, Valladolid, dating from 1526 (Valladolid Mus.) and a set of choir stalls with *alabaster figures above for the choir of Toledo Cathedral (1539–43). The emotional intensity and expressive *contrapposto* characteristic of his style reflected the influence of *Michelangelo (who refers to Berruguete in his letters) and of the *Laocoön*, which he had studied in Rome. He is generally considered the greatest Spanish sculptor of the 16th cent., his work having something of the spirit of El *Greco, who succeeded him as the outstanding artist in Toledo.

Bertoldo di Giovanni (*c.*1420–91). Florentine sculptor. He was a fairly minor talent, but he is remembered for three things. First, he was the pupil and assistant of *Donatello and teacher of *Michelangelo, thus forming the link between the greatest Florentine sculptors of the 15th and 16th cents. Secondly, he was described by *Vasari as the first head of the *academy of art which Lorenzo the Magnificent is said to have founded in the *Medici gardens by the Piazza di S. Marco. Thirdly, he developed a new type of sculpture— the small-scale bronze, intended, like the *cabinet picture, for the private collector. Bertoldo was responsible for the completion of the two pulpits in S. Lorenzo left unfinished by Donatello at his death. His own most noteworthy work is a bronze *relief of a battle scene in the Bargello, Florence, which inspired Michelangelo's *Battle of the Lapiths and Centaurs* (Casa

Buonarroti, Florence). Bertoldo was also recognized as one of the leading portrait medallists of his time.

Beuys, Joseph (1921–86). German sculptor, draughtsman, and *Performance artist, regarded as one of the most influential leaders of avant-garde art in Europe in the 1970s and 1980s. Like Yves *Klein, he was one of the leading lights in shifting emphasis from what an artist makes to his personality, actions, and opinions, and he succeeded in creating a kind of personal mythology. (As a Luftwaffe pilot he was shot down in the Crimea in 1943 and was looked after by nomadic Tartars who kept him warm with fat and felt— materials that came to figure prominently in his work. The hat that he habitually wore hid the head injuries he received in the crash.) Little of his work fits into conventional categories, but he is best known for his performances, of which the most famous was probably *How to Explain Pictures to a Dead Hare* (1965). In this he walked around an exhibition in the Schmela Gallery in Düsseldorf, his face covered in honey and gold leaf, carrying in his arms a dead hare, to which he gave an explanation of various pictures. He described the performance as 'A complex tableau about the problems of language, and about the problems of thought, of human consciousness and of the consciousness of animals.' Beuys was a prominent figure in Fluxus (an international group of artists, set up in Germany in 1962, which was opposed to tradition and professionalism in the arts), and he was also active in politics, aligning himself with the West German ecology party, the Greens. He was appointed Professor of Sculpture at the Kunstakademie in Düsseldorf in 1961, but was dismissed in 1972 after his teaching methods had aroused conflict with authority. The protests that followed included a strike by his students, and a settlement was eventually reached whereby he kept his title and studio but his teaching contract was ended. He devoted a good deal of his later career to public speaking and debate, and in 1982 he had a meeting with the Dalai Lama in Paris. By the end of his life he was an international celebrity and was regarded by his admirers as a kind of art guru.

Bevan, Robert (1865–1925). English painter. In the 1890s he studied in Paris and knew *Gauguin at Pont-Aven. Back in London he became a member of *Sickert's circle and he was a founding member of the *Camden Town Group (1911) and the *London Group (1913). Bevan painted in the *divisionist manner of Lucien *Pissarro, whom he admired, but modified it in the direction of the pure colour and flat patterning of Gauguin. He is best known for paintings featuring horses.

Bewick, Thomas (1753–1828). English wood engraver, active for most of his life in Newcastle upon Tyne. Bewick was a bird-watcher and a countryman and his finest works are natural history illustrations, particularly those to his celebrated books *A General History of Quadrupeds* (1790) and *A History of British Birds* (2 vols., 1797 and 1804). The animals and birds are characterized with great skill, but Bewick is as much admired for his tailpieces, which are miniature scenes of rural *genre, showing with a rare felicity the countryside in its varying moods in all weathers and seasons and shrewdly observed pictorial comment on incidents of rustic life. Bewick arrested the decline of engraving into a primarily reproductive technique and brought to it new expressive possibilities. He has been called the father of modern wood engraving and he established a school of engraving in Newcastle, his pupils and followers including his younger brother **John** (1760–95) and his son **Robert** (1788–1849). Bewick wrote an autobiography, which was published in an incomplete edition in 1862; the full text did not appear until 1975.

Beyeren, Abraham van (1620/1–90). Dutch painter, little regarded in his day but now considered one of the greatest of still-life painters. He initially specialized in fish subjects, but around the middle of the 17th cent. he began to devote himself to sumptuous banquet tables laden with silver and gold vessels, Venetian glassware, fine fruit, and expensive table coverings of damask, satin, and velvet. Works of this kind, in which he was rivalled only by *Kalf, gave him even greater opportunity than his fish pieces to demonstrate his ability to show the play of light on varied surfaces and organize forms and colours into an opulently blended composition.

He worked in various towns before settling in Overschie in 1678.

Bibiena (or **Galli-Bibiena**). Family of Italian architects, *quadraturisti, and stage-designers based in Bologna, members of which practised from the 1680s until the 1780s in practically every country of Europe. The founder of the dynasty was **Giovanni Maria Galli** (1625–65), who adopted the name of his birthplace, Bibiena, a small town in Tuscany. Other members of the family included **Alessandro** (1687–1769), **Antonio** (1700–74), **Carlo** (1728–87), **Ferdinando** (1657–1743), **Francesco** (1659–1739), and **Giuseppe** (1696–1757). They provided fantastically elaborate stage-settings for operas, balls, state occasions, and religious ceremonies, mainly in the service of the Austrian Imperial family in Vienna and of various German princelings. They also built several theatres in Italy and Germany, one of which survives: the Opera House at Bayreuth, decorated by Giuseppe in 1748. The most illustrious and prolific member of the family was Ferdinando, who produced several books on architecture and scenography.

Biedermeier. Term applied to German and Austrian art and interior decoration in the period roughly between the end of the Napoleonic Wars (1815) and the Year of Revolutions (1848). The name derives from a fictional character called Gottlieb Biedermaier (sic) from the journal *Fliegende Blätter* (Flying Leaves), who personified the solid yet philistine qualities of the bourgeois middle classes, and the art to which he lent his name eschewed flights of the imagination in favour of sobriety, domesticity, and often sentimentality. There were, as is to be expected, no major masters of Biedermeier but many excellent practitioners, such as *Waldmüller. The term is sometimes extended to cover the work of artists in other countries, for example, *Købke in Denmark.

Biennale (or **Bienale**). An international art exhibition held every two years and adjudicated by an international committee. The first and most famous was the Venice Biennale, instituted in 1895 as the 'International Exhibition of Art of the City of Venice', and claiming to represent 'the most noble activities of the modern spirit without distinction of country'. At this first Biennale artists from 16 different countries were represented, and the committee included such famous personalities as *Burne-Jones, *Israëls, *Liebermann, Gustave *Moreau, and *Puvis de Chavannes. The exhibition soon acquired world-wide prestige, and after it resumed in 1948 following the Second World War it became the leading show-place for the established international avant-garde. Other biennales have been inaugurated on the Venice model, notably the São Paulo Bienale, founded in 1951, and the Paris Biennale, founded in 1959.

Bierstadt, Albert (1830–1902). German-born American painter, active mainly in New York. He made several trips to the Far West and was one of the last of those painters (known collectively as the *Hudson River and *Rocky Mountain Schools) who specialized in grandiose pictures of awesome mountain scenery. His paintings—often huge in size—were immensely popular in his lifetime, but his on-the-spot sketches are now generally found much more appealing.

Bigot, Trophime (1579–1650). French *Caravaggesque painter, active in Rome (c.1600–34) and then in the Aix-en-Provence area. His career is obscure, but he has been identified as the author of a number of paintings, mainly intimate candlelit scenes, that were previously grouped under the name of 'the Candlelight Master'. *A Doctor Weighing Urine* (Ashmolean, Oxford) is an example of the unusual subjects he sometimes favoured.

Bill, Max (1908–). Swiss painter, sculptor, architect, designer, and writer. He studied at the *Bauhaus in 1927–9, and in 1932–6 belonged to the *Abstraction-Création group in Paris. In 1936 he took up the term *Concrete Art (*Konkrete Kunst*), proposed by van *Doesburg in 1930, and popularized it in Switzerland in place of 'abstract'. In 1941 he visited Brazil and Argentina, and introduced the concept of Concrete Art there. His work has been based upon the use of mathematical formulae to engender the relations between the parts from which a work is constructed, and his ultimate aim is to establish a unity among the individual branches of the visual arts. His sculptures have been considered precursors of the *primary structures of *Minimal art, although they are in fact derived from quite complicated mathematical formulae and his influence has been repudiated by Minimalists such as *Judd and Robert *Morris. Bill's influence has been acknowledged not only in Switzerland, however, but also in Argentina and Italy, where he has been the inspiration of a number of associations of Concrete Art. Bill has lived and worked mainly in Zurich, where he designed his own house (1932–3).

Bingham, George Caleb (1811–79). American painter. He worked mainly in Missouri (where he held several political posts), painting the life of the frontier people. Except for a short period studying at the Pennsylvania Academy of Fine Arts, he was self-taught. His finest canvases, particularly the celebrated *Fur Traders Descending the Missouri* (Met. Mus., New York, 1845), distil visual poetry from the commonplace, but after a trip to study in Düsseldorf in 1856–8 his work lost much of its racy freshness and charm, becoming overlaid with sentimentality.

biomorphic. A term applied to forms in abstract art that derive from organic rather than geometric shapes, as, for example, in the sculpture of Henry *Moore.

Bird, Francis (1667–1731). English sculptor. He trained in Brussels and later visited Rome and could work in a *Baroque idiom more convincingly than most of his English contemporaries, as is seen in his best-known work, *The Conversion of St Paul* (1706) in the west pediment of St Paul's Cathedral, London. His work is uneven, but he ranks as the most significant figure in English sculpture between *Gibbons (for whom he worked for a time) and *Rysbrack.

Birolli, Renato (1906–59). Italian painter who, because of his outspoken political views and his advanced and energetic artistic outlook, exercised an important influence on the Italian avant-garde. In 1938 he took a prominent part in founding the anti-Fascist *Corrente association, and was persecuted and imprisoned for his political activities. In 1947 he joined the *Fronte Nuovo delle Arti association. His work was varied in style, ranging from

*Expressionist pictures influenced by *Ensor and van *Gogh to abstracts reflecting his interest in the *Orphists.

Bissière, Roger (1888–1964). French painter, born in the province of Lot-et-Garonne. He came to Paris in 1910 and after a period of experimentation with *Cubism, he was for a time associated with *Ozenfant and *Le Corbusier. From 1925 to 1938 he taught at the Académie Ranson, where his influence on many of the younger abstract artists, such as *Manessier was great, but his own work during the 1920s and 1930s remained almost unknown. In 1938 he retired to Lot and during the war contracted an eye ailment that left him unable to paint. Instead, he produced compositions pieced together from tapestry and other materials. A successful operation in 1948 enabled him to resume painting and during the 1950s he achieved international recognition for his large, tapestry-like compositions in rich and glowing colours. Abstract in appearance, they resulted from the careful and sensitive reduction of natural scenes to scintillating patterns of interacting colours, and Bissière himself always refused to accept the term 'abstract' for his own work.

bistre. A transparent brown *pigment prepared by boiling the soot of burned wood. It is often used as a *wash for pen-and-ink drawings, water-colours, and *miniatures. *Rembrandt and *Claude were among the artists who exploited its potentialities. See also SEPIA.

bitumen (asphaltum). A transparent brown *pigment which at the time of use gives a rich glowing quality, but later becomes almost black and increasingly opaque. It never completely hardens and eventually develops a pronounced and often disfiguring *craquelure. It was most popular in the 18th cent., and its damaging effects can be seen in works by *Reynolds and other British painters of the period

black-figure vase painting. Technique of vase-painting, originating in Corinth in the 7th cent. BC, in which figures were painted in black silhouette on the light red clay background. Details were added by incising through the black pigment or sometimes by overpainting in red or white. The technique had its finest flowering around the mid 6th cent. BC, notably in the work of *Execias, but then began to give way to *red-figure painting.

Blake, Peter (1932–). British painter. With Richard *Hamilton he was the leading pioneer of *Pop art in Britain. His use of imagery from comics, pin-up magazines, consumer goods, and advertisements captures the flavour of the times in a manner that now evokes nostalgia for the 'swinging sixties', as was made clear during his enormously successful retrospective exhibition at the Tate Gallery in 1983 (his most famous work is the cover design for the Beatles LP *Sergeant Pepper's Lonely Hearts Club Band*, 1967). The engaging combination of sophistication and naïvety typical of Blake's style is seen particularly clearly in his work as a member of The Brotherhood of Ruralists, a small group of painters based in the West Country, of which Blake (then living near Bath) was a founder member in 1975. They took as their inspiration 'the spirit of the countryside'. A series of winsome fairy paintings are characteristic of this facet of his work. With other members of the Brotherhood (which includes David Inshaw (1943–), and Graham Ovenden (1943)), Blake has designed covers for the New Arden edition of Shakespeare's work.

Blake, William (1757–1827). English artist, philosopher, and poet, one of the most remarkable figures of the *Romantic period. From childhood he possessed visionary powers, and the engraving of *Joseph of Arimathea*, done at the age of 16, shows him already using a personal symbolism to express his mystical philosophy. His apprenticeship (1772–9) to the engraver James Basire (1730–1802), for whom he made drawings of the monuments in Westminster Abbey and other London churches, led him to a close study of *Gothic art and intensified his love of linear design and formal pattern. In 1779 he entered the *Royal Academy Schools, but his relations with *Reynolds were painful; later he was to find more sympathetic spirits in *Stothard, *Flaxman, *Fuseli, and *Barry. During the 1780s Blake worked as a commercial engraver, but from about 1787 he became engrossed in a new method of printing his own illustrated poems in colour, which he claimed to have been revealed to him in a vision by his brother

Robert, then recently deceased. The first of these major works of 'illuminated printing', in which handwritten text and illustration were engraved together to form a decorative unit, was *Songs of Innocence* (1789). In 1793 with his wife, Catherine Boutcher, he settled in Lambeth, where he engraved his principal prose work, *The Marriage of Heaven and Hell*. He had little material success and in 1800, at the suggestion of William Hayley, poet and man of letters, he left London to settle for three years at Felpham on the Sussex coast. Here he continued a series of water-colours illustrating biblical subjects for his first and most generous patron, Thomas Butts, and also began to engrave *Jerusalem*, the last and longest of his surviving mystical writings. On his return to London, Blake made a series of drawings for Robert Blair's poem *The Grave*, and in 1809 held a small one-man exhibition for which he issued *A Descriptive Catalogue*, eloquently summarizing his aims and convictions about art. In 1818 he met John *Linnell, whose sympathetic patronage ensured him a livelihood for the remainder of his life. For Linnell he carried out his engravings for *The Book of Job* and his magnificent designs for *The Divine Comedy*, on which he was working up to the time of his death. Linnell introduced to him a group of younger artists, including *Varley, *Calvert, and Samuel *Palmer, who were inspired and stimulated by Blake's imaginative power. He thus passed his last years surrounded by a group of admiring disciples, who formed themselves into a kind of brotherhood called the *Ancients.

In art as in life Blake was an individualist who made a principle of nonconformity. He had a prejudice against painting in oils on canvas and experimented with a variety of techniques in colour printing, illustration, and *tempera. His work as an artist is almost impossible to divorce from the complex philosophy expressed also through his poetry. He believed that the visible world of the senses is an unreal envelope behind which the spiritual reality is concealed and set himself the impossible task of creating a visual symbolism for the expression of his spiritual visions. He refused the easy path of vagueness and misty suggestion, remaining content with nothing less than the maximum of clarity and precision. To most of his contemporaries Blake seemed merely an eccentric, and his genius was not generally recognized until the second half of the 19th cent. (*Rossetti—another painter-poet with mystical leanings—was an early champion.) His output was enormous; there are important collections in the British Museum, the Tate Gallery, the Fitzwilliam Museum, Cambridge, and several American museums.

Blanchard, Jacques (1600–38). French painter, active mainly in his native Paris. He studied in Italy (1624–8) and his style reflects both *Baroque developments in Rome and the sensuous richness of the Venetian school. Back in France he gained a reputation for decorative work, but is now known chiefly as a painter of small religious and mythological subjects in a sensitive but sentimental manner (*Charity*, Courtauld Inst., London, 1637).

Blaue Reiter, Der (The Blue Rider). A loosely organized group of *Expressionist artists formed in Germany in 1911. The name, deriving from the title of a picture by *Kandinsky, was also used as the title of an 'Almanac' (a collection of essays and illustrations) published by Kandinsky and Franz *Marc in 1912. The members of the group (who included *Klee and *Macke) differed widely in their artistic outlooks, but they were linked by a desire to express spiritual values in their work. Two touring exhibitions brought the work of Der Blaue Reiter to several major cities of Germany, and the association had international affiliations; *Braque, *Derain, *Goncharova, *Larionov, and *Picasso were among those whose works were shown in the exhibitions. With the outbreak of the First World War the group disintegrated, but its short life is considered to mark the high point of German Expressionism.

Blaue Vier, Die (The Blue Four). A group of four painters formed in 1924 by *Kandinsky, *Jawlensky, *Klee, and *Feininger in succession to the *Blaue Reiter, with which they had all been associated. The members were united by a desire to publicize their work and ideas through exhibiting together rather than by stylistic similarity. Exhibitions were held in Germany, the USA, and Mexico between 1925 and 1934. Their patroness, Galka Scheyer, who suggested the formation of the group, formed a large collection of their work, which is now in the Norton Simon Museum in Pasadena.

Bles, Herri met de (*c*.1500/10–after 1550). Netherlandish painter of landscapes with figures. He is an enigmatic figure presumed to be one and the same as the Herri Patenier who entered the Antwerp Guild in 1535. Herri met de Bles, as van *Mander informs us, is simply a nickname meaning 'Herri with the white forelock', and it is generally assumed that he was a relation of Joachim *Patenier, who certainly had a decisive influence on his work. No signed or documented work by Herri exists, but a small group of distinctive works has been ascribed to him, characterized by panoramic landscapes dominating the figure groups in the manner of Patenier. His work was popular with Italian collectors, who called him 'Civetta' (little owl) because he often included owls in his pictures.

block book. A book printed from *woodcut blocks on which text and illustrations are combined, rather than by means of movable type. Block books were made in China probably as early as the 6th cent. AD, but in Europe the earliest known examples seem to date from around 1450, that is, at very much the same time that Gutenburg introduced printing from movable metal type. As the entire text had to be cut letter by letter on wood blocks, the process was extremely laborious and suitable only for short books in continuous popular demand. Very few block books were executed after 1480 and their place in the history of printing is as sterile descendants of the woodcut rather than as ancestors of printing from movable type.

Bloemaert, Abraham (1564–1651). Dutch historical and landscape painter and engraver, the son of a sculptor and architect, **Cornelis I Bloemaert** (*c*.1525–*c*.1595). Most of his life was spent in Utrecht, where for many years he was the leading painter and an outstanding teacher. *Both, *Honthorst, *Terbrugghen, and virtually all the Utrecht painters of the period who attained any kind of distinction trained with him. Bloemaert was a good learner as well as a good teacher and rapidly assimilated the new ideas his pupils brought back from Italy. For a time he became a *Caravaggesque painter and late in his career adopted some aspects of the *Classicism of the *Carracci. Although his landscape paintings are firmly in the *Mannerist tradition, his landscape drawings are naturalistic and his most original works. Many of his drawings were etched and published by his son **Frederick** (*c*.1610–69) in a well-known drawing book for the use of art students. Bloemaert had three other painter sons, who like Frederick were his pupils: **Hendrick** (*c* 1601–72), **Cornelis II** (*c*.1603–*c*.1684), and **Adriaen** (1609–66).

Blondeel, Lancelot (1496–1561). Netherlandish artist. He entered the Guild of Painters in Bruges in 1519, and also worked as an architect and designed sculpture, tapestries, and pageant decorations. In 1550 he and Jan van *Scorel were commissioned to restore the van *Eycks' celebrated Ghent Altarpiece. The *triptych of *The Martyrdom of SS. Cosmas and Damian* (S. Jacques, Bruges, 1523) is typical of his work as a painter in its profusion of Italianate ornament. Bruges had begun to decline in importance as its port silted up, and Blondeel was one of the last sparks of its great artistic tradition.

Bloomsbury Group A loosely knit association of writers, artists, and critics which had an important influence on cultural and intellectual life in Britain during the early decades of the 20th cent. The association stemmed from student friendships formed at Cambridge, where many of the group had been 'Apostles'—members of a semi-secret intellectual club—and took its name from the Bloomsbury district of London, where members frequently met at the houses of Clive and Vanessa *Bell or of Vanessa's sister, the writer Virginia Woolf. There was no formal membership and the group was unified by no common social or aesthetic ideology; its adherents were linked rather by attitudes and interests which have caused them to be represented as an intellectual élite in revolt against the artistic, social, and sexual restrictions of Victorian society. It was during the 1920s and early 1930s that the influence of Bloomsbury was most effective. The persistent propaganda of Roger Fry for *Cézanne and the *Post-Impressionists converted ridicule and outraged rejection into interest, if not full understanding, heralding the reaction from the anecdotal sentimentalism of 19th-cent. criticism and laying the foundation for a more just appreciation of the aims of contemporary art. After a period when the aims and achievements of the Bloomsbury Group fell out of favour and its members were attacked as dilettante and elitist, the late 1960s witnessed a great revival of interest.

blot drawing. A technique evolved by Alexander *Cozens and described in *A New Method for Assisting the Invention in Drawing Original Compositions of Landscape* (1785 or 1786). He prescribed the use of an accidental stain or 'blot' on the paper as a basis for an imaginative landscape composition. A similar suggestion had much earlier been made by *Leonardo da Vinci, who proposed that marks on wall surfaces might be used in this way. Somewhat similar techniques were used by the *Surrealists for stimulating subconscious imagery.

Blue Rider. See BLAUE REITER.

Blunt, Anthony (1907–83). English art historian. He was Director of the *Courtauld Institute of Art from 1947 to 1974, Surveyor of the King's (later Queen's) Pictures from 1945 to 1972, and one of the leading figures in establishing art history as an academic discipline in Britain. In 1979, however, his career was blighted when—amid clamorous publicity—it was revealed that he had spied for the Soviet Union during his service at the War Office in the Second World War. He wrote on a wide variety of subjects, but is best known for his contributions to the study of French and Italian art and architecture in the 16th cent. and 17th cent., above all for his numerous books and articles on *Poussin. His books include *Artistic Theory in Italy 1450–1600* (1940), *Art and Architecture in France 1500–1700* (1953 and subsequent editions), *The Art of William Blake* (1959), and *Guide to Baroque Rome* (1982). His brother **Wilfrid** (1901–87) was drawing master at Eton 1938–59, Curator of the *Watts Gallery at Compton 1959–85, and the author of numerous books on art and other subjects, notably *The Art of Botanical Illustration* (1950) and '*England's Michelangelo*' (1975), a biography of Watts.

Boccioni, Umberto (1882–1916). Italian *Futurist painter and theorist, and the only sculptor in the movement. He joined the Futurists in 1909, helped to draw up their manifestos of painting (1910) and sculpture (1912), and became the most energetic member of the group. Advocating a complete break with the art of the past, Boccioni was centrally concerned with the two main preoccupations of the Futurists— the production of emotionally expressive works and the representation of time and movement. He believed that physical objects have a kind of personality and emotional life of their own, revealed by 'force lines' with which the object reacts to its environment. These ideas are perhaps best shown in Boccioni's most famous piece of sculpture, *Unique Forms of Continuity in Space* (casts in Tate, London, MOMA, New York, and elsewhere, 1913), which vividly expresses bodily movement. His theories on sculpture were very forward-looking. He advocated the use of materials such as glass and electric lights and the introduction of electric motors to create movement. However, he died in an accident whilst serving in the Italian army before most of his ideas could be put into practice.

Böcklin, Arnold (1827–1901). Swiss painter. With *Hodler he ranks as the most important Swiss painter of the 19th cent., and in the 1880s and 1890s he was the most influential artist of the German-speaking world, even though from 1850 he had spent most of his time in Italy. He established his reputation with *Pan in the Reeds* (Neue Pinakothek, Munich, 1857), the beginning of his preoccupation with the world of nymphs and satyrs, naiads, and tritons, the results of which are sometimes slightly absurd. Later his style became more sombre and charged with mystical feeling, as in his best-known work, *The Island of the Dead* (Met. Mus., New York, 1880, and four other versions). Such works are considered among the most distinguished *Symbolist paintings produced outside France, and their morbid imagery appealed to the *Surrealists. A curious aspect of Böcklin's career is that like *Leonardo— whom he disliked—he spent much of his time experimenting with flying machines.

Bode, Wilhelm von (1845–1929). German art historian. His career was centred on the Berlin Museum; in 1872 he was appointed assistant in the department of sculpture, of which he became director in 1883, in 1903 he became director of the Gemäldegalerie (picture gallery), and in 1905 director general of all the royal museums of Prussia, a post he held until he retired in 1920. Under Bode's administration the Berlin Museum became one of the world's outstanding collections. Apart from being a noted scholar, Bode was one of the pioneers of modern museum organization and display, combining pictures, sculptures, and frames in harmonious arrangements and achieving a balance between creating an up-to-date setting for works of art and reconstructing their historical milieu. His main publications were in the field of Dutch and Flemish art (particularly *Rembrandt and his contemporaries), but he also wrote on Italian art and assisted *Burckhardt with his *Cicerone*.

bodegón. Spanish term, literally meaning 'tavern' or 'chophouse', applied strictly to domestic (particularly kitchen) scenes that have a prominent still-life element. *Velázquez painted several *bodegones* early in his career. More loosely, the term is used as a synonym for still life.

Body art. Type of art, related to both *happenings and *Conceptual art, in which the artist's body is used as the medium. Sometimes works of Body art are executed in private and communicated by means of photographs or films; sometimes the execution of the 'piece' is public. Sometimes the demonstration is pre-choreographed (as with *Gilbert and George); sometimes it is extemporaneous. Spectator participation is generally discounted rather than invited.

body colour. Paint that is opaque rather than transparent, more specifically *water-colour mixed with a white *pigment. *Gouache is an alternative name for body colour used in the more restricted sense.

Boilly, Louis-Léopold (1761–1845). French painter and engraver. He painted portraits, domestic and *genre scenes, and *scènes galantes*, which brought him into disrepute at the time of the Revolution. In 1823 he took up *lithography and used this technique to popularize his scenes from contemporary life. He was extremely prolific (claiming to have executed 5,000 portraits), and smooth and meticulous in his technique.

Bol, Ferdinand (1616–80). Dutch painter and etcher. He entered *Rembrandt's studio in the mid-1630s and in his early work imitated his master's style so well as to create occasional difficulty in distinguishing between them. The portrait of Elizabeth Bas in the Rijksmuseum, Amsterdam, is the best-known instance; it was acknowledged as a Rembrandt until 1911, when it was attributed to Bol by *Bredius, and although this opinion is still generally accepted, there has been renewed support for Rembrandt as the author (as well as some for Jacob *Backer). As Bol's career prospered, both as a portraitist and a painter of historical subjects, his style moved away from that of Rembrandt, becoming blander and more elegant in the manner of van der *Helst. In 1669 he married a wealthy widow and seems to have stopped painting. Sir Godfrey *Kneller was Bol's most distinguished pupil.

Boldini, Giovanni (1842–1931). Italian painter, one of the most renowned society portraitists of his day. His vivacious brushwork and gift for making his sitters look graceful and poised recalled the work of his even more successful contemporary, John Singer *Sargent, and like Sargent he had an international career, working mainly in Paris, but also in London (1869–72). Apart from portraits, his work includes some excellent street scenes of Paris. There is a Boldini museum in his native Ferrara. See also MACCHIAIOLI.

Bolotowsky, Ilya (1907–81). Russian-born painter who went to New York in 1923 and became an American citizen in 1929. From 1933 he painted in a manner of *Constructivist abstraction and during the 1940s he was one of the group of American artists who came most deeply under the influence of *Mondrian. He was a founding member of *American Abstract Artists in 1936 and his mural for the Williamsburgh Housing Project, New York, of that year was one of the first abstract murals to be commissioned. Bolotowsky was also a playwright and an experimental film maker.

Boltraffio, Giovanni Antonio (1466/7–1516). Italian painter, the pupil and assistant of *Leonardo and the most talented of his followers in Milan. He painted religious paintings and portraits (an example of each is in the National Gallery, London). The beautiful female portrait in the Louvre known as *La Belle Ferronnière* is attributed to Boltraffio by some authorities and to Leonardo by others.

Bomberg, David (1890–1957). British painter. He gave up an apprenticeship as a lithographer to devote himself to painting, studying under *Sickert and at the *Slade School. Whilst still a student he showed an advanced understanding of avant-garde Continental painting, particularly *Cubism and *Futurism (he visited Paris in 1913), and he became associated with the *Vorticists, although he disclaimed any formal connection with them. His best-known work of this time is probably *In the Hold* (Tate, London, 1913–14), a dazzlingly coloured abstraction of fragmented geometric forms. After early success, he became dismayed at the failure of a one-man show in 1919, and thereafter worked in isolation. From the 1920s he travelled widely, and at this time began moving away from abstraction to a heavily-worked, somewhat *Expressionist figurative style, painting mainly portraits and landscapes. Much of his later career was devoted to teaching, and he had a strong influence on pupils such as *Auerbach. At the time of his death he was little appreciated, but his reputation has since soared; a major exhibition was devoted to him at the Tate Gallery in 1988.

Bombois, Camille (1883–1970). French *naïve painter. He passed his childhood on barges along the canals of France and was afterwards a farmhand and a wrestler in a travelling circus. From 1907 he worked as a porter on the Paris Métro, as a navvy and a docker, and then took a night job in a printing establishment in order to have more time for painting. In 1922 a pavement exhibition of his pictures attracted the attention of Wilhelm *Uhde and other critics, and thereafter he was able to devote all his time to painting. His pictures have exceptional strength and vitality, particularly his scenes of circus life; a fine example is *Country Fair Athlete* (Mus. d'Art Moderne, Paris, c.1930).

Bone, Sir Muirhead (1876–1953). British draughtsman and etcher, mainly of architectural subjects. He studied architecture and painting in his native Glasgow, then settled in London in 1901 and became a member of the *New English Art Club. In 1916 he became the first official war artist to be appointed and he was also an official war artist in the Second World War. His son **Stephen** (1904–58) was a painter and art critic.

Bonheur, Rosa (1822–99). French animal painter. Trained by her father, **Raymond Bonheur** (d. 1849), she exhibited regularly at the Paris *Salon from 1841, where her pictures of lions, tigers, wolves, etc., were soon very popular. *The Horse Fair* (1853; Met. Mus., New York, reduced replica in NG, London) gave her an international reputation. She was a colourful and formidable character, outspoken in her feminine independence (she smoked cigarettes and wore trousers), and in 1865 was the first woman to be awarded the Grand Cross of the Legion of Honour. There is a small museum of her work at Fontainebleau.

Bonifazio Veronese (Bonifazio de' Pitati) (1487–1553). Italian painter. He was born in Verona, but all his recorded activity was in Venice, where he based his style on *Giorgione, *Titian, and *Palma Vecchio. There are few signed, dated, or documented works by him, but he appears to have run a prolific studio. Consequently he has become one of those artists whose names are used as dustbins for dumping difficult attributions.

Bonington, Richard Parkes (1802–28). English painter, active mainly in France, where his family moved when he was 15. In 1819 he went to Paris, where he became a pupil of *Gros and formed a friendship with *Delacroix. He was influenced by the medievalism and orientalism of the French *Romantics and produced paintings in their manner. However, he established his reputation as a landscapist, particularly with his works exhibited at the *Salon of 1822 and the so-called 'English' Salon of 1824, at which his own paintings (which won him a gold medal) and those of *Constable were the star attractions. In 1825 he accompanied Delacroix to England and sought out pictures by Constable, whose influence is apparent in his subsequent work, and in 1826 he visited Italy, producing some of his finest work in Venice. Bonington was overloaded with work and his delicate health suffered; he died of consumption in London a month before his 26th birthday. Although his career was so brief, Bonington was highly influential, the freshness and spontaneity of his fluid style in both oil and water-colours attracting many imitators. Delacroix wrote of him: 'Other artists were perhaps more powerful or more accurate than Bonington, but no one in the modern school, perhaps no earlier artist, possessed the lightness of execution which makes his works, in a certain sense, diamonds, by which the eye is enticed and charmed independently of the subject or of imitative appeal.' These qualities are particularly apparent in the *pochades* (oil sketches done rapidly on the spot as records of transitory effects in nature), a fashion which he together with *Turner and Constable was instrumental in establishing. The best collection of Bonington's work is in the Wallace Collection, London, and he is also well represented in the City Museum and Art Gallery at Nottingham, his home town.

Bonnard, Pierre (1867–1947). French painter and graphic artist. He studied first at the Académie Julian, where he met *Sérusier, Maurice *Denis, and others who formed the *Nabis group. Later at the École des *Beaux-Arts he came into contact with *Vuillard, who was to be his lifelong friend and with whom he developed the type of intimate domestic interior scene to which the term *Intimiste is applied. From 1891 he exhibited fairly regularly at the *Salon des Indépendants and in 1903 he was one of the founder members of the *Salon d'Automne, organized by the *Fauves, exhibiting there regularly from that date. Bonnard's life was as serene and uneventful as those of *Gauguin and van *Gogh were tempestuous; his exuberance was reserved for his art. Even in this he was never blatant, learning from every new experiment around him yet adapting all he learnt to the refinement of his personal style. In effect he became the most distinguished upholder of the *Impressionist tradition, adding his own lusciousness of colour without ever stepping over the boundaries of conventional taste into the world of the avant-garde. His finest works radiate a sense of well-being that won him great popularity with both collectors and the general public.

Bonnat, Léon (1833–1922). French painter and collector. Bonnat's early works were mainly religious paintings in a *tenebrist style influenced by 17th-cent. Spanish painting, but from about 1870 he turned increasingly to portraiture. His portraits are usually as glum as his religious paintings, but their almost photographic realism won them an appreciative audience and the fortune he earned painting them enabled him to form a superb art collection, particularly of Old Master drawings. He donated it to Bayonne, his native city, where it forms the nucleus of the Musée Bonnat, one of France's finest provincial galleries. His studio and personal effects can be seen in the nearby Musée Basque. Bonnat was a renowned teacher, his many pupils including *Toulouse-Lautrec and *Braque.

Bontemps, Pierre (c.1505/10–68). French sculptor, first documented in 1536 as an assistant to *Primaticcio at *Fontainebleau. By 1550 he was in Paris, working on two important monuments for the royal burial church at S. Denis—the reclining effigies and bas-*reliefs for the tomb of Francis I, designed by the great architect Philibert Delorme, and the monument for the heart of Francis I. Only one other work is documented as being by him—the tomb of Charles de Maigny (1557) in the Louvre—but other works of the period are confidently attributed to him on stylistic evidence, and he seems to have been the foremost French tomb sculptor of the mid 16th cent. His style was elegant and decorative.

Book of Hours. A prayer book used by laymen for private devotion, containing prayers or meditations appropriate to certain hours of the day, days of the week, months, or seasons. They became so popular in the 15th cent. that the Book of Hours outnumbers all other categories of *illuminated manuscripts; from the late 15th cent. there were also printed versions illustrated by *woodcuts. The most famous Book of Hours and one of the most beautiful of all illuminated manuscripts is the *Très Riches Heures du duc de Berry*

(Musée Condé, Chantilly), illuminated by the *Limburg Brothers for Jean de Berry.

Bordone, Paris (1500–71). Italian painter. Bordone was from Treviso, but by 1518 he had settled in Venice, where he was a pupil of *Titian. He found his master disagreeable (*Vasari says Titian stole his first commission) and soon left him. However, his work was strongly influenced by Titian and also by *Giorgione, 'for that master's style pleased him exceedingly' (Vasari). He painted Giorgionesque pastoral scenes and mythologies that now seem rather hard and conventional compared with their inspiration, but they won him great popularity. Commissions came from patrons all over Europe, and he visited France and Germany. His most impressive work is generally agreed to be *The Presentation of the Ring of St Mark to the Doge* (Accademia, Venice), a large ceremonial composition in Titian's grand manner.

Borduas, Paul-Émile (1905–60). Canadian painter, active mainly in Montreal but also in Paris and New York. He trained as a church decorator under Ozias *Leduc, then studied in Paris. In the early 1940s, under *Surrealist influence, he started to produce 'automatic' paintings (see AUTOMATISM), and with *Riopelle founded the radical *abstract group Les *Automatistes. His later paintings have an *all-over surface animation recalling the work of *Pollock, although the only American influence Borduas acknowledged was that of Franz *Kline. He ranks with Riopelle as one of the outstanding Canadian abstract painters of the post-war years.

Borghese Gallery, Rome. Italian state museum housed in the Villa Borghese. The villa was built (1613–15) for Cardinal Scipione Borghese (1576–1633), nephew of Pope Paul V (Camillo Borghese, 1552–1621), and their collections of paintings and sculpture form the nucleus of the museum. Scipione was *Bernini's first important patron, and the sculptor's early work has an unrivalled representation, including two busts of Scipione. The collection of paintings includes outstanding works by *Caravaggio (Scipione was an early admirer), *Raphael, and *Titian. The Borghese collection was one of the few Roman patrician collections not dispersed in the 18th cent. The villa and its contents were acquired by the Italian government from the Borghese family in 1902.

Borghese Warrior (*Borghese Gladiator*). Marble statue (Louvre, Paris) of a nude warrior in a vigorous attitude of combat (his sword and shield are missing, but he is apparently fighting an opponent on horseback). It was discovered in 1611 at Nettuno (near Anzio), had entered the *Borghese collection by 1613, and was bought by Napoleon (brother-in-law of Prince Camillo Borghese) in 1807. The statue is signed by 'Agasias, son of Dositheos, Ephesian' and is generally considered to be a copy of a *Hellenistic work done under the influence of *Lysippus. It became famous soon after its discovery and for two centuries it was one of the most admired and copied of antique statues, praised particularly for its anatomical mastery (*Bernini's *David* is an early instance of a derivation from it).

Borglum, Gutzon (1867–1941). American sculptor of Scandinavian descent. He carried to an extreme the American cult for the colossal (what his wife called 'the emotional value of volume') and gained notoriety with gigantic sculptures on mountain-sides executed with pneumatic drills and dynamite, particularly the huge portrait busts of Washington, Jefferson, Lincoln, and Theodore Roosevelt at Mount Rushmore in the Black Hills of South Dakota. The project, begun in 1930, was sponsored by the US Government and cost over $1,000,000; the final details were added in 1941 after Borglum's death by his son Lincoln. **Solon Hannibal Borglum** (1868–1922), Gutzon's brother, was also a sculptor, mainly of Wild West subjects.

Borrassá, Luís (d. *c*.1425). Spanish painter, active in Barcelona and its neighbourhood from 1388 to 1424. His style shows French and Sienese influences and is representative of the *International Gothic style. Several of his documented works survive, for example, the great composite altarpiece of Sta Clara, executed 1412–15, now in Vich Museum, Barcelona.

Bosboom, Johannes (1817–91). Dutch painter and lithographer, a member of The *Hague School. He specialized in paintings of church interiors and was much inspired by the works of Emanuel de *Witte—figures in many of his church interiors even wear 17th-cent. costumes.

Bosch, Hieronymus (*c*.1450–1516). Netherlandish painter, named after his native town of 'sHertogenbosch (Bois-le-Duc) in northern Brabant, where he seems to have lived throughout his life. His real name was Jerome van Aken. Bosch married well and was successful in his career (although his town was fairly isolated, it was prosperous and culturally stimulating). He was an orthodox Catholic and a prominent member of a local religious brotherhood, but his most characteristic paintings are so bizarre that in the 17th cent. he was reputed to have been a heretic. About forty genuine examples of Bosch's work survive, but none is dated and no accurate chronology can be made. It seems likely, however, that the conventional compositions, such as *The Crucifixion* (Musées Royaux, Brussels), are early works. The majority of his paintings are completely unconventional and immediately recognized by the elements of fantasy, such as half-human half-animal creatures, demons, etc., interspersed with human figures. The basic themes are sometimes quite simple, but heavily embroidered with subsidiary narratives and symbols. Scenes from the life of Christ or a saint show the innocent central figure besieged by horrific representations of evil and temptation—*The Temptation of St Anthony* (Museu Nacional de Arte Antiga, Lisbon) is the most spectacular instance. Other subjects were allegorical representations of biblical texts or proverbs, stressing in morbid vein the greed and folly of human beings and the fearful consequences of their sins. Of these, *The Haywain* and *The Garden of Earthly Delights*, both in the Prado, are perhaps his best-known paintings.

Although his father was a painter, the origins of Bosch's style and technique are far from clear. His manner had little in common with Jan van *Eyck or Rogier van der *Weyden, the two painters who most influenced the development of style in the Low Countries until *c*.1500. There is, indeed, something strangely modern about Bosch's turbulent and grotesque fantasy and it is no accident that his appeal to contemporary taste has been strong. But attempts to discover the psychological key to his motivation or to trace the origin of his imagery or find a coherent interpretation of the symbolism remain inconclusive. In his own time his fame stood high and a generation or so after his death his paintings were avidly collected by Philip II of Spain. Through the medium of prints his works reached a wider public and imitators appeared even in his lifetime. But it was not until Pieter *Bruegel the Elder that another Netherlandish artist appeared with a genius strong enough to extend Bosch's vision rather than simply pastiche it. Apart from the riot of fantasy and that element of the grotesque which caused the *Surrealists to claim Bosch as a forerunner of their school, the haunting beauty of his genuine works derives largely from his glowing colour and superb technique, which was much more fluid and painterly than that of most of his contemporaries.

Bosschaert, Ambrosius (1573–1621). Flemish flower and still-life painter, active mainly in the Netherlands, where he is recorded in Middelburg from 1593 to 1613 and later in the Utrecht Guild in 1616. Although he spent the major part of his life in Holland, Bosschaert's style was basically Flemish—similar to that of Jan *Brueghel, with whom he ranks in quality and as one of the pioneers of flower painting as an independent genre. His bouquets have a rich variety of flowers from different seasons arranged in a formal way. The degree of finish and exactitude, and the subtlety of the colour, are exceptional. His *Vase of Flowers* (Mauritshuis, The Hague, c.1620) is one of the most reproduced of all flower pieces. Bosschaert may fairly be said to have initiated flower painting in Holland and his style was continued by his three sons, **Ambrosius the Younger** (1609–45), **Abraham** (1613–43), and **Johannes** (c.1610–c.1650), and his brother-in-law, Balthasar van der *Ast.

Bosse, Abraham (1602–76). French engraver. His large output (more than 1,500 prints) provides a rich source of documentation on 17th-cent. French life and manners. Many of his engravings are *genre scenes, and even his religious works are in modern dress. Bosse taught perspective at the Académie Royale from its foundation in 1648 until 1661, when he was expelled for quarrelling with his colleagues over his opposition to *Lebrun's dogmatic

theories. He wrote treatises on engraving, painting, perspective, and architecture and he occasionally painted.

Botero, Fernando (1932–). Colombian painter. He has evolved a highly distinctive style in which figures look like grossly inflated dolls; sometimes his paintings are sardonic comments on modern life, but he has also made something of a speciality of parodies on the work of Old Masters. Botero has worked in New York and Paris as well as Colombia and has acquired an international reputation accompanied by extravagant prices for his paintings in the saleroom.

Both, Jan (c.1618–52). Dutch painter, with Nicolaes *Berchem the most celebrated of the Italianate landscape painters. He came from Utrecht, where he studied with *Bloemaert before moving to Italy for a period of about four years, c.1637–41. Although he died young, his output was large, but none of the more than 300 paintings attributed to him can be convincingly dated to his Italian sojourn. His landscapes are typically peopled by peasants driving cattle or travellers gazing on Roman ruins in the light of the evening sun. Such contemporary scenes were an innovation, for *Claude Lorraine and the earlier Dutch painters of the Italian countryside had populated it with biblical or mythological figures. They express the yearning of northerners for the light and idyllic life of the south, and proved immensely popular with collectors, not least in England, helping to shape ideas about Italy for two centuries. Jan's brother **Andries** (c.1612–41) lived with him in Rome from 1639 to 1641 and they are said to have collaborated; but Andries is best known for paintings and drawings of lively peasant scenes which have little in common with Jan's idyllic tone. He was drowned in an accident in Venice.

Botticelli, Sandro (Alessandro di Mariano Filipepi) (1444/5–1510). Florentine painter, long neglected but now probably the best-loved painter of the *quattrocento. The name 'Boticelli', meaning 'little barrel', was originally given to an older brother, presumably because he was portly, but it became adopted as the family surname. He trained with Filippo *Lippi, who was the most important influence on his style. By temperament he belonged to the current of late 15th-cent. art which reacted against the scientific naturalism of *Masaccio and his followers and revived certain elements of the *Gothic style—a delicate sentiment, sometimes bordering on sentimentality, a feminine grace, and an emphasis on the ornamental and evocative capabilities of line. Almost all Botticelli's life was spent in Florence, his only significant journey from the city being in 1481–2, when he worked on the decoration of the Sistine Chapel in the Vatican, where he painted side by side with *Perugino, *Rosselli, and *Ghirlandaio. The fact that he was called to Rome for such a prestigious commission shows that he must have had a considerable reputation, and by this time the most characteristic idiosyncrasies of his style had already gained shape in the celebrated poetic allegory known since *Vasari as the *Primavera* (Uffizi, Florence, c.1478). There is evidence that the patron who commissioned this and two of his other famous mythological paintings (*The Birth of Venus* and *Pallas and the Centaur*, both in the Uffizi) was Lorenzo di Pierfrancesco de' *Medici (second cousin of Lorenzo the Magnificent), a wealthy Florentine with strong interests in Platonic philosophy. It has been suggested that it was this philosophy that prompted the new idea of large-scale pictures with a secular content; the classical deities represented are not the carefree Olympians of Ovid's tales but the symbolic embodiment of some deep moral or metaphysical truth. Given that the Neo-Platonists regarded Beauty as the visible token of the Divine, there would be no blasphemy in using the same facial type and expression for Venus and for the Holy Virgin. According to Vasari, Botticelli later fell under the sway of Savonarola's sermons, repented of his 'pagan' pictures, and gave up painting. The second half of this statement is definitely incorrect and the first is doubtful, but it is certainly true that Botticelli's later paintings are more obviously 'serious'—solemn, intense, sometimes ecstatic—than his early work. The most telling example is the *Mystic Nativity* (NG, London, 1500), which bears a cryptic inscription seeming to imply that Botticelli expected the end of the world and the dawn of the millennium.

Botticelli ran a busy studio (his most important pupil was Filippino *Lippi) and his surviving output is large for a painter of his period. Apart from religious and mythological pictures, he produced some memorable portraits and also some marvellously delicate drawings—mainly in pen outline—for a lavish manuscript of Dante's *Divine Comedy* (now divided between the Staatsbibliothek, Berlin, and the Vatican Library). Although little is known of his life, it seems clear that at the peak of his career he was the most popular painter in Florence. After *Leonardo's return to the city in 1500, however, Botticelli's linear style must have looked archaic and he died in obscurity. His fame was not resurrected until the second half of the 19th cent., when the *Pre-Raphaelites imitated his wan, elongated types, *Ruskin sang his praises, and Walter *Pater dedicated to his art one of his most eloquent essays. At the end of the century his work was a major influence on *Art Nouveau.

Botticini, Francesco (Francesco di Giovanni) (c.1446–97). Florentine painter. His style consists almost entirely of elements drawn from his more illustrious contemporaries—*Botticelli, Domenico *Ghirlandaio, Filippino *Lippi, *Verrocchio. He painted one remarkable work, however, the *Assumption* (NG, London, c.1474), which has the distinction of being the only picture from the *quattrocento known to have been painted to illustrate a heresy. The *donor, Matteo Palmieri, believed that human souls are the angels who stayed neutral when Satan rebelled against God.

Bouchardon, Edmé (1698–1762). French sculptor, medallist, and draughtsman, whose work marks the beginning of the *Classical reaction against the *Rococo style. From 1723 to 1732 he worked in Rome, where the influence of the *antique inspired the severe Classicism of his bust of Philippe Stosch (Staatliche Museen, West Berlin, 1727). Although his style later softened somewhat, notably in the famous *Cupid Making a Bow from Hercules' Club* (Louvre, Paris, c.1750), it remained too severe for court taste. Bouchardon had many supporters, however, and his contemporary reputation stood high. His most important work, an equestrian statue of Louis XV, was left unfinished at his death, and was destroyed in the Revolution.

Boucher, François (1703–70). French *Rococo painter, engraver, and designer, who best embodies the frivolity and elegant superficiality of French court life at the middle of the 18th cent. He was for a short time a pupil of François *Lemoyne and in his early years was closely connected with *Watteau, many of whose pictures he engraved. In 1727–31 he was in Italy, and on his return was soon busy as a versatile fashionable artist. His career was hugely successful and he received many honours, becoming Director of the *Gobelins factory in 1755 and Director of the Academy and King's Painter in 1765. He was also the favourite artist of Louis XV's most famous mistress, Mme de Pompadour, to whom he gave lessons and whose portrait he painted several times (Wallace Coll., London; NG, Edinburgh). Boucher mastered every branch of decorative and illustrative painting, from colossal schemes of decoration for the royal châteaux of Versailles, Fontainebleau, Marly, and Bellevue, to designs for fans and slippers. In his typical paintings he turned the traditional mythological themes into wittily indecorous *scènes galantes*, and he painted female flesh with a delightfully healthy sensuality, notably in the celebrated *Reclining Girl* (Alte Pinakothek, Munich, 1751), which probably represents Louis XV's mistress Louisa O'Murphy. Towards the end of his career, as French taste changed in the direction of *Neoclassicism, Boucher was attacked, notably by *Diderot, for his stereotyped colouring and artificiality; he relied on his own repertory of motifs instead of painting from the life and objected to nature on the grounds that it was 'too green and badly lit'. Certainly his work often shows the effects of superficiality and overproduction, but at its best it has irresistible charm and great brilliance of execution, qualities he passed on to his most important pupil, *Fragonard.

Boucicaut (or **Boucicault**) **Master** (active early 15th cent.). Franco-Flemish manuscript *illuminator, named after a *Book of Hours (Musée Jacquemart-André, Paris) done for Jean II le Meingre Boucicaut (1365–1421). This manuscript, which was presumably commissioned before 1415, when Boucicaut was captured at the Battle of Agincourt, is a magnificent example of the *International Gothic style, but in its accomplished handling of space and *aerial perspective and its delightful *genre detail

it heralds the achievements of the 15th-cent. Netherlandish School. Many other manuscripts are attributed to the workshop of the Boucicaut Master.

Boudin, Eugène (1824–98). French painter. Son of a sailor, he ran a stationery and picture-framing business at Le Havre (1844–9), where his clients included Jean-François *Millet, who encouraged him to paint. *Courbet, *Jongkind, and *Corot were among his friends. He was a strong advocate of direct painting from nature, and had a great influence on the young *Monet, whom he introduced to *plein-air* painting. Boudin's own paintings consisted mainly of beach scenes and seascapes from the coast of northern France and were distinguished by the prominence given to luminous skies. He is regarded as a link between the painters of the generation of Corot and the *Impressionists, and he exhibited in the first Impressionist exhibition of 1874. There is a Boudin Museum in Honfleur, his native town.

Bouguereau, Adolphe-William (1825–1905). French painter. In 1850 he won the *Prix de Rome, and after his return to France in 1854 he became an immensely successful and influential exponent of academic art, upholding traditional values and contriving to exclude avant-garde work from the *Salon—*Cézanne once expressed regret at being excluded from the 'Salon de Monsieur Bouguereau'. He painted portraits of photographic verisimilitude, slick and sentimental religious works, and coyly erotic nudes. For many years damned unequivocally as a 'master in the hierarchy of mediocrity' (J.-K. Huysmans) and an opponent of all progressive ideas, Bouguereau has recently achieved something of a rehabilitation, his work becoming the subject of serious study and fetching huge prices in the saleroom.

Bourdelle, Émile-Antoine (1861–1929). French sculptor, born at Montauban. As a boy he obtained practical experience of carving in the workshop of his father, a cabinet maker. In 1876 he began to study at the École des Beaux-Arts, Toulouse, from where he won a scholarship to the École des *Beaux-Arts, Paris, in 1884. However, he shortly left the school and worked for a while with Jules *Dalou before becoming *Rodin's chief assistant.

Bourdelle's work has been somewhat over-shadowed by his association with Rodin, but he was already an accomplished artist when he started working for him and developed an independent style. His energetic, rippling surfaces owe much to Rodin, but his flat rhythmic simplifications of form, recalling *Romanesque art, are more personal. He was particularly interested in the relationship of sculpture to architecture, and his reliefs for the Théâtre des Champs-Élysées (1912) are among his finest works. Bourdelle had many other prestigious public commissions and also achieved great distinction as a teacher. He was a talented painter and draughtsman as well as a sculptor. The most representative collection of his work is in the Musée Bourdelle, Paris.

Bourdichon, Jean (*c.*1457–1521). French painter, the most important pupil of *Fouquet. He was active in Tours, where he worked for several royal patrons, including Charles VIII, Louis XII, and Anne of Brittany, who married each of them in turn. For this queen consort Bourdichon produced his most celebrated work—the *Hours of Anne of Brittany* (completed 1508), now in the Bibliothèque Nationale, Paris (see BOOK OF HOURS). It contains numerous exquisite borders of plants and insects, together with fifty-one large scenes—mainly from the New Testament and lives of the saints, but also including a portrait of Anne at prayer. Some of the religious scenes show such strong Italianate influence that it seems almost certain Bourdichon had visited Italy. Bourdichon is recorded as having painted works on a larger scale, but apart from a *triptych of *The Madonna and Child with Saints* in the Museo di Capodimonte, Naples, all his other known works are manuscript *illuminations. He effectively ends the great French tradition in this art.

Bourdon, Sébastien (1616–71). French painter. In 1634–7 he worked in Rome, where he developed a talent for imitating the work of other painters—*Claude, *Dughet, van *Laer—sometimes probably with intent to deceive. He continued in this vein when he returned to France and his *œuvre* is still ill-defined. From 1652 to 1654 he was court painter to Queen Christina of Sweden, of whom he did two

portraits (Prado, Madrid, and National-Museum, Stockholm), and after his return to France he worked mainly as a portraitist, developing a more personal style in which soft tonalities and skilful play with cascading draperies create a languorous, romantic effect (*Self-portrait*, Louvre, Paris).

Bourgeois, Louise (1911–). French-American sculptor, born in Paris, where part of her training was with *Léger. Bourgeois, started as a painter and engraver and turned to sculpture only in the late 1940s. She first achieved recognition in the 1950s for her wood constructions painted uniformly black or white, which preceded the similar works of Louise *Nevelson. Since then Bourgeois has worked in various materials, including stone, metal, and latex, and has built up a reputation as one of the leading contemporary American sculptors. Although her work is abstract, it is often suggestive of the human figure, and sexual significance is sometimes ascribed to it.

Boursse, Esaias (1631–72). Dutch painter, active mainly in his native Amsterdam. He joined the Dutch East India Company in 1661 and made two voyages to the Indies, on the second of which he died at sea. His few surviving paintings include some exquisite interior scenes that invite comparison with *Vermeer because of their tranquil beauty and subtle colour harmonies (*Interior: Woman Cooking*, Wallace Coll., London, 1656).

Bouts, Dirk (or **Dieric**) (d. 1475). Netherlandish painter, born probably in Haarlem and active mainly in Louvain, where he was city painter from 1468. His major commissions there were the *Last Supper* altarpiece for the church of S. Pierre (still *in situ*, 1464–7) and two panels (out of a projected set of four) on the *Justice of Emperor Otto* for the Hôtel de Ville (Musées Royaux, Brussels, 1470–5). Apart from these, there are no documented works, but his style is highly distinctive and a convincing œuvre has been built up for him. His static figures are exaggeratedly slender and graceful, and often set in landscapes of exquisite beauty. There is little action, but deep poetry of feeling. Sources for his work have been sought in the mysterious Albert van *Ouwater (who likewise seems to have had Haarlem connections), Rogier van der *Weyden, and

Petrus *Christus, but the individuality of Bouts's work transcends any models. His style was highly influential and was continued by his two sons, **Dieric the Younger** (c.1448–90/1) and **Aelbrecht** (c.1450/60–1549). Particularly popular were small devotional images of the *Mater Dolorosa* and *Christ Crowned with Thorns*.

Bowes, John (1811–85). English collector. The illegitimate son of the 10th Earl of Strathmore, he married Josephine Benoîte Coffin Chevallier (1825–1874), a French actress and amateur painter, in 1852, and they devoted much of their wealth and energy to collecting. In 1869 (the year after Josephine was created Countess of Montalbo), they began to build an enormous museum at Barnard Castle in County Durham (near to the Strathmore's home at Streatlam) and it was opened to the public in 1892 (by which time the founders were dead). The building was designed by a French architect, Jules Pellechet, and *Pevsner describes it as 'big bold, and incongruous, looking exactly like the town hall of a major provincial town in France ... gloriously inappropriate for the town to which it belongs'. The Bowes Museum is particularly rich in French paintings and applied art of the 18th cent. (it has been called 'the *Wallace Collection of the North'), but the most remarkable area of the collection is the fine representation of Spanish painting—the best in Britain outside London.

Boyd, Arthur (1920–). Australian painter, potter, etcher, lithographer, and ceramic artist, a member of a family who have made a name in many of the arts. His father was a sculptor and potter, his mother a painter, but he was largely self-taught as an artist. After holding his first one-man show at the age of 17, his artistic career was interrupted by the Second World War. Subsequently he became well known in Australia particularly for his large ceramic totem pole at the entrance to the Olympic Pool, Melbourne, and for his series (twenty pictures) *Love, Marriage and Death of a Half-Caste*. He moved to England in 1959 and soon established a reputation; with *Nolan he has become probably the best-known Australian artist of his generation.

Boydell, John (1719–1804). English engraver and print publisher. He made a fortune in the 1740s by publishing views of England and Wales, which he engraved from his own drawings. Later he published the work of other engravers and by developing a large foreign trade spread the fame of English artists and engravers on the Continent. In 1790 he was Lord Mayor of London. His most ambitious undertaking was the celebrated Shakespeare Gallery: from 1786 he commissioned from major artists (including *Fuseli, *Reynolds, and *Romney) 162 oil paintings illustrating Shakespeare's plays, exhibiting them in a purpose-built gallery in Pall Mall, opened in 1789. The engravings after them were published as illustrations to a nine-volume edition of Shakespeare in 1802 and separately in 1803. Boydell hoped by this venture to encourage the rise of a 'great national school of *history painting', and he intended to leave the collection to the nation, but he had heavy losses during the French wars and it was sold by lottery in 1804 shortly after his death. Boydell's nephew, **Josiah Boydell** (1752–1817), was a painter and engraver, his uncle's partner and successor in his engraving business.

Boys, Thomas Shotter (1803–74). English water-colour painter and lithographer. For some time he lived in France, where he was a friend of *Bonington, but he settled in England in 1837. He specialized in continental urban scenes and in 1839 he published *Picturesque Architecture in Paris, Ghent, Antwerp, Rouen, etc.*, a work which marked the transition from hand-tinted *lithography to chromolithography. In 1842 he published *Original Views of London as it is*, the plates of which constitute a fine topographical record of Regency London.

bozzetto. Italian term for a sculptor's small-scale model, usually in wax or clay, for a larger work in more durable material. The term is sometimes also applied to a painted sketch.

Bramante, Donato (Donato di Angelo) (1444–1514). Italian architect and painter. Bramante was the creator and greatest exponent of the High *Renaissance style in architecture, but most of his early career, which is ill-documented, seems to have been devoted to painting. He probably trained in Urbino and is first documented in 1477 working on fresco decorations at the Palazzo del Podestà in Bergamo. In about 1480 he settled in Milan, and in 1481 produced his earliest surviving dated work, the design of an engraving of an elaborate architectural fantasy (the British Museum, London, possesses one of only two known impressions). At about the same time he began his first building, Sta Maria presso S. Satiro, Milan, in which his knowledge of *perspective was used to create an illusion of recession in the choir, which is in reality only a few inches deep. His only certain surviving paintings are poorly preserved frescos of armed men (c.1480–5) in the Brera, Milan, which also houses the finest painting attributed to him (on the testimony of *Lomazzo), a sombre and poignant *Christ at the Column*, which shows some influence from his friend *Leonardo. In 1499 Bramante left Milan for Rome, where in 1506 he began the rebuilding of St Peter's. There is no evidence of any activity as a painter in Rome, but *Vasari says that Bramante designed the majestic architectural setting of *Raphael's fresco *The School of Athens* in the Vatican Stanze. Certainly Raphael paid tribute to Bramante by introducing his portrait into this painting as the mathematician Euclid. Bramante had an enormous influence as an architect, and his interest in perspective and *trompe-l'œil* left a mark on Milanese painting, notably in the work of his follower *Bramantino.

Bramantino (Bartolomeo Suardi) (c.1460–1530). Milanese painter and architect, a follower of *Bramante, from whom he takes his nickname. He was appointed court painter and architect to Duke Francesco *Sforza in 1525. His style as a painter is complex and eclectic, drawing on *Piero della Francesca and *Leonardo as well as Bramante; at its best is has a certain stolid dignity. Perhaps his most individual characteristic is his use of sombre Classical architectural backgrounds, as in *The Adoration of the Magi* (NG, London).

Bramer, Leonaert (1596–1674). Dutch *genre and history painter, active mainly in his native Delft. He travelled widely in Italy and France, 1614–28, and drew on a variety of influences for his most characteristic paintings—small nocturnal scenes with vivid effects of light. Works such as

the *Scene of Sorcery* (Musée des Beaux-Arts, Bordeaux) have earned him the reputation of 'an interesting independent who cannot easily be pigeonholed' (J. Rosenberg, S. Slive, and E. H. ter Kuile, *Dutch Art and Architecture, 1600–1800*). Bramer was also one of the few Dutch artists to paint frescos in Holland, but none of his work in the medium has survived. He evidently knew well the greatest of his Delft contemporaries, *Vermeer, for he came to the latter's defence when his future mother-in-law was trying to prevent him from marrying her daughter. In fact, it is likely that Bramer, rather than Carel *Fabritius, was Vermeer's teacher.

Brancusi, Constantin (1876–1957). Romanian sculptor, active mainly in Paris, one of the most revered and influential of 20th-cent. artists. After studying at Bucharest and afterwards at Vienna and Munich, in 1904 he settled in Paris, where he spent many years of poverty and hardship. In 1906 he was introduced to *Rodin, whose offer to take him on as assistant Brancusi refused, with the famous comment 'No other trees can grow in the shadow of an oak tree.' In 1909–10 he worked with *Modigliani in Montparnasse and about the same time abandoned modelling for direct carving. His craftsmanship was masterly and he would often let the nature of the stone dictate stylizations. He had a one-man show in 1926 at the Brummer Gallery, New York, which gained notoriety owing to a law case against the Customs authorities who proposed to assess his bronze *Bird in Space* for duty as raw metal (sculpture was exempt from duty). In 1937 he made sculpture (including the enormous *Endless Column*, nearly 30 m. high) for the public park at Tirgu Jiu near his birthplace and in the same year he visited India to design a Temple of Meditation for the Maharajah of Indore.

Brancusi's originality in reducing natural forms to their ultimate—almost abstract—simplicity had profound effects on the course of 20th-cent. sculpture. *Epstein and *Archipenko owed much to him and *Gaudier-Brzeska was his professed admirer. Later, Carl *Andre claimed to have been inspired by *Endless Column*, converting its repeated modules into his horizontal arrangements of identical units. More generally, Henry *Moore wrote of Brancusi: 'Since the Gothic, European sculpture had become overgrown with moss, weeds—all sorts of surface excrescences which completely concealed shape. It has been Brancusi's special mission to get rid of this undergrowth and to make us once more shape-conscious.' On his death Brancusi bequeathed to the French Government his studio and its contents, which included versions of most of his best works. The studio has now been reconstructed in the Pompidou Centre in Paris. There is another outstanding Brancusi collection in the Philadelphia Museum of Art.

Brangwyn, Sir Frank (1867–1956). British painter, etcher, and designer, born at Bruges of Welsh parentage. Brangwyn was apprenticed to William *Morris (1882–4), and like his master was active in a variety of fields. He was an official war artist in the First World War and was a skilful etcher and lithographer, but he became best known for his murals, the most famous of which, on the theme of the British Empire (1924–30) and originally commissioned for the House of Lords, is now in the Guildhall in Swansea. During his lifetime Brangwyn had a great reputation on the Continent, and there are museums devoted to him in Bruges and Orange. He was one of the finest draughtsmen of his time, though his painting tended to the decoratively sentimental.

Braque, Georges (1882–1963). French painter, with *Picasso the joint creator of *Cubism. Initially he followed his father's trade of house painter, but in 1900 he began to study at the École des *Beaux-Arts in Paris. In about 1906 he formed a friendship with Othon *Friesz and like him painted in the manner of the *Fauves, with pure pigments and bright colours. Braque, however, was not by temperament in harmony with the subjective and impulsive aspects of Fauvism and after being immensely impressed by the *Cézanne Memorial Exhibition at the *Salon d'Automne in 1907, he began painting in a geometrically analytical manner. Thus, when the dealer *Kahnweiler introduced him to Picasso in the same year he was ripe to join the latter in the researches that led to Cubism. Until Braque's mobilization in 1914 he and Picasso worked in close association. *The Portuguese* (Kunstmuseum, Basle, 1911) is one of the best-known paintings of this phase of his career, and the first picture to incorporate *stencilled lettering. Braque also took the lead with the *papier collé* technique of introducing pieces of imitation wood engraving, marbled surfaces, etc., stuck on to the canvas. After the First World War, in which he was seriously wounded, Braque's work diverged sharply from that of Picasso. His style became much less angular, lending towards graceful curves. He concentrated mainly on still life, using subtle muted colours and sometimes mixing sand with his paint to produce a textured effect. A mature expression of his late work is *The Studio* series of the 1950s. Braque also did much book illustration, designed stage sets and costumes, and did some decorative work. By the end of his career he enjoyed immense prestige.

Bratby, John (1928–). British painter and writer. Bratby is a versatile artist: he has done portraits, still lifes, figure compositions, landscapes, and flower pieces, and also designed film sets. In the years after the Second World War he was one of the group of harsh and austere painters of domestic life who were known as the *Kitchen Sink School. Later his work became lighter and more exuberant. Among his publications are the novel *Breakdown* (1960) and a book on Stanley *Spencer (1970).

Bray, Jan de (c.1627–97). Dutch painter, principally of portraits. He worked in Haarlem and his vigorously characterized work shows the lasting influence of *Hals in the city, although de Bray's handling is much smoother, in the manner of van der *Helst. Jan's father, **Salomon** (1597–1664), was an architect and painter of biblical and allegorical scenes. He wrote a book, *Architectura Moderna* (1631), describing the buildings of Hendrick de *Keyser.

Bredius, Abraham (1855–1946). Dutch art historian and collector. Bredius was particularly noted for his archival research and published a large amount of new documentation relating to 17th cent. Dutch artists. His best-known work is his complete illustrated catalogue of *Rembrandt's paintings, originally published in German in 1935 and then in an English edition in 1937; a second English edition, revised by Horst Gerson, Bredius's collaborator on the original edition, appeared in 1969. It is still a standard work (although the illustrations are of notably poor quality) and the Bredius numbering system is widely used in Rembrandt scholarship. Bredius made a choice collection of Dutch paintings; many were presented or bequeathed by him to the *Rijksmuseum in Amsterdam and the *Mauritshuis in The Hague (of which he was director from 1889 to 1909) and others are in the Bredius Museum in The Hague. His reputation as a connoisseur was somewhat blighted because he was deceived by the work of the Vermeer forger Han van Meegeren (1880–1947); however, Bredius was very old at the time (1937) and almost all his contemporaries were similarly deceived.

Breenbergh, Bartolomeus (1598/1600–1657). Dutch painter, with *Poelenburgh the leading pioneer of the taste for Italianate landscapes in the Netherlands. Breenbergh was in Italy for about a decade in the 1620s and thereafter worked in Amsterdam. His style as a painter is very similar to Poelenburgh's, his biblical and mythological characters set in well-balanced views of the Roman Campagna, often complete with Classical ruins. His drawings are much fresher and bolder, and have often passed under the name of *Claude, as is the case with two examples in Christ Church, Oxford. Late in his career Breenbergh turned to figure painting.

Breitner, George Hendrik (1857–1923). The leading Dutch *Impressionist painter. His most characteristic early works, influenced by the *Hague School, were pictures of horsemen, but a visit to Paris in 1884 brought him under the spell of Impressionism. In 1886 he settled in Amsterdam and became particularly associated with scenes of its busy harbour, its architecture, and its bustling street life. The unposed 'snapshot' compositions of many of these paintings reflects his interest in photography. After 1910, owing to ill health, he practically ceased to paint.

Breton, André (1896–1966). French poet, essayist, and critic, the founder and chief theorist of *Surrealism. He published the first *Manifesto of Surrealism* in 1924 and helped with the first number of the periodical *The Surrealist Revolution*, which he afterwards edited. His *Second Manifesto of Surrealism* was published in the final number of this journal, December 1929, and he wrote numerous other books and articles on Surrealism. Breton also made *assemblages of surrealistically juxtaposed objects, which he called 'Poemobjects'.

Brett, John (1830–1902). English painter, mainly of coastal scenes and landscapes. He was influenced by the *Pre-Raphaelites and *Ruskin, and a handful of his early paintings such as *The Stonebreaker* (Walker Art Gal., Liverpool, 1857–8) are remarkable *tours de force* of minute and brilliant detail. His later work, however, tended to degenerate into a prosaic catalogue of objects.

Breu, Jörg the Elder (1475/6–1537). German painter and designer of woodcuts, probably a pupil of Ulrich *Apt. Breu was one of the leading painters of his time in his native Augsburg, but his most important works there—a series of frescoes in the town hall—are no longer extant. He was patronized by the emperor Maximilian and by Duke William IV of Bavaria, for whom he painted *The Battle of Zama* (Alte Pinakothek, Munich) in the same series as Altdorfer's celebrated *Battle of Issus*. His style was complex, sharing something of *Altdorfer's passion and love of landscape, and showing strong influence from *Dürer and from a journey he made to Italy in about 1514. His son, **Jörg the Younger** (c.1510–47), was court painter at Neuburg, and a prolific book illustrator.

Breughel. See BRUEGEL.

Bril, Paul (1554–1626). Flemish landscape painter, active mainly in Rome, where he settled in about 1575. Bril painted frescos, but his fame rests on his small easel paintings. He lived long enough to assimilate some of the qualities of *Elsheimer's and Annibale *Carracci's landscapes and his work bridges the gap between the fantastic 16th-cent. Flemish *Mannerist style and the more plausible, idealized Italian landscapes of the 17th cent. He also made views of Rome for the tourist trade, and marine pictures. His conception of both of these subjects had considerable influence upon Agostino *Tassi, the teacher of *Claude Lorraine, and upon Claude himself. Paul's brother, **Matthew** or **Mattheus** (1550–

83), also worked in Rome, and their work is hard to distinguish.

British Museum, London. The national museum of archaeology and antiquities, which also houses the national library of manuscripts and printed books. It was established by Act of Parliament in 1753 when the government purchased the private collection of the physician and naturalist Sir Hans Sloane (1660–1753), consisting of 'books, manuscripts, prints, drawings, pictures, medals, coins, seals, *cameos and natural curiosities'. It was first housed in Montagu House, Bloomsbury, and for nearly 50 years it was necessary to make formal application for admission. With the acquisition of Sir William Hamilton's collection of Classical vases and antiquities (1772), a plethora of Egyptian antiquities (including the Rosetta Stone donated by George III) on the defeat of Napoleon at the turn of the century, the *Elgin Marbles, the magnificent library of George III (1823), and many other bequests and purchases, the Museum became established as one of the world's greatest treasure houses. The present structure (1823–47), one of the masterpieces of Greek Revival architecture, was built by Sir Robert Smirke and the great circular Reading Room was completed in 1857. Until 1881 the building also housed the collections now in the Natural History Museum, and one of its greatest attractions was a stuffed giraffe in the entrance hall. The Department of Prints and Drawings was originally part of the Library, but led a separate existence from 1808 onwards. It began with over 2,000 drawings from the Sloane collections, which included an album of *Dürer's drawings. Among the most important acquisitions since was the Richard Payne *Knight bequest (1824) of over 1,000 drawings, including 273 drawings by *Claude. It is now one of the largest and most comprehensive collections in the world containing more than two million items. The British Museum Library (as it was formerly known) was reconstituted by Act of Parliament as part of the British Library in 1973, and will eventually be housed in a new and separate building near St Pancras Station.

Briulov, Karl. See BRYULOV.

Broederlam, Melchior (active 1381–1409). Netherlandish painter, court painter to Philip the Bold, Duke of Burgundy, from 1387. Documents show that he was a busy and versatile artist, but his only surviving works are two wings from an altarpiece representing *The Annunciation and Visitation* and *The Presentation and Flight into Egypt* (Musée des Beaux-Arts, Dijon, 1394–9). They are among the first and finest examples of *International Gothic, combining lavish decorative display with realistic touches that look forward to the later development of the Netherlandish School. The figure of St Joseph in *The Flight into Egypt*, for example, is represented as an authentic peasant.

bronze. An alloy of copper (usually about 90 per cent) and tin, often also containing small amounts of other metals such as lead or zinc. Since antiquity it has been the metal most commonly used in cast sculpture because of its strength, durability, and the fact that it is easily workable—both hot and cold—by a variety of processes. It is easier to cast than copper because it has a lower melting-point, and its great tensile strength makes possible the protrusion of unsupported parts—an advantage over *marble sculpture. The colour of bronze is affected by the proportion of tin or other metals present, varying from silverish to a rich, coppery red, and its surface beauty can be enhanced when it acquires a *patina. See also CIRE-PERDUE.

Bronzino, Agnolo (Agnolo di Cosimo) (1503–72). Florentine *Mannerist painter, the pupil and adopted son of *Pontormo, who introduced his portrait as a child into his painting *Joseph in Egypt* (NG, London). The origin of his nickname is uncertain, but possibly derived from his having a dark complexion. Bronzino was deeply attached to Pontormo and his style was heavily indebted to his master. However, Bronzino lacked the emotional intensity that was such a characteristic of Pontormo's work and excelled as a portraitist rather than a religious painter. He was court painter to Duke Cosimo I de *Medici for most of his career, and his work influenced the course of European court portraiture for a century. Cold, cultured, and unemotionally analytical, his portraits convey a sense of almost insolent assurance. Bronzino was also a poet, and his most personal portraits are perhaps those of other literary figures (*Laura Battiferri*, Palazzo Vecchio, Florence, *c*.1560). He was less successful as a religious painter, his lack of real feeling leading to empty, elegant posturing, as in *The Martyrdom of S. Lorenzo* (S. Lorenzo, Florence, 1569), in which almost every one of the extraordinarily contorted poses can be traced back to *Raphael or to *Michelangelo, whom Bronzino idolized. It is the type of work that got Mannerism a bad name. Bronzino's skill with the nude was better deployed in the celebrated *Venus, Cupid, Folly, and Time* (NG, London), which conveys strong feelings of eroticism under the pretext of a moralizing allegory. His other major works include the design of a series of tapestries on *The Story of Joseph* for the Palazzo Vecchio. He was a much respected figure who took a prominent part in the activities of the Accademia del Disegno (see ACADEMY), of which he was a founder member in 1563. His pupils included Alessandro *Allori, who—in a curious mirroring of his own early career—was also his adopted son.

Brooking, Charles (1723?–59). English marine painter. Very little is known of his short career, but he was the finest British marine painter of his day, equally adept at calm or rough seas. He is said to have been employed at Deptford dockyard and had an intimate knowledge of the ships he painted.

Brotherhood of Ruralists. See BLAKE, PETER.

Brouwer, Adriaen (1605/6–38). Flemish painter who spent a great part of his short working life at Haarlem in Holland. He went to Haarlem in about 1623 and was probably a pupil of Frans *Hals. In 1631 he left Holland for Antwerp (where he was for a while detained by the Spaniards as a suspected spy) and apparently spent the rest of his career there. He perhaps died from the plague that swept the city in 1638. Brouwer was an important link between the Dutch and Flemish schools and played a major role in popularizing low life *genre scenes in both countries in which he worked. Early sources depict him as a colourful bohemian character and his most typical works represent peasants brawling and drinking. Although the subject-matter is humorously coarse, his

technique was delicate and sparkling. The virtuosity of brushwork and economy of expression are perhaps surpassed in his landscapes, which are among the greatest of his age. *Rembrandt and *Rubens were among the admirers and collectors of Brouwer's paintings (Rubens at one time owned seventeen), and Adriaen van *Ostade and David *Teniers the Younger were among his many followers.

Brown, Ford Madox (1821–93). English painter. He was born at Calais and trained at Antwerp (under *Wappers), in Paris, and at Rome, where he came into contact with the *Nazarenes. Settling in England in 1846, he became a friend of the Pre-Raphaelites and—with his taste for literary subjects and meticulous handling—an influence on their work, though he was never a member of the Brotherhood. *Rossetti studied briefly with him in 1848 and Brown's *Chaucer at the Court of Edward III* (Art Gallery of New South Wales, Sydney, 1851) contains portraits of several of the Brotherhood. His best-known picture, *The Last of England* (City Art Gallery, Birmingham, 1855), was inspired by the departure of *Woolner, the Pre-Raphaelite sculptor, for Australia. The other famous anthology piece that Brown painted, *Work* (Manchester City Art Gallery, 1852–63), shows his dedicated craftsmanship and brilliant colouring, but is somewhat swamped by its social idealism. In 1861 Brown was a founder member of William *Morris's company, for which he designed *stained glass and furniture. The major work of the later part of his career is a cycle of paintings (1878–93) in Manchester Town Hall on the history of the city. Brown was an individualist and a man of prickly temperament; he opposed the *Royal Academy and was a pioneer of the one-man show.

Brücke, Die (The Bridge). Group of German *Expressionist artists founded in 1905 by *Kirchner, *Schmidt-Rottluff, *Heckel, and Fritz Bleyl (1880–1966), who at the time were all architectural students at the Dresden Technical School. The name was chosen by Schmidt-Rottluff and indicated their faith in the art of the future, towards which their own work was to serve as a bridge. They were moved by an impulse of revolt and wanted, as others have wanted, to achieve 'freedom of life and action against established and older forces', but their aims remained vague. In practice they created an intense and sometimes angst-ridden version of Expressionism, influenced by van *Gogh, *Gauguin, *Munch, the *Nabis, and the *Fauves. Other artists associated with Die Brücke included *Nolde, *Pechstein, and van *Dongen. Most of the members of the group were without proper training and their handling of paint can have an almost crude vigour. Like the Fauves they were interested in *primitive art, which they saw in the Dresden Ethnological Museum, but the inspiration which they derived from it was different; forms were often harshly distorted and colours were used symbolically in a violently clashing manner. The achievement which seems to have most lasting value was their revival of graphic arts, in particular the *woodcut, for emotional expressive purposes. Strong contrasts of black and white, bold cutting, and simplified forms were used to great effect. In 1910 Die Brücke shifted its activities to Berlin where Otto Müller (1874–1930) joined the group. The members had for a time lived together as a community, but the personal rifts that had been present from the beginning became more intense and led to the dissolution of the group in 1913.

Bruegel (or **Breughel**), **Pieter** (*c.*1525–69). The greatest Netherlandish painter and draughtsman of the 16th cent. There is very little documentary evidence concerning his career, but van *Mander's laudatory biography, published in 1604, is a useful source of information, even though it misleadingly projects an image of Bruegel as above all else a comic painter. Far from being the yokel of popular tradition—'Peasant Bruegel'—he seems to have been a man of some culture, as is indicated by his friendship with the great geographer Abraham Ortelius. He joined the Antwerp Guild in 1551, having been the pupil of Pieter *Coecke van Aelst, whose daughter Bruegel later married. Between 1551 and 1553 he made a prolonged journey via France to Italy, where he travelled as far south as Naples and Sicily. On his return journey through the Alps he made extremely sensitive landscape drawings; the experience of the Alps affected him much more than the example of any art he had seen in Italy. Back in Antwerp he designed a series of landscapes which were engraved and published by Hieronymous *Cock, for whom Bruegel produced many drawings of various subjects, including parables like 'the Big Fish eat Little Fish'. The engraving after Bruegel's drawing of this subject (published in 1557), bears the inscription 'Hieronymus Bos Inventor', an attempt by Cock to cash in on the continued popularity of *Bosch, who influenced Bruegel considerably.

A drawing of Amsterdam dated 1562 probably indicates a visit there before his move to Brussels in 1563, where he married in that year. From this time until his death he concentrated on painting and produced his best-known works. His patrons included Cardinal Granvella, chief counsellor to Margaret of Parma, Philip II's regent in the Netherlands, and the wealthy banker Niclaes Jonghelinck, who in 1565 commissioned the series of *The Months*, of which five survive today. Three of these (including the celebrated *Hunters in the Snow*) are in the remarkable collection of fourteen paintings by Bruegel in the Kunsthistorisches Museum, Vienna, which comprises nearly one-third of his surviving paintings; the other two are in the Metropolitan Museum, New York, and the National Gallery, Prague. His style changed during the last six years of his life in Brussels; he abandoned the crowded panoramas of his earlier years, making his figures bigger and bolder, as is seen most notably in his novel treatment of proverbs, a genre that had previously been of minor account (*The Blind Leading the Blind*, Museo di Capodimonte, Naples, 1568). Bruegel enjoyed a considerable reputation in his lifetime, and his pictorial and spiritual influence, through his original works and the many prints after them, is incalculable in later Flemish painting, whether landscape or *genre. It is only in the 20th cent., however, that he has come to be recognized also as a profound religious painter and an artist whose human sympathy and understanding have hardly been excelled. Bruegel's two painter sons were infants when he died and so they had no training from him (they were reputedly taught by their grandmother—the widow of Pieter Coecke—Mayken Verhulst). Both sons spelled their surname 'Brueghel', retaining the letter 'h' that their father had dropped in 1559.

Brueghel, Jan (1568–1625). Flemish painter and draughtsman, second son of Pieter *Bruegel the Elder. Early in his career he visited Cologne and Italy, before settling in Antwerp in 1597. He enjoyed a highly successful and honourable career there, becoming Dean of the Guild, working for the Archduke Albert and the Infanta Isabella, and making frequent visits to the Brussels court. His specialities were still lifes, especially flower paintings, and landscapes, but he worked in an entirely different spirit from his father, depicting brilliantly coloured, lush woodland scenes, often with mythological figures, in the manner of *Coninxloo and *Bril. His exquisite flower paintings were rated the finest of the day, and his virtuoso skill at depicting delicate textures earned him the nickname 'Velvet' Brueghel. Often he collaborated with other artists (notably his close friend *Rubens), painting backgrounds, animals, or flowers for them. He had considerable influence, notably on his pupil Daniel *Seghers, his sons **Jan II** (1601–78) and **Ambrosius** (1617–75), and his grandson Jan van *Kessel. Further descendants and imitators carried his style into the 18th cent.

Brueghel, Pieter the Younger (1564–1638). Flemish painter, the elder son of Pieter *Bruegel. He was born in Brussels but made his career in Antwerp, where he became a guild master in 1585. He is best known for his copies and variants of his father's peasant scenes, which sold well and are often of high quality, in contrast to the work of lesser copyists such as his son **Pieter Brueghel III** (1589–c.1640). His other speciality was scenes of fires, which earned him the nickname 'Hell' Bruegel. Frans *Snyders was his most notable pupil.

Brunelleschi, Filippo (1377–1446). Florentine architect and sculptor. Brunelleschi was one of the most famous of all architects—a Florentine hero on account of the celebrated dome (1420–36) he built for the city's cathedral—and one of the group of artists, including *Alberti, *Donatello, and *Masaccio, who created the *Renaissance style. He trained as a goldsmith and was one of the artists defeated by another great goldsmith/sculptor, Lorenzo *Ghiberti, in the competition (1401–2) for the new baptistery doors for Florence Cathedral; their competition panels are in

the Bargello. The disappointment of losing is said to have caused Brunelleschi to give up sculpture and turn to architecture, but one other important sculptural work is attributed to him—a painted wooden Crucifix in Sta Maria Novella (1412). Although he was not a painter, Brunelleschi was a pioneer of *perspective; in his treatise on painting Alberti describes how Brunelleschi devised a method for representing objects in depth on a flat surface by means of using a single vanishing point.

Brunswick Monogrammist. See MASTER OF THE BRUNSWICK MONOGRAM.

brush. A painting or drawing implement usually consisting of flexible fibres set in a handle. Prehistoric artists used materials such as feathers and leaves and the Egyptians used a brush consisting simply of a reed with the end macerated to separate the fibres, but animal hairs have been used since the ancient Greeks and are still the most important materials. For watercolour painting the 'sable' brush (made from the fur of the Siberian mink) is the best type; the 'camel-hair' brush (usually made from squirrel hair) is cheaper, but lacks springiness and durability. For oil painting a stiffer type of brush is needed; the best quality ones are made of white hog bristles. See also PENCIL.

Brygos Painter. Greek red-figure vase-painter, active in Athens (c.500–c.475 BC), named after a potter called Brygos, several of whose signed works he decorated. He is best known for a cup in the Louvre depicting the Sack of Troy. Showing consummate mastery of composition and movement, it is regarded as one of the masterpieces of Greek painting and is sometimes referred to simply as 'the Brygos cup'. More than a hundred other pieces have work attributed to the artist.

Bryulov (or **Brülloff** or **Briulov**), **Karl** (1799–1852). Russian painter. He spent part of his life in Italy (1822–34 and 1849–52), where he painted his chief work, *The Last Day of Pompeii* (Russian Mus., Leningrad, 1830–3), inspired by a performance of the opera of that name by Giovanni Pacini. An enormous (6 m. wide) melodramatic composition, it brought him European fame and inspired Edward Bulwer-Lytton's novel *The Last Days of Pompeii* (1834).

Bueckelaer, Joachim (*c.*1535–74). Netherlandish painter of large still lifes—market and kitchen pieces—active at Antwerp. Bueckelaer was the nephew and pupil of Pieter *Aertsen, and he followed his uncle's preference for scenes in which a religious subject is relegated to the background by the still life or *genre content (*Christ in the House of Mary and Martha*, Musées Royaux, Brussels, 1565). He seems to have been the first painter to depict fish stalls.

Buffalmacco (Buonamico Cristofani) (active first half of 14th cent.). Italian painter, a tantalizingly enigmatic figure. Various early sources, not only *Ghiberti and *Vasari, but also the writers Boccaccio and Sacchetti, attest to his celebrity as an artist—evidently one of the leading painters of the post-*Giotto generation—and as a burlesque character. Their cumulative testimony is impressive, but as no works can be securely attributed to him, many critics have regarded him as a legendary rather than a historical figure. Recently, however, there have been attempts to give Buffalmacco a stature commensurate with his literary reputation by attributing to him the famous frescos of *The Triumph of Death* in the Campo Santo, Pisa, which are usually considered the work of Francesco *Traini. A rival school of thought has it that Buffalmacco may be identified with another obscure personality, the *Master of St Cecilia.

Buffet, Bernard (1928–). French painter. A precocious artist, he had developed a distinctive style and won considerable critical acclaim by the age of 20. His work is instantly recognizable, characterized by elongated, spiky forms with dark outlines, sombre colours, and an overall mood of loneliness and despair. It seemed to express the existential alienation and spiritual solitude of the post-war generation, and Buffet enjoyed enormous success in the 1950s. Later, as he found himself overwhelmed by commissions, his work became more stylized and decorative, losing much of its original impact.

Buon, Bartolommeo (*c.*1374–*c.*1465). Venetian sculptor and architect. With his father **Giovanni** (active 1382–d. *c.*1443), he ran the most successful Venetian sculpture workshop of the period. Major works of the shop include the decoration of the Cà

d'Oro (1422–34) and the Porta della Carta (1438–42) of the Doges' Palace. They epitomize the survival of the *Gothic style in Venice into the mid-*quattrocento.

Burchfield, Charles (1893–1967). American painter. During the 1920s and 1930s he was one of the leading *American Scene painters, portraying the bleakness of small-town life and the grandeur and power of nature. In the 1940s his style changed, as he turned to a more personal interpretation of the beauty and mystery of nature.

Burckhardt, Jacob (1818–97). Swiss historian, professor at the universities of Zurich (1855–8) and Basle (1858–93). He was a pioneer of the cultural approach to history and is best known for his *Die Kultur der Renaissance in Italien* (The Civilization of the Renaissance in Italy), published in 1860. In this survey of the arts, philosophy, politics, etc., of the period he propounds the view that it was at this time that man, previously conscious of himself 'only as a member of a race, people, party, family or corporation', became aware of himself as 'a spiritual individual'. This romanticized view has been highly influential but also much attacked. Burckhardt's other books included *Cicerone* (1855), a guidebook to Italian art that was a popular handbook for German tourists for many years, and *Erinnerungen aus Rubens* (Recollections of Rubens), published posthumously in 1898.

Bürger, W. See THORÉ.

Burgkmair, Hans, The Elder (1473–1531). German painter and designer of woodcuts. After learning his trade under *Schongauer in Colmar, he had settled in his native Augsburg by 1498. Before then he is presumed to have been to Italy, for his paintings, with their warm glow of colour, their decorative Classical motifs, and their intricate spatial composition, show how decisively he transformed his late *Gothic heritage with *Renaissance influence. Indeed, he occupied a place in Augsburg comparable to that of *Dürer in Nuremberg in introducing the new style. Like Dürer he contributed to the famous series of woodcuts for the Emperor, the *Triumph of Maximilian*. He was also employed to illustrate the Emperor's own writings, the *Teuerdank* and *Weisskunig*, moralizing knightly romances. A certain clarity of characterization, which is typical of all his works, not least his incisive portraits, seems to have influenced Hans *Holbein the Younger. His son, **Hans Burgkmair the Younger** (*c.*1500–59), was a painter and engraver.

burin (or **graver**). The engraver's principal tool. It is a short steel rod, usually lozenge-shaped in section, cut obliquely at the end to provide a point. Its short, rounded handle is pushed by the palm of the hand while the fingers guide the point.

Burliuk, David (1882–1967) and **Vladimir** (1886–1916). Russian artists, brothers. They studied at Munich from 1902 and were later friends of *Kandinsky there, associating themselves with him in the first *Blaue Reiter exhibition of 1911. In Russia they worked with *Goncharova and *Larionov, adopting a style of deliberate primitivism akin to theirs, and they exhibited at the first *Knave of Diamonds exhibition in 1910. Together with the poet Mayakovsky and with a third brother, **Nikolai** (1890–1920), David and Vladimir, but above all David, were instrumental in creating a Russian variant of *Futurism *c.*1911. Vladimir was killed in the First World War. David settled in the USA in 1922 and became an American citizen in 1930. He ran both an art magazine, *Color Rhyme*, and an art gallery.

Burne-Jones, Sir Edward Coley (1833–98). English painter, illustrator, and designer. He was destined for the Church, but his interest was turned to art first by William *Morris, his fellow divinity student at Oxford, and then by *Rossetti, to whom Burne-Jones apprenticed himself in 1856 and who remained the decisive influence on him. Like Rossetti, Burne-Jones painted in a consciously aesthetic style (see AESTHETICISM), but his taste was more Classical and his elongated forms owed much to the example of *Botticelli. He favoured medieval and mythical subjects and hated such modernists as the *Impressionists, describing their subjects as 'landscape and whores'. His own ideas on painting are summed up as follows: 'I mean by a picture a beautiful romantic dream, of something that never was, never will be—in a light better than any that ever shone—in a land no-one can define or remember, only desire—and the forms divinely beautiful.' He exhibited little before 1877, but then became quickly famous, with a remarkably wide following abroad. His work had considerable influence on the French *Symbolists and the ethereally beautiful women who people his paintings, like the more sensuous types of Rossetti, had a considerable progeny at the end of the century. Some of Burne-Jones's finest work was done in association with William Morris (he was a founder member of Morris and Co. in 1861), notably as a designer of stained glass and tapestries, and as an illustrator of some of the *Kelmscott Press books. The best collection of his work is in the City Art Gallery at Birmingham, his birthplace.

burr. In metal engraving, the rough, upturned edge of the furrow made in the plate by the *burin or needle. In *line engraving it is removed to obtain sharpness, but in *drypoint it is allowed to remain because the soft, rich quality it gives to the printed line is considered one of the attractions of the medium. Only a limited number of impressions can be taken before the burr wears down.

Burra, Edward (1905–76). English painter, draughtsman, and stage designer, one of the most delightfully eccentric figures in British art. He suffered chronic ill health continuously from childhood and lived almost all his life in the genteel Sussex seaside town of Rye (he called it an 'overblown gifte shoppe'), but he travelled indomitably and had a tremendous zest for life. His career, in fact, represents a revolt against his respectable middle-class background, for he was fascinated by low-life and seedy subjects, which he experienced at first hand in places such as the streets of Harlem in New York and the dockside cafés of Marseilles. From 1921 to 1925 Burra trained in various art schools, including the *Royal College in London. He early formed a distinctive style, depicting squalid subjects with a keen sense of the grotesque and a delight in colourful detail. Usually he worked in water-colour, but on a larger scale than is generally associated with this medium and using layer upon layer of pigment so that—in reproduction at any rate—his pictures appear to have the physical substance of oil paintings. Burra's work has been compared to that of George *Grosz, whom he admired, but whereas the satirical spirit of Grosz is linked with bitter castigation of evil and ugliness, Burra concentrated on the picturesque aspects of his subjects, which he depicted with warmth and humour. Particularly well known are his Harlem scenes of 1933–4, with their flamboyant streetwise dudes and other shady characters. Burra's style changed little, but about the mid 1930s his imagery underwent a radical change and he became fascinated with the bizarre and fantastic (*Dancing Skeletons*, Tate, 1934). Many of his recurrent images—such as the bird-man—and his manner of juxtaposing incongruous objects acquired overtones of *Surrealism, and although he generally kept aloof from groups he exhibited with the English Surrealists (he was also a member of *Unit One, organized by his friend Paul *Nash). The sense of tragedy evoked in him by the Spanish Civil War and the Second World War found expression in occasional religious pictures and during the 1950s and 1960s his interest turned from people to landscape. By this time he had achieved critical and financial success, but he reacted with sardonic humour towards his growing fame.

Burrell, Sir William (1861–1958). Scottish art collector. He made an immense fortune from the family shipping business, which he sold in 1917, and devoted most of his life to collecting. His interests were extremely diverse, but his collection became particularly strong in 19th-cent. French painting Burrell eventually amassed 8,000 objects, which he presented to the City of Glasgow in 1944, followed by the sum of £450,000 to build a new museum to house them. This was not opened until 1983 in Pollok Country Park, to the south of the city, and in the intervening years the Burrell Collection acquired something of a legendary reputation as a hidden treasure trove; it soon became one of the most popular museums in Britain. Apart from 19th-cent. French painting, it is particularly strong in medieval art. Burrell also gave paintings to the Museum and Art Gallery at Berwick-upon-Tweed; in his later years he lived nearby at Hutton Castle.

Burri, Alberto (1915–). Italian painter and *collagist. He was originally a doctor, but began to paint in 1944 as a prisoner of war in Texas. He used whatever materials were to hand, including sacking, and after his return to Italy in 1945 he frequently used the device of splashing red paint on cloth in a manner that suggested blood-soaked bandages (*Sacking with Red*, Tate, London, 1954). His later works including materials such as charred wood and rusty metal also reflect the direct experience of the carnage of war he had as an army doctor, even though they are elegantly constructed. Burri won international fame for these works, which were among the first to exploit the evocative force of waste and trash, and looked forward to *Junk art in America and *Arte Povera in Italy.

Bury, Pol (1922–). Belgian artist, best known as one of the leading exponents of *Kinetic sculpture. From 1947 he exhibited with the *Jeune Peinture Belge group and was also active in the *Cobra group. In 1953, however, he abandoned painting for Kinetic sculpture. His early works could be rotated at will, inviting spectator participation, but he later incorporated electric motors. The movement was usually very slow and the impression made was humorous and poetic, in contrast to the violent effects of *Tinguely.

Bush, Jack Hamilton (1909–77). One of Canada's leading abstract painters. His early work was in the tradition of the *Group of Seven, but in the early 1950s, inspired by Jock *Macdonald and by *Borduas's work, he began to experiment with automatic composition (see AUTOMATISM). In 1952 he made the first of what became regular visits to New York. The influence of these brought him, by the mid-1950s, to a type of *Abstract Expressionism. His later works, however, explore the unaffectedly direct use of colour in a more personal way, as in his most famous painting, *Dazzle Red* (Art Gal. of Ontario, 1965), in which the colour is placed in joyous, broadly brushed bands. Bush worked as a commercial designer for most of his career and did not devote his whole time to painting until 1968, but by the end of his life he had an international reputation.

Bushnell, John (*c.*1630–1701). English sculptor. He fled to the Continent when he was an apprentice, after his master, Thomas Burman (1618–74), forced him to marry a servant he had himself seduced. In Italy Bushnell assimilated much of the *Baroque style (he probably saw *Bernini's work in Rome) and executed a monument to Alvise Mocenigo (1663) in S. Lazzaro del Mendicanti, Venice. On his return to England, c.1670, he received important commissions including a *Sir Thomas Gresham* for the Royal Exchange (now in the Old Bailey), and would have received more but for his difficult and unstable temperament (he died insane). Bushnell's work is extremely uneven, but he is an important figure, for he showed untravelled Englishmen for the first time something of the possibilities of Baroque sculpture.

Butler, Elizabeth (Lady Butler, née Thompson) (1846–1933). British painter who concentrated almost exclusively on military scenes. During her heyday in the 1870s she was one of the most popular and talked-about artists in Britain. Her work appealed to popular patriotic sentiment, but she was also praised by critics such as *Ruskin, who said she had forced him to admit he had been wrong in believing that 'no woman could paint'. Lady Butler said 'I never painted for the glory of war, but to portray its pathos and heroism' and, although her pictures often have a glossy, Hollywood quality, they are sincerely felt, and she has been praised for trying to show the experience of the common soldier rather than concentrating—as was then traditional—on the heroic deeds of officers. Her best-known painting is probably *Scotland for Ever!*, showing the charge of the Royal Scots Greys at the Battle of Waterloo (Leeds City Art Gall., 1881).

Butler, Reg (1913–81). British sculptor. He was an architect by training (his work included the clocktower of Slough Town Hall, 1936), and architecture remained his main preoccupation until 1950. In 1953 he suddenly came to prominence on being awarded first prize in the International Competition for a monument to *The Unknown Political Prisoner* (defeating *Calder, *Gabo, and *Hepworth among other established artists). His design was characterized by harsh, spindly forms, suggesting in his own words 'an iron cage, a transmuted gallows or guillotine on an outcrop of rock'. The monument was never built (one of the models is in the Tate Gallery), but the competition established Butler's name and he won a high reputation among the generation of metal sculptors which followed Henry *Moore. He had learned iron-forging when he had worked as a blacksmith during the Second World War (he was a conscientious objector) and his early sculpture is remarkable for the way in which he used his feeling for the material to create sensuous textures. His later work, which was more traditional (and to many critics much less memorable), included some bronze figures of nude girls, realistically painted and with real hair, looking as if they had strayed from the pages of 'girlie' magazines. Butler was an articulate writer and radio broadcaster and he vigorously argued the case for modern sculpture. Five lectures he delivered to students at the *Slade School in 1961 were published in book form the following year as *Creative Development*. He was a widely read man, who numbered leading intellectuals among his friends, and his liberal sympathies were shown by his donation of works to such causes as the campaign against capital punishment.

Buytewech, Willem (1591/2–1624). Dutch painter and engraver, nicknamed 'Geestige Willem' (Witty Willem). He was active in his native Rotterdam and in Haarlem, where he was closely associated with Frans *Hals. Although his surviving output as a painter is tiny, he is one of the most interesting artists during the first years of the great period of Dutch painting. His pictures of dandies, fashionable ladies, topers, and lusty wenches are among the most spirited Dutch *genre scenes, and instituted the category known as the 'Merry Company' (*Merry Company*, Boymans Mus., Rotterdam). His engravings are more numerous, and include genre scenes, fashion plates, and etchings of the Dutch countryside. He had an important influence on painting in Haarlem. His son **Willem the Younger** (1625–70) was also a painter. An example of his very rare work—a landscape—is in the National Gallery, London.

Byzantine art. Art produced in or under the influence of the Eastern Roman (Byzantine) Empire; it was founded in AD 330 by the emperor Constantine (the first Christian emperor) and ended in 1453 when his capital Constantinople (originally named Byzantium) was captured by the Turks and under the name of Istanbul became the capital of the Ottoman Empire. The split between the Western and Eastern Empires became permanent in 395, when each adopted a separate ruler, and after the Western Empire was overrun by barbarians in the 5th cent. the Byzantine Empire became the great upholder of Christianity and of the cultural traditions of Greece and Rome. Byzantine territories varied greatly in extent; at one time they covered almost the entire Mediterranean basin, but from the 7th cent. many provinces were lost, first to the Arabs and later to the Turks. However, Byzantine art extended beyond the political or geographical boundaries of the Empire, penetrating, for example into the Slav countries, and in certain areas—where the Eastern Orthodox Church flourished—its tradition continued long after the collapse of the Empire.

Byzantine art was, above all, a religious art. It was serious, otherworldly, and conservative, and the Byzantine artist did not aspire to freedom of individual interpretation but was the voice of orthodox dogma. The choice of subjects and the attitudes and expressions of figures were determined according to traditional schemes charged with theological meaning. In the domes of churches, for example, Christ was usually shown as ruler of the universe (the Greek term is Pantocrater, meaning 'all-powerful'). Although Byzantine artists produced panel paintings, frescoes, manuscript illuminations, ivories, enamels, textiles, jewellery, and metalwork of high quality, Byzantine art is seen at its finest and most typical in the mosaic decoration of churches. Mosaics were applied to all available surfaces of the interior, the luminous shimmering of the colours and the remote, implacably staring figures creating—in the finest works—a truly awe-inspiring effect, raising the art to unprecedented levels of grandeur and expressive power. Figures are flat and arranged frontally, occupying a spiritual dimension rather than a realistic space. Also typical of Byzantine art is the *icon, which usually represented the head of Christ, the Virgin and Child, or a particular saint, although there are also much more complex figure groups of subjects such as the Crucifixion. Icons tended to become cult images, and the view that this was idolatrous led to the Iconoclast Controversy of 726 to 843, when many figurative works were destroyed and artists had to revert to ornamental forms or symbols such as the cross. The conventions of Byzantine art were eventually challenged by the more naturalistic ideals of artists such as *Giotto and *Duccio.

C

Cabanel, Alexandre (1823–89). French painter. The winner of the *Prix de Rome in 1845, he ranked with *Bouguereau as one of the most successful and influential academic painters of the period and one of the sternest opponents of the *Impressionists. *The Birth of Venus* (Musée d'Orsay, Paris) is his best-known work and typical of the slick and titillating (but supposedly chaste) nudes at which he excelled. It was the hit of the official *Salon of 1863, the year of the *Salon des Refusés, and was bought by the emperor Napoleon III, who gave Cabanel several prestigious commissions.

cabinet painting. Term applied to small *easel paintings intended to be viewed at close range. It has no precise limits, but is often applied, for example, to 17th-cent. Dutch *genre paintings, which were usually painted to fit into unpretentious bourgeois interiors.

Caillebotte, Gustave (1848–94). French painter and collector. A naval architect by profession, he was also a prolific painter of contemporary subjects, town and country views, still lifes, and boating scenes. He exhibited at five of the *Impressionist exhibitions, but is better known as a patron than as a painter, although his *Paris, A Rainy Day* (Art Institute of Chicago, 1877) has become a much reproduced favourite. He bought pictures from the other Impressionist painters and on his death he bequeathed his collection of sixty-five pictures to the State. Against the opposition of various academic artists representing the taste of the École des *Beaux-Arts and the official *Salon (*Gérôme called the works offered 'filth'), thirty-eight of the pictures were accepted after much wrangling and formed the nucleus of the Impressionist collection of the Luxembourg Museum. They are now in the Musée d'Orsay.

Calder, Alexander (1898–1976). American sculptor and painter, famous as the inventor of the *mobile. His grandfather, **Alexander Milne Calder** (1846–1923), and his father, **Alexander Stirling Calder** (1870–1945), were sculptors and his mother was a painter, but he began to take an interest in art only in 1922, after studying mechanical engineering. In 1923 he enrolled at the School of the Art Students' League, New York, where George *Luks and John *Sloan were among the teachers. Calder and his fellow students made a game of rapidly sketching people on the streets and in the subway and Calder was noted for his skill in conveying a sense of movement by a single unbroken line. From this it was but a step to his wire sculptures, the first of which was done in 1925. He also made animated toys in a similar vein. Calder lived mainly in Paris from 1928 to 1933. In 1931 he joined the *Abstraction-Création association and in the same year produced his first non-figurative moving construction. They were moved by hand or by motor-power and were baptized 'mobiles' in 1932 by Marcel *Duchamp; *Arp suggested 'stabiles' for the non-moving constructions in the same year. It was in 1934 that Calder began to make the unpowered mobiles for which he is most widely known. Constructed usually from pieces of shaped and painted tin suspended on thin wires or cords, these responded by their own weight to the faintest air currents and were designed to take advantage of effects of changing light created by the movements. They were described by Calder as 'four-dimensional drawings', and in a letter to Duchamp written in 1932 he spoke of his desire to make 'moving Mondrians'. Calder was greatly impressed by a visit to *Mondrian in 1930, but his pawky delight in the comic and fantastic, which obtrudes even in his large works, was at the opposite pole from the messianic seriousness of Mondrian. Calder continued to do both mobiles and stabiles until the 1970s, sometimes combining the two into one structure. Some of these works are very large: the motorized hanging mobile *Red, Black, and Blue* (1967) at Dallas airport is 14 m. wide. Calder's mobiles were among the forerunners of *Kinetic art and his great reputation depended in part on the fact that he was among the first to incorporate real movement into sculptural art. He worked in a variety of other fields, however, painting *gouaches and designing, for example, rugs and tapestries.

Callcott, Sir Augustus Wall (1779–1844). English painter, a pupil of *Hoppner. He became the most fashionable English landscape painter of his day, and was knighted in 1837. His early work had some freshness, which later subsided into a conventional Italianate manner with a carefully modulated reflection of *Turner, for the satisfaction of the larger public who could not yet stomach either Turner himself or *Constable. In 1827 he married **Maria Graham** (née Dundas, 1785–1842), author of numerous books on topography and painting, and the two formed a society salon for artistic London.

Callot, Jacques (1592/3–1635). French engraver and draughtsman. He went to Italy when he was in his teens and, working in Rome and then in Florence at the court of the Grand Duke Cosimo II, he learnt to combine the sophisticated techniques and exaggerations of late *Mannerism with witty and acute observation into a brilliantly expressive idiom. In 1621 he returned to France, and most of the remainder of his career was spent in his native Nancy, although he also worked in Paris and the Low Countries. He made a speciality of beggars and deformities, characters from the picaresque novel and the Italian *commedia dell' arte*. In this respect he comes close to *Bellange, also active in Nancy, but Callot's style was more realistic. His last great work, the series of etchings entitled the *Grandes Misères de la Guerre*, followed the invasion of Lorraine by Cardinal Richelieu in 1633, and is a harrowing depiction of the atrocities of war; its themes and imagery were used as a source by *Goya. Callot's output was prodigious; more than a thousand etchings and more than a thousand drawings by him are extant, and some of his plates are large, featuring scores of figures. He was one of the greatest of all etchers and one of the first major creative artists to work exclusively in the *graphic arts.

Calraet, Abraham. See CUYP.

Calvaert, Denys (called Dionisio Fiammingo) (*c*.1540–1619). Flemish painter from Antwerp who emigrated to Italy in about 1562 and remained there for the rest of his life. Calvaert settled in Bologna, and although his work is in an undistinguished *Mannerist style, he played an important role as a teacher. He established an *academy in 1572 and had more than 100 pupils, among whom were some of the most distinguished artists of the Bolognese School—*Albani, *Domenichino, and *Reni. The more celebrated academy of the *Carracci was probably inspired by Calvaert's.

Calvert, Edward (1799–1883). English painter and engraver. After five years in the navy, he began to study art, coming into contact with *Fuseli, Samuel *Palmer, who became his lifelong friend, and *Linnell, who introduced him to *Blake. He became one of the *Ancients, and under the influence of Blake his imagination was fired, like that of others in the group, to a poetic fervour which was unable to survive the death of the master. The tiny water-colour *The Visionary City* (BM, London) is perhaps the finest of the visionary works he produced during this period. In his later career he painted mostly in oils on paper and after visiting Greece in 1844 developed a sentimental pseudo-Hellenic arcadianism.

camaieu. A painting executed in several shades of a single colour; it is distinct from *grisaille, which is grey or greyish.

Cambiaso, Luca (1527–85). Genoese painter. He was a precocious artist (his highly accomplished frescos in the Doria Palace, now the Prefettura, in Genoa were done in 1544, when he was only 17) and he became the dominating figure in 16th-cent. Genoese painting. His style derives from *Michelangelo in the massiveness of his figures and *Correggio in the softness of his modelling, but the use of dry paint and the simplification of forms are his own. The latter is particularly noticeable in his drawings, which often utilize geometrical forms that give them a superficially *Cubist look. Another curious instance of antecedence is apparent in his night scenes, which have been claimed as sources for Georges de *La Tour, even though it is not clear by what route they could have become known to him. In 1583 Luca accepted an invitation from Philip II of Spain to decorate the *Escorial. He died there in 1585 and was succeeded by Federico *Zuccaro and then Pellegrino *Tibaldi.

Camden Town Group. Group of British painters formed in 1911 who took their name from the drab working-class area of London (as it was then) made popular as a subject by *Sickert. In addition to being the prime inspiration of the group, Sickert suggested the name. The leading members were Robert *Bevan, Harold *Gilman, Charles *Ginner, and Spencer *Gore; others included Duncan *Grant, Augustus *John, and Lucien *Pissarro. These artists were very different in their aims and styles. What they had in common was dislike for the romantic idealizations of the *Royal Academy and an inclination towards descriptive *realism in the depiction of ordinary things. Their subjects included not only street scenes in Camden Town, but also landscapes, portraits, interiors, and still lifes; their use of bold, flat colour was one of the earliest responses by British artists to the influence of *Post-Impressionism. After holding group exhibitions in 1911 and 1912, the members merged with a number of smaller groups to form the *London Group in November 1913.

cameo. Carving on gemstones, glass, ceramics, or similar materials in which the surrounding ground is cut away so that the design stands up in *relief above the surface. It is the opposite of *intaglio. Often, the term refers to a portrait cut in a gemstone; this form was highly popular among the Greeks and Romans for jewellery and it was revived during the Renaissance. Commonly a banded or multicoloured stone, such as agate, was used, in such a way as to exploit the different layers of colour—with one colour for the background and another for the carving, for example.

camera lucida (Latin: 'light chamber'). An apparatus for drawing and copying, patented in 1807 by William Hyde Wollaston (1766–1828), a well-known man of science. It received this misleading name—for it is not a 'chamber' at all—because it

performed the same function as the *camera obscura, but in full daylight. It consists essentially of a prism on an adjustable stand. The draughtsman sets the prism between his eye and the paper in such a way that he can see an image of the object apparently lying on the paper and can trace its outline. Various refinements were added to the basic format, including a lens to aid focusing.

camera obscura (Latin: 'dark chamber'). An apparatus which projects the image of an object or scene on to a sheet of paper or ground glass so that the outlines can be traced. It consists of a shuttered box or room with a small hole or lens in one side through which light from a brightly lit scene enters and forms an inverted image on a screen placed opposite the opening. The optical principle is essentially that of the photographic camera. For greater convenience a mirror is usually installed, which reflects the image the right way up on to a suitably placed drawing surface. The principle was known as early as Aristotle, but the first written account of its use for drawing must be ascribed to Giambattista della Porta, a physician of Naples. His description in his work on popular science, *Magiae Naturalis* (1558), did much to make the device widely known, and by the 18th cent. the camera obscura had become a craze. Both amateurs and professionals—such as *Canaletto—were using it for topographical painting, and we hear of an apparatus, somewhat like a sedan chair, inside which the artist could sit and draw, at the same time actuating bellows with his feet to improve the ventilation. More modest versions were easily portable and even pocketable.

Campagnola, Giulio (c.1482–c.1518). Italian artist, active mainly as an engraver. Born in Padua, he trained under *Mantegna in Mantua, and by 1499 was attached to the ducal court at Ferrara. In 1509 he was in Venice and it is with this city that he is chiefly associated, his engravings of idyllic landscape subjects playing a major role in spreading the style of *Giorgione and *Titian. His many copies after *Dürer likewise disseminated knowledge of this artist in Italy. Giulio's pupil and adopted son, **Domenico** (1500–after 1552), made some engravings in the manner of his master, but became better known as a painter and draughtsman. He sold his drawings (mainly landscapes) as finished compositions, sometimes passing them off as the work of Titian. In the 1520s he moved to Padua and became the city's busiest painter.

Campania, Pedro de (1503–80). Netherlandish painter, active mainly in Seville and known by the Spanish form of his name rather than the Flemish one, Pieter de Kempeneer. Before settling in Seville he had worked in Italy and he exercised a strong influence in Andalusia as a pioneer of *Mannerism and the style of *Raphael. Several of his paintings are in Seville Cathedral. In 1562 he left Spain to direct a tapestry factory at Brussels, his native city.

Campen, Jacob van (1595–1657). Dutch architect and painter. He was the greatest Dutch architect of the 17th cent. and occupied a role in his country similar to that of his contemporary Inigo *Jones in England by introducing a fully mature Classical style; the contemporary diplomat Constantin Huygens described him as the man 'who vanquished Gothic folly with Roman stateliness and drove old heresy forth before an older truth'. His most important building is Amsterdam Town Hall (begun 1648), a triumphant symbol of the city during its greatest period. The building was richly decorated; Artus *Quellin I led a team of sculptors, and *Rembrandt was among those who provided paintings, although his *Conspiracy of Julius Civilis* (Nationalmuseum, Stockholm, 1661–2) was removed soon after installation and replaced with a picture by his pupil Juriaen Ovens (1623–78). Van Campen's other buildings include the beautiful *Mauritshuis in The Hague (1633–5), designed as a royal palace and now a celebrated picture gallery. As a painter he concentrated on historical and decorative work and was one of the team, including *Jordaens and *Lievens, who worked on the decoration of the Huis ten Bosch, the royal villa on the outskirts of The Hague.

Campin, Robert. See MASTER OF FLÉMALLE.

Canadian Group of Painters. A group of 20th-cent. Canadian artists formed in Toronto as a successor to the *Group of Seven. Its policy was 'to encourage and foster the growth of art in Canada which has a national character'. Many of the best-known Canadian artists exhibited with the group between its first exhibition in 1933 and its disbanding in 1969.

Canaletto (Giovanni Antonio Canal) (1697–1768). Venetian painter, the most famous view-painter of the 18th cent. He began work painting theatrical scenery (his father's profession), but he turned to topography (see VEDUTA) during a visit to Rome in 1719–20, when he was influenced by the work of Giovanni Paolo *Panini. By 1723 he was painting dramatic and picturesque views of Venice, marked by strong contrasts of light and shade and free handling, this phase of his work culminating in the splendid *Stone Mason's Yard* (NG, London, c.1730). Meanwhile, partly under the influence of Luca *Carlevaris, and largely in rivalry with him, Canaletto began to turn out views which were more topographically accurate, set in a higher key, and with smoother, more precise handling—characteristics that mark most of his later work. At the same time he began painting the ceremonial and festival subjects which ultimately formed an important part of his work. His patrons were chiefly English collectors, for whom he sometimes produced series of views in uniform size. Conspicuous among them was Joseph Smith, a merchant, appointed British Consul in Venice in 1744. It was perhaps at his instance that Canaletto enlarged his repertory in the 1740s to include subjects from the Venetian mainland and from Rome (probably based on drawings made during his visit as a young man), and by producing numerous *capricci*. He also gave increased attention to the graphic arts, making a remarkable series of etchings, and many drawings in pen, and pen and wash, as independent works of art and not as preparation for paintings. This led to changes in his style of painting, increasing an already well-established tendency to become stylized and mechanical in handling. He often used the *camera obscura as an aid to composition. In 1746 he went to England, apparently at the suggestion of Jacopo *Amigoni (the War of the Austrian Succession drastically curtailed foreign travel, and Canaletto's tourist trade in Venice had dried up). For a time he was very successful, painting views of London and of various country houses. Subsequently, his work became increasingly lifeless and mannered, so much so that rumours were put about, probably by rivals, that he was not in fact the famous Canaletto but an impostor. In 1755 he returned to Venice and continued active for the remainder of his life. Legends of his having amassed a fortune in Venice are disproved by the official inventory of his estate on his death. Before this, Joseph Smith had sold the major part of his paintings to George III, thus bringing into the royal collection an unrivalled group of Canaletto's paintings and drawings. Canaletto was highly influential in Italy and elsewhere. His nephew Bernardo *Bellotto took his style to Central Europe and his followers in England included William *Marlow and Samuel *Scott.

Candlelight Master. See BIGOT.

Cano, Alonso (1601–67). Spanish sculptor, painter, architect, and draughtsman, sometimes called 'the Spanish *Michelangelo' because of the diversity of his talents. He was born and died in Granada, and worked there and in Seville and Madrid. His movements were partly dictated by his tempestuous character, for more than once he fled or was expelled from the city he was working in (once for the suspected murder of his wife). In spite of his violent temperament, his work tends to be serene and often sweet. He studied painting in Seville with *Pacheco (*Velázquez was his fellow-student) and sculpture with *Montañés, and stayed in the city from 1614 to 1638, when he moved to Madrid to become painter to the Count-Duke Olivares and was employed by Philip IV to restore pictures in the royal collection. Thus he became acquainted with the work of the 16th-cent. Venetian masters, whose influence is apparent in his later paintings; they are much softer in technique than his earlier pictures, which are strongly lit in the manner of *Zurbarán. From 1652 he worked mainly in Granada, where he designed the façade of the cathedral (1667), one of the boldest and most original works of Spanish *Baroque architecture. He was ordained a priest in 1658, as this was necessary for him to further his career at Granada Cathedral. The cathedral has several of Cano's works in painting and sculpture, including a *polychrome

wooden statue of the *Immaculate Conception* (1655) that is sometimes considered his masterpiece.

Canova, Antonio (1757–1822). Italian sculptor. He was the most successful and the most influential sculptor of the *Neoclassical movement, outdoing even *Thorvaldsen and *Flaxman in international fame and prestige. Born in Possagno, near Treviso, he began his career as a stonemason and took up sculpture after he moved to Venice in 1768. His early work is lively and naturalistic (*Daedalus and Icarus*, Museo Correr, Venice, 1779), but after he settled in Rome in 1781 his style became graver and thoroughly imbued with *antique influence. *Theseus and the Minotaur* (V&A, London, 1781–3) was his first major work in Rome, and he was soon followed this with the prestigious commission for the tomb of Pope Clement XIV in SS. Apostoli (1783–7). After this Canova never looked back. He ran a large studio and worked for a galaxy of European notables, including Napoleon (who tried unsuccessfully to bring him to Paris), the Duke of Wellington, and Catherine the Great of Russia; his portrait of Napoleon's sister (*Pauline Borghese as Venus*, Borghese Gal., Rome, 1805–7) is one of his most celebrated works, a marble equivalent to *David's *Madame Récamier*. Canova worked much for the papal court and in 1815 he became the Pope's representative in recovering works of art looted by Napoleon; on his visits to Paris and London he was fêted. In 1816 he was created Marchese d'Ischia by the Pope and he retired to Possagno, where he built a studio that is now a museum devoted to him. Canova was immensely influential and was renowned for his generosity to young sculptors. He went out of favour during the *Romantic period, when his work seemed cold and static, but his reputation has greatly revived in the 20th cent. His work, in fact, was always much more individual than that of many of his Neoclassical contemporaries and he placed great importance on the personal handling of his material.

canvas. A woven cloth used as a *support for painting. The best-quality canvas is made of linen; other materials used are cotton, hemp, and jute. It is now so familiar a material that the word 'canvas' has become almost a synonym for an *oil painting, but it was not until around 1500 that it began to rival the wooden *panel (which was more expensive and took longer to prepare) as the standard support for movable paintings (the transition came later in Northern Europe than in Italy). Canvas is not suitable for painting on until it has been coated with a *ground, which isolates the fabric from the paint; otherwise it will absorb too much paint, only very rough effects will be obtainable, and parts of the fabric may be rotted by the *pigments. It must also be made taut on a *stretcher or by some other means.

canvas board. Sheet of cardboard or pasteboard covered with sized and primed cloth, usually cotton. It was first made commercially in the second half of the 19th cent. and is chiefly used by amateurs as a cheap substitute for canvas or for outdoor sketching.

Čapek, Josef (1887–1945). Czech painter, graphic artist, designer, and writer. He was a member of the group of avant-garde artists formed in Prague in 1911 by Otto *Gutfreund and Emil *Filla with the object of combining *Cubism and German *Expressionism into a new national artistic style. The Expressionist current in his work prevailed. Like his brother, the celebrated writer Karel Čapek (several of whose books he illustrated), he was deeply concerned with fundamental moral and social questions. They fervently opposed the threat from Nazi Germany in the 1930s; Karel died the year before the Second World War began, but Josef lived to see its full horrors and died in a concentration camp.

Cappelle, Jan van de (c.1624–79). Dutch marine and landscape painter. He was a wealthy Amsterdam dyer who taught himself to paint during his spare time, but there is nothing of the Sunday painter in his work. Typically his paintings show handsome vessels on calm rivers or seas; they have a grandeur of composition, a limpid quality of light, and an exquisite silver-grey tonality that places them among the finest marine paintings of any time or place. Cappelle also painted winter landscapes and beach scenes. His work is rare; the best collection is in the National Gallery in London. He was affluent enough to make a distinguished art collection.

capriccio. Italian term, meaning 'caprice', that can be applied to any fantasy subject, but is most commonly used of a type of townscape popular in the 18th cent. in which real buildings are combined with imaginary ones or are shown with their locations rearranged. *Canaletto and *Guardi often painted pictures of this type, and there is a painting by William *Marlow in the Tate Gallery showing St Paul's Cathedral above a Venetian canal. *Goya's Los Caprichos are etchings of fantastic subjects of a completely different kind.

Caracciolo, Giovanni Battista (called Battistello) (1578–1635). Neapolitan painter. He was one of the greatest of *Caravaggio's followers, and his powerful work was an important factor in making Naples a stronghold of the Caravaggesque style. The decisive impact that Caravaggio made on his style can be seen from his Liberation of St Peter (1608–9), painted for the same church (the Chiesa del Monte della Misericordia, still in situ) as the master's Seven Acts of Mercy. It shows how Caracciolo, unlike so many of the *Caravaggisti, looked beyond the obvious trademarks of Caravaggio's style, emulating it in depth of feeling as well as in mastery of dramatic light and shade. He visited Rome and Florence in the second decade of the century and his later work shows a more Classical strain, influenced perhaps by the *Carracci. Unusually for a Caravaggesque artist he was an accomplished fresco painter, and his finest late works are decorations in the Certosa di S. Martino in Naples, finished in 1631.

Caravaggio, Michelangelo Merisi da (1571–1610). The most original and influential Italian painter of the 17th cent., named after his native town near Bergamo. His early experience of the works of *Lotto, *Savoldo, and the Venetians was more significant than his actual training under Simone Peterzano, a weak pupil of *Titian. By 1592 he was in Rome, where two phases in his career can be distinguished: an early experimental period (c.1592–9) and a mature period (1599–1606) in which he carried out several large commissions. The early works are usually small pictures of non-dramatic subjects with half-length figures, a preponderance of still life, and a frankly homo-erotic character (Young Bacchus, Uffizi, Florence, *c*.1595). Subsequently his figures gain greater plasticity, becoming clearly articulated and painted in rich deep colours with strongly accentuated shadows (*The Supper at Emmaus*, NG, London, *c*.1598–1600). The second Roman period began with a commission (probably gained through his first noteworthy patron, the hedonistic Cardinal Francesco Del Monte) for the Contarelli Chapel in S. Luigi dei Francesi (*Calling of St Matthew* and *Martyrdom of St Matthew*, 1599–1600), in which Caravaggio's extraordinary advance in mastery of construction, dramatic action, and handling of paint was achieved only after great effort, as X-rays of the paintings make clear. The altarpiece of *St Matthew and the Angel* was rejected because it was thought to lack decorum, but it was bought by the Marchese Vincenzo *Giustiniani, one of the most important patrons in Rome, who also paid for the replacement. (The first altarpiece was formerly in Berlin, but was destroyed in the Second World War; the replacement is still *in situ*. Both were painted in 1602.) Meanwhile Caravaggio had embarked on his second great public commission—two paintings for the Cerasi Chapel in Sta Maria del Popolo (*Crucifixion of St Peter* and *Conversion of St Paul*, 1600–1), which are astounding in the economy and force of the pictorial vision, seeing the old subjects in completely new ways. The Contarelli Chapel and Cerasi Chapel paintings changed the direction of Caravaggio's work, for thenceforth he devoted himself almost exclusively to large-scale religious pictures, among them the *Madonna de' Palafrenieri* (Borghese Gal., Rome, 1605) and *The Death of the Virgin* (Louvre, Paris, 1605–6). These two pictures were again refused on grounds of decorum or theological incorrectness. Despite this misunderstanding of his work, Caravaggio was not without powerful supporters and his rejected paintings found ready secular buyers.

Caravaggio's tempestuous character frequently caused scandals and in 1606 he fled Rome after killing a man in a brawl over a wager on a tennis match, spending the last four years of his life wandering from Naples to Malta and Sicily, and back to Naples again. He continued to paint large religious compositions in a new style shorn of all inessentials: little colour, thinly applied paint, the crowded drama and movement of the late Roman works replaced by a moving silence and contemplativeness. Remarkable among these is *The Beheading of St John the Baptist* (Valetta Cathedral, Malta, 1608), a work of the utmost tragic power. Caravaggio was not yet 40 when he died from malarial fever while returning to Rome in hope of a pardon, but his last works have all the ineffable qualities of the late works of an aged genius. In spite of his brief career and his fairly small output he made an enormous impact on painting throughout Europe. He had no pupils, but a legion of followers (the *Caravaggisti), and his work, together with that of the *Carracci, revived Italian painting from the nebulous unreality of late 16th-cent. *Mannerist art.

Caravaggio continued to be a famous name throughout the 17th cent., but he was regarded by many as an 'evil genius' (in the words of Vincenzo *Carducho, writing in 1633), whose influence on other artists was pernicious. Interest in him declined in the 18th cent. (he is not mentioned in *Reynolds's *Discourses*), but revived in the mid 19th cent. By this time his rejection of ideal beauty could be seen to have the advantage of truth, although there were still those, like *Ruskin, who saw in him 'perpetual seeking for and feeding upon horror and ugliness, and filthiness of sin'. Serious historical research on him began in the early years of the 20th cent., since when he has attracted an enormous amount of critical commentary and speculation, so much so that Ellis *Waterhouse has written that 'the innocent reader of art-historical literature could be forgiven for supposing that his place in the history of civilization lies somewhere in importance between Aristotle and Lenin.'

Caravaggisti. Term applied to painters who imitated the style of *Caravaggio in the early 17th cent. Caravaggio's methods, particularly his dramatic use of *chiaroscuro, had extraordinary influence in Rome in the first decade of the 17th cent., on both Italian painters and artists from other countries, who flocked to what was then the artistic capital of Europe. His fame was already widespread by 1603, when Karel van *Mander, in Haarlem, wrote of 'Michelangelo da Caravaggio, who is doing extraordinary things in Rome'. The most prominent of the Italian Caravaggisti included Orazio *Gentileschi, one of the few followers to have close personal contact with the master, and Bartolommeo *Manfredi, who popularized tavern and guard room scenes, subjects that Caravaggio himself had not painted. In Naples, where Caravaggio moved to in 1606, *Caracciolo, Artemisia *Gentileschi, and *Ribera, a Spaniard by birth, ensured that the style took firm root. In Rome, Caravaggism went out of favour in the 1620s, but it persisted elsewhere in Italy, and in other parts of Europe, particularly in Sicily (which Caravaggio visited), Utrecht, and Lorraine, lingering into the 1650s in all three places. *Baburen, *Honthorst, and *Terbrugghen were the three most important artists in making Utrecht the Dutch centre of Caravaggism, and in Lorraine George de *La Tour perfected perhaps the most personal and poetic interpretation of the style. Few major painters worked in a Caravaggesque style throughout their careers; some, such as Guido *Reni, had a brief flirtation with it, while others, such as Honthorst (who became a court portraitist), had a complete change of direction. Echoes of the Caravaggesque style can be found in the work of some of the giants of 17th-cent. art: *Rembrandt, *Rubens, and *Velázquez.

cardboard. A thin but stiff board made from paper pulp or sheets of paper, sometimes used as a *support for paintings. Some of *Etty's finest nudes were painted on the type called millboard. A large number of the best works of *Toulouse-Lautrec are on cardboard as, also, are many paintings by *Bonnard and *Vuillard.

Carducho, Vincente (c.1576–1638). Spanish painter and writer on art. He was a Florentine by birth (his name was originally Vincenzo Carducci), but he settled in Spain when he was 9, when his elder brother, **Bartolomé Carducho** (originally Bartolommeo Carducci, c.1560–1608), went to the *Escorial in 1585 as assistant to Federico *Zuccaro. Vincente was appointed a court painter in Madrid in 1609, and had a successful and prolific career, but he is now remembered mainly for his book *Diálogos de la Pintura* (1633). In this he defended the heroic Italian tradition (championing *Michelangelo in particular), and excoriated the naturalism of *Caravaggio. In a sense this was an attack on *Velázquez, who had completely eclipsed Carducho at

court. Bartolomé Carducho also had a successful career in Spain, becoming a court painter in 1598 and working on royal commissions in Madrid, Segovia, and Valladolid. He painted in oils and fresco, and was influential in introducing Italian ideas to Spain.

caricature. A form of art, usually portraiture, in which characteristic features of the subject represented are distorted or exaggerated for comic effect. The term is sometimes used more broadly to denote other forms of pictorial burlesque, *grotesque or ludicrous representation, such as the grotesque heads of *Leonardo. The invention of caricature in the more limited sense is usually credited to Annibale *Carracci, who defended it as a counterpart to idealization (see IDEAL): just as the serious artist penetrates to the idea behind appearances, so the caricaturist also brings out the essence of his victim, the way he should look if Nature wholly had her way. Many other leading 17th-cent. artists were brilliant caricaturists (notably *Bernini), but the first artist to earn a substantial part of his living by caricature was probably Pier Leone Ghezzi (1674–1755). Political caricature as we know it today emerged in the last three decades of the 18th cent. It was perfected by artists such as *Gillray and *Cruikshank and it has remained a field in which British artists have shone; however, the greatest of all political caricaturists was a Frenchman, *Daumier. Many leading artists of the 19th and 20th cents. have shown a gift for caricature, but mainly as a sideline.

Carlevaris, Luca (1665–1731). Italian painter, born in Udine and active mainly in Venice. He is regarded as the father of 18th-cent. Venetian view-painting (see VEDUTA), for although he was not (as is sometimes asserted) the first to specialize in the genre, he approached it with a new seriousness, his training as a mathematician being reflected in his rigorous perspective settings. His paintings, and his set of over 100 engraved views of the city published in 1703, are the foundation on which *Canaletto and *Guardi built. A collection of oil sketches from nature in the Victoria and Albert Museum reveals his powers of lively observation.

Caro, Sir Anthony (1924–). British sculptor. After training as an engineer and serving in the Navy during the Second World War he studied sculpture in London, then was assistant to Henry *Moore (1951–3). In his earlier work Caro preferred modelling and he never developed the technique of carving. From 1960, following his meeting with David *Smith in the USA in the previous year, he made metal sculpture using prefabricated elements such as I-beams, aluminium tubing, boiler tank tops, propeller blades, Z-shaped steel plates, etc. These elements, while retaining their individual identity, were linked together in a system of shapes which conveyed a distinctive mood, sometimes suggested by the title, e.g. *Early One Morning* (Tate, London), *Slow Movement* (Arts Council Coll.). He would paint the finished work in smooth, resonant, and saturated colours suggestive of the mood to be conveyed. Later work, however, has been rougher in texture. Among contemporary sculptors Caro has been prominent in challenging the 'pedestal' tradition, using the ground as his base in order to involve the spectators more intimately in the space occupied by the sculpture, instead of segregating it artificially on a pedestal or plinth. He is considered by many critics to have originated and developed a new sculptural aesthetic, and his work has had an important influence on younger artists.

Carolingian art. The art and architecture of the reign of Charlemagne (800–814), the first Holy Roman Emperor, and of his successors until about 900. Charlemagne's reign was noteworthy for reforms in many fields; his guiding principle was a renewal of the values of the Roman Empire, and this was felt in the arts no less than in administrative, judicial, and religious matters. His capital was at Aachen (Aix-la-Chapelle), which became the centre of a cultural revival following a bleak period for the arts in the Franco-German lands that formed the heart of his vast empire. Charlemagne recognized the value of the arts for the education of his subjects and was himself the principal initiator of the cultural revival. Little survives of Carolingian mural paintings or mosaics, but several manuscripts contemporary with Charlemagne are known, showing a classical, naturalistic figure style, but also at times a vivid expressiveness. There was no large-scale sculpture, but Carolingian ivory sculpture and metalwork (on book covers, for example) often reached a high level. Carolingian art had great influence on *Ottonian and *Romanesque art.

Carolus-Duran, Charles-Émile-Auguste (1838–1917). French painter. His early works were influenced by *Courbet, but from about 1870 he concentrated on portraiture, becoming a great fashionable success with his slick style. In 1905 he was appointed Director of the French School in Rome. *Sargent was the most important of his many pupils.

Caron, Antoine (*c*.1520–*c*.1600). French *Mannerist painter. He is one of the few French painters of his time with a distinctive artistic personality, and his work reflects the refined but unstable atmosphere of the Valois court during the Wars of Religion (1560–98). He worked at *Fontainebleau under *Primaticcio in the 1540s and later became court painter to Catherine de *Médicis, wife of Henry II of France. His few surviving works include historical and allegorical subjects in the manner of court ceremonies, scenes of magic and prediction, and massacres, as in *Massacres under the Triumvirate* (1566) in the Louvre, his only signed and dated painting. His style is characterized most obviously by extremely elongated, precious-looking figures set in open spaces that seem too large for them. He had a penchant for gaudy colours and bizarre architectural forms. Some of the works attributed to him may be by other hands, however, for French painting of his period is such an obscure area that Caron's name is liable to be attached to anything similar to his known *œuvre*.

Carpaccio, Vittore (*c*.1450/60?–1525/6). Venetian painter. His life is poorly documented, and it is not known with whom he trained, but it is generally agreed that the chief influence on his work was Gentile *Bellini. This is especially apparent in the first of the two great cycles of paintings that are his chief claim to fame—the *Scenes from the Life of St Ursula*, executed in the 1490s and now in the Accademia, Venice. Carpaccio's distinguishing characteristics—his taste for anecdote, and his eye for the crowded detail of the Venetian scene—found their happiest expression in these paintings, one of which, the *Miracle of the Cross*, looks forward to the 18th-cent. compositions of *Canaletto and *Guardi. His other cycle, *Scenes from the Lives of St George and St Jerome*, painted for the Scuola (or 'Society') of S. Giorgio degli Schiavone, Venice, in 1502–7 (still *in situ*), combines fantasy with detail minutely observed. After these two major commissions, however, Carpaccio's career declined, his work seeming old-fashioned, and he remained virtually forgotten until *Ruskin revived his reputation in the 19th cent. He is now rated as second only to Giovanni Bellini as the outstanding Venetian painter of his generation.

Carpeaux, Jean-Baptiste (1827–75). French sculptor and painter. The son of a mason, he worked for some months in the studio of *Rude and also studied at the École des *Beaux-Arts, where he won the *Prix de Rome in 1854. His *Ugolino* (Musée d'Orsay, Paris, 1860–2) earned him the acclaim of the French colony in Rome, and upon his return to Paris in 1862 he won favour with the court, receiving many commissions for portrait busts. He also made several large sculpture groups, of which the most famous is *La Danse* (1869) for the façade of the Paris Opéra (the original is now in the Musée d'Orsay). This uninhibitedly dynamic work caused a sensation, was denounced as immoral, and had ink thrown over it. Partially because of such attacks on his work he suffered from a persecution complex in his final years before his early death from cancer. Carpeaux was the outstanding French sculptor of his period and an influential figure. His exuberance of feeling and vivacious modelling made a decisive break with the *Neoclassical tradition and presaged the work of *Rodin. His paintings are well represented in the Petit Palais in Paris, and there are also good examples of his work in the Musée des Beaux-Arts in Valenciennes, his home town.

Carr, Emily (1871–1945). Canadian painter of *Expressionist landscapes. In 1910–11 she was in Paris, where she experienced the impact of the *Fauves and was probably also influenced by Frances *Hodgkins. After her return she painted the landscape of her native British Columbia with passionate feeling for the power of nature, executing much of her

work out of doors. Discouraged by years of neglect, she had almost ceased to paint when in 1927 she first saw the work of the *Group of Seven in Toronto and thereafter worked with renewed energy and deepened spirituality, her ardent spirit given free rein. She was the author of several autobiographical works and overcame her earlier neglect to attain the status of a national heroine.

Carrà, Carlo (1881–1966). Italian painter, a prominent figure in both *Futurism and *Metaphysical painting. After training on Classical lines in Milan, he joined the Futurists in 1909, and visits to Paris in 1911 and 1912 introduced a *Cubist influence into his work. In his best-known painting *The Funeral of the Anarchist Galli* (MOMA, New York, 1911), for example, he combined the dynamism typical of Futurism with a sense of Cubist structural severity. In 1915 he met Giorgio de *Chirico and turned to Metaphysical painting, producing about twenty works with de Chirico's paraphernalia of posturing mannequins, half-open doors, mysteriously significant interiors, etc., though generally without his typically sinister feeling. Carrà broke with de Chirico in 1918 and abandoned Metaphysical painting, devoting himself to trying to recapture the monumental grandeur of early Italian painters such as *Giotto and *Masaccio and becoming an influential teacher.

Carracci. Family of Bolognese painters, the brothers **Agostino** (1557–1602) and **Annibale** (1560–1609) and their cousin **Ludovico** (1555–1619), who were prominent figures at the end of the 16th cent. in the movement against the prevailing *Mannerist artificiality of Italian painting. They worked together early in their careers, and it is not easy to distinguish their shares in, for example, the cycle of frescos in the Palazzo Fava in Bologna (c.1583–4). In the early 1580s they opened a private teaching *academy, which soon became a centre for progressive art. It was originally called the Accademia dei Desiderosi ('Desiderosi' meaning 'desirous of fame and learning'), but later changed its name to Accademia degli Incamminati (Academy of the Progressives). In their teaching they laid special emphasis on drawing from the life (all three were outstanding graphic artists) and clear

draughtsmanship became a quality particularly associated with artists of the Bolognese School, notably *Domenichino
and *Reni, two of the leading members
of the following generation who trained
with the Carracci.

They continued working in close relationship until 1595, when Annibale, who
was by far the greatest artist of the family,
was called to Rome by Cardinal Odoardo
*Farnese to carry out his masterpiece, the
decoration of the Farnese Gallery in the
cardinal's family palace. He first decorated
a small room called the Camerino with
stories of Hercules, and in 1597 undertook
the ceiling of the larger gallery, where the
theme was *The Loves of the Gods*, or, as
*Bellori described it, 'human love gov-
erned by Celestial love'. Although the
ceiling is rich in the interplay of various
illusionistic elements, it retains fundamentally the self-contained and un-
ambiguous character of High *Renaissance
decoration, drawing inspiration from
*Michelangelo's Sistine Ceiling and *Raph-
ael's frescos in the Vatican Loggie and the
Farnesina. The full untrammelled stream
of *Baroque illusionism was still to come
in the work of *Cortona and *Lanfranco,
but Annibale's decoration was one of the
foundations of their style. Throughout the
17th and 18th cents. the Farnese Ceiling
was ranked alongside the Sistine Ceiling
and Raphael's frescos in the Vatican Stanze
as one of the supreme masterpieces of
painting. It was enormously influential, not
only as a pattern book of heroic figure
design, but also as a model of technical
procedure; Annibale made hundreds of
drawings for the ceiling, and until the age
of *Romanticism such elaborate preparatory work became accepted as a fundamental part of composing any ambitious
history painting. In this sense, Annibale
exercised a more profound influence than
his great contemporary *Caravaggio, for
the latter never worked in fresco, which
was still regarded as the greatest test of a
painter's ability and the most suitable
vehicle for painting in the *Grand Manner.

Annibale's other works in Rome also
had great significance in the history of
painting. Pictures such as *Domine, Quo
Vadis?* (NG, London, *c*.1602) reveal a
striking economy in figure composition
and a force and precision of gesture that
had a profound influence on *Poussin and
through him on the whole language of

gesture in painting. He developed landscape
painting along similar lines, and is regarded
as the father of *ideal landscape, in which
he was followed by Domenichino (his
favourite pupil), *Claude, and Poussin.
The Flight into Egypt (Doria Gal., Rome,
c.1604) is Annibale's masterpiece in this
genre. In his last years Annibale was over-
come by melancholia and gave up painting
almost entirely after 1606. When he died
he was buried according to his wishes near
Raphael in the Pantheon. It is a measure
of his achievement that artists as great and
diverse as *Bernini, Poussin, and *Rubens
found so much to admire and praise in his
work. Annibale's art also had a less formal
side that comes out in his *caricatures (he
is generally credited with inventing the
form) and in his early *genre paintings,
which are remarkable for their lively observation and free handling (*The Butcher's
Shop*, Christ Church, Oxford).

Agostino assisted Annibale in the Farnese
Gallery from 1597 to 1600, but he was
important mainly as a teacher and engraver.
His systematic anatomical studies were
engraved after his death and were used for
nearly two centuries as teaching aids. He
spent the last two years in Parma, where
he did his own 'Farnese Ceiling', decorating
a ceiling in the Palazzo del Giardino with
mythological scenes for Duke Ranuccio
Farnese. It shows a meticulous but somewhat spiritless version of his brother's lively
*Classicism.

Ludovico left Bologna only for brief
periods and directed the Carracci academy
by himself after his cousins had gone to
Rome. His work is uneven and highly
personal. Painterly and expressive con-
siderations always outweigh those of stability and calm Classicism in his work, and
at its best there is a passionate and poetic
quality indicative of his preference for
*Tintoretto and Jacopo *Bassano. His most
fruitful period was 1585-95, but near the
end of his career he still produced remarkable paintings of an almost *Expressionist force, such as the *Christ Crucified
above Figures in Limbo* (Sta Francesca
Romana, Ferrara, 1614).

The Carracci fell from grace in the 19th
cent. along with all the other Bolognese
painters, who were one of *Ruskin's pet
hates and whom he considered (1847) had
'no single virtue, no colour, no drawing,
no character, no history, no thought'. They
were saddled with the label *'eclectic' and

thought to be ponderous and lacking in originality. Their full rehabilitation had to wait until the second half of the 20th cent. (the great Carracci exhibition held in Bologna in 1956 was a notable event), but Annibale has now regained his place as one of the giants of Italian painting.

Agostino's illegitimate son **Antonio** (1589?–1618) was the only offspring of the three Carracci. He had a considerable reputation as an artist in his day, but after his early death was virtually forgotten, and it is only recently that his work has been reconsidered.

Carreño de Miranda, Juan (1614–85). Spanish painter, active mainly in Madrid. Until he was appointed one of the royal painters in 1669 he concentrated on religious works, but thereafter he worked mainly as a portraitist. Except for his friend *Velázquez, he was the most important court painter of 17th-cent. Spain; he was of noble birth and his paintings have an aristocratic dignity and something of Velázquez's sensitivity and taste. His religious paintings (which include several frescos, notably in Toledo Cathedral) are, however, more extravagantly *Baroque.

Carriera, Rosalba (1675–1757). Venetian *pastel portraitist and *miniaturist, the sister-in-law of *Pellegrini. She made pastel portraits fashionable and achieved spectacular success throughout the capital cities of Europe, her visits to Paris (1721–2) and to Vienna (1730) being in the nature of royal progresses. She had considerable influence in France and converted Maurice Quentin de *La Tour to the pastel medium. It is now hard to appreciate why her work, which is highly accomplished but generally rather insipid, should have aroused such enthusiasm. After becoming blind in 1745, she had her sight temporarily restored by an operation, but lost it permanently in 1749 and retired into a state of melancholy dejection.

Carstens, Asmus Jacob (1754–98). Danish-born German draughtsman and painter. Apart from some initial training at the Copenhagen Academy he was largely self-educated. He moved to Berlin in 1787 and taught at the Academy. After 1792 he lived in Rome with the help of a grant from the Prussian State. Carstens was totally committed to *Neoclassicism and

concentrated on heroic figure compositions. He was uninterested in colour and was much more prolific as a draughtsman than as a painter. His work has a pompous seriousness in tune with his own inflated idea of his genius, but he is a significant figure because of the strictness of his ideals and the influence he had on the next generation of artists, notably *Thorvaldsen and the *Nazarenes.

cartoon. A full-size drawing made for the purpose of transferring a design to a painting or tapestry or other (usually large) work. Cartoons were an essential part of the process of making stained glass, and it was perhaps from this art that painters borrowed the idea; they were used in painting certainly by the early 15th cent. The design was transferred either by pressing heavily along the outlines with a pointed metal implement called a stylus or by rubbing powdered charcoal through a series of pinpricks—a process called 'pouncing'. In the 19th century designs submitted in a competition for frescos in the Houses of Parliament in London were parodied in the magazine *Punch*. From this the word has acquired its most common meaning today—a humorous drawing or parody.

caryatid. A carved female figure, usually clad in long robes, serving as a column. They were first used in Greek architecture and the most famous caryatids are on the Erechtheum at Athens. The male equivalent of the caryatid is the *atlas; the term 'canephorae' is applied to caryatids with baskets on their heads.

casein. A substance with strong adhesive powers made from the curd of milk, used in art as a binding material for paints and *grounds and as a glue for joining parts of a wooden *panel together.

Cassatt, Mary (1844–1926). American painter and printmaker who worked mostly in Paris in the circle of the *Impressionists. Persuaded to exhibit with the Impressionists by *Degas, for whom she had a great admiration, she nevertheless retained the extremely personal character of her art and her affinities with them lay less in technique than in an interest in everyday subject matter. Paintings such as *Lady at the Tea Table* (Met. Mus., New York, 1885) evoke with a fragile and delicate beauty the elaborate refinement of the society described by the novelist Henry James. She had a distinguished gift for draughtsmanship and was as skilful with pastel and the tools of printmaking as she was with oils. Her prints, in which she often combined etching and *drypoint, show the influence of Japanese art (see UKIYO-E). Cassatt's eyesight began to fail when she was in her fifties and she had virtually stopped working by 1914. She came from a wealthy family and exercised an important influence on American taste by urging her rich friends to buy Impressionist works.

cassone. Italian term for a large chest which contained the bride's dowry or was given as a wedding present. Decorated *cassoni* became the fashion in *Renaissance Italy, and *quattrocento Florence saw the development of the painted *cassone* front. These paintings usually represented episodes from the Bible or Classical history or mythology which pointed a lesson or contained a happy augury for the newly-weds. Often the *cassoni* were made as pairs, bearing the coats of arms respectively of the bride and groom, as with a pair, dated 1472, in the Courtauld Institute Galleries, London (this pair is particularly noteworthy in retaining the original backboards—*spallieri*) *Cassone* paintings are rarely of high quality, although some major artists such as *Domenico Veneziano, *Uccello, and *Botticelli seem to have done them once in a while. The chief documented exponent was Apollonio di Giovanni (1415–65).

Castiglione, Giovanni Benedetto (called Il Grechetto) (*c.*1610–65). Genoese painter, etcher, and draughtsman. His style of painting owed something to *Rubens, van *Dyck, and Bernardo *Strozzi, all of whom worked in Genoa, whilst his etchings depend particularly on *Rembrandt. This openness to foreign influence was unusual for an Italian artist of this period. He was extremely versatile as well as eclectic, being equally at home with *Grand Manner history paintings and rustic genre scenes (he was a superb animal painter). Some of his best works have a sense of fantasy recalling Salvator *Rosa, notably the etching *The Genius of Castiglione* (1648). He was highly prolific as a graphic artist as well as a painter and is

credited with inventing the *monotype. From 1648 he was court painter at Mantua, a post in which he was succeeded by his son **Francesco** (d. 1716). His work had wide influence, for example, on *Fragonard and Giambattista *Tiepolo.

Catena, Vincenzo (*c.*1480–1531). Venetian painter of religious subjects and portraits. Catena was a man of good birth and independent means who moved in humanist circles and may have been the link between these circles and *Giorgione. He is first mentioned in 1506 in an inscription on the back of Giorgione's portrait *Laura* (Kunsthistorisches Mus., Vienna), according to which they had entered into some kind of partnership. Nothing else is known of this arrangement. His early works are awkward and stiff variants of compositions probably evolved in Giovanni *Bellini's studio in the 1490s. From *c.*1510 his work matured under the influence of the late Bellini, *Cima, and *Titian into a style that was derivative but handsome, with pleasing handling of diffused light and warm colours.

Catlin, George (1796–1872). American painter and writer, renowned for his portrayal of Red Indian life. He practised law before becoming an artist in the early 1820s (initially as a portraitist in Philadelphia) and was completely self-taught. In 1830 he began a series of visits to various Indian tribes (he had been fascinated with the subject since childhood) and from 1837 to 1845 he exhibited the resulting paintings as the 'Gallery of Indians' in the USA and Europe. He was better received in England and France than in his native country (*Baudelaire wrote about him enthusiastically) and he lived in Europe from 1858 to 1870. In addition to his paintings, he published various illustrated books on Indian life. Most of his work is in the Smithsonian Institution in Washington.

Cavallini, Pietro (active 1273–1308). Italian painter and mosaic designer, active mainly in Rome, where he must have been the leading artist of his day. His two major surviving works are mosaics of the *Life of the Virgin* (Sta Maria in Trastevere, signed and dated 1291) and a fragmentary fresco cycle, the most important part of which is a *Last Judgement* (Sta Cecilia in Trastevere, Rome). In 1308 Cavallini was in Naples serving the Angevin kings, and was probably responsible for the design and possibly some of the execution of a fresco cycle in Sta Maria Donnaregina. Although he is such an obscure figure, Cavallini occupies an important place in the history of Italian painting. He was the first artist to make a significant break with the stylizations of *Byzantine art, and his majestic figures have a real sense of weight and three-dimensionality. His work undoubtedly influenced his great contemporary *Giotto, whose Last Judgement in the Arena Chapel at Padua features Apostles enthroned exactly as in Cavallini's fresco of the subject.

Cavallino, Bernardo (1616–56?). Neapolitan painter. He was the most individual and sensitive Neapolitan painter of his time, but his career is somewhat obscure. About eighty paintings by him are extant, but only one is dated, St Cecilia in Ecstasy (Palazzo Vecchio, Florence, 1645; a *modello is in the Museo di Capodimonte, Naples). Usually small-scale religious works, they are peopled by exquisitely elegant and refined figures who evoke a feeling of tender melancholy. Their fragile sensitivity is in complete contrast to the earthy vigour of much of Neapolitan painting of his period. Cavallino trained with Massimo *Stanzione, but his style has more in common with that of van *Dyck, whose work was fairly well known in Naples. He is presumed to have died in the plague that devastated Naples in 1656.

Cellini, Benvenuto (1500–71). Florentine sculptor, goldsmith, and metal-worker. His autobiography, written in a racy vernacular, has been famous since the 18th cent. (it was first published in 1728) for its vivid picture of a *Renaissance craftsman proud of his skill and independence, boastful of his feats in art, love, and war, quarrelsome, superstitious, and devoted to the great tradition embodied in *Michelangelo. It has given him a wider reputation than could have come from his artistic work alone; but to modern eyes he also appears as one of the most important *Mannerist sculptors, and his statue Perseus is one of the glories of Florentine art. His life can be roughly divided into three periods. From the first, spent mainly in Rome, nothing survives but some coins and medals and the impressions of two large seals. During the second (1540–5), which he

spent in the service of Francis I of France (see FONTAINEBLEAU, SCHOOL OF), he created the famous salt-cellar of gold enriched with enamel (Kunsthistorisches Mus., Vienna), the most important piece of goldsmith's work that has survived from the Italian Renaissance. He also made for the king a large bronze *relief, the Nymph of Fontainebleau (Louvre, Paris). The remainder of Cellini's life was passed in Florence in the service of Cosimo I de' *Medici, and it was only in this period that he took up large-scale sculpture in the round. The bronze Perseus (Loggia dei Lanzi, Florence, 1545–54) is reckoned his masterpiece. His other sculptures include the Apollo and Hyacinth and the Narcissus (both in the Bargello, Florence) and the Crucifix (Escorial, near Madrid), all in marble. His two portrait busts, Bindo Altoviti (Gardner Mus., Boston), and Cosimo I (Bargello), are in bronze. Their somewhat dry, niggly quality shows that the exquisite precision of handling of his goldsmith's work did not always transfer easily to a larger scale. Because of his fame, many pieces of metalwork have been attributed to him, but rarely on secure grounds.

Cennini, Cennino (c.1370–c.1440). Florentine painter and writer. None of his paintings has survived, but he is remembered as the author of Il Libro dell' Arte (translated by Daniel V. Thompson as The Craftsman's Handbook, 1933), written in about 1400 and the most important source concerning artistic practice in the late Middle Ages. Cennini states in the book that he was a pupil of Agnolo *Gaddi, who learnt from his father Taddeo Gaddi, who in turn was a pupil of *Giotto, so his detailed descriptions of *tempera and *fresco painting no doubt reflect, even if at several removes, the technical procedures of the founder of the great tradition of Florentine painting.

Cercle et Carré (Circle and Square). A discussion and exhibition society for *Constructivist artists formed in Paris by *Seuphor and *Torres-García in 1929. A journal of the same name was founded, of which three numbers appeared in 1929–30. *Mondrian contributed an article. In Paris Cercle et Carré was superseded in 1931 by the more important *Abstraction-Création group, but some years later Torres-García formed an Asociación de

Arte Constructivo in Montevideo and edited a journal entitled *Círculo y Cuadrado*, of which seven numbers appeared between 1936 and 1938.

Cerquozzi, Michelangelo (1602–60). Italian painter, known as 'Michelangelo of the Battles' because of his predilection for battle scenes. He spent all his career in Rome, but had considerable contact with Northern painters; his friendship with the Dutchman Pieter van *Laer led to his becoming the leading Italian exponent of *bambocciate* (small pictures of low-life and peasant scenes).

César (**César Baldaccini**) (1921–). French sculptor. His work is highly varied, but he has become best known for his ingenious use of scrap material. In the mid 1950s he began to make sculptures from material that he found in refuse dumps—scrap iron, springs, tin cans, etc.—building these up with wire into strange winged or insect-like creatures. These had closer affinities, however, with the insect-creatures of Germaine *Richier than with the *Abstract Expressionism of the California *Junk school of sculpture. During the 1960s he became internationally known mainly for sculptures made by crushing car bodies.

Cesari, Giuseppe (also called **Cavaliere d'Arpino**) (1568–1640). Italian *Mannerist painter, active mainly in Rome. He had an enormous reputation in the first two decades of the 17th cent., when he gained some of the most prestigious commissions of the day, most notably the designing of the *mosaics for the dome of St Peter's (1603–12). Although some of his early work is vigorous and colourful, his output is generally repetitive and vacuous, untouched by the innovations of *Caravaggio (who was briefly his assistant) or the *Carracci. He was primarily a fresco painter, but he also did numerous *cabinet pictures of religious or mythological scenes in a finicky Flemish manner.

Cézanne, Paul (1839–1906). French painter, with *Gauguin and van *Gogh the greatest of the *Post-Impressionists and a key figure in the development of 20th-cent. art. He was born at Aix-en-Provence, son of a hat dealer who became a prosperous banker, and his financial security enabled him to survive the indifference to his work that lasted until the final decade of his life. His schoolfellow Émile Zola introduced him to *Manet and *Courbet, and persuaded him to take up the study of art in Paris. There at the Académie Suisse in 1861 he met Camille *Pissarro, and the following year he got to know *Monet, *Bazille, *Sisley, and *Renoir. His painting at this time was in a vein of unreserved *Romanticism, reflecting his admiration for *Delacroix, with a predilection for themes of violence or eroticism (*The Murder*, Walker Art Gallery, Liverpool). In 1869 he met Hortense Fiquet, a model and seamstress, who became his mistress and bore him a son, Paul, in 1872. Cézanne kept them a secret from his family—he was terrified of his domineering father—but eventually married Hortense in 1886, shortly before his father's death. From about 1870 Cézanne started painting directly from nature and began to impose a more disciplined restraint on his natural impetuosity. In 1872 he settled in Auvers-sur-Oise, near Pontoise, the home of Camille Pissarro, and entered upon a long and fruitful association with him (in the last year of his life he even described himself as a 'pupil of Pissarro'). He exhibited with the *Impressionists in 1874 and again in 1877, but never identified himself with the Impressionist group or wholly adopted their aims and techniques (he was a touchy character and hid his insecurities by posing as a provincial boor, once refusing to shake hands with the elegant *Manet because he claimed he had not washed for days and did not wish to dirty the great man). Cézanne was less interested in the realistic representation of casual and fleeting impressions and the fugitive effects of light, devoting himself rather to the structural analysis of nature, looking forward in this respect to the *Neo-Impressionists. His own aims are summarized in two of his sayings: that it was his ambition 'to do *Poussin again after nature' and that he wanted to make of Impressionism 'something solid and enduring like the art of the museums'. He trod a solitary and difficult path towards his goal of an art which would combine the best of the French *Classical tradition of structure with the best in contemporary naturalism, an art which appealed not superficially to the eye but to the mind.

After the death of his father in 1886 and his inheritance of the family estate (the Jas de Bouffan, which features in many of his paintings), Cézanne lived mainly in Aix. He devoted himself principally to certain favourite themes—portraits of his wife, still lifes, and above all the landscape of Provence, particularly the Monte Ste-Victoire. His painstaking analysis of nature differed fundamentally from Monet's exercises in painting repeated views of subjects such as *Haystacks* or *Poplars*. Cézanne was interested in underlying structure, and his paintings rarely give any obvious indication of the time of day or even the season represented. His later paintings are generally more sparsely composed and open, permeated with a sense of air and light. The third dimension is created not through perspective or foreshortening but by extraordinarily subtle variations of tonality. He worked in comparative obscurity until he was given a one-man show by the dealer *Vollard in 1895. From that time his painting began to excite younger artists and by the end of the century he was revered as the 'Sage' by many of the avant-garde; in 1904 the *Salon d'Automne gave him a special exhibition. Since his death his reputation has increased and he has exercised a profound influence among 20th-cent. artists, most notably the *Cubists. His work was introduced to England with the Post-Impressionist exhibitions organized by Roger *Fry in 1910 and 1912, and in 1914 Clive *Bell wrote that: 'He was the Christopher Columbus of a new continent of form.'

Although Cézanne was a laboriously slow worker—he is said to have had over 100 sittings for a portrait of Ambroise Vollard (Petit Palais, Paris, 1899) before abandoning it with the comment that he was not displeased with the shirt front—he left a substantial body of work (drawings and water-colours as well as oils). There are works in many major museums, with particularly fine collections in, for example, the Courtauld Institute Galleries, London, the Musée d'Orsay, Paris, and the Barnes Foundation, Merion, Pennsylvania. His studio in Aix is now a Cézanne museum.

Chadwick, Lynn (1914–). One of the leading English sculptors of his generation. He trained as an architect and took up sculpture after serving as a pilot in the Second World War. At first he experimented with *mobiles and these were followed by what he called 'balanced sculptures', ponderous metal structures supported on thin legs, bristling and rough-finished. His work has been shown in a number of international exhibitions and in 1956 he was awarded the International Sculpture Prize at the 28th Venice *Biennale. During the 1960s and 1970s his work became more block-like and monumental, and in his more recent sculpture he has exploited highly polished surfaces and facetings.

Chagall, Marc (1887–1985). Russian-born painter and designer, active mainly in Paris. He studied at St Petersburg under *Bakst, then came to Paris in 1910 and there became an intimate of the avant-garde circle which included *Apollinaire, *Soutine, *Léger, *Delaunay, and *Modigliani. In 1914 he was exhibited at the gallery of Der *Sturm in Berlin and returned to Russia. He founded an art school in Vitebsk and in 1917 was made director and Commissar of Fine Art for Vitebsk. But the element of fantasy in his work caused difficulties with the authorities, whose conception of art demanded traditional *realism with a social message, and he went to Moscow, where he designed for the newly founded Jewish Theatre. He returned to Paris in 1923, and among much other work illustrated Gogol's *Dead Souls* and La Fontaine's *Fables* for the dealer *Vollard. In 1941 he moved from occupied France to the USA, but returned to Paris in 1947; from 1950 he made his home at St-Paul-de-Vence near Nice. Chagall was prolific as a painter and also as a book illustrator and designer of stained glass and of sets and costumes for the theatre and ballet. His work was dominated by two rich sources of imagery: memories of the Jewish life and folklore of his early years in Russia; and the Bible. He derived some of his spatial dislocations and prismatic colour effects from *Cubism and *Orphism, but he created a highly distinctive style, remarkable for its sense of fairy-tale fantasy. This caused André *Breton to claim him as one of the precursors of *Surrealism, but Chagall himself stated in his autobiography *Ma vie* (1931) that however fantastic and imaginative his pictures appeared, he painted only direct reminiscences of his early years. There is a museum devoted to Chagall's religious art in Nice. The work there does not always show him at his best, for he could be sentimental and overblown, but his finest paintings reveal him as one of the greatest masters of the School of *Paris.

chalk. Drawing material made from various soft stones or earths. There are three main types; black chalk (made from stones such as carbonaceous shale); red chalk, also called sanguine (made from red ochre or other red earths); and white chalk (made from various limestones). Chalk drawings are known from prehistoric times, but the medium really came into its own in the late 15th cent., notably in the hands of *Leonardo, who made many drawings in red and black chalk. The terms 'chalk', 'crayon', and *'pastel' are not always clearly distinguished from one another. Crayons, as the term is now generally understood, are sticks of colour made with an oily or waxy binding substance, and pastels are sticks of powdered pigment bound with gum. In other words, they are both manufactured products, whereas chalk needs only to be cut to a suitable shape and size to be usable.

Champaigne, Philippe de (1602–74). Flemish-born painter who came to Paris with his master Jacques Fouquières (c.1580/90–1659) in 1621 and took French citizenship in 1629. He became the outstanding French portraitist of the 17th cent. and was patronized by Louis XIII, the Queen Mother (Marie de *Médicis), and Cardinal Richelieu. Two of his finest portraits of Richelieu (late 1630s) are in the National Gallery, London; they bring the personality of the cardinal vividly to life and show how Champaigne moderated the *Baroque idiom of *Rubens towards a Classical simplicity in line with French artistic trends of the middle of the 17th cent. He was a friend of *Poussin, and Anthony *Blunt has written that 'His portraits and his later religious works are as true a reflection of the rationalism of French thought as the classical compositions of Poussin in the 1640s.' His style became even more severe after he was influenced by the Jansenists—a Catholic sect of great austerity—in the early 1640s. Some of his finest work was done for the Jansenist convent at Port-Royal, where his daughter

became a nun: he commemorated her miraculous recovery from paralysis in his most celebrated work, the *Ex-Voto de 1662 (Louvre, Paris). His masterpiece in portraiture might well have been his self-portrait of 1676, which is lost, but survives in a copy by his nephew Jean-Baptiste de Champaigne (1631–81) in the Louvre and in a superb engraving by Gerard *Edelinck.

Chantrey, Sir Francis (1781–1841). English sculptor. The son of a carpenter, he was apprenticed to a wood carver in Sheffield but left to come to London, c.1802, to work in the *Royal Academy Schools. Until about 1804 his work included painted portraits, but after that date he confined himself to sculpture. His portrait bust of the Revd J. Horne-Took, exhibited at the Royal Academy in 1811 (Fitzwilliam, Cambridge), brought him fame, and he succeeded *Nollekens as the most successful sculptor of portrait busts in England. Once he was famous, Chantrey, like Nollekens, did little of the cutting of the marble himself. His enormous practice included statues and church monuments as well as busts; his monument to the Robinson children (1817) in Lichfield Cathedral and his bronze equestrian statue of George IV (1828) in Trafalgar Square are his best-known works in these fields. He became extremely wealthy, and besides being very generous during his life he left the bulk of his fortune of £150,000 to the Royal Academy, the interest to be used for the purchase of 'works of Fine Art of the highest merit executed within the shores of Great Britain'. These are now housed in the *Tate Gallery.

charcoal. Charred twigs or sticks used for drawing. Its use dates back to Roman times and possibly much earlier. An essential characteristic of charcoal is that it is easily rubbed off the drawing surface unless a *fixative is used, so it has been much favoured for preparatory work, either for sketches or *cartoons or for outlining on wall or panel a design that could be gone over with a more permanent medium. The soft-edged effect it produces has been notably exploited by the Venetian painters of the later 16th cent., *Baroque artists, and the *Impressionists. *Pencils and *chalks have now taken its place to some extent, but it remains well suited to large-scale work and broad, energetic draughtsmanship, and in the 20th cent. has been memorably used by *Barlach and *Kollwitz.

Chardin, Jean-Baptiste-Siméon (1699–1779). French painter of still life and *genre, in which fields he was one of the greatest masters of all time. He was the contemporary of *Boucher and he taught *Fragonard, but his work is a contrast to theirs in every way, representing the naturalistic tendency which persisted through the 18th cent. alongside the more fashionable *Rococo. He was received into the Académie in 1728 on the strength of a still life (*The Rayfish*, Louvre, Paris), which drew forth the extravagant praises of *Diderot for its realism, and he was Treasurer of the Académie for twenty years. His small canvases depicting modest scenes and objects from the everyday life of the middle classes to which he belonged were in the tradition of the Dutch *cabinet pictures, which were having a great commercial success in France at the time. Chardin, however, developed a technique of his own, achieving great depth of tone by successive applications of the loaded brush and a subtle use of *scumbled colour. He was praised for his verisimilitude of detail, but his work goes far beyond matter-of-fact realism and through its simplicity and directness of vision achieves a sense of deep seriousness, in spite of the humble objects he portrayed (*Pipe and Jug*, Louvre). His genre paintings, which usually contain only one or two figures, are likewise completely without sentimentality or affectation (*The Young Governess*, versions in the National Galleries of London and Washington). In his last years, when his sight was failing, he turned his hand to pastel portraits and in the 1775 Salon exhibited two self-portraits and a portrait of his wife (Louvre).

Charonton (or **Quarton**), **Enguerrand** (*c.*1410–66). French painter, born in Laon. His career is unusually well documented for a provincial artist of his date (he was active in Aix, Arles, and Avignon), but there are only two extant works that are certainly by him. These are the *Virgin of Mercy* (1452) in the Musée Condé at Chantilly, painted in collaboration with an obscure artist called Pierre Villatte, and the *Coronation of the Virgin* (1454) in the Musée de l'Hospice at Villeneuve-lès-Avignon.

They are both highly impressive works, uniting Flemish and Italian influence and having something of the monumental character of the sculpture of Charonton's region. Indeed, they show Charonton to have been a painter of such commanding stature that there is an increasing tendency to attribute to him the celebrated *Avignon Pietà* (Louvre, Paris), the greatest French painting of the period (see AVIGNON, SCHOOL OF).

Chase, William Merritt (1849–1916). American painter. He settled in New York in 1878 after five years studying in Munich and became the most important American teacher of his generation. He taught at the Art Students' League of New York and then at his own Chase School of Art, founded in 1896. The vigorous handling and fresh colour characteristic of much of the best American painting of the early 20th cent. owes a good deal to his example. His pupils (whom he encouraged to paint in the open air) included *Demuth, *O'Keefe, and *Sheeler. Chase was a highly prolific artist (his output of more than 2,000 paintings included still lifes, portraits, interiors, and landscapes), and his work is represented in many American museums. See also TEN, THE.

Chassériau, Théodore (1819–56). French painter. He was the most gifted pupil of *Ingres, whose studio in Rome he entered when he was 11, but in the 1840s he conceived an admiration for *Delacroix and attempted, with considerable success, to combine Ingres's *Classical linear grace with Delacroix's *Romantic colour. His chief work was the decoration of the Cour des Comptes in the Palais d'Orsay, Paris, with allegorical scenes of Peace and War (1844–8), but these were almost completely destroyed by fire. There are other examples of his decorative work, however, in various churches in Paris. Chassériau was also an outstanding portraitist and painted nudes and North African scenes (he made a visit there in 1846).

Cheere, Sir Henry (1703–81). English sculptor, possibly of French descent. He went into partnership with Henry *Scheemakers and after Scheemakers left England about 1733 Cheere extended the practice, his output including much work for Oxford University. Cheere was also prominent in public affairs and devoted efforts to an abortive scheme to found an academy of arts a decade before the *Royal Academy came into being. His art is markedly *Rococo in feeling, with an interest in small rhythms, and in his charming smaller monuments (*Dean Wilcocks*, Westminster Abbey, 1756) he often used coloured marbles. He was well thought of by his fellow artists and furthered the career of *Roubiliac by gaining him his first important commission in England—the statue of Handel for Vauxhall Gardens (now V&A, London, 1738). His brother **John** (1709–87) had a yard near Hyde Park Corner which turned out a great number of garden figures.

chiaroscuro (Italian: bright-dark). Term describing the effects of light and shade in a work of art, particularly when they are strongly contrasting. *Leonardo was a pioneer of bold chiaroscuro, but the term is most usually associated with 17th-cent. artists, particularly the *Caravaggisti and *Rembrandt.

chiaroscuro woodcut. A type of *woodcut in which tonal effects are created by printing successively on to the same sheet from different blocks of varying tone. Two or more tones of a single colour are used, or of two nearly related colours, one of which is darker than the other. The method dates from the early 16th cent., when it was chiefly used for the reproduction of drawings, and developed more or less simultaneously in Germany and Italy. The earliest dated example is *The Emperor Maximilian on Horseback* of 1508, designed by Hans *Burgkmair; other notable German exponents were *Cranach, *Baldung Grien, and *Altdorfer. In Italy, where the medium was used more extensively, *Ugo da Carpi (who is sometimes credited with inventing the technique) made many prints after designs by *Raphael and *Parmigianino, the latter artist being a prolific designer for the process.

Chinnery, George (1774–1852). English painter, active for almost all his career in the Far East. His movements after sailing for India in 1802 were: 1802–7 in Madras, 1807–27 in Calcutta, 1827–c.1830 in Canton, c.1830–52 in Macao. Chinnery painted a number of portraits while abroad and from time to time sent to *Royal Academy exhibitions, but his reputation rests today on the large number of landscapes and decorative studies he made of oriental scenes.

chinoiserie. The imitation or evocation of Chinese styles in Western art and architecture. The term is applied particularly to art of the 18th cent., when pseudo-Chinese designs in a whimsical or fantastic vein accorded well with the prevailing lighthearted Rococo style. By the middle of the 18th cent. the enthusiasm for things Chinese affected virtually all the decorative arts, and there was also a vogue for Chinese-style buildings in garden architecture. The taste for chinoiserie faded during the dominance of the *Neoclassical style in the second half of the century, but there was something of a revival in the early 19th cent.

Chirico, Giorgio de (1888–1978). Italian painter, the originator of *Metaphysical painting. He studied in Munich, where he was influenced by the works of *Böcklin and *Klinger, with their juxtaposition of the commonplace and the fantastic. In 1909–10, in Italy he painted his first 'enigmatic' pictures, which convey an atmosphere of strangeness and uneasiness through their empty spaces, illogical shadows, and unexpected perspectives. Soon he developed a more deliberate theory of 'metaphysical insight' into a reality behind ordinary things by neutralizing the things themselves of all their usual associations and setting them in new and mysterious relationships. In order to empty the objects of his compositions of their natural emotional significance he painted tailors' dummies as human beings (from 1914). In 1915 de Chirico was conscripted into the armed forces and sent to Ferrara. There he suffered a nervous breakdown, and in 1917 met *Carrà in the military hospital and converted him to his views, founding Metaphysical painting. The movement was short-lived, however, and although de Chirico found himself hailed as a precursor by the *Surrealists, he eventually repudiated his earlier work and set himself against modern art. In the 1920s he painted some of his most powerful and distinctive works, notably a series featuring horses on unreal sea-shores with broken Classical columns, but his later work became repetitive and obsessed with technical refinement.

Chodowiecki, Daniel Nikolaus (1726–1801). Polish-German painter and illustrator, born in Danzig (now Gdansk), and active mainly in Berlin. He began his career by painting *enamels. His early oil paintings were imitations of the French manner, and his fame rests on the more individual book illustrations and graphic work of all kinds which he produced prolifically from *c*.1770 onwards. Most attractive are the little intimate sketches he made of the bourgeois life around him, not least of his own family. In 1797 he became Director of the Berlin Academy.

Christie's. The popular name for the firm of Christie, Manson & Woods, the oldest fine art auctioneers in the world (*Sotheby's was founded earlier, but originally sold only books). It was founded by James Christie (1730–1803), who gave up a commission in the Navy to become an auctioneer and held his first sale on 5 December 1766 in rooms in Pall Mall, in the same premises in which the exhibitions of the *Royal Academy were held until 1779. He was a friend of *Reynolds and *Gainsborough, and Christie's developed a tradition of holding the studio sales of prominent artists. The firm acquired its present name in 1859, when James Christie's grandsons took new partners. Its headquarters are still in London and there are branches in New York, Amsterdam and Geneva.

Christo (**Christo Javacheff**) (1935–). Bulgarian-born sculptor and designer who settled in New York in 1964. He is chiefly known as the originator of 'packaging' art, which consists of wrapping familiar objects in canvas or semi-transparent plastic and dubbing them works of art. He made his first packaged objects in 1958. At first these were small in scale, but they gradually increased in size and pretentiousness through trees and motor cars to architectural monuments, including the Pont Neuf in Paris (1985).

Christus, Petrus (d. 1472/73). Netherlandish painter. He is first documented at Bruges in 1444, and he is thought by some authorities to have been the pupil of Jan van *Eyck and to have completed some of the works left unfinished by the master at his death in 1441 (e.g. *St Jerome*, Detroit Inst. of Arts). It is certainly true that he was overwhelmingly influenced by van Eyck, and his copies and variations of his work helped to spread the Eyckian style. Christus's work is more summary than van Eyck's, however, his figures sometimes rather doll-like and without van Eyck's feeling of inner life. The influence of Rogier van der *Weyden is also evident in Christus's work; the *Lamentation* (Musées Royaux, Brussels) is clearly based on van der Weyden's great Prado *Deposition*, but the figures have completely lost their dramatic impact. Christus's most personal works are his portraits, notably *Edward Grimston* (Earl of Verulam Coll., 1446) in which he abandons the dark backgrounds of van Eyck and van der Weyden and places his sitter in a clearly defined interior. His interest in representing space comes out also in his *Virgin and Child with Sts Jerome and Francis* (Städelsches Kunstinstitut, Frankfurt, 1457), the earliest dated example in the north of the use of geometric *perspective with a single vanishing point.

chromolithography. The process of making coloured prints by *lithography, using a separate stone or plate for each colour.

chryselephantine. Term describing statues in which the drapery is made of gold (Greek *chrysos*) and the flesh of ivory (Greek *elephantinos*). The technique was used on a small scale in ancient Egypt, Mesopotamia, and Crete, and in colossal statues by the Greeks from the 6th cent. BC. Most famous of chryselephantine statues were the enormous cult images of Athena and Zeus that *Phidias made respectively for the Parthenon at Athens and the Temple of Zeus at Olympia.

Church, Frederick Edwin (1826–1900). American landscape painter. He was a pupil and close friend of *Cole and continued the preoccupations of the *Hudson River School with the most spectacular aspects of natural scenery. Church looked and travelled beyond his native country, however, painting not only the Niagara Falls, for example, but also the tropical forests of South America, icebergs, and exploding volcanoes, often on a huge scale. He was immensely popular in his day, and after a period of neglect is returing to favour again. His house, Olana, on the Hudson River, is now a museum.

Churrigueresque. Term applied to an extravagant style of architecture and ornament popular in Spain (and also Latin America) in the 18th cent. and sometimes used more loosely to refer to the *Rococo period as a whole in Spanish architecture. It is named after the Churriguera family of architects and sculptors, who were active mainly in Seville. The most important member of the family was José Benito (1665–1725), whose work is well represented by the *retable (1693–1700) of the church of San Esteban in Salamanca, an important early example of the style, full of lavishly decorated barley-sugar columns. It still retains a sense of architectural solidity, however, and is restrained compared with later manifestations of the style, in which surface ornament runs riot to such a degree that the underlying structure is hidden. To *Neoclassical taste the Churrigueresque style represented the last word in decadence and it died out completely in the last quarter of the 18th cent.

Cibber, Caius Gabriel (1630–1700). English sculptor of Danish birth. He arrived in England before the Restoration in 1660, probably via Amsterdam, and worked for John Stone, son of Nicholas *Stone. His first important work was the large *relief (1674) on the base of the Monument erected in memory of the Great Fire of London (1666). Other works in London included the dramatic figures of *Raving* and *Melancholy Madness* (c.1675) for the gate of old Bedlam Hospital (now in the V&A, London). Much of his later career was taken up with decorative sculpture; he was much favoured by Sir Christopher Wren, who employed him at Hampton Court and St Paul's Cathedral. With the exception of the figures of *Raving* and *Melancholy Madness*, which are powerful and original pieces, and the dignified and moving tomb of Thomas Sackville at Withyham, Sussex (1677), Cibber's work is usually competent but uninspired; it is of interest, however, in reflecting *Baroque influence (still unusual in England at this time) from Italy (where Cibber is said to have studied early in his career) and also from the Netherlands. He was the father

of Colley Cibber (1671–1757), the actor-manager and dramatist.

ciborium. A term applied to both a liturgical vessel used for holding the consecrated Host and an altar canopy supported on columns, popular particularly in Italy in the *Romanesque and *Gothic periods. In the latter sense the word is not easily distinguished from *baldacchino.

Cignani, Carlo (1628–1719). Bolognese painter. He was a pupil of *Albani, but his style is closer to that of Guido *Reni and he became the main force in upholding the tradition of Bolognese Classicism into the 18th cent. In 1711 he became the first president of the Accademia Clementina in Bologna.

Cignaroli, Giambettino (1706–70). Italian historical, religious, and decorative painter, active mainly in and around Verona. He was the leading artist of his period there, working in an elegantly academic style.

Cigoli, Il (Ludovico Cardi) (1559–1613). Florentine painter, architect, and poet. A pupil of Alessandro *Allori, he was the outstanding Florentine painter of his generation and his work represents the complex stylistic crosscurrents in the period of transition from *Mannerism to *Baroque. His sensuous colour and handling show the influence of *Barocci, *Correggio, and the art of Venice, and his dramatic handling of light and shade that of *Caravaggio, especially after he moved to Rome in 1604 (*Ecce Homo*, Pitti, Florence, 1606).

Cimabue (Cenni di Peppi) (c.1240–1302?). Florentine painter. His nickname means 'Ox-head'. He was a contemporary of Dante, who refers to him in *The Divine Comedy* (*Purg.* xi. 94–6) as an artist who was 'believed to hold the field in painting' only to be eclipsed by *Giotto's fame. Ironically enough this passage, meant to illustrate the vanity of short-lived earthly glory, has become the basis for Cimabue's fame; for, embroidering on this reference, later writers made him into the discoverer and teacher of Giotto and regarded him as the first in the long line of great Italian painters. He was said to have worked in the 'Greek' (i.e. *Byzantine) manner, but to have begun the movement towards greater realism which culminated in the *Renaissance. Documentary evidence is insufficient to confirm or deny this estimate of Cimabue's art. The only work that can be proved to be by his hand is a *St John* forming part of a larger mosaic in Pisa Cathedral (1302), but tradition has tended to attribute to Cimabue many works of outstanding quality from the end of the 13th cent., such as the *Madonna of Sta Trinità* (Uffizi, Florence), a cycle of frescos in the Upper Church of S. Francesco in Assisi, and a majestic *Crucifix* in Sta Croce (badly damaged in the Florence flood of 1966). If these highly plausible attributions are correct, Cimabue was indeed the outstanding master of the generation before Giotto. The movement towards greater naturalism, however, may owe more to the school of Roman painters and mosaicists (*Cavallini, *Torriti) than to him; he is documented in Rome in 1272 and could have known their work.

Cima da Conegliano, Giovanni Battista (1459/60–1517/18). Italian painter, named after the town of his birth, and active mainly in nearby Venice. His paintings are mostly quiet devotional scenes, often in landscape settings, in the manner of Giovanni *Bellini. He has been called 'the poor man's Bellini', but because of his calm and weighty figures he was also known in the 18th cent. (rather incongruously) as 'the Venetian Masaccio'. Nine of his works are in the National Gallery, London.

cinquecento. See QUATTROCENTO.

Cione, Andrea, Nardo and **Jacopo di**. See ORCAGNA.

Cipriani, Giovanni Battista (1727–85). Florentine decorative painter and designer, active mainly in England. In 1756 he was brought to London by the architect Sir William Chambers and the sculptor *Wilton, whom he had met in Rome. He was employed in the decoration of many public buildings and private houses and in some cases designed such architectural details as plasterwork, woodwork, and stone carving. Good examples of his paintings are at Somerset House (where he worked for Chambers) and in the Philadelphia Museum of Art (a series originally executed for Lansdowne House, London). He was also active as a teacher at the *Royal Academy (he was a foundation member in 1768 and designed its diploma) and his numerous decorative designs (many engraved by *Bartolozzi, his friend since student days) had wide influence. Cipriani's work is accomplished rather than inspired, but he was, in the words of Sir Ellis *Waterhouse, 'one of the great backroom figures of the *Neoclassic style in England'.

Circle. A collective manifesto of *Constructivism edited by the architect Sir Leslie Martin, the painter Ben *Nicholson, and the sculptor Naum *Gabo, published in London in 1937. Sub-titled 'International Survey of Constructive Art', it is nearly 300 pages long with numerous illustrations and was originally intended as an annual. The volume contains Piet *Mondrian's seminal essay 'Plastic Art and Pure Plastic Art', and essays or statements by, among others, *Hepworth (who took much of the responsibility for the layout and production), *Le Corbusier, *Moholy-Nagy, *Moore, and *Read. The artists illustrated included (in addition to those already mentioned) *Malevich, *Lissitzky, Antoine *Pevsner, and many others, such as *Picasso, *Braque, *Brancusi, and *Giacometti, whose work did not conform with the theoretical concept of Constructivism.

cire-perdue (French 'lost wax'). Term used to describe a method of hollow metal casting in which a thin layer of wax corresponding to the shape of the final sculpture is encased within two layers of heat-resistant clay or plaster, melted and drained off and then replaced with molten metal poured into the cavity that the 'lost wax' has created. The technique, found in every continent except Australasia, was used by the Egyptians, Greeks, and Romans and is still the main means of casting used for traditional bronze sculpture. Casting sculptures of any size is an industrial process requiring great expertise, and there is a celebrated account in *Cellini's autobiography of the difficulties he encountered (and heroically overcame) with his figure of *Perseus*.

Claesz., Pieter (*c.*1597–1660). Dutch still life painter, born in Germany and active in Haarlem, where he settled in 1617. He and Willem Claesz. *Heda, who also worked in Haarlem, were the most important exponents of the *ontbijt* or breakfast piece. They painted with subdued, virtually monochromatic palettes, the subtle handling of light and texture being the prime means of expression. Claesz. generally chose objects of a more homely kind than Heda, although his later work became more colourful and decorative. The two men founded a distinguished tradition of still life painting in Haarlem, but Claesz.'s son, Nicolaes *Berchem, became a distinguished landscape painter.

Clark, Kenneth (Baron Clark) (1903–83). British art historian, administrator, patron, and collector. After working with *Berenson in Florence, he was Keeper of Fine Art at the *Ashmolean Museum in Oxford (1931–3), then Director of the *National Gallery, London (1934–45), and at the same time Surveyor of the King's Pictures (1934–44). Subsequently he held many other public posts, including that of Chairman of the Independent Television Authority, 1954–7. He published more than twenty books, his forte being appreciation and interpretation rather than exact scholarship, although his monographs on *Leonardo da Vinci (1939) and *Piero della Francesca (1951), both of which have been issued in revised editions, still remain standard works. His other books include *The Gothic Revival* (1928), *Landscape into Art* (1949), and *The Nude* (1956). He regarded *The Nude* as 'without question my best book, full of ideas and information, simplifying its complex subject without deformation, and in places eloquent'. A polished television performer as well as an elegant and stimulating writer, he did a great deal to popularize art history, most notably with his television series *Civilisation* (1969, also published then as a book), which was shown in over sixty countries. The part he played as a patron and collector (he inherited substantial wealth from his parents) is less well known, but was of considerable importance. He bought the work of *Moore, *Pasmore, *Piper, and *Sutherland in the 1920s and 1930s when they were little known and helped to establish their reputations (he also made a regular allowance—in strict secrecy—to several artists), and he had a major influence as chairman of the War Artists' Advisory Committee in 1939: 'We employed every artist whom we thought had any merit,

not because we supposed that we would get records of the war more truthful or striking than those supplied by photography, but because it seemed a good way of preventing artists being killed.' His two volumes of autobiography—*Another Part of the Wood* (1974) and *The Other Half* (1977)—are highly entertaining, if not always accurate in detail, but some of the pot-boilers that appeared in his old age would have been better left unpublished.

Classicism. Term that, with the related words 'classic' and 'Classical', is used in various (and often confusing) ways in the history and criticism of the arts. In its broadest sense, Classicism is used as the opposite of *Romanticism, characterizing art in which adherence to recognized aesthetic ideals is accorded greater importance than individuality of expression. The word often implies direct inspiration from *antique art, but this is not a necessary part of the concept, and according to context the word might be intended to convey little more than the idea of clarity of expression, or alternatively of conservatism. In the context of Greek art, the term 'Classical' has a more precise meaning, referring to the period between the *Archaic and *Hellenistic periods, when Greek culture is thought to have attained its greatest splendour. The term 'classic' is used to refer to the best or most representative example of its kind in any field or period. This is what *Wölfflin meant when he gave the title *Classic Art* to his book on the Italian High *Renaissance. Thus, in this sense, it would be legitimate, if wilfully confusing, to refer to *Delacroix as the classic Romantic artist. The three terms 'classic', 'Classical', and 'Classicism' are, then, often not used with discrimination or exactness, the conflation of historical term and value judgement reflecting the idea (dominant for centuries) that the art of the Greeks and Romans set a standard for all future achievement. To clear up (or perhaps add to) the confusion, the rather ungainly word 'classicistic' has also entered the lists—it conveys the idea of dependence on ancient models but without any sense of qualitative judgement.

Claude Gellée (1600–82). French painter, often called Le Lorrain (in France), or Claude Lorrain(e) (in the English-speaking world), after his place of birth, but usually referred to simply as Claude, a familiarity reflecting his enormous fame as the most celebrated of all exponents of *ideal landscape. When about 12 years of age he entered the household of the Roman painter Agostino *Tassi as a pastry-cook (a favourite trade of Lorrainers), but became Tassi's studio assistant. In his early twenties he made a two-year visit to Naples, where he was deeply impressed by the beauty of the Gulf of Naples; he used the coastline in his paintings to the end of his life. In 1625 he returned to Lorraine, and worked at Nancy with Claude *Deruet, but in 1627 he was back in Rome, where except for local journeys he remained for the rest of his life.

In Tassi's decorative paintings he came into contact with the conventionalized late *Mannerist style of landscape painting. The influence of the two leading exponents of the style, *Bril and *Elsheimer, comes out in the lively paraphernalia of architectural fragments, figures, and animals that often animates the foreground of his early paintings (*The Mill*, Mus. of Fine Arts, Boston, 1631). But his profound sensitivity to the tonal values of light and atmosphere lent an unpremeditated Classical harmony to his pictures which matured with the years. During the 1630s he became well known and successful, working for illustrious patrons, and as early as 1634 *Bourdon had thought it worthwhile to pass off a painting of his own as a work by Claude. To combat such forgeries Claude began to compile his *Liber Veritatis* (Book of Truth) in 1635–6; it contains drawings of virtually all his paintings made from that date, making his œuvre exceptionally well documented. It is now in the British Museum, which also has the greatest collection of Claude's drawings from nature, works that often show a freedom of brushwork that has led them to be compared to Chinese art. Claude was also an accomplished etcher, but not nearly as prolific as he was a painter and draughtsman.

From 1640 to 1660 Claude developed steadily towards the mature style of the poetic landscapes on which his enormous reputation was built. His painting shed the affectations of Mannerism and became an expression of his deep feeling for the beauty of the Roman countryside with its rich associations of *antique grandeur. He used this landscape not to create a heroic vision of ancient Rome, as did his friend *Poussin, but to evoke a sense of the pastoral serenity of a Golden Age. The ostensible subjects of his pictures, taken frequently from the Bible, Virgil, Ovid, or medieval epics, are subordinate to the real theme, which was the mood of the landscape presented poetically in terms of light and colour. In his earlier paintings Claude, like Elsheimer, used light for the sake of dramatic effects; as his style matured he began to use it for its own sake, letting it play on forms and explore their texture. In the landscapes of the last two decades of his life everything was depicted in terms of light: the eye-level was raised and the view kept as open as possible so that the eye can roam at will over a spacious panorama to the distant horizon and beyond it into infinity. Forms melt and lose their material solidity and the figures become unnaturally elongated and insubstantial, as in *Ascanius and the Stag* (Ashmolean, Oxford), painted in the last year of Claude's life.

Claude has nowhere been more admired and more influential than in England. Not only were his works keenly sought after by late 17th- and 18th-cent. collectors, but they had great influence on such artists as *Wilson and *Turner. His name became virtually synonymous with the ideals of the *picturesque, he inspired a revolution in English landscape gardening about the middle of the 18th cent., and much descriptive verse paid tribute to the ideal of beautiful natural scenery which derived from him.

Claude glass. A small black convex glass used for reflecting landscapes in miniature so as to show their broad tonal values, without distracting detail or colour. It was popular in the 17th and 18th cents., and not only with artists, for the poet Gray carried one with him in his travels round Britain in search of the *picturesque. *Claude Lorraine was said to have used such a glass, and in the 19th cent. the device was used by *Corot, who regarded tonal unity in painting as supremely important.

Clausen, Sir George (1852–1944). English painter of Danish parentage. In the late 1870s he visited Holland and Paris, where he came under the influence of *Bastien-Lepage and was converted to the methods of the *plein air* school (*The Girl at the Gate*,

Tate, London, 1889). Later he reverted to the habit of composing in the studio from open-air studies and developed a modified *Impressionist technique. He specialized in agricultural scenes, which have been likened to those of *Millet. A founder member of the *New English Art Club in 1886, he was made Professor of Painting to the *Royal Academy Schools in 1904.

Clerck, Hendrik de (c.1570–1630). Flemish painter, born in Brussels, where he spent the greater part of his successful career. He was the pupil of Martin de *Vos and carried the *Mannerist tradition far into the 17th cent. In 1606 he was appointed Court Painter to Archduke Albert. He was primarily a painter of altarpieces and a characteristic example of his style is the *Family of the Virgin* (Musées Royaux, Brussels, 1590), with its Italianate figures clad in restless draperies and placed in a coldly Classical building.

Clodion (1738–1814). French sculptor, whose real name was Claude Michel. He was the son-in-law of *Pajou and the nephew of L.-S. *Adam, and had his training with the latter and with *Pigalle. His best work is found in his small statuettes and *terracotta figures and groups. They are often of lighthearted Classical subjects nymphs and satyrs and so on—and have the wit and verve of the best *Rococo art. After the Revolution he changed his style completely to suit the sterner *Neoclassical taste and worked on the Arc de Triomphe du Carrousel (1806–9) in Paris, which was built to commemorate Napoleon's victories.

Cloisonnism. Style of painting associated with the *Pont-Aven School, characterized by dark outlines enclosing areas of bright, flat colour, in the manner of stained glass or cloisonné enamels (cloison is French for 'partition'). *Anquetin and *Bernard first developed the style, and *Gauguin also worked in it. The term was coined by the critic Edouard Dujardin in 1888.

Close, Chuck (1940–). American painter. He is one of the best-known *Superrealists, specializing in huge portrait heads done from photographs projected on to the canvas—his self-portrait (1968) in the Walker Art Center, Minneapolis, is almost 3 m. high.

Clouet. A family of painters descended from **Jean Clouet** (or **Jan Cloet**) **the Elder** (b. c.1420), a Fleming who came to France c.1460. Almost nothing is known for certain of his life and works. The more famous **Jean Clouet** (d. 1540/1) is thought to have been his son. He was celebrated in his lifetime, but no documented works survive. A handful of portraits, however, including *Man holding Petrarch's Works* (Royal Coll., Windsor), and a number of drawings (mainly in the Musée Condé, Chantilly) are attributed to him on fairly strong circumstantial evidence. The paintings belong to the school of Flemish *naturalism that dominated French portraiture at this time, but the drawings are more personal and often of very high quality. They have often been compared to those of Clouet's contemporary Hans *Holbein the Younger, with which they share a keenness of observation; whereas Holbein's drawings are overwhelmingly linear, however, Clouet's are subtly modelled in light and shade with a delicate system of *hatching that recalls *Leonardo, whose work he could well have known. Jean's son, **François** (c.1510–72), succeeded him as court painter in 1541. His work is somewhat better documented than his father's, but his career is still very obscure (they used the same nickname, 'Janet', which has caused much confusion, and one of the finest works attributed to him, the celebrated portrait of Francis I in the Louvre, showing the king in a lavish gold doublet, has also been given to Jean). François, too, was mainly a portraitist, his signed works including *Pierre Quthe* (Louvre, Paris, 1562), much more Italianate than any of his father's paintings, and *Lady in Her Bath* (NG, Washington, c.1570). This mysterious and captivating work has been traditionally identified as representing Diane de Poitiers, but it is more probably a likeness of Marie Touchet, mistress of Charles IX. A number of drawings, mostly in the Musée Condé, are also attributed to him.

Clovio, Giulio (1498–1578). Italian painter and *illuminator, born in Croatia, now part of Yugoslavia. He went to Rome in 1516 and spent most of the rest of his career there, though with frequent breaks when he worked in other cities. In his illuminations he made frequent use of motifs from the work of *Michelangelo and *Raphael, adapting the fashionable *Mannerist style to a miniature scale. Amongst them is the *Towneley Lectionary* (New York Public Library). He also did some work in oils (*Pietà*, Uffizi, Florence, 1553). Clovio enjoyed a very high reputation in his lifetime. *Bruegel worked with him when he visited Rome and El *Greco painted his portrait (Museo di Capodimonte, Naples).

Coade stone. An artificial stone manufactured in London in the late 18th and early 19th cents., used for figure sculpture, monuments, architectural dressings, and decorative work. It is not known who invented it or what the recipe was, but it was named after Mrs Eleanor Coade (d. 1821), who set up in business in Lambeth in 1769. She claimed that it resisted frost and therefore retained sharpness of outline better than natural stone, and time has proved her right. It was mixed into a kind of paste and formed into the required shape with moulds, so popular designs could be more or less mass produced. The business was an immediate success; Robert Adam was one of the notable architects who used the material and several good sculptors, particularly John *Bacon the Elder, worked for the firm. Monuments made of Coade stone exist in many English churches, and some garden sculpture remains. Mrs Coade's successor in the business, William Croggan, went bankrupt in 1833 and Coade stone abruptly vanished from the market.

Cobra. A group of *Expressionist painters formed in Paris in 1948 by a number of Netherlandish and Scandinavian artists. The name derived from the first letters of the capital cities of the three countries of the artists involved—Copenhagen, Brussels, and Amsterdam. The Dane Asgar *Jorn, the Dutchman Karel *Appel, and the Belgian *Corneille were the leading members. Their aims were to exploit free expression of the unconscious, unimpeded and undirected by the intellect. In their emphasis upon unconscious gesture the group had affinities with American *Action painting, but they tended to put more emphasis upon the development of strange and fantastic imagery, related in some cases to Nordic mythology and folklore, in others to various magical or mystical symbols of the unconscious. Their approach was similar to the exponents of *Art Informel, but was more savage and vigorously expressive. The group arranged Cobra exhibitions at Copenhagen (1948), Amsterdam (1949), and Liège (1951), before disbanding in 1951.

Cock, Jan de (d. *c*.1526). Netherlandish painter. He became a master in the Antwerp guild in 1503, and was dean of the guild in 1520. Although he is a fairly shadowy figure and the reconstruction of his œuvre is controversial, he is noteworthy as one of the earliest followers of *Bosch, his penchant seemingly being small pictures of hermits and saints in weird landscapes. He had two artist sons, **Matthys** (*c*.1509–48) and **Hieronymus** or **Jerome** (*c*.1510–70), both of whom worked in Antwerp. Matthys was renowned in his day as a landscapist and is mentioned by *Vasari as well as van *Mander, but little is known for certain of his work. Jerome was an engraver, printer, and editor who ran a printselling business, 'Aux Quatre Vents' (At the Sign of the Four Winds), that became internationally renowned. Pieter *Bruegel was much employed by Cock in the earlier part of his career, when he excelled at prints in the tradition of Bosch.

Codde, Pieter (1599–1678). Dutch *genre and portrait painter of the fashionable world and barrack-room life, active in Amsterdam. His best works are usually on a small scale, marked by subtle silvery-grey tonalities, but he achieved one memorable feat on a much larger scale. In 1637 he was called upon to finish the group portrait of the Amsterdam Civic guards known as the *Meagre Company* (Rijksmuseum, Amsterdam) that Frans *Hals began in 1633 and refused to finish because he would not come to Amsterdam for sittings, and Codde succeeded so well in capturing Hals's spirit and the touch of his brush that experts still disagree where the work of the one ends and the other begins. Codde also wrote poetry.

Coecke van Aelst, Pieter (1502–50). Netherlandish painter, architect, sculptor, designer of tapestries and stained glass, writer, and publisher. A pupil of Bernard van *Orley, he entered the Antwerp Guild in 1527. Some time before then he had been to Rome and in 1533 he visited

Constantinople. His mission to gain business there for the Brussels tapestry works was unsuccessful, but the drawings he made on his journey were later published by his widow Mayken Verhulst as woodcut illustrations in *Les Mœurs et Fachons de Faire des Turcz* (The Manners and Customs of the Turks, 1553). He ran a large workshop and was regarded as one of the leading Antwerp painters of his day, but his work is fairly run-of-the-mill and he is generally more important for his publishing activities. Like his paintings, his books are saturated in Italian influence, and the translation of the architectural treatise of Sebastiano Serlio that he issued in 1545 played a large part in spreading *Renaissance architecture in the Netherlands (it was from this edition, too, rather than from the Italian original, that the English translation of 1611 was made). Pieter *Bruegel the Elder was his son-in-law, and, according to van *Mander, his pupil, but there is no trace of Coecke's influence in his work.

Coello, Claudio (1642–93). Spanish painter, the last important master of the Madrid school of the 17th cent. In 1686 he succeeded *Carreño as court painter, and worked in Madrid and at the *Escorial. His masterpiece, *Charles II Adoring the Host* (Escorial, near Madrid, 1685–90), combines a mystical religious subject with realistic portraiture and is an outstanding example of *Baroque *illusionism, mirroring the architecture of the sacristy in which it hangs. He had other noteworthy successes, particularly in work he carried out for Toledo Cathedral, but he died a disappointed man because he was passed over in favour of the Italian Luca *Giordano for the commission to carry out a huge programme of decoration at the Escorial. Coello had travelled to Italy as a young man and also studied the work of *Titian in the royal collection, and his skill as a colourist and painterly brushwork reflect the influence of the great Venetian masters.

Coldstream, Sir William (1908–87). English painter. He was one of the founders of the *Euston Road School in 1937 and one of the perpetuators of the Euston Road style. In 1943 he was appointed an official war artist. Coldstream stood somewhat aloof from the aesthetic and stylistic concerns which moved his contemporaries and his own rather austere work developed in close contact with nature. In an article 'How I Paint' contributed to *The Listener*, 15 Sept. 1937, he wrote: 'I find I lose interest unless I let myself be ruled by what I see.' Kenneth *Clark described his attitude to art as one of 'dismal rectitude'. Coldstream was Professor of Fine Art at the *Slade School (where he himself had been a student) from 1949 to 1975 and exercised an important influence as a teacher. His work is well represented in the *Tate Gallery, London.

Cole, Thomas (1801–48). American *Romantic landscape painter, a founder of the *Hudson River School. His family migrated to America from England in 1819 and he became passionately devoted to the natural scenery of his new country. He spent two years at the Academy of Fine Arts in Pennsylvania and made his living as a portrait painter and engraver there and in New York until some of his landscapes attracted the attention of *Dunlap, *Durand, and *Trumbull, in 1825, assuring his success. In the following year he moved to Catskill on the Hudson River, journeying into the mountains, often on foot, to make sketches of the scenery and working his studies up into finished paintings in the studio. He had two stays in Europe, 1829–32 and 1841–2, living mainly in Florence with *Greenough. These European visits, during which he came under the influence of *Turner and John *Martin, turned him increasingly from the depiction of natural scenery towards grandiose historical and allegorical themes, notably the two great series *The Course of Empire* (New-York Hist. Society, 1836) and *The Voyage of Life* (Munson-Williams-Proctor Inst., Utica, 1840).

collage. A pictorial technique in which photographs, news cuttings, and other suitable objects are pasted on to a flat surface, often in combination with painted passages (*coller* is French for 'to gum'). Long popular as a leisure-time occupation for children and amateurs, it first became an accredited artistic technique in the 20th cent., when it drew its main material from the proliferation of mass-produced images in newspapers, advertisements, etc. The *Cubists were the first to incorporate real objects such as pieces of newspaper into their pictures, often deliberately giving them a dual function both as the real things they were and as contributing to the picture image (see PAPIER COLLÉ). Collage was given a social and ideological direction by the *Futurists and was used by the *Dadaists for their own anarchical purposes. It was adopted by the *Surrealists, who emphasized the juxtaposition of disparate and incongruous imagery. See also MONTAGE.

Collins, William (1788–1847). English painter. He was initially taught by *Morland (of whom his father wrote a biography) and specialized in sentimental rustic landscapes and *genre scenes that won him great popularity. As with Morland, his work became very repetitive. He was a lifelong friend of *Wilkie, after whom he named his elder son, the novelist Wilkie Collins, who published a biography of his father in 1848. His second son was **Charles Allston Collins** (1828–73), a friend of *Millais and painter of the well-known *Convent Thoughts* (Ashmolean, Oxford, 1851), which *Ruskin rated highly because of its botanical detail, done in a fastidious *Pre-Raphaelite manner. He married one of the daughters of Charles Dickens and abandoned painting for writing.

Collinson, James (1825–81). English painter. He was one of the original members of the *Pre-Raphaelite Brotherhood in 1848, but left it in 1850 and trained to be a Roman Catholic priest. Another change of heart followed, and in 1854 he returned to painting, specializing in pretty and sentimental *genre scenes, the best known of which is *The Empty Purse* of 1857 (versions in the Tate, London, and Graves Art Gallery, Sheffield). He is probably the least known of the PRB and the most remarkable talent he showed at their meetings was his ability to fall asleep at any time.

Colombe, Michel (c.1430–after 1512). French sculptor. He had a great name in his day, but only two works that are certainly by him survive, both from very late in his life. They are: the tomb of Francis II of Brittany and Marguerite de Foix (Nantes Cathedral, 1502–7), done in collaboration with Jean *Perréal and Girolamo da Fiesole, an Italian sculptor working in France; and a relief of *St George*

and the Dragon (Louvre, Paris, 1508–9), done for an altarpiece for the Château de Chaillon. The latter also was a work of collaboration, for the frame was carved by Jérôme Pacherot, another Italian expatriate. Colombe's fame rests mainly on the *St George*, for it is a captivating work, blending the fantasy of the French *Gothic style with elements of the Italianate *Renaissance taste that was coming into vogue in southern France at this time, yet without copying particular Italian models.

Colour Field painting. Term applied to certain abstract paintings that feature large expanses of unmodulated colour. This type of painting developed in the USA in the late 1940s and early 1950s, leading exponents including *Newman and *Rothko. From 1952 Helen *Frankenthaler developed colour field painting by soaking or staining very thin paint into raw unprimed canvas, so that the paint is integral with it rather than superimposed. The term colour stain painting is applied to paintings of this type.

Colquhoun, Robert (1914–62). British painter, graphic artist, and designer. On being invalided out of the army he settled in London with Robert MacBryde (1913–66), his friend since their student days at Glasgow School of Art, driving an ambulance in the Civil Defence Corps by day and painting by night. Within a few years their studio at Bedford Gardens, Campden Hill, had become a centre for a group of young artists and writers which included Keith *Vaughan and Rodrigo *Moynihan. In the 1940s Colquhoun won a reputation as one of the finest British painters of his generation, his characteristic angular figure compositions owing something to *Cubism, but having an expressive power of their own. After he and MacBryde were evicted from their studio in 1947, however, his fortunes declined and he died in relative obscurity. A Colquhoun Memorial Gallery was opened in 1972 in Kilmarnock, his home town.

Combine painting. A name given to a type of work devised by *Rauschenberg in the early 1950s in which a painted surface is 'combined' with various real objects, or sometimes photographic images, attached to it. It may be regarded as a very radical development of the technique of *collage used by *Schwitters. See also JUNK ART.

Conca, Sebastiano (1680–1764). Italian painter. A pupil of *Solimena at Naples, he moved to Rome in 1706, and with *Trevisani he was one of the most important decorative painters there during the first half of the 18th cent. Out of the High *Baroque tradition he developed a distinctively elegant Roman *Rococo style. Good examples of his work are the decorations in the churches of S. Clemente (1714) and Sta Cecilia (1725), Rome. *Batoni was the most important of his many students.

Conceptual art. Term embracing various forms of art in which the idea for a work is considered more important than the finished product, if any. The notion goes back to *Duchamp, but it was not until the 1960s that Conceptual art became a major international phenomenon. Its manifestations have been very diverse. Photographs, texts, maps, diagrams, sound cassettes, video, etc., have been used as communication media, and most Conceptual artists deliberately render their productions visually uninteresting in order to divert attention to the 'idea' they express. Exponents and admirers of Conceptual art see it as posing questions about the nature of art and provocatively expanding its boundaries; to the general public and to many critics it usually seems pretentious and hollow.

Concrete art. Term applied to abstract art that repudiates all figurative reference and uses only simple geometric forms. The term was coined by van *Doesburg, who in 1930 issued a manifesto entitled *Art Concret*, disguised as the first number of a review (no other numbers were issued), in answer to the formation of the *Cercle et Carré association, to which he had been vigorously opposed.

Condivi, Ascanio (d. 1574). Italian painter, sculptor, and writer, a pupil and friend of *Michelangelo. He was an insignificant artist and his only claim to fame is his *Life of Michelangelo*, published in 1553. Three years earlier the first edition of *Vasari's *Lives* had appeared, and Michelangelo seems to have taken exception to some of the statements made there. Condivi's *Life* was meant as a corrective, and he writes not only from intimate personal knowledge, but obviously at times almost at dictation from the master. Johannes *Wilde (*Michelangelo*, 1978, pp. 9–12) considers that Condivi was a 'simpleton' who could not have composed 'such an eminently readable book' unaided, and thinks that Annibale Caro (1507–66), a humanist man of letters, was probably the ghost writer.

Coninxloo, Gillis van (1544–1607). The most important member of a large and prolific family of Flemish painters, many of whom are not clearly distinguishable personalities. He was born at Antwerp and in 1587 emigrated to Frankenthal, where he became a leader of a group of landscape painters established there. In 1595 he settled permanently in Amsterdam. Coninxloo's early landscapes are panoramic views of vast valleys and great mountain ranges populated by biblical or mythological personages. In later works, such as the majestic *Forest* (Kunsthistorisches Mus., Vienna), he narrows his field of vision and takes as his subject the mood evoked by luxuriant nature. His younger countrymen, Roelant *Savery and David *Vinckboons, who had also come to Holland at about the same time, were influenced by Gillis's late works. Among his many pupils there were two major Dutch artists, Esias van de *Velde and Hercules *Seghers.

Constable, John (1776–1837). English painter, ranked with *Turner as one of the greatest British landscape artists. Although he showed an early talent for art and began painting his native Suffolk scenery before he left school, his great originality matured slowly. He committed himself to a career as an artist only in 1799, when he joined the *Royal Academy Schools and it was not until 1829 that he was grudgingly made a full Academician, elected by a majority of only one vote. In 1816 he became financially secure on the death of his father and married Maria Bicknell after a seven-year courtship and in the face of strong opposition from her family. During the 1820s he began to win recognition: *The Hay Wain* (NG, London, 1821) won a gold medal at the Paris *Salon of 1824 and Constable was admired by *Delacroix and *Bonington among others. His wife died in 1828, however, and the remaining years of his life were clouded by despondency.

After spending some years working in the *picturesque tradition of landscape and the manner of *Gainsborough, Constable developed his own original treatment from the attempt to render scenery more directly and realistically, carrying on but modifying in an individual way the tradition inherited from *Ruisdael and the Dutch 17th-cent. landscape painters. Just as his contemporary William Wordsworth rejected what he called the 'poetic diction' of his predecessors, so Constable turned away from the pictorial conventions of 18th-cent. landscape painters, who, he said, were always 'running after pictures and seeking the truth at second hand'. Constable thought that 'No two days are alike, nor even two hours; neither were there ever two leaves of a tree alike since the creation of the world', and in a then new way he represented in paint the atmospheric effects of changing light in the open air, the movement of clouds across the sky, and his excited delight at these phenomena, stemming from a profound love of the country: 'The sound of water escaping from mill dams, willows, old rotten planks, slimy posts and brickwork, I love such things. These scenes made me a painter.' He never went abroad, and his finest works are of the places he knew and loved best, particularly Suffolk and Hampstead, where he lived from 1821. To render the shifting flicker of light and weather he abandoned fine traditional finish, catching the sunlight in blobs of pure white or yellow, and the drama of storms with a rapid brush. Henry *Fuseli was among the contemporaries who applauded the freshness of Constable's approach, for C. R. *Leslie records him as saying: 'I like de landscapes of Constable; he is always picturesque, of a fine colour, and de lights always in de right places; but he makes me call for my great coat and umbrella.'

Constable worked extensively in the open air, drawing and sketching in oils, but his finished pictures were produced in the studio. For his most ambitious works—'six-footers' as he called them—he followed the unusual technical procedure of making a full-size oil sketch, and in the 20th cent. there has been a tendency to praise these even more highly than the finished works because of their freedom and freshness of brushwork. (The full-size sketch for *The Hay Wain* is in the V&A, London, which has the finest collection of Constable's work.) In England Constable had no real successor and the many imitators (who included his son **Lionel**, 1825–87) turned rather to the formal compositions than to the more direct sketches. In France, however, he was a major influence on *Romantics such as Delacroix, on the painters of the *Barbizon School, and ultimately on the *Impressionists.

Constructivism. Russian geometric abstract art movement, founded in about 1913 by Vladimir *Tatlin. He was joined by the brothers Antoine *Pevsner and Naum *Gabo, who in 1920 published their *Realist Manifesto*, in which one of the directives was 'to construct' art; it is from this that the name derives. Pevsner and Gabo rejected the idea that art must serve a socially useful purpose and conceived a purely abstract art that reflected modern machinery and technology and used industrial materials such as plastic and glass. Tatlin and Alexander *Rodchenko, on the other hand, were among those who applied Constructivist principles to architecture and design. Gabo and Pevsner left Russia in 1922 after Constructivism had been condemned by the Soviet regime, and they and other exiles helped to spread the ideals of the movement throughout Europe. They were influential, for example, on the *Bauhaus in Germany, De *Stijl in the Netherlands, and the *Abstraction-Création group in France, and Gabo was one of the editors of the English Constructivist manifesto, *Circle*, in 1937.

conté crayon. A very hard, grease-free type of crayon, named after Nicolas-Jacques Conté (1755–1805), the French scientist who invented it. Conté, who worked as a portrait painter in his youth, was also the inventor of the modern graphite *pencil.

continuous representation or **continuous narrative**. A pictorial convention whereby two or more consecutive incidents from a narrative are combined in the same image. It is most common in medieval art, but occasionally occurs later. In *Pontormo's *Joseph in Egypt* (NG, London, c.1515), for example, four episodes from Genesis are shown in the same panel and the figure of Joseph appears separately in each scene.

contrapposto. Term (Italian for 'set against') applied to poses in which one part of a figure twists or turns away from another part. It was originally applied, during the *Renaissance, to a relaxed asymmetrical pose characteristic of much Greek and Roman sculpture in which the body's weight is borne mainly on one leg, so that the hip of that leg rises relative to the other (the *Doryphoros* of *Polyclitus is a classic example). The term is now, however, used in a much broader sense and applied equally to painting as to sculpture. The acknowledged master of *contrapposto* was *Michelangelo, and his *Mannerist followers (for example *Bronzino) often devised poses of wilful complexity to demonstrate their skill in the field.

conversation piece. A portrait group in a domestic or landscape setting in which two or more sitters are engaged in conversation or other polite social activity. Conversation pieces are usually, though not always, small in scale. They were especially popular in Britain during the 18th cent., but the use of the term is not confined to British painting or to this period. Arthur *Devis and the young *Gainsborough were notable practitioners.

Cooper, Samuel (1609–72). English *miniaturist, the nephew and probably the pupil of John *Hoskins. Cooper was the greatest English miniaturist of the 17th cent. and he enjoyed a European reputation and the patronage of both Oliver Cromwell and Charles II. His portraits are almost always of the bust only, but within this limitation his range is remarkable: he presents each sitter with a force and individuality besides which the life-size portraits by contemporaries such as *Lely appear doll-like, and his ambitious composition and *Baroque sense of design mark a complete breach with the tradition of *Hilliard and Hoskins. His brother **Alexander** (before 1609–60) was also a miniaturist. He worked mainly on the Continent—in the Netherlands and at the Swedish court.

Coorte, Adriaen (active 1683–1707). Dutch still-life painter, active around Middelburgh. Nothing is known of his life,

and his work was completely forgotten for more than two centuries after his death. Only a handful of paintings by him survive, but they show him to have been one of the most individual still-life painters of his time. They are the complete opposite of the lavish pieces by such celebrated contemporaries as Jan van *Huysum and Rachel *Ruysch, for they are small in scale and depict a few humble objects, characteristically placed on a bare ledge. The intensity of his scrutiny is such, however, that they take on something of the mystical quality of the still lifes of *Sánchez Cotán or *Zurbarán, and the hovering butterfly that Coorte sometimes incorporates in his work may have allegorical significance. One of his favourite subjects was a bundle of asparagus (examples in the Rijksmuseum, Amsterdam, the Fitzwilliam, Cambridge, and the Ashmolean, Oxford).

Copley, John Singleton (1738–1815). The greatest American painter of the 18th cent. He was the stepson of the engraver Peter Pelham (c.1695–1751), from whose large collection of engravings he gained a considerable knowledge of European art, but he was virtually self-taught as a painter. While still in his teens he had set up as a painter in his native Boston and by his early twenties he was painting portraits that, in their sense of life and character, completely outstripped anything previously produced by Colonial portraitists (*Colonel Epes Sargent*, NG, Washington, c.1760). Though he became extremely successful, Copley was diffident and self-doubtful by nature and came to see himself as an artist afflicted with provincialism, cut off from the great European tradition of painting. For a long while he hesitated to leave the security of Boston (where he earned 'as much as if I were a *Raphael or a *Correggio') even after his portrait of his step-brother Henry Pelham (*The Boy with a Squirrel*, Mus. of Fine Arts, Boston, 1765) had been highly praised by both *Reynolds and *West when it was exhibited in London in 1766. He finally left in 1774, when revolutionary activity was beginning to threaten his practice, and settled in London in 1775 after a study trip to Italy.

In England his style changed radically, sacrificing the forthright vigour of his Colonial work for a more fashionable and ornate manner. He continued to paint fine portraits that were more than a match for the work of most of his contemporaries, but it is generally agreed that those he painted in America have much greater originality and conviction. In compensation for this decline as a portraitist, he was able to turn his hand to history painting, in which he had long been eager to make a success but for which the opportunities in America were severely limited. The first was *Brook Watson and the Shark* (NG, Washington, 1778; a copy Copley made for himself is in the Mus. of Fine Arts, Boston, and a smaller variant, 1782, is in the Detroit Institute of Arts). In this he followed the innovation of his countryman West in using modern dress, and went beyond him in choosing a subject not because it was of historical importance or moral significance, but merely because it was exciting. It was not until a generation later that the French *Romantics took up this revolutionary idea. His other history paintings took more conventional themes, mainly patriotic and military, such as *The Death of Major Peirson* (Tate, London, 1783). Copley revealed a magnificent gift for depicting heroic action in multi-figure compositions that none of his British contemporaries could approach, and his history paintings won him considerable acclaim. They also brought on him the wrath of the *Royal Academy (of which Copley had become a full member in 1779) when they were shown privately with great success, for this constituted a rival attraction to the Academy's own exhibitions. Copley's success in England, however, was fairly short-lived and his work gradually went out of favour. He spent his final years lonely and in ill-health, and he died leaving debts that had to be paid off by his son and namesake, who became Lord Chancellor.

Coppo di Marcovaldo (b. *c.*1225). Italian painter, one of the earliest about whom there is a body of documented knowledge. He served in the army of Florence and settled in Siena after his capture at the Battle of Montaperti (1260). In 1261 he painted the signed and dated *Madonna and Child Enthroned* (called the *Madonna del Bordone*) for the Servite church at Siena, and in 1274 he and his son **Salerno** painted a Crucifix for Pistoia Cathedral; both paintings still remain in their original

locations. On the basis of these documented works two other outstanding paintings are attributed to Coppo: a *Madonna and Child Enthroned* in Sta Maria dei Servi in Orvieto, and a Crucifix in the Pinacoteca at San Gimignano. He introduced new solidity and humanity to the *Byzantine tradition, in the way, for example, that he represents the Virgin with her head inclined towards the Child, and with *Guido da Siena he ranks as the founder of the Sienese School.

Coques, Gonzales (1618 or less likely 1614–84). Flemish *genre and portrait painter, known as the 'little van *Dyck', although his style is much closer to *Terborch. He was born in Antwerp and was mainly active there, but he also travelled to Holland and England. His best works, charming and daintily executed, are small-scale fashionable group portraits such as *A Family Group* (NG, London).

Corinth, Lovis (1858–1925). German painter and graphic artist. Part of his training was with *Bouguereau in Paris (1884–7), but he was more strongly influenced by the painterly work of French artists such as *Courbet and *Manet, as well as by *Hals, *Rembrandt, and *Rubens. On his return to Germany he lived mainly in Munich before settling in Berlin in 1901. With *Liebermann he became recognized as the leading representative of the German *Impressionist school. An apoplectic stroke incapacitated him in 1911, however, and when he began to paint again (with great difficulty) it was in a much looser and more powerful *Expressionist manner, to which he had previously been strongly opposed. Corinth was varied and prolific as a painter and graphic artist, his prints being mainly *drypoints or *lithographs. Apart from landscapes, portraits, and still lifes, he had a fondness for voluptuous allegorical and religious subjects.

Cormon, Fernand (pseudonym of Fernand-Anne Piestre) (1845–1924). French painter. He had a successful career both as a painter and a popular teacher (his pupils included *Matisse, *Toulouse-Lautrec, and van *Gogh), but his reputation has not lasted well. His work included decorations at the Museum of Natural History and the Petit Palais in Paris and some excellent portraits, and he also had a penchant for paintings of prehistoric history (*The Age of Stone*, Musée du Prieuré, Saint-Germain-en-Laye, 1884).

Corneille (Cornelis van Beverloo) (1922–). Belgian painter, active mainly in Paris. He was a founder member of *Cobra in 1948 and his paintings are marked by brilliant colour and vigorous brushwork.

Corneille de Lyon (active 1533–74). Netherlandish-born painter, active mainly at Lyons in France. He was a native of The Hague (in France he is still often known as 'Corneille de La Haye'), but he settled in Lyons in 1534 and in 1540 he became court painter to the Dauphin, later Henry II. Contemporary references to Corneille indicate that he had a considerable reputation as a portrait painter, but only one work survives that is unquestionably from his hand, a portrait of Pierre Aymeric (Louvre, Paris, 1553), authenticated by an inscription in the sitter's handwriting on the back of the picture. Many other works in a similar style go under his name. They are mostly small in scale and sharply naturalistic in manner, with the sitter usually set against a plain green or blue background.

Cornelis van Haarlem (1562–1638). Dutch painter who ranks with Hendrik *Goltzius and Carel van *Mander as one of the leading representatives of *Mannerism in the Netherlands. He is best known for his large biblical and historical pictures packed with athletic, life-size Italianate nudes in wrenched and sharply foreshortened positions. But he also did a few forceful portraits of individuals and groups which show that he was an important forerunner of Frans *Hals. Both facets of his work can best be seen in the Frans Hals Museum in Haarlem.

Cornelisz. van Oostsanen, Jacob (also called Jacob van Amsterdam) (*c*.1470–1533). Netherlandish painter and designer. He trained in Antwerp, but worked mainly in Amsterdam, where he was the leading designer of *woodcuts in his day, liberating the Dutch woodcut from the *miniature tradition and giving it a new power and breadth. Comparatively few of his works have been preserved: among the woodcuts is a famous series illustrating the *Passion* and among the paintings there is a *Self-portrait* (Rijksmuseum, Amsterdam, 1533) and an *Adoration of the Shepherds* (Museo di Capodimonte, Naples, 1512) which contains pudgy angels playing toy-like instruments, singing, and decorating with garlands an improbable *Renaissance manger. Although his work is somewhat provincial, he marks the beginning of the great artistic tradition of Amsterdam, and his keenness of observation was to be one of the trademarks of later Dutch art. Jan van *Scorel was his most important pupil.

Cornelius, Peter von (1783–1867). German painter, best known for the major part he played in the revival of *fresco in the 19th cent. After training at the Düsseldorf Academy Cornelius went to Italy in 1811 and joined the *Nazarenes. In 1819 he was called to Munich by Crown Prince Ludwig of Bavaria (later Ludwig I), for whom he worked extensively, notably on a series of frescos in the Ludwigskirche (1836–9), including a *Last Judgement* that is larger than *Michelangelo's in the Sistine Chapel. When this work was not well received Cornelius left Munich to work for Frederick William IV of Prussia in Berlin. His major undertaking there was a commission for frescos in a mausoleum for the royal family. The project was officially cancelled after the revolution in 1848, but Cornelius continued to work on his drawings for it for the rest of his life. Cornelius's work is undoubtedly impressive, but rather self-conscious in its desire to revive the heroic language of *Raphael and Michelangelo, and combine it with the didactic philosophy of German *Romanticism. He was director of the academies at Düsseldorf and Munich and his influence was considerable; it may well be claimed that his works in Munich sparked off the revival of large-scale fresco decoration in Germany and perhaps elsewhere. His advice was sought when frescos were painted in the Houses of Parliament, London, in the 1840s.

Cornell, Joseph (1903–72). American sculptor, one of the pioneers and most celebrated exponents of *assemblage. He had no formal training in art and his most characteristic works are his highly distinctive 'boxes'. These are simple boxes, usually glass-fronted, in which he arranged surprising collections of photographs or

Victorian bric-à-brac in a way that has been said to combine the formal austerity of *Constructivism with the lively fantasy of *Surrealism. Like Kurt *Schwitters he could create poetry from the commonplace. Unlike Schwitters, however, he was fascinated not by refuse, garbage, and the discarded, but by fragments of once beautiful and precious objects, relying on the Surrealist technique of irrational juxtaposition and on the evocation of nostalgia for his appeal (he befriended several members of the Surrealist movement who settled in the USA during the Second World War). Cornell also painted and made Surrealist films.

Corot, Jean-Baptiste-Camille (1796–1875). French painter. At the age of 26 he abandoned a commercial career for art, and from the first showed a strong vocation for landscape painting. He lived in Paris, but travelled about France making sketches from nature and from these he composed in his studio. In addition to his journeys in France, he visited England, the Low Countries, Switzerland, and Italy three times (1825–8, 1834, and 1843). Throughout his life Corot found congenial the advice given to him by his teacher Achille-Etna *Michallon 'to reproduce as scrupulously as possible what I saw in front of me'. On the other hand he never felt entirely at home with the ideals of the *Barbizon School, the members of which saw *Romantic idealization of the countryside as a form of escapism from urban banality, and he remained more faithful to the French *Classical tradition than to the English or Dutch schools. Yet although he continued to make studied compositions after his sketches done direct from nature, he brought a new and personal poetry into the Classical tradition of composed landscape and an unaffected naturalness which had hitherto been foreign to it. Though he represented nature realistically, he did not idealize the peasant or the labours of agriculture in the manner of *Millet and *Courbet, and he was uninvolved in ideological controversy.

From 1827 Corot exhibited regularly at the *Salon, but his greatest success there came with a rather different type of picture—more traditionally Romantic in its evocation of an Arcadian past, and painted in a misty soft-edged style that contrasts sharply with the luminous clarity of his more topographical work. Late in his career Corot also turned to figure painting and it is only fairly recently that this aspect of his work has emerged from neglect—his female nudes are often of high quality. It was, however, his directness of vision that was generally admired by the major landscape painters of the latter half of the century and influenced nearly all of them at some stage in their careers. His popularity was (and is) such that he is said to be the most forged of all painters (this in addition to an already prolific output). In his lifetime he was held in great esteem as a man as well as an artist, for he had a noble and generous nature; he supported Millet's widow, for example, and gave a cottage to the blind and impoverished *Daumier.

Correggio (Antonio Allegri) (c.1489–1534). Italian painter, named after the small town in Emilia where he was born. Little is known of his life, but his paintings suggest under whom he may have formed his style. Echoes of *Mantegna's manner in many of his early paintings indicate that he may have studied that master's work in Mantua, and he was influenced in these works also by Lorenzo *Costa and *Leonardo, adopting Costa's pearly Ferrarese colouring and, in the St John of the St Francis altarpiece (Gemäldegalerie, Dresden, 1514), his first documented work, Leonardo's characteristic gesture of the pointing finger. Later he initiated a style of sentimental elegance and conscious allure with soft *sfumato and gestures of captivating charm. Correggio may well have visited Rome early in his career, although *Vasari maintains that he never went there and the obvious inspiration of the paintings of *Raphael and *Michelangelo could be accounted for by drawings and prints which were known all over Italy.

He was probably in Parma, the scene of his greatest activity, by 1518. His first large-scale commission there was for the decoration of the abbess's room in the convent of S. Paolo. The theme of the decorations is Diana, goddess of chastity and the chase, and the vaulted ceiling uses Mantegna's idea of a leafy trellis framing *putti and symbols of the hunt. The S. Paolo ceiling was followed by two dome paintings in which Correggio developed the *illusionist conception—already used by Mantegna—of depicting a scene as though it were actually taking place in the sky above (see SOTTO IN SU). The first of these domes was commissioned for the church of S. Giovanni Evangelista in 1520. The twelve Apostles sit on clouds round the base, while Christ is shown in sharp foreshortening ascending to heaven. In the commission six years later for an *Assumption of the Virgin* in the dome of Parma Cathedral he used the same principle, but on a much larger scale and with still more daring foreshortening. These works reveal Correggio as one of the boldest and most inventive artists of the High *Renaissance and they were highly influential on the development of *Baroque dome painting (one of his most important successors, *Lanfranco, was a native of Parma). Other aspects of Correggio's work were even more forward-looking. His extraordinarily sensuous mythologies, notably the series on the *Loves of Jupiter* painted for Federigo *Gonzaga in c.1530–3 (*Ganymede* and *Jupiter and Io* in the Kunsthistorisches Mus., Vienna; *Leda* in the Staatliche Mus., Berlin; *Danaë* in the Burghese Gal., Rome), foreshadow the paintings of *Rococo artists such as *Boucher, and it was at this time that Correggio's reputation was at its height.

Corrente. An anti-Fascist association of young Italian artists formed by Renato *Birolli in Milan in 1938; *Guttuso, was among the members. The association had no fixed artistic programme beyond a desire to oppose what they regarded as the provincialism of the *Novecento and the official art. They stood for the defence of 'modern' art at a time when the Nazi campaign against *'degenerate' art (*entartete Kunst*) was spreading to Italy. The association's activities, which included exhibitions and the publication of a review of literature, politics, and the arts, were dissipated by the Second World War.

Cortese. See COURTOIS.

Cortona, Pietro da (Pietro Berrettini) (1596–1669). Italian painter, architect, decorator, and designer, second only to *Bernini as the most versatile genius of the full Roman *Baroque style. He was named after his birthplace in Tuscany and probably had some training with his father, a stonemason, before being apprenticed as a painter in Florence. In 1612 or 1613 he

moved to Rome. His first major works were frescos in Sta Bibiana, Rome (1624–6), commissioned by Urban VIII (Maffeo *Barberini), and the patronage of the Barberini family played a major part in his career. For their palace he painted his most famous work, the huge ceiling fresco, *Allegory of Divine Providence and Barberini Power*. This was begun in 1633, but he interrupted the work in 1637 to go to Florence and paint two of four frescos commissioned by the Grand Duke of Tuscany for the *Pitti Palace. He returned to finish the Barberini ceiling in 1639. This, one of the key works in the development of Baroque painting, is a triumph of *illusionism, for the centre of the ceiling appears open to the sky and the figures seen from below (*di *sotto in su*) appear to come down into the room as well as soar out of it. It demonstrates Pietro's belief, which came out in a celebrated controversy with Andrea *Sacchi in the Accademia di S. Luca, that a history painting could be compared with an epic and was entitled to use many figures; Sacchi, intent on *Classical simplicity and unity, argued for using as few figures as possible. In 1640–7 Pietro was back in Florence to finish his decorations in the Pitti Palace, where he received a new commission for seven ceilings. These *Allegories of Virtues and Planets* have elaborate *stucco accompaniments uniting the painted ceilings with the framework of the rooms, and this form of decoration was widely influential, not only in Italy, but also in France. (Pietro turned down an invitation to visit Paris from Cardinal Mazarin, but his style was taken there by his best pupil, *Romanelli.) From 1647 until his death Pietro again worked in Rome, his major paintings from this period being an extensive series of frescos in Sta Maria in Vallicella (the Chiesa Nuova, 1647–65), in which, as in his Pitti decorations, paint and stucco are magnificently combined. Throughout his career he also painted easel pictures of religious and mythological subjects.

Pietro once wrote that architecture was merely a pastime for him, but he ranks among the greatest architects of his period. His masterpiece is the church of SS. Martina e Luca in Rome (1635–50), which was the first Baroque church designed and built as a complete unity. Although his architecture has all the vigour of his painting, there is less correspondence between the two fields than might be imagined. He never decorated any of his own churches, and indeed they were not designed with fresco decoration in mind. Pietro's great contemporary reputation sank in the next century with that of many other Baroque artists. In a famous passage in his *Dizionario delle belle arti* (1797), Francesco Milizia wrote: 'Borromini in architecture, Bernini in sculpture, Pietro da Cortona in painting . . . represent a diseased taste—one that has infected a great number of artists.

Cosmati work. A type of coloured decorative inlay work of stone and glass that flourished mainly in Rome between *c.*1100 and 1300. It is characterized by the use of small pieces of coloured stone and glass in combination with strips of white marble to produce geometrical designs. The term derives from two craftsmen called Cosmas, whose names are inscribed on several works, but there were several families of 'Cosmati' workers and many individual craftsmen. Cosmati work was applied to church furnishings such as tombs and pulpits and was also used for architectural decoration. The style spread as far as England, for example in the tomb of Henry III in Westminster Abbey (*c.*1280), executed by imported Italian craftsmen.

Cossa, Francesco del (*c.*1435–*c.*1477). Italian painter, active mainly in Ferrara, where with Cosimo *Tura and Ercole de' *Roberti he was the leading artist of the period. His style has many affinities with that of Tura and the same background of development from *Mantegna and *Piero della Francesca, but Cossa's work reveals a more genial temperament and relaxed urbanity. This found expression in the delightful frescos of the *Months* in the Palazzo Schifanoia at Ferrara; Cossa, Roberti, and Tura are all thought to have contributed to the scheme, but Cossa seems to have been the leading master. In the early 1470s he moved to Bologna, where he painted an altarpiece for the Griffini Chapel in the church of S. Petronio (1473); the central panel is in the National Gallery, London.

Costa, Lorenzo (*c.*1460–1535). Italian painter. He began his career in Ferrara and his early work was much influenced by *Tura and Ercole de' *Roberti. In about 1483 he settled in Bologna, where he

entered into partnership with *Francia and worked for the ruling Bentivoglio family. In 1506 he succeeded *Mantegna as court painter at Mantua, where his work included two *Allegories* painted for Isabella d' *Este (Louvre, Paris). His mature style is often rather sweetly *Peruginesque, with a delicate feeling for landscape, and has been suggested as one of the sources of *Giorgione's work. There are good examples of Costa's work in the National Gallery, London, including *The Concert*, one of the first examples of a type of picture (a close-up of a group of musicians) that was later to have a considerable vogue.

Cosway, Richard (1742–1821). English *miniaturist, a pupil of *Hudson. A friend of the Prince of Wales (later Prince Regent), Cosway was by far the most fashionable miniature painter of his day, imparting to sitters an air of great elegance. The larger portraits in oils that he occasionally attempted have been judged less successful. In 1781 he married **Maria Hadfield** (1759–1838), who was also a miniaturist.

Cotes, Francis (1726–70). English portrait painter, a pupil of *Knapton. He began as a specialist in *pastel and never altogether gave up the medium, but in the 1760s he turned mainly to oils and became a great fashionable success, the only serious rival to *Gainsborough and *Reynolds. Like them, he was a founder member of the *Royal Academy. His work is charming and vivacious and totally unintellectual; in the words of Sir Ellis *Waterhouse, 'He went all out for health and youth and fine clothes, a strong likeness and no nonsense.' His studio in Cavendish Square in London (and something of his position in the market) was later taken over by *Romney.

Cotman, John Sell (1782–1842). English landscape painter (mainly in water-colour) and etcher. Son of a well-to-do Norwich merchant, he went to London in 1798 and was employed by Dr *Monro. In 1800 he was in Wales and became a member of the circle of artists around the collector Sir George *Beaumont, where he met *Girtin. From 1803 to 1805 he made tours in Yorkshire, where he painted some of his finest work. In 1806 he settled in Norwich, where, together with *Crome, he became the most important representative of the

*Norwich School. He made several trips to France, and in 1834 he was appointed Professor of Drawing at King's College, London. Throughout his life Cotman was subject to periods of melancholia and despondency. Cotman's early water-colours, such as the celebrated *Greta Bridge* (BM, London, c.1805, a later version, 1810, is in the Castle Museum, Norwich), include some of the greatest examples of the classic English water-colour technique, showing remarkable boldness and sureness of hand. He used large flat *washes to build up form in clearly defined planes and shapes of almost geometrical simplicity. In his later years, however, he tried to catch the public fancy by large and gaudily melodramatic water-colours, in which he used an *impasto obtained with rice-paste. Cotman also illustrated various books with his etchings, mainly works on architectural antiquities.

Courbet, Gustave (1819–77). French painter, born at Ornans, the son of a prosperous farmer. He was a man of independent character and obstinate self-assurance, and claimed to be self-taught. In fact he studied with various minor masters in Ornans, Besançon and in Paris, where he moved in 1839, but he avoided the official schools and learnt much from copying the work of 17th-cent. *naturalists such as *Caravaggio and *Velázquez. His earliest pictures (including several narcissistic self-portraits) were in the *Romantic tradition, but with three large canvases exhibited at the *Salon of 1850 he established himself as the leader of the *Realist school of painting: these are *The Burial at Ornans* (Musée d'Orsay, Paris), *The Peasants at Flagey* (Musée des Beaux-Arts, Besançon), and *The Stone Breakers* (formerly in Dresden, but destroyed in the Second World War). The huge burial scene in particular made an enormous impact; it was attacked in some quarters for its alleged crudity and deliberate ugliness, but also hailed for its powerful naturalism. Never before had a scene from everyday life been presented in such an epic manner and Courbet was cast in the role of a revolutionary socialist. He gladly accepted this role (although it is unlikely that he painted the picture with political intention) and he became a friend and follower of the anarchist philosopher Pierre-Joseph Proudhon, collaborating on his book *On

Art and its Social Significance (1863). Courbet's boldness and self-confidence are as evident in his technique as in his choice of subjects. He often used a palette knife to apply paint and his work shows an unprecedented relish for the physical substance of his materials.

His unconventionality and hatred of authority was expressed most forcefully in 1855, when, dissatisfied with the representation allotted to him at the Paris Universal Exhibition, he organized a pavilion for his own work, calling it 'Le Réalisme'. Included in the works he showed here was his most celebrated work, *The Painter's Studio* (Musée d'Orsay, Paris, 1854–5). This huge (6-m. wide) canvas was subtitled by Courbet 'a real allegory [a seeming contradiction in terms] summing up seven years in my artistic life'. He wrote a long (but not very clear) account of it, describing it as 'the moral and physical history of my studio' and saying it showed 'all the people who serve my cause, sustain me in my ideal and support my activity'. In it he presents himself as the artist-hero, and in taking as his subject the activity of creating art he sounded a note that reverberated into the 20th cent. Interpretations of the picture have been many and varied, and it has recently been shown that it has covert but carefully thought out political content, attacking Napoleon III. After 1855 his work became less doctrinaire. His colours were less sombre and he often chose more obviously attractive subjects—landscapes from the Forest of Fontainebleau, the Jura, or the Mediterranean, seascapes with distant vistas, or comely and sensual nudes. After the deposition of Napoleon III, Courbet was active in the Paris Commune of 1871 and was appointed head of the arts commission. When the Commune fell he was imprisoned for his role in the destruction of the Vendôme Column, and he fled to Switzerland in 1873, being unable to pay the fine imposed on him (see MEISSONIER). He stayed there for the remaining four years of his life, painting mainly landscapes and portraits. Courbet did not form a school, but he had an enormous influence on 19th-cent. art because of his resounding rejection of the doctrine of idealization and concentration on the tangible reality of things. 'Painting', he said, 'is an art of sight and should therefore concern itself with things seen; it should, therefore, abandon both the historical scenes of the *Classical school and poetic subjects from *Goethe and Shakespeare favoured by the Romantic school.' When asked to include angels in a painting for a church he replied: 'I have never seen angels. Show me an angel and I will paint one.'

Courtauld, Samuel (1876–1947). British industrialist and art collector. A wealthy director of the family silk firm, he was a pioneer in Britain in the appreciation of French *Impressionist and *Post-Impressionist painters. In 1923 he gave to the *Tate Gallery £50,000 for the purchase of works by French 19th-cent. painters, who were hardly represented in the gallery. Most of his own superb collection was presented to the University of London in 1932, a year after he had endowed the Courtauld Institute of Art, the first specialist centre in Britain for the study of art history. The co-founders of the Institute were Lord Lee of Fareham (1868–1947), a soldier and politician, who in 1921 had presented his country house—Chequers—to the nation to be the prime minister's country residence, and Sir Robert Witt (1872–1952), a lawyer who formed a library of reproductions of paintings and drawings that is now one of the cornerstones of the Institute's pre-eminence in art-historical studies. Both men left collections to the Courtauld Institute—Lee mainly of paintings, Witt of drawings and water-colours—and there have been several other important bequests, including that of the painter and critic Roger *Fry. The most recent of the major bequests, that of the Anglo-Austrian art historian Count Antoine Seilern (1901–78) in 1978, has raised an already outstanding collection to new heights. Seilern's bequest is varied, reflecting his own scholarly interests, but its chief glory is its superlative group of works by *Rubens. The Courtauld Institute was originally located in Courtauld's former house (a fine Robert Adam building) at 20 Portman Square, while the galleries occupied a building about a mile away next to the *Warburg Institute in Woburn Sqare. In 1989–90, however, all the Institute's activities and collections were brought together under one roof at Somerset House in the Strand, fulfilling Samuel Courtauld's intention that students should work in intimate contact with original works of art.

Courtois, Jacques (1621–76) and **Guillaume** (1628–79). French painters, brothers, active in Italy and often known by the Italian forms of the names, Giacomo and Guglielmo Cortese. They came from Burgundy and both had the nickname 'Il Borgognone' or 'Le Bourguignon'. Jacques was a prolific painter of battle scenes, fairly close in style to those of Salvator *Rosa, but more colourful. Guillaume was a pupil of Pietro da *Cortona and mainly painted altarpieces. He was also an engraver. Both brothers worked in Rome for much of their careers and they sometimes collaborated. Another brother, a Capuchin priest, Padre **Antonio**, and a sister, **Anna**, were also painters.

Cousin, Jean the Elder (c.1490–1560/61). French painter, engraver, and designer, active in his native Sens and from about 1538 in Paris. He had a successful career as a painter and a designer of stained glass and tapestries, but very little surviving work can be securely attributed to him. The only certain documented works are three tapestries from a series on the life of St Mammès, which he contracted to design in 1543 (two are in Langres Cathedral, for which they were woven, the other in a private collection). The painting *Eva Prima Pandora* (Louvre, Paris), however, can also be confidently given to him, as the attribution goes back almost to his lifetime, and two windows in Sens Cathedral are also traditionally attributed to him. In 1560 he published a treatise on *perspective. The career of his son **Jean the Younger** (c.1522–c.1594), a painter and engraver, follows a similar pattern. He too worked in Sens and Paris and had a great contemporary reputation, but again little documented work survives. His most important painting is a *Last Judgement* (Louvre), but he is best known as a book illustrator; his *Livre de Fortune*, a book of *emblem drawings, was published in 1568, and he also illustrated editions of the *Metamorphoses* of Ovid (1570) and the *Fables* of Aesop (1582). The work of both father and son shows strong Italian influence and is remarkable for its independence from the prevailing style of the École de *Fontainebleau.

Coustou, Guillaume I (1677–1746). The best-known member of a dynasty of French sculptors. He was trained by *Coysevox (his mother's brother), and like him worked a good deal for the court. His vigorous style was formed partly on the example of *Bernini, whose work he saw in Rome, where he studied 1695–1703. Guillaume's masterpieces are the celebrated pair of *Horse Tamers* (*The Marly Horses*), originally made for the royal Château at Marly and set up there in 1745, but now in the Place de la Concorde in Paris. **Nicolas** (1658–1733), Guillaume's brother, was also employed in court circles, and his work can be seen at Versailles and in the Tuileries Gardens in Paris. He was probably the teacher of *Roubiliac. **Guillaume II** (1716–77), the son of Guillaume I, inherited his father's technical skill but little of his originality. Nevertheless, he enjoyed a successful career, his most important work being the monument to the Dauphin in Sens Cathedral (*c.*1767). **François** (*c.*1657–90), the father of Guillaume I and Nicolas and the founder of the dynasty, was a minor wood-sculptor working in Lyons.

Couture, Thomas (1815–79). French historical and portrait painter, a pupil of *Gros and *Delaroche. He is chiefly remembered for his vast 'orgy' picture *The Romans of the Decadence* (Musée d'Orsay, Paris), which was the sensation of the *Salon of 1847. Like other 'one-picture painters', his reputation has sunk with that of his big work, which now is often cited as the classic example of the worst type of bombastic academic painting, impeccable in every detail and totally false in overall effect. His more informal works, however, are often much livelier in conception and technique, and as a teacher he encouraged direct study from landscape. *Manet was his best-known pupil, and others included *Puvis de Chavannes and *Fantin-Latour.

Cox, David (1783–1859). English landscape painter, mainly in water-colour. In his youth he worked as a scene painter in Birmingham and London, where he received lessons from John *Varley. He lived in Hereford, 1814–27, and in London, 1829–41, before retiring to Harborne, near Birmingham, from where he made annual sketching tours to the Welsh mountains. In spite of a certain anecdotal homeliness, his style was broad and vigorous, and in 1836 he began to paint on a rough Scottish wrapping paper that was particularly suited

to it. A similar paper was made commercially and marketed as 'Cox Paper'. He wrote several treatises on landscape painting in water-colour, and in the last two decades of his life also worked quite frequently in oils.

Coypel. Family of French painters of which **Noel** (1628–1707) was the head. He created a successful academic style on the example of *Poussin and *Lebrun, was much employed on the large decorative schemes of Louis XIV, notably at Versailles, and was director of the French *Academy in Rome (1672–6) and then director of the Académie Royale in Paris (1695). His son **Antoine** (1661–1722) went to Rome as a child with his father and there is a strong Italian element in his style. This comes out particularly in his most famous work, the ceiling of the Chapel at Versailles (1708), which derived from *Baciccio's ceiling in the Gesù in Rome. This and Coypel's decorations at the Palais Royal in Paris (1702, destroyed) rank as the two most completely *Baroque schemes found in French art of this period. The Versailles ceiling is more successful than much of Coypel's work, which often combines, in the words of Anthony *Blunt, 'the bombast of the Baroque and the pedantry of the *Classical style without the virtues of either'. His half-brother **Noel-Nicolas** (1690–1734) painted with much more charm, mainly mythological subjects, but he seems to have had a rather timid personality and did not achieve the worldly success of the other members of the family. Indeed, he was the best painter of the family, but is the least famous. *Chardin was briefly his assistant. Antoine's son **Charles-Antoine** (1694–1752) was a much more forceful character than Noel-Nicolas and had a resoundingly successful career, largely due to his administrative capacity in the various official positions that he held. In 1747 he became director of the Académie Royale and chief painter to the king. He also was an accomplished writer of verse and plays as well as art criticism. As a painter he was versatile and prolific, but the weakest member of the family; his *Supper at Emmaus* (1746) in Saint-Merry, Paris, has been described by Sir Michael Levey as 'pathetically inept'.

Coysevox, Antoine (1640–1720). French sculptor, with *Girardon the most successful of Louis XIV's reign. His style was more *Baroque than Girardon's and Coysevox overtook his rival in popularity towards the end of the 17th cent. as the king's taste turned away from the *Classical. By 1679 Coysevox was working at Versailles, where he made numerous statues for the gardens and did much interior decoration, including a striking *relief of Louis XIV in the Salon de la Guerre. His originality, however, is seen mostly in his portrait busts, which show a naturalism of conception and an animation of expression that look forward to the *Rococo. This is particularly so with his portraits of friends, but even his formal commissions can be remarkably lively. The Wallace Collection, London, has an outstanding example of both his formal and informal portraits: the bronze *Louis XIV (c.1686) and the terracotta *Charles Lebrun* (1676).

Cozens, Alexander (1717–86). English landscape draughtsman. He was born in Russia, the son of a shipbuilder employed by Peter the Great (it was rumoured that Peter was his real father) and did not settle in England until 1746. In 1785 or 1786 he published his famous treatise *A New Method of Assisting the Invention in Drawing Original Compositions of Landscape*, in which he explains his method of using accidental blots on the drawing paper to stimulate the imagination by suggesting landscape forms that could be developed into a finished work. Cozens mentions that 'something of the same kind had been mentioned by *Leonardo da Vinci, in his Treatise on Painting' and that reading the passage in question 'tended to confirm my own opinion'. He quotes Leonardo as saying 'If you look upon an old wall covered with dirt, or the odd appearance of some streaked stones, you may discover several things like landscapes, battles, clouds, uncommon atittudes, humorous faces, draperies &c. Out of this confused mass of objects, the mind will be furnished with abundance of designs and subjects perfectly new.' He worked almost exclusively in monochrome, and both his *'blot drawings' and his more formal compositions use intense lights and darks with masterly effect to suggest the power and mystery of nature. Cozens was the first major English artist to devote himself entirely to landscape, and he spent much of his career as a fashionable teacher.

His son, **John Robert Cozens** (1752–97), was also a landscape painter. Most of his work derived from two continental journeys in 1776–9 and 1782–3, during which he visited Italy and Switzerland. On the first he was probably draughtsman to Richard Payne *Knight, and on the second he was part of the entourage of William *Beckford (a former pupil of his father). In 1793 he became insane and was cared for by Dr *Monro. Although his watercolours were based on sketches made on the spot, he by no means restricted himself to topographical exactitude and he often transposed landscape features in the interests of a more poetical composition. But he does not seem ever to have composed wholly from imagination, as his father did. His narrow but subtly gradated range of subdued colour is intensely evocative of the serene natural effects which appealed so strongly to his poetic melancholy. He was the most talented of the English landscape artists in the *picturesque tradition and his work was admired and copied by *Constable (who called him 'the greatest genius that ever touched landscape'), *Girtin, and *Turner.

Cranach, Lucas the Elder (1472–1553). German painter. He takes his name from the small town of Kronach in South Germany, where he was born, and very little is known of his life before about 1500–1, when he settled in Vienna and started working in the humanist circles associated with the newly founded university. His stay in Vienna was brief (he left in 1504), but in his period there he painted some of his finest and most original works. They include portraits, notably those of *Johannes Cuspinian*, a lecturer at the university, and his wife *Anna* (Reinhart Coll., Winterhur), and several religious works in which he shows a remarkable feeling for the beauty of landscape characteristic of the *Danube School. The finest example of this manner is perhaps the *Rest on the Flight into Egypt* (Staatliche Museen, Berlin), which shows the Holy Family resting in the glade of a German pine forest. It was painted in 1504, just before Cranach went to Wittenberg as court painter to Frederick III (the Wise), Elector of Saxony.

Cranach remained in Wittenberg until 1550, when he followed John Frederick (the Unfortunate), the last Saxon Elector

113

of the Ernestine branch, into exile, in Augsburg. During his time in Wittenberg he became extremely wealthy and one of the city's most respected citizens, serving as burgomaster for several years. His paintings were eagerly sought by collectors, and his busy studio often produced numerous replicas of popular designs, particularly those in which he showed his skill at depicting female beauty—more than ten versions are known of his *Reclining Nymph*. He excelled at erotic nudes, which sometimes draw on Italian *Renaissance models but are totally different in spirit, and he also had a penchant for pictures of coquettish women wearing large hats, sometimes shown as Judith or the goddesses in the *Judgement of Paris*. The most innovative works of his Wittenberg period, however, are probably his full-length portraits (*The Duke* and *Duchess of Saxony*, Gemälde-galerie, Dresden, 1514). Cranach continued with his religious work, but his woodcut designs (notably those for the first German edition of the New Testament in 1522) are generally more interesting than his paintings in this sphere. He also painted several portraits of Martin Luther. Despite his allegiance to the Protestant cause, he continued to work for Catholic patrons and was a very astute businessman. During the last years of his life Cranach was assisted by his son, **Lucas the Younger** (1515–86), who carried on the tradition of the workshop and imitated his father's style so successfully that it is often difficult to distinguish between their hands.

Crane, Walter (1845–1915). English illustrator and designer. Best remembered today as an illustrator of children's books, he was also a painter and designer; he was associated with *Burne-Jones and William *Morris in their work for the reform of decorative and applied art, designing wallpapers, printed fabrics, and stained glass, and also making illustrations for Morris's *Kelmscott Press. His work was exhibited in the USA as well as in Europe and he achieved some prestige as a writer and educationalist. He was influential in the *Arts and Crafts Movement.

craquelure. The network of small cracks which appears on a painting when in the course of time the *pigment or *varnish has become brittle.

Crawford, Thomas (1813–57). American sculptor. He settled in Rome in 1835, studied with *Thorvaldsen and became the most thoroughgoing *Neoclassicist among American sculptors of his generation. Although he stayed in Rome, he attained an extraordinary reputation in America and received numerous prestigious public commissions, among them the equestrian *George Washington* (1857) in Richmond, Virginia, and the *Armed Liberty* on top of the Capitol dome at Washington, which was set in place in 1863 after his early death from cancer.

crayon. See CHALK.

crayon manner. An 18th-cent. engraving technique, a variant of *etching, used for the reproduction of crayon (or *pastel) drawings. Invented c.1750 in France, where a number of engravers made prints after *Boucher, *Fragonard, and others, the crayon manner was also widely used in England. It was rendered obsolete early in the 19th cent. by the invention of *lithography. See also PASTEL MANNER.

Credi, Lorenzo di (c.1458–1537). Florentine painter. He was a fellow pupil of *Leonardo in *Verrocchio's workshop and he seems to have stayed there until Verrocchio's death in 1488, managing the painting side of his master's varied business. He was a very fine craftsman, but his style was lacking in individuality. His early work is in an extremely prosaic version of Leonardo's youthful style. Later he absorbed some of the ideas of the High *Renaissance, his *Madonna and Saints* in Sta Maria delle Grazie in Pistoia (1510) recalling Fra *Bartolommeo. He had several pupils and seems to have had a fairly successful career with his solid, unspectacular skills. It is said that influenced by the teachings of Savonarola in 1497 he destroyed all his pictures with profane subjects.

Crespi, Daniele (c.1598–1630). Milanese painter. Although he died young of the plague, his output was large and his work is considered to be one of the most typical expressions of the zealous spirit of the Counter-Reformation that affected Milan at this time. *St Charles Borromeo at Supper* in Sta Maria della Passione is his best-known work and in its simple composition and emotional directness reflects the ideals of painting advocated by the Council of Trent. Many other examples of his work are in the church. He was probably a relative of Giovanni Battista *Crespi, whose work influenced him.

Crespi, Giovanni Battista (Il Cerano) (c.1575–1632). Italian painter, sculptor, engraver, architect, and writer. His nickname derived from his birthplace near Novaro, but he was active mainly in Milan, where he was one of the leading artists of his time. From 1586 to 1595 he was in Rome, where he was befriended by Cardinal Federico Borromeo (nephew of St Charles Borromeo), who became his major patron after they returned to Milan together. Borromeo appointed him head of the painting section of the Accademia *Ambrosiana, which he founded in 1620, and in 1629 put him in charge of the sculptural decoration of Milan Cathedral. Crespi's paintings, often mystical in feeling, are complex stylistically; there is a strong *Mannerist current in his colouring and in the elegant posturing of his figures, but his work also shows a solidity and a feeling for realistic details that give it a place in the vanguard of the *Baroque.

Crespi, Giuseppe Maria (called Lo Spagnuolo) (1665–1747), Bolognese painter. He reacted against the academic tradition in which he was trained (*Cignani was one of his teachers) and specialized in *genre subjects, with violent *chiaroscuro effects of brilliant colour against dark backgrounds. They are in the tradition of the everyday-life paintings of the *Carracci, but go far beyond them in their sense of unvarnished reality (*The Hamlet*, Pinacoteca, Bologna). He was an outstanding teacher, numbering *Piazzetta and Pietro *Longhi among his pupils, and he exercised a great influence on Venetian 18th-cent. painting. Rudolf *Wittkower called him 'the only real genius of the late Bolognese school'.

Crivelli, Carlo (active 1457–93). Italian painter. He was born in Venice and always signed himself as a Venetian, but he spent most of his career working in the Marches, particularly at Ascoli Piceno, and he also lived for some time at Zara (now in Yugoslavia). His paintings are all of religious subjects, done in an elaborate, old-fashioned style that owes much to the wiry Paduan tradition of *Squarcione and *Mantegna and yet is highly distinctive. Their dense ornamentation is often increased by the use of *gesso decoration combined with the paint. The finest collection of his works is in the National Gallery in London and includes the delightful and much reproduced *Annunciation* (1486). **Vittore Crivelli** (d. 1501/2), probably Carlo's brother, was a faithful but pedestrian follower.

Crome, John (1768–1821). English landscape painter and etcher, with *Cotman the major artist of the *Norwich School. He was born, worked, and died in Norwich and his only journey abroad was to Paris in 1814 to see the exhibition of the pictures which had been seized by Napoleon. Of humble origin, he was first apprenticed to a coach-and-sign painter and taught himself principally by copying works in the collection of Thomas Harvey of Catton, a collector and amateur painter who befriended him. The Dutch masters *Ruisdael and *Hobbema were particularly influential on his work and he also admired *Gainsborough and *Wilson. He earned a major part of his living as a drawing master. Together with Wilson, Crome represents the transition from the 18th-cent. *picturesque tradition to the *Romantic conception of landscape. His finest paintings, such as *The Poringland Oak* (Tate, London), are marked by a broad handling of the paint, a bold realization of space, and keen appreciation of local characteristics.

As an etcher Crome's accomplishment was modest, and during his life he never published his plates: they were published by his widow and his eldest son **John Bernay Crome** (1794–1842), 13 years after his death. The elder Crome is sometimes referred to as 'Old Crome' to distinguish him from his son, who painted in his manner but with inferior talent.

Crowe, Sir Joseph Archer (1825–96). English journalist, diplomat, and art historian. He had a distinguished career as a commercial attaché in Berlin, Paris, and Vienna and was also a war correspondent in the Crimea and elsewhere, but he is best known for his writings on art history done in collaboration with the Italian painter

Giovanni Battista Cavalcaselle (1819–97). They met by chance in 1847 and became firm friends when Cavalcaselle was later a political refugee in London; for a time they lived in the same house. Every detail of their books was discussed between them, but Crowe did all the actual writing because Cavalcaselle's English was inadequate. Their prodigious output included *The Early Flemish Painters* (1857), *A New History of Painting in Italy* (3 vols., 1864–8), *A History of Painting in North Italy* (2 vols., 1871), *Titian: His Life and Times* (2 vols., 1877) and *Raphael: His Life and Works* (2 vols., 1882). These works, all of which have appeared in subsequent editions, either in English or translation, set new standards of methodical research, bringing to light masses of new information, and they are still considered valuable.

Cruikshank, George (1792–1878). English painter, illustrator, and *caricaturist. The son of a caricaturist, **Isaac Cruikshank** (1756?–1811?), he was highly precocious and quickly established himself in succession to *Gillray as the most eminent political cartoonist of his day. The private life of the Prince Regent (later George IV) was one of his first targets. He began to turn to book illustration in the 1820s and his output was immense. In later life he took up the cause of temperance, producing moral narratives in *woodcut (*The Bottle*, 1847; *The Drunkard's Children*, 1848) and a vast painting *The Worship of Bacchus* (Tate, London, 1860–2). His brother, **Isaac Robert Cruikshank** (1789–1856), was a *miniaturist and caricaturist.

Cubism. Movement in painting (and to a lesser extent sculpture) developed by *Picasso and *Braque from about 1907 and recognized as one of the great turning points in Western art. Cubism made a radical break from the idea of art as the imitation of nature that had dominated European painting and sculpture since the *Renaissance, for Picasso and Braque aimed to depict objects as they are known rather than as they appear at a particular moment and place. To this end they broke down the subjects they represented into a multiplicity of facets, rather than showing them from a single, fixed viewpoint, so many different aspects of the same object could be seen simultaneously. The two

most important influences on the emergence of Cubism were African sculpture and the later paintings of *Cézanne. Picasso and Braque's work up to 1912 is generally called 'Analytical' Cubism; in this phase of the movement forms were analysed into predominantly geometrical structures and colour was extremely subdued. In a second phase, known as 'Synthetic' Cubism, colour became much stronger and shapes more decorative, and elements such as stencilled lettering and pieces of newspaper were introduced into paintings. Juan *Gris was as important as Braque or Picasso in this phase of the movement. The First World War brought an end to the collaboration of Braque and Picasso, but their work was immensely influential. Cubism, as well as being one of the principal sources of abstract art, was infinitely adaptable, giving birth to numerous other movements, among them *Futurism, *Orphism, *Purism, and *Vorticism.

Cullen, Maurice (1866–1934). Canadian painter, whose work was influential in introducing *Impressionism to his country. From 1889 to 1895 he worked in Paris and elsewhere in France, with trips to Venice and North Africa. After his return to Canada he specialized in landscapes and city scenes (*Old Houses, Montreal*, Montreal Mus. of Fine Arts, *c.*1900). He was a war artist in the First World War.

Cumberland Market Group. Group of painters formed when the *Camden Town Group merged with the *London Group in 1913; it was named after 49 Cumberland Market, where Robert *Bevan had his studio, and where he, *Gilman, and *Ginner used to meet. In 1915 they were joined by John *Nash and later by E. McKnight *Kauffer and C. R. W. *Nevinson.

Currier and Ives prints. Popular *lithographs published in New York by Nathaniel Currier (1813–88) and James M. Ives (1824–95), who went into partnership in 1857. These lithographs, advertised by their publishers as 'Coloured Engravings for the People', represented almost every aspect of contemporary America, including sporting, sentimental, patriotic, and political subjects, together with portraits, landscapes, disasters, scenes of city life, of railroads, of Mississippi steamboats, and so forth. A number of artists, most of whom specialized in particular subjects, were retained by the firm to draw the lithographs in black and white; afterwards the prints were coloured by hand on a production-line system (one assistant to each colour) and sold cheaply to the public by agents, print-sellers, and pedlars. The business was carried on until 1907 by the sons of the founders.

Curry, John Steuart (1897–1946). American painter. He came to public notice with realistic scenes of American life such as *Baptism in Kansas* (Whitney Mus., New York, 1928) and *Hog Killing a Rattlesnake* (Art Inst. of Chicago, 1930) and he became a leading artist of the *Regionalist group, dramatizing and romanticizing the life of the Middle West and the sagas of the American pioneers. Notable among his works are the murals he did for the Department of Justice in Washington, DC, and for the state capitol in Topeka, Kansas.

Cuyp. The name of a family of Dutch painters of Dordrecht, of which three members gained distinction. **Jacob Gerritsz. Cuyp** (1594–1651/2) was the son of a glass painter and a pupil of Abraham *Bloemaert at Utrecht. He is thought of today mainly as a portrait painter—his portraits of children are particularly fine—but in old biographies is lauded principally for his views of the countryside around Dordrecht. **Benjamin Gerritsz. Cuyp** (1612–52) was the half-brother of Jacob. He is noted principally for paintings of biblical and *genre scenes which use *Rembrandtesque light and shadow effects. **Aelbert Cuyp** (1620–91) is the most famous member of the family and now one of the most celebrated of all landscape painters, although he also painted many other subjects. He was the son and probably the pupil of Jacob Gerritsz. Cuyp. His early works also show the influence of Jan van *Goyen. Aelbert was born and died at Dordrecht, but he seems to have travelled along Holland's great rivers to the eastern part of the Netherlands, and he also painted views of Westphalia. A prodigious number of pictures are ascribed to him, but his *œuvre* poses many problems. He often signed his paintings but rarely dated them, and a satisfactory chronology has never been established. Although he had little influence outside Dordrecht, Cuyp had several imitators there, and some of the paintings formerly attributed to him are now given to Abraham Calraet (1642–1722), who signed himself 'AC' (the same initials as Cuyp). In 1658 Cuyp married a rich widow, and in the 1660s he seems to have virtually abandoned painting. He was almost forgotten for two generations after his death. Late 18th-cent. English collectors are credited with rediscovering his merits, and he is still much better represented in English collections, public and private, than in Dutch museums. His finest works—typically river scenes and landscapes with placid, dignified-looking cows—show great serenity and masterly handling of glowing light (usually Cuyp favoured the effects of the early morning or evening sun). He approaches *Claude more closely in spirit than any of his countrymen who travelled to Italy.

D

Dada. A movement in European and American art characterized by violent revolt against traditional values. It was founded in Zurich in 1915 by a group of artists and writers including Hans *Arp and the Romanian poet Tristan Tzara, and arose from the mood of disillusionment engendered by the First World War, to which some artists reacted with feelings of irony, cynicism, and anarchy. Emphasis was given to the illogical and the absurd, and the importance of chance in artistic creation was exaggerated. According to the most popular of several accounts of how the name (French for 'hobby-horse') originated, it was chosen by inserting a penknife at random in the pages of a dictionary, thus symbolizing the anti-rational stance of the movement. Dada artists did not cultivate a particular style, but went to extremes in the use of buffoonery and provocative behaviour to disrupt public complacency. *Montage, *collage, and the *ready-made were among the typical forms of expression, as was the nonsense poem in the field of literature. Dada spread quickly (notably to New York, where Marcel *Duchamp and *Man Ray were leading figures) and an international Dadaist exhibition was held in Paris in 1922, but it did not survive as an organized movement for much after this date. Its influence, however, was profound, notably on *Surrealism (particularly in its tendency towards absurdity and whimsicality), *Abstract Expressionism, and *Conceptual art.

Dadd, Richard (1817–86). English painter who murdered his father in 1843 and spent the rest of his life in Bedlam and Broadmoor asylums. Before his mental breakdown he was considered a promising young artist (his friend *Frith called him 'a man of genius that would assuredly have placed him high in the first rank of painters') and he continued painting after his incarceration. Although most of his work before the murder had been fairly conventional, he had begun to paint fairy and fantasy subjects and in the asylums he developed these along highly imaginative lines; *The Fairy Feller's Master-Stroke* (Tate, London, 1855–64) is probably the best known. Dadd was long forgotten, but became popular in the 1970s.

Daddi, Bernardo (d. 1348). Florentine painter, the outstanding painter in Florence in the period after *Giotto's death. He ran a busy workshop specializing in small devotional panels and portable altarpieces. His signed and dated works include a *polyptych of *The Crucifixion with Eight Saints* (Courtauld Inst., London, 1348) and the works attributed to him include frescos of the *Martyrdoms of SS. Lawrence and Stephen* in Sta Croce. Daddi's style is a sweetened version of Giotto's, tempering the latter's gravity with Sienese grace and lightness. He favours smiling Madonnas, teasing children, and an abundance of flowers and trailing draperies. His lyrical manner was extremely popular and his influence endured into the second half of the century.

Daguerre, Louis-Jacques-Mandé (1789–1851). French artist and inventor. He invented the *diorama (1822) and the daguerreotype, the first practicable photographic process (made public in 1839).

Dahl, Johan Christian (1788–1857). Norwegian painter, often called the discoverer of the Norwegian landscape. From 1824 until his death he was a professor at the Academy of Dresden, where he was a friend of *Friedrich. The landscapes of *Ruisdael were another influence on his *Romantic outlook. Through his deep feeling for the grandeur of the landscape of his native country he was a pioneer of the new spirit of nationalism which entered into Norwegian art.

Dahl, Michael (1659?–1743). Swedish portrait painter, active mainly in England. He first came to England in 1682 and settled permanently in London in 1689, becoming *Kneller's principal rival. His work has not the brilliance and dash of Kneller's, but at his best he surpasses him in sincerity and humanity beneath a somewhat *Rococo artificiality. There are several works by him or from his busy studio in the National Portrait Gallery in London.

Dalí, Salvador (1904–89). Spanish painter, sculptor, graphic artist, and designer. After passing through phases of *Cubism, *Futurism, and *Metaphysical painting, he joined the *Surrealists in 1929 and his talent for self-publicity rapidly made him the most famous representative of the movement. Throughout his life he cultivated eccentricity and exhibitionism (one of his most famous acts was appearing in a diving suit at the opening of the London Surrealist exhibition in 1936), claiming that this was the source of his creative energy. He took over the Surrealist theory of *automatism but transformed it into a more positive method which he named 'critical paranoia'. According to this theory one should cultivate genuine delusion as in clinical paranoia while remaining residually aware at the back of one's mind that the control of the reason and will has been deliberately suspended. He claimed that this method should be used not only in artistic and poetical creation but also in the affairs of daily life. His paintings employed a meticulous academic technique that was contradicted by the unreal 'dream' space he depicted and by the strangely hallucinatory character of his imagery. He described his pictures as 'hand-painted dream photographs' and had certain favourite and recurring images, such as the human figure with half-open drawers protruding from it, burning giraffes, and watches bent and flowing as if made of melting wax (*The Persistence of Memory*, MOMA, New York, 1931). In 1937 Dalí visited Italy and adopted a more traditional style; this together with his political views (he was a supporter of General Franco) led *Breton to expel him from the Surrealist ranks. He moved to the USA in 1940 and remained there until 1955. During this time he devoted himself largely to self-publicity; his paintings were often on religious themes (*The Crucifixion of St John of the Cross*, Glasgow Art Gallery, 1951), although sexual subjects and pictures centring on his wife Gala were also continuing preoccupations. In 1955 he returned to Spain and in old age became a recluse.

Apart from painting, Dalí's output included sculpture, book illustration, jewellery design, and work for the theatre. In collaboration with the director Luis Buñuel he also made the first Surrealist films—*Un chien andalou* (1929) and *L'Age d'or* (1930)— and he contributed a dream sequence to Alfred Hitchcock's *Spellbound* (1945) . He also wrote a novel, *Hidden Faces* (1944), and several volumes of flamboyant autobiography. Although he is undoubtedly one of the most famous artists of the 20th cent., his status is controversial; many critics consider that he did little if anything of consequence after his classic Surrealist works of the 1930s. There are museums devoted to Dalí's work in Figueras, his home town in Spain, and in St Petersburg in Florida.

Dalmau, Luis (active 1428–60). Spanish painter, active mainly in Valencia. He was court painter to Alfonso V of Aragon, under whose patronage he went to Bruges in 1431 to study tapestry weaving. Dalmau's visit to Flanders is the first recorded contact of a Spanish painter with the Netherlandish School, and the only surviving painting certainly by him, the *Virgin of the Councillors* (Barcelona Mus., 1445), is clearly inspired by Jan van *Eyck.

Dalou, Aimé-Jules (1838–1902). French sculptor, the most important pupil of *Carpeaux. Although his name is particularly associated with the *naturalistic movement in French sculpture, he produced many works of *Baroque inspiration, notably his largest completed monument, the allegorical *Triumph of the Republic* (Place de la Nation, Paris, 1879–99). His most ambitious work, a vast *Monument to Labour*, was left uncompleted at his death, but clay models for many of the figures, reminiscent of *Millet's peasants in their rather sentimental view of human toil, are preserved in the Petit Palais, Paris. Dalou's other work included the memorial to *Delacroix in the Luxembourg Gardens (1890). He spent the years 1871–9 as a political exile in England after taking part in the Paris Commune (1871).

Dalziel Brothers. Firm of English illustrators and wood engravers founded in London in 1839 by **George Dalziel** (1815–1902) and **Edward Dalziel** (1817–1905). Two other brothers, **John** and **Thomas**, worked for the firm, which was the most prolific source of book illustrations in Victorian England, producing more than 50,000 plates. George and Edward collaborated on the book *The Brothers Dalziel: A Record of Work, 1840–90* (1901).

Danby, Francis (1793–1861). Irish painter. He worked mainly in Bristol and London, but between 1829 and 1841, owing to domestic troubles, he settled in Switzerland. He is remembered mainly for his bombastic apocalyptic paintings, such as *The Delivery of Israel out of Egypt* (Harris Mus. and Art Gal., Preston, 1825), which were a direct challenge to John *Martin. However, his best works are now usually considered to be the romantic sunset landscapes of his later years, with their mood of melancholy and solemn serenity (*Temple of Flora*, Tate, London, 1840).

Dance, Nathaniel (1735–1811), English painter, primarily of portraits. He studied under *Hayman and spent the years 1755–64 in Rome, where he was much influenced by the sophisticated portrait style of Pompeo *Batoni. In 1768 he became a foundation member of the *Royal Academy, but on inheriting a fortune in 1776 he retired from professional practice. He later became an MP and was created a baronet with the surname Dance-Holland. One of his best-known portraits is *Captain Cook* (Nat. Maritime Mus., Greenwich, 1766). He was the son and brother of architects, both called **George Dance**.

Daniele da Volterra (Daniele Ricciarelli) (*c.*1509–66). Italian *Mannerist painter and sculptor, born in Volterra, where he was a pupil of *Sodoma. In about 1536 he moved to Rome, where he became a friend of *Michelangelo and one of his most gifted and individual followers. Michelangelo helped to gain him commissions and (as with *Sebastiano del Piombo) supplied him with drawings to work from, but Daniele's finest picture owes little to the direct influence of the master. This is his fresco of the *Deposition* (commissioned 1541) in the Cappella Orsini in SS. Trinità dei Monti, a powerful and moving work,

based compositionally on *Rosso Fiorentino's famous painting of the same subject in Volterra, but with an eloquent richness of its own. It was one of the most admired works of its generation in Rome and continued to be influential into the next century: *Domenichino (Hatton Gallery, Newcastle upon Tyne) was among the artists who copied it, and *Rubens was clearly inspired by it in his painting of the subject in Antwerp Cathedral. Daniele was present at Michelangelo's deathbed and his most famous work of sculpture is a bronze bust of him based on the death mask (casts are in the Casa Buonarroti, Florence, the Louvre, and elsewhere). Ironically, in view of his devotion to the master, Daniele is perhaps best remembered for painting draperies over the nude figures in Michelangelo's *Last Judgement*, a concession to Counter-Reformation ideals that earned him the nickname 'Il Bragghettone' (the breeches-maker).

Danti (or **Dante**), **Vincenzo** (1530–76). Italian sculptor, architect, theoretician, and poet, born in Perugia and active mainly in Florence. His work bears witness to his admiration for *Michelangelo, for whose funeral ceremonies in 1564 he supplied sculpture and paintings. Danti's style, however, is more elegant and much less powerful than the master's. His best-known works are (in Florence) the bronze group of *The Execution of the Baptist* over the south door of the Baptistry (finished 1571), and (in Perugia) the bronze figure of Pope Julius II outside the Cathedral (1555). From 1573 he resided in Perugia, where he was one of the first professors at the newly founded Accademia del Disegno and city architect. He was the author of a treatise on proportion, dedicated to the Grand Duke Cosimo de' *Medici (1567).

Danube School. Term applied to a number of German painters working in the Danube valley in the early 16th cent. who were among the pioneers in depicting landscape for its own sake. *Altdorfer, *Cranach the Elder (in his earlier work), and *Huber are the most important artists covered by the term. They worked independently of one another, so 'Danube School' (German *Donauschule*) is a term of convenience rather than an indication of any group affiliation.

Daret, Jacques (*c*.1400–68 or later). Netherlandish painter from Tournai. From 1427 to 1432 he was apprenticed along with Rogelet de la Pâture (assumed to be identical with Rogier van der *Weyden) to Robert Campin, and the similarity of Daret's style to that of the *Master of Flémalle is one of the main reasons for thinking that Campin and this master are one and the same. Four panels survive from Daret's main work, an altarpiece for the Abbey of St Vaast in Arras (1433–5), and one of these—the *Nativity* (Thyssen Coll., Lugano)—is obviously based on the Master of Flémalle's painting of the subject in Dijon (Musée des Beaux-Arts). Two of the other three panels from the St Vaast Altarpiece are in West Berlin (Staatliche Museen), and the fourth is in Paris (Petit Palais). Daret's other work included tapestry *cartoons and manuscript *illuminations.

Daubigny, Charles-François (1817–78). French landscape painter of the *Barbizon School, one of the earliest exponents of *plein air* painting in France. He received his introduction to painting from his father **Edmé-François** (1789–1843), also a landscape painter, and in 1838 joined the class of Paul *Delaroche at the École des *Beaux-Arts. Although closely associated with the Barbizon painters, he did not himself live at Barbizon. His landscapes reflect his love of rivers, beaches, and canals (he often painted from a specially fitted boat), and are notable for the uncrowded quality of the composition and an almost Dutch clarity of atmospheric effect. He seems to belong more to the generation of *Monet and *Boudin, who were in fact admirers of his work.

Daumier, Honoré (1808–79). French *caricaturist, painter, and sculptor. In his lifetime he was known chiefly as a political and social satirist, but since his death recognition of his qualities as a painter has grown. In 1830, after learning the still fairly new process of *lithography, he began to contribute political cartoons to the anti-government weekly *Caricature*. He was an ardent Republican and was sentenced to six months' imprisonment in 1832 for his attacks on Louis-Philippe, whom he represented as 'Gargantua swallowing bags of gold extorted from the people'. On the suppression of political satire in 1835 he began to work for *Charivari* and turned to satire of social life, but at the time of the 1848 revolution he returned to political subjects. He is said to have made more than 4,000 lithographs, wishing each time that the one he had just made could be his last. In the last years of his life he was almost blind and was saved from destitution by *Corot. Daumier's paintings were probably done for the most part fairly late in his career. Although he was accepted four times by the *Salon, he never exhibited his paintings otherwise and they remained practically unknown up to the time of an exhibition held at *Durand-Ruel's gallery in 1878, the year before his death. The paintings are in the main a documentation of contemporary life and manners with satirical overtones, although he also did a number featuring Don Quixote as a larger-than-life hero. His technique was remarkably broad and free. As a sculptor he specialized in caricature heads and figures, and these too are in a very spontaneous style. In particular he created the memorable figure of 'Ratapoil' (meaning 'skinned rat'), who embodied the sinister agents of the government of Louis-Philippe. (A similar political type in his graphic art was 'Robert Macaire', who personified the unscrupulous profiteer and swindler.)

In the directness of his vision and the lack of sentimentality with which he depicts current social life Daumier belongs to the *Realist school of which *Courbet was the chief representative. As a caricaturist he stands head and shoulders above all others of the 19th cent. He had the gift of expressing the whole character of a man through physiognomy, and the essence of his satire lay in his power to interpret mental folly in terms of physical absurdity. Although he never made a commercial success of his art, he was appreciated by the discriminating and numbered among his friends and admirers *Delacroix, Corot, *Forain, and *Baudelaire. *Degas was among the artists who collected his works.

David, Gerard (d. 1523). Netherlandish painter. He was born at Oudewater, now in southern Holland, but he worked mainly in Bruges, where he settled in 1484 and became acknowledged as the city's leading painter after the death of *Memlinc in 1494. At this time the economic importance of Bruges was declining, but it still maintained its prestige as a centre of art and David played an important role in the flourishing export trade in paintings that it developed in the first quarter of the 16th cent. His work—extremely accomplished, but conservative and usually rather bland—was very popular and his stately compositions were copied again and again. Among his followers were *Ysenbrandt and *Benson, who carried on his tradition until the middle of the 16th cent. Most of his work was of traditional religious themes, but his best-known paintings are probably the pair representing The Judgement of Cambyses (Groeningemuseum, Bruges, 1498), a gory subject to which his reflective style was not ideally suited.

David, Jacques-Louis (1748–1825). French painter, one of the central figures of *Neoclassicism. He had his first training with *Boucher, a distant relative, but Boucher realized that their temperaments were opposed and sent David to *Vien. David went to Italy with the latter in 1776, Vien having been appointed director of the French Academy at Rome, David having won the *Prix de Rome. In Italy David was able to indulge his bent for the *antique and came into contact with the initiators of the new Classical revival, including Gavin *Hamilton. In 1780 he returned to Paris, and in the 1780s his position was firmly established as the embodiment of the social and moral reaction from the frivolity of the *Rococo. His uncompromising subordination of colour to drawing and his economy of statement were in keeping with the new severity of taste. His themes gave expression to the new cult of the civic virtues of stoical self-sacrifice, devotion to duty, honesty, and austerity. Seldom have paintings so completely typified the sentiment of an age as David's The Oath of the Horatii (Louvre, Paris, 1784), Brutus and his Dead Sons (Louvre, 1789), and The Death of Socrates (Met. Mus., New York, 1787). They were received with acclamation by critics and public alike. *Reynolds compared the Socrates with *Michelangelo's Sistine Ceiling and *Raphael's Stanze, and after ten visits to the *Salon described it as 'in every sense perfect'.

David was in active sympathy with the Revolution, becoming a Deputy and voting for the execution of Louis XVI. His position was unchallenged as the painter of the Revolution. His three paintings of 'martyrs of the Revolution', though conceived as portraits, raised portraiture into the domain of universal tragedy. They were: The Death of Lepeletier (now known only from an engraving), The Death of Marat (Musées Royaux, Brussels, 1793), and The Death of Bara (Musée Calvet, Avignon, unfinished). After the fall of Robespierre (1794), however, he was imprisoned, but was released on the plea of his wife, who had previously divorced him because of his Revolutionary sympathies (she was a royalist). They were remarried in 1796, and David's Intervention of the Sabine Women (Louvre, 1794–9), begun while he was in prison, is said to have been painted to honour her, its theme being one of love prevailing over conflict. It was also interpreted at the time, however, as a plea for conciliation in the civil strife that France suffered after the Revolution and it was the work that re-established David's fortunes and brought him to the attention of Napoleon, who appointed him his official painter.

David became an ardent supporter of Napoleon and retained under him the dominant social and artistic position which he had previously held. Between 1802 and 1807 he painted a series of pictures glorifying the exploits of the Emperor, among them the enormous Coronation of Napoleon (Louvre, 1805–7). These works show a change both in technique and in feeling from the earlier Republican works. The cold colours and severe composition of the heroic paintings gave place to a new feeling for pageantry which had something in common with *Romantic painting, although he always remained opposed to the Romantic school. With the fall of Napoleon, David went into exile in Brussels, and his work weakened as the possibility of exerting a moral and social influence receded. (Until recently his late history paintings were generally scorned by critics, but their sensuous qualities are now winning them a more appreciative audience.) He continued to be an outstanding portraitist, but he never surpassed such earlier achievements as the great Napoleon Crossing the Alps (Kunsthistorisches Mus., Vienna, 1800, one of four versions) or the coolly erotic Madame Récamier (Louvre, 1800). His work had a resounding influence on the development of French—

and indeed European—painting, and his many pupils included *Gérard, *Gros, and *Ingres.

David, Pierre-Jean (1788–1856). French sculptor, known after his birthplace as David d'Angers. In 1811 he won the *Prix de Rome, and spent 5 years in Italy, where he met and admired *Ingres and was also influenced by *Canova and *Thorvaldsen. However, *Neoclassical influence was tempered by a strong inclination towards naturalism, and his contemporaries considered him a *Romantic. His most prestigious commission was the high-relief on the pediment of the Pantheon in Paris, which shows an allegorical figure of France distributing wreaths to great Frenchmen (1837), but his best works are to be found among his busts and medallions of famous men. He left a large collection of them to his native city to found the Musée des Beaux-Arts there.

Davie, Alan (1920–   ). Scottish painter, also a goldsmith and jazz musician. After early influences of *Klee and *Picasso, he was greatly impressed by post-war American painting, particularly Jackson *Pollock. His strongly ornamental style, which marks his preoccupations with Zen Buddhism, myths, and magic, has made him one of the most potent image-makers in post-war British painting.

Davies, Arthur Bowen (1862–1928), American painter, printmaker, and tapestry designer. Davies was a member of the circle of Robert *Henri, a member of the *Eight group and president of the Association of American Painters and Sculptors which was launched to organize the *Armory Show. He was a man of wide and liberal culture, and his enthusiasm for the project was largely responsible for the scope of the show and the force of its impact. His own work was varied and embraced remarkably diverse influences. In his early career he showed an enthusiasm for the *Pre-Raphaelites, *Whistler, and *Puvis de Chavannes, and specialized in idyllic landscapes inhabited by dreamlike, visionary figures of nude women or mythical animals (Unicorns, Met. Mus. of Art, New York, 1906). After the Armory Show his work showed superficial *Cubist influence, but in the 1920s he returned to a more traditional style.

Davis, Stuart (1894–1964). American painter. He grew up in an artistic environment, for his father was art director of a Philadelphia newspaper who had employed *Luks, *Glackens, and other members of the *Eight. He studied with Robert *Henri 1910–13, made covers and drawings for the social realist periodical The Masses, which was associated with the *Ash-can School, and exhibited watercolours in the *Armory Show, which made an overwhelming impact on him. After a visit to Paris in 1928–9 he introduced a new note into US *Cubism, basing himself on its Synthetic rather than its Analytical phase. Using natural forms, particularly forms suggesting the characteristic environment of American life, he rearranged them into flat poster-like patterns with precise outlines and sharply contrasting colours (House and Street, Whitney Mus., New York, 1931). He later went over to pure abstract patterns, into which he often introduced lettering, suggestions of advertisements, posters, etc. (Owh! in San Pao, Whitney Mus., 1951). The zest and dynamism of such works reflect his interest in jazz. Davis is generally considered to be the outstanding American artist to work in a Cubist idiom. He made witty and original use of it and created a distinctive American style, for however abstract his work became he always claimed that every image he used had its source in observed reality: 'I paint what I see in America, in other words I paint the American Scene.'

De Andrea, John (1941–   ). American *Superrealist sculptor. As with Duane *Hanson, his figures are made of fibreglass and are realistic to the last detail, but De Andrea specializes in nude figures and his models are usually young and attractive.

decorative arts. Term embracing *applied art and also including objects that are made purely for decoration.

Degas, Edgar (1834–1917). French painter, graphic artist, and sculptor. He was the son of a wealthy art-loving banker (the family name was originally de Gas, but Degas adopted the less pretentious form) and was initially trained for the law. In 1855, however, he entered the École des *Beaux-Arts and studied under Louis Lamothe (1822–69), a pupil and admirer of *Ingres, who laid the foundation of Degas's superb draughtsmanship. His real artistic education, however, was gained through assiduous study of the Old Masters, and between 1854 and 1859 he spent much of his time in Italy. Most of his early works were portraits or history paintings on Classical themes (*Young Spartans*, NG, London). In 1861 Degas met *Manet while copying a *Velázquez in the Louvre and was introduced by him to the circle of the young *Impressionists. During the next few years he abandoned historical pictures and turned to contemporary subjects, with a special predilection for racing scenes, ballet, theatre, circus, rehearsals, café scenes, and laundresses. Degas exhibited in seven out of the eight Impressionist exhibitions and is regarded as one of the prominent members of the Impressionist School. He was, however, Impressionist only in certain restricted aspects of his work and like Manet (who also came from an upper-middle-class background) stood somewhat aloof from the rest of the group. He had little interest in landscape and therefore did not share the Impressionist concern for rendering the effects of changing light and atmosphere. He was more interested in draughtsmanship than most of the others and—apart from Manet—he alone had a thoroughly academic background. As with the other Impressionists, he liked to give the suggestion of accidental, spontaneous, and unplanned scenes, and Degas's pictures often cut off figures in the manner of a badly executed snapshot or used unfamiliar viewpoints. Like them he was influenced by the new techniques of photography and by Japanese colour prints (see UKIYO-E) and he was interested in conveying the impression of movement. But he did not paint out of doors or directly from nature. The appearance of spontaneity and accidental effects was an appearance only; in reality his pictures were carefully composed. 'Even when working from nature, one has to compose,' he said, and 'No art was ever less spontaneous than mine.'

Degas always worked much in *pastel and when his sight began to fail in the 1880s his preference for this medium increased. His colours grew stronger and his compositions more simplified. He was a restless experimenter, mixing tempera and pastel, for example, and using a technique called *peinture à l'essence*, in which pigment from which the oil has been removed is thinned with turpentine to promote rapid drying. From 1880 Degas also modelled in wax, but he exhibited only one bronze in his lifetime, the famous *Little Fourteen-year-old Dancer* (1881) dressed in a real tutu (various casts exist, including one in the Tate, London). During the 1890s, as his fears of failing sight increased, he devoted more time to modelling, doing mostly horses in action, women at their toilet, or nude dancers in characteristic postures. These were cast after his death. For the last twenty years of his life Degas was virtually blind and lived a reclusive life. He was a formidable personality and his complete devotion to his art made him seem cold and aloof. His genius compelled universal respect among other artists, however; *Renoir ranked him above *Rodin as a sculptor, and in 1883 Camille *Pissarro wrote that he was 'certainly the greatest artist of our epoch'. He was the first of the Impressionist group to achieve recognition and his reputation as one of the giants of 19th-cent. art has endured undiminished.

degenerate art (*entartete Kunst*). A term coined in Germany in the 1930s to discredit all contemporary art that did not correspond to the ideology of the Nazi party. Adolf Hitler and Alfred Rosenberg (the chief theoretical spokesman of Nazism) linked art with political doctrines and racial theories, attacking modern art as 'political and cultural anarchy'. Nazi-approved art was thoroughly traditional in concept and technique and took as its subject-matter themes (often militaristic) that glorified Hitler and his ideals of Aryan supremacy. Hitler made his first speech against 'degenerate art' (in German Entartete Kunst) at Nuremberg in 1934, and a series of exhibitions designed to ridicule modern art culminated in an infamous show (also called Entartete Kunst) that opened in Munich in 1937 and then went on tour round Germany. The works on display were confiscated from German museums and were mocked by being shown alongside pictures done by inmates of lunatic asylums. Among the artists included were some of the giants of modern art— van *Gogh, *Matisse, and *Picasso, for example. As a propaganda exercise the exhibition was a huge success, more than two million people visiting it in Munich alone. German artists whose work was declared 'degenerate' were forbidden to exhibit or even to work, and people who sympathized with modern art were deprived of their posts in museums and teaching posts. Some of the confiscated works were sold for the enrichment of Nazi politicians, and others were burned in Berlin in 1939.

de Kooning, Willem (1904–   ). American *Abstract Expressionist painter. He was born in Rotterdam and emigrated to the USA in 1926. His early work was conservative, but his friendship with Arshile *Gorky drew him into the circle of artists who would later become prominent in the Abstract Expressionist movement, and in the 1930s he painted in several manners simultaneously, as he experimented vigorously. After his first one-man show in 1948 he was generally recognized as sharing with Jackson *Pollock the unofficial leadership of the Abstract Expressionist group. Unlike Pollock, de Kooning usually retained figurative elements in his painting, and he achieved notoriety with his *Women* series (*Women, nos. I–VI* were exhibited together at his third one-man show in 1953). *Woman I* (MOMA, New York, 1950–2), with its grotesque leer and frenzied brushwork, shocked the public and dismayed critics who believed in a rigorously abstract art. During the 1970s he began to make sculpture. His wife, **Elaine de Kooning** (1920–   ), whom he married in 1943, is also a painter, notably of *Expressionist portraits.

Delacroix, Eugène (1798–1863). The greatest French painter of the *Romantic movement. He was the son of a politician, Charles Delacroix, but there is some evidence to indicate that his real father was the diplomat Talleyrand, a friend of the family. His mother, Victoire Oeben, came of a family of notable craftsmen and designers. In 1816 he entered the studio of Pierre *Guérin, and was a fellow pupil of *Géricault. His basic artistic education was obtained, however, by copying Old Masters at the *Louvre, where he delighted in *Rubens and the Venetian School. He met *Bonington in the Louvre and was introduced by him to English *watercolour painting. *Constable's *Hay Wain*, exhibited in the 1824 *Salon, also made a great impression on him and in 1825 he

spent some months in England, admiring in particular *Gainsborough, *Lawrence, *Etty, and *Wilkie. In the Salon of 1822 he had his first public success with *The Barque of Dante* (Louvre, Paris). It was bought by the State (with Talleyrand perhaps pulling strings in the background), as was *The Massacre at Chios* (Louvre) two years later, ensuring the success of his career. *Gros called this painting 'the massacre of painting', but *Baudelaire wrote that it was 'a terrifying hymn in honour of doom and irremediable suffering'. In 1832 Delacroix visited Morocco in the entourage of the Comte de Mornay and there acquired a fund of rich and exotic visual imagery which he exploited to the full in his later painting (*Sultan of Morocco*, Musée, Toulouse, 1845). From the late 1830s his style and technique underwent a change. In place of luminous glazes and contrasted values he began to use a personal technique of vibrating adjacent tones and *divisionist colour effects in a manner of which *Watteau had been a master, making colour enter into the structure of the picture to an extent which had not previously been attempted. In spite of being hailed as the leader of the Romantic movement, his predilection for exotic and emotionally charged subject-matter, and his open enmity with *Ingres, Delacroix always claimed allegiance to the *Classical tradition, and for his large works followed the traditional course of making numerous preparatory drawings. In his later career he became one of the most distinguished monumental mural painters in the history of French art. His public commissions included: decorations in the Chambre des députés, Palais Bourbon (Salon du roi, 1833–7; Library, 1838–47); in the Library of the Luxembourg Palace (1841–6); and three paintings in the Chapelle des Anges of S. Sulpice (1853–61). In the last of these, his *Jacob and the Angel* and *Heliodorus Expelled from the Temple* are among the maturest expressions of his decorative richness of colour and grandiose structural integration. Baudelaire said of him that he was the only artist who 'in our faithless generation conceived religious pictures' and van *Gogh wrote, 'only *Rembrandt and Delacroix could paint the face of Christ'.

Delacroix's output was enormous. After his death his executors found more than 9,000 paintings, pastels, and drawings in his studio and he prided himself on the speed at which he worked, declaring 'If you are not skilful enough to sketch a man falling out of a window during the time it takes him to get from the fifth storey to the ground, then you will never be able to produce monumental work.' Among great painters he was also one of the finest writers on art. He was a voluminous letter writer and kept a journal from 1822 to 1824 and again from 1847 until his death—a marvellously rich source of information and opinion on his life and times. His influence, particularly through his use of colour, was prodigious, inspiring *Renoir, *Seurat, and van Gogh among others. Delacroix's studio in Paris is now a museum devoted to his life and work, but the Louvre has the finest collection of his paintings.

Delaroche, Paul (1797–1856). French painter, one of the leading pupils of *Gros. He achieved great popularity with his melodramatic history scenes, engravings of his work hanging in thousands of homes. Often he chose subjects from English history, as with two of his most famous works, *The Little Princes in the Tower* (Louvre, Paris, 1831) and *The Execution of Lady Jane Grey* (NG, London, 1853). They are *Romantic in flavour, but academically impeccable in their draughtsmanship and detailing. After a period when such pictures were totally out of favour, his work is once again being treated seriously.

Delaunay, Robert (1885–1941). French painter, who through most of his career experimented with the abstract qualities of colour. He began his researches c.1906 from the *Neo-Impressionist theories of *Seurat, but instead of using the *pointillist technique he investigated the interaction of large areas of juxtaposed and contrasting colour. He was particularly interested in the interconnections between colour and movement. By 1910 he was making an individual contribution to *Cubism, notably with his series of paintings of the Eiffel Tower, which combine fragmented forms with vibrant colour. *Apollinaire gave the name *Orphism to Delaunay's work, which by 1912 had moved on to become completely abstract, as in his lyrically beautiful *Circular Forms* series (an example is in the Kunsthaus in Zurich). In 1913 Delaunay exhibited at the galleries of Der *Sturm in Berlin, and his work was a major influence on German *Expressionists such as *Klee, *Macke, and *Marc. It also powerfully affected the *Futurists in Italy and the American *Synchromists. The period of Delaunay's greatest achievements was, however, fairly short-lived; he was in Spain and Portugal for much of the First World War and after his return to Paris his work lost its inspirational quality and became rather repetitive. His home became a meeting place for *Dada artists, but he continued with work related to colour theories.

Delaunay-Terk, Sonia (1885–1979). Russian painter and textile designer, the wife of Robert *Delaunay. She came to Paris in 1905, married Delaunay in 1910 (after a short-lived marriage to Wilhelm *Uhde) and became associated with him in the development of *Orphism. During the 1920s she worked mostly on hand-printed fabrics and tapestries; as a designer she made a strong impact on the international world of fashion, designing creations for such famous women as Nancy Cunard and Gloria Swanson. In 1930 she turned primarily to painting and became a member of the *Abstraction-Création association. After the death of her husband in 1941 she continued to work as a painter and designer.

de Loutherbourg, Philippe Jacques (1740–1812). French painter who settled in England in 1771. He became a designer of stage sets for David Garrick at Drury Lane (maquettes in the V&A, London) and is best known for his invention of the *Eidophusikon, a theatrical presentation of scenic pictures. Although a foreigner, de Loutherbourg is said to have declared that 'no English landscape painter needed foreign travel to collect grand prototypes for his study' and in his landscapes, which are indeed very varied in character, he exalted the English scenery as material for the *picturesque and the *sublime. He also painted battle scenes, and literary and biblical subjects in a lively style.

Delvaux, Paul (1897–). Belgian painter. After working in *Neo-Impressionist and *Expressionist manners, he began painting in a *Surrealist style in about 1935 under the influence of *Chirico and *Magritte. Although Delvaux was not formally a member of the Surrealist movement, and was not in sympathy with its political aims, he has become regarded as one of the foremost upholders of the tradition. In the mid 1940s, following *Ensor, he became interested in the skeleton as a theme, but more typically his works show an obsession with an ideal of abstracted female beauty, represented nude or semi-nude in incongruous settings. His work combines the unreal space of the dream with a hallucinatory precision of detail and a compelling sense of eroticism.

De Maria, Walter (1935–   ). American sculptor and experimental artist. He was one of the earliest exponents of *Minimal Art, producing examples of the type c.1960, before the term was current, and was also a pioneer in the art of *earthworks. Some of his work belongs to the category of *Conceptual art, as for example *Mile Long Drawing* of 1968, two parallel chalk lines 12 ft. (3.6 m.) apart in the Mojave Desert.

Demuth, Charles (1883–1935). American painter. In the first two decades of the century he spent several years in Paris (he also visited Berlin and London) and became an important channel for the transmission of modern European ideas into American art (he was a friend of *Duchamp). Demuth's work was varied, but he is best known as one of the leading *Precisionists. His most personal paintings, however, are what he called 'poster portraits' (pictures composed of words and objects associated with the person 'represented'). The most famous example is *I saw the Figure Five in Gold* (Met. Mus., New York, 1921), a tribute to the poet William Carlos Williams.

Denis, Maurice (1870–1943). French painter, designer, and writer on art theory. He was a member of the *Nabis and one of the chief exponents of the theories of *Symbolism. In his article *Definition of Neo-Traditionalism* (1890), he made his most famous pronouncement on art, which has often been regarded as the key to contemporary aesthetics of painting: 'Remember that a picture—before being a war horse or a nude woman or an anecdote—is essentially a flat surface covered with colours assembled in a certain order.' His own work, however, was very much concerned with subject-matter, for he was a devout

Catholic and set himself to revive religious painting. In 1917 he did frescos for the church of St Paul in Geneva, and he also designed stained glass and church furnishings. His writings on art are for the most part collected in *Théories* (1912) and *Nouvelles Théories* (1922). In 1939 he published a history of religious art.

de Piles, Roger (1635–1709). French art historian and amateur painter. De Piles was employed by Louis XIV on various diplomatic missions and was thus enabled to study the arts at first hand in many European countries. He was an admirer of *Rubens and in the famous controversy of the 'Rubénsistes' against the 'Poussinistes' (see POUSSIN) that split the French *Academy in the second half of the 17th cent. he took the side of those who held that colour and *chiaroscuro are of prime importance in painting against the upholders of the academic emphasis on drawing. He also recognized the value of genius, imagination, and 'enthusiasm' against the excessive domination of formalized rule. His best-known book is *Cours de peinture par principes avec une balance des peintres* (1708), which has become notorious for the section (the 'balance des peintres') in which he awarded marks to great artists of the past for their skill at composition, drawing, colour, etc., then added up the scores to form a sort of league table of genius. His criticism, however, is usually much less crude than this.

Derain, André (1880–1954). French painter, sculptor, and graphic artist. In the first two decades of the 20th cent. he was near the centre of avant-garde developments in Paris, but thereafter he based his work increasingly on that of the Old Masters and it became rather dry and academic. He was one of the creators of *Fauvism, an early adherent of *Cubism, and one of the first to 'discover' *primitive art, but although he is undoubtedly a figure of historical importance, his work does not approach in quality that of his great contemporaries such as *Matisse and *Picasso. He produced numerous book illustrations, and also designed for the stage, notably for *Diaghilev's *Ballets Russes*.

Desiderio da Settignano (1428/31–61). Florentine sculptor. He came to maturity while *Donatello was in Padua, but like most of his contemporaries he formed his style on Donatello's Florentine work of the 1430s. He learnt from Donatello the practice of carving in very low *relief, and the lively, thick-set figures of children on the *Singing Gallery* made by Donatello for Florence Cathedral (1433–8) provided models for Desiderio's own reliefs of the *Madonna and Child*. Desiderio's artistic personality, however, was more delicate than Donatello's, and for refinement of handling he is unsurpassed by any Italian sculptor of his period. His only important public work was the tomb of the Florentine humanist and statesman Gregorio Marsuppini in Sta Croce (after 1453). This is architecturally dependent on the tomb of Leonardo Bruni by Bernardino *Rossellino (probably Desiderio's teacher), executed for the same church about ten years earlier, but is sculpturally richer and more animated. His sensitive modelling is best exemplified by busts in Florence (Bargello) and Washington (NG).

Desportes, Alexandre-François (1661–1743). French painter of dogs, game, and emblems of the chase. In his early career he worked much as a portraitist, notably in 1695–6 at the court of Jan Sobieski (John III) in Poland, but on his return to France he took up hunting subjects and won the patronage of Louis XIV and Louis XV. He achieved considerable celebrity (he was well received on a visit to England in 1712) and in his field was rivalled only by *Oudry. Although he continued the lavish Flemish tradition exemplified by *Snyders, Desportes was among the first artists of the 18th cent. to make landscape studies from nature for his backgrounds, and because of this he was considered eccentric. His work is well represented in the Louvre (which has his *Self-portrait as a Huntsman*, 1699) and in the Wallace Collection, London.

Detroy. See TROY.

Deutsch, Niklaus Manuel (*c.*1484–1530). Swiss painter, designer, and poet, active mainly in his native Berne. Deutsch was one of the outstanding Swiss artists of his period, but much of his energy was expended in other activities. He fought as a mercenary in Italy and took an active part in the political and religious affairs of Berne as a passionate supporter of the

Reformation, writing satires against the Pope, whom he equated with Antichrist. His paintings are related to *Baldung Grien and *Grünewald in their love of the grotesque (*The Temptation of St Anthony*, Kunstmuseum, Berne, 1520). Deutsch also designed woodcuts and stained glass and a set of choir stalls for Berne Cathedral.

Deverell, Walter Howell (1827–54). British painter. He was a friend of *Rossetti, and was proposed for membership of the *Pre-Raphaelite Brotherhood (to replace *Collinson) but was never actually elected. In 1849 he 'discovered' Elizabeth Siddal, the archetypal Pre-Raphaelite model and Rossetti's future wife. Deverell was noted for his good looks and charm and Elizabeth was probably in love with him before he died aged 26 from Bright's disease. In his brief career he gave promise of becoming perhaps the most painterly of the Pre-Raphaelite followers (*A Pet*, Tate, London, 1853).

Devis, Arthur (1711–87). English painter, the best-known member of a family of artists. He was one of the first specialists in the small *conversation piece and also painted single portraits of similar scale. The sitters are usually in repose, often somewhat artificially posed, and the Devis type of portrait group was animated in the next generation by *Zoffany. Devis was a minor figure in his day and virtually forgotten until the 1930s, but since then his work has attained considerable popularity because of the doll-like charm of his figures and the delicate detail of his settings. It has also become of interest to social historians, as most of his clients were from the newly prosperous middle class. A small representative collection of his work is in the Art Gallery at Preston, his native town. He worked both in London and in Lancashire. **Anthony** (1729–1816), his half-brother, was a landscape painter. Arthur's son, **Arthur William** (1763–1822), spent the years 1785–95 in India, where he painted portraits and a series of pictures representing the arts, manufactures, and agriculture of Bengal (two examples are in the Ashmolean, Oxford), which were engraved. He lived in London from 1795, working mainly as a portraitist, but also painting *The Death of Nelson* (Nat. Maritime Mus., London, *c.*1806). Another son, **Thomas Anthony** (1757–1810), painted undistinguished portraits and *fancy pictures. Little of his work survives.

De Wint, Peter (1784–1849). English landscape painter of Dutch extraction. He served his apprenticeship with John Raphael *Smith, then studied at the *Royal Academy Schools and frequented the house of Dr *Monro. Although he was an admirable painter in oils, he is best known as one of the finest exponents of watercolour of his generation. He is particularly associated with views of the countryside around Lincoln (where his wife's parents lived), in which he often uses broad *washes of colour somewhat in the manner of *Cotman. De Wint was a popular figure and enjoyed considerable success as a teacher.

Diaghilev, Sergei Pavlovich (1872–1929). Russian ballet impresario, who exerted great influence on the visual arts as well as on dancing and music, and employed some of the finest painters of his time as designers of costumes and décor. He brought the *Ballets Russes* to Paris in 1909, and the many Russian artists whom he employed, most notably *Bakst, caused a revolution in European theatrical design. Diaghilev toured Europe and America with his ballet company until his death, and among the artists who designed for him were *Braque, *Picasso, and *Rouault. Before his involvement with the ballet, Diaghilev had been active in the *Mir Iskusstva group and had organized exhibitions in Russia and western Europe, including a representative exhibition of Russian painting at the *Salon d'Automne in Paris, which was the most comprehensive to have been seen in the West.

Diaz de la Peña, Narcisse-Virgile (1807–76). French painter, born at Bordeaux of Spanish parents. He began his career as a porcelain painter, and then painted *Romantic historical subjects, but after meeting Théodore *Rousseau in 1837 he became a member of the *Barbizon group of landscape painters. His style is distinct from that of his Barbizon colleagues, however, for his work lacks the sense of quiet communion with nature that was a characteristic feature of the school and his brushwork is heavy and restless (his detractors call it turgid). He never lost the Romantic leanings of his youth, and

continued to paint mythological pictures (typically featuring nymphs) throughout his career. He was helpful to the *Impressionists, and *Renoir stated that his meeting with Diaz led him to lighten his palette.

Dickinson, Edwin (1891–1978). American painter. His work, which often treats disquieting or enigmatic subject-matter in an academic technique, has been called *Surrealist, but is best regarded as a sophisticated culmination of the 19th-cent. *Romantic tradition. Paintings such as *The Fossil Hunters* (Whitney Mus., New York, 1926–8) contain superimposed and suggestive imagery but lack the special impact of material from the subconscious.

Dickinson, Preston (1891–1930). American painter. As a student in Paris he was influenced particularly by the structural features of *Cézanne's work and the high-keyed colour of the *Fauves, but in the 1920s his work became less experimental as he became associated with the *Precisionists. Like others of the school, he favoured subjects which were adapted to representation in terms of semi-geometrical abstract design, in particular the machine.

Diderot, Denis (1713–84). French philosopher and critic, mainly remembered in England as the chief editor of the *Encyclopédie* (1751–72), a work of fundamental importance in shaping the rationalist and humanitarian ideals of the Age of Enlightenment. His views on art appear in articles in the *Encyclopédie* and elsewhere, notably his reviews of the *Salons between 1759 and 1781, which are written in a lively conversational style and formed the model for the later criticism of *Baudelaire. Against the intellectualist bias of *Neoclassicism he maintained that our ideas of beauty arise from practical everyday experience of beautiful things. His views on the relation between poetry and painting provided a basis for *Lessing's famous book *Laokoön*.

Diller, Burgoyne (1906–65). American painter and sculptor. After passing through phases of *Impressionism and *Cubism, he became interested in *Neo-Plasticism and by the mid 1930s had become one of the earliest and most committed American followers of *Mondrian. He was a member of *American Abstract Artists and from 1935 to 1940 Head of the Mural Division of the *Federal Art Project. His sculpture, restricted to rectangular elements and *primary colours, was like his painting deeply influenced by Mondrian.

Dine, Jim (1935–). American painter, printmaker, and creator of *environments and *happenings. Dine was a prominent figure in American *Pop art and became well known for his combination of real objects—ties, lawn-mowers, household appliances, wash basins, etc.—set against backgrounds of painterly textures. In 1959–60 he came to the fore as one of the pioneers of happenings, sometimes collaborating with Claes *Oldenburg, and he also collaborated with the British Pop artist *Paolozzi in a series of *collages. He is considered to have been a pioneer of *Performance art of the late 1960s and early 1970s. Later he turned to representational painting of a traditional kind.

diorama. A large, partially translucent scenic painting, which by means of varied illumination simulates such effects as sunrise, changing weather, etc. The term is applied by extension to the building in which the display is housed. The diorama was invented by *Daguerre in 1822 and was exhibited in Regent's Park, London, in the following year. Nowadays the term diorama is more usually applied to a certain type of museum display. It consists of a miniature scene, viewed through a window in a screen or cabinet, in which the foreground details, modelled in the round, join imperceptibly with the more distant parts which are painted in perspective on a vertical panel.

dipper. A small metal container that clips on to the oil painter's *palette and holds *medium or diluent. They are often made in pairs—a 'double dipper'. The American term is 'palette cup'.

diptych. A picture or other work of art consisting of two parts facing one another like the pages of a book and usually hinged together. See also POLYPTYCH, TRIPTYCH.

Discobolus. See MYRON.

distemper. Type of paint in which the pigment is mixed with water and glue or *size. Its principal use is in scene-painting, as it is cheap but impermanent. Whitewash is a form of distemper.

divisionism. A method and technique of painting by which colour effects are obtained not by mixing pigments on the *palette but by applying small areas or dots of unmixed pigment on the canvas in such a way that to a spectator standing at an appropriate distance they appear to react together. This method, which produces greater luminosity and brilliance of colour than if the colours are physically mixed, has been employed to some extent by many artists in *alla prima painting, although it is contrary to the traditional principles of painting by superimposed *glazes and *scumbles. Notable precursors of divisionism were *Watteau and *Delacroix. It was also employed empirically by the *Impressionists, but it was not developed systematically and scientifically until *Seurat and the *Neo-Impressionists. Seurat (in common with other contemporaries) spoke of an 'optical mixture', but (contrary to what is usually stated) the dots do not really fuse in the viewer's eye to make different colours, for they remain visible as dots. Rather, they seem to vibrate, creating something of the shimmering effect experienced in strong sunlight. The effect is noted in Ogden Rood's *Modern Chromatics* (1879), a treatise on colour theory well known to Seurat. Camille *Pissarro, who was closely associated with Seurat at this time, said that the optimum viewing distance for a picture painted by the divisionist method was three times the diagonal measurement. The terms divisionism and *pointillism are not always clearly differentiated, but whereas divisionism refers mainly to the underlying theory, pointillism describes the actual painting technique associated with Seurat and his followers. 'Divisionism' (usually with a capital 'D') was also the name of an Italian movement, a version of *Neo-Impressionism, that flourished in the last decade of the 19th cent. and the first decade of the 20th cent. It was one of the sources of *Futurism.

Dix, Otto (1891–1969). German painter and printmaker. After serving in the First World War he studied at the academies of Dresden and Düsseldorf. In the 1920s he was, with George *Grosz, the outstanding artist of the *Neue Sachlichkeit movement, his work conveying his disillusionment and disgust at the horrors of war and the depravities of a decadent society with complete psychological truth and devastating emotional effect. *The Match Seller* (Staatsgalerie, Stuttgart, 1920), for example, is a pitiless depiction of indifference to suffering, showing passers-by ignoring a blind and limbless ex-soldier begging in the street, and Dix's fifty etchings entitled *The War* (1924) have been described by G. H. Hamilton (*Painting and Sculpture in Europe, 1880–1940*) as 'perhaps the most powerful as well as the most unpleasant anti-war statements in modern art'. Another favourite theme was prostitution and he was a brilliantly incisive portraitist. In 1927 he was appointed a teacher at the Dresden Academy, but his anti-military stance drew the wrath of the Nazi regime and he was dismissed from his academic posts in 1933 and his work declared *degenerate. In 1939 he was jailed on a charge of complicity in a plot on Hitler's life, but was soon released. He was conscripted into the *Volkssturm* (Home Guard) in 1945 and was a prisoner in France 1945–6. His work after the war lost much of the strength of his great Neue Sachlichkeit period and much of it was inspired by religious mysticism.

Dobell, Sir William (1899–1970). Australian painter. In 1929 he won a travelling scholarship that enabled him to study at the *Slade School under Henry *Tonks and did not return to Australia until 1938. His work reveals the broad artistic education he gained on his travels in Europe, and his rich textures and colours, show, in particular, a debt to the *Expressionism of Chaïm *Soutine. In 1943/4 he won the Archibald Prize for portraiture, awarded annually by the Art Gallery of New South Wales, with a portrait of his fellow-artist, Joshua Smith. The award, which was contested in the courts by two of the unsuccessful competitors on the grounds that it was not a portrait but a caricature, created a *cause célèbre* for modernism in Australia and Dobell (who won the case) became a household name. In 1949 and again in 1950 he visited the highlands of New Guinea, and as a result of this experience his work became broader in execution and more decorative. Dobell was unique among Australian artists in combining successfully a mastery of *Renaissance tradition (particularly in portraiture) with a profound insight into the character and values of 20th-cent. Australians.

Dobson, Frank (1886–1963). British sculptor. His early work consisted mainly of paintings, which show how impressed he was by the *Post-Impressionist exhibitions organized by Roger *Fry. After the First World War (when he was on active service with the Artists' Rifles), he turned increasingly to sculpture, and in the 1920s and 1930s gained an outstanding reputation: in 1925 Roger Fry described his work as 'true sculpture and pure sculpture . . . almost the first time that such a thing has been even attempted in England'. He worked in both metal and stone (he was one of the earliest to revive direct carving) and his sophisticated stylizations made him one of the pioneers of modern British sculpture. The monumental dignity of his work was in the Classical tradition of *Maillol, and like him Dobson found the female nude the most satisfactory subject for three-dimensional composition, as in *Cornucopia* (University of Hull, 1925-7), described by Clive *Bell as 'the finest piece of sculpture by an Englishman since—I don't know when'. He was also outstanding as a portrait sculptor, as witness his head of Sir Osbert Sitwell in polished brass (Tate, London, 1923). His craftsmanship was superb and he played an important role as a teacher as Professor of Sculpture at the *Royal College of Art, 1946–53. With the rise of a younger generation led by Henry *Moore, however, Dobson's prestige as an artist dropped and he was regarded as 'dated'; the memorial exhibition of his work organized by the Arts Council in 1966 was not well received. Since then he has again been recognized as one of the outstanding figures in 20th-cent. British sculpture.

Dobson, William (1611–46). English portrait painter. He is regarded as the most accomplished English painter before *Hogarth, and was described by John Aubrey in his *Brief Lives* (c.1690) as 'the most excellent painter that England hath yet bred'. Some sixty paintings by him are known, all from the years 1642–6, when he was painter to the wartime court at Oxford. He is thought to have returned to London after the surrender of Oxford in 1646. Said to have been 'somewhat loose and irregular in his way of living', he was thrown into prison for debt, and his early death followed shortly after his release. His style is superficially similar to van *Dyck's, but his colouring is richer and his paint texture rougher, very much in the Venetian tradition. He also had an uncompromisingly direct way of presenting character (as in his most celebrated work—*Endymion Porter*, Tate, London) that is considered quintessentially English. Various paintings by Dobson other than portraits are mentioned by early writers, but only two survive: *The Executioner with the Baptist's Head* (Walker Art Gallery, Liverpool); and an allegory, *The Civil Wars of France* (Rousham House, Oxfordshire).

Doesburg, Theo van (1883–1931). Dutch painter, architect, and writer on art. His early work was influenced variously by *Impressionism, *Fauvism, and *Expressionism, but in 1915 he met *Mondrian and rapidly underwent a transition to complete abstraction. In 1917 he founded the association of artists called De *Stijl and the periodical of the same name, and for the remainder of his life the propagation of the ideas of the group was his dominant interest. He went on an extended lecture tour outside the Netherlands in 1921 and his ideas made a considerable impression at the *Bauhaus, where he taught irregularly from 1922 to 1924. In 1930 he moved to Paris and built himself a studio at Meudon that became a new focus of the De Stijl movement. The movement collapsed with his death in 1931, but its influence survived in many fields. See also ELEMENTARISM.

Dolci, Carlo (1616–86). Florentine painter, active in his native city for virtually his whole career. He was intensely devout and most of his paintings are of religious subjects, done in a cloyingly sweet and meticulously smooth style. They were enormously popular in his lifetime (his reputation spread to England and elsewhere), but have been totally out of favour in the 20th cent. His portraits, on the other hand, are now much admired for their sober objectivity (*Sir Thomas Baines*, Fitzwilliam, Cambridge, c.1665–70).

Domenichino (properly Domenico Zampieri) (1581–1641). Bolognese painter. He was Annibale *Carracci's favourite pupil and one of the most important upholders of the tradition of Bolognese *Classicism. After studying with *Calvaert and Ludovico Carracci he went to Rome (1602) and joined the colony of artists working under Annibale Carracci at the Palazzo *Farnese. His only undisputed work there is the *Maiden with the Unicorn*, a charming, gentle fresco over the entrance of the Gallery. By the second decade of the century he was established as Rome's leading painter and had a succession of major decorative commissions, among them scenes from the life of St Cecilia in S. Luigi dei Francesi (1613–14). The dignified frieze-like composition of the figures reflects a renewed study of *Raphael's tapestries, and in turn influenced *Poussin. The frescos in the pendentives and apse of S. Andrea della Valle (1624–8), his chief work of the 1620s, show a move away from this strict Classicism towards an ampler *Baroque style; but compared with his rival *Lanfranco (who at this time was overtaking him in popularity) Domenichino never abandoned the principles of clear, firm drawing for the sake of more painterly effects. In 1631 Domenichino moved to Naples, and in his ceiling frescos of the S. Gennaro chapel in the cathedral he made even greater concessions to the fashionable Baroque. He met with considerable hostility in Naples from jealous local artists and was forced to flee precipitately in 1634. He later returned, but died before completing his work in the cathedral.

Domenichino was important in fields other than monumental fresco decoration, particularly as an exponent of *ideal landscape, in which he formed the link between Annibale Carracci and *Claude (four of his landscapes are in the Louvre). He was one of the finest draughtsmen of his generation (the Royal Library at Windsor Castle has a superb collection of his drawings) and also an excellent portraitist (*Monsignor Agucchi*, City Art Gallery, York, c.1610). In the 18th cent. his reputation was enormous—his *Last Communion of St Jerome* (Vatican, 1614) was generally regarded as one of the greatest pictures ever painted—but he fell from grace in the 19th cent. along with other Bolognese painters under the scathing attacks of *Ruskin.

Domenico Veneziano (d. 1461). Italian painter. His name indicates that he came from Venice, but he was active mainly in Florence. *Vasari credits him with introducing *oil painting into Tuscany. Although this is incorrect, it seems to be true that he was responsible for introducing a new interest in colour and texture to a tradition in which draughtsmanship normally ruled supreme. His fresco cycle *Scenes from the Life of the Virgin* (1439–45) in S. Egidio, Florence, on which *Piero della Francesca was one of his assistants, has disappeared, and only two fully authenticated works have survived. These are three much-damaged and repainted fragments from a frescoed street tabernacle (NG, London, c.1440) and the celebrated *St Lucy Altarpiece* of c.1445 (the central panel is in the Uffizi, Florence, and the *predellas dispersed in Cambridge (Fitzwilliam), Washington (NG), and Berlin (Staatliche Mus.)). The delicate beauty of its colouring, mastery of light, and airy lucidity of spatial construction are reflected in the work of his assistant Piero, and also, for example, in that of *Baldovinetti.

Donatello (Donato di Niccolo) (1386?–1466). Florentine sculptor. He was the greatest European sculptor of the 15th cent. and one of a remarkable group of artists—including his friends *Alberti, *Brunelleschi, and *Masaccio—who created the *Renaissance style in Florence. Between 1404 and 1407 he was working as an assistant to *Ghiberti, but he developed a style that was radically different to his master's *Gothic elegance. He was unconcerned with the surface polish or linear grace so typical of Ghiberti, and excelled rather in emotional force. His revolutionary conception of sculpture is exemplified in the great series of standing figures in niches which he made for Or San Michele and Florence Cathedral. The series began with the *St Mark* of 1411–13 (Or San Michele), included the celebrated *St George* (c.1415–17), now in the Bargello, Florence, and culminated in the so-called *Zuccone* ('bald-pate') in the Cathedral Museum (probably completed in 1436, although because various figures of prophets, of which this is one, are not identified unambiguously in the documents, some authorities think it was carved in 1423–5). *Vasari conveys the brilliance of Donatello's characterization in his description of

the *St George*: 'The head exhibits the beauty of youth, its spirit and valour in arms, a proud and terrifying lifelikeness, and a marvellous sense of movement within the stone.' With this acute psychological insight went a technique of daring originality that shows how concerned Donatello was with the optical effects of his works. He carefully took into consideration the position from which they would be viewed, adjusting the proportions of a figure when it would be seen from below, for example, and carving with almost brutal power and boldness when it was positioned to be seen at a distance. On the other hand, his relief of *St George and the Dragon* (Or San Michele, 1417), done for the base of his *St George* statue, is executed with great delicacy in the technique Donatello invented called *rilievo schiacciato* (*relief so low it is like 'drawing in stone'); situated on the north side of the building, the relief is seen in a soft, diffused light, so the subtlety of the carving can be appreciated.

In 1430–2 Donatello visited Rome, probably with Brunelleschi, and the impact of *antique art can be seen most clearly in his famous *Cantoria* (singing gallery) for Florence Cathedral (now Cathedral Mus., 1433–9), which makes a lavish show of freely interpreted Classical motifs. The bronze statue of *David* (Bargello), which is credited with being the first free-standing nude statue since antiquity, is also sometimes seen as a response to Donatello's visit to Rome and assigned to the 1430s, but some scholars date it much later. The subject as well as the date is controversial, for it has been proposed that it represents *Mercury with the Head of Argus* rather than *David*. From 1443 to 1453 Donatello was based in Padua, his reason for moving there presumably being the commission to execute the Gattamelata monument in the Piazza del Santo—the first life-size equestrian statue since antiquity. His other major work in Padua was the High Altar of the church of S. Antonio (the Santo), which features free-standing figures and reliefs that are not now in their original positions.

From 1454 until his death Donatello was based mainly in Florence, although he also worked in Siena on an abortive project for a set of bronze doors for the Cathedral. In his late work he gave more prominence to the element of emotional intensity that was already such a feature of his style. The most important works from his final years are *Judith and Holofernes* in the Piazza della Signoria, a harrowing and emaciated *Mary Magdalene* in wood (Baptistry), and two pulpits with bronze reliefs in S. Lorenzo, which were unfinished at his death. These sublime late works show how freely Donatello exploited the expressive possibilities of distortion, and in them he created what has been called 'the first style of old age in the history of art'. His work had enormous influence, on painters as well as sculptors, and his true spiritual heir was *Michelangelo.

Dongen, Kees van (1877–1968). Dutch-born painter who settled in Paris in 1897 and took French nationality in 1929. His early work was *Impressionistic, but he became a member of the *Fauvist group in 1906 and in 1908 exhibited with the German *Expressionist group Die *Brücke. Nudes and female portraits were his favourite themes. After the First World War he became well known for his fashionable female portraits and pictures of café society. He kept the brilliant colouring of his Fauve days, but his great facility led to repetition and banality.

Donkey's Tail. Title of an exhibition organized in Moscow in 1912 by *Larionov and *Goncharova after they had dissociated themselves from the *Knave of Diamonds group in 1911. They accused that group of being too much under foreign influence, and advocated a nationalist Russian art. At this time Larionov and Goncharova were painting in their 'primitivist' manner based upon Russian peasant art and *icon painting. *Malevich and *Tatlin also showed at the exhibition, which took its name from Larionov's having heard that a group of artists in Paris had exhibited a picture that a donkey had 'painted' by means of a brush tied to its tail. The exhibition caused an outcry because some of the pictures shown were regarded as sacrilegious. It was followed by the *Target exhibition in 1913.

Donner, Georg Raphael (1693–1741). The outstanding Austrian *Baroque sculptor, active mainly in Salzburg, Bratislava, and Vienna. His masterpieces are acknowledged to be the figures from the fountain in the Mehlmarkt, Vienna (Österreichisches Barockmuseum, Vienna,

1737–9), and the group of *St Martin and the Beggar* (Bratislava Cathedral, c.1735), in which the saint is dressed in hussar's uniform rather than the traditional armour. These works are in lead, which Donner preferred to the Austrian speciality of wood, and his smooth surfaces have led some critics to see his work as presaging *Neoclassicism, although his elongated figures seem to place him closer to Italian *Mannerism.

donor. The commissioner of a work of religious art whose portrait is incorporated in the work. By having themselves included in the picture donors sought to associate themselves in a special way with the sacred figures portrayed there, either in thanks for favours received, or in the hope of future protection and salvation.

Doré, Gustave (1832–83). The most popular and successful French book illustrator of the mid 19th cent. Doré became very widely known for his illustrations to such books as Dante's *Inferno* (1861), *Don Quixote* (1862), and the Bible (1866), and he helped to give European currency to the illustrated book of large format. He was so prolific that at one time he employed more than forty blockcutters. His work is characterized by a rather naïve but highly spirited love of the *grotesque and represents a commercialization of the *Romantic taste for the bizarre. Drawings of London done in 1869–71 were more sober studies of the poorer quarters of the city and captured the attention of van *Gogh. In the 1870s he also took up painting (doing some large and ambitious religious works) and sculpture (the monument to the dramatist and novelist Alexandre Dumas in the Place Malesherbes in Paris, erected in 1883, is his work).

Doryphorus. See POLYCLITUS OF ARGOS.

Dossi, Dosso (Giovanni Luteri) (c.1490?–1542). The outstanding painter of the Ferrarese School in the 16th cent. His early life and training are obscure, but *Vasari's assertion that he was born around 1474 is now thought unlikely. He is first recorded in 1512 at Mantua (the name 'Dosso' probably comes from a place near Mantua—he is not called 'Dosso Dossi' until the 18th cent.). By 1514 he was in Ferrara, where he spent most of the rest of his career, combining with the poet Ariosto in devising court entertainments, triumphs, tapestries, etc. Dosso painted various kinds of pictures—mythological and religious works, portraits, and decorative frescos—and he is perhaps most important for the part played in his work by landscape, in which he continues the romantic pastoral vein of *Giorgione and *Titian. The influence from these two artists is indeed so strong that it is thought he must have been in Venice early in his career. Dosso's work, however, has a personal quality of fantasy and an opulent sense of colour and texture that gives it an individual stamp (*Melissa*, Borghese Gal., Rome, *c*.1523). His brother **Battista Dossi** (*c*.1497–1548) often collaborated with him, but there is insufficient evidence to know whether he made an individual contribution.

dotted manner. See MANIÈRE CRIBLÉE.

Dou, Gerrit (1613–75). Dutch painter. He was born and active in Leiden and in 1628 became the first pupil of the young *Rembrandt, basing his early work closely on his master's. After Rembrandt moved to Amsterdam, Dou developed a style of his own, painting usually on a small scale, with a surface of almost enamelled smoothness. He was astonishingly fastidious about his tools and working conditions, with a particular horror of dust. Some of his pictures were painted with the aid of a magnifying glass. He painted numerous subjects, but is best known for domestic interiors. They usually contain only a few figures framed by a window or by the drapery of a curtain, and surrounded by books, musical instruments, or household paraphernalia, all minutely depicted. He is at his best in scenes lit by artificial light. With Jan *Steen, Dou was among the founders of the Guild of St Luke at Leiden in 1648. Unlike Steen he was prosperous and respected throughout his life, and his pictures continued to fetch big prices (consistently higher than those paid for Rembrandt's work) until the advent of *Impressionism influenced taste against the neatness and precision of his style. Dou had a workshop with many pupils who perpetuated his style (notably *Schalken)—and Leiden continued the *fijnschilder* (fine painter) tradition until the 19th cent.

Doughty, Thomas (1793–1856). American painter and lithographer, one of the first American artists to specialize exclusively in landscapes. He was born in Philadelphia and mainly lived there, but also in Boston and New York. In 1837 and again in 1845 he travelled to Europe, visiting England on both occasions. As one of the first to recognize the American landscape as a viable subject for painting, he is regarded as a forerunner of the *Hudson River School. His best-known painting is probably *In Nature's Wonderland* (Detroit Inst. of Arts, 1835).

Dove, Arthur (1880–1946). American painter. For most of his career he earned his living as a commercial illustrator and did not paint full-time until 1930. He visited Europe in 1907–9, coming into contact with *Fauvism and other avant-garde movements, and in 1910 began to paint abstract pictures. They were the first abstracts in American art and are somewhat similar to *Kandinsky's work of the same date. In 1910 he had his first one-man show at *Stieglitz's *291* Gallery and in 1913 he exhibited at the *Armory Show. His abstractions are based on natural forms, suggesting the rhythms of nature with their pulsating shapes (*Sand Barge*, Phillips coll., Washington, 1930). In the 1940s he experimented with a more geometric type of abstraction (*That Red One*, William H. Lane Foundation, Leominster, Mass., 1944).

Downman, John (*c*.1750–1824). English portrait painter. Most of his paintings are small society portraits, many of them being in a technique he perfected using pencil or charcoal lightly tinted with water-colour (four examples of the type are in the Wallace Collection, London). He practised in Cambridge, Chester, Exeter, London, Plymouth, and Wrexham and travelled widely about the country, staying in great houses and often painting a series of portraits of members of the family.

Dreier, Katherine S. (1877–1952). American painter, remembered more for her role in organizing exhibitions of modern art than for her own work. She became an ardent supporter of avant-garde art as a result of the *Armory Show, where she met Marcel *Duchamp, and in 1920 together with him and *Man Ray she founded the *Société Anonyme. The travelling exhibitions which she organized through the Société Anonyme were a potent factor in bringing a knowledge of European abstract painters to American artists and public. Her portrait of Duchamp (1918) is in The Museum of Modern Art, New York.

Drost, Willem (active mid 17th cent.). Dutch painter. Almost nothing is known of his life, and only about half a dozen paintings (and an even smaller number of etchings) are recognized as being by him. All the works that are dated are of the 1650s, and it would seem that at this time Drost was one of *Rembrandt's closest and most talented followers. His *Portrait of a Young Woman* in the Wallace Collection, London, bears a false Rembrandt signature.

Drouais, François-Hubert (1727–75). French portrait painter. He trained under *Boucher (among others) and became a rival to *Nattier as a fashionable portraitist. His portraits have a gracious and artificial charm and at their best bear comparison with those of Boucher. He was particularly successful with children, but his best-known painting is probably the very grand portrait of Mme de Pompadour in the National Gallery, London (1763–4), completed after the sitter's death. His father and his son were painters. **Hubert Drouais** (1699–1767) had a successful career as a *miniaturist and *pastel portraitist. **Germain Drouais** (1763–88) was a favourite pupil of *David's and won the *Prix de Rome, but his promising career was cut short when he died of malaria aged 25.

drying oils. Fatty oils of vegetable origin which harden into a solid transparent substance on exposure to air and are much used as *vehicles in paints and varnishes. They do not dry in the sense of losing moisture but by oxidation together with certain molecular changes. The vegetable oils which have been in commonest use since the Middle Ages are *linseed, *walnut, and *poppy. Almond and olive oil are not suitable as they do not harden. Sunflower oil has been used in Russia but has never become popular. Small amounts of castor oil have sometimes been used to give elasticity to *varnishes.

drypoint. A method of engraving on copper in which the design is scratched directly into the plate with a sharp tool that is held like a pen. It is a more spontaneous technique than *line engraving, but not so fluent as *etching. A distinctive feature of drypoint is the 'burr' or rough, upturned edge of the furrow made by the cutting tool. This produces a soft, rich quality in the print, but because it soon wears down only a limited number of good impressions can be taken. Drypoint, which seems to have originated in the last quarter of the 15th cent., has often been used in combination with other processes; *Rembrandt, for example, often touched up his etchings in drypoint.

Drysdale, Sir Russell (1912–81). Australian painter. He was born in England of a family that had long associations with Australia and he spent several years of his childhood there. The family settled in Melbourne in 1923 and Drysdale moved to Sydney in 1940. From then he devoted himself full-time to painting and his work became well known throughout Australia during the 1940s. It revived in a new fashion the tradition of hardship, tragedy, and melancholy associated with the Australian bush that had been obscured by the much more optimistic interpretation developed by the city-based painters of the *Heidelberg School during the 1890s. In 1949 Kenneth *Clark, on a visit to Sydney, encouraged Drysdale to exhibit in London and late in 1950 he held an exhibition at the Leicester Galleries. It is to this exhibition that the beginning of a new interest in Australian art in London, which reached a peak in the early 1960s, may be traced. During the 1950s Drysdale travelled widely throughout Australia, drawing and painting the life of the interior. The plight of the Australian Aborigines in contact with white settlement became an important and continuing theme in such paintings as *Mullaloonah Tank* (Art Gal. of South Australia, Adelaide, 1953). During the early 1960s he experienced periods of depression accentuated by the death of his son and his wife. From that time he continued to broaden and develop the themes and methods with which he began in the 1940s.

Dubois, Ambroise. See FONTAINEBLEAU, SCHOOL OF.

Dubreuil, Toussaint. See FOUNTAINE-BLEAU, SCHOOL OF.

Dubuffet, Jean (1901–85). French artist. He studied painting as a young man but was engaged mainly in the wine trade until 1942 when he took up art seriously again, his first exhibition coming in 1946. He made a cult of *Art Brut ('raw art'), the products of psychotics or wholly untrained persons, and of graffiti, preferring untrained spontaneity to professional skill. His own work is aggressively reminiscent of such 'popular' art. Often he incorporated materials such as sand and plaster into his paintings, and he has also produced large sculptural works made from junk materials. His work initially provoked outrage, and he stands out as the pioneer and chief representative of the tendencies in modern art to depreciate traditional artistic materials and methods and, as he himself said in 1957, to 'bring all disparaged values into the limelight'. There are several examples of his work in the Tate Gallery.

Duccio di Buoninsegna (active 1278–1318/19). The most famous painter of the Sienese School. Little is known of his life: records of several commissions survive and he is known to have been fined on several occasions for various minor offences (one perhaps involving sorcery), but only one fully documented work by him survives. This is the famous *Maestà commissioned by Siena Cathedral in 1308 and completed in 1311. Today most of this elaborate double-sided altarpiece is in the cathedral museum, but several of the *predella panels are scattered outside Italy—in London (NG), Washington (NG), and elsewhere. The whole of the front of the main panel is occupied by a scene of the Virgin and Child in majesty surrounded by angels and saints, and corresponding to this on the back are twenty-six scenes from Christ's Passion. Originally there were subsidiary scenes from Christ's life above and below the main panel. The whole work is of a superb standard of craftsmanship, and the exquisite colouring and supple draughtsmanship create effects of great beauty. Although Duccio drew much on *Byzantine tradition, he introduced a new warmth of human feeling that gives him a role in Sienese painting comparable to that of *Giotto in Florentine painting. He re-creates the biblical stories with great vividness, and as no one else before him he succeeds in making the setting of a scene—a room or a hillside—a dramatic constituent of the action, so that figures and surroundings are intimately bound up together. The other main work attributed to Duccio is the large *Rucellai Madonna* (Uffizi, Florence), which is probably the picture documented as having been painted by him for Sta Maria Novella, Florence, in 1285. Several other smaller panels can be attributed to him with a fair degree of confidence, but there is no evidence that he ever worked in fresco. His influence in Siena was enormous (*Simone Martini was his greatest disciple) and reached as far as France, notably in the work of *Pucelle.

Duchamp, Marcel (1887–1968). French artist and art theorist, the brother of Raymond *Duchamp-Villon and Jacques *Villon. Although Duchamp produced few works (most of them are now in the Philadelphia Museum of Art), he is regarded as one of the most potent figures in 20th-cent. art because of the originality and fertility of his ideas. He sprang into notoriety with his *Nude descending a Staircase* (Philadelphia), combining the principles of *Cubism and *Futurism, which had a *succès de scandale* at the *Armory Show in 1913. From this time he abandoned conventional media and became with *Picabia the leader of the New York *Dada movement. In 1912 he invented the *ready-made with a bicycle wheel mounted on a kitchen stool, and went on to show a bottle rack bought in a Paris store, and a urinal—the last was entitled *Fountain* and signed R. Mutt. Another of his celebrated provocative gestures was adding a moustache and beard and an obscene inscription to a reproduction of the *Mona Lisa*. So far as it is possible to derive a theoretical basis from the incoherences of Dadaism, the concept of the ready-made seems to derive from Duchamp's conviction that life is meaningless absurdity and from his repudiation of all the values of art. From 1915 to 1923 he was engaged on his major work, a painting and construct on glass with esoteric or obscure symbolism which he called *The Bride stripped bare by her Bachelors, even*, also known as *The Large Glass* (Philadelphia: a facsimile by Richard *Hamilton is in the Tate, London). During the 1920s he combined the idea of the machine

137   DUGHET, GASPARD

with that of futility, constructing elaborate mechanical gadgets which have been seen as forerunners of *Kinetic art. However, after leaving *The Large Glass* 'definitively unfinished' he virtually abandoned art for chess. He was a good enough player to represent France in four chess Olympiads and his obsession for the game intensified as he grew older. Of his marriage in 1927 his friend *Man Ray wrote: 'Duchamp spent most of the one week they lived together studying chess problems, and his bride, in desperate retaliation, got up one night when he was asleep and glued the chess pieces to the board. They were divorced three months later.' After his death it was discovered that Duchamp had worked in secret for twenty years on *Etant Donnés* (Given that . . .), a large mixed-media construction; it is now in Philadelphia. Duchamp became a legend in his own lifetime. By his life as much as his artistic achievements he did more than any other one man to change the concept of art in the 20th cent. He tried, unsuccessfully as he himself recognized, to destroy the mystique of taste, and in 1962 said: 'When I discovered ready-mades I thought to discourage aesthetics . . . I threw the bottle rack and the urinal in their faces and now they admire them for their aesthetic beauty.' Nevertheless, he revolutionized notions of art and beauty.

Duchamp-Villon, Raymond (1876–1918). French sculptor, the brother of Jacques *Villon and Marcel *Duchamp. After studying medicine he took up sculpture in 1898. From 1905 to 1913 he exhibited at the *Salon d'Automne with works of expressive naturalism which at first differed little from those of others who were seeking a way to escape from the influence of *Rodin. From about 1910, however, he came under the influence of the *Cubist group and by 1914 he was recognized as pre-eminent among the small number of Cubist sculptors. His most celebrated work is *The Horse* (casts in Tate, London, MOMA, New York, and elsewhere, 1914), which completed his move towards abstraction. This has been called by G. H. Hamilton (*Painting and Sculpture in Europe 1880–1940*) 'the most powerful piece of sculpture produced by any strictly Cubist artist', and has been compared to the work of the *Futurists, particularly that of *Boccioni, who had

met Duchamp-Villon in 1913. In the success with which it expresses the taut energy of muscular movement in static forms it certainly achieves at least one of the things at which the Futurists were aiming in their attempts to represent 'the dynamics of movement'. Duchamp-Villon served with the French army in the First World War and died from blood-poisoning after contracting typhoid fever.

Dufy, Raoul (1877–1953). French painter, graphic artist, and textile designer. His early work was in an *Impressionist manner, but he became a convert to *Fauvism in 1905 under the influence of *Matisse. In 1908 he worked with *Braque at L'Estaque in a more sober style influenced by *Cézanne, but thereafter he soon developed the highly personal manner for which he became famous. It is characterized by rapid calligraphic drawing on backgrounds of bright colours thinly washed on a white ground, and was well suited to the glittering scenes of luxury and pleasure he favoured. He was a well-established figure by the mid 1920s and the accessibility and *joie de vivre* of his work helped to popularize modern art. In 1910 he made friends with the fashion designer Paul Poiret, who interested him in textile design, and he worked as a designer for Bianchini-Férier, a silk manufacturer of Lyons, exerting a considerable influence on the world of fashion. He also made numerous book illustrations, notably for *Apollinaire's *Bestiaire* in 1910.

dugento. See QUATTROCENTO.

Dughet, Gaspard (called Gaspard Poussin) (1615–75). French landscape painter, draughtsman, and etcher, born and active in Rome. He was a pupil (c.1631–5) of Nicolas *Poussin, who married his sister in 1630 and whose surname he adopted. His work combines something of the romanticism of *Claude with the solidity of Poussin, although he preferred a more rugged type of scenery to that favoured by either of his great contemporaries. The combination brought him considerable success in his lifetime, and in the 18th cent. his reputation stood very high, particularly in England. His work was avidly sought by English collectors and he influenced painters such as Richard *Wilson and the supporters of the *picturesque. The only works by Dughet that are securely dated are his frescos (begun 1647) on the *History of the Carmelite Order* in S. Martino ai Monti, Rome (these too are landscapes), and it has proved difficult to establish a chronology for him.

Dujardin, Karel (*c*.1622–78). Dutch painter and etcher of landscapes, cattle, *genre scenes, portraits, and religious subjects, active mainly in Amsterdam. He is best known for his small paintings of humble bucolic scenes set in an Italianate or a Dutch landscape and diffused with a clear, warm light. These works reveal the impact of *Berchem (who was probably his teacher) and his admiration for Paulus *Potter and Adriaen van de *Velde. He was an excellent portraitist and his large religious pictures show that his long visit to Italy in the 1640s had made him *au fait* with the picture-making techniques of Italian *Baroque. In 1674 he made a second visit to Italy and died in Venice four years later. Like so many of the 17th-cent. Dutch artists who made the journey to Italy, Dujardin was a Catholic.

Dumonstier. Family of French portrait painters, who carried on the tradition of the *Clouets into the middle of the 17th cent. About a dozen members of the family are recorded and several of them held court appointments. The earliest of any significance was **Geoffroy** (*c*.1510–60), and the last and best-known member of the dynasty was **Daniel** (1574–1646).

Dunlap, William (1766–1839). American artist and writer. He had a varied career, much of it being spent as a successful dramatist and theatrical manager, but in the context of art history he is remembered mainly for his *History of the Rise and Progress of the Arts of Design in the United States* (1834). This is the most valuable source-book on the subject, rich in information and anecdote, and has earned him the nickname 'the American *Vasari'. His varied work as a painter and engraver is now virtually forgotten.

Dunoyer de Segonzac, André (1884–1974). French painter, designer, and graphic artist. Although he went through a period of *Cubist influence early in his career, he became an upholder of the

*naturalistic tradition in a period dominated by anti-naturalistic tendencies. His oil paintings (landscape, still life, and figures) were usually executed in thick paint with little or no *medium and emphasize the weight and earthiness of the forms. His water-colours and etchings, however, were more elegant and spontaneous, and had a wider range of subject-matter, including dancers and boxers. He was a prolific book illustrator, did theatre and ballet designs, and was in charge of a camouflage unit in the First World War.

Dupont, Gainsborough (1754–97). English painter and engraver, the nephew and only assistant of Thomas *Gainsborough. He made copies and *mezzotints of his uncle's pictures, completed others left unfinished at his death, and painted some original works in his manner, notably several portraits of actors, examples of which are in the Garrick Club, London.

Duquesnoy, François (1594–1643). Flemish sculptor, active mainly in Rome, where he settled in 1618. He was a friend of *Poussin, sharing a house with him for a time, and became a leading figure in circles devoted to Classical art. Alongside *Algardi he came to be recognized as the outstanding sculptor in Rome after the great *Bernini (who employed him on the decoration of the *Baldacchino in St Peter's in 1627–8), and as with Algardi, his style was much more restrained and less *Baroque than Bernini's. Duquesnoy's two major works are the statues of *Sta Susanna* (Sta Maria di Loreto, 1629–33) and *St Andrew* (St Peter's, 1629–40). He also produced many small bronzes that spread his fame. Duquesnoy was particularly renowned for his handling of *putti, and it is curious that someone who so unaffectedly depicted the beauty and charm of children seems to have been mentally unstable; he was a chronic procrastinator and the diarist John Evelyn, visiting Rome in 1644, said that he 'died mad' because his *St Andrew* 'was placed in a bad light'. Duquesnoy's father and brother were sculptors; **Jerome I** (before 1570–1641) and **Jerome II** (1602–54). His father is remembered mainly for the famous *Manneken-pis* fountain (1619) behind the town hall in Brussels. His brother worked with François in Rome and took a somewhat diluted Baroque style back to Flanders with him. The tomb of

Bishop Anton Trest in Ghent Cathedral (c.1640–54) is considered his finest work. He is perhaps best remembered, however, for his sticky end; he was executed by strangulation in Ghent for committing sodomy in a church.

Durand, Asher B. (1796–1886). American painter and engraver. His early work was mainly as an engraver and he established his reputation with his print after John *Trumbull's *Signing of the Declaration of Independence* and with portraits of eminent contemporaries. In the 1830s he turned increasingly to painting. At first he worked mainly as a portraitist, but then devoted himself to landscape, becoming a leading figure of the *Hudson River School. Thomas *Cole was a major source of inspiration, and Durand's most famous painting, *Kindred Spirits* (New York Public Library, 1849), was painted as a memorial to him; it shows Cole and the poet William Cullen Bryant admiring spectacular scenery in the Catskill Mountains, New York State.

Durand-Ruel, Paul (1831–1922). The best-known member of a family of French picture dealers, renowned as the first dealer to give consistent support to the *Impressionists. He took over the family firm in 1865 and established himself as the main dealer of the *Barbizon School painters. It was one of these—*Daubigny—who introduced him to *Monet and *Pissarro when all four had taken refuge in England from the Franco-Prussian War of 1870–1. For years Durand-Ruel was such a solitary champion of the Impressionists that he often came near to bankruptcy, but in 1886 he achieved a breakthrough with an exhibition of their work in New York, the success of which encouraged him to open a branch of his firm there. This played a major role in building up some of the great American collections of Impressionists. After Durand-Ruel's death, Monet wrote to the dealer's son: 'I shall never forget all that my friends and I owe to your father, in a very special way.'

Dürer, Albrecht (1471–1528). German graphic artist and painter, the greatest figure of *Renaissance art in northern Europe. Son of a goldsmith and godson of Anthony Koberger, one of Germany's foremost printers and publishers, he attended a Latin school where he met the humanist and poet Willibald Pirckheimer, who was to become his lifelong friend and correspondent, and then was apprenticed when 15 years old to the leading painter and book illustrator in his native Nuremberg, Michael *Wolgemut. These four men exercised a powerful influence on Dürer's genius and determined to some degree his artistic career. The father must not only have taught him the rudiments of drawing, as is borne out by the young boy's self-portrait (Albertina, Vienna, 1484), but also instilled into him that devotion to exact and meticulous detail which is the mark of a goldsmith's work. From Wolgemut, whose influence was mainly technical, he learned the painter's trade and the craft of *woodcut. Through Koberger he had access to the world of books and learning, and Pirckheimer directed these interests towards Italy and the new humanism. From the beginning Dürer's world reached well beyond the confines of the normal medieval workshop.

After completing his apprenticeship Dürer set out in 1490 on the usual bachelor's journey. He went to the Upper Rhine in search of Germany's leading painter and engraver Martin *Schongauer, who, however, had just died when Dürer reached Colmar in 1493, and he worked for a while as a book illustrator in Basle and Strasburg. After his return to Nuremberg and his marriage (1494) he went on a short visit to north Italy and then set up a workshop in his native town. Though also active as a painter—the self-portrait of 1500 and the *Paumgärtner Altar* of 1504 (both Alte Pinakothek, Munich) being the most important early works—he was for years preoccupied with woodcuts and engravings, among which the large series of the *Apocalypse* (1498), the *Great Passion* (1510), and the *Life of the Virgin* (1510) take first place. In spite of the traditional subject-matter, they are revolutionary in approach, size, and subtlety of technique. They are alive with dramatic tension and a pathos which is not only the result of his close study of *Mantegna's engravings but also an expression of his participation in the spiritual life of his day.

At the same time he began to be occupied by the *Renaissance problems of *perspective, of *ideal beauty, of proportion and harmony. In 1505–6 he made another visit to Venice, returning with a system of human proportions which he must have met with in circles close to *Leonardo. His great admiration for Giovanni *Bellini enhanced his sense of colour and the *Feast of the Rose-garlands* (NG, Prague, 1506), done in Venice, was meant to compete with the best Venetian painting. Most of his landscape water-colours also belong to this period. They are unique in several ways: as personal records, in their choice of medium and subject, but most of all since they seem to have been made for sheer pleasure and not—as was usual with sketches in those days—with larger works in view.

By now Dürer was a well-established artist. Commissions for large altar-paintings came not only from his home town of Nuremberg (*Adoration of the Trinity*, Kunsthistorisches Mus., Vienna, 1511), but from further afield, and after c.1512 his most important patron was the emperor Maximilian. For him Dürer designed an enormous triumphal arch laden with history and allegory, and a triumphal procession, executed in woodcut by members of Dürer's workshop and others. At the same time his creative spirit found outlets entirely of his own choosing in such celebrated engravings as *The Knight, Death and the Devil* (1513), *St Jerome in his Study* (1514), and the brooding and enigmatic allegory of the *Melencolia I* (1514). In these works he achieved a mastery of *line engraving that has never been surpassed, rivalling the richness and textures of painting. During these years he also experimented with a new technique, *etching, and found in it the means to convey, in an *Agony in the Garden* (1515), his troubled religious feelings. There is other evidence to tell us how deeply Dürer felt during the years of the Reformation and we know from one of his own letters that liberation and consolation came to him finally through Luther's writings.

In 1520–1 a journey to the court of the emperor Charles V to ask for a renewal of his pension took him to the Netherlands, where he was fêted as the acknowledged leader of his profession. The day-to-day diary that Dürer kept on this tour, together with his drawings showing the people and places he saw, is the first record of its kind in the history of art. After his return to Nuremberg Dürer was busy with portraits and with the designs for yet another *Passion* series, but his main task was the two panels with the *Four Apostles* (Alte Pinakothek, Munich) which he presented to his native town in 1526, an action without precedent. Here Dürer summed up his life's work: the study of the ideal human figure and the expression of a deeply felt religious message.

It was only natural that a man of Dürer's cast of mind should pursue theoretical studies throughout his life, and that among them—according to his own testimony—proportion should take first place, other things being attempted only 'if God should give me time'. The *Underweyssung der Messung* (Treatise on Measurement) (1525) was published by Dürer himself, but the *Vier Bücher von menschlicher Proportion* (Four Books on Human Proportion) (1528) was published posthumously. When Dürer died in 1528, though he was widely known as a painter, his real fame rested on his graphic work, which was used in the north and south very much as pattern-books had been. Erasmus called him 'the *Apelles of black lines', the highest praise that a student of the ancients could give to any artist.

Duveen, Joseph (Baron Duveen) (1869–1939). English art dealer, patron, and philanthropist. In 1886 he entered the firm of his father, Sir **Joseph Duveen** (1843–1908), and with his enormous energy and great gift for salesmanship expanded it into the largest firm of art dealers in the world, operating on an unprecedented scale. He employed Bernard *Berenson to give his seal of authenticity to the *Renaissance paintings he sold and he was the main agent in forming the collections of such fabulously wealthy Americans as *Frick, *Kress, and Andrew *Mellon. Duveen's benefactions to the arts were also on a princely scale. In addition to giving many pictures to national collections, he paid for extensions or new galleries at the *National Gallery, the *National Portrait Gallery, the *Tate Gallery, and the *British Museum (to house the *Elgin Marbles). He also bore the cost of decorations at the *Wallace Collection and of Rex *Whistler's murals at the Tate Gallery and endowed a chair for the history of art at London University.

Duvet, Jean (1485–1561/70). French engraver and goldsmith, sometimes called the Master of the Unicorn from his series of engravings (probably from the 1540s) on the medieval theme of the hunting of the unicorn. Little is known of his life (he lived mainly in his native Langres and in Dijon), but the *Renaissance influence in his early work strongly suggests that he spent some time in Italy. His most famous work, a set of twenty-four engravings illustrating the *Apocalypse*, published at Lyons in 1561, is, however, completely different in style. They borrow many features from *Dürer's series on the *Apocalypse*, but are a world apart in spirit, for Duvet treats the subject with a visionary intensity and expressive freedom that seems to anticipate *Blake (who may well have known Duvet's work). His work reflects the disturbed religious conditions which prevailed in Langres and is in complete contrast to the mannered elegance of the School of *Fontainebleau, then the dominant force in French art.

Duyster, Willem Cornelisz. (1599–1635). Dutch painter of *genre scenes and portraits, active mainly in his native Amsterdam. Most of his paintings depict soldiers, sometimes in action, but more usually drinking, gaming, or wooing. His delicate skill at painting textiles, his ability to characterize individuals, and his power to express subtle psychological relationships between them, suggest that if he had not been carried off by the plague in his mid 30s he might well have rivalled *Terborch. There are two examples of his fairly rare work in the National Gallery, London.

Dyce, William (1806–64). Scottish painter, designer, and art educationalist. He made several visits to Italy and was profoundly impressed by Renaissance painting, especially that of *Raphael, and by the problem of fresco in relation to its architectural setting. He also came into contact with the *Nazarenes, whose Christian primitivism he tried to acclimatize in Scotland. Dyce was widely talented; he was an accomplished musician and wrote a prize-winning paper on electromagnetism, but for some time he was successful mainly as a rather conventional portraitist and it was not until after 1840 that he was able to devote himself to more ambitious work, producing decorative schemes for the Houses of Parliament, several churches, and the royal residences Buckingham Palace and Osborne on the Isle of Wight (he

was a favourite of Prince Albert). He was commissioned by the Council of the newly founded Government School of Design, which included *Eastlake, *Chantrey, and *Callcott, to investigate state schools in France, Prussia, and Bavaria, and was appointed Director in 1840 on his return. His ideas on design were much respected, and although he had little influence on manufacturers, his training of teachers was important. As a painter he was versatile, for as well as portraits and history pictures he painted works as varied as the delightfully sentimental *Titian's First Essay in Colour* (Aberdeen Art Gallery, 1856–7) and *Pegwell Bay, Kent* (Tate, London, 1859–60), one of the most remarkable of all Victorian landscapes. His bright colours and naturalistic detail formed a bridge between the Nazarenes and the *Pre-Raphaelites, but his design is usually stronger and his high-mindedness more convincing than in the works of either.

Dyck, Sir Anthony van (1599–1641). Apart from *Rubens, the greatest Flemish painter of the 17th cent. In 1609 he began his apprenticeship with Hendrick van *Balen in his native Antwerp and he was exceptionally precocious. Although he did not become a master in the painters' guild until 1618, there is evidence that he was working independently for some years before this, even though this was forbidden by guild regulations. Probably soon after graduating he entered Rubens's workshop. Strictly speaking he should not be called Rubens's pupil, as he was an accomplished painter when he went to work for him. Nevertheless the two years he spent with Rubens were decisive and Rubens's influence upon his painting is unmistakable, although van Dyck's style was always less energetic. In 1620 van Dyck went to London, where he spent a few months in the service of James I (1566–1625), then in 1621 to Italy, where he travelled a great deal, and toned down the Flemish robustness of his early pictures to create the refined and elegant style which remained characteristic of his work for the rest of his life. His great series of *Baroque portraits of the Genoese aristocracy established the 'immortal' type of nobleman, with proud mien and slender figure. The years 1628–32 were spent mainly at Antwerp. From 1632 until his death he was in

England—except for visits to the Continent—as painter to Charles I, from whom he received a knighthood. During these years he was occupied almost entirely with portraits. Perhaps the strongest evidence of his power as a portraitist is the fact that today we see Charles I and his court through van Dyck's eyes. It is customary to accuse van Dyck of invariably flattering his sitters, but not all his patrons would have agreed. When the Countess of Sussex saw the portrait (now lost) van Dyck painted of her she felt 'very ill-favourede' and 'quite out of love with myself, the face is so bige and so fate that it pleases me not at all. It lokes lyke on of the windes puffinge—but truly I think tis lyke the originale.' Van Dyck's influence on English portraiture has been profound and lasting: *Gainsborough, in particular, revered him, but he was an inspiration to many others until the early 20th cent., when society portraiture ceased to be a major form of artistic expression. He also painted religious and mythological subjects, however, and a surprising facet of his activity is revealed by his landscapes in water-colour (BM, London). His *Iconography* (1645) is a series of etchings or engravings of his famous contemporaries. Van Dyck etched some of the plates himself, and many more were engraved after his drawings and oil sketches.

Dying Gaul. Marble statue in the Capitoline Museum, Rome, showing a wounded warrior supporting himself wearily on one arm. First recorded in Rome in 1623, it soon became one of the most celebrated and copied of *antique works. It is a Roman copy of a Greek work in the *Pergamene style of the late 3rd cent. BC. The statue is sometimes called the 'Dying Gladiator', but this is a misnomer as the hairstyle and accessories are scrupulously Gallic. It was among the works removed from Italy by Napoleon and was in Paris from 1798 to 1815. Unlike many once famous antique statues, the *Dying Gaul* is still admired, particularly for its sense of pathos.

E

Eakins, Thomas (1844–1916). American painter. Eakins is regarded by most critics as the outstanding American painter of the 19th cent. and by many as the greatest his country has yet produced. Born in Philadelphia, he passed the major part of his life there with the exception of a period of training in Europe, 1866–70. He studied in Paris with *Gérôme, but learnt most from the Spanish painters *Velázquez and *Ribera, absorbing a precise and un-compromising sense for actuality which he applied to portraiture and *genre pictures of the life of his native city (boating and bathing were favourite themes). He began teaching at the Pennsylvania Academy of Fine Arts in 1876 and was attacked for his radical ideas, particularly his insistence on working from nude models. In 1886 he was forced to resign after allowing a mixed class to draw from a completely nude male model. Eakins's quest for realism led him to study anatomy and make full use of *Muybridge's photographic researches, but the scientific bent in his work is of less importance than his honesty and depth of characterization. His portraits are often compared to Rembrandt's because of their dramatic play of sombre lighting and sense of inner truth. The most famous of his paintings is *The Gross Clinic* (Jefferson Medical Coll., Philadelphia, 1875), which aroused controversy because of its un-sparing depiction of surgery, an experience that was repeated with *The Agnew Clinic* (Univ. of Pennsylvania, 1889). Because of financial support from his father, Eakins could continue on his chosen course despite public abuse, but much of his later career was spent working in bitter isolation. It was only near the end of his life that he achieved recognition as a great master, and in the first two decades of the 20th cent. his desire to 'peer deeper into the heart of American life' was reflected in the work of the *Ash-can School and other Realist painters. As well as being a painter and photographer, Eakins also made a few sculptures. His wife, **Susan Hannah Mac-dowell Eakins** (1851–1938), whom he married in 1884, was also a painter and photographer, as well as an accomplished pianist.

Earl, Ralph (1751–1801). American painter, active in Connecticut, Mas-sachusetts, New York, and Vermont, and also in England (1778–85), when his loyalty to the British put his life in danger in his homeland. He painted landscapes and battle scenes of the Revolution, but was primarily a portraitist. Although his style became softer and more sophisticated after studying with *West in London, his work generally has a sincerity and freshness of vision that makes him one of the finest American artists of the 18th cent. His presentation of character is extremely forthright and his portraits convey the immense pride his New England sitters took in their pos-sessions. Earl's personal life was a disaster. He was imprisoned for debt and died an alcoholic after deserting both of his wives in turn. Other members of his family were artists, notably his brother **James** (1761–96) and his son **Ralph E. W. Earl** (c.1785–1838), who is remembered mainly for his portraits of President Andrew Jackson, whose niece he had married.

Early Christian art Term generally ap-plied to Christian art from the 3rd cent. AD until about 750, particularly in Italy and the Western Mediterranean. The art of the eastern Empire during this time is termed *Byzantine art, but there is no hard-and-fast demarcation between the two traditions.

Earthwork (or Land Art). Type of art in which instead of using the land as a site providing the environment for a work of art, the land itself is fashioned into the art work. It emerged in the late 1960s partly in consequence of growing dissatisfaction with the deliberate boredom cultivated by the simple, undetailed forms of *Minimal art and partly as an expression of dis-enchantment with the sophisticated tech-nology of an industrial culture. Earthworks art proper is obviously unsuitable for exhibition in a gallery except by photographs, and owing to the difficulty of putting Earthworks schemes into practice they often exist only as projects. Hence the affinity with *Conceptual art is close. Among those works of Land Art that have been carried out the best known is probably Robert *Smithson's *Spiral Jetty* (1970).

easel. Stand on which a painting is supported while the artist works on it. The oldest representation of an easel is on an Egyptian relief of the Old Kingdom (c.2600–2150 BC). *Renaissance illustrations of the artist at work show all kinds of contrivances, the commonest being the three-legged easel with pegs such as we still use today. Light folding easels were not made until the 18th and 19th cents., when painters took to working out of doors. The studio easel, a 19th-cent. invention, is a heavy piece of furniture which runs on castors or wheels, and served to impress the clients of portrait painters. Oil painters need an easel which will support the canvas almost vertically or tip it slightly forward to prevent reflection from the wet paint, whereas the water-colourist must be able to lay his paper nearly flat so that the wet paint will not run down. The term 'easel-painting' is applied to any picture small enough to have been painted on a standard easel.

Eastlake, Sir Charles Lock (1793–1865). English painter, art historian, and administrator. He studied under *Haydon and early became famous with his *Napoleon on board the Bellerophon* (Earl of Roseberry Coll., 1815), made from sketches when he witnessed Napoleon on board ship (in Eastlake's native Plymouth) *en route* to exile in St Helena. Using the proceeds from the sale of this work he lived in Rome 1816–30, and there painted picturesque scenes of the Roman Campagna, often peopled by *banditti*, that became very popular in England. After his return to England, however, he turned increasingly to administration and achieved a remarkable record as a public servant. Most notably he was President of the Royal Academy from 1850 and Director of the National Gallery (the first holder of this post) from 1855 until his death. Among his writings, *Materials for a History of Oil Painting* (1847) was a pioneer work. His informed purchases of early Italian paintings for the National Gallery were largely responsible for its outstanding representation in this area. His wife, **Elizabeth**, *née* Rigby (1809–93), was in her own right a figure in the literary-artistic world of the day. She wrote several books on art and translated *Waagen's *Treasures of Art in Great Britain*. Eastlake's nephew **Charles Lock Eastlake** (1836–1906) was Keeper of the National Gallery, 1878–98, and published several works on art and decoration, the best known of which was *Hints on Household Taste* (1868), in which he advocated quality of materials and workmanship. It was highly influential in England and even more so in America, although so-called 'Eastlake furniture' often has little to do with his ideas.

Eckersberg, Christoffer Wilhelm (1783–1853). Danish painter. After being trained in Copenhagen and studying in Paris (1810–13) under J.-L. *David, he continued his studies in Rome (1814), where he executed a masterly portrait of his friend *Thorvaldsen (Royal Academy, Copenhagen, 1815). Returning to Copenhagen in 1816, he occupied himself mainly with portraits, minutely rendering the features of his models with a *Neoclassic feeling for clarity and purity of line. He also painted many landscapes, however (as he had done in Rome), and as an influential teacher at the Copenhagen Academy (from 1818) he introduced painting from nature into the curriculum. His pupils included J. C. *Dahl and Christen *Købke.

eclectic, eclecticism. Terms in criticism for a person or style which conflates features borrowed from various sources. Such a style often arises from the overt or tacit doctrine that the excellences of great masters can be selected and combined in one work of art. After *Vasari had praised *Raphael for his skill in selecting the best from the art of his predecessors, it became commonplace to use the same formula in eulogies of other artists. Thus it was said that *Tintoretto had set himself to combine the drawing of *Michelangelo with the colour of *Titian. In the 18th cent. 'eclectics' became a label for the *Carracci family and their Bolognese followers, and gradually the term came to be used mainly pejoratively, implying lack of originality. Such usage has been abandoned in serious criticism, and it is clear that the Carracci never adopted eclecticism as the fundamental principle of their school. As Denis *Mahon has said: 'Annibale Carracci, the greatest member of the family and one of the founders of 17th-cent. painting, was . . . contemptuous of art theory, and (far from being a dispenser of learned recipes and synthetic systems) was in practice one of the most insatiable experimentalists known to the history of art.'

École de Paris. See PARIS, SCHOOL OF.

écorché figure (French: 'flayed'). A representation of a figure without the skin, displaying the muscles. Drawings, prints, and statues of such figures, both human and animal (horses were particularly popular), were much used in art teaching from the 16th cent. *Stubbs's *écorché* figures of animals are well known and *Houdon made a celebrated human *écorché* statue (Schlossmuseum, Gotha, 1767).

Edelfelt, Albert (1854–1905). Finnish painter, who with *Gallen-Kallela ranks as his country's leading artist in the 19th cent. He trained in Antwerp and then in Paris, where under the influence of his friend *Bastien-Lepage he took up *plein air naturalism. His paintings gave a fresh interpretation of Finnish country life and he sometimes set biblical scenes in the Finnish landscape (*Christ and Mary Magdalene*, Atheneum, Helsinki, 1890). Much of his later work was on themes from Finnish history, a type of patriotic work that was relevant to Russia's growing oppression of his country. Edelfelt was also an outstanding book illustrator and portraitist.

Edelinck, Gerard (1640–1707). Flemish engraver, active mainly in Paris. He was the son-in-law of *Nanteuil and like him was celebrated as a portrait engraver. His prints after the Old Masters are also highly distinguished, the best known being that of *Rubens's copy of *Leonardo's *Battle of Anghiari*.

Eeckhout, Gerbrandt van den (1621–74). Dutch painter, born and active in Amsterdam. He was a pupil of *Rembrandt and, according to *Houbraken, his 'great friend'. His religious paintings were deeply influenced by Rembrandt; *St Peter Healing the Lame* (M. H. De Young Memorial Mus., San Francisco, 1667), for example, shows how well he understood the broad touch and warm colours of the master's mature works. Eeckhout's *genre scenes, on the other hand, are close to *Terborch in style (*The Music Lesson*, Statens Museum for Kunst, Copenhagen, 1655). He was also a successful portraitist.

Egg, Augustus (1816–63). English painter. He painted historical, anecdotal, and literary themes (he was a friend of Dickens and a talented actor), and under the influence of the *Pre-Raphaelites he also turned to overtly moralizing subjects. The most famous of these is the series of three pictures *Past and Present* (Tate, London, 1858), which melodramatically illustrates the dire consequences of adultery.

Eidophusikon. An ingenious system of moving pictures within a proscenium arch which, by a clever disposition of lights, coloured gauzes, and the like imitated landscape and townscape views with varying atmospheric effects at different times of day, to the accompaniment of appropriate musical effects. The inventor was J. P. de *Loutherbourg, who exhibited the Eidophusikon (meaning 'image of nature') in London in 1782 with immediate popular success, appealing to lovers of romantic and *picturesque scenery and deeply impressing both *Gainsborough and *Reynolds.

Eight, The. A group of American painters who exhibited together in 1908, united by opposition to the National Academy of Design and a determination to bring painting back into direct touch with life. The original group consisted of: Arthur B. *Davies, Maurice *Prendergast, Ernest *Lawson, Robert *Henri, George *Luks, William J. *Glackens, John *Sloan, and Everett *Shinn. They were later joined by George Wesley *Bellows. The group came into being when the National Academy of Design rejected the work of Luks, Sloan, and Glackens, and Henri, the dominant personality in the group, in protest withdrew his own pictures from the exhibition of 1907. Arthur B. Davies was then asked to organize an independent exhibition at the Macbeth Gallery in New York. This exhibition, which took place in February 1908 and was the only occasion on which The Eight exhibited together, was subsequently shown by the Pennsylvania

Academy and circulated to eight other museums over a period of a year. The members of the group were not unified stylistically, but they mainly painted contemporary urban life. The exhibition is regarded as an important step in the development of a vigorous native school of American painting in the 20th cent. Glackens, Henri, Luks, Shinn, and Sloan went on to become part of the *Ash-can School.

Elementarism. A modified form of *Neo-Plasticism propounded by van *Doesburg in the mid 1920s. While continuing *Mondrian's restriction to the right angle, Elementarism abandoned his insistence on the use of strict horizontals and verticals. By introducing inclined lines and forms van Doesburg sought to achieve a more dynamic quality by an element of deliberate instability. Mondrian was so offended by this 'heresy' that he left De *Stijl.

Elgin Marbles. Those sculptures of the Parthenon in Athens (most of what had survived) and some other pieces (including a *caryatid from the Erechtheum) which the British diplomat Thomas Bruce, 7th Earl of Elgin (1766–1841), procured from the Turks in 1801–3 and sold to the nation in 1816. The price was £35,000, which was much less than his costs. They are now in the *British Museum. By their exhibition in London original Greek sculpture of the *Classical age first became generally accessible in modern times; until then people had been familiar only with Roman and late *Hellenistic copies. Their first impact was enormous: *Flaxman was bowled over, declaring that compared to the figure of Theseus from the Parthenon the *Apollo Belvedere was 'a dancing master', and *Haydon wrote 'I consider it truly the greatest blessing that ever happened to this country their being brought here.' Many other artists voiced similar opinions, although certain connoisseurs, led by Richard Payne *Knight, were unenthusiastic or even disparaging. 'You have lost your labour, my Lord Elgin', said Payne Knight. 'Your marbles are overrated: they are not Greek: they are Roman of the time of Hadrian.' Although the supporters of the marbles won the day and the sculptures have come to be universally recognized as one of the

summits of ancient art, they have continued to be the subject of controversy on another count—that of the morality or legality of their removal when Greece was under the dominion of a foreign power. Byron wrote of them as 'poor plunder from a bleeding land' (*Childe Harold's Pilgrimage*, Canto ii, 1812), and a campaign to have them restored to Greece is strongly active today. See also PHIDIAS.

Elsheimer, Adam (1578–1610). German painter, etcher, and draughtsman, active mainly in Italy. Although he died young and his output was small he played a key role in the development of 17th-cent. landscape painting. He was born in Frankfurt, where he absorbed the *Coninxloo tradition, and moved to Italy in 1598. In Venice he worked with his countryman *Rottenhammer, then settled in Rome in 1600. His early *Mannerist style gave way to a more direct manner in which he showed great sensitivity to effects of light; his nocturnal scenes are particularly original, bringing out the best in his lyrical temperament, and he is credited with being the first artist to represent the constellations of the night sky accurately (*The Flight into Egypt*, Alte Pinakothek, Munich, 1609). He painted a few pictures in which figures predominate, but generally they are fused into a harmonious unity with their landscape settings. They are invariably on a small scale and on copper (the only exception is a self-portrait in the Uffizi, Florence, of doubtful attribution), but although exquisitely executed they have a grandeur out of all proportion to their size. Elsheimer achieved fame during his lifetime and there are numerous contemporary copies of his works. His paintings were engraved by his pupil and patron, the Dutch amateur artist Count Hendrik Goudt (1585–1648), and Elsheimer himself made a number of etchings. In spite of his popularity he was personally unsuccessful and died in poverty. *Sandrart says he suffered from melancholia and was often unable to work, and Goudt had him imprisoned for debt. *Rubens was a friend of Elsheimer and after his death lamented his 'sin of sloth, by which he has deprived the world of the most beautiful things'; he also wrote 'I have never seen his equal in the realm of small figures, of landscapes, and of so many other subjects.' Both

Rubens (Staatliche Kunstsammlungen, Kassell) and *Rembrandt (NG, Dublin) made paintings of *The Flight into Egypt* inspired by Elsheimer's masterpiece, and his influence is apparent in the work of many other 17th-cent. artists.

emblem. A visual image carrying a symbolic meaning and often accompanied by texts to explain this meaning. In its most typical form the emblem consisted of a picture, a motto, and an explanatory verse called an epigram. For example, one of the most famous emblems depicted a dolphin and an anchor with the motto *Festina Lente* ('Make haste slowly'), to symbolize the idea that maturity is achieved by a combination of the speed and energy of the dolphin and the steadiness and gravity of the anchor. The aim of the emblem therefore was to give symbolic expression to a moral adage. Printed collections of emblems ('emblem books') enjoyed a great vogue in the 16th and 17th cents. and were often used as sources of pictorial imagery. In particular, Cesare Ripa's *Iconologia* (1593, first illustrated edition, 1603) became the standard handbook on *iconography for artists.

emulsion. A liquid in which water is combined with an oily or resinous substance in such a way that they will not separate out. Oil proverbially will not mix with water, but if an emulsifying agent—such as albumen—is added, it will surround the drops of oil and prevent them from coming together. The *medium of *tempera painting is always an emulsion. The natural emulsions used most commonly in painting are egg-yolk and *casein. Both have the advantage that once they have set they are not soluble in water.

enamel. A smooth, glossy material made by fusing glass to a prepared surface, usually of metal. The term is also applied to any object made with, or decorated by, this material. The study of enamelling belongs mainly to the history of jewellery and the decorative arts, but in the Middle Ages enamel was sometimes used for major works, notably *Nicolas of Verdun's Klosterneuburg Altar. Today the word 'enamel' is loosely used of any glossy protective covering such as durable paint or varnish applied to the surface of objects made from metal, wood, etc.

encarnado (Spanish: 'flesh-coloured'). Term applied in Spanish art to the painting of the flesh parts of wooden sculptures in more or less naturalistic colours. The term 'estofado' (literally 'quilted') is applied to the painting of draperies. In the 16th cent. the paint of both flesh and draperies was given a glossy finish, but in the 17th cent. a mat finish was adopted for greater realism. Such work was sometimes done by distinguished painters as well as specialist craftsmen—*encarnadores* and *estofadores*—and *Pacheco was one of the first artists to make this change. See also POLYCHROME.

encaustic painting. Technique of painting with *pigments mixed with hot wax. Its name derives from a Greek word meaning 'burnt in' and it was one of the principal painting techniques of the ancient world. *Pliny describes two methods which were already 'ancient' in his day (one of them on ivory), and a third newer method which had been devised since it became the practice to paint ships, and he records that it stood up to sun, salt, and winds. Encaustic painting was the commonest technique in the early centuries of the Christian era but fell into disuse in the 8th or 9th cent. Since then various attempts have been made to revive it (e.g. by Julius *Schnorr von Carolsfeld, who painted several scenes in encaustic in the Residenz at Munich in 1831). Jasper *Johns has used encaustic in his *Flag* and *Target* paintings, but the technique finds few exponents today, probably because it is too troublesome.

Engelbrechtsz., Cornelis (1468–1533). Netherlandish painter born at Leiden, where he was the leading artist of his day. He served his apprenticeship in Brussels and seems to have returned home through Antwerp. Although his style shows the influence of the Italianate tendencies prevalent at Antwerp, Engelbrechtsen's work has a deeper intensity of emotional feeling that is *Gothic rather than *Mannerist in spirit. Contorted linear rhythms and resonant colouring characterize his highly personal art, which is closer to the *Master of the Virgo inter Virgines than to any Antwerp artist. The altarpieces of *The Crucifixion* and *The Lamentation* in the Municipal Museum, Leiden, are typical of his work. *Lucas van Leyden was his greatest pupil and tends to overshadow his achievements. The other pupils in his large studio included his three sons, **Pieter**, **Cornelis**, and **Lucas**, as well as Lucas van Leyden's brother, Aertgen.

engraving. Term applied in its broadest sense to the various processes of cutting a design into a plate or block of metal or wood, and to the prints taken from these plates or blocks (see PRINT for a classification of these processes). In everyday usage, the term more usually applies to one of the processes, known more technically as *line engraving.

Ensor, James (1860–1949). Belgian painter and printmaker. One of the most original artists of his time, Ensor was one of the formative influences on *Expressionism and was claimed by the *Surrealists as a forerunner, but his work defies classification within any school or group. He was born at Ostend, where his parents (his father was English) kept a souvenir shop, and apart from his training in Brussels rarely left his home town. His early works were mainly bourgeois interiors painted in a thick and vigorous technique. When several were rejected by the Salon in Brussels in 1883, Ensor joined the progressive group Les *Vingt. During the 1880s his subject-matter changed and he began to introduce the fantastic and macabre elements which are chiefly associated with his name. He made much use of carnival masks, grotesque figures, skeletons, and bizarre and monstrous imaginings with a gruesome and ironic humour reminiscent of *Bosch and *Bruegel. The interest in masks probably originated in his parents' shop, but he was also one of the first European artists who appreciated African masks. His paintings, and even more his graphic work, took on a didactic or satirical flavour involving social or religious criticism and his most famous work, the huge *Entry of Christ into Brussels* (Getty Museum, Malibu, 1888) provoked such an outburst of criticism among his associates that he was expelled from Les Vingt. After this Ensor became a recluse and his outlook became misanthropic. His work changed little after about 1900, when he was content to repeat his favourite themes. In 1929 he was created a baron when his *Entry of Christ into Brussels* was first exhibited in public. There is an Ensor museum in Ostend.

entartete Kunst. See DEGENERATE ART.

Environment art. Type of art in which the artist creates a three-dimensional space pre-programmed or mechanically energized in order to enclose the spectator and involve him in a multiplicity of sensory stimulations—visual, auditory, kinetic, tactile, and sometimes olfactory. Environment art, which began to establish itself in the 1960s, was closely linked with spectator involvement, and environments were deliberately planned with a view to forcing the spectator to participate in the *happenings or the 'game'. Allen *Kaprow, who also pioneered the happening, is sometimes credited with originating Environment art, and other leading exponents include *Kienholz and *Oldenburg.

Epstein, Sir Jacob (1880–1959). American-born sculptor who settled in England in 1905 and became a British citizen in 1911. Before then, in 1902–5, he had studied in Paris and visits to the *Louvre aroused an interest in ancient and *primitive sculpture that lasted all his life and powerfully affected his work. His first important commission was executed in 1907–8: eighteen figures (destroyed) for the façade of the British Medical Association's headquarters in the Strand. The nude figures aroused a furore of abuse on the grounds of alleged obscenity and such attacks were to become a feature of his career. His tomb of Oscar Wilde (Père Lachaise Cemetery, Paris, 1912), for example, a magnificently bold and original piece featuring a hovering angel inspired by Assyrian sculpture, was banned as indecent until a bronze plaque had been fixed over the angel's sexual organs. (It was removed in a night raid by a band of artists and poets.) In Paris he met *Picasso, *Modigliani, and *Brancusi and was influenced by their formal simplifications. In England he associated with Wyndham *Lewis and the *Vorticists, and in *The Rock Drill* (Tate, London, 1913–14), a robot-like figure that was originally shown aggressively mounted on an enormous drill, he created his most radical work; he said it symbolized 'the terrible Frankenstein's monster we have made ourselves into'. Epstein's later work was generally much less audacious than this, but his public sculptures were still attacked with monotonous regularity, their expressive use of distortion being offensive to conservative critics even when they were immune to charges of indecency. *Rima*, a memorial to the naturalist W. H. Hudson in Hyde Park (1922), and the enormous bronze group of *St Michael and the Devil* (1958) at Coventry Cathedral are two of his most famous later works. From the 1920s Epstein devoted himself more and more to bronze portrait busts, and these—unlike his monumental works—have always had an appreciative audience. Many of the great figures of the time sat for him and he portrayed them with psychological insight and great mastery of expressive surfaces, carrying on the tradition of *Rodin.

Ernst, Max (1891–1976). German-born artist who became a French citizen in 1958, one of the major figures of *Surrealism. He studied philosophy and psychology at Bonn University, but he became fascinated by the art of psychotics (he visited the insane as part of his studies) and neglected academic work for painting. After serving in the First World War he made himself the leader of the Cologne *Dada group in 1919, working under the name of 'Dadamax', and was responsible for adapting the techniques of *collage and *photomontage to Surrealist uses. In 1922 he settled in Paris, bringing these techniques with him, and he joined the Surrealist movement on its formation in 1924. Even before then, however, he had painted works such as *The Elephant Célèbes* (Tate, London, 1921) that are regarded as Surrealist masterpieces. The irrational and whimsical imagery seen here, in part inspired by childhood memories, occurs also in his highly individual collages. In them he manipulated banal engravings so that the contrast between the archaic appearance of the engraving and the startling novelty he created from it made an impact of strangeness and unreality. In this vein he produced 'collage novels', the best known of which is *Une Semaine de Bonté* (1934). His work was always imaginative and experimental and he was a pioneering exponent of *frottage. In the 1930s sculpture also began to occupy a prominent place in his work. In 1938 he broke with the Surrealist movement, but without any stylistic consequences. He was interned for a short while after the German invasion of France and in 1941 went to New York,

remaining in America until 1948. While in the USA he collaborated with *Breton and *Duchamp in the periodical *VVV* and continued to paint. He was also briefly married (his third of four wives) to the American patron and art dealer Peggy *Guggenheim. After his return to France in 1949 his painting became more lyrical and abstract.

Escher, M. C. (Maurits Cornelis) (1898–1972). Dutch graphic artist. He became well known for his prints that make sophisticated uses of visual illusion, exploiting ambiguity between figure and ground, and between flat pattern and apparent three-dimensional recession. From c.1944 his work took on a *Surrealist flavour as he made brilliant play with optical illusion to represent, for example, staircases that appear to lead both up and down in the same direction. Mathematical concepts played a key role in many of these prints and they have been of considerable interest to mathematicians.

Escorial. A small village about 50 km. north-west of Madrid that gives its name to the palace and monastery built there by Philip II, containing one of the great treasure houses of Spanish art. Begun in 1563 by Juan Bautista de Toledo and finished in 1584 by Juan de Herrera, the huge complex of buildings is constructed entirely of granite and is overpoweringly austere. It comprises a royal palace and mausoleum combined with a Hieronymite monastery, college, and church. The plan is a large rectangle, roughly 160 m. × 200 m., and the layout has been compared to a gridiron, the attribute of St Lawrence, to whom the monastery was dedicated in acknowledgement of Philip II's victory over the French at St Quentin on St Lawrence's day, 1557. Philip II tried unsuccessfully to persuade *Titian to come to Spain to paint altarpieces for the Escorial; and El *Greco was rejected after his *St Maurice* had failed to obtain royal approval (1580). The Italian *Mannerists Pellegrino *Tibaldi and Luca *Cambiaso painted a number of altarpieces and large fresco decorations in the church, cloister, and library. Other altar paintings were executed by Federico *Zuccaro, *Navarrete, and *Sánchez Coello. A school of painting was thus established at the Escorial, in which younger artists such as *Ribalta were trained. The principal sculptors employed by Philip II included Leone and Pompeo *Leoni. In 1688 Claudio *Coello completed the sacristy altarpiece and a few years later Luca *Giordano painted the vaults of the church and the cloister staircase. In the 18th cent. Charles III used the Escorial as a hunting seat and furnished the hitherto unoccupied state rooms of the palace; many of the tapestries with which the walls were hung were designed by *Goya. Other outstanding works of art in the Escorial include a crucifix carved by Benvenuto *Cellini and paintings by *Dürer, *Bosch, Titian, El Greco, *Ribera, and *Velázquez.

Este. Italian family, Lords of Ferrara, Modena, and Reggio from the late 13th cent. until 1598 and thereafter of Modena and Reggio until the end of the 18th cent. They were notable patrons of the arts and letters. **Leonello** (1407–50) made Ferrara into an important cultural centre; he was the friend of *Alberti, and a patron of Jacopo *Bellini and *Pisanello; Rogier van der *Weyden painted his illegitimate son **Francesco** (Metropolitan Mus., New York). His brother **Borso** (1413–71) was in touch with the young *Mantegna and *Piero della Francesca, made Cosimo *Tura his chief court painter in 1458, and employed him, Francesco del *Cossa, and Ercole de *Roberti on the frescos in the Palazzo Schifanoia. **Isabella** (1474–1539), daughter of **Ercole I** (1431–1505), the half-brother of Leonello and Borso, was the greatest of the Este patrons and one of the most brilliant women of her time. She secured paintings from Mantegna, *Perugino, *Costa, and later *Correggio to decorate her famous Studiolo in Mantua (she was married to Francesco *Gonzaga) and is said to have implored art dealers not to show her their wares so she would not spend herself even further into debt. A portrait drawing of her by *Leonardo is in the Louvre. Her brother **Alfonso** (1476–1539) commissioned mythological paintings by Bellini and *Titian for his Studiolo. Dosso and Battista *Dossi, *Garofalo, *Girolamo da Carpi, and *Scarsellino were the painters principally employed by the Estes during the 16th cent. In the next century they continued their collections in Modena, and **Francesco I** (1610–58) commissioned portraits from *Bernini and *Velázquez. But in 1744 **Francesco III**

sold 100 of the most splendid pictures in his collection to Augustus III of Poland at Dresden.

estofado. See ENCARNADO.

etching. Term applied to a method of engraving in which the design is bitten into the plate with acid, and also to the print so produced. The design is drawn on a metal (usually copper) plate that has been coated with a waxy, acid-resistant substance. Where the waxy coating is scratched through with the etching needle the bare metal is exposed, and when the plate is placed in a bath of acid the acid bites only the lines so exposed. The depth to which the lines are bitten (and hence the darkness with which they will print) depends on how long the plate is immersed in the acid, and it is possible to achieve subtle variations of tone by 'stopping out' part of the design (covering it with a protective varnish) while other parts are bitten more deeply. Etching was developed in the early 16th cent. as a shortcut to engraving metal, but it soon became an independent art form, and it reached exalted heights in the hands of *Rembrandt, the greatest of all etchers. Etching is a much more spontaneous technique than *line engraving, as it is possible to draw on the waxy ground with virtually the same fluency as with pen or pencil. It is still a popular technique, and has been much used in 20th cent. book illustration.

Etty, William (1787–1849). English painter, one of the few British artists to specialize almost exclusively in the nude. He was born and died in York, but was active mainly in London, where he trained at the *Royal Academy Schools and then with *Lawrence, whose great influence on him was modified by subsequent visits to Italy. His paintings are often of mythological or historical subjects, sometimes on an ambitious scale, but he also made life studies in the RA Schools throughout his career, and these are now probably his most admired works. Etty was poor for much of his life and his pictures were often attacked for their alleged indecency, *The Times* considering them 'entirely too luscious for the public eye'. However, by the time of his death he was a celebrated figure and his works had begun to fetch high prices. He summed up his attitude to his favourite subject thus: 'Finding God's most glorious work to be Woman, that all human beauty had been concentrated in her, I dedicated myself to painting—not the Draper's or Milliner's work—but God's most glorious work, more finely than ever had been done.' His draughtmanship is often criticized, but it is generally agreed that he attained a glowing voluptuousness in the painting of flesh that few British artists have approached. The best collection of Etty's work is in the City Art Gallery, York.

Euston Road School. Group of painters centred round the 'School of Drawing and Painting' that opened in the Euston Road, London, in 1937. Its founding teachers were William *Coldstream, Victor *Pasmore, and Claude *Rogers; Graham *Bell and Lawrence *Gowing were also important members of the circle. These artists were united by a desire to return from abstract and esoteric styles of modernism to a more straightforward *naturalism. The onset of the Second World War caused the closure of the school, but the term 'Euston Road' was used for a decade or so afterwards as a generic description of work in a style similar to that in which the original exponents painted.

Everdingen, Allart van (1621–75). Dutch landscape and marine painter. He was born in Alkmaar and worked with *Savery in Utrecht and *Molyn in Haarlem. In the 1640s he visited Scandinavia, where he developed a taste for subjects inspired by the scenery there—above all mountain torrents—and helped to popularize such themes in the Netherlands. *Ruisdael, in his pictures of majestic waterfalls, was one of the artists influenced by him. Allart was also a fine etcher. His elder brother **Caesar** (1617–87), who painted portraits and historical pictures, was attracted by the south not the north. Although he never went to Italy but learned his *Classicism in Utrecht, he captured the spirit of Italian art better than many of his countrymen who crossed the Alps: witness his beautiful *Four Muses with Pegasus* (c.1650), part of the decoration of the royal villa—the Huis ten Bosch—at The Hague.

Evergood, Philip (1901–73). American painter. He was educated in England, at Eton and Cambridge, and much of his early life was spent travelling and studying in Europe. His early works were mainly of biblical and imaginative subjects, but returning to settle in New York in 1931 at the height of the Depression, he was drawn into the ambit of the Social *Realists, who looked upon their art as an instrument of social protest and propaganda. He was active in several organizations concerned with the civil rights of artists, and under the banner of the *Federal Art Project he produced militant paintings of social criticism, his best-known work in this genre being *American Tragedy* (Whitney Mus., New York, 1937), which commemorates a police attack on striking steel workers in Chicago. Even his allegorical religious painting *The New Lazarus* (Whitney Mus., 1954) has sociological overtones, with its figures of starving children. His inclination for the bizarre and grotesque brings his work close to *Surrealism, as is seen in what is perhaps his most famous painting, *Lily and the Sparrows* (Whitney Mus., 1939).

Evesham, Epiphanius (1570–after 1633). English sculptor. He was the first distinctive personality in English sculpture since the Reformation, but details of his career are scanty. From 1601 to c.1614 he was working as a sculptor and painter in Paris, but though he had a studio of some size and several works in both arts are recorded, none has survived. After his return to England he made a number of tombs that stand out for their humanity, freshness of invention, and refinement of handling at a period when most English tomb sculpture was mass-produced. His signed tomb of Lord Teynham (Lynsted, Kent c.1622), for example, has, in addition to the recumbent effigy, a distinguished kneeling figure of the widow and a series of touching *reliefs of mourning children. *Vertue called him 'that most exquisite artist'.

Eworth (or **Ewouts**), **Hans** (c.1520–after 1573). Netherlandish painter, active mainly in England, where he settled in the 1540s. About thirty of his paintings survive, almost all portraits (there are also a few allegories), dating from 1549 to 1570. He is known also to have painted for pageants and masques. Although his work is uneven, he was the outstanding figure in the history of English painting in the mid 16th cent.

He painted Queen Mary and Queen Elizabeth I, but his masterpiece is perhaps the striking allegorical portrait of Sir John Luttrell (Courtauld Inst., London, 1550).

Execias. The most famous of Greek *black-figure vase painters, active in the second half of the 6th cent. BC. Among the best-known works with his signature are an amphora (wine jar) showing Achilles and Ajax gaming (versions BM, London, and Vatican Mus.) and a splendid cup showing Dionysus in his boat (Antikensammlungen, Munich). Many of the works signed by Execias contain battle scenes, but he was able to impart an air of dignity and grandeur even to the most ordinary activities, and his greatest gift was perhaps for conveying pathos and psychological insight.

Expressionism. A term used in the history and criticism of the arts to denote the use of distortion and exaggeration for emotional effect. It is used in several different ways and can be applied to various art forms, but is chiefly associated with the visual arts. In its broadest sense it can be used of any art that raises subjective feeling above objective observation, reflecting the state of mind of the artist rather than images that conform to what we see in the external world. The paintings of *Grünewald and El *Greco, who conveyed intense religious emotion through distorted, unnaturalistic forms, are outstanding examples of expressionism in this sense (when used in this way the word is usually spelled with a small 'e'). In a narrower sense, the word Expressionism is applied to a broad trend in modern European art that traces its origin to van *Gogh, who used colour and line emotionally 'to express . . . man's terrible passions'. Among the great artists who represent Expressionism in this sense are *Ensor and *Munch. In its narrowest sense, the term Expressionism is applied to one aspect of the trend just described—a movement that was the dominant force in German art from about 1905 to about 1930. The *Brücke and *Blaue Reiter groups represent the high point of German Expressionism, and led, in the case of *Kandinsky, for example, to abstraction. Expressionism represented a rebellion against the naturalism of 19th cent. art, and its insistence on the supreme importance of

the artist's personal feelings has been one of the foundations of aesthetic attitudes in the 20th cent.

ex-voto (Latin: 'from a vow'). A painting or other work of art made as an offering to God in gratitude for a personal favour or blessing or in the hope of receiving some miraculous benefit. There is a famous example by Philippe de *Champaigne in the Louvre.

Eyck, Jan van (d. 1441). The most celebrated painter of the Early Netherlandish School. Within a short time of his death he had a reputation on both sides of the Alps as a painter of great stature and importance, and although he is no longer credited with being the 'inventor' of *oil painting, as was long maintained, his fame has continued undimmed to the present day. Nothing is known of his training and he is first recorded in 1422, entering the service of the Count of Holland, John of Bavaria, in The Hague. In 1425 John died and later in the same year van Eyck moved to Lille when he was appointed court painter and 'varlet de chambre' (equerry) to Philip the Good, Duke of Burgundy, a post he held until his death. Apparently he was highly esteemed by the Duke and he travelled on secret diplomatic missions to Spain and Portugal for him. About 1430 Jan moved from Lille to Bruges, where he lived until his death. In spite of the documentation on his life, which for a painter of his period is fairly rich, his *œuvre* presents many problems, especially in the reconstruction of his early career, for all his dated paintings come from the last 10 years of his life. The central problem of his career—and one of the most discussed in the history of art—concerns the work that has always been the basis of his resounding fame, the great altarpiece of the *Adoration of the Lamb* (completed 1432) in Ghent Cathedral. An inscription on the frame states that it was begun by 'the painter Hubert van Eyck, than whom none was greater', and completed by 'Jan, second in art'. Jan's brother **Hubert** (died 1426?) is such an obscure figure that some scholars have even denied his existence, and there is certainly no obvious division into the work of two hands in the altarpiece. Thus, Jan's contribution to the central masterpiece of Early Netherlandish painting is uncertain. *Dürer called the Ghent altarpiece 'a stupendous painting' and the comment is appropriate both to the majesty and *iconographical richness of the huge *polyptych, and also to its breathtaking technical mastery. Jan brought the new technique of oil painting to a sudden peak and his ability to depict minute detail and to create glowing effects of colour has never been surpassed. About two dozen other paintings are reasonably attributed to Jan. They are all either religious works or portraits, although he is known to have painted pictures of other subjects (including a nude woman at her bath), which are now lost. Outstanding among the surviving works are the famous double portrait *Giovanni Arnolfini and his Wife* (NG, London, 1434) and two paintings of the Virgin and Child with *donors—*The Madonna of Chancellor Rolin* (Louvre, Paris, c.1435) and *The Madonna with Canon van der Paele* (Groeningemuseum, Bruges, 1436). The Louvre painting, with large figures in the foreground set against a distant panoramic landscape, shows Jan's all-embracing vision of the natural world and his mastery of light and space, as well as detail and texture—in Erwin *Panofsky's words, 'his eye was at one and the same time a microscope and a telescope'. The *Man in a Red Turban* (NG, London, 1433) is generally considered to be a self-portrait. As a portrait painter Jan is preoccupied with the realities and textures of the human face, and in this as in his inanimate interiors he records the subtleties of appearances rather than commenting on them as did his great contemporary Rogier van der *Weyden. His portraits do, however, convey a sense of inner life and are not simply coldly objective records. Jan stands with the *Master of Flémalle as the founder of the Early Netherlandish School and his technique became the accepted model for his successors. His main follower was Petrus *Christus, but his influence was wide (it is seen, for example, in the work of Luis *Dalmau in Spain) and profound. In the Netherlands itself, however, the more emotional work of Rogier van der Weyden came to have even more influence and the very perfection of Jan's work must have made him the most daunting of models.

F

Fabritius, Carel (1622–54). Dutch painter. He was *Rembrandt's most gifted pupil and a painter of outstanding originality and distinction, but he died tragically young in the explosion of the Delft gunpowder magazine, leaving only a tiny body of work (much may have perished in the disaster). In his youth he worked as a carpenter (the name Fabritius was once thought to have derived from this profession, but it is now known that his father had used it) and he was probably in Rembrandt's studio in the early 1640s. He settled in Delft in about 1650. Although only about a dozen paintings by him survive, they show great variety. His earliest works (*The Raising of Lazarus*, National Mus., Warsaw, 1642) are strongly influenced by Rembrandt, but he broke free from his master and developed a personal style marked by an exquisite feeling for cool colour harmonies and (even though he often worked on a small scale) unerring handling of a loaded brush (*The Goldfinch*, Mauritshuis, The Hague, 1654). These qualities, together with an interest in *perspective, occur in the work of *Vermeer, the greatest of Delft painters, and Fabritius certainly influenced him, although it is not likely (as is sometimes maintained) that he was his master, this distinction perhaps belonging to *Bramer. Carel's brother **Barent** (1624–73) was also a painter, but of much lesser quality. He also may have studied with Rembrandt; he mainly painted portraits and religious works.

Faithorne, William (1616–91). English engraver. He fought as a Royalist and later spent some time in exile in France, where he worked with *Nanteuil; but by 1650 he was established in London and became the most distinguished of English 17th-cent. engravers, especially of portrait heads. He engraved the work of painters (van *Dyck, *Dobson, *Soest, *Lely) and also made engravings of his own drawings from the life, many published as frontispieces to books. He also drew very sensitive portrait heads as independent works (*John Aubrey*, Ashmolean, Oxford, 1666). In 1662 he published *The Art of Graving and Etching*. His son **William** (1656–1710) was also an engraver.

Falcone, Aniello (1607–56). Neapolitan painter. He was one of the most prominent artists in Naples in the generation before the plague of 1656 (in which he died), and did religious paintings, some in fresco, for several churches in the city. His only complete surviving fresco cycle, however, is the *History of Moses* in the Villa Roomer at Barra, and he is now remembered mainly as the first specialist in battle pieces, a genre that won him an international reputation and in which he inspired his pupil Salvator *Rosa. Falcone was also an outstanding draughtsman.

Falconet, Étienne-Maurice (1716–91). French sculptor and writer on art, a pupil of J. B. *Lemoyne. Falconet was perhaps the most quintessentially *Rococo of all French sculptors, his forté being gently erotic figures such as the celebrated *Bather* (1757) in the Louvre. Like many other of his works, this was reproduced in porcelain by the Sèvres factory, of which he was Director from 1757 to 1766, a position that he gained through the influence of his patron Mme de Pompadour. Falconet had other sides to his talent, however, and his masterpiece—the equestrian statue of Peter the Great in Leningrad—is in a completely different vein. He went to Russia in 1766, recommended to Catherine II by *Diderot, and left in 1778, the statue being unveiled in 1782. The huge horse is represented with its forelegs raised and unsupported—a daring technical feat—and the heroic vigour of the statue gives it a place among the greatest representatives of the genre. Falconet suffered a stroke in 1783 and thereafter produced no more sculpture, devoting himself to writing. A six-volume edition of his writings had already appeared in 1781 and in 1761 he had published his best-known literary work, *Réflexions sur la sculpture*. In this he was one of the first to argue that the modern artists were superior to those of the ancient world (it is significant that unlike most of his distinguished contemporaries he never saw the need to visit Italy).

fancy picture. A term applied in the 18th cent. to a type of sentimental rural *genre picture. Scenes in which idealized peasants behave rather more as if they were in the studio than the countryside are 'fancy pictures', and *Gainsborough's paintings of this type were so called in his own day. The term is elusive and cannot be defined with precision.

Fantastic Realism. A school of painting which arose in Vienna *c*.1945 and came to be regarded as typical of post-war Austrian painting. The artists involved combined minute realism with a fairy-tale world of fantasy and imagination. Though very different in their ways of painting and in the quality of their work, they had in common an interest in the art of the past, notably that of Pieter *Bruegel (supremely well represented in the Kunsthistorisches Museum in Vienna) and in the literary and anecdotal character of painting.

Fantin-Latour, Henri (1836–1904). French painter and lithographer. He is best known for his luxurious flower pieces, but he also painted several group portraits that are important historical documents and show his friendship with leading avant-garde artists. *Homage to Delacroix* (Musée d'Orsay, Paris, 1864) shows Fantin-Latour himself, with *Baudelaire, *Manet, *Whistler, and others grouped round a portrait of *Delacroix; and *A Studio at Batignolles* (sometimes called *Homage to Manet*) (Musée d'Orsay, Paris, 1870) shows *Monet, *Renoir, and others in Manet's studio. In spite of his associations with such progressive artists, Fantin-Latour was a traditionalist, and his portraits particularly are in a precise, detailed style. Much of his later career was devoted to *lithography; he greatly admired Richard Wagner and did imaginative lithographs illustrating his music and that of other *Romantic composers.

Farington, Joseph (1747–1821). English landscape painter and topographical draughtsman, best known today for his copious diary (1793–1821), which contains valuable information about the London art world of the time. Most of the original manuscript is in the Royal Library at Windsor Castle. Publication of the full text began in 1978; previous editions had been heavily abridged.

Farnese. Italian family of humanists and patrons of the arts who rose to importance with the election of Cardinal **Alessandro Farnese** (1468–1549) to become Pope Paul III in 1534. He was the most important patron of *Michelangelo's later years, commissioning from him *The Last Judgement* in the Sistine Chapel and the *Conversion of St Paul* and the *Crucifixion of St Peter* in the Cappella Paolina, and also appointing him architect to St Peter's. Michelangelo also had a hand in the design of the Palazzo Farnese, the finest palace built in Rome in the 16th cent. Pope Paul's grandson (or 'nephew' as he was known), another **Alessandro** (1520–89), was made a Cardinal in 1534 and was acknowledged to be the greatest patron of his day. He built up the largest collection of antiquities in Rome (now mainly in the Archaeological Museum in Naples; see FARNESE BULL; FARNESE HERCULES), was instrumental in bringing *Titian to Rome (1545–6), encouraged *Vasari to write his *Lives*, engaged Giacoma da Vignola to complete the Palazzo Farnese at Caprarola, and commissioned some of the most important *Mannerist frescos. He gave special support to the Jesuits and built for them the church of Il Gesù, one of the most influential buildings in the history of architecture. Alessandro's great-nephew, Cardinal **Odoardo** (1573–1626), great-great-grandson of Paul III, was responsible for employing Annibale and Agostino *Carracci to decorate the Farnese Gallery in the Palace in Rome. **Elisabetta**, second wife of the Bourbon King Philip V (1683–1746), was a Farnese and through this connection their son Charles III of Spain brought the majority of the Farnese collections to Naples, where they still are.

Farnese Bull. Ancient marble sculpture group (probably a Roman copy of a Greek original of *c*.150 BC), once part of the *Farnese collection and now in the Archaeological Museum in Naples. The subject, taken from Greek legend, shows the punishment of Dirce, who for her cruelty to Antiope was tied to the horns of a bull by Antiope's sons (Dirce's stepsons) and trampled to death. The figures are life-size, and the group, which was found in the Baths of Caracalla in Rome in 1545, is one of the most spectacular examples of the virtuosity and dramatic movement typical of *Hellenistic art.

Farnese Hercules. Gigantic marble statue of Hercules leaning sideways on his club and resting after his labours, once part of the *Farnese collection and now in the Archaeological Museum in Naples. It is signed by an Athenian sculptor named Glycon and is a copy of an original of the 4th cent. BC, probably by *Lysippus. The figure was discovered in the Baths of Caracalla in Rome in c.1546 and became highly influential and much copied. Its powerful musculature and realistic surface treatment . were particularly admired by *Baroque artists.

Fattori, Giovanni. See MACCHIAIOLI.

Fautrier, Jean (1898–1964). French painter and graphic artist. He came to England as a child in 1909 and studied at the *Royal Academy Schools and at the *Slade School, returning to Paris in 1917. Throughout his life he remained isolated from groups and movements, and his work is difficult to classify, although he is often seen as a forerunner of *Art Informel. His best-known works are the series of *Hostages* (1943), inspired by his horror of war. In these he developed his characteristic technique, building up by layer upon layer of paint, thickened with white, a heavy *impasto into which he worked the representation of his subject. The effect produced is both powerful and mysterious. From 1950 he was one of the first to develop the idea of *multiples.

Fauvism. Style of painting based on the use of intensely vivid non-naturalistic colours, the first of the major avant-garde developments in European art between the turn of the century and the First World War. The dominant figure of the Fauvist group was Henri *Matisse, and other artists involved included *Derain, *Marquet, *Rouault, and *Vlaminck. They exhibited together at the *Salon d'Automne of 1905 and their name was given to them by the critic Louis Vauxcelles, who pointed to a *quattrocento-like sculpture in the middle of the same gallery and exclaimed: 'Donatello au milieu des fauves!' (*Donatello among the wild beasts).The Fauves exhibited together again at the *Salon des Indépendants of 1906, but with most of the group Fauvism was a temporary phase through which they passed in the development of widely different styles, and at no later period did their work display again such a degree of similarity. Only Matisse continued to explore the beauty of pure colour. Although short lived, however, Fauvism was highly influential, particularly on the development of German *Expressionism.

Federal Art Project. A project instituted by the US Government in 1935, and lasting until 1943, with the dual purpose of assisting artists who had been hard hit by the Depression and of deploying the artistic potential of the country in the decoration of public buildings and places. There were also a Federal Writers Project, a Federal Theatre Project, and a Federal Music Project, and collectively they are known as the Federal Arts Projects. They were part of the Works Progress Administration (WPA), a work programme for the unemployed executed as part of President F. D. Roosevelt's New Deal. The Federal Art Project grew out of two previous schemes of a similar nature. In 1933 the Public Works of Art Project was set up to assist artists over the winter of 1933/4 by employing them on public works. The following year the Treasury Relief Art Project (July 1935–June 1943) was set up for a similar purpose, while a new section of Painting and Sculpture established in the Treasury Department commissioned artists for specific tasks in connection with the embellishment of Federal buildings. At its peak the Federal Art Project employed more than 5,000 people, not only decorating public buildings but also producing prints, posters, various works of craft, and setting up community art centres and galleries in areas where art was virtually unknown. The project also involved an *Index of American Design*, a gigantic documentation of the decorative arts in America. Virtually all the major American artists of the period were involved, either as teachers or practitioners. A huge amount of work was generated by the Federal Art Project, but most of it was unremarkable in quality.

Feininger, Lyonel (1871–1956). American painter of German origin. Feininger left America for Europe in 1887 with the intention of studying music, but he turned to art and worked as a cartoonist for German newspapers. In 1907 he turned seriously to painting and after 1912 was linked with the *Section d'Or branch of *Cubism. He evolved a personal Cubistic style in which natural forms were treated in terms of a rhythmic pattern of prismatically coloured interpenetrating planes bounded by straight lines—a manner which he applied particularly to architectural and marine subjects. Feininger exhibited with Der *Blaue Reiter in 1913, taught at the *Bauhaus 1919–33 and was one of the founders of Die *Blaue Vier in 1924. He returned to the USA in 1937.

Feke, Robert (active 1740s). American Colonial portrait painter. Nothing is known of his life until 1741 when he executed a large portrait group in Boston, *Isaac Royall and his Family* (Harvard Univ.). He was active from that time in Newport and Philadelphia until 1750, when his life is once more veiled in obscurity. There are about fifteen signed portraits from his hand and about fifty more are reasonably attributed to him. His works are somewhat lacking in characterization, but their strength and clarity of design and delicacy of touch give them a high place among Colonial portraits.

Félibien des Avaux, André (1619–95). French architect and writer, a friend of Nicholas *Poussin in Rome. His *Entretiens sur les vies et sur les ouvrages des plus excellens peintres anciens et modernes*, first published in 1666–88 and often reprinted, is a major source book and contains the best contemporary biography of Poussin. In 1676 he published a textbook on artists' techniques with a dictionary of art terms.

Fergusson, John Duncan (1874–1961). Scottish painter and, to a lesser degree, sculptor. He abandoned medicine to study painting and in 1905 settled in Paris. His early work was *Whistlerian, and he then came under the influence of *Manet, but by 1907 he had adopted the bold palette and firm outlines of *Fauvism and became

the most uncompromising adherent to the style among British artists (*Blue Beads*, Tate, London, 1910). In 1914 the war brought him back to Britain and the rest of his life was spent between London, Paris, and, after 1940, Glasgow.

Fernandez, Alejo (*c*.1470–1543). Spanish painter, probably of German extraction, as he is referred to as 'Maestro Alexos—pintor Aléman'. He married the daughter of a painter called Pedro Fernandez at Cordova and took her name, but he worked mainly at Seville, where he was the leading painter of the first third of the 16th cent. His work, which is represented in Seville Cathedral, was essentially Flemish *Mannerist in style, but it has a personal lyrical quality, and his treatment of architecture and *perspective suggests that he may have visited Italy. He had a busy studio and several followers, among them his son **Sebastián**.

Fernandez (or **Hernandez**), **Gregório** (*c*.1576–1636). Spanish sculptor, active at Valladolid from *c*.1605. Continuing the tradition of painted religious sculpture, he worked in the manner of *Juan de Juni but with greater realism of expressive gesture. He was one of the first and greatest masters of *Baroque naturalism in Spain, abandoning the earlier practice of using gold and brilliant colours and insisting upon realistic colouring from the *polychromists who painted his sculptures. Among the numerous altarpieces emanating from his workshop are those of S. Miguel, Valladolid (1606) and Plasencia Cathedral (1624–34). He is well represented in Valladolid Museum.

Ferrari, Gaudenzio (*c*.1471/81–1546). Italian painter, active in his native Piedmont and in Lombardy. His early work was strongly influenced by *Leonardo and his Milanese followers, and throughout his life he remained *eclectic, absorbing into his highly-charged, emotional style elements from *Pordenone and *Lotto and also, for example, from the engravings of *Dürer. He was an artist of considerable power and individuality, but his work has remained comparatively little known because much of it is in fairly remote situations. His most remarkable works are *The Stations of the Cross* in a series of chapels at the Sanctuary of Sacro Monte, Varallo, in which life-size foreground figures are carved in the round and the rest of the scene painted behind them.

fête champêtre (French: 'outdoor feast'). Type of *genre scene in which romantic figures are shown in an idealized outdoor setting, usually eating, dancing, flirting, or listening to music. Since the Gardens of Love represented in medieval manuscripts, the theme has had great popularity in European art, undergoing several transformations. It was particularly favoured in 16th-cent. Venetian painting and the *Concert Champêtre* in the Louvre (traditionally by *Giorgione, but now usually given to *Titian) is the most celebrated of all examples of the type. The term 'fête galante' ('courtship party') was invented by the French *Academy in 1717 to describe *Watteau's variants on the theme, in which figures in ball dress or masquerade costume disport themselves amorously in a parkland setting.

Feti (or **Fetti**), **Domenico** (*c*.1589–1623). Italian painter. He was born at Rome, where he studied under Ludovico *Cigoli, was court painter to Vincenzo *Gonzaga at Mantua from 1613 to 1622, and then settled in Venice. His most characteristic works are of religious themes turned into *genre scenes of contemporary life. They are broadly painted, with characteristic 'windswept' brushstrokes, though small in scale. Their great popularity is shown by the fact that they often exist in numerous very similar versions. Feti, who was also an excellent portraitist, was one of a group of non-Venetian artists (including the German *Liss and the Genoan *Strozzi) who revivified painting in the city when there was a scarcity of native talent. Consequently, he is often classed as a member of the Venetian School, even though he spent only the last two years of his life there.

Feuchtmayer, Joseph Anton (1696–1770). German *Rococo *stuccoist and sculptor, the most famous member of a family of artists from Wessobrunn in Bavaria. A virtuoso carver and stuccoist, he did a great deal of decorative work for buildings in the Lake Constance area. The greatest ensemble of his work is in the pilgrimage church of Neu-Birnau (1746–

53): it includes his most famous single figure, the *Honey-licking Putto*.

Feuerbach, Anselm (1829–80). German painter. He studied in Düsseldorf, Antwerp, and Paris (with *Couture), then lived in Italy from 1855 to 1873. His father was a professor of Classical archaeology (he had written a book on the *Apollo Belvedere*) and the son grew up in an atmosphere saturated with the high-minded ideals of humanistic philosophy. He wished to become the founder of a new school which was to combine noble, didactic, and idealistic subjects with a style derived from the *Grand Manner of Venetian 16th-cent. painting. His subjects are usually taken from Greek antiquity—in the case of his most celebrated painting, from one of Plato's Dialogues (*The Symposium*, Kunsthalle, Hamburg, 1869). Feuerbach's fervent desire to preach a philosophy through pictorial means was usually a source of weakness rather than strength, and his best works are now generally considered to be his portraits of his model and mistress Nanna Risi, which have a statuesque beauty lacking in his more elaborate paintings; she also posed for subject pictures such as *Iphigenia* (Hessisches Landesmuseum, Darmstadt, 1862). Feuerbach went to Vienna in 1873 to become Professor of History Painting at the Academy, but he returned to Italy in 1876 after criticism of his ceiling of *The Fall of the Titans* for the Academy. Throughout his life he complained that he was being misunderstood and not receiving the recognition due to a very great artist. It is this element of self-pity which makes his book *Ein Vermächtnis* (A Testament) one of the most pathetic and repellent autobiographies ever written. It was posthumously published in 1882.

Fielding, Anthony Vandyke Copley (1787–1855). English water-colour painter, a pupil of *Varley. He was a popular and prolific artist and much of his work is repetitive. Early in his career he specialized in scenes of Wales and the Lake District, but after 1814 he spent much of his time near the coast because of his wife's health, and turned increasingly to seascapes.

Field painting. A type of painting inaugurated in America by Barnett *Newman *c*.1950 in which the picture is no longer regarded as a structure of interrelated elements but as a total field. Field painting has affinities with *Systemic painting and with the *All-over style initiated by Jackson *Pollock. It has been known as *Colour Field painting when emphasis is placed upon brilliance and saturation of colour in monochromatic canvases. Rather than a specific style it may be regarded as an aspect of a very general tendency during the 1950s and 1960s to eschew traditional composition in favour of a single 'total' theme.

figurative art. Art in which recognizable figures or objects are portrayed. The term 'representational art' is used synonymously; the opposite is non-figurative or *abstract art.

Filarete (properly Antonio Averlino) (c.1400–c.1469). Florentine sculptor, architect, and writer on art. His nickname is derived from the Greek for 'lover of virtue'. He probably trained with *Ghiberti and his most important work in sculpture—the bronze doors of St Peter's in Rome (1433–45)—are heavily indebted to Ghiberti's doors for the Baptistery in Florence, although much less accomplished. After being expelled from Rome for allegedly stealing a relic, Filarete went to Florence and Venice, then in 1450 settled in Milan. There he worked mainly as an architect, his principal work being the Ospedale Maggiore (begun 1457, completed in the 18th cent.), which helped to introduce the *Renaissance style to Lombardy and created new standards of comfort and sanitation in hospital design. His novel ideas came out also in his *Treatise on Architecture*, written in 1461–4. It includes a vision of a new city, Sforzinda (named after his patron, Francesco *Sforza), which is the first symmetrical town-planning scheme of modern times. Among his ingenious proposals for his ideal city was a Tower of Virtue and Vice, a ten-storey structure accommodating a brothel on the ground floor and an astronomical observatory at the top.

Filla, Emil (1882–1953). Czech painter, sculptor, graphic artist, and writer on art. Between 1907 and 1914 he spent much of his time in France, Germany, and Italy, and during this period he turned from his early *Expressionist manner to *Cubism,

becoming the pioneer and one of the most distinguished exponents of the style in Czechoslovakia. He passed the First World War in the Netherlands and during the Second World War he was imprisoned in the concentration camp at Buchenwald. In his later work he moved to a more naturalistic style.

fine arts. Term applied to the 'higher' non-utilitarian arts, as opposed to *applied or *decorative arts. In its most common usage the term is taken to cover painting, sculpture, and architecture (even though architecture is obviously a 'useful' art), but it is often extended to cover poetry and music too. The term came into use in the 18th cent. See also LIBERAL ARTS.

Finiguerra, Maso (1426–64). Florentine goldsmith, engraver, designer, and craftsman in *niello (a type of decorative metal inlay). *Vasari asserts that he was the inventor of copper engraving and although this claim has been discredited, Finiguerra was certainly one of the earliest to use that medium, which was first developed in Italy as an extension of *niello* work, in which he was the most famous practitioner of his day. He was a pupil of *Ghiberti and seems to have collaborated with Antonio del *Pollaiuolo.

Fitzwilliam Museum. The museum and art gallery of the University of Cambridge. It was founded in 1816 and is one of the oldest public museums in Great Britain. Like the *Ashmolean Museum in Oxford it has been built up almost entirely from private benefactions. The founder, the 7th Viscount Fitzwilliam (1745–1816), bequeathed to the University a typical gentleman's collection of the 18th cent., which included Italian High *Renaissance paintings, and the best collection of *Rembrandt etchings then in England. He also left £100,000 for a building, which was begun in 1837 by George Basevi, continued by C. R. Cockerell, and finished by E. M. Barry in 1875. There have been several extensions. Among the bequests to the museum the most noteworthy after the founder's was that of Charles Brinsley Marlay (1831–1912), which enriched all departments. Sir Sydney Cockerell (1867–1962) has been the most remarkable director of the museum (1908–37). According to *The Dictionary of National Biography*, he 'transformed a dreary and ill-hung provincial gallery into one which set a new standard of excellence which was to influence museums all over the world. This he achieved by the skilful and uncrowded display of pictures against suitable backgrounds, and by the introduction of fine pieces of furniture, Persian rugs, and flowers provided and arranged by lady admirers, fired by his enthusiasm.' In Cockerell's own words, 'I found it a pig stye, I turned it into a palace.' The museum's collections are now extremely wideranging; the areas of greatest richness include Italian painting and Greek coins.

fixative. A liquid applied to drawings in *chalk, *charcoal, or *pastel (usually by means of spraying) to prevent the *pigments from rubbing off, by binding them together and securing them to the *ground. It is most needed for pastels, but it tends to reduce their brilliance.

Flandrin, Hippolyte (1809–64). French painter. He was one of the favourite pupils of *Ingres and won the *Prix de Rome in 1830. In Italy he was influenced by the monumental decorative tradition and after his return to Paris in 1838 he became the leading muralist of his day, painting vast compositions in such churches as St Vincent-de-Paul (1849–53) and St Germain-des-Prés (1856 61) in Paris. He was a zealous but rather frigid upholder of Ingres's theories. Flandrin was an excellent portraitist and also painted historical and mythological works. He came from a family of artists. His brothers **Auguste** (1804–43) and **Paul** (1811–1902) were pupils of Ingres, and concentrated mainly on portraiture and landscape respectively; his son **Paul-Hippolyte** (1856–1921) painted religious, historical, and *genre scenes.

Flaxman, John (1755–1826). English sculptor, draughtsman, and designer, an outstanding figure of the *Neoclassical movement. He was the son of a moulder of plaster figures, and after studying at the *Royal Academy School (where he met his life-long friend *Blake) he worked for the potter Josiah Wedgwood from 1775 to 1787. The designs he produced for Wedgwood not only strengthened his interest in *antique art but also developed the innate sensitivity to line that was his greatest gift. At the same time he gradually

built up a practice as a sculptor. In 1787 he went to Rome to direct the Wedgwood studio and stayed for seven years. While there he drew his illustrations, much influenced by Greek vase painting, to the *Iliad* and the *Odyssey*, engraved and published in Rome in 1793, followed by illustrations to Aeschylus (1795) and Dante (1802). These engravings, which are of exceptional purity of outline, were republished in several editions, and won him international fame. His later illustrations to Hesiod (1817) were engraved by Blake. He returned to England in 1794 with a well-established reputation and immediately became a busy sculptor. His monument to the poet William Collins (Chichester Cathedral, 1795) and the more important one to Lord Mansfield (Westminster Abbey, 1795–1801) were commissioned while he was in Rome. His enormous practice as a maker of monuments included large groups with free-standing figures (*Lord Nelson*, St Paul's Cathedral, 1809), but his most characteristic work appears in simpler and smaller monuments, sometimes cut in low *relief. In these his great gift for linear design was given full play. Flaxman was appointed the first Professor of Sculpture at the Royal Academy in 1810 and his reputation among Neoclassical sculptors was exceeded only by those of *Canova and possibly *Thorvaldsen. He was one of the first English artists to be famous outside his own country, although his reputation and influence was based principally on engravings after his drawings rather than his sculpture. University College London has a large collection of Flaxman's drawings and models, and examples of his monuments can be seen in churches throughout England.

Flinck, Govert (1615–60). Dutch painter, active mainly in Amsterdam. He studied with *Rembrandt in the early 1630s, and his early work was overwhelmingly influenced by his master. From the mid 1640s, however, he adopted the elegant style of van der *Helst, with which he had great success. In 1659 he was awarded the most important commission a Dutch painter of his time could receive: he was asked to paint twelve pictures for van *Campen's new Town Hall of Amsterdam, eight of which (each about 5 m. high) were to represent the story of *The Revolt of the Batavians*. But Flinck died three months after signing the contract and the commission was divided among Rembrandt, *Lievens, and *Jordaens.

Flint, Sir William Russell (1880–1969). British painter and graphic artist. He was trained as a lithographer and was a prolific book illustrator, but is now best remembered for his water-colours (particularly his mildly erotic nudes), painted in a distinctive and rather flashy style.

Floris (or **Floris de Vriendt**). Netherlandish family of artists active in Antwerp. The most important members were the brothers **Cornelis** (1514–75) and **Frans** (c.1516–70). They worked in Italy in the early 1540s and returned to Antwerp with a desire to emulate the Italian *Renaissance manner. Both ran flourishing workshops and became principal representatives of 'Romanism' in Flanders. Cornelis was an architect and sculptor and also published engravings of Italianate motifs, which were used by many northern artists. He is famous principally as the architect of Antwerp Town Hall (1561–5), the finest and most influential building of the 16th cent. in Flanders. Frans Floris was a painter and studied with Lambert *Lombard before going to Italy, where in 1541 he witnessed the unveiling of *Michelangelo's *Last Judgement* in the Sistine Chapel. This made an indelible impression on him and he concentrated on making large religious and mythological pictures crowded with athletic *Mannerist nudes (*Fall of the Rebel Angels*, Musée Royal, Antwerp, 1554). In his portraits, however, he combined powerful brushwork with forthright characterization in a way that anticipates *Hals (*Portrait of an Old Lady*, Musée des Beaux-Arts, Caen, 1558). According to van *Mander every Flemish youth with artistic leanings studied with him, but in spite of his success he died in debt because of his extravagant lifestyle.

Flötner, Peter (c.1495–1546). German sculptor and engraver, active mainly in Nuremberg. He was in Italy in 1530 (perhaps following an earlier visit) and his work was important in spreading the *Renaissance style in Northern Europe. His best-known work is the *Apollo Fountain* (Germanisches Nationalmuseum, Nuremberg, 1532), which is Classical in inspiration but with a flowing elegance that is Flötner's own.

Focillon, Henri (1881–1943). French art historian. He was a celebrated teacher and held various university appointments, notably at the Sorbonne in Paris, where in 1924 he succeeded Émile *Mâle in the chair of art history. He also taught in the USA. Focillon's work ranged from studies of medieval sculpture to 20th-cent. painting; he also wrote much on engraving (his father was an engraver), notably a book on *Piranesi (1918). His best-known work is *Art d'Occident* (The Art of the West, 1938), a study of *Romanesque and *Gothic art in which he placed great emphasis on the technical aspects of artistic creation, stressing how the artist responds to his raw materials, their potentialities, and limitations. This outlook also finds expression in his *Vie des formes* (1934), translated as *The Life of Forms in Art*.

Fontainebleau, School of. Term applied to artists working in a style associated with the French court at Fontainebleau in the 16th cent. The palace at Fontainebleau was the most brilliant expression of the ambition of Francis I (reigned 1515–47) to glorify the French crown by emulating the lavish patronage of the great humanist princes of Italy. As France lacked an indigenous tradition of mural painting adequate to his grandiose conceptions, he brought in Italian masters to lead the work, which was carried out between 1528 and 1558. The two most distinguished Italians to work at Fontainebleau were *Rosso, who came to France in 1531, and *Primaticcio, who followed in 1532. The Italian masters succeeded in adapting their own styles to the courtly ideals of the French taste and were assisted by French and Flemish artists. From the combination was born a distinctive style of *Mannerism, a composite of sensuality and decorative flair, of boudoir voluptuousness and etiolated elegance. Many engravings were made of the work at Fontainebleau and the union of *stucco ornament with mural painting introduced an original feature which had wide influence. Much of the stucco-work was in high *relief, but Rosso also developed a distinctive motif known as strapwork, in which the stucco is formed into shapes resembling leather or parchment that has been rolled and cut into decorative patterns; this became a particularly popular form of ornament in England and the Low Countries. Primaticcio's distinctive figure style—characterized by long limbs, small heads, and sharp, elegant profiles—became virtually canonical in French art until the end of the 16th cent. Other Italian artists who worked at Fontainebleau included Niccolò dell' *Abbate and *Cellini, but much of the work associated with the school is by unknown hands, although often of high quality, such as the celebrated painting of Diana the Huntress (c.1550) in the Louvre. The mythological subject-matter, elongated elegance, idyllic landscape setting, and air of sophisticated artificiality in this work are wholly typical of the School, the influence of which left few French artists of the time untouched. After the hiatus caused by the Wars of Religion (1562–98) the decorative painting of royal palaces was revived under the patronage of Henry IV (reigned 1589–1610). The name **Second School of Fontainebleau** is usually given to the artists who carried out this work for Henry IV, notably Ambroise Dubois (1542/3–1614), Toussaint Dubreuil (1561–1602), and Martin Fréminet (1567–1619). Their work was accomplished, but without the inventive brilliance of the best work of the First School.

Fontana, Lucio (1899–1968). Italian painter and sculptor, born in Argentina. His family moved to Milan in 1905 and his exhibition at the city's Galleria del Milione in 1930 was the first appearance of non-figurative sculpture in Italy. In 1934 he joined the *Abstraction-Création group in Paris. During the Second World War he lived in Argentina, where he issued his White Manifesto (1946), which introduced a new concept of art called Spatialism. This called for co-operation with scientists in synthesizing new ideas and materials. In 1947 he returned to Milan, and in the same year founded the Spatialist movement (*Spazialismo) and issued the Technical Manifesto of Spatialism. His most characteristic works are paintings in which completely plain surfaces are penetrated by gashes in the canvas, but he also made environments, for example using neon lights in blackened rooms.

Fontana, Prospero (1512–97). Italian painter, active mainly in his native Bologna, but also in other cities of Italy, notably Florence, Genoa, and Rome, assisting 16th-cent. decorative masters such as *Pierino del Vaga, *Vasari, and *Zuccaro. He also worked at *Fontainebleau (c.1560) under *Primaticcio. Fontana was a favourite artist of Gabriele Paleotti, Archbishop of Bologna, and was the leading painter in the city in the 1570s. Paleotti was one of the churchmen who, in line with the ideals of the Counter-Reformation, called for greater clarity in painting as an aid to devotion, but Fontana's work—elegant but rather spineless—is generally seen as exemplifying everything that the *Carracci opposed in their move towards naturalism. Most of Fontana's work is still in and around Bologna. His daughter and pupil **Lavinia Fontana** (1552–1614) was much esteemed in her day as a portraitist.

Foppa, Vincenzo (c.1427–1515). Italian painter, the leading figure in Lombard painting until the arrival of *Leonardo da Vinci in Milan in 1481/2. He was born and died in Brescia, but was active mainly in Milan. According to *Vasari he obtained his training in Padua, and his robust style owed much to *Mantegna, not least in his interest in *perspective. His major works include frescos in S. Eustorgio, Milan, and Sta Maria del Carmine, Brescia.

Forain, Jean-Louis (1852–1931). French painter, lithographer, and *caricaturist, born at Reims. He studied under Jean-Léon *Gérôme at the École des *Beaux-Arts, where he was particularly interested in *Rembrandt and *Goya. In his work, much of it done for Paris journals, he combined the *Realist eye of *Manet with the mordant satire of *Daumier, and he had the gift of expressing disposition in a few lines by a characteristic attitude or gesture. Forain was on good terms with Manet and *Degas and exhibited in four of the *Impressionist exhibitions between 1879 and 1886. As a painter he was uneven, sometimes influenced by Manet and Degas, sometimes adopting the restricted palette of Daumier, as in the court room scenes Le Tribunal (c.1902–3) and Counsel and Accused (1908), both in the Tate Gallery.

Forbes, Stanhope. See NEWLYN SCHOOL.

Forum exhibition. An exhibition arranged in New York in 1916 by the critic Willard Huntington Wright with the support of the magazine *Forum*, to which he was a regular contributor. The purpose of the exhibition was to pinpoint the best of American avant-garde painting in order to convince the public that it could stand up to the European avant-garde, which had captured public interest at the *Armory Show. Both Robert *Henri and Alfred *Stieglitz were on the selection committee. The exhibition consisted of about 200 pictures by seventeen artists, including *Benton, *Dove, *Marin, *Sheeler, and *Zorach.

Foster, Myles Birket (1825–99). English painter and engraver. He was trained as a wood engraver and designed many book illustrations. After *c*.1858 he devoted himself primarily to water-colour painting of rustic subjects in a sweetly sentimental style that has made him a favourite artist for manufacturers of greetings cards.

Foujita, Tsuguharu (or **Léonard**) (1886–1968). Japanese-French painter and graphic artist. He settled in Paris in 1913 and, except for a world tour in 1929 and residence in Tokyo during the Second World War, he lived in Paris for the rest of his life. In 1959 he became a convert to Roman Catholicism and changed his personal name to Léonard in memory of Leonardo da Vinci. He was a member of the circle of *émigré* *Expressionists in the School of *Paris—*Soutine, *Chagall, *Modigliani—and he developed from *c*.1925 a personal style of delicately mannered Expressionism which combined Western and Japanese traits. He began by doing Parisian landscapes and then became known for his nudes and for his compositions in which still life and figures were combined.

Fouquet (or **Foucquet**), **Jean** (*c*.1420–*c*.1481). The outstanding French painter of the 15th cent. He was born at Tours and is known to have been in Rome between 1443 and 1447, when he painted a portrait, now lost, of Pope Eugenius IV. Much has been made of this Italian journey, the influence of which can be detected in the *perspective essays and Classical architecture of his subsequent works, but the strongly sculptural character of his

painting, which was deeply rooted in his native tradition, did not succumb to Italian influence. On his return from Italy Fouquet entered the service of the French court. His first patron was Étienne Chevalier, the royal secretary and lord treasurer, for whom he produced a *Book of Hours (1450–60), now dismembered but mainly in the Musée Condé at Chantilly, and who appears in the *Diptych of Melun* (*c*.1450), now divided between Antwerp (Musée Royal) and Berlin (Staatliche Museen). The Virgin in this work, at Antwerp, is rumoured to be a portrait of Agnes Sorel, Charles VII's mistress, whom Chevalier had also loved. It was not until 1475 that Fouquet became Royal Painter (to Louis XI), but in the previous year he was asked to prepare designs for the king's tomb, and he must have been the leading court artist for many years. Whether he worked on *miniatures or on a larger scale in panel paintings, Fouquet's art had the same monumental character. His figures are modelled in broad planes defined by lines of magnificent purity. He was essentially a draughtsman, and it was his drawing that imparted to his compositions their balance and clarity. His sculptural sense of form went with a cool and detached temperament, and in his finest works the combination creates a deeply impressive gravity.

Fragonard, Jean-Honoré (1732–1806). French painter whose scenes of frivolity and gallantry are among the most complete embodiments of the *Rococo spirit. He was a pupil of *Chardin for a short while and also of *Boucher, before winning the *Prix de Rome in 1752. From 1756 to 1761 he was in Italy, where he eschewed the work of the approved masters of the High *Renaissance, but formed a particular admiration for *Tiepolo. He travelled and drew landscapes with Hubert *Robert and responded with especial sensitivity to the gardens of the Villa d'Este at Tivoli, memories of which occur in paintings throughout his career. In 1765 he became a member of the *Academy with his historical picture in the *Grand Manner *Coroesus Sacrificing himself to Save Callirhoe* (Louvre, Paris). He soon abandoned this style, however, for the erotic canvases by which he is chiefly known (*The Swing*, Wallace Coll., London, *c*.1766). After his marriage in 1769 he also painted children and family scenes. He stopped exhibiting at the *Salon in 1767 and almost all his work was done for private patrons. Among them was Mme du Barry, Louis XV's most beautiful mistress, for whom he painted the works that are often regarded as his masterpieces—the four canvases representing *The Progress of Love* (Frick Coll., New York, 1771–3). These, however, were returned by Mme du Barry and it seems that taste was already turning against Fragonard's lighthearted style. He tried unsuccessfully to adapt himself to the new *Neoclassical vogue, but in spite of the admiration and support of *David he was ruined by the Revolution and died in poverty. Fragonard was a prolific painter, but he rarely dated his works and it is not easy to chart his stylistic development. Alongside those of Boucher, his paintings seem to sum up an era. His delicate colouring, witty characterization, and spontaneous brushwork ensured that even his most erotic subjects are never vulgar, and his finest work has an irresistible verve and joyfulness.

Frampton, Sir George (1860–1928). British sculptor. Early in his career he was one of the leading avant-garde British sculptors of his day, experimenting with unusual materials and *polychrome and working in a style imbued with elements of *Art Nouveau and *Symbolism (*Mysteriarch*, Walker Art Gallery, Liverpool, 1892). Later his work became more traditional and he had a successful career with accomplished but uninspired monuments, the best known of which are *Peter Pan*, erected in Kensington Gardens in 1911, and the Edith Cavell memorial (1920) in St Martin's Place, London. His son **Meredith** (1894–1984) was a painter, primarily of portraits. He gave up painting in 1945 because his sight was failing and was almost entirely forgotten until an exhibition of his work was held at the Tate Gallery in 1982, revealing him as an artist of great distinction. His work is beautifully finished, with an almost hypnotic clarity, and he excelled in conveying the intellectual qualities of his sitters.

Francesco di Giorgio (1439–1501/2). Sienese painter, sculptor, architect, military engineer, and writer. He painted mainly during the early part of his career and few works certainly by him survive; the most important are a signed *Nativity* (1475) and a documented *Coronation of the Virgin* (1471), both in the Pinacoteca at Siena. As a sculptor, his major works are four bronze angels (1489–97) on the high altar of Siena Cathedral. Francesco was widely travelled, and the latter part of his career was spent mainly as an architect and engineer, particularly a specialist in fortifications. He is also said to have exploded the first mine. As a technological innovator he was second only to his friend *Leonardo, whom he certainly influenced. Among his patrons was Federico da *Montefeltro, and Francesco may have had a hand in the designing of his celebrated palace in Urbino. His only certain non-military building however, is Sta Maria del Calcinaio, near Cortona, begun 1484. Francesco wrote a treatise on architecture in the last years of his life.

Francia (Francesco Raibolini) (c.1450–1517/18). The outstanding Bolognese painter of his period, originally a goldsmith. He entered into a partnership with *Costa after the latter came to Bologna c.1483 and modified the harshness of the Ferrarese manner by a delicate and poetic if somewhat monotonous elegance. The strongest influence on his style, however, came from the Umbrians *Perugino and *Raphael, and his most characteristic works are sweet, softly rounded Madonnas, which his large workshop produced in some numbers. He was also an accomplished portraitist.

Franciabigio (Francisco di Cristofano) (1482–1525). Florentine painter, a minor master of the High *Renaissance style. He was a pupil of *Piero di Cosimo and collaborated with *Andrea del Sarto. His best works are generally considered to be his portraits, particularly those of young men (*A Knight of Rhodes*, NG, London).

Francis, Sam (1923–). American painter, one of the leading second-generation *Abstract Expressionists. After studying medicine he took up painting in 1945. He went to Paris in 1950, attended the Atelier Fernand *Léger and was friendly with *Riopelle and other *Art Informel painters, by whom his style was influenced as well as by the American artists such as Jackson *Pollock. In 1957 he made a world tour, including a long stay in Japan, and afterwards the thin texture of his paint, his drip and splash technique, and his asymmetrical balance of colour against powerful voids, caused critics to speak of influences from Japanese traditions of contemplative art. In the mid 1960s his sensitive feeling for oriental simplicity was enhanced to bring his work into closer affinity with certain *Minimalist trends.

Francken. Family of Flemish painters active in the 16th and 17th cents., mainly in Antwerp. The individual contributions of the many artists in the family are often difficult to assess, but the two most distinguished members were **Frans I** (1542–1616) and his son **Frans II** (1581–1642). The father mainly painted religious and historical compositions. His early works were frequently life-size; the late ones were small, usually done on copper, and crowded with exotic figures and accessories. Frans II frequently adopted his father's subjects and style, but his range was wider. He painted landscapes and *genre scenes as well as historical pictures, and was also one of the first artists to use the interior of a picture gallery as a subject, giving faithful miniature reproductions of the works in the collection. His paintings were even smaller and more crowded than his father's; they were also more colourful. Frans II was frequently employed by his fellow artists in Antwerp to paint the figures in their landscapes and interiors.

Frankenthaler, Helen (1928–). American painter. Under the influence of Arshile *Gorky and then Jackson *Pollock she evolved her own manner of *Abstract Expressionism. She was particularly interested in exploring new methods of colour combination and her style c.1950 was notable for small areas of abstract colour within a large expanse of naked canvas. Early in the 1950s she began to use thinned paint applied to unprimed canvas and her work is seen as transitional between Abstract Expressionism and *Colour Field painting. Although abstract, her work often evokes suggestions of landscape and is noted for its lyrical qualities. She was married to Robert *Motherwell from 1958 to 1971.

Fréminet, Martin. See FONTAINEBLEAU, SCHOOL OF.

French, Daniel Chester (1850–1931). American sculptor. He made his name with the famous statue of *The Minute Man* (1875) in Concord, Mass., a monument to commemorate the rising of the citizens of the town during the early years of the Revolution (the figure was ready to fight for his country in a minute). After this success, French went on to become the most illustrious sculptor of public monuments of his day, his best-known work being the seated marble figure of Abraham Lincoln (dedicated in 1922) on the Lincoln Memorial in Washington.

fresco. A method of wall-painting in which pure powdered *pigments mixed in water are applied to wet plaster freshly laid on the wall (the word 'fresco' is Italian for 'fresh'). The paint fuses with the plaster, making the picture an integral part of the wall. This technique is also called *buon fresco* or *fresco buono* (true fresco) to distinguish it from painting on dry plaster, which is called by analogy *fresco *secco* or simply *secco*. *Buon fresco* is exceptionally permanent in dry climates, but if damp penetrates the wall, the plaster is liable to crumble and the paint with it. Consequently the art has been practised chiefly in dry countries, particularly in Italy (though not in Venice), and seldom in northern Europe. The technique is of great antiquity, going back to Greek times, and it is also found outside Europe, for example in China and India. *Giotto was the first really great master of fresco, and thereafter many of the leading Italian masters produced works in the medium. It became less common in the 18th cent. and Giambattista *Tiepolo was the last in the line of great Italian painters who used it. It was revived in the 19th cent., notably by German painters such as the *Nazarenes and *Cornelius, but some notable decorators, such as *Delacroix and *Puvis de Chavannes, preferred to use the method of *marouflage. In the 20th cent. the greatest exponents of fresco have been the Mexican muralists *Orozco, *Rivera, and *Siqueiros.

Freud, Lucian (1922–). German-born British painter. He was born in Berlin, a grandson of Sigmund Freud, came to England with his parents in 1931, and acquired British nationality in 1939. His earliest love was drawing, and he began to work full time as an artist after being invalided out of the Merchant Navy in 1942. In 1951 his *Interior at Paddington* (Walker Art Gal., Liverpool) won a prize at the Festival of Britain, and since then he has built up a formidable reputation as one of the most powerful contemporary figurative painters. Portraits and nudes are his specialities, often observed in arresting close-up. His early work was meticulously painted, so he has sometimes been described as a *'Realist' (or rather absurdly as a *Superrealist), but the subjectivity and intensity of his work has always set him apart from the sober tradition characteristic of most British figurative art since the Second World War. In his later work (from the late 1950s) his handling became much broader.

Freundlich, Otto (1878–1943). German painter and sculptor. He went to Paris in 1909 and became a member of *Picasso's circle. After exhibiting with the *Cubists in Paris, Cologne, and Amsterdam, he began to do purely abstract painting c.1919, composing with interlocking swathes of pure colour. He was a member of *Cercle et Carré and of the *Abstraction-Création association. During the 1930s he was classed as a *degenerate artist in Germany (before being destroyed by the Nazis, his sculpture *The New Man* was reproduced on the cover of the catalogue of the infamous exhibition of 'Degenerate Art' held in 1937) and he died in a concentration camp at Lublin.

Frick, Henry Clay (1849–1919). American industrialist, art collector, and philanthropist. He made his fortune in coke and steel operations and assembled a collection of paintings, sculpture, and decorative art under the guidance of Roger *Fry and the dealer Joseph *Duveen. On his death he left his New York mansion and a large fund to form the Frick Collection, which was opened to the public in 1935. It is generally regarded as one of the finest small museums in the world, with a choice collection of works from the Middle Ages to the late 19th cent. *Rembrandt's *Polish Rider* and Giovanni *Bellini's *St Francis* are among the celebrated masterpieces in the collection. Attached to the Frick Collection is the Frick Art Reference Library, which has major collections of books and photographs. It was founded in 1920 by Frick's daughter, **Helen Clay Frick**. In 1970 she established the Frick Art Museum in Pittsburgh, the city where her father had made his fortune.

Friedlaender, Walter (1873–1966). German-born American art historian. He had a distinguished academic career in Germany and, as professor at the university of Freibourg, numbered Erwin *Panofsky among his pupils. In 1933 he was dismissed by the Nazis and emigrated to the USA, where he became professor at New York University and exercised a great influence on American art historians. His major publications include *Caravaggio Studies* (1955), *David to Delacroix* (1952), *Mannerism and Anti-Mannerism in Italian Painting* (1957), and monographs on *Poussin in German (1914) and English (1966).

Friedländer, Max J. (1867–1958). German art historian. The successor to Wilhelm von *Bode as director of the Gemäldegalerie in Berlin, he enriched the collection particularly in his own field of Early Netherlandish painting. In 1934 he retired to Holland. His *magnum opus* is *Die altniederländische Malerei* (14 vols., 1924–37). In a prefatory note to the English edition (*Early Netherlandish Painting*, 1967 76) Erwin *Panofsky described it as 'one of the few uncontested masterpieces produced by our discipline'. Friedländer covered the same ground in a much briefer format in *Die frühen niederländischen Maler von Van Eyck bis Bruegel* (1916), translated as *From Van Eyck to Bruegel* (1956).

Friedrich, Caspar David (1774–1840). The greatest German *Romantic painter and one of the most original geniuses in the history of landscape painting. He was born at Greifswald on the Baltic coast, and after studying at the Copenhagen Academy with *Juel and *Abildgaard from 1794 to 1798, he settled permanently in Dresden. There he led a quiet life, interrupted only by occasional excursions to the mountains or the coast of Pomerania, pursuing with a rare and instinctive single-mindedness his personal insight into the spiritual significance of landscape. He was intensely introspective and often melancholic (although his marriage at the age of 44 brought him much happiness), and he relied on deep contemplation to summon up mentally the images he was to put on canvas. 'Close your bodily eye, so that you may see your picture first with your spiritual eye', he wrote, 'then bring to the light of day that which you have seen in the darkness so that it may react on others from the outside inwards.' Friedrich began as a topographical draughtsman in pencil and sepia wash and did not take up oil painting until 1807. One of his first works in the new medium, *The Cross in the Mountains* (Staatliche Kunstsammlungen, Dresden, 1808), caused great controversy because it was painted as an altarpiece, and to use a landscape in this unprecedented way was considered sacrilege by some critics. His choice of subjects often broke new ground and he discovered aspects of nature so far unseen: an infinite stretch of sea and mountains, snow-covered or fog-bound plains seen in the strange light of sunrise, dusk, or moonlight. He seldom uses obvious religious imagery, but his landscapes convey a sense of haunting spirituality. Friedrich had a severe stroke in 1835 and returned to his small sepias. He was virtually forgotten at the time of his death and his immediate influence was confined to members of his circle in Dresden, notably G. F. *Kersting, who sometimes painted the figures in Friedrich's work. It was only at the end of the 19th cent., with the rise of *Symbolism, that his greatness began to be recognized. Most of his work is still in Germany; *Winter Landscape*, acquired by the National Gallery, London, in 1988, is the first Friedrich oil to enter a British public collection.

Frink, Dame Elisabeth (1930–). British sculptor and graphic artist. She trained under Bernard *Meadows, through whom she underwent some influence from Henry *Moore, and she was also influenced for a while by *Giacometti, some of her early work being angular and menacing. During the 1960s her figures—typically horses and riders or male nudes—became smoother, but she retained a feeling of the bizarre in the polished goggles that feature particularly in her over-life-size heads. She works mainly in bronze and has had numerous public commissions.

Frith, William Powell (1819–1909). English painter. He began with illustrative paintings of classics such as *The Vicar of Wakefield*, but c.1851 he turned to contemporary scenes, with which he had

a great commercial success. His crowded, anecdote-packed pictures of Victorian life, among them *Derby Day* (Tate, London, 1858) and *The Railway Station* (Royal Holloway and Bedford New College, Egham, 1862), are among the most familiar images of their age. Frith's *Reminiscences* (1887) and *Further Reminiscences* (1888) form a useful record of the conservative academic conception of art and of contemporary gossip.

Froment, Nicolas (active c.1450–c.1490). French painter, born at Uzès in Languedoc and active in Avignon. Two documented works by him—both *triptychs—survive: *The Raising of Lazarus* (Uffizi, Florence, 1461) and *The Burning Bush* (Aix-en-Provence Cathedral, 1476). They show that with *Charonton he introduced Netherlandish naturalism to French art. His figures have strong if sometimes clumsy expressions and gestures, while his draperies have a characteristic angularity reminiscent of some of the works of the Spanish and German followers of Rogier van der *Weyden.

Fromentin, Eugène (1820–76). French painter and writer. As a painter he was a specialist in oriental themes (he visited North Africa in 1846, 1848, and 1852), which were much admired in his day but are now known only to specialists. His reputation now rests on his book *Les Maîtres d'autrefois* (*The Masters of Past Time*, 1876), a study of Dutch and Belgian painting. He also wrote a lyrical novel, *Dominique* (1862).

Fronte Nuovo Delle Arti (New Art Front). An association of Italian artists founded in 1946 with the aim of combating the pessimism of the post-war world and advocating a return to an art concerned with human values. *Birolli and *Guttuso were the best-known figures in the group, which combined artists of very different styles and ideologies. The split between Abstractionists and Realists led to the dissolution of the association in 1948.

Frost, Terry (1915–). British painter, one of the leading *St Ives painters. He started painting in 1943 when a prisoner of war, then studied under Victor *Pasmore at the Camberwell School of Art, 1947–50. His work is abstract and in the 1950s he created screens of brightly striped colours; more recently he has used circles and ovals in high-pitched and saturated colours, often juxtaposing segments of closely related colour. Characteristically he draws on and transposes direct visual experiences of landscape, boats in harbour, and the human figure.

frottage (French: 'rubbing'). A technique of creating a design by placing a piece of paper over some rough substance such as grained wood or sacking and rubbing with a crayon or pencil until it acquires the surface quality of the substance beneath. The resulting design is usually taken as a stimulus to the imagination, the point of departure for a painting which expresses imagery of the subconscious. Max *Ernst pioneered the technique and it was much used by other *Surrealists.

Fry, Roger (1866–1934). English critic and painter. After taking a degree in natural sciences at Cambridge he took up painting and then turned to criticism. He was Curator of Paintings at the *Metropolitan Museum of Art, New York, 1906–10, but in the year he took up this appointment he 'discovered' *Cézanne and turned his attention away from the Italian Old Masters, with whom he had established his scholarly reputation, to become the ardent champion of modern French painting. He introduced the *Post-Impressionists to Great Britain by exhibitions which he arranged at the Grafton Galleries in 1910 and 1912, and from this time his critical writing was aligned with the aesthetic attitude which assigns pre-eminent importance to formal values. In 1913 he founded the *Omega Workshops for the production of well-designed objects of daily use instead of the pretentious and 'arty' objects which were then the fashion. He also supported the *London Group. As an artist, although he painted some abstracts, most of his work was carefully naturalistic within the general style of the *Bloomsbury Group; several of his portraits of eminent contemporaries (including a self-portrait) are in the National Portrait Gallery, London. Fry was a brilliant teacher and lecturer and probably did more than anyone else to awaken public interest and understanding of modern art in England. Kenneth *Clark called him 'incomparably the greatest influence on taste since

*Ruskin' and said: 'In so far as taste can be changed by one man, it was changed by Roger Fry.' His books include monographs on *Bellini (1899) Cézanne (1927) and *Matisse (1930), an edition of *Reynolds's *Discourses* (1905) and several collections of lectures and essays. Fry also helped to found the *Burlington Magazine* in 1903 and was later its editor.

Fuller, Isaac (c.1606–72). English decorative and portrait painter. He studied in France with F. *Perrier then worked in Oxford and London. Fuller painted altarpieces for Oxford colleges (that in All Souls was described by the diarist John Evelyn in 1644 as 'too full of nakeds for a chapel') and did decorative painting for taverns in London, including mythological scenes for the Mitre Tavern, Fenchurch Street, but these works have disappeared. His largest surviving works are five canvases, each about 3 m. wide, showing Charles II's escape after the Battle of Worcester in 1651 (NPG, London). Otherwise, Fuller is remembered for his highly idiosyncratic portraits. He was a notorious drunkard and his self-portraits (NPG, and Bodleian Lib., Oxford) are painted with a bravura worthy of a larger-than-life character.

Funk art. Term applied to a type of art that originated in California around 1960 in which tatty or sick subjects—often pornographic or scatological—are treated in a deliberately distasteful way. The word 'funky' originally meant 'smelly' and 'Sick art' is sometimes used as a synonym for 'Funk art'. Edward *Kienholz is the best-known practitioner of the genre.

Fuseli, Henry (Johann Heinrich Füssli) (1741–1825). Swiss-born painter, draughtsman, and writer on art, active mainly in England, where he was one of the outstanding figures of the *Romantic movement. He was the son of a portrait painter, **Johann Caspar Füssli** (1707–82), but he originally trained as a priest; he took holy orders in 1761, but never practised. In 1765 he came to London at the suggestion of the British Ambassador in Berlin, who had been impressed by his drawings. *Reynolds encouraged him to take up painting, and he spent the years 1770–8 in Italy, engrossed in the study of *Michelangelo, whose elevated style he sought to emulate for the rest of his life. On his return he exhibited highly imaginative works such as *The Nightmare* (Detroit Institute of Arts, 1781), the picture that secured his reputation when it was shown at the Royal Academy in 1782 (there is another version in the Goethe-museum, Frankfurt). An unforgettable image of a woman in the throes of a violently erotic dream, this painting shows how far ahead of his time Fuseli was in exploring the murky areas of the psyche where sex and fear meet. His fascination with the horrifying and fantastic also comes out in many of his literary subjects, which formed a major part of his output; he painted several works for *Boydell's Shakespeare Gallery, and in 1799 he followed this example by opening a Milton Gallery in Pall Mall with an exhibition of forty-seven of his own paintings. Fuesli was a much respected and influential figure in his lifetime, but his work was generally neglected for about a century after his death until the *Expressionists and *Surrealists saw in him a kindred spirit. His work can be clumsy and overblown, but at its best has something of the imaginative intensity of his friend *Blake, who described Fuseli as 'The only man that e'er I knew / who did not make me almost spew'. Fuseli's extensive writings on art include *Lectures on Painting* (1801) and a translation of *Winckelmann's *Reflections on the Painting and Sculpture of the Greeks* (1765).

Futurism. Italian avant-garde art movement founded in 1909 by the poet Filippo Tommaso Marinetti. It was originally a literary movement, but the dominant figures were painters (*Balla, *Boccioni, *Carrà, *Russolo, *Severini) and it also embraced sculpture, architecture, music, the cinema, and photography. The aim of the movement, which was outlined in various manifestoes, was to break with the past and its academic culture and to celebrate modern technology, dynamism, and power. The rendering of movement was one of the key concerns of Futurist painters, and their work at times approached abstraction. As an organized movement Futurism did not last much beyond the death of Boccioni—its greatest figure—in 1916 or the end of the First World War, but it had wide influence, notably in Russia, where there was a Russian Futurist movement (which included *Goncharova, *Larionov, and *Malevich), and also in England, on Vorticism and *Nevinson. In France Marcel *Duchamp and Robert *Delannay among others developed in their own ways Futurist ideas about the representation of movement, and the *Dadaist also owed something to Futurism, particularly in their noisy publicity techniques.

Fyt, Jan (1611–61). Flemish painter and etcher, primarily of still life and hunting pieces. He was born and mainly active in Antwerp, where he was a pupil of *Snyders, but in the course of his successful and prolific career he also travelled in France, the Netherlands, and Italy. Like Snyders, Fyt painted in the elaborate style of large decorative still life associated with the circle of *Rubens. His most characteristic paintings depict trophies of the hunt, dead stags, hares, and birds, all treated with a feeling for texture and detail akin to the manner of Dutch still life. The rare flower paintings by Fyt are exceptionally fine and more attuned, perhaps, to modern taste.

G

Gabo, Naum (Naum Neemia Pevsner) (1890–1977). Russian-born sculptor who became an American citizen in 1952, the most influential exponent of *Constructivism. He was the brother of Antoine *Pevsner, but began using the name Gabo in 1915. After studying medicine, natural sciences, and engineering in Munich, he was introduced to avant-garde art by his brother in Paris in 1913 and 1914, and in 1915 he began to make geometrical constructions in Oslo, where he had gone during the First World War. In 1917 he returned to Russia with Antoine and in 1920 they issued their *Realistic Manifesto*, which set forth the basic principles of European Constructivism. When it became clear that official policy favoured the regimentation of artistic activity in the direction of socially useful work (as exemplified by *Tatlin), rather than the pure abstract art conceived by Gabo, the latter left Russia for Berlin in 1922 and spent the next ten years there. In 1932 he moved to Paris and was active in the *Abstraction-Création association until 1935, when he went to England. He remained there until 1946, and in 1937 he was co-editor of the Constructivist review *Circle*. In 1946 Gabo settled in the USA. In the last three decades of his life he received many prestigious awards and carried out numerous public commissions in Europe and America. He often worked on themes over a long period; his *Torsion Fountain* outside St Thomas's Hospital in London, for example, was erected in 1975, but is a development from models he was making in the 1920s. (Small models are a feature of his work; there are numerous examples in the Tate Gallery, which has an outstanding collection of Gabo material.) Gabo never trained as an artist, but came to art by way of his studies of engineering and physical science, and was one of the first artists to embody in his work modern concepts of the nature of space. He was one of the earliest to experiment with *Kinetic sculpture and to make extensive use of semi-transparent materials for a type of abstract sculpture which incorporates space as a positive element rather than displacing or enclosing it. He was throughout his life an advocate of the Constructivist idea not merely as an artistic movement but as the ideology of a life-style.

Gaddi, Taddeo (c.1300–c.1366). Florentine painter, the son of a painter and mosaicist **Gaddo Gaddi** (c.1250–1327/30?). According to Cennino *Cennini, Taddeo was *Giotto's godson and worked with him for twenty-four years. In 1347 he headed a list of the best living painters compiled for the purpose of choosing a master to paint a new high altarpiece for Pistoia Cathedral. His best-known works were painted for Sta Croce, Florence: notably the frescos devoted to the *Life of the Virgin* in the Baroncelli Chapel (finished 1338), and the panels illustrating the *Life of Christ* (c.1330), originally meant for the doors of a sacristy cupboard and now scattered among museums in Florence (Accademia), Munich (Alte Pinakothek), and Berlin (Staatliche Museen). Many other panels are attributed to him and he must have had a flourishing workshop. Although transmitting the tradition of Giotto, his style is less heroic and more anecdotal. Gaddi's son **Agnolo** (active 1369–96) continued the Giotto tradition but modified it still further in the direction of decorative elegance. He is particularly notable for his cool pale colours, which influenced the refined late *Gothic art of artists of the next generation such as *Lorenzo Monaco. Agnolo's works include frescos on *The Story of the Cross* in the chancel of Sta Croce (after 1374) and on *The Story of the Virgin and her Girdle* in the Chapel of the Holy Girdle in Prato Cathedral (1392–5). Many panel paintings also are attributed to Agnolo.

Gainsborough, Thomas (1727–88). English painter of portraits, landscapes, and *fancy pictures, one of the most individual geniuses in British art. He was born at Sudbury, Suffolk, and went to London in about 1740, probably studying with the French engraver *Gravelot. He returned to Sudbury in 1748 and in 1752 he set up as a portrait painter at Ipswich. His work at this time consisted mainly of heads and half-lengths, but he also painted some small portrait groups in landscape settings which are the most lyrical of all English *conversation pieces (*Heneage Lloyd and his Sister*, Fitzwilliam, Cambridge). His patrons were the merchants of the town and the neighbouring squires, but when in 1760 he moved to Bath his new sitters were members of Society, and he developed a free and elegant mode of painting seen at its most characteristic in full-length portraits (*Mary, Countess Howe*, Kenwood House, London, *c*.1763–4). In 1768 he was elected a foundation member of the *Royal Academy, and in 1774 he moved permanently to London. Here he further developed the personal style he had evolved at Bath, working with light and rapid brush-strokes and delicate and evanescent colours. He became a favourite painter of the Royal Family, even though his rival *Reynolds was appointed King's Principal Painter. Gainsborough sometimes said that while portraiture was his profession landscape painting was his pleasure, and he continued to paint landscapes long after he had left a country neighbourhood. He produced many landscape drawings, some in pencil, some in charcoal and chalk, and he occasionally made drawings which he varnished. He also, in later years, painted fancy pictures of pastoral subjects (*Peasant Girl Gathering Sticks*, Manchester City Art Gal., 1782). Gainsborough's style had diverse sources. His early works show the influence of French engraving and of Dutch landscape painting; at Bath his change of portrait style owed much to a close study of van *Dyck (his admiration is most clear in *The Blue Boy*, Huntingdon Art Gal., San Marino, 1770); and in his later landscapes (*The Watering Place*, NG, London, 1777) he is sometimes influenced by *Rubens. But he was an independent and original genius, able to assimilate to his own ends what he learnt from others, and he relied always mainly on his own resources. With the exception of his nephew Gainsborough *Dupont, he had no assistants and unlike most of his contemporaries he never employed a drapery painter. He was in many ways the antithesis of Reynolds. Whereas Reynolds was

sober-minded and the complete professional, Gainsborough (even though his output was prodigious) was much more easy-going and often overdue with his commissions, writing that 'painting and punctuality mix like oil and vinegar'. Although he was an entertaining letter-writer, Gainsborough, unlike Reynolds, had no interest in literary or historical themes, his great passion outside painting being music (his friend William Jackson the composer wrote that he 'avoided the company of literary men, who were his aversion . . . he detested reading'). Gainsborough and Reynolds had great mutual respect, however; Gainsborough asked for Reynolds to visit him on his deathbed, and Reynolds paid posthumous tribute to his rival in his Fourteenth *Discourse*. Recognizing the fluid brilliance of his brushwork, Reynolds praised 'his manner of forming all the parts of a picture together', and wrote of 'all those odd scratches and marks' that 'by a kind of magic, at a certain distance . . . seem to drop into their proper places'.

Gallego, Fernando (*c*.1440–after 1507). Spanish painter. He worked mainly in Salamanca, where *Palomino says he was born, and was the major Castilian painter of his period. Gallego's sober, impassive style has affinities with that of Dirk *Bouts, and it has been suggested that he visited the Netherlands early in his career. His works include a *retable (*c*.1475–80) of *San Idelfonso* in the cathedral of Zamora, a *triptych of *The Virgin, St Andrew and St Christopher* in the new cathedral of Salamanca, and ceiling frescos on astrological subjects (much repainted) in the Old Library in the University of Salamanca. Gallego had considerable influence in Castile. One of his followers, **Francisco Gallego**, was presumably a relative.

Gallen-Kallela, Akseli (1865–1931). Finnish painter, graphic artist, and designer. After studying in Helsinki he worked in Paris under *Bouguereau and *Bastien-Lepage, 1884–90, and he later exhibited in Berlin with *Munch. His style developed through French *Symbolism and *Art Nouveau to a distinctive stylized and expressive manner. He is chiefly known for his romantic paintings illustrating the Finnish national epic *Kalevala*. He also painted a number of murals for public buildings (including the Finnish National Museum, 1928) and his designs for stained glass, fabrics, and jewellery gave an important stimulus to the development of Finnish crafts. In all its ramifications his work manifested strong leanings towards Finnish folklore and he is regarded not only as his country's outstanding artist, but also as the chief figure in the creation of a national art. His former house in Helsinki is now a Gallen-Kallela museum.

Garofalo (Benvenuto Tisi) (1481?–1559). Italian painter, active mainly in Ferrara. *Vasari says that he twice visited Rome, and his work—accomplished but derivative and repetitious—was heavily influenced by *Raphael. He was the first to paint in such a manner in Ferrara and was influential in spreading the High *Renaissance style. His output was large and there are many examples in Ferrarese churches and, for example, in the National Gallery, London. In 1550 he went blind.

Gaudier-Brzeska, Henri (Henri Gaudier) (1891–1915). French sculptor and draughtsman. In 1910 he started to work as a sculptor in Paris and met the Polish-born Sophie Brzeska, with whom he lived from that time, both of them adopting the hyphenated name. In 1911 they went to London, which Gaudier had visited briefly in 1906 and 1908, and lived for a while in extreme poverty. He became a friend of Wyndham *Lewis and other leading literary and artistic figures, and his work was shown in avant-garde exhibitions, such as the *Vorticist exhibition of 1915. In 1914 he enlisted in the French army and was killed in action the following year, aged 23. Gaudier developed with astonishing rapidity from a modelling style based upon *Rodin towards a highly personal manner of carving in which shapes are radically simplified in a manner recalling *Brancusi (*Red Stone Dancer*, Tate, London, 1913). In England, only *Epstein was producing sculpture as stylistically advanced as Gaudier-Brzeska at this time. In his lifetime his work was appreciated by only a small circle, but since his death he has become widely recognized as one of the outstanding sculptors of his generation and has acquired something of a legendary status as an unfulfilled genius. In addition to his sculptures he left behind some splendid animal drawings.

Gauguin, Paul (1848–1903). French *Post-Impressionist painter, sculptor, and printmaker, born in Paris of a journalist from Orleans and a Peruvian Creole mother. He spent his childhood in Lima, joined the merchant marine in 1865, and from 1872 worked successfully as a stockbroker. In the early 1870s he became a spare-time artist and in 1874 he met *Pissarro and saw the First *Impressionist Exhibition. At about the same time he began to make a collection of Impressionist pictures. He had a landscape accepted by the *Salon in 1876 and his work was shown in the Fifth to Eighth (and last) Impressionist Exhibitions. In 1883 he gave up his employment to become a full-time artist, but had little success and sold his collection to support himself and his family. After the last Impressionist Exhibition in 1886 he moved to Brittany, abandoning his family, and until 1890 he spent much of his time at *Pont-Aven, where he became the pivot of a group of artists who were attracted by his picturesque personality and new ideas in aesthetics. The most important work he produced there was *The Vision After the Sermon*, also known as *Jacob Wrestling with the Angel* (NG, Edinburgh, 1888), in which he broke away completely from the Impressionist style, using areas of pure, flat colour for expressive and symbolic purposes. In 1887–8 he went to Panama and Martinique, and in 1888 he spent a short time at Arles with van *Gogh, a visit which ended in a disastrous quarrel as van Gogh suffered one of his first attacks of madness.

Gauguin had had a taste for colourful, exotic places since his childhood in Peru and in 1891 he left France for Tahiti. In the book *Noa Noa*, which he wrote about his life there, he said: 'I have escaped everything that is artificial and conventional. Here I enter into Truth, become one with nature. After the disease of civilization life in this new world is a return to health.' His theory and practice of art reflected these attitudes. He was one of the first to find visual inspiration in the arts of ancient or primitive peoples, and reacted vigorously against the naturalism of the Impressionists and the scientific preoccupations of the *Neo-Impressionists. As well as using colour unnaturalistically for its decorative or emotional effect he reintroduced emphatic outlines forming rhythmic patterns suggestive of Japanese colour prints (see UKIYO-E) or the technique of stained glass. Gauguin also did woodcuts in which the black and white areas formed rhythmical, almost abstract, patterns and the tool marks were incorporated as integral parts of the design. He claimed to have revived the art of the woodcut, which had declined since it had had to compete with engraving in the 15th cent. His other work included carving and pottery. In Tahiti Gauguin endeavoured to 'go native' and despite the constant pressure of poverty he painted his finest pictures there. His painting became more profound, the colours more resonant, and the drawing more grandly simplified. In 1893, however, poverty and ill-health forced him to return to France, but he had a financial windfall when an uncle died and he was back in Tahiti in 1895. At the end of 1897 he painted his largest and most famous picture, the allegory of life, *Where Do We Come From? What Are We? Where Are We Going To?* (Mus. of Fine Arts, Boston) before attempting suicide (although he had deserted his family he had been devastated that year by the news of the death of his favourite daughter). In September 1901 he settled at Dominica in the Marquesas Islands, where he died two years later. Until his death he worked continuously in the face of poverty, illness (he had syphilis), and lack of recognition. During his time in the South Seas he was often unable to obtain proper materials and was forced to spread his colours thinly on coarse sacking, but from these limitations he forged a style of rough vigour wholly appropriate to the boldness of his vision.

At the time of his death few would have agreed with Gauguin's self-assessment: 'I am a great artist and I know it. It is because I am that I have endured such suffering.' His reputation was firmly established, however, when 227 of his works were shown at the *Salon d'Automne in Paris in 1906, and his influence has been enormous. The *Nabis were formed under his inspiration, he was a leading figure of the *Symbolist movement and one of the sources for *Fauvism. Later, he has been one of the major influences on the general non-naturalistic trend of 20th-cent. art. Because of the romantic appeal of his life and personality, particularly his willingness to sacrifice everything for his art, Gauguin has been with van Gogh the most common subject for popular and fictional biography, including the novel *The Moon and Sixpence* (1919) by Somerset Maugham, and the opera (1957) of the same title by John L. Gardner.

Gaulli, Giovanni Battista. See BACICCIO.

Geertgen tot Sint Jans (*c*.1460–*c*.1490). Netherlandish painter, born in Leiden but active in Haarlem. Almost nothing is known of his career, but van *Mander says that he was a pupil of *Ouwater and died when he was 28. His name means 'Little Gerard of the Brethren of St John', after the Order in Haarlem of which he was a lay-brother. For the monastery church of the Brethren he painted his only documented work, a *triptych of *The Crucifixion*, of which two large panels (originally two sides of a wing) survive (Kunsthistorisches Mus., Vienna): the *Lamentation of Christ* and the *Burning of the Bones of St John the Baptist*. Certain features of these paintings—particularly the slender, doll-like figures with smooth, rather egg-like heads—are highly distinctive, and a small *œuvre* of about fifteen paintings has been attributed to Geertgen on stylistic grounds. Unlike the Vienna panels, most of the other pictures given to him are fairly small. They include such remarkably beautiful works as *The Nativity* (NG, London), a radiant nocturnal scene, and *St John the Baptist in the Wilderness* (Staatliche Museen, Berlin), which shows an exquisite feeling for nature. The vein of tender melancholy that pervades Geertgen's work, the beguilingly innocent charm of his figures, and his sensitivity to light are perhaps the salient qualities that make him one of the most irresistibly attractive artists of the Early Netherlandish school.

Gelder, Aert de (1645–1727). Dutch painter, active mainly in his native Dordrecht. After studying there with *Hoogstraten, he became one of *Rembrandt's last pupils in Amsterdam. He was not only one of the most talented of Rembrandt's pupils, but also one of his most devoted followers, for he was the only Dutch artist to continue working in his style into the 18th cent. His religious paintings, in particular, with their imaginative boldness and preference for oriental types, are very much in the master's spirit, although de Gelder often used colours—such as lilac and lemon yellow—that were untypical of

Rembrandt, and his palette was in general lighter. One of his best-known works, *Jacob's Dream* (Dulwich College Picture Gal., London), was long attributed to Rembrandt.

Generalić, Ivan (1914–). Yugoslav *naïve painter, the outstanding figure of the school of peasant painters associated with his native village of Hlebine in Croatia. His repertory is extremely catholic, his favourite themes being scenes from village life, celebrations, festivals, etc., landscapes, still lifes in a landscape, figures, and portraits. Some of his pictures are quiet and almost idyllic depictions of peasant activities, but in others there is an element of grotesque fantasy reminiscent of *Bruegel or Hieronymus *Bosch, while still others have a *Surrealist air of the unexpected.

genre. Term in art history and criticism for paintings depicting scenes from daily life. It may be applied to appropriate art of any place or period, but most commonly suggests the type of domestic subject-matter favoured by Dutch 17th-cent. artists. In a broader sense, the term is used to mean a particular branch or category of art; landscape and portraiture, for example, are genres of painting, and the essay and the short story are genres of literature.

Gentile da Fabriano (*c.*1370–1427). Italian painter named after his birthplace, Fabriano in the Marches. He carried out important commissions in several major Italian art centres and was recognized as one of the foremost artists of his day, but most of the work on which his great contemporary reputation was based has been destroyed. It included frescos in the Doges' Palace in Venice (1408) and for St John Lateran in Rome (1427). In between he worked in Florence, Siena, and Orvieto. His major surviving work is the celebrated altarpiece of the *Adoration of the Magi* (Uffizi, Florence, 1423), painted for the church of Sta Trinità in Florence, which places him alongside *Ghiberti as the greatest exponent of the *International Gothic style in Italy. It is remarkable not only for its exquisite decorative beauty but also for the naturalistic treatment of light in the *predella, where there is a night scene with three different light sources. Gentile had widespread influence (much more so initially than his great contemporary *Masaccio), notably on *Pisanello, his assistant in Venice, Jacopo *Bellini, who worked with him in Florence, and Fra *Angelico, who was his greatest heir.

Gentileschi, Orazio (properly Orazio Lomi) (1563–1639). Italian painter. He was born in Pisa, but in about 1576 he settled in Rome. After working in a *Mannerist style he became one of the closest and most gifted of *Caravaggio's followers. He was one of the few *Caravaggisti who was a friend of the master, and in 1603 he and Caravaggio and two other artists were sued for libel by Giovanni *Baglione. Gentileschi's work does not have the power and uncompromising naturalism of Caravaggio, tending rather towards the lyrical and refined. His graceful figures are stately and clearly disposed, with sharp-edged drapery—qualities recalling his Tuscan heritage. In 1621 he moved to Genoa, where he stayed until 1623; while there he painted an *Annunciation* (Galleria Sabauda, Turin) that is often considered his masterpiece. After working for Marie de *Médicis in Paris, he settled in England in 1626 and became court painter to Charles I. He was held in great esteem in England and remained until his death. His travels were a factor in spreading the Caravaggesque manner, but by the end of his career he had long abandoned heavy *chiaroscuro in favour of light colours. His major works in England were a series of ceiling paintings commissioned by Charles I for the Queen's House at Greenwich, now in Marlborough House, London (probably after 1635). His daughter **Artemisia Gentileschi** (1593–*c.*1652/3) was one of the greatest of Caravaggesque painters and a formidable personality. She was precociously gifted, built up a European reputation, and lived a life of independence rare for a woman of the time. Born in Rome, she worked mainly there and in Florence until she settled in Naples in 1630 (she also visited her father in England in 1638–40). Artemisia's powerful style—totally different to that of her father—is seen at its most characteristic in paintings of *Judith and Holofernes*, a subject she made her own (one of the finest examples is in the Uffizi, Florence). Her predilection for the bloodthirsty theme has been related to events in her own life. At the age of 19 she was allegedly raped by Agostino *Tassi (who was eventually acquitted of the charge) and was tortured during the legal proceedings; thus the fierce intensity with which she depicted a woman decapitating a man has been seen as pictorial 'revenge' for her sufferings.

Gérard, François (1770–1837). French painter, born in Rome, a favourite pupil of J.-L. *David. In the *Salon of 1796 he won acclaim with his portrait of *Jean-Baptiste Isabey and his Daughter* (Louvre, Paris) and became the most sought after court and society portraitist of his day. He successfully negotiated the various political changes of the day and was made a Baron and a member of the Legion of Honour. In addition to portraits Gérard painted historical and mythological works. His style derived from David, but was much less taut and heroic, tending at times towards a rather mannered gracefulness.

Gerhaert van Leyden, Nicolaus (active 1462–73). The most powerful and original Netherlandish sculptor of the second half of the 15th cent. He is known to have worked in Strasburg, Trier, and Vienna, and several signed or documented works survive, in both stone and wood, but the details of his life are obscure. His work is extraordinarily vivid and unconventional, capturing an intense feeling of inner life, as in the celebrated bust of a man in Strasburg (Musée de l'Œuvre, Notre-Dame), which is usually considered to be a self-portrait. The voluminous style of his draperies and his boldness of approach suggest that he was trained in a Burgundian workshop where Claus *Sluter's style was still predominant, although his name indicates that he was born in the northern Netherlands. His work had considerable influence, particularly in Germany.

Géricault, Théodore (1791–1824). French painter, one of the prime movers and most original figures of *Romanticism. He studied in Paris with Carle *Vernet and Pierre *Guérin, but was influenced more by making copies of the Old Masters at the *Louvre, developing in particular a passion for *Rubens. In 1816–17 he was in Italy and there became an enthusiastic admirer of *Michelangelo and the *Baroque. On his return to Paris he exhibited the picture for which he is most famous, *The Raft of the Medusa* (Louvre, Paris,

1819), which, although it was awarded a medal at the *Salon, was to create a furore both on account of its realistic treatment of the macabre and because of its political implications (it depicts the ordeal of the survivors of the shipwreck of the *Medusa* in 1816, a disaster ascribed by some to government incompetence). The picture, which was remarkably original in treating a contemporary event with epic grandeur, also had a *succès de scandale* in England, where Géricault spent the years 1820–2. He painted jockeys and horse races (*Derby at Epsom*, Louvre, 1821) and was one of the first to introduce English painting to the notice of French artists (he was particularly enthusiastic about *Constable and *Bonington). Géricault was a passionate horseman and his death at the age of 33 was brought on by a riding accident. In his temperament and life-style as well as his work he ranks (like Byron, for example) as an archetypal Romantic artist. His tempestuous career lasted little more than a decade and in that time he displayed a meteoric and many-sided genius which never matured into a unified or settled bent. His love of stirring action, his sense of swirling movement, his energetic handling of paint, and his taste for the macabre were all to become features of Romanticism. He was, at the same time, virile and inspiring in his realism: he made studies from corpses and severed limbs for *The Raft of the Medusa* and painted an extraordinary series of portraits of mental patients in the clinic of his friend Dr Georget, one of the pioneers of humane treatment for the insane (*A Kleptomaniac*, Musée des Beaux-Arts, Ghent, *c*.1822–3). His work had enormous influence, most notably on *Delacroix.

Gérôme, Jean-Léon (1824–1904). French painter and sculptor. He was a pupil of Paul *Delaroche and inherited his highly finished academic style. His best-known works are his oriental scenes, the fruit of several visits to Egypt; two typical examples are in the Wallace Collection, London. They won Gérôme great popularity and he had considerable influence as an upholder of academic tradition and enemy of progressive trends in art; he opposed, for example, the acceptance by the state of the *Caillebotte bequest of *Impressionist pictures.

Gerstl, Richard (1883–1908). Austrian painter. His early painting was in the style of the Vienna *Sezession, influenced particularly by the decorative linearism of *Klimt. By 1905, however, he had advanced towards a personal style of *Expressionism, his finest works being portraits, including two groups of the family of the composer Arnold Schoenberg, remarkable for their psychological insight. He was a tormented character, and after running off with Schoenberg's wife he committed suicide. His work, which anticipates that of such painterly Expressionists as *Kokoschka, remained little known until the 1930s.

Gertler, Mark (1891–1939). English painter. Born of poor Polish–Jewish parents, he spoke only Yiddish up to the age of 8. He was a member of the *New English Art Club (1912–14) and became a member of the *London Group in 1915. Gertler was influenced by certain *Post-Impressionist trends, but worked in an individual manner that, particularly in his later paintings, has strong elements of folk art. His preferred subjects included still lifes and nudes, such as the earthy and voluptuous *The Queen of Sheba* (1922) in the Tate Gallery. The Tate also has his only piece of sculpture, *Acrobats* (1917). In fragile health and suffering from the fits of depression that had afflicted him since childhood, he committed suicide after an exhibition of his work proved unsuccessful.

gesso. Brilliant white preparation of chalky pigment mixed with glue, used during the Middle Ages and the Renaissance as a *ground to prepare a panel or canvas for painting or gilding. In preparing a ground the gesso was applied in several layers. When applied to frames and furniture it could be painted and gilded in the same way, and was often modelled (*gesso rilievo*). In the 20th cent. the term 'gesso' came to be used loosely for any white substance that can be mixed with water to make a ground; in reference to sculpture it often means *plaster of Paris.

Gestural painting. A term near synonymous with *Action painting, but used more broadly and not envisaging a specific school of American painting. It carries an implication that the artist's actions express his emotions and personality, just as in other walks of life gestures express a person's feelings. The name 'gestural' is applied particularly to painting in which the visible sweep and manner of applying pigment has been deliberately emphasized. It has sometimes been used as a synonym for *Art Informel or *Tachisme.

Getty, J. Paul (1892–1976). American oil magnate and art collector. Reputedly the richest man in the world, he amassed a large collection of works of art, his main areas of interest being, as he wrote in his book *The Joys of Collecting* (1966), 'Greek and Roman marbles and bronzes; Renaissance paintings; sixteenth-century Persian carpets; Savonnerie carpets and eighteenth-century French furniture and tapestries.' The J. Paul Getty Museum in Malibu, California, was opened in 1954, and in 1974 a new museum, housed in a re-creation of a Roman villa, was opened nearby. One of the archetypes of the eccentric, parsimonious millionaire, Getty lived in England from the 1950s and never saw his museum. On his death it became the most richly endowed museum in the world, and has become famous for its spectacular purchases (see LYSIPPUS), which have aroused fears that it would monopolize the world market for masterpieces. The J. Paul Getty Trust, founded in 1953 'for the diffusion of artistic and general knowledge', administers various bodies, including the Getty Center for the History of Art and the Humanities (founded 1983) in Santa Monica, California (a centre for advanced research with a large library of photographs and books), and a Grant Program, which assists, for example, with the publication of scholarly works. **J. Paul Getty Jr**. (1932–   ), one of Getty's five sons by his five wives, lives in England and has been a princely benefactor to British art institutions; most notably he gave £50,000,000 to the National Gallery, London, in 1985.

Gheeraerts, Marcus the Younger (1562–1636). Flemish-born portrait painter, who settled in England in 1568 with his father **Marcus the Elder** (c.1530–c.1590), an engraver and painter. Marcus the Younger was probably the leading society portraitist in London at the peak of his career (his popularity declined after about 1615), but it is not easy to disentangle his work from that of some of his contemporaries. The best-known work attributed to him is the splendid full-length portrait of Elizabeth I known as the 'Ditchley' portrait (NPG, London, c.1592), in which the queen is shown standing on a map of England.

Gheyn, Jacob de II (1565–1629). Dutch draughtsman, engraver, and painter. He was born at Antwerp and was probably a pupil of his father **Jacob de Gheyn I** (c.1530–82), a glass painter and *miniaturist. From c.1585 to 1590 he studied with Hendrick *Goltzius. He worked for the Court of Orange at The Hague, and designed the grotto (the earliest in the Netherlands) and other ornamentation of Buitenhof, the garden of Prince Maurice. His drawings and engravings are of greater importance than his paintings, for in their spontaneity and informality they are outstanding documents of the period of transition from *Mannerism to *naturalism in Dutch art. His son **Jacob de Gheyn III** (c.1596–1641) was also an engraver, specializing in mythological subjects.

Ghiberti, Lorenzo (1378–1455). Florentine sculptor, goldsmith, and designer. He came to prominence in 1401 when he competed successfully (defeating *Brunelleschi, Jacopo della *Quercia, and others) for a commission, offered by the merchant guild, to make a pair of gilded bronze doors for the Baptistery of Florence. His competition *relief of *The Sacrifice of Isaac* is in the Bargello, Florence. Work on the doors lasted until 1424 and in 1425 he was asked to make a second pair for the same building, which occupied him until 1452. These two commissions necessitated the formation of a large workshop in which some of the outstanding Florentine artists of the period, including *Donatello, *Masolino, and *Uccello, received at least part of their training. Ghiberti also served on the committee in charge of the architectural works of Florence Cathedral, designed stained-glass windows, goldsmiths' work, and reliquaries, and made several life-size bronze statues. He was also a writer and left a large incomplete manuscript under the title of *Commentarii*. Apart from a survey of ancient art based on *Pliny and notes on the science of optics, this manuscript contains valuable records of Italian painters and sculptors of the trecento, and also Ghiberti's autobiography, the first by an artist that has

survived. The same interest in the new humanist ideals that is reflected in Ghiberti's writings also prompted him to collect *Classical sculptures. Despite this prominent place which Ghiberti occupies in the Classical revival, his style was deeply rooted in the tradition of *Gothic craftsmanship. Not only was his first pair of Baptistery doors closely modelled on the pattern of Andrea *Pisano's earlier doors, but its twenty episodes from the Life of Christ and its eight saints reflect the *International Gothic style with its emphasis on graceful lines, lyrical sentiment, and minute attention to landscape detail. While these traits survive in Ghiberti's second pair of doors, they are here subordinated to the new principles of the *Renaissance. The doors are divided into ten large panels in which episodes from the Old Testament are represented on carefully constructed *perspective stages. As most of these reliefs were planned and laid out by 1437, they must rank among the most 'advanced' works of Florentine art, particularly in the mastery of composition within a spatial framework. The fame of these doors always stood high. *Michelangelo's dictum, recorded by *Vasari, that they were worthy to form the Gates of Paradise secured their prestige even in times less sympathetic to *quattrocento art.

Ghirlandaio, Domenico (1449–94). Florentine painter. He trained with *Baldovinetti and possibly with *Verrocchio. His style was solid, prosaic, and rather old-fashioned (especially when compared with that of his great contemporary *Botticelli), but he was an excellent craftsman and good businessman and had one of the most prosperous workshops in Florence. This he ran in collaboration with his two younger brothers, **Benedetto** (1458–97) and **Davide** (1452–1525). His largest undertaking was the fresco cycle in the choir of Sta Maria Novella, Florence, illustrating *Scenes from the Lives of the Virgin and St John the Baptist* (1486–90). This was commissioned by Giovanni Tornabuoni, a partner in the *Medici bank, and Ghirlandaio depicts the sacred story as if it had taken place in the home of a wealthy Florentine burgher. It is this talent for portraying the life and manners of his time (he often included portraits in his religious works) that has made Ghirlandaio popular with many visitors to Florence. But he also had considerable skill in the management of complex compositions and a certain grandeur of conception that sometimes hints at the High *Renaissance. Ghirlandaio worked on frescos in Pisa, San Gimignano, and Rome (in the Sistine Chapel) as well as in Florence, and his studio produced numerous altarpieces. He also painted portraits, the finest of which is *Old Man and his Grandson* (Louvre); this depicts the grandfather's diseased features with ruthless realism, but has a remarkable air of tenderness. Ghirlandaio's son and pupil **Ridolfo** (1483–1561) was a friend of *Raphael and a portrait painter of some distinction. His most famous pupil, however, was *Michelangelo.

Giacometti, Alberto (1901–66). Swiss sculptor and painter, son of the Swiss *Impressionist painter **Giovanni Giacometti** (1868–1933). After short periods at the École des Arts et Métiers, Geneva, and in Italy, he went to Paris and there worked under *Bourdelle from 1922 to 1925. He abandoned naturalistic sculpture in 1925, however, and went through a period of restless experimentation. In 1930 he attached himself to the *Surrealist movement and during the 1930s developed a highly individual attenuated manner and open-cage construction exemplified in *The Palace at 4 a.m.* (MOMA, New York, 1933). Throughout his career he was obsessed with the specifically sculptural theme of spatial relationships and it has been said by Sir Herbert *Read that in his work of this period the whole purpose and effect of Surrealist sculpture is expressed—'the construction in space of precise mechanisms that are of no use but are nevertheless profoundly disturbing'. Giacometti abandoned Surrealism in 1935, however, and began to work again from the model. In 1941–5 he lived in Geneva, but then returned to Paris, and his most characteristic style emerged in 1947, featuring 'transparent constructions' of human figures, sometimes disposed in groups, notable for their emaciated, extremely elongated, and nervous character (*Man Pointing*, Tate, London, 1947). His isolated figures often have a suggestion of existentialist tragedy, and he was indeed a friend of the existentialist philosopher Jean-Paul Sartre, who wrote on Giacometti's work. It had widespread influence, which can be seen, for example, in many of the entries for the

Unknown Political Prisoner competition of 1953 (see BUTLER, REG). Giacometti is generally considered one of the outstandingly original sculptors of the 20th cent., and from the 1950s his reputation as a painter began to increase. Most of his paintings and drawings are portraits of his family and friends; his brother Diego, who was a skilled technician and a life-long assistant, was a favourite model and the subject of dozens of sculptures, paintings, and drawings.

Giambologna (Giovanni Bologna or Jean Boulogne) (1529–1608). Flemish-born Italian sculptor. He was the greatest sculptor of the age of *Mannerism and for about two centuries after his death his reputation was second only to that of *Michelangelo. In about 1550 he went to Italy to study in and spent 2 years in Rome. On the way back he stopped in Florence and was based there for the rest of his life. The work that made his name, however, was for Bologna—the *Fountain of Neptune* (1563–6), with its impressive nude figure of Neptune which he had designed for a similar fountain in Florence (*Ammanati defeated him in the competition). Even before working on the fountain in Bologna, however Giambologna had begun in Florence the first of a series of celebrated marble groups that in their mastery of complex twisting poses mark one of the high-points of Mannerist art: *Samson Slaying a Philistine* (V&A, London, c.1561–2); *Florence Triumphant over Pisa* (Bargello, Florence, completed 1575); *The Rape of a Sabine* (Loggia dei Lanzi, Florence, 1581–2); *Hercules and the Centaur* (Loggia dei Lanzi, Florence, 1594–1600). Giambologna worked extensively for the *Medici and his monument to Duke Cosimo I (1587–95) was the first equestrian statue made in Florence and an immensely influential design, becoming the pattern for similar statues all over Europe (for example that of Charles I by Hubert *Le Sueur at Charing Cross in London). Giambologna's similar statue to Henry IV of France, formerly on the Pont Neuf in Paris, has been destroyed. It was for the Medici that he made his largest work—the colossal (about 10 m. high) figure of the mountain god *Appennino* (1577–81) in the gardens of the family's villa at Pratolino. Constructed of brick and stone, the god crouches above a pool and seems to have emerged from the earth, fusing brilliantly with the landscape. Giambologna was as happy working on a small scale as in a monumental vein. His small bronze statuettes were enormously popular (they continued to be reproduced almost continuously until the 20th cent.) and being portable helped to give his style European currency. Many of his preliminary models also survive (uniquely for an Italian sculptor of his period), giving insight into his creative processes. The best collection is in the Victoria and Albert Museum.

Gibbons, Grinling (1648–1721). Dutch-born wood-carver and sculptor who settled in England c.1667. He was discovered by John Evelyn (see *Diary*, 18 Jan., 1671) and introduced to King Charles II and to Sir Christopher Wren, who employed him on decorations at Hampton Court and St Paul's Cathedral. In 1714 he was made Master Carver to King George I. Gibbons was unsurpassed in his day for naturalistic decorative carving of fruits, flowers, and shells, strung together in garlands and festoons, with small animals, cherubs' heads, etc. Because of his fame an enormous amount of work has been attributed to him, but he lived in a great age of English craftsmanship and much of the carving that is connected with his name was done by artists influenced by his style. Apart from his work for Wren, his documented commissions include outstanding ensembles at Burghley House, Lincolnshire, and Petworth House, Sussex. His virtuosity in wood was not equalled in marble or bronze, and George *Vertue said of him: 'He was a most excellent carver in wood, he was neither well skill'd or practized in Marble or Brass for which works he employd the best artists he coud procure.' About 1684 he took as partner Artus *Quellin III, who is thought to have been responsible for some of the figure sculpture for which Gibbons was officially responsible.

Gibson, John (1790–1866). British *Neoclassical sculptor. His early years were spent as a monumental mason in Liverpool, where he became a protégé of the banker and connoisseur William Roscoe. In 1817 he moved to London, where he was taken up by *Flaxman, on whose encouragement he went to Rome the following year with an introduction to *Canova, whose pupil

he became. Later he was also taught by *Thorvaldsen. He spent nearly all the rest of his life in Rome apart from occasional visits to England, the longest being from 1844 to 1847. Gibson won recognition internationally as one of the outstanding Neoclassical sculptors, and in his enthusiasm for Greek art he experimented with the ancient practice of colouring statues (see POLYCHROMY), arousing much controversy. His best-known work of this type is the *Tinted Venus* (Walker Art Gal., Liverpool, 1851). He left the fortune he made from his work to the *Royal Academy.

Gilbert, Sir Alfred (1854–1934). British sculptor and metal worker. After beginning to train as a surgeon he studied art at the *Royal Academy Schools and the École des *Beaux-Arts, Paris, after which he spent six years in Rome. He returned to England in 1884 and worked on several major projects, the best known of which is his Shaftesbury Memorial Fountain in Piccadilly Circus (1887–93). The celebrated figure of *Eros* that surmounts the fountain was cast in the new light-weight aluminium, allowing Gilbert to achieve a much more delicately poised pose than if he had been restricted to the traditional medium of bronze. Although Gilbert was hard-working, respected, and sought-after, he was unworldly and a hopeless businessman; his refusal to delegate work or compromise his standards meant that he took on more work than he could handle and he sometimes lost money on commissions. In 1901 he became bankrupt, and in 1909 he moved into self-imposed exile in Bruges. However, in 1926 he returned to England at the request of King George V to complete his masterpiece, the tomb of the Duke of Clarence in St George's Chapel, Windsor Castle, which he had begun in 1892. The sinuous and labyrinthine detailing, crafted with consummate skill, reveals Gilbert as one of the major practitioners of *Art Nouveau, although he himself was disparaging about the style. Gilbert's reputation suffered after his death because he was so clearly outside the mainstream of 20th-cent. art, but he is now regarded as the greatest English sculptor of his generation.

Gilbert and George (Gilbert Proesch, 1943– , and George Passmore, 1942–).

British avant-garde artists who met whilst studying at St Martin's School of Art in London in 1967 and since 1968 have lived and worked together as self-styled 'living sculptures': 'Being living sculptures is our life blood, our destiny, our romance, our disaster, our light and life.' They have worked in various media, including painting, photographs, and *Performance art. In 1986 they won the prestigious Turner Prize (see MORLEY), an award that was widely criticized, for, although they are the darlings of a certain section of the art world, they are regarded by many critics as tedious poseurs.

Gill, Eric (1882–1940). British sculptor, engraver, typographer, and writer. He began to earn his living as a letter cutter in 1903 and carved his first figure piece in 1910. In 1913 he became a convert to Roman Catholicism and was commissioned to make the *Stations of the Cross* at West-minster Cathedral, fourteen *relief carvings which he did in 1914–18. These and the *Prospero and Ariel* group on Broadcasting House (1929–31) are his best-known sculptures. Gill was one of the chief protagonists in the movement for the revival of direct carving, and his work usually has an impressive simplicity of conception; he wrote that his 'inability to draw naturalistically was, instead of a drawback, no less than my salvation. It compelled me . . . to concentrate upon something other than the superficial delights of fleshly appearance . . . to consider the significance of things.' He tried to revive a religious attitude towards art and craftsmanship, and in life, as in his work and writing, he was a vigorous advocate of a romanticized medievalism. His unconventionality was famous in his own time, but the most bizarre and unpleasant aspects of his life were not revealed until the publication of Fiona MacCarthy's biography in 1989: he had incestuous relationships with two of his sisters and two of his daughters and sexual congress with a dog. Gill was a major figure in the revival of book design and typography. He illustrated many books, and his 'Perpetua' and 'Gill Sans-Serif' typefaces are among the classics of 20th-cent. typography. His books include *Christianity and Art* (1927), *Art* (1934), and *Autobiography* (1940).

Gillot, Claude (1673–1722). French painter, draughtsman, and etcher. Few of his paintings survive, but his predilection for scenes from the *commedia dell'arte* (*Quarrel of the Cabmen*, Louvre, Paris) was inherited by his pupil *Watteau. His work survives mainly in the form of drawings and etchings, and he excelled at designs in the elegant *Rococo manner of *Audran.

Gillray, James (1757–1815). One of the most eminent of English *caricaturists. He began his career as an engraver of letter-heads and although he later studied at the *Royal Academy Schools, he seems to have been largely self-trained. After the publication of *A New Way to Pay the National Debt* (1786), a satire on the royal family, he found his bent in caricature and achieved enormous popularity. He enlarged the scope of *Hogarth's satire, making his caricature more personal than Hogarth's general social comment, and he showed great fecundity and vividness of imagination. His career was cut short by insanity in 1811.

Gilman, Harold (1876–1919). English painter. He was a member of *Sickert's circle, a founder of the *Camden Town Group, and first President of the *London Group. His preference for working-class subjects derived from Sickert, but he differed from him in his brilliant palette and bold simplification of planes, which reflected his interest in the *Post-Impressionists. He was one of the most gifted English painters of his generation, but his career was cut short by the influenza epidemic of 1919.

Gilpin, Sawrey (1733–1807). English animal painter. He began his career as an apprentice to Samuel *Scott, the marine painter, but turned early to the painting of horses, making a name with 'portraits' of celebrated racers. In occasional large canvases (*The Election of Darius*, City Art Gal., York) he contrived his own admixture of horse and history painting. His son, **William Sawrey Gilpin** (1762–1843), was the first president of the Old Water-Colour Society. The Revd **William Gilpin** (1724–1804), brother of Sawrey Gilpin, was a writer and amateur draughtsman and one of the most important advocates of the *picturesque.

Ginner, Charles (1878–1952). English painter, born at Cannes. He studied in Paris and in 1910 settled in London, becoming a member of the informal group of artists who met in *Sickert's studio, and in 1911 a founder of the *Camden Town Group. His direct knowledge of French *Post-Impressionism made him a respected figure among his English contemporaries. Ginner is chiefly known for his urban scenes, usually featuring conventionally unattractive buildings, painted with highly ordered brush-strokes that create a sense of structural solidity.

Giordano, Luca (1634–1705). Neapolitan painter, the most important Italian decorative artist of the second half of the 17th cent. He was nicknamed '*Luca Fa Presto*' (Luke work quickly) because of his prodigious speed of execution and huge output. He began in the circle of *Ribera, but his style became much more colourful under the influence of such great decorative painters as *Veronese, whose works he saw on his extensive travels. Indeed, he absorbed a host of influences and was said to be able to imitate other artists' styles with ease. His work was varied also in subject-matter, although he was primarily a religious and mythological painter. He worked mainly in Naples, but also extensively in Florence and Venice, and his work had great influence in Italy. In 1692 he was called to Spain by Charles II and stayed there for 10 years, painting in Madrid, Toledo, and the *Escorial. His last work when he returned to Naples was the ceiling of the Treasury Chapel of S. Martino. In his personal self-confidence and courtliness, and in the open, airy compositions and light luminous colours of his work, Giordano presages such great 18th-cent. painters as *Tiepolo.

Giorgione (Giorgio Barbarelli or Giorgio da Castelfranco) (1476/8–1510). Venetian painter. Almost nothing is known of his life and only a handful of paintings can be confidently attributed to him, but he holds a momentous place in the history of art. He had achieved legendary status soon after his early death (probably from plague) and through succeeding centuries he has continued to excite the imagination in a way that few other painters can match. The extraordinary discrepancy between his enormous fame and the tiny scale of his œuvre is explained by the fact that he initiated a new conception of painting. He was one of the earliest artists to specialize in *cabinet pictures for private collectors rather than works for public or ecclesiastical patrons, and he was the first painter who subordinated subject-matter to the evocation of mood—it is clear that his contemporaries sometimes did not know what was represented in his pictures. *Vasari, who says that Giorgione earned his nickname—meaning 'Big George'—'because of his physical appearance and his moral and intellectual stature', ranked him alongside *Leonardo as one of the founders of 'modern' painting.

Giorgione was born in Castelfranco, about 30 km. north-west of Venice, and according to Vasari he trained with Giovanni *Bellini (although it has also been suggested that *Carpaccio may have been his teacher). He had two important public commissions in Venice; in 1507–8 he was working on a canvas (now lost without trace) for the audience chamber of the Doges' Palace, and in 1508 he collaborated with *Titian on frescos for the exterior of the Fondaco dei Tedeschi (the German warehouse), now known only through engravings and ruinous fragments. Apart from this, the only contemporary documentation on any of his surviving paintings is an inscription on the back of a female portrait known as *Laura* (Kunsthistorisches Mus., Vienna), which says it was painted by 'Master Zorzi da Castelfranco' in 1506; it also records that Giorgione was a colleague of Vicenzo *Catena, a partnership about which nothing else is known. The main document for reconstructing Giorgione's œuvre is the notebook of the Venetian collector and connoisseur Marcantonio Michiel, written between 1525 and 1543. Michiel, who is a scrupulous and reliable source, mentions a number of paintings by Giorgione, four of which can be identified with extant works: *The Tempest* (Accademia, Venice), *The Three Philosophers* (Kunsthistorisches Mus.), *Sleeping Venus* (Gemäldegalerie, Dresden), and (an oblique and less explicit reference than the others) *Christ Carrying the Cross* (S. Rocco, Venice). He says *The Three Philosophers* was finished by *Sebastiano del Piombo and the *Sleeping Venus* by Titian. The problem of attribution was, then, complicated from the start by the fact that Giorgione left works uncompleted that were finished by other hands, and confusion soon arose; in the first edition of his *Lives* (1550) Vasari attributed the S. Rocco painting to Giorgione, but in the second edition (1568) he gave it in one place to Giorgione and in another to Titian, even though 'many people believed it was by Giorgione'. Distinguishing between the work of Giorgione and the young Titian continues to be one of the knottiest problems in connoisseurship, the celebrated *Concert Champêtre* in the Louvre being the picture most hotly disputed between them.

Among the other paintings given to Giorgione are the *Castelfranco Madonna*, in the cathedral of his home town (first mentioned by *Ridolfi in 1648 and accepted by almost all critics), and several male portraits, including a self-portrait in the Herzog-Anton-Ulrich Museum in Brunswick (perhaps a copy). Giorgione is said to have been handsome and amorous, and he initiated a type of dreamily romantic portrait that became immensely popular in Venice. The powerful influence that his work exerted in the generation after his death (even the venerable Bellini succumbed to it) is one of the main factors in making the construction of a catalogue of his work so difficult, for there are scores of paintings of the period, particularly pastoral landscapes, that can be described as Giorgionesque, and many are of high quality. The problems of *iconography that Giorgione's paintings present are sometimes every bit as difficult as those of attribution. The most famous instance is *The Tempest*. Michiel saw it in 1530 and described it as a 'little landscape with the tempest with the gipsy and soldier', so he evidently did not know what subject, if any, was represented. X-rays have shown that Giorgione radically altered the figures in a way that suggests he was here indulging his imagination rather than illustrating a particular theme, although many ingenious attempts have been made to unravel a subject. This development of the 'landscape of mood' was, indeed, his great contribution to the history of art—an innovation of great originality and influence. Apart from the artists already mentioned, *Palma Vecchio, *Savoldo, and Dosso *Dossi were among the outstanding contemporaries who fell under the Giorgionesque spell, and among later artists *Watteau was his most sensitive heir.

Giottesques. A term applied to the 14th-cent. followers of *Giotto. The best-known of the 'Giotteschi' are the Florentines Taddeo *Gaddi, *Maso di Banco, Bernardo *Daddi, and to a lesser extent the *Master of St Cecilia. Giotto's most loyal follower was Maso, who concentrated on the essential and maintained Giotto's high seriousness.

Giotto di Bondone (*c.*1267–1337). Florentine painter and architect. Giotto is regarded as the founder of the central tradition of Western painting because his work broke free from the stylizations of *Byzantine art, introducing new ideals of naturalism and creating a convincing sense of pictorial space. His momentous achievement was recognized by his contemporaries (Dante praised him in a famous passage of *The Divine Comedy*, where he said he had surpassed his master *Cimabue), and in about 1400 Cennino *Cennini wrote 'Giotto translated the art of painting from Greek to Latin.' In spite of his fame and the demand for his services, no surviving painting is documented as being by him. His work, indeed, poses some formidable problems of attribution, but it is universally agreed that the fresco cycle in the Arena Chapel at Padua is by Giotto, and it forms the starting-point for any consideration of his work. The Arena Chapel (so-called because it occupies the site of a Roman arena) was built by Enrico Scrovegni in expiation for the sins of his father, a notorious usurer mentioned by Dante. It was begun in 1303 and Giotto's frescos are usually dated *c.*1305–6. They run right round the interior of the building; the west wall is covered with a *Last Judgement*, there is an *Annunciation* over the chancel arch, and the main wall areas have three tiers of paintings representing scenes from the life of the Virgin and her parents, St Anne and St Joachim, and events from the Passion of Christ. Below these scenes are figures personifying Virtues and Vices, painted to simulate stone *reliefs—the first *grisailles. The figures in the main narrative scenes are about half life-size, but in reproduction they usually look bigger because Giotto's conception is so grand and powerful. His figures have a completely new sense of three-dimensionality and physical presence, and in portraying the sacred events he creates a feeling of moral weight rather than divine splendour. He seems to base the representations upon personal experience, and no artist has surpassed his ability to go straight to the heart of a story and express its essence with gestures and expressions of unerring conviction.

The other major fresco cycle associated with Giotto's name is that on the Life of St Francis in the Upper Church of S. Francesco at Assisi. Whether Giotto painted this is not only the central problem facing scholars of his work, but also one of the most controversial issues in the history of art. The St Francis frescos are clearly the work of an artist of great stature (their intimate and humane portrayals have done much to determine posterity's mental image of the saint), but the stylistic differences between these works and the Arena Chapel frescos seem to many critics so pronounced that they cannot accept a common authorship. Attempts to attribute other frescos at Assisi to Giotto have met with no less controversy (see also MASTER OF THE ST FRANCIS LEGEND and MASTER OF ST CECILIA). There is a fair measure of agreement about the frescos associated with Giotto in Sta Croce in Florence. He probably painted in four chapels there, and work survives in the Bardi and Peruzzi chapels, probably dating from the 1320s. The frescos are in very uneven condition (they were whitewashed in the 18th cent.), but some of those in the Bardi Chapel on the life of St Francis remain deeply impressive. Nothing survives of Giotto's work done for Robert of Anjou in Naples, and the huge mosaic of the Ship of the Church (the Navicella) that he designed for Old St Peter's in Rome has been so thoroughly altered that it tells us nothing about his style. In Rome he would have seen the work of Pietro *Cavallini, which was as important an influence on him as that of his master Cimabue.

Several panel paintings bear Giotto's signature, notably the Stefaneschi Altarpiece (Vatican), done for Cardinal Stefaneschi, who also commissioned the Navicella, but it is generally agreed that the signature is a trademark showing that the works came from Giotto's shop rather than an indication of his personal workmanship. On the other hand, the Ognissanti Madonna (Uffizi, Florence, c.1305–10) is neither signed nor firmly documented, but is a work of such grandeur and humanity that it is universally accepted as Giotto's. Among the other panels attributed to him,

the finest is the Crucifix in Sta Maria Novella, Florence. On account of his great fame as a painter, Giotto was appointed architect to Florence Cathedral in 1334; he began the celebrated campanile, but his design was altered after his death. In the generation after his death he had an overwhelming influence on Florentine painting; it declined with the growth of *International Gothic, but his work was later an inspiration to *Masaccio, and even to *Michelangelo. These two giants were his true spiritual heirs.

Giovanni da Maiano. See BENEDETTO DA MAIANO.

Giovanni di Paolo (active 1420–82). One of the most attractive and idiosyncratic painters of the Sienese School, sometimes called Giovanni dal Poggio, from the district of the city where he lived. Little is known of his life, but there is a considerable number of surviving works by him—all small-scale religious panels. He may have been taught by *Taddeo di Bartolo and was influenced notably by *Gentile da Fabriano and *Sassetta, but his style is highly personal and engaging, with rather whimsical figures inhabiting strange landscapes. After centuries of neglect his reputation was revived by *Berenson, who called him 'the El *Greco of the *quattrocento'.

Girardon, François (1628–1715). French sculptor. He ranked with *Coysevox as the outstanding sculptor of Louis XIV's reign, but his style was more restrained and *Classical, embodying the ideas of the Academy. Much of his work was done for Versailles, where he collaborated with *Lebrun, and his group Apollo Tended by the Nymphs, commissioned in 1666, has been considered the most purely Classical work of French 17th-cent. sculpture. (The group was originally in a grotto room, but is now in the palace gardens.) His other work includes the monument to Cardinal Richelieu (1675–7) in the church of the Sorbonne, and an equestrian statue of Louis XIV made (1683–92) for the Place Vendôme but destroyed in the Revolution. Girardon died on the same day as Louis XIV.

Girodet de Roucy, Anne-Louis (1767–1824). French painter and illustrator, usually known as Girodet-Trioson, a name he adopted in honour of a benefactor, Dr Trioson. He studied with J.-L. *David and won the *Prix de Rome in 1789, returning to Paris in 1795. In style and technique he followed David, but for his choice of themes and his emotional treatment he was acclaimed by the young *Romantics. He was particularly interested in unusual colour effects and in the problems of concentrated light and shade, as in *The Sleep of Endymion* (1792) and *The Entombment of Atala* (1808), both in the Louvre. Girodet often favoured literary themes, but he also won renown for his paintings glorifying Napoleon (*The Revolt of Cairo*, Versailles Mus., 1810) and was a fine portraitist. One of his best-known portraits, *Mademoiselle Lange as Diana* (Minneapolis Institute of Arts, 1799), caused a scandal because of its satirical sexual allusions. His book illustrations included work for editions of Jean Racine and Virgil. In 1812 he inherited a fortune and thereafter devoted himself to writing unreadably boring poems on aesthetics.

Girtin, Thomas (1775–1802). English landscape painter in water-colours. His earlier works were tinted drawings in the 18th-cent. topographical tradition, but before the end of his short life he had developed a technique that revolutionized water-colour painting. He used strong colour in broad *washes, influenced to some extent by J. R. *Cozens, but going beyond him in the grandeur with which he created effects of space, the power with which he suggested mood, and the boldness of his compositions. His work stands at the beginning of the classic English tradition of water-colour painting, freed from its dependence on line drawing, and *Turner acknowledged his friend's greatness with the words 'If Tom Girtin had lived, I should have starved.' Girtin made tours in various parts of Britain, and spent six months in Paris in 1801–2, making a series of etchings of the city that were published in 1803. In 1802 he exhibited an enormous panorama of London, painted in oils—the *Eidometropolis*—but this is no longer extant.

gisant. French term used from the 15th cent. onwards for a lying or recumbent effigy on a funerary monument. The *gisant* typically represented a person in death (sometimes decomposition) and the *gisant* position was contrasted with the *orant*, which represented the person as if alive in a kneeling or praying position. In Renaissance monuments *gisants* often formed part of the lower register, where the deceased person was represented as a corpse, while on the upper part he was represented *orant* as if alive.

Gislebertus (active first half of 12th cent.). French *Romanesque sculptor. He was one of the great geniuses of medieval art, but his name has survived only because he carved his signature—*Gislebertus hoc fecit*—beneath the feet of the central figure of Christ in the tympanum of the west doorway of Autun Cathedral in Burgundy. The unusually prominent position of his signature suggests that his greatness was appreciated in his own time. The typanum represents the Last Judgement; it is a huge work (over 6 m. wide at the base) and a masterpiece of expressionistic carving, conveying both the horror of the damned and the serenity of the elect with awesome power. Most of the rest of the sculptural decoration of the cathedral can be confidently attributed to Gislebertus. It includes a carving of Eve, one of the few surviving fragments of the north doorway (now in the Musée Rolin, Autun), a large-scale reclining nude without parallel in medieval art, and the decoration of 60 or so capitals. These display his great fecundity of imagination and range of feeling. It is highly probable that Gislebertus was trained in the workshop that was responsible for the decoration of the abbey of Cluny, the most influential of all Romanesque monasteries, and that he worked at the nearby cathedral at Vézelay before going to Autun. He was already a mature artist when he started at Autun, where he worked c.1125–35, and his style changed little while he was there. His influence was felt in the sculpture of various Burgundian churches, and many of his ideas had a long-term effect on the development of French *Gothic sculpture.

Giuliano da Maiano. See BENEDETTO DA MAIANO.

Giulio Romano (prob. 1499–1546). Italian painter and architect, born in Rome and active mainly in Mantua. He was

*Raphael's chief pupil and assistant (although exactly what part he played is controversial) and one of the major figures of *Mannerist art. About 1515 he was working on Raphael's Stanza dell' Incendio in the Vatican and after the master's death in 1520 Giulio became his main artistic executor, completing a number of his unfinished works, including the *Transfiguration* (Vatican) and the decorations of the Villa Madama. His independent works of this time include the *Holy Family* in Sta Maria dell' Anima, Rome. He also designed some pornographic prints that caused such a scandal that their engraver Marcantonio *Raimondi was imprisoned (their notoriety was sustained by the sonnets that the poet Pietro Aretino wrote inspired by them soon after their publication). Giulio had moved to Mantua in 1524 and escaped Raimondi's fate. He remained there for the rest of his life and dominated the artistic affairs of the *Gonzaga court. The great monument to his genius is the Palazzo del Tè, begun in 1526 for Federico Gonzaga. This was one of the first Mannerist buildings, deliberately flouting the canons of Classical architecture as exemplified by *Bramante in order to shock and surprise the spectator. The same tendency is continued in Giulio's fresco decoration in the palace, especially in the *Sala de' Giganti*, where the whole room is painted from floor to ceiling to give an overall illusionistic effect, and the spectator feels himself overwhelmed by the rocks and thunderbolts hurled down on the rebellious Titans who attempted to storm Olympus. Giulio painted several other frescos in the Palazzo del Tè and in the Sala di Troia of the Ducal Palace at Mantua which testify to his Classical learning and exuberant invention. His muscular style owed much to *Michelangelo as well as to Raphael, but was less daunting than that of either and proved widely influential. Indeed, he became one of the most famous painters of his day and has the distinction of being the only artist mentioned by Shakespeare (in *The Winter's Tale*), who called him 'that rare Italian master Julio Romano', but mistakenly imagined him a sculptor.

Giusti, Giovanni (1485–1549). Italian-born sculptor who settled at Tours in France in about 1504, changing his name to Jean Juste. He was a leading figure in the introduction of the *Renaissance style

to France. His masterpiece is the tomb of Louis XII and Anne of Brittany, made at Tours in 1517–18 and set up in the Abbey of Saint-Denis by Francis I in 1531. He was probably assisted in the work by his brother **Antonio** (1479–1519). It features seated figures of the twelve Apostles in purely Italian style, allegorical figures of the Virtues, and *reliefs depicting the King's Italian victories.

Giustiniani. Prominent Italian family, branches of which were established in many parts of Italy, especially Genoa and Venice, where they played an important role in politics, literature, and religion. For the arts the most interesting member of the family was the enormously wealthy **Marchese Vincenzo** (1564–1638). He owned the finest collection of *antique sculpture in Rome—published in the *Galleria Giustiniana* (1631), the first ever illustrated catalogue of an art collection—and was an enthusiastic and discriminating patron of painters, especially *Caravaggio and his northern followers.

Glackens, William James (1870–1938). American painter and draughtsman. His early career was spent mainly as a newspaper illustrator, but he was encouraged to take up painting by Robert *Henri, whom he met in 1891. With Henri he became a member of The *Eight and of the *Ash-can school. Glackens, however, was less concerned with Social *Realism than with representing the life of the people as a colourful spectacle, and he was heavily influenced by the *Impressionists. By the time of the *Armory Show, which he helped to organize and in which he was represented, he was painting in the manner of the early *Renoir. In 1912 Glackens was employed as art consultant to Dr Albert C. *Barnes and toured Europe buying paintings by Renoir, *Degas, *Cézanne, van *Gogh, and others.

glair. White of egg when used as the *medium in *illuminating manuscripts, in *tempera painting, and in gilding with gold-dust. It is also used as an adhesive substance to fix gold leaf.

Glasgow School. Term applied to two quite distinct groups of Scottish artists active respectively in the late 19th and early 20th cents. The earlier group (who preferred to be known as the 'Glasgow Boys') was a loose association of painters (including *Lavery) centred in Glasgow who were in revolt against the conservatism of the *Royal Academy and were advocates of open-air painting (see PLEIN AIR). The school had reached its apogee before 1900 and did not outlast the First World War, but it had some influence on younger painters at the opening of the 20th cent. The later important group created a distinctive version of *Art Nouveau. Its most important member was the architect Charles Rennie Mackintosh.

glass prints (or **clichés-verre**). Prints made by exposing sensitized photographic paper to the sun beneath a glass plate on which the design has been drawn. Such prints resemble *etchings. The medium was popular in the 1850s, its practitioners including *Corot, *Daubigny, Jean-François *Millet, and Théodore *Rousseau.

glaze. A transparent layer of paint applied over another colour or *ground, so that the light passing through is reflected back by the under surface and modified by the glaze. The effect of an under-colour through a glaze is not the same as any effect obtainable by mixing the two *pigments in direct painting, for the glaze imparts a special depth and luminosity. From the 15th to the 19th cent. most oil paintings were built up as an elaborate structure of superimposed layers, glazes, and *scumbles over an *underpainting, but since *alla prima painting became the norm such a highly deliberate, craftsmanly approach has fallen into disfavour.

Gleizes, Albert (1881–1953). French painter, graphic artist, and writer. His early works were in an *Impressionist manner, but in 1909 he became associated with *Cubism, and in 1912 he wrote with *Metzinger the book *Du Cubisme*. This was the first book on the movement and is regarded as the most important exposition of the theoretical principles of the Cubist aesthetic. In 1912 he was among the founders of the *Section d'Or group and in 1913 he exhibited at the *Armory Show, New York. He spent the First World War in New York and in 1917 he experienced a religious conversion and subsequently wrote several books on spiritual meaning in art.

Gleyre, Charles (1808–74). Swiss painter, active mainly in Paris, where he enjoyed a successful career, particularly with anecdotal scenes, sometimes in an *antique setting, and portraits. He was a renowned teacher and when *Delaroche closed down his teaching studio in 1843, the majority of his students transferred to Gleyre. He taught *Whistler and several of the *Impressionists—*Bazille, *Monet, *Renoir, and *Sisley—and although his own paintings were conventional, he encouraged open-air painting (see PLEIN AIR). Renoir, however, said that his main strength as a teacher was that he left his pupils 'pretty much to their own devices'. Gleyre closed his studio in 1864 because of an eye ailment.

Gobelins. French tapestry manufactury, named after a family of dyers and clothmakers who set up business on the outskirts of Paris in the 15th cent. Their premises became a tapestry factory in the early 17th cent., and in 1662 it was taken over by Louis XIV, with Charles *Lebrun as Director. Initially it made not only tapestries but also every kind of product (except carpets, which were woven at the Savonnerie factory) required for the furnishing of the royal palaces—its official title was Manufacture royale des meubles de la Couronne. The celebrated tapestry designed by Lebrun showing *Louis XIV Visiting the Gobelins* (Gobelins Mus., Paris, 1663–75) gives a good idea of the range of its activities. In 1694 the factory was closed because of the king's financial difficulties, and although it re-opened in 1699, thereafter it made only tapestries. For much of the 18th cent. it retained its position as the foremost tapestry manufactory in Europe. *Oudry and *Boucher successively held the post of Director (1733–70). The Gobelins continues in production today and houses a tapestry museum.

Godefroid de Clair (Godefroid de Huy). *Mosan goldsmith and enamellist, active in the 12th cent. He may have trained in the workshop of *Renier of Huy. Early sources praise his great skill and suggest he was a prolific artist, but his career is obscure and the numerous attributions to him of reliquaries and *enamels are highly speculative. Peter Lasko (*Ars Sacra: 800–1200*, 1972) considers that 'On the whole, the introduction of the personality of Godefroid has hindered rather than helped our understanding of the development of the Mosan style.'

Godward, J. W. See ALMA-TADEMA.

Goes, Hugo van der (d. 1482). The greatest Netherlandish painter of the second half of the 15th cent. Nothing is known of his life before 1467, when he became a master in the painters' guild at Ghent. He had numerous commissions from the town of Ghent for work of a temporary nature such as processional banners, and in 1475 he became dean of the painters' guild. In the same year he entered a priory near Brussels as a lay-brother, but he continued to paint and also to travel. In 1481 he suffered a mental breakdown (he had a tendency to acute depression) and although he recovered, died the following year. An account of his illness by Gaspar Ofhuys, a monk at the priory, survives; Ofhuys was apparently jealous of Hugo and his description has been called by Erwin *Panofsky 'a masterpiece of clinical accuracy and sanctimonious malice'. No paintings by Hugo are signed and his only securely documented work is his masterpiece, a large *triptych of the Nativity known as the *Portinari Altarpiece* (Uffizi, Florence, c.1475–6). This was commissioned by Tommaso Portinari, the representative of the House of *Medici in Bruges, for the church of the Hospital of Sta Maria Nuova in Florence, and it exercised a strong influence on Italian painters with its masterful handling of the oil technique. There is a great variety of surface ornament and detail, but this is combined with lucid organization of the figure groups and a convincing sense of spatial depth. As remarkable as Hugo's skill in reconciling grandeur of conception with keen observation is his psychological penetration in the depiction of individual figures, notably the awe-struck shepherds. The other works attributed to Hugo include two large panels probably designed as organ shutters (Royal coll., on loan to NG of Scotland). His last work is generally thought to be the *Death of the Virgin* (Groeningemuseum, Bruges), a painting of remarkable tension and poignancy that seems a fitting swan-song for such a tormented personality.

Goethe, Johann Wolfgang von (1749–1832). German writer, scientist, and amateur artist, one of the giants of European literature and one of the major figures of the *Romantic movement. Throughout his life he devoted much time to the study of painting and was a prolific draughtsman. Although his talent as an artist was modest, his writings on art were very influential in the upsurge of Romantic ideas in Germany. Identifying art with 'nature', Goethe held that great art must simulate and carry on the blind creative force in nature. He also advocated the typically Romantic view that art should concentrate on what is individually 'characteristic' rather than the generic type. In 1786–8 he visited Italy, where he came into contact with German artists such as *Tischbein in Rome, and his taste changed to an appreciation of the *Classicism of the *Renaissance. Identifying art with 'style', he now maintained that beauty is symbolic expression of the inner laws of nature, and that this expression had been supremely achieved by the art of antiquity. His writings on art included a book on theory of colour (*Zur Farbenlehre*, 1810, English translation 1840), in which he purported to refute the *Optics* of Newton, and a translation into German of *Cellini's *Autobiography* (1798).

Gogh, Vincent van (1853–90). Dutch painter and draughtsman, with *Cézanne and *Gauguin the greatest of *Post-Impressionist artists. His uncle was a partner in the international firm of picture dealers Goupil and Co. and in 1869 van Gogh went to work in the branch at The Hague. In 1873 he was sent to the London branch and fell unsuccessfully in love with the daughter of his landlady. This was the first of several disastrous attempts to find happiness with a woman, and his unrequited passion affected him so badly that he was dismissed from his job. He returned to England in 1876 as an unpaid assistant at a school, and his experience of urban squalor awakened a religious zeal and a longing to serve his fellow men. His father was a Protestant pastor, and van Gogh first trained for the ministry, but he abandoned his studies in 1878 and went to work as a lay preacher among the impoverished miners of the grim Borinage district in Belgium. In his zeal he gave away his own worldly goods to the poor and was dismissed for his literal interpretation of Christ's teaching. He remained in the Borinage, suffering acute poverty and a spiritual crisis, until 1880, when he found that art was his vocation and the means by which he could bring consolation to humanity. From this time he worked at his new 'mission' with single-minded frenzy, and although he often suffered from extreme poverty and undernourishment, his output in the ten remaining years of his life was prodigious: about 800 paintings and a similar number of drawings.

From 1881 to 1885 van Gogh lived in the Netherlands, sometimes with his parents, sometimes in lodgings, supported by his devoted brother Theo, who regularly sent him money from his own small salary. In keeping with his humanitarian outlook he painted peasants and workers, the most famous picture from this period being *The Potato Eaters* (Van Gogh Museum, Amsterdam, 1885). Of this he wrote to Theo: 'I have tried to emphasize that those people, eating their potatoes in the lamp-light have dug the earth with those very hands they put in the dish, and so it speaks of manual labour, and how they have honestly earned their food.' In 1885 van Gogh moved to Antwerp on the advice of Antoine *Mauve (a cousin by marriage), and studied for some months at the Academy there. Academic instruction had little to offer such an individualist, however, and in February 1886 he moved to Paris, where he met *Pissarro, *Degas, Gauguin, *Seurat, and *Toulouse-Lautrec. At this time his painting underwent a violent metamorphosis under the combined influence of *Impressionism and Japanese woodcuts (see UKIYO-E), losing its moralistic flavour of social realism. Van Gogh became obsessed by the symbolic and expressive values of colours and began to use them for this purpose rather than, as did the Impressionists, for the reproduction of visual appearances, atmosphere, and light. 'Instead of trying to reproduce exactly what I have before my eyes,' he wrote, 'I use colour more arbitrarily so as to express myself more forcibly.' Of his *Night Café* (Yale Univ. Art Gal., 1888), he said: 'I have tried to express with red and green the terrible passions of human nature.' For a time he was influenced by Seurat's delicate *pointillist manner, but he abandoned this for broad, vigorous, and swirling brush-strokes.

In February 1888 van Gogh settled at Arles, where he painted more than 200 canvases in 15 months. During this time he sold no pictures, was in poverty, and suffered recurrent nervous crises with hallucinations and depression. He became enthusiastic for the idea of founding an artists' co-operative at Arles and towards the end of the year he was joined by Gauguin. But as a result of a quarrel between them van Gogh suffered the crisis in which occurred the famous incident when he cut off his left ear (or part of it), an event commemorated in his *Self-Portrait with Bandaged Ear* (Courtauld Inst., London). In May 1889 he went at his own request into an asylum at St Rémy, near Arles, but continued during the year he spent there a frenzied production of tumultuous pictures such as *Starry Night* (MOMA, New York). He did 150 paintings besides drawings in the course of this year. In 1889 Theo married and in May 1890 van Gogh moved to Auvers-sur-Oise to be near him, lodging with the patron and connoisseur Dr Paul Gachet. There followed another tremendous burst of strenuous activity and during the last 70 days of his life he painted 70 canvases. But his spiritual anguish and depression became more acute and on 29 July 1890 he died from the results of a self-inflicted bullet wound. He sold only one painting during his lifetime (*Red Vineyard at Arles*, Pushkin Mus., Moscow), and was little known to the art world at the time of his death, but his fame grew rapidly thereafter. His influence on *Expressionism, *Fauvism, and early abstraction was enormous, and it can be seen in many other aspects of 20th-cent. art. His stormy and dramatic life and his unswerving devotion to his ideals have made him one of the great cultural heroes of modern times, providing the most auspicious material for the 20th-cent. vogue in romanticized psychological biography.

Golden Section. A proportion in which a straight line or rectangle is divided into two unequal parts in such a way that the ratio of the smaller to the greater part is the same as that of the greater to the whole. Like the mathematical value pi, it cannot be expressed as a finite number, but an approximation is 8:13 or 0.618:1. The proportion has been known since antiquity and has been said to possess inherent aesthetic value because of an alleged correspondence with the laws of nature or the universe. It was much studied during the *Renaissance, and Luca Pacioli, the most famous mathematician of his day and a close friend of *Leonardo and of *Piero della Francesca, wrote a book on it called *Divina Proportione* (1509). In accordance with the tendencies of the time, Pacioli's book, illustrated with drawings by Leonardo, credits this 'divine proportion' with various mystical properties and exceptional beauties both in science and in art.

Goltzius, Hendrick (1558–1617). Dutch graphic artist and painter of German descent, the outstanding line engraver of his day. He was the leader of a group of *Mannerist artists who worked in Haarlem, where in 1583 he founded an academy with *Cornelis van Haarlem and Karel van *Mander. In 1590 he was in Rome and upon his return to the Netherlands he abandoned his Mannerist style for a more Classical one. Goltzius's right hand was crippled, but in spite of this handicap he was renowned for his technical virtuosity and his skill in imitating the work of other great engravers such as *Dürer and *Lucas van Leyden. In his early career much of his work was reproductive, but later he produced many original compositions, including a splendid series on *Roman Heroes* (1586). His *miniature portrait drawings were also outstanding, and the landscape drawings which he made after 1600 mark him as a forerunner of the great 17th-cent. landscape artists. His paintings are less interesting than his drawings and much less advanced stylistically.

Gombrich, Sir Ernst (1909–). Austrian-born British art historian. He came to England in 1936 and began a long association with the *Warburg Institute in the University of London, where he was Director and Professor of the History of the Classical Tradition from 1959 to 1976. He has also been *Slade Professor at both Oxford and Cambridge. His scholarly work, which shows a remarkable ability to combine great breadth of learning with lucidity and wit, has been devoted largely to the theory of art, the psychology of pictorial representation, and Renaissance symbolism, and has won him a position of the highest esteem in his profession. His writings bear witness to his interest in psychology and scientific method and have helped to break down barriers between art history and other disciplines. Gombrich's best-known book, however, is a popular work, *The Story of Art*, which was first published in 1950 and has ever since held its place as the most congenial introduction to the history of art. It reached its 15th English edition in 1989 and has been translated into 19 languages. Among his other books the best known is probably *Art and Illusion* (1960 and subsequent editions). This highly influential work deals with conventions of representation and examines how styles change and develop, challenging many orthodox views and received opinions about visual perception. In *Thinkers of the Twentieth Century* (ed. Elizabeth Devine, et al., 1983) J. M. Massing wrote: 'For his scholarly method, his theoretical approach and his defence of cultural values, Gombrich will be remembered as one of the leading art historians of this century. Through his study of the psychology of perception, he is also one of the very few to have widened our understanding of the visible world.'

Gonçalves, Nuño (active 1450–71). Portuguese painter, recorded in 1463 as court painter to Alfonso V (1437–81). No works certainly by his hand survive, but there is strong circumstantial evidence that he was responsible for the *St Vincent* *polyptych (Lisbon Mus., *c.*1460–70), the outstanding Portuguese painting of the 15th cent. The style is rather dry, but powerfully realistic, and the polyptych contains a superb gallery of highly individualized portraits of members of the court, including a presumed self-portrait. There are affinities with contemporary Burgundian and Flemish art, especially the work of *Bouts.

Goncharova, Natalia (1881–1962). Russian painter, graphic artist, and designer. After studying science and sculpture, she took up painting in 1904. While a student she met *Larionov and began a lifelong friendship and artistic collaboration with him. They contributed to the *Mir Iskusstva exhibition of 1906 and to the exhibition of Russian art organized by *Diaghilev at the *Salon d'Automne, visiting Paris together. She participated in Larionov's *Knave of Diamonds exhibition of 1910 and *Donkey's Tail exhibition of

1912. Goncharova was profoundly interested in Russian peasant art and in medieval *icon painting, and it was under the influence of these that she developed a cultivated primitivism in her painting of this time. In many of her paintings Goncharova managed to achieve a successful combination of this folk-art interest with *Fauvist and *Cubist influences. At the *Target exhibition of 1913 she, together with Larionov, showed works done under the influence of *Futurism which inaugurated the *Rayonist style. (*Cats*, Solomon R. Guggenheim Mus., New York, 1910). She left Russia in 1915 and after settling in Paris with Larionov in 1919 devoted herself mainly to designing settings and costumes for the theatre.

Goncourt, Edmond de (1822–96) and **Jules de** (1830–70). French authors, brothers, who wrote in close collaboration. They wrote on various artistic topics, their most important work of criticism being a collection of articles *L'Art du dix-huitième siècle* (1875), which helped to revive the reputation of 18th-cent. French artists such as *Watteau. The brothers inherited a substantial fortune when their mother died in 1848, and their lives were divided between their writing and self-indulgence; the *Journal* that they began in 1851, and which Edmond continued after Jules died until his own death, provides a richly detailed record of Paris in the second half of the 19th cent. Edmond's books on Utamaro (1891) and Hokusai (1896) helped to popularize Japanese art (see UKIYO-E). The brothers also wrote novels, and the Académie Goncourt, founded under Edmond's will, is a body of ten men or women of letters that awards an annual prize (the Prix Goncourt) for imaginative prose.

Gonzaga. Lords of Mantua between 1328 and 1708, who at several different periods attracted to their court some of the greatest Italian and other European artists. Under **Lodovico** (reigned 1445–78) and his immediate successors *Mantegna was employed as court painter and *Alberti began the church of S. Andrea. The presence of Isabella d'*Este, who married **Francesco II** in 1490, helped to make Mantua one of the greatest centres of art collecting and patronage. Under **Federico** (1519–40)

*Giulio Romano built and decorated the Gonzaga pleasure house, the Palazzo del Tè, and turned Mantua into one of the main centres of *Mannerist art. Under **Vincenzo I** (1587–1612) *Rubens was made court painter; and the reign of **Ferdinando** (1612–26) saw the employment of van *Dyck, Domenico *Feti, *Albani, and other artists. The spectacular collections built up over the years were sold by **Vincenzo II** in 1628 principally to Charles I of England, and important Gonzaga patronage came to an end after the sack of Mantua in 1630.

González, Julio (1876–1942). Spanish sculptor, the leading pioneer in the use of iron as a sculptural medium. He learnt to work metals under his father, a goldsmith and sculptor, but his early career was spent mainly as a painter. In 1900 he moved to Paris and formed a lifelong friendship with *Picasso, whom he had earlier met in his native Barcelona. His important works as a sculptor date from the last 15 years of his life, when he turned to welded iron as a material. His best-known work, *Montserrat* (Stedelijk Mus., Amsterdam, 1937), is a fairly naturalistic piece, showing a woman with a child in her arms, and commemorates the suffering of the people of Spain in the civil war (Montserrat is Spain's holy mountain). More usually, however, his sculptures are semi-abstract, as in his series of *Cactus People*. González' work had great influence, notably on Picasso, to whom he taught the techniques of iron sculpture, and on a generation of British and American artists exemplified by Reg *Butler and David *Smith.

Gore, Spencer (1878–1914). English painter of landscapes, music-hall scenes, and interiors. After studying at the *Slade School, he visited *Sickert at Dieppe in 1904, and returned to France in 1905 and 1906, acquiring the orthodox *Impressionist technique. But like many young painters of his time he was excited by the *Post-Impressionists (he exhibited in Roger *Fry's second Post-Impressionist exhibition in 1912) and his later works show simplified planes with decorative pattern and form built up by strong outlines in a manner acquired from *Gauguin and van *Gogh. Gore was the first president of the *Camden Town Group in 1911 and he became a member of the *London Group in 1913. He died young of pneumonia and was much lamented by his many artist friends, notably Sickert, who said Gore was 'probably the man I love and admire most of any I have known'. His son **Frederick** (b. 1913) is also a painter.

Gorky, Arshile (Vosdanig Manoog Adoian) (1905–48). American painter, born in Turkish Armenia, who formed a link between European *Surrealism and American *Abstract Expressionism. He emigrated to the USA in 1920 and adopted the pseudonym Arshile Gorky, the first part of the name being derived from the Greek hero Achilles, the second part (Russian for 'the bitter one') from the Russian writer Maxim Gorky, to whom the painter sometimes claimed he was related. In 1925 he settled in New York, where he first studied and then taught at the Grand Central School of Art. He was among the first to recognize the importance of the abstract work of Stuart *Davis, and owed a debt to *Picasso, seen both in his haunting *The Artist and his Mother* (Whitney Mus., New York, c.1926–9) and in the *Cubist abstractions which he did at this period. Gorky was never at home with geometrical abstraction, however, but preferred to adapt Cubist techniques to his own more painterly and expressive purposes. He came into his own when he became a friend of the circle of European immigrant Surrealists who during the early years of the 1940s lived in New York. Under this influence he worked out a style of abstraction using *biomorphic forms akin to those of *Miró. At the peak of his powers, however, Gorky suffered a tragic series of misfortunes. In 1946 a fire in his Connecticut studio destroyed a large proportion of his recent work. In the same year he was operated on for cancer. In 1948 he broke his neck in a motor-car accident and, when his wife left him soon after, he hanged himself. Gorky has been called both the last of the great Surrealists and the first of the Abstract Expressionists, and his work in the 1940s was a potent factor underlying the emergence of a specifically American school of abstract art.

Gossaert, Jan (also called Mabuse) (c.1478–c.1533). Netherlandish painter, probably from Maubeuge in Hainault, from which

his name 'Mabuse' derives. In 1503 he was registered in the Guild Master's list at Antwerp and in 1508/9 he went to Rome in the service of Philip Bastard of Burgundy, an ambassador to the Vatican. His work before his Italian journey is in the tradition of Hugo van der *Goes and Gerard *David, whose influences can be seen in the *Adoration of the Magi* (NG, London). On his return to Antwerp, however, his work was transformed by the experience of Italy, although the motifs he learned there were never thoroughly digested and co-existed with Flemish figures and details. *Vasari acclaimed him for being the first 'to bring the true method of representing nude figures and mythologies from Italy to the Netherlands', but in, for example, *Neptune and Amphitrite* (Staatliche Museen, Berlin, 1516), his first dated work, the life-size figures are in fact closer to *Dürer than to any Italian contemporary, and they are set in a curious, totally misunderstood Classical temple. Gossaert was highly thought of by his contemporaries. His commissions took him to various towns in the Netherlands, his patrons included the Royal House of Denmark, and his work was widely influential. However, to modern eyes there seems justice in Dürer's assessment of him as better in execution than in invention ('nit so gut im Haupstreichen als im Gemäl'). Jan van *Scorel was Gossaert's pupil for a short time in Utrecht.

Gothic. Style of architecture and art that succeeded *Romanesque and prevailed in Europe (particularly northern Europe) from the mid 12th cent. to the 16th cent. The word was, like many other stylistic labels, originally a term of abuse; it was coined by Italian artists of the *Renaissance to denote the type of medieval architecture which they condemned as barbaric (implying, quite wrongly, that it was the architecture of the Gothic tribes who had destroyed the Classical art of the Roman Empire). The Gothic style is still characterized chiefly in terms of architecture—in particular by the use of pointed arches, flying buttresses, and elaborate tracery. By extension, however, the term 'Gothic' is applied to the ornament, sculpture, and painting of the period in which Gothic architecture was built; it has less precise meaning in these contexts, although a swaying elegance is often considered typical of Gothic figures, which are generally much more naturalistic and less remote than those of the Romanesque period.

Gottlieb, Adolph (1903–74). American painter, one of the leading *Abstract Expressionists. He early worked in an *Expressionist style and in 1935 he was one of the founding members of the Expressionist group The *Ten. In 1936 he worked for the *Federal Art Project. His landscapes of the later 1930s were influenced by *Surrealism, and this tendency was enhanced by contact with expatriate European Surrealists from 1941 and an interest in Freudian psychology. As a member of the *New York School he is best known for his series of *Pictographs* done between 1941 and 1951. These pictures were divided into compartments, each of which was filled with schematic shapes operating as Freudian symbols or abstract mythological concepts endowed with universal significance from unconscious association. A series of *Imaginary Landscapes* in the first half of the 1950s consisted of a zone of astral shapes above loosely pictured foregrounds and was succeeded by a *Burst* series, which carried the artist's style still further in the direction of expressive abstraction but still suggested solar orbs and astral bodies hovering above violently coloured terrestrial explosions.

gouache. Opaque *water-colour, sometimes also known as *body colour. It differs from transparent water-colour in that the *pigments are bound with glue and the lighter tones are obtained by the admixture of white pigment. Its degree of opacity varies with the amount of white which is added, but in general is sufficient to prevent the reflection of the *ground through the paint and it therefore lacks the luminosity of transparent water-colour painting. It is, however, easier to use, as trials and errors can be painted over. The colours sold as poster paints by commercial colourmen are usually a form of gouache.

Goujon, Jean (c.1510 68). French sculptor. He ranks second only to Germain *Pilon as the greatest French sculptor of the 16th cent. and he created a distinctive *Mannerist style as sophisticated as the finest works of painting and decoration

of the contemporary School of *Fontainebleau. Nothing is known of his early life and he is first recorded in 1540 as the carver of the fine columns supporting the organ loft in the church of S. Maclou at Rouen. The pure *Classicism of these columns has caused some critics to assume that he had first-hand knowledge of Italian art. He had moved to Paris by 1544, when he was working on the screen of S. Germain-l'Auxerrois, in collaboration with the architect Pierre Lescot. Low-*relief panels (now in the Louvre) from this screen show that Goujon had evolved a style of extreme grace and delicacy, owing something to the influence of Benvenuto *Cellini. The style is seen at its most mature in his decorations (now in the Louvre) for the *Fontaine des Innocents*, Paris (1547–9). The six relief panels of nymphs from the fountain, with their exquisitely carved rippling draperies, are generally considered Goujon's masterpieces. Goujon's most extensive undertaking was on the sculptural decoration of the *Louvre; he worked there from 1549 to 1562 in collaboration with Lescot, mainly on decorative panels forming part of the architectural scheme. Unfortunately all Goujon's work there has been heavily restored, including the famous *caryatids (1550–1) in the Salle des Caryatides. Using caryatids on a monumental scale was a novelty, perhaps inspired by his reading of *Vitruvius (he made illustrations for the first French edition of his treatise in 1547). There is no indication of any work executed after 1562 and it is possible that Goujon left France because of religious persecution and died in Bologna (the documentation is ambiguous).

Gower, George (d. 1596). English portrait painter. He was appointed Serjeant-Painter to Queen Elizabeth in 1581 and seems to have been the leading English portraitist of his day. His *Sir Thomas Kitson* and *Lady Kitson* (Tate, London, 1573) show his clear and individual, if unsubtle, style. Gower was a gentleman by birth and his *Self-Portrait* (Earl Fitzwilliam Coll., 1579) shows his coat of arms outweighed in a balance by a pair of dividers, a symbol of the painter's craft.

Gowing, Sir Lawrence (1918–   ). British painter and writer on art. He has had a distinguished academic career, during which he has been Deputy Director of the *Tate Gallery (1965–67) and a professor at several universities (notably at the *Slade School, 1975–85), and he has published books and catalogues, valued for their critical insights, on numerous artists, among them *Cézanne, *Matisse, and *Vermeer. As a painter he began as a pupil of *Coldstream working in the *Euston Road tradition, and much of his subsequent work has been in this sombre vein. His work has also included abstracts, however, and in 1976 he began producing large pictures in which he traced the outline of his own naked body stretched on the canvas, the paint being applied by an assistant.

Goya, Francisco de (1746–1828). Spanish painter and graphic artist. He was the most powerful and original European artist of his time, but his genius was slow in maturing and he was well into his thirties before he began producing work that set him apart from his contemporaries. Born at Fuendetodos in Aragon, the son of a gilder, he served his apprenticeship at Saragossa, then appears to have worked at Madrid for the court painter Francisco *Bayeu. In about 1770 he went to Italy but he was back in Saragossa the next year. In 1773 he married Bayeu's sister, and by 1775 had settled at Madrid. Bayeu secured him employment making *cartoons for the royal tapestry factory, and this took up most of his working time from 1775 to 1792. He made sixty-three cartoons (Prado, Madrid), the largest more than 6 m. wide. The subjects range from idyllic scenes to realistic incidents of everyday life, conceived throughout in a gay and romantic spirit and executed with *Rococo decorative charm. During these years Goya also found time for portraits and religious works, and his status grew. He was elected to the Academy of San Fernando in 1780 and became assistant director of painting in 1785. In 1789 he was nominated a court painter to the new king, Charles IV. A more important turning point in his career than any of these appointments, however, was the mysterious and traumatic illness he developed in 1792. It left him stone deaf, and while convalescing in 1793 he painted a series of small pictures of 'fantasy and invention' in order, as he said, 'to occupy an imagination mortified by the

contemplation of my sufferings'. This marks the beginning of his preoccupation with the morbid, bizarre, and menacing that was to be such a feature of his mature work. It was given vivid expression in the first of his great series of engravings, *Los Caprichos* (Caprices), issued in 1799. The set (executed *c.*1793–8) consists of eighty-two plates in *etching reinforced with *aquatint, and their humour is constantly overshadowed by an element of nightmare. Technically revealing the influence of *Rembrandt, they feature savagely satirical attacks on social customs and abuses of the Church, with elements of the macabre in scenes of witchcraft and diabolism.

In 1795 Goya succeeded Bayeu as director of painting at the Academy of San Fernando and in 1799 he was appointed First Court Painter, producing his most famous portrait group, the *Family of Charles IV* (Prado), in the following year. The weaknesses of the royal family are revealed with unsparing realism, though apparently without deliberate satirical intent. Goya's early portraits had followed the manner of *Mengs, but stimulated by the study of *Velázquez's paintings in the royal collection he had developed a much more natural, lively, and personal style, showing increasing mastery of pose and expression, heightened by dramatic contrasts of light and shade. From about the same date as the royal group portrait are the celebrated pair of paintings the *Clothed Maja* and *Naked Maja* (Prado), whose erotic nature led Goya to be summoned before the Inquisition. Popular legend has it that they represent the Duchess of Alba, the beautiful widow whose relationship with Goya caused scandal in Madrid. Goya retained his appointment of court painter under Joseph Buonaparte during the French occupation of Spain (1808–14), but his activity as a painter of court and society decreased, and he was torn between his welcome for the regime as a liberal and his abhorrence as a patriot against foreign military rule. After the restoration of Ferdinand VII in 1814 Goya was exonerated from the charge of having 'accepted employment from the usurper' by claiming he had not worn the medal awarded him by the French, and he painted for the king the two famous scenes of the bloody uprising of the citizens of Madrid against the occupying forces—*The Second of May, 1808* and *The Third of May,*

1808 (Prado). Equally dramatic, and even more savage and macabre, are the sixty-five etchings *Los Desastres de la Guerra* (The Disasters of War, 1810–14)—nightmare scenes, depicting atrocities committed by both French and Spanish.

Goya virtually retired from public life after 1815, working for himself and friends. He kept the title of court painter but was superseded in royal favour by Vicente *López. Towards the end of 1819 he fell seriously ill for the second time (a remarkable self-portrait in the Minneapolis Institute of Arts shows him with the doctor who nursed him). He had just bought a country house in the outskirts of Madrid, the Quinta del Sordo (House of the Deaf Man); and it was here after his recovery in 1820 that he executed fourteen large murals, sometimes known as the *Black Paintings*, now in the Prado. Painted almost entirely in blacks, greys, and browns, they depict horrific scenes, such as *Saturn Devouring One of His Sons*, executed with an almost ferocious intensity and freedom of handling. In 1824 Goya obtained permission from Ferdinand VII to leave the country for reasons of health and settled at Bordeaux. He made two brief visits to Spain, on the first of which (1826) he officially resigned as court painter. In these last years he took up the new medium of *lithography (in his series the *Bulls of Bordeaux*), while his paintings illustrate his progress towards a style which foreshadowed that of the *Impressionists.

Goya completed some 500 oil paintings and murals, about 300 etchings and lithographs, and many hundreds of drawings. He was exceptionally versatile and his work expresses a very wide range of emotion. His technical freedom and originality likewise are remarkable—his frescos in San Antonio de la Florida in Madrid (1798), for example, were apparently executed with sponges. In his own day he was celebrated for his portraits, of which he painted more than 200; but his fame has since been greatly enhanced by the *Disasters of War*, the *Black Paintings*, and other works made public only many years after his death.

Goyen, Jan van (1596–1656). Dutch painter, one of the foremost pioneers of realistic landscape painting in the Netherlands. His earliest works are heavily indebted to his master Esaias van de *Velde, but he then created a distinctive type of monochrome landscape in browns and greys with touches of vivid blue or red to catch the eye; gnarled oaks; wide plains, usually seen from a height; low horizons and clouded skies. He was one of the first painters to capture the quality of the light and air in a scene and to suggest the movement of clouds. Most of his paintings seem to be based on drawings made as he travelled about the countryside, and he apparently used the same drawings again and again because the same motifs recur repeatedly in his works. His finest work has a sense of poetic calm as well as great freshness and luminosity of atmosphere. Van Goyen worked in his native Leiden, Haarlem, and The Hague, where he died. He was hugely prolific and had many pupils and imitators. With Salomon van *Ruysdael, whose paintings are often virtually indistinguishable from his, he was the outstanding master of the 'tonal' phase of Dutch landscape painting, when the depiction of atmosphere was the artist's prime concern.

Gozzoli, Benozzo (Benozzo di Lese) (c.1421–97). Florentine painter. Originally trained as a goldsmith, he worked in his early years with *Ghiberti on the doors of the Baptistery in Florence, but is mentioned as a painter in 1444 and subsequently became Fra *Angelico's assistant in Rome and Orvieto. His reputation rests on only one work—but one of the most enchanting in all Italian *Renaissance art: the decoration of the chapel of the Palazzo *Medici in Florence with frescos of *The Journey of the Magi* (1459–61). This is the most glittering fresco cycle of the century, recalling, and perhaps consciously rivalling, *Gentile da Fabriano's *Adoration of the Magi* of 1423. Its secular outlook is far removed in spirit from the work of his master Fra Angelico. The rest of Gozzoli's career was undistinguished. His other major work was a fresco cycle with scenes from the Old Testament, now badly damaged, in the Campo Santo at Pisa, begun in 1467. He also painted altarpieces, one of which (*Madonna and Child with Saints*, 1461) is in the National Gallery, London.

Graf, Urs (c.1485–1527/8). Swiss graphic artist, designer, and goldsmith, active mainly in Basle. He is best known for his drawings, which survive in considerable number, often signed and dated. They are done in a bold and energetic style, with virtuoso curling strokes of the pen; favourite subjects are soldiers (Graf himself spent some time as a mercenary in Italy), peasants, and flamboyantly dressed ladies of easy virtue. Graf also designed stained glass, made woodcuts, and executed the earliest extant dated etchings (1513).

Grand Manner. Term applied to the lofty and rhetorical manner of *history painting that in academic theory was considered appropriate to the most serious and elevated subjects. The classic exposition of its doctrines is found in *Reynolds's Third and Fourth *Discourses* (1770 and 1771), where he asserts that 'the *gusto grande* of the Italians, the *beau idéal* of the French, and the *great style*, *genius*, and *taste* among the English, are but different appellations of the same thing'. Cecil Gould (*An Introduction to Italian Renaissance Painting*, 1957) rightly points out that 'the Grand Manner is an attitude rather than a style' and goes on to give a lucid account of some of its characteristics. 'The general aim is to transcend Nature. . . . The Subject itself must be on an elevated and elevating plane. . . . Similarly, the individual figures in such a scene must be shown purged of the grosser elements of ordinary existence. . . . Landscape backgrounds or ornamental detail must be reduced to a minimum and individual peculiarities of human physiognomy absolutely eliminated. Draperies should be simple, but ample, and noble, and fashionable contemporary costume absolutely shunned. Alternatively, the figures should be nude.' The idea of the Grand Manner took shape in 17th-cent. Italy, notably in the writings of *Bellori. His friend *Poussin and the great Bolognese painters of the 17th cent. were regarded as outstanding exponents of the Grand Manner, but the greatest of all was held to be *Raphael.

Grand Tour. An extensive journey to the Continent, chiefly to France, the Netherlands, and above all Italy, sometimes in the company of a tutor, that became a conventional feature in the education of the English gentleman in the 18th cent. Such tours often took a year or more.

The practice reflects Dr Johnson's pronouncement (1776) that 'A man who has not been in Italy is always conscious of an inferiority.' It had a noticeable effect in bringing a more cosmopolitan spirit to the taste of connoisseurs and laid the basis for many collections among the landed gentry. It also helped the spread of the fashion for *Neoclassicism and an enthusiasm for Italian painting. Among the native artists who catered for this demand were *Batoni, *Canaletto, *Panini, and *Piranesi, and British artists (such as *Nollekens) were sometimes able to support themselves while in Italy by working for the dealers and restorers who supplied the tourist clientele. There was also a flourishing market in guide books (see RICHARDSON).

Granet, François-Marius (1775–1849). French painter. Granet was a pupil of J.-L. *David and subsequently spent the years 1802–19 in Rome. He made a speciality of sombre tonal effects and changing light in dimly lit interiors, his highly individualistic style recalling Dutch interiors rather than the *Neoclassical School in which he was trained. His *Choir of the Capuchin Church in Rome* was exhibited at the 1819 *Salon with such success that he made sixteen replicas of it. Granet also painted Italian landscapes, constructed with firm, cubic volumes in which some critics have seen a foreshadowing of *Cézanne. In 1826 he became curator of the *Louvre Museum and was made Keeper of Pictures at Versailles in 1830. During the Revolution of 1848 he retired to his native Aix-en-Provence, where he founded the museum which bears his name. It contains a celebrated portrait of him by *Ingres.

Grant, Duncan (1885–1978). British painter, decorator, and designer. Grant, who studied at the *Slade and in Italy and Paris, was a cousin of the writer Lytton Strachey and a member of the *Bloomsbury Group. He exhibited at the *New English Art Club and with the *London Group, and contributed to the second *Post-Impressionist Exhibition in 1912. His work of this period shows that he was among the most advanced of British artists in responding to recent trends in French painting. From about 1913 he was also influenced by African sculpture and he was one of the pioneers of abstract art in

Britain; in 1914 he made an *Abstract Kinetic Collage Painting*, which was meant to be unrolled while music by J. S. Bach was playing (this is now in the Tate Gallery, which has had a film made demonstrating the painting being unrolled in the desired fashion). Grant's later painting was generally much more traditional, and many critics consider that he was at his best as a designer. He was the most gifted of the designers who worked for *Fry's *Omega Workshops, and he collaborated much with Vanessa *Bell (they lived together from about 1914) in interior decoration after the workshops closed in 1919. His work included designs for textiles, pottery, stage scenery, and costumes.

Grant, Sir Francis (1803–78). Scottish painter. He was one of the most fashionable portrait painters of his day and succeeded *Eastlake as President of the *Royal Academy in 1866. His best works are generally considered to be his smaller sporting *conversation pieces.

graphic art. Term current with several different meanings in the literature of the visual arts. In the context of the *fine arts, it most usually refers to those arts that rely essentially on line or tone rather than colour—i.e. drawing and the various forms of engraving. Some writers, however, exclude drawing from this definition, so that the term 'graphic art' is used to cover the various processes by which prints are created. In another sense, the term—sometimes shortened to 'graphics'—is used to cover the entire field of commercial printing, including text as well as illustrations.

Grasser, Erasmus (*c*.1450–1518). German sculptor and wood-carver, active mainly in Munich. He worked in an animated and expressive late *Gothic style and was the leading sculptor of his day in south Bavaria, with a flourishing workshop and numerous pupils. His best-known works are the ten figures (originally sixteen) of morris dancers for the ballroom of the old town hall in Munich (Stadtmuseum, Munich, 1480). Grasser was also an architect and hydraulic engineer.

Gravelot, Hubert-François (1699–1773). French designer and engraver of book illustrations, active for much of his career in England. In London he became a friend of *Hogarth and probably taught *Gainsborough. He illustrated Gay's *Fables*, Shakespeare, and Dryden, and was one of the first artists to illustrate the novel, designing engravings for Richardson's *Pamela* (1742) and Fielding's *Tom Jones* (1750). Although not an artist of outstanding talent, he is important for helping to introduce the French *Rococo style to England.

Greco, El (1541–1614). Cretan-born painter, sculptor, and architect who settled in Spain and is regarded as the first great genius of the Spanish School. He was known as El Greco (the Greek), but his real name was Domenikos Theotocopoulos; and it was thus that he signed his paintings throughout his life, always in Greek characters, and sometimes followed by *Kres* (Cretan). Little is known of his youth, and only a few works survive by him in the *Byzantine tradition of *icon painting, notably the recently discovered *Dormition of the Virgin* (Church of the Koimesis tis Theotokou, Syros). In 1566 he is referred to in a Cretan document as a master painter; soon afterwards he went to Venice (Crete was then a Venetian possession), then in 1570 moved to Rome. The *miniaturist Giulio *Clovio, whom he met there, described him as a pupil of *Titian, but all of the Venetian painters *Tintoretto influenced him most, and *Michelangelo's impact on his development was also important.

Among the surviving works of his Italian period are two paintings of the *Purification of the Temple* (Minneapolis Institute of Arts, and NG, Washington), a much-repeated theme, and the portrait of Giulio Clovio (Museo di Capodimonte, Naples). By 1577 he was at Toledo, where he remained until his death, and it was there that he matured his characteristic style in which figures elongated into flame-like forms and usually painted in cold, eerie, bluish colours express intense religious feeling. The commission that took him to Toledo—the high altarpiece of the church of S. Domingo el Antiguo—was gained through Diego de Castilla, Dean of Canons at Toledo Cathedral, whom El Greco had met in Rome. The central part of the altarpiece, a 4-m. high canvas of *The Assumption of the Virgin* (Art Inst. of Chicago, 1577), was easily his biggest work to date, but he carried off the dynamic composition triumphantly. A succession of great altarpieces followed throughout his career, the two most famous being *El Espolio* (Christ Stripped of His Garments) (Toledo Cathedral, 1577–9) and *The Burial of Count Orgaz* (S. Tomé, Toledo, 1586–8). These two mighty works convey the awesomeness of great spiritual events with a sense of mystic rapture, and in his late work El Greco went even further in freeing his figures from earth-bound restrictions; *The Adoration of the Shepherds* (Prado, Madrid, 1612–14), painted for his own tomb, is a prime example.

El Greco excelled also as a portraitist, mainly of ecclesiastics (*Felix Paravicino*, Boston Mus., 1609) or gentlemen, although one of his most beautiful works is a portrait of a lady (Pollock House, Glasgow, *c.*1577–80), traditionally identified as a likeness of Jeronima de las Cuevas, his common-law wife. He also painted two views of Toledo (Met. Mus., New York, and Museo del Greco, Toledo), both late works, and a mythological painting, *Laocoön* (NG, Washington, *c.*1610), that is unique in his *œuvre*. The unusual choice of subject is perhaps explained by the local tradition that Toledo had been founded by descendants of the Trojans. El Greco also designed complete altar compositions, working as architect and sculptor as well as painter, for instance at the Hospital de la Caridad, Illescas (1603). *Pacheco, who visited El Greco in 1611, refers to him as a writer on painting, sculpture, and architecture. He had a proud temperament, conceiving of himself as an artist–philosopher rather than a craftsman, and had a lavish life-style, although he had little success in securing the royal patronage he desired and seems to have had some financial difficulties near the end of his life. His workshop turned out a great many replicas of his paintings, but his work was so personal that his influence was slight, his only followers of note being his son **Jorge Manuel Theotocopouli** and Luis *Tristán. Interest in his art revived at the end of the 19th cent. and with the development of *Expressionism in the 20th cent. he came into his own. The strangeness of his art has inspired various theories, for example that he was mad or suffered from astigmatism, but his rapturous paintings make

complete sense as an expression of the religious fervour of his adopted country.

Greek Revival and **Greek Taste**. See NEOCLASSICISM.

Green, Anthony (1939–). British painter. He specializes in scenes from his own middle-class domestic life portrayed with loving attention to detail and an engaging sense of whimsy. Often he uses oddly shaped canvases that accentuate his strange perspective effects, and his subjects are frequently erotic as well as humorous. His work, which is often on a large scale, is instantly recognizable and is generally highly popular with the public at the *Royal Academy summer exhibition.

Greenaway, Kate (1846–1901). English artist famous for her illustrations for children's books. Her delicate skill and fragile sentimentality, often imitated but never rivalled, won her many distinguished admirers, including *Ruskin, and (perhaps for her feeling for flat pattern) *Gauguin. She often illustrated her own texts, issuing for example a series of *Kate Greenaway's Almanacs*, and her work became so popular that the quaint clothes that are such a feature of her illustrations influenced children's costume.

Greenough, Horatio (1805–52). American *Neoclassical sculptor who spent the greater part of his working life in Italy. He is sometimes said to be the first professional American sculptor and his major work, the colossal marble figure of George Washington (1833–41), was the first important state commission given to an American sculptor. It was originally intended for the rotunda of the Capitol in Washington, but is now in the Smithsonian Institution. The seated figure is based on *Phidias' celebrated statue of Zeus at Olympia, but the head follows *Houdon's portrait of Washington—an uneasy mixture of idealism and naturalism. Greenough's work is in general rather stodgy and uninventive, and his writings on art are usually considered more interesting; his views on architecture have been claimed as precursors of modern functionalism. Greenough's brother, **Richard Saltonstall Greenhough** (1819–1904), was also a sculptor, best known for his statue of

Benjamin Franklin outside Boston City Hall.

Greuze, Jean-Baptiste (1725–1805). French painter. He had a great success at the 1755 *Salon with his *Father Reading the Bible to His Children* (Louvre, Paris) and went on to win enormous popularity with similar sentimental and melodramatic genre scenes. His work was praised by *Diderot as 'morality in paint', and as representing the highest ideal of painting in his day. He also wished to succeed as a history painter, but his *Septimius Severus Reproaching Caracalla* (Louvre, 1769) was rejected by the Salon, causing him acute embarrassment. Much of Greuze's later work consisted of titillating pictures of young girls, which contain thinly veiled sexual allusions under their surface appearance of mawkish innocence; *The Broken Pitcher* (Louvre), for example, alludes to loss of virginity. With the swing of taste towards *Neoclassicism his work went out of fashion and he sank into obscurity at the Revolution in 1789. At the very end of his career he received a commission to paint a portrait of Napoleon (Versailles, 1804 5), but he died in poverty. His huge output is particularly well represented in the Louvre, the Wallace Collection in London, the Musée Fabre in Montpellier, and in the museum dedicated to him in Tournus, his native town.

Grien, Hans Baldung. See BALDUNG.

Grimaldi, Giovanni Francesco (called Il Bolognese) (1606–80). Italian landscape painter. He developed an attractive landscape style in the manner of the mature Annibale *Carracci, and his work, which was popular with collectors and much engraved, helped to spread the tradition of *ideal landscape in Europe. Grimaldi worked mainly in Rome, painting frescos as well as easel paintings, notably at the Villa Doria Pamphili, where he was also employed as an architect. In 1649–51 he worked in Paris.

Grimmer. Two Flemish painters, **Jacob** (*c.*1526–90) and his son **Abel** (*c.*1570–*c.*1619), whose styles are so similar that it is often difficult to distinguish between their works. They worked in Antwerp, painting mainly landscape and *genre subjects in an attractive style, full of lively anecdote, that places them among the best followers of *Breugel. Jacob's work was praised by van *Mander and others.

Grimshaw, Atkinson (1836–93). English painter. He specialized in a distinctive type of nocturnal townscape, usually featuring gas lights and wet streets, and *Whistler said of him 'I considered myself the inventor of Nocturnes until I saw Grimmy's moonlit pictures.' Grimshaw's paintings, however, unlike Whistler's, are sharp in focus and rather acidic in colouring, although often remarkably atmospheric. They were very popular (in spite of the fact that he rarely exhibited at the *Royal Academy) and he was much imitated, not least by two of his sons, **Arthur** (1868–1913) and **Louis** (1870–1943?). Their father worked in his native Leeds and in other northern towns, as well as in London.

Gris, Juan (1887–1927). Spanish painter (real name José Victoriano González) active mainly in Paris, where he settled in 1906. After early work for illustrated papers in an *Art Nouveau style he came under the influence of *Picasso and his serious painting was almost entirely in the *Cubist manner. He is regarded as the chief originator of the 'Synthetic' type of Cubism and his work was generally more calculated than that of Picasso or *Braque, whose techniques of visual analysis were more intuitive. Gris himself summed up this difference: 'I try to make concrete that which is abstract . . . Cézanne turns a bottle into a cylinder, but I make a bottle—a particular bottle—out of a cylinder.' The use of *papier collé* (paper collage) was an important part of Gris's method (*The Sunblind*, Tate, London, 1914). In the 1920s his work became more painterly (*Violin and Fruit Dish*, Tate, 1924). His other work includes *polychrome sculpture, book illustrations, and sets and costumes for *Diaghilev.

grisaille. A painting done entirely in shades of grey or another neutral greyish colour. Grisaille is sometimes used for underpainting or for sketches (notably in the work of *Rubens), and particularly in the *Renaissance it was used for finished works imitating the effects of sculpture. See also CAMAIEU.

Gropius, Walter (1883–1969). German architect, designer, and teacher. In 1918 he founded the *Bauhaus, of which he was Principal, first in Weimar and from 1925 in Dessau, until 1928, when he resumed his architectural practice in Berlin. In 1934, after the National Socialists had come to power, he left Germany for England, where he practised in partnership with the British architect Maxwell Fry. In 1937 he went to the USA, where he taught at Harvard until 1951. He remained active until the end of his life and had an exceptional list of notable buildings to his credit. Although Gropius's practical work was in the field of architecture, his influence upon modernist trends in all the visual arts has probably not been exceeded by that of any other man. Nowhere else have so many major artists of outstanding originality been brought into collaboration as those whom Gropius induced to teach at the Bauhaus.

Gros, Antoine-Jean (1771–1835). French painter. He trained with his father, a *miniaturist and then with J.-L. *David. Although he revered David and became one of his favourite pupils, Gros had a passionate nature and he was drawn more to the colour and vibrancy of *Rubens and the great Venetian painters than to the *Neoclassical purity of his master. In 1793 Gros went to Italy, where he met Napoleon and was appointed his official battle painter. He followed Napoleon on his campaigns, and his huge paintings such as *The Battle of Eylau* (Louvre, Paris, 1808) are among the most stirring images of the Napoleonic era. Compared to the contemporary war scenes of *Goya, they are glamorous lies, but they are painted with such dramatic skill and panache that they cannot but be admired on their own terms. When David went into exile after the fall of Napoleon, Gros took over his studio, and tried to work in a more consciously Neoclassical style. He never again approached the quality of his Napoleonic pictures, however (although he painted excellent portraits), and haunted by a sense of failure he drowned himself in the Seine. Gros is regarded as one of the leading figures in the development of *Romanticism; the colour and drama of his work influenced *Géricault, *Delacroix, and his pupil *Bonington amongst others.

Grosz, George (1893–1959). German-born painter and draughtsman who became an American citizen in 1938. He began as a *caricaturist with a strong bent for social satire and through his drawings expressed his disgust at the depravity of the Prussian military caste. During the First World War he twice served in the German army and each time was discharged as being unfit for service. In 1917, with *Heartfield, he Anglicized his name (he was born Georg Groß) as a protest against the hatred being whipped up against the enemy. The most famous of the satirical anti-war illustrations he made at this time is the drawing *Fit for Active Service* (MOMA, New York, 1918), in which a fat, complacent doctor pronounces a skeleton fit for duty. From 1917 to 1920 he was prominent among the Berlin *Dada group and during the 1920s, while still working on Dadaist *montages, he became, with *Dix, the leading exponent of the *Neue Sachlichkeit. His collections of drawings *The Face of the Ruling Class* (1921) and *Ecce Homo* (1927) earned him an international reputation. In these and in his paintings he ruthlessly denounced a decaying society in which gluttony and depraved sensuality are placed beside poverty and disease; prostitutes and profiteers were frequently among his cast of characters. Grosz was prosecuted several times for obscenity and blasphemy, and in 1933, despairing at the political situation in Germany, he moved to America to take up the offer of a teaching post at the Art Students' League of New York. In America his satirical manner was largely abandoned for more romantic landscapes and still lifes with from time to time apocalyptic visions of a nightmare future. Although he won several honours in the last decade of his life, he regarded himself as a failure because he was unable to win recognition as a serious painter rather than a brilliant satirist, and he painted several self-portraits showing how isolated and depressed he was in his adopted country (*The Wanderer*, Memorial Art Gallery, the University of Rochester, New York, 1943). He returned to Berlin in 1959, saying 'my American dream turned out to be a soap bubble', and died there shortly after his arrival following a fall down a flight of stairs.

grotesque. A term originally used in the visual arts to describe a type of fanciful wall decoration (painted, carved, or moulded in *stucco) characterized by the use of interlinked floral motifs, animal and human figures, masks, etc. It was derived from the ornament found in certain Roman buildings (called *grotte*), and in the 16th century it spread from Italy to most of the countries of Europe. In France the word 'grotesque' was applied to literature and even people fairly early in the 17th cent., and later in the same century this meaning spread to England, and the word began to assume its current sense, suggesting the ridiculous, absurd, monstrous, or abnormal.

ground. The surface or *support on which a painting or drawing is executed, for example the paper on which a *watercolour is done or the plaster under a *fresco; or, more specifically, the prepared surface on which the colours are laid and which is applied to the panel, canvas, or other support before the picture is begun. The purpose of the ground in the second, more technical, sense is to isolate the paint from the support so as to prevent chemical interaction, to render the support less absorbent, to provide a satisfactory surface for painting or drawing on, and to heighten the brilliance of the colours. *Gesso is the ground that occurs most often in the literature of art history. In *etching the ground is the acid-resisting mixture which is spread over the plate before work is begun.

Groupe de Recherche d'Art Visuel (GRAV). An association of artists formed in Paris in 1960, the main purpose of which was to research into the aesthetic manipulation of light and movement (see KINETIC ART). The members, who included *Vasarely's son *Yvaral, adopted a scientific approach and investigated the use of modern industrial materials for artistic purposes. In common with other contemporary groups they made it one of their aims to produce works of art which called for closer collaboration on the part of the observer and they often collaborated

in the production of anonymous group works. The group disbanded in 1968.

Group of Seven. Group of 20th-cent. Canadian painters, based in Toronto, who found their main inspiration in the landscape of northern Ontario and created the first major national movement in Canadian art. The group was officially established in 1920, when it held its first exhibition in the Art Gallery of Toronto, the seven painters involved being Franklin Carmichael (1890–1945), Lawren *Harris, A. Y. *Jackson, Frank Johnston (1888–1949), Arthur Lismer (1885–1969), J. E. H. Macdonald (1873–1932), and Frederick Varley (1881–1969). Some members of the group had, however, been working together since 1913, and Tom *Thomson, who was one of the early leaders, had died in 1917. Other artists joined after the 1920 exhibition. The members made group sketching expeditions and worked in an *Expressionist style characterized by brilliant colour and bold brushwork. After initial critical abuse, they won public favour. The last group exhibition was held in 1931 and two years later the name was changed to the *Canadian Group of Painters; thereafter the members worked more as individuals and developed separately.

Grünewald, Mathis (*c.*1470/80–1528). German painter, the greatest of *Dürer's contemporaries. His real name was Mathis Gothardt or Neithardt, but this was not discovered until the 1920s; 'Grünewald' is an error of *Sandrart, who published the first biography of the artist in his *Teutsche Akademie* (1675), but it is now hallowed by usage. The obscurity into which he fell reflects the isolation and individuality of his work; he had no known pupils and (unlike most of his German contemporaries) he did not make woodcuts or engravings, which would have spread his name. He was successful for most of his career, working as court painter to two successive archbishops of Mainz, but his reputation did not survive, and in 1597, when the emperor Rudolf II tried to buy his masterpiece, the Isenheim Altarpiece, the name of the painter had already been forgotten. The first documentary reference to him (or what appears to be him) is of 1501, when a 'Master Mathis' is recorded working in Seligenstadt, a little town near

Frankfurt and within the diocese of the Archbishop of Mainz, Uriel von Gemmingen, for whom Grünewald began working in about 1508. Von Gemmingen died in 1514 and Grünewald was employed by his successor Albrecht von Brandenburg (who was also Archbishop of Magdeburg) from 1516 to 1526. Grünewald was employed as a hydraulic engineer and supervisor of architectural works as well as a painter, and in 1520 he accompanied Albrecht to Aix-la-Chapelle for the coronation of emperor Charles V, an occasion on which he met Dürer. The little that is recorded of his personal life comes from Sandrart, who says he was melancholy and withdrawn and made an unhappy marriage late in life. There is no documentary confirmation of his marriage, but he is known to have had an adopted son called Andreas Neithardt, whose surname he (the painter) sometimes used for himself in documents relating to the boy, thus creating one of the sources of confusion about the painter's identity.

Grünewald's work forms a complete contrast to that of Dürer. Whereas Dürer—an intellectual imbued with *Renaissance ideas—had limitless curiosity about the visual world, Grünewald concentrated exclusively on religious themes, and in particular the Crucifixion, a subject he was to make his own. His most famous treatment of it is the central panel of his masterpiece, the altarpiece for the hospital church of the Anthonite Abbey at Isenheim in Alsace, completed in about 1515 and now in the Musée d'Unterlinden, Colmar. The hospital at Isenheim cared particularly for plague victims, and the concentration on Christ's appalling physical agonies, his body gruesomely mangled and torn, was designed to bolster the faith of the sick by reminding them that he too had suffered horribly before triumphing over death. In the *Resurrection*, Christ displays his nail and lance wounds, but the lacerations that cover his body in the *Crucifixion* have disappeared, affirming that the patients at the hospital could be cleansed of their diseases and sins. The altarpiece is marked by extreme emotional intensity, brought about by expressive distortion and by colouring of an extraordinary incandescent beauty. Grünewald was familiar with Renaissance ideas of *perspective, but spiritually he belongs to the late medieval world.

His other work includes Crucifixions in Basle (Öffentliche Kunstsammlung), Karlsruhe (Staatliche Kunsthalle), and Washington (NG), and several drawings survive.

The end of Grünewald's career was marked by a decline in his fortunes. He had Protestant sympathies, and following the Peasants' War in 1525, in which Archbishop Albrecht narrowly escaped death, he was dismissed from his court post. He moved to Frankfurt, where he made a meagre living at a variety of jobs, including selling artists' colours and a curative balm, the latter presumably something he had learnt about at Isenheim. In 1527 he became convinced his life was in danger and fled to Halle, where he died of plague the following year. His effects included 'much Lutheran trash'. Grünewald's influence can be seen in the paintings of contemporaries such as *Baldung Grien and *Ratgeb, but it was not until the advent of *Expressionism in the early 20th cent. that his work started to arouse widespread interest and he began his rise to his present pinnacle of esteem as one of the most awe-inspiring artists of his, or any other, time.

Guardi, Francesco (1712–93). Venetian painter, the best-known member of a family of artists. He is now famous for his views of Venice, indeed next to *Canaletto he is the most celebrated view-painter (see VEDUTA) of the 18th cent., but he produced work on a great variety of subjects and seems to have concentrated on views only after the death of his brother **Gianantonio** (1699–1760). Until then Francesco's personality was largely submerged in the family studio, of which Gianantonio was head and which handled commissions of every kind. Francesco's career was unsuccessful in worldly terms; he was still working for other artists when he was over 40, he never attracted the attention of foreign visitors in the way Canaletto did, and he died in poverty. Recognition of his genius came in the wake of *Impressionism, when his vibrant and rapidly painted views were seen as having qualities of spontaneity, bravura, and atmosphere lacking in Canaletto's sharply defined and deliberate works. Francesco was enormously prolific and his work is in many public collections in Italy, Britain, and elsewhere. The major problem in Guardi studies concerns the authorship of paintings representing *The Story of Tobit* that decorate the organ loft of S. Raffaele in Venice. Critical opinion is sharply divided as to whether these brilliant works, painted with brushwork of breathtaking freedom, are by Francesco or Gianantonio (there is dispute also over the dating), but if they are indeed by the latter, he too must rank as a major figure. Giambattista *Tiepolo was married to the sister of the Guardi brothers, and it was possibly through his influence that Gianantonio became a founder member of the Venetian Academy in 1756. Francesco was not elected until 1784, during the presidency of his nephew Giandomenico Tiepolo.

Guercino, Il, (Giovanni Francesco Barbieri) (1591–1666). Italian painter, known as Il Guercino ('Squinting One') on account of an eye defect. He was born at Cento near Ferrara and his early work drew on a variety of north Italian sources, notably Lodovico *Carracci and Venetian painting, to create a highly individual style characterized by dramatic and capricious lighting, strong colour, and broad, vigorous brushwork. In 1621 Guercino was summoned to Rome by the Bolognese pope Gregory XV and among other commissions painted the celebrated ceiling fresco of *Aurora* in the Casino of the Villa Ludovisi for Gregory's nephew. This exuberant work, with its illusionistic architectural framework designed by Agostino *Tassi, is much more *Baroque in style than Guido *Reni's treatment of the subject of a decade earlier. Guercino returned to Cento in 1623 on the death of the pope, but his short stay in Rome introduced a more Classical feeling to his work. This trend became more pronounced when he moved to Bologna in 1642 to take over the studio of Reni, who died in that year. For the next quarter of a century, until his own death, he was Bologna's leading painter, and his late works can be remarkably similar to Reni's, calm and light in colouring, with little of the lively movement of his early style (*St Luke Displaying a Painting of the Virgin*, Nelson–Atkins Mus., Kansas City, 1652). Guercino was one of the most brilliant draughtsmen of his age; the finest collection of his drawings is in the Royal Library at Windsor Castle.

Guérin, Pierre-Narcisse (1774–1833). One of the most successful French painters of his period. He won the *Prix de Rome in 1797, and his later successes included becoming director of the French *Academy in Rome in 1822 and being created a baron in 1829. His style was derived mainly from *David, but his scenes from Classical history and mythology are less severe and more stagey. As the teacher of *Delacroix and *Géricault amongst others, he was an important figure in the transition from *Neoclassicism to *Romanticism. He laid particular emphasis on the painted sketch and as a professor at the École des *Beaux-Arts, he was instrumental in establishing a sketch competition as a preliminary to the Prix de Rome.

Guggenheim, Solomon R. (1861–1949). American industrialist, collector, and philanthropist, a member of a famous family of financiers whose fortunes were based on the mining and smelting of metals. Like other members of his family, he devoted much of his vast wealth to philanthropy and in 1937 he founded the Solomon R. Guggenheim Foundation 'for the promotion and encouragement of art and education in art'. In 1943 he commissioned Frank Lloyd Wright to design a museum in New York City to house his collection, and the Solomon R. Guggenheim Museum was opened in 1959. It is renowned not only for the outstanding collection of late 19th-cent. and 20th-cent. art it contains, but also for the radical nature of the architecture, which marks a complete departure from traditional museum design; the exhibition space is a continuous spiral ramp, six 'storeys' high, encircling an open central space. It is architecturally exhilarating, but its suitability for displaying paintings and sculptures has been much questioned. Guggenheim's niece, **Peggy Guggenheim** (1898–1979), was a noted patron, collector, and dealer, who did much to further the careers of many leading artists of the *New York School. She spent much of her time in Europe and founded a commercial gallery in Venice as well as in New York. In 1941 she married and divorced Max *Ernst.

Guglielmo della Porta (d. 1577). North Italian sculptor, who worked first in Genoa and then (from 1537) in Rome, where he succeeded *Sebastiano del Piombo at the Papal Mint (1547). Guglielmo had a prolific and varied career, his work including several papal busts and tombs in various Roman churches, the most important being that of Paul III in St Peter's (1549–75). He also produced numerous small devotional and pagan statuettes and was known as a restorer and copier of *antique works (both activities typical of his age). The major influence on his style was *Michelangelo and he had a penchant for reclining figures in the manner of the master's *Day* and *Night*, *Dawn* and *Evening* in the Medici Chapel, Florence.

Guido da Siena. Sienese painter active during the 13th cent. Nothing is known of his life, and his only certain work is a *Madonna and Child* in Siena Town Hall. The picture bears the date 1221, but this has been the subject of much controversy as stylistically the painting seems to be about half a century later. It may be a commemorative inscription the significance of which is now lost, rather than a record of the date of execution. Although the painting is majestic in effect and follows *Byzantine conventions of *iconography, the figures are more natural in posture, to some extent relaxing the stiff linear patterns which had been conventional in central Italian painting up to that time. The throne too is set in a deeper picture space, which adds to the realism of the figures. On the basis of this picture a number of other panels, most of which are in the Siena Pinacoteca, have been assigned to Guido or his school. Despite his great obscurity, he is regarded as sharing with *Coppo di Marcovaldo the honour of founding the Sienese school.

Guillaumin, Armand (1841–1927). French landscape painter, one of the minor figures of the *Impressionist group. Lack of success made him take a post with the department of bridges and causeways until he won a lottery in 1891 and was able to devote all his time to painting. Often his paintings are of industrial subjects, but he also painted seascapes. His style was bold and direct, often brilliantly coloured.

gum. A sticky liquid exuded by certain trees and shrubs, various types of which have been used as painting *media from ancient times. Gum is the normal medium of *water-colour paints and *pastel, and since it readily emulsifies with oil it has long been a medium in *tempera.

Günther, Ignaz (1725–75). Bavarian sculptor. After a varied training culminating in some years at the Vienna Academy he settled in Munich in 1754. His short career was productive of a considerable quantity of wood-carving combining a very elegant *Rococo style with a highly emotional religious content. In 1759–62 he produced his chief work, the almost entire furnishing of the church at Rott-am-Inn.

Guston, Philip (1913–80). American painter. He first came to prominence as a muralist working for the *Federal Art Project from 1935 to 1942. In the early 1940s he was painting in a figurative manner of fantasy bordering upon *Surrealism, but towards the end of the decade he began to experiment with abstractions vaguely suggestive of urban landscapes until c.1950 he eliminated the figurative element from his work. His most characteristic paintings feature luminous patches of overlapping colours delicately brushed in the central area of a canvas of light background (*Dial*, Whitney Mus., New York, 1956). This manner of his has been described as 'abstract Impressionism' and he was associated with the more lyrical group of *Abstract Expressionists. In the course of the 1960s shades of grey encroached on the earlier brilliance of colour and vague naturalistic associations crept in, until in the 1970s he introduced a new manner of figuration between satire and *Goya-like grotesquerie. Using a comic-strip technique and harsh discordant colours, and painting with a certain deliberate brutality, he depicted scenes of the Ku-Klux-Klan and fantastic social comment.

Gutfreund, Otto (1889–1927). Czech sculptor. After training in Prague, he worked with *Bourdelle in Paris, 1909–10, and was attracted by *Cubism. He was among the first to apply the principles of Cubism to sculpture and on his return to Prague in 1911 he formed one of a small group of avant-garde artists attempting a fusion of Cubism with *Expressionism. After the First World War he developed a more popular and naturalistic style based upon folk art.

Guttuso, Renato (1912–87). Italian painter. He was a forceful, vigorous personality and in 1938 became a founder member of the anti-Fascist association *Corrente. His subject-matter belonged to the field of Social *Realism, but his style was *Expressionist and he never subordinated artistic quality to political propaganda. He not only stigmatized Fascism in his work, but also, for example, pilloried the Mafia, and in 1943–5 published a series of drawings protesting against the massacres which took place under the German Occupation in Italy. After the war he was a member of the *Fronte Nuovo delle Arti. His interest in the history of art and in artists present and past provided him with another major theme in his work.

Guys, Constantin (1802–92). French illustrator. Little is known about his life. He was a soldier as a young man and travelled widely, leading a vagabond life. According to *Baudelaire, who immortalized him as the 'Painter of Modern Life' in his celebrated essay of that name (1863), Guys began to draw without instruction in 1847—but this is probably putting it too late. In 1854 he went to the Crimean War as Special Correspondent of *The Illustrated London News*, for which he had been working in London from 1848. He is most remembered, however, for his pictorial record of Paris life during the Second Empire in witty and lively drawings reinforced by thin washes of tone or colour.

H

Hackaert, Jan (*c.*1628–after 1685). Dutch landscape painter. He travelled extensively in Switzerland and Italy in the 1650s and is best known for Italian scenes. The finest is generally regarded as being *Lake Trasimene* (Rijksmuseum, Amsterdam), which shows how well he could capture the golden sunlight of Umbria. Little is known of his life. The figures in his paintings are often the work of other artists, notably *Berchem and Adrian van de *Velde.

Hackert, Jakob Philipp (1737–1807). German landscape painter, active in Italy from 1768. In 1786 he became court painter to Ferdinand IV of Naples. He was a sensitive upholder of the *ideal landscape tradition of *Claude, which he seasoned with touches of *Romanticism. Much of his prolific output was devoted to views of famous sites, which were eagerly sought by foreign visitors to Italy. He came from a family of artists and often collaborated with his brother **Johann Gottlieb Hackert** (1744–73). *Goethe met Hackert in 1787 and wrote his biography in 1811. His work is exceptionally well represented at Attingham Park in Shropshire.

Hague School. Group of Dutch artists who worked in The Hague between about 1860 and 1900. The group is particularly associated with landscapes and beach scenes, but the members also painted street scenes, views of everyday life, and church interiors. In some ways this was a *Romantic revival of the 17th-cent. tradition, and this romantically nostalgic strain—particularly in pictures made during the first years the group worked together—is one of the things which distinguishes them from their French counterparts, the painters of the *Barbizon School and the *Impressionists. They shared with the great Dutch landscapists of the 17th cent. a special sensitivity in recording light and atmospheric effects. Leading members of the Hague School included *Weissenbruch, *Bosboom, *Israëls, *Mauve, the *Maris brothers, and *Mesdag.

Hals, Frans (1580/5–1666). Dutch painter. He was probably born in Antwerp of Flemish parents who moved to Holland after the city fell to the Spaniards in 1585. His parents settled in Haarlem in 1591 and he spent his long life there. He was twice married, had at least ten children, and was constantly in financial trouble. *Houbraken says he was 'filled to the gills every evening', but there is little foundation for the popular image of him as a drunken wife-beater. His second wife, however, was more than once in trouble for brawling. During his last years he was destitute and the municipal authorities of Haarlem awarded him a small annual stipend four years before his death.

Hals was the first great artist of the 17th-cent. Dutch school and is regarded as one of the most brilliant of all portraitists. Almost all his works are portraits and even those that are not (some *genre scenes, and an occasional religious picture) are portrait-like in character. He is said to have been taught in Haarlem by Karel van *Mander, but there is no discernible influence from him in Hals's early works, which are not numerous or well documented. The earliest extant picture is the fragment of a portrait *Jacobus Zaffius* (Hals Mus., Haarlem, 1611), and upon the basis of stylistic evidence one or two paintings can be dated a year or so earlier. Nothing he did before 1616 suggested that he would shatter well-established traditions with his life-size group portrait *The Banquet of the Officers of the St George Militia Company* (Hals Mus.) painted during that year. There is no precedent in either his own work or that of his predecessors for the vigorous composition and characterization of this picture, which has become a symbol of the strength and healthy optimism of the men who established the new Dutch Republic. It demonstrates to the full his remarkable ability—his greatest gift as a portraitist—to capture a sense of fleeting movement and expression and thereby convey a compelling feeling of vivacity.

From 1616 onwards there is no shortage of dated or documented works and his artistic development is clear. He was at the height of his popularity in the 1620s and 1630s. During these decades he made five large group portraits of civic guards; one is in the Rijksmuseum and the others are in the Frans Hals Museum, Haarlem, the only place where one can get a comprehensive view of his range and power. In the 1630s his compositions became simpler and monochromatic effects took the place of the bright colours of the earlier paintings (*Lucas de Clercq* and *Feyntje van Steenkiste*, Rijksmuseum, Amsterdam, 1635). The group portrait of the *Regents of the St Elizabeth Hospital* (Hals Mus., 1641) sets the key for the sober restraint of the late period, when his pictures became darker and his brush-strokes more economical. The culmination of this phase—indeed of his entire career—are his group portraits of the *Regents* and the *Regentesses of the Old Men's Alms House* (Hals Mus., c.1664), which rank among the most moving portraits ever painted. By this time Hals was using in his commissioned portraits the bold brushwork and the *alla prima* technique which early in his career he reserved for genre pictures. No drawings by him are known and he presumably worked straight on to the canvas.

Hals had two painter brothers and five painter sons, but the only artist of substance among them was his brother **Dirk** (1591–1656), who painted charming small interior scenes. Apart from his sons, Hals taught numerous pupils, including such distinguished artists as Judith *Leyster, Jan Miense *Molenaer, Adriaen van *Ostade, Adriaen *Brouwer, and Philips *Wouwerman. His reputation did not long outlive him, however, and with rare exceptions—*Reynolds was one of them—few critics before 1850 praised him. It was only in the second half of the 19th cent. that there was a renewed appreciation of his genius. The spontaneity of his work appealed to the generation of the *Impressionists, and from about 1870 to about 1920 he was one of the most popular of the Old Masters, becoming a model for society portraitists. Lord Hertford's purchase of his most famous work, *The Laughing Cavalier* (Wallace Coll., London, 1624), for the then enormous sum of 51,000 francs in 1865, was a milestone in the revival of his fortunes, and the buoyant confidence of his paintings later made him a particular favourite with the new generation of fabulously rich American collectors—self-made men—who were beginning to dominate the picture market. This explains why so many works by him are in American collections.

Hamilton, Gavin (1723–98). Scottish painter, archaeologist, and picture-dealer, active mainly in Italy. He settled permanently in Rome in 1766, and was a leading member of the *Neoclassical circle of *Mengs and *Winckelmann. His archaeological excavations near Rome resulted in many important additions to contemporary collections, and his interest in antiquity exerted a decisive influence on the young *Canova. Hamilton's history paintings, mostly of Homeric subjects, were influenced by *Poussin as well as by the *antique (*Achilles Lamenting the Death of Patroclus*, NG, Edinburgh, 1763). They were never very numerous and today are generally regarded as rather tepid, but they became well known through engravings, and greatly influenced the development of the Neoclassical style amongst both his contemporaries and the younger generation, including *David. Indeed, Hamilton was much better known on the Continent than in Britain, where his name was more familiar for his activities in selling Old Masters and Classical antiquities. Together with *Barry, and the Anglo-Americans *West and *Copley, he is one of the few painters to have made a significant contribution to *history painting in Britain. Gavin Hamilton is not to be confused with **Gawen Hamilton** (1697?–1737), a minor portrait painter remembered for his *Conversation of Virtuosi . . . at the Kings Arms* (NPG, London, 1735), which shows himself and several other artists of the day.

Hamilton, Richard (1922–   ). British painter, one of the leading pioneers of *Pop art. As a young man he worked in the publicity department of an electrical firm and he is best known for his montages featuring scenes from the fields of advertisement and contemporary life, notably *Just what is it that makes today's homes so different, so appealing?* (Kunsthalle, Tübingen, 1956). This photomontage is sometimes considered to be the first Pop art work. Hamilton has had an influence on, among others, Peter *Blake and David *Hockney, and he has done much to popularize *Duchamp's work. See also INDEPENDENT GROUP.

Hammershøi, Vilhelm (1864–1916). Danish painter, active mainly in his native Copenhagen. He painted portraits, architectural subjects (including two murals for Copenhagen Town Hall), and landscapes, but is best known for his quiet interior scenes. They are painted in muted colours, and have a certain affinity with *Vermeer, often featuring a single standing or seated figure. Most of Hammershøi's paintings are in Denmark, but two of his interiors are in the Tate Gallery.

Hanson, Duane (1925–   ). American sculptor. Hanson is probably the best-known exponent of *Superrealism in sculpture, producing minutely detailed fibreglass resin figures dressed in real clothes and accompanied by real props. He concentrates pungently on the depressing or tasteless aspects of everyday American life—down-and-outs, exhausted shoppers, or in one of his most famous works, a pair of fat, ageing, and garishly dressed tourists (*Tourists*, NG of Modern Art, Edinburgh, 1970).

happening. A form of entertainment, often carefully planned but usually including some degree of spontaneity, in which an artist performs or directs an event combining elements of theatre and the visual arts. The term was coined by Allan *Kaprow in 1959 and has been used to cover a diversity of contrived artistic phenomena. The concept of the happening was closely bound up with Kaprow's deliberate rejection of the traditional principles of craftsmanship and permanence in the arts. He thought of the happening as a development mainly from the *assemblage and the *environment. It had close affinities with theatrical and *Performance art, and it was not restricted like the environment to the confines of a gallery or some other site. In conformity with the theories of the composer John Cage about the importance of chance in artistic creation, happenings were described as 'spontaneous, plotless theatrical events'. In America the artists chiefly responsible for the development of the happening in its early stages included, besides Cage and Kaprow, Jim *Dine, Claes *Oldenburg, Robert *Rauschenberg, and Roy *Lichtenstein, and it was widely exploited outside America. The idea of the happening was linked with the principle of spectator participation, and the term has often been employed to describe staged demonstrations for politico-social propaganda, as for example many of the happenings by Joseph *Beuys, or demonstrations intended to shock established moralities. The theory of the happening is as diverse as the practice.

Hard Edge painting. Term applied to a type of painting (predominantly abstract) in which forms, although not necessarily geometrical, have sharp contours and are executed in flat colours. The term was coined by the American critic Jules Langsner in 1958, and although it can be retrospectively applied to such styles as *Purism, it is used mainly of the type of painting that emerged as a reaction to the spontaneity and painterly handling of *Abstract Expressionism. Major exponents of Hard Edge painting have included Ellsworth *Kelly and Kenneth *Noland. See also POST-PAINTERLY ABSTRACTION.

Harnett, William Michael (1848–92). American still-life painter. He was born in Ireland and brought to America as a child, living mainly in Philadelphia until a stay in Europe in 1880–6, and thereafter in New York. He specialized in elaborate *trompe l'œil compositions, often involving firearms or musical instruments (*After the Hunt*, California Palace of the Legion of Honor, San Francisco, 1885). Although his works were long popular with the public, they were generally dismissed by critics as mere sleight of hand until about 1945, when they began to win favour for their strength of composition.

Harpignies, Henri (1819–1916). French landscape painter and engraver. He did not take up painting until 1846, but he was then very prolific and won considerable success and fame. He is sometimes classed with the *Barbizon School, but his work shows more specifically the influence of *Corot, with whom he went to Italy in 1860.

Harris, Lawren Stewart (1885–1970). Canadian painter. From 1904 to 1908 he studied in Berlin, and his work became imbued with bold *Expressionist colour. Until 1920 views of houses and cityscapes were his main interest, but after meeting J. E. H. *Macdonald in 1911 he turned as well to landscape and became one of the founder members of the *Group of Seven. In 1918 Harris had discovered Algoma, in northern Ontario, and the lushness of the countryside was suited to the dramatic and colourful style he had developed (*Autumn, Algoma*, Victoria University, Toronto, 1920). Later he sought out more spectacular scenery in the Rockies and even in the Arctic, his work expressing a desire for spiritual fulfilment through immersion in the vital forces of overpowering landscape. This transcendental quality was maintained when Harris turned to abstraction in the 1930s.

Hartley, Marsden (1877–1943). American painter, whose work represented an advanced response to modernist trends in European art. In 1912 he was sent to Europe by *Stieglitz (who had given him his first one-man exhibition in 1909), but finding *Cubist Paris little to his taste he went to Munich and Berlin, where the *Expressionism of *Kandinsky and *Jawlensky proved more congenial, and he exhibited with the *Blaue Reiter in Berlin in 1913. Later that year he returned to America and exhibited at the *Armory Show. From 1914 to 1916 he was again in Europe, visiting London, Paris, Berlin, and Munich. During these years he painted in an abstract manner with Expressionist overtones, as in the famous *Painting No. 5* (Whitney Mus., New York, 1914–15), a picture painted in rich Expressionist colours and incorporating military emblems and decorations of wartime Germany. Instead of continuing on this path, however, on his return to the USA in 1916, he began to paint near-*Constructivist abstracts in clear pastel hues. In 1917 he abandoned the abstract and from 1918 to 1920 did dramatic pastels of the New Mexico landscape, upon which in the early 1920s he based equally dramatic though more formalized oils. In the decade up to 1936 he led a wandering, unsettled life, visiting France, Italy, Germany, and New Mexico. In 1932–3 he began to paint in a sophisticated 'primitive' manner and continued in this vein to the end of his career.

Hartung, Hans (1904–   ). German-born painter who became a French citizen in 1946. Early in his career he met *Kandinsky and he began painting abstracts in 1922. In 1935 he fled from Germany and settled in Paris. He was afterwards imprisoned in Spain and during the war he served in the French Foreign Legion. After the war he returned to Paris, and developed a highly original and vibrant style of abstract painting in which thick black lines and blotches predominate in a manner superficially analogous to calligraphic scribbling. He has been regarded as one of the main precursors of *Art Informel.

Hassam, Childe (1859–1935). American painter and printmaker, one of the foremost American exponents of *Impressionism. He discovered Impressionism on his second trip to Europe in 1886–9, when he studied in Paris. On his return to the USA he settled in New York and the life of the city became his favourite subject-matter. His work is fresh and clear but sometimes rather saccharine. See also TEN, THE.

hatching. The use of finely spaced parallel lines to suggest shading. The technique is found mainly in drawing and engraving, but is also used, for example, in *tempera painting. When crossing sets of lines are used, the term cross-hatching is applicable.

Haydon, Benjamin Robert (1786–1846). English painter, who in reaction from the anecdotal pictures of *Wilkie and others aspired to redeem English painting by historical and religious work in the *Grand Manner preached by *Reynolds. His life was one of bombastic frustration and intransigent opposition to the establishment (particularly the *Royal Academy), fighting continuously for personal recognition and arguing for the social purpose of art. As a painter, however, his talents fell far short of his ambitions, his multi-figure compositions degenerating into turgid melodrama. His great monument, rather, is the massive collection of autobiographical writings he left behind him (various editions have been published), which gives fascinating insights into the contemporary artistic scene and paints a vividly detailed picture of his disturbed mind and tragicomical life. He was closely linked with the *Romantic movement in literature, particularly with William Wordsworth, who wrote a sonnet to him, and with John Keats, doing portraits of both of them (NPG, London), and but for his lack of talent he would exemplify all the traits traditionally ascribed to the Romantic concept of genius. In true Romantic fashion his death came by suicide.

Hayez, Francesco (1791–1882). Italian painter, active mainly in Milan. Hayez was the most important figure in the transition from *Neoclassicism to *Romanticism in Italian painting, but his Romantic leanings come out mainly in subject-matter rather than in technique, the clear outlines he favoured revealing his training in Rome in the circle of *Canova and *Ingres. He painted religious, historical, and mythological works in a vein owing something to *Delacroix and *Delaroche, and portraits that are sometimes thought worthy of comparison with those of Ingres. Many of the most eminent Italians of the day sat for him. For many years he taught at the *Brera in Milan (he became Director in 1860) and he exercised great influence on his pupils. The Brera has an outstanding collection of his work.

Hayman, Francis (1707/8–76). English painter and book illustrator. He was the most versatile British artist of his period, painting portraits, subjects from literature and the theatre (notably Shakespeare), and scenes of rural folklore; he also had the reputation of being 'unquestionably the best historical painter in the kingdom before the arrival of *Cipriani' (Edward Edwards, *Anecdotes of Painters . . .*, 1808), but little of his decorative work survives. In addition he was a prolific designer of book illustrations, sometimes collaborating with *Gravelot. His largest undertaking was the painting of decorations for the boxes and pavilions at Vauxhall Gardens, the fashionable London pleasure resort, of which two are now in the Victoria and Albert Museum. His *conversation pieces anticipated those of the early *Gainsborough, who almost certainly worked with him in Gravelot's studio. Hayman was President of the *Society of Artists, 1760–8, and became a foundation member of the *Royal Academy in 1768 and its librarian in 1771. His best work has a certain *Rococo charm, but there is some justification in Horace *Walpole's comment that his paintings are 'easily distinguishable by the large noses and shambling legs of his figures'.

Hayter, Sir George (1792–1871). English historical and portrait painter. The son of a *miniaturist **Charles Hayter** (1761–1835), he studied at the *Royal Academy Schools and in Rome, and was appointed portrait and history painter to Queen Victoria in 1837. On the death of *Wilkie in 1841 he was made 'principal painter in ordinary to the queen'. He is known chiefly for his royal portraits and his huge groups (*House of Commons*, NPG, London, 1833), unexciting in their handling, but composed with dexterity and accomplished grandiloquence. In spite of his royal favour he was never a member of the Royal Academy, seemingly because, after an unfortunate early marriage, he lived with a woman who was not his wife.

Hayter, S. W. (Stanley William) (1901–88). British engraver and painter, a descendant of Sir George *Hayter. He spent most of his life in Paris, where in 1927 he founded an experimental workshop for the graphic arts—Atelier 17—that played a central role in the 20th-cent. revival of the print as an independent art form. Hayter was a chemist by training and had an unrivalled knowledge of the technicalities of printmaking, on which he wrote two major books, *New Ways of Gravure* (1949) and *About Prints* (1962). Although his historical importance has long been acknowledged (probably no modern British artist has been so influential internationally), it is only recently that his own work has won him belated recognition as one of the outstanding graphic artists of his time. His prints are varied in technique and style, but most characteristically are influenced by the abstract vein of *Surrealism and are notable for their experiments with texture and colour.

Hazlitt, William (1778–1830). English essayist. He is known mainly for his literary criticism, but he also wrote much on the fine arts and he ranks as the most important British writer on the subject between *Reynolds and *Ruskin. Although he studied painting and did some portraits (one of Charles Lamb, 1804, is in the National Portrait Gallery, London), he lived mainly by journalism, publishing essays in various radical journals. Hazlitt was a *Romantic critic in placing much more importance on the role of genius in artistic creation than on rules or theories. Thus he admired

Reynolds's paintings, but attacked his ideas. A significant characteristic of Hazlitt's writing is that (unlike most previous art criticism) it was written for the general reader rather than for the connoisseur or practising artist.

Heartfield, John (Helmut Herzfelde) (1891–1968). German painter, graphic designer, and journalist, a founder of the Berlin *Dada group, best known as one of the pioneers and perhaps the greatest of all exponents of *photomontage. With *Grosz he Anglicized his name during the First World War as a protest against German nationalistic fervour and his finest works are brilliantly satirical attacks—often in the form of book covers and posters—against militarism and Nazism. Harassed by the Nazis he left Germany in 1938 and moved to London, where he lived until 1950. He died in Berlin, his native city.

Heckel, Erich (1883–1970). German painter and graphic artist, one of the founders of Die *Brücke. His work was somewhat more lyrical than that of the other members of Die Brücke and he showed a special concern for depicting sickness and inner anguish. His landscapes, too, sometimes displayed a decorative quality which was foreign to most German *Expressionism. In 1911 he settled in Berlin with *Kirchner and other members of Die Brücke. Here, as a result of contacts with *Feininger, *Macke, and Franz *Marc, the formal structure of his painting gained in strength and coherence. But his image of humanity became even more pessimistic, with harshly angular distortions, anguished expressions, and rigid, distracted gestures. From 1914 Heckel served as a medical orderly in Flanders and came into contact there with *Ensor and *Beckmann, by whom he was again influenced. His landscapes became more sombre in colour, expressing the agony of war through conflict of the elements, and the melancholic and tragic mood of his work was enhanced. After 1920 his work became more conventional and the verve and intensity of his Expressionist style was lost. His work was proscribed as *degenerate art in 1937. In 1944 his Berlin studio was destroyed by fire and he retired to Hemmenhofen on Lake Constance. From 1949 to 1955 he taught at the Karlsruhe Academy.

Heda, Willem Claesz. (1593/4–1680/2). Dutch still-life painter, active in Haarlem. He and Pieter *Claesz. are the most important representatives of *onthijt* (breakfast piece) painting in the Netherlands. His overall grey-green or brownish tonalities are very similar to those of Claesz., but Heda's work was usually more highly finished and his taste was more aristocratic. He showed a preference for ham, mincemeat pie, and oysters, and after 1629 never included a herring in his pictures. His son **Gerrit** (d. 1702) was his most important pupil.

Heem, Jan Davidsz. de (1606–83/4). Dutch still-life painter. He was born at Utrecht and his rare early pictures are in the style of Balthasar van der *Ast, who taught him there. Later he worked in Leiden and showed that he had studied the restrained and simple works of the Haarlem still-life artists *Claesz. and *Heda. In 1636 he moved to Antwerp, became a citizen of that city in 1637, and spent most of his very productive life there. The paintings he did in Flanders are the ones for which he is most renowned and are very different in spirit from his earlier works: splendid flower pieces and large compositions of exquisitely laid tables which breathe all the opulent exuberance of Flemish *Baroque painting. His work formed a link between the Dutch and Flemish still-life traditions and he is claimed by both schools. He came from a large family of painters and his many followers in Flanders and Holland included his son **Cornelis** (1631–95).

Heemskerck, Maerten van (1498–1574). Netherlandish *Mannerist painter, born at Heemskerck and active mainly in nearby Haarlem. His principal training was with Jan van *Scorel in Utrecht, c.1527–9. Although Heemskerck was only three years younger than Scorel and was a mature man when he entered his studio (he had already studied with two other teachers), the experience left a distinctive mark on him. In some pictures, particularly the portraits, experts still have difficulty distinguishing their hands. As a rule, however, Heemskerck's paintings are more crowded and nervous than Scorel's balanced and harmonious compositions. Equally important for Heemskerck's development was a visit to Italy (1532–5), where he was overwhelmed by *Michelangelo. When he returned to the Netherlands he emulated Michelangelo by painting large works packed with muscle-bound figures in vigorous movement (*Christ Crowned with Thorns*, Hals Museum, Haarlem). During his stay in Rome Heemskerck made drawings of ancient and modern buildings and sculpture; they áre valuable historical documents as well as sensitive impressions of the marvels of Rome. His interest in antiquity also comes out in his self-portrait of 1533 (Fitzwilliam, Cambridge), in which he shows the Colosseum in the background. Heemskerck was one of the leading Netherlandish painters of the 16th cent. and his work was much engraved and highly influential.

Heidelberg School. Group of Australian painters led by Tom *Roberts who met at the painting camp at Eaglemont, Heidelberg, Victoria. The art of the school, based on open-air *Impressionist painting, also featured local subject-matter and was associated with the emergence of a distinctive Australian literature. It flourished, appropriately enough, between 1888 (the centenary of Australia) and 1901 (the foundation year of the Commonwealth). Lack of patronage at home and desire for overseas training and experience had forced most of its members to Europe by 1900. But their vision of Australian life and landscape has had lasting influence.

Held, Al (1928–   ). American painter. After abandoning his early *Abstract Expressionist manner *c*.1960, he evolved during the 1960s a highly personal style which had affinities with both *Colour Field and *Hard Edge painting. Unlike other Colour Field painters such as Helen *Frankenthaler and Morris *Louis, he did not adopt the technique of thinly stained unprimed canvas but maintained a heavy *impasto, which he worked up into a massive over-all texture. He was much concerned with the expressive importance of scale. During the 1970s his work increased in stature and power with his well-known linear structures of white lines and a black ground (e.g. the *Flemish* series) and black lines on a white ground.

Hellenistic. A term applied to Greek culture in the late 4th to late 1st cent. BC, say from 323 BC, when Alexander the Great died, to 27 BC, when Augustus became the first Roman emperor. During this period Greece itself had lost its political importance as Rome rose to power, but Greek culture was adopted by diverse peoples in the Mediterranean world and beyond. Hellenistic art is more varied in inspiration than that of the *Classical age which preceded it, and the sculpture of the period is often remarkable for its technical bravura and overt display of emotion, as in the celebrated *Laocoön*, the most famous of Hellenistic works of art. After original Greek works of the Classical period became widely known in the course of the 19th cent. much Hellenistic art was generally dismissed as decadent, but it is now recognized as a rich field of study.

Helst, Bartholomeus van der (1613–70). Dutch portrait painter. He was born at Haarlem, settled in Amsterdam in 1636, and in the 1640s took over from *Rembrandt as the most popular portraitist in the city, his detailed, tasteful, and slightly flattering likenesses appealing more to the fashionable burghers than the master's more individual and introspective work. Van der Helst's influence during his lifetime was great. For example, Rembrandt's talented pupils *Bol and *Flinck abandoned the style of their master in order to follow his more popular manner. His reputation endured into the next century and as late as 1781 *Reynolds wrote that van der Helst's *Banquet of the Amsterdam Civic Guard in Celebration of the Peace of Munster* (Rijksmuseum, Amsterdam, 1648) 'is, perhaps, the first picture of portraits in the world', adding that it as far exceeded his expectations as Rembrandt's *Night Watch* fell below them.

Hemessen, Jan Sanders van (*c*.1500–*c*.1566). Netherlandish painter of religious and *genre scenes and portraits. The facts of his life are obscure, but in 1524 he was made a free master of the Antwerp Guild. He is reputed to have moved to Haarlem *c*.1550 and to have died there. His paintings illustrating popular proverbs and religious parables, and his satirical portraits, link him with Quentin *Massys and *Marinus van Reymerswaele, and Hemessen ranks with them as one of the founders of Flemish genre painting. An example of his work is *The Prodigal Son* (Musées Royaux, Brussels, 1536).

Henri, Robert (1865–1929). American painter. He studied first at the Pennsylvania Academy under Thomas Pollock Anshutz (1851–1912), a pupil of Thomas *Eakins, of whose work Henri became an ardent admirer, and then in Paris under *Bouguereau, 1888–91. In Paris he was influenced particularly by the 'Spanish' features of *Manet—his *realism, dark palette, and virtuoso brushwork. He returned to Philadelphia in 1891 and became the intellectual inspiration of The *Eight in their revolt against current academic dreariness. Henri's energetic propagation of the creed that the artist must be a social force, one whose 'work creates a stir in the world', and his sense of the dignity and importance of an art in touch with contemporary life, were the impulses which led to the emergence of a new school of American realism that blossomed in the *Ash-can School. From 1915 to 1928 Henri taught at the Art Students' League in New York and his importance in the history of 20th-cent. American art derives more from his influence as a teacher and a crusader than from the quality of his own work, which has a certain dash but is generally rather superficial. He was a powerful force in turning young American painters away from academism to look at the rich subject-matter provided by modern urban life, and his book *The Art Spirit* (1923), in which art was seen as an expression of love for life, enjoyed great popularity with artists and art students.

Hepworth, Dame Barbara (1903–75). English sculptor, one of the most important figures in the development of abstract art in Britain. She was trained at Leeds School of Art, where she became a friend of Henry *Moore, and at the *Royal College of Art. Her early sculptures were quasi-naturalistic and had much in common with Moore's work (*Doves*, Manchester City Art Gal., 1927), but she already showed a tendency to submerge detail in simple forms, and by the early 1930s her work was entirely abstract. She worked both in wood and stone, and she described an important aspect of her early career as being 'the excitement of discovering the nature of carving'—this at a time when there was a general antagonism to 'direct carving'. In this, too, she was united with Moore, but her work, unlike his, is not representational in origin but conceived as abstract forms.

Yet she consistently professed a *Romantic attitude of emotional affinity with nature, speaking of carving both as a 'biological necessity' and as an 'extension of the telluric forces which mould the landscape'. In 1931 she met Ben *Nicholson, who became her second husband a year later, and through him she became aware of contemporary European developments. They joined *Abstraction-Création in 1933, and *Unit One in the same year. During the 1930s Hepworth, Nicholson, and Moore worked in close harmony and became recognized as the nucleus of the abstract movement in England. In 1939 Hepworth moved to St Ives in Cornwall with Nicholson and lived there for the rest of her life (see ST IVES PAINTERS). During the late 1930s and 1940s she began to concentrate on the counterplay between mass and space in sculpture. In 1931 in *Pierced Form* (destroyed in the war) she first introduced into England the use of the 'hole', and she now developed this with great subtlety, making play with the relationship between the outside and inside of a figure, the two surfaces sometimes being linked with threaded string, as in *Pelagos* (Tate, London, 1946). *Pelagos* also shows her sensitive use of painted surface to contrast with the natural grain of the wood. In all her work she displayed a deep understanding of the quality of her materials and superb standards of craftsmanship. By the 1950s she was one of the most internationally famous of sculptors and she received many honours and prestigious public commissions, among them the memorial to Dag Hammerskjold—*Single Form*—at the United Nations in New York (1963). She now worked more in bronze, especially for large pieces, but she always retained a special feeling for direct carving. Hepworth died tragically in a fire at her studio in St Ives. The studio is now a museum dedicated to her work.

Herkomer, Sir Hubert von (1849–1914). Bavarian-born English painter. He came to England with his father, a wood-carver, in 1857 and was largely self-taught as a painter. He established himself as a master of sentimental *genre with his *Last Muster—Sunday at the Royal Hospital, Chelsea* (Lady Lever Art Gal., Port Sunlight, 1875), and then became a successful and prolific portrait painter. His best-known works today, however, are his scenes of social concern, which were then still something of a novelty in English art (*On Strike*, Royal Academy, London, 1891). Herkomer was a versatile artist and a man of many parts. He founded and directed a school of art at Bushey, Hertfordshire, 1883–1904, was *Slade Professor of Fine Art at Oxford, 1885–94, and published several books. In addition to paintings, his varied artistic output included set designs for the theatre and cinema, and he also acted and composed music.

Hermitage, Leningrad. The largest public museum and art gallery in the Soviet Union and one of the most important in the world. It takes its name from a pleasure pavilion adjoining the Winter Palace, built to the order of Catherine the Great in 1764–7 (the 'Little Hermitage') for the display of her treasures. In 1787 it was incorporated in a new building (the Old Hermitage). Catherine was one of the most voracious collectors of all time and at her death in 1796 the imperial collections were estimated to total nearly 4,000 pictures. From 1802 pictures by Russian artists began to be added to the imperial collections. In 1837 the Winter Palace was ravaged by fire and the New Hermitage was built by the Munich architect Leo von Klenze, 1840–9. It was opened to the public by Nicholas I in 1852. In the following year the Czar sold over 1,200 pictures, but the collection continued to grow, doubling the number of its pictures between 1910 and 1932 despite extensive sales by the Soviets. After the Soviet Revolution the imperial collections came into public ownership. The representation (only a fraction of the collection) of Western painting is rich in virtually every period and school, but perhaps most notably in 17th-cent. Dutch painting (the largest collection in the world) and in French painting of the late 19th and early 20th cents.

Heron, Patrick (1920–). British painter. He turned to abstraction in the late 1950s and evolved a style remarkable for the intense interaction of colour, which he thought should be the primary concern of painting. Heron has also written much art criticism. See also ST IVES PAINTERS.

Herrera, Francisco the Elder (*c.*1590–1656?). Spanish painter and engraver, a

representative of the transition from *Mannerism to *Baroque. With his older contemporary *Roelas, under whose influence he developed, he helped to prepare the way for the new naturalistic style of the School of Seville in the early 17th cent. *St Basil Dictating his Rule* (Louvre, Paris), which is generally considered his masterpiece, shows his work at its most bold and vigorous. About 1638 Herrera moved to Madrid, where he died. According to *Palomino, *Velázquez was briefly Herrera's pupil, but if this was so it could only have been for a short time. His son, **Francisco Herrera the Younger** (1627–85), painter and architect, spent many years in Italy, where he is said to have fled from his father's notoriously bad temper and may have studied architecture and fresco painting in Rome. Returning to Spain after his father's death, he was appointed *Murillo's deputy of the Academy of Seville when it was founded in 1660. Soon afterwards he moved to Madrid, where he was appointed Painter to the King (Charles II) in 1672 and Master of the Royal Works in 1677. His greatest achievement was the design (subsequently modified) of the church of El Pilar at Saragossa, begun in 1681. His work as a painter, airy and colourful, owed much to the example of Murillo.

Herring, John Frederick Sen. (1795–1865). British sporting and animal painter, the best-known member of a family of sporting artists. He had great success as a painter of racehorses, regularly doing portraits of the winners of the Derby and St Leger, and his work enjoyed wide popularity in engravings. His three painter sons included **John Frederick Jun.** (died 1907), and he also had a painter brother, **Benjamin Herring Sen.** (1806–30). It is often not easy to distinguish between the work of the various members of the family.

Heyden, Jan van der (1637–1712). Dutch painter, active in Amsterdam. He painted some landscapes and still lifes, but is celebrated as one of the greatest of all townscape painters. His views of towns are done with loving attention to detail, but the harmonious colours and sunny light of his elegantly composed pictures prevent the precise way he rendered foliage, bricks, and architectural detail from appearing dull or dry. In spite of the seemingly objective nature of his work, van der Heyden often took liberties with topographical accuracy and he also painted *capricci*. Painting was only a part of his activity, for he was also involved in civic administration in Amsterdam. The fire hose is said to have been his invention and it is included in his *Brandspuiten-boek* ('Fire Engine Book'), a volume about fire-fighting equipment, illustrated with his own engravings, that he published in 1690.

Heysen, Sir Hans (1877–1968). Australian landscape painter, mainly in water-colour. He was born in Hamburg and was taken to Australia as a child. A prolific artist, he became the most popular Australian landscape painter of his time.

Hicks, Edward (1780–1849). The best-known American primitive painter of the 19th cent., active in Bucks County, Pennsylvania. He was a coach- and sign-painter early in life, but for many years he devoted himself to preaching—the pleasure he derived from painting conflicted with his ascetic Quaker outlook and caused him much conscience-searching. Some of his pictures are farm scenes or landscapes, but he is best known for his many versions (he reputedly made more than 100) of *The Peaceable Kingdom*. Exemplifying the pacifism of the Quaker society in which he lived, they depict with a vivid and charming literalness the prophecy in the 11th chapter of Isaiah that all men and beasts will live in peace.

Highmore, Joseph (1692–1780). English painter, mainly of portraits. He studied at *Kneller's Academy and had a considerable practice as a portraitist by the 1720s. His early work is in the manner of *Richardson, but from the 1730s his portraits became more elegant as he responded to the *Rococo influences that began to pervade English painting at this time. Some of his more informal works, however, have a directness and freshness that recalls *Hogarth (*Mr Oldham and Friends*, Tate, London). Highmore was a friend of the novelist Samuel Richardson and painted a series of twelve illustrations to *Pamela* (Tate; Fitzwilliam, Cambridge; NG of Victoria, Melbourne), which link him with *Hayman and Hogarth as one of the initiators of a British school of narrative painting. He also painted Richardson's portrait (NPG, London). In 1761 he gave up painting and retired to Canterbury to devote himself to literary pursuits.

Hildebrand, Adolf von (1847–1921). German sculptor and writer on art. He spent much of his career in Italy, where he was closely associated with Hans von *Marées, and is regarded as one of the main upholders in his period of the Classical tradition in sculpture. He is now, however, better known for his treatise *Das Problem der Form in der bildenden Kunst* (1893) than for his highly accomplished but rather bland sculpture. The book went through many editions (an English translation, *The Problem of Form in Painting and Sculpture*, was published in 1907) and its credo of 'pure form' was influential in promoting a move against surface naturalism in sculpture.

Hilliard, Nicholas (1547–1619). The most celebrated of English *miniaturists. Son of an Exeter goldsmith, he was trained as a jeweller. In about 1570 he was appointed Court Miniaturist and Goldsmith by Elizabeth I, and he also worked for James I, but after the turn of the century his position as the leading miniaturist in the country was challenged by his former pupil Isaac *Oliver. These two were head and shoulders above their contemporaries and dominated the *limning of their era. Hilliard's reputation extended to France, which he visited *c.*1577–8. In his treatise *The Arte of Limning* (written in about 1600 but not published until 1912) Hilliard declared himself as a follower of *Holbein's manner of limning. In particular he avoided the use of shadow for modelling and in his treatise he records that this was in agreement with Queen Elizabeth's taste—'for the lyne without shadows showeth all to good jugment, but the shadowe without lyne showeth nothing'. But while for Holbein a miniature was always a painting reduced to a small scale, Hilliard developed in the miniature an intimacy and subtlety peculiar to that art. He combined his unerring use of line with a jeweller's exquisiteness in detail, an engraver's elegance in calligraphy, and a unique realization of the individuality of each sitter. His miniatures are often freighted with enigmatic inscription and intrusive allegory (e.g. a hand reaching from a cloud); yet this literary burden usually manages to heighten the vividness with which the sitter's face is impressed. Apart from the Queen herself, many other of the great Elizabethans sat for him, including Sir Francis Drake, Sir Walter Raleigh, and Sir Philip Sidney. The finest collection of his miniatures is in the Victoria and Albert Museum. He is known also to have worked on a large scale and among the paintings attributed to him are portraits of Elizabeth I in the National Portrait Gallery, London, and the Walker Art Gallery, Liverpool. In spite of his success, Hilliard had considerable financial problems and in 1617 was briefly imprisoned for debt. His son **Lawrence** (1582–after 1640) was also a miniaturist.

Hilton, Roger (1911–75). British painter of German extraction (Aby *Warburg was his father's cousin). He trained at the *Slade School, and in the 1930s also studied in Paris under *Bissière. In 1942–5 he was a prisoner of war. In Paris Hilton had absorbed a strong feeling for the sensuous qualities of paint, and in the 1950s he became one of the leading British abstract painters, using interlocking coloured shapes. From the mid-1950s he introduced a shallow sense of pictorial space into his work, and no longer eschewed figural elements. In the 1960s he did a series of exuberant, jokey, female nudes that are among his best-known works (*Oi yoi yoi*, Tate, London, 1963). Their sense of good humour is also present in the colourful gouaches he did in the last two-and-a-half years of his life, when he was bed-ridden.

history painting. A term applied not only to scenes representing actual historical events, but also to scenes from legend and literature of a morally edifying kind, treated in a suitably grand and noble way. Thus scenes from the Bible, Greek mythology, Dante, or Shakespeare would usually come under the heading 'history painting', whereas scenes drawn from a domestic novel might be considered as *genre pictures, even if set in a period before the painter's own. In conventional academic theory history painting was considered the highest branch of art, to which the *Grand Manner was appropriate. The American painters *West and *Copley were pioneers in painting history pictures in modern dress.

Hitchens, Ivon (1893–1979). British painter. He created a highly distinctive style on the borderline between abstraction and figuration in which broad, fluid areas of vibrant colour, typically on a canvas of wide format, evoke but do not represent the forms of the English countryside that were his main inspiration. From 1940, after being bombed in London, he lived in Sussex. By this time his characteristic manner was fully developed and subsequently his work altered little, apart from the fact that his palette changed from naturalistic browns and greens to much more vivid colours such as bright yellows and purples. Contrary to what often happens when an artist remains constant in one style over a period of decades, Hitchens's work did not become stereotyped or banal. Hitchens also painted flowers and figures, and did several large murals, for example at the University of Sussex (1963).

Hoare, William (c.1707–92). English portrait painter. He spent the formative years of his working life in Italy (1728–37), but his style is a continuation of *Richardson's. By 1738 he had settled in Bath, and until the arrival of *Gainsborough in 1759 he was the leading portrait painter of that city. Sir Ellis *Waterhouse has described his style as 'serious, but a little blank'. He worked much in *pastel, and in this was followed by his daughter Mary (c.1753–1820).

Hobbema, Meindert (1638–1709). Dutch landscape painter. He worked in his native Amsterdam, where he was the friend and only documented pupil of Jacob van *Ruisdael. Some of his pictures are very like Ruisdael's, but his range was more limited and he lacked the latter's power to capture the majesty of nature. He painted a narrow range of favourite subjects—particularly water-mills and trees around a pool—over and over again. In 1668 he became a wine gauger with the Amsterdam customs and excise, and thereafter seems to have painted only in his spare time. His most famous work, however, *The Avenue at Middelharnis* (NG, London), dates from 1689. Hobbema has long been a popular artist in England (his influence is clear in *Gainsborough's early landscapes) and he is outstandingly well represented in English collections.

Hockney, David (1937–). British painter, draughtsman, printmaker, photographer, and designer. After a brilliant prize-winning career as a student at the *Royal College of Art, Hockney had achieved international success by the time he was in his mid-20s, and has since consolidated his position as by far the best-known British artist of his generation. His phenomenal success has been based not only on the flair, wit, and versatility of his work, but also on his colourful personality, which has made him a recognizable figure even to people not particularly interested in art: a film about him entitled *A Bigger Splash* (1974) enjoyed considerable popularity in the commercial cinema. His early paintings, often almost jokey in mood, gained him a reputation as a leading *Pop artist, although he himself rejected the label. In the late 1960s he turned to a weightier, more traditionally representational manner, in which he has painted some striking portraits (*Mr and Mrs Clark and Percy*, Tate, London, 1970–1). He has spent much of his time in the USA, and the Californian swimming pool has been one of his favourite themes (*A Bigger Splash*, Tate, 1967). Often his work has a strong homo-erotic content. Hockney is a brilliant draughtsman and has been as outstanding as a graphic artist as he has as a painter, his work in this field including etched illustrations to Cavafy's *Poems* (1967) and *Six Fairy Tales of the Brothers Grimm* (1969). In the 1970s he came to the fore also as a stage designer, notably with his set and costume designs for Stravinsky's *The Rake's Progress* and Mozart's *The Magic Flute* produced at Glyndebourne in 1975 and 1978 respectively. The broader style demanded by stage design is reflected in his most recent easel paintings. In the 1980s he has experimented much with photography, producing, for example, photographic collages and—since 1986—prints created on photocopiers. Hockney is a perceptive commentator on art and in 1976 published a book on his own work, *David Hockney by David Hockney*.

Hodges, William (1744–97). English landscape painter and engraver. He was the pupil and assistant of Richard *Wilson *c.*1758–65 and became a skilful imitator of his style. His work took on a more personal character when he travelled as draughtsman with Captain Cook in 1772–75, and his finest paintings are those based on drawings he made of such exotic Pacific islands as Tahiti and Easter Island (examples are in the National Maritime Museum, London). In 1779–84 he was in India and in 1790 he visited the Continent, going as far as Russia. He did pictures for *Boydell's Shakespeare Gallery and also some allegorical subjects, but in 1795 he abandoned painting and opened a bank in Dartmouth. It failed shortly before he died.

Hodgkin, Howard (1932–). British painter and printmaker. His paintings, which are usually fairly small, sometimes look completely abstract, but in fact he bases his work on specific events, usually an encounter between people. He has travelled widely, making several visits to India, and his preference for flat colours and decorative borders reflects his admiration for Indian *miniatures. He is regarded as one of the outstanding colourists in contemporary painting. A well-known figure in the art world, he has been a Trustee of the Tate Gallery and the National Gallery, and in 1985 he was the second recipient (following *Morley) of the Turner Prize. His work is well represented in the Tate Gallery.

Hodgkins, Frances (1869–1947). New Zealand painter, active mainly in England, where she settled in 1913 after some time alternating between the two hemispheres. She was the daughter of **William Matthew Hodgkins** (1833–98), an amateur painter who had emigrated from England in 1859 and took a lead in the artistic life of Dunedin. Her father taught her water-colour painting, but she did not begin to paint in oils until 1915. Until that time her work had been conventional, but she gradually developed a more individual style, echoing *Matisse and *Dufy in its use of vibrant colour, which brought her prominence among the avant-garde in the 1930s. She painted mainly landscapes and still lifes.

Hodler, Ferdinand (1853–1918). Swiss painter active mainly in Geneva. He ranks alongside *Böcklin as the outstanding Swiss artist of the 19th cent., but his early work (till 1890) was rather unimaginatively naturalistic, and his landscapes were hardly more than rather ambitious colour postcards for tourists. But with his *Night*

(Kunstmuseum, Berne) of 1890 began a sudden change of style. From then on Hodler's canvases were filled with monumental and simplified flat figures, composed into a rhythmic and repetitive pattern of lines, forms, and colours—a method which the artist himself called 'Parallelism'. Contacts with the Rosicrucians (see SALON DE LA ROSE + CROIX) in Paris (1891/2) and possibly knowledge of the aims of Maurice *Denis gave a markedly *Symbolist flavour to his art (*The Disappointed*, Kunstmuseum, 1892). He applied the same principles to *history painting (*The Return from Marignano*, Kunsthaus, Zurich, 1896–1900) and to his Swiss landscapes. Hodler became immensely popular in the German-speaking world and ranks among the harbingers of *Expressionism.

Hofmann, Hans (1880–1966). German-born painter who became an American citizen in 1941. After training in Munich, he lived in Paris from 1904 to 1914 and knew many of the protagonists of *Fauvism, *Cubism, and *Orphism. In 1915 he founded another art school in Munich and taught there successfully until 1930, when he emigrated to the USA. He founded his own school in New York in 1934 and became a teacher of great influence on the minority group of American artists who practised abstract painting during the 1930s. In 1958, to counter opinions that he was merely an academic figure, he closed his school so he could concentrate on his own painting. He experimented with many styles during his career, and was a pioneer of the technique of dribbling and pouring paint that was later particularly associated with Jackson *Pollock. As a painter and teacher he was one of the most significant figures in the development of *Abstract Expressionism.

Hogarth, William (1697–1764). English painter and engraver. He trained as an engraver in the *Rococo tradition, and by 1720 was established in London independently as an engraver on copper of billheads and book illustrations. In his spare time he studied painting, first at the *St Martin's Lane Academy and later under Sir James *Thornhill, whose daughter he married in 1729. By this time he had begun to make a name with small *conversation pieces, and about 1730 he set up as a portrait painter. At about the same time he invented and popularized the use of a sequence of anecdotal pictures 'similar to representations on the stage' to point a moral and satirize social abuses. *A Harlot's Progress* (6 scenes, c.1731; destroyed by fire) was followed by *A Rake's Progress* (8 scenes, Sir John Soane's Mus., London, c.1735), and *Marriage à la Mode* (6 scenes, NG, London, c.1743), which each portray the punishment of vice in a somewhat lurid melodrama. Each series was painted with a view to being engraved, and the engravings had a wide sale and were popular with all classes. They were much pirated and Hogarth's campaigning against the profiteers led to the Copyright Act of 1735. 'I have endeavoured', he wrote, 'to treat my subjects as a dramatic writer: my picture is my stage, and men and women my players.' Hogarth, however, was much more than a preacher in paint. His satire was directed as much at pedantry and affectation as at immorality, and he saw himself to some extent as a defender of native common sense against a fashion for French and Italian mannerisms. In spite of his rabid xenophobia, Hogarth made some attempts to show he could paint in the Italian *Grand Manner (*Sigismunda*, Tate, London, 1759). These, however, are generally considered his weakest works, and apart from his modern morality subjects he excelled mainly in portraiture. *Captain Coram* (Coram Foundation, London, 1740), which he regarded as his highest achievement in portraiture, shows that he could paint a portrait in the *Baroque manner with complete confidence and without artificiality. However, he could not flatter or compromise and had not the disposition for a successful portraitist. From 1735 to 1755 he ran an academy in St Martin's Lane (independent of the one at which he had studied), and this became the main forerunner of the *Royal Academy. In 1753 he published *The Analysis of Beauty*, a treatise on aesthetic theory which he wrote with the conviction that the views of a practising artist should carry greater weight than the theories of the connoisseur or dilettante.

Hogarth was far and away the most important British artist of his generation. He was equally outstanding as a painter and engraver and by the force of his pugnacious personality as well as by the quality and originality of his work he freed

British art from its domination by foreign artists. Because so much of his work has a 'literary' element, his qualities as a painter have often been overlooked, but his more informal pictures in particular show that his brushwork could live up to his inventive genius. The vigour and spontaneity of *The Shrimp Girl* (NG, London, *c*.1740), for example, have made it deservedly one of the most popular British paintings of the 18th cent.

Holanda (or **Hollanda**), **Francisco de** (1517–84). Portuguese *miniaturist, draughtsman, and writer on art, the son of a Netherlandish miniaturist, **Antonio** (active *c*.1495–*c*.1540). He visited Rome in 1538–9 and produced a volume of drawings (now in the Escorial, near Madrid) which contains interesting portraits and drawings of Roman antiquities that are an important source of information about 16th-cent. collecting and archaeology. Although he was Court Painter in Lisbon, his influence in propagating the Italianate style in Portugal was exercised mainly through his writings. In 1548 he completed a manuscript entitled *Da Pintura Antigua* (*Of Ancient Painting*), which was not published until 1890–6. It contains four dialogues (Eng. trans., 1928) in which Holanda purportedly discusses theories of art with *Michelangelo, the miniaturist Giulio *Clovio, and others. As an appendage he completed in 1549 ten dialogues entitled *Do tirar polo natural* (*On Drawing from Nature*).

Holbein, Hans (1497/8–1543). German painter and designer, chiefly celebrated as one of the greatest of all portraitists. He trained in his native Augsburg with his father, **Hans Holbein the Elder** (*c*.1465–1524)—another son, **Ambrosius** (1494–*c*.1519), was also a painter—and in about 1514 moved to Basle. There he quickly found employment as a designer for printers, and in 1516 he painted the portraits of Burgomaster Meyer and his wife (Öffentliche Kunstsammlung, Basle). From 1517 to 1519 he was working in Lucerne, assisting his father on the decoration of a house for the von Hertenstein family (now destroyed). It is possible that during this time he crossed the Alps to Lombardy, for on his return to Basle, where he was to remain until 1526, his style was less harsh, his modelling softer, and his composition

more monumental. The harrowing *Christ in the Tomb* (Öffentliche Kunstsammlung, 1521 or 1522), for example, has a power of expression combined with a mastery of *chiaroscuro that almost rivals *Leonardo.

He was now the leading painter in Basle, and gained an important commission for decorating the Town Hall with scenes of *Justice* taken from Classical history. Apart from fragments in the Öffentliche Kunstsammlung, Basle, these are lost, but are known from copies. He also continued to work for printers, producing between 1523 and 1526 his best-known work in this field, the series on the *Dance of Death*. Since these reflected the new critical outlook of the Reformation, they were not published until 1538 in Lyons, when they enjoyed enormous popularity, running into many editions. His most notable portraits in these years are those of Erasmus (Louvre, Paris; Earl of Radnor Coll., Longford Castle, Wiltshire; and Öffentliche Kunstsammlung, Basle; all *c*.1523). In them, perhaps by the sitters' wish, he used for the first time the formula of the scholar in his study, first devised by Quentin *Massys, also for a portrait of Erasmus. A visit to France in 1524 gave Holbein further knowledge of *Renaissance painting, especially through the works of *Raphael in the royal collection, and the effect may be seen in the *Madonna of Burgomaster Meyer* (Schlossmuseum, Darmstadt, 1526). Mother and Child alike have an ideal beauty which is quite un-German, though the *donor portraits have a splendid naturalism.

The disturbances of the Reformation meant a decline of patronage in Basle, and in 1526, armed with an introduction from Erasmus to Sir Thomas More, Holbein sought work in England. His great group portrait of the More family (lost, but later copies in the NPG, London, and Nostell Priory, West Yorkshire) is a landmark in European art, for no previous artist had produced a group portrait of full-length figures in their own home. A number of single portraits date from this visit, but Holbein obtained no commissions for subject pictures and returned home in 1528. Basle, however, had changed. Religious pictures were banned and there was much religious strife. Holbein accepted the Reformed religion, continued his work at the Town Hall, and made many designs for stained glass. In 1532, leaving his family, he returned to England. More was now out of favour and Holbein found new patrons in the German Steelyard Merchants, for whom he painted several portraits and did decorative work.

Through the Steelyards he probably met Thomas Cromwell (portrait, Frick Coll., New York, 1532–3), who may have obtained for him the commission for his famous double portrait *The Ambassadors* (NG, London, 1533), and almost certainly helped him to gain royal patronage. By 1536 he was working for Henry VIII, and in the next year undertook his most famous English work, the wall-painting in Whitehall Palace of Henry VIII with his father and mother and his third wife, Jane Seymour. Though the picture perished in 1698, part of the *cartoon survives (NPG, London) and the formidable figure of the King standing four-square and staring at the spectator is well known through copies. The only portrait of the King indisputably from Holbein's hand is a bust-length picture in the Thyssen collection at Lugano, a type of which numerous replicas exist. The King also sent Holbein abroad to paint prospective brides—*Anne of Cleves* (Louvre, 1539), *Christina, Duchess of Milan* (NG, London, 1538). Numerous other members of the court are portrayed in paintings and in drawings, a marvellous collection of which is in the Royal Library at Windsor Castle. Many designs for decoration survive from Holbein's last years, when he also turned to *miniature painting, to which his exquisitely detailed craftsmanship was eminently suited. Holbein's portraits were much copied, but none of his followers approached the penetration of his characterization or the virtuosity of his technique. Only in miniature painting did he have a worthy successor in *Hilliard.

Hollar, Wenceslaus (or **Wenzel**) (1607–77). Bohemian engraver and watercolourist, born in Prague. He trained in the workshop of *Merian in Frankfurt, and became one of the foremost engravers of topographical views in the 17th cent. In 1636, while working in Cologne, he met the English connoisseur, the Earl of *Arundel, who took him on a tour of Europe to make views for his private collections. On account of his English connections Hollar finally settled in London—during the Civil War he fought on the Royalist side—and his views of the city form an invaluable record of its appearance before the Great Fire of 1666. He was very prolific and engraved a wide range of subjects apart from views.

Homer, Winslow (1836–1910). American landscape, marine, and *genre painter. He came to painting from illustration, chiefly for *Harper's Weekly*, and *Prisoners from the Front* (Met. Mus., New York, 1866), one of his first important oils, has a quality of vivid, unromanticized reportage. He aspired to naturalistic recording and expressed his attitude in the words: 'When I have selected the thing carefully, I paint it exactly as it appears.' In 1867 Homer visited Paris; he was influenced by *Manet's broad tonal contrasts, but he explored the rendering of light and colour in a direction other than that of the *Impressionists—instead of dissolving outline into light and atmosphere, he sought luminosity within a firm construction of clear outline and broad planes of light and dark (*Long Branch, New Jersey*, Mus. of Fine Arts, Boston, 1869). The sea was Homer's favourite subject, and after living near Tynemouth on the rugged coast of north-east England in 1881–2 he settled at Prout's Neck on the Maine coast, where he lived in isolation. His pictures of the Maine coast, which represent the power and solitude of the sea and the contest of man with the forces of nature, are his best-known works. Homer was an artist of considerable originality who, through a bold and vivid naturalism of his own interpretation, created an imaginative vision of nature which has come to be accepted as a reflection of American pioneering spirit. He used water-colour with the force and authority of oil (*Inside the Bar, Tynemouth*, Met. Mus., 1883).

Hondecoeter, Melchior d' (1636–95). Dutch painter, the best-known member of a family of artists. He was the Netherland's most renowned painter of birds, winning an international reputation with his vigorous and brightly coloured canvases. They show both domestic and exotic birds, often in action and sometimes pointing a moral. Hondecoeter also painted still lifes. He was a prolific artist and is represented in many museums. His father, **Gysbert** (1604–53), was also a bird painter and his grandfather, **Gillis** (d. 1638), was a landscapist. Melchior trained with his father and with his uncle, Jan Baptist *Weenix; he worked in Utrecht, The Hague, and Amsterdam.

Hone, Nathaniel (1718–84). Irish *miniaturist and portrait painter, who settled permanently in London after studying in Italy, 1750–2, and became a foundation member of the *Royal Academy. He is now remembered mainly for one painting, *The Conjurer* (NG, Dublin, 1775), in which he satirized *Reynolds's practice of borrowing poses from the Old Masters. The picture was accepted at the RA, but was withdrawn after Angelica *Kauffmann (whose name had been linked romantically with Reynolds's) objected that a nude figure in the background was meant to represent her. (Hone painted out the nude figures, but they can be seen in his sketch for the picture in the Tate Gallery.) In protest at the removal of his painting Hone exhibited it in a one-man show in St Martin's Lane, the first of its kind recorded in Britain. Hone's sons, **Horace** (1754–1825) and **Camillus** (1759–1836), were also painters, as was a brother, **Samuel** (born 1836). Camillus was the subject of some of his father's best portraits.

Honthorst, Gerrit van (1590–1656). Dutch painter of biblical, mythological, and *genre scenes, and of portraits. At Utrecht, his birthplace, he was a pupil of *Bloemaert, but his style was formed by a long stay in Italy (c.1610–20) and upon his return to Holland he became, along with *Baburen and *Terbrugghen, a leading representative in the Netherlands of the style of *Caravaggio. The candlelight effects he favoured in his early pictures (*Christ before the High Priest*, NG, London) earned him the nickname 'Gherardo delle Notti' (Gerard of the Night Scenes). During the last three decades of his career Honthorst abandoned his Caravaggesque style for a lighter manner in which he achieved international success (rare for a Dutch artist) as a court portraitist. He was employed by the Elector of Brandenburg and by King Christian IV of Denmark, and in 1628 Charles I called him to England, probably on trial as a court painter (his portrait of Charles is in the NPG, London). From 1637 to 1652 he was court painter at The Hague.

Hooch, Pieter de (1629–84). Dutch *genre painter. He is generally counted among the painters of the School of Delft, where he worked throughout most of the 1650s, although he was born in Rotterdam and died in Amsterdam. His very name evokes the quiet and peace of Dutch domestic scenes of the 17th cent. De Hooch is at his best when representing a sunny yard (*The Courtyard of a House in Delft*, NG, London, 1658) or light streaming into the interior of a corner of a burgher's house (*The Pantry*, Rijksmuseum, Amsterdam, c.1658). The small number of tranquil masterpieces of this type that he created in Delft give him a place among the finest Dutch genre painters, but after he moved to Amsterdam in the early 1660s the quality of his paintings was less remarkable than their quantity. Instead of the simple brick and plaster backgrounds of his earlier groups he chose sumptuous marble interiors, and towards the end these backgrounds acquired something of the harsh quality of a painted drop-scene. He died in a madhouse.

Hoogstraten, Samuel van (1627–78). Dutch painter and writer on art. He painted *genre scenes in the style of de *Hooch and *Metsu, and portraits, but he is best known as a specialist in *perspective effects. One of his 'perspective boxes', which shows a painted toy world through a peep-hole, is in the National Gallery, London (see PEEP-SHOW BOX). Only in his early works can it be detected that he was a pupil of *Rembrandt. Hoogstraten travelled to London, Vienna, and Rome, worked in Amsterdam and The Hague as well as his native Dordrecht, and was a man of many parts. He was an etcher, poet, director of the mint at Dordrecht, and art theorist. His *Inleyding tot de hooge schoole der schilderkonst* (Introduction to the Art of Painting, 1678) contains one of the rare contemporary appraisals of Rembrandt's work.

Hope, Thomas (1769–1831). British collector, patron, and writer. He was born in Amsterdam to a wealthy banking family, and travelled extensively before and after settling in England in 1795. In 1801 he was described as being reputedly 'the richest, but undoubtedly far from the most agreeable man in Europe', and he used his great wealth to spend lavishly on art for his London mansion in Duchess Street (to which the public could buy admission tickets) and his country seat at Deepdene, Surrey. He was a devotee of *Neoclassicism, and the artists he patronized included *Canova, *Flaxman, and *Thorvaldsen. Hope also had notable collections of paintings and antique statuary. He trained craftsmen to make furniture from his own Greek and Egyptian designs, and his publications included *Household Furniture and Interior Decoration* (1807).

Hopper, Edward (1882–1967). American painter, active mainly in New York. He trained under Robert *Henri, 1900–6, and between 1906 and 1910 made three trips to Europe, though these had little influence on his style. Hopper exhibited at the *Armory Show in 1913, but from then until 1923 he abandoned painting, earning his living by commercial illustration. Thereafter, however, he gained widespread recognition as a central exponent of *American Scene painting, expressing the loneliness, vacuity, and stagnation of town life. Yet Hopper remained always an individualist: 'I don't think I ever tried to paint the American scene; I'm trying to paint myself.' Paintings such as *Nighthawks* (Art Inst. of Chicago, 1942) convey a mood of loneliness and desolation by their emptiness or by the presence of anonymous, non-communicating figures. But of this picture Hopper said: 'I didn't see it as particularly lonely . . . Unconsciously, probably, I was painting the loneliness of a large city.' Deliberately so or not, in his still, reserved, and blandly handled paintings Hopper often exerts a powerful psychological impact distantly akin to that made by the *Metaphysical painter de *Chirico; but while de Chirico's effect was obtained by making the unreal seem real, Hopper's was rooted in the presentation of the familiar and concrete.

Hoppner, John (1758–1810). British portrait painter. He was trained as a chorister in the Chapel Royal, and later received an allowance from George III to study at the Royal Academy Schools. The royal favour he was shown led to rumours that he was the king's illegitimate son, but these were never proved. In 1789 he was appointed Portrait Painter to the Prince of Wales (later George IV) and from this time was associated with 'the Prince of Wales's Set'. After the death of *Reynolds he and *Lawrence were the leading portraitists in the country. In his attempts to emulate first Reynolds, then Lawrence, Hoppner rarely achieved striking individuality, but

his best work, particularly his portraits of women and children, often has great charm.

Hoskins, John (c.1595–1665). The leading English portrait *miniaturist between c.1625 and c.1640. His early work is a development of *Hilliard's style. He later became a specialist in miniature copies of van *Dyck's portraits in oils—a type which remained much in demand throughout the 17th cent.—but his miniatures often have a charm and originality of their own. He was *'limner' to Charles I in 1640, but thereafter was overshadowed by the work of his nephew and pupil, Samuel *Cooper.

Houbraken, Arnold (1660–1719). Dutch painter and writer on art. His paintings are now forgotten, but he is important for his large biographical work *De Groote Schouburgh der Nederlantsche Konstschilders en Schilderessen*, (The Great Theatre of Netherlandish Painters), 3 vols., 1718–21. This was the first comprehensive study of Netherlandish art since van *Mander published his *Schilderboeck* in 1604 and is the most important source-book on 17th cent. Netherlandish artists. Arnold's son **Jacobus** (1698–1780) was a leading portrait engraver. His work includes engraved plates after his father's designs for the *Groote Schouburgh*.

Houdon, Jean-Antoine (1741–1828). French sculptor. A pupil of Jean-Baptiste *Lemoyne and of Jean-Baptiste *Pigalle, he won the *Prix de Rome in 1761. He was in Rome 1764–8 and there produced two works of sculpture which assured his reputation: an *écorché figure (Schlossmuseum, Gotha, 1767), casts of which were widely used in art academies, and *St Bruno* (Sta Maria degli Angeli, 1767), executed in a direct and unpretentious Classical style. Returning to Paris in 1769, he was successful in the popular mythological style, becoming a member of the Academy in 1777 with his *Morpheus* (Louvre, Paris). His greatest strength, however, was in his portrait busts. By the middle 1780s he was acknowledged as the leading portrait sculptor of Europe and his fame spread also to America. In 1785 the State of Virginia commissioned from him a statue of George Washington, and he visited America in order to study his model face to face before doing his famous marble statue of Washington as the modern Cincinnatus, called from the ploughshare to wield the reins of government (Virginia State Capitol, Richmond, 1788, bronze copy outside the NG, London). In his portraiture Houdon had a knack of catching characteristic tricks of gesture and expression and a brilliant gift of depicting the marks of individuality, rather than a profound penetration into human character. His portraits of Voltaire (e.g. in the Comédie Français, Paris, and V&A, London) are among his most celebrated works. During the French Revolution Houdon narrowly escaped imprisonment and although he found favour again under Napoleon (a terracotta bust of the Emperor is in the Musée des Beaux-Arts, Dijon, 1806), he produced little of importance after the turn of the century. He became senile in 1823.

Huber, Wolfgang (or **Wolf**) (c.1490–1553). German painter, printmaker, and architect, active mainly in Passau, where he was court painter and architect to the prince-bishop. He was first and foremost a poetic interpreter of his native landscape and is usually counted among the masters of the so-called *Danube School. His landscape drawings are particularly delicate and his religious paintings often have landscape backgrounds.

Hudson, Thomas (1701–79). English portrait painter, a pupil of Jonathan *Richardson, whose daughter he married. From the mid 1740s to the mid 1750s he was the leading fashionable portraitist in London, rivalled only by *Ramsay. His studio produced a great deal of work, with much help from specialist assistants, and Hudson has been described by Sir Ellis *Waterhouse as 'the last of the conscienceless artists, of whom *Lely was the first in England, who turned out portraits to standard patterns and executed comparatively little of the work themselves'. Hudson went into semi-retirement in the late 1750s, when his former pupil *Reynolds (another Devonian) was rapidly rising in success.

Hudson River School. Term applied retrospectively to a number of American landscape painters, active c.1825–c.1875, who were inspired by pride in the beauty of their homeland. The early leaders and the three most important figures in the group were Thomas *Cole, Thomas *Doughty, and Asher B. *Durand, who painted with a reverential spirit the Hudson River Valley, the Catskill Mountains, and other remote and untouched areas of natural beauty. These three artists and many of those who followed had studied in Europe and part of their inspiration came from painters of the grandiose and spectacular such as *Turner and John *Martin. The patriotic spirit of the painters of the Hudson River School won them great popularity in the middle years of the century. Painters of a similar outlook who found their inspiration in the far West are known collectively as the *Rocky Mountain School.

Huet, Christophe (d. 1759). French *Rococo painter, engraver, and designer, best known for paintings and engravings involving animals, dressed up and acting like humans (see SINGERIE). Good examples of his work are in the Musée Condé at Chantilly.

Hughes, Arthur (1832–1915). English painter and illustrator. In the 1850s he was one of the most distinguished of the *Pre-Raphaelite sympathizers, remarkable for his lyrical delicacy of colour and drawing. Two paintings are particularly well known—*April Love* (Tate, London, 1856), which *Ruskin called 'exquisite in every way', and *The Long Engagement* (City Art Gal., Birmingham, 1859). After about 1870, however, his work declined in quality, although he did some good book illustrations. He was shy and withdrawn and in later life he lived in suburban obscurity.

Huguet, Jaime (active c.1448–92). Spanish painter, the most prominent figure in the Catalan School during the second part of the 15th cent. Huguet is thought to have settled in Barcelona about 1448. He continued the Catalan tradition of Bernardo *Martorell, but was highly individual in his characterization. His studio produced many sumptuous composite altarpieces of the type that became typical in Spanish art and his work exercised a wide influence on the painting of Catalonia and Aragón.

Humphry, Ozias (1742–1810). English portrait painter. He worked for a time as a *miniaturist in Bath, but settled in

London in 1763 on the encouragement of *Reynolds. In 1772 a riding accident which affected his eyes made it necessary for him to abandon miniatures and after a visit to Italy with *Romney in 1773–7 he practised in oils. From 1785 to 1788 he was in India, where he resumed miniature painting, but again he found the work too great a strain. He then took up pastel and in this medium was highly successful (being given the title of Portrait Painter in Crayons to His Majesty in 1792) until he went blind in 1797. Examples of his work are in the National Gallery, London.

Hundertwasser, Fritz (Friedrich Stowasser) (1928–   ). Austrian painter and graphic artist. He took the name Hundertwasser in 1949, translating the syllable 'sto' (which means 'hundred' in Czech) by the German 'hundert'. From c.1969 he signed his work 'Friedensreich Hundertwasser', symbolizing by 'Fried-ensreich' (Kingdom of Peace) his boast that by his painting he would introduce the observer into a new life of peace and happiness. He often added 'Regenstag' (Rainy Day) to the name—making it in full 'Friedensreich Hundertwasser Regen-stag'—on the ground that he felt happy on rainy days because colours then began to sparkle and glow. This exaggerated concern with the name is a symptom of the braggadocio, conceit, and talent for self-advertisement that are apparent in his work as well as his life. Standing outside most contemporary artistic movements, though borrowing from many, he works mainly on a small scale, often in water-colour. His work has sometimes been compared with that of *Klee and *Klimt, but although it is in the same tradition of figurative fantasy it lacks their elegance and wit. In his concern with the dehumanizing aspects of 20th-cent. society, he has been an outspoken critic of modern architecture and his recent work has included the design of an idiosyncratic, multi-coloured, fairytale-like housing unit in Vienna (completed 1986).

Hunt, William Holman (1827–1910). English painter, co-founder of the *Pre-Raphaelite Brotherhood in 1848. He was the only member of the Brotherhood who throughout his entire career remained faithful to Pre-Raphaelite aims, which he summarized as finding serious and genuine ideas to express, direct study from nature in disregard of all arbitrary rules, and envisaging events as they must have happened rather than in accordance with the rules of design. Hunt's work was remarkable for its minute precision, its accumulation of incident, and its didactic emphasis on moral or social symbolism, and from 1854 he made several journeys to Egypt and Palestine to paint biblical scenes with accurate local detail. *The Scape-goat* (Lady Lever Art Gal., Port Sunlight, 1854–5), showing the outcast animal on the shore of the Dead Sea, is one of the most famous paintings that resulted from his fanatical devotion to authenticity. Most of his works are now regarded as failures (his colouring tends to be painfully harsh and his sentiment mawkish), but his fervent devotion to his dogmas compels respect. His autobiographical *Pre-Raphaelitism and the Pre-Raphaelite Brotherhood* (1905) is the basic source book of the movement, though somewhat biased.

Huysum, Jan van (1682–1749). Dutch painter, with Rachel *Ruysch the most distinguished flower painter of his day. He had a European reputation and was much imitated. The light colours he used, the even lighter backgrounds, and the openness of his intricate compositions became dis-tinguishing features of 18th-cent. Dutch flower painting. He occasionally painted subjects other than flowers, including a self-portrait in the Ashmolean Museum, Oxford. His father, **Justus the Elder** (1659–1716), was a flower and landscape painter and he had three painter brothers: **Justus the Younger** (c.1684–1707); **Mi-chiel** (d. 1759); and **Jacob** (c.1687–1740?), who worked in England and imitated Jan's style.

Hyperrealism. See SUPERREALISM.

I

Ibbetson, Julius Caesar (1759–1817). English painter. His unusual Christian names were given to him because of his Caesarean birth. He specialized in fairly small landscapes with figures and animals, and his style has been characterized by Sir Ellis *Waterhouse as 'more natural than *de Loutherbourg's, and more civilized than *Morland's'; Benjamin *West called him 'the *Berchem of England'. Ibbetson worked mainly in his native Yorkshire, but also for a time in London and the Lake District, and he visited Java (1789). He worked in water-colour as well as oil and also made etchings. In 1803 he published a treatise on painting. Like his friend Morland, Ibbetson is said to have been given to dissipation, but his work did not obviously suffer because of this as Morland's did.

icon. An image of a saint or other holy personage, particularly when the image is regarded by the devotee as sacred in itself and capable of facilitating contact between him or her and the personage portrayed. The term, which derives from the Greek word *eikon*, meaning 'likeness', has been applied particularly to sacred images of the *Byzantine Church and the Orthodox Churches of Russia and Greece.

iconography. The branch of art history dealing with the identification, description, classification, and interpretation of the subject-matter of the figurative arts. In his book *Studies in Iconology* (1939) Erwin *Panofsky proposed that the term 'iconology' should be used to distinguish a broader approach towards subject-matter in which the scholar attempts to understand the total meaning of the work of art in its historical context. However, in practice an exact distinction between the two terms is rarely made, and 'iconography' is the much more commonly used of the two. The term 'iconography' can also be applied to collections (or the classification) of portraits. Van *Dyck, for example, made a series of etchings of famous contemporaries entitled *Iconography*.

iconostasis. In *Byzantine and Russian churches, a screen shutting off the sanctuary from the main body of the church on which *icons were placed.

ideal. A conception of something that is perfect, referring in the visual arts to works that attempt to reproduce the best of nature, but also to improve on it, eliminating the inevitable flaws of particular examples. The notion derives ultimately from Plato's Theory of Ideas, according to which all perceptible objects are imperfect copies approximating to unchanging and imperceptible Ideas or Forms. This idea reappeared with the revival of Platonism in the Italian *Renaissance, and throughout much of subsequent European art the model of ideal beauty was supplied by Classical statuary. Its most influential formation was in a lecture by *Bellori delivered before the *Academy of St Luke in Rome in 1664, and published as a Preface to his Lives in 1672. To Bellori, the contemporary artist who best exemplified the doctrine was *Poussin, whose example became binding for the French Academy of the 17th cent. The doctrine provided the philosophical justification for the *Grand Manner, and was the basis of criticism of anti-idealistic artists such as *Caravaggio and *Rembrandt, who were thought to have broken the 'rules' of good art. Although the doctrine has been responsible for much arid art, it has also been an inspiration to such great artists as *Raphael, who said, 'To paint a beautiful woman I must see several, and I have also recourse to a certain ideal in my mind', and Guido *Reni, who said 'The beautiful and pure *idea* must be in the mind, and then it is no matter what the model is.'

ideal landscape. A type of landscape painting, invented by Annibale *Carracci in the first decade of the 17th cent., in which the elements of the landscape are composed into a grand and highly formalized arrangement suitable as a setting for small figures from serious religious or mythological subjects. It was an extraordinarily influential invention, which was developed most memorably by *Claude and *Poussin.

illuminated manuscripts. Books written by hand, decorated with paintings and ornaments of different kinds. The word 'illuminated' comes from a usage of the Latin word *illuminare* in connection with oratory or prose style, where it means 'adorn'. The decorations are of three main types: (a) *miniatures* or small pictures, not always illustrative, incorporated into the text or occupying the whole page or part of the border; (b) *initial letters* either containing scenes (historiated initials) or with elaborate decoration; (c) *borders*, which may consist of miniatures, occasionally illustrative, or more often are composed of decorative motifs. They may enclose the whole of the text space or occupy only a small part of the margin of the page. Manuscripts are for the most part written on skin, *parchment, or vellum. From the 14th cent. paper was used for less sumptuous copies. Although a number of books have miniatures and ornaments executed in outline drawing only, the majority are fully coloured. By the 15th cent. illumination tended more and more to follow the lead given by painters, and with the invention of printing the illuminated book gradually went out of fashion. During the 15th and 16th cents. illuminations were added to printed books.

illusionism. Term applied in its broadest sense to the basic principle of *naturalistic art whereby verisimilitude in representation causes the spectator in various degrees to seem actually to be seeing the object represented, or the space in which it is represented, even though with part of his mind he knows that he is looking at a pictorial representation and not at the real object or scene. In a somewhat narrower sense 'illusionism' refers to the use of pictorial techniques such as *perspective and foreshortening to deceive the eye (if not the mind) into taking that which is painted for that which is real, or in architecture and stage scenery to make the constructed forms seem visually more extensive than they are. Two specific forms of illusionism in painting are *quadratura*, in which painted architecture appears to extend the real space of a room, and

trompe l'œil, in which the spectator is genuinely, if momentarily, tricked into thinking that a painted object is a real one.

impasto. Thickly applied opaque paint retaining the marks of the brush or other instrument of application.

Impressionism. A movement in painting originating in the 1860s in France and regarded as one of the most momentous phenomena in 19th-cent. art. The Impressionists were not a formal group with clearly defined principles and aims; rather they were a loose association of artists linked by some community of outlook who banded together for the purpose of exhibiting. The central figures involved in the movement were (in alphabetical order) *Cézanne, *Degas, *Manet, *Monet, Camille *Pissarro, *Renoir, and *Sisley. Monet, Renoir, and Sisley met as students, and the others came into contact with them through the artistic café society of Paris. There were friendly ties of varied degrees of intimacy linking each of them to most of the others, but Degas and even more Manet were set somewhat apart because they came from a higher stratum of society than the others, and the artists' commitment to Impressionism varied considerably (Manet was much respected as a senior figure, but he never exhibited with the group). The Impressionists reacted against academic teaching and conventions and also were in revolt from the basic principle of Romanticism that art should convey intense personal emotion. They repudiated imaginative art, including historical subjects, and were interested rather in the objective recording of contemporary life, trying to capture an 'impression' of what the eye sees at one particular moment. Landscape is considered the theme most typical of the Impressionists, but they painted many other subjects. Degas, for example, had little interest in landscape and made subjects such as horse races, dancers, and laundresses his own, and Renoir is famous for his pictures of pretty women and children.

The Impressionists' desire to look at the world with a new freshness and immediacy was encouraged by photography and by scientific research into colour and light. In trying to capture the effects of light on varied surfaces, particularly in open-air settings, they transformed painting, using bright colours and sketchy brushwork that seemed bewildering or shocking to traditionalists. The name 'Impressionism', in fact, was coined derisively, when it was applied to a picture by Monet, *Impression: Sunrise* (Musée Marmottan, Paris, 1872), which was shown at the first Impressionist exhibition, held in Paris in 1874. There were seven more Impressionist exhibitions (1876, 1877, 1879, 1880, 1881, 1882, and 1886), and after the final one the group broke up, only Monet continuing to pursue Impressionist ideals rigorously. Although Impressionism was at first greeted with great hostility and many of its practitioners had to endure great financial hardship early in their careers, it began to win critical acceptance in the 1880s (see DURAND-RUEL) and its influence was enormous—much of the history of late 19th cent. and early 20th cent. painting is the story of developments from it or reactions against it. The *Neo-Impressionists, for example, tried to give the optical principles of Impressionism a scientific basis, and the *Post-Impressionists began a long series of movements that attempted to free colour and line from purely representational functions and return to the emotional and symbolic values that the Impressionists had sacrificed in their concentration on the fleeting and the casual.

imprimatura. A thin layer of transparent colour applied to a †ground. It reduced the absorbent quality of the ground and could also be used as a middle tone in the painting.

Independent Group. A small and informal organization operating during the 1950s within the *Institute of Contemporary Arts, London. It was first convened in the winter of 1952/3 for the purpose of holding exploratory meetings to discuss techniques. The artists involved included Richard *Hamilton and Eduardo *Paolozzi and the first phase of English *Pop art grew out of the Independent Group.

Indiana, Robert (Robert Clark) (1928–). American painter, sculptor, and graphic artist. He is regarded as one of the leading American *Pop artists, and although he has done some figurative paintings he is best known for pictures involving geometric shapes emblazoned with lettering and signs.

Ingres, Jean-Auguste-Dominique (1780–1867). French painter, born at Montauban, the son of a minor painter and sculptor, **Jean-Marie-Joseph Ingres** (1755–1814). After an early academic training in the Toulouse Academy he went to Paris in 1796 and was a fellow student of *Gros in *David's studio. He won the *Prix de Rome in 1801, but owing to the state of France's economy he was not awarded the usual stay in Rome until 1807. In the interval he produced his first portraits. These fall into two categories: portraits of himself and his friends, conceived in a *Romantic spirit (*Gilibert*, Musée Ingres, Montauban, 1805), and portraits of well-to-do clients which are characterized by purity of line and enamel-like colouring (*Mlle Rivière*, Louvre, Paris, 1805). These early portraits are notable for their calligraphic line and expressive contour, which had a sensuous beauty of its own beyond its function to contain and delineate form. It was a feature that formed the essential basis of Ingres's painting throughout his life.

During his first years in Rome he continued to execute portraits and began to paint bathers, a theme which was to become one of his favourites (*The Valpinçon Bather*, Louvre, Paris, 1808). He remained in Rome when his four-year scholarship ended, earning his living principally by pencil portraits of members of the French colony. But he also received more substantial commissions, including two decorative paintings for Napoleon's palace in Rome (*Triumph of Romulus over Acron*, École des Beaux-Arts, Paris, 1812; and *Ossian's Dream*, Musée Ingres, 1813). In 1820 he moved from Rome to Florence, where he remained for 4 years, working mainly on his *Raphaelesque *Vow of Louis XIII*, commissioned for the cathedral of Montauban. Ingres's work had often been severely criticized in Paris because of its 'Gothic' distortions, and when he accompanied this painting to the *Salon of 1824 he was surprised to find it acclaimed and himself set up as the leader of the academic opposition to the new Romanticism. (*Delacroix's *Massacre of Chios* was shown at the same Salon.) Ingres stayed in Paris for the next ten years and received the official success and honours he had always craved. During this period he devoted much of his time to executing two large works: *The Apotheosis of Homer*, for a ceiling in the *Louvre (installed 1827), and *The Martyrdom of St Symphorian* (Salon, 1834) for the cathedral of Autun. When the latter painting was badly received, however, he accepted the Directorship of the French School in Rome, a post he retained for 7 years. He was a model administrator and teacher, greatly improving the school's facilities, but he produced few major works in this period. In 1841 he returned to France, once again acclaimed as the champion of traditional values. He was heartbroken when his wife died in 1849, but he made a successful second marriage in 1852, and he continued working with great energy into his 80s. One of his acknowledged masterpieces, the extraordinarily sensuous *Turkish Bath* (Louvre, 1863), dates from the last years of his life. At his death he left a huge bequest of his work (several paintings and more than 4,000 drawings) to his home town of Montauban and they are now in the museum bearing his name there.

Ingres is a puzzling artist and his career is full of contradictions. Yet more than most artists he was obsessed by a restricted number of themes and returned to the same subject again and again over a long period of years. He was a bourgeois with the limitations of a bourgeois mentality, but as *Baudelaire remarked, his finest works 'are the product of a deeply sensuous nature'. The central contradiction of his career is that although he was held up as the guardian of Classical rules and precepts, it is his personal obsessions and mannerisms that make him such a great artist. His technique as a painter was academically unimpeachable—he said paint should be as smooth 'as the skin of an onion'—but he was often attacked for the expressive distortions of his draughtsmanship; critics said, for example, that the abnormally long back of *La Grande Odalisque* (Louvre,1814) had three extra vertebrae. Unfortunately the influence of Ingres was mainly seen in those shortcomings and weaknesses which have come to be regarded as the hallmark of inferior academic work. He had scores of pupils, but *Chassériau was the only one to attain distinction. As a great calligraphic genius his true successors are *Degas and *Picasso.

ink. Coloured fluid used for writing, drawing, or printing. Inks usually have staining power without body, but printers' inks are pigments mixed with oil and varnish, and are opaque. The use of inks goes back in China and Egypt to at least 2500 BC. They were usually made from lampblack or a red ochre ground into a solution of glue or gums. These materials were moulded into dry sticks or blocks, which were then mixed with water for use. Ink brought from China or Japan in such dry form came to be known in the West as 'Chinese ink' or 'Indian ink'. The names are also given to a similiar preparation made in Europe.

Innes, James Dickson (1887–1914). Welsh painter. He is best known for his landscapes, especially those painted in Wales, where he worked with his friend Augustus *John. Usually painted on a small scale, they combine a strong sense of decorative pattern with a range of hot colour recalling *Derain and *Matisse.

Inness, George (1825–94). American landscape painter. He was without formal training but developed his style in the course of frequent visits to Europe, being particularly influenced by the *Barbizon School. His work falls into two fairly distinct periods. In the first he attempted to bring greater breadth to American *Romantic realism, dissolving hard outline into a play of atmosphere and colour, but with something of the ordered beauty of *Claude (*Peace and Plenty*, Met. Mus., New York, 1865). From *c.*1859, when he went to live in the village of Medfield outside Boston, his style began to change to a more intimate manner of landscape in which he chose deliberately unpicturesque subjects and relied for pictorial appeal on subtle harmonies of colour and broad massing of light and shade. Inness has often been considered the outstanding American landscape painter of the 19th cent. His son, **George Inness, Jun.** (1854–1926), was also a painter and published an account of his father's career.

Inshaw, David. See BLAKE, PETER.

installation. Term which came into vogue during the 1970s for an *assemblage or *environment constructed in the gallery specifically for a particular exhibition.

Institute of Contemporary Arts, London. Cultural centre founded by Roland

*Penrose and Herbert *Read in 1947 to cater for some of the functions fulfilled by the *Museum of Modern Art in New York, organizing exhibitions, lectures, films, and so on. Its original home was in Dover Street, but it moved to Nash House, the Mall, in 1968.

intaglio. Carving or engraving on a small scale, as for example on a gemstone or seal, in which the design is hollowed into the surface—the opposite of *cameo, in which the design projects above the surface. In the graphic arts, 'intaglio printing' refers to any process of printmaking in which the parts of the plate or block that will take the ink are incised into it rather than raised above it ('relief printing'). *Etching is thus a form of intaglio printing (see PRINT).

intarsia. Method of creating a picture or design on a wooden surface (typically a piece of furniture) by inlaying it with differently coloured woods and other materials such as mother-of-pearl and ivory.

International Gothic. Style in painting, sculpture, and the decorative arts that spread widely over western Europe between c.1375 and c.1425. The style was characterized by aristocratic elegance and delicate naturalistic detail and was formed by a blending of elements from Italy and northern Europe, a situation encouraged by the cultural rivalry of major courts and the growing frequency with which leading artists travelled between them. Lombardy, Franco-Flemish Burgundy and Bohemia were among the most important centres of the style, major exponents of which included *Gentile da Fabriano, *Pisanello, and the *Limburg Brothers. Elements of the style are present in the work of many of the leading artists of the early *Renaissance, such as Fra *Angelico, *Ghiberti, and *Uccello. In England, the finest work in the style is the celebrated Wilton Diptych (NG, London), which testifies to how genuinely international the International Gothic style was, for although it is a painting of extraordinary beauty and must be from the hand of an artist of the highest rank, authorities disagree as to whether he was English, French, or Italian. It shows Richard II being presented to the Virgin and Child by John the Baptist, Edward the Confessor, and Edmund, king and martyr

(his patron saints), but its purpose and significance are uncertain. It may date from late in Richard's reign (heraldic evidence suggests it cannot be earlier than c.1395), but some scholars think it is a posthumous memorial.

Intimisme. Term applied to a type of intimate domestic *genre painting, more or less *Impressionist in technique, that is particularly associated with *Bonnard and *Vuillard.

intonaco. The final layer of plaster on which *fresco painting is done.

Isenbrandt. See YSENBRANDT.

Israëls, Jozef (1824–1911). Dutch painter. He studied in Amsterdam and Paris and began his career as a portrait and historical painter, but in the 1850s he turned to the kind of work for which he is principally known—scenes of peasants and fishermen and the milieu in which they lived. In the 1870s he settled in The Hague and became one of the leading members of the *Hague School. He has been called 'the Dutch *Millet' and during his lifetime he won great popularity because of his piously sentimental approach. His son, **Isaäc** (1865–1934), also worked at The Hague, but in a style almost completely independent of his father's. His pictures of the social life of his time are influenced by *Breitner and characterized by the vivid colours and vigorous brushwork of the *Impressionists.

Itinerants. See WANDERERS.

Itten, Johannes (1888–1967). Swiss painter and designer, best remembered as a teacher. He studied at Stuttgart, 1913–16, and then opened his own school of art in Vienna. From 1919 to 1923 he taught at the *Bauhaus, where he introduced the important 'Preliminary Course' obligatory for all students. From 1923 he had his own art school in Berlin and from 1932 he taught at the Krefeld School of Textile Design. In 1938 he settled in Zurich, where he was appointed Director of the School and Museum of Arts and Crafts, the Rietberg Museum and the School of Textile Design. His own work as a painter belonged to the category of geometrical colour abstraction, exemplifying his researches into colour. As a teacher he not only emphasized the importance of knowledge of materials, but also encouraged his pupils to develop their imaginations through, for example, automatic writing (see AUTOMATISM). His ideas were opposed to the technological outlook of *Gropius (their quarrels caused Itten's departure from the Bauhaus) and he had something of a reputation as a crank, but his influence was considerable.

Ivanov, Alexander (1806–58). Russian painter. He was born in St Petersburg and studied there at the Academy of Fine Arts under his father, the painter **Andrey Ivanov** (1772–1848). Most of his career was spent in Rome, where he settled in 1827. Under the influence of the *Nazarenes he turned to religious painting, and his fame is inseparable from his main work, which occupied him for about 20 years, *Christ's First Appearance to the People* (Tretyakov Gal., Moscow). This enormous painting achieved European celebrity long before its completion, but proved disappointing when it was finally exhibited in St Petersburg in 1858, its *Raphaelesque composition being at odds with the naturalistic setting and details, the result of hundreds of preparatory studies. He also hoped by biblical illustrations to create a new religious art which was to combine his own mysticism with historical exactitude.

None of these illustrations got beyond the stage of drawings, but many of them show a strikingly original visual imagery. In 1858 he returned to Russia and died shortly afterwards. Little of his work can be seen outside the Soviet Union.

ivory. A hard, smooth, creamy white substance forming the main part of the tusks of elephants and some other animals, used as a carving material from the earliest times. Elephant (also mammoth) and walrus tusks have been the commonest source of ivory, but carvings made from narwhal and rhinoceros horn, stag-horn, and even bone, have been embraced by the term. True ivory is easily worked with saws, chisels, drills, and rasps, but the size and shape of a carving are usually limited by the dimensions of the tusk, the curvature of which has sometimes been exploited to give a graceful swing to the figure, notably in *Gothic statuettes of the Virgin. Though ivory was often painted in the Middle Ages, its natural lustre, translucence, and satin smoothness have always been appreciated. In the ancient world it was classed with gold and precious stones as a luxury material, and the Greeks used it for colossal *chryselephantine (gold and ivory) cult-statues. After the 14th cent. ivory-carving declined steadily, despite revivals in the 17th and 18th cents.

J

Jackson, Alexander Young (1882–1974). Canadian landscape painter. He was one of the leading artists in the *Group of Seven and in the latter part of his long career became a venerated senior figure in Canadian painting. Jackson visited virtually every region of Canada, including the Arctic, and responded particularly to the hilly region of rural Quebec along the St Lawrence River. From 1921 he returned there almost every spring, and the canvases he prepared from sketches made there are probably his finest work. Their easy, rolling rhythms, and rich and full colouring had a far-reaching impact on Canadian landscape painting.

Jamesone, George (c.1589/90–1644). Scottish portrait painter, active in Aberdeen and Edinburgh. His name has been indiscriminately applied to a great number of Scottish portraits of the period, as he is virtually the only 17th-cent. Scottish painter about whom anything is known. A now discounted tradition has it that he trained with *Rubens and he has been flatteringly called 'the Scottish van *Dyck', but his style was closer to Cornelius *Johnson's. It is difficult to assess, however, as most of the works that are certainly by him are in a bad state of preservation. John Michael *Wright was his pupil.

Janssens, Abraham (c.1575–1632). Flemish figure and portrait painter, active mainly in Antwerp. He was in Rome in 1598 and back in Antwerp by 1601. A second visit to Italy seems likely, for although in 1601 he was painting in a *Mannerist style (*Diana and Callisto*, Museum of Fine Arts, Budapest), by 1609 (*Scaldis and Antwerpia*, Musée Royal, Antwerp) his work had become much more solid, sober, and Classical, suggesting close knowledge of *Caravaggio in particular. For the next decade Janssens was one of the most powerful and individual painters in Flanders, but during the 1620s his work became less remarkable as he fell under the all-pervasive influence of *Rubens. His

pupils included Gerard *Seghers and Theodoor *Rombouts.

Jawlensky, Alexei von (1864–1941). Russian painter. After studying with *Repin in St Petersburg, he left Russia in 1896 dissatisfied with historical *realism and settled in Munich. There he met *Kandinsky and became closely associated with the *Blaue Reiter, although he did not participate in their exhibitions. In 1905 he travelled to Brittany and Provence, making contact with painters of the *Pont-Aven school. During a stay of some months in Paris he became acquainted with the paintings of *Gauguin and van *Gogh and worked for a short while with *Matisse. In this artistic environment he evolved the mode of expression suited to his passionate but naïvely religious temperament, painting in flat, strong hues with bold outlines in a manner akin to the *Fauves. Yet his work was in no sense derivative from the French school; rather it combined these influences with Russian traditions of *icon painting and peasant art to form a highly personal style. His synthesis of Russian and French elements is best seen in the series of heads which he began in 1910. From 1914 to 1921 he lived as a solitary at Saint-Prex, Switzerland, and there he painted a series of 'variations' on the view from his window. Like Kandinsky and others, Jawlensky was obsessed by a belief in the correspondence between colours and musical sounds and he named these small abstract landscapes, which have a meditative, religious aura, *Songs without Words*. From 1921 he lived in Wiesbaden, and in 1924 he joined with Kandinsky, *Klee, and *Feininger to form the *Blaue Vier, exhibiting with them for some years until he became crippled with arthritis and abandoned painting.

Jervas, Charles (c.1675–1739). Irish painter, active mainly in London. His surname was pronounced, and often spelled, Jarvis. After studying with *Kneller he spent several years in Italy, particularly Rome, before settling in London in 1709. Jervas had a great reputation and succeeded Kneller as Principal Portrait Painter to King George II in 1723, but his fame depended on his friendship with various literary figures, who trumpeted his praises, rather than on the quality of his work, which does not rise above the level of that of any other of Kneller's pupils or followers. He has perhaps more claim to literary distinction, for he made a well-regarded translation of Cervantes' *Don Quixote*, posthumously published in 1742. His conceit was enormous: once, having copied a painting by *Titian, he looked from one to the other and said complacently 'Poor Little Tit! How he would stare!'

Jeune Peinture Belge. An avant-garde artists' association founded in Brussels in 1945. Although the members of the group (which included *Alechinsky and *Bury) were strongly individualistic in their aims and had no common programme, they were basically abstract in their outlook and were influenced particularly by Flemish *Expressionism and by the expressive abstraction of the post-war École de *Paris. The group dissolved in 1948.

John, Augustus (1878–1961). British painter and graphic artist. He trained at the *Slade School, where he was the most brilliant student of his day, renowned for his outstanding draughtsmanship. During the first quarter of the 20th cent. John, who was identified with all that was most independent and rebellious in English art, was one of the most talked-of figures of his day. In 1911–14 he led a nomadic, bohemian life and he created a type of gypsy beauty romanticizing the gypsies of North Wales. At this time he also painted ambitious figure compositions that in their stylized forms bring him close to *Symbolist painters such as *Puvis de Chavannes. In the First World War he was an official war artist. It is as a portraitist, however, that John is best remembered. He was taken up by society and painted many of the leading literary figures of the day. Increasingly, however, the painterly brilliance of his early work degenerated into flashiness and bombast, and the second half of his long career added little to his achievement. He published *Chiaroscuro*, *Fragments of Autobiography* in 1952, and

Finishing Touches appeared posthumously in 1964.

John, Gwen (1876–1939). British painter. She was the sister of Augustus John, but his complete opposite artistically, as she was in personality, living a reclusive life and favouring introspective subjects. After studying at the *Slade School she took lessons in Paris from *Whistler, and adopted from him the delicate greyish tonality which characterizes her work. She lived in France for most of her life and was *Rodin's lover. In 1913 she became a Catholic, and she said 'My religion and my art, these are my life'. Most of her work consists of single figures (typically girls or nuns) in interiors, painted with great sensitivity and an unobtrusive originality. Good examples are her self-portraits in the Tate Gallery and National Portrait Gallery, London. She had only one exhibition devoted to her work during her lifetime (at the Chenil Galleries in London in 1936) and at the time of her death her work was little known. However, her brother's prophecy that one day she would be considered a better artist than him has been fulfilled, for as his star has fallen hers has risen.

Johns, Jasper (1930–). American painter, sculptor, and printmaker. He has been closely associated with Robert *Rauschenberg, and they are considered to have been largely responsible for the breakthrough from *Abstract Expressionism to the types of *Pop art and *Minimal art which succeeded it. In the early 1950s he worked as a commercial artist in New York, doing display work for shop windows. He began to emerge on the art scene in 1955 and had his first one-man show at the Leo Castelli Gallery in New York in 1958. This was an enormous success, and since then he has become one of the most famous living artists. Much of his work has been done in the form of series of paintings presenting commonplace two-dimensional objects—for example *Flags*, *Targets*, and *Numbers*—and his sculptures have most characteristically been of equally banal subjects such as beer-cans or brushes in a coffee tin. Such works—at one and the same time laboriously realistic and patently artificial—are seen by his admirers as brilliant explorations of the relationship between art and reality; to others, they are as uninteresting as the objects depicted.

Johnson, Cornelius (Cornelis Jonson van Ceulen) (1593–1661). Anglo-Dutch portrait painter born in London of Dutch parents. He perhaps trained in Holland, and he settled there in 1643, but he worked mainly in London, where he had an extensive practice. Johnson was at his best when working on a fairly small scale, showing a sensitive gift for characterization.

Jones, Allen (1937–). British painter and sculptor, one of the most successful of British *Pop artists. He is best known for his use of fetishistic or obsessive objects, often of a sexual character, particularly legs, stockings, shoes, etc., taken from women's fashion magazines.

Jones, David (1895–1974). British painter, engraver, and writer. A convert to Roman Catholicism in 1921, he met Eric *Gill in 1922 and under his influence achieved a sense of purpose (his studies at the Camberwell School of Art, 1909–15, had left him, as he said, 'completely muddleheaded as to the function of art in general'). Gill not only introduced him to the craft of engraving on wood, but also guided him to a conception of art that rejected the current concern with formal properties in favour of an art that aspired to reveal universal and symbolic truths behind the appearance of things. He worked mainly in pencil and water-colour, his subjects including landscape, portraits, still life, animals, and imaginative themes; Arthurian legend was one of his main inspirations. As a writer he is best known for *In Parenthesis* (1937), a long work of mixed poetry and prose on the subject of the First World War (in which he had fought). T. S. Eliot declared this to be a work of genius and it was awarded the Hawthornden Prize. After the Second World War Jones retired to Harrow and devoted himself mainly to calligraphic inscriptions in the Welsh language (he was of Welsh extraction). His work is well represented in the Tate Gallery.

Jones, Inigo (1573–1652). English architect, stage designer, draughtsman, and painter. Jones was one of the greatest of English architects and certainly the most influential, introducing a pure Classical style based on the work of the Italian architect Andrea Palladio to a country where *Renaissance influence had previously been fairly superficial. It was not until he was in his 40s, however, that he showed his genius as an architect, and the first known mention of him as an artist is as a 'picture maker' in 1603. No paintings certainly by him are known, but his drawings survive in large numbers (the finest collection is at Chatsworth). They are mainly costume and scenery designs for the court masques, on which he worked from 1605 to 1640, and in which he introduced movable scenery and the proscenium arch into England. Inigo's lively and fluent style as a draughtsman reflects his two visits to Italy (c.1600 and 1613–14), the second of them in the train of the great collector the Earl of *Arundel. He advised Arundel on the purchase of Italian antiques while developing his own knowledge of Italian and *antique architecture, and his knowledge as well as his skills gave him immense prestige in England at the courts of James I and Charles I. His principal collaborator in the masques was the formidable Ben Jonson, with whom he had a running feud about the rival claims of words and spectacle. Few of Jones's buildings survive in anything like their original state. The most important are the Queen's House at Greenwich (1616–35) and the Banqueting House in Whitehall (1619–22), with its painted ceiling by *Rubens.

Jones, Thomas (1742–1803). Welsh landscape painter, a pupil of Richard *Wilson. He was in Italy 1776–83, and although he painted some ambitious *Classical landscapes, he is now best known for his remarkably fresh and unaffected oil sketches done in and around Naples and Rome (good examples are in the National Museum of Wales at Cardiff). They are among the earliest British examples of this kind of open-air sketch and have a directness that looks forward to *Corot.

Jongkind, Johan Barthold (1819–91). Dutch landscape painter and etcher who had close affinities with the French *Impressionists. Although he was better appreciated during his lifetime than van *Gogh, in some ways his career is similar to that of his more famous countryman.

Both artists made a greater impression abroad than in their own country; both failed to adjust to the society of their time; both were troubled by serious psychological problems; and sensational aspects of their lives—in Jongkind's case it was alcoholism—have interfered with a balanced appraisal of their achievement. Jongkind studied in The Hague with *Schelfhout. In 1846 he moved to Paris, and from then onwards was in close touch with leading French artists. He worked and exhibited with members of the *Barbizon School, and during the 1860s played an important part in the development of Impressionism. His marine pictures and views of ports, which are beautiful studies of the effects of air and atmosphere, particularly influenced *Monet and *Boudin.

Joos van Cleve (c.1490–1540). Netherlandish painter, born presumably at Cleves in the lower Rhine region and active mainly in Antwerp, where he became a master painter in 1511. He was dean of the painters' guild in 1515 and 1525 and seems to have been one of the most productive Antwerp painters of his time, but his career is ill-defined. There is a flavour of *Leonardo in some of his works, and he may have visited Italy. Almost certainly he worked in France and there are several portraits of Francis I and his wife attributed to him, as is a portrait of Henry VIII of England (Royal Coll.). According to van *Mander he collaborated with Joachim *Patenier: a *Rest on the Flight into Egypt* (Musées Royaux, Brussels) is possibly a joint work. Joos's son, **Cornelis van Cleve** (1520–67), was also a painter. He was known as 'Sotte Cleve' (Mad Cleve) after becoming insane in 1554—a result of failing to win the post of Court Painter to Philip II of Spain.

Joos van Wassenhove (active c.1460–80). Netherlandish painter, part of whose career was spent in Italy, where he was known as Giusto da Guanto (Justus of Ghent). He became a member of the Antwerp Guild in 1460, but by 1464 had moved to Ghent, where he was a friend of Hugo van der *Goes. At some time after 1468 he went to Rome, and by 1472 had settled in Urbino, where he worked for Duke Federico da *Montefeltro. Joos's only documented work is *The Communion of the Apostles* (also known as *The Institution of the Eucharist*, 1472–4), which is still at Urbino, in the Galleria Nazionale. Like Hugo's Portinari Altarpiece, it was an important work in spreading knowledge of the Netherlandish oil technique in Italy. Of the other works attributed to Joos, the most important are a series of twenty-eight *Famous Men* (Galleria Nazionale, Urbino, and Louvre, Paris), commissioned for the Ducal Palace. Their authorship is controversial, and they may have been a work of collaboration between Joos and the Spanish painter Pedro *Berruguete.

Jordaens, Jacob (1593–1678). Flemish painter. He was the pupil and son-in-law of Adam van *Noort. Although Jordaens often assisted *Rubens, he had a flourishing studio of his own by the 1620s, and after Rubens's death in 1640 he was the leading figure painter in Flanders. His style was heavily indebted to Rubens, but was much more earthbound, using thick *impasto, strong contrasts of light and shade, and colouring that is often rather lurid. His physical types, too, are coarser than Rubens's and his name is particularly associated with large canvases of hearty rollicking peasants. Two of his favourite subjects, which he depicted several times, are *The Satyr and the Peasant*, based on one of Aesop's fables, and *The King Drinks*, which depicts a boisterous group enjoying an abundant Twelfth Night feast. Jordaens's prolific output, however, included many other subjects, including religious works and portraits, and he also etched and made designs for tapestries. He rarely left his native Antwerp, but commissions came from all over Europe, the most important being *The Triumph of Frederick Hendrik* (1651–2), an enormous composition painted for the Huis ten Bosch, the royal villa near The Hague. In about 1655 Jordaens became a Calvinist; he continued to paint pictures for Catholic churches, but the work of the last two decades of his life is more subdued.

Jorn, Asger (Asger Oluf Jørgensen) (1914–73). Danish painter and graphic artist, active in Paris for much of his career. He was one of the founders of the *Cobra group in 1948, and his mature works are highly coloured abstracts executed with violently expressive brushwork.

Jouvenet, Jean (1644–1717). French painter, the outstanding member of a family of artists from Rouen. He went to Paris in 1661 and joined the studio of *Lebrun. His early works, including decorations for the Salon de Mars at Versailles, were closely imitative of the style of Lebrun and Hubert *Le Sueur (*St Bruno in Prayer*, Nat. Mus., Stockholm). He was the most distinguished of the group of artists who collaborated with *La Fosse in the decorations at Trianon and Les Invalides, but he is now best remembered as the leading French religious painter of his generation, carrying out numerous major commissions for churches in Paris and elsewhere. His later work was marked both by *Baroque emotionalism and by a realistic treatment of details foreign to the principles encouraged by the Academy. It is recorded, for example, that before painting his *Miraculous Draught of Fishes* (Louvre, Paris, c.1706) he studied fishing scenes on the spot at Dieppe.

Juan de Flandes (d. c.1519). Flemish painter active in Castile from 1496. He was one of a number of north European artists employed by Queen Isabella, who appointed him court painter in 1498. A miniature altarpiece he painted for her was once much renowned, but is now dismembered and scattered; a characteristic panel from it, *Christ Crowned with Thorns* (Detroit Institute of Arts), shows his delicate *miniaturistic style. After Isabella's death in 1504 he worked for churches in Salamanca and Palencia.

Juan de Juanes. See MACIP.

Juan de Juni (c.1507–77). Sculptor, probably of Burgundian origin, active in Spain from c.1533. He worked at León and Salamanca before settling at Valladolid in 1540. He was a prolific sculptor of religious subjects, excelling in the dramatic expression of emotion, and is generally ranked with Alonso *Berruguete as the outstanding Spanish sculptor of his period. His most famous works are probably the two versions of the *Entombment* in Valladolid Museum (1539–44) and Segovia Cathedral (1571).

Judd, Donald (1928–   ). American sculptor, one of the most prominent of *Minimalist artists. His work consists characteristically of stainless steel or painted iron boxes or similar simple forms set side by side without emotional overtones.

Juel, Jens (1745–1802). Danish painter. He had a distinguished career both in Denmark and in his travels throughout Europe—he studied in Hamburg and in the 1770s worked in Rome, Paris, Dresden, and Geneva. After settling in Copenhagen he became court painter (1780) and a professor at the Academy, where *Friedrich and *Runge were among his pupils. Juel painted landscapes, *genre scenes, and still lifes (particularly flowers), but he is most renowned for his sensitive portraits.

Jugendstil. See ART NOUVEAU.

Junk art. Art constructed from worthless materials, refuse, rubbish, and urban waste. In so far as Junk art represented a revolt against the traditional doctrine of fine materials and a desire to show that works of art can be constructed from the humblest and most worthless things, it may be plausibly traced back to Kurt *Schwitters and the *collages of early Synthetic *Cubism. However, it is not possible to speak of a Junk movement until the 1950s, particularly with the work of Robert *Rauschenberg, who in the mid 1950s began to affix to his canvases rags and tatters of cloth, torn reproductions, and other waste materials (see COMBINE PAINTING). The name 'Junk art' was first applied to these by the critic Lawrence Alloway and was then extended to sculpture made from scrap metal, broken machine parts, used timber, and so on. The Junk art of the USA had its analogies in the work of *Tàpies and others in Spain, *Burri and *Arte Povera in Italy, and similar movements in most European countries and in Japan, where the litter and refuse left over from the war was sometimes converted to artistic use. In the case of Rauschenberg and others the use of Junk material was objective and unemotional. In other instances, including the Junk sculpture of California and the work of Burri and Tàpies, a nostalgic emotional suggestion was conveyed by the use of discarded machine parts, rotted beams and rusted metal, torn and dirty textile scraps, and the detritus generally of industrialized urban life.

Justus of Ghent. See JOOS VAN WASSENHOVE.

K

Kahlo, Frida. See RIVERA, DIEGO.

Kahnweiler, Daniel-Henri (1884–1976). German-born art dealer, publisher, and writer, who became a French citizen in 1937. In 1907 he opened a gallery in Paris, and became interested in the *Fauves—*Derain and *Vlaminck particularly. He is best known, however, as the friend and promoter of the *Cubists. From 1907 he was the chief dealer of *Picasso, remaining his lifelong friend. He was also a friend and supporter of Juan *Gris, of whom he wrote a standard biography (1947). As a publisher he brought out numerous books illustrated by his artist friends.

Kalf, Willem (1619–93). Dutch painter, one of the most celebrated of all still-life painters. He was born in Rotterdam and in 1642–6 worked in Paris. On his return to the Netherlands he lived in Hoorn and then in 1653 settled in Amsterdam. His early works were modest kitchen and courtyard scenes, but he soon became the outstanding exponent of a type of still life in which fruit and precious objects—porcelain, oriental rugs, Venetian glass—are arranged in grand *Baroque displays. His pictures have often been compared with those of *Vermeer because of his masterly handling of texture and his ability to manipulate warm and cool colours (he frequently contrasts the reddish browns in a carpet with the yellow of a peeled lemon and the blue and white of porcelain).

Kandinsky, Wassily (1866–1944). Russian-born painter and writer on art, one of the most important pioneers of *abstract art. He abandoned a promising university career teaching law, partly under the impact of an exhibition in Moscow of French *Impressionists, at which one of *Monet's *Haystack* pictures made a particularly lasting impression upon him, and in 1896 went to Munich to study painting. In 1901 he was one of the founders of an avant-garde exhibiting society called the Phalanx, the main forum for Jugendstil

(*Art Nouveau) in Germany and in 1902 he joined the Berlin *Sezession. Between 1903 and 1908 he travelled widely in western Europe and Africa. His pictures at the turn of the century combined features of Art Nouveau with reminiscences of Russian folk art, to which he added a *Fauve-like intensity of colour. In 1908 he returned to Munich and began to eliminate the representational element from his work, until, in a series of *Compositions, Improvisations*, and *Impressions*, done between 1910 and 1913, he arrived at pure abstraction. (The best collection of his work from this period is in the Lenbachhaus in Munich.) Kandinsky said that his understanding of the power of non-representational art derived from a night when he went into his studio in Munich and failed to recognize one of his own paintings that was lying the wrong way up, seeing in it a picture 'of extraordinary beauty glowing with an inner radiance'. From 1911 he was one of the most active figures in the *Blaue Reiter, editing with Franz *Marc the *Blaue Reiter* almanac. In 1914 he returned to Russia, where he gained several distinguished academic posts. However, being out of sympathy with the new ideas that subordinated fine art to industrial design, he left Russia in 1921 to take up a teaching post in the *Bauhaus, where he remained until it was closed in 1933. In 1927 he became a German citizen. He left Germany for France in 1933 and lived at Neuilly-sur-Seine. He became a French citizen in 1939. Kandinsky was one of the most influential artists of his generation both for his painting and for his writing. His progress towards abstraction proceeded alongside his philosophical views about the nature of art, which were influenced by theosophy and mysticism. He did not completely repudiate representation, but he held that the 'pure' artist seeks to express only 'inner and essential' feelings and ignores the superficial and fortuitous. His chief works setting forth his theories of abstract pictorial composition are *Über das Geistige in der Kunst*

(Concerning the Spiritual in Art, 1912), *Rückblicke* (Reminiscences, 1913), and *Punkt und Linie zu Fläche* (Point, Line and Surface, published in 1926 as a Bauhaus pamphlet).

Kane, John (1860–1934). American *naïve painter, born in Scotland. In 1879 he emigrated to Pittsburgh, where he was employed as a steelworker, and then worked from 1884 to 1890 as a coalminer in Alabama, during which time he first began to sketch. After losing a leg in 1891 he worked as a watchman on the railway. His first oil paintings were done c.1910, when he was working as a carpenter and housepainter in Ohio. He painted portraits—including a *Self-portrait* (1929) now in the Museum of Modern Art, New York—landscapes, interiors, and cityscapes of industrial Pittsburgh, combining meticulous detail with naïve stylization and imaginative reconstruction. Although he was the first naïve painter to win recognition in the United States, he died in poverty.

Kaprow, Allen (1927–   ). American artist, best known as the creator of *happenings. His studies included a period with the musician John Cage, from whom he took over the idea of chance and indeterminacy in aesthetic organization. In an article published in 1958 in *Art News* he argued for the abandonment of craftsmanship and permanence in the fine arts and advocated the incorporation of perishable materials. His first major exhibition was of a work called *18 Happenings in 6 Parts* at the Reuben Gallery, New York, and during the 1960s he developed the art of the happening in the direction of environmental theatre or *Performance art continuous with everyday life, breaking down the barriers between art and actual experience.

Kauffer, E. McKnight (1890–1954). American-born painter and illustrator who settled in England in 1914. He was a member of Wyndham *Lewis's Group X and of the *Cumberland Market Group, but is best known for his brilliant and witty poster designs, notably for the London Transport Board and the Great Western Railway.

Kauffmann, Angelica (1741–1807). Swiss painter. From an early age she travelled with her father, the painter **Joseph Johann Kauffmann** (1707–82), in Switzerland and Italy, and she formed her style in Rome. In 1766 she moved to London, where her work and her person were vastly admired. A foundation member of the *Royal Academy in 1768, she was a close friend of the President, Sir Joshua *Reynolds, their relationship giving rise to gossip and a satirical picture by Nathaniel *Hone. (*Canova, *Goethe, and *Winckelmann were among the other distinguished men charmed by her.) Kauffmann began in England as a fashionable portraitist, but then devoted herself more to historical scenes and also did decorative work for Robert Adam and other architects. Although her work owes much to the *Neoclassical tradition, it has a prettiness that can be described as *Rococo. At its best it has great charm, but it can be rather insipid, and she was much more successful with ladylike decorative vignettes than with scenes from Homer or Shakespeare. After an unhappy first marriage, she married the decorative painter Antonio Zucchi (1726–95) in 1781 and settled in Rome, where she continued her successful career.

Kelly, Ellsworth (1923–   ). American painter and sculptor. He is one of the most prominent of the *Hard Edge colour painters who succeeded the *Abstract Expressionists. His most characteristic paintings use large, bold shapes, simply arranged, and he was also among the first to develop the idea of the shaped canvas. During the 1940s he had done low-*relief constructions laced with cord and wire, sometimes deriving from natural shapes formalized into abstract patterns and sometimes incorporating *biomorphic *Surrealist forms. His later, highly coloured sculpture has close affinities with his own two-dimensional paintings.

Kelly, Sir Gerald (1879–1972). British painter. He was the leading society portraitist of his day and had many distinguished friends, among them Somerset Maugham, whose portrait by Graham *Sutherland Kelly wittily attacked. From 1949 to 1954 he was President of the *Royal Academy; in this position he devoted much of his time to organizing loan exhibitions, and became well known for his appearances in related television programmes. Apart from portraits Kelly painted landscapes and also pictures of Asian dancing girls (he had spent some time in Burma) that were once very popular in reproduction.

Kelmscott Press. A private printing-press founded in 1890 by William *Morris at Hammersmith and named after the village near Oxford where he had lived since 1871. Between 1891 and 1898, two years after Morris's death, the press issued more than fifty titles, including editions of several of Morris's own works. Deeply influenced by his study of early printing, Morris himself designed most of the type, borders, ornaments, and title-pages. The press's greatest book, and by common consent one of the world's masterpieces of book production, is the 1896 edition of Geoffrey Chaucer's works, with illustrations by *Burne-Jones. Although short-lived, the Kelmscott Press had enormous influence on the private presses that followed in its wake.

Kennington, Eric (1888–1960). British painter, sculptor, and graphic artist. He was an official war artist in the First and Second World Wars and was chiefly known for his studies of the daily life of ordinary soldiers and the RAF in the Second World War. Between the wars he worked mainly as a portraitist but also did book illustration, including illustrations to T. E. Lawrence's *Seven Pillars of Wisdom* (1926). His sculptures included the *Monument to the 24th Division* in Battersea Park, London (1924).

Kent, William (1685–1748). English architect, designer, landscape gardener, and painter. He began his career as a painter and studied in Rome, where in about 1717 he painted a ceiling in the church of S. Giuliano dei Fiamminghi (offering to work without payment for the chance to establish his reputation). As a guide and agent for Englishmen on the *Grand Tour he met the architect and patron Lord Burlington, who in 1719 invited him to return with him to London. From then until Kent's death in 1748 the two were inseparable partners. After some rather unsuccessful decorative painting at Burlington House and Kensington Palace in London, Kent began to find himself as an architectural impresario, interior decorator, and garden designer, and he abandoned his first profession. The richness and fantasy of his interior decoration and the imagination displayed in his garden designs are probably his chief claim to fame, and are the perfect complement to the somewhat rigid Classicism of Burlington's architecture. As an architect Kent's most important work is Holkham Hall, Norfolk, begun in 1734 for the first Earl of Leicester, whom he had first met in Rome. Although he was a painter of little talent, Kent has the distinction of painting the earliest medieval history subjects in British art—a series of three pictures for Queen Caroline depicting scenes from the life of Henry V (Royal Coll., c.1730). There is no attempt to re-create the scenes accurately, and in fact there is some doubt whether one of the pictures is intended to represent the Battle of Agincourt (1415) or the Battle of Crécy (1346).

Kersting, Georg Friedrich (1785–1847). German painter. After studying at the Copenhagen Academy he settled in 1808 at Dresden, where he specialized in small portraits set in delicately rendered interiors. He was a friend of *Friedrich and painted several versions of a portrait showing him in his studio (Kunsthalle, Hamburg, Staatliche Museen, Berlin, and Städtische Kunsthalle, Mannheim).

Kessel, Jan van (1626–79). Flemish still-life and flower painter active in Antwerp, where he became a Guild member in 1645. He continued the traditions of his grandfather, Jan 'Velvet' *Brueghel, and was also influenced by Daniel *Seghers. Van Kessel painted garlands and bouquets of flowers, but is best known for small, jewel-like pictures, often on copper, of insects or shells against a light background, executed with strong colour and great exactitude. Good examples of his prolific output are in Oxford (Ashmolean), Cambridge (Fitzwilliam), and Madrid (Prado).

Ketel, Cornelis (1548–1616). Dutch portrait and history painter. He worked mainly in Gouda, where he was born, and in Amsterdam, where he died, but also in France and in England, where he lived 1573–81. Van *Mander, who was well informed about him, mentions that he painted a portrait of Queen Elizabeth I for the Earl of Hertford in 1578, but the picture is not known. The portrait of Martin Frobisher (Bodleian Lib., Oxford), however, is a good example of his work from his English period. Ketel's finest works are his group portraits (examples in the Rijksmuseum, Amsterdam), which prefigure those of Frans *Hals.

Kettle, Tilly (1735–86). English portrait painter. After working in the Midlands and London, he became one of the first British painters to risk a long visit to India, where he spent the years 1769–76 and made a fortune painting nabobs and princes. He died on his way out a second time, having found it much harder to achieve success in England. Kettle's style was derivative from that of *Reynolds, *Cotes, and *Romney.

Key. Family of Netherlandish painters best known for their portraiture. **Willem Key** (c.1515–68) was a pupil of Lambert *Lombard c.1540 in Liège. In 1542 he was made a master of the Antwerp Guild, where he spent the rest of his working life. His nephew, **Adriaen Thomasz. Key** (c.1544–after 1589), was probably his pupil. The latter became a master of the Antwerp Guild in 1568. Both artists were highly regarded in their day and did assured and solid portraits of famous people. Their religious works are less well known, and many of Willem's are known to have perished at the hands of iconoclasts.

Keyser, Hendrick de (1565–1621). The outstanding Dutch sculptor and one of the leading Dutch architects of his period. Most of his career was spent in Amsterdam, where he was appointed municipal sculptor and architect in 1594. His most important buildings are the Zuiderkerk (South Church, 1606–14), Holland's first large Protestant Church, and the Westerkerk (West Church, 1620–38), which broke free from the *Mannerist tradition, looking forward to the *Classicism of Jacob van *Campen. The splendid towers of these two churches are still among Amsterdam's chief landmarks. As a sculptor, de Keyser excelled particularly as a portraitist in a soberly realistic style (*Unknown Man*, Rijksmuseum, Amsterdam, 1608), but his best-known work is the tomb of William the Silent (begun 1614) in the Niewe Kerk at Delft. **Thomas de Keyser** (1596/7–1667), Hendrick's son and pupil, was municipal architect to the City of Amsterdam from 1662 until his death (he added the cupola to van Campen's Town Hall), but

he is better known as a portrait painter. He was, indeed, Amsterdam's leading portraitist before being overtaken in popularity by *Rembrandt in the 1630s. His life-size portraits look stiff compared with Rembrandt's and he is more attractive and original on a small scale. *Constantin Huygens and His Clerk* (NG, London, 1627) is an excellent example of one of his small portraits of full-length figures in an interior, forerunners of the *conversation pieces. His small equestrian portraits were also a new type (*Pieter Schout*, Rijksmuseum, 1660). Two other sons of Hendrick, **Pieter** (1595–1676) and **Willem** (1603–after 1678), were sculptors. Willem worked for some years in England, probably with Nicholas *Stone, Hendrick's son-in-law and former pupil.

Kienholz, Edward (1927–   ). American sculptor, specializing in life-size three-dimensional tableaux. He belongs to the California school of *Funk art, using the bizarre and shoddy detritus of contemporary life to create horrific and brutal images of murder, sex, death, and decay. A typical example of his work is *The State Hospital* (Moderna Mus., Stockholm, 1964–6). In 1975 Kienholz began to work in Berlin and his work took on more precise social implications.

Kinetic art. Term describing art incorporating real or apparent movement. In its broadest sense the term can encompass a great range of phenomena, including cinematic motion pictures, *happenings and the animated clockwork figures found on clocktowers in many cities of Europe. More usually, however, it is applied to sculpture incorporating motors or driven by air currents, such as *Calder's mobiles. The term was first used in connection with *fine art by *Gabo and *Pevsner in their *Realistic Manifesto* of 1920, but it was not until the 1950s that the phrase 'Kinetic art' became established as a recognized addition to critical classification.

Kip, Johannes (1653–1722). Dutch topographical engraver who migrated to England in about 1690. He is best known for his engravings of country houses in the sumptuous *Britannia Illustrata* (1708 and subsequent volumes). They are of little artistic merit but of great historical interest.

Kiprensky, Orest (1782–1836). Russian painter, active for much of his career in Italy. He is best known for his *Romantic portraits in which he combined the then fashionable attitude of 'Byronic' melancholy with an integrity which earned him the epithet 'the Russian van *Dyck'.

Kirchner, Ernst Ludwig (1880–1938). German *Expressionist painter, sculptor, and graphic artist, the dominant figure in the *Brücke group. In his early woodcuts a reflection of the mannered linearism of the Jugendstil, the German version of *Art Nouveau, was soon displaced by the harsh contrast of planes and the abrupt angularity which he derived from his admiration for late *Gothic German woodcuts and which became characteristic of the style of the Brücke. Throughout his life he produced prints as well as paintings, and he also made coloured wooden sculpture. He was the first of the group to discover an enthusiasm for Polynesian and other *primitive art, but this had less apparent effect on his own painting or sculpture than on the work of other members of the Brücke. In painting he was first influenced by the Post-Impressionists and particularly by *Gauguin and van *Gogh. But under the influence chiefly of *Munch he developed a style similar to that of the *Fauves, with simplified drawing and boldly contrasting colours. By 1907–10 he had matured a manner of painting superficially similar to that achieved by *Matisse and his colleagues in 1905, but he was more impetuous and direct in his approach to his subjects. He was also more committed to theme than they and attempted to express in paint the emotional atmosphere distilled by the life of the circus and the music-hall, the gaiety and the sadness with its overtones of sexuality in the human detritus of the urban scene. In 1911 he went to Berlin and during 1912 and 1913 created the series of street scenes which are regarded as the most mature manifestation of German Expressionism. In a style which had become more frenzied, with more ruthless fragmentation of the object, he gave visible expression to the pace, the morbidity, the glare, and the exhibitionist eroticism of megapolitan man (*Street, Berlin*, MOMA, New York, 1913). Kirchner had always been highly strung and he was invalided out of the army in the First World War after suffering a physical and nervous breakdown. In 1917 he was sent to convalesce in Switzerland and stayed there for the rest of his life. Living in solitude among the Swiss mountains near Davos, Kirchner began to paint again, mainly monumental mountain landscapes and scenes from the life of mountain peasants. In the new environment his work gained in serenity what it lost in vigour. From 1928 his style underwent another change. It became more abstract as he painted less directly from nature. Kirchner's work was declared *degenerate by the Nazis in 1937, adding to his already acute depression at the political events in Germany, and in the following year he killed himself.

Kitaj, Ron B. (1932–). American painter and graphic artist, active mainly in England, where he has been one of the most prominent figures of the *Pop art movement. Before becoming a student at the *Royal College of Art Kitaj had travelled widely (he was a merchant seaman, then served in the US army) and his wide cultural horizons gave him an influential position among his contemporaries (he studied with *Hockney and Allen *Jones), particularly in holding up his own preference for figuration in opposition to the prevailing abstraction. After a visit to Paris in 1975 he was inspired by *Degas to take up pastel, which he has used for much of his subsequent work. Late 19th-cent. French art has been a major source of inspiration, as has a preoccupation with his Jewish identity, and he has said: 'I took it into my cosmopolitan head that I should attempt to do *Cézanne and Degas and Kafka over again, after Auschwitz.' Unlike the majority of Pop artists, Kitaj has had relatively little interest in the culture of the mass media and has evolved a multi-evocative pictorial language, deriving from a wide range of pictorial and literary sources—indeed he has declared that he is not a Pop artist.

kit-cat. A canvas measuring 36 × 28 in. (92 × 71 cm.). The name derives from *Kneller's portraits of the Kit-Cat Club (NPG, London, c.1702–21), all but one of which (there are forty-two) are of this size. Members of the club, which was founded in the last years of the 17th cent. and included many of the leading whigs of the day, met originally at a tavern near Temple

Bar kept by Christopher Cat (or Kat) that was famous for its mutton pies known as 'Kit-cats'. The kit-cat size canvas is particularly suited to life-size portraits showing the sitter's head and shoulders and one or both hands, and Kneller's portraits popularized the format.

Kitchen Sink School. A group of British Social *Realist painters active in the years immediately following the Second World War and in the early 1950s. By their choice of drab and sordid themes and their violently aggressive technique they expressed the post-war mood of the 'angry young men'. The mood did not last and the group, never tightly organized, ceased to cohere after a few years. John *Bratby was the best-known member.

Klee, Paul (1879–1940). Swiss painter and graphic artist, one of the most individual but also most influential figures in 20th-cent. art. He trained at the Academy of Fine Art, Munich, 1898–1901, and after travelling in Italy, 1901–2, and visiting Paris in 1905 with Louis *Moilliet he settled in Munich in 1906, in the same year marrying the pianist Lily Stumpf (he was himself a talented violinist). From 1911 he made contact with the *Blaue Reiter group at Munich and in the following year took part in the second Blaue Reiter exhibition. In 1914 he travelled with Moilliet and August *Macke to Tunisia, a journey which awakened him to a new sense of colour (most of his work before this date had been in black and white). During the war he served in the German army, being engaged for part of the time on painting aeroplane wings. In 1919 an exhibition in Munich of 362 of his works made Klee internationally famous. Invited by *Gropius to teach painting at the *Bauhaus, he moved to Weimar in 1921 and followed the Bauhaus to Dessau in 1926. In 1931 he left the Bauhaus to take up an appointment at the Düsseldorf Academy, but he was forced to abandon this in 1933 by the Nazi administration and left Germany for Berne. His works were included in the notorious exhibition of *Degenerate Art in 1937.

Although Klee was not politically inclined, there is no doubt that during his last years in Berne his mood was one of profound disappointment, perhaps bordering on acute depression. In 1935 he suffered the first symptoms of the illness which caused his death in 1940, a rare debilitating disease called scleroderma. Although he remained productive until the end, the predominance of a darker scale of colour in the paintings of the last seven years, their preoccupation with malign and malevolent forces and themes of corruption, and the appearance of a more bitter form of satire instead of his earlier playfulness all attest to the mental stress under which he lived during these years. Yet his technical and formal mastery remained unaffected and his sense of humour (albeit macabre humour) remained even when he was facing death (*Death and Fire*, Paul Klee Foundation, Kunstmuseum, Berne, 1940). Klee was one of the most inventive and prolific of the modern masters, his complete output being estimated at some 8,000 works. It is impossible to categorize his work stylistically as he moved freely between figuration and abstraction, absorbing countless influences and transforming these through his unrivalled imaginative gifts. In spite of this variety, his work—in whatever style—is almost always easily recognizable as his, revealing a joyous spirit that is hard to parallel in 20th-cent. art. Of Klee's writings the most important are: *On Modern Art* (1948), English translation of a lecture delivered in 1924 at Jena and published in 1945; and *Pedagogical Sketchbook* (1953), English translation of *Pädagogisches Skizzenbuch*, published in 1925 as the second of the Bauhaus Books.

Klein, Yves (1928–62). French painter and experimental artist, one of the most influential figures in European avant-garde art in the post-war period. He had no formal artistic training; among other things he was a jazz musician and in 1952–3 he lived in Japan, where he obtained the high rank of black belt, fourth dan for judo. On his return to Paris he wrote a textbook on the subject (1954) and he was a judo instructor for several years. In the mid 1950s he began exhibiting 'monochromes', non-objective paintings in which a canvas was uniformly painted a single colour, usually a distinctive blue that he called 'International Klein Blue'. He used this also for sculptured figures, reliefs of sponges on canvas, etc. In a lecture given at the Sorbonne in 1959, Klein explained his theory of monochrome painting as an attempt to depersonalize colour by ridding it of subjective emotion and so to give it a metaphysical quality. Klein also made pictures by a variety of unorthodox methods, including the action of rain on a prepared paper (these he called *Cosmogonies*), the use of a flame-thrower (*Peintures de Feu*), or imprints of the human body (*Anthropométries*). In 1958 he created a sensation (and almost a riot) at the Galerie Iris Clert in Paris by an 'exhibition of emptiness'—an empty gallery painted white. It was called *Le Vide* (The Void). In 1960 he gave his first public exhibition of the *Anthropométries*: girls smeared with blue pigment were dragged over canvas laid on the floor to the accompaniment of his *Symphonie monotone*—a single note sustained for ten minutes and alternating with ten minutes' silence. Klein died young of a heart attack, but his work had great influence, particularly on the development of *Minimal art. A great showman, he represents the tendency in 20th-cent. art for the personality of the artist to be of more importance than the things he makes.

Klimt, Gustav (1862–1918). Austrian painter and graphic artist. Early in his career he was highly successful as a painter of sumptuous decorative schemes in the grandiose tradition of *Makart, whose staircase decoration in the Kunsthistorisches Museum in Vienna Klimt completed after Makart's death in 1884. In spite of his official academic successes, Klimt was drawn to avant-garde art, and he came under the influence of *Impressionism, *Symbolism, and *Art Nouveau. Discontent with the conservative attitudes of the Viennese Artists' Association led him and a group of friends to resign in 1897 and set up their own organization, the *Sezession, of which he was elected President. His role as a leader of the avant-garde was confirmed when his allegorical mural paintings for Vienna University (1900–3) aroused great hostility, being called nonsensical and pornographic. (Klimt abandoned the commission in 1905 and the paintings were destroyed by fire in 1945.) Although official commissions dried up after this he continued to be much in demand with private patrons, as a portraitist as well as a painter of mythological and allegorical themes. He was highly responsive to female beauty (he was a great womanizer) and in both his portraits and his subject pictures he stresses the allure and mystery of womanhood. Notable examples

are the magnificent full-length portrait of Emilie Flöge (his sister-in-law and mistress) in the Historisches Museum der Stadt, Vienna (1902) and *Judith I* (Österreichische Galerie, Vienna, 1901), one of the archetypal images of the *femme fatale*. Characteristically, the figures in Klimt's paintings are treated more or less naturalistically but embellished—in the background or their clothing—with richly decorative patterns recalling butterfly or peacock wings, creating a highly distinctive style of extraordinarily lush sensuality. His work was particularly influential on *Kokoschka and *Schiele.

Kline, Franz (1910–62). American painter, generally considered one of the most individual of the *Abstract Expressionists. He began as a representational painter, notably of urban landscapes, but turned to abstraction at the end of the 1940s. This change of direction reflected the influence of *de Kooning and was also stimulated by his seeing some of his drawings enlarged by a projector, an experience that made him realize their potential as abstract compositions. From c.1950 he developed an extremely original style of expressive abstraction, converting the brush-strokes of these drawings into independent ideograms and using bold black patterns on a white ground reminiscent of oriental calligraphy. Towards the end of his life he sometimes incorporated vivid colours but for the most part remained constant in the black-and-white style perfected in the 1950s.

Klinger, Max (1857–1920). German painter, sculptor, and graphic artist, born at Leipzig. He studied at Karlsruhe and Berlin, then spent the years 1883–6 in Paris, 1886–8 in Berlin, and 1888–93 in Rome. His work is complex technically, stylistically, and intellectually, full of symbols and fantasy. As a sculptor he experimented with *polychromy in the manner of Greek *chryselephantine statues; the culmination was his statue of Beethoven (Mus. der Bildenden Künste, Leipzig, 1899–1902) in white and coloured marbles, bronze, alabaster, and ivory. As a painter he is best known for his enormous *Judgement of Paris* (Kunsthistorisches Museum, Vienna, 1885–7), in which the frame is part of the decorative scheme. It is as a graphic artist, however, that Klinger most clearly showed his originality, his etchings being considered forerunners of *Surrealism. The most remarkable are in the series *Adventures of a Glove* (1881), a grotesque exploration of fetishism that antedated the publication of Freud's theories.

Knapton, George (1698–1778). English portrait painter, a pupil of *Richardson. He was in Italy 1725–32 and in 1736 he became official painter to the Society of Dilettanti, of which he was a Foundation Member. His twenty-three portraits of his fellow members (still in the possession of the Society) are considered his finest works. From about 1737 Knapton worked much in pastels, but after the 1750s he appears to have virtually given up painting. In 1765 he was appointed Keeper of the King's Pictures. *Cotes was his most important pupil.

Knave of Diamonds (Bubnovyi Valet). An artists' association and exhibition group which was formed in Moscow in 1909 and for a short time became the most important of the avant-garde associations in Russia. In 1911 *Larionov, *Goncharova, and *Malevich broke away from the group, accusing it of being too dominated by the 'cheap orientalism of the Paris School' and the 'Munich decadence', and founded their own association, the *Donkey's Tail, to promote an art based upon native Russian inspiration. The Knave of Diamonds continued to function as an exhibition society until 1918.

Kneller, Sir Godfrey (originally Gottfried Kniller) (1646–1723). German-born painter who settled in England and became the leading portraitist there in the late 17th cent. and early 18th cent. He studied in Amsterdam under *Bol, a pupil of *Rembrandt, and later in Italy, before moving to England, probably in the mid 1670s. The opportune death of serious rivals (notably *Lely in 1680) and his own arrogant self-assurance enabled him to establish himself as the dominant court and society painter by the beginning of the reign of James II (1685). He was appointed Principal Painter jointly with *Riley on the accession of William III and Mary II in 1689 (becoming sole bearer of the title when Riley died in 1691), was knighted in 1692, and created a baronet in 1715. Kneller established a workshop-studio in London

with a large team of specialized assistants, many of them foreign, organized for the mass production of fashionable portraits. Sitters were required to pose only for a drawing of the face and efficient formulas were worked out for the accessories. He is said sometimes to have accommodated as many as fourteen sitters in a day. The average portrait turned out from his studio in this way was slick and mechanical (and the heavy wigs then fashionable make for great monotony in male portraits), but Kneller was capable of work of much higher quality when he had a sitter to whom he especially responded; outstanding examples are *The Chinese Convert* (Kensington Palace, London, 1687) and *Matthew Prior* (Trinity Coll., Cambridge, 1700). Many other examples of his work, including the portraits of the *Kit-Cat Club, are in the National Portrait Gallery, London. His style was less elegant and more forthright than Lely's, but the influence of his mass-produced work was stultifying. He was the last foreign-born artist to dominate English painting, but it needed a *Hogarth and a *Reynolds to break through the conventions that he had popularized.

Knight, Dame Laura (née Johnson 1877–1970). English painter. In the first half of the century she was one of the most highly regarded of British artists and in 1936 she became the first woman to be elected a *Royal Academician since the original women members Angelica *Kauffmann and Mary *Moser. At the height of her considerable fame (she was regarded as a 'character'—the nearest equivalent to a female Augustus *John) she won great popularity for her colourful scenes of circus life and the ballet, but these now often seem to hover close to kitsch. On the other hand, her early *Newlyn School landscapes, which at their best have a sparkling sense of *joie de vivre*, have recently come back into favour. Some of the work she did as an official war artist during the Second World War is also now highly regarded. In 1946 she went to Nuremberg to make a pictorial record of the War Criminals' Trial; she made scores of sketches and produced a large painting (Imperial War Mus., London). Her husband **Harold Knight** (1874–1961) was also a painter, mainly of portraits.

Knight, Richard Payne (1751–1824). English collector and connoisseur. His collections were highly varied, but particularly outstanding were his drawings and antique coins and bronzes, which he bequeathed to the *British Museum. He wrote a didactic poem in the manner of Pope entitled *The Landscape* (1794) and *An Analytical Inquiry into the Principles of Taste* (1805), both of which were important documents in the literature of the *picturesque, of which he was a leading advocate. His other publications included *An Account of the Remains of the Worship of Priapus* (1786), which was violently attacked as being obscene. See also ELGIN MARBLES.

Købke, Christen (1810–48). Danish painter, a pupil of *Eckersberg. Although he visited Italy, this had little influence on his work, which is narrow in range. He concentrated on everyday scenes in and around Copenhagen and on portraits of family and friends, displaying great sensitivity as a colourist and a warm intimacy of characterization. Købke was little appreciated in his lifetime, but he began to win recognition at the end of the 19th cent. and is now considered the outstanding Danish painter of his period.

Koch, Joseph Anton (1768–1839). Austrian painter, active mainly in Rome, where he settled in 1795. He was influenced by *Carstens and worked with the *Nazarenes on the decorations of the Casino Massimo (1825–9) in Rome, choosing Dante's *Inferno* for his subject, but is now best known for his landscapes. They were directly descended from the heroic and *ideal landscape of *Poussin, but have a distinctive *Romantic flavour, particularly in his paintings of mountains.

Koekkoek, Barend Cornelis (1803–62). The best-known member of a family of Dutch painters. He frequently travelled in Belgium and Germany, where he found inspiration for the *Romantic views of forests and mountains which he painted in a precise and detailed style, often with rosy light effects recalling the work of Jan *Both. Other members of his large and prolific family specialized mainly in seascapes.

Kokoschka, Oskar (1886–1980). Austrian-born painter, graphic artist, and writer who became a British citizen in 1947. His formative years were spent at Vienna amid the intellectual and artistic ferment brought about by the somewhat belated introduction of *Art Nouveau to Austria in the early years of the century. He made a name for himself *c*.1909–10 by his 'psychological portraits' in which the soul of the sitter was thought to be laid bare, and at the same time he produced striking and sometimes shocking lithographs and posters. He was seriously wounded in the First World War and after recovery taught at the Dresden Academy 1919–24. From this time he came to the fore as a painter of *Expressionist landscapes and a particular kind of 'portrait' picture of town scenes from a high viewpoint (*Jerusalem*, Detroit Institute of Arts, 1929–30). Outspokenly opposed to the Nazis, he moved to Prague in 1934 and then to England in 1938. From 1953 he lived mainly at Villeneuve in Switzerland. In his later years he continued to paint landscapes and portraits, but his most important works of this time are his *Prometheus* ceiling (1950) for Count Seilern's house at Princes Gate in London, and the *Thermopylae* *triptych for Hamburg University. Kokoschka remained steadfastly unaffected by modern movements and throughout his long life he pursued his highly personal and imaginative version of pre-1914 Expressionism. His writings include an autobiography (1971) and several plays.

Kollwitz, Käthe (née Schmidt, 1867–1945). German graphic artist and sculptor. She came from a family of strong moral and social convictions, and after marrying a doctor, Karl Kollwitz, in 1891 she lived in the poorer quarters of northern Berlin, where she gained first-hand acquaintance of the wretched conditions in which the urban poor lived. Much of her work was intended as a social protest against the working conditions of the day, and her series of etchings *Weavers' Revolt* (1897–8) and *Peasants' War* (1902–8) brought her notoriety. She concentrated on the great tragic and poignant themes of life (notably the Mother and Child), and many of her later works were pacifist in intention (her son was killed in the First World War and her grandson in the Second World War). In line with her left-wing views she visited the Soviet Union in 1927, but was subsequently disillusioned with Soviet Communism. In 1929 she was made the first woman member of the Prussian Academy in Berlin, but in 1933 she was expelled and suffered harassment from the Nazis. Soon after this (1934–5) she made a moving series of eight lithographs on the theme of Death. Her best-known sculpture is the war memorial at Dixmuiden, Flanders, completed in 1932. In its elimination of the accidental and its instinctive grasp of the tragic essential, her work represents in its purest and most poignant form the element of social protest which has been prominent in much German *Expressionist art. 'I should like', she wrote in 1922, 'to exert influences in these times when human beings are so perplexed and in need of help.'

Koninck (or **de Koninck**), **Philips** (1619–88). Dutch painter, the best-known member of a family of artists. He studied with his brother **Jacob** (1614/15–after 1690) in Rotterdam, and *Houbraken says he was also a pupil of *Rembrandt in Amsterdam, where he settled in 1641. Although he painted various subjects (the poet Vondel praised his portraits and history pictures) his fame now rests on his landscapes. He specialized in extensive views, and his work has a majesty and power that rivals the similar scenes of *Ruisdael; the National Gallery in London has four outstanding examples. Like many Dutch painters he had a second occupation; he ran a prosperous shipping firm and apparently painted little in the last decade of his life. His wealth enabled him to collect drawings. He was a prolific draughtsman himself and his sketchy penmanship can be deceptively close to Rembrandt's. **Salomon Koninck** (1609–56), the cousin of Philips and Jacob, was also a painter. He was a follower of Rembrandt, imitating him in pictures of hermits, old men, and philosophers in their studies, as well as in religious scenes, and exaggerating the master's early predilection for rich exotic costumes, emphatic gestures, and dramatic contrasts of light and shadow.

kore. Greek word for 'maiden', applied to the draped standing female statues characteristic of the *Archaic period. The plural is *korai*.

Kosuth, Joseph (1945–). American experimental artist who about the mid 1960s came to the fore as one of the chief pioneers of *Conceptual art. He has been much concerned with linguistic analysis of concepts of art, his best-known work being *One and Three Chairs* (MOMA, New York, 1965), which presents an actual chair alongside a full-scale photograph of a chair and an enlarged photograph of a dictionary definition of a chair. 'Actual works of art', he said, 'are little more than historical curiosities.'

kouros. Greek word for 'young man', applied to the nude standing male statues typical of the *Archaic period. The plural is *kouroi*.

Kraft, Adam (*c*.1460–*c*.1508). German sculptor, active in Nuremberg. He was a virtuoso stone carver and his most celebrated work, the tabernacle in St Lawrence, Nuremberg (1493–6), is a gigantic stone imitation (*c*.18 m. high) of a subtle piece of goldsmith's work. The richly decorated structure houses a multitude of human figures, animals, amphibia, etc. One of the supporting figures at the base is supposed to be a self-portrait. Other examples of Kraft's work can be seen in the Germanisches Nationalmuseum in Nuremberg.

Krasner, Lee. See POLLOCK.

Kress, Samuel H. (1863–1955). American businessman, art collector, and philanthropist. He became immensely wealthy from his chain of stores and in 1929 he established the Samuel H. Kress Foundation 'to promote the moral, physical and mental welfare of the human race'. His philanthropic work included contributions to medical research and restoring historic buildings in Europe after the Second World War, but he is best known for donations of works of art to American galleries. Above all, his donation of 375 paintings and eighteen sculptures to the newly formed National Gallery of Art in Washington in 1939 (together with subsequent gifts) formed one of the cornerstones of the collection. Kress was a friend of Bernard *Berenson and his main field of interest was Italian *Renaissance painting.

Krieghoff, Cornelius (1815–72). Dutch-born, Canadian painter. He studied in Düsseldorf, went to New York c.1837 and a few years later moved to Canada, where he worked mainly in Montreal and Quebec. His pictures of the Indians, French-Canadian life, and the landscape, done in a colourful, detailed, and often anecdotal style, proved highly popular, and he has been much imitated and forged.

Krøhg, Christian (1852–1925). Norwegian painter. He trained in Germany and worked in Paris 1881–2, and inspired by the ideas of *Realism he took his subjects mainly from ordinary life—often from its sombre or unsavoury aspects. Particularly well known are his paintings of prostitutes, and he wrote a novel, *Albertine* (1886), on the same subject. From 1902 to 1909 he taught in Paris and from 1909 until his death he was Director of the Academy in Oslo. Krohg's vigorous and straightforward style made him one of the leading figures in the movement from *Romanticism to *naturalism that characterized Norwegian art of his period. **Per Krohg** (1889–1965), son of Christian, grew up and was trained in Paris, where he developed in contact with contemporary French artistic trends. *Cubism, in particular, served him as a vehicle for his rich and fantastic imagination. He was best known as a muralist, decorating many public buildings, particularly in Oslo.

Krøyer, Peder Severin (1851–1909). Danish painter, Norwegian by birth. He studied in Paris and was a significant figure in introducing *Impressionism to Denmark. He used a broad technique and was particularly interested in capturing complex effects of light—the fusion of daylight and lamplight, for example. From 1882 he was an influential leader of a colony of Scandinavian artists at the seaside village of Skagen; his work is well represented in the museum there. He ceased painting after he became mentally ill in 1900.

Kubin, Alfred (1877–1959). Austrian graphic artist. In 1910 he became a member of *Kandinsky's circle at Munich and in 1911 joined the *Blaue Reiter. Kubin had a taste for the morbid and fantastic, which he combined with pessimistic social satire and allegory. In his earlier work elements from the macabre etchings of *Goya, the erotic obsessions of Félicien *Rops, and the tainted beauties of *Beardsley coalesced in the murky twilight space of *Redon, whom he met in 1905. The imagery of his work reflects his disturbed and traumatic existence. In 1896 he attempted suicide on his mother's grave and in 1903 he underwent a mental breakdown after the death of his fiancée. His works reveal an obsession with the theme of death and with female sexuality as a symbol of death. Primarily an illustrator, he created a haunted, nightmare, unhealthy world, many of the images in which acquired a historical importance as sources of later *Surrealist imagery. In 1909 he wrote a Kafkaesque novel *Die andere Seite* (The Other Side).

Kunsthistorisches Museum, Vienna. Museum of painting, sculpture, and decorative arts (the title means 'Museum of Art History') based on the acumulation of treasures by members of the Hapsburg dynasty from the 16th century onwards and first opened to the public in 1781. The Gemäldegalerie (picture gallery) has a world-famous collection of paintings, particularly rich in works by the great Venetian masters (*Giorgione, *Titian, *Tintoretto, *Veronese), *Rubens, and *Pieter Bruegel the Elder.

Kunstkammer. German term (literally 'art chamber') used to describe a type of collection of pictures and curios popular with *Renaissance princes. The cabinet pieces in such collections (which were by no means confined to Germany) might include anything from a watch to a fossil. In the 16th- and 17th-cent. inventories the term *Kunstkammerstück* means an object of art, a jewel, or a devotional article of particularly remarkable character or quality ordered specially for display in the *Kunstkammer*.

Kupka, František (**Frank, François**) (1871–1957). Czech painter and graphic artist, active mainly in France, a pioneer of *abstract art. He studied in Prague and Vienna, and settled in Paris in 1895, working first mainly as a satirical draughtsman and book illustrator. From an early age he had been interested in spiritualism and the occult (later in theosophy), and from this grew an interest in the spiritual symbolism of colour. He came to the realization that a picture need not have a 'subject' and this laid the roots of his ambition to create paintings whose linear rhythms and colour schemes would produce effects similar to those of music—in his letters he sometimes signed himself 'colour symphonist'. From 1909 (inspired by high-speed photography) he experimented—in a manner similar to that of the *Futurists—with ways of showing motion, and by 1912 this had led him to complete abstraction in *Amorpha: Fugue in Two Colours* (NG, Prague). This created something of a sensation when exhibited at the *Salon d'Automne in 1912. As with *Delaunay and the *Orphists, to whom his work is closely related, Kupka excelled at this stage in his career in the creation of lyrical colour effects. During the First World War Kupka enlisted in the Czech Legion and after the war he taught at the Prague Academy as Visiting Professor, 1918–20, while continuing to do book illustrations and to work in abstract art. In 1931 he was one of the founder members of the *Abstraction-Création group. His later work was in a more geometrical abstract style. Although Kupka established a considerable reputation, his pioneering role in abstraction was not generally realized before the 1960s.

L

Lachaise, Gaston (1882–1935). French-American sculptor. In 1906 he emigrated to the USA, where he became one of the pioneers of modern sculpture. He settled first in Boston, then in 1912 moved to New York, where he became assistant to Paul *Manship. Lachaise was a consummate craftsman in stone, metal, and wood (his father was a cabinet maker), but his most characteristic works are in bronze. He did a number of portrait busts remarkable for their psychological insight, but is best known for his female nudes—monumental and anatomically simplified figures, with voluptuous forms and a sense of fluid rhythmical movement (*Standing Woman*, Whitney Mus., New York, 1912–27). Their smooth modelling links them with the work of *Nadelman, who was also at this time helping to lead American sculpture away from the 19th-cent. academic tradition, but Lachaise's figures are more powerful than those of Nadelman and have an overt sexuality that has caused them to be compared with the nudes of *Renoir.

Laer, Pieter van (c.1592–1642). Dutch painter, active for much of his career (c.1625–39) in Rome. There he was nicknamed 'Il Bamboccio' (which may be translated as 'Little clumsy one') on account of his deformed body. His self-portrait in the Pallavicini Gallery in Rome suggests that he bore his handicap bravely and without bitterness, and he was one of the leaders of the *Schildersbent, a fraternal organization set up by the Netherlandish artists in Rome to protect their interests. Van Laer specialized in scenes of street life, and inspired numerous followers (mainly other Northern artists, but also Italians such as *Cerquozzi) who were known as the 'Bamboccianti'. Their pictures are called *bambocciate* (the singular is *bambocciata*—Italian for childishness)· or in French *bambochades*; an English equivalent—bambocciade—exists but is rarely used. In 1639 van Laer returned to his native Haarlem.

La Fosse, Charles de (1636–1716). French painter, one of the pre-eminent decorative artists of Louis XIV's reign. He was a pupil of *Lebrun and his assistant at Versailles, but his style was more strongly affected by his stay in Italy (1658–63), where he absorbed the *Baroque manner of Pietro da *Cortona and was influenced by the colour and warmth of such north Italian artists as *Correggio and *Veronese. In the 1680s he turned more to *Rubens as a source of inspiration. La Fosse was in London working for the first Duke of Montagu on the decoration of Montagu House (formerly on the site of the British Museum) from 1689 to 1692, in which year he returned to Paris to decorate the church of the Invalides. Originally he was commissioned to paint the entire building, but eventually he did only the dome and pendentives (1702–4), in a style that heralds something of the lightness and elegance of the ensuing *Rococo. La Fosse's work was much more free and colourful than that of most of his contemporaries, and Anthony *Blunt described him as 'almost the only 17th-cent. French artist whom *Watteau may have studied with profit'

La Fresnaye, Roger de (1885–1925). French painter. He was a member of the *Section d'Or group, and his work shows an individual response to *Cubism; his paintings were more naturalistic than those of *Braque and *Picasso, but he adopted something of their method of analysing forms into planes. The effect in La Fresnaye's work, however, is more decorative than structural, and his prismatic colours reflect the influence of *Delaunay (*The Conquest of the Air*, MOMA, New York, 1913). His health was ruined during his war service in the army and he never again had the physical energy for sustained work.

Laguerre, Louis (1663–1721). French decorative painter, active for almost all his career in England. After working for a short time under Charles *Lebrun in Paris he came to England in 1683/4, initially collaborating with *Verrio but soon branching out on his own, working mainly in country houses, notably Burghley House, Chatsworth, and Blenheim Palace. He was a better painter than Verrio (although still unexceptional judged by European standards) and was also a more attractive personality, but he never achieved the extravagant worldly success of the Italian. From about 1710 *Thornhill began to succeed him in popularity. Late in his career Laguerre turned increasingly to portraits and history paintings.

La Hyre, Laurent de (1606–56). French painter, active in his native Paris. He painted religious and mythological scenes, portraits, and landscapes and also made engravings. His earlier work was influenced by *Primaticcio and the *Fontainebleau schools, but from c.1638 his style became more Classical, under the influence of *Poussin and then Philippe de *Champaigne. *The Birth of Bacchus* (Hermitage, Leningrad, 1638) is a good example of his work—obviously indebted to Poussin, but showing a certain individuality in the soft and romantic treatment of the landscape that is the most attractive feature of La Hyre's style.

Lairesse, Gerard de (1641–1711). Dutch painter, etcher, and writer on art. Born in Liège, he settled in Amsterdam in 1665, and moved to The Hague in 1684. He was the leading decorative painter in Holland in the second half of the 17th cent., working in an academic *Classical style that inspired his over-enthusiastic contemporaries to call him 'the Dutch *Raphael' and 'the Dutch *Poussin'. In about 1690, however, he went blind and thereafter devoted himself to art theory. His lectures were collected in two books— *Grondlegginge der Teekenkunst* (Foundation of Drawing, 1701) and *Het Groot Schilderboek* (The Great Painting Book, 1707)—which were translated and much reprinted during the 18th cent. Lairesse's writings reveal the same academic approach as his paintings and he somewhat naïvely confessed that he had a special preference for *Rembrandt until he learned 'the infallible rules of art'. Rembrandt had painted a portrait of the young Lairesse in 1665 (Met. Mus., New York), sympathetically showing his disease-disfigured face.

Lam, Wifredo (1902–82). Cuban painter. His father was Chinese and his mother of mixed African, Indian, and European origin, and Lam's career was appropriately cosmopolitan. After studying in Havana, he went to Madrid in 1924, then in 1938 moved to Paris, where he became a friend of *Picasso. He also met André *Breton, whose book *Fata Morgana* he illustrated in 1940, and joined the *Surrealist association. He followed the group to Marseilles and in 1941 sailed for Martinique on the same ship as *Masson, Breton, and the French anthropologist Claude Lévi-Strauss. After his return to Cuba in 1942 he came increasingly under the spell of African and Oceanic sculpture, and following visits to Haiti in 1945 and 1946 he also began incorporating images of Voodoo gods and rites in his work. In 1952 he returned to Paris and from the 1960s also spent much of his time at Albisola Mare, near Genoa. In the 1970s he began making bronze sculpture. Lam's work successfully reconciles the artistic vigour of Latin America with the European avant-garde and with the powerful mystique of African and Oceanic tradition, fusing human, animal, and vegetable elements in menacing semi-abstract images. He won many prestigious prizes and his work is included in many leading collections.

Lamb, Henry (1883–1960). British painter. A member of the *Bloomsbury Group, he is best known for his sensitive portraits of fellow members, done in the restrained *Post-Impressionist style that characterized his work throughout his career (examples in the NPG and Tate, London). Before taking up painting he had studied medicine under parental pressure, and in the First World War he was a medical officer in France, Macedonia, and Palestine (winning the Military Cross) as well as an official war artist. He was an official war artist again from 1940 to 1945.

Lambert, George (1700–65). The leading English landscape painter of his day. He was a pupil of John *Wootton and learned something of the principles of *ideal landscape composition from him but more from studying the work of Gaspard *Dughet. As well as painting handsome works essentially in Dughet's manner, Lambert also did more realistic topographical views, two examples of which

(1733) are in the Tate Gallery. Sir Ellis *Waterhouse has written of him: 'Lambert was the first native painter to apply the rules of art to the English rural scene, and, in this sense, *Wilson followed him.' The figures in Lambert's paintings were done by other artists—sometimes, according to tradition, by *Hogarth. He also collaborated with Samuel *Scott (who painted the shipping) in views of the East India Company's settlements (India Office Library, London, 1732).

Lancret, Nicolas (1690–1743). French painter. He was a fellow student of *Watteau in *Gillot's studio and had considerable success in imitating the style and the themes which Watteau had made popular, though he lacked Watteau's sensitivity and subtlety. Several of his pictures are in the Wallace Collection, London.

Land Art. See EARTHWORK.

Landseer, Sir Edwin (1803–73). English painter, sculptor, and engraver of animal subjects. He was the son of an engraver and writer, **John Landseer** (1769–1852), and was an infant prodigy. His life was one of continuous professional and social success; he was the favourite painter of Queen Victoria (who considered him 'very good looking although rather short') and his friends included Dickens and Thackeray. The qualities in his work that delighted the Victorian public, however, have subsequently caused his reputation to plummet, for although he had great skill in depicting animal anatomy, he tended to humanize his subjects to tell a sentimental story or point a moral. His most familiar works in this vein include *The Old Shepherd's Chief Mourner* (V&A, London, 1837), *Dignity and Impudence* (Tate, London, 1839), and the celebrated *The Monarch of the Glen* (Guinness plc, Edinburgh, 1850). Other paintings by Landseer have been attacked for their cruelty (he made many visits to the Scottish Highlands and frequently painted scenes of deer-hunting). Apart from animal subjects, Landseer also painted portraits and historical scenes. As a sculptor he is best known for the lions at the base of Nelson's Column in Trafalgar Square, London, unveiled in 1867. Landseer's health broke down in the 1860s, and in his last years he suffered from bouts of madness, aggravated by alcohol. His

brother **Thomas** (1798–1880) was an engraver, whose prints played a great part in popularizing Edwin's work. Another brother, **Charles** (1800–79), bequeathed £10,000 to the Royal Academy to found Landseer scholarships.

Lanfranco, Giovanni (1582–1647). Italian painter, who with *Guercino and Pietro da *Cortona ranks as one of the founders of the High *Baroque style of painting. He was born in Parma, where he trained under Agostino *Carracci before going to Rome in 1602 to work under Annibale Carracci in the Palazzo Farnese. After Annibale's death in 1609, he returned for a while to Emilia, but by about 1612 was back in Rome, where he gradually superseded his arch-rival *Domenichino as the leading fresco decorator in the city. His ascendancy was confirmed when he took over from Domenichino the major commission for the decoration of the dome of S. Andrea della Valle; the *Assumption of the Virgin* (1625–7) that Lanfranco painted here is one of the key works of Baroque art and it ended the dominance of Bolognese Classicism in Rome. The heroic figure style derives from the Carracci, but the *illusionistic foreshortening is based on *Correggio's dome paintings in Lanfranco's native Parma, here carried to new extremes. *Bellori compared the way in which Lanfranco handles the multitude of figures to the harmonious blending of voices in a choir, and the dynamic design became a pattern for illusionistic decorators throughout Europe. Between 1633 and 1646 Lanfranco was in Naples, where his work was an inspiration to such Neapolitan masters as Mattia *Preti, Luca *Giordano, and *Solimena. In the S. Gennaro Chapel of the cathedral he painted an even more extravagant dome (1641–3) than his masterpiece in S. Andrea della Valle, and this inspired Pietro da Cortona in the Chiesa Nuova in Rome and *Mignard in the church of the Val-de-Grâce in Paris. He returned to Rome in 1646 and his last (unfinished) work in the apse of S. Carlo ai Catinari exemplifies the airy luminosity of his final style. Lanfranco is much less renowned as an easel painter, but he created some outstanding works in this field also. Particularly remarkable are his *Ecstasy of St Margaret of Cortona* (Pitti, Florence), on which *Bernini may have drawn for his

St Teresa, and *St Mary Magdalen Transported to Heaven* (Museo di Capodimonte, Naples), a bizarre and highly original work in which the rapturous saint is carried by angels above a poetically evoked view of the Roman Campagna.

Lanzi, Luigi (1732–1810). Italian art historian, archaeologist, and philologist. As a pioneer in the systematic study of the art of antiquity he ranks next to *Winckelmann, but he is best known for his history of Italian painting from the 13th cent. until his own time, *Storia pittorica dell' Italia* . . . (1792; 2nd edn., 1795–6; 3rd edn. 1800). Lanzi classified his material by regional schools and based his work on a thorough knowledge of previous writings on the subject and of the paintings themselves (he was keeper of the galleries of Florence from 1773 and also visited churches and collections throughout central and northern Italy in the course of his work). His methodical arrangement and his synthesis of solid research with sensitive analysis of style make his work a landmark in art historical writing, and Rudolf *Wittkower has described it as 'still unequalled for knowledge of the material and breadth of approach'. There have been several English translations and editions (the first in 1828), as well as numerous other Italian editions published after Lanzi's death. Lanzi published scholarly but controversial works on the Etruscan language and also a book on ancient vases (1806) in which he correctly perceived that vases traditionally called Etruscan were in fact Greek in origin.

Laocoön. An antique marble group (Vatican Mus.) representing the Trojan priest Laocoön and his two sons being crushed to death by snakes as a penalty for warning the Trojans against the wooden horse of the Greeks, an incident related by Virgil in the *Aeneid* ii. 264– 95. It is usually dated to the 2nd or 1st cent. BC or the 1st cent. AD, although whether it is an original *Hellenistic piece or a Roman copy is a matter of dispute. *Pliny states that in his time it stood in the palace of the emperor Titus in Rome, records that it was made by the sculptors Hagesander, Polydorus, and Athenodorus of Rhodes, and describes it as 'a work to be preferred to all that the arts of painting and sculpture have produced'. This praise echoed long after the sculpture had disappeared, and its dramatic rediscovery in a vineyard in Rome in 1506 made an overwhelming impression, particularly on *Michelangelo, who identified it immediately. Its liberating influence for the expression of the emotions continued to be important for *Baroque sculpture and until the 19th cent. it was ranked (with the *Apollo Belvedere* and the *Belvedere Torso*) as one of the greatest works of antiquity. (As early as about 1530 *Titian satirized the adulation it received in a woodcut showing the figures changed to monkeys.) It was given a new aesthetic significance by *Winckelmann, who saw it as a supreme symbol of the moral dignity of the tragic hero and the most complete exemplification of the 'noble simplicity and quiet majesty' which he regarded as the essence of Greek idealistic art and the key to true beauty. In 1766 *Lessing chose *Laokoon* as the title of the book in which he attacked Winckelmann's ideas. The sculpture was one of the prizes taken from Italy by Napoleon and was in Paris 1798–1815. Although no longer considered one of the world's greatest masterpieces, the *Laocoön* has slipped in esteem much less than some once-revered antique statues; it continues to be a work with a powerful hold over the imagination and still finds a place in almost all general histories of art. It has been restored several times since its discovery, and a complete renovation was made in the 1950s, when Laocoön's original right arm was returned to the figure and replaced in its correct position behind his head. In 1957 several groups of marble figures representing events in Homer's *Odyssey* were found in a cave that was once the Emperor Tiberius' summer banqueting hall at Sperlonga near Naples; the names Hagesander, Polydoros, and Athenodoros are inscribed on one of the groups (now in the museum at Sperlonga), which are close in style to the *Laocoön*. There is strong evidence suggesting that the Sperlonga sculptures date from the 1st century AD, so this date is now finding favour among classical archaeologists for the *Laocoön* also.

Largillière (or **Largillierre**), **Nicolas de** (1656–1746). French painter, mainly of portraits. He spent his youth in Antwerp and c.1674–80 worked as assistant to *Lely in London. Returning to Paris in 1682, he soon established his position as a leading portraitist, rivalled only by *Rigaud, his almost exact contemporary. The two men were friends and seldom in direct competition, for Largillière specialized in portraits of the rich middle classes and Rigaud painted the aristocracy. Largillière's long and successful career culminated when he was made Director of the *Academy in 1743 at the age of 87. His output of portraits was prodigious (contemporary sources indicate he painted about 1,500), and he also did religious works (once highly regarded), still lifes, and landscapes. At his best, his paintings are vigorous, forthright, and colourful; at his worst, they are pompous and vacuous.

Larionov, Mikhail (1881–1964). Russian painter and designer, one of the leading figures in the development of modernism in Russia in the period before the First World War. His early work represented a Russian version of *Post-Impressionism, but from 1908, together with his friend, artistic associate and, later, wife *Goncharova, he developed a form of cultivated *primitivism—his style more aggressive than hers—based upon an interest in Russian folk art. In a series of 'Soldier' and 'Prostitute' pictures done in 1908–13 this primitivism was exaggerated into crude distortions and a deliberate flouting of conventional good taste. He organized a series of exhibitions of avant-garde art (the *Knave of Diamonds, *Donkey's Tail, and *Target exhibitions) in 1910–13, and in 1912 he founded *Rayonism. In 1915 he and Goncharova left Russia, moving to Switzerland and then settling in Paris in 1919. From this time he practically abandoned easel painting and concentrated on designing for the Ballets Russes of *Diaghilev.

Larkin, William (d. 1619?). English portrait painter. He emerged from total obscurity in 1952 with the publication of his only documented works—a pair of oval portraits at Charlecote Park, Warwickshire. Subsequently several other portraits in a different vein—full-length featuring elaborate Turkey carpets, dazzling metallic curtains, and poses of a starched magnificence—have been attributed to him, including a breathtaking group at Ranger's House, London. If they are indeed all by Larkin he was the genius of Jacobean painting, but Sir Ellis *Waterhouse considered the Ranger's House portraits to be

the work of 'at least three different hands' and thought that Isaac *Oliver might be one of the artists responsible.

Laroon, Marcellus (1679–1772). English painter, the son of a Franco-Dutch painter of the same name (1653–1701/2) who came to England as a young man and was one of *Kneller's assistants. The younger Laroon was a colourful character who in his long and strenuous life was a musician, singer, professional soldier, and man of pleasure; he drew and painted 'for diversions', to use the words of *Vertue. He painted portraits, *conversation pieces, and *genre scenes, usually fanciful in character. His nearly monochromatic, feathery style added a touch of French daintiness to the stolid English manner and he anticipated *Gainsborough by his lightness of touch. After a long period of almost total obscurity he was rediscovered in the 20th cent.

Larsson, Carl (1853–1919). Swedish painter and graphic artist. Although he painted large-scale murals (the best known are in the Nationalmuseum, Stockholm, 1896), he is associated particularly with intimate water-colours of the idyllic everyday life of his own home in Dalecarlia. They became popular in colour reproductions and had a lasting influence on Swedish furnishing and interior decoration.

Lastman, Pieter (1583–1633). Dutch painter, highly esteemed in his day but now remembered mainly as the most significant of *Rembrandt's teachers. Most of his career was spent in his native Amsterdam, but in about 1603–7 he was in Italy, where *Caravaggio and *Elsheimer made a strong impact on his style. He specialized in religious, historical, and mythological scenes and often chose unusual subjects that proclaimed his status as a learned artist (*The Volscian Women and Children Beseeching Coriolanus not to Attack Rome*, Trinity College, Dublin, 1622). The glossy colours, the animated gestures and facial expressions, and the dramatic lighting of Rembrandt's early works all owe much to Lastman, and his *Balaam and the Ass* (Musée Cognacq-Jay, Paris, 1626), for example, is clearly based on a prototype by his master (private coll., 1622).

La Tour, Georges de (1593–1652). French painter, active at Lunéville in the duchy of Lorraine. He was patronized by the Duke of Lorraine and had a successful career, but his name sank into oblivion after his death and it is only in the 20th cent. that he has been rediscovered and hailed as the most inspired of *Caravaggesque painters. Little is known of his life (although he is known to have been arrogant and unpopular with his neighbours) and it is a matter of dispute whether he gained his knowledge of Caravaggio's style via painters of the Utrecht school such as *Honthorst or by travelling to Italy. Like Honthorst he is particularly associated with nocturnal scenes and the use of a candle as the light source in a painting. La Tour's handling of light is more subtle and sensitive, however, and he is grander in conception and more sombre in mood. In his mature work he smoothed the forms of his figures until they approached geometric simplicity and achieved a feeling of monumental stillness that is considered to represent the spirit of 17th cent. French *Classicism no less than the paintings of Philippe de *Champaigne and *Poussin in their different fields. Only three of La Tour's paintings are dated— *The Payment of Dues* (Museum Lvov, USSR, 1634); *Penitent St Peter* (Cleveland Mus. of Art, 1645); *The Denial of St Peter* (Musée des Beaux-Arts, Nantes, 1650)— and there is much scholarly debate about his chronology. The works associated with the beginning of his career are daylit scenes of such subjects as peasants and card-sharpers; they are very different in spirit from the calm and majestic religious images of his maturity and have become controversial as regards attribution as well as dating. It has been argued (and hotly disputed) that *The Fortune Teller* (Met. Mus., New York) is a modern fake, and although the status of most of the other early works as authentic (and high-quality) 17th-cent. French paintings is not denied, their attribution to La Tour (which rests almost entirely on stylistic evidence) has been questioned. Another problem in La Tour studies is that many of his undeniably authentic compositions exist in more than one version, and the studio replicas (as they appear to be) are sometimes of extremely high quality; the versions of *St Sebastian Tended by St Irene* in the Louvre and the Staatliche Museen, Berlin, for example, are

each extraordinarily beautiful. La Tour's son **Etienne** (1621–92) worked in his father's studio and may have been responsible for some of the replicas. No independent works certainly by him are known, but *The Education of the Virgin* (Frick Coll., New York), signed 'de la Tour', has been attributed to him.

La Tour, Maurice-Quentin de (1704–88). With *Perroneau the most celebrated and the most successful French *pastel portraitist of the 18th cent., active mainly in Paris. His portraits have great vivacity and exploit the resources of the technique to the full. Some are lightly sketched impressions, others elaborate and detailed studies. In both the essence of his art lies in his swift and accurate draughtsmanship; his colour, which is never very deep, and his superb velvet finish are always subordinate. La Tour portrayed many of the most famous men and women of his day and in 1750 he became portraitist to Louis XV, a position he held until he had a nervous breakdown in 1773.

Laurana, Francesco (c.1430–1502?). Italian sculptor, born near Zara in Dalmatia, at that time subject to Venice. In 1453 he is recorded working on decorations to the Triumphal Arch of Alfonso I at Castelnuovo, Naples. He was one of several sculptors who did so and his contribution is uncertain. Thereafter he divided his time between France and Italy, mainly the south of the country, including Sicily, although he also visited Urbino, and was possibly related to the architect Luciano Laurano, who designed the celebrated Ducal Palace there. In France his most important work was the chapel of St Lazare (1475–81) in the church of La Major at Marseilles, described by Anthony *Blunt as 'probably the earliest purely Italian work on French soil'. He is best known, however, for his portrait busts of members, mostly female, of the Neapolitan royal house and their relatives. In these remarkably sensitive works the forms of the face are subtly generalized in a search for basic geometric shapes, and their simple naturalism was sometimes enhanced by heightening the marble with colour, as in the bust of Isabella of Aragon in the Kunsthistorisches Museum in Vienna.

Laurens, Henri (1885–1954). Fench sculptor. His early work shows the influence of *Rodin, but in 1911 he became a friend of *Braque (he later met *Picasso, *Léger, and *Gris) and became one of the first artists to adapt the *Cubist style to sculpture. Much of his work was coloured, but although his output was more influenced than most by the painters with whom he associated, he retained a genuine sculptor's feeling for mass, which became more apparent in his later productions. His other work included stage designs for *Diaghilev and numerous book illustrations.

Lavery, Sir John (1856–1941). British painter. Born in Belfast, he studied at Glasgow and subsequently in Paris, where he was influenced by *Whistler and the *Impressionists. He was a member of the *Glasgow School before settling in London in 1895. Lavery had an immensely successful career as a fashionable portraitist (particularly of women), painting in a dashing and fluid, if rather facile, style.

Lawrence, Sir Thomas (1769–1830). The outstanding English portrait painter of his generation. Lawrence was a child prodigy and was almost entirely self-taught. He was also handsome and charming, and after a resounding early triumph with his portrait of Queen Charlotte (NG, London, 1789) he never looked back in terms of professional and social success. On the death of Reynolds in 1792 he succeeded him as Painter in Ordinary to the King, and on the death of *Hoppner in 1810 he was recognized as the leading portrait painter of the time, and also to some extent as head of the profession of painting in Britain. The high point of his career came in 1818, when he was sent to Europe as the envoy of the Prince Regent (later George IV) to paint the heads of state and military leaders who were involved with the allied victory over Napoleon. As a preliminary gesture he was knighted, and on his return in 1820 he succeeded Benjamin *West as President of the *Royal Academy. The portraits painted on this tour are now in the Waterloo Chamber, Windsor Castle. Lawrence was devoted to the memory and example of Reynolds and in some respects he was the last of the great portrait painters in the 18th-cent. tradition. In others he was a *Romantic, responding to the glamour of the historic years through which he lived. His fluid and lush brushwork won the admiration of French painters when his work was exhibited at the Paris *Salon of 1824 and after *Delacroix visited London in the following year he paid Lawrence the compliment of painting a portrait in his style (*Baron Schwiter*, NG, London). Lawrence's reputation declined after his death, however, and has never revived to its former heights. He was constantly in debt in spite of his success and took on too many commissions, so his work is uneven and sometimes careless (and like Reynolds he was a failure as a history painter), but at his best he has a feeling for paint that few British artists can rival. Lawrence was a man of great taste and made one of the finest collections of Old Master drawings ever assembled, particularly rich in works by *Michelangelo and *Raphael (these are now among the greatest treasures of the Ashmolean Museum in Oxford). He played a part in founding the National Gallery and in securing the *Elgin Marbles for the nation, and was noted for the unselfish help he gave to young artists.

Lawson, Ernest (1873–1939). American painter, the least distinguished member of the *Eight. Unlike the other members of the group he was primarily a landscapist (although he did also paint urban scenes), and his work was essentially *Impressionist in style.

lay figure. An articulated model of the human figure, jointed so that it can be given all kinds of poses. It may be anything from a few inches in height to life-size. Articulated dolls and marionettes were known in antiquity, but the first description of an artist's lay figure is given by *Filarete in his *Treatise on Architecture* (1461–4). Although *Vasari mentions a life-size wooden model made by Fra *Bartolommeo, the early lay figures were mostly small and were called manikins. The 18th-cent. portrait painter used a life-size model, completely jointed and covered with knitted fabric. He could arrange the costumes on it and work on that part of the picture in the absence of the sitter.

Lear, Edward (1812–88). English artist, author, and traveller. Although he is now remembered principally for his nonsense poems and as the popularizer of the limerick, he earned his living mainly through drawing and painting. He began his career as a draughtsman for the Zoological Society, but when the exacting work began to affect his eyesight he turned to topographical painting in the 1830s, initially in water-colour and later in oils. His style is very clear and brightly lit. He travelled widely and published several illustrated accounts of his journeys. In 1871 he settled in San Remo, Italy.

Lebrun, Charles (1619–90). French painter and art theorist, the dominant artist of Louis XIV's reign. After training with *Vouet he went to Rome in 1642 and worked under *Poussin, becoming a convert to the latter's theories of art. He returned to Paris in 1646. From 1661 he became established in the employ of Louis XIV, in 1662 he was raised to the nobility and named *Premier Peintre du roi*, and in 1663 he was made director of the reorganized *Gobelins factory. Also in 1663 he was made director of the reorganized Académie, which he turned into a channel for imposing a codified system of orthodoxy in matters of art (see ACADEMY). His lectures came to be accepted as providing the official standards of artistic correctness and, formulated on the basis of the *Classicism of Poussin, gave authority to the view that every aspect of artistic creation can be reduced to teachable rule and precept. In 1698 his small illustrated treatise *Méthode pour apprendre à dessiner les passions* . . . was posthumously published; in this, again following theories of Poussin, he purported to codify the visual expression of the emotions in painting. Despite the Classicism of his theories, Lebrun's own talents lay rather in the direction of flamboyant and grandiose decorative effects. Among the most outstanding of his works for the king were the Galerie d'Apollon at the *Louvre (1661), and the famous Galerie des Glaces (1679–84) and the Great Staircase (1671–8, destroyed in 1752) at Versailles. His importance in the history of French art is twofold: his contributions to the magnificence of the *Grand Manner of Louis XIV and his influence in laying the basis of academicism. Many of the leading French artists of the next generation trained in his studio. Lebrun was a fine portraitist and an extremely prolific draughtsman.

Leck, Barth (or **Bart**) **van der** (1876–1958). Dutch painter and designer. His early landscape work fell within the ambit of the *Hague School, but he developed a more personal style of simplified and stylized forms. In 1917 he joined the De *Stijl group and began to paint abstract compositions consisting of fragmentary lines and coloured rectangles into which figural scenes had been broken down. They were very similar to the paintings which *Mondrian was producing at this time and for a while the two artists worked closely together. But whereas Mondrian went on to 'pure' abstraction, van der Leck reverted to figural subjects. During the 1920s he became interested in textile design and during the 1930s and 1940s he extended his interests to ceramics and interior decoration. His work can best be seen at the Rijksmuseum Kröller-Müller, Otterlo.

Le Corbusier (Charles-Édouard Jeanneret) (1887–1965). Swiss-born architect, painter, designer, and writer who became a French citizen in 1930. Although chiefly celebrated as one of the greatest and most influential architects of the 20th cent., Le Corbusier also holds a small but distinguished place in the history of modern painting as one of the founders of *Purism. Up to 1929 he painted only still life, but from that time the human figure was occasionally introduced into his compositions. He adopted the pseudonym Le Corbusier in 1920, but continued to sign his paintings 'Jeanneret'. The pseudonym derives from the name of one of his grandparents and is also a pun on his facial resemblance to a raven (French, 'corbeau'). Apart from paintings and architecture, his enormous output included drawings, book illustration, lithographs, tapestry designs, furniture, and numerous books, pamphlets, and articles.

Leduc, Ozias (1864–1955). Canadian painter, active mainly in his native St. Hilaire, Quebec. He painted still lifes and *genre scenes, but is most notable for his church decorations. In 1897 he visited Paris, and his later work was affected by *Symbolist ideas. He became a much respected senior figure in Canadian art.

Leech, John (1817–64). English *caricaturist and illustrator, one of the leading artists of *Punch* from 1841 until his death. He made over 3,000 pictures for *Punch* alone (including 600 cartoons) and was also particularly associated with the sporting novels of R. S. Surtees. His other book illustrations included *The Ingoldsby Legends* by R. H. Barham and Charles Dickens's *Christmas Books*. Dickens said of his pictures that they were 'always the drawings of a gentleman'; he more than any other set the gentlemanly tone for *Punch*.

Le Fauconnier, Henri (1881–1946). French painter. From *c*.1910 he was in close contact with artists of the *Cubist school and exhibited with them in 1911. In about 1914 he moved to a more *Expressionist style, but he still retained structural features derived from Cubism. He passed the war years in the Netherlands, where he laid the basis of a European reputation and exercised considerable influence on the development of northern Expressionism. After his return to Paris in 1920 he gradually abandoned his Expressionist manner for a more restrained and austere style. He is not now generally highly regarded as a painter, but he played an important role in spreading the mannerisms of Cubism.

Léger, Fernand (1881–1955). French painter. From *c*.1909 he was associated with the *Cubists, but his curvilinear and tubular forms (he was for a time called a 'tubist') contrasted with the fragmented forms preferred by *Picasso and *Braque. After having been gassed in the First World War he was discharged in 1917 and formed a friendship with *Le Corbusier and *Ozenfant. During this period of his association with the leaders of *Purism his work exemplified the 'machine aesthetic' which the movement stood for. His paintings were static, with the precise and polished facture of machinery, and he had a fondness for including representations of mechanical parts. During the late 1920s and 1930s he also painted single objects isolated in space and sometimes blown up to gigantic size. He also busied himself with theatrical décors, and with the cinema. His *Ballet mécanique* (1924) was the first film without scenario. During the Second World War he lived in the USA, teaching at Yale University, and at Mills College, California. Acrobats and cyclists were favourite subjects in his paintings of this time. From his return to France in 1945 his painting reflected more prominently his political interest in the working classes. But its static, monumental style remained, with flat, unmodulated colours, heavy black contours, and a continuing concern with the contrast between cylindrical and rectilinear forms. In his later career Léger worked much on large decorative commissions. In 1949 he opened a studio for ceramics and there made his glass mosaic for the University of Caracas (1954). At the same time he was working on the windows and tapestries for the church at Audincourt (1951). Although in his Cubist years Léger started with the concept of art as an autonomous activity, during the First World War his contact with men of different social classes and different walks of life came as a revelation to him. 'I was abruptly thrust into a reality which was both blinding and new', he said. Henceforward he made it his ambition to create an art which should be accessible to all ranks of modern society. His views were best expressed in a lecture delivered in 1923 at the Collège de France: 'The Aesthetics of the Machine: Manufactured Objects, Artisan and Artist.' His influence on the artists of his day was far-reaching and very diversified. There is a Léger museum at Biot in France.

Legros, Alphonse (1837–1911). French-born painter and engraver who settled in England in 1863 (encouraged by *Whistler) and was naturalized in 1881, although he never acquired fluency in English. His chief importance was as an influential teacher at the *Slade School, where he was appointed Professor of Etching in 1876. He was a fine draughtsman but was overly given to sentimentality

Lehmbruck, Wilhelm (1881–1919). German sculptor. His early work was in a fairly conservative academic manner, but when he was living in Paris from 1910 to 1914 he found a much more personal style, influenced by the formal simplifications of *Archipenko, *Brancusi, and *Modigliani, although still essentially in the tradition of *Rodin and *Maillol. It is exemplified in the extremely attenuated forms, angular pose, and melancholic expression of his *Kneeling Woman* (MOMA, New York, 1911). On the outbreak of the First World War he returned to Germany and worked in a hospital, the suffering he witnessed being reflected in the poignancy of his last works. The war brought him to a state of acute depression and he committed suicide in 1919. Lehmbruck often worked in marble, but he was by temperament a modeller rather than a carver, working in clay over a spindly armature, and several of his works were cast in artificial stone to preserve the texture of the clay. With *Barlach he ranks as the outstanding German *Expressionist sculptor. Lehmbruck also did etchings and lithographs, painted, and wrote poetry. There is a museum dedicated to him in his native Duisburg.

Leibl, Wilhelm (1844–1900). German painter, one of the leading exponents of *Realism in his country. His meeting with *Courbet at Munich in 1869 exercised a decisive influence on his art in both style and subject-matter, and he moved to Paris to work with him, although only briefly because of the outbreak of the Franco-Prussian War in 1870. Disgusted with the intrigues of the Munich art world, from 1873 Leibl withdrew to the Bavarian countryside, where he found his favourite models in the simple country folk, as in his best-known work *Three Women in Church* (Kunsthalle, Hamburg, 1878–82). This is in the hard, objective manner of his so-called '*Holbein period'; later his technique became more fluid. Leibl also painted a number of portraits. His work is well represented in the Wallraf-Richartz-Museum in Cologne, his birthplace.

Leighton, Frederic (Baron Leighton) (1830–96). English painter and sculptor, one of the dominant figures of late Victorian art. He travelled widely in Europe as a boy and studied art in Frankfurt, Rome, and Paris. It was not until 1859 that he settled in London, but he had earlier made his name with *Cimabue's Madonna Carried in Procession through the Streets of Florence*, exhibited at the 1855 *Royal Academy exhibition and bought by Queen Victoria. Thereafter he was matched in worldly success perhaps only by *Millais, his almost exact contemporary; he became President of the Royal Academy in 1878, was made a baronet in 1886, and on the day before he died was raised to the peerage, the first English artist to be so honoured. Intelligent, cultured, and of distinguished appearance, he was one of the chief adornments of London society. Leighton's varied output included portraits and book illustrations, but he is best known for his paintings of Classical Greek subjects,

the finest of which are distinguished by magnificently opulent colouring as well as splendid draughtsmanship (*The Garden of the Hesperides*, Lady Lever Art Gal., Port Sunlight, 1892). As a sculptor he is best known for *Athlete Struggling with a Python* (Leighton House, London, 1874–7). The sumptuously decorated house and studio he built in Holland Park Road, Kensington, is now a Leighton museum.

Lely, Sir Peter (1618–80). Painter of Dutch origin who spent almost all his career in England and was naturalized in 1662. His family name was originally van der Faes, and the name Lely is said to have come from a lily carved on the house in The Hague where his father was born. Lely was born at Soest in Westphalia (where his father, a captain of infantry, was stationed) and trained in Haarlem. He came to England in the early 1640s (early biographers say 1641 or 1643), and although he first painted figure compositions in landscapes (*Sleeping Nymphs*, Dulwich College Picture Gallery), he soon turned to the more profitable field of portraiture. Fortune shone on him, for within a few years of his arrival the best portraitists in England disappeared from the scene; van *Dyck and William *Dobson died in 1641 and 1646 respectively, and Cornelius *Johnson returned to Holland in 1643. In 1654 he was described as 'the best artist in England'. Lely portrayed Charles I and his children, Oliver Cromwell and his son Richard, and other leading figures of the Interregnum, but he is associated chiefly with the Restoration court of Charles II. He was made Principal Painter to the King in 1661 and was able to enjoy a lavish lifestyle, described in Samuel Pepys's *Diary*. With the aid of a team of assistants he maintained an enormous output, and his fleshy, sleepy beauties clad in exquisite silks and his bewigged courtiers have created the popular image of Restoration England. Van Dyck was the strongest influence on his style, but Lely was more earthy and less refined. Much of his work is repetitive (it is sometimes hard to tell sitters apart), but he was a fluent and lively colourist and had a gift for impressive composition. He completely dominated portraiture in his time, and the tradition of the society portrait which he consolidated, developed by *Kneller, *Jervas, and *Hudson, endured for almost a century until it was challenged by *Hogarth. He amassed one of the finest collections of Old Master drawings, which was sold after his death.

Lemoyne. Family of French sculptors. **Jean-Louis Lemoyne** (1665–1755) was a pupil of *Coysevox and is remembered mainly for portrait busts in his master's manner. His brother **Jean-Baptiste the Elder** (1679–1731) was a figure and portrait sculptor of little distinction. Jean-Louis's son, **Jean-Baptiste the Younger** (1704–78), was the outstanding member of the family, becoming official sculptor to Louis XV. He did much large-scale work at Versailles and elsewhere, but is renowned particularly for the vivacity of his portraits. Among his pupils were *Falconet, *Houdon, and *Pigalle.

Lemoyne (or **Lemoine**), **Françoise** (1688–1737). French painter. He was one of the leading decorative artists of the day, continuing the grand tradition of *Lebrun but adapting it to the lighter taste of the court of Louis XV, to whom he became official painter in 1736. Much of his work can be seen at Versailles, notably in the Salon d'Hercule. He was a man of wide pictorial culture, learning from *Rubens in his use of colour and from Bolognese painters (see CARRACCI) in his clarity and grace of drawing. The easy fluency of his style belies his disturbed personality; he committed suicide a few hours after completing *Time Revealing Truth* (Wallace Coll., London, 1737).

Le Nain, Antoine (d. 1648), **Louis** (d. 1648), and **Mathieu** (1607–77). French painters, brothers, who were born at Laon but had all moved to Paris by 1630. The traditional birth-dates for Antoine and Louis are 1588 and 1593 respectively, but it is now thought likely that they were born shortly before and shortly after 1600, so that all three brothers were of much the same generation. Mathieu was made painter to the city of Paris in 1633, and all three were foundation members of the *Academy in 1648. Apart from this, little is known of their careers and the assigning of works to one or the other of them is fraught with difficulty and controversy, for such paintings as are signed bear only their surname, and of those that are dated none is later than 1648, when all were still alive. The finest and most original works associated with the brothers—powerful and dignified *genre scenes of peasants—are conventionally given to Louis; Antoine is credited with a group of small-scale and richly coloured family scenes, mainly on copper; and in a third group, attributed to Mathieu, are paintings of a more *eclectic style, chiefly portraits and group portraits in a manner suggesting influence from Holland. The brothers are also said to have collaborated on religious works. Examples of all these types are in the Louvre. In 1978–9 a major exhibition in Paris brought together most of the pictures associated with the brothers, but it raised as many problems as it solved. It also, however, confirmed the stature of 'Louis', whose sympathetic and unaffected peasant scenes are the main reason why the Le Nains have attracted so much attention. It has recently been proposed that the traditional description of the figures in these paintings as 'peasants' is a misnomer (they are said to be too well dressed for that) and that in fact they represent members of the bourgeoisie.

Lenbach, Franz von (1836–1904). German painter active in Munich and elsewhere. He painted various subjects, but is remembered as the most successful German portraitist of his day. His rich Venetian technique (he had been employed as a copyist of Old Masters in Italy) combined with his solid, respectful characterization appealed greatly to the prosperous ruling classes of Germany. He painted some eighty portraits of Bismarck, whom he first met in 1878 and with whom he had a reserved friendship. Lenbach was a dominant figure in Munich's artistic life in the late 19th cent. His splendid house there, which he designed himself, is now a museum.

Leochares. Greek sculptor active in the mid 4th cent. BC. He worked for Philip of Macedon and his son Alexander the Great and is recorded in several ancient sources, but is an elusive figure. In about 350 BC he worked with *Scopas and two other sculptors on the friezes of the celebrated Mausoleum of Halicarnassus, but it is not possible confidently to assign any of the surviving portions (BM, London) to him. On rather tenuous evidence, the original of the *Apollo Belvedere* is sometimes attributed to Leochares, and a seated marble figure of the goddess Demeter in the British

Museum (the *Demeter of Cnidus*) has been proposed as a work from his own hand. It is considered one of the finest Greek sculptures to survive from the fourth century.

Leonardo da Vinci (1452–1519). Florentine artist, scientist, and thinker, the most versatile genius of the Italian *Renaissance. Leonardo was born in or near the small town of Vinci in the Tuscan countryside. His father Piero was a Florentine notary and Leonardo was his illegitimate son by a peasant girl, Caterina. In 1472 he was enrolled as a painter in the fraternity of St Luke in Florence. Almost certainly, on traditional and stylistic evidence, he was the pupil of *Verrocchio, and *Vasari attributed to him one of the angels in Verrocchio's *Baptism of Christ (c.*1472), now in the Uffizi. The head of the angel on the left of the picture does indeed far surpass its companion in spirituality and beauty of technique, and gives the first demonstration of that combined languor and intensity which is the predominant mood of much of Leonardo's work. Verrocchio is said to have been so impressed that he gave up painting, and it is possible that he was content to entrust the painting side of his business to Leonardo, who was still living in his master's house in 1476. Leonardo stayed in Florence until 1481 or 1482, when he moved to Milan. Several paintings are reasonably attributed to this early Florentine period, notably an exquisite *Annunciation* in the Uffizi, and a portrait of Ginevra de Benci (NG, Washington), probably painted to mark her wedding in 1474, as well as the large altarpiece of *The Adoration of the Magi* (Uffizi, Florence), commissioned in 1481 by the monks of S. Donata a Scopeto and left unfinished when Leonardo moved to Milan. This painting and the numerous preparatory drawings for it show the astonishing fecundity of Leonardo's mind. The range of gesture and expression was unprecedented, and features such as the contrasting figures of wise old sage and beautiful youth who stand at either side of the painting, and the rearing horses in the background, became permanent obsessions in his work.

Leonardo lived in Milan until 1499 (when the French invaded), working mainly at the court of Duke Ludovico *Sforza (Il Moro). He is said to have been recommended primarily as a musician, and in a letter to the duke listing his accomplishments he gives some idea of his versatility, writing of himself first and foremost as a designer of instruments of war and adding his attainments as an artist almost as an afterthought. From then on schemes of applied science and investigations of all kinds into the natural world occupied much of his time and filled his notebooks. He never properly formulated his researches, and when he put theories into practice, whether methods of painting or diversions of rivers, the results were generally faulty. It was the quest which absorbed him, and there was never the dedication to his art that characterizes many great masters. Although he surpassed all of his contemporaries in the sheer beauty of his technique as a painter, this 'mechanical' aspect of his work was much less appealing to him than solving problems of composition and characterization in his drawings (incomparably the finest collection of which is at Windsor Castle). His dilatoriness infuriated his paymasters and although his *œuvre* as a painter is small, he left a high proportion of his pictures unfinished. This stress on the intellectual aspects of painting was one of the most momentous features of Leonardo's career, for he was largely responsible for establishing the idea of the artist as a creative thinker, not simply a skilled craftsman (see LIBERAL ARTS). Leonardo's main artistic undertakings in Milan were a project for a huge equestrian statue to Ludovico Sforza's father, now known only in preliminary drawings, and the wall-painting of the *Last Supper* (c.1495–7) in the refectory of Sta Maria delle Grazie. The *fresco method of mural painting was not flexible or subtle enough for the slow-working Leonardo, so he adopted an experimental technique that quickly caused the picture to deteriorate disastrously. It has been many times restored, but although it is only a shadow of Leonardo's original creation it still retains some of the immense authority that has made it, for almost five centuries, the most revered painting in the world. Leonardo's other works in Milan included portraits, notably the marvellous picture of Duke Ludovico's mistress Cecilia Gallerani known as the *Lady with an Ermine* (Czartoryski Gal., Cracow) and an altarpiece of the *Virgin of the Rocks*, which exists in two problematically related versions, the earlier

(Louvre, Paris) possibly painted when Leonardo was still in Florence, the later (NG, London) still being worked on in 1508. There may have been some studio assistance in the London version, but the finest passages, notably the heads of the Virgin and the angel, with their exquisitely curled hair and heavy-lidded eyes, can be by no one but Leonardo himself. The larger, bolder forms of the London picture show Leonardo's move towards the more monumental style of the High Renaissance, of which he was the main creator.

Between 1500, when he returned for a time to Florence, and 1516, when he left Italy for France, Leonardo's life was unsettled. In 1502–3 he worked as a military engineer for Cesare Borgia, in 1506–13 he was based again in Milan, and in 1513 he moved to Rome, but the artistic activity of his later years was chiefly centred in Florence in the years 1500–6. From this time dates his portrait of *Mona Lisa* (Louvre) and the wall painting of the *Battle of Anghiari* in the Palazzo Vecchio, Florence, where he worked in rivalry with *Michelangelo. The battle piece is destroyed, but is preserved in copies; fittingly, the most famous copy is a drawing by *Rubens (Louvre), for Leonardo's painting anticipated the dynamism of the *Baroque and influenced battle painters up to the 19th cent. In Florence also Leonardo worked out variations on a theme that fascinated him at this time and presented a great challenge to his skill in composing closely knit groups of figures. This was *The Virgin and Child with St Anne*, known today mainly through a painting in the Louvre and the incomparably beautiful *cartoon (which includes also the infant John the Baptist) in the National Gallery, London. The exact dates of these two famous works are controversial.

In 1516 Leonardo accepted an invitation from Francis I to move to France, and he died at Cloux, near Amboise, in 1519. He did little artistic work in the last decade of his life, the last paintings from his hand generally being accepted as two pictures of *St John the Baptist* (one later converted into a *Bacchus*), both in the Louvre (c.1515). They show the enigmatic smile, the dense shadow, the pointing finger, and the thick curling hair that rapidly became clichés in the work of his followers. In painting Leonardo had an enormous influence. His heroic figures and beautifully balanced compositions (particularly his use of pyramidical grouping) were the basis of the High Renaissance style, influencing particularly his two greatest contemporaries, Michelangelo and *Raphael, and his subtle modelling through light and shade (see SFUMATO) showed the potentialities of the *oil medium, which he was one of the first Italians to exploit. *Giorgione and *Correggio were among those most deeply influenced by this aspect of Leonardo's work. His writings on painting were influential too; they were first published from his scattered notes as the *Treatise On Painting* (in Italian and French) in 1651, but were well known before then. In sculpture and architecture no work that is indisputably by Leonardo survives, but his expertise and ideas were important in both fields. Leonardo is one of the very few artists whose reputation has from his own times onward constantly remained at the highest level, even though his output of completed works was tiny—a reflection of his extraordinary force of intellect and his virtually single-handed creation of the idea of the artist as genius.

Leoni, Leone (1509–90). Italian *Mannerist sculptor who worked in many parts of Italy and in the service of the emperor Charles V in Germany and the Netherlands. He was trained as a goldsmith, but none of his works in that medium survives. From 1538 to 1540 he was coin engraver to Pope Paul III (Alessandro *Farnese), but he was then condemned to the galleys for conspiring to murder the papal jeweller. He was released in 1541 and for most of the rest of his life was master of the imperial mint in Milan. His sculpture consists mainly of portraits—both medals and busts. Many of his works for the emperor were sent to Spain, where his son **Pompeo** (c.1533–1608), who moved there in about 1556, gave them the finishing touches. The most important was a group of twenty-seven bronze statues (finished 1582) for the high altar of the *Escorial. Pompeo executed several tombs in Spain on his own account, and was, like his father, a goldsmith and medallist. Again like his father, he had a dangerous brush with authority, being briefly imprisoned by the Inquisition.

Le Parc, Julio (1928–). Argentinian experimental artist, regarded as one of the leading exponents of *Kinetic art. In 1958 he went to Paris and after working for a while with Victor *Vasarely became a founder member of the *Groupe de Recherche d'Art Visuel (GRAV) in 1959. Le Parc professes to adopt a rational and objective attitude to his work, repudiating the ideas of artistic creativity or symbolic meaning and working according to scientific principles. He often uses the idea of spectator participation, but tries to eliminate subjective response on the part of the spectator, looking for an objective and predictable perceptual response to a planned stimulus. Much of his work consists of devices for disorienting the spectator (distorting glasses and so on), but he has also made some outstanding *mobiles, using perspex or metallic elements to scatter or reflect the light.

Lepicié, Nicolas-Bernard (1735–84). French painter of portraits, domestic *genre scenes, and historical subjects. His best works, although not entirely free from the sentimentality of the period, have something of the tranquil beauty associated with *Chardin (*The Reading Lesson*, Wallace Coll., London). His father **François-Bernard** (1698–1755) was an engraver and writer on art.

Leslie, Charles Robert (1794–1859). British painter and writer on art, of American parentage. In his day he was well known for his paintings of literary themes, but he is now remembered mainly as a writer, above all for his *Memoirs of the Life of John Constable* (1843), which is regarded as one of the classics of artistic biography (Constable was a close friend).

Lessing, Gotthold Ephraim (1729–81). German writer. He was a man of formidable intellect and great versatility who played a leading role in the development of German theatre, but he is known mainly for his treatise on aesthetics, *Laokoon* (1766). This takes as its starting-point a passage in *Winckelmann's writings in which he discussed the celebrated antique statue *Laocoön. Winckelmann contrasted what he considered the stoical beauty of Laocoon in the sculpture with the loud cries that Virgil causes him to utter in the *Aeneid*, interpreting the alleged difference (to most people he appears to be howling with pain in the sculpture too) as a superior serenity in Greek art. Lessing dissented, and argued that each art achieves its effects by the means appropriate to its medium and that the artist must exploit the potentialities of his medium to the full, whilst respecting its limitations. The impact of Lessing's book stemmed from its emphasis on the aesthetic functions of art in contrast with the traditional view of art as the handmaid of religion and philosophy, whose duty was primarily to instruct.

Lessing, Karl Friedrich (1808–80). German painter, one of the leaders of the Düsseldorf School of history painting. He combined earnestly melodramatic poses with studiously correct historical detail, so that many of his pictures look like scenes from plays or pageants. His best-known works have subjects taken from the Hussite Rebellion of the 15th cent. (*Hussite Prayer*, Staatliche Museen, Berlin, 1836) and were identified with the spirit of rebellion against the political and religious repression of the day. Lessing also painted landscapes. In 1858 he became Director of the gallery at Karlsruhe, and settled there permanently.

Le Sueur, Eustache (1616–55). French painter, active throughout his career in his native Paris. He was a pupil of *Vouet, whose influence is strong on his early works (*The Presentation of the Virgin*, Hermitage, Leningrad, c.1640). In the 1640s he was profoundly affected by the paintings of *Poussin (who visited Paris 1640–2) and his work became more *Classical. He lacked Poussin's heroic grandeur, but he added a tenderness of his own to the master's manner, as in his most important works, a series of paintings (begun 1648), illustrating the life of St Bruno, done for the Charterhouse of Paris and now in the Louvre. In the last years of his life his chief model became *Raphael, whom he imitated in an uninspired manner. Le Sueur was a founder member of the French *Academy in 1648. In his own day and throughout the 18th cent. he was almost as well thought of as Poussin, but he now has the status of an attractive but minor master.

Le Sueur, Hubert (c.1580–after 1658). French sculptor, active chiefly in England, where he is first recorded in 1626. He worked much for Charles I, his most famous work being the equestrian statue of the king (1633) at Charing Cross in London. This shows the skill as a bronze caster for which he was renowned, but also his smooth, lifeless surfaces, which give his works, in the words of Margaret Whinney (*Sculpture in Britain 1530 to 1830*, 1964), 'a curious, inflated appearance, as if they were not modelled, but blown up from within'. He was remarkably conceited, on occasions signing himself '*Praxiteles Le Sueur', but Charles recognized him as a second-rate artist and sometimes reduced the prices he asked for his work. By 1643 Le Sueur was back in Paris. His main influence in England was in popularizing the bust portrait.

Leutze, Emanuel Gottlieb (1816–68). German-born painter who lived in America from 1825 to 1841 and again from 1859 and is usually considered a member of the American School. He is remembered mainly for *Washington Crossing the Delaware* (Met. Mus., New York, 1851), painted in Düsseldorf, where he spent most of his career, and for another work which similarly appeals more for its patriotic sentiments than for any aesthetic merit—his large mural *Westward the Course of Empire Takes its Way* (1861–2) in the Capitol at Washington. His portraits and rare landscapes are more distinguished, but remain virtually unknown.

Lewis, (Percy) Wyndham (1882–1957). English painter, novelist, and critic, born on a yacht off Nova Scotia of British-American parentage. He came to England as a child, and studied at the *Slade School, 1898–1901, then lived on the Continent for seven years, mostly in Paris, where he was a friend of Augustus *John. In 1909 he returned to England and in the years leading up to the First World War emerged as one of the leading figures in British avant-garde art. He worked for a short while with Roger *Fry at the *Omega Workshops and in 1914 formed the Rebel Art Centre, from which grew *Vorticism, a movement of which he was the chief figure and whose journal *Blast* he edited. From 1911 he developed a semi-abstract style, angular, machine-like, and suggestive of mechanical impersonality. He carried this style into his war pictures as an official war artist (he also served during the war as a bombardier). In 1919 he founded the avant-garde Group X as an attempt to revive Vorticism, but this failed, and from the late 1920s he devoted himself mainly to writing, his books including novels and volumes of criticism and autobiography. He became blind in 1950. The best-known paintings of his later years are his incisive portraits; the rejection of that of T. S. Eliot (Durban Art Gal.) occasioned Augustus John's resignation from the *Royal Academy in 1938. Lewis was the most original and idiosyncratic of the major British artists working through the first decades of the century, and was among the first artists in Europe to produce completely abstract paintings and drawings. He took from both *Cubism and *Futurism features from which he built his personal style, but without accepting either. The Futurists, he wrote, had the vivacity and the quality of life which the Cubists lacked, but they themselves lacked the grandness and the 'great plastic qualities' which Cubism achieved. His own work, he declared, was 'electric with a mastered and vivid vitality'.

Lewitt, Sol (1928–). American sculptor. With Carl *André, Donald *Judd, and Robert *Morris, he is regarded as one of the leading exponents of *Minimal art, his work characteristically involving permutations of simple basic elements. He has also experimented with *Conceptual art.

Leyster, Judith (1609–60). Dutch painter of *genre scenes, portraits, and still life. She was a pupil of Frans *Hals in Haarlem, where she spent most of her career (she also worked in Amsterdam). In 1636 she married Jan Miense *Molenaer, with whom she shared a studio, using the same models and props. Leyster was one of Hals's most talented pupils and her work has sometimes passed as his, an example being the *Lute Player* in the Rijksmuseum, Amsterdam. Her monogram includes a star, a play on 'Ley/ster' (lode star).

Lhote, André (1885–1962). French painter, sculptor, and writer on art. He worked initially as a commercial woodcarver and was largely self-taught as a painter. His early work was *Fauvist in spirit, but from 1911 he adopted the stylistic mannerisms of *Cubism to his very varied range of subjects, including landscapes, still lifes, interiors, mythological scenes, and portraits. Lhote, however, was more important as a teacher and critic of modern art than as a practising artist. He exercised an extensive influence on younger artists both French and foreign through his own academy of art, the Académie Montparnasse, which he opened in 1922, and he founded a South American branch on a visit to Rio de Janeiro in 1952. His writings included treatises on landscape painting (1939) and figure painting (1950).

liberal arts. Term applied to those arts that were traditionally considered primarily as exercises of the mind rather than of practical skill and craftsmanship. The concept of a distinction between 'liberal' (worthy of a free man: Latin *homo liber*) and 'vulgar' arts goes back to Classical antiquity, and survived in one form or another up to the *Renaissance, forming the basis of secular learning in the Middle Ages. In the early Renaissance the lowly position accorded to the visual arts was increasingly contested, providing a theoretical basis for the social struggle which took place to raise them from the status of manual skill to the dignity of a liberal exercise of the spirit. The most formidable champion of the visual arts was *Leonardo, who more than anyone else was responsible for creating the idea of the painter as a creative thinker. By about 1500 painting and sculpture were generally accepted as liberal arts by Italian humanists (significantly so in Baldassare Castiglione's influential *Book of the Courtier* of 1528, which was translated into English in 1561). However, as Anthony *Blunt points out (*Artistic Theory in Italy 1450–1600*), 'As soon as the visual arts became generally accepted as liberal, the protagonists began to quarrel among themselves about which of them was the noblest and most liberal.' The acceptance came later in other parts of Europe.

Lichtenstein, Roy (1923–). American painter, sculptor, and graphic artist. After passing through an *Abstract Expressionist phase he changed to *Pop art and his first one-man exhibition of work in this style at the Leo Castelli Gallery, New York, in 1962 was a sensational success. In common with other Pop artists Lichtenstein adopted the vulgar and debased images of popular commercial art, but he did so in a highly distinctive manner. Taking his inspiration from comic strips, he blew up images to a large scale, reproducing the primary colours and dots of the cheap printing processes (*Whaam!*, Tate, London, 1963). Despite his use of popular kitsch, such paintings show an impressive mastery of composition and colour and he is widely recognized as one of the most eminent artists in his field. In the mid 1960s he turned to adaptations of works of art, which were turned into his comic-strip images, just as he had previously turned comic strips into art. His later work has also included sculpture, mostly in polished brass.

Liebermann, Max (1847–1935). German painter and graphic artist. His importance in his day lay in his openness to foreign influences, overcoming German parochiality. During a visit to France in 1874 he found himself more in sympathy with *Courbet, *Millet, and the *Barbizon School than with *Manet or *Renoir, but after his return to Germany in 1878 came to be considered the leading German *Impressionist painter together with *Corinth and *Slevogt. In 1899 he founded the Berlin *Sezession and became its President. He was unable, however, to keep abreast of developments and a decade later stood as the supporter of that old-fashioned traditionalism against which *Nolde, the members of the *Brücke and other German *Expressionists were at this time in revolt. Nevertheless, his work was declared *degenerate by the Nazis.

Lievens, Jan (1607–74). Dutch painter and graphic artist. He was extremely precocious, and after training in Amsterdam with *Lastman he was practising independently in ·his native Leiden by the time he was 13. From *c*.1625 to 1631/2 he worked in close collaboration with his friend *Rembrandt. They shared the same models (and probably a studio) and even worked together on the same pictures—a *Portrait of a Child* in the Rijksmuseum in Amsterdam, for example, is signed 'Lievens retouched by Rembrandt'. The diplomat and connoisseur Constantin Huygens visited them in 1629 and thought they showed equal promise of greatness. He wrote that Rembrandt surpassed Lievens in vivacity of expression, but that Lievens was superior in 'a certain grandeur of invention and boldness of subjects and forms'. That this was not excessive praise is borne out by Lievens's marvellously melodramatic

Raising of Lazarus (Brighton Museum and Art Gallery, 1631), in which the only parts of Lazarus shown are his arms emerging from the tomb. After the paths of the two young artists separated in 1631/2, however, Lievens did not sustain his early brilliance. From 1635 to 1644 he was in Antwerp, where under the influence of van *Dyck he adopted a more elegant and facile style that brought him renown as a portraitist. In 1644 he returned to the Netherlands, where he remained for the rest of his life and during the last three decades was popular in official circles in Amsterdam and The Hague. Lievens was a talented etcher and also made some woodcuts.

Limburg (or **Limbourg**) **Brothers**. Netherlandish manuscript *illuminators, **Herman**, **Jean (Jannequin)**, and **Paul (Pol)**, all three of whom died in 1416, presumably victims of the plague or other epidemic. Pol was probably the head of the workshop, but it is not possible to distinguish his hand from those of his brothers. They were born in Nijmegen, nephews of Jean *Malouel, and Herman and Jean are first documented in the late 1390s apprenticed to a goldsmith in Paris. In 1402 Jean and Pol were working for Philip the Bold, Duke of Burgundy, and after Philip's death all three Limburgs worked for his brother Jean, Duc de Berry, remaining in his service until their deaths and holding privileged positions at his court, which moved with him around France from one magnificent residence to the next. He was, indeed, one of the most extravagant patrons and collectors in the history of art, and the Limburgs illuminated two manuscripts for his celebrated library: the Belles Heures (Met. Mus., New York, *c*.1408) and the Très Riches Heures (Musée Condé, Chantilly), which was begun *c*.1413 and left unfinished at their deaths (it was completed by the French illuminator Jean Colombe (*c*.1440–93?) about seventy years later). The Très Riches Heures (see BOOK OF HOURS) is by common consent one of the supreme masterpieces of manuscript illumination and the archetype of the *International Gothic style. Its most original and beautiful feature is the series of twelve full-page illustrations of the months (the first time a calendar was so lavishly treated), full of exquisite ornamentation and beautifully observed naturalistic detail. The *miniatures are remarkable, too, for their mastery in rendering space, strongly suggesting that one or more of the brothers had visited Italy, and they occupy an important place in the development of the northern traditions of landscape and *genre painting.

limner. A word for a painter that has been used in different ways according to time and place. In the Middle Ages it was applied to manuscript *illuminators, and from the 16th cent. it was used of painters of *miniature portraits (Nicholas *Hilliard's treatise is called *The Arte of Limning*). In American usage it denotes the anonymous and often itinerant painters, particularly portraitists, of the 17th and 18th cents. Sometimes limners, in this last sense, are given invented names in the same manner in which the term 'Master of' is used in European painting—the Schuyler Limner, named after one of the families he portrayed, is an example.

Lindner, Richard (1901–78). German-born painter who became an American citizen in 1948. He fled from the Nazi regime in 1933 and settled in Paris, then moved to the USA in 1941. At first he worked as a magazine and book illustrator (in Germany he had been art director of a publishing firm), and he began to paint seriously in the early 1950s. His most characteristic works take their imagery from the vulgar and sordid aspects of New York life, often with overtly erotic symbolism, and are painted with harsh colours and hard outlines. The effects he created owed something to *Expressionist exaggeration, *Surrealist fantasy, and *Cubist manipulations of form, but his style is vivid and distinctive and anticipates aspects of *Pop art.

Lindsay. Family of Australian artists. The members included five of the children of Dr R. C. Lindsay of Creswick, Victoria: **Percy Lindsay** (1870–1952), painter and graphic artist; **Sir Lionel Lindsay** (1874–1961), art critic, water-colour painter, and graphic artist in pen, etching, and woodcut, who did much to arouse an interest in the collection of original prints in Australia; **Norman Lindsay** (1879–1969), graphic artist, painter, critic, and novelist; **Ruby Lindsay** (1887–1919), graphic artist; and **Sir Daryl Lindsay** (1889–1976), painter and Director of the National Gallery of Victoria (1942–56). Norman's son **Raymond** (1904–60) and Daryl's wife **Joan** (1896–1984) were also painters. For over half a century this family through one or the other of its members played a leading role in Australian art.

line engraving. Term applied to a method of making prints (and the print so made) in which the design is cut directly into the surface of a metal (usually copper) plate. In normal parlance the term *engraving usually refers to line engraving, but strictly the former is a generic term, covering a variety of processes. The line engraver cuts the design into a smooth metal (usually copper) plate with a tool called a *burin. Characteristically, line engravings have a quality of metallic hardness and austere precision, compared with the easy, spontaneous drawing of the *etcher or *lithographer. The essential nature of the medium is linear, though shading and tone may be suggested by parallel strokes, cross-*hatching, or textures compounded of various dots and flicks. Line engraving seems to have originated towards the middle of the 15th cent. in the workshops of goldsmiths, arising independently in Italy (see NIELLO) and Germany, though perhaps slightly earlier in the latter country. Martin *Schongauer, who died in 1491, was the first major artist to work mainly as an engraver, and the medium had its finest flowering in the early 16th cent. in the work of Albrecht *Dürer and *Lucas van Leyden. Active at the same time was Marcantonio *Raimondi, who was the great pioneer in the use of engraving as a means of reproducing the works of other artists. This soon became the primary function of line engraving, and until the invention of photomechanical methods in the 19th cent. it was the principal method of reproductive printing. In the 20th cent., however, line engraving has been revived as a means of original expression, the most important impetus coming from S. W. *Hayter.

Linnell, John (1792–1882). English painter. He made his reputation and his fortune as a fashionable portraitist and *miniaturist, but was devoted to landscape painting. His wealth enabled him to patronize *Blake, and some of his early landscapes have something of the visionary quality of the master and of Samuel *Palmer, who married Linnell's daughter. In 1852 he settled in Redhill and most of his prolific output thereafter was devoted to idyllic scenes in Surrey, done in a lush and more conventional pastoral idiom than his early work. Such works were highly popular and he became immensely wealthy. In spite of his success he was denied membership of the *Royal Academy, this being a reflection of his unpopularity with his fellow-artists (his admiration for Blake was the saving grace in an otherwise unsavoury character).

linocut. A technique of making a print from a piece of thick linoleum. It was introduced at the beginning of the 20th cent., but is essentially a development of the *woodcut, although linocuts are much simpler to make because the soft material is comparatively easy to work. Linocutting has been much used for teaching art in schools, and this has caused it to be somewhat lightly regarded, but artists of the stature of *Matisse and *Picasso have made memorable use of it. For colour prints it has obvious advantages, since a number of large blocks may be used without undue expense, while the fact that the surface can be cut rapidly and spontaneously means that the process is highly suitable for big prints boldly conceived.

linseed oil. Oil from the seeds of flax, the commonest *medium in *oil painting. Most modern painters have used raw linseed oil diluted with *turpentine as a medium, but the Old Masters generally preferred polymerized oil, known as 'stand oil', which was prepared by heating linseed oil or drying it in the sun. Linseed oil tends to turn yellow with age, but has less tendency to crack than *walnut or *poppy oil.

Liotard, Jean-Etienne (1702–89). Swiss *pastel painter and engraver. He travelled widely in Europe and also spent 4 years in Constantinople (1738–42), after which he adopted Turkish dress and beard, his eccentric appearance being familiar from his numerous self-portraits. His delicate and polished style brought him fashionable success in Paris, the Netherlands, and England, which he twice visited (1733–5 and 1772–4). The best collection of his work is in the Musée d'Art et d'Histoire in Geneva, his native city.

Lipchitz, Jacques (1891–1973). Lithuanian-born sculptor who worked mainly in France and then in the USA. After studying engineering in Lithuania he moved to Paris in 1909. In about 1912 he became intimate with the circle of avant-garde artists including *Matisse, *Modigliani, and *Picasso, and from 1914 he became one of the first sculptors to apply the principles of *Cubism in three dimensions (*Man with Guitar*, MOMA, New York, 1916). During the 1920s his style changed, as he became preoccupied with open forms and the interpenetration of solids and voids. He took French nationality in 1925 but settled in the USA in 1941, by this time an internationally renowned figure. In the USA he returned to greater solidity of form, but with a desire for greater spirituality. At times the tortured, bloated forms of his late work, as in *Prometheus Strangling the Vulture* (Walker Art Center, Minneapolis, 1944–53), look rather like inflated shrubbery.

Lippi, Filippino (*c*.1457–1504). Florentine painter, the son and pupil of Filippo *Lippi, who died when the boy was about 12. He also studied with *Botticelli and learned much from his expressive use of line, but Filippino's style, although sensitive and poetic, is more robust than his master's. His first major commission (1484) was the completion of *Masaccio's fresco cycle in the Brancacci Chapel of Sta Maria del Carmine, a task he carried out with such skill and tact that it is sometimes difficult to tell where his work begins and that of more than half a century earlier ends. Filippino painted several other frescos, the most important of which are cycles on the life of St Thomas Aquinas (1488–93) in the Caraffa Chapel, Sta Maria sopra Minerva, Rome, and the lives of SS. Philip and John (1495–1502) in the Strozzi Chapel, Sta Maria Novella, Florence. In these he strove for picturesque, dramatic and even bizarre effects that reveal him as one of the most inventive of late *quattrocento painters. Filippino also painted many altarpieces, the most famous of which is *The Vision of St Bernard* (Badia, Florence, *c*.1480), an exquisitely tender work, full of beautiful detail. Although he is now somewhat

overshadowed by Botticelli, Filippino enjoyed a great reputation in his lifetime, being described by Lorenzo de' *Medici as 'superior to *Apelles'.

Lippi, Fra Filippo (*c*.1406–69). Florentine painter. He was brought up as an unwanted child in the Carmelite friary of the Carmine, where he took his vows in 1421. Unlike the Dominican Fra *Angelico, however, Lippi was a reluctant friar and had a scandalous love affair with a nun, Lucrezia Buti, who bore his son Filippino and a daughter Alessandra. The couple were released from their vows and allowed to marry, but Lippi still signed himself 'Frater Philippus'. His biography (romantically embroidered to include capture by pirates) is one of the most colourful in *Vasari's *Lives* and has given rise to the picture of a worldly *Renaissance artist, rebelling against the discipline of the Church—an image reflected in Robert Browning's poem about Lippi ('Fra Lippo Lippi' in *Men and Women*, 1855). He must certainly have had a more eventful life than most, but there is little documentary evidence of his character and personality. Vasari writes that Lippi was inspired to become a painter by watching *Masaccio at work in the Carmine church, and his early work, notably the *Tarquinia Madonna* (Galleria Nazionale, Rome, 1437) is certainly overwhelmingly influenced by him. From about 1440, however, his style changed direction, becoming more linear and preoccupied with decorative motifs—thin, fluttering draperies, brocades, etc. Lippi is associated particularly with paintings of the Virgin and Child, which are sometimes in the form of *tondi, a format he was among the first to use—a beautiful example, showing the wistful delicacy and exquisite pale lighting that characterizes his best work, is in the Pitti, Florence. Another formal innovation with which Lippi is associated is the *sacra conversazione—his *Barbadori Altarpiece* (Louvre, Paris, begun 1437) is sometimes claimed as the earliest example of the type. As a fresco painter Lippi's finest achievement is his cycle on the lives of SS. Stephen and John the Baptist (1452–66) in Prato Cathedral. Lippi was highly regarded in his day (he was patronized by the *Medici, who came to his aid when he was imprisoned and tortured for alleged fraud) and his influence is seen in the work of numerous artists, most notably *Botticelli, who was probably his pupil. Four centuries later he was one of the major sources for the second wave of *Pre-Raphaelitism.

Liss (or **Lys**), Johann (*c*.1597–1631). German painter, active mainly in Italy. He trained in the Netherlands (probably in Amsterdam, possibly with *Goltzius) and visited Paris before moving to Italy by 1621, when he is documented in Venice, the main centre of his activity. In 1622 he visited Rome, and *Caravaggesque influence is clearly seen in such vivid and strongly lit works as *Judith and Holofernes* (NG, London). His work enjoyed considerable popularity in Venice (where there was a dearth of talented native painters at this time) and his *Vision of St Jerome* in the church of S. Nicolo da Tolentino was much copied. It shows the remarkably free brushwork and brilliant use of high-keyed colour that were the salient features of his style and which were influential on Venetian painting when its glory revived in the 18th cent. It was formerly assumed that Liss, who ranks second only to *Elsheimer as the most brilliant German painter of the 17th cent., perished in the Venetian plague of 1629–30, but it is now known that he died in Verona in 1631.

Lissitzky, El (Eliezer Markowich) (1890–1941). Russian painter, designer, and graphic artist. After studying engineering at Darmstadt and architecture in Moscow he worked in an architect's office and collaborated with *Chagall on the illustration of Jewish books. In 1918 Chagall became head of the art school at Vitebsk and in the following year he appointed Lissitzky as Professor of Architecture and Graphic Art. One of his colleagues at Vitebsk was *Malevich, whose advocacy of the use of pure geometric form greatly influenced Lissitzky, notably in his series of abstract paintings to which he gave the nonsense collective name 'Proun' and which he referred to as 'the interchange station between painting and architecture'. They do indeed look like plans for three-dimensional constructions, and at the same time Lissitzky made ambitious architectonic designs that were never realized. In 1921, after a brief period as professor at the state art school in Moscow, he went to Berlin, where he arranged and designed the important exhibition of abstract art at

the Van Diemen Gallery (later shown also in Amsterdam) that first comprehensively presented the modern movement in Russia to the West. While in Berlin he made contact with van *Doesburg and members of De *Stijl and with *Moholy-Nagy, who spread Lissitzky's ideas through his teaching at the *Bauhaus. In 1923 he went with *Gabo to a Bauhaus exhibition at Weimar and there met *Gropius. From 1923 to 1925 he was in Switzerland, and from 1925 to 1928 he lived in Hanover. He returned to Russia in 1928 and devoted himself mainly to typography and industrial design. His work included several propaganda and trade exhibitions, notably the Soviet Pavilion of the 1939 World's Fair in New York, and his dynamic techniques of *photomontage, printing, and lighting had wide influence. For a considerable time Lissitzky was the best known of the Russian abstract artists in the West. In his mature work he achieved a fusion between the *Suprematism of Malevich (often using his diagonal axis), the *Constructivism of *Tatlin and *Rodchenko, and features of the Dutch *Neo-Plasticism of *Mondrian.

lithography. A method of printing from a design drawn directly onto a slab of stone or other suitable material. The most recent of the major graphic techniques, it was invented in 1798 by Aloys *Senefelder. The process is based on the antipathy of grease and water, the design being drawn with a greasy crayon. After this has been chemically fixed, the stone is wetted and then rolled with oily ink, which adheres only to the greasy drawing, the rest of the surface, being damp, repelling the ink. Prints can then be taken in a press. Many distinguished artists of the 19th and 20th cents. have worked in the lithographic technique (beginning with *Goya in his old age), attracted by the freedom it allows (the artist need do nothing more than draw on the stone—the printer can handle all the technicalities), and *Daumier was the first great figure to execute the major part of his life's work in lithography.

Lochner, Stephan (active 1442–51). German painter, the leading master of his time in Cologne, where he worked from 1442 until his death. His early life is obscure, but stylistic evidence, particularly his eye for naturalistic detail, suggests he trained in the Netherlands. The most important of his surviving works is *The Adoration of the Magi*, painted for Cologne's town hall (where in 1520 *Dürer saw it 'with wonder and astonishment'), but now in the city's cathedral. It shows the exquisite colouring and delicate sentiment that was characteristic of his work.

Loggan, David (1633–92). British engraver and draughtsman. He is best known for his *Oxonia Illustrata*, 1675, and *Cantabrigia Illustrata*, 1688, topographical studies of the Universities, but he also made sensitive portrait drawings.

Lohse, Richard (1902–). Swiss painter and graphic artist. Like *Bill, he is a leading representative of *Concrete art in Switzerland, but his work, although mathematically based, is particularly noted for its beauty and refinement of colour, and has a certain resemblance to *Op art of the kind associated with Bridget *Riley.

Lomazzo, Giovanni Paolo (1538–1600). Milanese painter and writer. At the age of 33 he went blind and took to writing on the theory of art, publishing two treatises: *Trattato dell'Arte de la Pittura, Scoltura, et Architettura* (1584) and *Idea del Tempio della Pittura* (1590). The *Trattato* was the largest and most comprehensive treatise on art published in the 16th cent. and has been described as 'the Bible of *Mannerism'. It is divided into seven books, whose themes are Proportion, Motion, Colour, Light, *Perspective, Practice, and History, the last containing a complete prescriptive guide to Christian and Classical *iconography. Throughout the book runs the assumption that the arts can be taught by detailed precepts. It was widely influential and was translated into English (as *A Tracte containing the Artes of Curious Paintinge, Carvinge, and Buildinge*) by the Oxford physician Richard Haydocke in 1598. The translation adds details of English artists such as *Hilliard not mentioned in Lomazzo's original. Lomazzo also wrote poetry. An example of his rare surviving paintings is a self-portrait (1568) in the Brera, Milan.

Lombard, Lambert (1505–66). Netherlandish painter, draughtsman, engraver, architect, and antiquarian, active mainly in his native Liège. He was probably a pupil of *Gossaert and was influenced by Jan van *Scorel. A man of scholarly inclinations, Lombard was in Rome in 1537 (he also travelled in France and Germany) and made drawings of the *antique, some of which were engraved in the workshop of Jerome *Cock. He corresponded with *Vasari, providing him with information about Netherlandish artists, and Vasari said of him: 'Of all the Flemish artists I have named none is superior to Lambert Lombard of Liège, a man well versed in letters, a painter of judgement, a learned architect and—by no means his least title to merit— the master of Frans *Floris, and Willem *Key.' This opinion was confirmed by van *Mander, who wrote in 1604: 'One can confidently rank him among the best Netherlandish painters, past and present.' Unfortunately, very few paintings that can certainly be assigned to him survive to bear witness to his high contemporary reputation, and his work is known from drawings, copies, and engravings. A formidable *Portrait of the Artist* in the Musée de l'Art Wallon, Liège (another version is in the Staatliche Kunstsammlungen, Kassel) is among the best works given to him, but some critics think it is by his pupil Frans Floris. The portraits associated with Lombard—lively and strongly characterized— generally appeal more to modern taste than his somewhat academic religious paintings.

Lombardo. Family of Italian artists, the leading Venetian sculptors of their period: **Pietro** (*c*.1435–1515) and his sons **Tullio** (*c*.1455–1532) and **Antonio** (*c*.1458–1516). Pietro, who came from Lombardy, settled in Venice in about 1467. He was an architect as well as a sculptor, and his church of Sta Maria dei Miracoli (1481– 9), on the sculptural decoration of which he was assisted by his sons, has been called the choicest jewel of *Renaissance work in Venice. Of his numerous tombs in Venetian churches, the best known is that of Doge Pietro Mocenigo (SS. Giovanni e Paolo, *c*.1476–81). His style is distinguished by polished mastery of marble cutting and an interest in the *antique, features that recur in the work of Tullio. Tullio's most imposing work is the Vendramin monument (*c*.1493) in SS. Giovanni e Paolo; the figure of *Adam* from this—a sensuously beautiful freestanding nude—is in the Metropolitan Museum, New York. Antonio had less substance as an independent artist. His work included mythological reliefs for

Alfonso d'*Este (mainly in the Hermitage, Leningrad).

London Group. An exhibiting society of English artists formed in 1913 by an amalgamation of the *Camden Town Group with several smaller groups and various individuals. The first President was Harold *Gilman, and among the members were *Nevinson, *Wadsworth, John and Paul *Nash, and the sculptors *Gill and *Epstein. Roger *Fry became a member in 1918 and brought with him a number of his followers. The strong interest of the early members in *Post-Impressionism was deprecated by *Tonks, who said: 'The leaders of the London Group have nearly all come from me. What an unholy brood I have raised.' Thus began an opposition between 'advanced' art and the semi-academicism of the *Slade. Unlike most other associations the London Group survived opposition, was revived after the Second World War, and came to be looked on as something of an institution. It still exists.

Long, Edwin. See ALMA-TRADEMA.

Longhi, Pietro (properly Pietro Falca) (1702–85). Venetian painter. Although he carried out some fresco commissions he is known principally as a painter of small *genre scenes of contemporary patrician and low life. These charming and often gently satirical scenes were very popular, although surprisingly he does not seem to have been patronized by English visitors to Venice. A prolific artist, Longhi occasionally painted more than one version of his own compositions, and these again were often duplicated by pupils and followers. **Alessandro Longhi** (1733–1813), the son of Pietro, was a successful portraitist. He was the official portrait painter to the Venetian Academy, so that he was in a good position for compiling his *Compendio delle Vite de' Pittori Veneziani Istorici* (1762) with portraits etched by himself.

Longhi, Roberto (1890–1970). Italian art historian. Longhi was a scholar of great industry, and published much new material, particularly in the area with which he is most associated—*Caravaggio and Caravaggism (he catalogued the great exhibition of the work of Caravaggio and the *Caravaggisti held in Florence in 1951,

which is regarded as a landmark in this field). He was involved with various periodicals, and in 1950 founded a new periodical, *Paragone*, in Florence. In the same year he became professor of art history at Florence University. His villa in Florence is now an art-historical foundation, housing his library of books and photographs, and his picture collection.

Lopes, Gregório (c.1490–c.1550). Portuguese painter, court painter to Manuel I and John III. Among Portuguese painters of his period he was the most directly inspired by *Renaissance influence. His work is represented in the Museu Nacional de Arte Antiga, Lisbon.

López y Portaña, Vicente (1772–1850). Spanish painter. Primarily a portraitist, he was influenced by *Mengs, whose style he continued into the 19th cent. In 1815 he became first court painter to Ferdinand VII (who preferred him to *Goya), in 1817 director of the Academia of San Fernando, and in 1823 director of the *Prado.

Lorenzetti, Pietro (active 1320–48) and **Ambrogio** (active 1319–48). Sienese painters, brothers. They were among the outstanding Italian artists of their time, but their lives are poorly documented—both are assumed to have died in the Black Death of 1348. Pietro is usually said to have been the elder brother, but the evidence is not conclusive. His first dated work is of 1320—a *polyptych of *The Virgin and Child with Saints* in the Pieve di Sta Maria at Arezzo; Ambrogio's earliest reliably attributed work is of a year earlier—a *Virgin and Child* for a church at Vico l'Abate (Museo Diocesano, Florence). Apart from collaborating in a cycle of the *Life of Mary*, now lost, which they painted in fresco on the façade of Siena's public hospital in 1335, the brothers worked independently. They shared a certain affinity of style, however, the weightiness of their figures showing the influence of *Giotto and clearly setting them apart from the elegance of their greatest Sienese contemporary *Simone Martini. Ambrogio was the more innovative of the brothers, and his greatest work, the fresco series representing *Good and Bad Government* in the Town Hall at Siena (1338–9), is one of the most remarkable achievements in 14th-cent. Italian art. In it he broke new ground in the naturalistic painting of landscape and townscape, and the talkative crowds of figures show he was an acute observer of his fellow men. Ambrogio's other dated work includes altarpieces of *The Presentation in the Temple* (Uffizi, Florence, 1342) and *The Annunciation* (Pinacoteca, Siena, 1344). Pietro's work is noted for its emotional expressiveness, his fresco of *The Descent from the Cross* in the Lower Church of S. Francesco at Assisi having remarkable pathos and dramatic power. The extent and the date of Pietro's contribution at Assisi are matters of controversy, but his other work includes dated altarpieces of *The Virgin and Child Enthroned* (Uffizi, 1340) and *The Birth of the Virgin* (Cathedral Museum, Siena, 1342).

Lorenzo Monaco (*c.*1370–*c.*1425). Italian painter who, though born in Siena, seems to have spent all his professional life in Florence. In 1391 he took his vows as a monk of the Camaldolese monastery of Sta Maria degli Angeli. He rose to the rank of deacon, but in 1402 was enrolled in the painters' guild under his lay name, Piero di Giovanni (Lorenzo Monaco means 'Laurence the Monk'), and was living outside the monastery. The monastery was renowned for its manuscript *illuminations and several *miniatures in books in the Laurentian Library in Florence have been attributed to him, but he was primarily a painter of altarpieces, good examples of which are in the National Gallery in London and the Uffizi in Florence. His main works in fresco are the scenes of the *Life of Mary* in the Bartolini chapel of Sta Trinità, Florence. His style is distinguished by luminous beauty of colouring and a graceful, rhythmic flow of line. He stands in complete contrast to his great contemporary *Masaccio and represents the highest achievement of the last flowering of *Gothic art in Florence.

Lorrain, Claude. See CLAUDE.

Lotto, Lorenzo (*c.*1480–1556/7). Venetian painter. According to *Vasari and *Ridolfi, he trained with *Giorgione and *Titian in the studio of Giovanni *Bellini, but he worked in many places apart from Venice, had an idiosyncratic style, and stands somewhat apart from the central Venetian tradition. In 1508–12 he was in Rome, then lived mainly in Bergamo until 1526, when he returned to Venice. From 1530 he worked mainly in various towns in the Marches, and in 1554, when he was partially blind, he became a lay-brother at the monastery at Loreto, where he died. He had a nervous, difficult temperament and his work, with which he seems to have had difficulty earning a living, is extremely uneven. It draws on a wide variety of sources, from Northern Europe as well as Italy, but at the same time shows acute freshness of observation. He is now perhaps best known for his portraits, in which he often conveys a mood of psychological unrest (*Young Man in his Study*, Kunsthistorisches Museum, Vienna), but he worked mainly as a religious painter. An outstanding example of how original and poetic his altarpieces could be is *The Annunciation* in the church of Sta Maria sopra Mercanti at Recanati—a bizarre and captivating work full of brilliant colours and lighting effects, odd expressions and poses, and unusual and beautifully painted details.

Louis, Morris (Morris Louis Bernstein) (1912–62). American painter, considered the main pioneer of the movement beyond *Abstract Expressionism to *Colour Stain painting. The manner of his painting fundamentally changed in 1954, apparently as a result of a visit to the studio of Helen *Frankenthaler. From this time he used thinned-out *acrylic paint which, when poured on to unprimed or sometimes partially *sized canvas, acted as a stain and not as an overlaid surface of pigment. In his series of *Veils* done in 1954, and again in 1957–60, the paint was poured down the canvas in striated patterns of partially overlapping areas of translucent dyes. The technique is particularly exacting, allowing no possibilities for subsequent alteration or modification. For this reason, perhaps, Louis destroyed much of the work of this period. Louis painted the last of his *Veils* in the winter of 1959/60. But from the summer of 1959 he was experimenting— though still with the same technique—in a number of directions at once. These series of paintings are conventionally known as *Florals*, *Alephs*, *Columns*, *Omegas*, and *Japanese Banners* (Louis himself was disinclined to name his works and few of the titles originated with him) and led on to the series of *Unfurleds*, of which Louis painted 120 between the summer of 1960 and the spring of 1961. In these pictures the large central area of unpigmented canvas is given a curious positive quality by diagonal stripes of colour on the left and right in the form of half pyramids the other half of which lies outside the picture. In the spring of 1961 Louis stopped painting *Unfurleds* and began what was to be the last of his series—the *Stripes*. In these paintings bunched straight vertical bands of colour are surrounded by empty canvas. Louis's impact on the development of Colour Stain painting was immense.

Louvre, Paris. The national museum and art gallery of France, an epitome of the nation's history and culture. The first building on the site, begun c.1190 by Philip-Augustus as a fortress and arsenal, held the royal treasures of jewels, armour, illuminated manuscripts, etc. It became a royal residence c.1400, and was enlarged and beautified by Charles V, but was plundered by the British troops after Agincourt (1415). Francis I demolished the old Louvre and in 1546 commissioned the architect Pierre Lescot to build a new palace of four wings around a square court, roughly of the same size as the old castle and on the same site. Only the west and half of the south wings were completed by Lescot, but his work forms the heart of the present vast structure, and his elegant and sophisticated *Classical style set the tone for all the future additions, which were made by virtually every French monarch up to Napoleon III. Under Louis XIV the royal collection increased from some 200 pictures to over 2,000. In support of the policy for state control of the arts and taste some of the king's pictures were opened to public view in the Louvre from 1681 and the exhibitions of the new Académie were held there from 1673. The court had moved into the Louvre in 1652, but it transferred to Versailles in 1678. Under Louis XVI the conversion of the Grande Galerie into a museum was begun and as a result of the democratic fervour incidental to the Revolution the Louvre was opened as the first national public gallery in 1793 (though as a public gallery it was preceded by others including the *Ashmolean in Oxford and the *Vatican). Napoleon renamed the Louvre the Musée Napoléon in 1803 and exhibited there the works of art he had gathered from conquered territories. Most were restored after his fall from power. The Louvre was reopened by Napoleon III in 1851 with the addition of the *Rubens's Medici cycle from the Luxembourg Palace. To relieve congestion after the Second World War a special museum for Impressionist art was formed at the Jeu de Paume in the gardens of the Tuileries. The paintings from the Jeu de Paume, together with certain other works from the Louvre, have now been moved to the Musée d'Orsay in Paris (opened 1986), which is devoted to the art of the late 19th cent., c.1848–c.1905.

Lowry, L. S. (Laurence Stephen) (1887–1976). British painter. He lived all his life in or near Manchester (mainly in Salford) and worked as a rent collector and clerk for a property company until he retired in 1952. His painting was done mainly at night after his day's work, but he was not a *naïve painter, having studied intermittently at art schools from 1905 to 1925. It was during this period that he evolved the type of picture for which he is best known, featuring firmly drawn backgrounds of industrial buildings bathed in a white haze, against which groups or crowds of figures, painted in his characteristic stick-like manner, move about their affairs isolated in an intensely individual, personal life. His pictures embodied a consistent, disquieting vision, revealing a sense of alienation and man's inconsequence against the juggernaut of industrialism; he was a solitary character and said: 'Had I not been lonely I should not have seen what I did.' A comprehensive retrospective exhibition of his work at the Royal Academy in the year of his death brought considerable divergence of opinion among critics. Some thought of him as a great artist with an important original vision. Others represented him as a very minor talent, although interesting as a social commentator.

Lucas van Leyden (1494?–1533). Netherlandish engraver and painter, born and mainly active in Leiden. He was the pupil of his father, from whose hand no works are known, and of Cornelis *Engelbrechtsz., but both of these were painters whereas Lucas himself was principally an engraver. Where he learnt engraving is unknown, but he was highly skilled in that art at a very early age; the earliest known print by him (*Mohammed and the Murdered*

Monk) dates from 1508, when he was perhaps only 14, yet reveals no trace of immaturity in inspiration or technique. In 1514 he entered the Painters' Guild at Leiden. He seems to have travelled a certain amount, and visits are recorded to Antwerp in 1521, the year of *Dürer's Netherlandish journey, and to Middelburg in 1527, when he met *Gossaert. An unbroken series of dated engravings makes it possible to follow his career as a print-maker and to date many of his paintings, but no clear pattern of stylistic development emerges. Dürer was the single greatest influence on him, but Lucas was less intellectual in his approach, tending to concentrate on the anecdotal features of the subject and to take delight in *caricatures and *genre motifs. Van *Mander characterizes Lucas as a pleasure-loving dilettante, who sometimes worked in bed, but he left a large *œuvre*, in spite of his fairly early death, and must have been a prodigious worker. Lucas had a great reputation in his day (*Vasari even rated him above Dürer) and is universally regarded as one of the greatest figures in the history of *graphic art (he made etchings and woodcuts as well as engravings and was a prolific draughtsman). His status as a painter is less elevated, but he was undoubtedly one of the outstanding Netherlandish painters of his period. He was a pioneer of the Netherlandish genre tradition, as witness his *Chess Players* (Staatliche Museen, Berlin)—which actually represents a variant game called 'courier'—and his *Card Players* (Wilton House, Wiltshire), while his celebrated *Last Judgement* *triptych (Municipal Mus., Leiden, 1526–7) shows the heights to which he could rise as a religious painter. It eloquently displays his vivid imaginative powers, his marvellous skill as a colourist and his deft and fluid brushwork. Lucas left no pupils or direct followers, but his work was a stimulus to an even greater Leiden-born artist, *Rembrandt.

Luchism. See RAYONISM.

Luini, Bernardino (*c.*1485–1532). Milanese painter, one of the most prominent of *Leonardo's followers in Lombardy. Luini vulgarized Leonardo's style, but he had a successful and prolific career and his sentimentality ensured him great popularity with the Victorians. His work is well represented in the Brera in Milan and many of his frescos and altarpieces are in Lombard churches. He painted mythological as well as religious subjects, an example being *Cephalus and Procris* in the National Gallery, Washington.

Luks, George (1867–1933). American painter and graphic artist, a member of The *Eight and of the *Ash-can School. A flamboyant character who identified himself with the poorer classes and made a pose of bohemianism, he was much given to tall tales and sometimes posed as 'Lusty Luks', an ex-boxer. His work was uneven and unpredictable. It had vigour and spontaneity but too often lacked anything other than an ebullient superficial vitality.

Luminism. Term coined in 1954 by John Baur, director of the Whitney Museum in New York, to describe an aspect of mid 19th-cent. American landscape painting in which the study of light was paramount. He defined Luminism as 'a polished and meticulous realism in which there is no sign of brushwork and no trace of impressionism, the atmospheric effects being achieved by infinitely careful gradations of tone, by the most exact study of the relative clarity of near and far objects, and by a precise rendering of the variations in texture and color produced by direct or reflected rays' ('American Luminism', *Perspectives USA*, Autumn 1954). At their most characteristic, Luminist paintings are concerned chiefly with the depiction of water and sky. Leading Luminists included *Bingham and *Durand, and aspects of it can be seen in the work of the *Hudson River School. By about 1880 Luminism was becoming outmoded by French influences. In the field of 20th-cent. art the term 'luminism' has also been applied to work incorporating electric light.

Lurçat, Jean (1892–1966). French painter and designer. The most important and lasting influence on his work came from his extensive travels during the 1920s, in Spain in 1923 and from 1924 to 1929 in the Middle East, North Africa, and the Sahara. His painting was dominated by impressions of desert landscape, reminiscences of Spanish and Greek architecture and a love of fantasy that caused him to join the *Surrealist movement for a short period in the 1930s. Lurçat is chiefly remembered, however, for his work in the revival of tapestry. His designs were based on fantastic representations of the vegetable and insect worlds combined with exalted themes from human history, and he succeeded in combining the stylizations of medieval religious tapestry with modern modes of abstraction. His designs included the well-known *Apocalypse* for the church of Assy (1948). From 1930 onwards he did a number of coloured lithographs, stage designs, and book illustrations and in the 1960s he renewed his painting activities.

lyrical abstraction. A rather vague term, used differently by different writers, applied to certain aspects of the more intuitive (as opposed to geometric) forms of abstract painting associated with the *Abstract Expressionists and their followers. Generally it implies a lush and sumptuous use of colour.

Lysippus. Greek sculptor from Sicyon, active in the middle and later 4th cent. BC. He was one of the most famous of Greek sculptors, with a long and prolific career (he worked from perhaps as early as c.360 BC to as late as c.305 BC and *Pliny said he made 1,500 works—all in bronze), but nothing is known to survive from his own hand. However, there are numerous Roman copies that can be said with a fair measure of certainty to reproduce his works, the best and most reliable being the *Apoxyomenos* (a young athlete scraping himself with a strigil) in the Vatican Museum. The figure is tall and slender, bearing out the tradition current in antiquity that Lysippus introduced a new scheme of proportions for the human body to supersede that of *Polyclitus, and the pose—with one arm outstretched—is novel. Lysippus was famous also for his portraits of Alexander the Great, who is said to have let no other sculptor portray him; many copies survive, including examples in the British Museum and the Louvre. Among his other works was a colossal statue of Hercules at Sicyon, which was probably the original of the celebrated *Farnese Hercules* in the Archaeological Museum at Naples. It shows the realism that was said to be another hallmark of his work. Of the works associated with him on stylistic grounds, the best-known is a bronze statue of a victorious athlete found in the Adriatic Sea in 1964. This was bought by the Getty Museum, Malibu, in 1977 for $3,900,000, then the highest price ever paid for a piece of sculpture, and it is now sometimes known as 'the Getty Victor'. Even from the second-hand evidence that survives, it is clear that Lysippus was an outstandingly original sculptor whose stylistic innovations, like those of his great contemporary *Praxiteles, became common currency in the Greek world; J. J. Pollitt (*Art in the Hellenistic Age*, 1986) describes him as 'probably the single most creative and influential artist of the entire *Hellenistic period'.

M

Mabuse. See GOSSAERT.

MacBryde, Robert. See COLQUHOUN.

Macchiaioli. Group of Italian painters, active mainly in Florence c.1855 65, who were in revolt against academic conventions and emphasized painterly freshness through the use of blots or patches (*macchie*) of colour. They were influenced by the *Barbizon School, but they painted *genre scenes, historical subjects, and portraits as well as landscapes. Leading members included Giovanni *Boldini, Giovanni Fattori (1825–1908), and Telemaco Signorini (1835–1901). The Macchiaioli met with little critical or financial success, but they are now considered the most important phenomenon in 19th-cent. Italian painting. Sometimes the Macchiaioli are even claimed as proto-*Impressionists, but the differences between the two groups are as striking as the similarities; there is often a strong literary element in the work of the Macchiaioli, for example, and however bright their lighting effects they never lost a sense of solidity of form. See also NITTIS, GIUSEPPE DE.

McCubbin, Frederick (1855–1917). Australian painter, a founder of the *Heidelberg School. The melancholy mood and strong vein of national sentiment in his *genre painting recall the stories of Australian writers such as Marcus Clarke and Henry Lawson. After a visit to Europe in 1907 he worked in a more *Impressionistic style. His son **Louis** (1890–1952) was a painter and director of the National Gallery of South Australia 1936–50. His major work is a huge mural of battle scenes for the Australian National War Museum in Canberra (1920–9).

Macdonald, Jock (1897–1960). Canadian painter, born in Scotland. He emigrated to Canada in 1926 to teach at the new Vancouver School of Decorative and Applied Arts. His early work was in the *Group of Seven tradition, but in 1934 he painted his first abstract or *automatic work, *Formative Colour Activity* (NG of Canada, Ottawa). He became a friend of Emily *Carr, and in 1940 of Lawren *Harris, who encouraged him in his abstract experiments. During the last five years of his life Macdonald's output was prodigious, as he threw himself into experimenting with various techniques and media. He taught at various art colleges in the course of his career and is considered to have played a leading role in advancing the cause of modern art in Canada.

Macdonald-Wright, Stanton (1890–1973). American painter, one of the first American abstract artists. In 1907 he moved to Paris, where together with Morgan *Russell he evolved a theory of painting based upon the scientific deployment of colour. Their theory, which was parallel to the *Orphism of Robert *Delaunay and which they called *Synchromism, was put forward in statements made at a joint exhibition held first in Munich and then in Paris, in 1913. They claimed that they and not Delaunay and *Kupka were the originators of the new style of abstract colour painting. After spending part of 1914–16 in London, Macdonald-Wright returned to the USA in 1916 and in 1919 moved to California, where he abandoned Synchromist painting and became involved with experiments with colour film and various other projects. He was deeply interested in oriental art and from 1958 he spent part of every year in a Zen monastery in Japan.

McEvoy, Ambrose (1878 1927). English painter. A contemporary of Augustus *John and William *Orpen at the *Slade, he began as a painter of poetic landscapes and restful interiors, but from about 1915 he gained success as a portraitist. His most characteristic pictures are of beautiful society women, often painted in watercolour in a rapid, sketchy style. They can be merely flashy, but the finest have something of the romantic air of refinement of *Gainsborough, an artist McEvoy greatly admired.

Machuca, Pedro (d. 1550). Spanish architect and painter, active mainly in Granada. He worked in Italy in his early career (which is ill documented) and was one of the first Spanish artists to break entirely with medieval tradition and show a full understanding of *Renaissance ideals. His earliest dated work, *The Virgin with the Souls of Purgatory* (Prado, Madrid, 1517), was painted in Italy and is thoroughly *Raphaelesque in style. Machuca was back in Spain by 1520, and although he worked mainly as a painter, he is most important as the architect of the Palace of Charles V in the grounds of the Alhambra in Granada, begun in 1527, which is completely Italianate in style. Most of Machuca's work as a painter has disappeared.

Macip (or **Masip**), **Vicente** (c.1475–before 1550). Spanish painter, one of a dynasty of artists working in Valencia. Little is known of his life, but his major work, the main altarpiece of Segorbe Cathedral (completed 1535), shows him to have been a leading representative of the Italianate style. During his later years he collaborated with the outstanding member of the family, his son and follower **Juan Vicente** (better known as Juan de Juanes, c.1523–79). Juan's work combines figures in the Italian *Mannerist style with a polished Netherlandish technique. He was the leading painter of his time in Valencia and had many followers.

Macke, August (1887–1914). German *Expressionist painter. His training included a period studying with *Corinth. Between 1907 and 1912 he visited Paris several times and he evolved a personal synthesis of *Impressionism, *Fauvism, and *Orphism with which to display a basically Expressionist attitude, coming closer in spirit to French art than any other German painter of the time. In 1909–10 he met *Kandinsky and Franz *Marc in Munich and joined them in the formation of the *Blaue Reiter, but apart from a few experiments his work moved less towards abstraction than that of other members of the group. Early in 1914 he made a trip with Paul *Klee and Louis *Moilliet to Tunisia, and the water-colours he did on this trip are considered to be his most personal achievement. Macke was killed in action in the First World War.

Maclise, Daniel (1806–70). Irish painter and *caricaturist, active in London from 1827. An outstanding draughtsman, Maclise became the leading history painter of his period, his greatest works being two enormous murals in the House of Lords on *The Meeting of Wellington and Blücher at Waterloo* (completed 1861) and *The Death of Nelson at Trafalgar* (completed 1865). They were done in the *water-glass technique and are poorly preserved (a sketch for the *Nelson* in the Walker Art Gallery in Liverpool gives an idea of the original colouring), but they are powerful works and fully coherent in spite of the huge numbers of figures involved, and they remain the most stirring examples of his heroic powers of design. Maclise was handsome, charming, and popular with fellow artists, and *Frith wrote that he was spoken of in academic circles as 'out and away the greatest artist that ever lived'. Grandiose history painting was only one side to his talent, however, for he also excelled as a caricaturist, and is particularly noted for a series of character portraits of literary men and women. There are several examples of his conventional portraits in the National Portrait Gallery, London, including a well-known one of his close friend Charles Dickens (1839).

McTaggart, William (1835–1910). The leading Scottish landscape painter of his period. He has been called 'the Scottish *Impressionist', but although he was much concerned with light and atmosphere, the sense of the drama of nature in his work brings him closer in spirit to *Constable. He was an influential figure, his followers including his grandson, **Sir William MacTaggart** (1903–81).

Maderno, Stefano (c.1576–1636). Italian sculptor. He was one of the leading sculptors in Rome during the papacy of Paul V (1605–21) before *Bernini came into the ascendancy, working on statues and *reliefs in numerous churches, notably the chapel that the pope had built (the Cappella Paolina, begun 1605) in Sta Maria Maggiore. One of his works has attained lasting fame; the recumbent figure of St Cecilia (1600) in Sta Cecilia in Trastevere, a lyrical and poignant work which is said to show the body of the Early Christian martyr in the exact position in which it was discovered in the church in 1599.

Maes, Nicolaes (1634–93). Dutch painter. He was born in Dordrecht and in about 1648 became a pupil of *Rembrandt in Amsterdam, staying there until 1654 when he returned to his native town. In his early years he concentrated on *genre pictures, rather sentimental in approach, but distinguished by deep glowing colours he had learnt from his master. Old women sleeping, praying, or reading the Bible were subjects he particularly favoured. In the 1660s, however, Maes began to turn more to portraiture, and after a visit to Antwerp between 1665 and 1667 his style changed dramatically. He abandoned the reddish tone of his earlier manner for a wider, lighter, and cooler range (greys and blacks in the shadows instead of brownish tones), and the fashionable portraits he now specialized in were closer to van *Dyck than to Rembrandt. In 1673 he moved permanently to Amsterdam and had great success with this kind of picture. Maes was a fairly prolific painter and is well represented in, for example, the National Gallery, London, and the museum at Dordrecht.

Maestà. Term (Italian for 'majesty') used to describe a representation of the Virgin and Child in which the Virgin is enthroned as Queen of Heaven, surrounded by a court of saints and angels.

Maffei, Francesco (c.1600–60). Italian painter, born at Vicenza and active mainly in the Veneto. He had a refreshingly individualistic style, carrying on the great painterly tradition of *Tintoretto and *Bassano, reinforced by the example of *Liss, *Feti, and *Strozzi, to which he added his own note of mysterious and sometimes bizarre fantasy. He painted religious and mythological scenes and also allegorical portraits of local officials.

Magic(al) Realism. Term coined by the German critic Franz Roh in 1925 to describe the aspect of *Neue Sachlichkeit characterized by sharp-focus detail. In later criticism the term has been used to cover various types of painting in which objects are depicted with photographic naturalism but which because of paradoxical elements or strange juxtapositions convey a feeling of unreality, infusing the ordinary with a sense of mystery. The paintings of *Magritte are a prime example.

Magnasco, Alessandro (called Il Lissandrino) (1667–1749). Italian painter. He was born and died in Genoa, but spent most of his working life in Milan. At the beginning of his career he was a portraitist, but virtually nothing is known of this aspect of his career. Later he turned to the type of work for which he is now known—highly individual melodramatic scenes set in storm-tossed landscapes, ruins, convents, and gloomy monasteries, peopled with small, elongated figures of monks, nuns, gypsies, mercenaries, witches, beggars, and inquisitors. His brushwork is nervous and flickering and his lighting effects macabre. He was very prolific and his work is rarely dated or datable. Marco *Ricci and Francesco *Guardi were among the artists influenced by him.

Magritte, René (1898–1967). Belgian painter, one of the leading figures of the *Surrealist movement. Apart from three years living in a suburb of Paris (1927–30), his entire career was spent in Brussels. After initially working in a *Cubist–Futurist style, he turned to Surrealism in 1925 under the influence of de *Chirico and by the following year had already emerged as a highly individual artist with The Menaced Assassin (MOMA, New York), a picture that displays the startling and disturbing juxtapositions of the ordinary, the strange, and the erotic that were to characterize his work for the rest of his life. Apart from a period in the 1940s when he experimented with *Neo-Impressionist techniques, he worked in a precise, scrupulously banal manner (a reminder of the early days when he made his living designing wallpaper and drawing fashion advertisements) and he always remained true to Surrealism. *Iconographically he had a repertory of obsessive images which appeared again and again in ordinary but incongruous surroundings. Enormous rocks that float in the air and fishes with human legs are typical leitmotivs. He repeatedly exploited ambiguities concerning real objects and images of them (many of his works feature paintings within paintings), inside and out-of-doors, day and night. He also made Surrealist analogues of a number of famous paintings—for example *David's *Madame Récamier* and *Manet's *The Balcony*, in which he replaced the figures with coffins. For the fertility of his imagery, the unforced spontaneity of his effects, and not least his rare gift of humour, Magritte was one of the very few natural and inspired Surrealist painters. J. T. Soby summed this up felicitously when he wrote: 'In viewing Magritte's paintings . . . everything seems proper. And then abruptly the rape of commonsense occurs, usually in broad daylight.'

mahlstick. See MAULSTICK.

Mahon, Sir Denis (1910–). British art historian and collector. A private scholar with private means, he has devoted himself single-mindedly to the study of 17th-cent. Italian (particularly Bolognese) painting, and has not only built up a choice collection in this field, but also played a greater part than anyone else in the rehabilitation of such once-scorned artists as the *Carracci, *Guercino, and *Reni. His publications include *Studies in Seicento Art and Theory* (1947), a brilliant pioneering work, and catalogues of Carracci drawings (1956) and Guercino paintings (1968) and drawings (1969) for major exhibitions of their work held in Bologna. He is also regarded as a leading *Poussin scholar.

Maiano, Benedetto da. See BENEDETTO DA MAIANO.

Maillol, Aristide (1861–1944). French sculptor, painter, graphic artist, and tapestry designer. His early career was spent mainly as a tapestry designer, but he also painted, exhibiting with the *Nabis. Although he first made sculpture in 1895, it was only in 1900 that he decided to devote himself to it after serious eyestrain made him give up tapestry. In 1902 he had his first one-man exhibition, which drew praise from *Rodin; in 1905 came his first conspicuous public success at the *Salon d'Automne; and after about 1910 he was internationally famous and received a constant flow of commissions. With only a few exceptions, he restricted himself to the female nude, expressing his whole philosophy of form through this medium. Commissioned in 1905 to make a monument to the revolutionary Louis-Auguste Blanqui, and asked by the committee what

form he proposed to give it, he replied: 'Eh! une femme nue.' More than any artist before him he brought to conscious realization the concept of sculpture in the round as an independent art form stripped of literary associations and architectural context, and he ranks as the most distinguished figure of the transition from Rodin to the moderns. He rejected Rodin's emotionalism and animated surfaces, however, Maillol's weighty figures, often shown in repose, being solemn and broadly modelled, with simple poses and gestures. His work consciously continued the Classical tradition of Greek and Roman sculpture (Maillol visited Greece in 1908), but at the same time has a quality of healthy sensuousness (his peasant wife sometimes modelled for him). Maillol took up painting again in 1939 when he returned to his birthplace, Banyuls, but apart from his sculpture the most important works of his maturity are his book illustrations, which helped re-establish the art of the book in the 1920s and 1930s. His finest achievements in this field are the woodcut illustrations (which he cut himself) for an edition of Virgil's *Eclogues* (begun 1912 but not published until 1926), which show superb economy of line. Maillol's work is in many important collections of modern art.

Makart, Hans (1840–84). Austrian painter. He studied under *Piloty in Munich, then the chief centre of history painting, and from 1869 worked in Vienna, where he was enormously successful and a leading society figure. His exuberant, somewhat *Rubenesque style, which he applied to mythological, historical, and allegorical subjects, often on a huge scale, now seems overblown, but it had great influence in Austria and Germany.

Malatesta, Sigismondo (1417–68). Italian nobleman, effective lord of Rimini from 1422 until his death. A brilliant and totally unscrupulous *condottiere*, he is the prototype of the megalomaniac, paganizing tyrant once thought to be characteristic of the Italian *Renaissance (he was publicly consigned to hell while still alive—the only man ever to suffer this fate—by Pope Pius II, but modern research has watered down his image). His name is indissolubly linked to one of the most famous creations of 15th-cent. art—the conversion (begun 1457) of the church of San Francesco in

Rimini into a sort of temple to himself and his mistress (later wife) Isotta degli Atti. *Alberti was his architect and *Agostino di Duccio and *Piero della Francesca were among the artists who worked on the decoration of the building. It was never completed, but under Sigismondo's direct inspiration it became the most self-conscious return to the *antique yet seen.

Mâle, Émile (1862–1954). French art historian. A pioneer in the study of French medieval art, on which he published several books, he became Professor of the History of Art at the Sorbonne in 1912. His work is distinguished not only by great learning but also by literary merit, his style being praised by Marcel Proust amongst others.

Malevich, Kasimir (1878–1935). Russian painter and designer, with *Mondrian the most important pioneer of geometric *abstract art. He began working in an unexceptional *Post-Impressionist manner, but by 1912 he was painting peasant subjects in a massive 'tubular' style similar to that of *Léger as well as pictures combining the fragmentation of form of *Cubism with the multiplication of the image of *Futurism (*The Knife Grinder*, Yale Univ. Art Gal., 1912). Malevich, however, was fired with the desire 'to free art from the burden of the object' and launched the *Suprematist movement, which brought abstract art to a geometric simplicity more radical than anything previously seen. He claimed that he made a picture 'consisting of nothing more than a black square on a white field' as early as 1913, but Suprematist paintings were first made public in Moscow in 1915 and there is often difficulty in dating his work. (There is often difficulty also in knowing which way up his paintings should be hung, photographs of early exhibitions sometimes providing conflicting evidence.) Malevich moved away from absolute austerity, tilting rectangles from the vertical, adding more colours and introducing a suggestion of the third dimension and even a degree of painterly handling, but around 1918 he returned to his purest ideals with a series of *White on White* paintings. After this he seems to have realized he could go no further along this road and virtually gave up abstract painting, turning more to teaching, writing, and making three-dimensional models that were important

in the growth of *Constructivism. In 1919 he started teaching at the art school at Vitebsk, where he exerted a profound influence on *Lissitzky, and in 1922 he moved to Leningrad, where he lived for the rest of his life. He visited Warsaw and Berlin in 1927, accompanying an exhibition of his works and visited the *Bauhaus. In the late 1920s he returned to figurative painting, but he was out of favour with a political system that now demanded Socialist *Realism from its artists and he died in neglect. However, his influence on abstract art—in the west as well as Russia—was enormous. The best collection of his work is in the Stedelijk Museum, Amsterdam.

Malouel, Jean (d. 1419). Netherlandish painter. He is documented in Paris in 1396 and from 1397 to 1415 he was court painter to the Dukes of Burgundy. No documented works by him survive, but he has been suggested as the painter of several works, including part of the *Martyrdom of St Denis* (completed by *Bellechose), and a *tondo of the *Trinity*, both in the Louvre. They have all the refinement of French court art combined with a strength of modelling and a realistic naturalism derived from Flanders.

Malvasia, Count Carlo (1616–93). Italian painter, art historian, and antiquarian. His *Felsina pittrice: vite dei pittori bolognesi* (1678) is the most important source for knowledge of the great period of the Bolognese School that began with the *Carracci (Felsina was the Etruscan name for Bologna). His guide to the paintings of Bologna (1686) was one of the first books of its kind.

Mander, Karel van (1548–1606). Netherlandish painter and writer on art, born in Flanders and active mainly in Haarlem. He is sometimes known as the 'Dutch *Vasari', for his fame rests primarily on his work as a biographer of artists, published in *Het schilderboeck* (The Book of Painters) in 1604. The book is divided into three parts, the first and most important being made up of about 175 biographies of Netherlandish and German artists from van *Eyck to van Mander's own younger contemporaries. This section of the book is the first systematic account of the lives of northern European artists, and our only source of information about some of them.

The second part of the book contains the lives of Italian artists from *Cimabue up to his own time. Most of this material is a condensed translation into Dutch of Vasari, but it also has valuable information collected by van Mander himself when he was in Italy in 1573–7 or from friends and correspondents. The third part of the book, the *Lehrgedicht*, a long poem divided into fourteen chapters, gives practical advice to artists and sums up much of the theory and practice of 16th-cent. Netherlandish art. Van Mander's own pictures, which were mainly religious and allegorical, adopted the elongated forms of the *Mannerists, but his later works showed a tendency towards *naturalism. With *Cornelis van Haarlem and Hendrik *Goltzius, van Mander founded at Haarlem an *academy where artists could draw from nude models. Frans *Hals was his most important pupil.

Manessier, Alfred (1911–). French abstract painter, a pupil of *Bissière. After a retreat in a Trappist monastery during the Second World War he became increasingly concerned with expressing spiritual meaning through abstract art and designed stained-glass windows for numerous churches. He is regarded as one of the outstanding exponents of expressive abstraction in the post-war School of Paris and had great influence on *Tachiste artists.

Manet, Édouard (1832–83). French painter and graphic artist. He was the son of a senior civil servant in the Ministry of Justice and inherited considerable wealth when his father (who disapproved of his choice of career) died in 1862. His upper middle-class background was important, for although he was cast as an artistic rebel, he always sought traditional honours and success and he cut an impeccable figure as a man-about-town. He entered the studio of *Couture in 1850 and remained a pupil there for six years. His own painting style was, however, based mainly on a study of the Old Masters at the *Louvre, and particularly Spanish painters such as *Velázquez (his greatest artistic hero) and *Ribera. During the 1850s he visited museums in the Netherlands, Germany, Austria, and Italy and it is one of the ironies of Manet's career that a painter with such reverence for the art of the past should be so much attacked for his modernity. His first taste of official disfavour came when his first submission to the *Salon—*The Absinthe Drinker* (Ny Carlsberg Glyptothek, Copenhagen, 1859)—was rejected. He had two paintings accepted in 1861, but then in 1863 his *Déjeuner sur l'herbe* (Musée d'Orsay, Paris) caused a scandal. It was turned down by the Salon and was shown instead at the newly established *Salon des Refusés, set up specially for such rejected paintings. Its hostile reception was based on moral as well as aesthetic grounds, for nudity was considered acceptable only if it was sufficiently remote in time or place and this showed a naked woman having a picnic with two contemporary, clothed men. Manet caused even greater outrage two years later when his *Olympia* (Musée d' Orsay, 1863) was exhibited at the Salon. The reclining nude figure was based on *Titian's *Venus of Urbino* (which Manet had copied in Florence 10 years earlier), but her blatant sexuality was thought an affront to accepted standards of decorum, and one critic wrote 'Art sunk so low does not even deserve reproach.' Manet was denounced also for his bold technique, in which he eliminated the fine tonal gradations of academic practice and created vivid contrasts of light and shade: 'The shadows are indicated by more or less large smears of blacking', wrote another critic, 'The least beautiful woman has bones, muscles, skin, and some sort of colour. Here there is nothing.' From this time, Manet reluctantly found himself acquiring a reputation as a leader of the avant-garde. He was a respected and admired member of the group of young *Impressionists, including *Monet, *Renoir, *Bazille, *Sisley, and *Cézanne, who met at the Café Guerbois and elsewhere. But despite their admiration for him, Manet stood somewhat aloof from the group (although he enjoyed going to the races with *Degas, who was also from the upper middle class) and did not participate in the Impressionist exhibitions. He did, however, adopt the Impressionist technique of painting out of doors (persuaded by Berthe *Morisot, who became his sister-in-law in 1874), and his work became freer and lighter in the 1870s under their influence. In the late 1870s Manet became ill with a disease diagnosed as locomotor ataxia (associated with the late stages of syphilis), which caused him bouts of great pain and extreme tiredness. Increasingly he preferred to work in pastels, which were less physically demanding than oils, but in his last great painting, *A Bar at the Folies-Bergère* (Courtauld Inst. Galleries, London, 1882), Manet rose to heights of painterly brilliance that no other 19th-cent. artist surpassed. He died in appalling pain a week after having a gangrenous leg amputated. The official honours he had craved—in the form of a second-class medal at the Salon and the Legion of Honour—came too late (1881) to be enjoyed.

Manet was a varied and complex artist. He painted a great variety of subjects (he was also a skilled etcher and lithographer) and rarely repeated himself. His approach was completely undogmatic and he was reluctant to theorize; his friend Émile Zola wrote of him 'In beginning a picture, he could never say how it would come out.' In spite of the fact that his work often has a feeling of complete freshness and spontaneity, he would often repaint and rework pictures or even cut them into fragments. His greatest strength was with modern-life subjects (he sketched constantly in the boulevards and cafés of Paris), but although he is accused by some critics of having no imagination, of being able to paint something only if he had it in front of him, his pictures are anything but straight transcriptions of nature. They are, indeed, sometimes enigmatic and elusive, as with *A Bar at the Folies-Bergère*, and seem to be more concerned with the act of painting than with the ostensible subject. It is partly in this freedom from the traditional literary, anecdotal, or moralistic associations of painting that he is seen as one of the founders of 'modern' art, and it is significant that the official title of the first *Post-Impressionist Exhibition, organized by Roger *Fry in 1910–11, was *Manet and the Post-Impressionists*.

Manfredi, Bartolommeo (*c*.1587–1620/1). Italian painter, born in Mantua and active mainly in Rome, where he was one of the most important of *Caravaggio's followers. He specialized in low-life scenes of taverns, soldiers in guardrooms, card-playing, etc., and it was he rather than Caravaggio himself who was mainly responsible for popularizing this kind of work, particularly with painters from France and the Netherlands who came to Italy. In spite of his contemporary reputation, no works survive that are signed or documented as his, and several of the forty or so paintings now given to him were formerly attributed to Caravaggio, an example being the *Concert* in the Uffizi, Florence.

manière criblée (or **dotted manner**). An early type of metal engraving in which dots were stamped in the plate with a punch to create a textured effect, the dots showing as white against the inked background. The technique was not common after the end of the 15th cent., but there was something of a revival in the late 18th cent.

Mannerism. Term used in the study of the visual arts (and by transference in the study of literature and music) with a confused medley of combined historical and critical connotations. Even more than with most stylistic labels, there is little agreement amongst scholars as to its delimitations, and John Shearman begins his book on the subject (*Mannerism*, 1967) with the frank admission: 'This book will have at least one feature in common with all those already published on Mannerism; it will appear to describe something quite different from what all the rest describe.' The word derives from the Italian *maniera*, meaning 'style' or 'stylishness', and it was popularized mainly by the writings of *Vasari, who used it as a term of praise, signifying qualities of grace, poise, facility, and sophistication—characteristics that are indeed apparent in much of the art that he admired from his own time. From the 17th cent., however, most critics thought that Italian art of Vasari's period marked a decline from the peaks of grandeur and harmony reached during the High *Renaissance by *Leonardo, *Michelangelo, and *Raphael, and the term 'Mannerism' came to suggest an art characterized by artificiality, superficiality, and exaggeration, feebly plagiarizing and distorting the work of the masters. From being a stylistic label the term expanded its meaning to become a period label, so that 'Mannerism' came to designate the era in Italian art between the High Renaissance and the *Baroque—that is, from about 1520 to about 1600. The term is still applied mainly to Italian art and architecture, but it is also used of art in other countries.

It was not until the 20th cent.—and particularly the period between the two

world wars—that a more sympathetic attitude towards Mannerist art emerged, and
the word began to be used neutrally,
without the implication of decadence that
it had long carried. At this time, after the
revolutionary achievements of early 20th-
cent. art, Mannerist art was looked at with
new eyes, and the work of artists who had
long been ignored or disparaged began to
seem exciting and original to modern taste.
The qualities associated with Mannerist art
include tension, emotionalism, elongation
of the human figure, strained poses, unusual
or bizarre effects of scale, lighting, or
perspective, and vivid—sometimes harsh
or lurid colours. Often the subject is
approached in an unconventional way,
with the artist drawing attention to his
own learning or virtuosity. In the hands of
the greatest Mannerist artists (for example
*Pontormo or *Parmigianino) such pre-
occupations led to works that are not only
highly sophisticated but also powerful,
disturbing, and moving. The work of
less accomplished Mannerists (for example
Vasari as a painter) often degenerated,
however, into insipid or frenzied gesturing
and grimacing.

With Mannerism no longer receiving
blanket condemnation, more subtle issues
occupied the minds of historians, for example to what extent the term could be
applied to art outside Italy (e.g. El *Greco
in Spain, Romanist painters in the Netherlands, and the École de *Fontainebleau in
France, and *Hilliard in England) or to
architecture (where what might be taken
in one context as playful or capricious
disregard for the rules of Classical architecture might in another be regarded as
provincial clumsiness). While some critics
wish to expand the use of the term, others
wish to contract it, and still others seek to
distinguish what they regard as the central
elements of the style within the general
period label by using the term '*maniera*'.
The following sentence from S. J. Freedberg's *Painting in Italy, 1500–1600* in the
Pelican History of Art series shows how
potentially bewildering the terminology
can be: 'The first generation of Mannerism,
its inventors, thus could achieve *maniera*,
but this requires to be distinguished not
only chronologically but in degree and in
some respects of kind from the "high
Maniera" or Maniera proper.' Thus while
the term 'Mannerism' can generally be
taken to imply an elegant, refined, artificial,

self-conscious, and courtly style, the shade
of meaning to be attached to it varies very
much according to the context and the
outlook of the writer using it.

Man Ray (1890–1977). American painter,
draughtsman, sculptor, photographer, and
film maker. He was secretive about his
early life and neither his real name (it may
have been Emmanuel Rudnitsky) nor the
origin of his pseudonym is known. In 1915
he began a lifelong friendship with Marcel
*Duchamp, collaborating with him and
*Picabia in founding the New York *Dada
movement. He also collaborated with Duchamp and Katherine *Dreier in forming
the *Société Anonyme. In 1921 he went
to Paris and became a member of the
European Dada group and then of the
*Surrealist movement. In 1940 he went
back to America to escape the Nazi occupation of Paris and settled in Hollywood,
then in 1951 returned to Paris, where he
died. Man Ray is regarded as one of the
most inventive photographers of his time,
notably for his development of the technique of 'solarization' (the partial reversal
of the tones of a photographic image). He
gained an international reputation as one
of the most prominent figures in the Dada
and Surrealist movements, and several of
his constructions have become famous as
paradigms of Dada. Later critics, however,
have spoken of his 'jackdaw eclecticism'
and have been dismissive about his paintings. A large retrospective exhibition arranged in 1975 to coincide with his 85th
birthday in 1975 was shown at the New
York Cultural Center and later at the ICA
Galleries, London. While this exhibition
proved the enormous ingenuity and versatility of Man Ray, the general reaction
among critics was that it demonstrated the
poverty of Dada once the shock of novelty
had worn off.

Manship, Paul (1885–1966). American
sculptor. He worked in an elegant, streamlined style, his beautifully crafted figures
characterized by clarity of outline and
suave generalized forms, and he achieved
great success as a sculptor of public monuments. One of his best-known works is
the gilded bronze *Prometheus* (1933) in
Rockefeller Center Plaza, New York.
Manship was also an excellent portraitist.
Because of the stylization of his work,
derived partly from his interest in archaic

sculpture, he for a time had a reputation as a pioneer of modern sculpture in America, but his modernism was of a very facile kind and by about 1940 he was being labelled an academic artist.

Mantegna, Andrea (1431–1506). Italian painter. He was the pupil and adopted son of *Squarcione in Padua, growing up in a humanist atmosphere that was to colour his whole approach to art. Squarcione exploited his pupils for his own ends and at the age of 17 Mantegna gave an early indication of his formidable strength of character by taking him to court and forcing him to recognize his independence. He was remarkably precocious, and the distinctive style he created at the beginning of his career changed little over the next half century. It was a style characterized by sharp clarity of drawing, colouring, and lighting, a passion for archaeology that fed on the relative abundance of *Classical remains in northern Italy, and a mastery of *perspective and foreshortening unequalled in the 15th cent. These qualities were apparent in his first major commission (1448), the decoration of the Ovetari Chapel of the Eremitani Church in Padua with frescos on the lives of SS. Christopher and James (almost totally destroyed in the Second World War) and they can be seen in the celebrated *Agony in the Garden* (NG, London, c.1455).

In 1460 Mantegna was appointed court painter to Ludovico *Gonzaga at Mantua, and apart from a visit to Rome in 1488–90 he remained there for the rest of his life. Mantegna was held in the highest esteem by Ludovico, by his son and successor Federico, and by Isabella d'*Este, who married Federico's successor, Francesco. At this time Mantua was rising to take its place among the leading centres of humanist culture in Europe, and Mantegna glorified the Gonzaga family and court in his most famous work—the fresco decoration of the Camera degli Sposi (Bridal Chamber) in the Ducal Palace (completed 1474). Group portraits of the Gonzaga family, arranged in various courtly scenes, line the walls and above them are bust medallions of the Caesars, indicating that the reigning house was worthy of the Roman Empire. The most remarkable feature of the room, however, is the *illusionistic painting of the architecture (particularly of the ceiling), which appears to extend the real space of the room. This was the first time since antiquity that such a scheme had been carried out and Mantegna's work became the foundation for much subsequent decorative painting. Mantegna's other great work for the Gonzaga was his series of nine paintings on the *Triumph of Caesar* (Hampton Court, London, c.1480–95)—it is often said that they were done for Francesco, but in fact it is not known which member of the family commissioned them. These large and fragile canvases have suffered dreadfully at the hands of 'restorers' in former centuries, but they were successfully cleaned in the 1960s and 1970s, and although they are battered and faded they still give a marvellous picture of Mantegna's magnificent powers of invention and design and rank alongside *Raphael's tapestry *cartoons as one of the greatest ensembles of *Renaissance art outside Italy.

Mantegna was an engraver as well as a painter and was one of the first artists to use prints to disseminate his compositions. He also designed his own house in Mantua, and it is generally thought that he modelled the bronze bust of himself in his memorial chapel in the church of S. Andrea. At his death he was a venerated figure and his fame has never declined. His influence was profound, not only on Italian artists such as his brother-in-law Giovanni *Bellini, but also, for example, on *Dürer, one of the many northern artists who found his version of the *antique particularly easy to assimilate.

Manzoni, Piero (1933–63). Italian experimental artist. He worked in a conventional figurative style until 1956, when he turned to avant-garde work. In 1957 he began to produce *Achromes*, textured white paintings influenced by *Burri and *Klein, and from 1959 he devised a series of provocative works and gestures that included signing people's bodies and designating them works of art, a block on which is inscribed upside down 'The base of the world' (Herning Park, Denmark, 1961), and cans of his own excrement. He is regarded as one of the forerunners of *Arte Povera and *Conceptual art.

Manzù, Giacomo (1908–). Italian sculptor. The son of a sacristan in a convent, he was apprenticed to a wood-carver at the age of 11, then to a gilder and stucco-worker, beginning to draw, paint, and model in his spare time. His early work was influenced by Egyptian and Etruscan art, but then he turned to a more *Impressionistic style owing much to the example of *Rodin and Medardo *Rosso. In the 1940s he simplified his style, so that although the surface of his work is often animated, the feeling it produces is one of Classic calm. He has worked much on religious subjects, and is celebrated above all for the set of bronze doors he made for St Peter's in Rome after winning an international competition in 1950. In 1958 he also completed a set of doors for Salzburg Cathedral, and his work shows the possibility of producing sculpture that fits within a traditional religious context and yet is in a modern and personal idiom. Manzù has also worked as an etcher, lithographer, and painter.

maquette. A small preliminary model, often in clay or wax, for a work of sculpture. The word implies something in the nature of a rough sketch, not so fully worked out as a *bozzetto.

Maratta (Maratti), Carlo (1625–1713). Italian painter, the leading painter in Rome in the latter part of the 17th cent. As the pupil of Andrea *Sacchi he continued the tradition of the Classical *Grand Manner, based on *Raphael, and he gained an international reputation particularly for his paintings of the Madonna and Child, which are reworkings of types established during the High *Renaissance. The rhetorical splendour of his work is thoroughly in the *Baroque idiom, however, and the numerous altarpieces he painted for Roman churches (many still *in situ*) give whole-hearted expression to the dogmas of the Counter-Reformation. Maratta was also an accomplished fresco painter, and the finest portraitist of the day in Rome. He had a large studio and his posthumous reputation suffered when the inferior works of his many pupils and imitators were confused with his own paintings.

marble. Word loosely applied to any hard limestone which can be sawn into thin slabs and will take a good polish so that it is suitable for decorative work, and in a stricter sense to metamorphosed limestones whose structure has been recrystallized by heat or pressure. Marbles are widely disseminated and occur in a great variety of colours and patterns, but certain types have been particularly prized by sculptors. The most famous of Greek white marbles in the ancient world was the close-grained Pentelic, which was quarried at Mt. Pentelicon in Attica. The *Elgin Marbles are carved in Pentelic. Widely used also were the somewhat coarser-grained translucent white marbles from the Aegean islands of Paros and Naxos. Parian marble was used for the celebrated Mausoleum at Halicarnassus. The pure white Carrara marble, quarried at Massa, Carrara, and Pietra Santa in Tuscany from the 3rd cent. BC, is the most famous of all sculptors' stones. It was used for the *Apollo Belvedere*, and was much favoured in the *Renaissance, particularly by *Michelangelo, who often visited the quarries to select material for his work. *Neoclassical sculptors also favoured Carrara marble because of its ability to take a smooth, sleek surface, but it can look rather 'dead' compared to some of the finest Greek marbles.

Marc, Franz (1880–1916). German painter. The son of a Munich painter, he began working in an academic naturalistic style, but visits to Paris in 1903 and 1908 brought him into contact with *Impressionism and *Post-Impressionism, and responding particularly to van *Gogh he advanced towards a more *Expressionist style. In 1910 he entered into a close friendship with *Macke, who introduced him to the Expressionist use of colour. Through Macke he joined the *Neue Künstlervereinigung at Munich and found in *Kandinsky and *Jawlensky men of congenial artistic views. With them he founded the *Blaue Reiter in 1911–12. Marc was of a deeply religious disposition (he visited Mt. Athos in 1906) and was troubled by a profound spiritual malaise; through painting he sought to uncover mystical inner forces that animate nature. His ideas were expressed most intensely in paintings of animals, for he believed that they were both more beautiful and more spiritual than man. Using non-naturalistic symbolic colour and simplified, rhythmic shapes, he tried to paint animals not as we see them, but as they feel their own existence (*Blue Horses*, Minneapolis Institute of Arts, 1911). In 1912 Marc met *Delaunay in Paris and was influenced by the *Orphist experiments in the abstract use of colour. The culminating work of this period was *Animal Destinies* (Kunstmuseum, Basle, 1913), which uses panic-stricken animals to symbolize a world on the edge of destruction; on the back of the picture he wrote: 'Und alles sein ist flammend leid' (And all being is flaming suffering). By 1914, under the influence partly of *Cubism and *Futurism, his paintings had become still more abstract, losing almost entirely any representational content, as in *Fighting Forms* (Neue Pinakothek, Munich, 1914), an image of convulsive fury. These last paintings are considered among the culminating works of German Expressionism. Marc was killed in action in the First World War.

Marées, Hans von (1837–87). German painter, active mainly in Italy, where he settled in 1864. Like his friends *Böcklin, *Feuerbach, and *Hildebrand, he was one of the Germanic artists working in Italy who turned to the tradition of *ideal art at a time when naturalism was becoming dominant in their own countries. He devoted himself mainly to the theme of the human figure in a landscape setting (*Age*, Staatliche Mus., Berlin, 1873-8). In 1873 he received a major commission to paint a series of large frescos in the Zoological Institute in Naples, but he lacked self-confidence, and died disappointed and practically unknown. It was only at the beginning of the 20th cent. that the statuesque dignity of his work became appreciated and taken up as a symbol of a new spirit of modernity in German art.

Margarito (or **Margaritone**) **of Arezzo** (active *c*.1262). Italian painter from Arezzo. He is one of the very few 13th-cent. Italian painters and the only early Aretine by whom we have signed works (examples are in the NG, London, and the NG, Washington). Margarito's paintings are clumsy, but have something of the vividness and lucid brevity of the comic strip. *Vasari, who also came from Arezzo, wrote his biography in his *Lives* (saying he was an architect as well as a painter), and this is virtually the only source of knowledge on him, although a document of 1262 probably refers to him.

Marin, John (1870–1953). American painter. From 1905 to 1910 he worked in Europe, where he was influenced by *Whistler's water-colours and etchings, but he first came into contact with avant-garde movements after his return to America, when he became a member of *Stieglitz's circle. The *Armory Show also made a great impact on him. Responding especially to German *Expressionism, and the planimetric structure of the late work of *Cézanne, he developed a distinctive style that he used most characteristically in powerful water-colours of the Maine coast. His oil paintings are often similar in effect to water-colours, leaving parts of the canvas bare. During the 1920s he provided the dominant force in the movement away from naturalistic representation towards an art of expressive semi-abstraction.

Marini, Marino (1901–80). One of the outstanding Italian sculptors of the 20th cent., also a painter, lithographer, and etcher. Until *c*.1928 he worked mainly as a graphic artist. During the 1930s he travelled widely in Europe and also visited the USA, but he did not ally himself with any avant-garde movements, remaining essentially isolated in his artistic aims. Working mainly in bronze, he concentrated on a few favourite themes, most notably the Horse and Rider, a subject in which he seemed to express an obscure but poignant tragic symbolism. He also made numerous portrait busts, remarkable for their psychological penetration and sensuous exploitation of the surface qualities of the material. Often he *polychromed his bronzes, sometimes working with corrosive dyes. There is a Marini museum in Milan, where he spent much of his career, and his work is represented in many major collections of modern art.

Marinus van Reymerswaele (active *c*.1509– d. after 1567). Netherlandish painter, presumably from Romerswaele in Zealand. He specialized in two types of picture, both with more or less life-size half-length figures: representations of St Jerome in his study (seemingly deriving from *Dürer) and *genre scenes of bankers, usurers, misers, and tax-collectors. The genre scenes show the sin of avarice and the vanity of earthly possessions: according to a Flemish proverb a banker, a usurer, a tax-collector, and a miller were the four evangelists of the devil. These paintings must have been very popular, for they exist in numerous versions and copies, but it is not known what kind of clientele bought pictures of such unpleasant characters, grotesquely presented in a manner deriving (via *Massys) from *Leonardo's *'caricatures'. Marinus is last heard of in Middelburg in 1567, when he was condemned to walk in a penitential procession for taking part in the destruction of a church.

Maris. Family of three brothers who played a leading part in Dutch painting during the second half of the 19th cent. **Jacob (Jacobus Hendricus)** (1837–99) was one of the leaders of the *Hague School, painting principally views of the Dutch countryside, with some portraits and figure studies. **Matthias (Matthijs, Thijs)** (1839–1917) had an entirely different approach to art, specializing in figure compositions of visionary subjects. In 1869 he moved to Paris and then in 1877 to London, where he lived for the rest of his life and was influenced by the *Pre-Raphaelites in his choice of poetic subjects, although not in style. **Willem** (1844–1910) was a pupil of his two brothers and was influenced by *Mauve. His subjects are almost entirely confined to meadows and cattle. In his later years he became a leader of Dutch *Impressionism, urging his pupils—among them *Breitner—to paint in the open air and to use vivid colours.

Marlow, William (1740–1813). English landscape and marine painter, a pupil of Samuel *Scott and possibly also of Richard *Wilson. His early landscapes were topographical views, including pictures of country houses, but after a visit to the Continent (1765–8) he painted largely from his memories of France and Italy. He retired from professional practice c.1785, but continued to paint for his own pleasure. See also CAPRICCIO.

Marmion, Simon (d. 1489). Franco-Flemish manuscript *illuminator and painter. In 1449–54 he was at Amiens, where he may have been born, and he was a member of the Tournai guild in 1468, but the greater part of his working life was spent at Valenciennes. He had a great reputation in his day, but no works certainly from his hand survive. The main work attributed to him is the *retable of S. Bertin (1459; most of it in the Staatliche

Museen, Berlin, fragments in the NG, London). His style was very tender, with delicate, almost pastel colouring, and does not belong to the main-stream of either French or Netherlandish art.

Marochetti, Carlo (1805–67). Italian sculptor. He had an internationally successful career, being made a baron in his native country, awarded the Legion of Honour in France, and patronized by Queen Victoria and Prince Albert in England, where he worked from 1848. His dramatic style, exemplified in his equestrian statue of Richard the Lionheart (1851–60) outside the Houses of Parliament, was, however, considered rather flashy in England.

marouflage. Term for gluing a *canvas down, whether before painting it or afterwards, on to a wall. In French *maroufle* means a sticky mixture of the remains of paint left in the artist's pots, and *maroufler* may describe almost any operation which might be carried out with this powerful glue, for example lining one canvas with another to strengthen it.

Marquet, Albert (1875–1947). French painter. In 1897 he entered the studio of Gustave *Moreau, where he was a fellow student of *Matisse, with whom he became a member of the *Fauves. Subsequently, however, he abandoned the Fauvist style and turned to a comparatively naturalistic form of landscape painting. His favourite themes were ports and the bridges and quays of Paris, subjects he depicted with unaffected simplicity and great sensitivity to tone.

Marsh, Reginald (1898–1954). American painter. He was a newspaper illustrator in the 1920s, but after taking up painting seriously in 1923 he came to the fore during the 1930s as one of the leading painters of the shabbiness and tawdriness of city life in New York (*Tattoo and Haircut*, Art Institute of Chicago, 1932). He was also capable of bitter satire against the smug complacency of the wealthy, but in general his work shows a love of depicting teeming life through ugly but colourful subjects rather than a desire for social protest. Marsh painted mainly in *tempera and also worked as a book illustrator.

Marshall, Benjamin (1767–1835). English sporting painter, an able follower of *Stubbs. He was a pupil of the portrait painter L. F. *Abbot, but from c.1792 he turned to animal painting. In 1812 he settled in Newmarket, where he concentrated on pictures of horses and hunting and racing scenes.

Martin, John (1789–1854). English *Romantic painter and *mezzotint engraver, celebrated for his melodramatic scenes of cataclysmic events crowded with tiny figures placed in vast architectural settings. He caught the public imagination with spectacular paintings such as *Joshua Commanding the Sun to Stand Still* (United Grand Lodge of Great Britain, London, 1816), the work that made him famous, and in 1821 *Lawrence referred to him as 'the most popular painter of the day'. His work was indeed truly popular, for he made his living mainly through the sale of engravings of his pictures rather than the paintings themselves. He became famous in France as well as Britain, he was knighted by Leopold I of Belgium (1833), and his influence was felt by American artists such as *Cole. However, while he pleased a vast audience and was regarded by some admirers as one of the greatest geniuses who ever lived, Martin was reviled by *Ruskin and other critics, who considered his work vulgar sensationalism. Few artists, indeed, have been subject to such wide extremes of critical fortune, and his fame sank to such an astonishing degree after his death that very large and once famous paintings by him were sold in the 1930s for as little as £2. In the 1970s his reputation greatly revived. Martin made mezzotints not only as a means of reproducing his paintings but also as original compositions. Particularly noteworthy are his illustrations to the Bible and John Milton's *Paradise Lost*, which show that although he had great weaknesses as an artist, especially in his drawing of the human figure, he also had a vividness and grandiloquence of imagination not unworthy of such elevated subjects. He is sometimes called 'Mad Martin', but the sobriquet is undeserved and applies more to his brother Jonathan, who was insane and set fire to York Minster. John Martin was eminently sane and in the 1830s almost bankrupted himself with extremely ambitious but entirely practical plans for improving the water

supply and sewage system of London. They were unsuccessful, but reveal a heroic desire to put the architectural visions of his paintings into a concrete form. His work is best represented in the Tate Gallery, London, and the Laing Art Gallery, Newcastle upon Tyne.

Martin, Kenneth (1905–84). British painter and sculptor. In 1930 he married Mary Balmford, whose artistic development as Mary *Martin had very close affinities with his own. In the 1930s he painted in a naturalistic style and was in close touch with artists of the *Euston Road School, but during the 1940s the representational character of his work receded until in 1948–9 both he and Mary Martin made their first completely abstract paintings. With Victor *Pasmore the Martins were among the leaders of a new *Constructivist movement which burgeoned both in England and in America in the 1950s, making their first constructions at the beginning of the decade. Thereafter with great versatility he pioneered in England a number of different forms of geometrical abstraction.

Martin, Mary (*née* Balmford) (1907–69). British painter and sculptor, the wife of Kenneth *Martin, who was a fellow student at the Royal College of Art. She painted landscapes and still lifes, but during the 1940s her work, like that of her husband, moved towards geometrical abstraction. With Kenneth Martin and Victor *Pasmore she belonged to the group of post-war *Constructivists which continued the tradition of geometrical abstraction in England. Her major commissions included a Wall Construction for the University of Stirling (1969).

Martorell, Bernardo (active 1427–52). Spanish painter and *miniaturist. He worked in Barcelona and was the outstanding painter in Catalonia in the second quarter of the 15th cent., the successor to *Borrassá, who probably taught him. Only one surviving work is securely documented—the *Altarpiece of St Peter of Púbol* (Gerona Mus., 1437)—but on stylistic grounds a group of paintings formerly given to 'the Master of St George' has been attributed to him. The group includes (and formerly took its identity from) an altarpiece of St George; the central panel is in the Art Institute of Chicago and the four wings are in the Louvre. Martorell's work, influenced by Franco-Flemish painting and *illumination, was essentially *International Gothic in style, but reveals a highly distinctive personality, particularly in its vigorous sense of drama and delicate handling of light. Among the painters of the next generation *Huguet was most obviously indebted to him.

Marzal de Sax, Andrés (active 1393–1410). Painter, probably of German origin (Sax indicating Saxony), who worked in Valencia. Only one fragment survives of his documented works—the *Incredulity of St Thomas* in Valencia Cathedral, part of an altarpiece he completed for the cathedral in 1400. Among the works given to him on stylistic grounds the most important is the huge and sumptuous *retable of St George (V&A, London), featuring the varied tortures of the saint in grisly detail. The somewhat rough vigour of Marzal de Sax's style had considerable influence in Valencia; he is last mentioned in 1410, impoverished and ill, receiving free lodging from the city in recognition of the quality of his work and his generosity in training local painters.

Masaccio (Tommaso di Ser Giovanni di Mone) (1401–28). Florentine painter. Although he died in his mid-twenties he brought about a revolution in painting and he ranks alongside his friends *Alberti, *Brunelleschi, and *Donatello as one of the founding fathers of the *Renaissance. His affectionate nickname, which may be translated as 'Sloppy Tom', was given to him, so *Vasari says, because he was so devoted to art that 'he refused to give any time to worldly causes, even to the way he dressed'. He became a guild member in Florence in 1422, but nothing is known of his training, the tradition that he was taught by *Masolino, later his collaborator, now being discounted. The earliest work attributed to him is the San Giovenale *Triptych (Uffizi, Florence, 1422), which is somewhat uncouth but reveals a totally individual spirit in its rejection of all *Gothic elegance and concentration on the weight and bulk of the figures. Instead of learning from contemporary painters, Masaccio looked back to *Giotto for inspiration, recapturing the gravity and grandeur that characterized his work. But

whereas Giotto set his figures in space intuitively, Masaccio grappled with and solved the problem of creating a completely coherent and consistent sense of three dimensions on a two-dimensional surface, his work thus becoming one of the cornerstones of European painting. His enormous achievement was based on his mastery of the new science of *perspective and his use of a single constant light source to define the construction of the body and its draperies. Among contemporary artists he was closest in spirit to Donatello. Both artists were less concerned with surface appearances and isolated detail than with the underlying construction of objects and both excelled at the depiction of emotion with great force and directness. Masaccio has left three great works to posterity in which he enunciated his new principles: a *polyptych (1426) for the Carmelite church in Pisa (the central panel is in the National Gallery in London, and other parts in the Staatliche Museen, Berlin, and the Museo di Capodimonte, Naples); a fresco cycle, done in collaboration with Masolino, on the life of St Peter (with additional scenes of *The Temptation* and *The Expulsion from Paradise*) in the Brancacci Chapel of Sta Maria del Carmine, Florence (c.1425–8); and a fresco of the *Trinity* in Sta Maria Novella, Florence (probably 1428). Masaccio went to Rome in 1428, leaving the frescos in the Brancacci Chapel unfinished, and died so suddenly that Vasari said 'there were some who even suspected he had been poisoned'. Vasari adds that 'during his lifetime he had made only a modest name for himself', and certainly many of his Florentine contemporaries and successors were unmoved by his innovations. He was a great inspiration to the progressive masters of the next generation, however (Filippo *Lippi, *Piero della Francesca), and Vasari records a whole roster of great artists, including *Leonardo, *Michelangelo, and *Raphael, who studied his work with profit.

Masereel, Frans (1889–1972). Belgian *Expressionist painter and print-maker, best known for his *romans in beelden* (novels in pictures), which are series of woodcuts telling a story without a text.

Maso di Banco (active second quarter of the 14th cent.). Florentine painter. Almost nothing is known of his career (*Vasari does not mention him), but he is regarded as the greatest of *Giotto's followers on the strength of *Ghiberti's testimony that he was the painter of the frescos illustrating the legend of St Sylvester in the Bardi chapel of Sta Croce, Florence. The stately figures here are sometimes even more massive than Giotto's and the lucid and beautifully coloured compositions are of almost geometric clarity (although it has been argued that some of the effect of monumental simplicity may be due to restoration). On stylistic grounds other works have been attributed to Maso, including panels in Budapest (Mus. of Fine Arts), Chantilly (Musée Condé), and New York (Brooklyn Mus. and Met. Mus.).

Masolino da Panicale (c.1383–1447?). Italian painter. He is generally considered to be a member of the Florentine School, but he travelled a good deal and even went to Hungary. His career is closely linked to that of *Masaccio, but the exact nature of the association remains ill-defined. The tradition that he was Masaccio's master is now dismissed, for he became a guild member in Florence only in 1423 (a year after Masaccio) and although he was appreciably the older man it was he who was influenced by Masaccio rather than the other way round. They are thought to have collaborated on *The Madonna and Child with St Anne* (Uffizi, Florence, c.1425), but the major undertaking on which they worked together was the decoration of the Brancacci Chapel of Sta Maria del Carmine in Florence. Masolino's style was softer than Masaccio's and there is a fair measure of agreement about the division of hands. After Masaccio's death Masolino reverted to the more decorative style he had practised earlier in his career. At his best he was a painter of great distinction, his masterpiece perhaps being the fresco of the *Baptism of Christ* (c.1435) in the Baptistery at Castiglione d'Olona, near Como, a graceful and lyrical work that is a world away from Masaccio's *Baptism of the Neophytes* in the Brancacci Chapel.

Masson, André (1896–1987). French painter, engraver, sculptor, stage designer, and writer, one of the leading figures of *Surrealism. He was severely wounded in the First World War and deeply scarred emotionally. His pessimism was accompanied by a profound and troubled curiosity about the nature and destiny of man and an obscure belief in the mysterious unity of the universe, to which he devoted the whole of his artistic activity to penetrating and expressing. In the early 1920s he was influenced by *Cubism, but in 1924 he joined the Surrealist movement and remained a member until 1929, when he left in protest against *Breton's authoritarian leadership. His work belonged to the spontaneous, expressive variety of Surrealism, and included experiments with automatic drawings (see AUTOMATISM), chance effects, and the incorporation of sand in his paintings. Themes of metamorphosis, violence, psychic pain, and eroticism dominated his work. In 1934–6 he lived in Spain and in 1941–5 he took refuge from the Second World War in the USA. There his work formed a link between Surrealism and *Abstract Expressionism. In 1945 he returned to France and two years later settled at Aix-en-Provence, where he concentrated on landscape painting, achieving something of the spiritual rapport with nature seen in some Chinese paintings.

Massys (or **Matsys** or **Metsys**), **Quentin** (1465/6–1530). Netherlandish painter. He was born at Louvain but worked in Antwerp, where he became the leading painter of his day. Although he became a master in the guild there in 1491, his early career is obscure and his first dated works are the altarpiece of *St Anne* (Musées Royaux, Brussels, 1507–9) and the *Lamentation* (Musée Royal, Antwerp, 1508–11). Massys continued the tradition of the great masters of 15th-cent. Netherlandish art, but he was also clearly aware of Italian art (particularly the work of *Leonardo) and may well have crossed the Alps at some point in his career. In his exquisite *Madonna and Child with Angels* (Courtauld Inst., London), for example, the *iconographic type of the standing Virgin goes back to Jan van *Eyck, but the *putti with the garland reveal the influence of the *Renaissance. The landscape backgrounds of some of his religious works were possibly done by *Patenier. Massys also painted portraits and *genre scenes. The satirical quality in his pictures of bankers, tax-collectors, and avaricious merchants has been linked with the writings of the great humanist Erasmus.

Certainly the two met, for Massys painted a pair of portraits of Erasmus (Gal. Naz., Rome) and Petrus Egidius (Earl of Radnor Coll., Longford Castle, Wiltshire) as a gift for Sir Thomas More in 1517. They instituted a new type—the scholar in his study—that influenced *Holbein among others. Massys had two painter sons, **Jan** (1509–75) and **Cornelis** (1513–79).

Master E. S. (sometimes called the Master of 1466 from the date on one of his engravings). German engraver working in the mid-15th cent., named after the monogram on eighteen of his surviving prints. He was the most prolific and influential of the early German engravers, working on profane and fantastic subjects as well as religious images and producing more than 300 known prints. Earlier engravers had been content with pure outline, but E. S. managed to produce rich tonal effects by the ingenious use of *hatching, and cross-hatching.

Master Francke (early 15th cent.). German painter, active in Hamburg. His major surviving work is an altarpiece for the guild of merchants trading with England (Kunsthalle, Hamburg, 1424), showing Passion scenes and incidents from the life of St Thomas à Becket. Francke was a leader of the northern German version of *International Gothic. He had close links with the west and Burgundy in particular. His influence was widely spread over north Germany and along the shores of the Baltic.

Master of . . . Term used in art history to label the author of anonymous works for convenience in discussing them. This use of invented names is more common in the study of painting and the *graphic arts than of sculpture, and historians of architecture hardly ever resort to it. It began in Germany in the early 19th cent. with the description of early Netherlandish painting. The choice of names was then often more lyrical than descriptive: for instance the 'Master of the Pearl of Brabant' (who later was identified with *Bouts) got his name from a picture which had received that poetical title simply because it caught the imagination. Nowadays invented names are more prosaic and more directly appropriate. Often the anonymous master is named after a particular picture and/or the collection to which it belongs, e.g.

'Master of the Mansi Magdalen'. Alternatively, the name can refer to some aspect of the artist's style, as in the 'Master of the Anaemic Figures' (a 15th-cent. Spanish painter), which shows that the designation 'master' is used neutrally and is not a sign of approbation. The practice of creating artistic personalities in this way has been overdone, but is often useful.

Master of Alkmaar (active early 16th cent.). Netherlandish painter named after the altarpiece of the *Seven Works of Mercy* painted for the church of St Lawrence in Alkmaar in 1504 and now in the Rijksmuseum, Amsterdam. Attempts have been made to identify the painter with Cornelis Buys, who was the brother of Jacob *Cornelisz. van Oostsanen. The figure style is reminiscent of *Geertgen tot Sint Jans and the altarpiece is important as an early instance of the characteristically Dutch delight in the representation of everyday life.

Master of Flémalle. Netherlandish painter named after three paintings in the Städelsches Kunstinstitut in Frankfurt that were wrongly supposed to have come from Flémalle, near Liège. There is a strong consensus of scholarly opinion that he is to be identified with Robert Campin (active 1406–44), who was the leading painter of his day in Tournai but none of whose documented pictures survive. The identification depends on the similarity between the Master of Flémalle's paintings and those of Jacques *Daret and Rogier van der *Weyden, for Daret was Campin's pupil and Rogier almost certainly was. The hypothesis that the Master of Flémalle's paintings are early works by Rogier now has few adherents. While there is still doubt about the Master of Flémalle's identity, there is no argument about his achievement, for he made a radical break with the elegant *International Gothic style and ranks with van *Eyck as one of the founders of the Netherlandish school of painting. None of the paintings given to him is dated—with the exception of the wings of the Werl altarpiece of 1438 in the Prado, a doubtful attribution—but it seems likely that his earliest works antedate any surviving picture by van Eyck. The earliest of all is generally thought to be *The Entombment* (Courtauld Inst., London) of about 1410/20. This still has the decorative gold background of medieval tradition, but the influence of Claus *Sluter is clear in the sculptural solidity and dramatic force of the figures. The most famous work associated with the Master of Flémalle is the Mérode Altarpiece (Met. Mus., New York), and he is indeed sometimes referred to as the Master of Mérode. However, the attribution of this painting has also been questioned. Among the other works generally accepted as his are *The Marriage of the Virgin* (Prado, Madrid), *The Nativity* (Musée des Beaux-Arts, Dijon), and *The Virgin and Child before a Firescreen* (NG, London), which shows the homely detail and down-to-earth naturalism associated with the artist (the firescreen behind the Virgin's head forms a substitute for a halo). The National Gallery also has three portraits associated with the Master of Flémalle. In spite of the many problems that still surround him, he emerges as a very powerful and important artistic personality.

Master of Mary of Burgundy. Netherlandish manuscript illuminator, active in the last quarter of the 15th cent. He is named after two *Books of Hours painted for Mary of Burgundy, who married the emperor Maximilian I in 1477 and died in 1482 (Österreichische Nationalbibliothek, Vienna, and Kupferstichkabinett, Berlin). They are among the finest illuminated books of the period, with many charming everyday-life and still-life details, and other fine works in a similar style have been attributed to him, notably a Book of Hours in the Bodleian Library, Oxford. It has been suggested that he is to be identified with Alexander *Bening.

Master of Moulins (active *c*.1480–*c*.1500). French painter, named after a *triptych in Moulins Cathedral representing the Madonna with Saints and Donors and datable *c*.1498. The style of this work is quite distinctive, and has enabled a considerable *œuvre* to be built up around it. The Master of Moulins' sculptural precision of form (recalling *Fouquet), the poise of his individual figures, his brilliant palette, the harmony of his compositions, and his taste for splendid and meticulous details make him one of the outstanding painters of his period in northern Europe. Various attempts have been made to identify the Master of Moulins with named artists (for example Jean *Perréal), but none has met with general acceptance.

Master of St Cecilia (active *c*.1304). Italian painter named after the St Cecilia Altarpiece in the Uffizi, which was originally in the church of Sta Cecilia, destroyed by fire in 1304. Presumably he was a Florentine, but nothing is known about him. Other works have been attributed to him because of their resemblance to the Uffizi picture, the most important being the three concluding scenes of the great fresco cycle of the life of St Francis in the Upper Church of S. Francesco at Assisi (SEE MASTER OF THE ST FRANCIS LEGEND). The painter of these scenes resembles *Giotto in lucidity of presentation and the solid drawing of his figures, but he is more genial in feeling. His figures are more vivacious, his colour warmer and sweeter. The completion of the great cycle in the Upper Church would have been entrusted only to an established master and some critics have attempted to identify the painter of these scenes and the St Cecilia Altarpiece with the famous but tantalizingly elusive *Buffalmacco.

Master of St George. See MARTORELL.

Master of St Giles (active *c*.1480–*c*.1500). Netherlandish (?) painter named after two panels representing scenes from the life of St Giles (NG, London). Other paintings in the same style have been grouped round them. Their attention to detail and their meticulous finish have caused some to consider that the artist was trained in the Netherlands, but the inclusion of views of Paris in some of his works indicates that he worked there, whatever his origin. His work is of high quality and he must have been one of the best painters of the day in northern France.

Master of Segovia. See BENSON.

Master of the Brunswick Monogram (active *c*.1520–40). Netherlandish painter, named after a picture in the Herzog-Anton-Ulrich Museum in Brunswick of *The Parable of the Great Supper* (Luke 14). There is no agreement how the monogram should be read. A dozen or so small pictures have been attributed to the same hand; about half depict religious subjects in the open air, and most of the others scenes in brothels. The quality of the pictures is uniformly high. The artist's observation of nature, his fine drawing, and ability to integrate figures into a landscape make him an important forerunner of Pieter *Bruegel the Elder. Attempts have been made to identify him with various painters, including Jan Sanders van *Hemessen.

Master of the Housebook (late 15th cent.). German (or according to some authorities Netherlandish) engraver, so called from a number of drawings contained in a kind of commonplace book in Castle Wolfegg in Germany. He used to be called the Master of the Amsterdam Cabinet, since the largest collection of his engravings is in the Print Room of the Rijksmuseum. His *line engravings often represent very worldly subjects and his use of *drypoint gives them a curiously sketchy and lively character. *Dürer must have studied them fairly closely, as their influence can be traced in several of his early drawings. A few paintings have also been attributed to this master.

Master of the Life of the Virgin or **Master of the Life of Mary** (active c.1460–90). German painter, named after a series of eight panels illustrating the Life of the Virgin, of which the *Presentation in the Temple* is in the National Gallery, London, and the remainder in the Alte Pinakothek, Munich. He was one of the outstanding Cologne painters of his time, and his affinities with Dirk *Bouts and Rogier van der *Weyden suggest that he trained in the Netherlands. None of the pictures attributed to him is dated, but a *Crucifixion* in the hospital church at Cues on the Moselle, generally accepted as his work, is probably from 1465.

Master of the Playing-Cards (mid 15th cent.). German engraver, named after a set of playing-cards depicting human figures, animals, flowers, etc., now divided between the Kupferstichkabinett in Dresden and the Bibliothèque Nationale in Paris. They have been dated as early as the 1430s and he was one of the first distinct artistic personalities in the history of engraving. More than a hundred prints have been attributed to him, his style being characterized by closely observed naturalistic detail and the use of short, densely packed parallel strokes to create shading.

Master of the St Francis Cycle. A name for the unidentified painter of the famous cycle of frescos on the nave walls of the Upper Church of S. Francesco in Assisi, depicting the life of St Francis and probably dating from the 1290s, although some critics put them as late as the 1320s. This cycle was praised by *Vasari as one of the principal works of *Giotto and figures as such in many histories of art, but many scholars nowadays challenge this assertion, feeling that Giotto's undoubted works in Padua differ so thoroughly from those of Assisi in both sentiment and formal organization that it is hard to imagine that he should have painted both. The last three scenes differ in style from the rest and have been attributed to the *Master of St Cecilia.

Master of the Třeboň Altarpiece or of **Wittingau.** *Bohemian painter, active in the late 14th cent., named after his main work, three panels (c.1380–90) from an altarpiece originally in the monastery at Třeboň (Wittingau) in Czechoslovakia and now in the National Gallery, Prague. With him the art at the short-lived imperial court of Prague reached its climax. His style points west rather than south and shows particular affinities with Burgundian art and Melchior *Broederlam.

Master of the Virgo Inter Virgines (active c.1470–c.1500). Netherlandish painter, named after a picture representing the Virgin Mary surrounded by the virgin saints Barbara, Catherine, Cecilia, and Ursula (Rijksmuseum, Amsterdam). He worked in Delft, and his style is reflected in the woodcut illustrations (which he presumably designed) to several books published there between 1482 and 1498. About twenty paintings have been attributed to him, revealing a highly distinctive and distinguished artist of strong religious fervour, who obtained his dramatic effects through intense colours, desolate landscapes, and gaunt figures. His work is sometimes awkward but his emotional sincerity is always convincing. Two of his finest paintings are *The Crucifixion* (Bowes Museum, Barnard Castle) and *The Entombment* (Walker Art Gal., Liverpool).

Master of Vyšší Brod (or **of Hohenfurth**). Bohemian painter, so called after his main work, a large altarpiece with scenes from the life of Christ (NG, Prague, c.1350) painted for the monastery of Vyšší Brod (Hohenfurth). These panels show the beginnings of the Bohemian variant of *International Gothic. Another important painting from his workshop, a *Death of the Virgin*, is in the Museum of Fine Arts, Boston.

masterpiece. A term now loosely applied to the finest work by a particular artist or to any work of art of acknowledged greatness or of pre-eminence in its field. Originally it meant the piece of work by which a craftsman, having finished his training, gained the rank of 'master' in his guild.

Master Theoderic (active mid 14th cent.). Bohemian painter. He was first head of the painter's guild in Prague, founded in 1348, and was painter to the emperor Charles IV between 1359 and 1367. For Charles he decorated the Holy Cross Chapel of Karlstein Castle near Prague with more than a hundred panels of saints, prophets, and angels, most of them still *in situ*. He shows even more clearly than the *Master of Vyšší Brod the evolution of a distinct Bohemian School from Italian and French antecedents.

Mateo de Compostela (active late 12th cent.). Spanish *Romanesque sculptor and architect responsible for the Portico de la Gloria, signed and dated 1188, at the cathedral of Santiago de Compostela. A huge composition featuring a triple doorway, this is the greatest work of Spanish sculpture of this period.

Mathieu, Georges (1921–). French painter. After studying philosophy and law, he began to paint in 1942 and by 1944 had worked his way towards abstraction. He was, however, opposed to the geometrical abstraction then in vogue and became one of the originators of the Paris school of expressive abstraction. In 1947 he settled in Paris and his work was confirmed by the example of *Wols in the direction of *Art Informel. He worked at great speed, often on a large scale, and sometimes created *Action paintings in front of an audience. His reputation became international in the 1950s as the vogue for *Gestural painting grew.

Matisse, Henri (1869–1954). French painter, sculptor, graphic artist, and designer. From c.1920 he enjoyed an international reputation as, with *Picasso, the foremost painter of his time, and he was the supreme master in those trends in 20th-cent. art which are represented by calligraphic pattern and the abstract use of pure colour. In 1891 he abandoned a legal career for painting, studying under *Bouguereau and *Moreau, with whom he remained until 1896. During these years he painted still lifes and landscapes in a sober range of colour reminiscent of *Chardin and *Corot, but in the summer of 1896, painting in Brittany, he began to adopt the lighter palette of the *Impressionists. In 1899 he began to experiment with the *Neo-Impressionist technique, which was still applied in one of his first major works—the celebrated *Luxe, calme et volupté* (Musée d'Orsay, Paris, 1904–5), exhibited at the *Salon des Indépendants in 1905 and bought by *Signac. During the same years he had been painting with *Marquet, had met *Derain and through him *Vlaminck, and in 1905 together with these and other friends from Moreau's studio he took part in the sensational exhibition at the *Salon d'Automne which gave birth to the name *'Fauves'. He met Picasso as early as 1906 and like him was excited by African sculpture. Although he never allied himself to the *Cubist group, he was influenced by their work in the second decade of the century, when he painted some of his most austere and formal pictures (*Bathers by a River*, Art Institute of Chicago, 1916–17). In the 1920s, however, he returned to the luminous serenity that characterized his work for the rest of his long career.

From 1917 he spent much of his time on the Riviera, mainly at Nice and also at Vence. The luxuriously sensual works he painted there—odalisques, still lifes of tropical fruits and flowers, and glowing interiors—are irradiated with the strong sun and rich colours of the south. Following two major operations for duodenal cancer in 1941, Matisse was confined to bed or a wheelchair, but he worked until the end of his life and one of his greatest and most original works was created in 1949–51 in thanksgiving for the nuns at the Dominican convent at Vence who had nursed him during an illness. This is the Chapel of the Rosary at Vence, of which he designed every detail, including the priests' vestments. The stained-glass windows show his familiar love of colour, but the walls feature murals of pure white ceramic tiles, decorated with black line drawings of inspired simplicity. Matisse was not a believer, but he created here one of the most moving religious buildings of the 20th cent. and expressed what he called 'the nearly religious feeling I have for life'. In his bed-ridden final years Matisse also embarked on another kind of highly original work, using brightly coloured cut-out paper shapes (*gouaches découpées*) arranged into purely abstract patterns (*L'Escargot*, Tate, London, 1953). The colours he used in his cut-outs were often so strong that his doctor advised him to wear dark glasses. They must rank among the most joyous works ever created by an artist in old age. Unlike many of his great contemporaries, Matisse did not attempt to express in his work the troubled times through which he lived. 'What I dream of,' he wrote, 'is an art of balance, of purity and serenity devoid of troubling or disturbing subject-matter . . . like a comforting influence, a mental balm—something like a good armchair in which one rests from physical fatigue.'

Matisse made sculptures at intervals throughout his career, the best known probably being the four bronzes called *The Back I–IV* (casts in the Tate and elsewhere, 1909–*c*.1929), in which he progressively removed all detail, paring the figure down to massively simple forms. He also designed sets and costumes for *Diaghilev and was a brilliant book illustrator. His work is represented in most important collections of modern art, and there is also a Matisse Museum at his birthplace, Le Cateau in Picardy.

Matta (Roberto Sebastian Antonio Matta Echaurren) (1911–). Chilean painter who has worked principally in Paris, but also in Italy and the USA. He was trained as an architect in Santiago and in Paris under *Le Corbusier in 1934–5, but turned to painting in 1937. An active member of the *Surrealist movement from 1938 until 1947, he was in New York with *Breton, *Tanguy, *Ernst, *Masson, etc., during the Second World War and his

influence there was strong. He encouraged *Gorky, *Pollock, and others to experiment with *automatic techniques, for example. His most characteristic works border on abstraction and evoke fantastic subjective landscapes.

Matteo di Giovanni (active 1452–d. 1495). Sienese painter. He originally came from Borgo San Sepolcro and he painted the wings and *predella (Pinacoteca, Sansepolcro) of the altarpiece of which *Piero della Francesca's *Baptism of Christ* (NG, London) was the centre panel. His style was elegant, linear, and decorative, revealing affinities with *Pollaiuolo, and he seems to have been one of the most popular and prolific Sienese painters of the second half of the 15th cent. His major works include a large *Assumption of the Virgin* in the National Gallery, London.

Maulbertsch (or **Maulpertsch**), **Franz Anton** (1724–96). The outstanding Austrian decorative painter of the 18th cent. He was active (and extremely productive) over a wide area of Central Europe and most of his works (altarpieces as well as *frescos) are still in the churches and secular buildings in Austria, Czechoslovakia, and Hungary for which they were painted. Maulbertsch's vivacious, colourful, and emotional style was almost completely resistant to *Neoclassical influences, representing the last glorious flowering of the *Baroque and *Rococo tradition. His painterly dash is even more apparent in his oil sketches, which are well represented in the Barockmuseum, Vienna, and he was also an outstanding etcher.

maulstick (**mahlstick** or **rest-stick**). A stick with a padded knob at one end, used by painters to support and steady the brush hand, particularly when working on detailed passages. It is first recorded in the 16th cent., and often appears in artists' self-portraits.

Mauritshuis. The royal picture gallery in The Hague, opened to the public in 1820. The building, designed by Jacob van *Campen *c*.1633 as a palace for Prince John Maurice of Nassau, is one of the masterpieces of Dutch architecture. It houses one of the world's choicest collections of 17th-cent. Dutch painting (with pictures also from the 15th, 16th, and 18th cents.), including such celebrated works as *Rembrandt's *Anatomy Lesson of Dr Tulp* and *Vermeer's *View of Delft*.

Mauve, Antoine (1838–88). Dutch painter, one of the leading artists of the *Hague School. Influenced by the French painters *Millet and *Corot, he concentrated on small pictures of unpretentious subjects—dunes, meadows, and beaches— painted in light, silvery tones. His sincere and modest spirit made a deep impression upon van *Gogh, who was his wife's cousin and spent some time working with him. Mauve was a prolific and popular artist and is represented in many museums in the Netherlands and elsewhere.

Mayno (or **Maino**), **Juan Bautista** (1578– 1641). Spanish painter. There is a tradition that he was a pupil of El *Greco in Toledo, but there is no suggestion of this in Mayno's clear and firm style, which was formed in Italy c.1600–10. In about 1620 he moved from Toledo to Madrid, where he worked for Philip III and Philip IV (whose drawing master he had been) and was a friend of *Velázquez. Mayno was a Dominican priest as well as an artist, but although he painted religious works, he is most highly regarded for his portraits, outstanding among which is the formidably characterized *Dominican Monk* (Ashmolean, Oxford, c.1635).

Mazo, Juan Bautista Martínez del (c.1610/15–67). Spanish painter. He was a pupil of *Velázquez, married his daughter in 1633, and succeeded him as court painter in 1661. Among his very few signed works is a portrait of Queen Mariana (NG, London, 1666), and many of the works attributed to him were formerly given to Velázquez, whose mature style he imitated with some distinction.

Mazzoni, Sebastiano (c.1611–78). Italian painter, poet, and architect, born in Florence and active mainly in Venice, where he settled in 1648. He was one of the most individualistic of Italian *Baroque painters, often choosing unusual subjects and expressing a vivid sense of movement with his brilliantly free brushwork. His work looks forward to 18th-cent. Venetian painting and he may have been Sebastiano *Ricci's first teacher.

Meckenem, Israhel van the Younger (c.1450–1503). German engraver, the son of an engraver of the same name, active c.1450–65. He was trained by his father and probably by *Master E. S., whose work he copied. His œuvre is bigger than that of any other 15th-cent. engraver; he is known to have made more than 600 plates, and in some instances over a hundred prints have been preserved from each plate. Like many early engravers, he also worked as a goldsmith. Although he was a minor figure as a creative artist (much of his work consisted of copies), he is important in showing the growing popularity of engraving. He was the first artist to engrave his own features (in a double portrait together with his wife) and looks a very shrewd individual.

Medici. Italian family of bankers and merchants which was the ruling house of Florence and later Tuscany for most of the period from 1434 to 1737 and was famous for its patronage of learning and the arts throughout the *Renaissance. The name appears in Florentine records as early as the 12th cent., but the founder of the family fortune was **Giovanni di Bicci de' Medici** (1360–1429), who commissioned *Brunelleschi to build the Old Sacristy of San Lorenzo. His son **Cosimo** (1389–1464) spent lavishly on religious foundations and he had the family palace designed by *Michelozzo (begun 1444; now known as the Palazzo Medici-Riccardi). He also commissioned important works from *Donatello. His son **Piero** (1416–69) commissioned the sumptuous tabernacles of SS. Annunziata and San Miniato (Florence) and Benozzo *Gozzoli's frescos in the family palace. He was in contact with many of the leading painters of the day, including *Domenico Veneziano and Filippo *Lippi. His son and successor, **Lorenzo the Magnificent** (1449–92), was a humanist poet and the most famous member of the family, but his interest in art lay mainly in the collecting of Classical gems and coins. We have no record of any major painting he commissioned, but he was the first patron of *Michelangelo, whom he set to copy *antique sculpture in his garden near San Marco. His second cousin, **Lorenzo di Pierfrancesco** (1463–1503), seems to have been the principal patron of *Botticelli. Lorenzo the Magnificent's son **Giovanni** (1475–1521) and his nephew

Giulio (1479–1534) became pope as Leo X and Clement VII respectively, the artists they patronized including Michelangelo, *Raphael, *Giulio Romano, and *Sebastiano del Piombo. A member of another line of the family, **Cosimo I** (1519–74), became the first Grand Duke of Tuscany in 1569. He gathered around him the leading artists of the late Renaissance in Florence, notably *Pontormo, *Bronzino, *Ammanati, *Cellini, *Giambologna, and *Vasari, and he laid the basis for the *Uffizi collection. Of later members of the dynasty, **Leopoldo** (1617–75) made perhaps the most distinctive contribution to the arts, founding the great collection of artists' self-portraits in the Uffizi. **Maria de' Medici** (1573–1642), known in France as Marie de Médicis) was daughter of Francesco, Grand Duke of Tuscany, and queen of France (1600–10) by marriage to Henry IV. *Rubens painted a great cycle of paintings on her life (Louve, Paris).

Medici Venus. Marble statue of naked Venus (Uffizi, Florence), first recorded for certain in 1638 in the Villa Medici in Rome. It is signed by 'Cleomenes son of Apollodorus', but in the 18th cent. its fame as a model of female beauty was so great that the signature's authenticity was doubted and the statue was attributed to such illustrious names as *Phidias and *Praxiteles (to whose *Aphrodite of Cnidus it bears some resemblance in pose). Several other statues of similar type exist, but in spite of the *Medici Venus*'s quite severe restorations, it far outdid its rivals in fame, and it was one of the greatest prizes that Napoleon caused to be brought to France when Italy was under his dominion (it was in Paris between 1803 and 1815). As late as 1840 it was described by *Ruskin as 'one of the purest and most elevated incarnations of woman conceivable', but its reputation has since crumbled, Martin Robertson (*A History of Greek Art,* 1975) describing it as being 'among the most charmless remnants of antiquity'. It is now considered to be a copy of *c.*100 BC deriving from an original of the time of Praxiteles.

medium. Term used in its broadest sense to describe the various methods and materials of the artist; thus painting, sculpture, and drawing are three different media, and bronze, marble, and wood are three of the media of sculpture. In a more restricted

sense the term refers to the substance with which *pigment is mixed to make paint; for example, water in *water-colour, egg yolk in *tempera, *linseed oil (most usually) in *oil painting.

Meegeren, Han van. See BREDIUS.

megilp. A painting *medium consisting of mastic varnish mixed with *linseed oil. It makes paint glossy and easy to work, but it is a dangerous aid, in time rendering the paint yellow and brittle.

Meissonier, Ernest (1815–91). French painter, etcher, lithographer, and sculptor. He was immensely successful with his trite and nigglingly detailed historical paintings and historical *genre pieces (particularly scenes from the Napoleonic campaigns) and from the 1840s received the highest official honours, including the Grand Cross of the Legion of Honour—he was the first painter to win this award. Astonishingly conceited as well as mean-spirited, he cultivated a huge white beard and liked to be photographed or painted in attitudes of fiercely profound thought, as in his self-portrait of 1889 in the Musée d'Orsay. He had a personal enmity for *Courbet and may have been instrumental in inducing the government to impose a fine on him after the suppression of the Commune. Meissonier did his best work when he was at his least pretentious. His landscapes are attractive descriptive exercises and his *Rue de la Martellerie* (Musée d'Orsay, Paris, 1848), which shows a corpse-strewn street during the revolutionary events of 1848, has genuine pathos and impressed *Delacroix. There are large collections of Meissonier's work in the Musée d'Orsay and in the Wallace Collection, London.

Meit, Conrad (*c.*1475–1550/1). German sculptor. He was born at Worms and in 1506–10 worked at the court of Frederick the Wise, elector of Saxony, at Wittenberg, collaborating with *Cranach. Soon afterwards he moved to the Netherlands, where he worked as court sculptor to the Habsburg rulers for most of his career. His work included a number of large monuments, but his most characteristic sculptures are small figures and portraits, most notably sensuous free-standing nudes such as the well-known *Judith* (Bayerisches Nationalmuseum, Munich, *c.*1510–15). In these he created a distinctive type of German *Renaissance sculpture, combining Italian idealism with northern particularity of detail.

Meléndez, Luis (1716–80). Spanish still-life painter, active mainly in Madrid. He is regarded as the finest Spanish painter in his speciality in the 18th cent. and is sometimes called 'the Spanish *Chardin', but he spent much of his life in poverty. His work is rare outside Spain, but there is an example in the National Gallery in London and the Louvre has a striking self-portrait.

Mellan, Claude (1598–1688). French engraver. One of the most renowned and successful engravers of his period, he is best known for his portraits, but also made prints after *Poussin and *Vouet, for example. He was a technical virtuoso and instead of using cross-*hatching he obtained his effects of light and shade by varying the thickness of his lines. The most famous example of his prowess is his *Sudarium of St Veronica* (1642), a portrait of Christ made up of a single continuous line that goes round from the centre to the edge like the groove on a gramophone record. Mellan also painted, but few of his pictures survive.

Mellon, Andrew W. (1855–1937). American businessman, public official, art collector, and philanthropist. A banker and steel, coke, and oil magnate, he became secretary to the US treasury (1921–32), ambassador to England (1932–3), and one of the richest men in the world. In 1937 he donated his collection (particularly rich in Dutch and English painting) to the nation, together with funds to build a gallery to house them, thus creating the National Gallery of Art in Washington. His son, **Paul Mellon** (1907–), is also one of the greatest collectors of his generation, his main field of interest being British art. In 1966 he founded the Yale Center for British Art at New Haven. Opened in 1977, the Center is not only a major gallery, but also a research institution, with important collections of books and photographs. The Paul Mellon Foundation for British Art was established in London in 1962. It is a charitable trust whose purpose is to advance the study of British painting, sculpture, and the graphic arts, mainly by sponsorship of publications and support of research.

Melozzo da Forlì (1438–94). Italian painter from Forlì in the Romagna, active mainly in Loreto, Rome, and Urbino. He was an attractive and idiosyncratic painter who achieved a high reputation in his time, but little of his work survives intact and he has been a neglected figure until fairly recently. His style was indebted to *Piero della Francesca and he was renowned for his skill in *perspective and *illusionism; he was, indeed, credited with being the inventor of the extreme form of fore-shortening known as *sotto in su*, of which *Mantegna was another great exponent. Melozzo's skill in this field is seen in his fresco of the *Ascension* (1478–80) for the dome of SS. Apostoli in Rome, fragments of which are in the Quirinal Palace and the Vatican.

Memlinc (or **Memling**), **Hans** (c.1430/40–94). Netherlandish painter, active in Bruges from 1465. He was born in Seligenstadt, near Frankfurt, but nothing of his German heritage survived in his paintings, which show close connections with Rogier van der *Weyden, by whom according to tradition he was taught. Memlinc was a conservative artist, but his softened and sweetened version of Rogier's style (there is some influence also from *Bouts) made him the most popular Netherlandish painter of his day. Whereas Rogier excelled in the depiction of intense emotion, Memlinc's impeccably crafted paintings are quiet, restrained, and pious. Tax records indicate Memlinc was one of Bruges's wealthiest citizens and his large output shows he must have had a busy workshop. His style changed very little and it is difficult to place undated paintings in a chronological scheme. He painted numerous portraits and showed rather more originality in this field than in religious painting. Among his patrons were Italians then living in Bruges (*Tommaso Portinari and his wife*, Metropolitan Museum, New York, c.1468), and his portraits seem to have influenced artists such as Giovanni *Bellini in northern Italy. Memlinc's work is best seen in the museum devoted to him at Bruges.

Memmi, Lippo (active 1317–47). Sienese painter, *Simone Martini's brother-in-law and most able follower. They jointly signed the celebrated *Annunciation* (Uffizi, Florence, 1333) and their respective shares in it are uncertain. Several other works are signed by Memmi, including *Madonnas* in the Staatliche Museen, Berlin, and the Church of the Servites at Siena, showing his refined draughtsmanship, delicate palette, and extremely sensitive modelling. He was not an innovator, but an indication of the high quality of his work is that several paintings are disputed between him and Simone. Like Simone, Memmi worked at the papal court at Avignon.

Mengs, Anton Raffael (1728–79). German painter, the son of a court painter of Dresden, **Ismael Mengs** (d. 1764). His father brought him up with harsh severity to be a great painter on the models particularly of *Correggio and *Raphael (from which artists he gained his Christian names), and of the *antique. In 1741 he was taken to Rome and there established a reputation as a youthful prodigy. He returned to Germany in 1744 and became painter to the Saxon Court in Dresden in 1745. After another visit to Rome in 1748–9, when he married an Italian girl, he settled there in 1752 and became a close friend of *Winckelmann, who provided much of the theoretical inspiration for his work. It was for Winckelmann's patron, Cardinal *Albani, that Mengs painted his most famous work, the ceiling fresco *Parnassus* (1761) in the Villa Albani, Rome. This now seems flimsy and simpering, but it was the basis of Mengs's enormous reputation as the leader of the *Neoclassical reform in painting (he was widely regarded as the greatest living painter). It breaks completely with *Baroque *illusionism, treating the scene exactly as if it were to be seen at normal eye level, and is full of derivations from the most approved masters of the *Renaissance. In 1761–9 and 1773–7 he worked as court painter in Spain, decorating the royal palaces at Madrid and Aranjuez. His frescos there are dull and sterile, but it is a sign of the move in taste towards Neoclassicism that he prevailed over his rival, Giambattista *Tiepolo. Mengs was influential through his writings on art (which appeared in or soon after his lifetime in English, French, German, Italian, and Spanish) as well as his paintings. Today his portraits are considered vastly more successful than his history paintings,

and he was *Batoni's main rival as the leading portraitist in Rome.

Menzel, Adolf von (1815–1905). German painter and engraver, active mainly in Berlin, where in 1832 he took over his dead father's lithographic business. He was extremely industrious and achieved fame with 400 illustrations (wood engravings from his lively drawings) for Franz Kugler's *History of Frederick the Great* (1840–2). In painting he worked on similar themes and with comparable success, creating the popular image of the founder of the Prussian state. From the 1860s he turned to subjects from modern life and was one of the first German painters to note the picturesque qualities of industry (*The Steel Mill*, Staatliche Museen, Berlin, 1875). Today Menzel is most highly regarded not for the works that brought him contemporary acclaim, but for a series of informal landscapes and interiors dating from the 1840s that remained virtually unknown in his lifetime. They are remarkably free and fresh in technique, unorthodox in composition, and both bold and refined in their treatment of light, presaging the developments of *Impressionism (*The Artist's Sister with a Candle*, Neue Pinakothek, Munich, 1847). His attitude towards these paintings was strange; he kept them hidden and referred to Impressionism as 'the art of laziness', and when he visited Paris in 1855, 1867, and 1868 the artist he most admired was the tiresomely meticulous *Meissonier.

Merian, Matthäus (1593–1650). German engraver and publisher. He brought out hundreds of topographical prints of European towns which are of greater historical than artistic interest. Much of this vast output came from the hands of assistants. Among his pupils was Wenzel *Hollar. His daughter **Maria Sibylla Merian** (1647–1717) settled in Holland and visited Surinam in South America from 1699 to 1702. She is best known for her coloured drawings of insects and butterflies, which are as remarkable for their scientific accuracy as for their delicate beauty.

Merz. A variety of *Dada invented by Kurt *Schwitters and consisting initially of *collages made up of discarded refuse such as bus tickets, cigarette wrappers, and string. The name was reached by chance:

when fitting the word 'Commerzbank' into a collage Schwitters cut off some letters and used what was left. He called the collages *Merzbilden* ('merz pictures') and also went on to make a sculptural or architectural variant called the *Merzbau* ('merz building'). The original, which filled his house in Hanover, was destroyed by bombing in 1943; a second was left unfinished in Norway and destroyed by fire in 1951; a third, begun at Ambleside and unfinished at his death in 1948, is in the Hatton Gallery, Newcastle upon Tyne.

Mesdag, Hendrik Willem (1831–1915). Dutch painter and collector. He abandoned the family profession of banking in 1866 and became one of the leading artists of the *Hague School, particularly noted for his beach and sea scenes. His best-known work is the vast panorama (1881) of the fishing village of Scheveningen—about 120 m. in circumference—housed in a specially designed building in The Hague. The Mesdag Museum, in the same city, contains his excellent collection of paintings, rich in works by members of the *Barbizon and Hague Schools.

Mesens, E. L. T. (1903–71). Belgian musician, poet, and painter. His interest in the visual arts developed under the influence of *Duchamp and *Picabia, whom he met in Paris in 1921, and he was influenced towards *Surrealism by the paintings of de *Chirico. He helped to organize a number of international exhibitions which brought the various Surrealist groups in touch with one another and in 1938 he settled in London. Mesens was chiefly known for his highly original *collages; he created them from an eccentric assortment of materials—tickets, ribbons, pieces of paper and print, etc.—and made extensive use of printed words to create disconcerting or amusing ambiguities and suggested meanings.

Meštrović, Ivan (1883–1962). Yugoslavian-born sculptor who became an American citizen in 1954. He studied sculpture at the Academy in Vienna, 1900–4, attracted the attention of *Rodin in Paris, 1907–8, and on returning to Yugoslavia began to make his name as a monumental sculptor, working in a variety of Classicist styles furbished with a superficial air of modernity. He passed the

First World War in Rome, Geneva, Paris, and London. In 1919 he returned to Yugoslavia, where he received many public commissions, through which he expressed his ardent patriotism, and built up his fame internationally as a monumental sculptor, his works including an enormous mausoleum at Mt. Avala near Belgrade in commemoration of the Unknown Soldier (1934). During the Second World War he obtained several commissions from the Vatican and after living in Switzerland from 1943 to 1946 he went to the USA. There he obtained the post of Professor of Sculpture at Syracuse University and from 1955 was Professor of Sculpture at the University of Notre Dame, Indiana. He executed a number of monuments in the USA. The rhetoric of his large-scale works now seems rather ponderous and his smaller, more lyrical pieces have dated less. There are Meštrović museums at Split (his former house, which he designed himself) and Zagreb.

metal cut. A print made from a metal plate in which the design is cut in *relief (as in a *woodcut) rather than incised into the plate as in a *line engraving. Prints done in the *manière criblée are examples of the type.

metal point. Method of drawing using a small metal rod, pointed at one end, on specially prepared paper. The metal may be copper, gold, lead, or (most commonly) silver, which gives an attractive fine grey line that oxidizes to a light brown. The strength of tone can hardly be varied at all, so the technique depends on the quality of the drawn line and is best suited to work on a small scale. Moreover, it demands great certainty of purpose and hand, for the line cannot be removed except by disturbing the *ground, a coating of opaque white, often tinted by the addition of another pigment. Silver point first appeared in medieval Italy and was particularly popular in the 15th cent.; *Dürer and *Leonardo were perhaps the greatest exponents of the medium. It went out of fashion in the 17th cent., probably because the graphite *pencil was coming in, but was revived in the 18th cent. by *miniature painters, especially in France.

Metaphysical painting. A style of painting invented by de *Chirico in about 1913 and practised by him, *Carrà (from 1917), *Morandi (from 1918), and a few other Italian artists until about 1920. The term (*Pittura Metafisica*) was coined by de Chirico and Carrà in 1917, when both were patients at a military hospital in Ferrara, and the style is characterized by images conveying a sense of mystery and hallucination. This was achieved partly by unreal perspectives and lighting, partly by the adoption of a strange *iconography involving, for example, the use of tailor's dummies and statues in place of human figures, and partly by an incongruous juxtaposition of realistically depicted objects in a manner later taken over by some of the *Surrealists. Metaphysical painting had great influence on Surrealism, but the dreamlike quality conveyed by Metaphysical painters differed from that of the Surrealists because of their concern with pictorial structure and a strongly architectural sense of repose deriving from Italian *Renaissance art.

Metropolitan Museum of Art, New York. The most comprehensive collection of art in the USA and one of the greatest in the world. It was founded in 1870 and the present building in Central Park was opened in 1880. The museum is owned by the city, but is supported mainly by private endowment, and the history of its foundation and growth illustrates the rapid rise of New York at the end of the 19th cent. as the financial and cultural capital of North America, and the growing economic supremacy of America over Europe. Between 1880 and 1925, at a time when the major public collections in Europe were engaged in consolidation relying largely on their purchase grants and other state aid, the Metropolitan Museum was being built up out of the private fortunes of great businessmen, who collected rather for prestige than out of connoisseurship, but collected only first-class works of art. It could also profit from a number of endowed purchase grants, many of them unconditional, which have enabled it to progress not only as a collection of outstanding works, but as a comprehensive and representative one. The museum is rich in virtually every field of the *fine and *applied arts from all parts of the world and also houses one of the world's largest art libraries. Much of the collection of medieval art is housed in a separate

building called the Cloisters in Fort Tryon Park. Opened in 1938, the Cloisters incorporates parts of medieval buildings transported from Europe.

Metsu, Gabriel (1629–67). Dutch painter, active in his native Leiden, then in Amsterdam, where he had moved by 1657. *Houbraken says he trained with *Dou, but Metsu's early works are very different from his—typically historical and mythological scenes, broadly rather than minutely painted. Metsu also painted portraits and still lifes, but his most characteristic works are *genre scenes, some of which rank among the finest of their period. He concentrated on scenes of genteel middle-class life, fairly close to de *Hooch and *Terborch in style, but with a personal stamp. One of his best-known works, *The Sick Child* (Rijksmuseum, Amsterdam), is often compared with *Vermeer. His work is rarely dated, so his development and relationships with other artists are difficult to trace.

Metzinger, Jean (1883–1956). French painter and writer on art, one of the earliest devotees of *Cubism and a central figure of the *Section d'Or group. He was undistinguished as a painter and is remembered mainly as the co-author with *Gleizes of the book *Du Cubisme* (1912), an important statement of the principles of the movement.

Meulen, Adam Frans van der (1632–90). Flemish painter and tapestry designer. He moved to Paris in 1664, became an assistant to *Lebrun, and was made one of Louis XIV's court painters, specializing in military scenes. He accompanied the king on his campaigns, and his paintings and designs for *Gobelins tapestries are accurate historical documents of the battles which they represent. His work of this type is well represented at Versailles. He also made much less grandiose pictures of such subjects as hunting parties and landscapes.

mezzotint. A method of engraving that produces tonal areas rather than lines; the term also applies to a print made by this method. A metal (usually copper) plate is roughened with a tool called a rocker, which raises a 'burr' on the surface. The design is formed by scraping away the burr where the light tones are required and by polishing the metal quite smooth in the highlights. When the plate has been inked and then wiped, the ink is retained where the plate is rough and will print an intense black, but where it has been smoothed less ink is held and a lighter tone occurs. Mezzotint was invented in the Netherlands in the mid 17th cent. by Ludwig von *Siegen and soon spread to England, where it became an extremely popular method for reproducing portraits in particular. Its heyday was the 18th cent., but memorable use was made of it in the following century by John *Martin, one of the few artists who made original creative use of the medium rather than reproducing someone else's design. Like *drypoint, mezzotint yields only a small number of good impressions before the burr wears down. The technique became virtually extinct in the later 19th century with the development of photographic methods of reproduction.

Michallon, Achille-Etna (1796–1822). French landscape painter, the first artist to win the *Prix de Rome in the Historical Landscape category that was established in 1817. He was a pupil of *David and *Valenciennes and in his turn taught *Corot, who was influenced by his severe compositions and cool colour harmonies.

Michel, Georges (1763–1843). French landscape painter. Michel was a picture restorer at the *Louvre and was strongly influenced by 17th-cent. Dutch landscape painters. He was one of the earliest to paint in the open air (see PLEIN AIR) and because of this and his intimate, emotional depiction of nature he has sometimes been regarded as a forerunner of the *Barbizon School.

Michelangelo Buonarroti (1475–1564). Florentine sculptor, painter, architect, draughtsman, and poet, one of the greatest figures of the *Renaissance and, in his later years, one of the forces that shaped *Mannerism. His father was a member of the minor Florentine nobility and throughout his life Michelangelo was touchy on the subject; pride of birth had much to do with the family opposition to his apprenticeship as a painter as well as with Michelangelo's own insistence in later life on the status of painting and sculpture among the *liberal arts. In 1488 he was apprenticed for a term of three years to

Domenico *Ghirlandaio and from him he must have learnt the elements of *fresco technique. He could not have learnt very much else, however, since he seems to have transferred very quickly to the school set up in the *Medici gardens and run by *Bertoldo di Giovanni. More important than either master, however, was what he learned from the drawings he made of figures in the frescos of *Giotto and *Masaccio. After the death of his patron Lorenzo de Medici in 1492 the political situation in Florence deteriorated, and in October 1494 Michelangelo left for Bologna, where he carved three small figures for the tomb of S. Dominic (see NICOLO DELL' ARCA). On 25 June 1496 he was in Rome, where he remained for the next five years and where he carved the two statues which established his fame— the *Bacchus* (Bargello, Florence, c.1496–7) and the *Pietà* (St Peter's, Rome, 1498–9). The latter is the masterpiece of his early years—a tragically expressive and yet beautiful and harmonious solution to the problem of representing a full-grown man lying dead in the lap of a woman. There are no marks of suffering—as were common in northern representations of the period— and the carving has a flawless beauty and polish demonstrating his absolute technical mastery. Still in his mid-twenties, Michelangelo returned to Florence in 1501 to consolidate the reputation he had made in Rome. He remained there until the spring of 1505, the major completed work of the period being the *David* (Accademia, Florence, 1501–4), which has become a symbol of Florence and Florentine art. Soon after the *David* was completed, Michelangelo received a commission from the Signoria of Florence to paint a huge mural of the *Battle of Cascina* for the new Council Chamber in the Palazzo Vecchio; here he worked in rivalry with *Leonardo, who was engaged on the *Battle of Anghiari* for the same room. Neither painting was completed, but Michelangelo began work on the full-size *cartoon in the winter of 1504, and the fragment known as the *Bathers* was, while it existed, a model for all the young artists in Florence—including *Raphael—and was one of the prime causes of Mannerist preoccupation with the nude figure in violent action. It is now known from a copy (Earl of Leicester coll.) and an engraving, as well as some preliminary drawings (for example in the BM).

Michelangelo left the battlepiece unfinished when Pope Julius II summoned him to Rome in 1505 to make him a tomb. Julius died in 1513, but the project dragged on until 1545 and was rightly described by *Condivi as the 'Tragedy of the Tomb'. It was originally conceived on the most grandiose scale, but was whittled down in successive contracts with Julius's heirs, and of the monument finally erected in S. Pietro in Vincoli in 1545 only the celebrated *Moses* (c.1515) was from Michelangelo's own hand. (Two figures of *Slaves*, c.1513, carved by Michelangelo for the tomb are now in the Louvre.) The other great work commissioned from Michelangelo by Julius—the frescoing of the ceiling of the Sistine Chapel—was equally daunting, but was brought to sublime fruition. The contract was signed on 10 May 1508 and the finished ceiling was unveiled on 31 October 1512. Michelangelo, who always regarded himself as a sculptor first and foremost, was reluctant to undertake the work, but he made of it his most heroic achievement, not only for its quality as a work of art, but also in terms of the endurance and stamina he showed in completing so quickly and virtually unaided such a huge and physically uncomfortable task. There is still much debate about the exact interpretation of the scores of figures that adorn the ceiling, but the main panels represent scenes from Genesis, from the Creation to the Drunkenness of Noah, forming the background to the frescos on the life of Moses and of Christ on the walls below by a number of 15th-cent. artists. Prophets and Sibyls who foretold Christ's birth are at the sides of the ceiling, and at each corner of the central scenes are figures of beautiful nude youths (usually called the *Ignudi*), whose exact significance is uncertain. They have been thought to represent the Neoplatonic ideal of humanity, and as Kenneth *Clark wrote, 'Their physical beauty is an image of divine perfection; their alert and vigorous movements an expression of divine energy.' From the moment of its completion the Ceiling has always been regarded as one of the supreme masterpieces of pictorial art (the recent cleaning has revealed anew the beauty of the colouring), and Michelangelo was, at the age of 37, recognized as the greatest artist of his day, a position he retained unchallenged until his death.

In December 1516 he was commissioned by the new pope, Leo X (Giovanni de' Medici), to design a façade for the Medici parish church in Florence, S. Lorenzo, which had been left unfinished by *Brunelleschi. The project came to nothing and wasted a good deal of Michelangelo's time, but it led to two other works for S. Lorenzo—the Medici Chapel, or New Sacristy, planned as a counterpart to Brunelleschi's Old Sacristy, and the Biblioteca Laurenziana. Both were left unfinished, but they nevertheless rank among Michelangelo's finest creations. The Medici Chapel was planned from November 1520 as a mortuary chapel for the family to contain the monuments of four members, but it was abandoned when the Medici were again expelled from Florence in 1527, restarted in 1530, and left incomplete in 1534 when Michelangelo finally settled in Rome. It was intended to be a union of architecture and sculpture (like the projected S. Lorenzo façade), with the view from the altar leading to the climax of the whole composition in the figures of the *Madonna and Child* (unfinished) and with the Active and Contemplative Life symbolized by figures on the wall-tombs of Giuliano and Lorenzo de' Medici. The figures of the Medici are set above the reclining figures symbolizing *Day* and *Night* (for *Vita activa*) and *Dawn* and *Evening* (for *Vita contemplativa*).

In the thirty years that remained to him in Rome, Michelangelo worked mainly for the papacy. He was at once commissioned to paint the *Last Judgement* in the Sistine Chapel and began the actual painting in 1536. It was unveiled on 31 October 1541, twenty-nine years to the day after the unveiling of the Sistine Ceiling but a whole world away from it in feeling and meaning, with its massive and menacing figures and mood of wrathful desolation. In the interval the world of Michelangelo's youth had collapsed in the horror of the Sack of Rome (1527), and its confident humanism had been found insufficient in the face of the rise of Protestantism and the new, militant spirit of the Counter-Reformation. For Paul III (Alessandro *Farnese), who commissioned the *Last Judgement*, Michelangelo also executed his last works in painting, the *Conversion of St Paul* and the *Crucifixion of St Peter* (1542–50), frescos in the Cappella Paolina in the Vatican. The figures here are even more blunt, heavy, and unconcerned with physical allure, totally repudiating his own early ideals. Something of the same deep and troubled spirituality is seen in his late drawings of the Crucifixion and two sculptures of the Pietà. One (now in Florence Cathedral) was intended for his own tomb and contains a self-portrait as Nicodemus; it was begun c.1546 and mutilated and abandoned by Michelangelo in 1555. The other (Castello Sforza, Milan) was his last work, left unfinished at his death.

For the last thirty years of his life, however, Michelangelo devoted most of his attentions to architecture, and in this field his stature is just as great as in sculpture and painting. His most important commission—indeed the most important in Christendom—was the completion of St Peter's, which had been begun under Julius II in 1506. When Michelangelo became architect in 1546, the building had advanced little since *Bramante's death in 1514. As with the Sistine Ceiling, he was initially unwilling to undertake the task, but he then proceeded with formidable energy and by the time of his death work had advanced so far that the drum of the dome was nearly complete. Michelangelo also designed the dome itself, but this was executed after his death and is probably a good deal steeper in outline than he intended. The addition of a long nave in the early 17th cent. altered Michelangelo's plan for a centralized church, but nevertheless the exterior of the building owes more to him than to any other architect and forms a fitting conclusion to his titanic career. In architecture, Michelangelo's decorative vocabulary soon attained widespread currency, but it was only in the 17th cent., however, that his massive and dynamic style was fully appreciated and emulated; it is fitting that *Bernini, the great sculptor-architect of the age, should complete St Peter's with his glorious piazza. In painting and sculpture Michelangelo's means of expression was limited almost entirely to the heroic male figure, usually nude, but in this field he reigned supreme as no artist has done before or since. The awe that his contemporaries felt for him has not diminished through the centuries and his influence, for good and ill, has been enormous.

Michelozzo di Bartolommeo (sometimes incorrectly called Michelozzo Michelozzi) (1396–1472). Florentine architect and sculptor. As a sculptor he worked for *Ghiberti (on both his sets of doors for the Baptistery of Florence Cathedral) and in partnership with *Donatello (1425–c.1433). With Donatello he produced three major tombs—those of anti-pope John XXIII (Baptistery, Florence), Cardinal Brancacci (S. Angelo a Nilo, Naples), and Bartolommeo Aragazzi (Montepulciano Cathedral, but now disassembled; two angels are in the V&A, London). His style was vigorous and forthright. In his later career Michelozzo worked mainly as an architect, and he ranks as one of the leading figures of the generation after *Brunelleschi, whom he succeeded as *capomaestro* at Florence Cathedral (1446). His most famous building is the Palazzo Medici-Riccardi in Florence (begun 1444), often described as the first *Renaissance palace. Michelozzo was influential in spreading the Renaissance style; he worked in Milan, Yugoslavia, and the island of Chios.

Miereveld (or **Mierevelt**), **Michiel van** (1567–1641). Dutch portrait painter, active mainly in his native Delft and The Hague. He was portrait painter to the House of Orange, highly successful, and enormously prolific: *Sandrart reports that Mierevelt himself estimated that he made about 10,000 portraits. His portraits are dull and repetitive, but they are meticulously crafted and of great value as historical records.

Mieris, Frans van (1635–81). Dutch painter, the most distinguished member of a family of artists who worked in Leiden. He was one of the best pupils of Gerrit *Dou and followed his master in choice of subjects (mainly domestic *genre scenes) and in his highly polished technique. The tradition was continued by his sons **Jan** (1660–90) and **Willem** (1662–1747) and by Willem's son **Frans II** (1689–1763).

Mignard, Pierre (1612–95). French painter, one of the most successful of *Vouet's pupils. His career culminated in 1690, when, on the death of *Lebrun, he became Director of the Académie and first painter to the king. He was one of the principal supporters on the side of *De Piles and the 'Rubensistes' in their battle against the *Classicism of the 'Poussinistes'. His own historical and religious paintings, however, did not exemplify his theories but fitted into the scheme of academic Classicism in the tradition of *Domenichino and *Poussin (he was in Italy 1635–57). His best works are his portraits; he painted many of the members of Louis XIV's court, sometimes fitting out his sitters with allegorical trappings. Pierre's brother, **Nicolas** (1606–68), also trained with Vouet and had a successful career painting portraits and religious subjects.

Millais, Sir John Everett (1829–96). English painter and book illustrator. A child prodigy who was hardworking as well as naturally gifted, he became the youngest ever student at the *Royal Academy Schools when he was 11, and although he suffered some temporary setbacks in his twenties, his career was essentially one of the great Victorian success stories. In 1848, with *Rossetti and Holman *Hunt, he founded the *Pre-Raphaelite Brotherhood and had his share of the abuse heaped against the members until *Ruskin stepped in as their champion. (Millais married Effie Gray, formerly the wife of John Ruskin, in 1854 after this first marriage had been annulled.) In the 1850s Millais's style changed, as he moved away from the brilliantly coloured, minutely detailed Pre-Raphaelite manner to a broader and more fluent way of painting—with a family to support he said he could not afford to spend a whole day working on an area 'no larger than a five shilling piece'. His subjects changed also, from highly serious, morally uplifting themes to scenes that met the public demand for sentiment and a good story (*The Boyhood of Raleigh*, Tate, London, 1870). He became enormously popular, not only with subject pictures such as this, but also as a portraitist and a book illustrator, his drawings for the novels of Anthony Trollope being such a success that Trollope said they influenced the way he developed the characters in sequels. Millais lived in some splendour on his huge income, in 1885 became the first artist to be awarded a baronetcy, and in the year of his death was elected President of the Royal Academy. To some contemporaries it seemed that he wasted his talents pandering to public taste, and many 20th-cent. critics have presented him as a young genius who sacrificed his artistic conscience for money. Millais, an easy-going and much-liked man, certainly enjoyed his success, but he was anything but a cynic.

He was always proud of his skills (near the end of his career he wrote 'I may honestly say that I have never consciously placed an idle touch upon canvas'), and few of his contemporaries could match his late works for sheer beauty of handling (*Bubbles*, A. & F. Pears Ltd., 1886).

millboard. See CARDBOARD.

Milles, Carl (1875–1955). Swedish-American sculptor. Originally inspired by *Rodin, with whom he came into contact in 1900, he turned (*c*.1912) to a more abrupt manner in which a great many influences, from ancient, medieval, and *Renaissance art, may be discerned. His international reputation was based mainly on the numerous monumental fountains he created in Sweden and the USA, where he spent much of his career. They are distinguished by rhythmic vitality and inventive figure types (he would fuse Classical and Nordic types such as tritons and goblins), and sometimes by a grotesque humour. From 1931 to 1945 he was Professor of Sculpture at the Cranbrook Academy at Bloomfield Hills, Michigan, and he became an American citizen in 1945. His home at Lindingo, near Stockholm, is now an open-air museum of his work, known as Millesgården.

Millet, Jean-François (often known by his nickname, 'Francisque') (1642–79). French landscape painter of Flemish birth. Active mainly in Paris, he is also said to have visited England and Holland. No signed or documented works are known, but several are authenticated by early engravings. He worked in a style related to *Poussin and *Dughet, sometimes enlivened by touches of the *picturesque in the manner of Salvator *Rosa, as in *Mountain Landscape with Lightning* (NG, London), one of the most original works of an artist usually content to be an able follower. His son **Jean** (1666–1723) was a landscape painter, and he too had a painter son, **Joseph** (1697?–1777).

Millet, Jean-François (1814–75). French painter and graphic artist, born of a peasant family at Gruchy, near Cherbourg in Normandy. He studied locally, then in 1837 entered the studio of *Delaroche in Paris. His early pictures consisted of conventional mythological and anecdotal *genre scenes and portraits, but with *The Winnower* (Musée d'Orsay, Paris), exhibited at the *Salon in 1848, he turned to the scenes of rustic life from which his name is now inseparable. He emphasized the serious and even melancholy aspects of country life, emotionalizing the labours of the soil and the sad solemnities of toil. Hostile critics accused him of being a socialist, but Millet's concerns were aesthetic rather than political and he said his desire was 'to make the trivial serve to express the sublime'. In 1849 he settled at Barbizon, where he remained for the rest of his life apart from a stay in Cherbourg during the Franco-Prussian War of 1870–1. Late in his career he turned increasingly to pure landscape, influenced by his close friend Théodore *Rousseau. Millet passed much of his life in poverty, but his work began to bring him success in the 1860s and *The Angelus* (Musée d'Orsay, 1859) became perhaps the most widely reproduced painting of the 19th cent. This has had a harmful effect on his subsequent critical fortunes, for largely on the strength of it he has been pigeon-holed as a purveyor of pious sentimentality. His greatness lies rather in his drawing, which for its elimination of the inessential, investing the ordinary with weight and dignity, has been compared with that of *Seurat. Van *Gogh and Camille *Pissarro were among those who admired Millet's work.

Mills, Clark (1810–83). American sculptor, a jack-of-all-trades, who was self-taught as an artist. In 1848 he won a competition for the monument to President Andrew Jackson (1765–1845) in Lafayette Square, Washington, and worked for five years on this, the first equestrian statue in the USA. He built his own foundry to cast the statue, which daringly has the rearing horse supported only by hind legs, and succeeded only at the seventh attempt. The ecstatic response when the statue was unveiled in 1853 brought him great financial rewards and the commission for an equestrian statue to George Washington in Washington Circle (1860). He spent his final years under a cloud, however, suspected of dishonesty in handling the metal assigned to him.

miniature. A very small painting, particularly a portrait that can be held in the hand or worn as a piece of jewellery. The word is applied to manuscript *illuminations as well as portraits and derives from the Latin *minium*, the red lead used to emphasize initial letters, decorated by the *miniator*. Since the 17th cent. the term has been applied to all types of manuscript illustration on account of a mistaken etymology: the word was connected with 'minute' (small). What we today call a 'miniature' was called *historia* in the Middle Ages and the portraits painted by *Hilliard and others were named 'limnings' or 'pictures in little' by the Elizabethans. They were painted on vellum (see PARCHMENT), or occasionally on ivory or card, and in the 17th and 18th cents. there was a vogue for miniatures done in an *enamelling technique. The portrait miniature developed from a fusion of the traditions of medieval illumination and the *Renaissance medal and flourished from the early 16th cent. to the mid 19th cent., when photography virtually killed it as a serious art form.

Minimal art. A trend in painting and more especially sculpture, arising during the 1950s, in which only the most elemental geometric forms were used. Minimal art is associated particularly with the USA and its impersonality is seen as a reaction against the emotiveness of *Abstract Expressionism. Carl *Andre, Don *Judd, and Tony *Smith are among the best-known Minimal artists.

Mino da Fiesole (1429–84). Florentine sculptor, active in Rome as well as Florence. He is best known for his strongly characterized and sensitively handled male portrait busts of which perhaps the finest is the *Diotisalvi Neroni* (Louvre, Paris, 1464). He also executed a number of tombs (e.g. that of Francesco Tornabuoni in Sta Maria sopra Minerva, Rome, 1480), the arrangement of which derives from *Desiderio da Settignano, under whom he possibly trained.

Mir Iskusstva (The World of Art). The title of a Russian periodical, founded in 1898 and edited by *Diaghilev; it ran until 1905 and among his contributors and collaborators were Léon *Bakst and Alexander *Benois. The name of the periodical has come to stand for a whole movement in art running parallel to *Art Nouveau in western Europe, with which

MIRÓ, JOAN

308

there were many ties (many articles in *Mir Iskusstva* had previously been published in Western journals). The artists of this group were chiefly responsible for the new ballet décors which revolutionized European stage design when Diaghilev brought them to Paris in 1909.

Miró, Joan (1893–1983). Spanish painter, graphic artist, and designer. From 1919 he spent much of his time in Paris, but he always kept close links with Spain, where he frequently returned. His early work shows the influence of various modern movements—*Fauvism, *Cubism (he was a friend of *Picasso) and *Dadaism—but he is particularly associated with the *Surrealists, whose manifesto he signed in 1924. Throughout his life, whether his work was purely abstract or whether it retained figurative suggestions, Miró remained true to the basic Surrealistic principle of releasing the creative forces of the unconscious mind from the control of logic and reason. However, even though *Breton wrote that he was 'probably the most Surrealistic of us all', Miró stood apart from the other members of the movement in the variety, geniality, and lack of attitudinizing in his work. It contains elements of *primitivism, a personal mythology and magic, and innovations in the field of abstraction which take it outside all classification, and shows none of the superficial devices beloved of other Surrealists. Much of his work has a delightful quality of playfulness about it, but he was inspired to much more sombre and even savage imagery by the Spanish Civil War. In 1940 Miró returned to Spain to avoid the German invasion and thereafter lived mainly in Majorca. From 1944 he turned to ceramics and also took up *terracotta, which absorbed the major part of his energies in the 1950s. He visited the USA in 1947 and did a mural at Cincinnati, followed by a large mural for Harvard University in 1950 (now replaced by a ceramic copy; the original is in MOMA, New York). From then until 1958 he worked on two immense ceramic wall decorations, *Mur du Soleil* and *Mur de la Lune*, for the Unesco building, Paris. During this time he was also engaged on etchings and lithographs, and he continued to explore new techniques into his old age, taking up stained glass design when he was in his eighties. The Foundation Joan Miró

was opened in 1975 on the heights of Montjuic overlooking Barcelona, his native city. It is designed both as a memorial museum housing a collection of Miró's works and as a centre of artistic activity.

mobile. Term coined by Marcel *Duchamp to designate certain sculptures by Alexander *Calder, exhibited in 1932, that consisted typically of flat metal parts suspended on wires and moved by a combination of air currents and their own structural tension. The term has been extended to cover other sculptures of this type (which may also be motor-driven); many other sculptors (for example Lynn *Chadwick) have experimented with the genre and since the mid-century it has even become a popular article of interior decoration sold in novelty shops, etc.

modello. A preparatory drawing or painting for a larger work, usually made to be shown to a patron. Since the object was to impress the patron and give him a clear idea of the picture which the artist had in mind, the *modello* was more elaborate and fully worked out than the sketch. *Rubens's work is particularly rich in *modelli*.

Modersohn-Becker, Paula (1876–1907). German painter and graphic artist, born Paula Becker. After studying in London and Berlin and travelling in Norway and Switzerland, she joined the artists' colony at *Worpswede in 1898. In 1901 she married **Otto Modersohn** (1865–1943), another member of the group. She shared in a high degree the poetic sensibility for nature which was cultivated by the Worpswede School and she was a friend of the poet Rilke. But she was dissatisfied with the sentimentalized idealization of the Worpswede manner, and made it her object to express by means of the utmost simplicity and economy of form 'the unconscious feeling that often murmurs so softly and sweetly within me'. She visited Paris in 1900 and on three subsequent visits before her early death in 1907, and in the last years of her life, under the influence of *Gauguin, van *Gogh, *Cézanne, and the *Pont-Aven painters, she found the 'great simplicity of form' for which she had been searching. Up to about 1900 she painted landscapes and scenes of peasant life; thereafter she concentrated on single figures, including self-portraits and portraits of peasants, and also still lifes. In her self-portraits she typically shows herself with wide, staring eyes and often in the nude. Her symbolic use of colour and pattern, her highly subjective vision, and the almost primitive force of some of her work place her among the most important precursors of German *Expressionism.

Modigliani, Amedeo (1884–1920). Italian painter, sculptor, and draughtsman, active in Paris from 1906. Although virtually his whole career was spent in France, he laid the foundations of his style in Italy with his study of the masters of the *Renaissance. In particular, he is often seen as a spiritual heir of *Botticelli because of the linear grace of his work. In Paris Modigliani immersed himself in the café and night life of the artistic quarter and was influenced by, for example, the *Fauves and *Cézanne. In 1909 he met *Brancusi and devoted himself mainly to sculpture until 1914, when the war made it impossible for him to get materials. He returned to painting and his finest works were produced in the last five years of his short life. Both as a sculptor and as a painter his range was limited. With few exceptions his sculptures are heads or crouching caryatid figures and the paintings are portraits or female nudes. Common to virtually all his work are extremely elongated, simplified forms and a superb sense of rhythmic vitality, but there is a great difference in mood between, for example, his sculpted heads (*Head*, Tate, London, c.1911–12), which have the primitive power of the African masks that inspired them, and his gloriously sensual nudes (*Reclining Nude*, MOMA, New York, c.1919), which were censured for their open eroticism. Modigliani's early death from tuberculosis was hastened by his dissolute lifestyle, and his mistress Jeanne Hébuterne, pregnant with their second child, committed suicide the day after he died. In the popular imagination he is the archetypal romantic genius, starving in a garret, the victim of drugs and alcohol, an inveterate womanizer, but painting and carving obsessively.

Moholy-Nagy, László (1895–1946). Hungarian born painter, sculptor, experimental artist, and writer who became an American citizen in 1944. After qualifying in law at Budapest University and

serving in the First World War, he went to Vienna in 1919 and came under the influence of *Malevich, *Lissitzky, and *Gabo. He moved to Berlin in 1921, experimented with *collage and *photomontage and exhibited at the *Sturm Gallery in 1922. From 1923 to 1928 he taught at the *Bauhaus while showing unusual versatility in experimental films, theatre, industrial design, photography, and typography as well as painting and sculpture. On resigning from the Bauhaus together with *Gropius in 1928 he worked for some years in Berlin chiefly on stage design and experimental film, then lived in Paris and Amsterdam before moving in 1935 to London, where he was a member of the *Constructivist group represented by the publication *Circle*. In London he also began the constructions which he named 'Space Modulators' and worked on designs for the Alexander Korda film *Things to Come* (1936). In 1937 he emigrated to Chicago, where he became Director of the New Bauhaus and founded the Institute of Design, which he directed until his death. Moholy-Nagy was one of the most inventive and versatile artists in the Constructivist school, pioneering especially in the artistic uses of light, movement, photography, film, and plastic materials, and he was one of the most influential teachers of the 20th cent. He also was an emphatic advocate of the Constructivist doctrine that so-called *fine art must be integrated with the total environment. His views were most fully expressed in his posthumously published book *The New Vision and Abstract of an Artist* (1947).

Moilliet, Louis (1880–1962). Swiss painter. From 1911 he was closely associated with the *Blaue Reiter group to which he introduced Paul *Klee, and in 1914 he accompanied Klee and *Macke to Tunisia on a journey whose repercussions on the development of expressive abstraction have become famous in the history of 20th-cent. art. He passed the war years in Switzerland and then in 1919 began extensive travel after which he lived in seclusion at La Tour de Peiltz on Lake Geneva. Moilliet was at his best as a water-colourist, achieving a brilliant transparency of colour in his landscapes. He also designed stained glass for churches.

Mola, Pier Francesco (1612–66). Italian *Baroque painter, active mainly in Rome. Although he trained there with *Cesari and in Bologna with *Albani, his style, characterized by warm colouring and soft modelling, was formed mainly on the example of *Guercino and Venetian art (his early career is not well documented, but he probably spent most of the period 1633–47 in north Italy). He painted frescos in Roman churches and palaces, and his best-known painting is the striking *Barbary Pirate* (Louvre, Paris, 1650), but his most characteristic works are fairly small canvases with religious or mythological figures set in landscapes (two examples are in the National Gallery, London). They are somewhat reminiscent of Albani, but much freer, and closer in spirit to Salvator *Rosa, with whom Mola was one of the chief representatives of a distinctively Romantic strain in Roman painting in the mid 17th cent.

Molenaer, Jan Miense (c.1610–68). Dutch painter, active in his native Haarlem and in Amsterdam. In 1636 he married Judith *Leyster; both belonged in their youth to the circle of Frans *Hals. He and his wife probably collaborated and sometimes it is difficult to differentiate their work. Molenaer specialized in *genre scenes, but his range was wide, from pictures of the crude, indecorous activities of peasants to small, exquisitely finished domestic scenes of well-to-do families. He also did portraits and religious scenes. His early works (which are considered his best) have a grey-blond tonality and touches of bright colour, but his later ones are darker, in the manner of *Brouwer or *Ostade. He had two painter brothers, **Bartholomaeus** (d. 1650) and **Claes** (d. 1676), both active in Haarlem.

Molyn, Pieter de (1595–1661). Dutch landscape painter, born in London and active mainly in Haarlem. With van *Goyen, and S. van *Ruysdael, also active in Haarlem, he ranks as one of the pioneers of naturalistic landscape painting in Holland. It is not known if these three painters worked together, if they arrived at similar solutions independently, or if one of them began experiments with monochromatic pictures of dunes and cottages and the others followed his lead.

However, *The Sand Dune* (Herzog-Anton-Ulrich Museum, Brunswick, 1626) by Molyn is earlier than any comparable dated picture by van Goyen or Ruysdael. Molyn's later career was less distinguished, and he seems then to have worked more as a draughtsman than a painter. He also etched.

Momper, Joos (or **Jodocus**) **II de** (1564–1634/5). Flemish landscape painter, the outstanding member of a family of artists. He worked in his native Antwerp, where he became a master in the guild in 1581, but mountains are so much a prevailing theme in his work that it seems likely he crossed the Alps to Italy at some time in his career. His chief inspiration was *Bruegel and his work stands half-way between the constructed landscapes of the 16th cent. and the naturalistic landscapes of the 17th cent. He enriched the traditional colour scheme of 16th cent. landscape painting, hitherto largely confined to cool blues and greens, until it ranged from brown to grey via green, yellow, and blue. Judging by the great number of extant pictures in his manner, his work must have enjoyed great popularity. They vary greatly in quality, but the best works that are indisputably from his own hand, for example the majestic *Winter Landscape with the Flight into Egypt* (Ashmolean, Oxford), show that he was one of the greatest landscape painters of his period and worthy to be mentioned in the same breath as Bruegel. His style seems to have changed little and his work is difficult to date. Figures in his paintings are often the work of other artists, notably Jan *Brueghel I.

Mondrian, Piet (originally Pieter Mondriaan) (1872–1944). Dutch painter, one of the most important figures in the development of *abstract art. His early painting was naturalistic and direct, delicate in colour, but between 1907 and 1910, partly under the influence of *Toorop and perhaps partly owing to his conversion to theosophy, his painting took on a *Symbolist character and he began to work with *primary colours. In 1911 he went to Paris, where he came into contact with *Cubism and executed a now famous series of paintings on the theme of a tree, in which the image became progressively more abstract (*Flowering Apple Tree*, Gemeente Mus., The Hague,

1912). He returned to Holland in 1914 and remained there during the war, continuing his study of abstraction and developing theories about the horizontal–vertical axes. With Theo van *Doesburg he founded the periodical De *Stijl in 1917 and became the main exponent of a new kind of rigorously geometrical abstract painting that he named *Neo-Plasticism, in which he limited himself to rectangular forms and a range of colours consisting of the three primaries plus black, white, and grey. In 1919–38 Mondrian lived in Paris, where in 1931 he joined the *Abstraction Création group. In 1938–40 he was in London, living near *Gabo and Ben *Nicholson, and in 1940 he settled in New York, where he died. In America he developed a more colourful style, with syncopated rhythms that reflect his interest in jazz and dancing (Broadway Boogie-Woogie, MOMA, 1942–3). Mondrian's concept of 'pure plasticity' consisted partly in the simplification of the means of expression to the bare essentials. He not only banished representation and three-dimensional picture-space but also the curved line, sensuous qualities of texture and surface, and the sensuous appeal of colour. This restrictedness he regarded as a sort of mystical pursuit of the Absolute, which he justified in terms of his theosophical beliefs. His extensive influence—expressed through his writings as well as his paintings—was not limited to artists whose style had direct affinities with his own. He also had a profound influence on much industrial, decorative, and advertisement art from the 1930s onwards.

Monet, Claude (1840–1926). French *Impressionist painter. He is regarded as the archetypal Impressionist in that his devotion to the ideals of the movement was unwavering throughout his long career, and it is fitting that one of his pictures—Impression: Sunrise (Musée Marmottan, Paris, 1872)—gave the group its name. His youth was spent in Le Havre, where he first excelled as a *caricaturist but was then converted to landscape painting by his early mentor *Boudin, from whom he derived his firm predilection for painting out of doors. In 1859 he studied in Paris at the Atelier Suisse and formed a friendship with *Pissarro. After two years' military service in Algiers, he returned to Le Havre and met *Jongkind, to whom he said he owed 'the definitive education of my eye'.

He then, in 1862, entered the studio of *Gleyre in Paris and there met *Renoir, *Sisley, and *Bazille, with whom he was to form the nucleus of the Impressionist group. Monet's devotion to painting out of doors is illustrated by the famous story concerning one of his most ambitious early works, Women in the Garden (Musée d'Orsay, Paris, 1866–7). The picture is about 2·5 m. high and to enable him to paint all of it outside he had a trench dug in the garden so the canvas could be raised or lowered by pulleys to the height he required. *Courbet visited him when he was working on it and said Monet would not paint even the leaves in the background unless the lighting conditions were exactly right.

During the Franco-Prussian War (1870–1) he took refuge in England with Pissarro: he studied the work of *Constable and *Turner, painted the Thames and London parks, and met the dealer *Durand-Ruel, who was to become one of the great champions of the Impressionists. From 1871 to 1878 Monet lived at Argenteuil, a village on the Seine near Paris, and here were painted some of the most joyous and famous works of the Impressionist movement, not only by Monet, but by his visitors *Manet, Renoir, and Sisley. In 1878 he moved to Vétheuil and in 1883 he settled at Giverny, also on the Seine, but about 40 miles from Paris. After having experienced extreme poverty, Monet began to prosper. By 1890 he was successful enough to buy the house at Giverny he had previously rented and in 1892 he married his mistress, with whom he had begun an affair in 1876, three years before the death of his first wife. From 1890 he concentrated on series of pictures in which he painted the same subject at different times of the day in different lights—Haystacks or Grainstacks (1890–1) and Rouen Cathedral (1891–5) are the best known. He continued to travel widely, visiting London and Venice several times (and also Norway as a guest of Queen Christiana), but increasingly his attention was focused on the celebrated water-garden he created at Giverny, which served as the theme for the series of paintings on Water-lilies that began in 1899 and grew to dominate his work completely (in 1914 he had a special studio built in the grounds of his house so he could work on the huge canvases). In his final years he was troubled by failing eyesight, but he painted until the end. He was enormously prolific and many major galleries have examples of his work.

monotype. A method of making a print (and the print so made) in which a design is painted (usually in oil colours) on a flat sheet of metal or glass and is then transferred directly to a sheet of paper. With glass plates it is necessary to apply the pressure to the back of the paper by hand; in other cases monotypes may be printed in a press. Strictly speaking, only one print may be taken by this process (hence the term 'monotype'); in practice the colour on the slab may be reinforced after printing and another one or two impressions taken, although they will differ considerably from the first. Various modifications of the principle are known. G. B. *Castiglione is generally credited with the invention of the monotype in the 17th cent. *Blake and *Degas are two artists who have made memorable use of the technique.

Monro, Dr Thomas (1759–1833). English collector, patron, and amateur painter, a physician by profession. He played an important role in encouraging some of the outstanding water-colour painters of his period, his protégés including *Turner, *Girtin, *Cotman, *De Wint, and many others. They used his houses in London and Bushey, Hertfordshire, as places to meet and work, and were given the run of his superb collection. Late in life Turner recalled how he and Girtin had often made 'drawings for good Dr Monro at half a crown apiece and a supper'.

montage (French: 'mounting'). Term applied to a pictorial technique in which cut-out illustrations, or fragments of them, are arranged together and mounted, and to the picture so made. Ready-made images alone are used, and they are chosen for their subject and message; in both these respects montage is distinct from *collage and *papier collé. *Photomontage is montage using photographs only. In cinematic usage, the term 'montage' refers to the assembling of separate pieces of film into a sequence or a superimposed image.

Montagna, Bartolomeo (d. 1523). Italian painter. He probably trained in Venice, but he worked mainly in Vicenza, where he was the leading painter of his day. His

style has been well characterized by S. J. Freedberg (*Painting in Italy: 1500–1600*) as 'gloomily impressive'.

Montañes, Juan Martínez (1568–1649). The greatest Spanish sculptor of the 17th cent., known as 'el dios de la madera' (the god of wood) on account of his mastery as a carver. He worked for most of his long and productive career in Seville (*Pacheco often painted his figures), his most famous work being the *Christ of Clemency* (1603–6) in the cathedral there, which shows the new naturalism he brought to the *polychromed wooden statue. In this he occupied a role comparable to Gregorio *Fernández in Valladolid, but Montañes was more aristocratic in style, tempering *Baroque emotionalism with a Classical sense of dignity. In 1635–6 he was in Madrid to undertake his only recorded secular work, a portrait head (now lost) of Philip IV to serve as model for the equestrian statue of the king executed by Pietro *Tacca in Florence, and it was on this occasion that *Velázquez painted his well-known portrait of Montañes (Prado, Madrid). His work influenced painters such as Velázquez and *Zurbarán as well as sculptors such as *Cano (whom he taught), and his style was spread by his flourishing workshop.

Montefeltro. Italian noble family that ruled Urbino from 1234 with short intervals until 1508, when the family became extinct. Under the guidance of **Federico da Montefeltro** (b. 1422, ruled 1444–82) the city became one of the most important centres of *Renaissance culture. He was a brave *condottiere* and the implacable enemy of Sigismondo *Malatesta, but is significant chiefly as an enlightened patron of literature and the arts. His library was the finest in Italy and his palace is one of the most beautiful buildings of the Renaissance. For us he chiefly survives—broken nose, warts, and all—in the famous portrait by *Piero della Francesca (Uffizi, Florence), who was one of the leading lights of his court. Federico's ideals lived on in his son **Guidobaldo** (1472–1508), whose court is commemorated in Castiglione's famous book *The Courtier* (1528). Guidobaldo was dispossessed by Cesare Borgia in 1502, but recovered Urbino in 1503. When he died childless in 1508 Urbino passed to the family of his nephew Francesco Maria della Rovere.

Monticelli, Adolphe (1824–86). French painter, active in his native Marseilles and in Paris. He was a pupil of Paul *Delaroche, but he learned more from his studies of Old Masters in the Louvre; he was also influenced by his friends *Delacroix and *Diaz de la Peña. His subjects included landscapes, portraits, still lifes, *fêtes galantes* in the spirit of *Watteau, and scenes from the circus, painted in brilliant colours and thick impasto that influenced van *Gogh. He enjoyed great success in the 1860s, but after the Siege of Paris in 1870 he returned to Marseilles and led a retiring life. His work is represented in many French museums, and he has been much forged.

Moore, Albert (1841–93). English painter, son of a portrait painter, **William Moore** (1790–1851). His early works were in a *Pre-Raphaelite vein, but in the mid 1860s, under the influence particularly of the *Elgin Marbles, he turned to Classical subjects. He specialized in elaborately, and sometimes diaphanously, draped female figures, singly or in groups—'subjectless' pictures akin to those of his friend *Whistler. The two men met in 1865 and influenced each other. Like Whistler, Moore was a colourist of great sensitivity, although his colours tend to be much higher-keyed, and he ranks with him as one of the leading figures of *Aestheticism. Moore's brother, **Henry** (1831–95), was a successful marine painter.

Moore, Henry (1898–1986). English sculptor and graphic artist. He is recognized as one of the greatest sculptors of the 20th cent. and from the late 1940s until his death was unchallenged as the most celebrated British artist of his time. Son of a Yorkshire miner, after service in the British Army in the First World War, he trained at Leeds School of Art and from there obtained a scholarship to the *Royal College of Art (1919–23). He taught at the Royal College 1925–32 and at Chelsea School of Art 1932–9. During the 1930s he lived in Hampstead in the same area as Ben *Nicholson, Barbara *Hepworth, the critic Herbert *Read, and others of the avant-garde. In 1940, after the bombing of his studio, he moved to Much Hadham in Hertfordshire, where he lived for the rest

of his life. Most of Moore's early work was carved, rejecting the academic tradition of modelling in favour of the doctrine of truth to material, according to which the nature of the stone or wood—its shape, texture, and so on—was part of the conception of the work. He also rejected the *Classical and *Renaissance conception of beauty and put in its place an ideal of vital force and formal vigour which he found exemplified in much ancient sculpture (Mexican, Sumerian, etc.), which he studied in the British Museum, and also in the frescos of *Giotto and *Masaccio, which he saw in Italy in 1925 in the course of a travelling scholarship. During the 1930s his work was more directly influenced by European avant-garde art particularly the *Surrealism of *Arp. Although he produced some purely abstract pieces, his work was almost always based on forms in the natural world—often the human figure, but also, for example, bones, pebbles, and shells. The reclining female figure and the mother and child were among his perennial themes. By the late 1930s Moore was well known in informed circles as the leading avant-garde sculptor in England, but his wider fame was established by the poignant drawings he did as an official war artist (1940–2) of people sheltering from air-raids in underground stations. Subsequently his reputation grew rapidly (particularly after he won the International Sculpture Prize at the 1948 Venice *Biennale), and from the 1950s he carried out many public commissions in Britain and elsewhere. During this time there were major changes in his way of working. Bronze took over from stone as his preferred medium and he often worked on a very large scale. Some critics discerned a falling away of his powers in his later work, marked in particular by a tendency towards inflated rhetoric, but for others he remained a commanding figure to the end. A man of great integrity and unaffected charm, Moore was held in almost universally high regard. The tributes paid after his death made it clear that he was widely regarded not only as one of the greatest artists of the century, but also as one of the greatest Englishmen. He was a lucid and perceptive commentator on his own and other people's sculpture, and his writings have been collected as *Henry Moore on Sculpture* (1966). His work is represented in collections of modern art throughout the world; among those with particularly fine holdings are the Tate Gallery, London, and the Henry Moore Sculpture Study Centre at Leeds City Art Gallery.

Mor, Anthonis (*c.*1517/20–1576/7). Netherlandish portrait painter, a pupil of Jan van *Scorel in his native Utrecht. He was the most successful court portraitist of his day, leading an international career that took him to England, Germany, Italy, Portugal, and Spain. In England he painted a portrait of Mary Tudor (Prado, Madrid, 1554, and other versions), for which he is said to have been knighted—he is sometimes known as Sir Anthony More (it is thus he appears in *The Dictionary of National Biography*) and the Spanish version of his name, Antonio Moro, is also commonly used. His work shows little variation throughout his career; sitters are shown life-size or a little larger, half-, three-quarter-, or full-length, turned slightly to the side, with an air of unruffled dignity. His composition is simple and strong and his grasp of character firm but undemonstrative. He owed much to *Titian, but his surfaces are much more detailed and polished in the northern manner. Mor had great influence on the development of royal and aristocratic portraiture, particularly in Spain, where his ceremonious but austere style ideally suited the rigorous etiquette of the court. *Sánchez Coello was his pupil.

Morales, Luís de (d. *c.*1586). Spanish painter. He worked for most of his life in Badajoz, a town on the Portuguese border, and his style—formed away from the influence of the court or great religious and artistic centres such as Seville—is highly distinctive. His pictures are usually fairly small and he concentrated on devotional images such as the *Mater Dolorosa* or *Ecce Homo* painted with intense spirituality. The piety of his work has earned him the nickname 'El Divino'. His style owes something to Netherlandish art, but his misty modelling seems to derive more from *Leonardo da Vinci.

Morandi, Giorgio (1890–1964). Italian painter and etcher. He was born at Bologna and lived there all his life, standing aloof from the intellectual turmoil and aesthetic experiments of the 20th cent. apart from a brief association with *Futurism, and

his adhesion to de *Chirico's idea of *Metaphysical painting for a few years from 1918. After early landscapes he painted almost exclusively still lifes, eschewing literary and symbolic content, and using subtle combinations of colour within a narrow range of tones. His style has something in common with *Purism, but is more subtle and intimate, breathing an air of serenity and cultivated sensibility. His work won great respect among younger Italian artists for its pure devotion to aesthetic values and its poetic quality.

Moreau, Gustave (1826–98). French painter, one of the leading *Symbolist artists. He was a pupil of *Chassériau and was influenced by his master's exotic *Romanticism, but Moreau went far beyond him in his feeling for the bizarre and developed a style that is highly distinctive in subject and technique. His preference was for mystically intense images evoking long-dead civilizations and mythologies, treated with an extraordinary sensuousness, his paint encrusted and jewel-like. Although he had some success at the *Salon, he had no need to court this as he had private means, and much of his life was spent in seclusion. In 1892 he became a professor at the École des *Beaux-Arts and proved an inspired teacher, bringing out his pupils' individual talents rather than trying to impose ideas on them. His pupils included *Marquet and *Matisse, but his favourite was *Rouault, who became the first curator of the Moreau Museum in Paris (the artist's house), which Moreau left to the nation on his death. The bulk of his work is preserved there.

Moreelse, Paulus (1571–1638). Dutch painter and architect, active in Utrecht, where he helped found the St Lucas guild in 1611. He is best known for his portraits, which are similar to those made by his teacher *Mierevelt, but less severe. His portraits of shepherds and blonde shepherdesses with a deep *décolletage* were popular during his lifetime. He designed the Catherine Gate (destroyed) and possibly the façade of the Meat Market in Utrecht.

Morelli, Giovanni (1816–91). Italian critic. He trained as a physician, but from 1873 he began to write on Italian art. As a student at Munich he had acquired such a command of German that he preferred to write in that language, and at first he published his work as supposed translations from the Russian of Ivan Lermolieff (an anagram of his surname with a Russian termination). Morelli concentrated mainly on the problems of *attribution and claimed to have reduced this to scientific principles. He maintained that an artist's method of dealing with subordinate details, such as the treatment of the hands or the ears (here his anatomical training was useful), is tantamount to a signature and that by systematic study of such technical details attribution can be put beyond doubt. This method, still sometimes referred to as 'Morellian criticism', was influential on connoisseurs such as *Berenson, but it has proved much less productive of scientific certainty than Morelli hoped; he himself made some brilliant attributions, but also some noteworthy blunders. He was a patriot and a politician as well as a writer (he declined the directorship of the *Uffizi because he did not want to be distracted from his political duties), and he secured the passing of an act forbidding the sale of works of art from religious or public institutions. His own collection of pictures was left to the Pinacoteca of his adopted city of Bergamo.

Moretto da Brescia (Alessandro Bonvicino) (c.1498 1554). Italian painter, active mainly in his native Brescia and the neighbourhood. *Ridolfi says he was a pupil of *Titian and certainly his influence is apparent in Moretto's work. He was the leading Brescian painter of his day and had a large practice as a painter of altarpieces and other religious works, the best of which display an impressive gravity and a poetic feeling for nature (*St Giustina with a Donor*, Kunsthistorisches Museum, Vienna, c.1530). However, his portraits, although much less numerous, are considered to be generally of higher quality and of greater importance historically. It seems likely that he introduced the independent full-length portrait to Italy, for although *Vasari credits Titian with this distinction, Moretto's *Portrait of a Gentleman* of 1526 in the National Gallery, London, antedates any known example by Titian by several years. The National Gallery has an outstanding collection of works by Moretto, including two other portraits, which show the thoughtful qualities he passed on to his pupil *Moroni.

Morgan, John Pierpont (1837–1913). American financier, industrialist, and art collector. The son of a financier and head of one of the most powerful banking houses in the world, Morgan used his personal fortune to spend lavishly on works of art. His main collecting activities were in manuscripts and rare books and after his death his son, also **John Pierpont Morgan** (1867–1943), endowed the Pierpont Morgan Library in New York as a research institute and museum in memory of his father. It has superb collections of *illuminated manuscripts and Old Master drawings and also contains stained glass, sculpture, and metalwork. The *Metropolitan Museum in New York also received an important bequest from the elder Morgan, who was chairman of its governing board for many years.

Morisot, Berthe (1841–95). French *Impressionist painter. *Fragonard was her grandfather and she was brought up in a highly cultured atmosphere. She was a pupil of *Corot, but the chief formative influence on her work was *Manet, whom she met in 1868, and whose brother she married in 1874. In her turn she is said to have persuaded Manet to experiment with the Impressionist 'rainbow' palette and with *plein air* painting. After Manet's death in 1883 she came under the influence of *Renoir. Her pictures were regularly accepted for the *Salon, but she was a strong opponent of conventional academic teaching and a champion of the Impressionist ideals; she exhibited in all the Impressionist exhibitions except the fourth (1879), when she was prevented by ill health. She specialized in gentle domestic scenes, painted in a delicate, feathery technique, and was also an excellent marine painter. Her water-colours are as accomplished as her oils. She was renowned for her beauty and charm and often posed for Manet.

Morland, George (1762/3–1804). English painter, mainly of scenes from rural life, the son and pupil of **Henry Morland** (1719?–97), a painter of portraits and *fancy pictures who was also a dealer, forger, and restorer. George was precocious and a fluent worker and produced a huge amount of work, in spite of leading a dissolute life and often being drunk, in hiding from his creditors, or in prison. His name is particularly associated with small scenes of middle- and lower-class rural life, usually drawn more from the tavern and the stable than the cottage. The quality of his work is uneven, but at his best he showed a spirited technique and a sure sense of tone. His paintings became extremely popular and he was much imitated and forged; his brother-in-law William *Ward made *mezzotints of many of his pictures. With *Wheatley and *Ibbetson he established the village scene in the English painter's repertory.

Morley, Malcolm (1931–). British painter. In the 1960s he was one of the pioneers of *Superrealism (a term he coined), but his later work has become increasingly loose in handling, often depicting animals in lush landscapes. In 1984 he was the first winner of the Turner Prize, administered by the *Tate Gallery and awarded for 'the greatest contribution to art in Britain in the previous 12 months'. The decision occasioned much controversy as Morley had been in New York since 1964.

Moroni, Giovanni Battista (*c.*1520/5–1578). Italian painter. He trained under *Moretto in Brescia and worked mainly in his home town of Albino and in nearby Bergamo. His style was based closely on that of his master, but whereas his religious and allegorical paintings are generally heavy-handed, his portraits are worthy successors to Moretto's. They are remarkable for their psychological penetration, dignified air, and exquisite silvery tonality. The National Gallery, London, has the best collection of his work, including the celebrated portrait known as '*The Tailor*'.

Morrice, James Wilson (1865–1924). Canadian landscape and figure painter, active mainly in Paris. Quitting law school, he went to Paris about 1890. He was a pupil of the Académie Julien and later studied with *Harpignies, but his first inspiration came from *Whistler and *Conder. Later, his style became gently *Fauvist, and he was the friend and associate of *Matisse and *Marquet. He was widely travelled and his work was important in introducing modern trends to Canada.

Morris, Robert (1931–). American sculptor, *Conceptual artist, and writer. He is regarded as one of the most prominent exponents and theorists of *Minimal art, and has also experimented in the fields of *Performance, *Earthworks, and *Environment art, and temporary structures of miscellaneous materials. His most characteristic sculptures consist of large-scale, hard-edged geometric forms, but he has also made 'anti-form' pieces in soft, hanging materials.

Morris, William (1834–96). English writer, painter, designer, craftsman, and social reformer. As a student at Oxford University he formed a lifelong friendship with *Burne-Jones and began to write poetry and to study medieval architecture. In 1856 he was apprenticed to the architect G. E. Street, but soon left to paint under *Rossetti's guidance—his only completed oil painting, *Queen Guenevere* (Tate, London, 1858), is strongly *Pre-Raphaelite. Morris married Jane Burden, who appears in numerous paintings by Rossetti as the archetypal *femme fatale*, in 1859, and for him and his bride the famous Red House, Bexley Heath, was built by his friend Philip Webb. With Webb, Rossetti, Burne-Jones, Ford Madox *Brown, P. P. Marshall (a surveyor), and Charles Faulkner (an accountant), Morris founded the manufacturing and decorating firm of Morris, Marshall, Faulkner & Co. in 1861. After a shaky start, the firm prospered, producing furniture, tapestry, stained glass, furnishing fabrics, carpets, and much more. Morris's wallpaper designs are particularly well known (they are still produced commercially today) and Burne-Jones did some superb work for the firm, particularly in stained glass and tapestry design. Morris repudiated the concept of *fine art and his company was based on the ideal of a medieval guild, in which the craftsman both designed and executed the work. He defined art as 'man's expression of his joy in labour', and saw it as an essential part of human well-being. As a socialist he wished to produce art for the masses, but there was an inherent flaw in his ambition, for only the rich could afford his expensive hand-made products. His ideal of universal craftsmanship and his glorification of manual skill thus proved unrealistic in so far as it ran counter to or failed to come to terms with modern machine production. But his work bore lasting fruit, in England (see ARTS AND CRAFTS MOVEMENT) and abroad, in the emphasis which it laid upon the social importance of good design and fine workmanship in every walk of life. He also had an important part in the development of the private printing-press, through the founding of the *Kelmscott Press. Morris's homes at Walthamstow in London and Kelmscott Manor in Oxfordshire contain good examples of work designed by him and his associates.

Morse, Samuel Finley Breese (1791–1872), American painter and inventor. He had ambitions as a history painter and studied with *West in London 1811–15, but had, to his discontent, to work mainly at portraiture for financial reasons. After his return to the USA he worked in Boston and then in New York, where he was a founder member of the National Academy of Design and its first President from 1826 to 1845. Disenchanted by his failure to achieve major commissions as a history painter, however, he turned to invention, and in the 1830s conceived the idea of the telegraph and developed the Morse Code, which eventually made him a fortune. His first telegraph line was established between Washington and Baltimore in 1844, by which time Morse had abandoned painting as a profession.

Mortimer, John Hamilton (1740–79) English painter, a pupil of *Hudson at the same time as his friend Joseph *Wright. Like Wright, he worked both at portraiture and at subject pieces of a pioneering *Romantic nature. His *conversation pieces bear comparison with those of *Zoffany, but he found his true bent in the 1770s with pictures representing the exploits of soldiers and *banditti* in the 'savage' style of Salvator *Rosa (*Bandit Taking up his Post*, Detroit Institute of Arts). Many of his paintings have disappeared and are now known only through engravings. Mortimer led an eccentric and irregular life, but he became more settled after marrying in 1775 and his early death cut short the career of one of the most individual British painters of his generation.

mosaic. The art of making patterns and pictures by arranging coloured fragments of glass, marble, and other suitable materials and fixing them into a bed of cement or plaster. It was first developed extensively by the Romans in pavements. But it is also well suited to the adornment of walls and vaults, and great use was made of wall mosaic by the Christian churches of Italy and the *Byzantine Empire throughout the Middle Ages. As an exterior decoration it has sometimes appeared on the façades of medieval churches and in modern architecture. More rarely it has been made into portable pictures, or inlaid in furniture and small objects, as in the Aztec art of Mexico.

Mosan School. School of manuscript illumination, metalwork, and enamelwork flourishing from the late 11th to the early 13th cents. in the valley of the Meuse (or Maas). The river rises in France and empties into the Rhine estuary in the Netherlands, but in the context of medieval art the term Mosan refers to the stretch of river and its tributaries in present-day Belgium, particularly the area around Liège and the Benedictine monastery of Stavelot. The most important artists of the school are *Godefroid de Claire, *Nicolas of Verdun, and *Renier of Huy. The Mosan style is part of *Romanesque art, but is distinctive because of its more naturalistic, if idealized, attitude towards the human figure. In Renier of Huy's font at Liège, for example, the figures are three-dimensional and well proportioned and their draperies are notably *antique-like. Mosan art is also noteworthy for its sheer sumptuousness, and Mosan metal-workers in particular were famed throughout Europe; *Suger employed a number at Saint-Denis.

Moser, Lukas (active 1432). German painter, known only from one work, the *Magdalen* Altarpiece in the church at Tiefenbronn (signed and dated 1432—not 1431, as had previously been read). The altarpiece is remarkably advanced stylistically, showing a detailed naturalism in the treatment of figures and landscape and an interest in light that have much in common with the paintings of *Witz, who worked in nearby Switzerland. Also remarkable is the enigmatic inscription the altarpiece bears (perhaps no more than the lament of an underpaid artist); 'Schri kunst schri vnd klag dich ser din begert iecz niemen mer' ('Cry out, art, cry out and wail! No one wants you now').

Moser, Mary (1744–1819). English flower painter, the daughter of **George Moser** (1704–83), a Swiss goldsmith, enameller, and medallist who settled in England and became the first Keeper of the *Royal Academy. Like her father she was a foundation member of the Academy and in 1805 her name was put forward as a candidate for the presidency. Her small flower pieces in the Dutch manner were highly popular.

Moses, Anna Mary Robertson (called Grandma Moses) (1860–1961). The most famous of American *naïve painters. She took up painting seriously only in the 1930s after arthritis made her unable to continue with embroidery, initially copying postcards and *Currier & Ives prints. Her first exhibition was held in a drugstore at Hoosick Falls, NY, in 1938. She was then 'discovered' by a collector, Louis J. Calder, and had her first 'one-man' show in New York in 1940 at the age of 80. In 1949 she was received at the White House by President Harry Truman and in 1960 Governor Nelson Rockefeller proclaimed her 100th birthday, 7 September, 'Grandma Moses Day' in New York State. She produced more than a thousand pictures (working on a sort of production line system, three or four at a time, painting first the skies and last the figures), her favourite subjects being scenes of what she called the 'old-timey' farm life she had known in her younger days. From 1946 her works were reproduced on Christmas cards and elsewhere and achieved widespread popularity for their brightly coloured freshness and charm. Examples are in many American collections.

Mostaert, Jan (c.1475–1555/6). Netherlandish painter. He was born in Haarlem and the influence of *Geertgen tot Sint Jans can clearly be seen in his rather stiff and gangling figures. As painter to Margaret of Austria (1480–1530), Regent of the Netherlands, he accompanied her on her travels, making portraits of her courtiers. He also painted religious works. His most remarkable painting, however, is a *Landscape of the West Indies* (Frans Hals Mus., Haarlem, c.1525–30). Many of his paintings were destroyed in the Great Fire of Haarlem in 1576, and little is known in detail of his career.

Motherwell, Robert (1915–). American painter, collagist, and writer on art, one of the pioneers and principal exponents of *Abstract Expressionism. He took up painting seriously in 1941 after studying aesthetics at Stanford and Harvard universities and his writings have played a large part in setting the serious intellectual tone of the Abstract Expressionist movement. Motherwell is unusual among Abstract Expressionists in that his work was essentially abstract from the beginning of his career. There is often a suggestion of figuration in the large amorphous shapes and bold austere colours of his paintings, however, and the intellectual sensibilities he brings to his work are reflected in the inspiration from literature, history, or his personal life. He has, for example, painted a series of works (more than a hundred pictures) entitled *Elegy to the Spanish Republic*. By the late 1960s his style had veered more towards *Colour Field painting than Abstract Expressionism. He is an extremely prolific artist and his work as a writer, teacher, and lecturer has also shown great energy. From 1958 to 1971 he was married to Helen *Frankenthaler.

Mucha, Alphonse (1860–1939). Czech painter and designer. He had a highly varied career, but is best known for his luxuriously flowing poster designs, which rank among the most distinctive products of the *Art Nouveau style. They often feature beautiful women, but have nothing of the morbid sexuality typical of the period. Some of the best known were made in Paris in the 1890s for the celebrated actress Sarah Bernhardt. Mucha also designed sets, costumes, and jewellery for her. He was successful in the USA also, making four journeys there between 1903 and 1922. A Chicago industrialist and Slavophile, Charles Richard Crane, sponsored his series of twenty huge paintings entitled *Slav Epic*. In 1922 Mucha returned to Czechoslovakia, where his work included designing banknotes and stamps. After a period of neglect a revival of interest in his work culminated in a large exhibition of paintings, posters, drawings, furniture, and jewellery at the Grand Palais, Paris, in 1980.

Mulready, William (1786–1863). Irish-born painter, active in England, the pupil and brother-in-law of John *Varley. After

319   **MUNCH, EDVARD**

undistinguished beginnings with historical *genre and landscape he turned with great success to scenes of contemporary life in the vein made popular by *Wilkie. *The Fight Interrupted* (V&A, London, 1816), which shows a vicar intervening between two boys who have come to blows, made his reputation and set the course for his career. Although at first his meticulous brushwork showed the influence of 17th-cent. Dutch painting, in the 1820s he began to develop a more distinctive technique, using light clear colours over a white ground. This, together with his clear draughtsmanship and the poetic quality of some of his later paintings (*The Sonnet*, V&A, 1839), has led him to be seen as a precursor of the *Pre-Raphaelites, although they themselves rejected his work as trivial. Mulready also designed the first penny postage envelope (1840).

multiples. Term used from about the middle of the 20th cent. to designate works other than *graphic art or cast sculpture which are planned to be produced by a variety of industrial processes in unlimited numbers. In principle they are not industrially produced copies of an original work hand-made by the artist himself. Indeed, in some cases the artist produces only a blueprint or instructions for the industrial process. The concept of the multiple represents a revolution of aesthetic attitude according to which craftsmanship is disparaged and works of art are no longer regarded as items for connoisseurs but as consumer goods for the masses like any other industrial product.

Multscher, Hans (documented 1427–d. before 1467). German sculptor, active in Ulm. The solid *naturalism of his style, reminiscent of *Sluter, suggests that he trained in the Netherlands or northern France. He ran a large workshop, which was influential in spreading this manner in Swabia. Paintings were often integral to his altarpieces, but it is a matter for debate whether he practised painting himself. Among his most important works was the high altar for the church at Sterzing in the Tyrol (1456–8), parts of which are now in the Multscher museum there.

Munch, Edvard (1863–1944). Norwegian painter, lithographer, etcher, and wood-engraver, his country's greatest artist. He began painting in a conventional manner, but by 1884 was part of the world of bohemian artists in Christiania (now Oslo) who had advanced ideas on ethics and sexual morality, Christian *Krohg being his early mentor. In 1885 he made the first of several visits to Paris, where he was influenced by the *Impressionists and *Symbolists and, above all, by *Gauguin's use of simplified forms and non-naturalistic colours. Munch had a traumatic childhood (his father was almost dementedly pious and his mother and eldest sister died of consumption when he was young). 'Illness, madness and death were the black angels that kept watch over my cradle,' he wrote, and in his paintings he gave expression to the neuroses that haunted him. Certain themes—jealousy, sickness, the awakening of sexual desire—occur again and again, and he painted extreme psychological states with an unprecedented conviction and an intensity that sometimes bordered on the frenzied.

From 1892 to 1908 he lived mainly in Germany, mostly Berlin, with frequent stays in Norway and visits also to France and Italy. In 1892 he exhibited more than fifty pictures at the Kunstlerverein (Artists' Union) in Berlin and these caused such an uproar that the exhibition had to be withdrawn. It was one of the elements which led to the formation of the Berlin *Sezession group. In the 1890s much of his effort went into an ambitious series of pictures that never had a definitive form and which he called the 'Frieze of Life'—'a poem of life, love and death'. The most famous of the paintings from the series, *The Shriek* (Munch Mus. Oslo, 1895), and several others were translated by Munch into etching, lithography, or woodcut—arts in which his summary manner was to be felt as revolutionary. The woodcuts in particular had a wide influence. In 1908 he suffered what he called 'a complete mental collapse', the legacy of heavy drinking, overwork, and a wretched love-affair, and after recuperating he returned permanently to Norway. Munch realized that his mental instability was part of his genius ('I would not cast off my illness, for there is much in my art that I owe to it'), but he made a conscious decision to devote himself to recovery and abandoned his familiar imagery. The anguished intensity of his art disappeared and his work became much more extroverted. In landscapes, portraits, and pictures of workmen in the snow his technique grew more and more sketchy and energetic, his palette bright and vigorous. The great achievement of this period is a series of large oil paintings for the University Hall of Oslo (1910–15) exalting the positive forces of nature, science, and history. In 1916 he settled at Ekely, Oslo, thenceforth living a solitary life. In some of his later work, however, he rekindled the passion and profundity of his great period, as in the last of his numerous self-portraits, *Between the Clock and the Bed* (Munch Mus., 1940–2), in which he shows himself old and frail, hovering on the edge of eternity. At his death he left the large body of his work still in his possession to the City of Oslo to found the Munch Museum.

Munch ranks as one of the most powerful and influential of modern artists. His influence was particularly strong in Scandinavia and Germany, where he and van *Gogh are regarded as the two main sources of *Expressionist art. In the intensity with which he symbolized and communicated mental anguish through an unrestrained and violent distortion of colours and forms, he was the embodiment of that spirit which has animated the more tortured exponents of German Expressionism. 'Just as *Leonardo da Vinci studied human anatomy and dissected corpses,' he said, 'so I try to dissect souls.'

Munkácsy, Mihály von (1844–1900). Hungarian painter. After training in Budapest, Munich, and Düsseldorf he lived mainly in Paris. He had a resounding early success when he won a gold medal at the 1870 *Salon with *The Last Day of a Condemned Man* (NG, Budapest) and won an international reputation with his *Milton and his Daughters* (Lenox Library, New York, 1877–8). These theatrical costume pieces were enormously popular with rich collectors and Munkácsy became one of the wealthiest artists of his day. His best works are now, however, considered to be his landscapes, in which although he did not paint out of doors, he continued the tradition of the *Barbizon School. He despised the *Impressionists, but his work is often very free in handling. The National Gallery in Budapest has the best collection of Munkácsy's work and he is regarded as his country's greatest painter.

Munnings, Sir Alfred (1878–1959). English painter, a specialist in scenes involving horses. He was an artist of considerable natural ability, but he became rather slick and repetitive and his great popularity is more with lovers of horses than lovers of painting. He was President of the *Royal Academy, 1944–9, and was one of the most outspoken opponents of modern art in England. There is a museum dedicated to him in Dedham, Essex, where he lived for much of his life.

Murillo, Bartolomé Esteban (1617/18–82). Spanish painter, active for almost all his life in his native Seville. His early career is not well documented, but he started working in a naturalistic *tenebrist style, showing the influence of *Zurbarán. After making his reputation with a series of eleven paintings on the lives of Franciscan saints for the Franciscan monastery in Seville (1645–6, the pictures are now dispersed in Spain and elsewhere), he displaced Zurbarán as the city's leading painter and was unrivalled in this position for the rest of his life. Most of his paintings are of religious subjects, appealing strongly to popular piety and illustrating the doctrines of the Counter-Reformation church, above all the Immaculate Conception, which was his favourite theme. His mature style was very different to that seen in his early works; it is characterized by idealized figures, soft, melting forms, delicate colouring, and sweetness of expression and mood. The term *estilo vaporoso* ('vaporous style') is often used of it. Murillo also painted *genre scenes of beggar children that have a similar sentimental appeal, but his fairly rare portraits are strikingly different in feeling—much more sombre and intellectual (an outstanding self-portrait is in the NG, London). In 1660, with the collaboration of *Valdés Leal and Francisco *Herrera the Younger, Murillo founded an *academy of painting at Seville and became its first president. He died at Seville in 1682, apparently from the after-effects of a fall from scaffolding. He had many assistants and followers, and his style continued to influence Sevillian painting into the 19th cent. His fame in the 18th cent. and early 19th cent. was enormous. With *Ribera he was the only Spanish painter who was widely known outside his own country and he was ranked by many critics amongst the greatest artists of all time. Later his reputation plummetted, and he was dismissed as facile and sugary, but now that his own work is being distinguished from that of his numerous imitators his star is rising again.

Musée d'Orsay. See LOUVRE.

Museum of Modern Art, New York. The world's pre-eminent collection of art from the late 19th cent. to the present day, privately founded in 1929 by a group of collectors. It operated first in rented premises, holding loan shows, but the nucleus of the permanent collection was established with the bequests of Lillie P. Bliss (including nine *Cézannes) and other founders. The present building, in 53rd Street, was opened in 1939 and there have been several major extensions. Apart from painting, sculpture, and the graphic arts, the museum has collections of photographs, films, and architectural documentation, and a large library. Through its permanent collections, exhibitions, and many other activities it exercises a strong influence both on taste and on artistic production. The many publications it has produced include some of the standard works on modern art, several of them written by Alfred H. *Barr, jun., the first director of the museum.

Muybridge, Eadweard (1830–1904). British-born photographer and pioneer of motion photography who emigrated to the USA as a young man. He became Director of Photographic Surveys to the US Government, and while surveying the Pacific coast in 1872, he was asked by the railroad magnate Leland Stanford, then Governor of California, to photograph a horse in motion, apparently to settle a bet as to whether a horse ever had all four legs off the ground simultaneously. Muybridge experimented with a battery of cameras with high-speed shutters operated by the horse itself passing across trip threads (he worked at Stanford's stud farm, and at his expense), and succeeded in proving that all four legs of a horse are indeed at times in the air simultaneously. He published his photographs in *The Horse in Motion* (1878), and then went on to study the movement of other animals, including humans, publishing his results in volumes such as *Animal Locomotion* (1887). In 1880 he invented the zoopraxiscope to project the pictures and recreate the movements he had photographed, and this he showed to scientific bodies all over Europe and America. This predecessor of the modern cinema caused a sensation. Muybridge's photographs were much used as a source by artists, among them *Eakins and the *Futurists.

Myron. Greek sculptor active in Athens in the mid 5th cent. BC. He was one of the leading Greek sculptors of the period and is now remembered mainly for his bronze *Discobolus* (Discus Thrower), which survives in Roman marble copies; the best of them is in the Terme Museum in Rome. As an example of compositional equilibrium it achieved a fame comparable to the *Doryphorus* of *Polyclitus. Copies also exist of Myron's group of *Athena and Marsyas*, but no visual record survives of the work for which he was most renowned in his own time—the bronze *Cow* in the market-place at Athens, which was said to display remarkable naturalism. See also SEVERE STYLE.

Mytens, Daniel (c.1590–1647). Anglo-Dutch portrait painter. He was born in Delft and trained in The Hague (probably under *Mierevelt), but almost all of his known career was spent in England, where he is first recorded in 1618 working for the Earl of *Arundel. By 1620 he was working for James I and in 1625 he was appointed 'one of our Picture Drawers' by Charles I. Mytens introduced a new elegance and grandeur into English portraiture, especially in his full-lengths, and he was the dominant painter at court until the arrival of van *Dyck in 1632. Van Dyck completely outclassed him, however, and he returned to The Hague in about 1634. Few paintings are known from his final years, but he continued to work as Arundel's agent. His finest picture is acknowledged to be *The First Duke of Hamilton* (Scottish NPG, Edinburgh, 1629), described by Sir Ellis *Waterhouse as 'the great masterpiece of pre-Vandyckian portraiture in England'. Mytens was one of a dynasty of painters active into the 18th cent. Among the other members was his great nephew, **Daniel Mytens the Younger** (1644–88), also a portraitist.

N

Nabis. Group of French painters, active in Paris in the 1890s, whose work was inspired by *Gauguin's expressive use of colour and rhythmic pattern. The name 'Nabis' was coined by the poet Henri Cazalis (1840–1909) from a Hebrew word meaning 'prophets' because of their half-serious, half-burlesque pose as adepts and their attitude to the new Gauguin style as a kind of religious illumination. *Sérusier, who met Gauguin at *Pont Aven in 1888, provided the initiative for the group and with *Denis was its main theorist. *Bonnard and *Vuillard were among the other members of the group, the activities of which included theatre, poster and stained-glass design, and book illustration as well as painting. The first Nabis exhibition was held in 1892. After a successful exhibition held in 1899 together with certain of the *Symbolists in the gallery of the dealer *Durand-Ruel, the members of the group gradually drifted apart.

Nadelman, Elie (1882–1946). Polish-born sculptor who became an American citizen in 1927. After brief studies in his native Warsaw and in Munich he settled in Paris by 1903 and lived there until 1914. With the outbreak of the First World War, Nadelman moved to London and then New York. There he was patronized by Helena Rubinstein, who commissioned him to make sleek marble heads for her beauty salons. He married a wealthy widow in 1919 and his work has a witty sophistication appropriate to the high society world he moved in, as with the delightful bowler-hatted *Man in the Open Air* (MOMA, New York, 1915). With his humour went a bold simplification and distortion of forms that places him alongside *Lachaise as one of the pioneers of modern sculpture in America. Much of his work was accidentally destroyed in 1935, bringing his career to an end.

naïve art. Term applied to painting (and to a much lesser degree sculpture) produced in more or less sophisticated societies but lacking conventional expertise in representational skills. Colours are characteristically bright and non-naturalistic, perspective non-scientific, and the vision childlike or literal-minded. The term *'primitive' is sometimes used more or less synonymously with naïve, but this can be confusing, as 'primitive' is also applied loosely to paintings of the pre-Renaissance era as well as to art of uncivilized societies. Moreover, naïve artists are not necessarily untrained or amateurs. Sophisticated artists may also deliberately affect a naïve style. Interest in the freshness and directness of vision of outstanding naïve artists such as Henri *Rousseau developed first in France in the early years of the 20th cent. (Wilhelm *Uhde was a notable figure in promoting it), and since then many other naïve artists, for example, Grandma *Moses in America and Alfred *Wallis in England, have received critical recognition.

Nanni di Banco (d. 1421). Florentine sculptor, one of the major figures of the transition from *Gothic to *Renaissance. Much of his work was designed for one or other of two architectural settings, the cathedral and Or San Michele, which together formed the chief source of demand for sculpture in Florence during the first quarter of the 15th cent., and he often worked alongside *Donatello. His work has a Gothic elegance, but also shows the influence of the *antique; his masterpiece, the group of the *Quattro Santi Coronati* (Four Crowned Saints) at Or San Michele, for example, features grave and dignified figures modelled on Roman senator statues. Because this and other major works are of controversial dating, however, it is uncertain whether he was in advance of Donatello in his use of *Classical exemplars.

Nanteuil, Robert (1623–78). French engraver and draughtsman, almost exclusively of portraits. He is considered the greatest European portrait engraver of the 17th cent., and in France stands as the counterpart of Philippe de *Champaigne among painters. He often engraved the work of Champaigne and other painters, but also made original compositions, in which he showed both great technical mastery and penetrating characterization. Louis XIV appointed him royal draughtsman in 1658 and he made many pastel portraits as well as engravings of the king and royal family.

Nash, Paul (1889–1946). English painter and graphic artist. Nash was one of the most individual British artists of his period, taking a distinguished place in the English tradition of deep attachment to the countryside whilst at the same time responding imaginatively to European modernism. He saw himself as a successor of *Blake and *Turner. After training at the *Slade he served in the First World War, was wounded, and worked as an official war artist, creating memorable images of the devastation the war wrought on the countryside. In the 1920s and 1930s he was influenced particularly by *Surrealism (above all de *Chirico, an exhibition of whose work he saw in London in 1928) and often concentrated on mysterious aspects of the landscape (*Monster Field*, Durban Art Gallery, 1939). He was the prime mover in the formation of *Unit One (1933), and he helped to organize and exhibited in the London Surrealist exhibition in 1936. In the Second World War he was again an official war artist, painting one of the best-known works to be inspired by the conflict, *Totes Meer* (*Dead Sea*) (Tate Gal., London, 1940–1), which portrays shotdown aircraft with their wings looking like undulating waves. Nash was regarded as one of the finest book illustrators of his time; he also designed scenery, fabrics, and posters, and was a photographer and writer. His brother **John** (1893–1977) was also a painter and illustrator, excelling in meticulous flower drawings for botanical publications.

Nasmyth, Alexander (1758–1840). Scottish painter. He worked mainly in his native Edinburgh, but he was a pupil and assistant of *Ramsay in London 1774–8, and in 1782–5 he visited Italy. There he became interested in landscape painting, which eventually took over from portraiture as his main concern. In his landscapes he blended *Classical elements stemming from *Claude with naturalistic observation and became the founder of the Scottish landscape tradition, influencing many younger painters. He was a man of wide culture, interested in science as well as art, and he worked as a stage designer and architectural consultant. One of his friends was the poet Robert Burns, whose portrait he painted against a romantic landscape background (NPG, Edinburgh, c.1787). Nasmyth had several artist sons, of whom the most important was the eldest, **Patrick** (1787–1831). He worked mainly in London and achieved great popularity with his prolific output of landscapes in the manner of the 17th-cent. Dutch masters, earning the nickname 'the English *Hobbema'.

National Gallery, London. The national collection of European paintings from c.1300 to c.1900 (it also includes a few earlier pictures and has recently started to acquire works from the early 20th cent.). It was founded in 1824 when the government purchased thirty-eight paintings from the collection of John Julius Angerstein, a merchant who died in 1823. They were first displayed in his former house at 100 Pall Mall. Further bequests (including that of Sir George *Beaumont) soon necessitated larger premises, and the present building in Trafalgar Square, designed by William Wilkins, was opened in 1838; a major extension—the Sainsbury Wing—was begun in 1988. The National Gallery shared its premises with the *Royal Academy until 1869, by which time it had grown into one of the great collections of the world. It now has about 2,000 pictures. This is a fairly small number compared with some of the great Continental galleries based on former royal collections, but the National Gallery's paintings surpass those of any other gallery in giving a comprehensive view of the mainstream of European painting from *Giotto to *Cezánne. Best represented of all are the earl Italian and Dutch Schools. The representation of the British School is selective because of the existence of the *Tate Gallery as a separate National Gallery of British art. Other well-known national galleries, with their dates of foundation, are: the National Gallery of Scotland in Edinburgh (1859); the National Gallery of Victoria in Melbourne (1859); the National Gallery of Ireland in Dublin (1864); the

National Gallery of Canada in Ottawa (1880); the National Gallery of Art in Washington (1937); and the Australian National Gallery in Canberra (1976).

National Portrait Gallery, London. The national collection of portraits of eminent British men and women. It was founded in 1856 at the urging of Philip Henry Stanhope, 5th Earl Stanhope, who was the first chairman. The collection was originally housed at 29 Great George Street, and the present premises, adjoining the National Gallery, were opened in 1896. The criterion for inclusion in the gallery is the celebrity of the sitter rather than the quality of the portrait, so as works of art the pictures in the collection vary enormously, from an acknowledged masterpiece such as *Holbein's cartoon of Henry VIII to the wholly amateurish representation of the three Brontë sisters by their brother Branwell. Nevertheless, because portraiture has played such a great part in the history of British art, many illustrious artists are well represented there. Recently the NPG has begun to commission portraits of living sitters, and since 1980 it has organized a series of annual portrait awards for artists under 40 years old. The NPG has four outstations: Montacute House in Somerset, Beningbrough Hall in Yorkshire, Gawthorpe Hall in Lancashire, and Bodelwyddan Castle in Wales. The Scottish National Portrait Gallery was established in Edinburgh in 1882, and the National Portrait Gallery in Washington in 1962.

Nattier, Jean-Marc (1685–1766). French portrait painter. His father, **Jean** (c.1642–1705), was a painter and his mother, **Marie Courtois** (c.1655–1703), was a *miniaturist. He was one of the most successful artists at the court of Louis XV excelling in the vogue for painting women in mythological or allegorical fancy dress—or undress—transforming his matrons into goddesses (*Mme de Lambesc as Minerva*, Louvre, Paris, 1737). His portraits are little concerned with individual characterization, but they show fluency, vivacity, and a relaxed charm. He was at his best with women and has been accused of 'painting with make-up', a comment that suggests the pastel-like delicacy of his handling. Taste was turning against him towards the end of his career and some of his later

work shows signs of fatigue. His brother **Jean-Baptiste** (1678–1726) was also a painter; he committed suicide after being expelled by the Académie.

naturalism. Term denoting an approach to art in which the artist endeavours to represent objects as they are empirically observed, rather than in a stylized or conceptual manner. As applied to a particular school of painting the term was first used by *Bellori (1672) of the followers of *Caravaggio, with reference to their doctrine of copying nature faithfully whether it seems to us ugly or beautiful. Naturalism, however, is not inconsistent with the *idealization of nature, for Greek sculpture may be naturalistic in its command of anatomy, but idealistic in that it sets up a standard of physical beauty remote from the everyday world. Nor need the term imply minute attention to detail, although this is often part of a naturalistic approach. The shade of meaning to be attached to the word can thus vary greatly according to context; when used in its broadest sense it may suggest little more than that a work is representational rather than *abstract. The terms 'naturalistic' and 'realistic' are often used more or less synonymously, but *Realism with a capital 'r' has a specific meaning in the history of art and should not be used loosely.

Navarrete, Juan Fernández de (c.1526–79). Spanish painter from Navarre, called 'El Mudo' (the mute) because he was deaf and dumb. After studying for many years in Italy (traditionally as a pupil of *Titian) he returned to Spain shortly before 1568 and was appointed court painter to Philip II. He was commissioned to paint thirty-two altarpieces for chapels in the *Escorial, but at the time of his death had completed only eight (still *in situ*). His eclectic style was influential in spreading Italian influence in Spain.

Nazarenes. A group of young, idealistic German painters of the early 19th cent. who believed that art should serve a religious or moral purpose and desired to return to the spirit of the Middle Ages. The nucleus of the group was established in 1809 when six students at the Vienna Academy formed an association called the Brotherhood of St Luke (*Lukasbrüder*), named after the patron saint of painting.

The name Nazarenes was given to them derisively because of their affectation of biblical dress and hairstyles. They wished to revive the working environment as well as the spiritual sincerity of the Middle Ages, and lived and worked together in a quasi-monastic fashion. In 1810 *Overbeck, *Pforr, and two other members moved to Rome, where they occupied the disused monastery of S. Isidoro. Here they were joined by Peter von *Cornelius and others. One of their aims was the revival of monumental *fresco and they obtained two important commissions which made their work internationally known (Casa Bartholdy, 1816–17, the paintings are now in the Staatliche Museen, East Berlin; and Casino Massimo, Rome, 1817–29). Stylistically they were much indebted to *Perugino, and their work is clear and prettily coloured, but often insipid. In general, modern taste has been more sympathetic towards the Nazarenes' simple and sensitive landscape and portrait drawings than to their ambitious, didactic figure paintings. The Nazarenes broke up as a group in the 1820s, but their ideas continued to be influential. Cornelius had moved in 1819 to Munich, where he surrounded himself with a large number of pupils and assistants who in turn carried his style to other German centres. The studio of Overbeck (the only one to remain permanently in Rome) was a meeting-place for artists from many countries; *Ingres admired him and Ford Madox *Brown visited him. William *Dyce introduced some of the Nazarene ideals into English art and there is a kinship of spirit with the *Pre-Raphaelites.

Neeffs (or Neefs), **Pieter the Elder** (c.1578–1656/61). Flemish painter, active in Antwerp. Most of his pictures are interiors of *Gothic churches, some of them night scenes illuminated by artificial light. They are generally small, painted on copper, and executed in a precise, neat way similar in style to those of the *Steenwycks, but more mechanical. His son **Pieter Neeffs the Younger** (1620–after 1675) painted the same subjects, and it is very difficult to distinguish between their hands. Another son, **Lodewijk** (b. 1617), was also a painter, but little is known of his work.

Neer, Aert (or **Aernout**) **van der** (1603/4–77). Dutch landscape painter, active in his native Amsterdam. He had two specialities: moonlit scenes, of which he is the acknowledged master among Dutch painters; and winter landscapes with skaters, as an exponent of which he is in the first rank. In both types he displayed his mastery of light effects and subtle modulations of colour. He was a prolific painter and his work was much copied and imitated, but he had difficulty earning a living as an artist. In 1658 he opened a wine shop in Amsterdam, but this venture was also a failure and in 1662 he became bankrupt. Two of his sons were artists. **Eglon** (1634?–1703) is best known for *genre pieces done in the style of *Terborch and *Metsu. He was conspicuously more successful than his father and became court painter at Düsseldorf. The few works which can be attributed to **Jan** (1638–65) show that he was an imitator of his father.

Neoclassicism. The dominant movement in European art and architecture in the late 18th and early 19th cents., characterized by a desire to re-create the spirit and forms of the art of Greece and Rome. A new and more scientific interest in *Classical antiquity, greatly stimulated by the discoveries at Pompeii (where excavations began in 1748) and Herculaneum, was one of the features of the movement, and it is also seen as mounting a reaction against the light-hearted and frivolous *Rococo style. The order, clarity, and reason of Greek and Roman art appealed greatly in the Age of Enlightenment, and the Neoclassical style could have moral as well as aesthetic implications, particularly in France, where it is associated with the Revolution and a desire to restore ancient Roman values into civil life. It is, indeed, in the paintings of *David, with their antique grandeur and simplicity of form, and their heroic severity of tone, that Neoclassicism finds its purest expression, but the style was born and had its centre in Rome. *Mengs and *Winckelmann were in the vanguard of the movement there, and other leading figures from all over Europe—*Canova, *Flaxman, Gavin *Hamilton, *Thorvaldsen—spent the main or important parts of their careers in the city. Many American artists worked there too—notably the sculptor Horatio *Greenough, who was a pupil of Thorvaldsen—and took the Neoclassical style back to their country. Because Neoclassicism placed respect for approved models above personal expression it was a style that particularly lent itself to having this kind of international currency. The 18th cent. saw a great growth in the publication of lavishly illustrated volumes on classical art, architecture and antiquities, and this helped to spread the ideals of the movement. There was, however, considerable stylistic variation within Neoclassicism, Angelica *Kauffmann, for example, painting in a delicate and pretty manner. Moreover, there is no firm dividing line between Neoclassicism and *Romanticism, even though in some ways they appear to be at opposite spiritual poles. In the revival of interest in antique art, archaeological zeal could easily give way to a nostalgic yearning for a lost Golden Age, and the term 'Romantic Classicism' is sometimes used to characterize an aspect of Neoclassicism in which an interest in antiquity is tinged with Romantic feeling. In fact the antipathy between Classics and Romantics (exemplified by *Ingres and *Delacroix, for example) was unknown before the 19th cent., and it was only in the mid 19th cent., at a time when the antique revival style was out of fashion, that the word 'Neoclassicism' was coined—originally a pejorative term with suggestions of lifelessness and impersonality. These negative connotations have clung tenaciously to the term, and the ardent aspirations of the founders of Neoclassicism have been obscured by the fact that the more decorative aspects of the movement—Wedgwood pottery, for example—have become more closely associated with the word in the public consciousness than have the great masterpieces of David and Canova.

Neoclassicism is related to but can be distinguished from Greek Taste, which was a fairly superficial fashion for Greek-inspired decoration, and from the Greek Revival, which in architecture was a movement expressing a new interest in the simplicity and gravity of ancient Greek buildings. It began seriously in the 1790s and culminated in the 1820s and 1830s. Greek architecture became widely known in the west only around 1750–60 and in the early days of Neoclassicism it was regarded as primitive and few architects cared to imitate it.

Neo-Impressionism. Term coined by the critic Félix Fénéon in 1886 for a movement in French painting that was both a development from *Impressionism and a reaction against it. Like the Impressionists, the exponents of Neo-Impressionism were fundamentally concerned with the representation of light and colour, but whereas Impressionism was empirical and spontaneous, Neo-Impressionism was based on scientific principles and resulted in highly formalized compositions. *Seurat was the outstanding artist of the movement; *Signac (who was its main theoretician) and (for a while) Camille *Pissarro were the other leading adherents. All three showed Neo-Impressionist pictures at the final Impressionist exhibition in 1886. The theoretical basis of Neo-Impressionism was *divisionism, with its associated technique of *pointillism—the use of dots of pure colour applied in such a way that when seen from an appropriate distance they achieve a maximum of luminosity. In each painting the dots were of a uniform size, chosen to harmonize with the scale of the work. In Seurat's paintings, this approach combined solidity and clarity of form with a vibrating intensity of light; in the hands of lesser artists, it often produced works that look rigid and contrived. Neo-Impressionism was short-lived, but it had a significant influence on several major artists of the late 19th and early 20th cents., notably *Gauguin, van *Gogh, *Matisse, and *Toulouse-Lautrec.

Neo-Plasticism. Term coined by Piet *Mondrian for his style of austerely geometrical *abstraction. He claimed that art should be 'denaturalized', by which he meant that it must be freed from any representational relation to the individual details of natural objects, being built up solely from abstract elements. In this way he thought that one might escape the individualism of the particular and achieve expression of an ideal of universal harmony.

Neo-Romanticism. A term applied to a movement in British painting and other arts c. 1935–55, in which artists looked back to certain aspects of 19th-cent. *Romanticism, particularly the 'visionary' landscape tradition of *Blake and Samuel *Palmer, and reinterpreted them in a more modern idiom. Painters and graphic artists whose work is embraced by the term include Michael *Ayrton, John *Piper, and

Graham *Sutherland, who all worked in a landscape tradition that was regarded as distinctly national, and projected a Romantic image of the countryside at a time when it was under threat from Nazi Germany. Other artists whose work has been dubbed Neo-Romantic include the poet Dylan Thomas, the film director Michael Powell, and photographers such as Bill Brandt and Edwin Smith. The term Neo-Romanticism has also been applied to certain painters working in France in the 1930s, notably *Berman and *Tchelitchew, who typically painted dreamlike imaginary landscapes with rather mournful figures. Their work influenced the British Neo-Romantics.

Neroccio dei Landi (1447–1500). Sienese painter and sculptor. He was a pupil of *Vecchietta and worked in partnership with *Francesco di Giorgio until 1475. Most of his paintings are representations of the Virgin and Child with Saints, but one of his finest works is a *Portrait of a Girl* in the National Gallery in Washington. He continued the elegant and refined Sienese tradition that stretched back to *Duccio and is particularly noted for his delicate colouring.

Netscher, Caspar (?1635/9–84). Dutch painter. *Houbraken makes inconsistent statements about his birthplace, mentioning both Heidelberg and Prague, and there is similar doubt about his birth date. Most of his career was spent in The Hague, where he settled in 1661/2, but he trained in Deventer with *Terborch. From his master he took his predilection for depicting costly materials—particularly white satin. He painted *genre scenes and some religious and mythological subjects, but from about 1670 he devoted himself almost exclusively to portraits, often for court circles in The Hague. His reputation was such that Charles II invited him to England (*Vertue says he came, *de Piles and Houbraken that he declined). His work, elegant, Frenchified, small in scale, and exquisitely finished, influenced Dutch portraiture into the 18th cent., his followers including his sons **Constantijn** (1688–1723) and **Theodoor** (1661–1732).

Neue Künstlervereinigung (NKV), Munich. An association of artists founded in 1909 by *Kandinsky, *Jawlensky, and Gabriele Munter (1877–1962). These artists were at that time imbued with the ideas and techniques of the *Fauves and their association was in opposition to the academic schools of Munich. The NKV held its first exhibition in 1909, limited to the works of members, and in 1910 it staged a much larger exhibition, European in character, which included works by *Rouault, *Picasso, and *Le Fauconnier, and by members of the *Fauves, some of whom (for example *Derain) had already advanced towards *Cubism. The *Blaue Reiter came into existence as a splinter group from the NKV.

Neue Sachlichkeit (New Objectivity). Movement in German painting of the 1920s and early 1930s reflecting the resignation and cynicism of the post-war period. It continued the interest in social criticism which characterized much of the prevalent *Expressionism, but repudiated the abstract tendencies of the *Brücke. The name was coined in 1923 by Gustav Hartlaub, director of the Kunsthalle, Mannheim, in connection with an exhibition, held in 1925, of 'artists who have retained or regained their fidelity to positive, tangible reality'. The movement was not characterized by a unified stylistic outlook, but the major trend was towards the use of meticulous detail to portray the face of evil for the purposes of violent social satire. *Dix and *Grosz are the greatest figures of the movement, which was dissipated in the 1930s before a State-imposed *naturalism for the glorification of Nazism.

Nevelson, Louise (1899–1988). Russian-born American sculptor, painter, and graphic artist. She was taken to the USA in 1905 and settled in New York in 1920. Her serious study of art began at the Art Students' League in 1929–30 and she then studied under Hans *Hofmann at Munich. In 1932–3 she worked with Ben *Shahn as assistant to Diego *Rivera on his frescos in New York. She started to make sculpture in 1932 and it was towards the end of the 1950s that she began the 'sculptured walls' for which she became internationally famous. These are wall-like *reliefs made up of many boxes and compartments into which abstract shapes are assembled together with commonplace objects such as chair legs, bits of balustrades, and other 'found objects' (*An American Tribute to*

329 NICCOLÒ DELL' ARCA

the British People, Tate, London, 1960–4). These constructions, painted a uniform black, or afterwards white or gold, won her a reputation as a leader in both *assemblage and *environment sculpture. They have great formal elegance, but also a strange ritualistic power. In the late 1960s she started working in a greater variety of materials and also began to receive commissions for large open-air and environmental sculptures, which she executed in aluminium or steel.

Nevinson, C. R. W. (Christopher Richard Wynne) (1889–1946). English painter. In 1912–13 he shared a studio with *Modigliani in Paris and at this time met several of the *Futurists. He became the outstanding British exponent of Futurism in painting, finding his ideal subjects in the First World War in harsh, steely images of life and death in the trenches. Stylistically they drew on certain *Cubist and Futurist ideas, but are closer to the *Vorticism of Wyndham *Lewis. At the end of the war Nevinson renounced Futurism and his later, more conventional paintings are a sad anticlimax; an example is *Twentieth Century* (Laing Art Gal., Newcastle upon Tyne) a turgid attempt to portray a world on the brink of catastrophe.

New English Art Club. Artists' society founded in London in 1886 in reaction against the conservative and complacent attitudes of the *Royal Academy. The founders were largely artists who had worked in France and had been influenced by the *plein air school and *Bastien-Lepage. They included *Clausen, *Steer, and *Sargent. In 1889 the Club came under the control of a minority group led by *Sickert, who had joined in 1888, and he and his associates later formed the nucleus of the *Camden Town Group. They were interested in the *Impressionists, particularly *Monet and *Degas, rather than in Bastien-Lepage, and in 1889 they held an independent exhibition under the name 'The London Impressionists'. From 1887 to 1904 the Club held regular annual exhibitions, and from c.1889 to the first *Post-Impressionist exhibition in 1910 it contained most of the noteworthy painters in England. After the First World War the Club occupied a position midway between the Academy and the avant-garde groups. With the gradual liberalization of the

Academy exhibitions its importance diminished, but the Club still exists.

Newlyn School. Group of artists who worked in the Cornish fishing village of Newlyn in the 1880s and 1890s and were leading pioneers of *plein air painting in Britain. The mild climate made Newlyn particularly suitable for outdoor work. Many of the Newlyn artists were associated with the *New English Art Club, but they also showed their work at the *Royal Academy. The leading figure was Stanhope Forbes (1857–1947) and other artists who worked there included Laura and Harold *Knight.

Newman, Barnett (1905–70). American painter. He was one of the most written about artists of the *New York School, but although he was associated with the *Abstract Expressionists his work was more austere than theirs, with much less painterly handling. He gradually found his own style of mystical abstraction during the second half of the 1940s, achieving a breakthrough with *Onement I* (private coll., 1948), a monochromatic canvas of dark red with a single stripe of lighter red running down the middle. Newman was an important influence on younger artists such as Larry *Poons and Frank *Stella and was the forerunner of various features of American painting that followed Abstract Expressionism: monochromatic *Colour Field painting; certain aspects of the work of Jasper *Johns and Kenneth *Noland; and the shaped canvas.

New York Realists. Informal name given during the early years of the 20th cent. to Robert *Henri and his disciples.

New York School. Name given to the innovatory painters, particularly the *Abstract Expressionists, who worked in New York during the 1940s and 1950s.

Niccolò dell' Arca (active 1462–94). Italian sculptor. He was of south Italian origin, but his known career was spent in Bologna, where he is first documented in 1462. His name comes from his work on the Arca di S. Domenico (shrine of St Dominic) in S. Domenico Maggiore, Bologna, for which he carved a marble canopy and small free-standing figures (1469 onwards). The work was unfinished at his death and *Michelangelo carved three missing figures. Niccolò's greatest work is a highly emotional group of the *Lamentation over the Body of Christ* in Sta Maria della Vita, Bologna, executed in *terracotta and originally painted. It is of uncertain date. According to tradition the figure of Nicodemus is a self-portrait.

Nicholson, Ben (1894–1982). British painter and maker of painted *reliefs, one of the most distinguished pioneers of abstract art in Britain. From his father, Sir William *Nicholson, he inherited a feeling for simple and fastidious still lifes, which with landscapes made up the bulk of his early work. They show him responding to the innovations of *Cubism, using the standard Cubist repertoire of objects such as jugs and glasses and arranging them as flat shapes on the picture plane. In 1933, during one of the several long stays in Paris he made at this time, Nicholson made the first of a series of white reliefs using only right angles and circles (*White Relief*, Tate, London, 1935). They show the influence of *Mondrian (whom Nicholson met in Paris in 1934) and were the most uncompromising examples of abstract art that had been made by a British artist up to that date. At the forefront of the modern movement in England, he was a member of *Unit One and one of the editors of *Circle*. In 1932 he married Barbara *Hepworth (they were divorced in 1951) and in 1940 moved with her to *St Ives, where with John *Piper and others he became the centre of a local art movement. After the war his international reputation grew and he won many prestigious awards. From the late 1950s he spent much of his time in Switzerland. Nicholson's first wife, **Winifred Nicholson** (1893–1981), was a painter of distinction. She is best known for her flower paintings, but she also did other subjects and abstracts, all her work showing her joy in colour and light.

Nicholson, Sir William (1872–1949). English painter and graphic artist. He is perhaps best remembered for his brilliant work as a poster designer, done in collaboration with his brother-in-law James *Pryde under the name 'the Beggarstaff Brothers'. His finest works as a painter are his still lifes, usually small, unpretentious, and sensitively handled.

Nicolas of Verdun (active late 12th cent.–early 13th cent.). *Mosan goldsmith, enameller, and metal-worker. He is considered the greatest goldsmith and enameller of his day and a major figure in the transition from *Romanesque to Gothic. Two signed works by him survive: an *enamelled pulpit frontal made for the abbey church at Klosterneuburg, near Vienna (completed in 1181, damaged in 1320, and then remodelled into its present *triptych-altar form); and the Shrine of St Mary for Tournai Cathedral (1205). Among the works attributed to him the most important is the Shrine of the Three Kings, made for Cologne Cathedral in about 1290 and the largest and most sumptuous reliquary of the period. All three works still belong to the churches for which they were commissioned. The Klosterneuburg altar is his masterpiece, featuring forty-five enamel plaques in an elaborate *typological programme, events from the New Testament being paralleled by ones in the Old Testament. His figure style is expressive and dynamic, with individualized faces and richly articulated drapery suggesting influence from the *antique.

niello. Term referring to a black compound (typically sulphur, silver, lead, and copper) used as a decorative inlay on metal surfaces, to the process of making such an inlay, and to a surface or object so decorated. Niello prints are impressions taken from such surfaces and are invariably Italian work of the second half of the 15th cent. They were probably taken as proofs by niellists who wanted to see their work clearly. But it appears that these craftsmen then took to engraving plates with the express purpose of taking impressions from them, and many early examples of Italian *line engraving show the influence of the niello craft. Maso *Finiguerra, whom *Vasari credits with the invention of line engraving, was both niellist and line engraver.

Nittis, Giuseppe de (1846–84). Italian painter, mainly of landscapes and scenes of city life. Early in his career he was associated with the *Macchiaioli. He settled in Paris in 1867, became a friend of *Degas and *Manet, and exhibited with the *Impressionists in 1874 (because de Nittis had had some success at the *Salon, Degas thought the presence of his work among the Impressionists would mean that critics 'won't be able to say that ours is an exhibition of rejected artists'). The best collection of his work is in the Pinacoteca Communale at Barletta, his native town.

NKV. See NEUE KÜNSTLERVEREINIGUNG.

Nolan, Sir Sidney (1917–   ). The most internationally famous of Australian painters. He turned from odd jobs to art after attending night classes in his native Melbourne, and became a full-time painter when he was 21. His early work was abstract, but while serving in the Australian army (1941–5) he painted a series of landscapes of the Wimmera District of Victoria that gave the first unmistakable signs of the originality of his vision, capturing the heat and emptiness of the bush. In 1946 he began a series of paintings on the notorious bushranger Ned Kelly, who had become a legendary figure in Australian folk history, and it was with these works that he made his name. He has returned to the Kelly theme throughout his career, and he has also drawn on other events from Australian history. In such works Nolan created a distinctive idiom to express this novel Australian *iconography and memorably portrayed the hard, dry beauty of the desert landscape. Technically, his work is remarkable for the lush fluidity of his brushwork and sometimes he paints on glass or other smooth materials. Nolan first visited Europe in 1951 (in that year he had his first London exhibition) and since then he has travelled widely. Apart from Australian themes, he has been inspired by, for example, the legend of Leda and the Swan.

Noland, Kenneth (1924–   ). American abstract painter. In the early 1950s he was one of the pioneers of *Colour Field painting but during the 1950s and 1960s, he tended to employ more precisely articulated geometrical forms, which brought him within the ambit of *Hard Edge painting. In the late 1950s and early 1960s he used concentric circles on a square canvas. This was followed by a chevron motif, sometimes on a diamond or lozenge-shaped canvas, and this again was gradually lengthened into horizontal stripes running across a canvas of a very long rectangular format.

Nolde, Emil (1867–1956). German painter and graphic artist, one of the most powerful representatives of *Expressionism. Born of a peasant family, he was originally trained as a wood-carver and came late to artistic maturity. His studies took him from his native North Germany to Munich and Paris, and from 1905 to 1907 he was a member of the *Brücke in Dresden, but he was essentially an isolated figure, standing apart from his great German contemporaries. He was well travelled (in 1913–14 he visited Russia, the Far East, and the South Sea islands as part of an ethnographic expedition), but at times he lived almost like a hermit. His travel broadened his knowledge of the kind of *primitive art that was then beginning to excite avant-garde artists, but Nolde had already established the essential features of his style before his contact with such art, and when the term 'primitive' is applied to his work it refers to its brutal force, not to any exotic trappings. He was a deeply religious man and is most famous for his paintings of Old and New Testament subjects, in which he expresses intense emotion through violent colour, radically simplified drawing, and grotesque distortion. The majority of his pictures, however, were landscapes, and he was also one of the greatest 20th-cent. exponents of flower painting, working with gloriously vivid colour. He was also a prolific etcher and lithographer. Although he was an early advocate of the National Socialist Party, he was declared a *degenerate artist by the Nazis and forbidden to paint. He did, however, execute small water-colours in secret (these are called the 'unpainted pictures') and from these made larger oils after the war. From 1926 he lived at Seebüll, where there is now a Nolde Foundation that has an outstanding collection of his work.

Nollekens, Joseph (1737–1823). English sculptor, the son of an Antwerp painter of the same name (1702–47) who came to London in 1733. He was a pupil of *Scheemakers. From 1760 to 1770 he worked in Rome, making a handsome living copying, restoring, faking, and dealing in *antique sculpture. He also made a few portrait busts including that of Lawrence Sterne (NPG, 1766), a splendid character study in the antique manner, and on his return to England it was chiefly as a portraitist that he built up his great reputation and fortune (he left £200,000 at his death). His finest portraits are vivacious and brilliantly characterized, but there are many inferior studio copies of his more popular works. He also made statues in a slightly erotic antique manner, and had a large practice as a tomb sculptor. Nollekens and his wife were well-known figures in London's artistic circles and were notorious skinflints. The life by his pupil and disappointed executor J. T. Smith (1766–1833), *Nollekens and his Times* (1828), gives a remarkable picture of their meanness and has been described by Rupert Gunnis (*Dictionary of British Sculptors 1660–1851*) as probably 'the most candid, pitiless and uncomplimentary biography in the English language'.

Non-Objective art. General term for all abstract art that does not depend on the appearance of the visual world as a starting-point. The term seems to have been first used by *Rodchenko, but it was given currency in the West by *Kandinsky in his book *Über das Geistige in der Kunst* (Concerning the Spiritual in Art) in 1912.

Noort, Adam van (1562–1641). Flemish history and portrait painter, remembered chiefly as one of the teachers of *Rubens. Too little is known of the style of either man at the time to know what influence he may have had. Another famous pupil was *Jordaens, who became van Noort's son-in-law in 1616.

Northcote, James (1746–1831). English portrait and history painter, *Reynolds's pupil, assistant, and biographer. He spent the years 1777–80 in Rome and settled in London in 1781. Rome had given him ambitions to history painting, but his exercises in this field, notably for *Boydell's Shakespeare Gallery, are ponderous and awkward. As a portraitist he was an uninspired follower of Reynolds, and it is as a writer that he has the main claim to distinction; he was something of a character and a lively commentator on the artistic scene. *Memoirs of Sir Joshua Reynolds* (1813–15) is his major publication.

Norwich School. English regional school of landscape painting, associated with the Norwich Society of Artists, which was founded in 1803, with *Crome as president. From 1805 until 1825 exhibitions

were held every year in Norwich—the first instance of a provincial institution holding regular exhibitions. When Crome died in 1821, his place as president was taken by *Cotman, and the activities of the Society continued until his departure for London in 1834. The Norwich artists consisted almost entirely of landscape painters in oil and water-colour, working chiefly under Crome's influence with a bias in favour of Norfolk scenery.

Nost (or **Van Ost**), **John** (d. 1711/13). Flemish-born sculptor who settled in England in about 1678. By 1686 he was foreman to Artus III *Quellin, whose widow he later married. He is chiefly notable as a maker of lead garden statues, some based on Italian or *antique models but others of his own creation. Examples remain at Derbyshire, Hampton Court, and many other places. His tombs are less interesting. His son—not, as long thought, his nephew—of the same name (d. 1780) continued the practice.

Notke, Bernt (d. 1509). German sculptor, the leading wood-carver in the Baltic area during his period. He worked mainly in Lübeck, where he is first recorded (as a painter) in 1467, but his masterpiece was executed in Sweden, where he was summoned in 1483 to make a monument commemorating a victory by the Regent, Sten Sture, over the Danes. The victory was attributed to the assistance of St George, and Notke's stirring group of *St George and the Dragon* (completed 1489) in the Storkyrka (Stockholm's main church) is one of the greatest of all votive images. Its spiky forms represent the most expressionistic strain in late *Gothic art and the vividly naturalistic details include the use of real elk antlers for the dragon's horns.

novecento. See QUATTROCENTO.

Novecento Italiano. Group of Italian artists, founded in 1922, which aimed to reject European avant-garde movements and revert to a naturalistic type of art based upon Classical Italian traditions. The *Novecento* had no clear artistic programme and numbered within its ranks artists of very different styles and temperaments. *Carrà and *Marini were among the most significant artists associated with the group, but it came more and more to be identified with the empty formalism and idealized propaganda encouraged by the Fascist *Sindicati delle Belle Arti* and during the 1930s it was the main bulwark of reaction. It finally disbanded in 1943.

November Group. An association of Finnish artists founded in Helsinki in 1917. The members showed a sometimes aggressive nationalism and were responsible for the emergence of a recognizably Finnish form of Expressionism.

Novembergruppe. A group of radical left-wing German artists formed in Berlin in November 1918 with the professed object of renewing national life by means of a closer relation between progressive artists and the public. Max *Pechstein was among the prime movers. In 1919 the founders of the association created the Arbeitsrat für Kunst (Workers' Council for Art) in an attempt to bring about a dialogue between art and the masses, but interest and support came mainly from the middle classes. Artistically the group covered a wide spectrum. Exhibitions staged during the early 1920s did much to foster an artistic revival, but it broke up around 1924 with the swing of public opinion towards the right, leaving its aims to be more fully realized at the *Bauhaus.

O

objet trouvé (French: found object) An object found by an artist and displayed with no, or minimal, alteration as a work of art. It may be a natural object, such as a pebble, a shell, or a curiously contorted branch, or a man made object such as a piece of pottery or old piece of ironwork or machinery. The practice began with the *Dadaists and *Surrealists and was cultivated for a time in England chiefly by Paul *Nash. See also READY-MADE.

Ochtervelt, Jacob (1634–82). Dutch *genre painter. He was born and mainly active in Rotterdam, but he is said to have been a pupil of *Berchem (presumably in Haarlem) and from 1674 he lived in Amsterdam. Apart from a few portraits and some early hunting party and 'merry company' scenes, his paintings are almost all elegant upper-class interiors, in which he showed off a skill in painting silks and satins to rival that of *Terborch. His figures are extremely refined, but there is often a sexual element in his paintings—a couple eating oysters (believed to be an aphrodisiac) was a favourite subject.

offset. A reproduction, also called a counterproof, made from a drawing by dampening it and/or a sheet of paper and pressing them together by machine or hand. The image is therefore reversed left to right. Offsets were often made for working purposes by designers of ornament who needed to have a copy of a design in reverse, or to complete one half of a symmetrical design, and they have also been used to create forgeries.

O'Gorman, Juan (1905–82). Mexican architect and painter. Early in his career he designed a series of houses in Mexico City (notably those for himself and for Diego *Rivera) that were among the first in the Americas to show the functionalist ideas of *Le Corbusier. In the 1930s, however, he abandoned architecture for painting. His work was strongly nationalistic and his anti-fascist, anti-church frescos at Mexico City airport (1937–8) were destroyed in 1939 during a political swing to the right. In the 1950s he returned to architecture, now advocating a more 'organic' approach inspired in part by Frank Lloyd Wright. His most celebrated work in this vein is the Library of the National University in Mexico City (1951–3) in which a modern structural design is completely covered externally in mosaics of his own design symbolically representing the history of Mexican culture. He committed suicide.

oil paint. Paint in which *drying oils are used as the medium; *linseed oil is the best known, but others that have been used in painting include *poppy oil and *walnut oil. It was long believed that oil painting was invented by Jan van *Eyck, but it is now known that its origins are older and obscurer. There is no doubt, however, that van Eyck revolutionized the technique and brought it to a sudden peak of perfection. He showed the medium's flexibility, its rich and dense colour, its wide range from light to dark, and its ability to achieve both minute detail and subtle blending of tones. Other painters soon took up his innovations—first in Northern Europe, then in Italy—and from the 16th century oil colour has been the dominant medium in Europe for serious painting. Its success has been largely on account of its versatility and ability to show an artist's personal 'handwriting', for its can attain any variety of surface from violent impasto to porcelain smoothness. Its versatility was increased still further in the 19th century with the invention of the collapsible metal tube (devised in 1841), which made it convenient to work out of doors. In the 20th century, however, *acrylic has become a serious rival to oil paint.

O'Keeffe, Georgia (1887–1986). American painter. One of the pioneers of modernism in America, she was a member of the circle of *Stieglitz, whom she met in 1916 and married in 1924. She is best known for her near-abstract paintings based on enlargements of flower and plant forms, works of great elegance and rhythmic vitality, whose sensuous forms are often sexually suggestive (*Black Iris*, Met. Mus., New York, 1926). Her other work included townscapes of New York in a manner close to that of the *Precisionists and landscapes done in broad, simple forms. From the 1930s she spent each winter in New Mexico and she settled there after Stieglitz's death in 1946, the desert landscape appearing frequently in her paintings. She began to travel widely in the 1950s and many of her later paintings were inspired by views of the earth, sky, and clouds seen from an aeroplane.

Oldenburg, Claes (1929–). Swedish-born sculptor and graphic artist who became an American citizen in 1953. He was educated at Yale University and studied at the Art Institute of Chicago (earning his living with part-time jobs as a reporter and illustrator) before settling in 1956 in New York. There he came into contact with a group of young artists, including *Kaprow, *Segal, and *Dine, who were in revolt against *Abstract Expressionism and from c.1958 he became interested in arranging *happenings, ensembles, *environments, 'situations', etc. His inspiration was drawn largely from New York's street life—shop windows, graffiti, advertisements, and so on—and in 1961 he opened 'The Store', at which he sold painted plaster replicas of foods and other domestic objects. This led to the work with which his name is most closely associated—giant-size sculptures of foodstuffs and 'soft sculptures' of normally hard objects (*Dual Hamburger*, MOMA, New York, 1962). With these he was hailed as one of the leaders of American *Pop art. Oldenburg is also well known for his projects for colossal monuments—for example, *Lipsticks in Piccadilly Circus, London* (Tate, London, 1966), consisting of a magazine cutting of an array of lipsticks pasted on to a picture postcard.

oleograph. A coloured lithograph impressed with a canvas grain to make it look like an oil painting. Oleographs were popular—but often considered rather vulgar—in the second half of the 19th cent.

Olitski, Jules (1922–). Russian-born American painter and sculptor. In reaction from *Abstract Expressionism Olitski took up and developed the stained canvas technique initiated by Helen *Frankenthaler and Morris *Louis. His so-called 'Core' pictures of the early 1960s combined the concentricity of *Noland with a weighted contour which has been compared with the *Unfurleds* of Louis. In 1964 he began *All-over sprayed paintings, which did away with contour drawing and prepared the way for the monochromatic sprayed *Colour Field paintings of the second half of the 1960s, for which he became chiefly known. During the 1970s his colours were reduced to delicately vibrant modulations of greys and browns, often in water-based *acrylic, and an expressive modelling of surface texture introduced a new note into his work. Olitski took up sculpture seriously in 1968 and has worked mainly with painted metal.

Oliver, Isaac (before 1568–1617). English *miniaturist of French origin, the son of a refugee Huguenot goldsmith who settled in England in 1568. He trained under *Hilliard (whose main rival he later became) and by 1590 was established in his own practice. Although Hilliard continued to receive royal favour under James I, Oliver was made *Limner to the Queen, Anne of Denmark, in 1604, and was patronized by Henry, Prince of Wales, and his circle. His style was more naturalistic than that of Hilliard, using light and shade to obtain modelling and generally dispensing with the emblematic trappings so beloved of the Elizabethan age. He was in Venice in 1596, and unlike Hilliard he did history paintings in miniature. Contemporary sources indicate that he probably also painted life-size portraits, and some of the pictures attributed to William *Larkin have been put forward rather as possible works by Oliver. His son, **Peter** (1594–1647), continued in his style, but specialized also in miniature copies after the Old Masters.

Omega Workshops. Decorative arts company founded by Roger *Fry in 1913. Inspired by the ideals of *Ruskin and *Morris, it was an attempt to bring modern art into touch with daily life by the production of decorative art. Among his chief associates in this enterprise were Duncan *Grant and Vanessa *Bell, and Fry encouraged amateur as well as professional artists to participate. In general the work was done by painters and consisted of decorating manufactured objects rather than designing products from scratch. Bright colour predominated in the designs, many of them abstract. The workshops, which operated from 33 Fitzroy Square, London, were a financial failure and they closed in 1919.

Oostsanen. See CORNELISZ. VAN OOSTSANEN.

Op art (abbreviation of Optical art on the analogy of *Pop art). A type of *abstract art that exploits certain optical phenomena to cause a work to seem to vibrate, pulsate, or flicker. Many of the devices employed by practitioners of Op art are elaborations upon the well-known visual illusions to be found in standard textbooks of perceptual psychology, and maximum geometrical precision is sought in the control of surfaces and edges in order to evoke an exactly prescribed retinal response. Leading exponents of Op art include *Vasarely and *Riley.

Opie, John (1761–1807). English painter. He was something of a child prodigy and was discovered by the political satirist John Wolcot (better known by his pen name Peter Pindar), who in 1781 successfully launched him in London as an untaught genius ('The Cornish Wonder'). Opie was then painting strongly modelled portraits and rustic *fancy pictures with *Rembrandtesque lighting which were praised by *Reynolds. He soon lost the rather rugged freshness of his early work and his later paintings were undistinguished and repetitive. His career continued to prosper, however, and he became Professor of Painting at the *Royal Academy in 1805, his lectures being posthumously published in 1809 (prefaced with a memoir by his wife, the novelist and poet Amelia Opie). Apart from portraits and *genre scenes, he also painted history pictures, notably for *Boydell's Shakespeare Gallery.

Oppenheim, Meret (1913–85). German-Swiss artist. She was introduced to the *Surrealist group by *Giacometti, was for a time the model and the disciple of *Man Ray (who called her 'one of the most uninhibited women I have ever known'), and was celebrated among the Paris Surrealists as the 'fairy woman' whom all men

desire. About 1936 she became known for her Surrealist 'objects', mainly everyday utensils made of fur, leather, etc. The best known is *Object* (MOMA, New York, 1936), a fur-lined tea cup and saucer.

orant. See GISANT.

Orcagna, Andrea (Andrea di Cione) (d. 1368/9). The leading Florentine artist of the third quarter of the 14th cent., a painter, sculptor, architect, and administrator. His nickname 'Orcagna' was apparently local slang for 'Archangel' (*Arcangelo*). In 1343/4 he was admitted to the guild of the painters and nine years later to that of the masons. His only certain work as a painter is the altarpiece of *The Redeemer with the Madonna and Saints* (1354–7) in the Strozzi Chapel of Sta Maria Novella. This is the most powerful Florentine painting of its period, and in spite of the massiveness of the figures it represents a reversion from *Giotto's naturalism to the hieratic ideals of *Byzantine art. Colours are resplendent, with lavish use of gold, and the figures are remote and immobile. The major work attributed to Orcagna is a fragmentary fresco trilogy of the *Triumph of Death, Last Judgement*, and *Hell* in Sta Croce. As a sculptor and architect he is known through one work, the tabernacle in Or San Michele (finished 1359), a highly elaborate ornamental structure housing a painting of the *Virgin Enthroned* by Bernardo *Daddi. Orcagna was *capomaestro* of Orvieto Cathedral from 1358 to 1362, supervising the mosaic decoration of the façade. He was also an adviser on the construction of Florence Cathedral. During 1368 Orcagna fell mortally ill while painting the *St Matthew* altarpiece (Uffizi, Florence) and this work was finished by his brother **Jacopo di Cione** (active 1365–98), who worked in his style and continued it to the end of the century. Another brother, **Nardo di Cione** (active 1343/6–65/6), was also a painter. *Ghiberti attributes to him the series of frescos of *The Last Judgement, Hell*, and *Paradise* in the Strozzi Chapel, Sta Maria Novella, which houses Andrea's great altarpiece. Orcagna's style was the dominant influence in late 14th-cent. Florentine painting.

Orchardson, Sir William Quiller (1832–1910). Scottish painter of *genre subjects and portraits, active in London from 1862.

He made his name with historical costume pieces, but later did his most memorable work in modern-day scenes of upper-class married life. In these he used large empty spaces to create feelings of psychological tension or despair. The best-known are *The First Cloud* (Tate Gallery, London, 1887) and a pair representing *A Marriage of Convenience* (City Art Gallery, Glasgow, 1883, and Aberdeen Art Gallery, 1886).

Ordóñez, Bartolomé (d. 1520). The first Spanish sculptor to show clearly the impact of the Italian High *Renaissance. On stylistic grounds, he is presumed to have trained in Florence, perhaps with Andrea *Sansovino, and in 1514–15 he was in Naples, working with Diego de *Siloe on the marble *reredos of the Caracciolo Chapel in the church of S. Giovanni a Carbonara. In 1517 he undertook part of the carved decoration for the choir of Barcelona Cathedral, executing in wood and marble a series of *reliefs in a pure Renaissance style. There followed a number of contracts for tombs, including that of Charles V's parents, Philip I and Juana of Castille, commissioned by Charles himself for the chapel royal at Granada. Ordóñez died while carrying out these commissions with Italian assistants at Carrara; but his testament records that he had completed the greater part of the work, including most of the royal tomb. Although he died young (he was perhaps born *c*.1490), his elegant and imaginative style was highly influential.

Orley, Bernard (or **Bernaert** or **Barend**) **van** (*c*.1490–1541). Netherlandish painter of religious subjects and portraits and designer of tapestries and stained glass. He was the leading artist of his day in Brussels, becoming court painter to Margaret of Austria, regent of the Netherlands, in 1518 and to her successor Mary of Hungary in 1532. His work is characterized by the use of ill-digested Italianate motifs. There is no evidence that he visited Italy, and his knowledge presumably came from engravings and from *Raphael's tapestry *cartoons, which were in Brussels *c*.1516–19; he has (very flatteringly) been called 'the Raphael of the Netherlands'. His best-known work is the turbulent *Job* altarpiece (Musées Royaux, Brussels, 1521). As a portraitist his style was quieter and more thoughtful (*Georg Zelle*, Musées Royaux,

Brussels, 1519). None of van Orley's paintings bears a date later than 1530; after that time he was chiefly occupied with designing tapestries and stained-glass windows.

Orozco, José Clemente (1883–1949). Mexican painter. With his contemporaries Diego *Rivera and David *Siqueiros he was one of the trio of politically and socially committed fresco painters who were the dominant force in modern Mexican art. In the years immediately following the revolution of 1910 he was doing political cartoons and bordello scenes in a vein of social satire. From the same years are usually dated his famous *wash drawings *Mexico in Revolution*, in which he worked with a deliberate practical aim of converting the illiterate masses to a realization of the miseries and futilities of war. From 1917 to 1919 Orozco lived in the USA, returning to Mexico in time to participate in the artistic revival inaugurated by the Obregón regime. In 1923–4 he did controversial murals in the National Preparatory School, all of which, except the *Maternity* and *The Rich Banquet while the Workers Quarrel*, were subsequently destroyed or altered. Their caricatural manner matured into his monumental style of more philosophical and generalized symbolism, manifested for example in a second series of frescos at the Preparatory School (1926–7). From 1927 to 1934 Orozco worked in the USA, and besides easel paintings and drawings in a more *Abstract Expressionist manner executed a number of important commissions for murals. These included frescos at Pomona College, Claremont and the New School for Social Research, New York. Returning to Mexico in 1934, he was occupied through the 1930s on the most stupendous of his mural paintings, outstanding both for the grandeur of their symbolic message and for their technical virtuosity. The *Katharsis* in the Palacio de Bellas Artes, Mexico City (1934), was followed by a series in the University, the Palace of Government, and the Cabañas Orphanage of Guadalajara, the latter covering some 1,200 square metres. He continued to be extremely active in the 1940s, and his last work, *Hidalgo and the Liberation of Mexico*, for the Senate Chamber of the Palace of Government in Guadalajara, was finished shortly before his death in 1949. During this last period his work became ever more violent emotionally, while the symbolic grandeur of his humanistic and sociological conceptions increased in profundity, moved by his passionate concern for the suffering and miseries of mankind.

Orpen, Sir William (1878–1931). Irishborn painter, active mainly in London. He succeeded *Sargent as the leading fashionable portraitist of the day and had a brilliant and prolific career. His portraits, painted in a vigorous but often flashy style, are frequently compared with those of his friend Augustus *John, and as with John, his enormous contemporary reputation has faded badly. When he was not painting his standard boardroom and drawing-room fare, however, Orpen could be a much more interesting artist. His numerous self-portraits are often particularly engaging, as he pokes fun at himself in character roles, and his *Homage to Manet* (City Art Gal., Manchester, 1909) is an admirably composed group of some of the leading figures in the art world informally arranged around a tea-table beneath Manet's portrait of his pupil Eva Gonzales. Orpen also did memorable work as a war artist.

Orphism (or **Orphic Cubism**). A short-lived movement in French painting that developed out of *Cubism c.1912. The word 'Orphism', which had previously been used by the *Symbolists, was applied to the movement by *Apollinaire and the reference to Orpheus, the singer and poet of Greek mythology, reflected the desire of the artists involved to bring a new element of lyricism and colour into the austere intellectual Cubism of *Picasso, *Braque, and *Gris. The painters mentioned by Apollinaire as practitioners of Orphism were *Delaunay, *Léger, *Picabia, and Marcel *Duchamp; *Kupka was the main member of the movement not named by Apollinaire. They made colour the principal means of artistic expression and Delaunay and Kupka were among the first to paint totally non-representational pictures, seeing an analogy between pure abstraction and music. Although it was short-lived, Orphism had a strong influence on German painting (notably *Macke, *Marc, and *Klee) and on *Synchromism.

Orsi, Lelio (c.1511–87). Italian *Mannerist painter and architect. He worked mainly in his birthplace Novellara and in Reggio

Emilia, and he is counted a member of the Parmesan School. His large-scale decorative work has almost all perished and he is now known mainly by *cabinet pictures of religious subjects. He drew on many different influences (*Correggio, *Giulio Romano, *Michelangelo, *Parmigianino, and perhaps also German woodcuts), but his style has a leaning towards the bizarre, with dramatic stage-lighting effects, that gives it a distinctly personal touch.

Os, van. Dutch family of painters active during the late 18th and 19th cents. **Jan** (1744–1808) was the founder. He and his daughter **Maria Margrita** (1780–1862) and his son **Georgius Jacobus Johannes** (1782–1861) specialized in painting flowers and fruits in the lavish detailed manner of Jan van *Huysum. Another of Jan's sons, **Pieter Gerardus** (1776–1839), specialized in pictures of cattle. His son and pupil, **Pieter Frederik** (1802–92), taught *Mauve.

Osona, Rodrigo de (active 1476–84). Spanish painter. He was one of the leading painters of his day in Valencia, introducing both Netherlandish and Italian *Renaissance influence to the area. His most important work is the Crucifixion in St Nicholas, Valencia (1476). On the basis of an altarpiece of *The Adoration of the Magi* in the Victoria and Albert Museum signed 'the son of Master Rodrigo', several works have been attributed to **Rodrigo de Osona the Younger**, who is documented from 1505 to 1513. He continued his father's style in a weaker more Italianate manner.

Ostade, Adriaen van (1610–85). Dutch painter, active in his native Haarlem. Although he turned his hand to most types of subject, he was principally a *genre painter. He was a very prolific painter and also made water-colours, etchings, and drawings. According to *Houbraken, both he and *Brouwer (whose work is similar) were pupils of Frans *Hals. His early pictures depict lively scenes of peasants carousing or brawling in crowded taverns or hovels. In his later works (after c.1650) his peasants learn better manners and the rooms they live in are tidier. These later pictures are lighter in key and more colourful; thus they follow the general trend of Dutch painting around this time. Ostade was successful, popular, and much imitated. His most talented pupil was his brother **Isaak** (1621–49), who also worked in Haarlem. As well as painting genre scenes in the manner of Adriaen, Isaak was an outstanding practitioner of the winter landscape, and his early death cut short a career of great promise. Good examples of the work of both brothers are in the National Gallery, London.

ottocento. See QUATTROCENTO.

Ottonian art. Term applied to art of the Holy Roman Empire in the 10th cent. and most of the 11th cent. The emperor Otto the Great (936–73), who re-established a strong royal authority, gave his name to the dynasty and the period. The Ottonian period saw the revival of large-scale bronze casting (see BERNWARD OF HILDESHEIM) and of life-size sculpture (in the celebrated Gero Crucifix of 969–76 in Cologne Cathedral), but the most typical sculptural products of the time were in ivory and metalwork, notably for book covers and altar reliefs. Though wall paintings still survive, the character of Ottonian art is better seen in a rich store of *illuminated manuscripts. In spite of differences in local schools, all Ottonian illumination has certain things in common, notably the pre-eminence given to the human figure, which is often imbued with strong expression and marked by exaggerated gestures. Ottonian art was widely influential and was one of the sources out of which *Romanesque grew.

Oudry, Jean-Baptiste (1686–1755). French painter, tapestry designer, and illustrator. He was a pupil of *Largillière and painted some portraits, but he is renowned chiefly as one of the outstanding animal painters of the 18th cent. With *Desportes he was the foremost exponent of hunting scenes and still lifes with dead game. Some of his best work was done as a tapestry designer, and he was head of the Beauvais and *Gobelins factory from 1734 and 1736 respectively. He also did book illustrations, notably for an edition of La Fontaine's *Fables* (1755–9). His son **Jacques-Charles** (1720–78), a flower and animal painter, sometimes collaborated with him.

Ouwater, Albert van (active mid 15th cent.). Netherlandish painter. Only one documentary reference to him is known (it refers to the burial of his daughter in 1467) and otherwise knowledge depends on what van *Mander wrote about him. He said Ouwater was the founder of the Haarlem school and the master of *Geertgen tot Sint Jans. He also praised his skill as a landscapist, so it is ironic that the only painting that can be identified as Ouwater's from van Mander's descriptions of his work is an interior scene—*The Raising of Lazarus* (Staatliche Museen, Berlin). The thoughtful, unemotional style has some affinities with the work of Dirk *Bouts, who was a native of Haarlem.

Ovenden, Graham. See BLAKE, PETER.

Ovens, Juriaen. See CAMPEN.

Overbeck, Friedrich (1789–1869). German painter, the leading member of the *Nazarenes. He moved to Rome in 1810 and was based there for the rest of his life, although he made several visits to Germany. In 1813 he was converted to Roman Catholicism and apart from a few portraits (there is a self-portrait in the Uffizi) his work was almost exclusively on religious themes. He painted in a consciously archaic style—clear and sincere but rather pallid—based on the work of *Perugino and the young *Raphael. *The Rose Miracle of St Francis* (Portiuncula Chapel, Assisi, 1829) is perhaps his best-known painting. The high-minded and didactic tone of his work won it a more sympathetic acceptance (particularly in England) than its artistic quality alone merited. William *Dyce and Ford Madox *Brown were among his supporters and there were affinities between his aspirations and those of the *Pre-Raphaelite Brotherhood.

Ozenfant, Amédée (1886–1966). French painter and writer. He founded *Purism with *Le Corbusier, but is more important as a writer and teacher than a painter. In 1937 he opened a school in London and in 1938 left Europe for New York, where he formed the Ozenfant School of Fine Arts. His *Foundations of Modern Art* (1931) has been widely read.

P

Pacheco, Francisco (1564–1644). Spanish painter and writer, active in Seville. He was a man of great culture, a poet and scholar as well as a painter, and his house was the focus of Seville's artistic life. As a painter he was undistinguished, working in a stiff academic style (though his portraits are fresher than his religious works). He was an outstanding teacher, however, for (in spite of his own limitations) he was sympathetic to the more naturalistic style that was then developing, holding that in the imitation of nature art should have a spiritual purpose in the service of religion. And he was generous enough in spirit to acknowledge openly that his greatest pupil, *Velázquez (who became his son-in-law in 1618), was a much better painter than himself: 'I consider it no disgrace for the pupil to surpass the master.' Alonso *Cano was his other outstanding pupil, and Pacheco often collaborated with the great sculptor *Montañés, painting his wooden figures. In 1649 there was posthumously *El Arte de la Pintura* (The Art of Painting), part theoretical, part biographical and a major source of information for the period (it includes accounts of his meeting with El *Greco in Toledo in 1611 and of Velázquez's early career). He was an official art censor to the Inquisition and the highly detailed *iconographical prescriptions in his book were often strictly adhered to by contemporary artists.

Pacher, Michael (active 1465?–98). Austrian painter and sculptor. He died at Salzburg, but most of his career was spent at Bruneck in the Tyrol. Nothing is known of his training, and the earliest recorded work by him (a signed and dated altarpiece of 1465) is now lost. He worked mainly for local churches, carrying out the carving as well as the painting of his altarpieces, and much of his work is still *in situ*. His most celebrated work is the St Wolfgang altarpiece (1471–81) in the church of S. Wolfgang on the Abersee, a huge *polyptych with some astonishingly intricate woodcarving. Although Pacher's sculpture is thoroughly late *Gothic in spirit, his painting is strongly influenced by Italian art. He is particularly close to *Mantegna, especially in the way dramatic effects are obtained by using a low viewpoint and setting the figures close to the picture plane. There is no documentary evidence that Pacher visited Italy, but because of its proximity to the Tyrol it seems overwhelmingly likely that he did. Pacher's work had wide influence and he was the most important interpreter of *Renaissance ideas for German painting before *Dürer. A **Friedrich** and a **Hans Pacher**, presumably related, were active in the Tyrol at the same time as Michael, and Friedrich collaborated with him.

Palamedesz., Anthonie (1601–73). Dutch portrait and *genre painter, active mainly in his native Delft. He was a pupil of *Mierevelt and Dirk *Hals and his paintings resemble those of his masters—his portraits rather wooden, his 'merry company' groups of soldiers, cavaliers, and their ladies livelier and pleasantly coloured. His brother **Palamedes I Palamedesz.** (1607–38) and his nephew **Palamedes II Palamedesz.** (1633–1705) were both painters.

palette. A flat board, usually rectangular, ovoid, or kidney-shaped, with a hole for the thumb, on which artists arrange their paints ready for use. Palettes first appeared in the 15th cent.; before then individual containers (sometimes shells) were used for mixing colours. For oil painting, mahogany is traditionally considered the best material for palettes, although other close-grained hardwoods have been used. Materials such as porcelain or ivory have been used by water-colour or *miniature painters and also sometimes by oil painters—*Millais, for example, used a porcelain palette early in his career, when he painted with fastidious detail and wished to avoid muddying his colours. For many artists choice of their pigments and the order in which they are set out on the palette is a very important and personal matter and much advice was published on how to 'set' a palette in handbooks of the 17th and 18th cents. By extension, the term 'palette' thus refers to the range of colours characteristic of an artist; *Caravaggio has a dark or restricted palette, *Monet a bright or rich palette.

palette knife. A thin, flexible, dull-edged blade, set in a handle, used for mixing paint, scraping it off the *palette or canvas and also as a painting instrument (although more delicate tools—'painting knives'— are often preferred for this purpose). Palette knives became popular in the 18th cent., ordinary knives being used for the purpose before this. The trowel shape commonly used today is said to have been invented by *Courbet.

Palma Giovane (Jacopo Palma) (c.1548– 1628). Venetian painter, great-nephew of *Palma Vecchio. He was trained by *Titian, whose Pietà (Accademia, Venice) he completed after the master's death. In the late 1560s and early 1570s he worked in central Italy, mainly Rome, but thereafter he spent the rest of his life in Venice, and after the death of *Tintoretto in 1594 he was the leading painter in the city. His style was influenced by several of his great Venetian predecessors—*Veronese as well as Titian and Tintoretto—and by central Italian *Mannerism. He was extremely prolific, fulfilling many commissions from abroad as well as for Venetian churches, and his later work is often mechanical.

Palma Vecchio (Jacomo Palma) (c.1480– 1528). Italian painter, born near Bergamo, but active for all his known career in Venice, where he is first documented in 1510. His original name was Jacomo Negreti, but he was using the name Palma by 1513. He is called Palma Vecchio (Old Palma) to distinguish him from *Palma Giovane (Young Palma), his great-nephew. Nothing is known of his training, and there is indeed very little secure knowledge about his life and works, none of his pictures being dated or reliably signed and very few of them being certainly identifiable from early sources. His style is distinctive, however, and in practice the

definition of his œuvre is much less problematic than with many of his contemporaries. He painted a few altarpieces for Venetian churches, but most of his work was done for private clients, his speciality being half-length portrayals of beautiful and voluptuous blonde-haired women, sometimes in religious or mythological guise. In opulence of colour and beauty of handling they show the influence of the early work of *Titian, and the finest, such as the celebrated La Bella (Thyssen coll., Lugano), are worthy of his name. Palma also painted some *Giorgionesque reclining nudes and some male portraits.

Palmer, Erastus Dow (1817–1904). American sculptor. Self-taught, he rarely left Albany in his native New York State, and he was the most successful American sculptor of his period to work in the USA rather than in Europe. He began with *cameo portraits and had a flourishing business with portrait busts and bas-*reliefs on religious subjects, but his most celebrated work, now as in his own day, is The White Captive (Met. Mus., New York, 1858). Inspired by *Powers's Greek Slave, it shows a naked young girl who has been captured by Red Indians but is sustained by her Christianity—this accompanying storyline undoubtedly contributed to its popularity. The statue is fresher in observation than Powers's Greek Slave, for although the marble surfaces are impeccably smooth, the chubby proportions of the figure are unidealized and the strikingly characterized head is a portrait of Palmer's daughter.

Palmer, Samuel (1805–81). English landscape painter and etcher. He showed a precocious talent and exhibited landscape drawings at the *Royal Academy when he was 14. In 1822 he met *Linnell, who introduced him to William *Blake in 1824. Palmer had had visionary experiences from childhood and the effect of Blake upon him was to intensify an inherent mystical bent. In 1826 he moved to Shoreham, near Sevenoaks, Kent, where he was the central figure of the group of artists known as the *Ancients and produced what are now his most famous works—landscapes charged with a sense of pantheistic fecundity and other-worldly beauty. In about 1832 what he called his 'primitive and infantine feeling' for landscape began to fade, and after returning to London in 1835, marrying Linnell's daughter in 1837, and spending a two-year honeymoon in Italy, the break with his visionary manner was complete. His later paintings were in a much more conventional topographical or pastoral mode, highly-wrought and often sentimental in feeling. In his etchings, however, something of his early genius remained; at his death he was working on an edition of Virgil's *Eclogues*, translated and illustrated by himself. His early work was virtually forgotten until the 1920s, but it has subsequently influenced modern romantic landscape artists such as Paul *Nash and Graham *Sutherland.

Palomino y Velasco, Antonio (1655–1726). Spanish painter and writer on art, active mainly in Madrid, where in 1688 he was appointed a painter to the king. Famous in his day for the frescos which he executed in churches at Madrid, Salamanca, Granada, etc., he is now best known for his book *Museo Pictórico y Escala Óptica* ('Pictorial Museum, and Optical Scale', Vol. 1, 1715; Vols. 2 and 3, 1724). The first two volumes are devoted respectively to the theory and the practice of art, and the third volume is a collection of biographies, the most important source for the history of Spanish art from the 16th to the early 18th cents.

panel. Term in painting for a *support of wood, metal, or other rigid substance, as distinct from *canvas. Until the adoption of canvas in the 15th cent. nearly all the movable paintings of Europe were executed on wood, and even up to the beginning of the 17th cent. it is probable that as much painting was done on the one support as on the other. Painters who worked on a small scale often used copper panels (*Elsheimer is a leading example), and in the colonial art of South America copper and tin and even lead and zinc were used. On a larger scale, *Sebastiano del Piombo sometimes used stone as a support, and *Rubens used slate for his altarpiece for Sta Maria in Vallicella (the Chiesa Nuova) in Rome; the picture he originally painted was said to reflect the light unpleasantly and slate was used for the replacement to produce a more matt finish. For wood panels the Italian masters of the *Renaissance preferred white poplar; the French used the planks of many other trees

on occasion. Analysis of the contents of art galleries has yielded a long list of woods, including beech, cedar, chestnut, fir, larch, linden, mahogany, olive, and walnut. In the 20th cent. cedar, teak, and dark walnut are favourites, and modern painters have also used plywood, fibre-board, and other synthetic materials as supports (see also ACADEMY BOARD).

Panini (or **Pannini**), **Giovanni Paolo** (or **Gianpaolo**) (1691/2–1765). Italian painter, born in Piacenza and trained in the school of stage designers at Bologna, possibly under one of the *Bibiena family. By 1711 he was in Rome, where he became the pre-eminent painter of real and imaginary views of the city. He was the first painter to make a special feature of ruins—an aspect of his work which links him with Hubert *Robert and *Piranesi—and also did paintings of public festivities and events of historical importance. Panini taught *perspective at the French Academy in Rome and his influence was strong with French as well as Italian artists. He was a prolific painter and many galleries have examples of his work.

Panofsky, Erwin (1892–1968). German art historian. He was a professor at Hamburg University 1926–33, then was dismissed by the Nazis. He settled in the USA, where he had been a visiting professor at New York since 1931, and was then visiting professor at Princeton University, 1934–5, and from 1935 professor at the Institute for Advanced Study, Princeton. Kenneth *Clark described him as 'unquestionably the greatest art historian of his time', and he is renowned particularly for his immensely learned contributions to the study of *iconography. His many books include *Studies in Iconology* (1939), *Albrecht Dürer* (1943), *Early Netherlandish Painting* (1953), and *Tomb Sculpture* (1964). Panofsky enjoyed teaching and was influential through his work in the classroom and lecture hall as well as through his writings. Many scholars have tried to emulate his way of analysing works of art as part of a broad philosophical, intellectual, and cultural pattern, but few have rivalled his learning or finesse, and some of his followers have been accused of 'over-interpreting' pictures in their desire to uncover 'hidden symbolism'.

panorama. 'A picture of a landscape or other scene, either arranged on the inside of a cylindrical surface round the spectator as a centre (a *cyclorama*), or unrolled or unfolded and made to pass before him, so as to show the various parts in succession' (*OED*). In 1787 a patent for such a device was granted to Robert Barker (1739–1806), an Irish-born painter working in Edinburgh, and it soon became a popular form of entertainment: 'Panorama painting seems all the rage', *Constable wrote in 1803. Panoramas were indeed a kind of forerunner of the popular cinema and tended to be remarkable for sheer spectacle rather than artistic merit. Distinguished artists were sometimes associated with them, however; notably *Girtin, who made a panorama of London, now lost, and *Mesdag, whose panorama of Scheveningen can still be seen in The Hague. In more general parlance, the term 'panorama' is used of any wide, uninterrupted view over a scene, particularly a landscape.

pantograph. An instrument, known since the 17th cent., for copying a drawing on a larger or smaller scale. By a simple system of levers the outline of the original work traced with a point attached to one arm can be repeated on to another surface by a drawing instrument that is attached to another arm.

Paolozzi, Sir Eduardo (1924–). British sculptor and printmaker of Italian parentage. From the mid 1940s Paolozzi became interested in *Dada and *Surrealism, and first came to notice as a maker of *collages embodying the Surrealist conception of the juxtaposition of incongruities, using cuttings from American magazines, etc. (*I was a Rich Man's Plaything*, Tate, London, 1947). Paolozzi regarded these collages as 'ready-made metaphors' representing the popular dreams of the masses, and they have been seen as forerunners of *Pop art. From the 1950s he has worked primarily as an abstract sculptor, often on a large scale. His early heavy rough-cast figures in bronze and square, box-like forms with mechanistic overtones looked forward towards the 'mechanical men' of the 1960s—large totem-like figures made up from casts of pieces of machinery and often brightly painted. In the 1970s he made solemn machine-like forms and also box-like low *reliefs, both small and large, in wood or bronze, sometimes made to hang on the wall, compartmented and filled with small carved items. His more recent work has included several large public commissions, for example mosaic decorations for Tottenham Court Road underground station in London (installed 1983–5). See also INDEPENDENT GROUP.

paper. A tissue of vegetable fibres used for writing, drawing, and printing on. It is an oriental invention carried from the Far to the Middle East by the Turks during the Dark Ages. In Europe it is first traceable in the 12th cent. among the Moors in Spain, where it was made as well as imported. It was known in southern Italy at much the same time. France, southern Germany, and Switzerland had well-developed industries in paper by the end of the 14th cent. White paper was first made in England in 1495, but not on a large scale until the 18th cent. Until 1800 European paper was made entirely of rags pulped in water, and drawing-paper of the best quality is still made by hand in the traditional way. Writing-papers, less expensive drawing-papers, and some book papers are machine-made of a mixture of cotton, hemp, esparto, and wood, with a good deal of china clay added to make them smooth and opaque, *size to make them non-absorbent, and starch to make them stiff. Cheaper papers are machine-made wholly of wood. Oriental papers made of bamboo, rice straw, and mulberry bark are imported for artists' use.

papier collé (French: 'pasted paper'). A variety of *collage in which pieces of decorative paper are incorporated into a picture or, stuck on a ground such as canvas, themselves constitute the picture. The technique was invented by *Braque in 1913 when he used in a still life pieces of wallpaper simulating wood graining, and was almost immediately adopted by *Picasso. *Matisse was perhaps the greatest exponent of the technique.

papyrus. A writing material prepared from the stem of the marsh plant of the same name, growing in antiquity principally in Egypt and now in the Sudan. It was used in Egypt from the third millennium BC onwards and was the standard writing material in ancient Greece and throughout the Roman empire. From the 4th cent. AD onwards it was increasingly replaced by *parchment.

parchment. Writing material made from the skins of sheep or calf, less frequently pig, goat, and other animals; it has also been used for painting, and occasionally for printing and bookbinding. *Pliny says that it was invented in the second cent. BC in Pergamum; hence the name 'parchment' from the Latin *pergamena*, 'of Pergamum'. Skin had been used as a writing material before this, but the refined methods of cleaning and stretching involved in making parchment enabled both sides of a leaf to be used, leading eventually to the supplanting of the manuscript roll by the bound book. Vellum is a fine kind of parchment made from the delicate skins of young (sometimes stillborn) animals. *Paper began to replace parchment from about the 14th cent., but parchment is still used for certain kinds of documents, and the name is often applied to high-quality writing paper.

Pareja, Juan de See VELÁZQUEZ

Paris, Matthew (d. 1259). English chronicler and *miniaturist. He became a monk at St Albans in 1217 and was appointed monastery chronicler in 1236. In 1248 he visited Norway to reform the monastery of St Benet Holme, but otherwise seems never to have travelled further than London (the surname Paris is found elsewhere in England in the 13th cent. and does not necessarily imply that he had any French associations). Matthew carried on the abbey's *Chronica Majora* from 1235 until his death (it is now divided between Corpus Christi College, Cambridge, and the BL, London) and also wrote a summary of the chief events between 1200 and 1250 that is known as the *Historia Minor* or *Historia Anglorum* (BL). His historical manuscripts are almost unique in being illustrated with numerous marginal scenes and symbols from his own hand. He also composed several Lives of the Saints (the *Life of St Alban*, Trinity College, Dublin, is autograph) in which the illustrations occupy the upper half of the page and are of equal importance with the text. The frontispiece to his *Historia Anglorum* is his only signed work—a self-portrait showing him on his knees dedicating the manuscript to the

Virgin. It is a tinted outline drawing, and because of his fame there has been a mistaken tendency to assign all mid 13th-cent. English work of this character to St Albans in general and, if at all plausible, to his hand.

Paris, School of. Very general term applied to those movements in modern painting— *Fauvism, *Cubism, *Surrealism, etc.—that had their focus in Paris although many of their exponents were from other countries. The term reflects the intense concentration of artistic activity, supported by critics, dealers, and connoisseurs, which made Paris the world centre of advanced art during the first 40 years of the 20th cent. After the Second World War, New York replaced Paris as the world capital of avant-garde art. In the context of manuscript *illumination, the term 'School of Paris' is applied to the manuscript illuminators who in the 13th cent. made Paris the leading centre of book illustration in Europe.

Parler, Peter (c.1330–99). German architect and sculptor, the most famous member of a dynasty of masons active in the 14th cent. and early 15th cent. In 1353 he was appointed architect of Prague Cathedral and much of the present structure was designed by him. He also built the celebrated Charles Bridge over the River Vltava in Prague. As a sculptor he is best known for a series of portrait busts in the triforium of Prague Cathedral, including a self-portrait and one of the emperor Charles IV.

Parmigianino (Girolamo Francesco Mazzola) (1503–40). Italian *Mannerist painter and etcher, born in Parma, from which he takes his nickname. He was a precocious artist, and as early as 1522–3 painted accomplished frescos in two chapels in S. Giovanni Evangelista, Parma, showing his admiration for *Correggio, who had worked in the same church a year or two before. The originality and sophistication he displayed from the beginning, particularly his love of unusual spatial effects, is, however, most memorably seen in his celebrated *Self-Portrait in a Convex Mirror* (Kunsthistorisches Museum, Vienna, 1524), in which *Vasari said he looks 'so beautiful that he seemed an angel rather than a man'. In 1524 Parmigianino travelled to Rome, possibly via Florence, and his work became both grander and more graceful under the influence of *Raphael and *Michelangelo. *The Vision of St Jerome* (NG, London, 1526–7) is his most important work of this time, showing the disturbing emotional intensity he created with his elongated forms, disjointed sense of space, chill lighting, and lascivious atmosphere. Parmigianino left Rome after it was sacked by German troops in 1527 and moved to Bologna. In 1531 he returned to Parma and contracted to paint frescos in Sta Maria della Steccata. He failed to complete the work, however, and was eventually imprisoned for breach of contract. Vasari says he neglected the work because he was infatuated with alchemy—'he allowed his beard to grow long and disordered . . . he neglected himself and grew melancholy and eccentric.' His later paintings show no falling off in his powers, however, and his work reaches its apotheosis in his celebrated *Madonna of the Long Neck* (Uffizi, Florence, c.1535). The forms of the figures are extraordinarily elongated and tapering and the painting has a refinement and grace that place it among the archetypal works of Mannerism. Parmigianino's range extended beyond religious works. He painted a highly erotic *Cupid Carving his Bow* (Kunsthistorisches Museum, Vienna, 1535), and was one of the subtlest portraitists of his age (two superb examples are in the Museo di Capodimonte, Naples). The landscape backgrounds to his religious works have a mysterious and visionary quality that influenced Niccolò dell' *Abbate and through him French art (see FONTAINE-BLEAU, SCHOOL OF). Parmigianino, whose draughtsmanship was exquisite, also made designs for engravings and for *chiaroscuro woodcuts and appears to have been the first Italian artist to produce original etchings from his own designs.

Parrhasius. Greek painter from Ephesus, active in the later 5th cent. BC. He is said to have been particularly skilful in the use of contour and in depicting character through facial expression, and his mastery of illusionism is recorded in one of *Pliny's most famous anecdotes. It concerns a contest Parrhasius had with *Zeuxis, who painted some grapes so naturalistically that birds came to peck at them. Victory seeming to be his, he called on Parrhasius to draw back the curtain concealing his

picture, but this turned out to be a painted curtain. Zeuxis conceded the contest; he had deceived the birds, but Parrhasius had deceived him.

Pascin, Jules (Julius Pincas), (1885–1930). Bulgarian-born painter and draughtsman. He led a wandering life, and although he acquired American citizenship when he moved to New York during the First World War, he is chiefly associated with Paris, where he belonged to the circle of artists at Montmartre who gravitated around *Soutine, *Modigliani, and *Chagall. Although he did portraits of his friends and began a number of large paintings with biblical themes, most of his work consists of erotically charged studies of the female nude. They have been compared with the work of *Degas and *Toulouse-Lautrec, but Pascin's paintings are less penetrating and more obviously posed. He can be rather repetitive, but his best work has great delicacy of colour and handling and a poignant sense of lost innocence. Pascin had an unstable emotional life and he committed suicide (slashing his wrists and then hanging himself) in spite of his financial success.

Pasmore, Victor (1908–). English painter. After early experiments with abstraction he reverted to naturalistic painting, and in 1937 he combined with *Coldstream and Claude *Rogers in forming the *Euston Road School. Characteristic of his work at this time and in the early 1940s are the lyrically sensitive Thames-side landscapes which have been likened to those of *Whistler (*Chiswick Reach*, NG of Canada, Ottawa, 1943). In the late 1940s he underwent a dramatic conversion to pure abstract art, and by the early 1950s he had matured a personal style of geometrical abstraction. At the same time he made abstract *reliefs partly under the influence of Ben *Nicholson. His earlier reliefs had a hand-made quality but later, through the introduction of transparent perspex, he gave them the impersonal precision and finish of machine products (examples are in the Tate Gallery). Through work in this style he came to be regarded as one of the leaders of the *Constructivist revival in Britain. Later paintings are less austere and more organic. Pasmore has been an influential teacher and has been much concerned with bringing abstract art to the general public. In 1955, for example, he was appointed Consulting Director of Architectural Design for Peterlee New Town, County Durham, and designed an urban centre in the form of a Pavilion which integrated architectural design with abstract relief painting.

Passarotti, Bartolommeo (1529–92). Italian painter, who except for some years in Rome (*c.*1551–*c.*1565) worked in his native Bologna. There he had a large studio, which became the focal point of the city's artistic life. The religious paintings that were the basis of his success were fairly conventional and undistinguished, and he is now remembered for his pioneering *genre scenes of butchers' shops (one of the few surviving examples is in the Galleria Nazionale, Rome). They reflect the influence of northern painters such as *Aertsen and in their lively observation broke free from the prevailing *Mannerism. Annibale *Carracci (whose brother Agostino studied with Passarotti) was influenced by these genre scenes in his early career. In addition to his religious and genre works, Passarotti painted excellent portraits throughout his career. His son **Tiburzio** (d. *c.*1612) imitated his style, and he in turn had two artist sons, **Gaspare** and **Archangelo**.

Passeri, Giovanni Battista (1610–79). Italian painter and writer on art. He is of no significance as a painter, but he is important for his collection of biographies of contemporary artists, *Vite de' Pittori, Scultori ed Architetti che anno lavorato in Roma morti dal 1641 fino al 1673*, not published until 1772. His accounts are detailed and on the whole accurate, forming one of the most important sources for the study of Roman *Baroque art.

pastel. A drawing or painting material consisting of a stick of colour made from powdered *pigments mixed with just enough *resin or *gum to bind them. Pastel is applied directly to paper, with no *medium, and a significant difference between this and other methods of painting is that the colour as applied represents the final result—no allowance has to be made for changes during drying. Pastel has the disadvantage, however, of being very fragile and easily dislodged from the paper.

This can be counteracted by using a *fixative, but fixing is apt to reduce the brilliance of the colour. As they are so delicate, pastels are usually used on a small scale, and they developed in the 16th cent. from the use of coloured chalks for drawing. The heyday of pastel was the 18th cent., when it was particularly popular for portraits, and it had a second great flowering in the late 19th cent., when several of the *Impressionists took it up.

pastel manner. An 18th-cent. engraving technique, a development of the *crayon manner, in which a number of plates were inked with different colours to give the appearance of *pastel drawings.

pastiche (or **pasticcio**). A picture or other work of art that (often with fraudulent purpose) imitates the style of a particular artist by copying and recombining parts of his authentic works.

Patch, Thomas (1725–82). English painter and engraver who lived in Italy from 1747. In Rome he first made a reputation, especially among the English tourists, as a view painter, but after settling in Florence in 1755 was best known for good-humoured *caricature *conversation pieces by which he is chiefly remembered today. Patch knew *Reynolds, who included a portrait of him in his own well-known caricature of *Raphael's *School of Athens* (NG, Dublin, 1751), and it is uncertain who influenced whom in the genre.

Patel, Pierre (*c.*1605–76). French landscape painter. He was a pupil of *Vouet but worked in the manner of *Claude, with whose paintings his own have sometimes been confused. In his day he was well known for his panels set into the decoration of rooms, notably in the Cabinet de l'Amour of the Hôtel Lambert in Paris. His son, **Pierre-Antoine** (1648–1708), painted in his father's manner. Both men often featured Classical ruins in their paintings, looking forward to the *picturesque.

Patenier, Herri. See BLES.

Patenier (or **Patinier**, or **Patinir**), **Joachim** (d. 1524). Netherlandish painter, a pioneer of landscape as an independent genre. Nothing is known of his early life, but in 1515 he became a member of the Antwerp Guild. In 1521 he met *Dürer, who made a drawing of him and described him as a 'good landscape painter'. There are only a very few signed paintings, but a great many others have been attributed to him with varying degrees of probability. Patenier also painted landscape backgrounds for other artists and *The Temptation of St Anthony* (Prado, Madrid) was done in collaboration with his friend Quentin *Massys (who after Patenier's death became guardian of his children). Although landscape never constitutes the subject of his pictures, Patenier was the first Netherlandish artist to let it dwarf his figures in religious and mythological scenes. His style combines naturalistic observation of detail with a marvellous sense of fantasy, forming a link between *Bosch and *Bruegel.

Pater, Jean-Baptiste-Joseph (1695–1736). French painter, the only pupil of *Watteau (a fellow native of Valenciennes), with whom he had a somewhat touchy relationship. An unlikely legend has it that Watteau dismissed him from his studio (c.1713) because he was disturbed by the threat offered by his progress to his own pre-eminence; they were reconciled soon before Watteau's death. Like Watteau's other imitator, *Lancret, Pater repeated the master's type of *fêtes galantes* (see FÊTE CHAMPÊTRE) in a fairly stereotyped fashion. He showed more originality in scenes of military life and groups of bathers (in which he gave freer rein to the suggestiveness often seen in his *fêtes galantes*). Examples of all types of his work are in the Wallace Collection, London.

Pater, Walter (1839–94). English critic and essayist. A fellow of Brasenose College, Oxford, he led an uneventful life and was regarded as an apostle of *Aestheticism, which set a supreme value upon the enjoyment of beauty. His best-known book is *Studies in the History of the Renaissance* (1873), which includes essays on *Winckelmann and the then neglected *Botticelli, and his celebrated evocation of the *Mona Lisa* in his essay on *Leonardo da Vinci: 'She is older than the rocks among which she sits ...'. This volume (which concludes 'To burn always with this hard gem-like flame, to maintain this ecstasy, is success in life'), though attacked by some as

unscholarly and morbid, had a profound influence on the undergraduates of the day and was acclaimed by Oscar Wilde as 'the holy writ of beauty'.

patina. Incrustation, usually green, on the surface of a metal (typically bronze) object, caused by oxidation. Such discoloration occurs naturally with age through exposure to the atmosphere and can be accelerated or modified when an object is buried in the sea or soil, where the particular substances present will cause various chemical reactions. Patination can produce an attractive, mellowing effect, and since the *Renaissance bronze statues have often been artificially patinated, usually by treatment with acid. By extension, the term 'patina' can be applied to any form of surface discoloration or mellowing, for example dirty varnish on a painting.

Paton, Sir Joseph Noël (1821–1901). Scottish painter. A friend of *Millais (a fellow student at the *Royal Academy), he had a kinship with the *Pre-Raphaelites early in his career. He painted mythological and historical scenes and later gained great success with his rather portentous and sentimental religious pictures, which went on tour and were much reproduced.

Pausanias (2nd cent. AD). Greek traveller and geographer, the author of a *Description of Greece* in ten books that is the single most important literary source for the history of Greek art (painting and sculpture as well as architecture). It is a guidebook written for tourists—simple, unpretentious, detailed, and in the main reliable, as is frequently attested by the remains of the monuments he describes. Sir James Frazer, who produced one of the many English translations of the work (6 volumes, 1898), said of Pausanias: 'without him the ruins of Greece would for the most part be a labyrinth without a clue, a riddle without an answer.'

Peale, Charles Willson (1741–1827). American painter, inventor, naturalist, and patriot, the founder and most distinguished member of a family of artists. A highly versatile craftsman, Peale was a saddler, watchmaker, silversmith, and upholsterer before working briefly in *Copley's studio in Boston. He then spent two years in London (1767–9), where he studied under

Benjamin *West. In 1775 he settled in Philadelphia, where he became the most fashionable portraitist in the Colonies, Copley having left for England in 1774. He fought as a colonel of the militia in the War for Independence and became a Democratic member of the Pennsylvania Assembly. In 1782 he opened an exhibition gallery next to his studio, the first art gallery in the United States, and there displayed his own portraits of leading personalities of the Revolutionary War (he painted George Washington several times). This expanded into a natural history museum, which attained a vast size and included as its star exhibit the first mastodon skeleton to be exhumed in America. Two of his most famous paintings celebrate his scientific interests—*The Exhumation of the Mastodon* (1806) in the Peale Museum, Baltimore, and *The Artist in his Museum* (1822) in the Pennsylvania Academy of the Fine Arts, an institution he helped to found in 1805. His inventions included new types of spectacles and false teeth. As a painter, Peale generally worked in a solid, dignified style, but his most celebrated work is a witty piece of *trompe-l'oeil*. This is *The Staircase Group* (Philadelphia Museum of Art, 1795), a life-size portrait of two of his sons mounting a staircase, with a real step at the bottom and a real door jamb as a frame; George Washington is said to have been deceived into doffing his hat to the boys' images. Peale married three times and had seventeen children, of whom several became artists. The most important were **Raphaelle** (1774–1825), one of America's most distinguished still-life painters, **Rembrandt** (1778–1860), a gifted though uneven portraitist, and **Titian Ramsay II** (1779–1885), who continued his father's tradition as an artist-naturalist. Apart from his portraits, Rembrandt won fame with his huge picture *The Court of Death* (Detroit Inst. of Arts, 1821), which toured the country with success for over half a century. Charles Willson's brother **James** (1749–1831) was also a painter and his son and four daughters carried on the family tradition. The Peales were largely responsible for establishing Philadelphia as one of the country's leading cultural centres.

Pearlstein, Philip (1924–). American painter, a leading proponent of the return to *naturalism and interest in the human

figure that came in reaction from *Abstract Expressionism. He specializes in starkly unidealized portrayals of the nude figure, usually set in domestic surroundings. Because of the clarity of his compositions and the relentlessness of his recording of anatomical detail, he is sometimes described as a *Superrealist, but his work has an emotionalism and vigour of handling that put him outside this classification. He uses harsh lighting, oblique angles, and cropping of the image (heads are often excluded and the body is seen in voyeuristic close-up) in a way that suggests candid photography.

Pechstein, Max (1881–1955). German *Expressionist painter and graphic artist. He studied in Dresden and in 1906 became a member of the *Brücke. In 1908 he moved to Berlin and became one of the founders of the Neue *Sezession. Pechstein had a facile gift for reproducing the superficial features of the French *Fauvists—*Matisse in particular. His love of the exotic, shared by other members of the Brücke, led him to make a visit in 1913–14 to the Palau Islands in the Pacific and he painted bright and lively anecdotal pictures depicting the paradisal life of the island fishermen in a near-Fauvist manner. For these reasons, perhaps, Pechstein was the first member of the Brücke to achieve popularity and win general recognition, but his reputation has not lasted. He was also known for his portraits and his opulent flower pieces. In 1918 he was one of the founders of the *Novembergruppe and he taught in the Berlin Academy from 1923, being dismissed in 1933 by the Nazis and reinstated in 1945.

peep-show box. A cabinet with scenes portrayed on the interior walls which, when viewed through a small opening or eyepiece, give a strong illusion of three-dimensional reality. *Alberti may have been the inventor of the peep-show box, for some such device is ascribed to him in a contemporary, anonymous biography, but they had their greatest popularity in the 17th cent. Samuel van *Hoogstraten was a noted exponent.

Peeters, Bonaventura the Elder (1614–52). Flemish marine painter. He was virtually the only noteworthy practitioner in the genre in his country, seascapes being much more a Dutch than a Flemish speciality. In his early works Peeters was influenced by Dutch masters, such as Simon de *Vlieger, but later he tended to introduce elaborate motifs and bright colour in a decorative vein less impressive than his earlier style. Various other members of the family were artists, including his sister **Catharina** (1615–76), a seascape and still-life painter, but **Clara Peeters** (1594–1657?), one of the outstanding Antwerp still-life painters of her time, was no relation.

peinture à l'essence. See DEGAS.

Pelham, Peter. See COPLEY.

Pellegrini, Giovanni Antonio (1675–1741). Venetian painter, the brother-in-law of Rosalba *Carriera. Pellegrini played a major part in the spread of the Venetian style of large-scale decorative painting in northern Europe, working in Austria, England, France, Germany, and the Netherlands. He was the first Venetian artist to visit England, arriving in 1708 in the train of the fourth Earl of Manchester, for whose country seat, Kimbolton Castle, he painted what are generally regarded as his finest works. His airy, *illusionistic compositions, with their bright, flickering colour and purely decorative intention, set a new standard of *Rococo elegance for English decoration, but he was an extremely prolific painter, and by European standards most of his work is routine. *Thornhill defeated him in competition for the commission to decorate the dome of St Paul's Cathedral, London.

pen. Writing and drawing instrument used with ink or a similar coloured fluid. From Early Christian times until the 19th cent. the standard form of pen in Europe was the quill, made from bird feathers, and most of the pen drawings of the Old Masters were done with the quill. Goose, swan, and turkey quills have commonly been used for writing and crow quills provide a very fine point for drawing. The reed pen, made from stems of bamboo-like grasses, was already in use in Classical antiquity and is probably older than the quill. The point is much coarser, producing a bold, angular line sometimes slightly blurred at the edges. For drawing it has been used much less than the quill, though

*Rembrandt, for example, was a master of the broad energetic technique appropriate to it. The metal pen dates back at least to Roman times, but steel nibs of the modern type were not made until late in the 18th cent. and began to replace the quill only when they were produced by machine, *c*.1822. No other drawing tool can produce such a variety of texture or reveal so intimately the personal 'handwriting' of an artist. The pen is the ideal medium for rapidly noting down the first idea and has been used in this way by masters of drawing as different as *Pisanello, *Michelangelo, *Dürer, and Rembrandt. But apart from its use for the hasty or inspired *sketch, in which the fire of execution is reflected in the line, the pen has been used with great effect in a careful, calligraphic manner, as in *Botticelli's illustrations to Dante's *Divine Comedy*.

pencil. Writing or drawing instrument consisting of a slender rod of graphite or similar substance encased in a cylinder of wood (or less usually metal or plastic). Although the material is graphite (a form of carbon), the 'lead' pencil took its name from the lead point (see METAL POINT) which it superseded, and is first heard of in the 1560s. Pencils of predetermined hardness or softness were not produced until 1790, however, when Nicolas-Jacques *Conté undertook to solve the problem of making pencils when France was cut off from the English supply of graphite (the mines in Borrowdale, Cumbria, which had opened in 1664, being the main source). He found that the graphite could be eked out with clay and fired in a kiln, and that more clay meant a harder pencil. Conté obtained a patent for his process in 1795. It was only then that the pencil became the universal drawing instrument that it is today. Although the *Oxford English Dictionary* records the usage of the phrase 'a pencil of black lead' as early as 1612, until the end of the 18th cent. the word 'pencil' more commonly meant a brush (particularly a small brush). 'Pencilling' could mean 'colouring' or 'brushwork' as well as 'drawing'.

Pencz, Georg (Jörg Bencz) (*c*.1500–50). German painter and engraver of religious and mythological subjects and portraits, active in his native Nuremberg, where he was an assistant of *Dürer. He travelled in

Italy early in his career and again in 1539, when he is recorded in Florence and Rome, and his work is deeply imbued with Italian influence. The sharp outlines and glossy textures of his portraits show, in particular, a kinship with *Bronzino (*Man Holding a Mirror*, Hessisches Landesmuseum, Darmstadt, 1544). In 1525 Pencz was expelled from Nuremberg with the *Beham brothers, two other 'godless artists', for their radical Protestant views, but the sentence was soon revoked and he returned to the city. In 1550 he was appointed painter to Duke Albrecht of Prussia, but died in the same year.

Penni, Francesco (*c.*1488–*c.*1528). Italian painter, nicknamed 'il Fattore' (the maker). He was born in Florence and died in Naples, but worked mainly in Rome, where with *Giulio Romano he was *Raphael's main assistant. Various parts of the works of the master have been attributed to him (*Vasari says he worked on the tapestry *cartoons for the Sistine Chapel), but he is a shadowy figure. After Raphael's death he collaborated with Giulio. A rare signed work by Penni is the *Portrait of a Young Man* in Dublin (NG).

Penrose, Sir Roland (1900–84). English painter, collector, and writer on art. As an artist he holds a distinguished place among British *Surrealists (he produced collages and 'objects' as well as paintings), but he is remembered mainly for the missionary zeal with which he promoted Surrealism and contemporary art in general in England. He was one of the organizers of the 1936 Surrealist exhibition in London, and he was closely involved with many leading artists, such as *Ernst, *Man Ray, *Miró, and *Picasso. During the Second World War he was a camouflage instructor. In 1947 he was cofounder and first chairman of the *Institute of Contemporary Arts in London. His books include *Picasso. His Life and Work* (1958, 3rd edition 1980), regarded as a standard work on the artist. Penrose's second wife, whom he married in 1947, was the photographer Lee Miller, a pupil and favourite model of Man Ray.

pentimento. Term (Italian for 'repentance') describing a part of a picture that has been overpainted by the artist but which has become visible again (often as a ghostly outline) because the upper layer of pigment has become more transparent through age. The presence of pentimenti is often used as an argument in matters of attribution, as it is felt that such evidence of an artist's second thoughts is much more likely to occur in an original painting than in a copy.

Pereda, Antonio de (1611–78). Spanish painter, active mainly in Madrid. He began as a history painter—his *Relief of Genoa* (Prado, Madrid, 1635) was painted for the Buen Retiro Palace in Madrid as part of the same series as *Velázquez's *Surrender of Breda*—but he is now best known for his still lifes. His most famous painting is *The Knight's Dream* (also called *The Dream of Life* or *Life is a Dream*, Academy, Madrid, *c.*1655), a splendidly sensuous composition, full of brilliantly painted still-life details, in which worldly pleasures and treasures are seen to be as insubstantial as a dream. It was a key work in the development of the moralizing still life in Spain, influencing *Valdés Leal in particular.

Performance art. An art form combining elements of theatre, music, and the visual arts. It is related to the *happening (the two terms are sometimes used synonymously), but Performance art is usually more carefully programmed and generally does not involve audience participation.

Pergamene School A trend in *Hellenistic sculpture, associated with the city of Pergamum in Asia Minor, whose great period coincided with the Attalid dynasty (241–133 BC). The works associated with the Pergamene school are characterized by an exaggeration of the general tendency of Hellenistic sculpture towards emotional display and virtuoso naturalistic detail. They include a series of Dying Gauls (the most famous is in the Capitoline Museum, Rome) that have been identified as copies of statues dedicated by Attalus I to celebrate a victory over the Gauls, and the Great Altar of Zeus (Staatliche Museen, East Berlin, *c.*180–150 BC), which features relief carvings of the fight between gods and giants depicted with an extraordinary sense of movement and dramatic tension. It is perhaps the 'Satan's seat' of Revelation 2: 13. Other Hellenistic works from places other than Pergamum (above all the celebrated *Laocoön) are clearly similar in their restless energy and some scholars deny that there is adequate reason for supposing there is a separate Pergamene School. T. B. L. Webster in his *Hellenistic Poetry and Art* (1964), however, maintains that although the artists employed by the Attalid kings came from various places, they 'achieved a unity of style which justifies the name Pergamene'.

Permeke, Constant (1886–1952). Belgian painter and sculptor, with Gustave de *Smet and Frits van den *Berghe the creator of the Belgian school of *Expressionism. His subjects were taken mainly from coastal cities and he is best known for his strong and solemn portrayals of sailors and fishermen with their women (*The Fiancés*, Musées Royaux, Brussels, 1923). From 1935 he also made sculpture. The studios he constructed at Jabbeke near Bruges are now a museum of his work.

Permoser, Balthasar (1651–1732). German sculptor. He was in Italy 1675–89 and his lively *Baroque style was much influenced by *Bernini. In 1689 he became court sculptor at Dresden and spent most of the rest of his life there. His most important work was the sculptural decoration of the Zwinger—Augustus the Strong's pleasure palace in Dresden, designed by the architect M. D. Pöppelmann (begun 1711, badly damaged in the Second World War). Permoser carved in wood and ivory as well as stone and also made ingenious use of coloured marble (*Damned Soul*, Museum der Bildenden Künste, Leipzig, *c*.1715). *Roubiliac is said to have studied with him.

Perréal, Jean (or **Jehan de Paris**) (*c*.1455–1530). French painter, architect, sculptor, and decorator of very considerable reputation in his day. He was in the service of Charles VIII, Louis XII, and Francis I and visited Italy on three occasions, with Charles VIII in 1494 and with Louis XII on his campaigns of 1502 and 1509 (on one of these journeys he met *Leonardo, who mentions Perréal in his notebooks). His activities were manifold, but little work survives that can confidently be attributed to his own hand—a portrait of Louis XII (1514) at Windsor Castle and a few *miniatures. They show him as a master of a scrupulously observed *naturalism. It has been suggested that he is to be identified with the *Master of Moulins.

Perrier, François (1590?–1650). French history painter and engraver. He visited Rome on two occasions and his style was formed on the example of *Lanfranco (in whose studio he worked), Pietro da *Cortona and the *Carracci. His decorative work helped to introduce the grand *Baroque style to France, but almost all of it has been destroyed or altered. His influence, however, can be seen in the work of Charles *Lebrun, who was briefly his pupil.

Perronneau, Jean-Baptiste (1715?–83). French painter and engraver. He worked mainly as a portraitist and mainly in *pastel. In this medium he was overshadowed in his lifetime by Maurice Quentin de *La Tour, whose style was more vivacious, but posterity has judged the more sober but more penetrating Perronneau to be at least his equal. From about 1755 he led a wandering life, visiting England, the Netherlands several times (he died in Amsterdam), Italy, Poland, and Russia. He was a prolific artist and is represented in many galleries.

perspective. Method of representing spatial extension into depth on a flat or shallow surface, utilizing such optical phenomena as the apparent diminution in size of objects and the convergence of parallel lines as they recede from the spectator. Perspective is by no means common to the art of all epochs and all peoples. For example, the pictorial art of the ancient Egyptians, although a richly developed tradition, did not take account of the optical effects of recession. Systematic, mathematically founded perspective, based initially on a fixed central viewpoint, was developed in Italy in the early 15th cent., when it was invented by *Brunelleschi, described by *Alberti in his treatise *De Pictura*, and put into majestic practice by *Masaccio. Various names are given to this type of perspective—geometric, linear, mathematical, optical, *Renaissance or scientific perspective—which remained one of the foundations of European painting until the late 19th cent. In pre-Renaissance Europe and in the East more intuitive systems of representing spatial recession were used. In medieval paintings, for example, lines that would in strict perspective converge are often shown diverging (this 'inverted perspective' can look much more convincing in practice than it sounds in theory); and in Chinese art 'parallel perspective' was a common convention in the depiction of buildings. See also AERIAL PERSPECTIVE.

Perugino, Pietro (Pietro Vannucci) (c.1445/50–1523). Italian painter, active mainly in Perugia, from which his nickname derives. His early career is obscure, but he seems to have formed his style chiefly in Florence, where *Vasari says he studied with *Verrocchio (another tradition has it that he was a pupil of *Piero della Francesca). By 1481 he had made himself sufficiently well known to be commissioned to paint frescos at the Sistine Chapel along with *Rosselli, *Ghirlandaio, and *Botticelli. His main work there, *Christ Delivering the Keys to St Peter*, established his reputation and in 1500, when he decorated the Audience Chamber of the Collegio del Cambio at Perugia, he was called by Agostino Chigi, the wealthy Sienese banker and patron, the best painter in Italy. Perugino was a fine portraitist as well as a fresco painter, but he is best known for his altarpieces, which are usually gentle, pious, and rather sentimental in manner. His style does not seem to have been a reflection of his personality, for Vasari says he 'was not a religious man' and that he 'would have gone to any lengths for money'. In about 1505 he left the competitive atmosphere of Florence, where his work now seemed old-fashioned, and settled permanently in Perugia; his later work is often routine and repetitive. At his best, however, as in the Vatican fresco, he has the authority of a great master. The harmony and spatial clarity of his compositions and his idealized physical types had great influence on the young *Raphael, who worked in his busy studio, so Perugino can be seen as one of the harbingers of the High *Renaissance. A second wave of his influence came in the 19th cent., when he was glorified by the *Pre-Raphaelites.

Peruzzi, Baldassare (1481–1536). Sienese architect, painter, and stage designer, active mainly in Rome, where he settled in 1503. He worked under *Bramante on St Peter's, and eventually became architect to the building after *Raphael's death in 1520. Amongst High *Renaissance architects he ranks almost alongside these two great contemporaries, but his style was very different—sophisticated and delicate rather than monumental and grave. In spite of his genius he had little material success according to *Vasari because of his 'retiring nature'. His greatest work—indeed the greatest secular building of the High Renaissance—is the Villa Farnesina (1500–11) in Rome, built for the Sienese banker Agostino Chigi. The Farnesina contains decorations by Raphael, *Sebastiano del Piombo and *Sodoma, as well as Peruzzi's own masterpiece in painting—the Sala delle Prospettive, a brilliant piece of feigned architectural painting that confirms early accounts of his skill in perspective and stage-design.

Peters, Matthew William (1741/2–1814). English painter of portraits, *genre and historical scenes, and *fancy pictures. He studied with *Hudson in the late 1750s and travelled to Italy and France in 1772–6 and again to Paris in 1783. Foreign influence is clearly seen in the richness of his technique (admirers called him 'the English *Titian') and in the pin-up type of picture of pretty women—distinctly reminiscent of *Greuze—with which he caused a mild scandal and attained great popularity in engravings. He took Holy Orders in 1782 and retired from professional practice in 1788, but continued to paint for his own pleasure. His later works include some mawkish religious paintings and some dull pictures for *Boydell's Shakespeare Gallery.

Peto, John Frederick (1854–1907). American still-life painter. With his friend *Harnett he is now considered the outstanding American still-life painter of his period, but he was little known during his lifetime and after his death was completely forgotten until rediscovered in 1947 by the critic Alfred Frankenstein. His work was strongly influenced by Harnett (whose signature has sometimes been fraudulently added to paintings by Peto), but his style was softer and more anecdotal, often depicting discarded objects. Peto worked in his native Philadelphia, then from 1889 in seclusion at Island Heights, New Jersey.

Pevsner, Antoine (1886–1962). Russian-born sculptor and painter who became a French citizen in 1930. He was the elder brother of Naum *Gabo and like him one of the pioneers of *Constructivism. In

1911–14 he lived in Paris, where he associated with *Archipenko and *Modigliani. After a period in Norway with Gabo he returned to Russia in 1917, and became professor at the Academy of Fine Arts, Moscow, where *Malevich and *Kandinsky also taught. In 1920 he was associated with Gabo in drawing up the manifesto of Constructivism and in 1922 he helped to organize the exhibition of Soviet art in Berlin. He moved back to Paris in 1923 because of official disapproval of abstract art. Up until this time he had been a painter, but he now turned to sculpture, at first working mainly in plastic, then in welded metal.

Pevsner, Sir Nikolaus (1902–83). German-born British art historian. He worked at the Gemäldegalerie in Dresden and taught at Göttingen University (1929–33) before moving to England because of the rise of Nazism. In England he was *Slade Professor at both Oxford and Cambridge universities and also professor at Birkbeck College in the University of London. He is best known for his writings on architecture, above all for the celebrated series of county-by-county guides *The Buildings of England* (46 vols., 1951–74), which he conceived, edited, and largely wrote himself. Companion series on the buildings of Ireland, Scotland, and Wales began publication in 1978. Pevsner's many books included important studies on painting, sculpture, and design as well as architecture. They include *Academies of Art, Past and Present* (1940), *An Outline of European Architecture* (1942 and numerous other editions), and *The Englishness of English Art* (1956). He also conceived and edited the *Pelican History of Art* (which began publication in 1953), the largest, most comprehensive, and most scholarly history of art ever published in English, many of the individual volumes of which have become classics. Anthony *Blunt, Sir Ellis *Waterhouse, and Rudolf *Wittkower are among the scholars who have written volumes in the series.

Pforr, Franz (1788–1812). German painter. He was one of the founders of the *Nazarenes and went to Rome with other members of the group in 1810. His work evokes a fairy-tale type of medievalism, with bright colours and picturesque details.

It is best represented in the Städelsches Kunstinstitut of his native Frankfurt.

Phidias (d. *c*.432 BC). Greek sculptor, active mainly in Athens, the most famous artist of the ancient world. No work survives that is certainly from his own hand, but through copies, descriptions, and above all the surviving sculpture of the Parthenon at Athens, which Phidias supervised, a fair idea can be gained of his style. In antiquity he was most celebrated for two enormous *chryselephantine cult statues—of Athena, inside the Parthenon, and of Zeus in the temple dedicated to the god at Olympia. The statue of Zeus, a seated figure about 12 m. high and one of the Seven Wonders of the World, is known through reproductions on Roman coins. The statue of Athena (dedicated 438 BC), a standing figure about 9 m. high, is known through several (much smaller) copies. Phidias made another statue of Athena for the Acropolis in Athens—the *Lemnian Athena* (so called because it was dedicated by Athenian colonists going to Lemnos between 451 and 448 BC) and this can be partially reconstructed from two fragmentary copies: a remarkably sensitive head in Bologna (Museo Civico Archeologico) and a substantially complete figure in Dresden (Albertinum). Other copies have been credibly associated with works of Phidias mentioned in ancient sources, and recently the two bronze statues of warriors found in the sea near Riace in 1972 ('The Riace bronzes') and now in the archaeological museum at Reggio di Calabria have been linked with his name because of their superlative quality. The greatest testimony to his genius, however, is the sculpture of the Parthenon (447–432 BC), the most ambitious sculptural undertaking of the age, consisting of a low-*relief frieze about 160 m. long, ninety-two metopes (decorative panels) in high relief, and groups of free-standing figures on both pediments. The quality is variable, as a team of sculptors was involved and Phidias could not have carved more than a tiny fraction of the work himself, but the finest parts (see ELGIN MARBLES) exemplify the harmony and serene majesty that earned the raptures of ancient commentators and stand as the greatest surviving examples of the *Classical period in Greek art.

The end of Phidias' career is something of a mystery. When the great statesman Pericles, his friend and patron, fell out of favour Phidias was accused of misappropriating gold supplied to him for the statue of Athena. Then, according to Plutarch, having cleared himself of this charge, he was thrown into prison for 'impiety' on the ground that he had introduced portraits of Pericles and himself on the shield of the goddess (a copy of the shield—the 'Strangford Shield'—is in the British Museum). Plutarch says that Phidias died in prison, but according to another ancient source he escaped and went to Olympia to work on his statue of Zeus, the date of which is uncertain. In 1954-8 Phidias' workshop at Olympia was excavated. Moulds, scraps of ivory, and other fragments were discovered, and—remarkably—a cup bearing the inscription 'I belong to Phidias'—the great man's tea-mug, as it were. This poignant relic is in the Olympia Museum. Phidias is said to have been a painter, engraver, and worker in embossed metalwork. His influence is seen in the best of contemporary vase-painting as well as in the sculpture of his successors.

Phillip, John (1817–67). Scottish painter. He began as a specialist in paintings of Scottish life and character in the manner of *Wilkie, but following visits to Spain in 1851, 1856, and 1860 he became celebrated for picturesque Spanish *genre scenes and was known as 'Spanish' Phillip or 'Phillip of Spain'. His style was fluent and colourful, often with a picture postcard flavour. He also painted portraits.

Phillips, Duncan (1886–1966). American collector and writer on art. He devoted much of his substantial inheritance (the family fortune had been made in steel and glass) to collecting, following his own judgement and refusing to operate through dealers. Mainly he bought the work of late 19th and 20th cent. artists, and when he opened his Washington home to the public (three afternoons a week) in 1921 it represented the first permanent museum of modern art in the USA. It proved so popular that Phillips made the house over completely as a gallery and moved to another home. The Phillips Collection retains its intimate, domestic air, and is widely regarded as one of the world's finest

small museums. Its star exhibit is *Renoir's celebrated *Luncheon of the Boating Party* (1880–1). As a writer on art Phillips is best known for his book *The Leadership of Giorgione* (1937).

Photographic Realism. See SUPER-REALISM.

photomontage. Term applied to a technique of making a pictorial composition from parts of different photographs and to the composition so made. Photomontage was popularized by the *Dadaists as a method for making a political propaganda, social criticism, and generally to assist the shock tactics in which they indulged. *Heartfield was perhaps the most brilliant of all exponents of the technique. Photomontage has also been memorably used by, for example, Max *Ernst and other *Surrealists and by *Pop artists such as Richard *Hamilton, but it is now mainly associated with advertising.

Piazzetta, Giovanni Battista (1683–1754). Venetian painter and graphic artist. After preliminary training in Venice he worked under G. M. *Crespi in Bologna, then settled permanently in his native city by 1711. He was one of the most individual Venetian painters of his period, his sombre and dramatic style looking back to work done a century earlier by *Liss, *Strozzi, and *Feti. Apart from a ceiling fresco of the *Glory of St Dominic* (c.1727) in SS. Giovanni e Paolo, he painted in oils and he was a notoriously slow worker, but his pictures seem fresh and spontaneous rather than laboured. He had a large family and although he was not without wealthy patrons (*Algarotti among them) he relied much on drawings and book illustrations to earn money. As a painter he did religious and historical works and portraits, as well as some hauntingly enigmatic *genre scenes that reflect his training with Crespi. In 1750 Piazzetta became the first Director of the Venice Academy of Fine Arts, but in his last years he was eclipsed by the new generation. The young *Tiepolo was greatly influenced by him, but later the influence was reversed, as Piazzetta's style became softer and lighter—more *Rococo—in feeling.

Picabia, Francis (1879–1953). French painter of Cuban-Spanish extraction. After painting in an *Impressionist manner he came under the influence of *Cubism in 1909 and in 1911 was one of the group which founded the *Section d'Or. He visited the USA and exhibited in the *Armory Show in 1913. In New York again in 1915 he collaborated with Marcel *Duchamp and contributed to the magazine *291*. Anarchistic, subversive, and highly individualistic by temperament, he was one of the most active and original members of the *Dadaist movement both in Europe and in the USA. At Barcelona in 1916 he founded the Dadaist periodical *391*, which continued to appear irregularly until 1924. He was associated with the Dadaist group in Zurich, returned to Paris in 1919, and for a time associated with the *Surrealists. Without himself remaining for long within the confines of any one school or movement, Picabia had a great influence on many artists and helped to disseminate avant-garde ideas through the magazines with which he was involved.

Picasso, Pablo (1881–1973). Spanish painter, sculptor, graphic artist, ceramicist, and designer, the most famous, versatile, prolific, and influential artist of the 20th cent. Although it is conventional to divide his work into certain phases, all such divisions are to some extent arbitrary, as his energy and imagination were such that he was at all times working on a wealth of themes and in a variety of styles. He himself said: 'The several manners I have used in my art must not be considered as an evolution, or as steps toward an unknown ideal of painting. When I have found something to express, I have done it without thinking of the past or future. I do not believe I have used radically different elements in the different manners I have used in painting. If the subjects I have wanted to express have suggested different ways of expression, I haven't hesitated to adopt them.'

Picasso was the son of a painter and drawing master and was remarkably precocious, mastering academic draughtsmanship when he was still a child. In 1900 he made his first trip to Paris and by this time had already absorbed a wide range of influences. Between 1900 and 1904 he alternated between Paris and Barcelona, and this time coincides with his Blue Period, when he took his subjects from the

poor and social outcasts, and the predominant mood of his paintings was one of slightly sentimentalized melancholy expressed through cold ethereal blue tones (*La Vie*, Cleveland Mus. of Art, 1903). He also did a number of powerful engravings in a similar vein (*The Frugal Repast*, 1904). In 1904 Picasso settled in Paris and became the centre of an avant-garde circle of artists and writers including *Apollinaire. The two or three years from 1905 are known as his Rose Period. The predominant blue tones of his earlier work gave way to pinks and greys and the mood became less austere. His favourite subjects were acrobats and dancers, particularly the figure of the harlequin. During these years he produced his first sculptures and some of his painted nudes took on a sculptural solidity which foreshadowed the majestic nudes of the early 1920s. In 1906 he met *Matisse, but although he seems to have admired the work being done by the *Fauves, he did not himself follow their method in the decorative and expressive use of colour. During the years 1907 to 1909, called his Negro Period, he pursued an independent path, concentrating on the analysis and simplification of form and taking his direction from his studies of *Cézanne and African sculpture. The researches of these early years culminated in *Les Demoiselles d'Avignon* (MOMA, New York, 1906–7), which in its treatment of form was as violent a revolt against traditional *Impressionism as the paintings of the Fauves in the realm of colour. At the time the picture was incomprehensible to artists, including Matisse and *Derain, and it was not publicly exhibited until 1937. It is now seen not only as a crucial achievement in Picasso's personal development but as the most important single landmark in the development of contemporary painting and as the herald of *Cubism, which he developed in close association with *Braque and then *Gris from 1907 up to the First World War.

In 1917 Picasso went with his friend Jean Cocteau to Rome to design costumes and scenery for the ballet *Parade* and in the following years he designed for other *Diaghilev productions. The visit to Italy was one factor in introducing the strain of monumental Classicism that was one of the features of Picasso's work in the 1920s (*Mother and Child*, Art Institute of Chicago, 1921), but at this time he was also involved with *Surrealism—indeed André *Breton hailed him as one of the initiators of the movement. But his predominant interest in the analysis and synthesis of forms and his conviction that painting should be conceptual rather than purely visual were at bottom opposed to the irrationalist elements of Surrealism, their exaltation of chance, and equally to the direct realistic reproduction of dream or subconscious material. From about 1925 he began to make more violently expressive works, fraught with emotional tension, a mood of foreboding, and an almost clinical pre-occupation with anguish and despair. He was concerned with the mythological image of the Minotaur and images of the Dying Horse and the Weeping Woman. It was a period which culminated in his most famous work, *Guernica* (Casón del Buen Retiro, Madrid, 1937), produced for the Spanish Pavilion at the Paris Exposition Universelle of 1937 to express horror and revulsion at the destruction by bombing of the Basque capital Guernica during the civil war (1936–9). It was followed by a number of other great paintings, including *The Charnel House* (MOMA, New York, 1945), attacking the cruelty and de-structiveness of war. 'Painting is not done to decorate apartments,' he said: 'it is an instrument of war against brutality and darkness.' Picasso remained in Paris during the Occupation, but from 1946 lived mainly in the South of France, where he added pottery to his many activities. His later output as a painter does not compare in momentousness with his pre-war work, but it remained vigorous, varied, and continuously inventive of new modes for the solution of new problems. It included a number of variations on paintings by other artists, including forty-four on *Las Meninas* of *Velázquez. The theme of the artist and his almost magical powers is one that exercised him greatly throughout his long career.

Picasso's status as a painter has perhaps overshadowed his work as a sculptor, but in this field too (although his interest was sporadic) he ranks as one of the outstanding figures in 20th-cent. art. He was one of the first artists to make sculpture that was assembled from varied materials rather than modelled or carved, and he made brilliantly witty use of found objects (see OBJET TROUVÉ). The most celebrated example is *Head of a Bull, Metamorphosis* (Musée

Picasso, Paris, 1943), made of the saddle and handlebars of a bicycle. Alan Bowness has written (*Modern Sculpture*, 1965) 'Picasso's sculpture sparkles with bright ideas—enough to have kept many a lesser man occupied for the whole of a working lifetime . . . it is not inconceivable that the time will come when his activities as a sculptor in the second part of his life are regarded as of more consequence than his later paintings.' As a graphic artist (draughtsman, etcher, lithographer, lino-cutter), too, Picasso ranks with the great-est of the century. He was a prolific book illustrator, and as few other artists had the power to concentrate the impress of his genius even in the smallest and slightest of his works. Picasso's emotional range is as wide as his varied technical mastery. By turns tragic and playful, his work is suffused with a passionate love of life, and no artist has more devastatingly exposed the cruelty and folly of his fellow men or more rapturously celebrated the physical pleas-ures of love.

picture plane. In the imaginary space of a picture, the plane occupied by the physical surface of the work. *Perspective appears to recede from the picture plane, and objects painted in *trompe-l'œil may appear to project from it.

picturesque. Term covering a set of at-titudes towards landscape, both real and painted, that flourished in the late 18th and early 19th cents. It indicated an aesthetic approach that found pleasure in roughness and irregularity, and an attempt was made to establish it as a critical category between the 'beautiful' and the '*sublime'. Pic-turesque scenes were thus neither serene (like the beautiful) nor awe-inspiring (like the sublime), but full of variety, curious details, and interesting textures—medieval ruins were quintessentially picturesque. Natural scenery tended to be judged in terms of how closely it approximated to the paintings of favoured artists such as Gaspard *Dughet, and in 1801 the *Supplement* to Samuel Johnson's *Dictionary* by George Mason defined 'picturesque' as: 'what pleases the eye; remarkable for sin-gularity; striking the imagination with the force of painting; to be expressed in painting; affording a good subject for a landscape; proper to take a landscape from.' The Picturesque Tour in search of suitable subjects was a feature of English landscape painting of the period, exemplified, for example, in the work of *Girtin and (early in his career) of *Turner, and the picturesque generated a large literary output; much of it was pedantic and obsessive and it became a popular subject for satire.

Pierce (or **Pearce**), **Edward** (c.1635–95). English sculptor and mason, son of a painter (d. 1658) of the same name, some of whose decorative work survives at Wilton House, Wiltshire. Little is known of his youth, but by 1671 he was well established in London and was much employed by Sir Christopher Wren on the rebuilding of the City churches, both as a mason and as a stone-carver. He was also a wood-carver, and his work in this field is of such quality that it has sometimes been credited to Grinling *Gibbons. His best work, however, is as a sculptor of portrait busts, the most notable being the splendid marble bust of Wren (Ashmolean, Oxford, c.1673), brilliantly characterized and more convincingly *Baroque than anything else of the date in English art. Pierce also worked as an architect, the Bishop's Palace, Lichfield (1686–7), being his chief known work.

Pierino del Vaga (Piero Buonaccorsi) (1500/1–47). Florentine painter. He took his name (del Vaga) from a local painter with whom he worked after studying with Ridolfo *Ghirlandaio. In about 1518 he went to Rome, where he became one of *Raphael's assistants working on the Vatican Loggie. After the Sack of Rome in 1527 he moved to Genoa, where he was based until the late 1530s and where his *Mannerist style had great influence. His major work there was a series of mythological frescos in the Palazzo Doria. By 1539 he was back in Rome, where he became the principal decorative artist employed by Pope Paul III (Alessandro *Farnese), his work for him including frescos on the history of Alexander the Great (1545–7) in the Sala del Consiglio of the Castel S. Angelo. Pierino's style derives from Raphael and *Giulio Romano, but is ornamental rather than monumental. He was one of the leading decorative artists of his generation, and his work has been aptly described by S. J. Freedberg (*Painting in Italy: 1500–1600*) as 'intelligent but facile'. He also did a number of devotional pictures

in a Raphaelesque vein, notably the unfinished *Holy Family* (Courtauld Inst., London).

Piero della Francesca (Piero dei Franceschi) (c.1410/20–1492). Italian painter, virtually forgotten for centuries after his death, but regarded since his rediscovery in the early 20th cent. as one of the supreme artists of the *quattrocento. He was born in Borgo San Sepolcro (now Sansepolcro) in Umbria and spent much of his life there. We hear of him also at various times in Ferrara, Rimini, Arezzo, Rome, and Urbino. But he found the origins of his style in Florence, and he probably lived there as a young man for some time during the 1430s, although he is documented there only once, in 1439 (the first known reference to him), when he was assisting *Domenico Veneziano on frescos (now lost) in S. Egidio. His first documented work, the *polyptych of the *Madonna della Misericordia* (Pinacoteca, Sansepolcro), commissioned in 1445 but not completed until much later, shows that he had studied and absorbed the artistic discoveries of his great Florentine predecessors and contemporaries—*Masaccio, *Donatello, Domenico Veneziano, Filippo *Lippi, *Uccello, and even *Masolino, who anticipated something of Piero's use of broad masses of colour. Piero unified, completed, and refined upon the discoveries these artists had made in the previous 20 years and created a style in which monumental, meditative grandeur and almost mathematical lucidity are combined with limpid beauty of colour and light. His major work is a series of *frescos on the *Legend of the True Cross* in the choir of S. Francesco at Arezzo (c.1452–c.1465). The subject was a medieval legend of great complexity, but Piero made from its fanciful details some of the most solemn and serene images in western art—even the two battle scenes have a feeling of grim deliberation rather than violent movement. He was a slow and thoughtful worker and often applied wet cloths to the plaster at night so that—contrary to normal fresco practice—he could work for more than one day on the same section.

Much of Piero's later career was spent working at the humanist court of Federico da *Montefeltro at Urbino. There he painted the portraits of Federico and his wife (Uffizi, Florence, c.1465) and the celebrated *Flagellation* (still at Urbino, in the Ducal Palace). The *Flagellation* is his most enigmatic work, and it has called forth varied interpretations; *Gombrich has suggested that the subject is rather *The Repentance of Judas* and *Pope-Hennessy that it is *The Dream of St Jerome*. Piero is last mentioned as a painter in 1478 (in connection with a lost work) and his two final works are probably *The Madonna and Child with Federigo da Montefeltro* (Brera, Milan, *c.*1475) and the unfinished *Nativity* (NG, London). Thereafter he seems to have devoted himself to mathematics and *perspective, writing treatises on both subjects. *Vasari said Piero was blind when he died, and failing eyesight may have been his reason for giving up painting, but his will of 1487 declares him to be 'sound in mind, in intellect and in body' and is written in his own clear hand. After his death, Piero was remembered mainly as a mathematician rather than as a painter. Even Vasari, who as a native of Arezzo must have known the frescos in S. Francesco well, is lukewarm in his enthusiasm for his work. However, he had considerable influence, notably on *Signorelli (in the weighty solemnity of his figures) and *Perugino (in the spatial clarity of his compositions). Both are said to have been Piero's pupils.

Piero di Cosimo (*c.*1462–1521?). Florentine painter, a pupil of Cosimo *Rosselli, whose Christian name he adopted as a patronym. There are no signed, documented, or dated works by him, and reconstruction of his *œuvre* depends on the account given in *Vasari's *Lives*. It is one of Vasari's most entertaining biographies, for he portrays Piero as a highly eccentric character who lived on hard-boiled eggs, 'which he cooked while he was boiling his glue, to save the firing'. The paintings for which he is best known are appropriately idiosyncratic—fanciful mythological inventions, inhabited by fauns, centaurs, and primitive men. There is sometimes a spirit of low comedy about these delightful works, but in the so-called *Death of Procris* (NG, London) he created a poignant scene of the utmost pathos and tenderness. He was a marvellous painter of animals and the dog in this picture, depicted with a mournful dignity, is one of his most memorable creations. Piero also painted portraits, the finest of which is that of

Simonetta Vespucci (Musée Condé, Chantilly) in which she is depicted as Cleopatra with the asp around her neck. His religious works are somewhat more conventional, although still distinctive, and Frederick Hartt (*A History of Italian Renaissance Art*, 1970) has written that 'His whimsical Madonnas, Holy Families, and Adorations provide a welcome relief from the wholesale imitation of *Raphael in early Cinquecento Florence'. One of his outstanding religious works is the *Immaculate Conception* (Uffizi, Florence), which seems to have been the compositional model for the *Madonna of the Harpies* by his pupil *Andrea del Sarto.

Pietà. Term (Italian for 'pity') applied to a painting or sculpture showing the Virgin Mary supporting the body of the dead Christ on her lap. Other figures, such as St John the Evangelist or Mary Magdalene, may also be included. The theme, which has no literary source, originated in the early 14th cent. in Germany (where it was called *Vesperbild*) and was more popular in northern Europe than in Italy. However, the most celebrated of all Pietàs is that by *Michelangelo in St Peter's, Rome; and one of the most sublime is that painted by *Titian for his own tomb (Accademia, Venice). The subject is not always clearly distinguished from the scene known as the Lamentation. However, whereas the Lamentation represents a specific moment from Christ's Passion, between the Descent from the Cross and the Entombment, the Pietà is a timeless devotional image.

Pigalle, Jean-Baptiste (1714–85). French sculptor. He studied under J.-B. *Lemoyne and then in Rome (1736–9). In his early career he endured poverty and sickness (his studies in Rome were made at his own expense and he walked there from Paris), but after he was received into the Académie Royale in 1744 with his rapturously acclaimed *Mercury* (Louvre, Paris; *terracotta model in the Met. Mus., New York), he rapidly went on to become the most successful French sculptor of his period. He was a superb craftsman and highly versatile and inventive, equally adept at small *genre pieces and the most grandiloquent tomb sculpture. As a portraitist he was noted for his warmth and vivacity. His most famous works are the startling nude figure of Voltaire (Institut de France, Paris, 1770–6) and the spectacular and majestic tomb of Maurice of Saxony (designed 1753) in St Thomas, Strasburg.

pigment. Any substance used as a colouring agent, particularly the finely ground particles that when held in suspension in a *medium constitute a paint. Most pigments are now manufactured synthetically, but historically they have been made from a great variety of mineral, plant, and animal sources: the brown colour *sepia, for example, comes from the inky secretions of the cuttlefish, and ultramarine blue was originally made from the semi-precious stone lapis lazuli. The history of pigments is a highly specialized field with little practical importance today for artists who use commercial paints, but it is often vitally important to the expert in relation to authentication and attribution.

Pillement, Jean-Baptiste (1728–1808). French painter and designer. As a painter he is best known for his charming landscapes, which are strongly indebted to *Boucher but more atmospheric. His importance, however, lies more in the engravings made after his drawings, which were popular throughout Europe and of influence in spreading the *Rococo style, particularly the taste for *chinoiserie. Pillement himself was well travelled, visiting Austria, England, Poland, Portugal, and Spain.

Pilon, Germain (c.1525–90). The most powerful and original French sculptor of the 16th cent. He was born in Paris, the son of a sculptor, **André Pilon**, and spent most of his career there. His first known work is the group of *Three Graces* on the monument for the heart of Henry II (Louvre, Paris, 1561–2), which shows that his early manner was based on the elegant decorative style of the École de *Fontainebleau, in particular *Primaticcio's *stucco-work. Although his work never lost its tendency towards graceful *Mannerist elongation, it developed in the direction of greater naturalism and emotional intensity. These qualities are seen most memorably in his marble *gisants on the tomb of Henry II and Catherine de Médicis at St Denis (1563–70), poignant works in which the semi-nude figures are shown relaxed in death. The kneeling effigies on the tomb are of bronze and Pilon excelled in this medium as well as marble, both as

a portrait sculptor (*Charles IX*, Wallace Coll., London) and a medallist—he was appointed Controller General of the Paris Mint in 1572. Pilon's early work was influential on his successors, but the deeply felt emotion of his later style proved too personal to inspire imitation. Several examples of his sublime late work are in the Louvre, notably the tomb of Valentine Balbiani (before 1583).

Piloty, Karl von (1826–86). German painter. After training in Antwerp and Paris, Piloty settled in Munich, where in 1856 he became a professor at the Academy and in 1874 its Director. He was highly successful with large, opulent history paintings in which the settings, furnishings, and costumes were reconstructed with great accuracy. They gave the public the same kind of feast for the eye as Hollywood epics and now have a distinctly hollow ring. Piloty's influence was felt by many of his pupils.

Pintoricchio (or **Pinturicchio**) (Bernardino di Betto) (c.1454–1513). Italian painter, born in Perugia. He was probably a pupil of *Perugino and it is likely that he assisted him with his frescos in the Sistine Chapel, Rome (1481/2). His style was strongly influenced by Perugino, especially in his sweet, elegant figure types, but Pintoricchio lacked Perugino's lucidity of design and was more interested in decorative effects. His chief works are frescos in the Borgia rooms in the Vatican (1492/5) and the colourful *Scenes from the Life of Aeneas Sylvius Piccolomini* (i.e. Pope Pius II) in the Piccolomini Library of Siena Cathedral (1503). In these he showed the brilliant colours, ornamental detail, and fanciful charm that make him at his best, in the words of Frederick Hartt (*A History of Italian Renaissance Art*, 1970), 'one of the most endearing masters of the *Quattrocento . . . a kind of Perugian Benozzo *Gozzoli'. Pintoricchio was a prolific painter of panels as well as frescos—there are several examples of his work in the National Gallery, London.

Piper, John (1903–). English painter, graphic artist, designer, and writer. After beginning a law career he took up the study of art in 1926 at the Richmond School of Art and then at the *Royal College, where Henry *Moore was a teacher. From 1928 to 1933 he wrote as an art critic for the *Listener* and the *Nation* and was among the first to recognize such contemporaries as William *Coldstream, Ivon *Hitchens, Victor *Pasmore, and Ceri *Richards. By the mid 1930s he was one of the leading British abstract artists, but by the end of the decade he had become disillusioned with non-representational art and reverted to naturalism. He concentrated on landscape and architectural views in a subjective emotionally charged style that continued the English *Romantic tradition. Some of his most memorable works were done as a war artist when he made pictures of bomb-damaged buildings. A similar stormy atmosphere pervades his famous views of country houses of the same period. Piper's work diversified in the 1950s and he became recognized as one of the most versatile British artists of his generation. He has done much work as a stage designer and designer of stained glass and has been a prolific printmaker. In addition he has made book illustrations and designed pottery and textiles. As a writer he is probably best known for his book *British Romantic Artists* (1942).

Piranesi, Giovanni Battista (1720–78). Italian etcher, archaeologist, and architect, born in Venice but active for almost all his career in Rome, where he settled in 1740. In Venice he had studied perspective and stage design and in Rome he achieved great popularity with his dramatically conceived etchings of the ancient and modern city—the *Vedute*—published from 1745 onwards. He often altered the scale of buildings to make them look even grander than they are in actuality (Horace *Walpole said he 'conceived visions of Rome beyond what it boasted even in the meridian of its splendour') and his work played a major role in shaping the popular mental image of the city. Piranesi produced numerous other plates of Roman antiquities and architectural details, but his most original works are a series of *Carceri d'Invenzione*, fantastic imaginary prisons, begun c.1745 and reworked in 1761. These striking and obsessive works were later claimed by the *Surrealists as an anticipation of their principles and their influence can be seen in 20th-cent. horror movies. Only one of Piranesi's architectural designs was built (Sta Maria del Priorato, Rome, 1764–6), but he was important as an architectural

polemicist, most notably in his *Della magnificenza ed architettura de' Romani* (1761), in which he championed the superiority of Roman architecture over Greek. Piranesi's influence was felt not only by architects, but also by stage designers and painters of *capricci* such as his friend Hubert *Robert, and perhaps most of all on the literary imagination. William *Beckford, for example, said that in writing his Gothic novel *Vathek* (1786) 'I drew chasms, and subterranean hollows, the domain of fear and torture, with chains, racks, wheels and dreadful engines in the style of Piranesi.' His etchings continued to be published for many years after his death and his work was continued by his son **Francesco** (1758–1810).

Pisanello (Antonio Pisano) (c.1395–1455?). Italian painter and medallist. He presumably came from Pisa (hence his nickname), but he spent his early years in Verona, a city with which he kept up his association for most of his life. His successful career also took him to the Vatican and numerous courts of northern Italy. With *Gentile da Fabriano, Pisanello is regarded as the foremost exponent of the *International Gothic style in Italian painting, but most of his major works have perished, including frescos in Venice in which he collaborated with Gentile, and in Rome in which he completed work left unfinished by Gentile at his death. His surviving documented frescos are *The Annunciation* (S. Fermo, Verona, 1423–4) and *St George and the Princess of Trebizond* (Sta Anastasia, Verona, 1437–8), and attributed to him are some fragments of murals of jousting knights in the Palazzo Ducale in Mantua, uncovered in 1968 and one of the most spectacular art discoveries of recent years. A very small number of panel paintings is also given to him, two being in the National Gallery, London. On the other hand, a good many of his drawings survive, those of animals being particularly memorable. They show his keen eye for detail and his ability to convey an animal's personality. Pisanello was also the greatest portrait medallist of his period and arguably of the whole *Renaissance, his work setting standards of delicacy, precision, and clarity that have not been surpassed.

Pisano, Andrea (c.1290–1348/9?). Italian sculptor and architect, not related to Nicola and Giovanni *Pisano. He probably came from Pontedera near Pisa (he is sometimes called Andrea de Pontedera), but he is first documented in Florence in 1330, when he received the commission to make a pair of bronze doors for the Baptistery. The doors, finished in 1336, are the first of the three great sets for the Baptistery (the other two are by *Ghiberti), and represent twenty scenes from the life of St John the Baptist and eight Virtues. They show a melodious line and a jeweller's refinement of execution. By 1340 Andrea was architect to Florence Cathedral (succeeding *Giotto) and the only other works certainly by him or from his workshop are *reliefs and statues for the cathedral's campanile. In their clear-cut designs the reliefs show the influence of Giotto's painting. In 1347 Andrea was appointed master of works at Orvieto Cathedral, where he was succeeded by his son **Nino** (d. 1368) in 1349. Nino is known from documents to have been active as goldsmith and architect, but all his surviving works are sculptures in marble. He was much less distinguished as an artist than his father, but noteworthy in being one of the first sculptors to specialize in free-standing life-size statues.

Pisano, Nicola (d. 1278/84) and **Giovanni** (d. after 1314). Italian sculptors and architects, father and son. They were the greatest sculptors of their period and stand at the head of the tradition of Italian sculpture in the same way that *Giotto stands at the head of the tradition of Italian painting. They often worked together, but their styles are distinctive. Nicola came from Apulia, where the emperor Frederick II (d. 1250) had encouraged a *Classical revival, and his first known work, the pulpit in the Baptistery at Pisa (dated 1260 Pisan style, i.e. 1259) shows his brilliant adaptation of *antique forms to a new context. He transformed a Dionysus into Simeon at the Presentation of Christ, a nude Hercules into a personification of Christian Fortitude, and a Phaedra into the Virgin Mary. But instead of following the *Romanesque convention of separating episodes into compartments arranged in bands, he combined them into the formal unity of single pictures on each side of the pulpit with great power and dramatic effect. Several of the figures were directly inspired by ancient sarcophagi that Nicola saw in the Campo Santo in Pisa, but they

are much more than simple borrowings, for he made them the vehicle for expressing richly varied human feeling. Nicola followed the Pisa pulpit with a similar but more complex work for Siena Cathedral (1265–8). The carving is deeper, the contrasts between light and shadow sharpened, the *reliefs more densely packed and full of movement. By then Nicola had a large workshop, his assistants including his son Giovanni and *Arnolfo di Cambio. His last great project was the large fountain in the public square of Perugia, which he and Giovanni finished in 1278. The dozens of reliefs are a typical medieval mixture: biblical scenes, heraldic beasts, personifications of seasons and places, and local dignitaries; but the vigour and spontaneity of the carving express a new freedom and naturalness.

By 1284 Nicola was dead. Between the Perugia fountain and this date, Giovanni, alone or in company with his father, had carved the sculpture for the outside of the Pisa Baptistery (now in the Museo Nazionale). Here for the first time in Tuscany a scheme of monumental statuary was incorporated into architecture. Giovanni developed this much further in Siena, where from 1284 onwards he designed the façade of the cathedral and carried out much of the sculptural decoration (some of the figures have been transferred to the cathedral museum and a magnificent fragment is in the Victoria and Albert Museum). It is the most richly decorated of all the great Italian *Gothic cathedral façades, and the statuary has tremendous energy and inner life. Giovanni's last two great works were pulpits for S. Andrea, Pistoia (1300–1), and Pisa Cathedral (1302–10). They are modelled on those of his father, but more elegant in style (showing French Gothic influence) and also more emotionally charged. The Pisa pulpit was damaged in a fire in 1599, then dismantled and reassembled, some parts being dispersed; several museums, including the Metropolitan Museum, New York, have fragments that are said to come from it. Giovanni also made a number of free-standing statues, the best known of which is the *Madonna and Child* on the altar of the Arena Chapel in Padua (c.1305). Its grandeur and humanity suggests a close kinship with Giotto, amid whose celebrated frescos it stands.

Pissarro, Camille (1830–1903). French painter and graphic artist. He was born in the West Indies of a Jewish father and a Creole mother, and in 1855 moved to Paris, where he was initially strongly influenced by *Corot. In 1859 he met *Monet, and with him became a central figure of the *Impressionist group. Pissarro in fact was the only artist who exhibited at all eight Impressionist exhibitions and was a much-respected father figure to other members of the group. His talents as a teacher made him influential even among artists of greater stature than himself *Cézanne and *Gauguin, for example, spoke glowingly of him. During the Franco-Prussian War of 1870–1, when his home at Louveciennes was overrun by the invaders and his paintings destroyed, he joined Monet in England and came under the influence of the English landscape school, particularly *Turner and *Constable. In 1872 he settled at Pontoise, where he had lived 1866–9, and for some years painted there in close friendship with Cézanne, who had settled at Auvers-sur-Oise. From 1884 he lived at Eragny, near Gisors, and there met *Signac and came to know *Seurat. For some years during the 1880s he flirted with the *pointillist technique and the optical methods of the *Neo-Impressionists under Seurat's influence, but later reverted to his earlier style. From about 1895 deterioration of his eyesight caused him to give up painting out of doors and many of his late works are town views painted from windows in Paris. He died blind. Pissarro was extremely prolific not only as a painter but also in various graphic techniques.

Lucien Pissarro (1863–1944), eldest son of Camille, was taught by his father and other leading members or associates of the Impressionist group. He exhibited in the final Impressionist exhibition (1886) and with Seurat in the Second *Salon des Indépendants, adopting the pointillist technique for a time. In 1890 he settled in England, where he became an associate of *Sickert and *Shannon. As a member of the *Camden Town Group and afterwards of the *London Group, he helped to diffuse an understanding of Impressionism and *Post-Impressionism in England.

Pitti Palace, Florence. Art gallery, originally built as a palace for Luca Pitti, a wealthy rival of the *Medici. It was probably begun in the 1450s, so the traditional attribution of its design to *Brunelleschi (who died in 1446) is unlikely; it has also been attributed to *Alberti. It remained unfinished until it was acquired in 1549 by Duke Cosimo I, who made it the Medici residence and had it enlarged by *Ammanati. Most of the present vast structure dates from the 16th and 17th cents. The interior includes opulent decoration by Pietro da *Cortona. The Pitti Gallery on the upper floor in the left wing contains about 500 masterpieces from the Medici collections which rival those of its sister institution, the *Uffizi. The State Apartments contain a profusion of art treasures including sculptures and tapestries, and on the ground floor is the Museo degli Argenti, which contains outstanding collections of plate, goldsmiths' work, ivories, *enamels, vestments, etc.

Pittoni, Giovanni Battista (1687–1767). Venetian painter of religious, historical, and mythological pictures. He was very popular in his day and ranks as one of the best contemporaries of *Tiepolo, whom he succeeded as President of the Venice Academy of Painting, 1758–61. Pittoni never left Italy, but he nevertheless received important foreign commissions from the Swedish, Austrian, and German courts. His early work was much indebted to *Piazzetta and Sebastiano *Ricci, but his style later became lighter and more colourful under the influence of Tiepolo.

Place, Francis (1647–1728). English gentleman artist, active mainly in York. He was a close friend of *Hollar, and his topographical and architectural drawings are near to his in style. His later drawings rely on a fuller use of *wash and are among the more important anticipations of English 18th-cent. water-colour style. Place also made portraits and was one of the pioneers of the *mezzotint technique. His work is best represented in the City Art Gallery, York.

Plamondon, Antoine (1804–95). Canadian painter of portraits, religious subjects, and figure compositions, active mainly in Quebec. He was the first Canadian to study in France after Quebec was ceded to Britain in 1763, training in Paris, 1826–30. His portraits, which are his best work, are painted in an austerely Classical style. Plamondon also executed numerous church commissions in Quebec.

plaquette. Small decorative *relief in metal, usually bronze or lead. They were almost always cast by the *cire-perdu* process and new editions could be made from the wax image of an existing plaquette; if this wax were altered a new 'state' would result. A very few were struck like coins. After casting, the best plaquettes were usually chiselled and chased, and finished with a *patina or gilding. Plaquettes were mounted as sword-hilts, ink-wells, or caskets, and applied as decoration to a variety of objects; small ones served as buttons. Plaquettes were easily transportable, and during the brief period in which they flourished (the end of the 14th to the middle of the 16th cent.) they were copied both in their country of origin and abroad, and not only in other minor arts but in important sculptural works as well. Like the engravings of which they are the plastic counterpart, they helped to disseminate the taste of the Renaissance. *Flötner's plaquettes, for example, helped to make his designs common property among German artists. *Donatello is the greatest name connected with the art, but most are of unknown authorship.

plaster of Paris. A fine white or pinkish powder, made by the calcination or dehydration of gypsum (see ALABASTER), which when mixed with water forms a quick-setting paste that dries to form a uniform, solid, and inert mass. It is used in sculpture for making moulds and casts.

plein air (French: open air). Term used for a painting done in the open air rather than in the studio, or more generally for a picture that gives a strong feeling of the open air. Although there are earlier instances, painting out of doors did not become common until the 19th cent., when the development of portable equipment made it much easier in practical terms. It became a central feature of *Impressionism and is especially associated with *Monet.

Pleydenwurff, Hans (d. 1472). German painter. He was active in Nuremberg and his work is typical of the kind of painting produced there by the generation before *Wolgemut (who married Pleydenwurff's

widow). The springs of *International Gothic were drying up and a new naturalism was beginning to come in from the Netherlands. A large *Crucifixion* (Alte Pinakothek, Munich) is characteristic of his work. Pleydenwurff's son **Wilhelm** (d. 1494) was a painter and engraver, also active in Nuremberg.

Pliny the Elder (Gaius Plinius Secundus) (AD 23 or 24–79). Roman encyclopaedist. As a side-line to his career in public office, Pliny produced (among many other things) the *Historia Naturalis* (Natural History), a massive compilation in thirty-seven books intended to embrace not only the whole of the natural sciences but also their application to the arts and crafts of civilized life. His only extant work, it has been condemned as uncritical, unreliable, and superficial, but it contains much information that would otherwise have been completely lost. The chapters on the history of painting and sculpture are especially interesting because earlier treatises on Classical art have perished. It is typical of Pliny's thirst for knowledge that he perished through asphyxiation when making observations of the eruption of Vesuvius that destroyed Pompeii and Herculaneum.

pochade. See BONINGTON.

Poelenburgh, Cornelis van (1594/5–1667). Dutch painter, mainly of landscapes. He studied in his native Utrecht with *Bloemaert and from about 1617 to 1625 was in Rome, becoming one of the leading members of the first generation of Dutch painters of Italianate landscapes. His paintings are typically small scale (he often painted on copper) with biblical or mythological figures set in Arcadian landscapes, sometimes scattered with antique remains. They are strongly influenced by *Elsheimer, but cooler in colour than the German artist's work and without his sense of mystery. After returning to Utrecht he enjoyed a career of great success. He was *Rubens's guide when he visited Utrecht in 1627, was popular in aristocratic and even royal circles (Charles I called him to England in 1637), and was imitated until the early 18th cent. There are examples of Poelenburgh's work (and by imitators) in the Fitzwilliam Museum, Cambridge, including a portrait of Jan *Both, in whose landscapes he sometimes painted the figures (an example of their collaboration is in the National Gallery, London).

pointillism. Technique of using regular small touches of pure colour in such a way that when a picture is viewed from a suitable distance they seem to react together optically, creating more vibrant colour effects than if the same colours were physically mixed together. The term ('peinture au point') was coined in 1886 by the French critic Félix Fénéon in reference to *Seurat's *La Grande Jatte*, but Seurat, and also *Signac, preferred the word *'divisionism'.

pointing. A method of creating an exact copy of a statue or of enlarging a model into a full-size sculpture by taking a series of measured points on the original and transferring them by means of mechanical aids to the copy or enlargement. An elementary method of pointing using callipers was developed in the 1st cent. BC, when the copying of Greek statues for Roman patrons had become an industry, and various more sophisticated techniques, using for example a frame and plumb-line, have been used since the *Renaissance. It was not until the early 19th cent., however, that the task was rationalized by the perfection of a pointing machine. This device consists of an upright stand carrying movable arms, each arm having attached to it an adjustable measuring rod which shows the depth to which each point must be drilled. Sometimes hundreds and even thousands of points will be taken. In the late 19th and early 20th cents. most stone sculpture was produced by this mechanical method, but modern sculptors increasingly reject it in favour of direct carving.

Poliakoff, Serge (1906–69). Russian-born painter who became a French citizen in 1962. He moved to Paris in 1923 and took up painting in 1930 (from 1935 to 1937 he studied in London, first at the Chelsea School of Art and then at the *Slade School), but it was not until 1952 that he was able to devote himself full time to painting and give up his career as a professional musician. By this time he had matured his style of abstract painting, begun in 1937 on his meeting with *Kandinsky, and his position was established as one of the most important painters in the French school of expressive abstraction. He adopted an almost religious attitude

towards painting, saying: 'You've got to have the feeling of God in the picture if you want to get the big music in.'

Polidoro da Caravaggio (Polidoro Caldara) (c.1500–43). Italian painter, named after his birthplace, Caravaggio in Lombardy. At an early age he moved to Rome, where he assisted *Raphael in the decoration of the Vatican Loggie and then achieved great success painting palace façades with monochrome scenes imitating *Classical sculpture. They have almost all perished (only the heavily restored decoration of the Palazzo Ricci remains *in situ*), but they became well known through engravings and drawings and were much imitated. Polidoro's other claim to fame is his decoration of the chapel of Fra Marino Fetti in S. Silvestro al Quirinale (1525) with two murals—oil not fresco—(one each from the life of St Mary Magdalene and St Catherine of Siena) in which he gave an entirely new prominence to the landscape, which dominates the figures. In this he foreshadowed the 'heroic landscape' of *Claude and *Poussin. Polidoro fled Rome after the sack of the city in 1527, moving to Naples and then Messina, where he was murdered.

Pollaiuolo, Antonio (c.1432–98) and **Piero** (c.1441–c.1496). Florentine artists, brothers, who jointly ran a flourishing workshop. They are both recorded as being painters, sculptors, and goldsmiths, but there are considerable problems in attempting to disentangle their individual contributions. Antonio was apparently primarily a goldsmith and worker in bronze, Piero primarily a painter. Several documented paintings by Piero are known, all of fairly mediocre quality, but none by Antonio, and as certain pictures from the studio of the two brothers are so much better than Piero's independent work, Antonio's collaboration, at least, has usually been assumed. The most important of these pictures is the *Martyrdom of St Sebastian* in the National Gallery, London, probably painted in 1475. The figures of the archers in the foreground reveal a mastery of the nude paralleled in certain bronzes generally accepted as Antonio's (e.g. the *Hercules and Antaeus* in the Bargello, Florence, c.1475–80), in his only surviving engraving (*The Battle of the Nude Men*, c.1460), and in his numerous pen drawings in which his typically wiry figures are seen in vigorous and expressive movement. His main contribution to Florentine painting lay in his searching analysis of the anatomy of the body in movement or under conditions of strain, but he is also important for his pioneering interest in landscape, seen in the National Gallery *St Sebastian* and other works. He is said to have anticipated *Leonardo in dissecting corpses in order to study the anatomy of the body. Antonio's two principal public works were the bronze tombs of Pope Sixtus IV (signed and dated 1493) and Pope Innocent VIII (*c.*1492–8), both in St Peter's, Rome. The latter contains the first sepulchral effigy that simulated the living man.

Pollock, Jackson (1912–56). American painter, the commanding figure of the *Abstract Expressionist movement. He began to study painting in 1929 at the Art Students' League, New York, under the *Regionalist painter Thomas Hart *Benton. During the 1930s he worked in the manner of the Regionalists, being influenced also by the Mexican muralist painters (see OROZCO; RIVERA; SIQUEIROS) and by certain aspects of *Surrealism. From 1938 to 1942 he worked for the *Federal Art Project. By the mid 1940s he was painting in a completely abstract manner, and the 'drip and splash' style for which he is best known emerged with some abruptness in 1947. Instead of using the traditional easel he affixed his canvas to the floor or the wall and poured and dripped his paint from a can; instead of using brushes he manipulated it with 'sticks, trowels or knives' (to use his own words), sometimes obtaining a heavy *impasto by an admixture of 'sand, broken glass or other foreign matter'. This manner of *Action painting had in common with Surrealist theories of *automatism that it was supposed by artists and critics alike to result in a direct expression or revelation of the unconscious moods of the artist. Pollock's name is also associated with the introduction of the *All-over style of painting which avoids any points of emphasis or identifiable parts within the whole canvas and therefore abandons the traditional idea of composition in terms of relations among parts. The design of his painting had no relation to the shape or size of the canvas—indeed in the finished work the canvas was sometimes docked or

trimmed to suit the image. All these characteristics were important for the new American painting which matured in the late 1940s and early 1950s. During the 1950s Pollock continued to produce figurative or quasi-figurative black and white works and delicately modulated paintings in rich impasto as well as the paintings in the new all-over style. He was strongly supported by advanced critics, but was also subject to much abuse and sarcasm as the leader of a still little comprehended style (in 1956 *Time* magazine called him 'Jack the Dripper'). By the 1960s, however, he was generally recognized as the most important figure in the most important movement of this century in American painting, but a movement from which artists were already in reaction (see *Post-Painterly Abstraction). His unhappy personal life (he was an alcoholic) and his premature death in a car crash contributed to his legendary status. In 1944 Pollock married Lee Krasner (1911–84), who was an Abstract Expressionist painter of some distinction, although it was only after her husband's death that she received serious critical recognition.

polychrome. Term meaning 'painted in many colours' applied in art historical writing particularly to sculpture treated in this fashion. Until the *Renaissance the practice was extremely common, whether the colours were conventionalized, as in much ancient art, or more or less naturalistic, as became more common during the Middle Ages, but because of fading of the pigments the colouring is rarely obvious today. Spain has a particularly rich tradition of polychrome sculpture (see ENCARNADO).

Polyclitus (or **Polycletus**) **of Argos** (active *c.*450–*c.*420 BC). One of the most celebrated of Greek sculptors. No original works by him survive, but several are known through Roman copies. He is now best known for his *Doryphorus* (Spear Carrier), the best copy of which is in the Archaeological Museum in Naples. In this figure he is said to have embodied the system of mathematical proportions on which he wrote a book, and the statue—long regarded as a standard for ideal male beauty—is sometimes referred to as 'The Canon'. Copies also exist of a *Diadumenus* (a youth wreathing a band round his head) by Polyclitus and of an Amazon with which, according to *Pliny, he defeated *Phidias in a competition. In antiquity his greatest work was held to be the colossal *chryselephantine statue of Hera in her temple—the Heraeum—near Argos. It is now known only through descriptions and representations on coins, but ancient writers compared it favourably with Phidias' statue of Zeus at Olympia. Strabo said the Zeus was more magnificent but the Hera more beautiful in workmanship.

polyptych. A picture or other work of art, typically an altarpiece, consisting of four or more leaves or panels, usually hinged together. See also DIPTYCH, TRIPTYCH.

pompier, l'art. A term applied pejoratively to French academic art (more particularly pretentious *history painting) of the late 19th cent. It is said to derive from the habit of posing nude models wearing firemen's helmets to substitute for ancient helmets ('pompier' is French for 'fireman').

Pompon, François (1855–1923). French sculptor. He worked for fifteen years as an assistant of *Rodin and success came to him very late. His speciality was animal sculpture and he was considered the greatest exponent of the genre since *Barye.

Pont-Aven, School of. Term applied to painters associated with *Gauguin during his period at the town of Pont-Aven in Brittany, 1886–91, and inspired by his anti-naturalistic style. Émile *Bernard was among them, and he and Gauguin together developed *Synthetism.

Pontormo (Jacopo Carucci) (1494–1556). Italian painter, born in the Tuscan village of Pontormo, near Empoli, and active in and around Florence. According to *Vasari, he studied successively with *Leonardo da Vinci, *Albertinelli, *Piero di Cosimo, and *Andrea del Sarto, whose workshop he is said to have entered in 1512. Pontormo was precocious (he was praised by *Michelangelo whilst still a youth) and by the time he painted his *Joseph in Egypt* (NG, London) in about 1515 he had already created a distinctive style—full of restless movement and disconcertingly irrational effects of scale and space—that put him in the vanguard of

*Mannerism. The emotional tension apparent in this work reaches its peak in Pontormo's masterpiece, the altarpiece of the *Entombment* (c.1526–8) in the Capponi Chapel of Sta Felicità, Florence. Painted in extraordinarily vivid colours and featuring deeply poignant figures who seem lost in a trance of grief, this is one of the key works of Mannerism. Pontormo was primarily a religious painter, but he was also an outstanding portraitist (he was a major influence on his pupil and adopted son *Bronzino) and in 1520–1 for the *Medici villa at Poggio a Caiano he painted a memorable mythological work (*Vertumnus and Pomona* according to Vasari, but the identification is disputed) in which an apparently idyllic scene reveals a strong undercurrent of neurosis. In Pontormo's later work his style was enriched by the study of Michelangelo and *Dürer's prints, but this stage of his career is known mainly through his superb drawings (best represented in the Uffizi), as the great fresco scheme in S. Lorenzo, Florence, that occupied him from 1546 until his death was destroyed in the 18th cent. Pontormo's diary for part of 1554–6 remains, giving a day-to-day account of his progress. It tells us much of his neurotic character, melancholy and introspective, dismayed by the slightest illness.

Pop art. Term coined by the English critic Lawrence Alloway to describe a modern art movement based on the imagery of consumerism and popular culture; it flourished from the late 1950s to the early 1970s, chiefly in the USA and Britain. Comic books, advertisements, packaging, and images from television and the cinema were all part of the *iconography of the movement, and it was a feature of Pop art that it rejected any distinction between good and bad taste. In the USA Pop art was initially regarded as a reaction from *Abstract Expressionism because its exponents brought back figural imagery and made use of hard-edged, quasi-photographic techniques. Their most immediate inspiration was the work of Jasper *Johns and Robert *Rauschenberg, which opened a wide new range of subject-matter. While often using similar subjects, however, the Pop artists generally employed commercial techniques in preference to the painterly manner of Johns and Rauschenberg. Examples are Andy *Warhol's silkscreens of soup-tins, etc. and Roy *Lichtenstein's paintings of comic strips. Claes *Oldenburg, whose subjects include ice-cream cones and hamburgers, has been the major Pop art sculptor. In England, Pop art, in the hands of such exponents as Peter *Blake and Richard *Hamilton, has generally been less aggressive, expressing a more romantic view of the subject-matter, which can now strike a note of nostalgia. (The erotic sculptures of Allen *Jones, however, are completely different in feeling.) Hamilton defined Pop art as 'popular, transient, expendable, low-cost, mass-produced, young, witty, sexy, gimmicky, glamorous, and Big Business'. In spite of the tongue-in-cheek jokiness revealed in much Pop art, however, it also has a darker side, some of Warhol's repetitions of the same banal image, for example, creating a disturbing effect.

Pope-Hennessy, Sir John (1913–). English art historian. He was Director of the *Victoria and Albert Museum, 1967–73, Director of the *British Museum, 1974–6, and from 1977 to 1987 was Consultative Chairman, Department of European Paintings, *Metropolitan Museum, New York, and Professor of Fine Arts at New York University. His many publications have made him perhaps the doyen in the field of Italian Renaissance art among English writers. They include the magisterial *An Introduction to Italian Sculpture* in three parts (all of which have subsequently appeared in revised editions), *Italian Gothic Sculpture* (1955), *Italian Renaissance Sculpture* (1958), and *Italian High Renaissance and Baroque Sculpture* (1963), an edition of *Cellini's *Autobiography* (1949), and monographs on *Giovanni di Paolo (1937), *Sassetta (1939), *Uccello (1950, revised 1972), Fra *Angelico (1952, revised 1974), *Raphael (1970), Luca della *Robbia (1980), and Cellini (1985). In 1986 he received the Galileo Galilei Prize, awarded annually for contributions to Italian culture.

poppy oil. Oil extracted from poppy seeds, one of the most popular of the *drying oils used as a *medium for *oil painting. It is less viscous than *linseed and *walnut oil and does not easily turn rancid. It is, however, slow drying. This turned out to be an advantage rather than a disadvantage when the method of *alla prima* painting came into vogue about the middle of the 19th cent. and for a time during the second half of that century poppy oil was much used by commercial colourmen.

Porcellis (or **Percellis**), **Jan** (c.1584–1632). Flemish painter and etcher of marine subjects, active in Holland. He was regarded as the greatest marine painter of his day and his work marks the transition from the busy and brightly coloured seascapes of the early 17th cent., with their emphasis upon the representation of ships, to monochromatic paintings which are essentially studies of sea, sky, and atmospheric effects. His favourite theme was a modest fishing-boat making its way through a choppy sea near the shore. *Rembrandt and Jan van de *Cappelle collected his works. His son **Julius** (c.1609–45) was also a marine painter.

Pordenone (Giovanni Antonio de Sacchis) (c.1483?–1539). Italian painter, named after the town of his birth, Pordenone in the Friuli, and active in various parts of northern Italy. After working in a provincial style at the very start of his career (his master is unknown and *Vasari says he was self-taught), by the beginning of the second decade of the 16th cent. he had come close to the contemporary Venetian (specifically *Giorgionesque) manner of painting. In the second half of the decade, however, he was in central Italy, and his style changed under the impact particularly of *Michelangelo, acquiring great weight and solidity. Pordenone was influenced also by *Mantegna's illusionism and by German prints, and the style he forged from these diverse influences was highly distinctive and original. He always retained something of provincial uncouthness—at times vulgarity—but he was, in Vasari's words, 'very rich in invention . . . bold and resolute', and he excelled at dramatic spatial effects. These qualities are seen at their most forceful in his fresco of the *Crucifixion* (1520–1) in Cremona Cathedral; the densely packed, bizarrely expressive figures are seen as if on a stage through a painted proscenium arch and they lunge violently out into the spectator's space. From 1527 Pordenone was based in Venice and for a while was a serious rival to *Titian. His major works in Venice have been destroyed, however. Pordenone died in

Ferrara, where he had gone to design tapestries for Ercole II d'*Este.

Portinari, Cândido (1903–62). Brazilian painter of Italian descent. He is best known for his portrayals of Brazilian workers and peasants, but he dissociated himself from the revolutionary fervour of his Mexican contemporaries, and painted in a style that shows affinities with *Picasso's 'Classical' works of the 1920s (Portinari was in Paris 1928–31). In the 1940s his work acquired greater pathos and he also turned to biblical subjects. He acquired an international reputation and his major commissions included murals for the Library of Congress in Washington and for the United Nations Building in New York.

Posada, José Guadalupe (1851–1913). Mexican graphic artist. His enormous output was largely devoted to political and social issues, revealing, for example, the dreadful conditions in which the poor lived. From 1890 he made his studio in Mexico City an open shop fronting the street, and turned out sensational broadsheets and cheap cartoons which spread among the illiterate throughout the country. His work had the vigour and spontaneous strength of genuinely popular art with the inborn Mexican taste for the more gruesome aspects of death—one of his recurring motifs is the *calavera* or animated skeleton. He made a lasting impression on *Orozco and *Rivera.

Post, Frans (c.1612–80). Dutch landscape painter, born in Leiden and active mainly in Haarlem. In 1637–44 he was a member of the Dutch West India Company's voyage of colonization to Brazil and became the first European to paint landscapes in the New World. He observed the unfamiliar flora and fauna with an appropriate freshness, creating scenes of remarkable vividness and charm, and he continued to paint Brazilian landscapes after his return to the Netherlands (indeed he is not known to have painted any other type of picture). Because of his *'naïve' style, he has been called the Douanier *Rousseau of the 17th cent., and he was virtually forgotten or regarded as a curiosity until the 20th cent. Examples of his fairly rare work are in the Louvre, the National Gallery of Ireland, and Ham House, London. His brother

Pieter (1608–69) was one of the outstanding Dutch architects of the 17th cent. (the Huis ten Bosch near The Hague is his most famous work) and also occasionally painted.

Post-Impressionism. Term applied to various trends in painting, particularly in France, that developed from *Impressionism or in reaction against it in the period c.1880–c.1905. Roger *Fry coined the term as the title of an exhibition, *Manet and the Post-Impressionists*, held at the Grafton Galleries, London, in 1910–11. The exhibition was dominated by the work of *Cézanne, *Gauguin, and van *Gogh, who are considered the central figures of Post-Impressionism. The ways in which Post-Impressionist artists rejected the naturalism and preoccupation with momentary effects of Impressionism varied greatly: Georges *Seurat and the *Neo-Impressionists, for example, concentrated on a more scientific analysis of colour; Cézanne, who wished 'to make of Impressionism something solid and durable, like the art of the museums', was concerned with pictorial structure; Gauguin renounced 'the abominable error of naturalism' to explore the symbolic use of colour and line; and van Gogh was the fountainhead of *Expressionism.

Post-Painterly Abstraction. Term introduced in 1964 by the American critic Clement Greenberg to cover a generation of artists who, despite a wide variety of individual styles, represented a breakaway from *Abstract Expressionism without reverting to figural painting. Among the most prominent representatives of this new trend, which began about the mid 1950s, were Morris *Louis, Kenneth *Noland, Frank *Stella, Ellsworth *Kelly, Al *Held, and Jules *Olitski. They had in common the repudiation of 'painterly' qualities such as the expressive brush-stroke, and for the spontaneous and impulsive method of *Action painting they substituted coolly planned and clearly defined areas of unmodulated colour.

Potter, Paulus (1625–54). Dutch painter and etcher of animals in landscapes, active in Delft, The Hague, and Amsterdam. His best-known work, the life-size *Young Bull* (Mauritshuis, The Hague, 1647), was in the 19th cent. one of the most famous paintings in Dutch art. Subsequent taste has found its detailed and precise manner a trifle dry and laboured and preferred his smaller, more typical work. His speciality was scenes of cattle and sheep in sunlit meadows.

pouncing. A method of transferring a drawing or design to another surface (typically a *cartoon to a wall for *fresco painting) by dabbing pounce (a fine powder of charcoal or similar substance) through a series of pinpricks in the outlines of the drawing, thus creating a 'join up the dots' replica of it on the surface below.

Pourbus. Family of Netherlandish painters, distinguished mainly as portraitists. **Pieter** (c.1523–84) was born in Gouda and settled c.1543 in Bruges, where he became the pupil and son-in-law of Lancelot *Blondeel. He was a civil engineer, surveyor, and cartographer as well as painter. Van *Mander wrote 'I have never seen a better equipped studio than his.' As well as portraits he painted religious and allegorical scenes, one of the most splendid of which is the *Love Feast* (Wallace Coll., London). Pieter's son, **Frans the Elder** (1545–81), was active in Antwerp and one of the chief pupils and a close follower of Frans *Floris. The most famous member of the family is his son **Frans the Younger** (1569–1622), who was one of the principal court portraitists of Europe. He first worked for the court at Brussels, and from 1600 to 1609 was employed in Mantua (at the same time as *Rubens) by Vincenzo I *Gonzaga. In 1609 he was called to Paris by Marie de *Médicis and worked as her court painter until his death. His style—more concerned with the meticulous reproduction of rich costumes and jewellery than with interpretation of character—was typical of international court portraiture of the day.

Poussin, Gaspard. See DUGHET.

Poussin, Nicolas (1593/4–1665). French painter, active mainly in Rome. He is regarded not only as the greatest French painter of the 17th cent., but also as the mainspring of the *Classical tradition in French painting. His interest in painting was aroused by the visit to his home town, Les Andelys, in 1611 of Quentin Varin (c.1570–1634), a mediocre late *Mannerist painter, and in 1612 he settled in Paris,

where his early years are obscure. Between commissions of various kinds—the most notable being for work for the Luxembourg palace, with Philippe de *Champaigne (c.1621)—Poussin made two unsuccessful attempts to go to Rome. He was also commissioned by the Italian poet Marino to make drawings to illustrate Ovid's *Metamorphoses* (Royal Library, Windsor, c.1623), and these are the first surviving works certainly by him. In 1623 he once more set out for Rome; travelling via Venice, he arrived early in 1624. Through Marino he came to the notice of Cardinal Francesco *Barberini and his secretary Cassiano dal Pozzo, who became his patrons. He worked for a time in the studio of *Domenichino and under the influence of Cassiano, who had a keen interest in antiquity, he studied Roman sculpture. With the predominance of these interests his manner began to shed earlier Mannerist influences and to evidence a Classical bent and a quality of restraint. He was never at home with the *Baroque style that was coming to the fore in Rome, and the only public picture he painted in Rome, the altarpiece of *The Martyrdom of St Erasmus*, commissioned by Cardinal Barberini for St Peter's (Vatican Pinacoteca, 1628), was coolly received. His most personal work during this period is the *Inspiration of the Poet* (Louvre, Paris, c.1628), Classical in design but Venetian in rich colouring.

In 1629–30 Poussin was seriously ill and was nursed back to health by the family of Jacques Dughet, a French chef working in Rome, whose daughter he married. The illness coincided with a change of direction in his work. Abandoning the competition for public commissions and rivalry with the current Baroque, he gave himself up to his dominating passion for the *antique. Instead of religious subjects he painted themes from ancient mythology seen through the eyes of Ovid or Torquato Tasso, which he treated in a pastoral and poetic mood. Until about 1633 the influence of *Titian was paramount. During the latter part of the 1630s he turned to Old Testament and historical subjects which afforded scope for more elaborate pageantry (*The Worship of the Golden Calf*, NG, London, c.1635). In the paintings of these years the influence of Titian waned and he moved towards a more austere Classicism which echoed the later Raphael and *Giulio Romano. He was preoccupied with the depiction of emotion by the gestures, pose, and facial expression of his figures, and pondered a literary and psychological conception of painting which he elaborated in a letter sent to his friend Paul Fréart de Chantelou, a civil servant, with the picture *The Gathering of the Manna* (Louvre, 1639).

His reputation was very high by the end of the 1630s and in 1640 he reluctantly succumbed to strong pressure and returned to Paris. He was commissioned to superintend the decoration of the Grande Galerie of the *Louvre (work wholly alien to his temperament), to paint altarpieces, and to design frontispieces for the royal press. His visit was ruined by jealousy and intrigue, and in September 1642 he left again for Rome, remaining there for the rest of his life. The most important outcome of the visit for Poussin was that he had come into contact with the intellectual bourgeoisie of Paris, the public of Pierre Corneille and René Descartes, who patronized him for the remainder of his life. During the next decade he painted for such patrons the works that in his own day were considered to be his finest achievement and are still recognized as the purest exemplification of the Classical spirit. The emphasis is on clarity of conception, moral solemnity, and obedience to rule. Poussin made it his endeavour to achieve a rational unity of mood in each picture and developed a theory of *modes* (later taken up by the Académie) akin to the current theory of musical 'modes' supposed to be derived from antiquity. According to this theory the subject of the picture and the emotional situations depicted dictate the appropriate treatment, which can be worked out rationally and consistently according to principles expressible in language. His working procedure was as methodical as his theoretical approach, for he not only made numerous drawings but also employed wax models on a kind of miniature stage-set so he could study the composition and lighting with great deliberateness. The series of paintings on the *Seven Sacraments* (Earl of Ellesmere Coll., on loan to NG, Edinburgh, 1644–8), painted for Chantelou, show the solemnity and rational economy of his work at this time, and make a fascinating comparison with an earlier, more sensuous series on the same subjects, painted for Cassiano dal Pozzo in 1636–40 (five in collection of Duke of Rutland, Belvoir; one in NG, Washington; one destroyed).

During the second half of the 1640s Poussin displayed a new interest in landscape, applying to animate and inanimate nature the principles of quasi-mathematical lucidity and order he sought elsewhere. He achieved an impression of monumental simplicity and calm, exemplified in two great works of 1648 illustrating the story of Phocion (Earl of Plymouth Coll., on loan to National Mus. of Wales; and Walker Art Gal., Liverpool). Together with the work of his friend *Claude and his brother-in-law *Dughet, Poussin's paintings in the genre were the basis for *ideal landscape for the next two centuries. By 1650 Poussin had become something of a hermit, but he had achieved European fame and his position in the world of art was unique. Between 1653 and his death in 1665 his style underwent yet a further development. Psychological expression, even if rationally controlled, was underplayed and his compositions took on a timeless allegorical quality. A motionless solemnity took the place of action and gesture and his pictures became symbols of eternal truths instead of representations of historical events. In some of the works figures attain a superhuman grandeur (*The Holy Family*, Hermitage, Leningrad, *c*.1655), and in others nature takes on a new wildness and splendour, as in his last great works, *The Four Seasons* (Louvre, 1660–4). The cold rationalism of his earlier works was left behind, and a poetical, imaginative, almost mystical approach took its place.

Poussin's example was the basis of *Lebrun's academic doctrine and has been of enormous influence on the development of French art. In the later 17th cent. Poussin's name was used in the Académie to give support to those who believed in the superior importance of design in painting (Poussinistes) in opposition to that of *Rubens, who stood for the importance of colouring, and although the Rubensistes won the day, Poussin continued to be the inspiration of Classically minded artists right into the early 19th cent. In the *Romantic era his influence declined, but his spirit was revived again by *Cézanne, who declared that he wanted 'to do Poussin again, from Nature'.

Powers, Hiram (1805–73). American sculptor, active in Italy from 1837. He first achieved success with portrait busts, but his great international fame came with his marble statue *The Greek Slave* (Corcoran Gal., Washington, 1843), which caused a sensation at the Great Exhibition in London in 1851 and was for a time one of the most talked about and reproduced works of art of the 19th cent. The naked girl is bound in chains and the astonishing popularity of the statue (which now seems rather insipid) no doubt depended on the way in which its sentimentality licensed its eroticism.

Poynter, Sir Edward (1836–1919). English painter and administrator, son of the architect Ambrose Poynter. He formed his academic style in Italy (1853), where he met Frederic *Leighton and admired *Michelangelo above all other artists, and in Paris (1856–9), where he studied with *Gleyre. His reputation was made with the huge *Israel in Egypt* (Guildhall, London, 1867) and he became one of the most popular painters of the day with similar elaborate historical tableaux in which he displayed his great prowess as a draughtsman. In the latter part of his career, however, he confined himself to much smaller works, similar to *Alma-Tadema's Classical *genre scenes, as he devoted himself much more to administration; most notably he was first *Slade Professor of Fine Art at University College, London, 1871–5; Director of the National Gallery, 1894–1904; and President of the Royal Academy, 1896–1918.

Pozzo, Andrea (1642–1709). Italian painter and architect, one of the greatest exponents of the *Baroque style of *illusionist ceiling decoration. He became a lay brother in the Jesuit order in 1665 (he is sometimes given the courtesy title 'Padre Pozzo') and worked much for Jesuit churches, both as a painter and architect. His masterpiece is the huge ceiling fresco, *Allegory of the Missionary Work of the Jesuits* (1691–4), in S. Ignazio, Rome, perhaps the most stupendous feat of *quadratura ever painted. Pozzo worked in several other Italian cities apart from Rome, and from 1702 until his death he was in Vienna, where he decorated the Jesuit Church, the University Church, and the Liechtenstein Garden Palace. His influence was spread not only by his paintings, but also by his treatise *Perspectiva pictorum et architectorum* (2 vols., 1693 and 1700), which was soon translated into several European languages and also (by Jesuit missionaries) into Chinese. As an architect, he designed several churches and numerous altars, but his work in this field was unexciting compared with his paintings and engraved designs.

Prado, Madrid. Spain's national museum of art, founded in 1818 by Ferdinand VII and opened to the public in 1819. The building, one of the finest examples of Spanish *Neoclassical architecture, had been intended for a Museum of Natural Science but had never served that purpose. The major part of the collection derives from the royal collections made in the course of three centuries by the Habsburg and Bourbon kings of Spain, who were some of the most discriminating and lavish patrons in Europe. The museum is remarkable less for comprehensiveness than for unequalled representation in certain fields. Above all, it contains what is far and away the world's greatest collection of Spanish painting, El *Greco, *Velázquez, and *Goya, being supremely well represented. It is among the richest of all museums in works by Hieronymus *Bosch and *Titian, and has superb collections of *Tintoretto, *Veronese, *Rubens, and van *Dyck.

Praxiteles. Greek sculptor, active in the mid 4th cent. BC. His fame among Greek sculptors, to posterity as in his own time, is second only to that of *Phidias. Various works by him described by ancient authors are known through Roman copies, and a marble statue of *Hermes and the Infant Dionysus*, found at Olympia in 1877 in the position where it was described by *Pausanias (now in the Olympia Museum), is considered by many authorities to be from his own hand. If this is so, it can be claimed as the only surviving original by a Greek sculptor of the first rank. Certainly it has a delicacy in the modelling of forms and a subtlety of finish far removed from the workmanship seen in most Roman copies, and it shows the sensuous charm and gentle grace for which he was renowned. In antiquity his most famous work was the *Aphrodite of Cnidus*, known through several copies. This much imitated work was the first free-standing life-size female nude in Greek art and *Pliny described it as 'the finest statue not only by Praxiteles but in the whole world'. Praxiteles' influence was profound. The tenderness and intimacy of his work marked a move away from the remote idealization of the *Classical period, to an art more concerned with human emotion, and his graceful, sinuous poses, with the figure often shown leaning on a support, became part of the general currency of *Hellenistic sculptors. His preference for working in marble made the material popular again after it had long been eclipsed by bronze.

Precisionism. A movement in American painting, originating c.1915 and flourishing throughout the 1920s, in which urban and especially industrial subjects were depicted with a very smooth, and precise technique, creating clear, sharply defined, sometimes quasi-*Cubist forms. The terms 'Cubist-Realists', 'Immaculates', and 'Sterilists' are also applied to Precisionist painters. They were not a formal group, but they often exhibited together. *Demuth, *O'Keeffe, and *Sheeler were among the leading figures. In Precisionist painting the light is often brilliantly clear, and frequently forms are chosen for their geometric interest. Human presence is excluded and there is no social comment. Rather, the American industrial and technological scene is endowed with an air of epic grandeur. Precisionism was influential in both imagery and technique on American *Magic Realism and *Pop art.

Preda (or **Predis**), **Ambrogio da** (c.1455–after 1508). Milanese painter. He was appointed court painter to the *Sforza in 1482 and worked mainly as a portraitist, but he is chiefly remembered for his association, together with his elder half-brother **Evangelista da Preda** (d. after 1490), with *Leonardo da Vinci in the 1483 contract for *The Virgin of the Rocks* (NG, London). The wings of this altarpiece, depicting angels with musical instruments, are of much lower quality than the centre panel and are presumed to be by Ambrogio and/or Evangelista. The National Gallery also has two portraits by Ambrogio, showing his rather wooden imitation of Leonardo's style.

predella. A subsidiary picture forming an appendage to a larger one, especially a small painting or series of paintings beneath an *altarpiece.

Prendergast, Maurice (1859–1924). American painter. He was a member of the *Eight, but stood somewhat apart from the rest of the group. He was a Bostonian and spent much of his career travelling and painting abroad, and it was only in the last few years of his life that he lived in New York, the centre of the Eight's activities. The main thing he had in common with the other members was a desire to move American art away from academic stagnation, and his work is notable for its brilliant decorative colour. His paintings were often of people enjoying themselves in innocent pleasures (*Central Park in 1903*, Met. Mus., New York, 1903).

Pre-Raphaelite Brotherhood. The name adopted in 1848 by a group of young English artists who shared a dismay at what they considered the moribund state of British painting and hoped to recapture the sincerity and simplicity of early Italian art (i.e. before the time of *Raphael, whom they saw as the fountainhead of academism). The nucleus of the group was formed by three fellow students at the *Royal Academy—John Everett *Millais, William Holman *Hunt, and Dante Gabriel *Rossetti (to whom, son of an Italian ex-revolutionary, the sealing of the group into a secret Brotherhood was due). The other four original brethren were James *Collinson, the sculptor Thomas *Woolner, and the art critics W. M. Rossetti (1829–1919) and F. G. Stephens (1828–1907). Ford Madox *Brown was closely allied with them, though not at any time a member of the Brotherhood. The movement had a strong literary flavour from the start, and the members published a journal called *The Germ*.They chose religious or other morally uplifting themes and had a desire for fidelity to nature that they expressed through detailed observation of flora, etc., and the use of a clear, bright, sharp-focus technique. The kind of pictures they hated were academic 'machines' and trivial *genre scenes. The initials PRB were first used on Rossetti's picture *The Girlhood of Mary Virgin* (Tate, London), exhibited in 1849, and were adopted by the other members of the Brotherhood. When their meaning became known in 1850 the group was subjected to violent criticism and abuse. Charles Dickens led the attack in his periodical *Household Words*, calling Millais's *Christ in the House of His Parents* (Tate) 'mean, odious, revolting and repulsive'. He was outraged by the implied rejection of Raphael (still unquestioningly thought of by many critics as the greatest painter who ever lived), and he regarded the claim to go behind Raphael as an antiprogressive reversion to primitivism and ugliness. The fortunes of the Pre-Raphaelites improved after they were publicly defended by *Ruskin in 1851, and they attracted numerous followers, including *Deverell and *Hughes. By 1853, however, the group had virtually dissolved. Apart from their youthful revolutionary spirit (they were very young in 1848) and their romantic if uninformed medievalism, the prime movers had little in common as artists and they went their separate ways. Of the original members only Hunt remained true to PRB doctrines. Millais adopted a much looser style and went on to become the most popular and successful painter of the day. Curiously, however, it was Rossetti, the least committed to PRB ideals (he never cultivated painstaking detail), who continued the name. Although his later work, made up principally of languorous depictions of *femmes fatales*, is entirely different from his Pre-Raphaelite pictures, the name stuck to him and to his followers such as *Morris and *Burne-Jones. Thus in the popular imagination the term 'Pre-Raphaelite' conjures up pictures of medieval romance, and ironically a movement that began as a rebellion against artificiality and sentimentality is now itself identified with a kind of escapism. This second wave of pseudomedieval Pre-Raphaelitism began in the 1860s and was long-lived; a painter such as John Melhuish Strudwick (1849–1937) was still producing work in this vein well into the 20th cent.

Preti, Mattia (also called Il Cavaliere Calabrese) (1613–99). Italian *Baroque painter. He came from Taverna in Calabria (hence his nickname) and his prolific career took him to many different parts of Italy (and according to an early biographer to Spain and Flanders). His early work includes groups of musicians and cardplayers, strongly *Caravaggesque in style, but later he excelled mainly in frescos on religious subjects. In this field his main

model was *Lanfranco, whom he succeeded in the decoration of S. Andrea della Valle in Rome (1650–1). After the plague of 1656 carried off virtually a whole generation of artists in Naples, Preti worked with great success there, gaining many important commissions. They included a series of seven frescos commemorating the plague for the city gates; they no longer survive, but two *modelli* for them are in the Museo di Capodimonte in Naples and give some idea of how powerful the huge frescos must have been. In 1661 Preti moved to Malta, where he lived for the rest of his life. Several churches on the island, including the cathedral of Valletta, have decorations by him.

Primary Structures. Style of sculpture which came to prominence in the mid-1960s, characterized by a preference for drastically simplified geometrical structures and frequent use of industrially fabricated elements. Among the artists who worked in this style were Carl *Andre, Robert *Morris, and Tony *Smith. The movement was included within the scope of *Minimal art and indeed the term 'Primary Structures' was sometimes used as a synonym of 'Minimal art'.

Primaticcio, Francesco (1504/5–70). Italian painter, architect, and decorator, mainly active in France. He was born in Bologna and developed his all-round skills as *Giulio Romano's assistant in Mantua. In 1532 he was called to France by Francis I and worked with *Rosso at Fontainebleau. Together they provided the main impetus for the distinctive French type of *Mannerism known as the School of *Fontainebleau. Their respective shares in the creation of the new manner—particularly the highly influential combination of paintings with *stucco ornament—are uncertain. Rosso is often accorded primacy, but *Vasari said 'the first works in stucco that were done in France, and the first labours in fresco of any account, had their origin, it is said, in Primaticcio.' His elongated figure style also had wide influence in France. Primaticcio took over the direction of the work at Fontainbleau on Rosso's death in 1540 and in the 1540s he twice visited Rome to buy antiquities or have casts made for Francis. In his later years Primaticcio turned more to architecture and his work helped to introduce *Renaissance elements into France.

priming. A thin layer applied on top of the *ground to make it more suitable to receive paint. For example, if the ground is too absorbent the priming may make it less so, or the priming may supply a tint.

primitive. Term used with various meanings in the history and criticism of the arts. In its widest sense it is applied to art of societies outside the great Western and Oriental civilizations—thus Pre-Columbian American art is embraced by the term, even though much of it was produced by highly sophisticated peoples. By extension it has been applied to other fields of art that appear unsophisticated relative to some particular standard. Thus the term was once widely used of pre-*Renaissance European painting, particularly of the Italian and Netherlandish schools, but this usage (as in the expression 'the Flemish primitives') is now much less common and no longer has derogatory implications. The term 'primitive' is also used more or less as a synonym for *naïve.

print. A picture or design made (usually on paper) from an inked impression of an engraved metal plate, wooden block, etc. Prints are made by a great variety of processes, which fall into three main groups.

(a) *Relief Methods*. In these, the parts of the wood block or metal plate which are to print black are left in relief and the remainder is cut away. The principal methods are *woodcut, *wood engraving, and *linocut. To these may be added certain techniques such as *metal cut, *manière criblée, and *relief etching, in which metal plates are engraved and printed like woodcuts.

(b) *Intaglio Methods*. In intaglio printing the principle is the reverse of that which operates in the relief methods, for the surface of the plate does not print, the ink being held only in the engraved furrows. The techniques are: *line engraving, in which the design is engraved on the metal plate with a *burin; *drypoint, where the lines are drawn by scratching the plate with a strong steel needle; *etching, *soft-ground etching, and *aquatint, where the designs are bitten into the plate by means of acid. In addition there are the defunct,

or nearly defunct, reproductive processes of *mezzotint, *stipple, and *crayon manner. The various intaglio processes are frequently used in combination with one another on the same plate.

(c) *Surface or Planographic Methods*. These are *lithography and its variants. Lithographs are neither incised nor raised in relief, but are printed from a perfectly flat slab of limestone or from prepared metal plates. The process utilizes the antipathy of grease and water to separate those areas which receive and those areas which reject the printing ink.

The *stencil is related to printmaking, and two other processes which cannot be classified with the rest may be added, namely the *monotype, and the *glass print. The term print is also more loosely applied to reproductions of works of art made by photomechanical methods.

Prix de Rome. A scholarship, founded concurrently with the French *Academy in Rome (1666), that enabled prize-winning students at the Académie Royale de Peinture et de Sculpture in Paris to spend a period (usually 4 years) in Rome at the state's expense. Prizes for architecture began to be awarded regularly in 1723, and prizes for engravers and musicians were added in the 19th cent. The prizes were meant to perpetuate the academic tradition and during the 18th and 19th cents. winning the award was the traditional stepping stone to the highest honours for painters and sculptors. Many distinguished artists (as well as many nonentities) were Prix de Rome winners, notably *David, *Fragonard, and *Ingres among painters and *Clodion, *Girardon, and *Houdon among sculptors. The prizes are still awarded and the system has been adopted by other countries.

Procaccini, Giulio Cesare (1574–1625). Italian painter and sculptor, the most distinguished member of a family of artists. He was born in Bologna and worked mainly in Milan, where the family settled in about 1590, and also in Modena and Genoa. Initially he worked mainly as a sculptor, but after about 1600 he concentrated on painting and became one of the leading painters in Milan. His style was eclectic but often very powerful, combining something of the emotional tension of *Mannerism with the dynamism and sense of physical presence of the *Baroque. His colours tend to be acidic, his handling of light and shade dramatic. Many of his paintings are still in Milan, but two large scenes from Christ's Passion (perhaps part of a series) are in Edinburgh (NG) and Sheffield (Graves Art Gal.). His father, **Ercole** (1515–95), and his brothers, **Camillo** (*c*.1560–1629) and **Carlo Antonio** (1555–1605), were also painters.

Prout, Samuel (1783–1852). English painter best known for his water-colour views of picturesque buildings and streets in Normandy, many of which appeared as engravings in illustrated books. He was an important popularizer of picturesque landscape and helped to build up the English *Romantic image of the Continent. His work was greatly admired by *Ruskin.

provenance. The record of the ownership of a work of art. A complete provenance accounts for the whereabouts of a work from leaving the artist's studio to the present day, and the nearer a work's pedigree approaches this ideal, the more secure its attribution is likely to be.

Provost, Jan (*c*.1465–1529). Netherlandish painter. He was born at Mons and worked in Valenciennes and briefly in Antwerp before settling in Bruges in 1494. His style was fairly close to Gerard *David, then the leading painter in Bruges, but Provost, although clumsier, was more inventive. In 1521 Provost met and entertained *Dürer, who is reputed to have drawn his portrait.

Prud'hon, Pierre-Paul (1758–1823). French portrait and historical painter. He was trained at the Dijon Academy and in 1784 went to Rome, where he was a friend of *Canova and formed his style on the example of the *sfumato and sensuous charm of *Leonardo and *Correggio. In 1787 he returned to Paris and after working in obscurity for some time he became a favourite of both empresses of the French, Josephine and Marie-Louise, designing the decorations for the bridal suite of the latter. His friendship with the statesman Talleyrand enabled him to remain in favour even after the fall of Napoleon in 1815, but he painted little in his final years. He had a neurotic personality and the shock of the suicide of his mistress—his pupil

Constance Mayer—in 1821 led to his own death. Prud'hon belongs both to the 18th and to the 19th cents. In his elegance, his grace, and his exquisite fancy he is akin to the epoch of Louis XVI, and David referred to him slightingly as 'the *Boucher of his time'. But his deep personal feeling aligns him with the *Romantics. *Gros said of him: 'He will bestride the two centuries with his seven league boots.' Among his best-known pictures are *Justice and Divine Vengeance pursuing Crime* (Louvre, 1808), for which he received the Legion of Honour, and *Venus and Adonis* (Wallace Coll., London, commissioned 1810, but still in Prud'hon's studio at his death). Prud'hon was an outstanding draughtsman, but many of his paintings are in poor condition because of his use of *bitumen.

Pryde, James (1866–1941). English painter and designer, best known for his collaboration in designing posters with his brother-in-law Sir William *Nicholson, under the name the Beggarstaff Brothers. His best paintings are dramatic and sinister architectural views, with figures dwarfed by their gloomy surroundings. They have something of the spirit of *Piranesi's prison etchings, but are broadly handled (*The Slum*, Ashmolean, Oxford).

psalter. A manuscript (particularly one for liturgical use) or a printed book containing the text of the Psalms. The great popularity and copious illustration of the psalter make it the most important *illuminated book from the 11th to the 14th cents. Thereafter the *Book of Hours became the most important channel for illuminations.

Pucelle, Jehan (*c*.1300–*c*.1350). French manuscript *illuminator. Little is known of his career, but his large workshop dominated Parisian painting in the first half of the 14th cent. He enjoyed court patronage and his work commanded high prices. Certain features of his work—particularly his mastery of space—indicate that he probably travelled in Italy early in his career, and he was also familiar with Flemish developments. It was the synthesis of these two elements, allowing for an increasing penetration of naturalistic representation into traditional *iconography, which formed the basis for Pucelle's individual style.

Puget, Pierre (1620–94). The greatest French sculptor of the 17th cent. He worked mainly in his native Marseilles and in Toulon, for although he sought success at court, his work was much too impassioned to fit into the scheme of *Lebrun's artistic dictatorship. Moreover, he was arrogant and headstrong in temperament and he fell victim to the intrigues of fellow artists. His *Baroque style was formed in Italy, where in 1640–3 he worked with Pietro da *Cortona in Rome and Florence. Subsequently he made several journeys to Genoa, where he established a considerable reputation. His first major work was a pair of *atlas figures for the entrance to Toulon Town Hall (1656) and in these he showed the physical vigour and emotional intensity that were the hallmarks of his style. They occur most memorably in his celebrated *Milo of Crotona* (Louvre, Paris, 1671–82), which was one of his few works accepted for the palace at Versailles. Puget spent his final years embittered by his failures. He worked as a painter, architect, and decorator of ships as well as a sculptor, and was an outstanding draughtsman. His son **François** (1651–1707) was a painter, working mainly in Toulon and Marseilles. He did a few religious works but was mainly a portraitist; a portrait by him of his father is in the Louvre.

Purism. A movement in French painting linked with the new aesthetic of 'machine art' and flourishing *c.*1918–25. Its founders and protagonists were Amédée *Ozenfant and *Le Corbusier. Feeling that *Cubism had missed its path and was degenerating into an art of decoration, they regarded their association as 'a campaign for the reconstitution of a healthy art', and held that emotion and expressiveness should be strictly excluded apart from the 'mathematical lyricism' which is the proper response to a well-composed picture. Their characteristic paintings are still lifes—cool, clear, and impersonally finished. Despite the anti-emotionalism of this Functionalist outlook, it was advocated by Ozenfant with passionate missionary fervour. The Purist aesthetic was expounded in the books *Après le Cubisme* (1918) and *La Peinture Moderne* (1925), joint works of Ozenfant and Le Corbusier, and in the journal *L'Esprit Nouveau*, which they ran from 1920 to 1925. It won a considerable measure of support from artists and writers of widely different persuasions, but Purism did not establish a continuing school of painting. Its main sequel is to be found in the architectural theories and achievements of Le Corbusier and more generally in the field of design.

putto (Italian: 'little boy'). Term applied to a representation of a chubby, naked child, sometimes winged, appearing—usually as a subsidiary figure—in a work of art. Putti have been a frequent motif of decorative art since Classical antiquity and may have a pagan, human, or divine status. They derived from a type of figure used in ancient art to represent Eros, the Greek god of love, and from the *Renaissance onwards a putto has often been used to represent his Roman counterpart, Cupid. More commonly, putti are anonymous figures pictured attending Classical gods, or, for example, the Virgin Mary.

Puvis de Chavannes, Pierre (1824–98). The foremost French mural painter of the second half of the 19th cent. He decorated many public buildings in France (for example, the Panthéon, the Sorbonne, and the Hôtel de Ville, all in Paris) and also Boston Public Library. His paintings were done on canvas and then affixed to the walls (see MAROUFLAGE), but their pale colours imitated the effect of *fresco. He had only modest success early in his career (when a private income enabled him to work for little payment), but he went on to achieve an enormous reputation, and he was universally respected even by artists of very different aims and outlook from his own. *Gauguin, *Seurat, and *Toulouse-Lautrec were among his professed admirers. His reputation has since declined, his idealized depictions of antiquity or allegorical representations of abstract themes now often seeming rather anaemic. He remains important, however, because of his influence on younger artists. His simplified forms, respect for the flatness of the picture surface, rhythmic line, and use of non-naturalistic colour to evoke the mood of the painting appealed to both the *Post-Impressionists and the *Symbolists.

Pynacker, Adam (1622–73). Dutch landscape painter, active chiefly in Delft (he was born in nearby Pijnacker) and in

Amsterdam. He was in Italy for three years (before 1649) and he was one of the outstanding Dutch exponents of Italianate landscapes. His style resembles that of Jan *Both and Jan *Asselyn, but his mature work often has a distinctive and attractive silvery tonality. A splendid example of his work, showing his ability to compose boldly on a large scale, is *Landscape with Sportsmen and Game* (Dulwich College Picture Gallery), which features some unnaturalistically (but attractively) blue leaves, caused by yellow pigment fading in the greens.

Pynas, Jan (1583/4–1631) and **Jacob** (c.1585–1650?). Dutch painters, brothers. They worked in Rome in the first decade of the 17th cent. and brought back a style of small-scale history painting in the manner of *Elsheimer. This in turn may have had some influence on *Rembrandt, who is said to have studied briefly with Jacob.

Q

quadratura. A type of *illusionistic decoration in which architectural elements are painted on walls and/or ceilings in such a way that they appear to be an extension of the real architecture of a room into an imaginary space. It was common in Roman art, was revived by *Mantegna, and reached its peaks of elaboration in *Baroque Italy. The greatest of all exponents of *quadratura* was probably *Pozzo, in whose celebrated ceiling in S. Ignazio, Rome, architecture and figures surge towards the heavens with breathtaking bravura. Unlike Pozzo, many artists relied on specialists called *quadraturisti* to paint the architectural settings for their figures (see GUERCINO and TIEPOLO, for example).

quadro riportato (Italian: 'carried picture'). Term applied to a ceiling picture that is painted without *illusionistic foreshortening, as if it were to be viewed at normal eye level. *Mengs' *Parnassus* (1761) in the Villa Albani, Rome, is a famous example—a kind of *Neoclassical manifesto against *Baroque illusionism.

Quarton, Enguerrand. See CHARONTON.

quattrocento Term (literally 'four hundred') applied to the 15th cent. (the 1400s) in Italian art. It can be used as a noun ('painting of the quattrocento') or as an adjective ('quattrocento sculpture'). Terms used in the same way for other centuries are: dugento (or duecento) for the 13th cent.; trecento for the 14th cent.; cinquecento for the 16th cent.; seicento for the 17th cent.; settecento for the 18th cent.; ottocento for the 19th cent.; and novecento for the 20th cent.

Quellin (or **Quellinus**), **Artus I (Arnoldus)** (1609–68). The most distinguished member of a family of Flemish sculptors. He was born in Antwerp and was a pupil of François *Duquesnoy in Rome. He was back in Antwerp c.1640, then moved to Amsterdam, where from c.1650 to 1664 he

directed the sumptuous sculptural decoration of the Town Hall. His dignified style was singularly appropriate for van *Campen's great building, and the decoration forms the most impressive sculptural ensemble of the time in northern Europe. The high quality of his portrait busts can be seen in the Rijksmuseum. His collaborators at Amsterdam Town Hall included his cousin, **Artus II Quellin** (1625–1700), whose independent work was more *Baroque in style. The commanding figure of *God the Father* (1682) for the rood screen at Bruges Cathedral is perhaps his finest work. **Artus III Quellin** (1653–86), usually called Arnold, son of Artus II, settled in England about 1678. By 1684 he was working with Grinling *Gibbons, and the drop in quality of Gibbons's large-scale figure work (not his forte) after Quellin's death indicates that the latter was probably the dominant personality in producing such fine statues as the bronze *James II* (1686) outside the National Gallery in Trafalgar Square. Quellin's outstanding independent work is the tomb of Thomas Thynne (Westminster Abbey, 1682), which features a *relief of Thynne's murder in his coach in Pall Mall. Other artist members of the Quellin family included **Erasmus I** (c.1584–1639/40), father of Artus I and likewise a sculptor, and Artus I's two brothers, **Erasmus II** (1607–78), a painter who was a pupil and collaborator of *Rubens, and **Hubert** (1619?–87), an engraver.

Quercia, Jacopo della (Jacopo di Piero di Angelo) (c.1374–1438). The greatest sculptor of the Sienese school, the son of an undistinguished goldsmith and woodcarver, **Piero di Angelo** (Quercia, from which he takes his name, is a place near Siena). He was one of the outstanding figures of his generation in Italian sculpture, alongside *Donatello and *Ghiberti, but his career is difficult to follow, as he worked in numerous places and sometimes left one commission unfinished while he took up another elsewhere. Contrary to

*Vasari's assertions that he led a 'well-ordered life', he seems to have been inveterately dilatory. He is first heard of unsuccessfully competing for the commission for the Baptistery doors at Florence in 1401. His first surviving work is usually considered to be the tomb of Ilaria del Carretto, wife of the ruler of Lucca, Paolo Guinigi (Cathedral, Lucca, c.1406), which was eulogized by *Ruskin. There are Renaissance *putti and swags round the sides of the coffin, but the serene and graceful effigy is in the northern manner and suggests Quercia had knowledge of work done in the circle of Claus *Sluter in Burgundy. His major work for his native city was a fountain called the *Fonte Gaia* (commissioned in 1409, executed in 1414–19), which is now—much damaged—in the loggia of the Palazzo Pubblico. Its *relief carvings include some beautifully draped female figures and a terribly battered but still awesomely powerful panel of *The Expulsion from Paradise*. Between 1417 and 1431 he worked together with Donatello and Ghiberti on reliefs for the font in the Baptistery at Siena, and in 1425 he received the commission for his last great work (left unfinished at his death), the reliefs on the portal of S. Petronio, Bologna, with scenes from Genesis and the nativity of Christ. The figures—usually only three to a relief, in contrast to the crowded panels of Ghiberti—have a directness and strength which won the admiration of *Michelangelo, who visited Bologna in 1494. Several of the motifs are to be found, reinterpreted, on the Sistine Ceiling.

R

Rackham, Arthur (1867–1939). British artist, celebrated for his illustrations to children's books. He said he believed in 'the greatest stimulating and educative power of imaginative, fantastic and playful pictures and writings for children in their most impressionable years', and he worked in a striking vein of Nordic fantasy, creating a world populated by goblins, fairies, and weird creatures.

Raeburn, Sir Henry (1756–1823). The leading Scottish portrait painter of his period, active mainly in his native Edinburgh. On leaving school he was apprenticed to a goldsmith, then worked as a *miniaturist, and appears to have been largely self-taught as a painter in oils. Between 1784 and 1787 he had periods in London (where he met *Reynolds) and Italy, but his distinctive style was by this time already formed—one of his finest works, the *Rev. Robert Walker Skating* (NG, Edinburgh), is traditionally said to have been painted in 1784. He painted directly on to the canvas without preliminary drawings, and his vigorous, bold handling—sometimes called his 'square touch'—could be extraordinarily effective in conveying the character of rugged Highland chiefs or bluff legal worthies. He also had a penchant for vivid and original lighting effects (*William Glendonwyn*, Fitzwilliam Mus., Cambridge, c.1795) and could be remarkably sensitive when painting women (*Isabella McLeod, Mrs James Gregory*, National Trust for Scotland, Fyvie Castle, Aberdeenshire, c.1798). At times, however, his technical facility can degenerate into empty virtuosity. In 1822, on the occasion of George IV's visit to Edinburgh, he was knighted and in 1823 he was appointed His Majesty's *Limner for Scotland. Since he had all the sitters he needed in Scotland, there was no need for him to compete with *Lawrence and *Hoppner in London (although he did consider moving there after Hoppner's death in 1810), and in the history of British portraiture he is an isolated and perhaps underrated figure.

Raggi, Antonio. See BACICCIA.

Raimondi, Marcantonio (c.1480–1534). Italian engraver, a pioneer in the use of prints to reproduce the work of other artists. He was born near Bologna, studied there with *Francia and learned much from *Dürer's engravings in Venice (Dürer is said to have complained to the Venetian senate about being plagiarized). In about 1510 he settled in Rome, and thereafter worked mainly for *Raphael, his engravings helping to spread the master's style throughout Europe. Apart from his association with Raphael, Raimondi is best known for his series of obscene engravings (after designs by *Giulio Romano) that led to his imprisonment. He left Rome after the Sack of 1527 and died in obscurity in Bologna.

Ramsay, Allan (1713–84). Scottish portrait painter, active mainly in London. He was the outstanding portraitist there from about 1740 to the rise of *Reynolds in the mid 1750s. Ramsay studied in London, in Rome, and in Naples (under *Solimena), and when in 1739 he settled in London he brought a cosmopolitan air to British portrait painting. His portraits of women have a decidedly French grace (*The Artist's Wife*, NG, Edinburgh, 1754/5) and in this field he continued to be a serious rival to Reynolds, who was upset when Ramsay was appointed Painter-in-Ordinary to George III in 1760. Ramsay, however, gradually gave up painting during the 1760s to devote himself to his other interests. He was the son of Allan Ramsay the poet, and inherited his father's literary bent. Political pamphleteering, Classical archaeology (he revisited Rome in 1754–7), and conversation took up much of his later years. He was successful in literary circles and Dr Samuel Johnson said of him, 'You will not find a man in whose conversation there is more instruction, more information, and more elegance.'

Raphael (properly Raffaello Sanzio) (1483–1520). Italian painter and architect, the artist in whose works the ideals of the High *Renaissance find their most complete expression. He was born in Urbino, where in the court of Federico da *Montefeltro Italian culture had found one of its most distinguished settings, and his father, Giovanni *Santi, was a writer as well as a painter, who would have introduced his son to humanist ideas. *Vasari says that 'Raphael came to be of great help to his father in the numerous works that Giovanni executed in the state of Urbino', but Santi died in 1494, when Raphael was only 11, and the overwhelming influence on his early work was *Perugino. It is often said that Raphael was Perugino's pupil, but this is probably not strictly true. He was highly precocious and working as an independent artist by 1500; his close contact with Perugino came a little later (c.1502–3), when he was probably his colleague rather than assistant. That he soon completely outstripped Perugino is best seen by comparing Raphael's *Marriage of the Virgin* (Brera, Milan, 1504) with Perugino's painting of the same subject (Musée des Beaux-Arts, Caen). The two compositions are closely similar in many ways, but Raphael far surpasses Perugino in lucidity and grace.

In his early career Raphael worked in various places in Tuscany and Umbria. From 1504 to 1508 he worked much in Florence, and this is usually referred to as his Florentine period, although he never took up permanent residency in the city. Under the influence particularly of *Leonardo and *Michelangelo his work became grander and more sophisticated. To the Florentine period belong many of his most celebrated depictions of the Virgin and Child. In these and his paintings of the Holy Family he showed his developing mastery of composition and expression. He paints the sacred figures as splendid, healthy human beings, but with a serenity, a sense of some deep inner integrity, that removes any doubt as to the holiness of the subject. This sense of well-being distinguishes the art of Raphael from the more disturbingly intellectual work of Leonardo or the overwhelmingly powerful creations of Michelangelo, and evidently reflects his own balanced nature. Unlike his two great contemporaries, he was not a solitary genius but a sociable and approachable figure, whom Vasari describes as 'so gentle and so charitable that even animals loved

him'. In 1508, though he was only 25 years old, his reputation was sufficiently established for him to be summoned to Rome by Pope Julius II and entrusted with the frescos for one of the papal rooms in the Vatican, the Stanza della Segnatura. He continued to work in Rome till his death in 1520 although he is known to have returned briefly to Florence in 1515.

The Stanza della Segnatura is based on a complex theological programme of the relationship between classical learning and the Christian revelation. On one main wall, in the celebrated painting known as *The School of Athens*, are shown the ancient philosophers, led by Plato and Aristotle, enclosed in a great architectural setting, a masterpiece of *perspective drawing. Opposite, is the painting called the *Disputà* (the Disputation over the Sacrament); the doctors of the church adore the Sacrament, while above the Trinity is surrounded by the saints and martyrs. Here the setting is a wide open space. They are works in which grandeur and gracefulness seem effortlessly combined and they have had a profound and continuing influence on European art. After the completion of the Stanza della Segnatura in 1511 Raphael was entrusted with three other apartments in the Vatican, but by the time he had completed the first of these—the Stanza d'Eliodero—in 1514, his services were so much in demand that he had to rely increasingly on assistants (of whom *Giulio Romano was the most distinguished) for the execution of the work. The *cartoons for tapestries in the Sistine Chapel (Royal Coll., on loan to V&A, London, 1515–16), for example, rank among his noblest designs, but probably comparatively little of the execution is from his own hand. In addition to the tapestries Raphael supervised various other great decorative schemes in Rome: the Villa Farnesina with its ceiling showing the story of Psyche, and a wall fresco, *Galatea* (1511–12), which is from Raphael's own hand at its most expert; the Chigi Chapel in Sta Maria del Popolo (begun c.1512), where he designed the entire scheme, comprising architecture, sculpture, painting, mosaic, stuccowork, and marble inlay; and the ceiling and wall arabesques of the Vatican Loggie (c.1515 onwards), which left a permanent imprint on European interior decoration. The richness of effect in the Chigi Chapel was an important source for similar works in the

*Baroque era, and it is fitting that the chapel was in fact completed by *Bernini.

Raphael also painted many portraits and it is in these that the quality of his own workmanship in his later years is best seen. They rival Leonardo in subtlety of characterization and *Titian in richness of colouring, show great inventiveness in creating psychological situations, and provide a remarkable record of the intellectual circles in which he moved (*Baldassare Castiglione*, Louvre, Paris, *c*.1515). Other important commissions from his Roman period that are largely from his own hand are the *Sistine Madonna* (Gemäldegalerie, Dresden, *c*.1512–14), his most famous painting of the Virgin and Child, and the great altarpiece of the *Transfiguration* (Vatican Gal.), on which he was working at his death, and which presages the *Mannerist style. In his last years he was employed in architecture and in a survey of ancient Rome as well as in painting. After the death of *Bramante in 1514 he became architect to St Peter's, and Raphael ranks second only to him among High Renaissance architects. It is difficult to appreciate his status, however, as little of his work survives as he designed it.

Vasari says that Raphael's early death (on his 37th birthday) 'plunged into grief the entire papal court'. He was rich, famous, and honoured (Vasari says the Pope, 'who wept bitterly when he died', had intended making him a cardinal), and his influence was widely spread even during his own lifetime through the engravings of Marcantonio *Raimondi. His posthumous reputation was even greater, for until the later 19th cent. he was regarded by almost all critics as the greatest painter who had ever lived—the artist who expressed the basic doctrines of the Christian Church through figures that have a physical beauty worthy of the *antique. *Reynolds said: 'It is from his having taken so many models that he became himself a model for all succeeding painters: always imitating and always original.' He became the ideal of all *academies (it was against his authority that the *Pre-Raphaelites revolted), and today we approach him through a long tradition in which Raphaelesque forms and motifs have been used with a steady diminution of their values. Many lesser artists have imitated him emptily, but he has been a major inspiration to great

*Classical painters such as Annibale *Carracci, *Poussin, and *Ingres.

Ratgeb, Jörg (*c*.1480–1526). German painter, active in Swabia. His few surviving paintings show him to have been closer in spirit to *Grünewald than practically any of his contemporaries. The most important is the Herrenberg Altarpiece (Staatsgalerie, Stuttgart, 1519), which has some harrowing Passion scenes. Ratgeb himself met a gruesome end—executed at Pforzheim for his part in the Peasants' War.

Rauschenberg, Robert (1925–). American artist, one of the most influential figures in avant-garde art since the 1950s. He studied at the Kansas City Art Institute, the Académie Julian in Paris, Black Mountain College in North Carolina (with *Albers), and the Art Students' League in New York. His earliest works included minimalist monochromatic paintings, but in the mid 1950s he began to incorporate three-dimensional objects into what he called *'combine paintings'. The best-known example is probably *Monogram* (Moderna Museet, Stockholm, 1959), which features a stuffed goat with a rubber tyre around its middle. Other objects he has used include Coca-Cola bottles, fragments of clothing, electric fans, and radios. In the 1960s he returned to working on a flat surface and was particularly active in the medium of *silk screen. He has been interested in combining art with new technological developments, and was active in forming EAT (Experiments in Art and Technology), an organization to help artists and engineers work together. His other work has included theatre design and choreography and involvement in *happenings. With his friend Jasper *Johns, Rauschenberg is regarded as one of the most important figures in the move away from the *Abstract Expressionism that dominated American art in the late 1940s and early 1950s.

Ravilious, Eric (1903–42). British painter, graphic artist, and designer. His highly varied output included (apart from paintings) book illustrations and book-jackets, designs for the *Wedgwood pottery factory (including a mug commemorating Edward VIII's coronation in 1937), and designs for furniture, glass, and textiles. He was one of the outstanding wood engravers of his time, his book illustrations in this medium making striking use of bold tonal contrasts and complex patterning. In 1940–2 he was an official war artist, and he produced some memorable watercolours of naval scenes off Norway (*Norway, 1940*, Laing Art Gal., Newcastle upon Tyne). His plane disappeared on a flying patrol near Iceland, in 1942, and he was officially presumed dead the following year.

Ray, Man. See MAN RAY.

Rayonism (Rayonnism, Rayism, Luchism). A painting style practised by the Russian artists *Goncharova and *Larionov and a few followers in the years 1912 to 1914 and representing their own adaptation of *Futurism. The movement was launched with a manifesto thought to have been written by Larionov and forming part of a Miscellany issued at the *Target exhibition held in Moscow in 1913. The manifesto stated: 'Rayonism is a synthesis of *Cubism, Futurism and *Orphism.' The style was bound up with a very unclear theory of invisible rays, in some ways analogous to the 'lines of force' which were postulated by Italian Futurist theory, emitted by objects and intercepted by other objects in the vicinity: the artist, it was said, must manipulate these rays to create form for his own aesthetic purposes. Many Rayonist paintings are very similar in style to those of the Futurists, with particular emphasis on breaking up the subject into bundles of slanting lines. In other works the subject virtually or completely disappears. The movement was short-lived, as both Goncharova and Larionov virtually abandoned easel painting after 1914 and they founded no school.

Read, Sir Herbert (1893–1968). British poet and critic, regarded as his period's foremost interpreter of modern art to the general public. During the 1930s Read was a close friend of the group of artists around Henry *Moore, Barbara *Hepworth, and Ben *Nicholson and acted as their public mouthpiece (see UNIT ONE). He was also concerned with the organization of the London *Surrealist Exhibition in 1936. With Roland *Penrose he was joint founder of the *Institute of Contemporary Arts in 1947. Among his best-known books were: *The Meaning of Art* (1931), *Art Now* (1933), *Art and Industry* (1934), *Art and*

Society (1936), *Surrealism* (1936). His most influential work is sometimes considered to be *Education through Art* (1943), which promoted the idea of teaching art as an aid to the development of the personality. His personal philosophy of art was expressed most consistently in *Icon and Idea* (1958) and *The Forms of Things Unknown* (1960). Two of his books—*A Concise History of Modern Painting* (1959) and *A Concise History of Modern Sculpture* (1964)—are much used as introductory surveys by art history students. Apart from his writing activities, Read worked in the ceramics department of the Victoria and Albert Museum and taught at various universities (he was Watson Gordon Professor of the History of Art at Edinburgh University, 1930–3).

ready-made. A name given by Marcel *Duchamp to a type of work he invented consisting of a mass-produced article selected at random and displayed as a work of art. His first ready-made (1912) was a bicycle wheel placed on a chair. Duchamp himself distinguished the 'ready-made' from the *objet trouvé* (found object), pointing out that whereas the *objet trouvé* is discovered and chosen because of its interesting aesthetic qualities, its beauty and uniqueness, the 'ready-made' is one—that is any one—of a large number of indistinguishable mass-produced objects without any individuality or uniqueness. Therefore the *objet trouvé* implies the exercise of taste in its selection, but the 'ready-made' does not.

Realism. Term used with various meanings in the history and criticism of the arts. In its broadest sense the word is used as vaguely as *naturalism, implying a desire to depict things accurately and objectively. Often, however, the term carries with it the suggestion of the rejection of conventionally beautiful subjects, or of idealization, in favour of a more down-to-earth approach, often with a stress on low life or the activities of the common man. In a more specific sense the term (usually spelled with a capital R) is applied to a movement in 19th-cent. (particularly French) art characterized by a rebellion against the traditional historical, mythological, and religious subjects in favour of unidealized scenes of modern life. The leader of the Realist movement was *Courbet, who said 'painting is essentially a concrete art and must be applied to real and existing things'. Since the 1950s the term has also been used in a contrasting sense, of art which eschews representation and depiction altogether and avoids all forms of illusionism. In this sense art is called 'Realist' when the materials or objects from which the work is constructed are presented for exactly what they are and are known to be. The term 'Social Realism' has been applied to 19th- and 20th-cent. works that are realistic in the second sense described above and make overt social or political comment. It is to be distinguished from 'Socialist Realism', the name given to the officially approved style in the USSR and some other Communist countries; far from implying a critical approach to social questions, it involves toeing the Party line in an academic style. *Magic Realism and *Superrealism are names given to two 20th-cent. styles in which extreme realism—in the sense of acute attention to detail—produces a markedly unrealistic overall effect. See also VERISM.

Recco, Giuseppe (1634–95). Neapolitan still-life painter, the outstanding member of a family of artists. He specialized in pictures of fish, painted in an impressively grand style, but more austere than those of *Ruoppolo, with whom he ranks as the most distinguished Italian still-life painter of his period.

red-figure vase painting. One of the two major divisions of Greek vase painting, the other being *black-figure. In the red-figure technique, the background was painted black, leaving the figures in the unpainted red colour of the pottery. Details of the figure could thus be added with a brush rather than incised through the black paint, allowing much greater flexibility and subtlety of treatment. Because of this advantage the red-figure technique, which developed in Athens from about 530 BC, rapidly superseded the black-figure technique.

Redgrave, Richard (1804–88). English painter, writer, and art administrator. He began as a painter of anecdotal literary subjects, often in 18th-cent. costume, but in the 1840s he became a pioneer of scenes of contemporary social concern (*The Poor Teacher*, Shipley Art Gal., Gateshead, 1845). 'It is one of my most gratifying feelings', he wrote, 'that many of my best efforts in art have aimed at calling attention to the trials and struggles of the poor and the oppressed.' Much of his later career was taken up with administration—the posts he held included surveyor of crown pictures and keeper of pictures at the South Kensington (later Victoria and Albert) Museum—and as a painter he turned mainly to landscapes done in his spare time. His brother, **Samuel Redgrave** (1802–76), was a writer on art, the author of a still-useful *Dictionary of Artists of the English School* (1874). The brothers collaborated on *A Century of Painters of the English School* (1866), a valuable source of information on 18th- and 19th-cent. British artists.

Redon, Odilon (1840–1916). French painter and graphic artist, one of the outstanding figures of *Symbolism. He led a retiring life, first in his native Bordeaux, then from 1870 in Paris, and until he was in his fifties he worked almost exclusively in black and white—in charcoal drawings and lithographs. In these he developed a highly distinctive repertoire of weird subjects—strange amoeboid creatures, insects, and plants with human heads and so on, influenced by the writings of Edgar Allen Poe. He remained virtually unknown to the public until the publication of J. K. Huysmans's celebrated novel *A Rebours* in 1884; the book's hero, a disenchanted aristocrat who lives in a private world of perverse delights, collects Redon's drawings, and with his mention in this classic expression of decadence, Redon too became associated with the movement. During the 1890s Redon turned to painting and revealed remarkable powers as a colourist that had lain dormant. Much of his early life had been unhappy, but after undergoing a religious crisis in the early 1890s and a serious illness in 1894–5, he was transformed into a much more buoyant and cheerful personality, expressing himself in radiant colours in mythological scenes and flower paintings. He showed equal facility in oils and pastel. The flower pieces, in particular, were much admired by *Matisse, and the *Surrealists regarded Redon as one of their precursors. He was a distinguished figure by the end of his life, although still a very private person.

Regionalism. Movement in American painting—part of the wider category of

*American Scene painting—in which artists concentrated on realistic depiction of scenes and types from the American Midwest and deep South. The movement flourished during the 1930s and early 1940s. The motivation of the Regionalists, like that of all the American Scene painters, derived from a patriotic desire to establish a genuinely American art by the utilization of American subject-matter and the repudiation of innovative artistic styles. In addition they were moved by a nostalgic desire to glorify, or at the least to record, rural and small-town America as distinct from the new industrial urbanization, and it was from this that their widespread popularity drew its sustenance. Thomas Hart *Benton was the vociferous mouthpiece of the group and prominent in the movement were Grant *Wood, Andrew *Wyeth, Edward *Hopper, and John Steuart *Curry, with Charles *Burchfield and Ben *Shahn on the fringes.

Reinhardt, Ad (1913–67). American painter. From the beginning his painting was abstract, although it changed radically in style over the years. Through the 1930s he used a crisp, boldly contoured geometrical style which owed something both to *Cubism and to the *Neo-Plasticism of *Mondrian. In the 1940s he passed through a phase of *all-over painting which has been likened to that of Mark *Tobey, and in the late 1940s he was close to certain of the *Abstract Expressionists, particularly *Motherwell, with whom he jointly edited *Modern Artists in America* (1950). During the 1950s he turned to monochromatic paintings. At first they were usually red or blue, but from the late 1950s he devoted himself to all-black paintings with geometrical designs of squares or oblongs barely perceptibly differentiated in value from the background colour. This reduction of his work to 'pure aesthetic essences' reflects his belief in the complete separation between art and life—'Art is Art. Everything else is everything else.' Reinhardt was particularly influential on the development of *Minimalism. His views were extremely uncompromising and he was a noted critic of trends in modern art of which he did not approve, both as a polemical writer and a satirical cartoonist.

relief (or **relievo**). Term, from the Italian *rilevare* (to raise), applied to sculpture that projects from a background surface rather than standing freely. According to the degree of projection, reliefs are usually classified as high (*alto rilievo*), medium (*mezzo rilievo*), or low (*basso rilievo* or bas-relief). The name *rilievo stiacciato* (also *schiacciato*) is given to a form of very low relief that was invented by *Donatello and memorably used also by *Desiderio da Settignano.

relief etching. A method of *etching plates for relief printing (ordinary etching being in *intaglio). The design is drawn on the plate in an acid-resisting *varnish. The plate is then immersed in acid, which eats away the unprotected parts so that the design stands out in relief and prints can be taken in the same way as from a *woodcut block. The method dates from the 18th cent., but was little used except by *Blake, who called it 'woodcut on copper'. In the 20th cent. the process has been revived and combined with intaglio printing by S. W. *Hayter and Joan *Miró.

Rembrandt Harmensz. van Rijn (1606–69). Dutch painter, etcher, and draughtsman, his country's greatest artist. He was born at Leiden, where he studied at a Latin school and was enrolled for a few months at the University, before leaving (c.1620) to study painting under the mediocre Jacob van Swanenburgh (c.1571–1638), with whom he worked for about three years. More decisive for his development were six months spent with Pieter *Lastman, c.1624, at Amsterdam. From Lastman he took not only his predilection for mythological and religious subjects, but also his manner of treating them, with dramatic gestures and expressions, vivid lighting effects, and a meticulous, glossy finish, as in his earliest dated work—*The Stoning of St Stephen* (Musée des Beaux-Arts, Lyons, 1625). *Houbraken says that Rembrandt also studied with Jacob *Pynas and Joris van Schooten (1587–1651), but this can have been only briefly, for by 1625 he was working as an independent master in Leiden. There he had a close association with Jan *Lievens, and both artists were highly praised by the scholar and diplomat Constantin Huygens, who visited them in 1629. Rembrandt's paintings of his Leiden period (which lasted until he settled permanently in Amsterdam in 1631/2) are mainly figure subjects, often involving old men depicted as philosophers or biblical characters. He also did portraits of himself and of members of his family, but it is not until 1631 that he painted his earliest known formal commissioned portrait. The sitter was Nicolaes Ruts, a prosperous Amsterdam merchant (Frick Coll., New York), and Rembrandt no doubt realized that here he had a recipe for success, as this type of work dominated his output in his early years in Amsterdam. It was the busiest period of his life, as he quickly established himself as the leading portraitist in the city—about fifty of his paintings are dated 1632 or 1633 and all but a handful are portraits. The most important—the work that most clearly demonstrated his superiority to rivals such as Thomas de *Keyser—is the *Anatomy Lesson of Dr Tulp* (Mauritshuis, The Hague, 1632), which brought a wholly new vitality to the group portrait. Rembrandt's great energy in his early years in Amsterdam comes out also in his religious works. The most important commission he received during the 1630s was from the Stadholder Prince Frederick Henry of Orange for five pictures depicting scenes of the Passion (Alte Pinakothek, Munich), and the *Baroque tendencies of his work at this time are even more emphatically expressed in his sensational, life-size *Blinding of Samson* (Städelsches Kunstinstitut, Frankfurt, 1636). Rembrandt presented this painting to Huygens, who probably had secured the commission from the Stadholder. Rembrandt's success in the 1630s was personal as well as professional. In 1634 he married Saskia van Uylenburch, cousin of a picture-dealer associate, and from the evidence of his marvellously tender portraits of her it must have been a blissful union. In 1639 he bought an imposing house (now a Rembrandt museum), and he spent lavishly on works of art and anything else that took his fancy or looked as if it might be useful as a prop—armour, old costumes, etc. His domestic happiness was, however, marred by a succession of infant deaths; of the four children Saskia bore him, only his son Titus (1641–68), who became one of his favourite models, lived longer than two months.

Saskia died in 1642, and in this year Rembrandt painted his most famous picture, *The Night Watch* (Rijksmuseum, Amsterdam), which Jacob Rosenberg, in his standard monograph on the artist, calls 'a thunderbolt of genius'. The erroneous title dates from the late 18th cent. when the painting was so discoloured with dirty varnish that it looked like a night scene. Its correct title is *The Militia Company of Captain Frans Banning Cocq and Lieutenant Willem van Ruytenburch*, and it is the culminating work of the Dutch tradition of civic guard portraits (a genre particularly associated with Frans *Hals). Rembrandt showed remarkable originality in making a pictorial drama out of an insignificant event. To do this he subordinated the individual portraits to the demands of the composition, and according to popular legend the sitters who had paid for the picture were appalled at this and demanded that Rembrandt make radical changes, paint a new picture, or refund their money. Rembrandt's refusal is supposed to have been his downfall and to have led him into penniless obscurity. There is, however, no basis in fact for the story, which is a 19th-cent. invention; indeed all the available evidence suggests that the picture was well received by contemporaries. Samuel van *Hoogstraten, for example, wrote 'It is so painter-like in thought, so dashing in movement, and so powerful' that the pictures beside which it hung were made to seem 'like playing cards'.

Nevertheless, in the 1640s Rembrandt's worldly success did decline as the direction of his art changed. Formal portraiture took up much less of his time and he concentrated more on religious painting, while his style grew less flamboyant and more introspective. The change has been explained as a response to the death of Saskia (and of his mother in 1640), and religion may well have been a solace to him in this difficult period. At the same time, some of his market in portraiture must have gone to pupils such as *Bol and *Flinck, who imitated his style so well. It seems just as likely, however, that Rembrandt was tired of routine portraiture and wanted to return to his first love—painting subjects from the Bible. In the 1640s Rembrandt also developed an interest in landscape and it has been suggested that he spent more time in the countryside during this period to escape from the domestic problems he encountered after Saskia's death. A widow called Geertge Dircx was employed as Titus's nurse, and she sued Rembrandt for breach of promise after his affections turned to Hendrickje Stoffels, a servant some 20 years his junior who entered the household in about 1645. After some unpleasant legal proceedings Geertge was placed in an asylum. Hendrickje remained with Rembrandt for the rest of her life and bore him two children, including a daughter, Cornelia, born in 1654, who was the only one of his children to outlive him. Rembrandt's portrayals of Hendrickje are just as loving as those of Saskia, but he was unable to marry her because of a clause in Saskia's will.

After he turned his back on fashionable portraiture, Rembrandt's extravagance led him into financial difficulties, which became acute by the early 1650s. In 1656 he was declared insolvent; his collections were sold and in 1660 he had to leave his house and move to lodgings in a poorer district of the city. Houbraken says that 'in the autumn of his life he kept company mainly with common people and such as practised art', but the romantic image of him as a pauper and a recluse is grossly exaggerated. He continued to be a respected figure who received important commissions (his patrons included the Sicilian nobleman Don Antonio Ruffo), and Hendrickje and Titus established an art firm with Rembrandt technically their employee, a device that protected him from his creditors. Indeed, with some weight thus lifted from his shoulders, Rembrandt may well have felt renewed energy, and there are more dated paintings from 1661 than from any year since the early 1630s. In 1661–2 he painted two of his greatest works—*The Sampling Officers of the Cloth-Makers' Guild* (sometimes called *The Syndics*, Rijksmuseum) and *The Conspiracy of Claudius Civilis*, painted for Amsterdam Town Hall, but for unknown reasons removed in 1663 and cut down (apparently by Rembrandt himself)—the magnificent fragment is now in the Nationalmuseum, Stockholm. Rembrandt's final years were clouded by the deaths of Hendrickje in 1663 and Titus in 1668, but his art was in no way impaired. On the contrary, his work seemed to grow in human understanding and compassion to the very end, and his last self-portraits, the culmination of an incomparable series that began 40 years earlier, show him facing his hardships with the utmost dignity— someone who has no illusions about life,

but equally no bitterness. Two self-portraits date from the last year of his life (NG, London, and Mauritshuis). At his death he left unfinished *Simeon with the Christ Child in the Temple* (Nationalmuseum, Stockholm), but the painting that best stands as his spiritual testimony is perhaps *The Return of the Prodigal Son* (Hermitage, Leningrad, c.1669), a work of the utmost tenderness and poignancy, which Kenneth *Clark described as 'a picture which those who have seen the original in Leningrad may be forgiven for claiming as the greatest picture ever painted'. The emotional depth and range of Rembrandt's work was matched by the total expressive mastery of his technique. Even as a young man, when surface polish and attention to detail were a necessary part of his skill as a fashionable portraitist, he had experimented boldly in his more private works, sometimes, for example, using the butt end of the brush to scrape through the paint. When he began to paint much more to please himself in the 1640s, his handling grew much broader, and Houbraken wrote that 'in the last years of his life, he worked so fast that his pictures, when examined from close by, looked as if they had been daubed with a bricklayer's trowel'.

It is not only the quality of Rembrandt's work that sets him apart from all his Dutch contemporaries, but also its range. Although portraits and religious works bulk largest in his output, he made highly original contributions to other genres, including still life (*The Slaughtered Ox*, Louvre, Paris, 1655), and he painted some pictures, such as *The Polish Rider* (Frick Coll., New York, c.1655), that virtually defy classification. Rembrandt was prodigious, too, as an etcher and draughtsman. He is universally regarded as the greatest etcher who ever lived, capable of expressing the airy breadth of the Dutch countryside with a few quick strokes, but also prepared to radically rework a complex religious scene such as *The Three Crosses* perhaps a decade after he had begun it in 1653 to create one of the most awesome of all images of Christ's Passion. His drawings were done mainly as independent works rather than as studies for paintings and often with the thick bold strokes of the reed pen, of which he was an unsurpassed master.

Rembrandt was a great teacher; Gerard *Dou became his first pupil in 1628 and

Aert de *Gelder, who was with him in the 1660s, continued his master's style into the 18th cent. Between these two, Rembrandt taught such illustrious names as Carel *Fabritius (his greatest pupil), Philips de *Koninck and Nicolaes *Maes, but often his pupils later abandoned his exacting standards for a more facile popularity. Rembrandt continued to have many admirers after his death, and his work often fetched high prices in the 18th cent. He was generally regarded as incomparable in his mastery of light and shade, but most critics considered him a flawed genius, whose failing was his 'vulgarity' and lack of decorum. It was during the age of *Romanticism, when it was felt that artists should give expression to their innermost feelings and flout conventions, that his reputation began to rise towards its present supremely exalted heights. In 1851 *Delacroix suggested that one day Rembrandt would be rated higher than *Raphael—'a piece of blasphemy that will make every good academician's hair stand on end'; his prophecy came true within 50 years.

Remington, Frederic (1861–1909). American painter, sculptor, and illustrator, the most famous portrayer of the 'Wild West'. He was a burly, athletic man and after attending Yale University he travelled widely in the West, prospecting and cowpunching as he worked to establish himself with his illustrations. Reproductions in *Harper's Weekly* and other popular journals made him a household name, and with his success he was able to turn more to painting and sculpture. He continued to travel (to Europe and North Africa as well as in America), and he wrote as well as working as an artist, covering the Indian Wars of 1890–1 and the Spanish-American War (in Cuba) of 1898 as a war correspondent. There is a collection of his work at the Remington Art Memorial, Ogdensburg, New York State.

Renaissance. Term meaning 'rebirth' applied to an intellectual and artistic movement that began in Italy in the 14th cent., culminated there in the 16th cent., and influenced other parts of Europe in a great variety of ways. The notion of a rebirth refers to a revival of the values of the classical world, and the concept was used as early as the 15th cent., by Italians who

thought they were living at a time when the qualities of ancient art and literature were blossoming anew after centuries of barbarism. In the following century *Vasari gave the idea of such a revival a systematically developed form; he thought that art had declined in the Middle Ages, had been set once again on its true path by *Giotto, and had risen to its greatest heights in the work of his friend and hero *Michelangelo. To modern historians this picture seems much too simplistic, and the Renaissance is seen more as a period of gradual change than as a sudden break with the past. Nevertheless, the intellectuals of the Renaissance were the first people to coin a period indentity for themselves, and this in itself gives the label a certain coherence. Scholars may debate endlessly over the exact interpretation of many aspects of the period, but in the general historical scheme of things, the Renaissance has come to represent the time when 'Medieval' turns into 'Modern' and the religion-dominated world of the Middle Ages gives way to a culture more responsive to the individual.

In the visual arts, the revival of the antique can be seen most clearly in architecture, for classical architecture uses a 'vocabulary' of forms that distinguishes it unambiguously from the Gothic style, and there can be no doubt that *Brunelleschi is entitled to rank as the first Renaissance architect. He was interested in Roman buildings probably more for what he could learn about engineering problems than for stylistic reasons, and he was undogmatic and unarchaeological in his use of antique detail, but he had an instinctual understanding of classical design, and his buildings—based on simple mathematical ratios—have a lucidity and harmony worthy of comparison with the finest ancient models. In sculpture, the beginnings of the Renaissance are sometimes traced as far back as Nicola *Pisano in the late 14th cent. because he is known to have been directly influenced by Roman sarcophagi. However, it is not until *Donatello, in the early 15th cent., that we find a sculptor who had thoroughly assimilated the spirit of ancient sculpture, rather than simply borrowing motifs from it. In paining, it is harder to define the Renaissance in terms of antique influence, as very little ancient painting survived compared with the fairly abundant remains of Roman architecture and sculpture to be found in Italy. From the writings of ancient authors, however, classical painters were known to have excelled in fidelity to nature, so this quality was seen as a keynote of Renaissance painting. Because Giotto made such great advances in naturalism he is sometimes put at the head of the Renaissance tradition in painting, but it is more consistent to give this position to *Masaccio, who brought a new scientific rigour to the problems of representation.

Masaccio, like his friends Brunelleschi and Donatello, was a Florentine, and it is thus reasonable to see Florence as the cradle of the Renaissance, and the period around 1425, when they were producing some of their most innovative works, as a major turning point in European art. Florence continued to be of pre-eminent importance throughout the 15th cent., but in the 16th cent. Rome and Venice were equally significant centres for the arts. The culmination of the Renaissance came in the period from about 1500 to 1520—a time which is now known as the High Renaissance. During this time the three most famous artists of the age—*Leonardo, Michelangelo, and *Raphael—produced works that have for centuries been regarded as touchstones of perfection and the fulfilment of all the ideals that artists had pursued since Giotto. In architecture, *Bramante represents a similar peak, and his noble and grave designs were regarded in his own time as having truly recaptured the majesty of Roman buildings.

The ideals and imagery of the Italian Renaissance did not generally begin to spread to the rest of Europe until about 1500. Albrecht *Dürer was the outstanding artist of the 'Northern Renaissance', making it his mission to transplant the new Italian ideas onto German soil. His work was of enormous importance in spreading Italian ideas, and during the 16th cent. it became a normal part of the career of ambitious young artists from northern Europe to follow in his footsteps across the Alps. By this time, however, Italian art had entered the phase called *Mannerism, and much Italian-inspired art of this period in Germany, France, and the Netherlands can be classified as Mannerist rather than Renaissance. Most northern artists imitated only the superficial characteristics of Italian art, and only a few—such as Jan van *Soorel—absorbed something of the order,

poise, and dignity associated with the High Renaissance. In England, Renaissance ideas made only superficial impact during the 16th century, Italian influence being mainly confined to decorative motifs (and many of these were used in debased or misunderstood forms). It was not until the 17th century that there emerged an English artist—Inigo *Jones—who thoroughly understood Renaissance ideals, and by this time Italian art had progressed through Mannerism to the *Baroque.

Reni, Guido (1575–1642). Bolognese painter. From about 1584 to 1593 he was a pupil of *Calvaert, then he entered the *Carracci academy, where he inherited their tradition of clear, firm draughtsmanship. Reni's style was also strongly influenced by the several visits he made to Rome, the first of them soon after 1600. He flirted briefly with the *Caravaggesque manner (*Crucifixion of St Peter*, Vatican, 1603), but *Raphael and the *antique were the main inspiration for his graceful Classical style, as is seen in his most celebrated work, *Aurora* (1613–14), a captivatingly beautiful ceiling fresco in the Casino Rospiglioso in Rome. After Ludovico Carracci's death in 1619, Reni became the most important painter in Bologna, running a large and prosperous studio, whose products (mainly religious works) were sent all over Europe. He cut an impressive, aristocratic figure, always fashionably and expensively dressed and usually attended by servants, but he was noted for his modesty and hated profanities and obscenities. According to his biographer *Malvasia 'It was generally thought that he was a virgin . . . When observing the many lovely young girls who served as his models, he was like marble.' His fame in his lifetime was great and in the 18th and early 19th cents. many critics went into raptures, ranking him second only to Raphael. *Winckelmann, for example, compared him to *Praxiteles, and *Reynolds wrote that 'his idea of beauty . . . is acknowledged superior to that of any other painter.' He fell from favour under the scornful attacks of *Ruskin (who detested the Bolognese painters in general), and until well into the 20th cent. a just appreciation of his stature was prevented by the failure to distinguish between his own works and those by his countless (often extremely insipid) imitators. The great exhibition devoted to him in Bologna in 1954 was a turning point in his critical fortunes, and his status as one of the greatest Italian painters of the 17th cent. is now firmly re-established. His late works in particular show an ethereal beauty of colouring that sets him apart from any of his contemporaries. The best collection of his work is in the Pinacoteca in Bologna.

Renier of Huy. *Mosan metal-worker active in the early 12th cent. Only one work is documented as being by him, but this is one of the great masterpieces of the period—a bronze font (1107–18) originally made for Notre Dame des Fonts, Liège, and now in St Bartholomew, Liège. It is a large bowl supported on ten (originally twelve) oxen (a reference to the 'sea of cast metal . . . mounted on twelve oxen' made for King Solomon (1 Kings 7: 23–5)) and adorned with scenes appropriate to the sacrament of baptism. The figures are much more naturalistic and classical than in most *Romanesque art. Very little other work can be attributed to Renier or his workshop, but he had great influence on Mosan art.

Renoir, Pierre-Auguste (1841–1919). French *Impressionist painter, born at Limoges. In 1854 he began work as a painter in a porcelain factory in Paris, gaining experience with the light, fresh colours that were to distinguish his Impressionist work and also learning the importance of good craftsmanship. His predilection towards light-hearted themes was also influenced by the great *Rococo masters, whose work he studied in the Louvre. In 1862 he entered the studio of *Gleyre and there formed a lasting friendship with *Monet, *Sisley, and *Bazille. He painted with them in the *Barbizon district and became a leading member of the group of Impressionists who met at the Café Guerbois. His relationship with Monet was particularly close at this time, and their paintings of the beauty spot called La Grenouillière done in 1869 (an example by Renoir is in the Nationalmuseum, Stockholm) are regarded as the classic early statements of the Impressionist style. Like Monet, Renoir endured much hardship early in his career, but he began to achieve success as a portraitist in the late 1870s and was freed from financial worries after the dealer Paul *Durand-Ruel began buying

his work regularly in 1881. By this time Renoir had 'travelled as far as Impressionism could take me', and a visit to Italy in 1881–2 inspired him to seek a greater sense of solidity in his work. The change in attitude is seen in *The Umbrellas* (NG, London), which was evidently begun before the visit to Italy and finished afterwards; the two little girls on the right are painted with the feathery brush-strokes characteristic of his Impressionist manner, but the figures on the left are done in a crisper and drier style, with duller colouring. After a period of experimentation with what he called his 'manière aigre' (harsh or sour manner) in the mid 1880s, he developed a softer and more supple kind of handling. At the same time he turned from contemporary themes to more timeless subjects, particularly nudes, but also pictures of young girls in unspecific settings. As his style became grander and simpler he also took up mythological subjects (*The Judgement of Paris*, Hiroshima Museum of Art, *c*.1913–14), and the female type he preferred became more mature and ample. In the 1890s Renoir began to suffer from rheumatism, and from 1903 (by which time he was world-famous) he lived in the warmth of the south of France. The rheumatism eventually crippled him (by 1912 he was confined to a wheelchair), but he continued to paint until the end of his life, and in his last years he also took up sculpture, directing assistants (usually Richard Guino, a pupil of *Maillol) to act as his hands (*Venus Victorious*, Tate, London, 1914).

Renoir is perhaps the best-loved of all the Impressionists, for his subjects—pretty children, flowers, beautiful scenes, above all lovely women—have instant appeal, and he communicated the joy he took in them with great directness. 'Why shouldn't art be pretty?', he said, 'There are enough unpleasant things in the world.' He was one of the great worshippers of the female form, and he said 'I never think I have finished a nude until I think I could pinch it.' One of his sons was the celebrated film director **Jean Renoir** (1894–1979), who wrote a lively and touching biography published in both French and English (*Renoir, My Father*) in 1962.

Repin, Ilya (1844–1930). The most celebrated Russian painter of his day. He received his first training from a provincial *icon painter, but later studied at the St Petersburg Academy, and became involved with the *Wanderers. His *Volga Boatmen* (Russian Mus., Leningrad), exhibited in Vienna in 1873, made him internationally famous. Repin excelled at scenes from Russian history, such as *Ivan the Terrible with the Body of his Son* (Tretyakov Gal., Moscow, 1885), which although often seeming anecdotal or melodramatic to modern taste are still admired for their vigour and colour. He could also handle modern social themes, however, as in *They Did Not Expect Him* (Tretyakov Gal., 1884), showing the unexpected return of a political exile from Siberia. But it is as a portraitist that he is now most highly regarded. He painted Tolstoy several times and numerous other distinguished contemporaries. Repin became professor of history painting at the St Petersburg Academy in 1894 and was an influential teacher.

repoussoir (French: to push back, set off). A figure or object in the foreground of a picture (and usually at the side) used to 'push back', give depth to, and enhance the principal scene or episode.

reredos. An altarpiece that rises from ground level behind an altar. See also RETABLE.

resin. An adhesive substance, insoluble in water, secreted by many trees and plants and used in art particularly as a constituent of *varnish. The resins used by painters in the past are not always easy to identify, but they include both soft resins from living trees, such as mastic, dammar, sandarac, Canada balsam, *turpentine, and hard fossil resins, such as copal and amber.

retable. An altarpiece that stands on the back of an altar or on a pedestal behind it, rather than rising from ground level. See also REREDOS.

Rethel, Alfred (1816–59). German painter and graphic artist. His biggest work, a cycle of frescos from the life of Charlemagne (Town Hall, Aachen), was once much admired as a great achievement of heroic *history painting, but today seems hollow and theatrical. The cycle was begun in 1847 but left unfinished because of the madness that ended his career in 1853. Rethel is now mainly remembered for his series of woodcuts *Another Dance of Death* (1849), much in the spirit of *Holbein's famous depictions of the subject, but satirizing the revolutionary events of 1848, with Death seen as the embodiment of anarchy. Two related woodcuts, *Death as a Strangler* (1847) and *Death as a Friend* (1851), were once extremely popular.

Rewald, John (1912–). German-born American art historian; a professor at the University of Chicago 1963–71 and thereafter at the City University, New York. He is the doyen of the field of *Impressionist and *Post-Impressionist scholarship, and is famous for two magisterial works, *The History of Impressionism* (1946, 4th edn. 1973) and *Post-Impressionism: From Van Gogh to Gauguin* (1956, 3rd edn. 1978). These show his total command of the voluminous material and his remarkable powers of organization and exposition in forming it into a highly readable narrative, and are, by common consent, among the greatest works of art history ever written; *The History of Impressionism* used to enjoy the 'distinction' of being the most stolen book from the *Courtauld Institute library. Rewald's other writings include studies of many leading 19th-cent. French artists, particularly *Cézanne (he received a gold medal from Cézanne's home town, Aix-en-Provence, in 1984), and two collections of his articles have appeared, *Studies in Impressionism* (1985) and *Studies in Post-Impressionism* (1986).

Reynolds, Sir Joshua (1723–92). English painter and writer on art, the first President of the *Royal Academy, the leading portraitist of his day, and perhaps the most important figure in the history of English painting. Reynolds was born at Plympton in Devonshire, the son of a scholarly clergyman, and he was brought up in an atmosphere of learning. He studied painting in London under *Hudson (another Devonshire man) 1740–3, but set up independently in Devon as a portraitist before his apprenticeship was officially ended. In 1750–2 he was in Italy, where he made an intensive study of the great masters of the 16th and 17th cents. and also of the *antique (it was while copying *Raphael in the cold of the Vatican that he contracted his deafness). He not only absorbed the formal language of his models, but also developed a deliberate cult of learning and Classical allusion that coloured his whole approach to art. In tune with established art theory, he thought that *history painting was the highest branch of art, but he believed that portraiture could rise above its traditional status as mere 'face-painting' by improving on the deficiencies of nature and using poses and gestures that allude to the great art of the past. Thus, in the work that established his reputation after he settled in London in 1753—*Commodore Keppel* (National Maritime Mus., London, 1753–4)—the sitter's heroic pose is based directly (albeit in reverse) on that of the *Apollo Belvedere*, then regarded as the matchless ideal of male beauty.

Reynolds quickly achieved a leading position in his profession. He had 150 sitters a year by 1758, and by 1764 was earning the enormous sum of £6,000 a year. His success was achieved through hard work and careful business management as well as talent; on the day he was knighted (21 April 1769) his visit to St James's Palace was fitted in between two sittings with clients. Moreover, although he always retained traces of his provincial origins (notably his Devonshire accent), he was completely at home with his eminent sitters. His pupil James *Northcote said that 'His general manner, deportment and behaviour were amiable and prepossessing; his disposition was naturally courtly. He . . . contrived to move in a higher sphere of society than any other English artist had done before. Thus he procured for the Professors of the Arts a consequence, dignity and reception which they never possessed in this country.' Reynolds's elevation of the status of the artist depended, then, not only on the intellectual quality of his work, but also on his social acceptability, and it is significant that his friends were mainly men of letters—notably Dr Johnson and Oliver Goldsmith—rather than other painters (James Boswell dedicated his celebrated *Life of Johnson* to Reynolds). On the foundation of the Royal Academy in 1768, he was the obvious choice for President, and he arranged for Johnson and Goldsmith to be appointed to the honorary positions of Professors of Ancient History and Literature. For the next twenty years, until his blindness stopped him painting in 1790, his authority in the Academy was paramount and his fifteen *Discourses* delivered over that period have become the

classic expression of the academic doctrine of the *Grand Manner, the doctrine of the rational *ideal as against the incipient *Romanticism inherent in the new emphasis on feeling, sentiment, and emotion as the basis of aesthetic judgement.

As a portraitist Reynolds is remarkable above all for his versatility—his inexhaustible range of response to the individuality of each sitter, man, woman, or child. The celebrated remark of his rival *Gainsborough, 'Damn him! How various he is!', is echoed in the praise of *Ruskin: 'Considered as a painter of individuality in the human form and mind, I think him the prince of portrait painters. *Titian paints nobler pictures and van *Dyck had nobler subjects, but neither of them entered so subtly as Sir Joshua did into the minor varieties of human heart and temper.' In spite of his impressive weight of learning Reynolds could at times be utterly direct, and although his huge output necessitated the employment of assistants and drapery painters, and his experimentation with *bitumen has resulted in some of his pictures being in poor condition, there is much beauty of handling in his work. His finest pictures undoubtedly take their place among the great masterpieces of British portraiture. On the other hand, his history paintings, dating mainly from the end of his career, are generally considered failures. Reynolds's work is in numerous public collections, great and small, in Britain and elsewhere, and many of his finest pictures are still in the possession of the families for which they were painted. His work was so varied that no single collection can be regarded as fully representative.

Riace bronzes. See PHIDIAS.

Ribalta, Francisco (1565–1628). Spanish painter. He was probably trained at the *Escorial and during most of the 1580s and 1590s he worked in Madrid. His earlier paintings are *Mannerist in character, notably his first known work, *The Nailing to the Cross* (Hermitage, Leningrad, 1582). By 1599 he was settled in Valencia and there his style became much more sombre and naturalistic. According to *Palomino, Ribalta had studied in Italy and he is known to have made a copy of *Caravaggio's *Martyrdom of St Peter*, but his late *tenebrist style may have been influenced more by

*Ribera than by direct knowledge of painting in Rome. In their turn, Ribalta's dramatically lit and powerfully austere mature works (*Christ Embracing St Bernard*, Prado, Madrid) had considerable influence on Spanish painting, notably on *Zurbarán. His son **Juan** (1596/7–1628) was also an able painter in the Caravaggesque manner, but died young.

Ribera, José (Jusepe) de (1591–1652). Spanish painter, etcher, and draughtsman, active for all his known career in Italy, where he was called 'Lo Spagnoletto'. Little is known of his life before he settled in Naples (at the time a Spanish possession) in 1616. Naples was then one of the main centres of the Caravaggesque style, and Ribera is often described as one of *Caravaggio's followers. However, although his early work is markedly *tenebrist, it is much more individual than that of most Caravaggesque artists, particularly in his vigorous and scratchy handling of paint. Similarly, his penchant for the typically Caravaggesque theme of bloody martyrdom has been overplayed, enshrined as it is in Byron's lines: 'Spagnoletto tainted/His brush with all the blood of all the sainted' (*Don Juan*, xiii. 71). He undoubtedly painted some powerful pictures of this type, notably the celebrated *Martyrdom of St Bartholomew* (Prado, Madrid, *c*.1630), but he was equally capable of great tenderness, as in *The Adoration of the Shepherds* (Louvre, Paris, 1650), and his work is remarkable for his feeling for individual humanity. Indeed, he laid the foundation of that respect for the dignity of the individual which was so important a feature of Spanish art from *Velázquez to *Goya. This feature of his work is evident also in the secular subjects, such as *The Clubfooted Boy* (Louvre, 1642). He was the first to breach the traditional Spanish dislike for mythological themes (*Apollo and Marsyas*, Musées Royaux, Brussels, 1637), and he broadened the *Baroque repertory by his series of philosophers depicted as beggars or vagabonds (*Archimedes*, Prado, 1630), done to flout the humanistic pedantry of the Academies and heralding the anti-Classical pictures of Velázquez. Ribera gradually moved away from his early tenebrist style, and his late works are often rich in colour and soft in modelling. He was the leading painter in Naples in his period (Velázquez visited him during his second visit to Italy and probably during his first) and his work was influential in Spain (where much of it was exported) as well as in Italy. His reputation has remained high, and until the Napoleonic Wars (1803–15) he and *Murillo were virtually the only Spanish painters who were widely known outside their native country.

Ricci, Sebastiano (1659–1730). Italian decorative painter. He was born at Belluno and is considered a member of the Venetian school, but before he settled in Venice in 1717 he led a peripatetic life, working in numerous Italian cities and also in England, Flanders, France, and Germany. His unsettled existence is a reflection not only of the demand for his talents but also of his penchant for illicit love affairs, which often led to his having to move in haste, and once almost resulted in his execution. In view of this it is not surprising that his work is uneven and sometimes shows signs of carelessness, but he had a gift for vivid, fresh colouring, and his itinerant career was important in spreading knowledge of Italian decorative painting. Little of the decorative work he did in England survives except the *Resurrection* in the apse of the Chelsea Hospital Chapel and some large but damaged canvases on the staircase at Burlington House (now the Royal Academy). He is, however, extremely well represented in the Royal Collection. **Marco Ricci** (1676–1729), Sebastiano's nephew, was also born in Belluno and travelled extensively. He made two visits to England, and worked there in partnership with his uncle, the collaboration continuing after they returned to Venice in 1717. Examples of their joint works are in the Royal Collection. He was primarily a landscape painter, working in a freely handled style that owed something to *Magnasco.

Riccio, Il (Andrea Briosco) (1470–1532). Italian sculptor, born in Trento, and active in and around Padua, where he was probably trained by Bartolommeo Bellano (*c*.1440–96/7), who in turn is assumed to have been one of *Donatello's assistants. His nickname means 'curly head'. Riccio was a virtuoso bronze-worker and his masterpiece is the great bronze Easter candlestick in the Santo (S. Antonio) at Padua (1507–16), which with its relief scenes of Classically draped figures, its satyrs, sphinxes, and decorative conceits, is an endlessly inventive work. He is best known, however, for his small bronze figures, which are done in an *antique manner and greatly appealed to humanist circles in Padua and Venice (he was on intimate terms with leading scholars). They were much imitated, but works from Riccio's own hand are distinguished by a vivacity and delicacy of surface that none of his rivals could match.

Richards, Ceri (1903–71). British painter, born at Dunvant, near Swansea, of a Welsh-speaking family. He was an artist of great versatility, able to absorb many influences without sacrificing his originality. From 1933, under the influence of *Picasso, he worked on a series of *relief constructions and *assemblages which were described by John *Rothenstein as 'original creations of a rare order, and unlike anything else done in Britain at the time'. He was influenced by the London *Surrealist Exhibition of 1936, which in his own words 'helped me to be aware of the mystery, even the "unreality", of ordinary things'. After the Second World War his painting drew inspiration from the large exhibition of Picasso and *Matisse at the Victoria and Albert Museum (1945). His love of music showed itself in the many pictures with musical themes done during this time—e.g. *Cold Light. Deep Shadow* (Tate, London, 1950)—culminating in his *Cathédrale engloutie* series illustrating Debussy's music on this theme. He was also inspired by the poetry of Dylan Thomas and one of his finest paintings is entitled '*Do not go gentle into that good night*' (Tate, 1956). Richards also did work for churches, designed for the stage, and made murals for ships of the Orient Line.

Richardson, Jonathan the Elder (1665–1745). English portrait painter, writer, and collector. John *Riley's most important pupil, he was one of the leading portraitists in the generation after *Kneller's death. This period, however, has been described by Sir Ellis *Waterhouse as 'the most drab in the history of British painting', and Richardson is remembered today more for his writings than his pictures. His most important book is *An Essay on the Theory of Painting* (1715), which made claims for the intellectual seriousness of painting and inspired the young *Reynolds. *An Account of Some of the Statues, Bas-Reliefs, Drawings,*

and Pictures in Italy (1722), which he wrote in collaboration with his son, **Jonathan the Younger** (1694–1771), also a portraitist, was much used as a guide-book by young Englishmen making the *Grand Tour. Richardson the Elder made a superb collection of Old Master drawings.

Richier, Germaine (1904–59). French sculptor. She had a traditional training as a carver, working under *Bourdelle from 1925 to 1929, but from about 1940 she began to create a distinctive type of bronze sculpture. Influenced by *Giacometti, her compositions became more open and often had slender, elongated limbs or fibrils suggestive of insect life, while her figures seemed half animal or half insect. Her surfaces have a tattered and lacerated effect, creating a macabre feeling of decomposition, and she was one of the pioneers of an open form of sculpture in which enclosed space becomes as important and alive as the solid material. Her international prestige grew steadily in the years after the Second World War.

Richmond, George (1809–96). The best-known member of a family of English painters. He was a pupil of his father, the *miniaturist **Thomas Richmond Sen.** (1771–1837), and also studied at the *Royal Academy, where he became a friend of Samuel *Palmer. With Palmer and others he was one of the group of *Blake's followers known as the *Ancients. His imitation of Blake's mannerisms was heavy-handed and he had nothing of the master's spirit (*The Eve of Separation*, Ashmolean, Oxford, 1830). From about 1830 he turned from poetic and religious themes to portraiture and became a great fashionable success. His brother, **Thomas Richmond Jun.** (1802–74), and his son, **Sir William Blake Richmond** (1842–1921), were also painters. They were principally portraitists, but Sir William was also a sculptor and medallist, and painted ambitious Classical scenes.

Ricketts, Charles (1866–1931). English painter, designer, sculptor, collector, and writer on art. While a youth he met *Shannon, who became his lifelong companion. Trained as an illustrator, in 1896 he founded a private printing press—the Vale Press—for which he designed founts, initials, borders, and illustrations in the tradition of William *Morris. But after 1904 he turned instead to painting, modelling, and theatrical design. Much of the excellent and varied collection he made with Shannon was bequeathed to the Fitzwilliam Museum, Cambridge.

Ridolfi, Carlo (1594–1658). Italian painter, etcher, and art historian. He is insignificant as an artist, and best remembered as the author of *Le Miraviglie dell' arte* (Marvels of the Painter's Art), published in two volumes in 1648. This is a source of great importance for the history of Venetian art, which was somewhat scantily treated by *Vasari. Ridolfi also wrote a life of *Tintoretto (1642).

Riemenschneider, Tilman (*c.*1460–1531). German sculptor, active in Würzburg, where he is first recorded in 1483. With *Stoss, he was the outstanding German late *Gothic sculptor, and his workshop was large and productive. He was primarily a wood-carver (he was the first German sculptor to leave the wood unpainted), but he also worked in stone. His style was intricate, but also balanced and harmonious, with none of the extreme emotionalism often seen in German art of the period. He held various offices in city government, and in 1525 he was tortured and briefly imprisoned because he was one of the councilmen who refused to support the use of force against the rebels in the Peasants' War. Much of Riemenschneider's work is still in the churches for which it was carved, but he is also well represented in the Mainfränkisches Museum in Würzburg. Two of his sons, **Jörg** and **Hans**, were sculptors, and two others, **Bartholomäus** (a pupil of *Dürer) and **Tilman**, were painters.

Rigaud, Hyacinthe (1659–1743). French portrait painter, the friend and rival of *Largillière. He was born in Perpignan and after working in Montpellier he settled in Paris in 1681. His reputation was established in 1688 with a portrait (now lost) of Monsieur, Louis XIV's brother, and he became the outstanding court painter of the latter part of Louis's reign, retaining his popularity after the king's death. He was less interested in showing individual character than in depicting the rank and condition of the sitter by nobility of attitude and expressiveness of gesture.

These qualities are seen most memorably in his celebrated state portrait of Louis XIV (Louvre, Paris, 1701), one of the classic images of royal majesty. Louis so admired this portrait that, although he had intended it as a present to Philip V of Spain, he kept it himself. Rigaud's unofficial portraits are much more informal and show a debt to *Rembrandt (*The Artist's Mother*, Louvre, 1695), several of whose works he owned. The output from Rigaud's studio was vast and examples are in many collections.

Rijksmuseum, Amsterdam. The Dutch national art collection. It had its origin in the Royal Museum erected by Louis Bonaparte (Napoleon's brother) as King of Holland in 1808. The idea of the Royal Museum was to assemble Netherlandish paintings of national importance and also to stimulate contemporary art. In 1815 the collection was transferred to the Trippenhuis, where it was opened in 1817 as the Rijksmuseum (State Museum). The present building, a large Gothic Revival building designed by P. J. H. Cuypers, the outstanding Dutch architect of the 19th century, was opened in 1885. In 1922 Schmidt Degener, formerly of the Boymans Museum at Rotterdam, became Director of the Rijksmuseum, modernized the display, and began the acquisition of foreign works of art. The Rijksmuseum has the most comprehensive collection of 17th-cent. Dutch art in the world, and although representation in other areas is uneven, it is strong in certain fields, such as oriental art. Associated with the Rijksmuseum is the Rijksprentenkabinet, which possesses one of the world's finest collections of prints and drawings.

Riley, Bridget (1931–). English painter and designer, the leading British exponent of *Op art. Her interest in optical effects came partly through her study of *Seurat's technique of *pointillism, but when she took up Op art in the early 1960s she worked initially in black and white. She turned to colour in 1966. By this time she had attracted international attention (one of her paintings was used for the cover to the catalogue of the exhibition 'The Responsive Eye' at the Museum of Modern Art, New York, in 1964, the exhibition that gave currency to the term 'Op art'), and the seal was set on her reputation when she won the International Painting Prize at the *Venice Biennale in 1968. Her work shows a complete mastery of the effects characteristic of Op art, particularly subtle variations in size, shape, or placement of serialized units in an all-over pattern. It is often on a large scale and she frequently makes use of assistants for the actual execution. Although her paintings often create effects of vibration and dazzle, one of her most recent works (1983) is a decorative scheme for the interior of the Royal Liverpool Hospital that uses soothing bands of blue, yellow, pink, and white and is reported to have caused a drop in vandalism and graffiti. She has also worked in theatre design, making sets for a ballet called *Colour Moves* (first performed at the Edinburgh Festival in 1983). Unusually, the sets preceded the composition of the music and the choreography. Riley has travelled widely (a visit to Egypt in 1981 was particularly influential on her work, as she was inspired by the colours of ancient Egyptian art) and she has studios in London, Cornwall, and Provence.

Riley, John (1646–91). English portrait painter. His early career is obscure, but he emerged as the most distinguished figure in English portraiture in the interval between the death of *Lely in 1680 and the domination of *Kneller. Although he was appointed Principal Painter to William III and Mary II jointly with Kneller in 1688, his finest works are not court portraits but depictions of sitters from humble callings; the two best known are *The Scullion* (Christ Church, Oxford) and *Bridget Holmes* (Royal Coll., 1686), a full-length portrayal of a nonagenarian royal housemaid who brandishes her broom at a mischievous pageboy. He was generally more successful painting men than women (he was no rival to Lely in depicting fine clothes and soft complexions) and his unassuming sincerity of presentation exemplifies a typically English approach to portraiture that he passed on to his pupil *Richardson.

Rimmer, William (1816–79). English-born American sculptor, painter, teacher, and writer. His family emigrated in the year he was born and eventually settled in Boston, which with New York was his main place of work. Rimmer was an off-beat character and had an eccentric career. He believed he was the heir to the

French throne and taught himself medicine, being licensed as a physician in 1855. As an artist too he was self-taught, and although he showed brilliantly precocious talent with his gypsum figure of *Despair* (Mus. of Fine Arts, Boston, c.1830), he struggled for recognition, and for years earned his living mainly as a sign and scenery painter and as a cobbler. In his later years, however, he became famous as a teacher, notably for his instructional books, *Elements of Design* (1864) and *Art Anatomy* (1877). Rimmer's output as an artist was very small, but he was the most powerful and original American sculptor of his time, his work, which excels in dramatic force, vividly displaying his anatomical mastery (*Falling Gladiator*, Mus. of Fine Arts, 1861). As a painter, his best-known work is the nightmarish *Flight and Pursuit* (Mus. of Fine Arts, 1872), which, like his sculptures, shows the freshness and unconventionality of his approach and the richness of his imagination.

Riopelle, Jean-Paul (1923–   ). Canadian painter, sculptor, and graphic artist. He is considered the leading Canadian abstract painter of his generation, although since 1947 he has lived in Paris. Riopelle's early abstracts were in a lyrical manner, but in the 1950s his work became tauter, denser, and more powerful, often with paint applied with the palette-knife. International attention came to his work with pictures such as the huge *triptych *Pavane* (NG of Canada, Ottawa, 1954). He is prolific, and renowned for his use of various media.

Ripa, Cesare. See EMBLEM

Rivera, Diego (1886–1957). Mexican painter, the most celebrated figure in the revival of monumental fresco painting that is Mexico's most distinctive contribution to modern art. He spent the years 1907–21 mainly in Europe and became familiar with modern movements, but although he made some early experiments with, for example, *Cubism (he knew *Picasso in Paris), his mature art was firmly rooted in Mexican tradition. In 1921 Alvaro Obregón, an art-lover as well as a reformist, was elected President of Mexico, and Rivera, who was an extremely forceful personality, swiftly emerged as the leading artist in the programme of murals he initiated glorifying the history and people of the country in a spirit of revolutionary fervour. Many examples of his work are in public buildings in Mexico City, and they are often on a huge scale, a tribute to his enormous energy. The most ambitious scheme of all, in the National Palace, covering the history of Mexico, was begun in 1929 and left unfinished at Rivera's death, but it contains some of his most magnificent work. Rivera's murals are frankly didactic, intended to inspire a sense of nationalist and socialist identity in a still largely illiterate population; their glorification of creative labour or excoriation of capitalism can be crude, but his best work has astonishing vigour. His skill in choreographing his incident- and figure-packed compositions, in combining traditional and modern subject-matter and stylized and realistic images is formidable. In 1930–4 Rivera also painted frescos in the USA, where he was influential on the muralists of the *Federal Art Project. His *Man at the Crossroads* in the Rockefeller Center, New York, occasioned controversy because it included a portrait of Lenin, and it was replaced with a mural by *Brangwyn. His main work in the USA is a series of frescos on *Detroit Industry* (1932–3) in the Detroit Institute of Arts, commissioned by William *Valentiner. Throughout his career Rivera also painted a wide range of easel pictures, and he experimented with the *encaustic technique. Rivera was an enormous man (standing over 6 ft. and weighing over 20 stones), and although he was notoriously ugly he had great charm and humour and was irresistibly attractive to women. He had numerous love affairs and was three times married, his second wife being a painter, Frida Kahlo (1907–54). Her parents said 'it was like a marriage between an elephant and a dove'.

Rivers, Larry (1923–). American painter, sculptor, graphic artist, and designer, considered one of the leading figures of the movement towards figurative art that succeeded *Abstract Expressionism in the *New York School. He was a professional jazz saxophonist in the early 1940s and began painting in 1945, studying at the Hans *Hofmann School, 1947–8, and then at New York University under *Baziotes in 1948. His work of the 1950s continued the vigorous painterly handling associated with Abstract Expressionism, but

featured subject-matter that earned him a place in the first generation of American *Pop artists. *Washington Crossing the Delaware* (MOMA, New York, 1953), based on the picture by *Leutze, is one of his best-known works of this period. Rivers also took up sculpture in the 1950s and from the mid 1960s he broadened his range considerably, his work embracing constructions, including painted sculptures and shaped canvases, *collages, and prints. He has also designed for the stage, acted, and written poetry.

Robbia, Luca della (1399/1400–82). Florentine sculptor, the most famous member of a family of artists. Nothing is known of his early career, and he was a mature artist by the time of his first documented work—a *Cantoria* (Singing Gallery, 1431–8) for Florence Cathedral, now in the Cathedral Museum. It is a work of considerable originality as well as enormous charm, antedating by a year or two the companion gallery by *Donatello (now also in the Cathedral Museum). Its marble *reliefs of angels and children singing, dancing, and making music reflect *antique prototypes, but conceived in a more cheerful, less heroic spirit than Donatello's figures. In his own time Luca had the reputation of being one of the leaders of the modern (i.e. *Renaissance) style, comparable to Donatello and *Ghiberti in sculpture and *Masaccio in painting, but he is now remembered mainly for his development of coloured, glazed *terracotta as a sculptural medium—in particular for his highly popular invention of the type of the half-length Madonna and Child in white on a blue ground. The family workshop seems to have kept the technical formula a secret and it became the basis of a flourishing business; among the major works by Luca in the medium are the roundels of Apostles (c.1444) in *Brunelleschi's Pazzi Chapel in Sta Croce. Luca's business was carried on by his nephew **Andrea** (1435–1525), and later by Andrea's five sons, of whom **Giovanni** (1469–after 1529) was the most important. The famous roundels of infants on the façade of the Foundling Hospital in Florence (1463–6) were probably made by Andrea. His successors tended to sentimentalize Luca's warm humanity, and in course of time the artists' studio became a potters' workshop-industry.

Robert, Hubert (1733–1808). French landscape painter. From 1754 to 1765 he was in Italy (mainly Rome), and in 1761 he travelled to south Italy and Sicily with *Fragonard. He made a vast quantity of drawings in Italy, on which he based his pictures after his return to Paris. His particular interest was in ruins and he was the first to make them the main theme of a picture rather than to use them as *picturesque accessories. He romanticized the vision of *Panini and *Piranesi, whom he knew in Rome, and often set his ruins in idealized surroundings (although he also painted topographical views). His work was highly successful, satisfying the vogue for rather artificial, idealized landscape that was one aspect of *Rococo taste. Under Louis XVI Robert became Keeper of the King's Pictures and one of the first curators of the *Louvre, but he was imprisoned during the Revolution. He owed his life to an accident whereby another person of the same name was guillotined in his stead.

Roberti, Ercole de' (c.1450–96). Italian painter, active mainly in Ferrara. He succeeded *Tura as court painter to the *Este in 1486, but little is known of his life. Earlier he appears to have assisted *Cossa for some years, and with Cossa and Tura he ranks as the leading artist of the 15th cent. Ferrarese school. The only picture reasonably certainly his is the altarpiece with a *Madonna Enthroned with Saints* (1480) painted for Sta Maria in Porto at Ravenna and now in the Brera, Milan. Other works, however, can be confidently given to him because of his distinctive style. He inherited the tradition of Tura and Cossa with their precise line and metallic colours against elaborately fanciful ornamentation, but he developed this manner with great originality, modifying it with a subtlety of handling that seems to derive from Giovanni *Bellini. His work is often remarkable for its almost mystical intensity of feeling, as in a moving *Pietà* in the Walker Art Gallery, Liverpool.

Roberts, David (1796–1864). Scottish painter. He was apprenticed to a house painter, then worked as a scene painter for a travelling circus and Glasgow and Edinburgh theatres. In 1822 he settled in London and worked at the Drury Lane Theatre with his friend Clarkson *Stanfield. From 1831 he travelled widely in Europe and the Mediterranean Basin and made a fortune with his topographical views. He worked in oil and water-colour and published lavishly illustrated books, among them the six-volume *The Holy Land, Syria, Idumea, Arabia, Egypt & Nubia* (1842–9). His work can be monotonous when seen *en masse*, but at his best he combines bold design with precise observation.

Roberts, Tom (1856–1931). Australian painter. He was born in England and first went to Australia as a child in 1869. In 1881 he returned to England to study at the *Royal Academy, where he came under the influence of the art of *Bastien-Lepage. In 1883 during a walking tour of Spain he acquired some knowledge of *Impressionism, and when he returned to Melbourne in 1885 he gathered several other painters about him and founded what came to be known as the *Heidelberg School. In 1903 he left for England, not returning permanently until 1923. During the mid to late 1880s his work in pure landscape was considerable and influential, but from the 1890s onwards Roberts was essentially a portraitist and *genre painter, particularly of Australian rural life, and his work is regarded as beginning the growth of an indigenous school of Australian art.

Roberts, William (1895–1980). British painter. He was a member of the *Vorticist movement, signing the manifesto in the first number of *Blast*, and his work is close to that of *Bomberg in the way he depicts stiff, stylized figures through geometrically simplified forms. He continued working in a similar style for the rest of his career (*The Vorticists at the Restaurant de la Tour Eiffel*; Tate Gal., London, 1961–2). In the late 1950s he issued a number of privately printed pamphlets on his early works in refutation of the claim made by Wyndham Lewis in 1956 that 'Vorticism, in fact, was what I, personally, did, and said, at a certain period.'

rocaille. Term applied from the mid 16th cent. onwards to fancy rock-work and shell-work for fountains and grottoes, and later to ornament based on such forms. From about 1730 it began to acquire a wider connotation, being applied to the bolder and more extravagant flights of the *Rococo style. Indeed, it preceded the word 'Rococo' itself as an indication of style and the two terms have sometimes been used synonymously by French art historians.

rocker. The tool used to prepare the surface of the plate in *mezzotint.

Rocky Mountain School. Term applied to 19th-cent. American artists who painted the Rocky Mountains in a spirit similar to that adopted by the *Hudson River School. Alfred *Bierstadt is the best-known artist of the school.

Rococo. Style of art and architecture, characterized by lightness, grace, playfulness, and intimacy, that emerged in France c.1700 and spread throughout Europe in the 18th cent. The Rococo was both a development from and a reaction against the weightier *Baroque style. It shared with the Baroque a love of complexity of form, but instead of a concern for solidity and mass, there was a delicate play on the surface, and sombre colours and heavy gilding were replaced with light pinks, blues, and greens, with white also often being prominent. Elegance and convenience were the qualities demanded by a society tired of the excessive grandiloquence of Louis XIV's court at Versailles, and the Rococo style was intially mainly one of decoration. The word is said to derive from a combination of *barocco* (Baroque) and *rocaille*; like many stylistic labels in the history of art, it was originally a term of abuse, meaning 'tastelessly florid or ornate', but it is now used without any pejorative connotations.

In painting, the first great master of the Rococo style was *Watteau and the painters who most completely represent the lighthearted (often gently erotic) spirit of the mature Rococo style are *Boucher and *Fragonard. *Falconet is perhaps the best representative of the style in French sculpture, but generally the Rococo spirit is seen more clearly in small porcelain figures than in large-scale statues (Falconet himself was Director of the famous porcelain factory at Sèvres). In architecture the Rococo style was much more suitable for interior decoration, with asymmetrical curves and pretty decorative motifs prevailing, than for exteriors, but something of the Rococo spirit—of its refinement and charm—can be seen even in such a regular and relatively unadorned building as Ange-Jacques Gabriel's Petit Trianon (1763–9) at Versailles.

From Paris the Rococo was disseminated by French artists working abroad and by engraved publications of French designs. It spread to Germany, Austria, Russia, Spain, and northern Italy (*Tiepolo, *Longhi, *Guardi). In England it had somewhat less of a vogue, although a substantial exhibition of English Rococo art was held at the Victoria and Albert Museum in 1984 and there are clear reflections of the style even in the work of so xenophobic an artist as *Hogarth. *Gainsborough's delicacy of characterization and sensitivity of touch (although completely personal) are also thoroughly in the Rococo spirit. In each country it took on a national character and in addition many local variants may be distinguished. Outside France, it had its finest flowering in Germany and Austria, where it merged with a still vigorous Baroque tradition. In churches such as Vierzehnheiligen (1743–72) by Balthasar Neuman, the Baroque qualities of spatial variety and of architecture, sculpture, and painting working together are taken up in a breathtakingly light and exuberant manner. Rococo flourished in central Europe until the end of the century (as in the work of *Maulbertsch), but in France and elsewhere the tide of taste had begun to turn from frivolity and lightheartedness towards the sternness of *Neoclassicism by the 1760s.

Rodchenko, Alexander (1891–1956). Russian painter, sculptor, industrial designer, and photographer, one of the leading *Constructivists. His production was prolific and his artistic evolution was rapid, as he moved from *Impressionistic pictures in 1913 to pure abstracts, made with a ruler and compass, in 1914. He was influenced by *Malevich's *Suprematism, his *Black on Black* (Met. Mus., New York, 1918) being a response to Malevich's *White on White* paintings. Rodchenko, however, was without Malevich's mystical leanings, and he coined the term 'Non-objective' to describe his own more scientific approach. In 1917 he began making three-dimensional constructions under the influence of *Tatlin, and some of these developed into graceful hanging sculptures. Like Tatlin and other Constructivists, however, Rodchenko came to reject pure art as a parasitical activity, and after 1922 he devoted his energies to industrial design, typography, film and stage design, propaganda posters, and photography. It was perhaps in photography that his originality was most evident. In sharp reaction from his abstract work, his photography was geared towards reportage and a pictorial record of the new Russia. But much of this work was outstanding for its exploitation of unusual perspectives and angles of vision, and his innovative use of light and shadow influenced, for example, the great Soviet film director Sergei Eisenstein. In the mid 1930s Rodchenko returned to easel painting, and in the early 1940s he produced a series of abstract canvases in an expressionist vein.

Rodin, Auguste (1840–1917). French sculptor, one of the greatest and most influential European artists of his period. He was the first sculptor since the heyday of *Neoclassicism to occupy a central position in public attention and he opened up new possibilities for his art in a manner comparable to that of his great contemporaries in painting—*Cézanne, *Gauguin, and van *Gogh. His beginnings, however, were not auspicious. He came from a poor background, was rejected by the École des *Beaux-Arts three times and for many years worked as an ornamental mason. In 1875 he went to Italy, where (as he later wrote to *Bourdelle) '*Michelangelo freed me from academism.' Michelangelo was the inspiration for his first major work, *The Age of Bronze*, which was exhibited in 1878. (Like many of Rodin's statues, this exists in several casts; the Rodin Museum in Paris has examples of virtually all his work. There is also a Rodin museum in Philadelphia.) It caused a sensation because the *naturalistic treatment of the naked figure was so different from the idealizing conventions then current that he was accused of having cast it from a live model. Two years later, in 1880, his reputation now established, Rodin was commissioned by the state to make a bronze door for a proposed Musée des Arts Décoratifs. Rodin never finished the huge work—*The Gates of Hell*—in a definitive form (he worked on it on and off until 1900 and the museum never came into being in its proposed form), but he poured

some of his finest creative energy into it, and many of the nearly 200 figures that are part of it formed the basis of famous independent sculptures, most notably *The Thinker*. The several casts of the complete structure that exist were made after Rodin's death. The overall design is a kind of *Romantic reworking of *Ghiberti's *Gates of Paradise* for the Florence Baptistery, the twisted and anguished figures, irregularly arranged, reminiscent of Michelangelo's *Last Judgement* and Gustav *Doré's illustrations for the *Divine Comedy*. His modelling is often rough and 'unfinished' and anatomical forms are exaggerated or simplified in the cause of intensity of expression.

These traits were taken further in some of Rodin's monuments, for example the famous group of *The Burghers of Calais* (1885–95), commissioned by the city of Calais for a site in front of the town hall (another cast is in Victoria Tower Gardens, London). In the figures of the six hostages who face the threat of death Rodin created a profound image of a variety of responses to an extreme emotional crisis. The civic authorities had wanted something in a more traditional heroic-patriotic vein, and the monument was eventually unveiled only after years of wrangling. Even worse hostility was aroused a few years later by his statue of Balzac. This was commissioned by the Société des Gens de Lettres in 1891, but Rodin's design was so radical—an expression of the elemental power of genius rather than a portrait of an individual— that it was rejected. The monument, which ranks as the most original piece of public statuary created in the 19th cent., and which Rodin said was 'the sum of my whole life', was not finally cast and set up—at the intersection of the Boulevards Raspail and Montparnasse—until 1939. In spite of this kind of controversy, by 1900 Rodin was widely regarded as the greatest living sculptor, and in that year a pavilion was devoted to his work at the Paris World Fair. Apart from his monuments, he did a large number of portraits of eminent personalities and he was a prolific graphic artist, some of his later work especially being notably erotic. Although the literary and symbolic significance he attached to his work has been out of keeping with the conception of 'pure' sculpture that has predominated in the 20th cent., Rodin's influence on the development of modern art has been immense, for single-handedly he rescued sculpture from a period of stagnation and made it once again a vehicle for intense personal expression.

Roelas, Juan de las (1558/60–1625). Spanish painter, the leading painter of his period in Seville. He was a priest and virtually all his work was done for churches and religious houses in and around Seville. Roelas has been called 'the Spanish *Tintoretto' and 'the Spanish *Veronese', and the painterly richness of his large multifigure compositions suggests he had studied in Italy. His work, however, has a religious fervour that is typically Spanish rather than Italian, and his blending of mysticism with *naturalism was deeply influential in Seville. Most of his work remains there; his masterpiece is perhaps the huge *Martyrdom of St Andrew* (Seville Mus., 1609).

Roger of Helmarshausen. See THEOPHILUS.

Rogers, Claude (1907–79). British painter. He exhibited with the *London Group in 1931 and became a member in 1938. With *Coldstream and Victor *Pasmore he was a founding member of the *Euston Road School in 1937 and he became one of the main upholders of its tradition. A distinguished teacher, he lectured at the *Slade School from 1948 to 1963 and was Professor of Fine Art in the University of Reading, 1963–72.

Rohlfs, Christian (1849–1938). German painter and graphic artist. Until he was over 50 he worked in a fairly traditional *naturalistic manner, but he then discovered the work of the *Post-Impressionists and became one of the pioneers of *Expressionism in Germany. He made sensitive experiments in the manners of various artists, and his favourite themes were visionary views of old German towns, colourful landscapes, and flower pieces.

Roldán, Pedro (1624–99). Spanish *Baroque sculptor. He was a fellow student of Pedro de *Mena in Granada under the latter's father, Alonso de Mena. By 1656 he had settled at Seville, where he became the leading sculptor of his period and where from 1664 to 1672 he was director of sculpture at the Academy. His greatest

work is the spectacular *reredos for the high altar of the Church of the Hospital de la Caridad (1670–5), which was *polychromed by *Valdés Leal. Roldán's daughter and pupil, **Luisa** (c.1656–c.1704), was also a sculptor, principally active at Cadiz and Madrid. She was the only woman to hold the position of royal sculptor (to Charles II of Spain).

Romanelli, Giovanni Francesco (c.1610–62). Italian painter and tapestry designer. He was Pietro da *Cortona's outstanding pupil, and like his master a protégé of the *Barberini family. Romanelli's graceful style was less energetic than Cortona's (he owed much to his first teacher *Domenichino) and his restrained type of Baroque proved particularly popular and influential in France, where he worked 1645–7 and 1655–7. He introduced to Paris Cortona's characteristic manner of decoration, consisting of paintings combined with richly gilded *stuccowork, and this was one of the sources for the great schemes of *Lebrun at Versailles and elsewhere. Examples of Romanelli's work survive in the Bibliothèque Nationale (painted for Cardinal Mazarin) and (much altered) in the Salle des Saisons of the Louvre (painted for Anne of Austria, mother of Louis XIV).

Romanesque. Style of art and architecture prevailing throughout most of Europe in the 11th and 12th cents., the first style to achieve such international currency. The dominant art of the Middle Ages was architecture, and 'Romanesque', like '*Gothic', is primarily an architectural term which has been extended to the other arts of the period. As the name suggests, it indicates a derivation from Roman art, and sometimes 'Romanesque' is used to cover all the developments from Roman architecture in the period from the collapse of the Roman Empire until the flowering of the Gothic—roughly AD 500–1200. More usually, however, it is applied to a distinctive style that emerged, almost simultaneously, in several countries—France, Germany, Italy, Spain—in the 11th cent. It is characterized most obviously by a new massiveness of scale, reflecting the greater political and economic stability that followed a period when Christian civilization seemed in danger of extinction. Romanesque painting and sculpture are generally strongly stylized, with little of the *naturalism and humanistic warmth of *Classical or later Gothic art. The forms of nature are freely translated into linear and sculptural designs which are sometimes majestically calm and severe and at others are agitated by a visionary excitement which can become almost delirious. Because of its expressionistic distortion of natural form, Romanesque art, as with other great non-naturalistic styles of the past, has had to wait for the revolution in sensibility brought about by the development of modern art in order to be widely appreciated.

Romantic Classicism. See NEOCLASSICISM and ROMANTICISM.

Romanticism. Movement in the arts flourishing in the late 18th and early 19th cents. Romanticism is so varied in its manifestations that a single definition is impossible, but its keynote was a belief in the value of individual experience. In this it marked a reaction from the rationalism of the Enlightenment and the order of the *Neoclassical style. The Romantic artist explored the values of intuition and instinct, exchanging the public discourse of Neoclassicism, the forms of which had a common currency, for a more private kind of expression. Romanticism is commonly seen as the antithesis of *Classicism, and the two concepts are sometimes used in a very general sense to designate polarities in attitude that may be seen in the art of any age—thus *Raphael might be described as a 'classical' artist, whereas his contemporary *Giorgione is a 'romantic' one. However, the exponents of both Romanticism and Classicism share a concern with the *ideal rather than the real, and that there is sometimes no firm dividing line between the two approaches is shown by the use of the term 'Romantic Classicism' to describe certain works that show a Romantic response to antiquity. Both Romanticism and Classicism embrace concepts of nobility, grandeur, virtue, and superiority. But where the Classical seems a possible ideal which will adapt man to his society and mould that society into an orderly setting for him, the Romantic envisages the unattainable, beyond the limits of society and human adaptability. The

Classical hero accepts the fate over which he has no control and triumphs nobly in this acquiescence, otherwise he would not be a hero. The Romantic hero pits himself against a hostile environment and at no time comes to terms with it even if he reaches his goal, otherwise he would not be Romantic.

Romanticism represents an attitude of mind rather than a set of particular stylistic traits and involves the expression of an idea that tends to have a verbal rather than a visual origin. It lends itself more easily to expression through music and literature than through the visual arts, as a sense of the infinite and the transcendental, of forces exceeding the boundaries of reason, must necessarily be vague—suggestive rather than concrete, as it must be in painting and even more so in sculpture. Almost by definition, the leading Romantic artists differ widely from one another—*Blake and *Turner in Britain, *Delacroix and *Géricault in France, *Friedrich and *Runge in Germany. The movement of which they were a part died out in the mid 19th cent., but in a broader sense the Romantic spirit has lived on, representing a revolt against conservatism, moderation, and insincerity and an insistence on the primacy of the imagination in artistic expression.

Rombouts, Theodoor (1579–1637). Flemish painter, mainly of religious and *genre scenes. He was a pupil of *Janssens in his native Antwerp, then from about 1616 to about 1625 he was in Italy. There his work became strongly *Caravaggesque and he established himself as one of the leading Flemish exponents of the style. Later, he fell under the all-pervasive influence of *Rubens and his work became much lighter in tonality.

Romney, George (1734–1802). English painter, mainly of portraits. Born in Lancashire, the son of a builder and cabinet-maker, he worked in the north of England until 1762, when he settled in London. There he became the most successful portraitist of the day apart from *Reynolds and *Gainsborough. His posthumous reputation was once almost the equal of theirs, but has faded greatly. Much of his work is now considered facile and he was probably at his best with portraits of young people, when his delicate colour sense and graceful line were used to good effect. As with many successful portraitists, his heart lay elsewhere and he had aspirations to be a history painter. His visit to Italy in 1773–5 made a lasting effect on him, but his plans for grandiose literary and historical works rarely advanced beyond his sepia drawings (a large collection is in the Fitzwilliam Museum, Cambridge), although he painted for *Boydell's Shakespeare Gallery. Introspective and nervous by temperament, Romney was attracted to literary circles and associated little with his fellow artists, never exhibiting at the *Royal Academy. His friends among artists tended to be others of literary temperament, such as *Flaxman. In about 1781 Romney became infatuated with Emma Hart, later Lady Hamilton (1761?–1815), Nelson's mistress, and he painted her many times in various guises. He retired to Kendal in 1798 and died insane. Romney was a fast and prolific worker, and his paintings are in many collections in Britain and the USA.

Ronald, William (William Ronald Smith) (1926–). Canadian painter and performer. In 1955 he moved to New York, where he enjoyed considerable success among the second generation of *Abstract Expressionists. Although he continued to live in the USA, becoming an American citizen in 1963, he retained a large following in Toronto and exerted a strong influence on painters there. With the decline of Abstract Expressionism his popularity waned, but he achieved success as a television and radio celebrity, sometimes painting before an audience.

Roncalli, Cristoforo (1552–1626). Italian painter also called Il Pomarancio (after his birthplace near Volterra). With *Cesari he was one of the leading fresco decorators of his time in Rome. Although he adapted somewhat to the innovations of the *Carracci he remained essentially in the *Mannerist tradition and his work is generally undistinguished. His unbiased, commonsense views on art, however, known from a lecture he gave to the Academy of St Luke in 1594, commended him to Vincenzo *Giustiniani, one of the most enlightened patrons of his time, and Roncalli became his artistic adviser.

Rooker, Michael Angelo (1743–1801). English painter, scene designer, and book illustrator. He studied engraving with his father **Edward** (1712?–1774), who specialized in architectural subjects, and painting with Paul *Sandby. From 1788 he travelled extensively in the southern and midland counties and was one of the most assiduous topographers of his time. For many years he was also scene painter at the Haymarket Theatre in London.

Rops, Félicien (1833–98). Belgian graphic artist and painter, active mainly in Paris. Rops was primarily a printmaker—one of the most brilliant and technically resourceful of his period—and his work is highly distinctive because of his vividly licentious imagination, which took delight in the morbid, perverse, and erotic. Much of his work was done as illustrations for books or for his own satirical journal *Uylenspiegel*. He was a member of the avant-garde Brussels group Les *Vingt and his work was notably influential on *Ensor.

Rosa, Salvator (1615–73). Neapolitan painter and etcher, active mainly in Rome. He was a flamboyant character—a poet, actor, and musician as well as an artist—and in the 1640s he lived mainly in Florence (where he worked for the *Medici) after he had been rash enough to satirize the great *Bernini. His colourful personality and unswerving belief in his own genius made him a prototype of the *Romantic artist and his fame was greatest in the 18th and 19th cents. (the story that he was a bandit seems to be a 19th-cent. invention). He was a prolific artist and painted various subjects (including spirited battle-pieces in which he surpassed his teacher, *Falcone), but he is best known for the creation of a new type of wild and savage landscape. His craggy cliffs, jagged, moss-laden trees, and rough bravura handling create a dank and desolate air that contrasts sharply with the serenity of *Claude or the Classical grandeur of *Poussin (a situation summed up in the famous lines from James Thomson's *The Castle of Indolence* (1748): 'Whate'er Lorraine light-touched with softening hue,/Or savage Rosa dashed, or learned Poussin drew'). Rosa is also well known for his macabre subjects (notably of witches), but he himself set most store by his large historical and religious compositions, which are now considered his least attractive works. In the 1660s he turned with great success to etching. Rosa was highly influential on the development of the *picturesque and the *sublime, and he had a great vogue in England, where *Mortimer was particularly taken with his pictures of bandits. *Ruskin, however, was responsible for the fall of his reputation, condemning his landscapes as artificial.

Rose + Croix, Salon de la. See SALON DE LA ROSE + CROIX.

Roslin, Alexander (1718–93). Swedish portrait painter, active mainly in France. He left his country in 1745, worked at the courts of Bayreuth (1745–7) and Parma (1751–2), and in 1752 finally settled in Paris. There he rapidly became one of the leading portraitists of the day, esteemed particularly for his skilful rendering of expensive fabrics and delicate complexions ('Satin, skin? Go to Roslin'). He visited St Petersburg, Vienna, and Warsaw (as well as Stockholm) in the 1770s, but in spite of his international travels his elegant work was entirely French in style. His wife, **Marie-Suzanne Giroust** (1734–72), was a pastellist. One of Roslin's finest works is an enchanting portrait of her entitled *The Lady in a Black Veil* (Nationalmuseum, Stockholm, 1768).

Rosselli, Cosimo (1439–1507). Florentine painter. His successful career (the highpoint of which was painting frescos in the Sistine Chapel along with *Botticelli, *Ghirlandaio, and *Perugino) was based on his facility and high standards of craftsmanship rather than on any great distinction or originality as an artist. His pupils included Fra *Bartolommeo and *Piero di Cosimo.

Rossellino, Bernardo (1409–64) and **Antonio** (1427–79). Florentine sculptors, brothers. Bernardo worked as an architect as well as a sculptor and he combined both arts in his chief work—the tomb of the great humanist and Chancellor of the Florentine Republic, Leonardo Bruni, in Sta Croce, Florence (1444–50). It is based on the monument of the antipope John XXIII (Baldassare Cossa) by *Donatello and *Michelozzo in the Baptistery in Florence, and although less powerful is more graceful and harmonious; the pilasters framing the serene effigy, lying on a bier, have a dignity and elegance almost worthy

of *Brunelleschi. It became the model for the niche tomb for the rest of the century.

Antonio was trained by his brother, and his most ambitious work—the tomb of the Cardinal Prince of Portugal in S. Miniato al Monte, Florence (1461–6)—is based on Bernardo's Bruni tomb. It is more elaborate and concerned with movement than Bernardo's masterpiece, but also a less coherent design, and Antonio was a more distinguished artist when working on a smaller scale. He was a fine portraitist (*Giovanni Chellini*, V&A, London, 1456) and also made charming reliefs and statuettes of the Madonna and Child, in which he continued the tradition of Luca della *Robbia of stressing the naturalness and humanity of the Virgin.

Rossetti, Dante Gabriel (1828–82). English painter and poet. He came from a remarkable and talented family, his father being an exiled Italian patriot and Dante scholar and his sister the poet Christina Rossetti. Growing up in modest circumstances but a strongly literary environment, he at first found it hard to decide whether he should devote himself to poetry or painting. Although painting became his profession (following the advice given to him by the poet and critic Leigh Hunt: 'If you paint as well as you write, you may be a rich man'), he continued to write poetry and make translations from the Italian, and he is accorded a distinguished position as a literary figure. In 1848 he formed the *Pre-Raphaelite Brotherhood with *Hunt, *Millais, and others. His *Girlhood of Mary Virgin* (Tate, London, 1849), the first picture to be exhibited bearing the Brotherhood's initials, was warmly praised and sold well, but the subsequent abuse that the Pre-Raphaelites received hurt him so much that he rarely again exhibited in public. In the 1850s he virtually gave up oils and concentrated on water-colours of medieval subjects. These found ready buyers (often contacts of *Ruskin, whom Rossetti met in 1854), and Rossetti, who was a hard and skilful businessman, proved Leigh Hunt's prediction true—by the 1860s he was earning the very substantial sum of £3,000 a year.

In 1860 Rossetti married the beautiful but sickly Elizabeth Siddal, the archetypal Pre-Raphaelite 'stunner', after a long and sometimes vexed liaison. Her melancholy face haunted his imagination, and he portrayed 'Guggums' (as he called her) again and again—'It is like a monomania with him', wrote Ford Madox *Brown in 1855. Rossetti immortalized her mainly in drawings, for in spite of the hatred for academic discipline that made him so disdainful of the official art world, he was an outstanding draughtsman. Elizabeth died from an overdose of laudanum, possibly deliberate, in 1862, and Rossetti was devastated; as a gesture of his grief he had the only complete manuscript of his poems placed in her coffin, but he was persuaded to have them exhumed in 1869 and they were published the following year. Rossetti also painted the intensely spiritual *Beata Beatrix* (Tate) as a memorial to Elizabeth, expressing his love for her as a parallel to Dante's for Beatrice (the picture is dated 1864, but was worked on over a period of several years). By the time of Elizabeth's death Rossetti had returned to oil painting, and in the last two decades of his life, his subject-matter was confined almost exclusively to beautiful women, portrayed in a richly sensuous manner and often evoking literary or mythological references. Elizabeth was replaced as his favourite model by William *Morris's wife Janey, who became in Rossetti's pictures one of the archetypal *femmes fatales*—all cascading curls, pouting lips, and smouldering eyes. Rossetti had met Morris and *Burne-Jones in 1856 and entered into partnership with them in 1861 (in the decorative arts firm later known as Morris & Co.), but both business and personal relationships became strained; Rossetti was in love with Janey and he and Morris parted amid rancour in 1875. In his later years Rossetti became an eccentric recluse (he had a menagerie of unusual animals, including a wombat, the death of which occasioned a poem); he fought a losing battle against drugs and alcohol and he died paralysed and prematurely aged. Rossetti was nevertheless a commanding personality and his work was highly influential; his romantic medievalism inspired the second wave of Pre-Raphaelitism associated with Burne-Jones and other followers, and his *femmes fatales* appealed to the *Symbolists and had a legion of descendants during the turn-of-the-century taste for 'decadence'.

Rosso, Giovanni Battista (called Rosso Fiorentino) (1495–1540). Florentine painter and decorative artist. *Vasari says that he 'would not bind himself to any master' (a story that fits in with his individuality of temperament), but in his youth he learned most from *Andrea del Sarto, and with Andrea's pupil *Pontormo (Rosso's friend and exact contemporary) he was one of the leading figures in the early development of *Mannerism. His work was highly sophisticated and varied in mood, ranging from the refined elegance of the *Marriage of the Virgin* (S. Lorenzo, Florence, 1523) to the violent energy of *Moses and the Daughters of Jethro* (Uffizi, Florence, *c*.1523) and to the disquieting intensity of the *Deposition* (Galleria Pittorica, Volterra, 1521). In 1523 Rosso left Florence for Rome, where he worked until the sack of 1527, and he then worked briefly in several Italian towns until 1530 when he was invited to France by Francis I. With *Primaticcio he was the most important artist to work on the decoration of the royal palace at Fontainebleau and one of the creators of the distinctive style of French Mannerism associated with the School of *Fontainebleau. Rosso's principal work there is the Gallery of Francis I. Many engravings were made from his designs and his influence on French art was great. Vasari, whose biography of Rosso also includes an entertaining story about his pet baboon, says that he killed himself in remorse after falsely accusing a friend of stealing money from him, but this may well be apocryphal.

Rosso, Medardo (1858–1928). Italian sculptor. In his early career he was a painter, and was virtually self-taught as a sculptor—he was dismissed from the Brera Academy in Milan in 1883 after only a few months' training when he appealed for more liberal instruction in the nude and anatomy. He went to Paris in 1884, where he worked in the studio of *Dalou and knew *Rodin, and from 1889 he spent most of his career there. It is indeed with French rather than with Italian art that his work has affinity, for in reaction from the Italian *Renaissance tradition of three-dimensional solidity, Rosso applied to sculpture the *Impressionist aesthetic by which atmospheric effects and transitory conditions of light break up the permanent identity of the object. He was essentially a modeller rather than a carver and he made subtle use of his preferred medium of wax to express his view that matter was malleable by atmosphere: 'We are mere consequences of the objects which surround us.' He also anticipated later trends by his occasional incorporation of real objects in a sculptural work. His subjects included portraits and single figures and groups in contemporary settings (*The Bookmaker*, MOMA, New York, 1894; *Conversation in a Garden*, Gal. Nazionale d'Arte Contemporanea, Rome, 1893).

At the turn of the century Rosso enjoyed an international reputation second only to that of Rodin. Then after a period of neglect he was 'rediscovered' by the *Futurists, who took over and developed many of his ideas. In his 1912 manifesto of Futurist sculpture *Boccioni called him 'the only great modern sculptor who has attempted to open up a larger field to sculpture, rendering plastically the influences of an ambiance and the atmospheric ties which bind it to the subject'. Today he is regarded as a sculptor of remarkable originality (not even Rodin challenged so decisively the traditional preoccupations of his art) and one of the precursors of the modern movement because of the emphasis he gave to the direct representation of visual experience and his realization that the ordinary and commonplace could have sculptural expressiveness. His output was fairly small; replicas of several of his works, together with a collection of his drawings, are in the Museo Medardo Rosso at Barzio in Italy.

Rothenstein, Sir William (1872–1945). British painter, draughtsman, writer, and teacher. He studied for a year at the *Slade School (1888–9) under Alphonse *Legros and afterwards at the Académie Julian, Paris. There he became a close friend of *Whistler and was encouraged by *Degas and *Pissarro. His best works are generally considered to be his early Whistlerian paintings such as *A Doll's House* (Tate, London, 1899), which shows Augustus *John and Rothenstein's wife as characters in a tense scene from Ibsen's play of that title. From about 1898, however, he specialized in portraits of the celebrated and those who later became celebrated. In the latter part of his career he was much more renowned as a teacher than a painter. His outlook was conservative (he regarded pure abstraction as 'a cardinal heresy') and

as Principal of the *Royal College of Art, 1920–35, he exercised an influence second only to that of *Tonks at the Slade School in earlier decades. His son, **Sir John Rothenstein** (1901–), has had a distinguished career as an art historian (he was Director of the *Tate Gallery, 1938–64); another son, **Michael Rothenstein** (1908–), is a painter, print-maker, and writer on art.

Rothko, Mark (1903–70). Russian-born American painter, one of the outstanding figures of the *New York School and in particular one of the creators of *Colour Field painting. He went to the USA as a child in 1913, studied at Yale University, and was largely self-taught as an artist. In the 1930s and 1940s he went through phases influenced by *Expressionism and *Surrealism, but from about 1947 he began to develop his mature and distinctive style. Typically his paintings feature large rectangular expanses of colour (often layers of thin washes of different hues) arranged parallel to each other, usually in a vertical format. The edges of these shapes are softly uneven, giving them a hazy, pulsating quality as if they were suspended and floating on the canvas. His paintings are often very large and the effect they produce is one of calmness and contemplation. Rothko's late works tend to be very sombre in colour, perhaps reflecting the state of depression that led to his suicide. Examples are his murals for the non-denominational chapel in Houston, Texas (1967–9), which have an appropriately transcendental quality and which Rothko regarded as his masterpieces.

Rottenhammer, Hans (or **Johann**) (1564–1625). German painter. In 1589–96 he worked in Rome and in 1596–1606 in Venice. He specialized in mythological scenes in landscape settings, working on a small scale and often on copper, and his paintings form a link between the styles of Paul *Bril, whom he knew in Rome, and Adam *Elsheimer, with whom he worked in Venice.

Rouault, Georges (1871–1958). French painter, graphic artist, and designer who created a personal kind of *Expressionism that gives him a highly distinctive place in modern art. In his youth he was apprenticed in a stained-glass workshop, and the vivid colours and strong outlines characteristic of the medium left a strong imprint on his work. In 1892 he became a fellow pupil of *Matisse and *Marquet under Gustave *Moreau at the École des *Beaux-Arts. He was Moreau's favourite pupil and in 1898 became the first curator of the Musée Moreau in Paris. At about the same time he underwent a psychological crisis and although he continued to associate with the group of artists around Matisse who were later known as *Fauves, he did not adopt their brilliant colours, but painted clowns, prostitutes, outcasts, and judges in sombre but glowing tones. These subjects expressed his hatred of cruelty, hypocrisy, and vice, depicting the ugliness and degradation of humanity with passionate conviction. Initially they disturbed the public, but during the 1930s he gained an international reputation. From about 1940 he devoted himself almost exclusively to religious art. He was a prolific painter, and his work also included numerous book illustrations, ceramics, designs for tapestry and stained glass and for *Diaghilev's ballet *The Prodigal Son* (1929).

Roubiliac, Louis-François (c.1705–62). French-born sculptor, active in England for virtually his entire career. Little is known of his life before he settled in London in the early 1730s, although he is said to have trained under Balthasar *Permoser in Saxony and Nicolas *Coustou in Paris. He made his reputation with a full-length seated statue of the composer Handel (V&A, London, 1738), remarkable for its lively informality, and quickly became recognized as the most brilliant portrait sculptor of the day. His busts have great vivacity, stressing small forms and rippling movement in a manner very different from the broader treatment of his contemporary Michael *Rysbrack. He was especially successful with portraits of old and ugly men, and in his series of busts at Trinity College, Cambridge, and the celebrated statue of Newton (1755) there, he showed a remarkable gift for producing lively portraits of men long dead. Roubiliac was also outstanding as a tomb sculptor, several notable examples being in Westminster Abbey, including the marvellously dramatic tomb of Lady Elizabeth Nightingale (1761), who is shown being attacked with a spear by Death (a hideous skeleton emerging from

a vault), while her husband vainly tries to keep him at bay (the skeleton was carved by Roubiliac's assistant Nicholas Read, c.1733–87). The Nightingale monument clearly shows the influence of *Bernini, whose work so impressed Roubiliac when he visited Rome in 1752; he said that compared to Bernini's his own sculptures looked 'meagre and starved, as if made of nothing but tobacco pipes'. Roubiliac is generally regarded as one of the greatest sculptors ever to work in England, certainly the greatest of his period. He had a vivid imagination, he was a superb craftsman, and, as Gerald Randall observes (*Church Furnishing and Decoration in England and Wales*, 1980), 'Unlike even the best of his rivals, Roubiliac seems to have been incapable of indifferent work, and even his most modest commissions are designed and executed with a master's touch.'

Rousseau, Henri (known as Le Douanier Rousseau) (1844–1910). French painter, the most celebrated of *naïve artists. His nickname refers to the job he held with the Paris Customs Office (1871–93), although he never actually rose to the rank of 'Douanier' (Customs Officer). Before this he had served in the army, and he later claimed to have seen service in Mexico, but this story seems to be a product of his imagination. He took up painting as a hobby and accepted early retirement in 1893 so he could devote himself to art. His character was extraordinarily ingenuous and he suffered much ridicule (although he sometimes interpreted sarcastic remarks literally and took them as praise) as well as enduring great poverty. However, his faith in his own abilities never wavered. He tried to paint in the academic manner of such traditionalist artists as *Bouguereau and *Gérôme, but it was the innocence and charm of his work that won him the admiration of the avant-garde: in 1908 *Picasso gave a banquet, half serious half burlesque, in his honour. Rousseau is now best known for his jungle scenes, the first of which was *Surprised!* (*Tropical Storm with a Tiger*) (NG, London, 1891) and the last *The Dream* (MOMA, New York, 1910). These two paintings are works of great imaginative power, in which he showed his extraordinary ability to retain the utter freshness of his vision even when working on a large scale and with loving attention to detail. He claimed such scenes were inspired by his experiences in Mexico, but in fact his sources were illustrated books and visits to the zoo and botanical gardens in Paris. His other work ranges from the jaunty humour of *The Football Players* (Philadelphia Museum of Art, 1908) to the mesmeric, eerie beauty of *The Sleeping Gypsy* (MOMA, 1897). Rousseau was buried in a pauper's grave, but his greatness began to be widely acknowledged soon after his death.

Rousseau, Théodore (1812–67). French landscape painter, the central figure of the *Barbizon School. He was one of the pioneers of landscape painting in the open air (see PLEIN AIR), and because of the non-academic outlook of his work it was consistently rejected by the *Salon, earning him the nickname 'le grand refusé'. From 1836 he worked regularly in the Forest of Fontainebleau, specializing in wooded scenes, and in 1848 he settled permanently in the village of Barbizon, where he was a close friend of *Millet and *Diaz. Success came to him during the 1850s. His output was prolific.

Rowlandson, Thomas (1756–1827). English *caricaturist, whose pre-eminence in social satire matched that of *Gillray in political satire. He began as a painter, mainly of portraits, but he turned to caricature to supplement his income (he was a notorious gambler), and finding his sideline highly successful he gave his career over to it completely. His talent for exuberant and flowing line had affinities with the French *Rococo of *Fragonard (Rowlandson had studied in France), but his rollicking humour and delicate tonal effects were distinctively English; the marvel of his art is that there is no inconsistency between the bawdiness or boisterousness of the subject-matter and the beauty of the technique. He created an instantly recognizable gallery of social types, such as the old maid, the hack writer and the crabbed antiquarian, and his buxom wenches have their descendants in the fat ladies of today's saucy seaside postcards. His repertory of themes was inexhaustible and his œuvre has been termed the English equivalent of Balzac's *Comédie humaine*. He was a friend of George *Morland and travelled about England and also in France, Germany, and the Low Countries making rapid and brilliantly illuminating sketches of country life. In addition he produced series of illustrative drawings for publishers, notably *The Comforts of Bath* (1798) and the series on *The Tours of Dr Syntax* (1812–20). Rowlandson's output was huge, but it was only towards the end of his career that the quality of his work suffered because of overproduction.

Royal Academy of Arts, London. The national art *academy of England, founded in 1768. Membership was limited to forty Academicians, who had to be artists by profession, and thirty-six were named in the Instrument of Foundation, signed by George III. Their motive in founding the Academy was to raise the status of their profession by establishing a sound system of training and expert judgement in the arts and to arrange for the free exhibition of works attaining an appropriate standard of excellence. Behind this conception was the desire to foster a national school of art and to encourage appreciation and interest in the public based on recognized canons of good taste. In 1769 a new class of Associates was instituted, from whom the number of Academicians was recruited.

The Royal Academy first functioned in Pall Mall. The Schools and the Exhibition were transferred to Somerset House in 1780, shared with the *National Gallery its premises in Trafalgar Square 1837–69, and moved to the present site of Burlington House in 1869. The first President of the Royal Academy was Sir Joshua *Reynolds, who held the office until his death in 1792. His famous *Discourses*, delivered over a period of twenty years, laid down the basic conception of the Academy as a body of professional men which, 'besides furnishing able men to direct the student', was to form a repository for the great examples of the Art'. The latter function was important, since until the foundation of the National Gallery in 1824 there was no public collection of masterpieces available to students and schools. Although the most celebrated work owned by the Academy is a marble *tondo by *Michelangelo of the Virgin and Child with St John the Baptist (the Taddei Tondo, *c*.1505), the collections are chiefly important for their representation of work by Academicians, the custom being that each new Academician deposits a work (called a Diploma Work) on admission.

Regarding itself as the main depository of national tradition in the arts and the safeguard of sound standards of professional competence in execution, the Royal Academy, in common with other official establishments, has been cautious of innovation. During the latter decades of the 19th cent. the reputation of the Academy sank very low and it began to be regarded as the bulwark of orthodox mediocrity in opposition to creative and progressive art. Other organizations, such as the *New English Art Club, and later the *London Group, were formed to accommodate progressive trends. Since the presidency (1944–9) of *Munnings, who was notorious for his opposition to modern art, its policy has become more liberal and the conflict between official 'Academy' art and creative art has narrowed.

Royal College of Art, London. Postgraduate university institution, now Britain's pre-eminent training school for artists and designers. It was founded in 1837 as the School of Design and was originally a school of industrial design, the fine arts being the province of the *Royal Academy. In 1852 it moved from its original home in Somerset House to Marlborough House and was renamed the Central School of Practical Art. It became part of the Government Department of Science and Art in 1853 and in 1857 it moved to join the Museum of Ornamental Art (later the *Victoria and Albert Museum) in South Kensington. In 1863 it moved to new buildings in Exhibition Road, and in 1896 it was renamed the Royal College of Art by Queen Victoria and allowed to grant diplomas. The College moved again to new buildings in Kensington Gore in 1961 and in 1967 was given a Royal Charter and empowered to award degrees. Some of the most illustrious British artists of the 20th cent. have been students at the Royal College of Art, among them Barbara *Hepworth, David *Hockney, and Henry *Moore.

Rubens, Sir Peter Paul (1577–1640). Flemish painter and designer, the greatest and most influential figure in *Baroque art in northern Europe. He was born at Siegen in Westphalia, the son of a protestant lawyer from Antwerp who moved to Germany to escape religious persecution, and he returned to Antwerp in 1587 with his mother soon after his father's death. He had been baptized a Calvinist in Germany, but he became a devout Catholic. His fairly undistinguished masters were three painters of Antwerp, Tobias *Verhaecht, Adam van *Noort, and Otto van *Veen. The first two could teach him no more than the local tradition, but van Veen was a man of some culture, who had spent about five years in Rome, and he no doubt inspired his pupil with a desire to visit Italy. Rubens became a master in the Antwerp painters' guild in 1598, and after working with van Veen for two more years he set out for Italy in 1600. Very little of Rubens's early work survives, and his style was largely formed in Italy, where he was based until 1608. He worked for Vincenzo *Gonzaga, Duke of Mantua, visiting most of the principal art centres of Italy to make copies for the ducal collection and also in 1603–4 travelling to Spain when he accompanied gifts from Vincenzo to Philip III. The most important centres of Ruben's activity in Italy, however, were Genoa and Rome. In Genoa he painted some stately aristocratic portraits (*Marchesa Brigida Spinola-Doria*, NG, Washington, 1606) that inspired van *Dyck when he worked in the city, and in Rome he found the basis of his own grandiose style in the *antique, the great masters of the *Renaissance, and Annibale *Carracci.

On learning that his mother was seriously ill, Rubens returned to Antwerp in 1608, but she died before he arrived. Italy had become Rubens's spiritual home (he usually signed himself 'Pietro Pauolo') and he must have intended returning, but his success in Antwerp was so immediate and great that he remained there, and in spite of his extensive travels later in his career he never saw Italy again. In 1609 Rubens was appointed court painter to the Archduke Albert and his wife the Infanta Isabella, the Spanish Viceroys in the Netherlands, and in the same year he married the 17-year-old Isabella Brant, the daughter of an eminent Antwerp lawyer. The portrait of himself and his wife (Alte Pinakothek, Munich) that he painted presumably to mark the occasion gives a marvellous picture of Rubens on the threshold of his great career—handsome, vigorous, and dashingly self-confident. In the next few years he established his reputation as the pre-eminent painter in northern Europe, his first two resounding successes being the huge *triptychs of the *Raising of the Cross* and the *Descent from the Cross* (Antwerp Cathedral, 1610–11 and 1611–14), which showed his mastery of history painting in the *Grand Manner and the immense vigour of his style.

The demand for Rubens's work was extraordinary, and he was able to meet it only because he ran an extremely efficient studio. It is not known how many pupils or assistants he had because as court painter he was exempt from registering them with the guild. The idea of his running a sort of picture factory has been exaggerated, but even a man of his seemingly inexhaustible intellectual and physical stamina (he habitually rose at 4 a.m.) could not carry out all the work involved in his massive output with his own hands. Rubens both collaborated with established artists ('Velvet' *Brueghel, van Dyck, *Jordaens, Daniel *Seghers, *Snyders, and others) and retouched pictures by pupils, the degree of his intervention being reflected in the price. Generally his assistants did much of the work between the initial oil sketch and the master's finishing touches. Modern taste has tended to admire these sketches and his drawings (in which his personal touch is evident in every stroke of brush, chalk, or pen) more than the large-scale works, but Rubens himself would surely have found this attitude hard to comprehend, for the sheer scale and grandeur of the finished paintings gives them an extra, symphonic dimension.

Rubens not only painted virtually every type of subject, but also designed tapestries, book illustrations, and decorations for festivals, as well as giving visual directives for sculptors, metalworkers, and architects. 'My talents are such', he wrote in 1621, 'that I have never lacked courage to undertake any design, however vast in size or diversified in subject.' So huge was his output, indeed, that it is difficult to put a figure on it; the *Corpus Rubenianum*, the first attempt in the 20th cent. at a complete scholarly catalogue of his work, began publication in 1968 and is expected to be completed in about thirty volumes. His biggest commission in Flanders was for the decoration of the Jesuit church (a building he may also have had a hand in designing), but almost all his work there was destroyed by fire in 1718. From outside Flanders, those who sought his services included the royal families of France, England, and Spain. For Marie de' *Médicis (mother of Louis XIII of France) he did a series of twenty-five enormous paintings on her life (Louvre, Paris, 1622–5); for Charles I of England he painted a series of canvases representing the reign of his father James I (completed 1635) for the ceiling of the Banqueting House in London (the only one of his major decorative schemes still in the position for which it was painted); and for Philip IV of Spain he embarked in 1636 on a series of more than a hundred mythological pictures for his hunting lodge, the Torre de la Parada (the series was incomplete when Rubens died and most of the finished paintings—executed by assistants from his *modelli—were destroyed in 1710 when the building was sacked during the War of the Spanish Succession).

After the death of the Archduke Albert in 1621, Rubens became a trusted adviser to the Infanta Isabella, and she sent him on diplomatic missions to Spain (where he met *Velázquez) in 1628–9 and to England (where Charles I knighted him) in 1629–30. In this role his polished manners and his prodigious linguistic skills were put to good advantage—apart from Flemish and Italian, he spoke French, German, Latin, and Spanish. Rubens's wife died in 1626 and in 1630 he remarried; his bride was the 16-year-old Hélène Fourment, daughter of a rich silk merchant and the niece of his first wife. The second marriage was as happy as the first, and Rubens's love of his family shines through many of his late paintings (*Hélène Fourment with Two of her Children* (Louvre, c.1637). In 1635 he bought a country house, the Château de Steen, between Brussels and Malines, and in his final years he developed a new passion for painting landscapes—marvellously ripe works that led *Constable to declare 'In no branch of the art is Rubens greater than in landscape.' Superb examples are in the National Gallery and the Wallace Collection, London.

Rubens's influence in 17th-cent. Flanders was overwhelming, and it was spread elsewhere in Europe by his journeys abroad and by pictures exported from his workshop, and also through the numerous engravings he commissioned of his work. In later centuries, his influence has also been immense, perhaps most noticeably in France, where *Watteau, *Delacroix, and

*Renoir were among his greatest admirers. Because of the unrivalled variety of his work, artists as different in temperament as these three could respond to it with equal enthusiasm.

Rublev, Andrei (1360?–1430). The most famous of Russian *icon painters. The 600th anniversary of his birth was celebrated by Soviet Russia in 1960, but there is some evidence that he may have been born a decade later and there is little secure knowledge of his life or works. In 1405 he worked as assistant to *Theophanes in the Cathedral of the Annunciation in the Kremlin at Moscow, but it has not been possible to distinguish his share there or in the Cathedral of the Dormition at Vladimir, where he is also said to have painted murals. The work that stands at the centre of his *œuvre* is the celebrated icon of the Old Testament Trinity (that is Abraham's three angels) in the Tretyakov Gallery, Moscow (c.1411). In its gentle lyrical beauty this marks a move away from the hieratic *Byzantine tradition, and other icons in a similar style have been attributed to Rublev.

Rude, François (1784–1855). French *Romantic sculptor. He was a fervent admirer of Napoleon Bonaparte and his emotionally charged work expresses the martial spirit of the Napoleonic era more fully than that of any other sculptor. In 1812 he won the *Prix de Rome, but he was unable to take it up because of the Napoleonic Wars, and when Napoleon abdicated in 1814 he went into exile in Brussels with *David. On his return to Paris in 1827 he became highly successful with public monuments, most notably his celebrated high *relief on the Arc de Triomphe, *Departure of the Volunteers in 1792*, popularly known as *The Marseillaise* (1833–6). None of Rude's other works matches the fire, dynamism, and heroic bravura of this glorification of the French Revolution, but he created another strikingly original work in his monument *The Awakening of Napoleon* (1845–7) in a park at Fixin, near his native Dijon, which shows the emperor casting off his shroud. In spite of the dramatic movement of his work, it always has a solidity that reveals his Classical training and his lifelong admiration of the *antique.

Ruisdael, Jacob van (1628/9–82). The greatest and most versatile of all Dutch landscape painters. He was born in Haarlem, traditionally called the home of Dutch landscape painting, where he probably received training from his father **Isaac**, who was a painter as well as a frame-maker and picture-dealer (no works by him are known to survive). His uncle Salomon van *Ruysdael (this distinction in spelling occurs consistently in their own signatures) presumably also played a part in his artistic education. Ruisdael was extremely precocious, however; his earliest known paintings date from 1646 and already reveal a mature and distinctive artistic personality. He was also versatile and prolific (about 700 paintings are reasonably attributed to him); he painted forests, grain fields, beaches and seascapes, watermills and windmills, winter landscapes and Scandinavian torrents influenced by Allart van *Everdingen; he could conjure poetry from a virtually featureless patch of duneland as well as from a magnificent panoramic view. Even more than his range, however, it is the emotional force of his work that distinguishes him from his contemporaries. He moved away decisively from the 'tonal' phase of Dutch landscape represented by his uncle; in place of subtle atmospheric effects he favoured strong forms and dense colours and his brushwork is vigorous and *impasted. His emotional, subjective approach found its most memorable expression in *The Jewish Cemetery* (versions in the Detroit Institute of Arts and the Gemäldegalerie in Dresden, c.1660), where tombstones and elegiac ruins, symbols of man's transitory and ephemeral existence, are contrasted with nature's power of renewal.

Ruisdael travelled to the Dutch/German border with his friend Nicolaes *Berchem in the early 1650s, and one of the pictures that resulted was the celebrated *Bentheim Castle* (Beit Coll., Blessington, Ireland, 1653), in which the castle heroically crowns the top of a steep, rugged hill, transformed by Ruisdael's imagination from the mild slope it is in actuality. In about 1656 he moved to Amsterdam, where he lived for the rest of his life (although he was buried in St Bavo's Cathedral in Haarlem). He evidently had a reasonably prosperous career, but little is known about his life and it was long thought he had died insane in the workhouse at Haarlem, a fate that is now known to have befallen his cousin and near namesake Jacob van *Ruysdael. There is still uncertainty, however, concerning the story, reported by *Houbraken and supported by other tantalizing evidence, that Ruisdael practised as a surgeon. It seems unlikely that he could have found the time for this (he is said to have taken a medical degree at Caen in Normandy in 1676, when he was in his late 40s), but other prolific Dutch painters, for example *Steen (who ran a tavern), managed to pursue two careers. Ruisdael's only documented pupil was *Hobbema, but his influence was resounding, both on his Dutch contemporaries and on artists in other countries in the following two centuries—*Gainsborough, *Constable, and the *Barbizon School for example. Examples of his work are in many public collections, the finest representation being in the National Gallery, London.

Runciman, Alexander (1736–85) and **John** (1744–68). Scottish painters, brothers, who painted religious, literary, and historical subjects in a proto-*Romantic manner. John, the more brilliantly gifted, died young during a sojourn by both brothers in Italy. His masterpiece, *King Lear in the Storm* (NG, Edinburgh, 1767), has freshness and originality, with nothing of the staginess of most 18th-cent. Shakespearian pictures. Alexander's major work, the decoration of Penicuik House near Edinburgh with romantically treated subjects from Ossian and the history of Scotland, ranked with *Barry's paintings in the Society of Arts as the most ambitious British decorative scheme of the time, but it was destroyed by fire in 1899. Some of its compositions survive in a series of spirited etchings he based on them.

Runge, Philipp Otto (1777–1810). German painter and draughtsman. Although he made a late start to his career and died young, he ranks second only to *Friedrich among German *Romantic artists. He studied under Jens *Juel at the Copenhagen Academy (1799–1801), then moved to Dresden, where he knew Friedrich. In 1803 he settled in Hamburg. Runge was of a mystical, pantheistic turn of mind and in his work he tried to express notions of the harmony of the universe through symbolism of colour, form, and numbers. To this end he planned a series of four paintings

called *The Times of the Day*, designed to be seen in a special building and viewed to the accompaniment of music and poetry. He painted two versions of *Morning* (Kunsthalle, Hamburg, 1808 and 1809), but the others did not advance beyond drawings. Runge was also one of the best German portraitists of his period; several examples are in Hamburg. His style was rigid, sharp, and intense, at times almost *naïve. In 1810 he published *Die Farbenkugel* (The Colour Sphere) after doing several years of research on colour, during which he corresponded with *Goethe.

Ruoppolo, Giovanni Battista (1629–93). Neapolitan still-life painter. He specialized in pictures of flowers and food (especially fruit and seafood), depicted in an exuberant and succulent style. With *Recco he was the finest Italian still-life painter of his period.

Rupert, Prince (1619–82). Bohemian-born soldier and amateur artist. Famous as a dashing cavalry commander for his uncle Charles I in the English Civil War, he was also an active dilettante of science and the arts. He was an amateur etcher and introduced to England *mezzotint engraving, which he may have learnt from Ludwig von *Siegen (Rupert was himself long credited as the inventor). He demonstrated the technique to the diarist John Evelyn, who publicized it in his book *Sculptura* (1662) under the auspices of the Royal Society.

Ruralists, Brotherhood of. See BLAKE, PETER.

Rusconi, Camillo (1658–1728). Italian sculptor. He was the outstanding sculptor in Rome during his period, a figure comparable to his friend *Maratta in painting. The vigour and boldness of his style derive from *Bernini, but Rusconi was more restrained and Classical. His most important works are four over life-size statues of Apostles in S. Giovanni in Laterano (1708–18) and the tomb of Pope Gregory XIII (1719–25) in St Peter's.

Rush, William (1756–1833). American sculptor, active in his native Philadelphia. His father was a ship's carpenter and Rush worked mainly in wood, progressing from ships' figureheads to free-standing figures, such as the *Nymph of the Schuylkill* (1812), a work which almost perished through exposure to the elements in Fairmount Park, Philadelphia, and was preserved only when it was belatedly cast in bronze. His work is vigorous and naturalistic and he marks the transition from the un-selfconscious folk carver to the professional artist. He was one of the prime movers in the foundation of the Pennsylvania Academy of the Fine Arts, which has many examples of his work. Thomas *Eakins, another native of Philadelphia, greatly admired Rush's work.

Ruskin, John (1819–1900). The most influential English art critic of his time, also a talented water-colourist. His output of writing was enormous and he had a remarkable hold over public opinion, as he showed when he successfully defended the *Pre-Raphaelites against the savage attacks to which they were being subjected. He was the son of a wealthy wine merchant and his artistic education was gained through frequent travel in Britain and on the Continent. Ruskin belonged to the *Romantic School in his conception of the artist as an inspired prophet and teacher. He advocated a revival of the *Gothic style, his rejection of the *Classical tradition following from his assumption that art and architecture should mirror man's wonder and delight before the visual creation of God and that this demanded a freely inspired and *naturalistic style to which he felt that Gothic alone was really suited. Although his worship of beauty for its own sake brought him into affinity with the advocates of 'art for art's sake' (see *Aestheticism), his strong interest in social reform and ever-increasing concern with economic and political questions during the second half of his life (he used much of his large inheritance for philanthropic work) kept him from accepting a doctrine of the autonomy of the arts in divorce from questions of social morality. His eloquence in linking art with the daily life of the workman had affinities with the views of William *Morris and his insistence on regarding the state of the arts as a 'visible sign of national virtue' and his constant emphasis on their moral function have sometimes been regarded as a conspicuous instance of the 'moral fallacy' in aesthetics and criticism. He set himself obstinately and short-sightedly against the effects of the Industrial Revolution in supplanting the older craftsmanship and opposed all efforts to raise the standard of design in industry and to institute schools for the application of good principles of design to mass-production.

Ruskin's personal life was deeply unhappy. His marriage was annulled in 1854 on the grounds of non-consummation (his ex-wife married *Millais in the following year) and in middle and old age he made many young girls the objects of his unhealthy affection. He proposed to one of them, the 18-year-old Rose La Touche, in 1866, but was refused; she died mad in 1875. In 1878 he lost a famous libel case against *Whistler, whom he had accused of 'flinging a pot of paint in the public face', and soon after showed the first signs of the mental illness that made his final years wretched. After 1889, living in isolation in the Lake District, where he was cared for by his cousin, John Severn, Ruskin wrote nothing and rarely spoke.

Ruskin's complete works were edited in thirty-nine volumes (1903–12). His most important works of art criticism are: *Modern Painters* (5 vols., 1843–60, epilogue 1888), which began as a defence of *Turner and expanded into a general survey of art; *The Seven Lamps of Architecture* (1849); and *The Stones of Venice* (3 vols., 1851–3). He is accorded a distinguished place amongst English prose writers of the 19th cent., and his finest flights of rhetoric, such as his descriptions of the *Tintorettos in the Scuola di San Rocco in Venice, are classics of their kind.

Russell, Morgan (1886–1953). American painter, with *Macdonald-Wright the founder of *Synchronism. He studied painting under *Henri in New York, then in 1908 moved to Paris, where he studied sculpture under *Matisse. Paris was his home for most of the rest of his life. By 1910 he was devoting himself increasingly to painting, and in 1911 he met Macdonald-Wright, with whom he developed colour theories with analogies to musical patterns. In 1913 they launched Synchronism, and Russell's *Synchrony in Orange: To Form* (Albright-Knox Art Gall., Buffalo, 1913–14), one of the first pure abstract pictures, won him considerable renown in Paris. His later work, in which he retreated from pure abstraction, was less memorable.

Russolo, Luigi (1885–1947). Italian painter and musician. He was one of the signatories of the *Futurist painters' manifestos in 1910, but he is remembered more as a theorist than a painter. His background was musical and he was so interested in the idea of developing a Futurist music that he gave up painting for several years to devote himself to it. In 1913 he published a manifesto, *The Art of Noises*, and constructed *intonarumori* ('noise-makers'), which produced a startling range of sounds. He gave concerts in London (1914) and Paris (1921), attracted the interest of Igor Stravinsky and other composers, and has been regarded as a pioneer of today's electronic music. As a painter he made rather crude use of the Futurist device of 'lines of force', and after the war his style moved towards *Surrealism.

Ruysch, Rachel (1664–1750). Dutch still-life painter, with van *Huysum the most celebrated exponent of flower pieces of her period. The daughter of a botanist and the pupil of Willem van *Aelst, she worked mainly in her native Amsterdam, but also in The Hague (1701–8) and Düsseldorf, where from 1708 to 1716 she was court painter to the Elector Palatine. Her richly devised bouquets were painted in delicate colours with meticulous detail, and their artistry and craftsmanship are worthy of the finest tradition of Dutch flower painting. She continued to use the dark backgrounds characteristic of van Aelst and the older generation long after van Huysum and other contemporaries had gone over to light backgrounds.

Ruysdael, Salomon van (c.1600/3–70). Dutch landscape painter, active in his native Haarlem, where he became a member of the painters' guild in 1623. His earliest works show the influence of Esaias van de *Velde and in the 1630s he was so close in style to Jan van *Goyen that it is sometimes difficult to differentiate between the work of the two artists. They both excelled in atmospheric, virtually monochromatic river scenes and are the leading masters of this type of picture. In the 1640s his landscapes became somewhat more solid and colourful, perhaps reflecting influence from his nephew, Jacob van *Ruisdael. Late in his career he occasionally painted still lifes. He was immensely prolific and many galleries have examples of his work. His son **Jacob Salomonsz. van Ruysdael** (1629/30–81) was also a landscape painter. An example of his rare work is *A Waterfall by a Cottage* (NG, London), which shows he worked in a style similar to that of his illustrious cousin and near-namesake, with whom he has sometimes been confused in documentary references.

Ryder, Albert Pinkham (1847–1917). American painter of imaginative subjects. He lived and worked most of his life as a solitary and dreamer in New York, and his methods and approach were largely self-taught. His pictures reflect a rich inner life, with a haunting love of the sea (he was born at the fishing port of New Bedford, Mass.) and a constant search to express the ineffable: 'Have you ever seen an inch worm crawl up a leaf or twig, and then clinging to the very end, revolve in the air, feeling for something to reach something? That's like me. I am trying to find something out there beyond the place on which I have a footing.' This imaginative quality and eloquent expression of the mysteriousness of things is expressed typically through boldly simplified forms and eerie lighting (*The Race Track* or *Death on a Pale Horse*, Cleveland Museum of Art). In spite of his self-imposed isolation Ryder's works became well known in his lifetime and he has been much imitated and faked. His own paintings have often deteriorated because of unorthodox technical procedures.

Rysbrack, John Michael (1694–1770). Flemish-born sculptor, a member of an Antwerp family of artists, who settled in England about 1720. He soon achieved success and in the 1730s was the leading sculptor in the country. The highpoint of his career was winning the commission for the monument to William III in Queen Square, Bristol (1735), in preference to *Scheemakers. This is generally regarded as the finest equestrian statue made in England in the 18th cent. However, from about 1740 (the year of Scheemakers's acclaimed Shakespeare monument in Westminster Abbey), Rysbrack began to lose ground to Scheemakers and also to *Roubiliac. He was a versatile and prolific artist, hard-working and popular. His output included tombs, statues, and portraits (often in the form of busts in the *antique manner, a fashion he introduced to England), and he also made architectural elements such as chimney-pieces. His style was vigorous and dignified, less sombre than that of Scheemakers. He did not match the brilliant vivacity that characterizes Roubiliac's work, but he could sometimes rival him in beauty of handling. Rysbrack's best-known work is perhaps the monument to Sir Isaac Newton (designed by *Kent) in Westminster Abbey (1731), with its eloquent figure of the scientist.

Rysselberghe, Théo van (1862–1926). Belgian painter and designer. He was a founder of the avant-garde group of Les *Vingt (XX) in 1883. This group encouraged an interest in innovative art largely through contact with France, and Rysselberghe, who met *Seurat in Paris, became the leading Belgian exponent of *Neo-Impressionism. In 1898 he moved to Paris and was associated with the *Symbolist circle of writers and artists. Later he settled in Provence.

S

Sacchi, Andrea (1599–1661). Italian painter. He was a pupil of *Albani in Rome and Bologna, but he was inspired chiefly by *Raphael, and with the sculptors *Algardi and *Duquesnoy he became the chief exponent of the style sometimes called 'High *Baroque Classicism'. In defence of the *Classical principles of order and moderation, Sacchi engaged in a controversy in the Academy of St Luke with Pietro da *Cortona on the question of whether history paintings should have few figures (as Sacchi maintained) or many (Cortona). Sacchi's ideas were more immediately influential, but his ponderous ceiling fresco of *Divine Wisdom* (1629–33) in the Palazzo Barberini in Rome is completely outshone by Cortona's exhilarating ceiling of the Gran Salone in the same building. Sacchi, indeed, was at his best on a much smaller scale—in altarpieces such as the grave, introspective *Vision of St Romuald* (Vatican, c.1631) and in portraits. His most important pupil was *Maratta. Sacchi also worked as an architect, designing the Chapel of St Catherine of Siena (1637–9) in the Sacristy of Sta Maria sopra Minerva, a work of austere Classical purity. He was a fine draughtsman.

sacra conversazione (Italian: 'holy conversation'). A representation of the Virgin and Child with Saints in which all the sacred personages are disposed in a single scene rather than in the separate compartments of a *polyptych. The type originated in Italy in the first half of the 15th cent.: Filippo *Lippi's Barbadori Altarpiece (Louvre, Paris, begun 1437) is perhaps the first dated example.

Saenredam, Pieter Jansz. (1597–1665). Dutch painter of architectural subjects, particularly church interiors, active in Haarlem. Saenredam, the son of an engraver, was a hunchback and a recluse, but he was acquainted with the great architect Jacob van *Campen, who may have played a part in determining his choice of subject. He was the first painter to concentrate on accurate depictions of real buildings rather than the fanciful inventions of the *Mannerist tradition. His pictures were based on painstaking drawings and are scrupulously accurate and highly finished, but they never seem pedantic or niggling and are remarkable for their delicacy of colour and airy grace. The Cathedral of St Bavo (where he is buried) and the Grote Kerk in Haarlem were favourite subjects, but he also travelled to other Dutch towns to make drawings, and Utrecht is represented in several of his paintings. He also made a few views of Rome based on drawings in a sketchbook by Maerten van *Heemskerck that he owned. His work had great influence on Dutch painting.

Saftleven, Cornelis (1607–81) and **Herman III** (1609–85). Dutch painters, brothers, the best-known members of a family of artists. Cornelis, who was influenced by *Brouwer and *Teniers, painted *genre scenes of peasants and satirical pictures of animals dressed and acting like theologians and jurists. He also did landscapes with sheep and cattle grazing. There are examples in the Fitzwilliam Museum, Cambridge. Herman travelled in Germany and is best known for his highly finished panoramic views of the Moselle and Rhine, done in a distinctive misty blue tonality (*View on the Rhine*, Dulwich College Picture Gallery, 1656).

Sage, Kay (1898–1963). American *Surrealist painter. She lived in Italy, 1900–14 and 1919–37, and there painted pictures under the influence of de *Chirico. In 1937 she went to Paris, where she met *Tanguy, with whom she returned to the USA in 1940. Later they married. From the time of her return to America architectural motifs became prominent in her work—strange steel structures depicted in sharp detail against vistas of unreal space—and she incorporated draperies from which faces and figures sometimes mistily emerged. Sage also made mixed-media constructions.

Saint-Gaudens, Augustus (1848–1907). The leading American sculptor of his period. Born in Dublin of a French father and an Irish mother, Saint-Gaudens was brought to America in infancy. He began his career as a *cameo-cutter in New York, then studied for three years in Paris (1867–70) and three in Rome (1870–3), returning to America in 1874. His first important commission was the *Admiral Farragut Monument* (1878–81) in Madison Square Park, New York, and following its successful reception he quickly achieved a leading reputation among American sculptors and retained this throughout his life. Saint-Gaudens was an energetic artist and he produced a large amount of work in spite of the high standards of craftsmanship he set himself. His preferred material was bronze and he excelled particularly at memorials. Although his style is generally warmly naturalistic, his most celebrated work, the Adams Memorial (1891) in Rock Creek Cemetery, Washington, is a powerful allegorical figure. It is a monument to a wife of a friend of Saint-Gaudens who had committed suicide, and the mysterious female figure, swathed in magnificent voluminous draperies, has been interpreted as 'Grief', although the sculptor himself saw the elegiac work as embodying 'the Peace of God'. Saint-Gaudens was a highly important figure in the development of American sculpture; he turned the tide against *Neoclassicism and made Paris, rather than Rome, the artistic mecca of his countrymen.

St Ives Painters. Name given to a group of painters who concentrated their activities on St Ives, Cornwall. The group originated when Barbara *Hepworth and Ben *Nicholson moved to St Ives in 1939, just before the outbreak of the Second World War. They later formed a nucleus around which congregated a number of painters, including Patrick *Heron. The painters had little in common stylistically.

St Martin's Lane Academy. A name of two successive organizations in London that were the most important training ground for English artists in the half century before the *Royal Academy was established in 1768. The original St Martin's Lane Academy was a drawing and painting class rather than a professional institution and grew out of the academy (London's

first) established in 1711 in Great Queen Street, of which *Kneller was the head. *Thornhill replaced Kneller in 1716, and in 1720, when Thornhill himself was deposed, the academy moved to St Martin's Lane. It soon became defunct, but *Hogarth reconstituted it in 1735.

Saint Phalle, Niki de (1930–). French sculptor, one of the most entertaining figures in modern art. She came to prominence during the 1960s chiefly for her *assemblages and for sculptures which incorporated containers of paint intended to be burst and spattered when shot with a pistol. Also well known are her grotesque and gaudily painted female figures which she called *Nanas*. She has collaborated with *Tinguely, notably in the enormous sculpture *Hon* (Swedish for 'she') erected at the Moderna Museet, Stockholm, in 1963. It was in the form of a reclining woman (more than 25 m. long) whose interior was a giant *'environment' reminiscent of a fun-fair: visitors entered through the crutch. Saint Phalle has also worked as a painter and film-maker. Since 1979, she has worked on a huge sculpture garden at Garavicchio in Italy.

Sallinen, Tyko (1879–1955). The outstanding Finnish *Expressionist painter. He was the son of a tailor belonging to the strict puritan and fundamentalist religious sect of the Hihhulit, and the unhappy background of his early years later formed the basis for some of his paintings. After spending several years as an itinerant jobbing tailor in Sweden, he studied art in Helsinki and in 1909 and 1914 visited Paris, where he was influenced by French modernism, particularly *Fauvism. His favourite subjects were the harsh Karelian landscapes and simple, unsophisticated peasant people of Finland, whom he painted in brilliant but firmly organized colours. He was a member of the *November Group and became regarded as the nationalist Finnish painter *par excellence*.

Salon. France's official art exhibition, first held in 1667 and originally limited to members of the Academie Royales de Peinture et de Sculpture. The name derived from the fact that exhibitions were held in the Salon d'Apollon in the *Louvre. They were originally held annually, then from

1737 to the Revolution they were two-yearly, and afterwards once again annually. The jury system of selection was introduced in 1748. As these were the only public exhibitions in Paris the official academic art obtained through them a stranglehold on publicity, and in the 19th cent. a number of rival Salons were organized by progressive artists. In 1881 the government withdrew official sponsorship and a group of artists organized the Société des Artistes Français to take responsibility for the show with a jury elected from each previous year's exhibitors. It still remained hostile to new and creative artists, but from this time the Salon began to lose its prestige and influence in the face of the various independent exhibitions. The *Salon des Indépendants, for example, appeared in 1884, and the *Salon d'Automne in 1903.

Salon d'Automne. Annual exhibition, held in the autumn in Paris, founded in 1903 as an alternative to the official *Salon and the *Salon des Indépendants. *Bonnard, *Rouault, *Matisse, and *Marquet were foundation members and the Salon d'Automne is best remembered for its 1905 exhibition, when Matisse and his associates won notoriety as the *Fauves. Also noteworthy were the memorial exhibitions of *Gauguin (1903, the inaugural exhibition) and *Cézanne (1907).

Salon de la Rose + Croix. An exhibition held annually in Paris from 1892 to 1897. It was organized by the Rosicrucians, an esoteric brotherhood (allegedly founded in the 15th cent. by one Christian Rosenkreuz) which in the late 19th cent. had close connections with the *Symbolist movement. The order's symbol, reflecting the name, was a rose and cross combined. Joséphin Péladan (1859–1918), a man of letters who called himself Sâr (i.e. High Priest) Péladan, founded a lodge of the brotherhood in France and this organized the exhibitions. They became a focal point of Symbolism, and the catalogue to the first exhibition said its objects were 'to destroy *Realism and to bring art closer to Catholic ideas, to mysticism, to legend, myth, allegory, and dreams'.

Salon des Indépendants. Name given to the annual exhibitions held in Paris by the Société des Artistes Indépendants, an association formed in 1884 by *Seurat,

*Signac, and other artists in opposition to the official Salon. There was no selection committee and any artist could exhibit on payment of a fee. The Salon des Indépendants became the main showcase of the *Post-Impressionists and was a major art event in Paris up to the beginning of the First World War.

Salon des Refusés. Exhibition held in Paris in 1863 to show work that had been refused by the selection committee of the official *Salon. In that year there were especially strong protests from artists whose work had been rejected, so the emperor Napoleon III ordered this special exhibition. It drew huge crowds, who came mainly to ridicule, and *Manet's *Déjeuner sur l'herbe* was subjected to furious abuse. Other major artists represented included *Cézanne, Camille *Pissarro, and *Whistler. In spite of the unfavourable reaction to the works shown there, the Salon des Refusés was of great significance in undermining the prestige of the official Salon. After this, artists began to organize their own exhibitions (notably the *Impressionists in 1874) and art dealers became of increasing importance. The Salon des Refusés is thus regarded as a turning point in the history of art and 1863 is, in the words of Alan Bowness (*Modern European Art*, 1972), 'the most convenient date from which to begin any history of modern painting'.

Salviati, Francesco (Francesco de' Rossi) (1510–63). Florentine *Mannerist painter, a pupil of *Andrea del Sarto. He went to Rome c.1530 and entered the service of Cardinal Salviati, whose name he adopted and for whom he painted the work that established his reputation—the fresco of the *Visitation* (1538) in S. Giovanni Decollato. In 1539 he travelled to Venice, and from the 1540s led a restless life, working mainly in Florence and Rome but also visiting Fontainebleau in 1554. He was one of the leading fresco decorators of his day, specializing in learned and elaborate multi-figure compositions, typically Mannerist in their artificiality and abstruseness, and similar in style to those of his friend *Vasari. His finest works are perhaps the frescos on the story of the ancient tyrant Furius Camillus (1543–5) in the Sala dell' Udienza of the Palazzo Vecchio, Florence, intended as an allegory of Cosimo de'

*Medici's reign. Salviati also made designs for tapestries and was noted for his portraits, which were Florentine in their direct characterization but North Italian in their richness of colour.

Samaras, Lucas (1936–). Greek-born sculptor and experimental artist who obtained US citizenship in 1955. His work has been extremely varied in scale, medium, and approach. At the end of the 1950s he was making figures from rags dipped in plaster and also did pastels combining *Surrealist fantasy and *Pop art *iconography. During the 1960s he developed an original style in the use of mixed media, employing thousands of pins, yarns, nails, etc., and he has experimented with *assemblages of diverse objects. He experimented also with light and reflection in his *Mirrored Room* (1966), a man-high room walled with mirrors in which the spectator was reflected endlessly. Perhaps his best-known works are his 'Autopolaroids'—photographs of the most intimate parts of the artist's own body that brought him considerable notoriety.

Sánchez Coello, Alonso (1531/2–88). Spanish painter of Portuguese parentage, principally a portraitist. He studied under Anthonis *Mor in Flanders in the early 1550s and by 1555 was working at the court of Philip II of Spain, where he was to remain for the rest of his life, achieving great success and becoming a personal favourite of the king, who was godfather to his two daughters. His dignified and sober style was strongly influenced by Mor, but was more sensuous, showing his admiration for *Titian, and it is regarded as marking the beginning of the great tradition of Spanish formal portraiture. He also painted religious works, but these are much less distinguished.

Sánchez Cotán, Juan (1560–1627). Spanish painter. He was a still-life painter in Toledo until 1603, when he decided to become a monk, and in the following year he entered the Carthusian monastery at Granada as a lay-brother. The religious works he painted after this date are unexceptional, but as a still-life painter he ranks with the great names of European painting. Characteristically he depicts a few simple fruits or vegetables, arranged on a ledge or shelf with an almost geometric clarity and standing out against a dark background (*Quince, Cabbage, Melon, Cucumber*, San Diego Museum of Art, 1602). Each form is scrutinized with such intensity that the pictures take on a mystical quality, conveying a feeling of wonder and humility in front of the humblest items in God's creation. Sánchez Cotán's austere style had considerable influence on Spanish painting, notably on *Zurbarán.

Sandby, Paul (1730/1–1809). English topographical water-colourist and graphic artist. He and his brother **Thomas** (1721–98) trained at the Military Drawing Office of the Tower of London and were engaged as draughtsmen on the survey of the Highlands of Scotland after the rebellion of 1745. In 1751 Paul went to live with his brother at Windsor Park, where Thomas held the position of Deputy Ranger (they did many views of Windsor and its environs, and the Royal Library at Windsor Castle has an outstanding Sandby Collection). Their work is similar in many respects, but Paul was more versatile as well as a better artist, his work including lively figure subjects as well as an extensive range of landscape subjects. In his later work he often used *body-colour (he also sometimes painted in oils) and he was the first professional artist in England to publish *aquatints (1775). He was singled out by *Gainsborough as the only contemporary English landscape artist who painted 'real views from nature' instead of artificial *picturesque compositions. Sandby has rather unjustifiably been called 'the father of water-colour art', but certainly his distinction won prestige for the medium. He was a founder member of the *Royal Academy and his brother was its first Professor of Architecture.

Sandrart, Joachim von (1606–88). German painter, engraver, and writer on art. He travelled widely and was the most highly regarded German artist of his day (he was ennobled in 1653), but he is now remembered almost exclusively for his treatise *Teutsche Academie der Edlen Bau-, Bild- und Mahlerey-Künste* (German Academy of the Noble Arts of Architecture, Sculpture and Painting), published in Nuremberg in 1675 (a Latin edition followed in 1683). This treatise, which is divided into three parts, is a source-book of major importance. The first part is an introduction to the arts of architecture, painting, and sculpture put together largely from material taken from earlier sources such as *Vasari and van *Mander. The second part, consisting of biographies of artists, likewise contains much material borrowed from previous writers but also much that is original, in particular about German artists (it was Sandrart who was the first to use the name *Grünewald) and on contemporary artists that the author knew personally. The third part contains information about art collections and a study of *iconography, and remarkably Sandrart also included in his book a chapter on Far Eastern art. Sandrart was the first director (1662) of the Academy at Nuremberg (the earliest such in Germany).

sanguine. Another name for red *chalk.

Sansovino, Andrea (c.1467/70–1529). Italian sculptor and architect, named after his birthplace near Monte San Savino, his real name being Contucci. He called himself a Florentine, but although Florence contains much of his sculpture his fame rests on what he did elsewhere, notably in Rome, where the companion tombs of Cardinals Sforza and Basso (Sta Maria del Popolo, between 1505 and 1509) and the group of The Virgin and Child with St Anne (S. Agostino, 1512) display Classical grace combined with human tenderness. Sansovino spent much of the period 1513–27 in Loreto in charge of the sculpture (and for part of the time the architecture also) of the shrine of the Holy House, originally designed by *Bramante. *Vasari says that Andrea also worked in Portugal, but his statement is doubted by some scholars. Jacopo *Sansovino was Andrea's main pupil.

Sansovino, Jacopo (Jacopo Tatti) (1486–1570). Florentine sculptor and architect, active mainly in Venice. He trained under Andrea *Sansovino, whose name he adopted as a sign of his admiration. In 1505/6 he followed Andrea to Rome, where he moved in the circle of *Bramante and *Raphael and worked on the restoration of ancient sculpture. From 1511 to 1517 he was again in Florence, where he shared a studio with *Andrea del Sarto, and he then returned to Rome until the Sack of 1527, when he moved to Venice. There

he was appointed state architect (1529), formed a close friendship with *Titian and became a dominant figure in the art establishment. Sansovino played a major role in introducing the High *Renaissance style to Venice in both architecture and sculpture, and his sculptures are often important decorative elements of his buildings. His most celebrated work, one of Venice's most familiar sights, is the glorious Library of San Marco (begun 1537). As a sculptor he is best known for the colossal figures of Mars and Neptune (commissioned 1554) on the staircase of the Doges' Palace. Sansovino's sculptural style was firmly rooted in his study of antiquity, but it was in no way academic and possessed great vitality. He studied assiduously from the life as well as from the *antique, and legend has it that the model for his Bacchus (Bargello, Florence, 1511–12) went mad through being made to pose for hours on end with his arm raised and one day was found in this position standing naked on top of a chimney. Sansovino's son **Francesco** (1521–86) was a scholar of diversified interests. His Venetia città nobilissima (Venice, most noble city), published in 1581, is an important source-book—the first attempt to give a systematic account of a city's artistic heritage.

Santi, Giovanni (d. 1494). Italian painter, the father of *Raphael, active mainly in Urbino, where he worked for the court. He was 'a mediocre painter but an intelligent man' (*Vasari) and no doubt gave his illustrious son his introduction to humanist culture. Santi is now remembered less for his paintings than for his verse chronicle in twenty-three books recounting the exploits of the dukes of Urbino, which he dedicated to the young Duke Guidobaldo da *Montefeltro. This work is interesting to the art historian because it includes incidental comments on the reputations of contemporary artists. Santi's house in Urbino is now a museum—the Casa di Raffaello. It contains a small fresco of the Virgin and Child that some authorities consider to be Santi's portrayal of Raphael and his mother, and others claim as a very early work by Raphael himself.

Saraceni, Carlo (c.1579–1620). Venetian painter, active mainly in Rome. There he formed his style under the influence of *Caravaggio and *Elsheimer, painting small luminous pictures of figures in land-scapes as well as much larger altarpieces, including the replacement for Caravaggio's *Death of the Virgin* (Louvre, Paris), which the church of Sta Maria della Scala had rejected in 1606. Saraceni's picture is still *in situ*. His style was sensitive and poetic, showing a delicate feeling for colour and tone. His liking for turbans, tasselled fringes, and stringy drapery folds, and his richly *impasted paint may have influenced Dutch artists in Rome such as *Lastman and *Pynas, and through them *Rembrandt.

Sargent, John Singer (1856–1925). American painter, chiefly famous as the outstanding society portraitist of his time. He was born in Florence, the son of wealthy parents, and he had an international upbringing and career—indeed, he has been described as 'an American born in Italy, educated in France, who looks like a German, speaks like an Englishman, and paints like a Spaniard' (William Starkweather, 'The Art of John S. Sargent', *Mentor*, October 1924). His 'Spanishness' refers to his deep admiration for *Velázquez, for although he was encouraged to paint directly by his teacher *Carolus-Duran in Paris (1874–6), the virtuoso handling of paint that characterized his style derived more particularly from Old Masters such as Velázquez and *Hals (he visited Madrid and Haarlem to study their work in 1879–80). In 1884 he became famous when his portrait of Madame Gautreau (Met. Mus., New York) caused a sensation at the Paris *Salon because of what was felt to be its provocatively erotic character. It was exhibited as *Madame X*, but the sitter, a society beauty of strikingly unconventional looks, was unmistakable, and her mother wrote to Sargent imploring him to withdraw the picture, which she said had made her daughter a laughing-stock. The scandal persuaded Sargent to move to London, and he remained based there for the rest of his life; he continued to travel extensively, however, and often visited America. The lavish elegance of his work brought him unrivalled success, and his portraits of the wealthy and privileged convey with brilliant bravura the glamour and opulence of high society life. Even in his lifetime he was deprecated by critics and artists (who no doubt found it easy to be jealous of his success) for superficiality of characterization, but although psychological penetration was certainly not his strength, he was admirably varied in his response to each sitter's individuality. As with many successful portraitists, Sargent's heart lay elsewhere and after about 1907 he took few commissions. Despite his sophistication and charm and the entrée to high society that his success gave him, he was a very private person, who never married and led a quiet life. He loved painting landscape water-colours, showing a technique as dashing in this medium as in his oil paintings, and from the 1890s he devoted much of his energies to ambitious allegorical mural schemes in the Public Library and Museum of Fine Arts in Boston. The most unexpected side to his talents is revealed in the enormous *Gassed* (Imperial War Mus., London, 1918), which he painted as an official war artist. It has remarkable tragic power and is one of the greatest pictures inspired by the First World War.

Sarrazin, Jacques (1588–1660). The leading French sculptor of the mid-17th cent. He was in Rome 1610–c.1627, during which time he formed his style on the example of the *antique and *Classicizing artists such as *Domenichino and *Duquesnoy. On his return to Paris he established himself as head of his profession, running an important workshop through which passed many of the leading sculptors of the following generation (those who worked at Versailles). Much of Sarrazin's best work was done as architectural decoration, the finest example being his *caryatids (1641) on the Pavillon de l'Horloge at the *Louvre. Sarrazin also supervised the decoration (1652–60) of the Château de Maisons, the masterpiece of François Mansart, the greatest French architect of the 17th cent. Although it does not rank on the same level, Sarrazin's dignified work forms a kind of sculptural parallel to the architecture of Mansart or the paintings of *Poussin.

Sassetta (Stefano di Giovanni) (1392?–1450). With *Giovanni di Paolo the outstanding Sienese painter of the 15th cent. His work continues Sienese tradition in its beautiful colouring and elegant line, but he was also influenced by the *International Gothic style and by contemporary Florentine developments, combining them into a highly personal manner expressive of his mystical imagination. His most important work was the St Francis altarpiece (1437–44) painted for the church of S. Francesco at Borgo San Sepolcro and now dispersed. The central panel, St Francis in Ecstasy (Berenson coll., Florence), has a monumental dignity that must have impressed *Piero della Francesca (a native of Borgo), and some of the other panels (seven are in the National Gallery, London) show him at his most lyrical.

Sassoferrato (Giovanni Battista Salvi) (1609–85). Italian painter, known by the name of his town of birth—Sassoferrato—and active in nearby Urbino and other cities of central Italy, notably Rome (where he was a pupil of *Domenichino) and Perugia. He did some portraits, but specialized in religious works painted in an extremely sweet, almost *Peruginesque style. They are very clearly drawn and pure in colouring and totally un-*Baroque in feeling—indeed, they have a deliberately archaic quality that brings the paintings of the *Nazarenes to mind. Little is known of his life (in the 18th cent. it was apparently generally believed he was a contemporary of *Raphael) and few of his pictures are dated or datable; they seem to have been in great demand, however, as his compositions often exist in numerous very similar versions. Most of them were presumably done for private collectors, as few are in churches. Examples of his work are in many galleries, and a fine collection of his drawings (virtually his entire surviving output as a draughtsman) is in the Royal Library at Windsor Castle.

Saura, Antonio (1930–). Spanish painter. He was self-taught and began painting during a long illness in 1947. During two years in Paris, 1953–5, he made contact with members of the *Surrealist movement, including André *Breton. After his return to Spain, however, Saura quickly abandoned Surrealism and worked in a semi-abstract *expressionist vein, his powerful, stormy, and thickly textured figures creating a feeling of tortured humanity (Great Crucifixion, Boymans Mus., Rotterdam, 1963). His work has been seen as one of the most forceful protests against the Franco regime.

Savery, Roelandt (1576?–1639). Flemish painter and etcher of landscapes, animal subjects, and still life, the best-known member of a family of artists. His successful and prolific career included periods working for Henry IV in France, Rudolf II in Prague, and the emperor Matthias in Vienna. He also worked in Amsterdam, and in 1619 settled in Utrecht. Savery is best known for his association with Rudolf, whose famous menagerie allowed him to study in detail the exotic animals that became the trademark of his work. He painted and drew creatures such as pelicans, ostriches, camels, and the now extinct dodo, and was one of the first artists in the Netherlands to do pictures of animals alone. His favourite subjects, however, were Orpheus and the Garden of Eden, which allowed him to include any number of colourful beasts. Savery's bright and highly finished style is similar to that of Jan 'Velvet' *Brueghel, but is somewhat more archaic. His rare flower paintings are sometimes of outstanding quality, and with *Bosschaert he was an influential Flemish exponent of this genre in Holland. *Houbraken says that Savery died insane.

Savoldo, Giovanni Girolamo (active 1508–after 1548). Italian painter, born in Brescia, first documented in Florence in 1508, and active mainly in Venice. His output was small and his career is said to have been unsuccessful, but he is now remembered as a highly attractive minor master whose work stands somewhat apart from the main Venetian tradition. His forté was night scenes, in which he gave his lyrical sensibility and liking for unusual light effects full play. One of the best-known examples is Mary Magdalen Approaching the Sepulchre, of which several versions exist, one in the National Gallery, London. The writer Pietro Aretino described Savoldo as 'decrepit' in 1548 and he is not heard of thereafter.

Scarsellino, Lo (Ippolito Scarsella) (1551–1620). The leading Ferrarese painter of his period. His best works are his small mythological or religious scenes set in landscapes, several of which are in the Borghese Gallery, Rome. Their romantic feeling and spirited technique recall Venetian painting and they were particularly influential on the young *Guercino.

Schadow, Johann Gottfried (1764–1850). German sculptor, graphic artist, and writer on art. He travelled in Italy, 1785–7, and in 1788 he settled in Berlin, where he became head of the Academy in 1816. His style was *Neo-classical (he knew *Canova in Italy), but retained a degree of *Baroque liveliness. He was active mainly as a portraitist and tomb sculptor, but his best-known work is the *quadriga* (four-horse chariot) (1793) surmounting the Brandenburg Gate in Berlin, which was badly damaged in the Second World War. His finest achievement is perhaps the charming and sensitive group of *The Princesses Luise and Frederika of Prussia* (Staatliche Mus., East Berlin, 1795–7). From the 1820s his sight deteriorated and he turned more to graphic work (he was a draughtsman, engraver, and lithographer) and to writing on art theory. He had three artist sons; **Felix Schadow** (1819–61), **Rudolf Schadow** (1786–1822) and, most importantly, **Wilhelm von Schadow** (1788–1862). Wilhelm was in Italy 1811–19 and a member of the *Nazarenes. He taught at the Berlin Academy, then in 1826 became Director of the Düsseldorf Academy, which he helped to make into a leading centre of history painting.

Schalken, Godfried (1643–1703). Dutch painter of biblical, allegorical, and anecdotal subjects and of portraits, active mainly in Leiden. He was taught by *Hoogstraten and *Dou, and was one of Dou's most distinguished successors in the Leiden *fijnschilder* (fine painter) tradition. His surfaces are as smooth, glossy, and delicately finished as Dou's, but Schalken differed from his master in his lighting effects (he had a strong preference for the red glow of candle-light) and in his penchant for scenes involving coquettish women. As with Dou, Schalken's great popularity lasted throughout the 18th cent.

Scheemakers, Peter (1691–1781). Flemish sculptor, active mainly in England, where he settled around 1720. Apart from a visit to Rome (1728–c.1730) he was based in London until 1771, when he returned to his native Antwerp. In the 1730s he became the main rival to *Rysbrack, whose prices he undercut. Rysbrack defeated him in competition for the equestrian statue of William III in Bristol, but Scheemakers gained a great success in 1740 with his Shakespeare monument in Westminster Abbey and thereafter received numerous commissions and controlled a large studio with many assistants. He was, indeed, perhaps the most prolific of mid 18th-cent. sculptors, particularly as a maker of monuments, ranging from small tablets to large multi-figure compositions. Rysbrack also made portrait busts, and these, like his monuments, are often severely Classical, reflecting his love of the *antique. Scheemakers' brother **Henry** (d. 1748) and his son **Thomas** (1740–1808) were also sculptors working in England.

Scheffer, Ary (1795–1858). Dutch painter, engraver, and book illustrator, active for almost all his career in Paris. His work was immensely popular in his lifetime, but is now generally considered sentimental. Early in his career he favoured literary themes (*Francesca da Rimini*, Wallace Coll., London 1835, and other versions), but later he turned to mawkishly treated religious subjects (*SS. Augustine and Monica*, NG, London, 1854, and other versions). He also painted many portraits. His work is well represented in the museum at Dordrecht, his native town.

Schelfhout, Andreas (1787–1870). Dutch landscape painter, a forerunner of the *Hague School. He is best known for carefully depicted winter scenes reminiscent of those made by 17th-cent. Dutch artists, but he also painted seascapes and was an accomplished water-colourist. His work was influential particularly on *Jongkind, his most famous pupil.

Schiavone, Andrea (Andrea Meldolla) (*c.*1510/15–1563). Italian painter and etcher, born in Zara, Dalmatia (then under Venetian jurisdiction), and associated with the Venetian school. He was influenced particularly by *Parmigianino and *Titian and he usually worked on fairly small-scale religious or mythological scenes for private patrons in a colourful, painterly style.

Schiele, Egon (1890–1918). Austrian painter and draughtsman. He studied at the Vienna Academy, where he met *Klimt, who was a strong influence on his early *Art Nouveau style. By 1909, however, he had begun to develop his own highly distinctive style, which is characterized by an aggressive linear energy expressing acute nervous intensity. He painted portraits, landscapes, and semi-allegorical works, but he is best known for his drawings of nudes (including self-portraits), which have a disturbing and explicit erotic power—in 1912 he was briefly imprisoned on indecency charges, and several of his drawings were burnt. The figures he portrays are typically lonely or anguished, their bodies emaciated and twisted, expressing an aching intensity of feeling. His work was much exhibited, and he was beginning to receive international acclaim when he died in the influenza epidemic of 1918. He has since come to be recognized as one of the greatest *Expressionist artists.

Schildersbent (Dutch: 'band of painters'). A fraternal organization founded in 1623 by a group of Netherlandish artists living in Rome for social intercourse and mutual assistance. Its members called themselves *Bentvueghels* or 'birds of a flock' and they had individual *Bentnames*—for example Pieter van *Laer, one of the early leaders, was called Bamboccio. In 1720 the Schildersbent was dissolved and prohibited by papal decree because of its rowdiness and drunkenness.

Schinkel, Karl Friedrich (1781–1841). German architect, painter, and designer, active mainly in Berlin. Schinkel was the greatest German architect of the 19th cent., but until 1815, when he gained a senior appointment in the Public Works Department of Prussia (from which position he effectively redesigned Berlin), he worked mainly as a painter and stage designer. His paintings are highly *Romantic landscapes somewhat in the spirit of *Friedrich, although more anecdotal in detail (*Gothic Cathedral by a River*, Staatliche Museen, Berlin, 1813–14). He continued working as a stage designer until the 1830s, and in this field ranks among the greatest artists of his period. His most famous designs were for Mozart's *The Magic Flute* (1815), in which he combined the clarity and logic of his architectural style with a feeling of mystery and fantasy.

Schjerfbeck, Helène (1862–1946). Finnish painter. She studied in Paris in the 1880s, her teachers including *Bastien-Lepage, and made her mark with *plein air* scenes notable for their fresh colouring. From about 1900 her health began to fail and she lived a solitary life, almost forgotten, developing a much more simplified style. Late in life she was recognized as one of the pioneers of modernism in Finland. She painted landscapes, still lifes, figure compositions, and portraits, including an outstanding series of self-portraits.

Schlemmer, Oskar (1888–1943). German painter, sculptor, stage designer, and writer on art. He was an important teacher at the *Bauhaus (1920–9), in the metalwork, sculpture, and stage-design workshops, and later taught in Breslau and Berlin, before he was dismissed by the Nazis, who declared his work *degenerate. Schlemmer had a mystical temperament and his ideas on art were complex. Some of his early work was influenced by *Cubism and he showed a deep concern for pictorial structure; characteristically his paintings represent rather mechanistic human figures, seen in strictly frontal, rear, or profile attitudes set in a mysterious space (*Group of Fourteen Figures in Imaginary Architecture*, Wallraf-Richartz-Museum, Cologne, 1930). He rejected what he considered the soullessness of pure abstraction, but he wished to submit his intuition to rational control. His cool, streamlined forms are seen also in his sculpture. Schlemmer did much work for the theatre, notably designs for the *Constructivist *Triadic Ballet*, to music by Paul Hindemith, which was performed at the Bauhaus in 1923.

Schlüter, Andreas (c.1660–1714). German sculptor and architect, active mainly in Berlin. He was the leading *Baroque sculptor in northern Germany, and his masterpiece is the splendid equestrian monument to the Great Elector Friedrich-Willem (Charlottenburg Castle, Berlin, 1696–1708). He fell under a cloud when some of his architectural work collapsed, and he moved to St Petersburg, where he died soon after arriving.

Schmidt-Rottluff, Karl (*né* Schmidt) (1884–1976). German *Expressionist painter and graphic artist born at Rottluff near Chemnitz, one of the founders of the *Brücke. His style was harsher than that of the other members of the Brücke, and it was particularly forceful in his superb woodcuts. Their abrupt manner was reflected in his paintings with their flat ungraduated planes of contrasting colours. In 1906 he stayed with *Nolde on the island of Alsten, Norway, and derived from him the 'monumental Impressionism' which was exemplified in landscapes painted at Dangaster, which he visited with *Heckel in 1907. In 1911 he moved to Berlin, where his work was influenced by the stylized forms of African sculpture (*Dr Rosa Schapire*, Tate, London, 1919). Later his style became somewhat more naturalistic. His work was declared *degenerate by the Nazis and in 1941 he was forbidden to paint. In 1947 he became a professor at the Berlin Hochschule für Bildende Künste. The Brücke-Museum in Berlin was founded on his initiative in 1967 and he gave sixty of his own works to the collection.

Schnorr von Carolsfeld, Julius (1794–1872). German painter and illustrator. After studying at the Vienna Academy he joined the *Nazarenes in Rome (1817–25) and with them painted frescos in the Casino Massimo. In 1827 he moved to Munich, where he worked for Ludwig I, painting mainly frescos in the royal palace. As head of the Dresden Academy from 1846 onwards, Schnorr exercised a considerable influence in Germany as a representative of Nazarene ideals. He was famous in his day for his Bible illustrations, which were also published in England (*Schnorr's Bible Pictures*, 1860).

Schönfeldt, Johann Heinrich (1609–82). German painter and etcher. His early career is not well documented; he spent about a decade in Italy (mainly Rome and Naples) as a young man, but it is only after he settled in Augsburg in 1652 that his development can be traced through dated works. He was versatile and prolific, painting historical and *genre subjects as well as many altarpieces for churches in southern Germany. His style was lively and *eclectic, drawing on various Italian influences, and in his delicate colouring and lightness of touch he anticipates elements of German *Rococo art.

Schongauer, Martin (d. 1491). German engraver and painter, active in Colmar, Alsace. In his day he was probably the most famous artist in Germany; it was in his workshop that the young *Dürer hoped to study, but when he arrived in Colmar in 1492 the master had recently died. Only one painting certainly by Schongauer survives—*Madonna in the Rose Garden* (St Martin's, Colmar, 1473)—and he is remembered chiefly as an engraver, the greatest of his period. His work was strongly influenced by Netherlandish art, above all by Rogier van der *Weyden, but Schongauer had a powerful imagination of his own. He concentrated on religious subjects and about 115 plates by him are known. In them he brought a new richness and maturity to engraving, expanding the range of tones and textures, so that an art that had previously been the domain of the goldsmith took on a more painterly quality. The gracefulness of his work became legendary, giving rise to the nicknames 'Hübsch ('charming') Martin' and 'Schön ('beautiful') Martin'.

Schwind, Moritz von (1804–71). Austrian painter, graphic artist, and designer, trained in Vienna and in Munich under *Cornelius. Schwind represents the tail-end of Germanic *Romanticism and his most characteristic works depict an idealized fairy-tale Middle Ages, with knights in armour, damsels in distress, enchanted woods and castles, and much loving depiction of costume, architecture, etc. He was at his best working on a small scale, as in his numerous book illustrations and his woodcuts for *Fliegende Blätter*, a humorous Munich periodical. In his young days Schwind, who was an accomplished violinist, had been friendly with Franz Schubert and late in his own life he depicted Schubert's Vienna circle in a number of drawings.

Schwitters, Kurt (1887–1948). German *Dadaist artist and writer. He is best known for his invention of *Merz, a form of art made from refuse. *Merz* was also the title of a Dadaist magazine he founded in 1923 and which ran until 1932. He emigrated to Norway in 1937 and after the German invasion of 1940 fled to England, where he passed the rest of his life.

Scopas of Paros. One of the most celebrated Greek sculptors, active in the mid 4th cent. BC. He is recorded as working on the Mausoleum of Halicarnassus, the temple of Artemis at Ephesus, and the temple of Athena Alea at Tegea, of which

*Pausanias says he was the architect. Sculptural remains from all three buildings have survived, and although none of them can be certainly associated with Scopas, it is likely that he is the author of certain pieces that show a distinctive style and are of a quality consonant with his elevated reputation. Among them are three slabs from the Mausoleum (BM, London) showing the Battle of Greeks and Amazons, which display the intensity of expression and the characteristically deep-set eyes that are considered typical of his work. Several other pieces have been associated with him on stylistic grounds. In spite of the lack of solid evidence, Scopas is presumed to have ranked with *Praxiteles and *Lysippus as the leading Greek sculptor of the mid to late 4th cent. BC, his work heralding the emotionalism of *Hellenistic sculpture.

Scorel, Jan van (1495–1562). Netherlandish painter, the first artist to bring the ideals of the Italian *Renaissance to the area we today call Holland. He was born in Schoorel near Alkmaar, and after a varied artistic training worked in Utrecht with *Gossaert, who probably encouraged him to visit Italy. Scorel set out in 1519: stopping at Speyer, Strasburg, Basle, and Nuremberg, he eventually reached Venice, where he joined a group of pilgrims and sailed to Cyprus, Rhodes, Crete, and on to Jerusalem. He returned to Venice the following year and finally made his way to Rome, where he found favour with Pope Adrian VI, a native of Utrecht. By 1524 Scorel was back in Utrecht, where he spent the rest of his life. His countrymen immediately ranked him as one of their leading artists, and he had contact with the courts of France, Spain, and Sweden. Most of Scorel's great altarpieces have been lost or destroyed, but enough of his work survives to show how he had studied *Classical sculpture and the works of *Raphael and *Michelangelo while he lived in Rome. His treatment of landscape and portraiture reveals that he was impressed by the Venetian masters *Giorgione and *Palma Vecchio. Unlike the works of many other Netherlandish masters, however, his pictures are no mere jumble of Renaissance motifs. The *Presentation in the Temple* (Kunsthistorisches Museum, Vienna) is set in a *Bramantesque building and the proportion, movement, and drapery of the figures indicate that he

understood what his Italian contemporaries were trying to achieve. On the other hand, his interest in atmospheric effects, in the play of light and shadow, and his fine landscape drawings are part of his Netherlandish heritage. The degree to which he was able to synthesize northern and southern elements in his figure compositions varies, but the quality of his portraits is uniformly high.

Scott, Samuel (1702?–72). English marine and topographical painter and etcher. He began as a marine painter in the tradition of the van de *Veldes, but he turned to topographical views in the manner of *Canaletto, who was then enjoying great success in England. He was not simply a mechanical imitator, however, and had a feeling for the English atmosphere that is lacking in Canaletto, who brought the Venetian light with him to England. Scott also could achieve a distinctive grandeur of design, as in *An Arch of Westminster Bridge* (Tate, London, c.1750), which is often considered his masterpiece. He left London in 1765 and settled in Bath for reasons of health, apparently painting little in his later years.

Scott, William (1913–). British painter. In 1937–9 he lived in France, and he said: 'I picked up from the tradition of painting in France that I felt most kinship with the still life tradition of *Chardin and *Braque, leading to a certain kind of abstraction which comes directly from that tradition.' His work continued to be mainly based on still life with increasing abstraction, and by the late 1950s he was painting pure abstractions. Although forms such as circles and squares feature in his work, they are not geometrically exact but bounded by sensitive, painterly lines. In the late 1960s and 1970s his paintings became more austere. Scott has won many prizes and is regarded as one of the leading British painters of his generation.

Scott, William Bell (1811–90). Scottish painter and poet. He was head of the Government School of Design in Newcastle upon Tyne, 1843–64, and his best-known works are at Wallington Hall, Northumberland, a series (begun 1855) representing Northumbrian history and including the well-known *Iron and Coal*, one of the earliest representations in art of heavy industry. Bell was a close friend of *Rossetti, and his work has affinities with Pre-Raphaelitism in its Romanticism and love of historical detail. His literary output included much poetry and several books on art, among them a memoir (1850) of his brother **David Scott** (1806–49), a *history painter and book illustrator. Their father, **Robert Scott** (1777–1841), was an engraver.

Scrotes, Guillim (William Stretes) (active 1537–53). Netherlandish portrait painter. He is first heard of in 1537, when he became court painter to Mary of Hungary, Regent of the Netherlands, and by 1546 he was King's Painter to Henry VIII in England, earning a very high salary. His appointment continued under Edward VI. Only a handful of paintings, all done in England, can be confidently attributed to him, among them a full-length portrait of Edward VI in the Royal Collection (several other versions exist). They show Scrotes to have been a highly accomplished practitioner in the international *Mannerist court style and he was an important figure in introducing the full-length portrait to England. He is last heard of in 1553 and may have left England after Edward's death in that year.

scumbling. Painting technique in which a layer of opaque colour is brushed lightly over a previous layer of another colour in such a way that the lower layer is only partly obliterated and shows through irregularly. With *glazing, scumbling allows a range of textural and colouristic effects that ensured *oil painting's dominance over other media. The same effects can now be obtained with *acrylic.

Sebastiano del Piombo (properly Sebastiano Luciani) (c.1485–1547). Venetian painter, active mainly in Rome. According to *Vasari, he trained with Giovanni *Bellini, but his early work was most strongly influenced by *Giorgione, whose *Three Philosophers* (Kunsthistorisches Mus., Vienna) Sebastiano is said to have completed after the master's death. Their styles, indeed, can be so close as to cause paintings to be disputed between them, most notably *The Judgement of Solomon* (National Trust, Kingston Lacy). This large and boldly original work was attributed to Giorgione by *Ridolfi, but scholarly opinion now

increasingly tends towards giving it to Sebastiano. The half-length figure of *Salome* (NG, London, 1510) shows the magnificent painterly skills of an undoubted work of Sebastiano at this date; it has a sensuous beauty reminiscent of Giorgione, but also a statuesque vigour that is Sebastiano's own. In 1511 Sebastiano moved to Rome on the invitation of the banker Agostino Chigi, and he remained there for the rest of his life apart from a visit to Venice in 1528–9 after the Sack of Rome. For Chigi he painted mythological frescos at the Villa Farnesina, where *Raphael also worked. It was with *Michelangelo rather than Raphael, however, that Sebastiano formed a friendship and a professional relationship. Michelangelo not only recommended him to people of influence, but also made drawings for him to work from, as with *The Raising of Lazarus* (NG, London, 1517–19). This was painted in competition with Raphael's *Transfiguration* (Vatican), both being intended for Norbonne Cathedral, and Vasari suggests that Michelangelo helped Sebastiano in order to discredit the Raphael faction, who had denigrated his powers as a colourist. Under Michelangelo's guidance Sebastiano's work became grander in form whilst losing much of its beauty of handling, the lack of sensuous appeal being accentuated when he began experimenting with painting on stone *supports, as in *The Flagellation* (S. Pietro in Montorio, Rome). Some of the finest works of Sebastiano's Roman years are his portraits, and after Raphael's death (1520) he had no rival in the city in this field, his work attaining a distinctive sombre grandeur. Clement VII (Giulio de' *Medici), the subject of one of Sebastiano's finest portraits (Museo di Capodimonte, Naples, 1526), appointed him keeper of the papal seals in 1531 and after this he was less active as a painter. The seals were made of lead, 'piombo' in Italian, hence Sebastiano's nickname.

secco (Italian: dry). Term applied to a technique of mural painting in which the colours are applied to dry plaster, rather than wet plaster as in *fresco. The colours were either *tempera, or *pigments ground in lime-water; if lime-water was used, the plaster had to be damped before painting, a method which was described by *Theophilus and which was popular in northern Europe and in Spain. In Italian

*Renaissance art the finishing touches to a true fresco would often be painted *a secco*, as it is easier to add details in this way; because the secco technique is much less permanent, such passages have frequently flaked off with time. Thus in *Giotto's *Betrayal* in the Arena Chapel, Padua, the details of many of the soldiers' weapons are now missing.

Section d'Or. Group of French painters who worked in loose association between 1912 (the date of their first exhibition) and 1914, when the war brought an end to their activities. The name, which was also the title of a short-lived magazine published by the group, was suggested by Jacques *Villon in reference to the treatise on the *Golden Section by Luca Pacioli, reflecting the interest of the artists involved in questions of proportion and pictorial discipline. Other members of the group included *Delaunay, *Duchamp, *Duchamp-Villon, *Gleizes, *Gris, *Léger, *Metzinger, and *Picabia. The common stylistic feature of their work was a debt to *Cubism.

Segal, George (1924–). American sculptor. He began as a painter, but turned to sculpture in the late 1950s. His most characteristic work consists of unpainted plaster casts taken from life, sometimes a single figure and sometimes a group, set in a context (*The Gas Station*, National Gal. of Canada, Ottawa, 1963). Segal has been classified with *Pop art and *Environment art, but his work is highly distinctive and original, his figures and groups capturing the spiritual isolation and the sense of alienation of modern man which constitute the central theme of existentialist philosophy.

Segantini, Giovanni (1858–99). Italian *Divisionist painter. He lived and worked mainly in the Swiss Alps and is best known for his views of mountain scenery. In later life, from c.1890, he often painted weirdly symbolic and mystical pictures (*The Bad Mothers*, Walker Art Gal., Liverpool), but most of his work is a more straightforward celebration of nature. There is a Segantini museum at St Moritz.

Seghers, Daniel (1590–1661). The leading Flemish flower painter of the generation after Jan *Brueghel, who was his master.

He worked in his native Antwerp, where he joined the Jesuit Order in 1614. The words 'Society of Jesus' usually follow his signature and in 1625–7 he stayed with the Order in Rome. The records of his community in Antwerp, which still survive, give an account of his considerable fame and the distinguished persons who visited him—among them the future Charles II of England. His works could not be sold like those of an ordinary artist, but were presented as gifts by the Order, and the princely patrons in return sent lavish treasures including holy relics and a gold palette and brushes. Seghers's work consists mainly of garlands or 'swags' (festoons) of flowers, often painted around a Madonna and Child or a *Pietà by another artist. He collaborated with his friend *Rubens in this way. Much rarer are his bouquets of flowers in a glass vase, where brilliant colours stand out against a dark background. Their simplicity makes it easier to appreciate his lovely creamy touch (his brushwork was broader than Brueghel's but unerringly sure) and they rank among the most beautiful flower pieces ever painted.

Seghers, Gerard (1591–1651). Flemish painter of religious subjects, active mainly in his native Antwerp, where he is said to have been taught by *Janssens. At some time between 1611 and 1620 he travelled in Italy (and probably also in Spain) and he became one of the very few noteworthy Flemish *Caravaggesque artists. By the time he painted *The Assumption of the Virgin* (Musée de Peinture et de Sculpture, Grenoble, 1629), however, he had fallen under the all-pervasive influence of *Rubens. Seghers had a successful career supplying altarpieces for churches in Antwerp and Ghent and also enjoyed considerable Spanish patronage.

Seghers (or **Segers**), **Hercules Pietersz**. (1589/90–1633/8). Dutch painter and etcher of landscapes, one of the most original but also most enigmatic figures in the history of Dutch art. Very few details of his life are known. He was born in Haarlem, studied with Gillis van *Coninxloo in Amsterdam, and worked also in Utrecht and The Hague, where he is last mentioned in 1633. The woman who was apparently his second wife is described as a widow in 1638. Hardly more than a dozen surviving paintings can be securely attributed to him, although contemporary documents show he certainly painted more. None of the paintings are dated and his chronology is difficult to reconstruct. He painted almost exclusively mountainous scenes, fantastic or *Romantic in conception but advanced in the naturalistic treatment of light and atmosphere. They are usually fairly small, but they suggest vast distances, and with their jagged rocks, shattered tree trunks, and menacing skies convey a sense of almost tragic desolation. Only *Rembrandt and *Ruisdael among Dutch artists attained a similar degree of emotional intensity in landscape painting, and Seghers certainly influenced Rembrandt, who owned no less than eight of his paintings. Seghers's etchings, are also rare (the latest catalogue lists 54, with 183 known impressions) and are perhaps even more original than his paintings. He experimented with coloured inks and dyed papers, so that extraordinarily different impressions could be made from the same plate, a dark paper printed with pale ink transforming a daylight scene into a haunting nocturnal view. Sometimes he printed on linen, which emphasized the vigorous and grainy quality of his work. Every print was an individual work rather than an item in a standardized commercial edition: *Hoogstraten said that he 'printed paintings'. They are unique in European art of the time, and it is often pointed out that some of them have a strange spiritual kinship with Chinese art. The best collection of his etchings is in the Print Room at Amsterdam. In 1678 Hoogstraten wrote a highly coloured account of Seghers's unhappy career, his desperate experiments with etchings, and his eventual poverty and drunkenness, adding that he was killed by falling downstairs when intoxicated. Although the account may be exaggerated, Seghers certainly had financial problems (he was forced to sell his house in Amsterdam in 1631), and it seems likely that he was little appreciated in his day.

seicento. See QUATTROCENTO.

Seisenegger, Jacob (1504/5–67). Austrian painter, chiefly a portraitist. In 1531 he became court painter to the emperor Ferdinand I at Augsburg and he worked much for the Habsburg family. He was a painter of modest talent, but has some importance in the development of the full-length portrait; his most famous work is the full-length of Charles V (Kunsthistorisches Mus., Vienna, 1532), which served as a model for the much more famous one by *Titian (Prado, Madrid). Seisenegger travelled widely, working in Italy, the Netherlands, and Spain, as well as in various cities in Central Europe—Innsbruck, Prague, Vienna.

Seligmann, Kurt (1900–62). Swiss-born American painter and graphic artist. He lived in Paris 1929–38 and became a member of the *Surrealist movement in 1934. His paintings had a magical and apocalyptic character with hazy shapes and swirling draperies indistinguishable from the landscape. He was also known for his Surrealist 'objects'. In 1939 he went to the USA and became an American citizen. In America he painted a series of visionary works which he called 'Cyclonic Forms' and which purported to express his reactions to the American landscape. He made a serious study of magic and wrote a book entitled *The Mirror of Magic* (New York, 1948).

Senefelder, Aloys (1771–1834). German writer who in 1798 invented *lithography as a cheap means of reproducing his plays. He soon realized the artistic possibilities of his invention and wrote of them in his *Vollständiges Lehrbuch der Steindruckerey* (1818), translated into English as *A Complete Course of Lithography* in 1819.

sepia. A brown pigment made from the ink of cuttlefish and other marine creatures. It is used for ink drawings and, because of its semi-transparent quality, in *washes. Its warm, reddish colour distinguishes it from the cooler, more greenish *bistre.

Sequeira, Domingos António de (1768–1837). Portuguese painter, graphic artist, and designer. He formed his *Neoclassical style in Rome 1788–95 and in 1802 he was appointed first court painter in Lisbon. He was a prolific painter of religious and historical compositions as well as portraits (*Dr Neves*, Ashmolean, Oxford, 1825). After 1823, thinking his talent was unappreciated in Portugal, he lived in Paris and Rome.

Séraphine (or **Séraphine de Senlis**) (Séraphine Louis) (1864–1934). French *naïve painter. She passed her youth as a farmhand and later entered domestic service in Senlis. 'Discovered' by Wilhelm *Uhde in 1912, she won recognition as one of the most interesting of the French naïve painters. She painted fantastic compositions of fruit and leaves and flowers worked with minute accuracy of detail into a visionary world of imagination. Towards 1930 her reason failed and she became obsessed with visions of the end of the world.

Sergel, Johan Tobias (1740–1814). German-born Swedish sculptor, active mainly in Stockholm. His early works are in a French *Rococo style, but he abandoned this during the period he spent in Rome (1767–78) and became the leading Swedish exponent of *Neoclassicism. He was a much livelier artist than many Neoclassical sculptors, however, and although his mature work has impressive clarity of form, it also possesses warmth and vitality. In Rome he was best known for his spirited sketches in clay and *terracotta, but after his return to Sweden he was mainly a portraitist. He was court sculptor to Gustavus III and his most important work is a bronze statue of the king (1790–1808) in front of the Royal Palace in Stockholm. Sergel was a prolific draughtsman, many of his drawings being *Romantic in spirit, in a style similar to those of *Fuseli, who was a friend during his period in Rome.

Serial art. A branch of *Systemic Art, in which simple, uniform elements, which may be commercially available objects such as bricks, cement blocks, etc., are assembled in accordance with a strict modular principle. Carl *Andre is a noted exponent of Serial art.

serigraphy. See SILK-SCREEN PRINTING.

Serpotta, Giacomo (1656–1732). Sicilian sculptor in *stucco. He was the greatest of all virtuosi in his medium and with the exception of *Antonello da Messina, the most distinguished artist to come from Sicily. Unlike Antonello, he spent almost all his life on the island (although he may have trained in Rome) and his work is mainly found in the churches of his native Palermo. Serpotta's icing-sugar-white figures—elegant, delicate, charming, and joyous in spirit—are amongst the finest expressions of the *Rococo in Italian art. He is particularly well known for his playful *putti, but his finest single figure is generally acknowledged to be the enchantingly coquettish *Fortitude* (1714–17) in the Oratoria del Rosario di San Domenico, Palermo. His brother **Giuseppe** (1653–1719) and his son **Procopio** (1679–1755) were also stuccoists.

Sérusier, Paul (1863–1927). French painter and art theorist. In 1888 he met *Gauguin and Émile *Bernard at Pont-Aven, was converted to their *Symbolist views and founded the *Nabi movement with *Denis, *Bonnard, *Vuillard, and others. He became the principal theorist of the group, and after visiting the school of religious painting at the Benedictine monastery at Beuron in Germany in 1897 and 1903 his ideas were permeated with concepts of religious symbolism. His theories were set out in his influential book *ABC de la Peinture* (1921), which deals with colour relationships and systems of proportion. Sérusier's paintings, which largely feature Brittany peasants and after about 1900 religious subjects, are generally considered of less interest than his writings.

sottecento. See QUATTROCENTO.

Seuphor, Michel (1901–). Belgian painter, graphic artist, and writer, a founder of *Cercle et Carré and *Abstraction-Création. His artistic work is in a geometrical abstract style, but he is better known for his writings. They include dictionaries of abstract painting (1957) and modern sculpture (1959), both of which have been translated into English.

Seurat, Georges (1859–91). French painter, the founding figure of *Neo-Impressionism. Seurat was the son of comfortably-off parents and his career took an unusual course; he never had to worry about earning a living and pursued his artistic researches with single-minded dedication. In 1878 he entered the École des *Beaux-Arts in Paris, but his studies were interrupted by military service in 1879. He returned to Paris in 1880 and for the next 2 years devoted himself to drawing (he was one of the subtlest and most original draughtsmen of the 19th cent., typically working with very broad, velvety areas of tone, using a *conté crayon on textured paper). In spite of this mastery of black and white, as a painter he turned for inspiration to artists in the colourist tradition—*Delacroix, the *Barbizon School, and the *Impressionists. As well as the work of such painters, Seurat studied aesthetic and scientific treatises, and he made it his aim to establish a rational system for achieving the kind of vibrant colour effects that the Impressionists in particular had arrived at instinctively. The method he evolved was to place small touches of unmixed colour side by side on the canvas, producing an effect of greater vibrancy and luminosity by this 'optical mixture' than if the colours had been physically mixed together on the palette. In his first major painting, *Bathers, Asnières* (NG, London, 1883–4, reworked 1887), Seurat was still experimenting with his technique, but his next large work, *Sunday Afternoon on the Island of La Grande Jatte* (Art Institute of Chicago, 1884–6), is a completely mature statement of his ideals. *La Grande Jatte* was shown at the final Impressionist exhibition in 1886 and led to the recognition of Seurat as a leader of the avant-garde. The critic Félix Fénéon coined the term *pointillism in reference to this painting to describe the technique of using a myriad of tiny dots of colour, but Seurat preferred the term *divisionism. From 1887 Seurat began to turn his attention to the significance of line in painting, believing that certain directions of lines could express specific emotions: horizontal lines represented calmness, for example, while upward- and downward-sloping lines represented happiness and sadness respectively. He embodied his beliefs in paintings such as *Le Chahut* (Rijksmuseum Kröller-Müller, Otterlo, 1890), in which the raised legs of the dancers performing 'Le Chahut' (a sort of can-can) express 'happiness'. Seurat died very suddenly at the age of 31, apparently from meningitis, although his friend *Signac said that he 'killed himself by overwork'. He was so dedicated to his work and kept himself to himself to such an extent that until his death few people knew he had a mistress and son. His mistress, Madeleine Knobloch, is represented in *Woman Powdering Herself* (Courtauld Inst., London, 1890). Seurat's work was highly influential, but his disciples rarely approached his skill, and even less his level of inspiration, in applying his theories; their paintings often look mechanical and lack his gently satirical humour. In power of composition Seurat stands above not only his followers, but also virtually all other painters of his period. He planned his pictures with extraordinary care, and they have nothing of the sense of the passing moment associated with Impressionism. Rather, they have a highly formalized quality and a conscious grandeur that has caused Seurat to be compared to such revered masters as *Piero della Francesca and *Poussin.

Severe style. A term applied to the style characteristic of much Greek sculpture in the period *c.*480 BC–*c.*450 BC, transitional between the *Archaic and *Classical periods. Winckelmann had used the term 'severe' of work of the time before *Phidias, but the term 'severe style' did not come into general usage until Vagn Poulsen's book *Der strenge Stil* of 1937. The characteristics of the severe style include simplicity and severity of form, grandeur and elevation of spirit, and an increase in characterization compared with the Archaic period. *Myron is the best-known sculptor of the period, but his work is sometimes described as early Classical rather than severe.

Severini, Gino (1883–1966). Italian painter. In 1906 he settled in Paris, and he played an important role in transmitting the ideas of French avant-garde to the *Futurists, whose *Technical Manifesto of Painting* he signed in 1910. His work was strongly influenced by *Cubism and he concerned himself with the problem of conveying a sense of movement and action by breaking up his picture space into contrasting and interacting rhythms (*Suburban Train Arriving in Paris*, Tate, London, 1915). He was influenced by theories of mathematical proportion and in 1921 published a book on the subject, *Du Cubisme au Classicisme*. In the 1920s his style became more traditional and he carried out several decorative commissions, including murals for churches in Switzerland. He also worked as a theatrical designer. In the late 1940s his style once again became semi-abstract.

Sezession. Name adopted by several groups of painters in Germany and Austria who in the 1890s broke away ('seceded') from the official academies, which they regarded as tradition-bound, and organized their own, more avant-garde exhibitions. The first of these groups came together in Munich in 1892, and there were Sezessionen also in Vienna (1897) and Berlin (1899). When in 1910 a number of young painters were rejected by the Berlin Sezession—among them members of Die *Brücke—they started the Neue Sezession.

Sezessionstil. See ART NOUVEAU.

Sforza. Italian family, the effective rulers of Milan from 1450, when the *condottiere* **Francesco** (1401–66) seized power, until 1499 when his son **Lodovico** (1452–1508)—the third to succeed him—was expelled by the French. During that time they were lavish patrons of the arts, and the court of Lodovico (who was known as 'Il Moro'—the Moor—because of his dark complexion) was one of the most splendid in Europe. The greatest artists to work for him were *Bramante and *Leonardo da Vinci.

sfumato (from Italian *fumo*: smoke). Term used to describe the blending of tones or colours so subtly that they melt into one another without perceptible transitions—in *Leonardo's words, 'without lines or borders, in the manner of smoke'. Leonardo was a supreme exponent of *sfumato* and *Vasari regarded the capacity to mellow the precise outlines characteristic of the earlier *quattrocento as one of the distinguishing marks of 'modern' painting.

Shahn, Ben (1898–1969). American painter and graphic artist, born at Kovno, Lithuania. He came to the USA in 1906 and worked as a lithographer until 1930. In the early 1930s he attracted attention by a series of gouaches illustrating first the Dreyfus case and then (1931–2) the Sacco and Vanzetti trials. From this time his work showed a pronounced leaning towards social criticism, notably in a series of gouaches and tempera panels concerned with another political scapegoat, Tom Mooney (1932–3). In 1933 he was engaged as assistant to Diego *Rivera on the latter's murals for the Rockefeller Center, New York, and subsequently undertook a number of commissions for murals, including the Bronx Post Office, New York (1938–9). From 1935 to 1938 he worked as an artist and photographer for the Farm Security Administration, depicting rural poverty. After the war his interest turned to easel painting and poster design. From the 1950s he gave more time to lecturing and teaching, and in 1956–7 he was Charles Eliot Norton Professor of Poetry at Harvard University, which published a book of his essays under the title *The Shape of Content* (1957). He illustrated a number of books, notably on Jewish festivals and Hebrew script.

Shannon, Charles (1863–1937). English lithographer and painter, best known for his lifelong association with Charles *Ricketts.

Shee, Sir Martin Archer (1769–1850). Irish portrait painter, active from 1788 in London. There he became second only to *Lawrence as the leading society portraitist, and in 1830 he succeeded him as President of the *Royal Academy, which he guided through a difficult period. Examples of his work—which in style lies between the bravura of Lawrence and the precision of *West—are in the National Portrait Gallery, London. His *Rhymes on Art* (1805), urging the claims of art on national support, enjoyed a considerable popularity. He also published *Elements of Art* (1809).

Sheeler, Charles R. (1883–1965). American painter and photographer, the outstanding exponent of *Precisionism. Between 1904 and 1909 he made several trips to Europe, and abandoned the bravura handling of *Chase (his teacher at the Pennsylvania Academy of the Fine Arts) for a manner influenced by European modernism—the paintings he exhibited at the *Armory Show of 1913, for example, were much indebted to *Cézanne. In 1912 Sheeler took up commercial photography for a living while continuing to paint, and the polished, streamlined forms of the architectural paintings for which he is famed reflect the precision of his photographic style and the formal structure of *Cubism. He himself said: 'In these paintings I sought to reduce natural forms to the borderline of abstraction, retaining only those forms which I believed to be indispensable to the design of the picture.' International acclaim came in the 1920s, not only for his paintings, but also for his photographs, notably a series he took of the Ford motor plant at River Rouge in 1927. During the 1930s and through the 1940s Sheeler's interest turned in the direction of country scenes and interiors and he had this in common with the American *Regionalist painters, although his style remained Precisionist in essence. While retaining this interest in regional themes, during the 1940s and 1950s he recovered his interest in industrial architecture, machinery, and urban scenes. In 1959 he suffered a stroke and had to abandon painting and photography.

Shinn, Everett (1876–1953). American painter and graphic artist. While employed as an illustrator on the *Philadelphia Press* he became a member of the group of friends who were inspired by Robert *Henri, and after he moved to New York in 1896 he became a member of The *Eight and of the *Ash-can School. Shinn differed from his associates in his choice of subject, preferring scenes from the theatre and music-hall to low-life imagery. In 1911 he was commissioned to do murals for Trenton City Hall, New Jersey, and these were the earliest use of Social *Realist themes in public mural decoration. He also did decorations for the interior of the Belasco Theatre, New York. In addition Shinn painted fashionable portraits, illustrated numerous books, wrote plays, and worked as an art director for motion pictures.

Siberechts, Jan (1627–1703). Flemish landscape painter who settled in England in the early 1670s. His landscapes are somewhat *Rubensian, but he is best known for his 'portraits' of English country houses, done in a simple, rather archaic manner; two views of Longleat, Wiltshire (1675 and 1676), are still preserved in the house. He was the first professional exponent of the genre.

siccative. A substance added to oil paint to make it dry more quickly. Siccatives are dangerous aids as they may cause cracking or darken a picture.

Sickert, Walter Richard (1860–1942). English painter, one of the outstanding British artists of his generation. He was born in Munich of Danish and Anglo-Irish parentage (his father and grandfather were painters) and he remained cosmopolitan. The family settled in London in 1868 and Sickert worked as an actor for several years (he toured with the actor-manager Henry Irving) before becoming a student at the *Slade School in 1881. In the following year he became a pupil of *Whistler, and in 1883 he worked in Paris with *Degas. Between 1885 and 1905 Sickert spent much of his time in Dieppe and also visited Venice several times. In 1918–22 he again lived in Dieppe. From 1905, when he returned to England, Sickert became the main link between French avant-garde and progressive English art, his studio in Fitzroy Street, Bloomsbury, becoming a centre for a group of artists who later formed the nucleus of the *Camden Town Group and the *London Group. Sickert took the elements of his style from many sources, but moulded them into a highly personal *œuvre*. From Whistler he derived his characteristic method of painting in a narrow range of low tones, but Sickert's colour effects are richer. To Degas he was indebted in particular for his method of painting from photographs. Sickert mainly painted urban scenes and figure compositions, particularly pictures of the theatre and music-hall and drab domestic interiors. He avoided fashionable good taste and the conventionally picturesque, eliciting rare beauty from the sordid and lending enchantment to the commonplace and dull: in 1910 he wrote 'The more our art is serious, the more will it tend to avoid the drawing-room and stick to the kitchen.' This attitude permeates Sickert's most famous painting *Ennui*, a compelling image of a stagnant marriage, of which he painted at least four versions, that in the Tate Gallery (c.1914) being the largest and most highly finished. In his etchings he continued the tradition of *Hogarth and *Rowlandson, depicting the pathetic and the ridiculous with a penetrating but unmalicious eye. Sickert was a stimulating talker and an articulate writer on art; Osbert Sitwell edited a posthumous collection of his writings entitled *A Free House!* in 1947.

One of the more eccentric theories about the Jack the Ripper murders of 1888 has it that Sickert (against his will) was part of a team that carried out the killings to cover up a scandal about an illegitimate child born to the Duke of Clarence (Queen Victoria's grandson) (see Stephen Knight, *Jack the Ripper: The Final Solution*, 1976, revised edition, 1984).

Siegen, Ludwig von (1609–*c*.1680). German soldier and amateur artist who probably invented the technique of *mezzotint. The earliest of his few surviving prints, a portrait of the Landgravine Amelia Elizabeth of Bohemia, dated 1642, was sent by Siegen to the Landgrave with a letter stating that the invention was his. Prince *Rupert, whom he probably met in Brussels in 1654, learnt the technique from him.

Signac, Paul (1863–1935). French *Neo-Impressionist painter. He began in the *Impressionist manner, but met *Seurat in 1884 and became an ardent disciple of his views and technical method. After the death of Seurat in 1891 he became the acknowledged leader of the Neo-Impressionist group, and in 1899 he published *D'Eugène Delacroix au néo-impressionnisme*, which was long regarded as the authoritative work on the subject. The book was, however, more in the nature of a manifesto in defence of the movement than an objectively accurate history. It reflected changes which had taken place in Signac's own style since 1890 towards greater brilliance of colour, and his best works are generally considered to be those in which he moved away from the scientific precision advocated by Seurat towards a freer and more spontaneous manner. His work had a great influence on *Matisse.

significant form. See BELL, CLIVE.

Signorelli, Luca (1441?–1523). Italian painter from Cortona, active in various cities of central Italy, notably Arezzo, Florence, Orvieto, Perugia, and Rome. According to *Vasari (who was related to him and met him 'as a child of eight') he was a pupil of *Piero della Francesca and this seems highly probable on stylistic grounds, for Signorelli's solid figures and sensitive handling of light echo the work of the master. Signorelli differed from Piero, however, in his interest in the representation of action, which put him in line with contemporary Florentine artists such as the *Pollaiuolo brothers. He must

have had a considerable reputation by about 1483, when he was called on to complete the cycle of frescos on the walls of the Sistine Chapel in Rome, left unfinished by *Perugino and others. His finest works, however, are in Orvieto Cathedral, where he painted a magnificent series of six frescos illustrating the end of the world and the Last Judgement (1499–1504). In these grand and dramatic scenes he displayed a mastery of the nude in a wide variety of poses surpassed at that time only by *Michelangelo. Vasari says that 'Luca's works were always highly praised by Michelangelo' and several instances of close similarity between the work of the two men can be cited; perhaps most interesting is the enigmatic seated nude youth in Signorelli's *Last Acts and Death of Moses* in the Sistine Chapel, which is remarkably close to some of the *Ignudi* painted by Michelangelo on the ceiling of the chapel a quarter of a century later. By the end of his career, however, Luca had become a conservative artist, working in provincial Cortona, where his large workshop turned out numerous altarpieces. Several examples of his work are in the National Gallery, London.

Signorini, Telemaco. See MACCHIAIOLI.

silhouette. An outline image in one, solid, flat colour, giving the appearance of a shadow cast by a solid figure. The term is applied particularly to profile portraits in black against white (or vice versa), either painted or cut from paper, which were extremely popular from about 1750 to about 1850, when photography virtually killed the art. The word silhouette derives from Etienne de Silhouette (1706–67), French finance minister under Louis XV, who was notorious for his parsimony and cut shadow portraits as a hobby; hence the phrase 'à la silhouette' came to mean 'on the cheap'. In England silhouette portraits were generally called 'shades' or 'profiles' up to the end of the 18th cent.

silk-screen printing (or **serigraphy**). A modern colour printing process based on stencilling. A cut *stencil is attached to a silk screen of fine mesh which has been stretched on a wooden frame, and the colour is forced through the unmasked areas of the screen on to the paper beneath by means of a squeegee. This method is an improvement on the simple stencil where, for example, a letter O required connecting pieces to prevent the centre from falling out—a problem which does not arise if the stencil is supported by the silk mesh. By a further improvement in the process the cut stencil is dispensed with altogether, its equivalent being painted directly on to the screen with opaque glue or *varnish. The process, which originated in the early 20th cent., has been widely used for commercial textile printing, but in the 1930s it was developed, particularly in the United States, as an artists' medium. Andy *Warhol was a notable exponent.

Siloe, Diego de (c.1495–1563). Spanish architect and sculptor, one of the leading figures in the transition from *Gothic to *Renaissance in Spanish art. He was the son of **Gil de Siloe** (d. c.1501), who is of uncertain origins (contemporary references suggest both Orleans and Antwerp as his native city) but who settled in Burgos and is regarded as the outstanding Spanish sculptor of the 15th cent. and the last great exponent of the Gothic tradition. His extant work includes the tombs of John II of Castille and Isabella of Castille and of Prince Alfonso (1489–93) for the monastery of Miraflores, Burgos. Diego presumably trained with his father, but he formed his style in Italy, where he collaborated with Bartolomé *Ordóñez. By 1519 he had returned to Burgos, where he carried out several important commissions in the cathedral. They included the tomb of Bishop Luis de Acuña (1519) in the Chapel of St Anne and the altarpiece for the same chapel (1522), but his greatest work there is the *Escalera Dorada* (Golden Stairway) of 1519–23, and it was as an architect rather than as a sculptor that he emerged as one of the great figures of Spanish art. His masterpiece is Granada Cathedral, where he took over as architect in 1528.

silver point. See METAL POINT.

Silvestre, Israël (1621–91). French etcher, the best-known member of a family of artists active from the 16th to the 18th cent. He worked much for Louis XIII and was drawing-master to Louis XIV. His etchings of architectural subjects and of ceremonies and fêtes are generally considered more valuable as historical records than as works of art.

Simone Martini (c.1285–1344). Next to *Duccio, the most distinguished painter of the Sienese School. He was probably trained in Duccio's circle, and he developed further the decorative use of outline, colour, and patterning that were the marks of Duccio's work. The main features of his style are present in his earliest surviving work, the large fresco of the *Maestà* (1315; reworked 1321) in Siena Town Hall: the sumptuous materials and the aloofness of the Madonna derive from the *Byzantine style of the older generation; the decorative line, gesture, and expression are informed by the gracious *Gothic fashion that was now current in Siena; and the use of foreshortening to create depth shows the awakening desire for more lifelike effects. In 1317 Simone was in Naples, where he executed for Robert of Anjou (king of Naples, 1309–43) a painting (Museo di Capodimonte, Naples) showing his elder brother St Louis of Toulouse, newly canonized, resigning his crown to him. The *predella scenes of this altarpiece contain the boldest compositions in *perspective that had been produced up to that date. The next major work associated with Simone is a fresco, dated 1328, on the wall opposite his *Maestà* in Siena Town Hall, commemorating the *condottiere* Guidoriccio da Fogliano, who in that year had won a great victory for the Sienese and liberated the towns of Montemassi and Sassoforte, shown in the background. This highly original work, which shows the general riding in stately but solitary triumph, is generally regarded as one of the first equestrian portraits since antiquity, but recently it has been the subject of great controversy, some scholars considering that it is not by Simone and considerably later than assumed. The work that is generally regarded as the epitome of Simone's style is the *Annunciation* (Uffizi, Florence, 1333), although this is jointly signed with his brother-in-law Lippo *Memmi. It is a ravishing blend of etiolated grace and sweet sentiment and for sheer beauty of craftsmanship is unsurpassed in its age. Simone's work is more fully Gothic in spirit than that of any other major Italian painter and it is not surprising that he was appreciated in France. In 1340/1 he went to Avignon to serve the papal court, where he painted the unusual subject *Christ Reproved by his Parents* (Walker Art Gal., Liverpool, 1342) and the frontispiece to a

Virgil manuscript which was then owned by the poet Petrarch (Ambrosiana Lib., Milan). He also did a portrait of Petrarch's beloved Laura; it is lost, but mentioned in one of the poet's sonnets. Simone's style and compositions were taken over by *illuminators from France and Flanders and generations of Italian *panel and fresco painters copied him too. He was one of the main sources of the *International Gothic style.

singerie. A depiction of monkeys (French: *singes*) engaged in playful activities, often dressed in human clothes and acting out human roles. The conceit of monkeys involved in human occupations goes back to medieval manuscripts, but the term *singerie* is usually restricted to a type of decorative painting associated with the French *Rococo. Claude *Audran and his pupil *Watteau were noted exponents.

sinopia. Term applied to a reddish-brown chalk used for the underdrawing of a *fresco and also to the drawing itself. Sinopie are often uncovered during restoration work when the upper layer of a fresco is removed (see, for example, TRAINI).

Siqueiros, David Alfaro (1896–1974). Mexican painter, one of the trio of muralists (with *Orozco and *Rivera) who have dominated 20th-cent. Mexican art. He was a political activist from his youth and at the age of 15 joined the revolutionary army fighting against President Huerta. In appreciation of his services the victorious General Venustiano Carranza sponsored him to study art in Europe. On returning to Mexico in 1922 he took a leading part in the artistic revival fostered by the regime of President Álvaro Obregón. Siqueiros was active in organizing the Syndicate of Technical Workers, Painters and Sculptors and was partly responsible for drafting its Manifesto which set forth the idealistic aims of the revolutionary artists. His political activities led to his being imprisoned several times; he also had a period of exile and fought in the Spanish Civil War. In 1925–30 he completely abandoned painting for political activity. Nevertheless, his output was prodigious, and he painted many easel pictures as well as murals—and though he himself insisted that they were subordinate to his murals, they proved a major factor contributing to his international fame as an artist. His murals are generally more spectacular even than those of Orozco and Rivera—bold in composition, striking in colour, freely mixing realism with fantasy, and expressing a raw emotional power. In contrast with the sense of disillusionment and foreboding sometimes featured in Orozco's work, Siqueiros always expressed the dynamic urge to struggle. He often experimented technically—working on carved surfaces and using air-brushes and synthetic pigments. Siqueiros worked in the USA, Chile, and Cuba, but most of his work is in Mexico City.

Sisley, Alfred (1839–99). French *Impressionist painter of English parentage. He was intended by his parents to have a commercial career, but he turned to painting. In 1862 he entered the studio of *Gleyre and there met *Renoir, *Monet, and *Bazille, his friendship with Monet proving particularly important. Like Monet, Sisley devoted himself almost exclusively to landscape, but his work was much less varied. He made several visits to England, but otherwise rarely travelled, and most of his pictures are of scenes in and around Paris. The best are among the most lyrical and gently harmonious works of Impressionism, delicate in touch and with a beautiful feeling for tone. Sisley was given a generous allowance by his wealthy father and his early life was happy: Renoir described him as 'a delightful human being' and said he 'could never resist a petticoat'. After the family business failed in 1871, however, his father was unable to support him and thereafter he spent much of his life in poverty, never winning the success or renown of his former colleagues. He still remains something of a Cinderella among the Impressionists, claimed as their own by neither the French nor the English. His work is in many public collections, including the National Gallery, the Tate Gallery, and the Courtauld Institute in London.

size. Glue made from animal skins, or, more loosely, any fairly weak glue. It is used in art mainly for filling the porous surface of wooden *panels or *canvases to provide a suitable foundation for the *priming (see GROUND). Size is also used as a *medium—paint mixed with it is called *distemper.

sketch. 'A rough drawing or delineation of something, giving the outlines or prominent features without the detail, especially one intended to serve as the basis of a more finished picture, or to be used in its composition . . .' (*OED*). This was the original meaning of the word, and it was not until the latter part of the 18th cent. that it acquired the additional sense of 'a drawing or painting of a slight or unpretentious nature'. A sketch should be distinguished from a 'study', which is a representation of a detail to be used in a large composition and may be highly finished. A *modello* is more elaborate than an ordinary sketch.

Slade, Felix (1790–1868). English art collector and philanthropist. He left a great part of his collection, notable particularly for glass, to the *British Museum and in his will endowed chairs of fine art at the universities of London (University College), Oxford, and Cambridge. The professorships at Oxford and Cambridge involve only the giving of lectures, intended for a general audience, but in London the Slade School of Fine Art, opened in 1871, is an institution giving practical instruction in painting, sculpture, and the graphic arts. The first professor was Sir Edward *Poynter, who founded the Slade tradition of emphasis on drawing from the nude. Rapidly taking over from the *Royal Academy (where the teaching methods were considered arid and academic) as the most important art school in the country, the Slade had its heyday in the period from about 1895 to the First World War. Its students then included some of the most illustrious names in 20th-cent. British art—Augustus and Gwen *John, Wyndham *Lewis, Paul *Nash, Ben *Nicholson, Stanley *Spencer, and so on. After Poynter, the Slade Professors in London have included *Tonks, *Coldstream, and *Gowing. The first Slade Professors at Oxford and Cambridge respectively were *Ruskin and the architect Matthew Digby Wyatt. Their successors have included many eminent art historians.

Slevogt, Max (1868–1932). German painter and graphic artist, with *Corinth and *Liebermann one of the leading artists in his country to show the impact of *Impressionism. He was born in Bavaria and studied in Munich, making visits later

to Paris (1889), Italy, the Netherlands, and Egypt. Although he took over from the Impressionists their fresh, bright palette, he never adopted their fragmentation of colours, and his work always retained something of the Bavarian *Baroque tradition. His loose handling of paint, bold effects of light, and energetic sense of movement give his work great dash, and he was much in demand as a decorative artist. He also made a name for himself as a book illustrator. As a painter his work included landscapes, portraits, and scenes of contemporary life; he loved the theatre and is perhaps best known for portrayals of the singer Francisco d'Andrade in the role of Don Juan. He also painted religious pictures, his last work being a fresco of *Golgotha* in the Friedenskirche at Ludwigshafen (1932) sometimes considered his masterpiece.

Sloan, John (1871–1951). American painter and graphic artist. He learned painting from Robert *Henri during the late 1890s while working as an illustrator for the Philadelphia *Press* and *Enquirer*. In 1904 he settled permanently in New York, where he and Henri were among the members of The *Eight. Sloan was interested in social reform and as well as finding his most characteristic subjects among everyday lower-class New York life, he did illustrations for the socialist periodical *The Masses*. His paintings are generally marked by a warm humanity, but he could also be sharply satirical and occasionally expressed himself in a totally different vein, as in *Wake of the Ferry* (Phillips Coll., Washington, 1907), which has a romantic, melancholy mood. He taught at the Art Students' League and became its director in 1931, but he was not accepted by many of the Social *Realists of the 1930s because although he always maintained his liberal sympathies he refused to incorporate what he called 'socialist propaganda' into his art.

Slodtz. Family of French sculptors, designers, and decorators. They were **Sébastien** (1655–1726), who was Flemish by birth, and his three sons: **Sébastien-Antoine** (*c.*1695–1754), **Paul-Ambroise** (1702–58), and **René-Michel** called **Michel-Ange** (1705–64). They all worked for the Menus Plaisirs (the office that designed costumes, festivities, etc. for the court), as did another son of Sébastien, the painter **Dominique Slodtz** (1711–64), and Michel-Ange was the only member of the family to attain great distinction as a sculptor. From 1728 to 1747 he was in Rome, where his admiration for *Michelangelo won him his nickname. His best-known work is *St Bruno* (St Peter's, Rome, 1744), which shows the nervous sensitivity of his style. In France he made several major tombs, notably that of Languet de Gergy (S. Sulpice, Paris, completed 1753), which shows the influence of *Bernini in its *Baroque rhetoric and use of different coloured marbles. *Houdon was Slodtz's most important pupil.

Sluter, Claus (d. 1405/6). Netherlandish sculptor, active mainly in Dijon. He was the greatest sculptor of his time in northern Europe and a figure of enormous importance in the transition from *International Gothic to a more weighty and naturalistic style. Sluter is first mentioned in Brussels (c.1379) in a document that says he came from Haarlem. In 1385 he entered the service of Philip the Bold, Duke of Burgundy, in his capital, Dijon. All of Sluter's surviving work was done for Philip, and almost all of it remains in Dijon. For the Chartreuse de Champmol, a monastery founded by Philip, Sluter carved figures for the portal of the chapel in the early 1390s, and made a fountain group, of which only the base survives intact, known as the *Well of Moses* (1395–1403). The monastery was destroyed during the French Revolution, and the portal and the *Well of Moses* are now part of the psychiatric hospital that occupies its site. The Well features six full-length figures of prophets of monumental dignity; they convey an intense sense of physical presence, and as character studies rival the prophets of *Donatello, which they preceded by about 20 years. Originally Sluter's figures were painted (by *Malouel) and the figure of Jeremiah is known to have worn copper spectacles, the record of payment for which still survives. Of the Calvary group that surmounted the Well (symbolizing the 'Fountain of Life') only fragments survive in the Archaeological Museum in Dijon; they include the head and torso of the figure of Christ—one of Sluter's noblest works, in which the expression of suffering stoically endured is deeply moving. Sluter's last work was the tomb of Philip the Bold, begun in 1404 and unfinished at the sculptor's death (Musée des Beaux-Arts, Dijon). Most of the work on it was carried out by Sluter's nephew and assistant Claus de Werve, but the figures of *pleurants* (weepers or mourners) that form a frieze around the sarcophagus are from the master's own hand, and although they are only about 40 cm. high they possess massive solemnity. They show Sluter's extraordinary ability to use the heavy folds of drapery for expressive effect; indeed some of the mourners are so completely enveloped in their voluminous cowls that they are in effect nothing else but drapery. Sluter's influence was enormous—on painters as well as sculptors. The emphatic plasticity of the *Master of Flémalle's figures, for example, has Sluter as its source, and in his *Entombment* (Courtauld Inst., London, c.1410/20), which stands at the head of the early Netherlandish tradition of painting, the angel that wipes away a tear with the back of his hand is a quotation from the *Well of Moses*.

Sluyters, Jan (1881–1957). Dutch painter, one of the best-known artists in the Netherlands in the inter-war period, and the one in whom French modernism is most variously reflected. His early works show the influence of van *Gogh and *Breitner, and of *Toulouse-Lautrec and *Matisse. Like many other 20th-cent. painters he also experimented with *Cubism. He finally worked out a lively personal style of colourful *Expressionism which is best seen in his nudes—he had a predilection for painting nude children.

Smart, John (1742/3–1811). One of the leading British *miniaturists of his period. His style was meticulous, bright, and pretty. He worked mainly in London but was in India 1785–c.1796.

Smet, Gustave de (1877–1943). With van den *Berghe and *Permecke, one of the leading Belgian *Expressionist painters. He began working in an *Impressionist style, but was influenced towards Expressionism by Jan *Sluyters and Henri *Le Fauconnier when he was in Holland during the First World War. Typically he painted scenes of rural and village life in which forms are treated in a schematic way owing something to *Cubism, and there is often an air of unreality reminiscent of that in

*Chagall's work (*Village Fair*, Musée des Beaux-Arts, Ghent, c.1930).

Smibert, John (1688–1751). Scottish-born portrait painter who emigrated to America in 1728 and settled in Boston in 1730. Previously he had travelled in Italy and practised successfully in London in an uninspired style derived from *Kneller. After he settled in America his work became somewhat more vigorous. He brought with him a small collection of copies, casts, and engravings and opened a shop where he sold English engravings from the works of well-known artists. These, together with his own paintings, became the corner-stone of the New England Colonial portrait style, and Smibert encouraged the young *Copley.

Smith, David (1906–65). The most original and influential American sculptor of his generation. He began to study art at Ohio University in 1924 and in the summer of 1925 worked at the Studebaker motor plant at South Bend, Indiana, where he acquired the skills in metalwork which stood him in good stead later in his career. From 1926 to 1930 he studied painting at the Art Students' League, New York, while supporting himself by a variety of jobs. Among his associates were Arshile *Gorky and Willem *de Kooning. He turned to sculpture in the early 1930s, making his first welded iron sculpture in 1933, although he always maintained that there was no essential difference between painting and sculpture and that although he owed his 'technical liberation' to Julio *González, his aesthetic outlook was more influenced by *Kandinsky, *Mondrian, and *Cubism. During the 1930s he was already doing sculpture of considerable originality, constructing compositions from steel and 'found' scrap, parts of agricultural machinery, etc. He had a love of technology, and wrote: 'The equipment I use, my supply of material, comes from factory study, and duplicates as nearly as possible the production equipment used in making a locomotive . . . What associations the metal possesses are those of this century: power, structure, movement, progress, suspension, destruction, brutality.'

In 1940 he exhibited a set of fifteen bronze *relief plaques entitled *Medals of Dishonour* stigmatizing the prevalence of violence and greed throughout the world.

After being employed as a welder on defence work, he returned to sculpture c.1945. His sculpture during the 1940s and 1950s was open and linear, like three-dimensional metal calligraphy. Perhaps the most noted work in this style is *Hudson River Landscape* (Whitney Mus., New York, 1951). From the end of the 1950s up to his death in a car accident he did the more structural and massive work for which he is best known, often working in series such as *Zig*, *Tank Totem*, *Agricola*, *Cubi*, *Voltri*. Although monumental and intended to be seen in the open, these last works—characteristically consisting of boxes and cylinders of polished metal—were not heavy but had an unstable, dynamic quality which contradicted their sense of density. They initiated a new era in American sculpture, ushering in the sort of objectivity which characterized *Post-Painterly Abstraction. Smith's work is in many major collections.

Smith, Sir Matthew (1879–1959). English painter. He studied at the *Slade School and for a short time in Paris (1911) under *Matisse. Thereafter he identified strongly with French art and spent much of his time in France. He was delicate in health and of a nervous disposition, but this is hardly apparent from his work, which uses colour in a bold, unnaturalistic manner echoing the *Fauves. His lush brushwork, too, has great vigour, and he was one of the few English painters to excel in painting the nude, his dark saturated colours and opulent fluency of line creating images of great sensuousness. He also painted landscapes (most notably a series done in Cornwall in 1920) and still lifes. Frank *Auerbach and Francis *Bacon are among the many artists who have admired Smith's painterliness. His work is in many public galleries, the best collection being in the Guildhall Art Gallery, London.

Smith, Tony (1912–80). American sculptor, painter, and architect. After studying at the Art Students' League, 1933–6, and the New Bauhaus, Chicago, 1937–8, he practised as an architect from 1940 to 1960, during which time he also painted. He began to interest himself in sculpture around 1940 and emerged in the early 1960s as one of the pioneers of *Minimal sculpture. His work was large in scale and composed of simple geometrical shapes to be made in steel, sometimes painted.

Smithson, Robert (1938–73). American sculptor and experimental artist. In the 1960s his work belonged mainly to the category of *Minimal art, and he experimented particularly with reflections and mirror images. From the late 1960s he turned to *earthworks and became the best-known artist working in this field. He visited the abandoned quarries and old mine trailings of Pennsylvania and New Jersey, collecting rock fragments, gravel, and geological refuse, which he arranged into random heaps or in metal or wood bins. With these and mirrors, combined with site plans, geological maps and Instamatic colour photographs, he built up his well-known 'Non-sites', using natural waste for artistic purposes in a manner similar to that in which *Junk artists had previously used urban waste. His later work, verging towards *Conceptual art, included *in situ* structures, the best-known of which is the enormous *Spiral Jetty* (1970), a spiral road (now submerged) running out into Great Salt Lake, Utah. Smithson was killed in a plane crash while surveying a site for an earthwork in Texas.

Smithsonian Institution. A research institution and educational centre founded by the bequest of the English scientist James Smithson (1765–1829) 'for the increase and diffusion of knowledge' and established by congressional act in Washington D.C. in 1846. Smithson was an illegitimate son of the Duke of Northumberland and it is thought to have been resentment over the circumstances of his birth that caused him to make the bequest to the USA rather than his native country. 'My name shall live . . . when the titles of the Northumberlands . . . are extinct and forgotten.' The Smithsonian administers many prestigious cultural organizations in Washington, including the National Gallery of Art, the National Portrait Gallery, and the Joseph H. Hirshhorn Museum and Sculpture Garden.

Snyders, Frans (1579–1657). Flemish painter of animals, hunting scenes, and still life, active mainly in his native Antwerp. He was a pupil of Pieter *Brueghel the Younger and travelled in Italy 1608–9. Back in Antwerp, he became a close friend

of *Rubens, also recently returned from Italy (Rubens eventually made him executor of his will). Snyders often collaborated with Rubens; he painted animals, fruits, and flowers in Rubens's pictures, and Rubens painted figures in his. He later worked out the same kind of reciprocal arrangement with *Jordaens, and collaborated with his brother-in-law Cornelis de *Vos, van *Dyck, and Abraham *Janssens. His independent works show he was the finest animal painter of his time: the best are his scenes of fighting wild animals and hunts, which have a tremendous sense of *Baroque vitality.

Social Realism and **Socialist Realism**. See REALISM.

Société Anonyme, Inc. (or A Museum of Modern Art). An association formed in 1920 by Katherine *Dreier together with Marcel *Duchamp and *Man Ray for the promotion of contemporary art in America by lectures, publications, and travelling exhibitions. It had the first museum in the USA, and one of the earliest anywhere, to be devoted entirely to modern art. The Société arranged more than eighty exhibitions between 1920 and 1940, and it was through its efforts that such artists as *Klee, *Miró, *Malevich, and *Schwitters were first exhibited in America. To some extent, therefore, the Société carried on the tradition which had been started by the 291 Gallery of *Stieglitz in the years before the *Armory Show. It also built up a permanent collection of modern painting and sculpture, the greater part of which passed to Yale University Art Gallery in 1941. The Société came to an end in 1950.

Society of Artists. An association of artists formed in London in the 1750s and incorporated by Royal Charter in 1765. It emerged in response to the desire for a state-run academy that would provide public exhibitions of contemporary art, and was the main forerunner of the *Royal Academy. Its leaders were *Hayman and *Lambert. It survived until 1791.

Society of Independent Artists. An American association formed in 1916 to succeed the Association of American Painters and Sculptors, which was dissolved after the *Armory Show. Its object was to hold annual exhibitions in rivalry with the

National Academy of Design and to afford progressive artists an opportunity to show their works. It was organized on the model of the French *Salon des Indépendants without jury or prizes, giving anyone the right to exhibit on payment of a modest fee. The first President was William *Glackens, followed by John *Sloan. The first exhibition, in the spring of 1916, comprised more than 2,000 exhibits and included both American and European artists. Although the Society continued to arrange exhibitions until the mid 1940s, subsequent exhibitions were smaller and inferior in quality and its importance diminished. In 1917 *Duchamp, who was one of the first Directors, resigned after the refusal to exhibit his *ready-made in the form of a urinal signed 'R. Mutt'. Although much recondite aesthetic theory has been read into this gesture, it is likely that the main purpose of it was to demonstrate the artistic incongruity of a Society with the professed purpose of allowing anyone to exhibit anything.

Sodoma, Il (Giovanni Antonio Bazzi) (1477–1549). Italian painter, born at Vercelli and active chiefly in and around Siena, where he settled in 1501. *Vasari, who disliked him, explains the origin of his nickname—'the sodomite'—in this fashion: 'His manner of life was licentious and dishonourable, and as he always had boys and beardless youths about him of whom he was inordinately fond, this earned him the nickname of Sodoma; but instead of feeling shame, he gloried in it, writing stanzas and verses on it, and singing them to the accompaniment of the lute.' Sodoma (who was married and had children) himself used the name in his signature, and Vasari's story has been questioned. Vasari also tells us that Sodoma kept a menagerie of strange animals 'so that his home resembled a veritable Noah's ark'. He was a prolific painter of frescos and easel pictures, and he drew on a variety of sources that were not always fully digested; consequently his work often has incongruous juxtapositions and a general air of uncoordination, but it also possesses charm and a flair for decoration. His fresco of the *Marriage of Alexander and Roxane* (1516–17), painted for the Sienese banker Agostino Chigi in his Villa Farnesina in Rome, is often cited as his finest work. In his time Sodoma was considered the leading artist in Siena, but later critics have come to rank *Beccafumi above him.

Soft art. Term applied to sculpture using non-rigid materials, a vogue of the 1960s and 1970s. The materials employed have been very diverse: rope, cloth, rubber, leather, paper, canvas, vinyl—anything in fact which offers a certain persistence of form but lacks permanent shape or rigidity. Perhaps the earliest example of 'Soft art' in this century was the typewriter cover which Marcel *Duchamp mounted on a stand and exhibited in 1916. But this belongs rather to the category of *ready-mades, which he introduced. 'Soft art' as a movement is usually traced to Claes *Oldenburg's giant replicas of foodstuffs (ice-cream sundaes, hamburgers, pieces of cake, etc.) made from stuffed vinyl and canvas. Other artists who have experimented with soft materials have been many and diverse, from many different movements, including *Arte Povera, *Pop art, and *Surrealism.

soft-ground etching. A method of *etching, invented in the late 18th cent., that produces prints characterized by softness of line or a grainy texture. The *ground used to coat the etching plate is softer and stickier than in normal etching, so that it adheres to anything pressed into it. Over this ground was laid a sheet of paper on which the artist drew with a pencil. Under the pressure of the pencil strokes the ground stuck to the back of the paper, so that when it was lifted the wax immediately underneath the lines came away with it, while the rest remained in place. The plate was then immersed in acid, and printed in the normal way. The printed lines were granulous, coarse, or fine according to the texture of the paper used for the drawing: thus if the paper had been smooth, the lines resembled pencil, but if rough, they were more like chalk. Soft-ground etchings bear a strong likeness to prints in the *crayon manner, but are generally a little softer and less regular. Although the technique was used in the late 18th and early 19th cents. chiefly for reproduction, a number of excellent original soft-ground etchings were produced by *Gainsborough, *Cotman, and *Girtin. Interest in the technique has revived among some modern artists.

Solimena, Francesco (1657–1747). The leading Neapolitan painter of the first half of the 18th cent. In a long and extremely productive career he painted frescos in many of the greatest churches in Naples, and he became one of the wealthiest and most famous European artists of his day. His vigorous style, often marked by dramatic lighting, owed much to the example of such *Baroque artists as Luca *Giordano (his great predecessor in Naples), *Lanfranco and *Preti, but it also has a firmness of structure and a clarity of draughtsmanship that shows his allegiance to the *Classical tradition of *Raphael and Annibale *Carracci. Solimena's paintings were in demand all over Europe, and his international influence was spread also by his celebrity as a teacher. *Ramsay was among his pupils and *Fragonard copied his work in S. Paolo Maggiore.

Solomon, Simeon (1840–1905). British painter and graphic artist, a member of a well-known family of artists. He was a member of *Rossetti's circle and a friend of *Burne-Jones, and his work shows strong *Pre-Raphaelite influence. In the 1860s he built up a reputation as a book illustrator, but then sank into a life of idleness and dissipation (in 1871 he was arrested on homosexual charges). His later years were spent in a pathetically Bohemian existence, and he died of alcoholism. His sister **Rebecca** (1832–86), who painted portraits and anecdotal historical scenes, also died an alcoholic. Their brother **Abraham** (1824–62) painted scenes from literature and contemporary life scenes, some of which attained great popularity, and were much reproduced as prints.

Somer, Paul van (c.1577–1622). Flemish portrait painter and engraver who settled in England in 1616 and became—with Cornelius *Johnson and Daniel *Mytens— the leading portraitist at the court of James I (1566–1625). His finest work is *Queen Anne of Denmark* (Royal Coll., 1617), an imposing full-length, but more archaic in style than similar portraits by Mytens.

Sorolla y Bastida, Joaquin (1863–1923). Spanish painter and graphic artist, active mainly in Valencia. He was a prolific and popular artist, working on a wide variety of subjects—*genre, portraits, landscapes, historical scenes—and producing many book illustrations. His pleasant and undemanding style was marked by brilliant high-keyed colour and vigorous brushwork, representing a kind of conservative version of *Impressionism. He was well known outside Spain, and in 1910–20 he painted a series of fourteen mural panels for the Hispanic Society of America in New York, representing scenes typical of the various provinces of Spain. There is a Sorolla Museum in Madrid.

Sotheby's. The oldest and largest firm of auctioneers in the world. It was founded by the London bookseller Samuel Baker, who held his first auction in 1744. On his death in 1778, his estate was divided between his partner George Leigh and his nephew John Sotheby. The last of the Sotheby family to be involved in the firm died in 1861. Although Sotheby's extended its range to take in prints, coins, medals, and antiquities of various kinds, books long remained the primary concern of the company, and it was not until after the First World War that paintings and other works of art became a major part of its business (before this time most important picture sales were held by *Christie's). In 1964 Sotheby's bought Parke Bernet, America's largest fine art auctioneers, and it now has major sale rooms in London, New York, Geneva, and Monaco, with numerous branches throughout the world.

sotto in su (Italian: from below upwards). Term applied to an extreme form of *illusionistic foreshortening in which figures or objects painted on a ceiling appear to be floating or suspended in space above the viewer. *Mantegna's Camera degli Sposi in the Palazzo Ducale in Mantua is the first major example, but the device is associated particularly with *Baroque decoration.

Soutine, Chaïm (1893–1943). Lithuanian-born painter who settled in France in 1913 and became one of the leading *Expressionists of the School of *Paris. Soutine suffered from depression and a lack of confidence in his own work (he was reluctant to exhibit and sometimes destroyed his pictures), and he endured years of poverty until the American collector Dr Albert C. *Barnes bought a number of his paintings in 1923. His style is characterized by thick, convulsive brushwork, through which he could express tenderness as well as turbulent psychological states. There is something of an affinity with van *Gogh, although Soutine professed to dislike his work and felt more kinship with the Old Masters whose work he studied in the Louvre; his pictures of animal carcasses, for example, are inspired by *Rembrandt's *Flayed Ox*. The gruesome intensity of works such as *Side of Beef* (Albright-Knox Art Gallery, Buffalo, c.1925) was not gained simply through study of similar pictures, however, for Soutine visited abattoirs and even brought a carcass into his studio. His neighbours complained of the smell of the rotting carcass and called the police, whom Soutine harangued on the subject of how much more important art was than sanitation. Soutine also painted landscapes, portraits, and studies of choir-boys, page-boys, pastry-cooks, etc. He was one of a circle of expatriate artists in Paris, his friends including *Modigliani, who painted a memorable portrait of him (NG, Washington, 1917).

Soyer, Moses (1899–1974) and **Raphael** (1899–1987). Russian-born painters, twins. They emigrated to America in 1912 as exiles from tsarist Russia. During the 1930s their work was typical of the Social *Realism practised by the *American Scene painters, depicting the lives of working people with sympathy and at times a touching air of melancholy, as in Raphael's well-known *Office Girls* (Whitney Mus. of American Art, New York, 1936). Another brother, **Isaac** (1907–81), who came to America in 1914, was also a painter.

Spazialismo (or **Spatialism**). A movement founded by Lucio *Fontana in Milan in 1947. The main ideas of the movement were anticipated in his *Manifesto Blanco* (White Manifesto) published in Buenos Aires in 1946. In it he spoke of a new 'spatial' art in keeping with the spirit of the post-war age. On the negative side it repudiated the illusory or 'virtual' space of traditional easel painting; on the positive side it was to unite art and science to project colour and form into real space by the use of up-to-date techniques such as neon lighting and television. Several more manifestos followed, more specific in their negative than their positive aspects, and carried the concept of Spazialismo little

further than the statement that its essence consisted in 'plastic emotions and emotions of colour projected upon space'. In 1947 Fontana created a 'Black Spatial Environment', a room painted black, which was considered to have foreshadowed *Environment art. His holed and slashed canvases (*Spatial Concept 'Waiting'*, Tate, London, 1960) are also considered to exemplify Spazialismo.

Spencer, Sir Stanley (1891–1959). English painter, one of the most original figures in 20th-cent. British art. He was born in Cookham in Berkshire and lived for most of his life in the village, which played a large part in the imagery of his paintings. His education was fairly elementary, but he grew up in a family in which literature, music, and religion were dominant concerns and his imaginative life was extremely rich. He said he wanted 'to take the inmost of one's wishes, the most varied religious feelings . . . and to make it an ordinary fact of the street', and he is best known for his pictures in which he set biblical events in his own village; his visionary attitude has been compared to that of William *Blake. Spencer was a prizewinning student at the *Slade School (1908–12) and served in the army from 1915 to 1918, first at the Beaufort War Hospital in Bristol, then in Macedonia. He was appointed an official war artist in 1918, but his experiences during the war found their most memorable expression a decade later when he painted a series of murals for the Sandham Memorial Chapel at Burghclere in Hampshire (1927–32), built to commemorate a soldier who had died from an illness contracted in Macedonia. The arrangement of the murals consciously recalls *Giotto's Arena Chapel in Padua, but Spencer painted in oil, not fresco, and he concentrated not on great events, but on the life of the common soldier, which he depicted with deep human feeling. There is no violence, and Spencer said that the idea for one of the scenes—*The Dug-Out*—occurred to him 'in thinking how marvellous it would be if one morning, when we came out of our dug-outs, we found that somehow everything was peace and the war was no more'. By this time Spencer was a celebrated figure, his greatest public success having been *The Resurrection: Cookham* (Tate, London, 1924–6), which when exhibited in 1927 was hailed by the critic of *The Times* as 'the most important picture painted by any English artist in the present century'. He continued: 'What makes it so astonishing is the combination in it of careful detail with modern freedom of form. It is as if a *Pre-Raphaelite had shaken hands with a *Cubist.'

Spencer was again an official war artist during the Second World War, when he painted a series of large canvases showing shipbuilding on the Clyde (Imperial War Mus.) that memorably capture the heroic teamwork that went into the war effort. His career culminated in a knighthood in the year of his death, but his life was not a smooth success story, and in the 1930s he somewhat alienated his public with the expressive distortions and erotic content of his work. In 1935 he resigned as an Associate of the *Royal Academy when two of his pictures, considered caricature-like and poorly drawn, were rejected for the annual summer exhibition, but rejoined the Academy in 1950. In 1937 he divorced his first wife, Hilda Carline, and married Patricia Preece, but Hilda continued to play a large part in his life, and he painted pictures in memory of her and even wrote letters to her after her death. Some of his nude paintings of Patricia vividly express not only the sexual tensions of his life, but also his belief in the sanctity of human love; the best known is the double nude portrait of himself and Patricia known as *The Leg of Mutton Nude* (Tate, 1937). In his later years Spencer acquired a reputation as a landscapist as well as a figure painter. There is a gallery devoted to Spencer at Cookham, containing not only paintings, but also memorabilia such as the pram that the eccentric figure used for pushing his painting equipment around the village. His younger brother **Gilbert Spencer** (1892–1979) was also a painter of imaginative subjects and landscapes, working in a style close to that of Stanley.

Spinario (Latin: spina, a thorn). Ancient bronze statue of a seated boy extracting a thorn from his left foot (Capitoline Museum, Rome). It is recorded in Rome as early as the 12th cent. and during the *Renaissance it was one of the most influential and copied of ancient sculptures. Its fame endured and it was one of the ancient works taken by Napoleon to Paris, where it remained from 1798 to 1815.

Various stories grew up from the Renaissance onwards to explain the subject, the most popular being that the statue commemorates a shepherd boy called Martius who delivered an important message to the Roman Senate and only when his task was accomplished stopped to remove a thorn from his foot. It is now generally thought that the *Spinario* is a Roman pastiche of about the 1st cent. BC, combining a *Hellenistic body with a head of earlier date (the way in which the hair falls indicates that the head was meant to be in an upright position rather than looking down as it is now).

Spinello Aretino (active 1373–1410/11). Italian painter. He was born at Arezzo (hence the name Aretino) and probably trained in Florence, perhaps under Agnolo *Gaddi. He was the most prolific muralist of his time and undertook large fresco cycles all over Tuscany. His last series was the cycle devoted to the Sienese pope Alexander III in Siena Town Hall (1408–10). He also painted altarpieces. Spinello borrowed ideas freely from other painters, notably *Giotto, but his style was sturdy and vigorous. His son **Parri Spinelli** (d. 1452) was his assistant. Several fresco fragments by Spinello are in the National Gallery, London.

Spitzweg, Karl (1808–85). German painter and graphic artist, active in his native Munich. He began his career as a pharmacist, and turned fairly late to art, first as a newspaper *caricaturist, then as a painter. Although he travelled widely (England, France, Italy, and elsewhere), he was provincial in his choice of subjects and is an outstanding representative of the *Biedermeier style. His pictures are generally small, humorous in content, and full of lovingly depicted anecdotal detail (*The Poor Poet*, Neue Pinakothek, Munich, 1839, and other versions). He also painted excellent landscapes that show a debt to the *Barbizon School.

Spranger, Bartholomeus (1546–1611). Flemish *Mannerist painter. He trained in his native Antwerp, where he came under the influence of Frans *Floris, then travelled widely in Italy and France and also visited Vienna before finally settling in Prague in 1581 at the court of the emperor Rudolf

II. His paintings, although not representational, are often of mythological or allegorical subjects and are highly polished and sophisticated. Spranger met van *Mander in Rome and through him his style was carried to Haarlem, where it became a formative influence in the Haarlem Academy. His work was also widely known in engravings.

Squarcione, Francesco (1397–c.1468). Italian painter, active in Padua. He is an enigmatic figure, who is important in terms of the pupils he trained, rather than for his own work. A Paduan writer of 1560 patriotically described him as a famous and benevolent master, with many pupils and a large collection of antique sculpture gathered on youthful journeys through Greece and Italy. More recent research, however, gives a picture of a tailor who, turning painter in his middle thirties, was for many years discreditably involved in a series of lawsuits with pupils who, resentful of his exploitation of their talents, had broken their apprenticeships with him (*Mantegna was the most famous litigant). No traces of his collection remain, but it is likely that something of the antiquarian erudition of the university town of Padua rubbed off on the young men who spent time in his workshop. It is impossible to assess any stylistic debt to Squarcione himself, however, as so little is known about his work, and his traditional role as the founder of a distinctive 'Paduan style' is highly questionable.

Stael, Nicolas de (1914–55). Russian-French painter, born at St Petersburg, son of Baron Vladimir Ivanovich de Staël-Holstein. In 1919 he emigrated with his family to Poland and in 1922, on the death of his parents, was sent to school in Brussels. In 1932 he began to study at the Académie des Beaux-Arts there, winning a first prize, but left for the Netherlands, where he discovered *Rembrandt, *Vermeer, and others of the Dutch school. After travelling in Spain, Italy, and North Africa he went to Paris in 1938 and joined the Foreign Legion on the outbreak of war. In 1943 he settled in Paris, where he knew *Braque and studied under *Léger, and in the 1940s and 1950s he gained an international reputation as one of the outstanding abstract painters of the School of Paris, his work having a delight in handling the sensuous qualities of paint that was unrivalled at the time. His paintings were usually derived from natural appearances as, for example, in *The Roofs* (Mus. National d'Art Moderne, Paris, 1952), and from 1953 he reverted to figurative painting, although not in a realistic style. In his *Footballers* series, landscapes, and still lifes, the subject was extremely simplified into patches of contrasting colour. He committed suicide.

staffage. Term applied to small figures and animals in a painting that are not essential to the subject but are used to animate the composition. Landscape painters, notably in 17th-cent. Flanders and Holland, have often employed other artists to paint their staffage (see, for example, POELENBURGH).

stained glass. Glass that has been given translucent colour in any of various ways, used particularly for creating pictorial designs in church windows. The art began in the service of the Christian Church and is of Byzantine origin, but in its most characteristic development and its highest achievements it is essentially an art of Western Christendom, practised most splendidly in the west and north of Europe as an adjunct to *Gothic architecture. Its early history is obscure, and the first surviving complete windows—in Augsburg Cathedral and dated c.1050–1150—show an art already nearly perfect in technique. Medieval windows are generally made up of hundreds of small pieces of glass of varied colours and shapes held together by strips of lead—somewhat like a jigsaw puzzle with dark outlines around the pieces. Windows of any size were made up of several panels so treated, and these were set in a framework of iron ('armature') that served not only as a support against wind pressure, but also to accentuate the main lines of the design of the window. The period from roughly 1150 to 1250 was the greatest age of stained glass: colours were strong and simple; designs were bold and fresh; and the feelings conveyed were lofty and awe-inspiring. From the 15th cent. stained glass tended towards a greter pictorialism, imitating the effects of oil painting, and this trend reached its height in the 18th cent., when some artists painted on glass more or less as they would on canvas. With the Gothic Revival in the 19th cent.

there came a return to medieval principles, and William *Morris and his associates (notably *Burne-Jones) were among the foremost designers in this spirit. In the 20th cent. many noteworthy artists have designed stained-glass windows, in both figurative and abstract veins—among them *Chagall, *Matisse, and *Piper.

Stanfield, Clarkson (1793–1867). English painter, best known for his marine subjects. From 1808 to 1818 he was a sailor, first in the merchant service and then, after being press-ganged in 1812, in the Royal Navy. He was invalided after being disabled in a fall from the rigging, and took up painting as a career on the advice of his captain at the time, the novelist Frederick Marryat. His initial success came as a scene painter (he won renown for his spectacular *dioramas at the Drury Lane Theatre), but from the 1830s he concentrated on easel paintings. With these, too, he gained a considerable reputation. He has been called 'England's van de *Velde', but the 'poor man's *Turner' might be a better description, as his work often looks flat and stagy compared with that of his great contemporary. Nevertheless, Stanfield's skill in depicting light and atmosphere is admirable. His work is represented in numerous British collections, including the National Maritime Museum and the art gallery of his native Sunderland.

Stantons of Holborn. A family of mason sculptors with a large workshop managed successively by **Thomas** (1610–74), his nephew **William** (1639–1705), and the latter's son **Edward** (1681–1734). They were much patronized by the lesser aristocracy and the professional classes, and their monuments are widespread in England. Their designs are usually conservative, but William was one of the most accomplished English sculptors of his generation.

Stanzione, Massimo (1585/6–1656). Neapolitan painter. Like so many artists in his city at this time, he was strongly influenced by *Caravaggism, but his style has a distinctive refinement and grace that has earned him the nickname 'the Neapolitan Guido *Reni'. He was head of the busiest studio in Naples, and many of his works are still in the churches of the city, his masterpiece being the eloquent *Lamentation*

(1638) in the Certosa di San Martino. His most important pupil was *Cavallino. Stanzione died in the terrible plague that struck Naples in 1656.

state. Term applied to any of the stages through which a *print may pass as an artist alters the design. The first state is represented by the first proof taken from the plate. If no alterations are made this can also be described as the 'only state'. Often, however, particularly in *etching, the artist will alter the design several times before reaching the final state; several impressions may be taken from the printing surface each time it is altered, but sometimes only a unique impression may exist. Differences in states may be so subtle that experts can disagree as to whether they are in fact intentional or are simply the result of chance or wearing of the plate. Some of *Rembrandt's etchings, however, exist in radically different states involving a major rethinking of the design.

Steen, Jan (1625/6–79). Dutch painter. He is best known for his humorous *genre scenes, warm-hearted and animated works in which he treats life as a vast comedy of manners. In Holland he ranks next to *Rembrandt, *Vermeer, and *Hals in popularity and a 'Jan Steen household' has become an epithet for an untidy house. But Steen, one of the most prolific Dutch artists, has many other facets. He painted portraits, historical, mythological, and religious subjects (he was a Catholic), and the animals, birds, and still lifes in his pictures rival those by any of his specialist contemporaries. As a painter of children he was unsurpassed. Steen was born in Leiden and is said to have studied with Adriaen van *Ostade in Haarlem and Jan van *Goyen (who became his father-in-law) in The Hague. He worked in various towns—Leiden, The Hague, Delft, Warmond, and Haarlem— and in 1672 he opened a tavern in Leiden. His father had been a brewer, and in the popular imagination Steen was a drunken profligate, but there is nothing in the known facts of his life to justify this reputation. Many of his pictures represent taverns and festive gatherings, but they often feature moralizing allusions, and he also painted scenes of impeccable genteelness. Apart from his versatility, richness of characterization, and inventiveness in composition, Steen is remarkable also for his skill as a colourist, his handling of salmon-red, rose, pale yellow, and blue-green being highly distinctive. He had no recorded pupils, but his work was widely imitated.

Steenwyck, Hendrick van the Elder (d. 1603?) and **Hendrick van the Younger** (d. 1649). Flemish painters, father and son, specialists in architectural views. Little is known of the career of either man, but the father, who was probably a pupil of Vredeman de *Vries, is credited with developing the church interior as a special branch of painting. Both father and son painted small pictures of real and imaginary *Gothic churches, sometimes as eerie nocturnal scenes. There are several examples of the work of Hendrick the Younger in the National Gallery, London; in two of them the figures are credited to Jan *Brueghel the Elder.

Steer, Philip Wilson (1860–1942). English painter, son of a portrait painter **Philip Steer**. With *Sickert (his friend and exact contemporary), Steer was the leader in his generation of those progressive English artists who looked to France for inspiration. He trained in Paris 1882–4 (revisiting France four times between 1887 and 1891), and was a founder member of the *New English Art Club in 1886. In 1892 the Anglo-Irish novelist George Moore wrote 'it is admitted that Mr Steer takes a foremost place in what is known as the modern movement' and around this time Steer was indeed at his peak, producing the beach scenes and seascapes that are regarded not only as his finest works but also as the best *Impressionist pictures painted by an Englishman. They are remarkable for their great freshness and their subtle handling of light, and unlike Sickert's paintings they are devoid of any social or literary content. After about 1895 his work became more conventional and more closely linked to the English tradition of *Gainsborough, *Turner, and *Constable. In the 1920s he turned increasingly to water-colour. His sight began to fail in 1935 and he had stopped painting by 1940.

Stella, Frank (1936–). American painter, who during the 1960s came to the fore as one of the most inventive of the new school of *Post-Painterly Abstraction in reaction from *Abstract Expressionism. The tenor of his work has been to emphasize the idea that a painting is a physical object rather than a metaphor for something else; he said he wanted to 'eliminate illusionistic space' and that a picture was 'a flat surface with paint on it—nothing more'. In 1958 he settled in New York and in 1958–60 he announced his intentions with a series of all-black paintings in which the figure–ground relationship was almost completely eliminated, the pinstripes which constituted the 'image' echoing the contours of the format. To identify the patterning more completely with the shape of the picture as a whole he began to use notched and shaped canvases, often painting in flat bands of bright colour. In the 1970s he began to experiment with paintings that included cut-out shapes in *relief. His paintings are often very large and they deliberately eschew any personal character in the handling—sometimes he uses commercial pigment such as house paint. Stella has been an influential figure not only in painting, but also on the development of *Minimal sculpture (he is a friend of *Andre and *Judd).

stencil. A thin sheet of metal, paper, or other suitable material perforated with a design (or often lettering) that is reproduced on paper or fabric when the sheet is laid on them and colour is brushed through the openings. Until the *silk screen was devised only simple shapes could be printed by the stencil technique; yet from the aesthetic point of view its very simplicity and sharpness of outline may become major virtues, and the process has a long history both for fabric printing and for the colouring of prints, especially *woodcuts. In France, where it is called *pochoir*, stencilling has been much employed in book illustration.

Stern, Irma (1894–1966). South African painter. She developed an *Expressionist style in Germany 1913–20 and was the most important figure in introducing European modernism to South Africa. She is represented in many collections in South Africa and in Europe.

Stevens, Alfred (1817–75). English sculptor, painter, and designer, born at Blandford in Dorset, the son of a housepainter. With the assistance of the Rector of Blandford, Stevens was sent to study in Italy when he was 15 and remained there until 1842. He worked with *Thorvaldsen in Rome, and laid the foundations of his style in the study of the masters of the *Renaissance, above all *Raphael. After his return to England he taught at the Board of Trade's School of Design, and worked as chief artist to a firm of bronze- and metal-workers in Sheffield, then settled in London in 1852. In 1856 he entered the competition for the Wellington Monument to be erected in St Paul's Cathedral, and although his design was placed sixth, he was eventually awarded the commission. It occupied him for the rest of his life and was plagued with bureaucratic delays and misunderstandings. It was not finally completed until 1912, when the equestrian group at the top was cast from Stevens's model. Nevertheless, it is not only Stevens's masterpiece (indeed, the only one of his large schemes to come to fruition and survive), but also the greatest piece of sculpture produced in England in the 19th cent. The architectural elements form a splendid, bold composition, and the two bronze groups *Valour and Cowardice* and *Truth and Falsehood* have an almost *Michelangelesque grandeur and vigour.

Apart from the Wellington Monument, Stevens's finest work was the decoration for the Dining Room at Dorchester House, London (c.1856), a sumptuous residence built for the millionaire R. S. Holford. It was demolished in 1929 (the Dorchester Hotel now occupies the site), but a fireplace is in the Victoria and Albert Museum, London, and many of the fittings are in the Walker Art Gallery, Liverpool, which has an outstanding Stevens collection. He was a masterful craftsman in numerous media—marble, bronze, silver, porcelain— and was also a painter, although he destroyed much of his work because it did not satisfy him. His unexecuted designs included schemes for the decoration of the interior of the dome of St Paul's Cathedral and the Reading Room at the British Museum, recorded in his superb drawings, which are particularly well represented in Cambridge (Fitzwilliam), Liverpool (Walker), London (Tate), Oxford (Ashmolean), and Sheffield (Mappin). These drawings are very much in the High Renaissance tradition, and it is to this era that Stevens belonged in spirit.

Stevens, Alfred-Émile (1823–1906). Belgian painter, active mainly in Paris, where he settled in 1844. From about 1860 he achieved immense success with his pictures of young ladies in elegant interiors dressed in the height of fashion. His skill in rendering fine materials earned him the title 'the *Terborch of France'. He was a friend and supporter of *Manet and influenced *Whistler, with whom he was one of the first enthusiasts for Japanese art. Stevens also painted coastal and marine scenes in a rather freer, more *Impressionistic style, similar to that of *Boudin or *Jongkind. His brother **Joseph** (1819–92) was also a painter, mainly of animals, and in his day was almost as famous and successful as Alfred (both brothers received the Legion of Honour). Another brother, **Arthur**, was an art critic and dealer.

Stieglitz, Alfred (1864–1946). American photographer and art dealer who was mainly responsible for bringing the works of the European avant-garde before the American public during the first two decades of the 20th cent. His 291 Gallery (at 291 Fifth Avenue, New York), which he opened in 1905, presented the first American exhibitions of *Matisse (1908), *Toulouse-Lautrec (1909), the Douanier *Rousseau (1910), *Picabia (1913), *Severini (1917), and the first one-man exhibition of *Brancusi anywhere (1914). It also gave the first major exhibition of African art in America. Stieglitz also championed American artists, among them Georgia *O'Keeffe, whom he married. From 1903 to 1917 Stieglitz edited the journal *Camera Work*, which he published from the 291 Gallery. At first devoted to photography, it was later extended to cover all the visual arts, including reviews and criticisms, and opened its pages to avant-garde American writers. The 291 Gallery was closed in 1917 when the building was pulled down, but Stieglitz continued his work with the Intimate Gallery (1925–9) and An American Place (1929–46), both of which promoted American artists of what had come to be known as the Stieglitz group. Stieglitz was a brilliant innovative artist in his own medium of photography. Learning from the avant-garde paintings which he exhibited, he experimented with various modes of abstraction and his work went a long way to revolutionize the concept of the photographic image and to establish photography as an independent art form. He formed a fine collection of art, much of which was donated to the Art Institute of Chicago.

Stifter, Adalbert (1805–68). Austrian writer and painter. He is now regarded as one of the outstanding Austrian novelists of the 19th cent., but he enjoyed little success in his lifetime, and full recognition of his stature came only after the First World War. For much of his career he worked as a tutor, then an educational administrator. His later years were clouded by the suicide of an adopted daughter in 1859 and he took his own life, cutting his throat with his razor, whilst suffering agonizing pain from what was thought to be cancer. As a painter he was self-taught, and as in his writing eschewed heroic events in favour of simple, everyday happenings. His sensitive perception of nature comes out in his remarkably fresh landscapes. There is a museum devoted to his work in Vienna.

Stijl, De (Dutch: 'the style'). The name of a group of Dutch artists founded in 1917 and of the journal they published to set forth their ideas. Members of the group included painters (most notably *Mondrian and van *Doesburg), sculptors (*Vantongerloo), architects and designers (Rietveld), and the poet Antony Kok. They sought laws of equilibrium and harmony that would be applicable to life and society as well as art, and their style was one of austere abstract clarity (see NEO-PLASTICISM). The journal was founded by van Doesburg and Mondrian in 1917 and van Doesburg continued to edit it until 1928. A final number was published in 1932 by Mme van Doesburg in memory of her husband. Mondrian ceased to contribute to De Stijl after 1924 and in 1926 van Doesburg published the manifesto of a splinter movement which he called *Elementarism. Despite this lack of cohesion, De Stijl was probably the most influential of the many avant-garde publications in Europe between the two wars on both ideas and artistic practice. It was, however, in architecture and the applied arts (including furniture design and typography), rather than painting and sculpture, that it had its greatest influence—

notably at the *Bauhaus and in the architectural style known as 'International Modern'.

Still, Clyfford (1904–80). American painter. After experimenting in a number of styles he found his own place among the *Abstract Expressionists, and became one of the pioneers of the very large, virtually monochromatic painting. But unlike *Newman and *Rothko, who employed thin unmodulated pigment, Still used heavily loaded, expressively modulated *impasto in jagged forms. His work can have a raw, aggressive power, but in the 1960s it became more lyrical. His paintings were included in many important collective exhibitions both in America and abroad, but from the 1950s he worked in increasing isolation. He considered himself something of a visionary who needed solitude to give expression to his high spiritual and aesthetic purpose, and he gained a reputation for cantankerousness and pretentiousness.

Stimmer, Tobias (1539–84). Swiss painter and graphic artist, active in his native Schaffhausen, in Strasburg (where he died) and in various German towns. He was a versatile artist, whose work included façade decorations (notably that of the Haus zum Ritter, 1568–70, now in the Museum zu Allerheiligen, Schaffhausen), portraits in a *Holbeinesque style, and numerous book illustrations. He also decorated the astronomical clock in Strasburg Cathedral. There is often strong Italian influence in his work and he may have visited Italy.

stipple engraving. A method of engraving in tone, in which the design is made up of small dots or flecks. It was a popular reproductive technique in the late 18th and early 19th cents., when it was often used in conjunction with the *crayon manner, from which it differs little. Both were rendered obsolete by *lithography. Stipple engraving, which produces prints characterized by softness and delicately graded tones, was almost entirely confined to England, where Francesco *Bartolozzi was an outstanding exponent.

Stokes, Adrian (1902–72). English writer on art and painter. An intensely subjective writer with an interest in psychoanalysis,

Stokes responded passionately, even ecstatically, to art, believing its task was to show the 'utmost drama of the soul as laid-out things'. Many admirers regard him as the most eloquent and poetic English art critic since *Ruskin, although others find his prose hard going. His best known books are *The Quattro Cento* (1932) and *The Stones of Rimini* (1934); *The Critical Writings of Adrian Stokes*, edited by Lawrence *Gowing, appeared in three volumes in 1978. Stokes began to paint in 1936 and became a student at the *Euston Road School in 1937. From 1939 to 1946 he lived near St Ives, Cornwall, with its flourishing group of painters.

Stone, Nicholas (1587–1647). English sculptor, mason, and architect. The son of a Devonshire quarryman, he trained in London, then in 1606 he went as a journeyman to the Amsterdam workshop of Hendrik de *Keyser, whose daughter he married. On his return to London in 1613 he quickly established himself as the outstanding tomb sculptor in the country. He surpassed his contemporaries in technical skill as a marble cutter and outdid them in introducing new ideas: the monument to Francis Holles (d. 1622; Westminster Abbey) has the first English example of a figure in Roman armour, and that to John Donne (made from Donne's own design, St Paul's Cathedral, 1631) shows the great preacher and poet standing erect in his shroud. In 1619 Stone became Master Mason for Inigo *Jones's Banqueting House at Whitehall, and in 1632 Master Mason to the Crown. His contact with the court gave him a knowledge of the *antique sculpture in Charles I's collection and his work after c.1630 shows a change in style, marked by an attempt to imitate antique drapery (Lyttelton Monument, Magdalen Coll., Oxford, 1634). His large workshop produced monuments of many types, and we are unusually well informed about its activities, as an office notebook covering the period 1614–41 and an account book for the period 1631–42 still survive (Soane Mus., London). Much less of his work as an architect is extant (and it is sometimes not clear whether he was the designer as well as the mason of the buildings on which he worked), but he is recognized as the creator of 'a vernacular classical architecture of considerable charm and accomplishment' (H. M. Colvin, *A Biographical Dictionary of British Architects 1600–1840*, 1978). The youngest of Stone's three sons, **John Stone** (1620–67), ran the family practice after his father's death, even though he does not appear to have been a sculptor himself.

stopping-out varnish. An acid-resisting varnish used in *etching, *aquatint, and similar processes.

Stoss, Veit (c.1450–1533). German sculptor, with *Riemenschneider the greatest wood-carver of his age. He is first recorded in 1477, when he moved from Nuremberg to Cracow in Poland. There he carved his largest work, the huge altarpiece for St Mary's Church (1477–89), and also made the red marble tomb of King Casimir IV in the cathedral (1492). In 1496 he returned to Nuremberg, where his successful career was blighted when (in an attempt to recoup some money he regarded as having been misappropriated in an investment) he forged a document in 1503 and was convicted and branded through both cheeks. He was also confined to the city limits of Nuremberg (he fled but returned), and although he was to some extent rehabilitated, he never regained his former position. He died a wealthy man, but his old age was embittered by disputes with the city authorities.

A good many documented and signed works by Stoss survive and his style is distinctive—bold and powerfully characterized, with exaggerated gestures and expressions and draperies rendered in an ornate, almost calligraphic manner. Indeed, Stoss's work is so individual that the famous figure of *St Roch* in SS. Annunziata, Florence, is almost universally accepted as his, even though it is undocumented and was attributed by *Vasari to 'Janni Francese' (Janni the Frenchman). Vasari wrote eloquently of the virtuosity of the carving, describing the draperies as 'cut almost to the thinness of paper, and with a beautiful flow in the arrangement of the folds, so that nothing more wonderful is to be seen'. Stoss sometimes, as here, left his figures unpainted, but otherwise his work is entirely in the late *Gothic spirit. He is recorded as being a painter and engraver as well as a sculptor and he also declared himself competent as a civil engineer.

Stoskopff, Sébastien (1597–1657). French still-life painter, active mainly in Strasburg. He painted in a spare, stiff, almost archaic style that has appealed greatly to modern taste—most of his paintings have come to light since the 1930s. The best collection is in the Musée de l'œuvre de Notre Dame, Strasburg.

Stothard, Thomas (1755–1834). English painter, book illustrator, and designer. He was a prolific and versatile artist, his designs ranging from monuments to jewellery, and although his paintings were mainly small-scale historical pieces in a sentimentalized Classical manner, he also did occasional more ambitious works, e.g. the decoration of the staircase at Burghley House (begun 1794) and the cupola of the upper hall of the Advocates' Library, Edinburgh (1822).His book illustrations were mainly in the field of English novels and poetry.

Streeter, Robert (1621–79). English painter, appointed Serjeant-Painter to Charles II in 1660. In the words of Sir Ellis *Waterhouse, 'he left no branch of painting untried and would have been a universal genius had he been endowed with the requisite talent.' The most important of his few surviving works is the allegorical ceiling painting representing *The Triumph of Truth and the Arts* (1668–9) in the Sheldonian Theatre, Oxford. This is a heavy-handed work, but noteworthy as the most ambitious attempt at a piece of *Baroque decoration by any Englishman before *Thornhill (Streeter had travelled in Italy during the Commonwealth). His reputation was evidently high in his day, for Samuel Pepys in his celebrated *Diary* calls him a 'famous history painter . . . who lives handsomely', and Robert Whitehall, whose ability as a poet happily matched that of Streeter as a painter, eulogized the Sheldonian ceiling in the immortal lines '. . . future ages must confess they owe / To Streeter more than Michael Angelo' (*Urania, or a Description of the Painting of the Top of the Theatre at Oxford*, 1669). Streeter's son **Robert** (d. 1711) succeeded him as Serjeant-Painter.

Streeton, Arthur (1867–1943). Australian painter, the most important landscapist of the *Heidelberg School. His work, featuring dominant notes of gold and blue, gave the lead to a popular school of Australian landscape. Between 1898 and 1924 he spent most of his time abroad—during 1918 as an official war artist with the Australian forces in France.

stretcher. The wooden frame or chassis on which a *canvas is stretched and fixed. Wedges or keys in the inner corners of the stretcher enable the canvas to be tightened if it slackens.

Strozzi, Bernardo (1581–1644). The leading Genoese painter of his period. He entered the Capuchin Order in about 1597, hence his nicknames, Il Prete Genovese (the Genoese priest) and Il Cappuccino (the Capuchin). In about 1610 he was allowed to leave his community to look after his sick and widowed mother, and after she died in 1630 he is said to have been pressurized to return, this accounting for his move to Venice (where he spent the rest of his life) in 1631. Strozzi was successful and prolific in both Genoa and Venice, painting portraits and allegorical and *genre scenes (often of musicians) as well as religious works. The sensuous richness of his style was influenced by *Rubens (who worked in Genoa), but his work is highly distinctive, with an air of refinement and tenderness that recalls van *Dyck (who also worked in Genoa). Strozzi worked in Venice when there was a dearth of native talent in the city, and with two other 'foreigners', *Feti and *Liss, he kept alive the painterly tradition of the 16th cent.

Stuart, Gilbert (1755–1828). American portrait painter. With *Copley he was the outstanding American portraitist of his period and he is regarded as the creator of a distinctively American style of portraiture. Much of his early career was spent in Scotland (*c.*1771–2), England (1775–87), and Ireland (1787–92). After he settled permanently in America in 1792, he worked briefly in New York City, then moved to Philadelphia, and finally settled in Boston in 1805. He quickly established himself as the outstanding portraitist in the country and painted many of the notables of the new republic. His portraits of George Washington are his most famous works—he created three types, all of which were endlessly copied: the 'Vaughan' type (NG, Washington, 1795), the 'Lansdowne' type

(Pennsylvania Academy of Fine Arts, Philadelphia, 1796), and the 'Athenaeum' type (Mus. of Fine Arts, Boston, 1796), which is one of the most famous images in American art, being used on the country's one-dollar bill. Stuart's style is notable for its strength of characterization (Benjamin *West said he '*nails* the face to the canvas') and fluent brushwork. His work had great influence on the next generation of American painters.

Stubbs, George (1724–1806). English animal painter and engraver, celebrated as the greatest of all horse painters. He was born at Liverpool, the son of a currier and leather-seller, and his life up to his mid-30s (which is poorly documented) was spent mainly in the north of England. Virtually self-taught as a painter and engraver, he seems to have earned his living mainly as a portraitist early in his career, and he also made the illustrations (based on his own dissections) for Dr John Burton's treatise on midwifery (1751). In 1754 he visited Rome, then spent 18 months dissecting and drawing horses in preparation for a book on equine anatomy. He moved to London in about 1758 and, unable to find an engraver to do the work, he made the plates himself, and in 1766 published his famous book—*The Anatomy of the Horse*. It was a great success, prized for its beauty as well as its scientific accuracy and Stubbs was soon in demand as a painter, not only for his 'portraits' of horses with their owners or grooms, but also for his conversation pieces in which the sitters were grouped in and around a carriage. His command of anatomy was matched by his ability to depict the beauty and grace of his equine subjects without sentimentalizing them and his range of feeling was wide, extending from the lyrical calm of *Mares and Foals in a River Landscape* (Tate, London, c.1763–8) to the full-blooded *Romanticism of his series of pictures on the theme of a horse attacked by a lion (the largest—c.1762—is in the Yale Center for British Art). Stubbs is said to have derived his fascination for the subject from having witnessed a lion attacking a horse in Morocco on his way back from Italy, but he may also have been familiar with a much copied *antique statue on the theme. Stubbs painted many other animals apart from horses—among them a moose, a rhinoceros, and a zebra. At his death he

was working on *A Comparative Anatomical Exposition of the Structure of the Human Body with that of a Tiger and a Common Foal*, the drawings for which are in the Yale Center for British Art. His scientific curiosity extended to the materials he used and he experimented with painting in *enamel on earthenware panels manufactured for him by the great potter Josiah Wedgwood. Stubbs's work became less popular during the 1780s and by the end of his life he was in financial difficulties. He kept his great powers until the end, however, and one of his finest works, painted when he was 75, is the enormous *Hambletonian, Rubbing Down* (National Trust, Mount Stewart, 1799), showing the champion horse looking strained and exhausted after winning a race in which it was 'much cut with the whip' and 'shockingly goaded' with the spur. It is a magnificent, heroic, almost tragic image. Stubbs was for long classified as a superior sporting painter, but he is now ranked alongside *Gainsborough and *Reynolds in the front rank of English painters of his age.

stucco. A type of light, malleable plaster made from dehydrated lime (calcium carbonate) mixed with powdered *marble and glue and sometimes reinforced with hair. It is used for sculpture and architectural decoration, both external and internal. In a looser sense, the term is applied to a plaster coating applied to the exterior of buildings, but stucco is a different substance from plaster (which is calcium sulphate). Stucco in the more restricted sense has been known to virtually every civilization. In Europe it was exploited most fully from the 16th cent. to the 18th cent., notable exponents being the artists of the School of *Fontainebleau and Giacomo *Serpotta. By adding large quantities of glue and colour to the stucco mixture *stuccatori* were able to produce a material which could take a high polish and assume the appearance of marble. Indeed, sometimes it is difficult to distinguish from real marble except that it is warmer to the touch.

Sturm, Der (The Assault). Name of a magazine and an art gallery in Berlin, both of which were founded and owned by Herwarth Walden (1878–1941), a writer and composer whose aim was to promote avant-garde art in Germany. The gallery ran from 1912 until 1924 and the magazine from 1910 to 1932. They became the focus of modern art in Berlin, introducing the work of the *Futurists to Germany, for example, and publicizing the *Expressionism of the *Blaue Reiter group.

Subleyras, Pierre (1699–1749). French painter who settled permanently in Rome after winning the Prix de Rome in 1727. He painted a variety of subjects, including portraits and still lifes, but he is most highly regarded for his religious paintings, which are much more serious in spirit than most French works of the *Rococo period. His most famous work is the *Mass of St Basil*, painted for St Peter's, but now in Sta Maria degli Angeli. This huge picture was highly acclaimed when it was unveiled in 1748, but Subleyras died before he could follow up his success. He has subsequently been something of an underrated figure, but a major exhibition of his work in Paris and Rome in 1987 did much to establish his reputation as one of the outstanding French painters of his period.

sublime. Term that came into general use in the 18th cent. to denote a new *aesthetic concept that was held to be distinct from the beautiful and the *picturesque and was associated with ideas of awe and vastness. The outstanding work on the concept of the sublime in English was Burke's *Philosophical Enquiry into the Origin of our Ideas of the Sublime and Beautiful* (1757). This book was one of the first to realize (in contrast with the emphasis on clarity and precision during the Age of Enlightenment) the power of suggestiveness to stimulate imagination. Speaking of painting Burke says that 'a judicious obscurity in some things contributes to the effect of the picture', because in art as in nature 'dark, confused, uncertain images have a greater power on the fancy to form the grander passions than those which are more clear and determinate.' The cult of the sublime had varied expressions in the visual arts, notably the taste for the 'savage' landscapes of Salvator *Rosa and the popularity among painters of subjects from Homer, John Milton, and Ossian (the legendary Gaelic warrior and bard, whose verses— actually fabrications—were published in the 1760s to great acclaim). In literature, the 'Gothic novel', in which mystery and

horror were the essential ingredients, appealed to the same sentiments. The first Gothic novel was Horace *Walpole's *The Castle of Otranto* (1764), and when crossing the Alps in 1739 Walpole expressed the essence of the imaginative appeal of the sublime in his memorable exclamation: 'Precipices, mountains, torrents, wolves, rumblings—Salvator Rosa.' The vogue for the sublime, with that for the picturesque, helped shape the attitudes that led to *Romanticism.

Suger, Abbot (*c*.1081–1151). French churchman and statesman, one of the greatest patrons of the Middle Ages. He was adviser to Louis VI and Louis VII, acting as regent in 1147–9 during the latter's absence on the Second Crusade, but he is remembered mainly for the rebuilding of the abbey of Saint-Denis, near Paris, of which he was abbot from 1122 until his death. Suger's reconstruction and redecoration of the abbey was the most important landmark in the emergence of the *Gothic style in architecture and sculpture. He wrote an autobiographical account of the work between 1144 and 1147—a unique document of the time. It was edited and translated by Erwin *Panofsky, who wrote that Suger was 'frankly in love with splendour and beauty in every conceivable form: it might be said that his reponse to ecclesiastical ceremonial was largely aesthetic'. He thought that through the splendour and brilliance of material treasure men were led away to an appreciation of the spiritual glories of the divine Being. Suger commissioned numerous items of church furnishing and sacred vessels for the abbey, several of which survive.

Sully, Thomas (1783–1872). The preeminent American portrait painter of his period, active mainly in Philadelphia. He was born in England, but went to America as a child. Subsequently he made two visits to England, in 1809, when he studied with *West, and in 1837–8, to paint Queen Victoria for the St George Society of Philadelphia (a preliminary version is in the Wallace Coll., London). His style, distinguished by fluid, glossy brushwork and romantic warmth and dash, betrays his great admiration for *Lawrence. In his later work, however, he tended towards a genteel sentimentality. Sully was highly successful and extremely productive. He is said to have painted some 2,000 portraits (he also made *miniatures), but his best-known work is probably one of his (also very numerous) history paintings—*Washington Crossing the Delaware* (Mus. of Fine Arts, Boston, 1819).

Superrealism. Style of painting and sculpture, popular particularly in Britain and the USA from the late 1960s, in which subjects are depicted with a minute and impersonal exactitude of detail. Hyperrealism and Photographic Realism (or Photorealism) are alternative names, and some artists who practise the style (such as Chuck *Close) do indeed work from photographs, the sharpness and precision of detail being evenly distributed over the whole picture (except where out-of-focus effects in the photograph are faithfully recorded). (Some critics prefer to use the terms 'Photographic Realism' or 'Photorealism' only when a picture has been painted direct from a photograph, but most are not so restrictive.) Superrealist sculptors, such as *De Andrea or *Hanson often use real clothes or props and attend to minutiae such as body hair. The effect of this indiscriminate attention to detail is generally—somewhat paradoxically—to create a strong feeling of unreality.

support. The material—*canvas, wooden *panel, *paper, or other substance on which a painting is executed; it is usually distinguishable from the *ground.

Suprematism. Russian abstract art movement, developed by *Malevich from about 1913 and officially launched by him in 1915. His Suprematist paintings were the most radically pure abstract works created up to that date, for he limited himself to basic geometric shapes—the square, rectangle, circle, cross, and triangle—and a narrow range of colours, reaching the ultimate distillation of his ideas in a series of paintings of a white square on a white ground (c.1918) after which he announced the end of Suprematism. In contrast to *Constructivism, where the stress was on the utilitarian function of art, Suprematism was a vehicle for Malevich's spiritual ideas; he wrote that 'The Suprematists have deliberately given up the objective representation of their surroundings in order to reach the summit of the 'unmasked' art and from this vantage point to view life

through the prism of pure artistic feeling.' Although his direct followers in Russia were of minor account, Malevich had great influence on the development of art and design in the West.

Surrealism. Movement in art and literature originating in France and flourishing in the 1920s and 1930s, characterized by a fascination with the bizarre, the incongruous, and the irrational. It was conceived as a revolutionary mode of thought and action—a way of life rather than a set of stylistic attitudes—and in this resembled *Dadaism, its principal source. However, although both movements were anti-rationalist, Surrealism was positive in spirit rather than nihilistic like Dada. André *Breton, the principal theoretician of the movement, said its purpose was 'to resolve the previously contradictory conditions of dream and reality into an absolute reality, a super-reality'. He and other members of the movement drew liberally on Freud's theories about the subconscious and its relations to dreams, but the way in which they set about exploration of submerged impulses and imagery varied greatly (in spite of Breton's demands there was little doctrinal unity, and defections, expulsions, and personal attacks are a feature of the history of the movement). Broadly speaking, however, there were three contrasting approaches. Some artists, for example, *Ernst, *Masson, and *Miró, cultivated various spontaneous techniques such as *frottage in an effort to eliminate conscious control. At the other extreme, *Dalí, *Magritte, and others painted in a scrupulously detailed manner to give an hallucinatory sense of reality to scenes that make no rational sense. Finally, in Surrealist constructions and *assemblages, as well as in some paintings, the unexpected and startling juxtaposition of unrelated objects was used to create a sense not so much of unreality as of a fantastic but compelling reality outside the everyday world. The text quoted to justify this search for the unexpected combination of incompatibles was a sentence from the poet Lautréamont, whom the Surrealists regarded as one of their precursors: 'Beautiful as the chance encounter of a sewing machine and an umbrella on an operating table.'

Surrealism became the most widely disseminated and most controversial aesthetic movement between the First and Second

World Wars. It spread throughout Europe (a major Surrealist exhibition, opened by Breton, was held in London in 1936) and also to the USA, where many artists migrated during the war years. Although it broke up as an organized movement during the war and by this time had spent its main force, the spirit of Surrealism lived on. With its stress on the marvellous and the poetic, Surrealism offered an alternative approach to the formalism of *Cubism and various types of abstract art, and its methods and techniques continued to influence artists in many countries. It was, for example, a fundamental source for *Abstract Expressionism.

Sutherland, Graham (1903–80). English painter, graphic artist, and designer. He abandoned an apprenticeship as a railway engineer to study engraving and etching, 1920–5, and up to 1930 worked exclusively as a graphic artist. His etchings of this period are in the *Romantic and visionary tradition of Samuel *Palmer. In the early 1930s he began experimenting with oils, and by 1935 he had turned mainly to painting. His paintings of the 1930s show a highly subjective response to nature, inspired mainly by his visits to Pembrokeshire. He had a vivid gift of visual metaphor and his landscapes are not scenic, but semi-abstract patterns of haunting and monstrous shapes (*Entrance to a Lane*, Tate, London, 1939). During the war years he was employed as an official war artist to record the effects of bombing, and his work matured as he wrestled with the problems of finding a visual surrogate for the devastation and the destruction of man-made things. Soon after the war he took up both religious painting and portraiture, with a *Crucifixion* (1946) for St Matthew's, Northampton (the idea came to Sutherland at the dedication of Henry *Moore's *Madonna and Child* in this church), and *Somerset Maugham* (Tate, 1949). It was in these two fields that he chiefly made his mark in his later career. The Maugham portrait has an almost *caricature quality (Maugham's friend Sir Gerald *Kelly said he made him look 'like an old Chinese madam in a brothel in Shanghai'), and his most famous portrait, that of Winston Churchill (1954), was so hated by the sitter that Lady Churchill destroyed it. Sutherland's most celebrated

work, however, has become widely popular—it is the immense tapestry of *Christ in Glory* (completed 1962) in Coventry Cathedral. Sutherland continued to paint landscapes—his first love—and from 1947 he lived for part of every year on the French Riviera. Apart from paintings and graphic art, his work included ceramics and designing posters and stage costumes and decor.

Swart van Groningen, Jan (*c.*1500–after 1553). Netherlandish painter, book illustrator, and designer of stained-glass windows. He came from Gröningen, worked in Antwerp and Gouda, and also travelled to Italy early in his career. His works show that he was familiar with those of *Dürer, *Holbein, *Scorel, and other northern artists who were impressed by Italian *Renaissance art, but in spite of this his style has a certain archaic charm. He had a predilection for showing people wearing high hats, turbans, and other odd headgear.

Sweerts, Michiel (1618–64). Flemish painter, an enigmatic and exceedingly attractive artist. Nothing is known of his training or early career. From about 1646 to about 1656 he was in Rome, where he came into contact with the *Bamboccianti* (see LAER, PIETER VAN). He painted *genre scenes in their manner, but his work is in a class apart because of the quiet, melancholy dignity of his figures and his exquisite silvery tonality. His other pictures in Rome included views of artists' studios (an example dated 1652 is in the Detroit Institute of Arts). By 1656 Sweerts had returned to his native Brussels, where in 1659 he became a member of the painters' guild. In 1661 he was in Amsterdam, where he joined a missionary group, and he sailed from Marseilles to the Orient in the following year. Sweerts was found quarrelsome and unsuitable, however, and was dismissed; he died at Goa in India. Towards the end of his career, Sweerts seemed to have worked mainly as a portraitist. Like his genre scenes, his portraits are distinguished by delicate and subdued colour harmonies and great sensitivity of expression and handling. They have often been compared with the work of *Vermeer, to whom Sweerts's *Portrait of a Girl* (Leicestershire Museum and Art Gallery, Leicester) was once attributed.

Symbolism. A loosely organized movement in art flourishing in the 1880s and 1890s in close connection with the Symbolist movement in French poetry. It came as a reaction from the naturalistic aims of *Impressionism and still more from the principles of *Realism as formulated by *Courbet who declared that painting should deal only with 'real and existing things'. In contrast the Symbolists tried to give visual expression to the mystical and the occult. As the poets thought there was a close correspondence between the sound and rhythm of the words they used and their meaning, so Symbolist painters thought that colour and line in themselves could express ideas. Symbolist critics were much given to drawing parallels between the arts, and *Redon's paintings, for example, were compared with the poetry of *Baudelaire and Edgar Allan Poe and with the music of Claude Debussy. Thus, the Symbolists stressed the priority of suggestion and evocation over direct description (or depiction) and explicit analogy. Stylistically, Symbolist artists varied greatly. *Moreau, for example, painted exotic pictures of a jewel-like richness, whereas *Puvis de Chavannes's murals are pale, serene, and melancholy. Many artists were inspired by the same kind of imagery as Symbolist writers (the *femme fatale* is a common theme), but *Gauguin and his followers (see NABIS and SYNTHETISM) chose much less flamboyant subjects, often peasant scenes. Religious feeling of an intense, mystical kind was a feature of the movement, but so was an interest in the erotic and the perverse—death, disease, and sin were favourite subjects. Although chiefly associated with France, Symbolism had international currency, and such diverse artists as *Burne-Jones and *Munch are regarded as part of the movement in its broadest sense.

Synchromism. Movement in modern painting founded in 1912–13 by Stanton *Macdonald-Wright and Morgan *Russell, two American artists living in Paris. The term 'synchromism' means literally 'colours together' and both Russell and

Macdonald-Wright were concerned with the purely abstract use of colour; in 1912 Russell said that he wished to do 'a piece of expression solely by means of colour and the way it is put down, in showers and broad patches, distinctly separated from each other, or blended . . . but with force and clearness and large geometric patterns'. Synchromism was very close to *Orphism and the two Americans protested in manifestos that they had primacy. Although the movement petered out with the First World War, Synchromism influenced several American artists, and its founders hold distinguished places in the vanguard of abstract art.

Synthetism. Term applied to a manner of painting associated with *Bernard, *Gauguin, and their associates at Pont-Aven. It involved the simplification of forms into large-scale patterns and the expressive purification of colours. Bernard believed that form and colour must be simplified for the sake of more forceful expression, and Gauguin spoke much of 'synthesis', by which he meant an intensification and concentration of our primary impressions of nature. He advised his disciples to 'paint by heart' because in memory coloured by emotion natural forms become more integrated and meaningful. Bernard and Gauguin each claimed credit for developing Synthetism and they probably acted as mutual catalysts. Synthetism was influential on the *Nabis and has affinities with the more literary *Symbolism. See also CLOISONNISM.

Systemic art. Term originated by the critic Lawrence Alloway in 1966 to refer to a type of abstract art characterized by the use of very simple standardized forms, usually geometric in character, either in a single concentrated image or repeated in a system arranged according to a clearly visible principle of organization. The chevron paintings of *Noland are examples of Systemic art. It has been described as a branch of *Minimal art, but Alloway extended the term to cover *Colour Field painting.

T

Tacca, Pietro (1577–1640). Florentine sculptor in bronze, the chief pupil and follower of *Giambologna. After the latter's death Tacca completed a number of his works and succeeded him as sculptor to the Grand Dukes of Tuscany. Tacca's works for the *Medici include his masterpieces, the four *Slaves* (1615–24) at the foot of *Bandinelli's statue of Ferdinand I de' *Medici at Leghorn. His last work was the equestrian statue of Philip IV of Spain (1634–40) for the Plaza de Oriente, Madrid, in which the King is shown on a rearing horse. This *Baroque pose was imposed on Tacca, having been already used in pictures of the King by *Rubens and *Velázquez (a copy of a painting by one or the other of these artists was sent to Florence to act as a model). The smooth, generalized treatment of the work shows, however, that Tacca remained essentially a *Mannerist sculptor. Tacca's son **Pietro** (1619–86) was also a sculptor; his best works are his graceful bronze statuettes.

Tachisme. Term coined in 1952 by the French critic Michel Tapié to designate a style of painting popular in the 1940s and 1950s characterized by irregular dabs or splotches of colour (*tache* is French for spot or blotch). Tachisme had affinities with *Abstract Expressionism in that it strove to be completely spontaneous and instinctive, excluding deliberation and formal planning. It was primarily a French movement (Jean *Fautrier, Georges *Mathieu, and the German-born but Paris-based *Wols were among the leading exponents), and Tachiste paintings are characteristically more elegant and less aggressive than the work of the American Abstract Expressionists. The terms '*abstraction lyrique*' (*lyrical abstraction) *'Art Autre' (other art), and *'*Art Informel*' (art without form) are sometimes used synonymously with Tachisme, although certain critics use them to convey different nuances. To add to the confusion of terminology, the word 'tachisme' was used differently in the 19th cent., being applied pejoratively to the *Impressionists and the *Macchiaioli.

tactile values. Term introduced into art criticism by Bernard *Berenson in his *Florentine Painters of the Renaissance* (1896) to describe those qualities in a painting that stimulate the sense of touch. He thought that *Giotto was the first master since *Classical antiquity whose painting demonstrated these qualities, which he considered to be a distinctive feature of Florentine painting and held to be 'life enhancing'. His theories were not very cogent, and the term is now little used.

Taddeo di Bartolo (c.1362/3–1422). Sienese painter, active in Pisa, Perugia, San Gimignano, and Volterra, his native city. He was a conservative artist, but is noteworthy for his series of frescos on Roman Republican heroes and civic Virtues (1406–14) in the Palazzo Pubblico, Siena, which are early examples of a type that became popular in the Renaissance.

Taeuber-Arp, Sophie (*née* Taeuber) (1889–1943). Swiss artist, the wife of Jean *Arp. She met Arp in Zurich in 1915 and married him in 1922. Her prolific output included *collages, embroideries, paintings, puppets, sculpture, and stage designs, much of her work being in an abstract style distinguished by its rhythmic vitality. She died in 1943 from an accident with a leaking stove.

Takis (Panayotis Vassilakis) (1925–   ). Greek experimental artist, best known for his highly original work in *kinetic sculpture. His creations often employ magnetic fields in which various metal objects produce changing patterns—the magnet's 'live force and vibration gives life to what has seemed to be dead material'. In 1960 he suspended the poet Sinclair Beiles in a magnetic field at the Galerie Iris Clert in Paris. Sometimes he combines light effects and music with movement. Since 1954 Takis has lived mainly in Paris.

Tamayo, Rufino (1899–   ). Mexican painter and graphic artist. Although he has painted many murals as well as easel paintings, his work is opposed to the creed of the revolutionary mural painters, *Orozco, *Rivera, and *Siqueiros, who set greater store by the message and theme of a picture than its pictorial qualities, and for many years his reputation was higher abroad than in Mexico. From 1938 he has lived mainly in New York. Tamayo's fervent and highly distinctive style blends influences from modern European movements such as *Surrealism with the *folk-art traditions of the indigenous Mexican Indians (his parents were Zapotec Indians and in the 1920s he was head of the Department of Ethnographic Drawing at the National Museum of Archaeology in Mexico City). His subjects include animals, still lifes, and portraits, many of his pianist wife, Olga. In 1974 he donated his fine collection of pre-Hispanic art to his native city of Oaxaca.

Tanguy, Yves (1900–55). French-born American painter. Originally a merchant seaman, he was impelled to take up painting after seeing pictures by de *Chirico and in 1925 joined the *Surrealist group. In 1939 he emigrated to the USA, where he lived for the rest of his life, marrying the American Surrealist painter Kay *Sage in 1940 and becoming an American citizen in 1948. Tanguy's most characteristic works are painted in a scrupulous technique reminiscent of that of *Dalí, but his imagery is highly distinctive, featuring half marine and half lunar landscapes in which amorphous nameless objects proliferate in a spectral dream-space (*The Invisibles*, Tate Gallery, London, 1951).

Tàpies, Antoni (1923–   ). The most important Spanish painter to emerge in the period since the Second World War. He studied law at the university in his native Barcelona from 1943 to 1946 and was largely self-taught as an artist. His early works were in a *Surrealist vein, but in about 1953, after turning to abstraction, he began working in mixed media, in which he has made his most original contribution to art. He incorporated clay and marble dust in his paint and used discarded materials such as paper, string, and rags, and then (from about 1970) more substantial objects such as parts of furniture. He explained his belief in the validity of commonplace materials in his essay *Nothing is Mean* (1970). Tàpies has travelled extensively and his ideas have had worldwide influence.

Target exhibition. Exhibition organized in Moscow by *Larionov, *Goncharova, and *Malevich in March 1913, at which *Rayonism was launched.

Tassi, Agostino (properly Agostino Buonamici) (*c.*1580–1644). Italian painter, born in Rome and mainly active there. He was one of the outstanding *quadratura* specialists of the period, his most famous work being the illusionistic architectural setting for *Guercino's celebrated *Aurora* fresco (1621–3) in the Casino Ludovisi, Rome. Tassi also painted small landscapes in the manner of *Bril and *Elsheimer, and for centuries he was remembered because he taught *Claude (who entered his service as a pastry-cook), his significance as a decorative painter being forgotten. His other claim to fame is that he was accused of raping Artemisia *Gentileschi; he was eventually acquitted after spending some time in prison.

Tate Gallery, London. The national collection of British art and of modern art from *c.*1870 to the present day. It is named after Sir Henry Tate (1819–99), the millionaire inventor of the sugar cube, who in 1890 offered his collection, consisting mainly of the work of Victorian contemporaries, to the nation on condition that the Government found a suitable site for a gallery. After many difficulties the Tate Gallery was opened at Millbank in 1897 in an undistinguished neo-Baroque building designed by Sidney R. J. Smith. On formation, however, it was not an independent gallery of British art as had been envisaged by Henry Tate. It was subordinate to the *National Gallery and it was intended only for modern British art. It began to be established as a historical collection of British art in 1910 when a collection of works by Alfred *Stevens was added and a wing was opened to accommodate most of the paintings bequeathed to the nation by *Turner, which had previously been housed (but in the main unexhibited) at the National Gallery. The Turner wing was the gift of Sir Joseph *Duveen, the art dealer. His son, Lord Duveen was an equally generous benefactor, financing extensions for modern foreign art (1926) and modern sculpture (1937). This expansion of the gallery's range was in line with the ideas of the Curzon Committee, which, reporting in 1915, recommended that the Tate should be converted from a Gallery of Modern British Art to a Gallery of British Art, that a Gallery of Modern Foreign Art should be formed in connection with the Tate, and that the administration of the Tate should be separate from that of the National Gallery. It was not until 1954, however, that the Tate Gallery became completely independent of the National Gallery (although transfers are still made between the two institutions). A major extension to the building was opened in 1979, and in 1987 a new gallery—the Clore Gallery (named after Sir Charles Clore, 1904–79, a businessman and philanthropist who was one of the Tate's greatest benefactors)—was opened to house the Turner bequest, including not only the oil paintings already at the Tate, but also the water-colours and drawings from the *British Museum. In 1988 a new branch of the Tate Gallery was opened in Liverpool.

Tatlin, Vladimir (1885–1953). Russian painter, designer, and maker of abstract constructions, the founder of *Constructivism. He ran away to sea at the age of 18 and until 1914 combined painting with the life of a merchant seaman; many of his earlier pictures are of maritime subjects, notably *The Sailor* (Russian Mus., Leningrad, 1911–12), a self-portrait. From 1910 he exhibited at several avant-garde exhibitions in Russia and worked in close association with *Goncharova and *Larionov, who had known him as a boy. In 1914 (not 1913 as long believed) Tatlin visited Berlin and Paris, and met *Picasso, who inspired his revolutionary *Painted Reliefs, Relief Constructions*, and *Corner Reliefs* of 1914 onwards. Only one or two of these survive and most are known only from photographs. It appears that he used a variety of materials—tin, glass, wood, plaster, etc.—with the object of doing away with pictorial illusion. After the October Revolution of 1917 Tatlin's constructions from real materials in real space were felt to be in accordance with the new doctrines and he threw himself wholeheartedly into support of the demand for socially oriented art. In 1919 he was commissioned by the Revolutionary Department of Fine Arts to design the *Monument to the Third International* (i.e. the Third International Communist Congress, to be held in Moscow in 1921). The huge monument was intended for a position in the centre of Moscow; it was to be in glass and iron, and the central glass cylinder was to revolve. A model was exhibited in December 1920 at the exhibition of the VIIIth Congress of the Soviets. The design was condemned by *Gabo as impracticable and it was never executed (it was intended to be much bigger than the Eiffel Tower), but it is recognized as the outstanding symbol of Soviet Constructivism. The *Monument* was the culmination of Tatlin's artistic career, and the rest of it is something of an anticlimax. He taught and was active in the Soviet programme for the organization of museums, schools, etc. for the propagation of modern artistic culture. His own work was mainly in the field of *applied art, designing furniture, workers' clothes, etc. In the late 1920s and early 1930s he devoted his energies to designing a glider, which he called *Letatlin* (a compound of his name and the Russian word for 'to fly'). From the 1930s his main activity was theatre design, and his later years were spent in lonely obscurity. There has even been some suspicion that he lived for some years after his official death date.

Tchelitchew, Pavel (1898–1957). Russian-born American painter. In 1918 he fled Moscow because of the Revolution and in 1923 settled in Paris, where he did theatrical designs, circus pictures, landscapes, and portraits, and was regarded as a leading exponent of *Neo-Romanticism. He went to the USA in 1934 and became an American citizen in 1952. His interest in theatrical and ballet design was reflected in a certain decorative and mannered quality of his painting with traits of a superficial *Surrealism. His best-known work is probably *Hide and Seek* (MOMA, New York, 1942), in which strangely coloured children's heads weirdly metamorphose into vegetable forms.

Teerlinc, Levina. See BENING.

tempera. A term originally applied to any paint in which the pigment is dissolved in water and mixed (tempered) with an organic gum or glue, but now generally confined to the most common form of the medium—egg tempera. Usually only the yolk of the egg is used, but the white by itself or both yolk and white together have also been used. Egg tempera was the most important technique for panel painting in Europe from the beginning of the 13th cent. until the end of the 15th cent., when it began to be overtaken by *oil. After being neglected for about 400 years, tempera painting has had a limited revival in the 20th cent., Andrew *Wyeth being a noted exponent.

Ten, The. Group of American painters from New York and Boston who exhibited together for about 20 years from 1898. Most of them had studied in Paris in the 1880s and the common factor in their work was an interest in *Impressionism. Childe *Hassam and W. M. *Chase were the best-known members. The Ten was also the name of a group of American *Expressionist painters who exhibited together from 1935 to 1940. *Gottlieb and *Rothko were among the members.

tenebrism. Term describing predominantly dark tonality in a painting. It derives from the Italian 'tenebroso' (obscure) and is applied mainly to the 17th-cent. followers of *Caravaggio in Italy and elsewhere.

Teniers, David the Younger (1610–90). Flemish painter, the most important of a family of Antwerp artists. His output was huge and varied (about 2,000 pictures have been attributed to him), but he is best known for his peasant scenes—similar to those of *Brouwer, but less hearty. In 1651 he was appointed court painter to Archduke Leopold Wilhelm of Austria, Governor of the Austrian Netherlands in Brussels, and was also made custodian of the Archduke's art collection. Teniers was an unusual curator. He not only compiled a first-rate catalogue of the Archduke's pictures but he also made paintings of the galleries in which the works of art were installed, and painted small copies of some of the pictures (examples of the latter are in the Courtauld Inst. and Wallace Coll., London). Teniers' father, **David the Elder** (1582–1649), was primarily a painter of religious scenes. Few pictures are known that are certainly by him, and many formerly attributed to him are now given

to his son, with whom he may have collaborated. David the Younger's son, **David III** (1638–85), was one of the many artists who imitated his father's work. Other members of the family were **Julien I** (1572–1615), the brother of David I, **Julien II** (1616–79), the brother of David II, and **Abraham** (1629–70), the brother of David III.

Tenniel, Sir John (1820–1914). English illustrator. He is remembered chiefly for his brilliant illustrations to Lewis Carroll's *Alice's Adventures in Wonderland* (1865) and *Through the Looking-Glass* (1872), which now seem inseparable from the text, and for his long association with *Punch*. He worked for *Punch* from 1850 to 1901, succeeding *Leech as chief cartoonist in 1864.

Terborch (or **Ter Borch**), **Gerard the Younger** (1617–81). Dutch painter and draughtsman of interiors and small portraits. A highly precocious artist—his earliest dated drawing (in the Rijksmuseum, Amsterdam) is from 1625—Terborch studied with his father, **Gerard the Elder** (1584–1662), in his native Zwolle, and with Pieter de *Molyn in Haarlem. Unlike most of the Dutch artists of his time he travelled extensively. In 1635 he was in London, and from c.1636 to 1640 he was in Italy. From Italy he probably went to Spain and then to Flanders. In 1648 he was in Germany, where he painted *The Swearing of the Oath of Ratification of the Treaty of Münster* (NG, London, 1648), a group portrait of the signatories to the treaty that gave the Dutch independence from the Spanish. In 1654 he finally settled in Deventer, where he won both professional and social success. After beginning his career with guardroom scenes, he turned to pictures of elegant society, to which his gifts for delicate characterization and exquisite depiction of fine materials were ideally suited. His best-known work, the subject of a charming passage by *Goethe, is the so-called *Parental Admonition* (versions in the Rijksmuseum, Amsterdam, and the Staatliche Museen, Berlin). It is symptomatic of Terborch's unvaryingly tasteful decorum that the true theme of this picture is a man making a proposition to a courtesan, the coin that he proffers to his 'daughter' having been partially erased.

Terborch's most important pupil was Caspar *Netscher.

Terbrugghen, Hendrick (1588?–1629). Dutch painter, one of the earliest and finest exponents of *Caravaggism in northern Europe. Born in Deventer, he trained with *Bloemaert in Utrecht, then spent about a decade in Rome (c.1604–14). On his return to the Netherlands he became with *Honthorst the leader of the Caravaggism associated with the Utrecht School. A second journey to Italy has been postulated as his later works are generally more thoroughly Caravaggesque than his earlier ones. Terbrugghen was chiefly a religious painter, but he also produced some remarkable *genre works, notably a pair of paintings of Flute Players (Staatliche Kunstsammlungen, Kassel, 1621), which in their subtle tonality—with dark figures placed against a light background—anticipated by a generation the achievement of painters of the Delft School such as *Fabritius and *Vermeer. Although he was praised by *Rubens, who visited Utrecht in 1627, Terbrugghen was neglected by 18th- and 19th-cent. collectors and historians. The rediscovery of his sensitive and poetic paintings has been part of the 20th cent. reappraisal of Caravaggesque.

terracotta (Italian: baked earth). Clay baked to become hard and compact. Figures and architectural ornaments have been made of it since very early times and it is to these, rather than pottery vessels, that the word 'terracotta' usually refers. Clay is found all over the world in many different colours and qualities. Coloured clay is commoner than white. The presence of certain chemicals, such as iron oxide, affects the colour of the baked product, so terracotta works are not necessarily of the reddish-brown colour that is normally associated with the word. Firing may produce a wide range of colour from light buff to deep red or black. The hardness and strength of the baked clay vary according to the temperature at which it has been fired. During the firing the clay shrinks by about one-tenth of its volume, sometimes more, sometimes less, according to its quality and the amount of moisture.

Testa, Pietro (called Il Lucchesino) (1611–50). Italian engraver and painter active in Rome. He trained with *Domenichino and was employed by Nicolas *Poussin's patron Cassiano dal Pozzo to make antiquarian drawings, but his bizarre imagination brings him closer in spirit to his more Romantic contemporaries such as *Castiglione and *Rosa. His paintings are rare and he is better known as an etcher. Testa died by drowning, and it was rumoured that he killed himself.

Theed, William (1804–91). English sculptor. He was the son of a painter and sculptor of the same name (1764–1817), best known for his pediment group Hercules Taming the Thracian Horses (Royal Mews, London, c.1816), one of the earliest works to show the influence of the *Elgin Marbles. Theed the Younger trained under E. H. *Baily and at the *Royal Academy Schools. In 1826 he went to Rome and worked under *Thorvaldsen and *Gibson. He returned to London in 1848 and became one of the most distinguished and prolific of Victorian sculptors. His work includes numerous busts and statues and the colossal group of Africa for the Albert Memorial.

Theophanes the Greek (in Russian Feofan Grek, c.1330–c.1405). Painter from Constantinople, active mainly in Russia. He is said to have been a prolific decorator of churches, but only one fresco cycle survives that is certainly from his own hand, in the church of the Transfiguration at Novgorod (1378). This is one of the outstanding monuments of Russian medieval art, showing the highly personal version of the *Byzantine style that Theophanes brought to Russia; his figures are vigorous and strongly characterized, and his brushwork has an almost impressionistic freedom and dash. Theophanes is known to have carried out major commissions in Moscow between 1395 and 1405, but none of his work there survives except some *icons for the Cathedral of the Annunciation, which were painted with the help of assistants and are poorly preserved. According to a contemporary source Theophanes was also famous as a book-*illuminator. No signed or documented work in this field is known by him, but several examples have been attributed to him. Theophanes made a great impression on the Novgorod and Moscow Schools of painting in the 15th cent., notably on *Rublev.

Theophilus. The pseudonym adopted by the author of a medieval treatise on arts and crafts entitled *De Diversis Artibus*. It has been variously dated from the 9th to the 13th cent. C. R. Dodwell, who made the standard English translation (1961), assigns it to a date between 1110 and 1140. It is the most important source of information on medieval arts and techniques and is unusual for its time in its references to the artist's attitude to his work. Various medieval manuscripts are extant, but the treatise did not become generally known until the late 18th cent. *Lessing produced the first printed edition, posthumously published in 1781, and an English edition, made from another manuscript, appeared in the same year. Little or nothing is known with certainty about the writer, but internal evidence suggests that he was a German Benedictine monk and also a practising craftsman whose primary interest lay in metal-work. He has been plausibly identified with Roger of Helmarshausen, a goldsmith and monk at the abbey of Helmarshausen, who is documented as the maker of a portable altar (Paderborn Cathedral Treasury, 1100) for Bishop Henry of Werl. Other works have been attributed to him.

Thoma, Hans (1839–1924). German painter. His early landscapes—usually scenes from his native Black Forest—are his finest and freshest works, showing the influence of *Courbet and the *Barbizon School. Later, under the impact of *Böcklin, he turned to more ponderous symbolic subjects. Thoma was immensely popular during his lifetime, but has fallen greatly in critical esteem. The largest collection of his works is in the Karlsruhe Kunsthalle, of which he was Director.

Thomson, Tom (1877–1917). Canadian landscape painter, one of the main creators of an indigenous Canadian school of painting. Most of his career was spent as a commercial artist, and it was only in 1914 that he was able to take up painting full time. Much of his painting was done out of doors, notably the fluently spontaneous oil sketches he produced in Algonquin Park. Among his more finished paintings, the most famous is the bold and brilliantly coloured *Jack Pine* (NG, Ottawa, 1917), which has become virtually a national symbol of Canada. Thomson's career ended tragically when he was mysteriously drowned in Algonquin Park, but his ideals were continued by the artists who formed the *Group of Seven, to whom he was an inspiration.

Thoré, Théophile (1807–69). French writer on art. He ranks alongside *Baudelaire as the most perceptive art critic of his time (he was among the first to acclaim *Courbet, *Daumier, *Manet, *Monet, and *Renoir and to see the weakness of *Meissonier), and he also made memorable contributions to the study of earlier art. Above all, he is remembered for virtually rediscovering *Vermeer, a brilliant feat of connoisseurship and historical detective work. He was originally a political journalist and he published much of his work under the pseudonym W. Bürger when he was living in exile.

Thornhill, Sir James (1675/6–1734). English decorative painter. He was the only British painter of his day successfully to emulate the European formulas for wall and ceiling painting and to challenge on their own ground the many foreign decorative painters then at work in England. His two finest works are the *grisaille paintings on the Life of St Paul (1716–19) in the dome of St Paul's Cathedral, London (he beat *Pellegrini and Sebastiano *Ricci in the competition for the commission), and the Painted Hall at Greenwich Hospital, on which he worked intermittently from 1708 to 1727. Thornhill was appointed History Painter to George I in 1718 and Serjeant Painter in 1720, was knighted in 1722, and elected Member of Parliament in the same year. He started an *academy in London at which *Hogarth was a pupil and from which he eloped with Thornhill's daughter.

Thorn-Prikker, Johan (1868–1932). One of the leading Dutch *Symbolist artists, best known as a designer of large murals, mosaics, and stained glass for churches and public buildings. After 1904 he worked and taught in Germany. The church of Neuss and the Folkwang-Museum at Hagen have windows designed by him. His paintings are noteworthy for their elaborate *Art Nouveau line and often have a strong erotic charge.

Thorvaldsen (or **Thorwaldsen**), **Bertel** (1768 or 1770–1844). Danish sculptor, next to *Canova the most celebrated sculptor of the *Neoclassical movement. After five years at the Academy in his native Copenhagen, he reached Rome in 1797 on 3 March, a day which he henceforth considered as his birthday. He made his name with the statue *Jason* (Thorvaldsens Mus., Copenhagen, 1802–3), which was based on the *Doryphoros* of *Polyclitus, and his growing reputation resulted in so many commissions that by 1820 he had forty assistants in his Roman workshop. In that year, when visiting Copenhagen, he began planning the decoration of the newly built church of Our Lady with marble statues and *reliefs, a scheme which was to be his principal task for several years. His other major works include the tomb of Pius VII at St Peter's in Rome (1824–31) and a monument to Lord Byron (Trinity College, Cambridge, 1829). He returned finally to Denmark in 1838, a celebrity whose authority in the arts was sovereign. In Copenhagen a museum was built for him (1839–48), itself a remarkable piece of neo-antique architecture, the courtyard of which was to contain his tomb. Thorvaldsen aimed at reviving the sublimity of Greek sculpture, but he never went to Greece and (in common with other artists of his time) bestowed his admiration mainly on late *Hellenistic or Roman copies. He did, however, gain close knowledge of Greek sculpture from the restorations he made to the recently excavated sculptures from the Temple of Aphaia in Aegina, which in 1816 passed through Rome on their way to Munich (they are now in the Glyptothek there); Thorvaldsen's restorations have only recently been removed. Compared with Canova he is cool and calculating; his sculptures are more logically worked out and have great precision and clarity, but they lack Canova's sensitive surfaces. According to the taste of the time, critics have tended either to praise his work for its nobility and Classical calm or to dismiss it as insipid and empty.

Thulden, Theodor van (1606–69). Flemish painter, engraver and designer of tapestries, a pupil and collaborator of *Rubens. Although like most contemporary painters of historical and religious themes he was strongly influenced by Rubens, he did

succeed in working out a personal idiom. His appealingly sweet style won him numerous commissions both inside and outside Flanders, and he worked in The Hague and Paris, as well as Antwerp, where he was mainly based.

Tibaldi, Pellegrino (1527–96). Italian *Mannerist painter, sculptor, and architect. He was in Rome in the late 1540s and early 1550s, and his style in painting, distinguished by grand, if sometimes rather ponderous, figures, was based mainly on the work of *Michelangelo, for whom he had a lifelong admiration. His finest paintings are frescos illustrating the story of Ulysses (*c*.1555) in the Palazzo Poggi (now University), Bologna. From the mid 1560s Tibaldi worked mainly as an architect, chiefly in and around Milan, where he was much employed by the Archbishop, Charles Borromeo, and was appointed chief architect to the cathedral in 1567. In 1587 he went to Madrid in order to superintend building operations at the *Escorial and did sculpture and a vast amount of paintings for its decoration. His work there was influential in the development of Spanish Mannerism. He returned to Milan, ennobled by Philip II, in the year of his death.

Tiepolo, Giovanni Battista (Giambattista) (1696–1770). The greatest Italian (and arguably the greatest European) painter of the 18th cent. His work sums up the splendours of Italian decorative painting, and with him the monumental fresco tradition which had begun with *Giotto is brought to an end. He revived the glories of the Venetian School, especially of *Veronese, and enriched them with the experience of the Roman and Neapolitan *Baroque and the new *perspective techniques of theatre decoration. His deep pictorial culture was drawn from a wide variety of sources, including *Rubens, *Rembrandt, and *Dürer. Tiepolo trained with the history painter Gregorio Lazzarini (1655–1730), but according to his earliest biographer, Vincenzo da Canal, he soon departed from his master's 'diligent manner, and, being all fire and spirit, adopted one which was rapid and free'. After making his name in Venice with some works in the 'dark' manner of *Piazzetta, he carried out his first important fresco cycle in the Archbishop's Palace in

Udine (c.1727–8) and with the change from oil to fresco he broke away from the dark tonality of his earliest work and established the clear, sunny palette which became one of his foremost characteristics. In the 1730s much of his work was done outside his native city, and by 1736 his fame was such that he was invited to Stockholm to decorate the Royal Palace—an invitation he declined because the fee offered was too small. Between 1741 and 1750 Tiepolo was active mainly in Venice, where his chief work was the decoration of the Palazzo Labia (1745), in which he was assisted by his expert in *quadratura, Gerolamo Mengozzi Colonna (c.1688–1766).

The next decade represents the peak of Tiepolo's career. In 1750–3 he was in Würzburg to decorate the Kaisersaal and the grand staircase of the Prince Archbishop's palace, and this work is the masterpiece of his maturity. Like *Rubens, Tiepolo could make even the most ponderous allegory come alive, and here the unpromising task of paying tribute to the lack-lustre Prince Archbishop brought forth his most glorious work—full of light and colour and perfectly attuned to the superb architectural setting. In 1757 Tiepolo decorated a series of rooms in the Villa Valmarana near Vicenza, with scenes from Homer, Virgil, Ariosto, and Tasso, and this work gives perhaps the most immediate experience of his qualities: grandeur, rich and glowing colour, and fancifulness warmed by humanity in the narrative. His last large-scale work in Italy was the ceiling of the ballroom in the Villa Pisani at Strà. While there he was called by Charles III to Madrid, where he spent the last eight years of his life. The *Apotheosis of Spain* (1764) on the ceiling of the throne room in the royal palace was his principal commission. Intrigue and jealousy embittered these last years in Madrid, and the final blow was dealt posthumously when his seven altarpieces for the church of S. Pascal Baylon at Aranjuez were displaced, by seven canvases done by *Mengs, the champion of *Neoclassicism (Mengs is said to have fallen from a tree whilst lying in wait to attack the aged Tiepolo, but Tiepolo—with characteristic nobility—saw to it that his rival was treated in hospital). Tiepolo's altarpieces are now divided between the Prado and the Royal

Palace in Madrid, and the surviving oil-sketches for them are mainly in the Courtauld Institute Galleries, London. They display a pathos and psychological intensity that was new to his art. He had painted easel pictures as well as frescos throughout his career, and a work such as the ravishing *Young Woman with a Macaw* (Ashmolean Mus., Oxford, c.1760) shows the masterly fluency of his brushwork. Tiepolo was as prolific a draughtsman as he was a painter (an outstanding collection of his drawings is in the Victoria and Albert Museum, London) and was one of the finest etchers of his period; *Goya was especially indebted to his graphic work.

Tiepolo was married to Cecilia Guardi, sister of the *Guardi brothers. They had two painter sons. **Giandomenico Tiepolo** (1727–1804) began to assist his father c.1745 and accompanied him to Madrid. He was so faithful to his father's work that it is sometimes impossible to say exactly where he has collaborated. In his independent work he has a clearly defined style with a marked bias towards *genre and *caricature, e.g. at the Villa Valmarana. He is noteworthy also for his etchings, especially the twenty-two variations on the theme of the *Flight into Egypt* (1753). **Lorenzo Tiepolo** (1736–before 1776) also assisted his father, but unlike his brother Giandomenico he has no individual substance as an artist.

Tinguely, Jean (1925–). Swiss sculptor and experimental artist. Tingueley's work has been concerned primarily with movement and the machine, satirizing technological civilization. His boisterous humour has been most fully demonstrated in his auto-destructive works, which turned *Kinetic art into *Performance art. The most famous was *Homage to New York* (1960), which was built and demonstrated at The Museum of Modern Art, New York, but failed to destroy itself as programmed and caused a fire. The object was constructed of an old piano and other junk. Tinguely has been an innovator not only in his combination of Kineticism with the *Expressionism of *Junk sculpture, but also in the impetus he gave to the principle of spectator participation, as in his *Rotozazas*, in which the spectator plays ball with the machine.

Tino di Camaino (c.1285–1337). Sienese sculptor, chiefly of tombs, active in Pisa, Florence, and Naples, as well as his native city. He probably trained with Giovanni *Pisano, but his style was more calm and reserved, with an imposing block-like massiveness. His early career was spent in Pisa and Siena, but his chief works are in Florence (where he worked 1321–4) and Naples (where he worked from 1324 until his death). In Florence his work included the tomb of Bishop Orso in the cathedral—possibly the earliest example of the seated effigy. In Naples, where he is known to have been in touch with *Giotto, who was court painter there at the time, and with the Sienese painter Pietro *Lorenzetti, his work included tabernacled tombs for the Angevin court (e.g. for Queen Mary of Hungary in Sta Maria Donnaregina). He somewhat modified his own rigorous style in the direction of the more decorative grace of the *Gothic style, but none the less his influence was significant as one of the Tuscan artists who carried the new northern developments to the southern parts of Italy.

Tintoretto (Jacopo Robusti) (1518–94). Venetian painter. His nickname derives from his father's profession of dyer (*tintore*). Although he was prolific and with *Veronese the most successful Venetian painter in the generation after *Titian's death, little is known of his life. He is said to have trained very briefly with Titian, but the style of his immature works suggests that he may also have studied with *Schiavone, Paris *Bordone, or *Bonifazio. Almost all of his life was spent in Venice and most of his work is still in the churches or other buildings for which it was painted. He appears to have been unpopular because he was unscrupulous in procuring commissions and ready to undercut his competitors. By 1539 he was sufficiently mature to be established independently, painting pictures composed in a traditional Venetian manner with the figures arranged parallel to the picture plane and unlinked by any strong movement or variation in the arrangement (*The Adoration of the Golden Calf*, Kunsthistorisches Mus., Vienna, c.1545). His early masterpiece is the *Miracle of the Slave* (Accademia, Venice, 1548), in which many of the qualities of his maturity, particularly his love of foreshortening, begin to be distinguishable. To help him with the complex poses he favoured, Tintoretto used to make small wax models which he arranged on a stage and experimented on with spotlights for effects of light and shade and composition. This method of composing explains the frequent repetition in his works of the same figures seen from different angles. He was a formidable draughtsman and, according to *Ridolfi, he had inscribed on his studio wall the motto 'The drawing of *Michelangelo and the colour of Titian'. However, he was very different in spirit from either of his avowed models—more emotive, using vivid exaggerations of light and movement. His drawings, unlike Michelangelo's detailed life studies, are brilliant, rapid notations, bristling with energy, and his colour is more sombre and mystical than Titian's.

Tintoretto's greatest works are the vast series of paintings he did for the Scuola di San Rocco from 1565 to 1587—scenes from the life of Christ in the upper hall and scenes from the life of the Virgin in the lower hall. The complicated system, starting in the upper hall, was probably not conceived by Tintoretto himself, but he interpreted it with a vividness and economy of colour and detail which gives a miraculous cohesion to the whole scheme. Its personal conception of the sacred story overwhelmed *Ruskin, who devoted eloquent pages to it, and Henry James wrote of the stupendous *Crucifixion*: 'Surely no single picture in the world contains more of human life; there is everything in it, including the most exquisite beauty.' The unorthodox rough brushwork incurred the censure of *Vasari, but later generations recognized it as a means of heightening the drama and tension. As well as religious works, Tintoretto painted mythological scenes and he was also a fine portraitist, particularly of old men (a self-portrait in old age is in the Louvre). Some of the weaker portraits that go under his name may be the product of his large workshop. His son **Domenico** (c.1560–1635) became his foreman and is said to have painted many portraits, although none can be attributed to him with certainty. Another son, **Marco** (1561–1637), and a daughter, **Marietta** (c.1556–90), were among his other assistants. The later paintings can thus be divided into those which are largely studio productions on the one hand and the visionary inspirations from Tintoretto's own hand on the other. A prime example of the latter is *The Last Supper* (S. Giorgio Maggiore, Venice, 1592–4), the culmination of a lifetime's development of this subject, from the traditional frontal representation to this startling diagonally viewed composition. Tintoretto had great influence on Venetian painting, but the artist who most fruitfully absorbed the visionary energy and intensity of his work was El *Greco.

Tischbein. Family of German 18th-cent. painters. The best-known of them, **Johann Heinrich Wilhelm Tischbein** (1751–1829), was most important for his engravings of Classical antiquities, but is now remembered almost solely for his famous portrait *Goethe in the Roman Campagna* (Städelsches Kunstinstitut, Frankfurt, 1786–7). Tischbein was *Goethe's friend and he is usually called 'Goethe' Tischbein. The two other leading members of the family, his uncle and cousin, were nicknamed after their main place of work: **Johann Heinrich the Elder**, 'Kassel' Tischbein (1722–89) and **Johann Friedrich** 'Leipzig' Tischbein (1750–1812). They were principally portraitists.

Tissot, James (1836–1902). French painter and graphic artist. Early in his career he painted historical costume pieces, but in about 1864 he turned with great success to scenes of contemporary life, usually involving fashionable women. Following his alleged involvement in the turbulent events of the Paris Commune (1871) he took refuge in London, where he lived from 1871 to 1882. He was just as successful there as he had been in Paris and lived in some style in St John's Wood; in 1874 Edmond de *Goncourt wrote sarcastically that he had 'a studio with a waiting room where, at all times, there is iced champagne at the disposal of visitors, and around the studio, a garden where, all day long, one can see a footman in silk stockings brushing and shining the shrubbery leaves'. His pictures are distinguished most obviously by his love of painting women's costumes: indeed, his work—which has a fashion-plate elegance and a chocolate-box charm—has probably been more often reproduced in works on the history of costume than on the history of painting. He also, however, had a gift for wittily

observing nuances of social behaviour. In 1882, following the death of his mistress Kathleen Newton (the archetypal Tissot model—beautiful but rather vacant), he returned to France. In 1888 he underwent a religious conversion when he went into a church to 'catch the atmosphere for a picture', and thereafter he devoted himself to religious subjects. He visited the Holy Land in 1886–7 and 1889, and his illustrations to the events of the Bible were enormously popular, both in book form and when the original drawings were exhibited. For many years after his death Tissot was considered a grossly vulgar artist, but there has been a recent upsurge of interest in him, expressed in sale-room prices for his work as well as in numerous books and exhibitions devoted to him.

Titian (Tiziano Vecellio) (c.1485–1576). The greatest painter of the Venetian school. The evidence for his birthdate is contradictory, but he was certainly very old when he died. He received the more important part of his training in the studio of Giovanni *Bellini, then came under the spell of *Giorgione, with whom he had a close relationship. In 1506–8 he assisted him with the external fresco decoration of the Fondaco dei Tedeschi, Venice, and after Giorgione's early death in 1510 it fell to Titian to complete a number of his unfinished paintings. The authorship of certain works (some of them famous) is still disputed between them.

Titian's first great commission was for three frescos in Padua (Scuola del Santo, 1511), noble and dignified paintings suggesting an almost central Italian firmness and monumentality. When he returned to Venice, Giorgione having died and *Sebastiano gone to Rome, the aged Bellini alone stood between him and supremacy, and that only until 1516 when Bellini died and Titian became official painter to the Republic. Meanwhile he was gradually winning free from the stylistic domination of Giorgione and developing a manner of his own. Something of a fusion between Titian's worldliness and Giorgione's poetry is seen in the enigmatic allegory known as *Sacred and Profane Love* (Villa Borghese, Rome, c.1516). This work inaugurated a brilliant period in Titian's creative career during which he produced splendid religious, mythological, and portrait paintings, original in conception and vivid with colour and movement. A series of great altarpieces opens with the *Assumption* (Sta Maria dei Frari, Venice, 1516–18), which in the soaring movement of the Virgin, rising from the tempestuous group of Apostles towards the hovering figure of God the Father, contradicts the stable basis of *quattrocento and High *Renaissance composition and looks forward to the *Baroque. The strong, simple colours used here, and the artist's evident pleasure in the silhouetting of dark forms against a light background, reappear throughout the work of this period. There followed the Pesaro altarpiece (Sta Maria dei Frari, Venice, 1519–26), a bold diagonal composition of great magnificence in which architectural motifs are used to enhance the drama of the scene, and the altarpiece of St Peter Martyr (now destroyed but known to us from several copies and engravings), where trees and figures together form a violent centrifugal composition suited to the action (*Vasari described it as 'the most celebrated, the greatest work . . . that Titian has ever done'). Titian's finest mythological works from this period are three pictures (1518–23) for Alfonso d'*Este—the *Worship of Venus*, the *Bacchanal* (both in the Prado, Madrid), and the *Bacchus and Ariadne* (NG, London)—and outstanding among his portraits is the exquisite *Man with a Glove* (Louvre, Paris, c.1520).

About 1530, the year in which his wife died, a change in Titian's manner becomes apparent. The vivacity of former years gave way to a more restrained and meditative art. He now began to use related rather than contrasting colours in juxtaposition, yellows and pale shades rather than the strong blues and reds which shouldered each other through his previous work. In composition too he became less adventurous and used schemes which, compared with some of his earlier works, appear almost archaic. Thus his large *Presentation of the Virgin* (Accademia, Venice, 1534–8) makes use of the *relief-like frieze composition dear to the *quattrocento. During the 1530s Titian's fame spread throughout Europe. In 1530 he first met the emperor Charles V (in Bologna, where he was crowned in that year) and in 1533 he painted a famous portrait of him (Prado) based on a portrait by the German *Seisenegger. Charles was so pleased with it that he appointed Titian court painter and

elevated him to the rank of Count Palatine and Knight of the Golden Spur—an unprecedended honour for a painter. At the same time his works were increasingly sought after by Italian princes, as with the celebrated *Venus of Urbino* (Uffizi, Florence, c.1538), named after its owner, Guidobaldo, Duke of Camerino, who later became Duke of Urbino. The pose is based on Giorgione's *Sleeping Venus* (Gemäldegalerie, Dresden), but Titian substitutes a direct sensual appeal for Giorgione's idyllic remoteness.

Early in the 1540s Titian came under the influence of central and north Italian *Mannerism, and in 1545–6 he made his first and only journey to Rome. There he was deeply impressed not only by modern works such as *Michelangelo's *Last Judgement*, but also by the remains of antiquity. His own paintings during this visit aroused much interest, his *Danaë* (Museo di Capodimonte, Naples) being praised for its handling and colour and (according to Vasari) criticized for its inexact drawing by Michelangelo. Titian also painted in Rome the famous portrait of *Pope Paul III and his Nephews* (Museo di Capodimonte). The decade closed with further imperial commissions. In 1548 the emperor summoned Titian to Augsburg, where he painted both a formal equestrian portrait (*Charles V at the Battle of Mühlberg*, Prado) and a more intimate one showing him seated in an armchair (Alte Pinakothek, Munich). He travelled to Augsburg again in 1550 and this time painted portraits of Charles's son, the future Philip II of Spain and the greatest patron of his later career. Titian's work for Philip included a series of erotic subjects: in 1554 the *Danaë*, the *Venus and Adonis* (both in the Prado), and the *Perseus and Andromeda* (Wallace Coll., London), and in 1559–60 the *Rape of Europa* (Isabella Stewart Gardner Mus., Boston) and *Diana and Actaeon* (Ellesmere Coll., on loan to NG, of Scotland). Titian referred to these pictures as *poesie*, and they are indeed highly poetic visions of distant worlds, quite different from the sensual realities of his earlier mythological paintings.

During the last twenty years of his life Titian's personal works, as opposed to those which busy assistants produced under his supervision and with his intervention, showed an increasing looseness in the handling and a sensitive merging of colours which makes them more and more im-material. Autumnal tones reflected the artist's meditative spirit. About the same time his interest in new pictorial conceptions waned. About 1550-5 he had painted a powerful *Martyrdom of St Lawrence* (Gesuiti, Venice), which had affinities with Mannerism in the types and movements of the figures. In 1564-7 he repeated the picture (Escorial, Madrid), but now the light, which had played a dramatic part in the first version, became the chief feature, creating and dissolving forms. His powers remained undimmed until the end, and his career closed with the awe-inspiring *Pietà* (Accademia, Venice, 1573-6), intended for his own tomb and finished after his death by *Palma Giovane.

Titian's influence on later artists has been profound: he was supreme in every branch of painting and revolutionized the oil technique with his free and expressive brushwork. Vasari wrote of this aspect of his late works that they 'are executed with bold, sweeping strokes, and in patches of colour, with the result that they cannot be viewed from near by, but appear perfect at a distance . . . The method he used is judicious, beautiful, and astonishing, for it makes pictures appear alive and painted with great art, but it conceals the labour that has gone into them.' His greatness as an artist, it appears, was not matched by his character, for he was notoriously avaricious. In spite of his wealth and status, he claimed he was impoverished, and his exaggerations about his age (by which he hoped to pull at the heartstrings of patrons) are one of the sources of confusion about his birthdate. Jacopo *Bassano caricatured him as a moneylender in his *Purification of the Temple* (NG, London). Titian, however, was lavish in his hospitality towards his friends, who included the poet Pietro Aretino and the sculptor and architect Jacopo *Sansovino. These three were so close that they were known in Venice as the triumvirate, and they used their influence with their respective patrons to further each other's careers.

Tobey, Mark (1890-1976). American painter. Tobey was a convert to the Baha'i religion and much of his work was inspired by his interest in oriental art and thought. He is best known for his 'white writing' paintings, which he developed in the

1930s—calligraphic white patterns overlying dimly discerned suggestions of colour beneath. Tobey painted both representational and abstract pictures in the style. Their '*all-over' manner anticipated *Pollock, but unlike *Action painters, Tobey believed that 'painting should come through the avenues of meditation rather than the canals of action'. Unusually for an American painter, he was more highly esteemed abroad than in his own country, and he exercised considerable influence on French *Tachisme in the 1950s.

Tommaso da Modena (*c*.1325-79). Italian painter, one of the leading artists of his day in northern Italy. His earthy, humane, and naturalistic style is well seen in his series of frescos of famous Dominicans (signed and dated 1352) in the Chapter House of S. Niccolò in Treviso. The saintly figures are shown meditating, writing, and reading (the first dated example of spectacles being worn appears here) and Tommaso shows a remarkable ability to depict intellectual activity. His reputation was such that work was commissioned from him by the emperor Charles IV in Bohemia, and two panels by Tommaso are still in Karlstein Castle, near Prague. It is unlikely that he visited Bohemia, but there is some kinship between his work and that of his leading Bohemian contemporary. *Master Theoderic.

tondo. A painting or *relief carving of circular shape: the word is Italian for 'round'.

Tonks, Henry (1862-1937). English painter, draughtsman, and teacher. He gave up a successful medical career for art in 1893 when he became a teacher at the *Slade School in London. From 1918 to 1930 he was Slade Professor and was highly influential as a teacher, helping to make the Slade the dominant teaching institution in Britain, the main channel through which the ideas of the *New English Art Club were disseminated to students. He set high standards for his pupils, particularly in draughtsmanship (his own forte) and he got on well with them, in spite of being notorious for his sarcasm and abruptness. However, he had not the gift of recognizing talent easily, as witness his unfavourable attitude towards Augustus

*John, Matthew *Smith, and Harold *Gilman. He was unable to move with the times, and after the *Post-Impressionist exhibitions of Roger *Fry, which he roundly condemned, he was looked upon as a back number by more progressive artists and students. His own paintings often look rather laborious, partly because of his technique of 'Tonking', which involved using an absorbent material to soak excess oil from the canvas after each day's work and so produce a dry surface for subsequent work. He was at his best in his conversation pieces e.g. *Saturday Night in the Vale* (Tate, London, 1928–9)—and his slighter satirical works. As a man, Tonks was secretive, touchy, suspicious, and resentful of criticism, though capable of close friendships, as, for example, with *Steer.

Tooker, George (1920–). American painter. He works mainly in egg *tempera, with a precise and polished surface in a style of exact but unemphatic *realism. His subjects, however, express the dehumanized and communal hopelessness of modern institutional man and a particularly poignant tension is set up between the superficial facility of the presentation and the profound existentialist message of the subject. *Subway* (Whitney Mus. of American Art, New York, 1950) is perhaps his most famous work—a terrifying vision of Kafkaesque isolation.

Toorop, Jan Theodoor (1858–1928). Dutch artist, born in Java, a leading figure in the *Symbolist and *Art Nouveau movements. His most characteristic paintings are literary subjects depicted with flowing lines, as in his masterpiece, *The Three Brides* (Rijksmuseum Kröller-Müller, Otterlo, 1893), a ghostly scene with an exotic feeling that recalls his origin in Java. In 1905 he was converted to Catholicism and thereafter concentrated mainly on religious works. Toorop's prolific output included book illustrations, designs for stained glass, and posters. His daughter, **Charley Toorop** (1891–1955), was a painter. Her early work was influenced by her father's Symbolism, but her later work was more solid and naturalistic.

Topolski, Feliks (1907–89). Polish-born painter and draughtsman who settled in England in 1935 and became a British subject in 1947. A versatile and prolific artist, he is perhaps best known for his large murals, notably *The Coronation of Elizabeth II* (30 m. × 1.5 m.) in Buckingham Palace. He was a war artist 1940–5, and his other work includes portraits and book illustrations. His style is marked by the use of vigorous swirling line.

Torres-García, Joaquin (1874–1949). Uruguayan painter and art theorist. Most of his life was spent in Spain, where he moved in 1891. After a visit to New York (1920–2) he settled in Paris (1924–32), where he developed a symbolic, severely geometrical, two-dimensional *Constructivist style, and founded the review *Cercle et Carré* in conjunction with the artist and critic Michel *Seuphor. In 1934 he returned to Uruguay, where he opened an art school. He wrote various works on art theory and by his example and teaching did much to promote Constructivist and *Kinetic art in South America. There is a Torres-García Museum in his native Montevideo.

Torrigiano, Pietro (1472–1528). Florentine sculptor. He was trained under *Bertoldo in the *Medici 'academy' and there broke the nose of his fellow student *Michelangelo and permanently disfigured him. Quitting Florence to escape the wrath of Lorenzo de' Medici, he wandered round Italy, producing no work of importance, and serving as a soldier. He visited the Netherlands, and c.1511 he came to England, where he executed his most important works, chief among them the tomb of Henry VII and his wife Elizabeth of York (1512–18) in Westminster Abbey. The two sensitive effigies, made with the aid of death masks, have a *Gothic elegance, but the figures of angels at the corners of the tomb and the exquisite decorative work introduced a pure *Renaissance style into England. It had little immediate influence, however. By 1522, Torrigiano left England for Spain, abandoning his projected tomb for Henry VIII. He was arrested by the Inquisition on a charge of heresy and died in prison.

Torriti, Jacopo (active late 13th cent.). Italian mosaicist and painter. Nothing is known of his life, but he signed two mosaics commissioned by Pope Nicholas IV for the apses of S. Giovanni in Laterano (1291), and Sta Maria Maggiore (1295?),

Rome, and must have been one of the leading contemporaries of *Cavallini. The mosaic in S. Giovanni in Laterano appears to have been a reworking of an earlier design and was reconstructed in the 19th cent., so Torriti's style can best be assessed from the less restored mosaic in Sta Maria Maggiore. Here, in the main scene of the *Coronation of the Virgin* and subsidiary scenes from the life of the Virgin, Torriti recaptures something of the vitality of late *antique mosaics; he was clearly influenced in his choice of colour by the pale delicate harmonies and silvery lights of the 5th-cent. mosaic on the triumphal arch of the same church. A small series of frescos in the Upper Church of S. Francesco, Assisi, has been attributed to Torriti on stylistic grounds.

Toulouse-Lautrec, Henri de (1864–1901). French painter and graphic artist, one of the most colourful of 19th-cent. artists. The son of an outrageously eccentric nobleman, he grew up with a love of sport, but as a result of two falls when he was in his early teens the bones in his legs atrophied and he became permanently stunted. (Accounts of his height vary, but he was certainly not the midget of the popular imagination. He was about 5 ft tall, but his large head made him appear grotesquely misproportioned. Lautrec was stoical about his condition, never mentioning it except in jest, and it did not prevent him from attracting women as beautiful as Suzanne *Valadon.) He showed an early talent for drawing (his father and uncle were amateur artists) and in 1882 he became a pupil of *Bonnat and in 1883 of *Cormon. At the age of 21, in 1885, he was given an allowance and set up in a studio of his own at Montmartre. He also began to draw for illustrated journals. He met van *Gogh at Cormon's school in 1886 and came into contact with *Impressionist and *Post-Impressionist painters. From the age of 15 until he was 24 he painted mainly sporting subjects. From c.1888 he began to illustrate the theatres, music-halls (particularly the Moulin Rouge), cafés, and low life of Paris; circuses and brothels were among the subjects he returned to again and again. He collected the etchings of *Goya and his painting came much under the influence of *Degas.

In 1888 he had come into contact with *Gauguin and began a continuing enthusiasm for Japanese colour prints (see UKIYO-E). The influence of Gauguin's flat rhythmic patterning and calligraphic use of strong outline became dominant chiefly in Lautrec's famous posters and in the lithographs. In spite of his notoriously dissipated lifestyle, he was a dedicated craftsman, and would arrive early at the workshop—even after a hard night's drinking—to supervise the printing of his lithographs. His work, with its masterfully bold and arresting forms, was one of the most important influences in gaining acceptance for both lithography and the poster as major art forms. Lautrec's alcoholism and dissolute life (he had syphilis) led to a breakdown in 1899 and the paintings he produced in the brief period between his recovery and his premature death, aged 36, are more sombre in style than his earlier work. In 1922 the Lautrec family presented some 600 of his works to his native town of Albi, where the Musée Toulouse-Lautrec was created to house them. The museum houses not only works by Lautrec but also memorabilia, notably his walking stick, which ingeniously opens up to reveal a tiny glass and flask of brandy.

Tournier, Nicolas (1590–1638/9). French painter. Very little is known of his life and most of the attributions to him are speculative, but he seems to have been—with the exception of Georges de *La Tour—the most individual and sensitive of French *Caravaggesque painters. He was in Rome c.1619–26, then is recorded in Carcassonne in 1627 and in Toulouse from 1632. The works attributed to him in his Roman period are *genre scenes of music making, dice-playing, etc. (*A Musical Party*, City Art Mus., St Louis), but after he returned to France he concentrated on religious pictures. There are examples in the Louvre and the Musée des Augustins, Toulouse, including a remarkable *Battle of Constantine* influenced by *Piero della Francesca's battle scenes at Arezzo—this at a time when Piero was virtually forgotten. More typical of Tournier's paintings in the museum at Toulouse are *The Lamentation* and *The Entombment*, which show the grace and refinement of his style.

Towne, Francis (1739/40–1816). English water-colour painter, active in London and

Exeter. He earned his living mainly as a drawing master and his work was little known to his contemporaries, but he is now regarded as being one of the most individual water-colourists of his period. His method of painting in flat *washes over a brown pen-and-ink outline was employed with a severe economy of means and he had an eye for geometrical structure that gives his pictures an almost abstract feel and an affinity with such 20th-cent. work as that of John *Nash. His best works are considered to be those done when he passed through Switzerland in 1781 when returning from a visit to Italy. He also visited Wales and the Lake District.

Traini, Francesco (documented 1321–63). Pisan painter. Only one work is certainly known to be by him—the signed *polyptych of *St Dominic and Scenes from his Life* (Mus. Naz., Pisa, 1345). The most important works attributed to him are frescos in the Campo Santo in Pisa—the celebrated *Triumph of Death*, with accompanying scenes of the *Last Judgement*, *Hell*, and *Legends of the Hermits*. These, among the outstanding Italian paintings of the 14th cent., were badly damaged by bombs in the Second World War, but this brought to light, by way of partial compensation, the beautiful *sinopie, which are now shown in the Museo delle Sinopie. The frescos include many telling details of death's victims and are usually seen as a reflection of the horrors of the Black Death of 1348, but some authorities consider them earlier, and recently there have been attempts to attribute them to the mysterious *Buffalmacco.

trecento. See QUATTROCENTO.

Tretyakov, Pavel (1832–98). Russian businessman and art collector. From an early age he conceived the idea of a national gallery of Russian art, and he not only bought great numbers of paintings, but also commissioned contemporary artists to produce work (he gave much encouragement and assistance to the *Wanderers). In 1892 he and his brother **Sergei** presented their collections to the city of Moscow, and the building in which they are housed was completed in 1902. The Tretyakov Gallery became the property of the State in 1918. It originally displayed foreign as well as Russian paintings, but

since 1925 it has been devoted exclusively to Russian art, of which it has the finest collection in the world. In the 1980s a major rebuilding and expansion of the gallery was carried out.

Trevisani, Francesco (1656–1746). Neapolitan painter, trained in Venice and working in Rome from 1678. He specialized in altarpieces and *cabinet pictures and was one of the most popular and prolific Italian painters of his day, his sweet and colourful *Rococo style challenging the Classicism of *Maratta.

triptych. 'A picture or carving (or set of three such) in three compartments side by side, the lateral ones being usually subordinate, and hinged so as to fold over the central one' (*OED*). Like the *diptych, this form lent itself to the making of portable religious images, whose delicate inner surfaces were protected by the outer leaves, which might, however, also be painted or carved on their outer as well as their own inner surfaces. See also POLYPTYCH.

Tristán, Luis (*c.*1586–1624). Spanish painter, active mainly in Toledo, where he was a pupil of El *Greco from 1603 to 1606. He is also known to have visited Italy, probably between 1606 and 1613. His style (notably his characteristically elongated proportions) owes much to El Greco, but Tristán is more sober, marking the transition from *Mannerism to a more naturalistic approach (*The Adoration of the Shepherds*, Fitzwilliam, Cambridge, 1620).

trompe-l'œil. Term (French for 'deceives the eye') applied to a painting (or detail of one) that is intended to deceive the spectator (if only briefly) into thinking that it is a real object rather than a two-dimensional representation of it. Such virtuoso displays of skill often have a humorous intent, and anecdotes of almost miraculous feats of *trompe-l'œil* by which some of the most famous painters of the past are said to have tricked and astonished their contemporaries are typical of periods in which *naturalism has been cultivated, such as the *Classical age in Greece (see PARRHASIUS) and the Italian *Renaissance. *Vasari, for example, records in evidence of *Giotto's precocity that as a boy he painted on the nose of a figure on which his master *Cimabue was engaged 'a fly so lifelike that when Cimabue returned to carry on with his work he tried several times to brush it off with his hand, under the impression that it was real, before he realized his mistake'. Petrus *Christus's *Portrait of a Carthusian* (Met. Mus., New York, *c*.1446) is an example of a painting with such a *trompe-l'œil* fly, here on a painted ledge at the bottom of the picture, rather than on the sitter's nose. Sometimes the term *trompe-l'œil* is used loosely to refer to any type of pictorial illusionism (for example *quadratura*), but such usage deprives a useful term of its precision.

Troost, Cornelis (1697–1750). The outstanding Dutch painter of the 18th cent. He made his name early with a lively group portrait of the *Amsterdam Inspectors of the Collegium Medicum* (Rijksmuseum, Amsterdam, 1724) and continued to enjoy success as a formal portraitist and painter of *conversation pieces. He is best known for his pictures of actors in famous roles and for his witty *genre scenes. His most famous work—made in his favourite technique of pastel and water-colour—is a series of five pictures entitled *NELRI* (Mauritshuis, The Hague, 1740); the name is derived from the first letters of the Latin inscriptions which accompany the five views of the activities of a group of men during the night of a reunion. Troost has much in common with his contemporary *Hogarth, but unlike Hogarth, Troost is a humorist without an ulterior motive; he never attempted to teach or preach.

Troy, Jean-François de (1679–1752). French painter and tapestry designer. His successful career was based initially on large historical and allegorical compositions (*Time Unveiling Truth*, NG, London, 1733), but he is now most highly regarded for his smaller and more spirited scenes of elegant social life. They are among the best of those that rode on the wave of *Watteau's success—indeed *The Alarm* (V&A, London, 1723) was attributed to Watteau in the 19th cent. In 1738 he was appointed Director of the French Academy in Rome, and spent the rest of his life there. He was one of a family of painters, his father and teacher, **François de Troy** (1645–1730), being a successful painter of fashionable portraits and Director of the Academy in Paris.

Troyon, Constant (1810–65). French painter. He was born in Sèvres and began his career as a porcelain decorator (the family trade) at the famous factory there. In the 1830s, however, he took up landscape painting, and became one of the leading figures of the *Barbizon School. He visited Holland in 1847, and the influence of *Cuyp and *Potter is seen in his predilection for including cows in his pictures. Late in his career he turned to seascapes, the freshnesss and freedom of his work influencing *Boudin and *Monet in this genre. Troyon was a prolific and successful painter, and his work is in many public collections in France and elsewhere.

Trumbull, John (1756–1843). American painter. Trumbull fought in the American War of Independence (for a time he was aide-de-camp to George Washington) and his career was devoted mainly to depicting the outstanding events and personalities of the Revolution. He was strongly influenced by Benjamin *West, with whom he studied in London (he made several visits there, and during the first of them, 1780–3, was imprisoned in reprisal for the hanging of a British agent in America). In 1817 he became President of the American Academy of Fine Arts in New York, but his tyrannical attitude, especially towards young painters, led to many members leaving to set up the National Academy of Design in 1825. His pictures did not sell well, so in 1831 he assigned those in his studio to Yale University Art Gallery in exchange for an annuity. The most famous of his works there, and one of the most reproduced images in American art, is *The Declaration of Independence* (1786–97), in which most of the portraits were painted from life. His larger works are usually fairly stodgy, but his smaller pictures and sketches can be much livelier. Trumbull, who died an embittered old man, published an autobiography in 1841.

Tucker, William (1935–   ). British abstract sculptor. He was among the pupils of Anthony *Caro who created a new British sculptural avant-garde in the latter half of the 1960s. His work is in various materials and often makes striking use of colour. In 1974 he published *The Language of Sculpture*.

Tura, Cosmè (or **Cosimo**) (*c.*1430–95). Italian painter, the first major artist of the School of Ferrara, where he was appointed court painter to the *Estes in 1452. His sculptural figure style was derived in the first place from *Mantegna, though its tortuous, metallic quality was a product of Tura's own feverish imagination. He also acquired a feeling for monumentality from *Piero della Francesca, who was painting in Ferrara *c.*1449. Tura was mainly a religious painter, his work including two huge shutters (1469) for the organ of Ferrara Cathedral, now in the Museo del Duomo; they represent *The Annunciation* and *St George and the Princess*. Good examples of his work on a smaller scale are in the National Gallery, London. Tura was an important influence on the other two major painters of the 15th cent. Ferrarese School—*Cossa and *Roberti. The latter replaced him as court painter in 1486 and Tura died poor.

Turner, Joseph Mallord William (1775–1851). English painter, the most original genius in landscape painting during the 19th cent. A precocious artist, he was admitted to the *Royal Academy Schools in 1789 and exhibited his first water-colour at the Academy in 1790. From 1792 he began the practice of sketching tours, making topographical drawings of *picturesque and architectural subjects, views, and landscape, which he was able to sell to engravers or later work up into water-colours. At this time his work was more accurate but less personal and inventive than that of his friend *Girtin (with whom he worked for Dr *Monro). His first exhibited oil at the Academy was *Fishermen at Sea* (Tate, London, 1796), a work showing the influence of 17th-cent. Dutch marine painting.

The Dutch influence in Turner's work soon gave way to that of *Wilson and *Claude, but already in the early 1800s it was recognized that he was introducing a new and revolutionary approach to landscape. Besides showing attention to luminosity and atmosphere his painting became increasingly *Romantic in its dramatic subject-matter and sense of movement, culminating in the powerful *Shipwreck* (Tate, 1805). During these years he was also exhibiting pictures in a more conventional manner and was still working for engravers. From 1807 to 1819 he

published the seventy plates of his famous *Liber Studiorum*, conceived in emulation of Claude's *Liber Veritatis*. Between 1814 and 1830 he made a great many drawings, the result of systematic tours in England and abroad studying the effects of landscape. Turner had made his first journey to the Continent in 1802, visiting Paris like so many other painters to see the pictures looted by Napoleon, which were then on exhibition, and travelling through France to Switzerland. His next trip was in 1817; he visited Italy two years later and thereafter made periodic trips until 1845. The mountains and lakes of Switzerland and the haunting beauty of Venice were to provide him with the subjects for some of his most original compositions. He continued throughout life his habit of making rapid shorthand pencil jottings which he used later as reminders for imaginative compositions.

Turner's work was highly controversial and violently attacked by some, but he had many admirers and there were those who regarded him as the outstanding genius of the day. His most important patron was the third Earl of Egremont (1751–1837), who was unusual among collectors of the time in buying contemporary British art (sculpture as well as painting) on a large scale. Turner had a studio at Petworth, Egremont's country house in Sussex, and several of his paintings are still to be seen there (although their ownership was transferred to the Tate Gallery in 1984). Turner's other great champion was the young *Ruskin, who discovered his work in the 1830s and wrote eloquently of him in the first volume of *Modern Painters*, published in 1843. By this time Turner's brushwork had become breathtakingly free and some of his compositions were almost abstract, the forms dissolved in a haze of light and colour: 'He seems to paint with tinted steam, so evanescent and so airy,' wrote Constable. But his originality lay not only in those features in which he anticipated the *Impressionists. He went further than the Impressionists in his abstract organization of the phenomena of luminosity and he went further than any Romantic before him in the dramatic symbolization of the elements conceived as abstract forces. Late in life Turner became more and more of a recluse, sometimes calling himself Mr Booth (assuming the name of his mistress Sophia

Booth). The mystery surrounding his private life was increased when, after Turner's death, Ruskin destroyed many erotic drawings that he found among his works and which he thought tainted his hero's memory. Turner left a vast bequest of his work to the nation—some 300 paintings and more than 19,000 drawings and watercolours. These were principally divided between the Tate Gallery and British Museum, but in 1987 a new gallery—the Clore Gallery—was opened at the Tate to house the entire Turner Collection.

Turner Prize. See MORLEY.

turpentine. A *resinous liquid exuded from various species of pine, which in its distilled form ('spirits of turpentine') is the usual *diluent, or thinner, for *oil paint. There is no definite evidence that it was used before the 16th cent.

Twombly, Cy (1929–). American abstract painter and draughtsman, based in Rome since 1957. His distinctive style is characterized by apparently random scrawls and scribbles on white or black grounds. In his rejection of traditional ideas of composition he shows an affinity with the *All-over style initiated by Jackson *Pollock, though Twombly's work is looser and more disorganized than that of Pollock.

typology. In Christian *iconography a system whereby figures and scenes from the Old Testament were thought of as prefiguring those of the New Testament. It became the custom in biblical illustration for Old Testament 'types' to be juxtaposed with or subordinated to New Testament 'antitypes', to demonstrate visually that the promise of the Old Testament was fulfilled in the New. Thus Abraham's willingness to sacrifice his son Isaac was seen as foreshadowing God's sacrifice of Christ, and David was seen as a 'type' of Christ, his fight with Goliath prefiguring Christ's struggle with Satan. Occasionally Classical myths or other secular sources were also accepted as types. Typological illustration is found not only in book illustration, but in virtually every field of art throughout the Middle Ages (the earliest examples date from the 3rd cent.), and occasionally afterwards.

Uccello, Paolo (properly Paolo di Dono) (1396/7–1475). Florentine painter, one of the most distinctive artists of the early *Renaissance. *Vasari says he got his nickname (*uccello* means 'bird') because he loved animals, and birds in particular. His career is not well documented, and although he lived long he had few major commissions; to his contemporaries, as well as to many later critics, he appeared an eccentric figure. He is first documented in 1407 in the workshop of *Ghiberti, but he is not known to have worked as a sculptor. In 1425 he went to Venice, where he worked as a mosaicist, but nothing survives there that can be certainly associated with him. By 1432 he was back in Florence, and in 1436 he painted his first dated surviving work—a huge fresco in Florence Cathedral depicting an equestrian statue, a monument to the English *condottiere* Sir John Hawkwood (d. 1394). It demonstrated the fascination with *perspective that was central to his style. His two other large-scale works are a series of frescos on Old Testament themes (probably 1430s and 1440s) in the 'Green Cloister' of S. Maria Novella and a series of three panels (c.1455) on the *Battle of San Romano*, a minor Florentine victory against the Sienese in 1432. The pictures were painted for the Palazzo *Medici and are now separated, with one panel each in the National Gallery, London, the Louvre, Paris, and the Uffizi, Florence. Uccello's other works include the decoration of the clock-face and designs for stained-glass windows in Florence Cathedral, and two enchanting paintings that are generally considered to date from late in his career— *St George and the Dragon* (NG, London), one of the earliest known Italian paintings on canvas, and *The Hunt in the Forest* (Ashmolean, Oxford). Vasari says that 'he came to live a hermit's life', and in his tax return of 1469 Uccello described himself as 'old, without means of livelihood . . . and unable to work'.

Uccello's work presents a striking—and often captivating—combination of two seemingly opposing stylistic currents: the decorative tradition of *International Gothic and the scientific involvement with perspective of the early Renaissance. Vasari maintained that Uccello wasted his time 'on the finer points of perspective' and presents him as an amiable fanatic who worked into the night and when told to come to bed by his wife would reply: 'What a sweet mistress is this perspective!' He undoubtedly took his enthusiasm to extraordinary lengths (in the *Battle of San Romano* the broken weapons and even the corpses recede neatly in accordance with the perspective scheme), but his effects were appropriate to his subjects and to the decorative charm of his pictures rather than mere technical exercises. In *The Hunt in the Forest*, for example, he creates not only an atmosphere of fairy-tale romance, but also, through the way in which the horses and dogs move swiftly back into space, an exhilarating sense of darting energy. Uccello's name became so identified with the subject of perspective that he was often said to have invented it: *Ruskin, for example, wrote in a letter to Kate *Greenaway 'I believe the perfection of perspective is only recent. It was first applied in Italian art by Paul Uccello. He went off his head with love of perpective.'

Uden, Lucas van (1595–1672). Flemish landscape painter and engraver, active mainly in his native Antwerp. Although there is no firm evidence for the tradition that he worked in *Rubens's studio and painted landscape backgrounds for him, he was certainly strongly influenced by the master. His pictures are often large and have something of Rubens's sweep and richness. The figures were often added by other artists.

Udine, Giovanni da (1487–1561/4). Italian painter, decorative artist, and architect, born at Udine near Venice. He was one of *Raphael's leading assistants and is chiefly important for reviving antique techniques of *stucco and the ancient taste for *grotesques, inspired by archaeological discoveries in Rome. His light and graceful style, seen best in the Vatican Loggie (1517–19), was imitated all over Europe, particularly by *Neoclassical designers. From the 1530s he was based in Udine, but also worked in Florence, Venice, and Rome again.

Uffizi, Florence. The chief public gallery of Florence. The nucleus of the collection derives from the collections of the *Medici family, and the Uffizi Palace was begun by *Vasari in 1560 for Cosimo I, Grand Duke of Tuscany. The ground floor housed government offices (Italian *uffizi*), hence the building's name. In 1565 Vasari built the corridor over the Ponte Vecchio connecting the Uffizi with the *Pitti Palace. Subsequently the building has been much altered, enlarged, and restored (it was damaged in the Second World War and by flooding in 1966). The last of the Medici line, Maria Ludovica, Grand Duchess of Tuscany, bequeathed the family collections to the State of Tuscany in 1737, and in 1789 they were reorganized to allow regular public visiting. In the 19th cent. the Uffizi was subjected to radical reorganization. Much archaeological material was placed in the Archaeological Museum in the Palazzo della Crocetta, while the medieval and *Renaissance sculpture and the rich collection of *applied art was transferred to the *Bargello. The Uffizi collection on the other hand was enriched by early Italian paintings resulting from suppressions of churches and monasteries and confiscations of religious property. Although it is primarily famous for its incomparable representation of Florentine Renaissance painting, the Uffizi also has outstanding works from other Italian and non-Italian schools (for example, Hugo van der *Goes's Portinari Altarpiece) and important examples of *antique sculpture. The collection of prints and drawings in the Gabinetto dei Disegni e Stampe is one of the finest in the world, and the gallery of artists' self-portraits, begun by Cardinal Leopoldo de' Medici in the 17th cent., is unrivalled.

Ugo da Carpi (d. 1532). Italian painter and wood engraver, a pioneer of the *chiaroscuro woodcut. In 1516 he requested from the Venetian senate a patent for his method 'of making from woodcuts prints that seem as though painted', and although there are German examples earlier than any known by Ugo, he may have discovered the technique independently. Certainly his prints achieve their pictorial effect better than those of the Germans. They are often based on designs by *Raphael and *Parmigianino.

Ugolino di Nerio (active 1317–27). Sienese painter, a close follower of *Duccio. His only certain work is the high altarpiece for Sta Croce, Florence, which formerly bore the signature 'Ugolino da Siena' and is now widely dispersed. Several panels are in the National Gallery, London. *Vasari says he painted 'many pictures and chapels in all parts of Italy' and several paintings are attributed to him on stylistic grounds. His style was charming, but must have been something of an anachronism in the Florence of *Giotto's day.

Uhde, Wilhelm (1874–1947). German collector and writer on art. After studying at Munich and Florence, he settled in Paris in 1904. In 1905 he was buying pictures by *Picasso and *Braque at a time when these artists were practically unknown and in 1906 he was one of the first to discover the Douanier *Rousseau. He published the first monograph on Rousseau in 1910 and in 1912 organized the first retrospective exhibition of his works. Subsequently he was best known for discovering and encouraging other *naïve artists, such as *Bombois and *Séraphine.

Ukiyo-e. Japanese term, meaning 'pictures of the floating world', applied to the dominant movement in Japanese art of the 17th to 19th cents. It refers to the subjects from transient everyday life, with its ever-shifting fashions, favoured by printmakers at this time. Favourite subjects were theatre scenes, actors in well-known roles, and prostitutes and bath-house girls. Japanese prints first came to Europe in the 19th cent., and they had a great influence on avant-garde French artists, to whom their flat decorative colour and expressive pattern came as a revelation.

Underwood, Leon (1890–1975). British sculptor, painter, graphic artist, and writer. A versatile and original figure, Underwood was out of sympathy with the main trends of modernism, describing abstraction as 'artfully making emptiness less conspicuous'. Nevertheless, from the 1960s critics began to speak of him as the 'father of modern sculpture in Britain', in view of the streamlined stylized quality of bronzes such as *Torso: The June of Youth* (Tate, London, 1937) and the influence of his teaching at the *Royal College of Art and his own school, opened in 1923. Henry *Moore was among his pupils.

Unit One. A group of avant-garde British artists formed in 1933, its members including Barbara *Hepworth, Henry *Moore, Paul *Nash, and Ben *Nicholson. The group held one exhibition, in 1933, and a book, *Unit One: The Modern Movement in English Architecture, Painting and Sculpture*, edited by Herbert *Read, was published in 1934. The group had no common doctrine or programme and was breaking up by 1935. Despite its short life, however, it made a considerable impact on British art of the 1930s.

Utrillo, Maurice (1883–1955). French painter. The illegitimate son of Suzanne *Valadon, he was given the name by which he is known by the Spanish art critic Miguel Utrillo (1863–1934), who recognized him as his son in order to help him (*Puvis de Chavannes was said by some to have been his real father). He began to paint in 1902 under pressure from his mother, who hoped that it would remedy the alcoholism to which he had been a victim since his boyhood (in 1934 the Tate Gallery wrongly said that he had died of drink in that year, thus bringing on the Trustees' heads a libel suit, settled out of court). Valadon gave him his first lessons, but he was largely self-taught. He became highly successful in the 1920s and in his later years became deeply involved in religion. Utrillo was highly prolific, painting mainly street scenes in Montmartre. The period from about 1909 to the First World War is known as his 'white period' because of the predominance of milky tones in his pictures, and his best works are generally agreed to have come from this time. They subtly convey solitude and emotional emptiness and have a delicate feeling for tone and atmosphere, even though he often worked from postcards. His later work is livelier but less touching. Utrillo's work is in many museums and (no doubt because of the deceptive simplicity of his paintings) he is among the most forged of modern artists.

Uytewael, Joachim. See WTEWAEL.

V

Valadon, Suzanne (1865 or 1867–1938).
French painter. As a girl she worked as a
circus acrobat, but had to abandon this
after a fall and then became a model and
the reigning beauty of Montmartre. The
artists she posed for included *Renoir,
*Puvis de Chavannes, and *Toulouse-
Lautrec (each of whom numbered among
her lovers). Toulouse-Lautrec brought her
drawings to the attention of *Degas, who
encouraged her to develop her artistic
talent and she eventually became a successful painter. She owed little to formal
training or to the influence of the artists
with whom she associated and her painting
has a fresh and personal vision. Her subjects
included portraits and still lifes, but she
was at her best in figure paintings, which
often have a splendid earthy vigour and a
striking use of bold contour and flat colour.
A child of the people, she has been compared with the writer Colette for her
sharpness of eye and avidity for life. Maurice *Utrillo was her son.

Valdés Leal, Juan de (1622–90). Spanish
painter and engraver, born in Seville,
where he worked from 1656 after some
early years in Cordova. With *Murillo he
helped to found an *academy of painting
there in 1660, and after Murillo's death in
1682 he was the leading artist in the city.
Like Murillo, he was primarily a religious
painter, but he was very different in style
and approach. He had a penchant for
macabre or grotesque subject-matter, and
his style is characterized by feverish ex-
citability, with a vivid sense of movement,
brilliant colouring, and dramatic lighting.
His most remarkable works are two large
Allegories of Death (commissioned 1672) in
the Hospital de la Caridad, Seville. He also
*polychromed *Roldán's great altarpiece
in the Caridad.

Valenciennes, Pierre-Henri de (1750–
1819). French landscape painter and writer
on art. From 1769 to 1777 he lived in Italy
and his grand formal style was influenced
most notably by Nicolas *Poussin. He
became a leading upholder of the Classical
tradition in landscape painting, but he also
encouraged studying direct from nature.

Valentin, Moïse (*c.*1591–1632). French
*Caravaggesque painter active in Rome
from about 1612. His life is obscure; the
name 'Moïse' (the French form of Moses)
by which he was called was not his
Christian name (which is unknown) but a
corruption of the Italian form of 'monsieur'. He did, however, have one major
public commission—*The Martyrdom of SS.*
Processus and Martinian (Vatican, 1629–30),
painted for St Peter's as a pendant to
*Poussin's *Martyrdom of St Erasmus*. About
fifty works are attributed to him. They
vary in subject—religious, mythological,
and *genre scenes and portraits—but the
same models often seem to reappear in
them, and all his work is marked by an
impressively solemn, at times melancholic,
dignity. He was one of the finest of
Caravaggio's followers and one of the most
dedicated, still painting in his style when
it had gone out of fashion. *Baglione says
that he died after taking a cold bath in a
fountain following a drinking bout; his
death was much lamented in the artistic
community.

Valentiner, William (1880–1958). German-
American art historian, one of the foremost
connoisseurs of Dutch painting, on which
he published numerous books. From 1906
to 1908 he worked at the Berlin Museum
under *Bode, then moved to the *Metropolitan Museum in New York, where
one of his innovations was to ban the
attendants from smoking cigars while they
were on duty. He stayed there until 1914,
then served in the German army in the
First World War. At this time he knew
various German *Expressionist artists, notably *Schmidt-Rottluff, and helped to
make their work known in the USA. In
1921 Valentiner began working at the
Detroit Institute of Arts, of which he was
director from 1924 to 1945 and where he
commissioned murals from Diego *Rivera.

He was then director of the County Museum of Art in Los Angeles (1946–54) and the first director of the North Carolina Museum at Raleigh (1955–58). Valentiner also founded the periodical *The Art Quarterly* (1938).

Valkenborch (or **Valkenborgh**). Family of Netherlandish landscape and *genre painters, the most important members of which were **Lucas** (*c.*1530–97) and his younger brother **Marten** (1535–1612). Lucas joined the Malines Guild in 1560 and in 1565 was in Antwerp, whence he fled to Aix-la-Chapelle to avoid persecution (he was a Protestant). He worked for Archduke Matthias and accompanied him to Linz before settling in Frankfurt in 1593. Marten fled with his brother and returned to Antwerp before going to Frankfurt, Venice, and Rome. Both worked in the *Bruegel tradition, and both favoured the subject of the *Tower of Babel*. They also painted series of *The Seasons*, and their winter scenes are especially notable.

Vallotton, Félix (1865–1925). Swiss-born painter, graphic artist, sculptor, and writer who became a French citizen in 1900. In 1882 he settled in Paris and became a friend of *Bonnard and *Vuillard, exhibiting several times with the *Nabis. He painted portraits, nudes, interiors, and landscapes in a style that is essentially naturalistic but shows an almost abstract feeling for simplified form, influenced by his enthusiasm for Japanese prints (see UKIYO-E]. In about 1890 he began to make woodcuts, and with artists such as *Gauguin and *Munch he played a part in the revival of interest in the technique that took place in the early years of the 20th cent.

Vanderbank, John (1694–1739). English portrait painter. He had a considerable practice in London in the years immediately succeeding the death of *Kneller, and *Vertue says he started the fashion for depicting ladies in Rubens costume. His best work is vigorous, but often marred by sloppy handling. With Louis Chéron (1660–1725), a French painter, he deposed *Thornhill as head of the *St Martin's Lane Academy in 1720, but it became defunct within a few years.

Vanderlyn, John (1775–1852). American painter. He spent much of his career in Paris (he also visited Rome), and his style was nearer to the mainstream of European *Neoclassicism and *Romanticism than that of almost any other American painter of his generation. His best-known painting is *Ariadne Asleep on Naxos* (Pennsylvania Academy of Fine Arts, Philadelphia, 1814), a reclining figure in the tradition of the Venuses of *Giorgione and *Titian that is regarded as the finest American nude before *Eakins. Although such works won him considerable renown in France, he was much less successful in America, where he worked mainly as a portraitist, and he became embittered in his final years.

Vantongerloo, Georges (1886–1965). Belgian sculptor and painter. After being wounded in the First World War he was interned from 1914 to 1918 in the Netherlands. There he joined the De *Stijl group in 1917 and turned from the conventionally naturalistic style he had practised to abstract sculptures in which he applied the principles of *Neo-Plasticism to three dimensions. In 1919–27 he lived at Menton and then for the rest of his life in Paris, where he was involved in the *Cercle et Carré and *Abstraction-Création groups. From 1928 he designed architectural projects and in the 1940s he began using wire and perspex in his sculpture, exploring effects of light. His paintings were based on horizontal and vertical lines until 1937, when he introduced rhythmic curving lines, rejecting *Mondrian's idea that only constructions based on the right angle reflect the harmony of the universe.

Varley, John (1778–1842). English landscape painter in water-colour. A protégé of Dr *Monro and later a member of *Blake's circle, he represents the transition between tinted topographical drawing and the bolder, more fully developed manner of water-colour painting characteristic of the 19th cent. He was perhaps the most influential teacher of his day; his pupils included *Cox, *Linnell, and *Palmer, and he published several handbooks on technique. His brothers **Cornelius** (1781–1873) and **William** (1785?–1856) were also water-colourists and several descendants carried on the family tradition.

varnish. Solution, usually of *resin in oil or a synthetic equivalent, used in art either as a protective coat over the paint or as a *medium. Ideally varnish used as a protective coating should be colourless, transparent, without effect on the colours of the paint, and easily removed if it deteriorates. Varnishes have seldom possessed these qualities, and most have deteriorated and darkened with age. The removal of old and impacted varnishes without damage to the paint layers is one of the hardest tasks of the restorer.

Vasarely, Victor (1908–). Hungarian-born painter, active in France from 1930, the main originator and one of the leading practitioners of *Op art. *Moholy-Nagy was one of his teachers in Budapest before he moved to Paris in 1930. For the next decade he worked mainly as a commercial artist, particularly on the designing of posters, showing a keen interest in visual tricks such as *trompe-l'œil and space illusions. From 1943 he turned to painting and c.1947 he adopted the method of geometrical abstraction for which he is best known, exploring methods of creating a hallucinatory impression of movement through visual ambiguity, using for this purpose alternating positive–negative shapes interrupted in such a way as to suggest underlying secondary shapes. His fascination with the idea of movement led him to experiment with *Kinetic art and he also collaborated with architects in such works as his relief in aluminium for Caracas University (1954), and the French Pavilion at 'Expo' 67' in Montreal, hoping to create a kind of urban folk art. He has written a number of manifestoes, which, together with his paintings, have been a major influence on younger artists in his field. Vasarely has lived mainly in the south of France since 1961 and there are two museums dedicated to the artist in Provence: the Fondation Vasarely at Aix-en-Provence, which he designed himself, and the Château et Musée Vasarely at Gordes. There is also a Vasarely museum at Pécs, his home town in Hungary. Vasarely's son, **Jean-Pierre** (1934–), who works under the name Yvaral, is also an Op and Kinetic artist.

Vasari, Giorgio (1511–74). Italian painter, architect, and biographer, born at Arezzo and active mainly in Florence and Rome. In his day he was a leading painter, architect, and artistic impresario, but his activities in these fields have been completely overshadowed by his role as the most important of all biographers of Italian art. His great book, generally referred to as *Lives of the Artists*, is not only the fundamental source of information on Italian *Renaissance art, but also a key document in shaping attitudes about the period for centuries afterwards. (The book was first published in 1550 as *Le Vite de' più eccelenti architetti, pittori, et sculteri italiani*—The Lives of the Most Eminent Italian Architects, Painters, and Sculptors; a second, much enlarged edition appeared in 1568, in which the painters are mentioned first in the title.) Vasari wrote with a definite philosophy of art and art history. He believed that art is in the first instance imitation of nature and that progress in painting consists of the perfecting of the means of representation. He accepted the belief of Italian humanism that these had been taken to a high level of perfection in *Classical antiquity, that art had passed through a period of decline in the Middle Ages, and that it was revived and set once more on its true path by *Giotto. The main theme of the *Lives* was to set forth the revival of the true art in Tuscany by Giotto and *Cimabue, its steady progress at the hands of such artists as *Ghiberti, *Brunelleschi, and *Donatello, and its culmination with *Leonardo, *Raphael, and above all *Michelangelo, whom Vasari idolized and whose biography was the only one of a living artist to appear in the first edition of his book (the second edition includes accounts of several artists then living, as well as Vasari's own autobiography). The idea of artistic 'progress' he promulgated subsequently coloured most writing on the period. Although Vasari's testimony has often been impugned on particular points (see, for example, *Andrea del Sarto), he gathered together an enormous amount of invaluable information and presented it in a lively style, full of memorable anecdotes. Moreover, his qualitative judgements have generally stood the test of time well.

As a painter, Vasari was one of the most prolific decorators of his period, but he is not now highly regarded, his work representing the most in-bred and affected kind of *Mannerism. As an architect he has a higher reputation; his most important building is the *Uffizi in Florence. He designed and decorated his own house in

Arezzo, now a Vasari museum. Vasari was also the first important collector of drawings, using them partly as research material for his biographies, for the insight they gave into the creative process.

Vatican Museums. Institutions housing the enormous collections of antiquities and works of art accumulated by the papacy since the beginning of the 15th cent. As the leaders of the Christian Church the popes were continually showered with gifts; as political rulers they were, paradoxically, chief guardians of the remains of pagan Rome until Italy was unified in 1870. The Vatican collections are now among the largest and most important in the world, housed in a complex of buildings in the papal palace and elsewhere in the Vatican. There are several separate museums and the visitor to them is also admitted to the exhibition rooms of the Vatican Library and to various suites of *Renaissance painting, of which the most important are the Sistine Chapel, decorated by *Michelangelo and others, and the Stanze, decorated by *Raphael and others. The museums had their origin with Julius II (pontificate 1503–13), who placed some of the most famous works of *Classical sculpture in the Cortile del Belvedere (Belvedere Court), accessible to artists, connoisseurs, and scholars. However, it was not until 1734 that a museum proper was set up by Clement XII. Now, as then, the Vatican Museums are most famous for their Classical statues, including the *Apollo Belvedere, the *Belvedere Torso, and the *Laocoön, but they also contain great riches in, for example, Egyptian art, jewellery, and vestments. The Pinacoteca (picture gallery) has an impressive if somewhat haphazard collection, devoted mainly to Italian painting of the 13th cent. to the 17th cent. There is also a collection of modern religious art, most of it merely of curiosity value.

Vaughan, Keith (1912–77). British painter. In the 1940s he was one of the leading exponents of *Neo-Romanticism. His later work became grander and more simplified, moving towards abstraction (*Leaping Figure*, Tate, London, 1951). Vaughan also designed textiles and book-jackets.

Vecchietta (Lorenzo di Pietro) (c.1412–80). One of the outstanding Sienese artists of the 15th cent., a painter, sculptor, architect, and military engineer. He was probably trained by *Sassetta, but he also came under the influence of Florentine art and his large-scale paintings have a monumentality rare in Siena in the *quattrocento. As a sculptor he worked in wood and marble and late in his career in bronze, this change in medium reflecting the influence of *Donatello, who was in Siena 1457–9. *The Risen Christ* (Sta Maria della Scala, Siena, 1476) has something of Donatello's sinewy expressiveness. Donatello's influence may also account for the strength and plasticity of Vecchietta's later paintings, such as the *St Catherine* in the Town Hall, Siena, and the *Assumption* in Pienza Cathedral, both dating from 1461/2. Another side to Vecchietta's talent is seen in his delightful *illuminations in a manuscript of Dante's *Divine Comedy* (BL, London, c.1440).

veduta. Term (Italian: 'view') applied to a representation of a town or landscape that is essentially topographical in conception, specifically one that is faithful enough to allow the location to be identified (an imaginary but realistic-looking view can be called a *veduta ideata*). Painters of *vedute* (for example *Canaletto and *Guardi) are called *vedutisti*.

Veen, Otto van (1556–1629). Flemish painter born in Leiden. From c.1575 to c.1580 he was in Italy, where he was a pupil of Federico *Zuccaro, and after working in various places in Germany and Flanders he settled in Antwerp in 1592. He was an uninspired *Mannerist painter, but he had a successful career by modelling his work on Italian masters such as *Correggio and *Parmigianino (*The Mystic Marriage of St Catherine*, Musées Royaux, Brussels, 1589). His love of Italian art and his scholarly inclinations (he often Latinized his name to Vaenius) must have been appreciated by *Rubens, who had his final training in van Veen's studio.

vehicle. The liquid in which *pigment is suspended—the 'carrier'. The word can be applied to either the *medium or the *diluent, or to a mixture of both; thus the vehicle of *oil painting might be either *linseed oil, or *turpentine, or both together.

Velázquez (or **Velasquez**), **Diego** (1599–1660). The greatest painter of the Spanish School. He was born in Seville, where in 1610/11 he was apprenticed to *Pacheco (possibly following a brief period of study with *Herrera the Elder). In 1617 he qualified as a master painter and in the following year he married Pacheco's daughter. Velázquez was exceptionally precocious and while he was still in his teens he painted pictures that display commanding presence and complete technical mastery. Pacheco's style in religious works was Italianate, dry, and academic; Velázquez revitalized it by following his master's advice to 'go to nature for everything', and in works such as *The Immaculate Conception* (NG, London, c.1618) he developed a *naturalistic religious art in which the figures are portraits rather than *ideal types (his wife may be the model for the Virgin in both these pictures) and in which the light, while realistically observed, has a mysterious, spiritual quality. In their strong *chiaroscuro as well as their naturalism these pictures show an affinity with the work of *Caravaggio and his followers. The clotted but supple brushwork is, however, already entirely Velázquez's own. Contemporary with these religious works were a series of *bodegones, a type of *genre scene to which he brought a new seriousness and dignity, as in *The Waterseller of Seville* (Wellington Mus., London, c.1620).

In 1622 Velázquez paid a short visit to Madrid, during which he painted a portrait of the poet Luis de Góngora (Museum of Fine Arts, Boston). In the following year he was recalled to the capital by Philip IV's chief minister, the Count-Duke Olivares, who like Velázquez was a Sevillian. Velázquez painted a portrait of the king (now lost) that pleased Philip so much that he appointed him one of his court painters and declared that now only Velázquez should paint his portrait. Thus, at the age of 24, Velázquez had suddenly become the country's most prestigious painter, and he kept his position as the king's favourite unchallenged for the rest of his life. With his appointment as court painter, the direction of Velázquez's work changed. He entirely abandoned *bodegones*, and although he painted historical, mythological, and religious pictures intermittently throughout his career, he was from now on primarily a portraitist. Technically, too, his work changed as a result of his move to Madrid, his brushwork becoming broader and more fluid under the influence particularly of the *Titians in the royal collection. Although his portraits of the king and his courtiers are grand and dignified, he humanized the formal tradition of Spanish court portraiture derived from *Mor and *Coello. To this end he set his models in more natural poses, gave them greater life and character, and eliminated unnecessary accessories. The king (who was six years younger than Velázquez) had an extremely high opinion of the artist's personal qualities as well as his artistic skills, and the warmth with which he treated him was considered astonishing, given the stiff etiquette for which the Spanish court was renowned. In 1627 Philip made Velázquez 'Usher of the Chamber', the first of a series of appointments that brought him great prestige but took up much of his time in trivial bureaucratic matters, thus partially accounting for his fairly small output as a painter. He was conscientious in his duties, however, and apparently well suited to them temperamentally.

In 1628–9 *Rubens visited Spain on a diplomatic mission and he and Velázquez became friends. *Palomino records that the contact with Rubens 'revived the desire Velázquez had always had to go to Italy', and the king duly gave him permission to travel there. Velázquez was in Italy from 1629 to 1631, visiting Genoa, Venice, and Naples, but spending most of his time in Rome. Two major paintings date from this period—*Joseph's Coat* (Escorial, Madrid) and *The Forge of Vulcan* (Prado), works that show how his brushwork loosened still further under the influence of the great Venetian masters and how his mastery of figure composition matured. The 1630s and 1640s (before he again left for Italy) were the most productive period of Velázquez's career. His series of royal and court portraits continued and he expanded his range in a series of glorious equestrian portraits (Prado). In these he showed an unprecedented ability to attain complete atmospheric unity between foreground and background in the landscape. Their rhetorical poses are in the *Baroque tradition, but they are without bombast or allegorical embellishments and as portraits are characteristically direct. The same ability to look beyond external trappings to the human mystery beneath is seen in his incomparable series of portraits of the pitiful court fools (Prado)—dwarfs and idiots whom Philip, like other monarchs, kept for his amusement. Velázquez presents them without any suggestion of caricature, but with pathos and human understanding, as if they too are worthy of his respect. During the 1630s and 1640s Velázquez continued to paint religious and mythological works, but they are all eclipsed by his great masterpiece of contemporary history painting, *The Surrender of Breda* (Prado, 1634–5), one of a series of twelve paintings by various court artists glorifying the military triumphs of Philip's reign that were executed for the new Buen Retiro Palace in Madrid. The composition is highly organized, but Velázquez creates a remarkable sense of actuality and no earlier picture of a contemporary historical event had seemed so convincing. Characteristically, he concentrates on the human drama of the situation, as Ambrogio Spinola, the chivalrous Spanish commander, receives the key of the town from Justin of Nassau, his Dutch counterpart, with a superb gesture of magnanimity.

Between 1648 and 1651 Velázquez paid another visit to Italy in order to purchase paintings and antiques for the royal collection (he may have been there briefly in 1636 but the evidence is inconclusive). Again, he spent most of the time in Rome, where he painted several portraits, including two of his most celebrated works—*Juan de Pareja* (Met. Mus., New York, 1650) and *Pope Innocent X* (Doria Gal., Rome, 1650). Juan de Pareja (*c.*1610–*c.*1670), who was himself a painter, was Velázquez's mulatto slave (he granted him his freedom while they were in Rome), and Velázquez painted this portrait because he felt he needed some practice before tackling that of the pope. The *Innocent X* is by common consent one of the world's supreme masterpieces of portraiture, unsurpassed in its breathtaking handling of paint and so incisive in characterization that the pope himself said the picture was 'troppo vero' (too truthful). While in Rome Velázquez fathered an illegitimate son, Antonio, by a widow named Martha, but nothing is known of what became of mother or child. They may have been on Velázquez's mind when he applied for (and was refused) permission to return to Italy in 1657, but his life and work continued to unfold with the same serious dignity and the skeleton in his cupboard remained hidden until 1983, when the documentation was published.

In his final years in Madrid, Velázquez continued to acquire new honours (the greatest was being made a knight of the Order of Santiago in 1659) and to reach new heights as a painter. His last portraits of the royal family are mainly of the new young Queen, Mariana of Austria, and of the royal children. In these works his brushwork has become increasingly sparkling and free, and the gorgeous clothes the sitters wore (such a change from the sombre costumes of the king and male courtiers) allowed him to show his prowess as a colourist (several examples are in the Kunsthistoriches Museum, Vienna). Velázquez never ceased to base his work on scrutiny of nature, but his means grew increasingly subtle, so that detail is entirely subordinated to overall effect. Thus in his late works space and atmosphere are depicted with unprecedented vividness, but when the pictures are looked at closely the individual forms dissolve into blurred brush-strokes. As Palomino put it, 'one cannot understand it if standing too close, but from a distance it is a miracle'.

The culmination of his career is *Las Meninas* (The Maids of Honour) (Prado, *c.*1656). It shows Velázquez at his easel, with various members of the royal family and their attendants in his studio, but it is not clear whether he has shown himself at work on a portrait of the king and queen (who are reflected in a mirror) when interrupted by the Infanta Margarita and her maids of honour or vice versa. Velázquez's prominence in the picture seems to assert his own importance and his pride in his art, but in the background he has included two pictures by Rubens showing the downfall of mortals who challenge the gods in the arts. Apparently spontaneous but in the highest degree worked out, it is both Velázquez's most complex essay in portraiture and an expression of the high claims he made for the dignity of his art. Luca *Giordano called it 'the Theology of Painting' because 'just as theology is superior to all other branches of knowledge, so is this the greatest example of painting'. Posterity has endorsed his verdict, for in a poll of artists and critics in *The Illustrated London News* in August 1985, *Las Meninas* was voted — by some margin — 'the world's greatest painting'.

The number of good contemporary copies of Velázquez's work indicates that he ran a busy studio, but of his pupils only his son-in-law *Mazo achieved any kind of distinction. As with most Spanish painters, Velázquez remained little known outside his own country until the Napoleonic Wars, but from the early 19th cent. the technical freedom of his work made him an inspiration to progressive artists, above all *Manet, who regarded him as the greatest of all painters. Most of Velázquez's work is still in Spain, and his genius can be fully appreciated only in the Prado, which has most of his key masterpieces. Outside Spain, he is best represented in London—in the National Gallery, which has his only surviving female nude, the *Rokeby Venus* (c.1648), in the Wellington Museum, and in the Wallace Collection.

Velde, Esaias van de (c.1591–1630). Dutch painter, one of the most important figures in the development of the tradition of naturalistic landscape painting in his country. He was born in Amsterdam, where he was perhaps the pupil of Gillis van *Coninxloo, and worked in Haarlem and The Hague. His earliest works are in the *Mannerist tradition, but by 1615 he had already moved away from the panoramic effect and high point of view of his predecessors. His fresh brushwork and directness of vision herald the subsequent accomplishment of his pupil Jan van *Goyen and of Salomon van *Ruysdael. Esaias was also an excellent etcher and draughtsman. There were other artists in his family, but he was not related to Willem van de *Velde.

Velde, Willem van de the Elder (1611–93). Dutch marine painter. He was the son of a naval captain, his brother was a skipper of merchant vessels, and he himself spent part of his youth as a sailor before devoting himself to the drawing and painting of ships. His pictures, which are frequently *grisailles, contain faithful and detailed portraits of ships (of much value to naval historians) and for a time he was an official artist for the Dutch fleet. In 1672, when the Netherlands were at war with England, he went to London and entered the service

of Charles II; why he left his country at a critical moment in its fortunes remains a mystery. **Willem the Younger** (1633–1707), his son, is one of the most illustrious of all marine painters. He was the pupil of his father and Simon de *Vlieger. Like his father, he gave very accurate portrayals of ships, but is distinguished from him by his feeling for atmosphere and majestic sense of composition. Father and son left Amsterdam for England in 1672 and in 1674 Charles II gave them a yearly retaining fee of £100 each; the father received his 'for taking and making draughts of seafights' and the son 'for putting the said draughts into colours for our own particular use'. They did not switch their allegiance to England completely; both subsequently painted pictures of naval battles for the Dutch as well as the English market. Willem the Younger's influence, however, was particularly great in England, where the whole tradition of marine painting stemmed from him. **Adriaen** (1636–72), Willem II's younger brother, was a versatile and prolific artist in spite of his short life. His father and Jan *Wijnants were his teachers. He painted various types of landscapes (most notably some fresh and atmospheric beach scenes) and also religious and mythological works, portraits, and animal pictures. He also did exceptionally fine etchings of landscapes with cattle and often painted the figures into the landscapes of other artists, notably *Hobbema and *Ruisdael.

vellum. See PARCHMENT.

Venus de Milo. A marble statue of Aphrodite, the best-known of all ancient statues, found on the island of Melos (or Milos) in 1820 and now in the Louvre. A plinth found with the statue was signed '. . . andros [Alexandros or Agasandros] of Antioch on the Maeander', but nothing is known of the sculptor. Originally the statue was thought to date from the *Classical age of Greek sculpture, but it is now put appreciably later—c.100 BC—and is thought to be a sophisticated combination of older styles—the goddess's head derives from the later 5th cent. BC, her nudity from the 4th cent., and her spiral, omnifacial posture from the *Hellenistic age. The *Venus de Milo* arrived in the Louvre (1821) soon after the *Medici Venus* had been returned to Italy (1815), and its enormous fame stemmed from French determination to persuade the world that they had gained a greater treasure than they had lost; Martin Robertson (*A History of Greek Art*, 1975) writes that its reputation 'which started by propaganda has become perpetuated by habit'. Many 19th-cent. critics went into raptures about the figure, which was thought to represent the apogee of female beauty, combining grandeur with gracefulness, but *Renoir described it as a 'big gendarme'. The statue's arms are missing and many conjectures have been made as to what the goddess might have been holding: it has been suggested for example that she is intended as Venus Victrix, and so would have been shown with the golden apple presented to her by Paris when he adjudged her more beautiful than her rivals Juno and Minerva.

Verhaecht, Tobias (1561–1631). Flemish painter, now remembered almost solely because he was *Rubens's first teacher. Apart from a sojourn in Italy as a young man, Verhaecht spent his career in his native Antwerp. He was a landscape specialist, working in a style similar to Paul *Bril's, and had no detectable influence on his great pupil.

Verhulst, Rombout (1624–98). Flemish sculptor active mainly in Holland. In the 1650s he was the most important assistant to Artus *Quellin in the sculptural decoration of the Town Hall in Amsterdam. In 1663 he settled in The Hague, where he became a leading sculptor of busts and tombs. The noble and sensitively cut monument to Admiral Michiel de Ruyter (1681) in the Niewe Kerk in Amsterdam is perhaps his masterpiece.

verism. An extreme form of *realism, in which the artist makes it his aim to reproduce with rigid truthfulness the exact appearance of his subject and repudiates idealization and all imaginative interpretation. The term has been applied, for example, to the most realistic Roman portrait sculpture. It has also been applied to that form of *Surrealism which claims to reproduce hallucination in exact and unselective detail.

Vermeer, Jan (1632–75). Dutch painter. Among the great Dutch artists of the 17th cent., he is now second in renown only to

*Rembrandt, but he made little mark during his lifetime and then long languished in obscurity. Almost all of the contemporary references to him are in colourless official documents and his career is in many ways enigmatic. Apart from a visit to The Hague in 1672 (to act as an expert witness concerning a group of Italian paintings of disputed authenticity), he is never known to have left his native Delft. He entered the painters' guild there in 1653 and was twice elected 'hooftman' (headman), but his teacher is not known. His name is often linked with that of Carel *Fabritius, but it is doubtful if he can have formally taught Vermeer, and this distinction may belong to Leonaert *Bramer, although there is no similarity between their work. Only about thirty-five to forty paintings by Vermeer are known, and although some early works may have been destroyed in the disastrous Delft magazine explosion of 1654, it is unlikely that the figure was ever much larger; this is because most of the Vermeers mentioned in early sources can be identified with surviving pictures, whilst only a few pictures now attributed to him are not mentioned in these sources—thus there are few loose ends. This small output may be at least partially explained by the fact that he almost certainly earned most of his living by means other than painting. His father kept an inn and was a picture-dealer and Vermeer very likely inherited both businesses. In spite of this he had grave financial troubles (he had a large family to support—his wife bore him eleven children), and his widow was declared bankrupt in the year after his death.

Only three of Vermeer's paintings are dated—*The Procuress* (Gemäldegalerie, Dresden, 1656), *The Astronomer* (private coll., 1668), and its companion piece *The Geographer* (Städelsches Kunstinstitut, Frankfurt, 1669)—and it is difficult to fit the others into a convincing chronology. (Another signed and dated work, *St Praxedis mopping up the Blood of the Martyrs* of 1655, has recently been discovered, but is of doubtful authenticity. It is in a private collection.) Nevertheless, his work divides into three fairly clear phases. The first is represented by only two works—*Christ in the House of Mary and Martha* (NG of Scotland, Edinburgh) and *Diana and her Companions* (Mauritshuis, The Hague)—both probably dating from a year or two before *The Procuress*. They are so different from Vermeer's other works—in their comparatively large scale, their subject-matter, and their handling—that *Diana and her Companions* was long attributed to the obscure Jan Vermeer of Utrecht (*c.*1630–after 1692), in spite of a genuine signature. *The Procuress* marks the transition to the middle phase of Vermeer's career, for although it is fairly large and warm in tonality—like the two history paintings—it is a contemporary life scene, as were virtually all Vermeer's pictures from now on. In the central part of his career (into which most of his work falls) Vermeer painted those serene and harmonious images of domestic life that for their beauty of composition, handling, and treatment of light raise him into a different class from any other Dutch genre painter. The majority show one or two figures in a room lit from the onlooker's left, engaged in domestic or recreational tasks. The predominant colours are yellow, blue, and grey, and the compositions have an abstract simplicity which confers on them an impact out of relation to their small size. In reproduction they can look quite smooth and detailed, but Vermeer often applies the paint broadly, with variations in texture suggesting the play of light with exquisite vibrancy—the critic Jan Veth aptly described his paint surface as looking like 'crushed pearls melted together'. From this period of Vermeer's greatest achievement also date his only landscape—the incomparable *View of Delft* (Mauritshuis), in which he surpassed even the greatest of his specialist contemporaries in lucidity and truth of atmosphere—and his much-loved *Little Street* (Rijksmuseum, Amsterdam). Another painting of this period is somewhat larger in scale and unusual in subject for him—*The Artist's Studio* (Kunsthistorisches Mus., Vienna), in which Vermeer shows a back view of a painter, perhaps a suitably enigmatic self-portrait. In the third and final phase of his career Vermeer's work lost part of its magic as it became somewhat harder. There are still marvellous passages of paint in all his late works, but the utter naturalness of his finest works is gone. The only one of his paintings that might be considered a failure, the *Allegory of Faith* (Met. Mus., New York), belongs to this period. His wife was a Catholic and he may well have been converted to her religion, but this rather lumbering figure shows he was not at ease with the trappings of *Baroque allegory. There are symbolic references in other of his paintings, but they all—except for this one—make sense on a straightforward naturalistic level.

No drawings by Vermeer are known and little is known of his working method. It seems likely, however, that he made use of a *camera obscura, as the exaggerated perspective in some of his pictures (in which foreground figures or objects loom unexpectedly large) and the way in which sparkling highlights sometimes appear slightly out of focus are effects duplicated by unsophisticated lenses. The scientist Antony van Leeuwenhoek (1632–1723), celebrated for his work with microscopes, became the executor of Vermeer's estate and it may well have been an interest in optics that brought them together.

Vernet. Family of French painters, three members of which attained distinction. **Claude-Joseph Vernet** (1714–89) was one of the leading French landscape painters of his period. From 1733 to 1753 he worked in Rome, where he was influenced by the light and atmosphere of *Claude and also by the more *picturesque and dramatic art of Salvator *Rosa. With Hubert *Robert, he became a leading exponent of a type of idealized and somewhat sentimental landscape that had a great vogue at this time. Vernet was particularly celebrated for his paintings of the sea-shore and ports, and on returning to Paris in 1753 he was commissioned by Louis XV to paint a series of the sea-ports of France. The sixteen which he did are in the Louvre. **Antoine-Charles-Horace**, known as 'Carle' (1758–1836), son of the foregoing, painted large battle pictures for Napoleon (*The Battle of Marengo; Morning of Austerlitz*; both at Versailles), and after the restoration of the monarchy he became official painter to Louis XVIII, for whom he did racing and hunting scenes. **Émile-Jean-Horace Vernet** (1789–1863), known as Horace Vernet, son of the foregoing, was one of the most prolific of French military painters, specializing in scenes of the Napoleonic era. A portrait of Napoleon and four battle-pieces by him are in the National Gallery, London. He also did animal and oriental subjects. From 1828 to 1835 he was Director of the French Academy in Rome.

Veronese, Paolo (Paolo Caliari) (*c.*1528–88). Italian painter, born at Verona (from which his nickname derives), but active in Venice from about 1553 and considered a member of the Venetian school. With *Tintoretto he became the dominant figure in Venetian painting in the generation after *Titian and he had many major commissions, both religious and secular. He soon established a distinctive style and thereafter developed relatively little. Few of his paintings are dated or can be reliably dated, so his chronology is difficult to construct. Similarly, because he had such a highly organized studio and his output was so large, there can be problems in distinguishing the work of his own hand. Nevertheless, his status and achievement are clear. He was one of the greatest of all decorative artists, delighting in painting enormous pageant-like scenes that bear witness to the material splendour of Venice in its Golden Age. Marble columns and costumes of velvet and satin abound in his work, and he used a sumptuous but delicate palette in which pale blue, orange, silvery white, and lemon yellow predominate. He painted many religious scenes as well as mythological and allegorical works (and portraits), but his penchant was for feast scenes from the Bible rather than incidents from Christ's Passion. His love of richness and ornament got him into trouble with the Inquisition in a famous incident when he was taken to task for crowding a painting of the *Last Supper* with such irrelevant and irreverent figures as 'a buffoon with a parrot on his wrist . . . a servant whose nose was bleeding . . . dwarfs and similar vulgarities'. Veronese staunchly defended his right to artistic license: 'I received the commission to decorate the picture as I saw fit. It is large and, it seemed to me, it could hold many figures.' He was instructed to make changes, but the matter was resolved by changing the title of the picture to *The Feast in the House of Levi* (Accademia, Venice, 1573).

Veronese's other great works include the delightfully light-hearted frescos (including *illusionistic architecture and enchanting landscapes) decorating the Villa Barbaro at Maser, near Treviso (*c.*1561) and the resplendent *Triumph of Venice* (*c.*1585) in the ceiling of the Hall of the Great Council in the Doges' Palace, Venice. His studio was carried on after his death by his brother and sons. He had no significant pupils, but his influence on Venetian painting was important, particularly in the 18th cent., when he was an inspiration to the masters of the second great flowering of decorative painting in the city, above all *Tiepolo.

Verrio, Antonio (*c.*1639–1707). Italian decorative painter who settled in England in about 1671 after working in France and enjoyed an enormously successful and well-remunerated career. He was much employed by the Crown—at Whitehall Palace, Windsor Castle, and Hampton Court—and also worked at great houses such as Burghley and Chatsworth. His success was based on his self-assertiveness and the lack of native talent in his field rather than on his skills as an artist, for his work is at best mediocre (and often dismal) judged by European standards. *Laguerre, his one-time assistant, was a better painter but had less worldly success.

Verrocchio, Andrea del (Andrea di Cioni) (*c.*1435–88). Florentine sculptor, painter, and metalworker, one of the outstanding Italian artists of his period. His nickname—Verrocchio means 'true eye'—refers not to his sharpness of vision, but to the fact that as a youth he had been the protégé of an ecclesiastic of that name. He is said to have studied in *Donatello's workshop, but his main training was as a goldsmith, and delicacy of craftsmanship is one of the salient features of his work. Only one work in precious metal by him survives, however—a silver *relief of the *Beheading of John the Baptist* (1477–80), done for the Baptistery in Florence and now in the Cathedral Museum. His major activity was as a sculptor, principally in bronze, but also in marble and *terracotta, and his two most famous works rank with the statues of Donatello that inspired them among the great masterpieces of Italian sculpture, whilst also showing the great differences in approach between the two artists. Verrocchio's *David* (Bargello, Florence, *c.*1475) is more refined, but less broodingly intense than Donatello's *David* in the same museum, and Verrocchio's masterpiece, the equestrian statue of the *condottiere* Bartolomeo Colleoni in Venice (begun 1481, completed after Verrocchio's death), has a magnificent sense of movement and swagger, but less of the heroic dignity of Donatello's *Gattemelata* statue

491 VIEN, JOSEPH-MARIE

in Padua. It is much harder to assess Verrocchio's stature as a painter as very few works exist that can be convincingly assigned to his own hand. Nevertheless numerous paintings came from his workshop, which was the largest in Florence at this time, and he trained distinguished painters, most notably *Leonardo da Vinci, who assisted his master with the *Baptism of Christ* (Uffizi, Florence, c.1470), one of the few paintings indisputably by Verrocchio. Leonardo took his superb craftsmanship from Verrocchio and also shared his fascination with two contrasting types—the tough old warrior (as in the *Colleoni* monument) and the epicene youth (as in the *David*). Leonardo's enormous fame has tended to cast a shadow over Verrocchio, but he is generally regarded as the greatest Italian sculptor between Donatello and *Michelangelo.

Vertue, George (1684–1756). English engraver and antiquarian. He was a prolific engraver of portraits and antiquarian subjects (he was official engraver to the Society of Antiquaries, 1717–56), but is important chiefly for the voluminous notes he collected for a history of art in England (now in the BM, London). A marvellously rich storehouse of information, they were used by Horace *Walpole as a basis for his *Anecdotes of Painting in England* (1762–71) and have been published separately (6 vols., 1930–55).

Victoria and Albert Museum, London. One of the world's greatest and most varied collections of *fine and *applied art. It was the brainchild of Prince Albert and developed out of the Great Exhibition (1851), the profits from which were used to buy a site in South Kensington for a cultural centre of museums and colleges. The Museum of Ornamental Art (as it was originally called) was opened by Queen Victoria on the present site in 1857. The nucleus of the collection consisted of objects of applied art bought from the Great Exhibition, which had been temporarily displayed in a Museum of Manufacturers in Marlborough House. Albert's ideal was to improve the standard of design in Britain by making the finest models available to study. A new building on the same site was begun in 1899, designed by Sir Aston Webb, and the name of the Museum was changed to 'The Victoria and Albert

Museum' at the ceremony of laying the foundation-stone by Queen Victoria. The new buildings were opened by King Edward VII in 1909. At this time the scientific collections were assigned to a separate Science Museum. The collections of the V&A are exceedingly rich, incorporating the national collections of post-*Classical sculpture (excluding modern), of British *miniatures, of *water-colours, and English silversmiths' work. The National Art Library is also part of the museum. There are great collections of, for example, ceramics, furniture, and musical instruments, and Oriental art is strongly represented. The highlights of the collection include the tapestry *cartoons by *Raphael (on loan from the Royal Collection), which form the most important ensemble of High *Renaissance art outside Italy; the representation of Italian Renaissance sculpture (again the finest outside Italy); and the collection of *Constable's work—the largest anywhere. The V&A has five branch museums in London: the Bethnal Green Museum of Childhood; Ham House; Osterley Park House; the Theatre Museum; and the Wellington Museum.

Victory of Samothrace. Celebrated larger-than-life Greek marble statue (Louvre, Paris) representing winged Victory (Nike) alighting on the bows of a galley. The figure, discovered on the island of Samothrace in 1863, is lithely outstretched and draped with magnificent swirls. Erected around 200 BC above a rocky pool, it showed its best view obliquely and from below, and now is appropriately and dramatically placed at the top of the main staircase in the Louvre.

Vien, Joseph-Marie (1716–1809). French painter. A winner of the *Prix de Rome, he was in Rome at a time (1743–50) coinciding with excavations at Herculaneum and Pompeii, and in his lifetime he gained a great reputation (partly self-promoted) as a pioneer of the *Neoclassical style. He was enthusiastic for the ideas of *Winckelmann, but his *Classicism was of a very superficial kind, consisting of prim and sentimentalized anecdote or allegory with pseudo-antique trappings (*The Cupid Seller*, Château de Fontainebleau, 1763). Nevertheless, he gauged the taste of the time well and had a career of exemplary success, becoming director of the French

Academy in Rome (1776) and First Painter to the King (1789). He was made a senator by Napoleon after the Revolution, a count in 1808, and was buried in the Panthéon. *David was his most important pupil. His son, **Joseph-Marie the Younger** (1762–1848), was also a painter, mainly of portraits.

Vigée-Lebrun, Élisabeth (1755–1842). French portrait painter, daughter and pupil of the pastellist **Louis Vigée** (1715–67). She was also taught by Claude-Joseph *Vernet and *Greuze and in 1776 she married the picture dealer Jean-Baptiste Lebrun. Renowned for her beauty, wit, and charm as well as for her talent, she had a highly successful career, becoming a friend of Queen Marie-Antoinette, whom she portrayed many times. On the outbreak of the Revolution she left France (1789), travelling to Italy (1789–93), Vienna (1793–4), and St Petersburg (1795–1802), before returning to Paris (1802). Disliking the Napoleonic regime she left almost immediately and stayed in England (1802–5), the Netherlands, and Switzerland (1805–9) before returning once again to Paris. She received distinguished patronage wherever she went and was admitted to several *academies. Her work is graceful, charming, pleasingly sentimental, and delicately executed. There are good examples in the Louvre. Her memoirs (3 vols., 1835–7) give a lively picture of the Europe of her day as well as an account of her own works, and vividly demonstrate what a redoubtable woman she was: 'on the day that my daughter was born I never left my studio and I went on working ... in the intervals between labour pains.'

Vigeland, Gustav (1869–1943). The most famous of Norwegian sculptors. He studied in Oslo and Copenhagen and then (1892–5) in Paris and Italy, spending a few months with *Rodin. The painstakingly naturalistic style he developed at this time developed in the direction of expressive stylization when he devoted himself in 1900 to the study of medieval sculpture in preparation for restoration work on Trondheim Cathedral. In the same year he made his first sketches for the massive project that occupied him for the rest of his life and which he left unfinished at his death—a series of allegorical groups centred on a fountain at Frogner Park, Oslo. The symbolism of the scheme is not clear, but essentially it represents 'a statement of the doubt, disillusion, and physical decline that beset humanity in its passage through this world' (G. H. Hamilton, *Painting and Sculpture in Europe: 1880–1940*). Reactions to the whole megalomaniac conception, involving scores of bronze and granite figures, have been mixed since the figures were finally installed in 1944, some critics finding it stupendous, others tasteless and monotonous.

Vignon, Claude (1593–1670). French painter and engraver. His richly eclectic style was formed mainly in Italy, where he worked c.1616–c.1623, and his openness to very diverse influences was later fuelled by his activities as a picture dealer. Paradoxically, in view of his varied sources of inspiration, his style is the most distinctive of any French painter of his generation—highly coloured and often bizarrely expressive. *Elsheimer and the *Caravaggisti were strong influences on his handling of light, and his richly encrusted brushwork has striking affinities with *Rembrandt, whose work he is known to have sold. There are examples of his work in the Louvre. Vignon is said to have fathered more than twenty children by his two wives, and his sons **Claude the Younger** (1633–1703) and **Philippe** (1638–1701) were also painters.

Villon, Jacques (Gaston Duchamp) (1875–1963). French painter, the elder brother of Raymond *Duchamp-Villon and Marcel *Duchamp. He changed his name because of his admiration for the 15th-cent. poet François Villon. As a young man he studied law and worked as a newspaper illustrator. From 1904 he exhibited at the *Salon d'Automne of which he was a founding member. His painting was influenced by *Cubism and he became a leader of the *Section d'Or group. In the late 1920s he evolved a technique of abstraction in which he claimed to represent the essence of objects by 'signs' rather than by reproducing their properties; his work became more naturalistic from c.1934 and it was not until the 1950s that he developed a style of abstraction without relation to natural appearances. Villon lived much of his life in comparative obscurity, but after the Second World War he achieved recognition and honours.

Vinckboons, David (1576–1631/3). Flemish-born painter active in Amsterdam. He painted landscapes and *genre scenes and is a transitional figure between the decorative and imaginative *Mannerist tradition and the more naturalistic style associated with 17th-cent. Dutch painting. His early genre pictures depicting village festivals reveal the influence of Pieter *Bruegel, and Vinckboons is credited with introducing some of his motifs into Holland. It has been asserted that Vinckboons's works can always be identified by the presence of a finch (*vinck*) in a tree (*boom*), but the painstaking student usually finds that the bird has flown.

Vingt, Les (**Les XX**). Group of twenty progressive Belgian painters and sculptors who exhibited together from 1884 to 1893. The members included James *Ensor and Jan *Toorop. They showed not only their own work, but also paintings by non-Belgian artists such as *Cézanne, van *Gogh, and *Seurat. The group was influential in spreading the ideas of *Neo-Impressionism and *Post-Impressionism and became the main Belgian forum for *Symbolism and *Art Nouveau.

Vischer. Family of German sculptors active in Nuremberg. **Hermann the Elder** (d. 1488) established the family bronze-foundry, and the business was inherited by his son **Peter the Elder** (c.1460–1529), the best-known of the Vischers. He was assisted by four sons: **Hermann the Younger** (1486–1517), **Peter the Younger** (1487–1528), **Hans** (c.1489–1550), and **Georg** (1520–92). The masterpiece of the Vischer workshop is the spectacular bronze shrine over the sarcophagus of St Sebald in the church dedicated to him in Nuremberg. The first design by Peter the Elder (Academy, Vienna) dates from 1488, but actual work began only in 1508 and was carried on till 1519. Through journeys of the younger generation the workshop had by that time gained a good deal of knowledge of Italian bronzes and in particular the work of north Italian sculptors. Thus the Sebald tomb became a fascinating mixture of *Gothic and *Renaissance styles. The canopy remained Gothic, as also the main figures of the Apostles standing before the supports; but both the base and the *baldacchino* were inhabited by biblical, mythological, and decorative figures conceived in a genuine Renaissance spirit. Peter the Elder included a celebrated self-portrait (complete with tools and leather apron) among these figures. Peter the Elder also made two splendid free-standing figures (1512–13) of Theodoric and King Arthur for the tomb of the emperor Maximilian I in the Hofkirche, Innsbruck. **Georg** (c.1520–92), a son of Hans, seems to have specialized in small decorative bronzes such as ink-wells.

Vittoria, Alessandro (1525–1608). Italian sculptor, born at Trent and active from 1543 in Venice. There he was the pupil of Jacopo *Sansovino, whom he succeeded as the leading monumental sculptor in the city, continuing his master's style but giving it a more *Mannerist character. He worked extensively in the Doges' Palace both before and after the fire of 1577, executing, for example, the *stuccoed ceiling of the Scala d'Oro (1555–9) and three statues in the Sala delle Quattri Porte (1587). Other examples of his work are in many Venetian churches. He also produced small elongated bronze figures of great elegance and realistic portrait busts of Venetian personalities.

Vivarini. Family of Venetian painters. **Antonio** (c.1420–76/84) seldom worked independently. He collaborated first with his brother in law, **Giovanni d'Alemagna** (active 1441–49/50), and secondly with his own younger brother, **Bartolomeo** (c.1432–c.1499). Their pictures usually took the form of large-scale *polyptychs with stiff, archaic-looking figures and very elaborate carved and gilded frames in the *Gothic tradition. Bartolomeo's independent works date from the 1460s onwards. He continued to paint polyptychs, but he modernized his style to a certain extent by imitating *Mantegna. **Alvise** (c.1445–1503/5), son of Antonio, was probably trained by his uncle, but later adopted the manner of Giovanni *Bellini, with whom he worked (1488) on paintings (now lost) for the Doges' Palace in Venice. None of the three had much originality. There are examples of the work of all three in the National Gallery, London.

Vivin, Louis (1861–1936). French *naïve painter. He worked in the Post Office from 1881 until his retirement at the age of

62, but had a passion for painting from childhood. In 1925 he was 'discovered' by Wilhelm *Uhde and won wide recognition. He painted *genre scenes, hunting scenes, flower pieces, and latterly views of Paris in a meticulously realistic manner, depicting every brick with precise neatness.

Vlaminck, Maurice de (1876–1958). French painter, graphic artist, and writer. As a young man he earned his living mainly as a violinist, painting in his spare time virtually without instruction. Indeed, he delighted to inveigh against all forms of academic training and boasted that he had never set foot inside the *Louvre. In 1901 the exhibition of van *Gogh's work in Paris overwhelmed him, intensifying his love of pure colour, and with *Matisse and *Derain he became a leading exponent of *Fauvism, often using paint straight from the tube in vigorous and exuberant compositions—mainly landscapes. From 1908 his palette darkened and he sought to achieve volume and a more solid basis of composition from a study of *Cézanne. After the First World War he moved from Paris and worked in isolation in the countryside. His style in his later work became rather slick and mannered. Vlaminck was a colourful character. He wrote novels and memoirs and was a pioneer collector of African art, although it had no influence on his style.

Vlieger, Simon de (c.1600–53). Dutch painter, mainly of marine subjects, active in his native Rotterdam, Delft, and Amsterdam. One of the outstanding marine painters of his period, he moved from stormy subjects in the manner of *Porcellis to serene and majestic images that influenced van de *Cappelle and Willem van de *Velde the Younger. De Vlieger also painted a few landscapes and *genre pictures.

Vollard, Ambroise (1865–1939). French dealer, connoisseur, art publisher, and writer on art, famous as a champion of avant-garde art. In 1893 he opened a gallery in Paris and in 1895 he gave the first important exhibition of *Cézanne. From that time the gallery became the centre of innovative art in the city, other landmark events including the first one-man exhibitions of *Picasso (1901) and *Matisse (1904). Vollard was the first to commission prominent artists to illustrate literary classics and contemporary works, publishing volumes which were of interest primarily for the illustrations. His portrait was painted many times, among others by Cézanne, *Renoir, Picasso, *Rouault, and *Bonnard. Vollard's writings included books on Cézanne and *Degas and the autobiographical *Recollections of a Picture Dealer* (1936).

Vorticism. A short-lived British avant-garde art movement originating just before the First World War. The central figure of Vorticism was Wyndham *Lewis, who edited its review—*Blast*—and later claimed that 'Vorticism . . . was what I, personally, did, and said, at a certain period.' His harsh, angular, mechanistic style was, however, shared by other artists in his circle, among them the painters *Nevinson, *Roberts, and *Wadsworth, and sculptors *Epstein and *Gaudier-Brzeska. Vorticism was strongly influenced by *Cubism and *Futurism; the name was coined by the poet Ezra Pound, perhaps in reference to a statement by the Futurist artist *Boccioni that all artistic creation must originate in a state of emotional vortex. Only one Vorticist exhibition was held, in 1915, and the movement did not survive the First World War (an attempt to revive it in 1920 as Group X proved abortive). However, it is of great significance as the first organized movement towards abstraction in English art and it subsequently had a strong influence on the development of British modernism.

Vos, Cornelis de (1584?–1651). Flemish painter, active in Antwerp. He painted historical, allegorical, mythological, and religious works, but excelled chiefly as a portraitist, in a style derived from *Rubens and van *Dyck. His finest paintings are his portraits of children, which have great sensitivity and charm without lapsing into sentimentality. A splendid self-portrait of *The Artist with his Family* (Musées Royaux, Brussels, 1621) shows him looking happy and proud with his own children. His brother **Paul de Vos** (c.1596–1678) painted hunting scenes and still lifes in the style of Frans *Snyders, who was the brother-in-law of the de Vos brothers. In 1637 all three helped Rubens execute pictures for the Torre de la Parada, Philip IV of Spain's hunting-lodge near Madrid.

Vos, Martin de (1531/2–1603). Netherlandish painter, active mainly in his native Antwerp, where he was a pupil of Frans *Floris. In 1552 he went to Italy and studied in Rome, in Florence, and with *Tintoretto in Venice. By 1558 he was back in Antwerp, and after the death of Floris in 1570 he became the leading Italianate artist in that city. The altarpieces that make up the bulk of his output are typically *Mannerist in their strained, slender elegance. His much rarer portraits, on the other hand, are notably direct and more in the Netherlandish tradition (*Antoine Anselme and his Family*, Musées Royaux, Brussels, 1577).

Vouet, Simon (1590–1649). The leading French painter in the first half of the 17th cent. He spent the years 1613–27 in Italy (mainly in Rome) and achieved a considerable reputation, being made President of the Roman Academy of St Luke in 1624. His early work in Italy was much influenced by *Caravaggio, but he later developed an *eclectic style in which *Baroque tendencies were tempered by the *Classicism of Guido *Reni and *Domenichino. In 1627 Louis XIII recalled Vouet to Paris and made him his court painter, launching him on an extremely busy and prosperous career. His compromise style proved exactly to the taste of a French public brought up in the *Mannerist tradition and seeking something new, but unprepared for the dramatic naturalism of the Caravaggesque or the full emotionalism of the Baroque. Only when *Poussin returned from Rome to Paris in 1640–2 was Vouet's dominance threatened. He painted religious and allegorical works and portraits and was employed on many important decorative schemes, sometimes in conjunction with Jacques *Sarrazin. Little of his best decorative work is extant, however. Vouet was a versatile and hardworking artist rather than a great one and his success and influence depended on his having hit upon a style which accorded with the taste of the day at a time when French painting was at a low ebb. He introduced new life and a tradition of solid competence and most of the leading members of the next generation of artists passed through his studio, including *Lebrun, *Le Sueur, and *Mignard. Examples of Vouet's work are in many French museums.

Vrel, Jacobus (active 1654–62). Dutch *genre painter, an enigmatic figure who has only recently gained recognition as one of the most charmingly idiosyncratic masters of his time. Nothing at all is known of his life, and his paintings—either sparse interiors or quiet street scenes—are very rare. They show a remarkably fresh, almost *naïve vision and have a sense of tranquil poetry that has led them to be compared to the work of *Vermeer. Several of his paintings have, indeed, formerly gone under Vermeer's name, for example *Street Scene* in the Getty Museum, Malibu, which was once owned by *Thoré, who considered it a Vermeer. Because of the similarity of spirit, it is surmised that Vrel, too, worked in Delft.

Vries, Adriaen de (1545–1626). Netherlandish sculptor, born in The Hague, who trained in Italy under *Giambologna and worked mainly in Central Europe, notably for the emperor Rudolf II in Prague. He was a fine craftsman in bronze and his sleek and elegant figures imitated his master's style with great accomplishment; their popularity showed the international currency of the courtly *Mannerist style. His major works included fountains for Augsburg (1598, 1602) and Copenhagen (1617). The figures made for the fountain in Copenhagen were taken by the Swedes as war booty in 1660 and are now in the Palace of Drottningholm near Stockholm. None of de Vries's commissions came from the Low Countries.

Vries, Hans Vredeman de (1526/7–1606). Netherlandish painter, architect, engineer, and designer, active in Germany and Prague, as well as Amsterdam, Antwerp, and The Hague. He was famous in his lifetime for his skill in *illusionistic architectural decoration, but much of his work was of a temporary nature (triumphal arches for festivities and so on) and few paintings are known by him (one of them is *Christ in the House of Mary and Martha* in the Royal Collection, which is set in an extremely elaborate interior). He is now remembered primarily for his many books and prints containing *perspective studies of fanciful palaces, courts, gardens, furniture, and decorative work. They had wide circulation in northern Europe and had great influence on architecture and decoration.

Vrubel, Mikhail (1856–1910). Russian painter and designer, the outstanding exponent of *Symbolism in his country. His first important work was the restoration of murals in the Church of St Cyril, Kiev, and in his subsequent career he showed an affinity with the spirituality of medieval religious art. In 1889 he moved from Kiev to Moscow and there was taken up by the wealthy art patron Savva Mamontov. In 1890 he began to do interpretations of Mikhail Lermontov's poem *The Demon* and the theme became central to his work. In treating it he passed from fairly naturalistic depictions to highly idiosyncratic anguish-ridden images rendered in brilliant fragmented brushwork that recalls the effects of medieval mosaics. The obsessive treatment of the theme reflected his own emotional instability; in 1902 the first symptoms of approaching insanity became apparent, in 1906 he went blind, and he died in a lunatic asylum.

Vuillard, Édouard (1868–1940). French painter and lithographer. In 1888 under the influence of *Sérusier he became a member of the *Nabis together with his friends *Denis and *Bonnard. He painted intimate interiors and scenes from Montmartre, his sensitive patterning of flattish colours owing something to *Gauguin and something to *Puvis de Chavannes, but creating a distinctive manner of his own. From about 1900 he turned to a more naturalistic style and with Bonnard became the main practitioner of *Intimisme. He made use of the camera to capture fleeting, informal groupings of his friends and relatives in their homes and gardens. There are examples of his work in many collections of modern art.

W

Waagen, Gustav Friedrich (1794–1868). German art historian. In 1822 he published a book on the van *Eycks that made his reputation and led to his appointment as director of the newly founded Berlin Museum in 1832. Waagen had studied art history at the universities of Breslau and Heidelberg and was one of the first trained art historians in the museum profession. In 1844 he became the first holder of a university chair in art history when he was appointed professor at Berlin University. A frequent traveller, with a great reputation as a connoisseur, Waagen is best remembered for his notes on works of art in public and private collections in various countries, which are a mine of information. Outstanding among them is *Treasures of Art in Great Britain* (3 vols., 1854); a supplementary volume entitled *Galleries and Cabinets of Art in Great Britain* was published in 1857.

Wadsworth, Edward (1889–1949). English painter and graphic artist. He worked for a short time with Roger *Fry at the *Omega Workshops, then was associated with Wyndham *Lewis in the *Vorticist group. At this time he produced completely abstract works such as the stridently geometrical *Abstract Composition* (Tate, London, 1915). In the First World War he served with the Royal Naval Volunteer Reserve and worked on designing dazzle camouflage for ships, turning his harsh Vorticist style to practical use. He documented this war work in the large *Dazzle-Ships in Drydock at Liverpool* (NG, Ottawa, 1919). The lucidity, precision, and clarity of his work were enhanced when in 1922/3 he changed from oil painting to *tempera, and during the rest of the 1920s, abandoning *Cubist leanings, he painted in a more straightforwardly naturalistic manner, showing a penchant for maritime subjects and developing a distinctive type of highly composed marine still life that often has a hypnotic, *Surrealistic flavour (*Satellitium*, Castle Museum, Nottingham, 1932). In 1933 he became a member of *Unit One and again painted abstracts (influenced by *Arp), but he reverted to his naturalistic style. In 1938 he painted mural decorations for the liner *Queen Mary*. His graphic work included collections of drawings and engravings published in books as *The Black Country* (1920) and *Sailing-Ships and Barges of the Western Mediterranean and Adriatic Seas* (1926).

Waldmüller, Ferdinand Georg (1793–1865). One of the leading Austrian painters of his period. He painted portraits, *genre subjects, and still life, but is perhaps best known for his landscapes, which in their loving attention to detail illustrate his belief that the close study of nature should be the basis of painting. His views were in opposition to the official doctrines of *ideal art promulgated by the Vienna Academy, where he became Professor of Painting in 1829, and he was dismissed in 1857.

Walker, Dame Ethel (1861–1951). British painter, trained at the *Slade School and one of the leading figures in the *New English Art Club from 1900. She painted portraits, flowerpieces, interiors, and seascapes in an attractive *Impressionist style, but her most individual works are decorative compositions inspired by her vision of a Golden Age. They show the influence of *Puvis de Chavannes as well as of her interest in philosophy and religion.

Walker, Robert (c.1605/10–56/60). English portrait painter. He has a certain niche in history as he was the portraitist most favoured by Oliver Cromwell and the Parliamentarians during the Interregnum (1649–60), but his work is generally dull and derivative (mainly of van *Dyck). His last dated pictures are of 1656 and he is said to have died 'a little before the Restoration'.

Wallace Collection, London. National museum consisting of the collection built up in the 18th and 19th cents. by the Seymour-Conway family, Earls and later

Marquesses of Hertford; it was bequeathed to the nation in 1897 by Lady Wallace, widow of Sir Richard Wallace, the illegitimate son of the 4th Marquess of Hertford, and opened to the public in 1900. It is housed in Hertford House, the former London residence of the family. The collection, the largest of its date to be preserved intact, reflects the tastes of various members of the family, but particularly of the 4th Marquess (Richard Seymour-Conway, 1800–70) and his son Sir Richard Wallace (1819–90), who each spent much of their lives in Paris. The Marquess bought most of the superb representation of 18th-cent. French art (furniture as well as paintings) that is the collection's chief glory; Sir Richard added much *Renaissance decorative art and the magnificent collection of armour, rivalled in Britain only by that in the Tower of London. Other areas in which the Wallace Collection is particularly rich are 17th-cent. Dutch and Flemish painting; 18th-cent. English portraits; and the works of *Bonington (the best representation anywhere).

Wallis, Alfred (1855–1942). British *naïve painter of sailing ships and landscapes. He went to sea as a cabin boy and cook at the age of 9, and from about 1880 worked as a fisherman in Cornwall. In 1890 he opened a rag and bone store in St Ives. He began to paint in 1925 to ease the loneliness he felt after his wife's death and was discovered by Ben *Nicholson and Christopher *Wood in 1928, the unselfconscious vigour of his work making a powerful impression on them. Wallis painted from memory and imagination, usually working with ship's paint on odd scraps of cardboard or wood. Although he rapidly became the best known of British naïve artists, he died in a workhouse.

walnut oil. *Drying oil obtained from the common walnut. It was one of the earliest oils used in painting, and perhaps the commonest *medium in the early days of *oil painting, but it is little used today. It dries more slowly than *linseed oil but has less tendency to turn yellow.

Walpole, Horace (1717–97). English collector, connoisseur, man of letters, and amateur architect. He was the fourth son of Sir Robert Walpole, Britain's first prime minister, and in 1791 he became fourth Earl of Orford. In 1739–41 he made the *Grand Tour, travelling in France and Italy with the poet Gray. His own literary fame rests on his voluminous correspondence and on *The Castle of Otranto* (1764), the first 'Gothic novel'. In the history of taste he is primarily important for his house at Twickenham, Strawberry Hill, which he bought in 1747 and extended into a showpiece of the Gothic Revival, employing professional architects to work from his sketches. He filled the building with his collections and it became such a tourist attraction that he had to issue tickets. In 1757 Walpole established his own printing press at Strawberry Hill, from which he issued his *Anecdotes of Painting in England* (4 vols., 1762–71), based on *Vertue's notebooks.

Wanderers (or **Itinerants**). Group of Russian painters associated with the Society of Wandering (Travelling) Exhibitions, a body founded in 1870 by a number of artists who resigned from the Academy in St Petersburg because of its rigid traditionalism. The Wanderers (in Russian *Peredvizhniki*), who eventually included *Repin and most of the other leading Russian painters of the last quarter of the 19th cent., were united by their belief that art should express humanitarian ideals and encourage social reforms. Thus they painted realistic pictures of peasant and middle-class life, often scenes arousing pity or inspiring the oppressed to better themselves. Their exhibitions travelled about the country, bringing art to a new public. The society officially lasted until 1923, but by then the once radical group had become conservative.

Wappers, Gustav (1803–74). Belgian painter. He was an enormous success in his day with his elaborate historical costume pieces, catching the public imagination with patriotic themes that appealed to the Belgian people, who had just won their independence (*Episode from the Belgian Revolution of 1830*, Musées Royaux, Brussels, 1834). Such works have dated badly, however. In 1845 he was created a baron, and in 1853 he settled in Paris.

Warburg, Aby (1866–1929). German art historian. His main field of study was the art of the Florentine *quattrocento, and opposing the *Aestheticism of the late 19th cent. he tried to understand the art of the period not in terms of formal values but as part of the intellectual history of the time. In particular Warburg was impressed by the hold that religious loyalties and astrological superstition retained on the minds of Renaissance merchants and princes, indicating that the subject-matter of the paintings they commissioned was no mere pretext for the display of artistic fancies. Warburg published little, but his aim of understanding every work of art in terms of a tradition modified by the psychological needs of the moment had great influence on his followers. The superb library that he built up in his home in Hamburg developed into a research institute, which was transferred to London in 1933 to escape the Nazi regime and in 1944 was incorporated in the University of London as the Warburg Institute. Its field of study is now officially defined as 'the history of the *Classical tradition' (das Nachleben der Antike), but its intellectual range encompasses, in *Panofsky's words, 'the history of art, the history of religion and superstition, the history of science, the history of cultic practices (including pageantry) and the history of literature'. Ernst *Gombrich, who wrote a biography of Warburg (1970, 2nd revised edn. 1986), is one of the many distinguished scholars associated with the Institute.

Ward, James (1769–1859). English painter and engraver. Until about the end of the century he painted mainly anecdotal *genre scenes in the manner of his brother-in-law George *Morland, but he then turned to the paintings of animals in landscape settings for which he is remembered. They are often dramatic and *Romantic in character and their rich colouring was influenced by *Rubens (*Bulls Fighting*, V&A, London, c.1804). His taste for natural grandeur and the *sublime often led him to work on a large scale, as in the enormous *Gordale Scar* (Tate, London, 1811–15). Ward had many admirers, including *Delacroix and *Géricault, but he lived in retirement from the 1830s and ended his life in poverty. His brother **William** (1766–1826) was an engraver.

Ward, John Quincy Adams (1830–1910). American sculptor. He was the most prolific and successful sculptor of public monuments of his period. His portrait statues,

equestrian figures, allegorical groups, war memorials, and architectural decorations have solid dignity but none of the genius of his contemporary *Saint-Gaudens.

Warhol, Andy (1928?–87). American painter, graphic artist, and film-maker. He settled in New York in 1949 and in the 1950s was a successful commercial artist (his shoe advertisements won a medal in 1957). In 1962 he achieved sudden notoriety when he exhibited stencilled pictures of Campbell's soup cans and sculptures of Brillo soap pad boxes. He was soon widely known as the most controversial figure in American *Pop art, embarking on a seemingly endless succession of pictures of Marilyn Monroe, Elvis Presley, and other celebrities, Coca-Cola bottles, and so on, often using rows of repeated images. The *silk-screen process that he favoured allowed infinite replication, and he was opposed to the concept of a work of art as a piece of craftsmanship, hand-made for the connoisseur and expressing the personality of the artist. 'I want everybody to think alike. I think everybody should be a machine.' In keeping with this outlook he used clippings of 'dehumanized' illustrations from the mass media, turned out his works like a manufacturer, and called his studio 'The Factory'. In 1965 he announced his retirement as an artist in order to devote himself to films and to managing the rock group *The Velvet Underground*, but he continued to work as a draughtsman and maker of constructions. As a film-maker, Warhol became perhaps the only 'underground' director to be well known to the general public. His first films were silent and virtually completely static: *Sleep* (1963)—a man sleeping for six hours; and *Empire* (1964)—the Empire State Building seen from one viewpoint for eight hours. Later films, such as the two-screen *Chelsea Girls* (1966), gained widespread attention because of their voyeuristic concentration on sex. In 1968 Warhol was shot and severely wounded by a bit-part player in one of his films, a member of SCUM (The Society for Cutting up Men), an incident that added to his legendary status. In spite (or perhaps because) of his impersonal persona he remained a cult figure and it could be argued that his advertising skills were nowhere more brilliantly employed than in promoting himself.

wash. An application of diluted *ink or transparent *water-colour to paper. The term usually refers to a uniform broad area done with a full brush.

water-colour. Term that can, in its broadest sense, be applied to any paint bound with a *medium (generally *gum arabic) soluble in water. In normal parlance, however, the term 'water-colour' generally refers specifically to a type of painting in which the lighter tones are not obtained by adding white pigment but by thinning with water so that the light is given by the paper or other support showing more strongly through the thinner layers of paint. It can thus be distinguished from other kinds of painting, such as *gouache, that use water as a medium but are opaque. Although there are isolated earlier examples of leading artists making memorable use of water-colour (*Dürer and van *Dyck, for example), its chief development took place in 18th-cent. and early 19th-cent. England, particularly in landscape. In the wake of *Impressionism the capacity of water-colour to achieve spontaneous effects was more widely appreciated and it ceased to be so much of an English speciality. Among the modern artists who have been great exponents of the technique (in their very different ways) are *Cézanne, *Sargent, *Dufy, *Grosz, and *Klee.

water-glass painting. A method of mural painting. The *pigments are mixed with plain water and painted on the plaster, which is then coated with a solution of water-glass (potassium or sodium silicate). Potassium silicate was first made commercially as a painting *medium in 1825. When the water-glass dries it leaves a thin film which seals the painting. As water-glass is strongly alkaline it can be used only with certain pigments. Some of the mural paintings in the House of Lords (see MACLISE) were executed in it, because it was thought that they would be proof against the damp and dirty atmosphere of London, but they deteriorated within ten years. Afterwards, in the 1880s, Adolf Keim of Munich improved the process, which he called *Mineral-malerei*, 'mineral painting'. The Victorian name for it was 'stereochromy'.

Waterhouse, Sir Ellis (1905–85). English art historian. In a highly distinguished career he was director of the National Galleries of Scotland (1949–52), director of the Barber Institute of Fine Arts, Birmingham (1952–70), and held many other prestigious posts in Britain and the USA. His publications were centred on two main areas, British painting of the 18th cent. and Italian *Baroque painting, his chief books being *Baroque Painting in Rome* (1937, revised edn. 1976), *Painting in Britain 1530–1790* (1953 and several revised edns.), *Italian Baroque Painting* (1962), a monograph on *Gainsborough (1958), and two on *Reynolds (1941 and 1973), *The Dictionary of British 18th-Century Painters* (1981), and *The Dictionary of British 16th- and 17th-Century Painters* (published posthumously 1988). He wore his great erudition lightly and was one of the most entertaining writers among art historians.

Waterhouse, John William (1849–1917). English painter. Early in his career he painted Greek and Roman subjects, but in the 1880s he turned to literary themes, painted in a distinctive, dreamily romantic style. In approach he was influenced by the *Pre-Raphaelites, but his handling of paint is quite different from theirs—rich and sensuous. His work includes such classic Victorian anthology pieces as *The Lady of Shalott* (Tate Gallery, London, 1888) and *Hylas and the Nymphs* (City Art Gallery, Manchester, 1896).

Watteau, Jean-Antoine (1684–1721). The greatest French painter of his period and one of the key figures of *Rococo art. He was born at Valenciennes, which had passed to France from the Spanish Netherlands only six years before his birth, and he was regarded by contemporaries as a Flemish painter. There are indeed strong links with Flanders in his art, but it also has a sophistication that is quintessentially French. He moved to Paris in about 1702 and *c*.1703–7 he worked with *Gillot, who stimulated his interest in theatrical costume and scenes from daily life. Soon afterwards he joined Claude *Audran, Keeper of the Luxembourg Palace, and thus had access to the *Rubens *Marie de Médicis* decorations, which were of enormous influence on him, even though Rubens's robustness was far removed from the fragile delicacy that characterized Watteau's art. Rubens was one of the prime inspirations for the type of picture with which Watteau is most associated—the *fête galante* (see FÊTE CHAM-PÊTRE), in which exquisitely dressed young people idle away their time in a dreamy, romantic, pastoral setting. The tradition of lovers in a parkland setting goes back via *Giorgione to the medieval type known as the Garden of Love, but Watteau was the first painter to make the theme his own, and his individuality was recognized by his contemporaries. In 1717 he submitted a characteristic work, *The Pilgrimage to the Island of Cythera* (Louvre, Paris; a slightly later variant is in Schloss Charlottenburg, Berlin), as his reception piece to the Academy, and owing to the difficulty of fitting him into recognized categories was received as a 'peintre de fêtes galantes', a title created expressly for him. He was, indeed, a highly independent artist, who did not readily submit to the will of patrons or officialdom, and the novelty and freshness of his work delivered French painting from the yoke of Italianate academicism, creating a truly 'Parisian' outlook that endured until the *Neoclassicism of *David. Watteau's world is a highly artificial one (apart from scenes of love he took his themes mainly from the theatre), but underlying the frivolity is a feeling of melancholy, reflecting the certain knowledge that all the pleasures of the flesh are transient. This poetic gravity distinguishes him from his imitators, and parallels are often drawn between Watteau's own life and character and the content of his paintings. He was notorious for his irritable and restless temperament and died early of tuberculosis, and it is felt that the constant reminder of his own mortality that his illness entailed 'infected' his pictures with a melancholic mood. In 1719 he travelled to London, almost certainly to consult the celebrated physician Dr Richard Mead, but the hard English winter worsened his condition. His early death came when he may have been making a new departure in his art, for his last important work combines something of the straightforward naturalism of his early pictures in the Flemish tradition with the exquisite sensitivity of his *fêtes galantes*: it is a shop sign painted for the picture dealer Edmé Gersaint and known as *L'Enseigne de Gersaint* (Staatliche Mus., Berlin, 1721).

Watteau was careless in matters of material technique and many of his paintings are in consequence in a poor state of preservation. A complete picture of his

genius depends all the more, then, on his numerous superb drawings, many of them scintillating studies from the life. He collected his drawings into large bound volumes and used these books as a reference source for his paintings (the same figure often appears in more than one picture). In spite of his difficult temperament, Watteau had many loyal friends and supporters who recognized his genius, and although his reputation suffered with the Revolution and the growth of Neoclassicism, he always had distinguished admirers. It is perhaps as a colourist that he has had the most profound influence. His method of juxtaposing flecks of colour on the canvas was carried further by *Delacroix and reduced to a science by *Seurat and the *Neo-Impressionists. Watteau's principal, but much inferior, followers were *Lancret and *Pater. He also had a nephew and a great-nephew (father and son) who worked more-or-less in his manner. They are both known as 'Watteau de Lille' after their main place of work—**Louis-Joseph Watteau** (1731–98) and **François-Louis-Joseph Watteau** (1758–1823).

Watts, George Frederic (1817–1904). English painter and sculptor. In 1843 he won a prize in the competition for the decoration of the Houses of Parliament and used the money to visit Italy, where the great *Renaissance masters helped shape his high-minded attitudes towards art. Returning to England in 1847, he established a solid reputation in intellectual circles, but popular fame did not come until about 1880. Thereafter he was the most revered figure in British art, and in 1902 became one of the original holders of the newly instituted Order of Merit. His style was early influenced by *Etty, but the *Elgin Marbles, the great Venetian painters (notably *Titian), and *Michelangelo were his avowed exemplars in his desire 'to affect the mind seriously by nobility of line and colour'. He tried to invest his work with moral purpose and his most characteristic paintings are abstruse allegories that were once enormously popular but now seem vague and ponderous (*Hope*, Tate, London, 1886; and other versions). His portraits of great contemporaries (*Gladstone, Tennyson, J. S. Mill*, etc., NPG, London) have generally worn much better. As a sculptor, he is remembered chiefly for his equestrian piece *Physical Energy* (1904). A cast of it forms the central feature of the Cecil Rhodes Memorial, Cape Town, and another is in Kensington Gardens, London. Watts was twice married, his first wife being the celebrated actress Ellen Terry. She was thirty years his junior and the marriage ended in divorce. His former house at Compton, near Guildford, Surrey, is now the Watts Gallery, devoted to his work. Wilfrid *Blunt was Curator 1959–85.

Weber, Max (1881–1961). Russian-born American painter. Weber's work more than that of any other American painter synthesized the latest developments in European art at the beginning of the 20th cent. In Paris, 1905–8, he was influenced by *Fauvism (he studied with *Matisse in 1908) and the early *Cubism of *Picasso and *Braque. He was also interested in primitive and oriental art. After 1917 his work became more naturalistic. During the 1940s he painted scenes with rabbis and Jewish scholars—mystical recollections of his Russian childhood. He published several books, including *Cubist Poems* and the autobiographical *Max Weber* (1945).

Weenix, Jan Baptist (1621–before 1663). Dutch painter. In 1642–6 he was in Italy, and on his return to his native Amsterdam he painted Italianate landscapes close in style to those of *Berchem, who is said to have been his cousin. Later he turned mainly to pictures of still life with dead game; he also painted portraits. His son, **Jan Weenix** (1642?–1719), specialized in hunting trophy subjects similar to those of his father; indeed, it is often difficult to tell their work apart. Most of his career was spent in Amsterdam, but from 1702 to 1712 he worked at Düsseldorf for the Elector Palatine. Both artists were prolific (Jan told *Houbraken that his father could paint three half-length life-size portraits in a day) and are represented in many public collections.

Weissenbruch, Hendrik Johannes (1824–1903). Dutch landscape and marine painter, a pupil of *Schelfhout and one of the outstanding artists of the *Hague School. His work is distinguished by its subtle handling of tone and feeling for atmosphere. His cousin **Johannes (Jan) Weissenbruch** (1822–80) painted town views in the detailed manner of 17th-cent. artists such as *Saenredam.

Werenskiold, Erik (1855–1938). Norwegian painter and graphic artist. He was one of the leading personalities in Norwegian art, the friend of numerous writers and intellectuals and a symbol of national culture. Influenced by French *plein air painters such as *Bastien-Lepage (he was in Paris 1881–3), Werenskiold developed an unsentimental yet affectionate approach to the Norwegian landscape. He also did portraits of many of the leading Norwegians of his day (*Henrik Ibsen*, NG, Oslo, 1895). But his finest works are perhaps his book illustrations, notably those to *Norwegian Fairy-Tales* by Asbjørnsen and Moe (1879–87).

Werff, Adriaen van der (1659–1722). Dutch painter of religious and mythological scenes and portraits, active mainly in Rotterdam. He combined the precise finish of the Leiden tradition (learned from his master Eglon van der *Neer) with the Classical standards of the French Academy and became the most famous Dutch painter of his day, winning international success and earning an enormous fortune. *Houbraken, writing in 1721, considered him the greatest of all Dutch painters and this was the general critical opinion for about another century. He is now considered an extremely accomplished, rather sentimental and repetitive minor master. Van der Werff also worked as an architect in Rotterdam, designing elegant house façades. His brother, **Pieter van der Werff** (1655?–1722), was his principal pupil and assistant, imitating Adriaen's style closely and making many copies of his work.

Wesselmann, Tom (1931–). American painter, one of the best-known exponents of *Pop art. He abandoned *Abstract Expressionism for *collages and *assemblages in mixed media, bringing representation and reality together to create a tension or ambiguity between the real world and the world of art. He is best known for his series *Great American Nude*, in which the nude became a depersonalized sex symbol set in a realistically depicted commonplace environment. During the 1970s the image became more and more explicitly sexual, concentrating attention on lips, breasts, and genitalia. He has also made painted Plexiglas sculptures and anatomical fragments set against large schematized landscapes.

West, Benjamin (1738–1820). American history and portrait painter who spent almost all his career in England. After early success as a portraitist in New York, he sailed for Italy in 1760. He spent three years studying there, chiefly in Rome, and in 1763 he settled in London. Here he soon repeated the professional and social success he had enjoyed in Italy, in part due to the novelty value of his being an American (a blind cardinal supposed he was a Red Indian). He became a founder member of the *Royal Academy in 1768 (in 1792 he succeeded *Reynolds as President) and in 1772 he was appointed historical painter to George III, with whom he had a long and lucrative association. Initially West had set up as a portraitist in London, but it was as a history painter that he made his mark. In Rome he had been in contact with the circle of Gavin *Hamilton and *Mengs, and his early work is in a determined but rather flimsy *Neoclassical style (*Agrippina Landing at Brundisium with the Ashes of Germanicus*, Yale Univ., 1768). With his famous *Death of Wolfe* (NG, Ottawa, 1770), however, he made a radical innovation by depicting the figures in contemporary costume. At first he was attacked for breaking with the conventions of the *Grand Manner, but his idea was soon adopted by other artists, most notably his countryman *Copley, and it marks an important turning-point in taste. As his style grew away from Neoclassicism, West was in the vanguard of the *Romantic movement with paintings such as the melodramatic *Saul and the Witch of Endor* (Wadsworth Atheneum, Hartford, 1777), and his *Death on a Pale Horse* (Philadelphia Museum of Art, 1802) has been hailed as a forerunner of *Delacroix. Following *Kent, he was also one of the pioneers of medieval subjects; in 1787–9 he did a series of paintings for Windsor Castle showing events from the life of Edward III (1312–77). West's historical importance far outweighs the quality of his work, which (in spite of its modernity in ideas) is generally pedestrian. He was the first American painter to achieve an international reputation and his influence on his successors, such as *Trumbull, was great.

Westall, Richard (1765–1836). English painter and graphic artist. His history paintings (he contributed to *Boydell's Shakespeare Gallery) are typical of the work of a second-class artist of the generation which was trained in the 18th-cent. tradition and lived to adapt itself to the *Romanticism of the new century. He was more successful in pastoral scenes and particularly in book illustration, in which field he was one of the most prolific artists of the day. As a water-colourist he was noted for his unusually rich colour effects.

Westmacott, Sir Richard (1775–1856). English *Neoclassical sculptor. The son of a sculptor also called **Richard** (1747–1808), he trained first under his father and then in Rome under *Canova (1793–7). On his return to London, he soon had a very large practice, second only to *Chantrey. Among his best-known works are the monument to Charles James Fox (Westminster Abbey, 1810–23), the *Achilles* statue in Hyde Park (1814–22), and the pediment sculpture on the British Museum (finished 1847). His work is dignified but often rather pedestrian and dead in handling. He was Professor of Sculpture at the *Royal Academy from 1827 to 1854. Two of his brothers, **George** (active 1799–1827) and **Henry** (1784–1861), were sculptors, as was his son, another **Richard Westmacott** (1799–1872).

Weyden, Rogier van der (1399/1400–64). The leading Netherlandish painter of the mid-15th cent. In spite of his contemporary celebrity (his work was appreciated in Italy as well as north of the Alps) and his continuing fame, there is little secure knowledge about his career. There are, in fact, no paintings that can be given to him indisputably on the basis of signatures or contemporary documentation, but several are mentioned in early sources, and the style these show is so distinctive that a coherent *œuvre* has been built up around them. His early life is still somewhat problematic, however. In 1427 a certain Rogelet de la Pâture entered the workshop of Robert Campin at Tournai and left as Maistre Rogier in 1432. It is generally accepted that this is Rogier van der Weyden (the French and Flemish forms of the name both meaning 'Rogier of the Meadow'), although it is uncertain why he should have started his apprenticeship so late. There are no documented pictures surviving from Campin's hand, but he is generally agreed to be identical with the *Master of Flémalle, so the whole question of Rogier's relationship with his master is based on stylistic analysis. Some scholars have assumed that the Master of Flémalle should be identified with the young Rogier rather than with Campin, but the prevailing opinion is now that Rogier's work shows a development from the powerfully naturalistic and expressive style of his master towards greater refinement and spirituality. Rogier's celebrated *Deposition* (Prado, Madrid), for example, is close to the Master of Flémalle's *Crucified Thief* fragment (Städelsches Kunstinstitut, Frankfurt) in its dramatic power and use of a plain gold background, but it has a new poignancy and exaltedness. *The Deposition*, like all of Rogier's works, is undated, but it must be earlier than 1443, when a copy was made.

By 1436 Rogier had moved to Brussels and been appointed official painter to the city. Apart from making a pilgrimage to Rome in 1450, he is never known to have left Brussels again. His work for the city included secular work—four large panels (destroyed in 1695) on the theme of justice for the court room of the town hall, for example—but all his surviving paintings are either religious pictures or portraits. He was extremely inventive *iconographically and compositionally, and was a master of depicting human emotion. Unlike Jan van *Eyck he seems to have had a large workshop with numerous assistants and pupils, and many of his compositions are known in several versions. His influence was strong and widespread; in his own lifetime his paintings were sent all over Europe, and his emotional and dramatic style found more followers than the quiet perfection of van Eyck. Rogier's portraits, usually serene and aristocratic, were also much imitated, influencing Netherlandish art until the end of the 15th cent.

Wheatley, Francis (1747–1801). English painter. He first practised in London as a painter of small full-length portraits and *conversation pieces in the manner of *Zoffany. After working in Dublin in 1779–83 he returned to London and began to specialize in scenes of rural and domestic life, imparting a certain 18th-cent. elegance to a genre in which *Hogarth had excelled,

and exploiting a facility for popular moral sentiment. Engravings of his *Cries of London* (1795), showing street-vendors, milkmaids, and so on had a great sale and it is by these that he is generally remembered. The originals are now dispersed; examples are at Upton House (National Trust) and in the Geffrye Museum, London.

Whistler, James Abbott McNeill (1834–1903). American-born painter and graphic artist, active mainly in England. He spent several of his childhood years in Russia (where his father had gone to work as a civil engineer) and was an inveterate traveller. His training as an artist began indirectly when, after his discharge from West Point Military Academy for 'deficiency in chemistry', he learnt etching as a US navy cartographer. In 1855 he went to Paris, where he studied intermittently under *Gleyre, made copies in the *Louvre, acquired a lasting admiration for *Velázquez, and became a devotee of the cult of the Japanese print (see UKIYO-E) and, in general, oriental art and decoration. Through his friend *Fantin-Latour he met *Courbet, whose *Realism inspired much of his early work. The circles in which he moved can be gauged from Fantin-Latour's *Homage to Delacroix*, in which Whistler is portrayed alongside *Baudelaire, *Manet, and others. He settled in London in 1859, but often returned to France. His *At the Piano* (Taft Mus., Cincinnati, 1859) was well received at the *Royal Academy exhibition in 1860 and he soon made a name for himself, not just because of his talent, but also on account of his flamboyant personality. He was famous for his wit and dandyism, and loved controversy. His life-style was lavish and he was often in debt. Dante Gabriel *Rossetti and Oscar Wilde were among his famous friends.

Whistler's art is in many respects the opposite to his often aggressive personality, being discreet and subtle, but the creed that lay behind it was radical. He believed that painting should exist for its own sake, not to convey literary or moral ideas, and he often gave his pictures musical titles to suggest an analogy with the abstract art of music: 'Art should be independent of all claptrap—should stand alone, and appeal to the artistic sense of eye or ear, without confounding this with emotions entirely foreign to it, as devotion, pity, love, patriotism, and the like. All these have no kind of concern with it, and that is why I insist on calling my works "arrangements" and "harmonies".' He was a laborious and self-critical worker, but this is belied by the flawless harmonies of tone and colour he created in his paintings, which are mainly portraits and landscapes, particularly scenes of the Thames. No less original was his work as a decorative artist, notably in the Peacock Room (1876–7) for the London home of the Liverpool shipping magnate Frederick Leyland (now reconstructed in the Freer Gal., Washington), where attenuated decorative patterning anticipated much in the *Art Nouveau style of the 1890s.

In 1877 *Ruskin denounced Whistler's *Nocturne in Black and Gold: The Falling Rocket* (Detroit Institute of Arts), accusing him of 'flinging a pot of paint in the public's face', and Whistler sued him for libel. He won the action, but the awarding of only a farthing's damages with no costs was in effect a justification for Ruskin, and the expense of the trial led to Whistler's bankruptcy in 1879. His house was sold and he spent a year in Venice (1879–80), concentrating on the etchings—among the masterpieces of 19th-cent. graphic art—that helped to restore his fortunes when he returned to London. He made a happy marriage in 1888 to Beatrix Godwin, widow of the architect E. W. Godwin, with whom Whistler had collaborated, but she died only eight years later. In his fifties Whistler began to achieve honours and substantial success. His portrait of Thomas Carlyle was bought by the Corporation of Glasgow in 1891 for 1,000 guineas and soon afterwards his most famous work, *Arrangement in Grey and Black: Portrait of the Painter's Mother* (1871), was bought by the French state (it is now in the Musée d'Orsay, Paris) and he was made a member of the Légion d'Honneur.

Whistler's paintings are related to *Impressionism (although he was more interested in evoking a mood than in accurately depicting the effects of light), to *Symbolism, and to *Aestheticism, and he played a central role in the modern movement in England. His aesthetic creed was explained in his *Ten O'Clock Lecture* (1885) and this, and much else on art and society, was republished in *The Gentle Art of Making Enemies* (1890).

Whistler, Rex (1905–44). English painter, graphic artist, and stage designer. He is best known for his decorations in a light and fanciful style evocative of the 18th cent., notably the series of murals *In Pursuit of Rare Meats* (1926–7) in the restaurant of the Tate Gallery. He did numerous book illustrations and much work for the stage, including ballet and opera. He was killed in action in the Second World War. His brother **Laurence Whistler** (1912–   ) a writer and glass engraver, has published several books on him.

Wiertz, Antoine (1806–65). Belgian painter, one of the great eccentrics in the history of art. He painted enormous religious, historical, and allegorical canvases in a staggeringly bombastic and almost dementedly melodramatic style and he thought that he had surpassed the masterpieces of his models—*Michelangelo and *Rubens. The Belgian government built him a special studio in Brussels (now the Wiertz Museum) to produce these bizarre (and often macabre and erotic) works, and he said they were painted for honour and his portraits for bread.

Wijnants, Jan (active 1643). Dutch landscape painter, active in his native Haarlem and from about 1660 in Amsterdam, where he also ran an inn. He specialized in landscapes with dunes and sandy roads, inspired by the countryside around Haarlem—unpretentious, naturalistic views that were favourites with collectors in the 17th and 18th cents. The figures in his paintings were apparently always painted by other artists, among them *Wouwerman. He, too, was an excellent painter of dunescapes and it is uncertain if one influenced the other. Wijnants was prolific and his work is in many public collections. Adriaen van de *Velde was his pupil and *Gainsborough was among the artists he influenced.

Wilde, Johannes (1891–1970). Hungarian-born art historian who became an Austrian citizen in 1928 and a British citizen in 1947. From 1923 to 1938 he was on the staff of the Kunsthistorisches Museum in Vienna and he gained an international reputation with his work on the Italian (particularly the Venetian) paintings there. He made many contributions to the attribution and dating of pictures, and one of his most important achievements was the systematic use of X-rays not only as a tool for discovering the physical condition of a painting but also as a guide to the individual artist's creative process. Following the annexation of Austria by Nazi Germany in 1938, Wilde resigned from the Kunsthistorisches Museum and moved to England. From 1948 to 1958 he taught at the *Courtauld Institute, where he was an inspirational figure—Kenneth *Clark described him as 'the most beloved and influential teacher of art history of his time'. Wilde published comparatively little, and as Anthony *Blunt wrote 'his wisdom was mainly dispensed in lectures, supervisions and private conversation'. During his lifetime only two of his major contributions appeared in book form in English, both on *Michelangelo's drawings—in the catalogue of the 15th- and 16th-cent. drawings at Windsor Castle (1949, with A. E. Popham) and in his catalogue of Michelangelo's drawings in the *British Museum (1953). In these two works, which demonstrate his keen sensibility as well as his great learning, Wilde effectively reversed the 'revisionist' tendency whereby many genuine drawings by Michelangelo had been rejected. After his death, two collections of lectures were published: *Venetian Art from Bellini to Titian* (1974) and *Michelangelo* (1978).

Wildens, Jan (*c*.1586–1653). Flemish landscape painter born at Antwerp, where he became a master in 1604. He is best known for painting landscape backgrounds for *Rubens and for many artists in his circle, but his finest independent work—the *Winter Landscape with a Hunter* (Gemäldegalerie, Dresden, 1624)—shows he was an accomplished master in his own right.

Wiligelmo (active *c*.1100). Italian *Romanesque sculptor. His name is known from an inscription on the façade of Modena Cathedral—'Among sculptors, your work shines forth, Wiligelmo. How greatly you are worthy of honours.' He must have been the main sculptor of the *reliefs on the façade (scenes from Genesis together with figures of prophets), which date from soon after 1099, when the cathedral was begun. Nothing else is known of him, but he created a distinctive style (his figures are squat and full of earthy vigour) that was the fountainhead of Romanesque sculpture in northern Italy.

Wilkie, Sir David (1785–1841). Scottish painter. He was trained in Edinburgh and then in 1805 moved to London, where he studied at the *Royal Academy Schools. His *Village Politicians* (private coll.) was the hit of the RA exhibition of 1806 and he established himself as the most popular *genre painter of the day. He was strongly influenced in technique and subject-matter by 17th-cent. Netherlandish artists such as *Ostade and *Teniers, and the public loved the wealth of lively and often humorous incident in his paintings. In 1825–8 he travelled abroad for reasons of health and his style changed radically under the influence particularly of Spanish painting, becoming grander in subject-matter and broader in touch. The change was regretted by many of his contemporaries. In 1840 Wilkie went to the Holy Land to research material for his biblical paintings and on the return journey died at sea; *Turner commemorated him in *Peace: Burial at Sea* (Tate, London). Wilkie's success did much to establish the popularity of anecdotal painting in England and many Victorian artists were influenced by him. The esteem in which he was held was possible only in an age which looked first to the 'story' of a painting and the moral lesson it contained.

Williams, Frederick (1927–82). Australian painter and graphic artist. After studying at the National Gallery School in Melbourne, 1944–9, he worked at the Chelsea Art School and the Central School of Arts and Crafts, London, 1951–6. His earliest etchings, often with music-hall subjects, were produced about this time. He returned to Australia in 1957, and from the late 1950s began his paintings revealing a distinctly personal vision of the Australian landscape such as *Charcoal Burner* (NG of Victoria, 1959). By increasing reductivism, his paintings in the 1970s became uniquely evocative of the primeval mystery and remoteness of Australian landscape, and he was regarded as the most original of Australian landscape painters. His work is represented in all Australian state galleries.

Willumsen, Jens Ferdinand (1863–1958). Danish painter, sculptor, architect, engraver, and potter. He was in Paris in 1888 and again in 1890–4, abandoning his early naturalistic manner under the impact of *Gauguin (whom he met) and *Symbolism. His work became highly individual, notable for its obscure and disturbing subject-matter and glaringly bright colours (*After the Tempest*, NG, Oslo, 1905). His sculpture is often *polychromatic, using mixed media, showing the influence of *Klinger. Willumsen was also influenced by El *Greco, on whom he wrote a long book (2 vols., 1927). There is a museum devoted to Willumsen at Frederikssund in Denmark.

Wilson, Richard (1713/14–82). British painter, born in rural North Wales, the son of a well-connected clergyman who encouraged his interest in art as well as giving him a good education. Wilson became the first major British artist to specialize in landscape, but after moving to London in 1729 he seems to have initially worked mainly as a portraitist. The decisive change in his career did not come until his visit to Italy in 1750–6, when he decided to devote himself exclusively to landscape. He is said to have done this at the urging of Francesco *Zuccarelli, whom he met in Venice and whose portrait (Tate, London, 1751) he painted, but he was more obviously influenced by the painting of *Claude and by the natural surroundings of Rome where Claude had worked. Here he found subject-matter suited both to his own taste and to that of his patrons, who were for the most part English noblemen, for whom he made chalk and charcoal drawings as well as paintings.

Back in England Wilson became successful with his Italian landscapes and applied the same Classical compositional principles to English and Welsh views, as in his celebrated *Snowdon from Llyn Nantlle* (versions are in the Walker Art Gallery, Liverpool, and the Castle Museum, Nottingham, c.1765). He also painted large historical landscapes more or less in the manner of *Dughet or Salvator *Rosa, trying to establish himself as a master of the *Grand Manner (*The Destruction of the Children of Niobe*, Yale Center for British Art, 1760). Wilson, however, had a prickly nature and a problem with drink, and in the early 1770s his career went into a sharp decline. The *Royal Academy (of which he had been a founder member in 1768) helped him out by appointing him librarian, but in 1781 his family took him (now

a pitiable figure) back to Wales. His work is of great importance in the history of British art, for he transformed landscape from an art that was essentially topographical to one that could be a vehicle for ideas and emotions. The only one of his pupils to attain distinction was Thomas *Jones, but he had many imitators and was admired by such later artists as *Cotman, *Crome, *Constable, and *Turner.

Wilson, Scottie (1889–1972). British self-taught painter of imaginative subjects, born in Glasgow of working-class parents. A colourful character, he ran away from home at the age of 16, did military service in India and South Africa and lived for some years in Canada. He started to draw in the 1930s. Unlike the work of most *naïve artists (with whom he is sometimes grouped), his pictures (which are often in coloured inks) were not 'realistic' renderings of scenes from the daily life with which he was familiar but pure decorative fantasies incorporating stylized birds, fishes, butterflies, swans, flowers, self-portraits, and totem heads. The last of these he saw at Vancouver, and they were rather fancifully thought by some commentators to represent the powers of evil in contrast to the powers of good symbolized in the images taken from nature. All his work, however, was decorative rather than symbolic or profound.

Wilton Diptych. See INTERNATIONAL GOTHIC.

Wilton, Joseph (1722–1803). English sculptor. He trained in Flanders and with *Pigalle in Paris, then was in Italy from 1747 till 1755. On his return to London he rapidly became successful, carved the state coach (still in use) for the coronation of George III (1760), and was then appointed sculptor to the King (1764). He was an intimate friend of the architect Sir William Chambers, with whom he often collaborated, and he was one of the original members of the *Royal Academy. His portraits are generally regarded as his best works, his monuments showing him hesitating between various styles. Much of his work was executed by assistants. His talents were considerable, but he was more interested in social life than his work; he inherited a fortune from his father (a manufacturer of ornamental plaster) but dissipated it and became bankrupt in 1793. Considering the quality of his training and his friendship with key figures in the art world, his career is a story of wasted opportunity.

Winckelmann, Johann Joachim (1717–68). German art historian and archaeologist, a key figure in the *Neoclassical movement, and in the development of art history as an intellectual discipline. He impressed contemporaries and later generations as much through his romantic life-story as by his writing. The son of a poor cobbler, he early developed a fervent love for *Classical antiquity and ancient art. After studying theology and medicine he held lowly positions as a schoolmaster and tutor whilst he taught himself Greek and absorbed himself in ancient culture. Eventually, in 1755, he managed to reach Rome (his conversion to Catholicism in 1754 was allegedly to facilitate this), where he became librarian to the famous collector Cardinal *Albani and soon established himself as a scholar and antiquarian of European fame. In 1768 he was murdered in Trieste, perhaps for the sake of some gold coins he had shown to a fellow guest at his inn.

Winckelmann's two most important books are *Gedanken über die Nachahmung der griechischen Werke in der Malerei und Bildhauerkunst*, published in 1755, shortly before he left for Rome (*Fuseli published an English translation in 1765 under the title *Reflections on the Painting and Sculpture of the Greeks*), and *Geschichte der Kunst des Altertums* (History of Ancient Art), published in 1764 (this is the first occurrence of the phrase 'history of art' in the title of a book). In these immensely influential works he proclaimed the superiority of Greek art and culture, combining rapturous descriptions of individual works (above all the *Apollo Belvedere*) with historical analysis. He never went to Greece and unwittingly based most of his observations on Roman copies, but his account of the stylistic development of Greek sculpture was a milestone in archaeological writing, and he is regarded as having laid the foundations of modern methods of art history. His analysis of ancient Greek culture as a unity, and his interpretation of art as an index of the spirit of the time were novel (he thought that when social conditions in general were good, then art was good, and when one

declined the other did also); these ideas were subsequently developed into a proper philosophy of culture by 19th-cent. German writers. He refined the notions of how a work may be dated or its place of origin located and explained the character of works of art by reference to such factors as climate, religious customs and social conditions. His influence on contemporary artists—above all *Mengs—was enormous, and his interpretation of Classical antiquity determined aspects of German education right into the 20th cent.

Winterhalter, Franz Xaver (1805–73). German painter, the most successful court portraitist of his period. He was based in Paris for most of his career, but he painted most of Europe's royalty and was a particular favourite of Queen Victoria. His style was romantic, glossy, and superficial and his portraits have until recently generally been valued more as historical records than as works of art. However, a major exhibition of his work at the National Portrait Gallery, London, in 1987 brought him into the limelight again. Winterhalter was also an accomplished lithographer. His brother **Hermann** (1808–91) was his assistant. A water-colour by him, *A Girl of Frascati* (signed but until recently given to his brother), is in the Wallace Collection, London.

Wit, Jacob de (1695–1754). The outstanding Dutch decorative painter of the 18th cent., active mainly in his native Amsterdam. He had his principal training in Antwerp and learned much from *Rubens's ceiling paintings in the Jesuit church there (his drawings became valuable records after the paintings were destroyed by fire in 1718). De Wit's style, however, was much lighter than Rubens's, with a *Rococo delicacy and charm. He was a Catholic and was the first Dutch artist since the 16th cent. to carry out a good deal of decorative work for Catholic churches, but he was at his best in domestic ceiling decorations (*Bacchus and Ceres in the Clouds*, Huis Boschbeek, Heemstede, 1751). His name has entered the Dutch language to describe a kind of *trompe-l'œil* imitation of marble *reliefs for which he was renowned; such pictures, usually set over a chimney-piece or door, are called 'witjes' (*wit* is Dutch for 'white'). De Wit was also an engraver and a noted collector of Old Master drawings.

Witte, Emanuel de (1615/17–91/2). Dutch painter, born at Alkmaar and active there, then in Delft (by 1641) and Amsterdam (by 1652), where he died. His range was wide, including history paintings, *genre scenes (notably of markets) and portraits, but after he settled in Amsterdam he concentrated on architectural paintings (primarily church interiors—both real and imaginary). *Houbraken wrote that 'in the painting of churches, no one was his equal with regard to orderly architecture, innovative use of light and well-formed figures', and this verdict has been endorsed by posterity, for his paintings are very different in spirit from the sober views of most Dutch architectural specialists, making powerful use of the dramatic play of light and shadow in the lofty interiors. His life was unhappy (he was constantly in debt) and when his body was found in a canal it was suspected that he had committed suicide.

Wittkower, Rudolf (1901–71). German-American art historian. He studied in Berlin, then worked at the Biblioteca Hertziana in Rome from 1923 to 1933. From 1934 to 1956 he was on the staff of the *Warburg Institute in London and from 1949 to 1956 was also professor of history of art at University College, London. In 1956 he moved to Columbia University, New York, as head of the Department of Fine Arts and Archaeology, which under his direction became one of the leading centres of art historical scholarship in the USA. After he retired in 1969 he was *Kress Professor at the National Gallery in Washington and *Slade Professor at Cambridge. Wittkower's many books and articles were devoted mainly to Italian art and architecture of the 16th and 17th cents., and his writings form one of the cornerstones in the study of Italian *Baroque art. His major books, several of which have appeared in revised editions, include: *Architectural Principles in the Age of Humanism* (1949), *Gian Lorenzo Bernini* (1955), *Art and Architecture in Italy 1600–1750* (1958), *Sculpture* (1977), and (with his wife **Margot Wittkower**) *Born under Saturn: The Character and Conduct of Artists* (1963).

Witz, Konrad (*c*.1400–44/6). German-born painter from Rottweil in Swabia, active in Switzerland and generally considered a member of the Swiss school. He entered the painters' guild in Basle in 1434 and apparently spent the rest of his career there and in Geneva. Little else is known of him and few paintings by him survive. These few, however, show that he was remarkably advanced in his *naturalism, suggesting a knowledge of the work of his contemporaries Jan van *Eyck and the *Master of Flémalle. In place of the soft lines and lyrical qualities of *International Gothic we find in Witz's work heavy, almost stumpy, figures, whose ample draperies emphasize their solidity. Witz's most famous works are the four surviving panels (forming two wings) from the altarpiece of St Peter he painted for the cathedral in Geneva. These are now in the Musée d'Art et d'Histoire there; the central panel is lost. One of the panels, the *Miraculous Draught of Fishes*, is Witz's masterpiece and his only signed and dated work (1444). The landscape setting depicts part of Lake Geneva (one of the earliest recognizable landscapes in art) and Witz's naturalism is even more remarkable in his observation of reflection and refraction in the water.

Wölfflin, Heinrich (1864–1945). Swiss art historian, professor at the universities of Basle (1893 1901), Berlin (1901 12), Munich (1912–24), and Zurich (1924–34). He was one of the most influential art historians of his period, and several of his books are still widely read. They include *Die klassische Kunst* (Classic Art, 1899), on the art of the High *Renaissance, *Kunstgeschichtliche Grundbegriffe* (Principles of Art History, 1915), and a monograph on *Dürer (1905). Most of his work was devoted to stylistic analysis, and he attempted to show that style—in painting, sculpture, and architecture—follows evolutionary principles. *Principles of Art History* presents his ideas in the most completely developed form, discussing the transformation from *Renaissance to *Baroque in terms of contrasting visual schemes—for example the development from linear to painterly ('malerisch'). Wölfflin's view that style was a force in its own right rather than an intellectual abstraction and his lack of interest in *iconography are out of tune with much modern thinking on art history, and his approach is often over-rigid; however, he was a figure of great importance in establishing his subject as an intellectually demanding discipline. Herbert *Read wrote: 'it could be said of him that he . . . found art criticism a subjective chaos and left it a science.'

Wolgemut, Michael (1434–1519). German painter and woodcut designer, active in his native Nuremberg. In 1472 he married the widow of Hans *Pleydenwurff and took over his workshop, the most prosperous in the city. It produced numerous large altarpieces in which there is little sign of a distinctive individual personality, and Wolgemut is more important for his book illustrations. Amongst many other books he illustrated was Hartman Schedel's *Weltchronik* (1493), the most enterprising attempt of its time at combining letterpress with woodcut illustration. Hitherto woodcuts had often been embellished by *illumination, but Wolgemut tried to refine the technique of woodcut so that it could achieve its own proper effects without hand painting. His pupils included *Dürer.

Wols (pseudonym of Alfred Otto Wolfgang Schulze) (1913–51). German-born painter active mainly in France. He went to Paris in 1932, where he earned a living by photography under the name Wols. He was interned at the outbreak of war but liberated in 1940 and lived in poverty in the south of France. On the termination of war he returned to Paris and was befriended by the writers Jean-Paul Sartre and Simone de Beauvoir, for whom he did illustrations. In the late 1940s he began to make a name for himself as a painter, but his irregular life, poverty, and excessive drinking undermined his health and he died in 1951. His posthumous fame far outstripped his reputation during his lifetime and he came to be regarded as the 'primitive' of *Art Informel and one of the great original masters of expressive abstraction. His work had an important influence on the *Tachiste art of the late 1940s and 1950s.

Wood, Christopher (1901–30). English painter. He studied at the Académie Julian in Paris in 1921 and subsequently travelled widely on the Continent. To influences from the modern French school (*Picasso and *Diaghilev were among his friends), he brought an entirely personal lyrical freshness and intensity of vision, but he was emotionally unstable and his early death was probably suicide (he was killed by a train). After this he became something of a legend as a youthful genius cut off before his prime. Much of Wood's best work was done in Cornwall, where he and his friend Ben *Nicholson discovered the *naïve painter Alfred *Wallis in 1928.

Wood, Grant (1892–1942). American painter, active mainly in Iowa, his native state. In 1927 he obtained a commission to make stained-glass windows for the Cedar Rapids Veteran Memorial Building and went to Munich in 1928 to supervise their manufacture. Influenced by the early Netherlandish paintings he saw in museums there, he abandoned his earlier *Impressionist style and began to paint in the meticulous, sharply detailed manner for which his work is chiefly known. Adapting this style to the depiction of the ordinary people and everyday life of Iowa, he came within the category of the *Regionalist group of the Painters of the *American Scene. He first came to national attention in 1930 when his painting *American Gothic* won a bronze medal at an exhibition of the Art Institute of Chicago, which now owns the painting. Although at the time it aroused violent controversy and was deplored as an insulting caricature of plain country people, the painting gradually gained great popularity. In 1931 Wood introduced an element of humorous fantasy in *The Midnight Ride of Paul Revere* (Met. Mus., New York) and in 1932 he painted his famous satirical picture *Daughters of the Revolution* (Cincinnati Art Museum), described as 'three sour-visaged and repulsive-looking females, represented as disgustingly smug and smirking because of their ancestral claim to be heroes of the American Revolution'. His other work includes some vigorous stylized landscapes, and during the 1930s he supervised several Iowa projects of the *Federal Art Project. In 1934 he became assistant professor of fine arts at the University of Iowa. A combination of perceptive insight and dry caricature make Wood's figure paintings outstanding among the works of the American Regionalist school.

woodcut. The technique of making a print from a block of wood sawn along the grain (the term is also applied to the print so made). It is the oldest technique for making prints and its principles are very simple. The design is drawn on a smooth block of wood (almost any wood of medium softness can be used) and the parts that are to be white in the print are cut away with knives and gouges, leaving the design standing up in relief. This is then inked and pressed against a sheet of paper. The origins of woodcut are obscure (the principle was employed in fabric printing in the Middle East at least as early as the 5th cent. AD), but woodcut as we know it appeared in Europe in the early 15th cent.; the earliest dated print is perhaps the *St Christopher* (1423) by an unknown artist in the John Rylands Library, Manchester. It was much used as an illustrative technique in the early days of printed books, but in the 16th cent. it lost ground to *line engraving, which could produce much subtler effects. In the late 19th and early 20th cents., however, there was a major revival of interest in the woodcut as a medium of original artistic expression, artists such as *Munch, *Gauguin and the German *Expressionists realizing the potential of the rugged boldness that is characteristic of the technique. The coloured woodcut, using different blocks for each colour, was particularly popular in Japan (see UKIYO-E).

wood engraving. Term applied to the technique of making a print from a block of hardwood sawn across the grain and to the print so made. It derives from the *woodcut, but because of the harder and smoother surface and the use of the *burin and other tools associated with the copperplate engraver, the effect is generally finer and more detailed. Though not the inventor of wood engraving, Thomas *Bewick was the first fully to exploit its possibilities and he succeeded in making it the most popular medium for book illustration until it was superseded by photo-mechanical processes at the end of the 19th cent.

Woolner, Thomas (1825–92). English sculptor, the only sculptor member of the *Pre-Raphaelite Brotherhood. His early career was unsuccessful, so he decided to try his hand at gold-prospecting in Australia. His departure in 1852 inspired Ford Madox *Brown's picture *The Last of England* (City Art Gallery, Birmingham, 1852–5). Woolner found little gold, but he began to prosper as a portrait sculptor, and after returning to England made a name for himself with his marble bust of Alfred Tennyson of 1857 (Trinity College, Cambridge, and replicas in Westminster Abbey and the NPG). His work was praised for its lifelikeness and he did portraits of many other distinguished sitters. Woolner also did a few figure subjects, occasionally painted, and wrote poetry.

Wootton, John (c.1682–1764). English landscape and sporting painter. He specialized very successfully in horse subjects, but his main contribution to British painting was the introduction of the *Classical landscape—Horace *Walpole said his works in this vein 'approached towards Gaspar Poussin [i.e. *Dughet], and sometimes imitated happily the glow of *Claude Lorrain'. His landscape manner was continued by his pupil George *Lambert.

Worpswede. A north German village near Bremen that in the last decade of the 19th cent. became the centre of a group of landscape painters who settled there, following the example of the *Barbizon group. The most famous artist to work there was Paula *Modersohn-Becker, and the 'Worpswede School' is sometimes regarded as one of the roots from which German*Expressionism sprang.

Wotruba, Fritz (1907–75). Austrian sculptor. In 1938 he emigrated to Switzerland and remained there during the war. He returned to his native Vienna in 1945 and was made Professor and later Rector of the Academy. Wotruba carved directly in stone, preferring a hard stone with a coarse texture. Starting from a naturalistic style reminiscent of *Maillol, he advanced towards abstraction by reducing the figure to bare essentials. It was the method used by *Brancusi, but unlike the subtle abstractions of Brancusi, Wotruba's figures are solid, blocklike structures. These carvings, which he left in a rough state, carried a suggestion at once of the monumental and the primitive. He brought about a revival of sculpture in Vienna and was the founder of the new Austrian school of abstract sculpture.

Wouters, Rik (1882–1916). Belgian painter and sculptor whose great talents reached incomplete development owing to his early death following operations for cancer of the eye. He is regarded as the leading Belgian exponent of *Fauvism, but his work is less violent in colour than that of the French exponents of the style and often (as in his portraits of his wife) has a quality of serene intimacy.

Wouwerman (or **Wouwermans**), **Philips** (1619–68). The most celebrated member of a family of Dutch painters from Haarlem, where he worked virtually all his life. He became a member of the painters' guild in 1640 and is said by a contemporary source to have been a pupil of Frans *Hals. The only thing he has in common with Hals, however, is his nimble brushwork, for he specialized in landscapes of hilly country with horses—cavalry skirmishes, camps, hunts, travellers halting ouside an inn, and so on. In this genre he was both immensely prolific and immensely successful—*Houbraken says he left his daughter a dowry of 20,000 guilders. He had many imitators, including his brother **Peter** (1623–82), and his great popularity continued throughout the 18th cent., when he was a favourite with princely collectors and engravings after his work had wide circulation. Subsequently he has perhaps been underrated, for although his work generally follows a successful formula, he maintained a high quality; his draughtsmanship is elegant, his composition sure, his colouring delicate, and his touch lively.

Wright, John Michael (1617–94). English portrait painter. He was apprenticed to George *Jamesone in Edinburgh in 1636, then spent a long period abroad, chiefly in Rome, where he became a member of the Accademia di S. Luca (see ACADEMY), the only British painter of the 17th cent. to have this distinction. On his return to England in 1656 he won many patrons among his fellow Catholics and became *Lely's chief rival, although he never had his great worldly success and died in modest circumstances. His style was less glossy than Lely's but more penetrating and individual in characterization, his sitters tending to look thoughtful rather than merely glamorous (*Magdalen Aston*, Castle Museum, Nottingham). Wright's most unusual work is an allegorical ceiling painting (Castle Museum) done for Charles II's bedroom at Whitehall Palace; it cannot be considered a success, but it is interesting as an attempt at *Baroque decoration by someone who was familiar with the works of Pietro da *Cortona (whom he described as 'the greatest master of his time'). Wright was a collector, antiquarian, and scholar, a man of considerable culture; in 1685–7 he accompanied an embassy from James II to Pope Innocent XI and wrote an account of it in Italian, published in 1687 (English translation, 1688).

Wright, Joseph (1734–97). English painter, born and principally active in Derby and generally known as 'Wright of Derby'. He was one of the most original, versatile, and accomplished British artists of the 18th cent. and the first major English painter whose career was based outside London. In 1751–3 and again in 1756–7 he trained under *Hudson in London, and returning to Derby he made a name as a portraitist in the Midlands, displaying a firm grasp of character. In the 1760s he began to paint candlelit scenes of various types, showing the fascination with unusual lighting effects that was to run throughout his career. He was influenced in some of these by Dutch painting, but in his depictions of the contemporary scientific world he broke new ground—his finest work, *An Experiment on a Bird in the Air Pump* (NG, London, 1768), has been described by Sir Ellis *Waterhouse as 'one of the wholly original masterpieces of British art'. Such works won him a considerable reputation, and in 1772 James *Northcote called him 'the most famous painter now living for candle-lights'. In 1768–71 Wright worked in Liverpool, and in 1774–5 was in Italy, where he assiduously studied the *antique but was even more impressed by the eruption of Vesuvius he witnessed and by a kind of man-made equivalent—the great fireworks display held annually at the Castel Sant' Angelo in Rome (he painted several pictures of both subjects). On his return to England in 1775 he moved to Bath, hoping to fill the gap left by *Gainsborough's departure for London, but his more forthright style did not please sophisticated society and in 1777 he returned to Derby. There he remained for the rest of his life apart from short journeys when he made tours of the Lake District in 1793 and 1794 (landscape became increasingly important towards the end of his career). Appropriately, Derby Art Gallery has far and away the finest collection of his work.

Wtewael (or **Uytewael**), **Joachim** (1566–1638). Dutch figure painter. After travelling in Italy and France 1586–90, he settled in his native Utrecht, where he became one of the leading Dutch exponents of *Mannerism. His highly distinctive, charmingly artificial style, which remained untouched by the naturalistic developments happening around him, was characterized by acidic colours and elegant figures in wilfully distorted poses. The best collection of his work, including a self-portrait (1601), is in the Centraal Museum, Utrecht.

Wyeth, Andrew (1917–). American painter, son and pupil of a well-known muralist and illustrator of children's books,

Newell Convers Wyeth (1882–1944). Wyeth's work consists almost entirely of depictions of the people and places of the two areas he knows best—the Brandywine Valley around his native Chadds Ford, Pennsylvania, and the area near Cushing, Maine, where he has his summer home. He usually paints in water-colour or *tempera with a precise and detailed technique, and often he conveys a sense of loneliness or nostalgia. He first came to general attention with his painting *Christina's World* (MOMA, New York, 1948), and since then has become enormously successful. There is a wide disparity of critical opinion about his status, however: J. Carter Brown, Director of the National Gallery in Washington, has called him 'a great master', whereas Professor Sam Hunter, one of the leading authorities on 20th-cent. American art, has written 'What most appeals to the public, one must conclude, apart from Wyeth's conspicuous virtuosity, is the artist's very banality of imagination.'

Y

Yáñez (or **Yáñez de la Almedina**), **Fernando** (active 1506–26). Spanish painter. He is first documented in 1506 in Valencia, where in 1507–10 he collaborated with Fernando de los Llanos (active 1506–25) in painting twelve panels of the *Life of the Virgin* for the main altarpiece of the cathedral. From the style of these paintings it is inferred that the 'Fernando spagnuolo' who was working in 1505 with *Leonardo da Vinci on the *Battle of Anghiari* was either Yáñez or Llanos. Yáñez is credited with being the more gifted artist and one of the most important influences in introducing the High *Renaissance style to Spain. Examples of his work are in the museum at Valencia and the Prado in Madrid.

Yeats, Jack Butler (1871–1957). The best-known Irish painter of the 20th cent., son of **John Butler Yeats** (1839–1922), a barrister who became a successful portrait painter, and brother of the poet William Butler Yeats. Until about 1910 he worked mainly as an illustrator, then turned to oils. His early work as a painter was influenced by French *Impressionism, but he then developed a more personal *Expressionistic style characterized by vivid colour and extremely loose brushwork. He painted scenes of Celtic myth and everyday Irish life, contributing to the upsurge of nationalist feeling in the arts that followed the winning of Irish independence.

Ysenbrandt (or **Isenbrandt**), **Adriaen** (d. 1551). Netherlandish painter. He became a master in Bruges in 1510 and is said by an early source to have been a pupil of Gerard *David. Otherwise, virtually nothing is known of him and there are no signed or documented works. However, in 1902 the Belgian art historian Georges Hulin de Loo proposed Ysenbrandt as the author of a large group of paintings deriving from David, and the identification has generally been accepted. Previously the paintings had been attributed to Jan *Mostaert and the anonymous Master of the Seven Sorrows of the Virgin, named after a *diptych of that subject divided between the church of Notre-Dame in Bruges and the Musées Royaux in Brussels. Some authorities prefer to use the name Ysenbrandt in inverted commas.

Yvaral. See VASARELY.

Z

Zadkine, Ossip (1890–1967). Russian-born sculptor who worked mainly in Paris and became a French citizen in 1921. He moved to Paris in 1909 after spending some time in England (to learn English) as a boy. Although he deeply admired *Rodin, *Cubism had a greater impact on his work. His experiments with Cubism, however, had none of the quality of intellectual rigour and restraint associated with *Picasso and *Braque, for although Zadkine was a learned artist, his primary concern was with dramatically expressive forms. The individual style he evolved made great use of hollows and concave inflections, his figures often having openings pierced through them. In 1915 he joined the French army but was invalided out after being gassed. He worked in Paris through the 1920s and 1930s, and spent the Second World War in New York, returning to Paris in 1944. Often Zadkine's work can seem merely melodramatic, but for his greatest commission—the huge bronze *To a Destroyed City* (1953) standing at the entry to the port of Rotterdam—he created an extremely powerful figure that is widely regarded as one of the masterpieces of 20th-cent. sculpture. With its jagged, torn shapes forming an impassioned gesture mixing defence and supplication, it vividly proclaims anger and frustration at the city's destruction and the courage which made possible its rebuilding.

Zeuxis (active latter 5th cent. BC). Greek painter from Heraclea (probably meaning the town of that name in southern Italy, rather than the one on the Black Sea). None of his works survives, but ancient writers describe him as one of the greatest of Greek painters and there are many anecdotes about his remarkable powers of verisimilitude (see PARRHASIUS). Another story tells how when called upon to paint a picture of Helen of Troy for a temple at Croton he assembled the five most beautiful maidens of the city and combined the best features of each into one figure of *ideal beauty—an early example of an idea that later became commonplace in aesthetic theory. He is said to have specialized in *panels rather than murals. According to legend, Zeuxis died laughing while painting a picture of a funny-looking old woman, and the story has occasionally formed the basis for later artists' self-portraits. Aert de *Gelder painted himself as Zeuxis (Städelsches Kunstinstitut, Frankfurt, 1685) and *Rembrandt's 'Laughing' Self-Portrait (c.1665) in the Wallraf-Richartz-Museum, Cologne has also been interpreted in this way.

Zoffany, Johann (1733–1810). German-born painter who settled in England in about 1760 after working in Rome. He was patronized by the famous actor David Garrick and made his name with paintings representing scenes from plays, usually showing Garrick in one of his favourite parts. They show how quickly he adapted to English taste, and he also painted *conversation pieces of much the same small scale and in the same relaxed vein. No doubt because of his German background, he was taken up by George III and Queen Charlotte and he painted numerous works for the royal family. The two most important (still in the Royal Collection) are *The Academicians of the Royal Academy* (1772) and *The Tribuna of the Uffizi* (1772–8). For the latter he made a long visit to Florence (1772–9) and when he returned to England he found that the demand for conversation pieces had slumped. He went to India in 1783 and made a fortune painting Indian princes and expatriate Britons before returning to England in 1789. The remainder of his career was undistinguished. For a long time Zoffany's paintings were valued chiefly as historical records (they are sharp and clear in detail and contain a wealth of information about costume, etc.), but he is now also appreciated for his charm and recognized as an artist who brought new life to the conversation piece.

Zorach, William (1887–1966). Lithuanian-born American sculptor. Zorach emigrated to the USA in 1891. Initially he worked as a painter, but he became involved in sculpture in 1917 and abandoned painting for it about 5 years later. Although he was not at any time a *Cubist, the salient characteristics of his work were solid contours, block-like bulk, and an emphasis on essential volumes with suppression of details, and in his formal austerity, as in his practice of direct carving, he exercised a powerful influence on the course of American sculpture.

Zorn, Anders (1860–1920). Swedish painter and etcher. After leaving the Stockholm Academy in 1881 because of its restrictive and out-dated ideas, he travelled widely, becoming the most cosmopolitan of Scandinavian artists and an international success. He was based in London (1882–5), then Paris (1888–96), and visited Spain, Italy, the Balkans, North Africa, and (on several occasions) the USA, where he painted three Presidents. Originally he worked almost exclusively in water-colour, but in 1887–90 he abandoned the medium for oils. In 1896 he settled permanently at Mora in Sweden, building his own house, which is now a museum dedicated to him. He painted three main types of pictures: portraits, *genre scenes (often depicting the life and customs of the area in which he lived), and female nudes. It is for his nudes—unashamedly healthy and voluptuous works—that he is now best known. He often painted them in landscape settings and delighted in vibrant effects of light on the human body, depicted through lush brushwork that recalls the handling of his friend Max *Liebermann. Zorn also gained a great reputation for his etchings and he occasionally made sculpture.

Zuccarelli, Francesco (1702–88). Italian painter of landscapes, often featuring mythological subjects. He was born near Florence and studied in Rome, but is associated chiefly with Venice, where he settled in 1732 and worked in the vein of pastoral landscape popularized by Marco *Ricci. Like *Canaletto, Zuccarelli was patronized by the English entrepreneur Joseph Smith and his work found a ready market in England. When Richard *Wilson (still primarily a portrait painter) visited Venice in 1751 he painted Zuccarelli's portrait and it was perhaps Zuccarelli's encouragement which induced him to turn his attention

to landscape. In 1752–62 and again in 1765–71 Zuccarelli worked in England, where his delicate *Rococo style met with great success. He was made a foundation member of the *Royal Academy in 1768, and on his return to Venice he became President of the Venetian Academy.

Zuccaro, Taddeo (1529–66) and **Federico** (c.1540–1609). Italian *Mannerist, painters, brothers, from the neighbourhood of Urbino. Taddeo worked mainly in Rome and although he was only 37 when he died he had made a great name for himself as a fresco decorator, working notably for the *Farnese family in their palace at Caprarola. His style was based on *Michelangelo and *Raphael and tended to be rather dry and wooden. Federico took over his brother's flourishing studio, continuing the work at Caprarola and also the decoration of the Sala Regia in the Vatican (begun by Taddeo in 1561). His talent was no more exceptional than Taddeo's, but he became even more successful and won himself a European reputation—indeed for a time he was probably the most famous living painter. In 1573/4 he travelled via Lorraine and the Netherlands to England, where he is said to have painted portraits of the Queen and many courtiers, although only two drawings in the British Museum portraying Elizabeth I and Robert Dudley, the Earl of Leicester, can safely be attributed to him. (Many anonymous portraits of the period are improbably attributed to him.) After working in Florence, Rome, and Venice, he was invited to the *Escorial by Philip II of Spain, where he painted a number of altarpieces (1585–8). Back in Rome he was elected the first President of the new Accademia di S. Luca, founded in 1593 (see ACADEMY), to which he later gave his house as headquarters. Like many of his contemporaries he believed that correct theory would produce good works of art and himself wrote L'Idea de' Scultori, Pittori e Architetti (1607). Zuccaro also worked as an architect, designing a doorway in the form of a grotesque face (one enters through the open mouth) for his own house in Rome (the Palazzo Zuccaro, now the Biblioteca Hertziana).

Zucchi, Antonio. See KAUFFMANN, ANGELICA.

Zuloaga y Zabaleta, Ignacio (1870–1945). Spanish painter, the son of **Placido Zuloaga**, a well-known metalworker and ceramicist. He spent much of his career in Paris, where he was on friendly terms with *Rodin, *Gauguin, and *Degas, but his art is strongly national in style and subject-matter. Bull-fighters, gypsies, and brigands were among his subjects, and he also painted religious scenes and portraits. His inspiration came from the great Spanish masters of the past, notably *Velázquez and *Goya, and he is credited with being one of the first to 'rediscover' El *Greco. He was highly popular during his lifetime (he had a resoundingly successful one-man show in New York in 1925), but his work now often looks rather stagy. There is a Zuloaga museum in Madrid.

Zurbarán, Francisco (1598–1664). Spanish painter, born at Fuente de Cantos and active mainly in Seville. He trained there 1614–17 and after a period at Llerena near his birthplace returned in 1629 as town painter. In 1634–5 he was in Madrid working for Philip IV on a series of ten pictures on *The Labours of Hercules* and a large historical scene, *The Defence of Cadiz* (all now in the Prado, Madrid), but apart from these pictures, a few portraits, and some masterly still lifes, he devoted himself almost entirely to religious works. He worked for churches and monasteries over a wide area of southern Spain and his paintings were also exported to South America. His compositionally simple and emotionally direct altarpieces, combining austere *naturalism with mystical intensity, made him an ideal Counter-Reformation painter. The most characteristic of his works are the single figures of monks and saints in meditation or prayer, most of which seem to have been executed in the 1630s. The figures are usually depicted against a plain background, standing out with massive physical presence. Many of these monumentally solemn figures are conceived in great series, such as *The Members of the Mercedarian Order* (Academy, Madrid), or *The Carthusian Saints* (Cadiz Mus.). But there are single pictures of the same kind. He painted numerous pictures of *St Francis*, for example (two in the NG, London), and a number of virgin saints. Towards the end of his career Zurbarán's work lost something of its power and simplicity as he tried to come to terms with the less ascetic style of *Murillo, who in the 1640s overtook him as the most popular painter in Seville. In 1658 he moved to Madrid, where he spent his final years. His son **Juan** (1620–49) is known from a few still-life paintings.